CORPORATIONS
LAW AND POLICY
MATERIALS AND PROBLEMS
Third Edition

By

Lewis D. Solomon
Arthur Selwyn Miller Research Professor of Law
George Washington University National Law Center

Donald E. Schwartz
Late Professor of Law
Georgetown University

Jeffrey D. Bauman
Professor of Law
Georgetown University Law Center

Elliott J. Weiss
Charles E. Ares Professor of Law
University of Arizona College of Law

AMERICAN CASEBOOK SERIES®

WEST PUBLISHING CO.
ST. PAUL, MINN., 1994

COPYRIGHT © 1982, 1988 WEST PUBLISHING CO.

COPYRIGHT © 1994 By WEST PUBLISHING CO.
                        610 Opperman Drive
                        P.O. Box 64526
                        St. Paul, MN 55164–0526
                        1–800–328–9352

All rights reserved
Printed in the United States of America
Solomon, Lewis, D.
    Corporations, law and policy, materials and problems / by Lewis D. Solomon . . . [et al.] — 3d. ed.
     p. cm. — (American casebook series)
  Includes index.
  ISBN 0–314–03717–9
  1. Corporation law—United States—Cases. I. Title. II. Series.
KF1413. S631994
346.73'066—dc20
[347.30666]   94–16098
                           CIP

ISBN 0–314–03717–9

(S., S., B. & W.) Corp.Law 3rd ACB
1st Reprint—1996

For Don, with love.
Lew
Jeff
Elliott

*

Preface to the Third Edition

All students and teachers of corporate law realize that there are many valid and varied ways to present the subject. The case method, standing alone, cannot fully encompass the diverse influences which are brought to bear on the field. We believe that a casebook which uses the problem method as an organizing principle is more effective for the task than a more traditional casebook. Using such a method also permits greater use of non-case materials which illuminate the questions which invariably arise in the study of corporate law, regardless of the depth in which such study is undertaken. Thus the emphasis in this edition of the book, as it was in previous editions, is on the development of the skill of learning how to solve problems. Because corporate lawyers most often engage in counseling rather than litigation, we believe that our approach is especially suitable for a course in corporate law. Hopefully, it will also enable the student to appreciate where matters of judgment become paramount.

We appreciate that not all of our colleagues in the field share our view on the use of problems. We respect their approaches and we have designed the book so that it may be used in a more conventional form, making little or no use of the problems. We are aware of many splendid teachers who use the book in precisely that way.

We should also note that while cases do comprise the largest part of the materials, we also have made extensive use of other materials. To integrate problems of public policy, legal ethics, accounting and economic analysis, we rely heavily on non-case material, consisting of secondary sources or our own textual notes. All of these subjects are vital to the understanding of corporate law and its place in our legal, economic, political and cultural system.

The organizing principle of the book is to introduce certain basic themes in the first few chapters and develop those themes throughout the book with increasing depth and sophistication. Chapter 2 uses a simple fact pattern to present an economic analysis of a business enterprise. In basic terms, we look at questions of risk-bearing, monitoring and incentives as they affect the parties to the enterprise. The analysis of these questions provides a reference point to which recurrent use may be made. We remind students of that analysis when we study the financial structure of the corporation, the duties of directors and officers, the governance of the corporation, derivative suits and changes in control. Thus we use the lessons from this early chapter throughout the course. When we reach the study of publicly held corporations, we present additional materials on agency costs, market efficiency, and the debate over the concept of the corporation as a nexus of contracts among competing interests.

This is not advanced economics material. We do not employ sophisticated graphs or calculus. Rather we seek to present fundamental economic concepts in order to develop in our students a deeper understanding about the nature of the corporation and the role of law and lawyers. Some of the material, particularly in the later chapters, is controversial, and we have provided ample space to the trenchant criticisms of the law and economics viewpoint. Corporate law is increasingly influenced by these ideas; they may have contributed as much to the development of corporate law in recent years as the formal acts of lawmakers. That influence is manifested in actions by courts, legislators and regulators. It is also clear that lawyers in their practice apply the learning from several disciplines solving problems. Some particularly interesting examples of the latter are seen in two provocative articles: Gilson, *Value Creation by Business Lawyers: Legal Skills and Asset Pricing,* 94 Yale L.J. 239 (1984); Klein, *The Modern Business Organization: Bargaining Under Constraints,* 91 Yale L.J. 1521 (1982).

After this introduction, we deal with the fact that many students lack a basic understanding of corporations and how they function. The Chesapeake Marine Services problem in Chapter 3 presents some of the fundamental concepts in corporate law, including the duty of care, the business judgment rule and the duty of loyalty. The chapter also illustrates judicial attitudes toward the interaction between the common law and a corporate statute and, perhaps most important, provides the student with a basic understanding of the structure of the corporation. Chapters 4 and 5 discuss the corporation and the Constitution and the role of corporation in society in contexts that emphasize the representative nature of the corporate governance system, the centrality of the business judgment rule, the power of managers, and the mechanisms available to shareholders who disagree with managers' actions. These chapters provide students with a framework that will allow them to understand better the issues that arise in connection with choosing an organizational form, organizing a corporation, designing a capital structure, and allocating power between shareholders and managers—materials that otherwise often seem unrelated.

Chapters 7 and 8 introduce the student to the issues that arise in connection with the decision to incorporate and in the incorporation process itself. Chapters 6 and 9 deal with valuation and corporate finance. Taken together, these chapters are intended to show the interplay between a statutory regime, the economics of a business, and the needs of the parties to the venture. Chapter 13 revisits this theme in the specific context of close corporations; the chapter illustrates the tension between legal rules and the desire for private ordering.

This edition reflects the extensive developments in themes of corporate governance that have burgeoned in the last five years. These themes begin in Chapter 12 which explores the theoretical governance structure of a corporation and the allocation of power among shareholders, directors and officers. It uses a reorganization transaction to demonstrate the potential conflicts that can arise from such allocation. Chapter 12 also highlights the increased importance that courts attach to shareholder voting, particularly in the election of directors.

Chapters 14 and 15, which are almost completely new, present a detailed discussion of the roles of individual shareholders, institutional investors and outside directors in the governance of the publicly held corporation. These chapters include a summary of the theory of the firm debate, discussion of the recently revised SEC proxy materials, and materials describing the emergence and increasing activism of institutional investors. They are intended to provide a working matrix for discussing the materials in subsequent chapters dealing with fiduciary duties, derivative suit litigation, and transactions involving corporate control.

The first edition of this book appeared as the American Bar Association was nearing the completion of the Revised Model Business Corporation Act and the American Law Institute was beginning serious deliberation of its Principles of Corporate Governance. The ABA completed the RMBCA in 1984, but has made, and continues to make, important and controversial changes to that statute. The ALI has just published the final version of the Principles of Corporate Governance; the influence of that work on corporate law makers and lawyers is one of the themes that will be played out in the coming years. Both works are featured prominently in this edition.

There is another focus to this book that we have sought to retain: its concern for issues of public policy relating to corporations. All teachers of corporation law understand that this is not a course in corporate mechanics; we are not simply training technicians. Law students study corporation law, not simply because they intend to practice in that field (some would never dream of doing so) but because all lawyers need to be educated about the phenomenon of the corporation and how the law deals with its impact. All of us constantly raise policy questions with our students: why should the law provide limited liability; why should we delegate enormous powers over other people's money to agents over whom we exercise so little control; why should persons with minimal interests in a corporation be allowed to bring suit in its name; whether our systems of management accountability are adequate; why should insider trading be prohibited; and countless other questions that go to the core of the subject. If anything, we have updated and expanded the materials to assist in this respect.

A corporate law casebook can be written from several perspectives; we have written this book to be helpful primarily to students. We have written many lengthy notes which are designed to provide a fuller understanding of discrete areas, especially where knowledge of the way in which the corporate world operates is needed in order for cases and statutes to make any sense. We have also found that students seek not mere recital of rules, but demand explanations for why things are the way they are and whether they should be that way. Our notes attempt to provide guidance in reaching those explanations. We find ourselves comfortable writing in that environment. While practitioners may also find our approach useful, the reader on whom we have focused our attention is the intelligent novice, no matter what his or her age.

This book is designed to be supplemented by the West Publishing's Selected Corporation and Partnership Statutes, Regulations and Forms which contains in convenient form the Revised Model Business Corporation Act (with official comment at strategic places), the Delaware General Corporation Law, various other relevant statutes, applicable portions of the federal securities laws and rules, and sample articles of incorporation, by-laws, and other forms.

As to editorial details, citations in the texts of cases and other materials, as well as the footnotes of courts and commentators, have been omitted without so specifying. We use the pronoun "she" for "he or she" in most places out of concern for simplicity, not out of bias. The footnotes of decisions and excerpts from books and articles bear the original number; those of the authors are indicated by asterisks and similar symbols.

A teacher's manual for this edition is available from the publisher. It contains further details and suggestions as to how the book and the problems might be used.

We owe thanks to many people. The spirit of our late colleague, co-author and friend, Don Schwartz, permeates the entire book; we have tried to be true to his memory and his ideas. Russ Stevenson co-authored the first edition before moving from teaching to practice. Professor Joel Seligman of the University of Michigan co-authored one of the earlier supplements and has been a source of ideas and information for which we are grateful. Professors Warren Schwartz and Steven Salop of Georgetown were extremely helpful in their suggestions and reviewing the economics material, particularly in Chapter 2. Professor Richard Diamond of Georgetown gave us many useful suggestions that we have been able to incorporate into this edition. We have been extremely fortunate in having a number of our colleagues at various law schools teach and comment on drafts of this edition. We owe a deep debt of gratitude to Professors James Cox of Duke, Reinier Kraakman of Harvard, Randall Thomas of Iowa, Junius Hoffman of Arizona, Sam Thompson of UCLA, and John Beckerman and Larry Cunningham of Cardozo for the time and effort they have spent in helping us bring this edition to fruition. Our classes have served as guinea pigs for this edition, and their comments have assisted us in keeping our attention focused on our student users.

We also owe special thanks to Justice Andrew G.T. Moore II of the Delaware Supreme Court. One of the authors of this book has had the privilege of teaching a seminar with Justice Moore for six years and has benefited immeasurably from his insights into Delaware corporate law. In addition, Justice Moore has taught some of the materials in this edition in his own courses and has provided us with invaluable comments. For the deficiencies that may remain, however, we readily acknowledge that the buck stops with us.

Finally, we have had invaluable assistance from our student research assistants. In particular, we owe thanks to Shannen Coffin, Robert Duffy, Ross Greenberg, David Lankford, Jeff LeForce, Mary Mulvaney and Carl Settlemyer of Georgetown, L. Darren Goldberg and Mary Ita Snyder of George Washington, Ted Burke of Cardozo and Sarah Jeffries Johnson, Sue Ellen Schuerman, and Marianne Susong of Arizona. They have provided substantive help and have borne the brunt of the difficult mechanical chores with ability and grace. Without them, our work would have been far more difficult.

LEWIS D. SOLOMON
JEFFREY D. BAUMAN
ELLIOTT J. WEISS

May 1994

*

Acknowledgements

William T. Allen, Independent Directors in MBO Transactions: Are They Fact or Fantasy?, 45 Bus.Law. 2055 (1990).

William T. Allen, Our Schizophrenic Conception of the Business Corporation, 14 Cardozo L.Rev. 261, 263–64, 278–79 (1992).

American Bar Association, Model Rules of Professional Conduct, Rules 1.6, 1.7, 1.13, 2.1 and Comments (1983). Reprinted by permission of the American Bar Association. Copies of the Model Rules are available from Order Fulfillment, American Bar Association, 750 North Lake Shore Drive, Chicago, IL 60611.

American Law Institute, Principles of Corporate Governance: Analysis and Recommendations, § 2.01; Comment e and f to § 2.01; Comment d(2)(a) to § 5.04; § 1.23 and Comment; § 3.02; § 4.01 and comment to § 4.01(a)(1)–(2); § 5.02 and Comment to § 5.02(a)(2)(B); comment to § 7.01; and pp. 324, 587–89 (1994). Copyright © 1994 by The American Law Institute. Reprinted with the permission of The American Law Institute.

Lucian A. Bebchuk, Federalism and the Corporation: The Desirable Limits on State Competition in Corporate Law, 105 Harv.L.Rev. 1484, 1485, 1501 (1992). Copyright © (1992) by the Harvard Law Review Association.

Adolf A. Berle, Jr., The Theory of Enterprise Entity, 47 Colum.L.Rev. 343, 348 (1947). This article originally appeared at 47 Colum.L.Rev. 343, 348 (1947). Reprinted by permission.

Reprinted with the permission of Macmillan Publishing Company from THE MODERN CORPORATION AND PRIVATE PROPERTY by Adolf A. Berle, Jr. and Gardiner C. Means. Copyright © 1932 by Macmillan Publishing Company, renewed 1960 by Adolf A. Berle, Jr. and Gardiner C. Means.

Norwood P. Beveridge, Jr., The Corporate Director's Fiduciary Duty of Loyalty: Understanding the Self-Interested Director Transaction, 41 DePaul L.Rev. 655, 659–62 (1992). Reprinted by permission of the DePaul Law Review.

Bernard Black, Agents Watching Agents: The Promise of Institutional Investor Voice. Originally published in 38 UCLA L.Rev. 811, 821–22, 822–24 (1992). Copyright © (1992), The Regents of the University of California. All rights reserved. Reprinted with the permission of the author, The Regents of the University of California, and Fred B. Rothman & Co.

William W. Bratton, The Economic Structure of the Post-Contractual Corporation, 87 Nw.U.L.Rev. 180–197 (1992).

Victor Brudney & Marvin A. Chirelstein, A Restatement of Corporate Freezeouts, 87 Yale L.J. 1354, 1356–57 n. 9 (1977). Reprinted by permission of The Yale Law Journal Company and Fred B. Rothman & Company from The Yale Law Journal, vol. 87, pp. 1354, 1356–57 n. 9.

Warren Buffet, Letters to Shareholders from Berkshire Hathaway Inc. Annual Reports of 1978, 1981, 1983, 1984 and 1986. Reprinted by permission. Copyright © Warren Buffet and/or Berkshire Hathaway Inc. All rights reserved.

Diedre A. Burgman & Paul N. Cox, Corporate Directors, Corporate Realities and Deliberative Process: An Analysis of the Trans-Union Case, 11 J.Corp.L. 311, 359–65 (1986).

Henry N. Butler, The Contractual Theory of the Corporation, 11 George Mason L.Rev. 99 (1989).

Henry N. Butler and Larry E. Ribstein, Opting Out of Fiduciary Duties: A Response to the Anti-Contractarians, 65 Wash.L.Rev. 1, 12–18 (1990). Reprinted with permission of Washington Law Review and Fred B. Rothman & Co.

Robert Charles Clark, Agency Costs Versus Fiduciary Duties, in John W. Pratt and Richard J. Zeckhauser, Principals and Agents: The Structure of Business (1985) 55–64, 66–69. Reprinted by permission of the Harvard Business School Press.

Robert Charles Clark, Corporate Law 389–94 (1986). Reprinted by permission of the author.

John C. Coffee, Jr., Liquidity Versus Control: The Institutional Investor as Corporate Monitor, 91 Colum.L.Rev. 1277, 1281–89 (1991). This article originally appeared at 91 Colum.L.Rev. 1277 (1991). Reprinted by permission of the author and Columbia Law Review.

Comment, "Corporate Opportunity," 74 Harv.L.Rev. 765, 770–71 (1961).

Comment, Law for Sale: A Study of the Delaware Corporation Law of 1967, 117 U.Pa.L.Rev. 861, 861–62 (1969). Copyright © (1969) University of Pennsylvania Law Review.

James D. Cox, Financial Information, Accounting and the Law 181, 183–88 (1980).

James D. Cox, Insider Trading and Contracting: A Critical Response to the "Chicago School," 1986 Duke L.J. 628, 635, 646, 648.

James D. Cox & Harry Munsinger, Bias in the Boardroom: Psychological Foundations and Legal Implications of Corporate Cohesion, 48 L. & Contemp.Prob., Summer 1985, at 83, 103–4. Reprinted by permission of Duke University School of Law.

Developments in the Law—Conflicts of Interest in the Legal Profession, 94 Harv.L.Rev. 1244, 1339–42 (1981).

Frank H. Easterbrook and Daniel R. Fischel, The Economic Structure of Corporate Law 232, 242, 247, 248, 250–51, 252 (1991). Reprinted by permission of the publishers from THE ECONOMIC STRUCTURE OF CORPORATE LAW by Frank H. Easterbrook and Daniel R. Fischel, Cambridge, Mass.: Harvard University Press, Copyright © 1991 by the President and Fellows of Harvard College.

Frank H. Easterbrook and Daniel R. Fischel, Limited Liability and the Corporation, 52 U.Chi.L.Rev. 89 (1985), reprinted in The Economic Structure of Corporate Law, 41–44 (1991). Copyright © 1985, The University of Chicago Law Review. Reprinted with permission of University of Chicago Law Review.

Melvin Eisenberg, The Structure of the Corporation: A Legal Analysis 56–58 (1976).

Milton Friedman, Capitalism and Freedom 133–34 (1962).

Ronald Gilson & Renier Kraakman, The Mechanics of Market Efficiency, 70 Va.L.Rev. 549, 549–50 (1984).

Roberto C. Goizueta, Letter to the Editor, Harvard Business Review, (Nov.-Dec. 1990).

James J. Hanks, Jr., Evaluating Recent State Legislation on Director and Officer Liability Limitation and Indemnification, 43 Bus.Law. 1207, 1231–36 (1988). Copyright © 1988 by the American Bar Association. Reprinted with permission.

Geoffrey C. Hazard, Jr., Ethics in the Practice of Law 58, 60–61, 63–68 (1978). Yale University Press. Copyright © 1978 by Seven Springs Farm Center, Inc.

Leo Herzel and Leo Katz, Smith v. Van Gorkom: The Business of Judging Business Judgment, 41 Bus.Law. 1187, 1188–91 (1986). Copyright © 1986 by the American Bar Association. Reprinted with permission.

John A.C. Hetherington, Bargaining For Fiduciary Duties: Preserving the Vulnerability of the Disadvantaged?, 70 Wash.U.L.Q. 341, 351 (1992).

John A.C. Hetherington and Michael P. Dooley, Illiquidity and Exploitation: A Proposed Statutory Solution to the Remaining Close Corporation Problem, 63 Va.L.Rev. 1, 26–27 (1977).

Michael C. Jensen, Eclipse of the Public Corporation, Harvard Business Review 61 (Sept.-Oct. 1989). Reprinted by permission of the Harvard Business Review. Copyright © 1989 by the President and Fellows of Harvard College; all rights reserved.

Michael C. Jensen, Letter to the Editor, Harvard Business Review (Nov.-Dec. 1990).

Lyman P.O. Johnson, The Delaware Judiciary and the Meaning of Corporate Life and Corporate Law, 68 Tex.L.Rev. 865, 892–96 (1990). Copyright © (1990) by the Texas Law Review Association. Reprinted by permission.

Bayless Manning, A Taxonomy of Corporate Law Reform, in Commentaries on Corporate Structure and Governance, 120–122 (D. Schwartz ed. 1979); Copyright 1979 by the American Law Institute. Reprinted with the permission of the American Law Institute—American Bar Assocation Committee on Continuing Professional Education.

Bayless Manning, The Business Judgment Rule and the Director's Duty of Attention: Time for Reality, 39 Bus.Law. 1477, 1481–92, 1492–95 (1984). Copyright © 1984 by the American Bar Association. All rights reserved. Reproduced with the permission of the American Bar Association and its Section of Corporation, Banking and Business Law.

Bayless Manning with James J. Hanks, Jr., Legal Capital 5–40 (3d ed. 1990).

Harold Marsh, Are Directors Trustees? Conflict of Interest and Corporate Morality, 22 Bus.Law 35, 36–44, 48–49 (1966). Copyright © 1966 by the American Bar Association. All rights reserved. Reproduced with the permission of the American Bar Association and its Section of Corporation, Banking and Business Law.

David Millon, Redefining Corporate Law, 24 Ind.L.Rev. 223, 277 (1991).

Ira M. Milstein, Letter of the Editor, Harvard Business Review (Nov.-Dec. 1990).

Model Business Corporation Act Annotated, Comment to § 7.31. Reprinted with the permission of Prentice Hall Law & Business.

Andrew G.T. Moore II, The 1980s—Did We Save the Stockholders While the Corporation Burned?, 70 Wash.Univ.L.Q. 277, 281–82 (1992).

Allan Nevins & Frank E. Hill, Ford: Expansion and Challenge, 97, 99–100 (1957).

A New Perspective on Corporate Governance: Second Compact for Owners and Directors, Corporate Governance Advisor 1, 4–7 (August/September 1993). Reprinted with permission of The Corporate Governance Advisor.

William C. Norris, Letter to the Editor, Harvard Business Review (Nov.-Dec. 1990).

Charles R. O'Kelley, Jr., Filling Gaps in the Close Corporation Contract: A Transaction Cost Analysis, 87 Nw.U.L.Rev. 216, 231, 234–35, 238, 240–41 (1992).

Richard A. Posner, Economic Analysis of Law 392–93, 406–409 (4th ed. 1992). Reprinted by permission of Little, Brown and Company.

Alfred Rappaport, The Staying Power of the Public Corporation, Harvard Business Review 96 (Jan.-Feb. 1990). Reprinted by permission of the Harvard Business Review. Copyright © 1990 by the President and Fellows of Harvard College; all rights reserved.

Norman Redlich, Lawyers, The Temple, and the Market Place, 30 Bus.Law. 65 (1975). Copyright © 1975 by the American Bar Association. All rights reserved. Reprinted by permission of the American Bar Association.

Edward B. Rock, The Logic and (Uncertain) Significance of Institutional Shareholder Activism, 79 Geo.L.J. 445, 469–76 (1991). Reprinted with the permission of the publisher. Copyright © 1991 The Georgetown Law Journal Association and Georgetown University.

Mark J. Roe, Strong Managers, Weak Owners: The Political Roots of the Separation of Ownership from Control (forthcoming 1994). Reprinted with the permission of the author.

Roberta Romano, Public Pension Fund Activism in Corporate Governance Reconsidered, 93 Colum.L.Rev. 795, 796–852 (1993). Reprinted by permission of Columbia Law Review and the author.

Christopher Paul Saari, Note, The Efficient Capital Market Hypothesis, Economic Theory and the Regulation of the Securities Industry, 29 Stan.L.Rev. 1031, 1035–40 (1977). Copyright © 1977 by the Board of Trustees of Leland Stanford Junior University.

Carl W. Schneider, Joseph M. Manko & Robert S. Kant, Going Public—Practice Procedure and Consequences, 27 Vill.L.Rev. 1, 10–17, 19–20, 25–31, 33 (1981). Reprinted with permission from Villanova Law Review Volume 27, #1, pp. 1–51. Copyright © 1981 by Villanova University.

David J. Schulte, The Debatable Case for Securities Disclosure Regulation, 13 J.Corp.L. 535, 537–47 (1988).

E. Norman Veasey, Jesse A. Finkelstein & C. Stephen Bigler, Delaware Supports Directors with a Three-Legged Stool of Limited Liability, Indemnification and Insurance, 42 Bus.Law. 399, 404–12 (1987). Copyright © 1987 by the American Bar Association. All rights reserved. Reproduced with the permission of the American Bar Association and its Section of Corporation, Banking and Business Law.

Elliott J. Weiss, The Board of Directors, Management and Corporate Takeovers: "Opportunities and Pitfalls," in Arnold W. Sametz (ed.), The Battle for Corporate Control: Shareholder Rights, Stakeholder Interests and Managerial Responsibilities 36–38 (1991). (Leonard Stern School of Business, New York University).

Elliott J. Weiss, Social Regulation of Business Activity: Reforming the Corporate Governance System to Resolve an Institutional Impasse, 28 U.C.L.A. L.Rev. 343 (1981). Originally published in 28 U.C.L.A. L.Rev. 343. Copyright © 1981, The Regents of the University of California. All rights reserved.

Elliott J. Weiss, Whose Rules Should Govern Takeovers: Delaware's, the ALI's or Martin Lipton's?, 33 Ariz.L.Rev. 761 (1991). Copyright © 1991 by the Arizona Board of Regents. Reprinted by permission.

John W. Welch, Shareholders' Individual and Derivative Actions: Underlying Rationales and the Closely Held Corporation, 9 J.Corp.L. 147 (1984).

Ralph K. Winter, Jr., State Law, Shareholder Protection and the Theory of the Corporation, 6 J. Legal Studies 251, 256–57, 259, 275, 276 (1977).

Summary of Contents

Table of Contents

Table of Cases

The principal cases are in bold type. Cases cited or discussed in the text are roman type. References are to pages. Cases cited in principal cases and within other quoted materials are not included.

*

CORPORATIONS
LAW AND POLICY
MATERIALS AND PROBLEMS
Third Edition

*

Chapter 1

INTRODUCTION

A. AN HISTORICAL SKETCH OF THE CORPORATION

All modern business corporations, be they giant, well-known firms like Exxon or Coca–Cola or local companies that operate a single taxicab or grocery market, have four basic attributes:

(1) Separate entity with perpetual existence. Every corporation is a legal entity with an unlimited life that exists separate from those who provide it with risk capital (generally called "shareholders" or "stockholders") and those who manage its business (its "directors" and "officers," sometimes referred to collectively as its "managers").

(2) Limited liability. While a corporation is liable for its debts and obligations, the corporation's shareholders are responsible for the corporation's debts and obligations only to the extent of the resources they have invested in the corporation. Put differently, liability for a corporation's debts and obligations is limited to the assets the corporation owns.

(3) Centralized management. Shareholders elect a corporation's directors, but are deemed to have delegated to those directors (operating collectively as a "board of directors") the power to manage the corporation's business.

(4) Transferability of ownership interests. Shareholders can transfer to others their ownership interests in a corporation.

The history of corporation law is largely a chronology of the evolution of these attributes. However, legal scholars disagree on the nature of that history and the importance of earlier business organizations to the modern business corporation. What seems most likely is that, as with other organisms, the evolution of the business corporation is an eclectic process in which those characteristics that reflect contemporary policies and needs survive, and those that do not gradually are discarded. Alfred F. Conard, Corporations in Perspective 126 (1976).

1

1. DEVELOPMENTS IN ENGLAND

Some scholars contend that the development of the corporation in England (which is the forerunner of the modern American corporation) has early historical roots: Solon's Greece; the trading practices of the Assyrians or those in early Europe; or the Church's recognition (based on Roman law) of the concepts of juristic personality and collective entity. Others argue that these antecedents simply present analogies to later developments, and that English corporations are *sui generis*, having developed in response to English experience. See, e.g., James Willard Hurst, The Legitimacy of the Business Corporation in the Law of the United States 2 (1970).

Early English corporate law dealt with ecclesiastical, municipal and charitable bodies; only later did it focus on commercial associations. The early ecclesiastical corporation emerged partly as a device for the church to hold property. It was to these ecclesiastical, municipal and charitable bodies that the concession theory of corporate existence was first applied, i.e., that corporate existence could only be conferred by a grant of the sovereign.

The principal medieval commercial associations were the merchant guilds. Many of these guilds obtained royal charters as a means of obtaining special privileges, especially monopolies of trade. While the royal charter thus conferred privileges, it also served an important function to the sovereign. "The major impetus derived from the need of the national authority to assert itself and to establish its superiority in law over otherwise divisive local governments or interest groups." Id. at 3.

To a large extent, the merchant guilds served different purposes than modern corporations and lacked many of the characteristics that we commonly think of as essential to business corporations. Each member of a guild continued to trade on her own account, subject to the regulations of the guild, and remained individually liable for her own acts. The guilds functioned primarily to regulate trade by their members and to protect the monopoly against the intrusion of nonmembers.

During the period in which the guilds remained active, the Company of the Staple and the Company of the Merchant Adventurers were organized for trading overseas, the former handling the raw commodities of a town and the latter handling the export of manufactured products. These companies were virtually extensions of the guild principle to foreign trade. Their members remained individually liable and traded on their own accounts, subject to the regulations of the company, as enforced by a governor and assistants elected by the members. While royal charters for these early regulated companies have been found as early as the fourteenth century, they did not become common until the sixteenth century, with the expansion of foreign trade and settlement. Charters were obtained "largely because of the need to acquire a monopoly of trade for members of the company and governmental power over the territory for the company itself." Id. See also, L.C.B. Gower, The Principles of Modern Company Law 24 (4th ed. 1979)

In the sixteenth and early seventeenth centuries, the principle of trading on joint stock, previously confined to partnerships, was introduced into regulated companies, which gradually became joint commercial enterprises rather than trade protection associations. The East India Company, first chartered in 1600, best typifies the transition to joint stock. Its members could subscribe to joint stock or could carry on trade privately. Initially, each voyage was separately funded, and the proceeds were divided at the end of each voyage. Beginning in 1614, subscriptions to joint stock were taken for a period of years rather than for each voyage, and in the 1650s permanent joint stock was introduced. The shares were freely transferable and individual liability was limited to the amount of shares owned. The Company kept a stock transfer book. The capital stock grew to an enormous size, and in 1709 the Company made a large loan to the English government. It appears that the Company was the first corporation engaged in large state operations with a perpetual charter and, most significantly, a permanent capital.

By 1692, England had three large joint stock companies, the East India Company, the Royal African Company, and the Hudson's Bay Company. They were treated as extensions of the state and expected to perform important public functions, notably trade. They were given a monopoly in carrying on a particular trade and the right to make regulations with regard to it. In 1692, private trading was finally forbidden to members of joint stock companies.

The transition from the early trading companies to the permanent joint stock company also involved a shift in the function served by incorporation. According to a noted legal historian:

> From the late sixteenth century royal chartering of companies to develop foreign trade and colonies was a prominent feature of national policy. A royal charter was essential to such ventures. In times of political uncertainty merchants who combined for a foreign venture without explicit royal sanction risked prosecution for criminal conspiracy against the national interest. Moreover, the royal charter legitimized a range of public functions performed by such trading organizations in organizing terms of trade, setting up local governments, controlling customs, and, in effect, making foreign policy in their areas of operation. Thus, in this early phase such corporate privileges as served private profit seeking were an incidental return for the public jobs the corporation undertook. But throughout the late seventeenth century trade began to bulk larger than public functions in the activities of such companies. By the eighteenth century English lawmakers and businessmen alike had come to regard the corporation mainly as a structure useful to private trading operations; public responsibilities receded so far into the background as to become of secondary account.

Hurst, supra, at 4.

Trading on joint stock became increasingly frequent during the seventeenth century and was extended to companies for domestic operation. The practice of conducting business on a joint stock basis was not confined to incorporated companies. Unincorporated joint stock companies were able to obtain many of the advantages commonly associated with incorporation through use of complex deeds of settlement, which provided for transferability of shares, continuity of life, and central management. Some writers have suggested that these unincorporated associations, rather than the monopolistic trading companies, were the real forerunners of the modern business corporation, see, e.g., Ballantine on Corporations 33 (rev. ed. 1946), but it seems more likely that each form of association borrowed from the other as the two developed side by side. E. Merrick Dodd & Ralph J. Baker, Cases and Materials on Corporations 14 (2d ed. 1951).

The beginning of the eighteenth century was characterized by a boom of promotion and speculation in both incorporated and unincorporated companies, stimulated by the grandiose scheme of the South Sea Company to acquire virtually the entire English national debt by buying out the debt holders or exchanging the Company's stock for their holdings. When the flood of speculative enterprises was at its height in 1720, Parliament enacted the famous "Bubble Act," "An Act to Restrain the Extravagant and Unwarranted Practice of Raising Money by Voluntary Subscriptions for Carrying on Projects Dangerous to the Trade and Subjects of this Kingdom." The Bubble Act was aimed at restricting unincorporated joint stock companies with transferable shares; it forbade individuals to act as a corporation without a charter. The Act permitted incorporation, and some companies succeeded in obtaining charters. But the Act reflected a general distrust of corporations and had the effect of making both the Crown and Parliament hesitant to grant charters. This, plus vagueness in the Bubble Act's prohibitions, encouraged formation of unincorporated associations of the kind the Act was designed to destroy. In particular, entrepreneurs began to use deeds of settlement. This device "pooled resources in the control of trustees to manage them for designated business purposes. Equity would recognize the transferability of shares in such a pool. By the early nineteenth century such an arrangement might even include limited liability for debts * * *." Hurst, supra at 3. By 1825, when it was repealed, the Bubble Act had become a dead letter.

2.   DEVELOPMENTS IN THE UNITED STATES

The principles of the Bubble Act were extended to the American colonies, precluding the formation of unincorporated joint stock companies. Although the Act did not preclude the formation of duly chartered corporations, there was initial resistance to such entities which were perceived as instruments of royal prerogative and antithetical to the ideals of economic equality. In the late eighteenth century, however, corporations became more readily accepted. The earliest corporations were non-business entities such as charities, churches, cities and boroughs; these were followed shortly by the incorporation of banks, stage and navigation companies, turnpikes and canals and other financial and transportation businesses. During this period charters were granted by special acts of state legislatures, which, although the matter was not free of doubt, were tacitly understood to have acceded to the power of the Crown in the granting of corporate status.

By 1800 there were about 335 incorporated businesses, all of which had been created by such acts. For this reason, corporate policy during this period was shaped primarily by legislative practice. But the number of corporations formed in the early 1800s grew geometrically, and to cope with the increased legislative burden, charters became increasingly standardized. A corporate charter was also considered a valuable privilege, and the legislative monopoly on the conferral of this privilege created certain obvious temptations, to which some legislators and entrepreneurs inevitably yielded, to their mutual profit. Criticism of the resulting corruption resonated with a growing feeling on the part of the business community that incorporation was a right rather than a privilege, and that there should be equality of opportunity to acquire corporate status, rather than reserving it for a select few. In addition, incorporation was becoming a matter of economic necessity. As industrial and manufacturing concerns grew, individuals no longer had resources adequate to finance such enterprises. The combination of these factors eventually led states to enact general corporation laws that allowed any group of persons to organize themselves into a corporation by complying with the prescribed conditions. New York was the pioneer; in 1811, it enacted a law that gave the privilege of self-incorporation to the organizers of certain manufacturing companies, but limited the capital of those companies to $100,000 and their existence to 20 years.

This rapid growth of corporations in size and number did not occur without opposition. Throughout its history, some in America have feared the aggregations of capital and the growing power in American society that corporations seemed to represent. But this opposition did little to stem the tide of corporate growth; other states soon followed New York's lead and encouraged incorporation by enacting general corporation laws. Many of the restrictions on size and duration were lifted; a state had little incentive to enact stringent laws, for they would only encourage would-be corporations to seek charters in other states.

It was not uncommon in the early nineteenth century for states themselves to become partners in corporate enterprises, in part because many of the early corporations were involved in transportation and other business that the state traditionally had conducted. In addition, joining a corporation was a good way for a state to give financial support to an enterprise while providing some public accountability. Lawrence M. Friedman, A History of American Law 448 (1973). State involvement fell off in the 1830s and '40s. Many of the states' investments went bad in the Panic of 1837. In addition, the feeling grew that states had no business meddling in what was properly the sphere of private enterprise.

Thus the period from 1800 to 1850 saw substantial changes in the law of corporations. From its early form as an ad hoc organization that was as much a vehicle for conferring monopoly privileges on a small group of investors as it was a legal form for conducting business, the corporation evolved into a distinctive entity legally available to all, which could be shaped to suit the needs of particular businesses with few restrictions on entry, duration or management. Id. at 170.

Unleashed from the constraints imposed by special charters, corporations continued to flourish during the latter half of the nineteenth century. The burgeoning of the railroad industry did much to shape their growth. Management of a railway company required a larger central organization, and capital requirements often exceeded the resources of any single individual. A variety of financial instruments, for which the corporate form proved convenient, were devised to meet the railways' capital requirements. Corporations gradually became more dependent on the availability of an open market for corporate securities. Also during this era, men such as Cornelius Vanderbilt, Jay Gould and James Fisk became known for their "tawdry battles" in the stock market.

But once again the rapid growth of corporate power and the unchecked abuses which seemed to follow disturbed many Americans. Pressure grew to reform the internal corporate mechanism and to impose limits on corporations' power. By the 1860s, the device of the shareholder derivative suit had been developed to deal with managers' fraud, and other doctrines were emerging aimed at imposing greater control over corporate management. Railway regulation was a leading public issue in the 1870s, and in the 1880s the Interstate Commerce Commission was created, primarily for the purpose of controlling the railroads. In 1890 the Sherman Act was passed to combat "trusts" that dominated major industries. Thus, while during this period businesses by and large had a free hand to adapt the corporate instrument to their will, regulatory efforts also were initiated to circumscribe some of the power and impact of large corporations and their managers.

In 1888, New Jersey enacted an innovative new enabling statute, a general corporation law that authorized creation of corporations but included none of the traditional limitations on corporations' size, scope or duration. New Jersey further "modernized" its general corporation law in 1896.

Delaware entered the competition in 1899. A small state, Delaware passed an enabling statute with a view to attracting incorporations and thereby generating substantial franchise tax revenues. When New Jersey, under the leadership of Governor Woodrow Wilson, amended its corporation law in 1913 to reimpose a number of restrictive provisions, Delaware emerged as the venue of choice, at least for publicly traded corporations. It has retained that position ever since, and currently is the domicile of more than half the Fortune 500 companies and more than 40% of companies listed on the New York Stock Exchange.

More generally, the availability of enabling statutes in Delaware and elsewhere led other states to abjure efforts to use general corporation laws to regulate corporate activities. "Enablingism" became the dominant statutory mode. Today, state corporation laws almost universally allow any person to form a corporation, grant all corporations broad powers, and establish frameworks for corporate operations that include few regulatory restrictions. As one commentator has described it, these laws enable the organizers of a corporation to pour into an empty vessel the brew of their choice, free of almost all state-imposed constraints. Elvin R. Latty, Why Are Corporation Laws Largely "Enabling?" 50 Corn.L.Q. 599 (1965).

At this point, a student beginning the study of corporation law might well wonder about the role of federal law. After all, many corporations, especially publicly traded corporations, operate on a national or international basis. Doesn't it seem logical that federal law would regulate these national and multi-national organizations?

We address this question at greater length in Chapter 8. At this point, suffice it to say that almost all American corporations are creatures of state law. There is no general federal corporation law. However, certain provisions of the federal securities laws do regulate significant aspects of the relationship among participants in corporations, especially publicly owned corporations, largely by requiring the managers of publicly owned corporations to disclose to shareholders and prospective investors important information about those corporations and their activities.[1] See Chapters 10, 14, 18 and 19.

B. REGULATING THE MODERN CORPORATION: THE SEARCH FOR ACCOUNTABILITY

In the mid-twentieth century, the prevalence and increasing uniformity of state enabling laws led some to conclude that all interesting questions of corporation law had been answered. In 1962, then-Professor Bayless Manning wrote that "corporation law, as a field of intellectual endeavor, is dead in the United States. * * * We have nothing left but our great empty corporation statutes—towering skyscrapers of rusty girders, internally welded together and containing nothing but wind." Bayless Manning, The Shareholder's Appraisal Remedy: An Essay for Frank Coker, 72 Yale L.J. 223, 245 (1962).

From a certain perspective, Manning was right. Debate had raged for decades about the nature of the corporation, especially the large, publicly traded corporation. At times, the dominant concept was of the corporation as strictly private property, owned by and operated exclusively for the benefit of its shareholders. At other times, the corporation

---

1. The federal government also regulates corporations through a variety of substantive laws, including antitrust, banking, civil rights, environmental, labor and product safety laws.

was seen as a creation of the state, formed for, and obligated to advance, the broader interests of the public, whose interests included both increasing shareholders' wealth *and* taking some account of other groups affected by a corporation's activities.

When Manning wrote, corporation law had not resolved this debate, but seemed to have successfully papered it over by relying on notions of long-run profit maximization. On the one hand, courts paid lip service to the idea that corporations were to be operated exclusively for shareholders' benefit; on the other hand, they allowed managers to engage in conduct that advanced the interests of non-shareholder groups whenever the managers claimed such action would benefit shareholders in the long run. This rationalization survived tolerably well into the 1960s. Then, dramatic economic and social changes began to subject it to considerable stress.

Increasing concerns about social values and social justice led to renewed debate about the extent of corporations' social responsibilities. A faltering economy, industries that seemed unable to compete with foreign rivals, and disclosures that many well-known companies had made illegal domestic political contributions and paid bribes to foreign government officials, generated concern about how effectively American corporations were being managed. And then came the 1980s, summarized as follows by William T. Allen, chief judge of the Delaware Court of Chancery (the nation's preeminent trial court specializing in corporate law issues):

> The evolution of the junk bond market and takeover entrepreneurs, the growth of institutional investors, and the striking emergence of a global economy came together in the 1980s to force massive changes in the private sector of our economy. In that process, tensions and antinomies in corporation law theory that had been lying beneath the surface for a very long time, were forced out into the open. As a result, during the 1980s, corporation law became not boring and marginal, but important, even fascinating. * * * Basic questions excited argument, and the *most* basic questions—"What *is* a corporation? What purpose does it serve?"— became the stuff of wide discussion and statutory activity. Everything old became new again.

William T. Allen, Our Schizophrenic Conception of the Business Corporation, 14 Cardozo L.Rev. 261, 263–64 (1992).

The goals of corporation law include promoting the efficient operation of business corporations and providing fairly for the interests of those who participate in corporations. If every participant in a corporation had the same goals, had access to all relevant information, and was able to process that information in a perfectly rational fashion, little need would exist for a body of law to govern their relationships. The participants would reach agreement at every juncture, no matter what structure they used to reach those decisions, because their information and reasoning processes would be identical.   See Kenneth J. Arrow, The Limits of Organization 68–70 (1974).

But in the real world, participants in corporations operate in an environment characterized by uncertainty, limited information and "bounded rationality."   Participants' goals also often differ.   Consequently, the principal task of corporation law is to create a governance structure for corporations that promotes an appropriate degree of accountability among the participants.   In addressing this task, the following questions must be considered.

     1.   To what extent is it reasonable to rely on market forces and contractual arrangements to promote management accountability to the shareholders and prevent overreaching?

     2.   If legal intervention is desirable, should it be in the form of mandating structural devices, such as meetings and voting; imposing fiduciary obligations on those who hold positions of power; requiring disclosure of information; or providing additional protection to those, such as creditors, whose relationship with the corporation is primarily contractual?

     3.   How is, and how should, responsibility for regulating corporations be divided between federal and state law?

Albert O. Hirschman, an economist, has developed a conceptual framework that is helpful when analyzing these questions.   In Exit, Voice and Loyalty (1970), Hirschman addressed the problems posed by organizations that operate at less than peak efficiency, as almost all organizations do.   He was concerned primarily with large organizations, but developed concepts that are relevant to small organizations as well.

Hirschman postulated that two fundamentally different strategies are available to a person who is dissatisfied with an organization.   One strategy is "exit": the person can sever her connection with the organization.   A motorist can decide not to buy the same brand of car again after having suffered with a "lemon;" a shareholder can sell her stock in a corporation that pays its executives bonuses she believes are grossly excessive; a law student can move out of her parents' home to escape their incessant questions about why she spends so much time studying.

The other strategy is "voice": a person can remain within the organization and attempt to remedy the situation.   The motorist can write a letter of complaint; the shareholder can attend the annual meeting and question the company's bonus plan; the law student can try to explain that her professors' demands are unreasonable.

Hirschman pointed out that a combination of exit and voice frequently will lead to more improvement in the organization's performance than exclusive reliance on one or the other.   However, a participant's willingness to rely on voice will depend heavily on her estimates of the prospects for success and,

> while exit requires nothing but a clearcut either-or decision, voice is essentially an *art* constantly evolving in new directions.   The situa-

tion makes for an important bias in favor of exit when options are present: customer-members [or shareholders] will ordinarily base their decisions on *past* experience with the cost and effectiveness of voice even though the possible *discovery* of lower cost and greater effectiveness is of the very essence of voice. The presence of the exit alternative can therefore tend to *atrophy the development of the art of voice.*

Id. at 43.

Economists generally favor exit. They argue that either exit will force the organization to eliminate inefficiency or the organization will be replaced by a more efficient competitor. As applied to corporation law, this view implies that legal rules should be directed primarily at sustaining market forces and enforcing contractual arrangements, and that legal intervention to advance other goals generally is unnecessary and inefficient.

As the above quotation indicates, Hirschman suggests a different approach. In some circumstances, voice will be more effective, either eliciting a positive response from those who control the corporation or causing new leaders to be chosen. Moreover, Hirschman notes that if exit is the only available option, the most quality-conscious participants in the organization are likely to exit first. But those participants often will be more qualified to help the organization identify and overcome its problems than those who remain. Consequently, structuring the organization to promote voice may advance the socially important goal of preventing the organization's deterioration from becoming cumulative.

Hirschman also points out that a third factor, "loyalty," may determine whether a participant chooses to pursue exit or voice. People tend to have stronger feelings of loyalty toward social or political organizations, such as their family or political party, than toward economic organizations such as corporations. Thus, they generally are more reluctant to sever ties with their families or to change political parties than to trade-in a Chevy for a Toyota or to sell General Motors stock.

Loyalty is more intangible than exit and voice. But how an organization is structured and what strategy the organization employs to deal with participants' dissatisfactions can have a powerful influence over their feelings of loyalty and whether they choose exit or voice when they become dissatisfied.

For students of corporation law, Hirschman's analytic structure provides a useful frame of reference. To what extent does a given rule facilitate exit or voice? Does the law establish an appropriate balance between exit and voice? How might exit or voice operate in any given situation, and how should the availability of one or the other influence the rights and remedies of the participants? How does the size of the corporation (public or closely-held) affect the need to create different exit and voice mechanisms and the rules that facilitate each?

Hirschman's work also reminds us of the need to take account of intangibles such as loyalty. Although the extent to which they influence an individual's decision in any specific situation often are difficult to predict, Hirschman reminds us that intangibles often dominate an individual's decision making. Economic analysis has many virtues. But the analyst who treats every person as an interchangeable "rational utility maximizer" overlooks the fact that people differ in all sorts of very human ways. These differences should be taken into account in many contexts, of which corporate law is but one.

Chancellor Allen made much the same point when he gave the following advice to students embarking on the study of corporation law:

* * * As a system of rules, the legal system is astonishingly complex, with an enormous variety of rules regulating our conduct and other rules regulating the legal system itself. When we start out in our study of law, we think that to become a lawyer it is necessary to learn these rules, especially the rules concerning the operation of the legal machinery. We are right to think that, but we would be badly wrong to think that knowledge of legal rules is all that we need to understand the legal world.

When we study corporation law we surely must learn the content of the corporation law statutes and the rules announced in court decisions. We must learn the analytical and theoretical tools of a lawyer, so that we can manipulate these rules within the permissible zone of their ambiguity in order to guide and protect clients. But if we were to learn the content of legal rules alone we would achieve only a dry and brittle power that would quickly snap under the dynamic cross-pressures of complex and contradictory real life.

In corporation law, as in every area of law, learning the rules, and the permissible manipulation of the rules, is the crucial beginning. But it is only the beginning. We must discover and understand the principles that stand behind the rules. But even that step is not yet enough. To approach understanding, we must be able to see legal rules and principles as social constructs, affected by their internal logic, but affected even more profoundly by the social world in which they exist.

Legal ideas are not static abstractions; the legal process is not simply a deductive exercise, and the evolution of law is not an inevitable working out of anything. In the judicial process the law of each case is constructed from generalities. In explaining that process everything counts. Ideas about efficiency certainly count. But ideology also counts. And social forces that judges feel but can only vaguely articulate may be important. In this process, the internal logic of the legal system itself will serve as an important constraint, even if it is not determinative in the way our naive selves first thought.

The law, like ourselves, is always in flux, always 'becoming.'
* * *

Allen, supra, at 278–79.

Chapter 2

INTRODUCTION TO THE
ECONOMICS OF
THE FIRM

This chapter introduces economic concepts fundamental to the analysis of business ventures. Every business venture involves potential tensions between the participants. By obtaining a grasp of the economic concepts discussed in this chapter, a student of corporation law should be able to better identify and understand those tensions, and thus to better understand what is at stake in the settings to which corporation law applies.

To facilitate students' exploration of these fundamental concepts, this chapter makes the simplifying assumption that the venture in question involves only two parties: a person who owns the business but wishes to do little or no work in it, and a second person who will do most or all of the work. We will refer to the first person as the "owner" or "employer" and to the second person as the "employee," even though they may not have a traditional "employer-employee" relationship. The principles used to analyze their relationship, however, apply equally to more complex settings. You will have frequent occasion to recall them as you work with problems involving more complex ventures in succeeding chapters of this book.

In any business venture, the parties have a shared interest in agreeing on a structure that produces the largest total return to the venture at the lowest cost. In the real world, however, such a structure is difficult to achieve because each of the parties probably will want to receive as large a share as possible of the venture's total profits. Moreover, the parties will not know what the future holds, and may have different preferences concerning which risks of the business they are willing to bear as well as different capacities to bear or insure against those risks. In addition, if the employee does not receive all the profits of the business, she will not work as hard as she would if she owned the business herself. Because of these conflicts, the self-interest of each party, viewed from an *ex post* perspective (after the venture has begun or when it is finished) will not always coincide with the interest of the venture as a whole.

Despite these conflicts, both parties see gains from entering into the venture together. The goal of the analysis in this chapter is to understand how the parties try to minimize the effects of the conflicts and maximize the value of the transaction for each of them. To achieve those ends, they must decide how to distribute the risks of the future uncertainties of the business and how to create incentives that will encourage the employee to work for the best interest of the venture rather than exclusively for her own interest. As we shall see, there is a fundamental tension between these objectives that makes it impossible to achieve them completely. The owner will also have to obtain information so that he can see whether the employee is doing what he is supposed to, and establish sanctions for the employee's failure to do so (these supervisory procedures often are referred to as "monitoring"). All these steps must be taken *before* the venture begins; i.e., the problem must be viewed from an *ex ante* perspective. The parties are willing to take these steps because, as noted above, they believe that they will each gain more from working together than they would if they worked separately.

PROBLEM
OF WINE AND WINEMAKING *

Ann Jones has recently purchased a vineyard in the middle of California's Napa Valley. The vineyard produces grapes which she proposes to sell to winemakers throughout the area. She does not anticipate making wine on her own. She is unable to farm the land herself because she lives in Los Angeles. Ann is aware that growing grapes is a risky activity. Her crop yields and profits will depend on unpredictables such as the weather and the price of grapes at harvest time (which, in turn, will be influenced by the availability of grapes from other sources). The size and quality of her crop also will depend upon the effort and ability of the person who does the farming.

Ann has recently met Bill Smith, a young man who has the necessary equipment, expertise and inclination to do the work necessary to grow grapes. Ann and Bill wish to negotiate an advantageous contract whereby Bill will handle the farming at Ann's vineyard. For the moment, they intend to cover only the coming growing season in the contract; they are proceeding on the assumption that thereafter, they will not deal with each other again.

At the outset, a number of issues must be decided: the level of compensation paid to Bill, the structure of the compensation plan, and the nature and extent of Bill's duties. The first issue on which they intend to negotiate is the compensation structure, although they recog-

---

* We are indebted to Professors Steven C. Salop and Warren F. Schwartz of the Georgetown University Law Center. Professor Salop is the principal author of this problem. Both he and Professor Schwartz assisted us greatly in the following notes.

nize that all the issues are closely related. Two alternatives have been proposed:

(i) *Employment* : Bill will be paid a monthly salary. Ann will retain the entire proceeds of the harvest (less the salary to Bill).

(ii) *Tenancy* : Bill will lease the land from Ann for a yearly rent in exchange for the right to receive the entire proceeds of the harvest.

Although the subsequent sections of the chapter formally analyze the determinants of the structure which the parties might adopt, consider, as a matter of your own intuition and experience, how the following factors might influence Ann and Bill in choosing one of these plans or a variant of one of them?

(a) Ann is rich and Bill is poor or vice versa.

(b) Ann owns a number of other vineyards in the same area.

(c) Ann owns a number of other vineyards in other areas of the state or in different states.

(d) Bill is young and intends to grow grapes under annual arrangements like this one (but with other local owners) for the next 20 years.

(e) Ann has experience growing grapes herself and visits the area frequently.

(f) Growing grapes in this region is not difficult and requires little expertise or judgment—only hard work.

A. RISK

1. INTRODUCTION

When someone other than the owner of an enterprise is brought in to do some or all of the work of the business, one question affecting the structure of their agreement is how they will allocate the various risks of the venture. Such risks can be broken down into two categories. One type is "non-controllable" risk. A non-controllable risk is one which, although it may affect some businesses more than others, is always present to some extent: the weather, the general state of the economy, the level of interest rates, market prices, war and peace, etc. These risks cannot be completely eliminated. The other type of risk is "controllable" risk, i.e., a risk which relates to the specific business: its competitive position, its product line, the quality of its management, the adequacy of its physical plant, etc. The extent to which such risks can be controlled depends on how well the people assigned to perform specific tasks in a business actually perform them. As we will see, successful performance depends in part on the incentives the performers have to act in the best interest of the business and in part on the monitoring and sanctioning devices which have been created to reduce the likelihood that they will not perform well.

2. NON-CONTROLLABLE RISKS

When we refer to the non-controllable risks of a venture, we actually mean two things: those risks that are truly beyond control (war and peace) and those that will remain after all reasonable efforts at controlling them have been exercised.

The question of who should bear these non-controllable risks is best approached by first looking at the means available to each party to avoid bearing the risk. One such means is to pool the cost of the risk with others who bear the same risk—by purchasing insurance, for example. Essentially, risk pooling reduces the risk for the members of the pool because each member bears a pro rata share of the total loss suffered by the pool. The total loss likely to be suffered by a large number of people subject to the same or similar risk is easier to predict than the loss that any one of them is likely to suffer. A person growing grapes, for example, can limit her non-controllable risks by purchasing insurance against floods, tornados, hurricanes and drought.

A second means of limiting these risks is to invest in a number of ventures, each of which involves risks different from the others. A simple example of this kind of diversification is provided by considering an investor in the stock market. The investor can reduce the effect of a decline in the value of any given stock by diversifying the number and nature of the stocks which he owns. Although such diversification will not completely eliminate the risk of loss in any given stock, it will reduce the total risk because the performance of the entire portfolio is more likely to be balanced between gains and losses. Thus the diversified portfolio will offer a more certain return than can be obtained from any particular stock.

Diversification can take many forms. If the principal variable affecting the harvest in a vineyard is the amount of rainfall, an owner can diversify her risk by investing in ten vineyards, each of which is expected to have different rainfall. The owner also can diversify by investing her other capital in stocks and bonds, a strawberry patch (see Chapter 6), baseball trading cards and Impressionist paintings, each of which involves risks that are of a completely different nature from, and are independent of, the risks of a vineyard.

The third way of protecting against non-controllable risks is to place the burden of the risk on the person who is best able to bear it. For example, if A is richer than B, it may be desirable for A to bear the risk because a large loss will have less catastrophic consequences for her.

In thinking about the vineyard problem, also consider Bill's investment. Unlike Ann, Bill is investing human capital. Because he cannot work for more than one employer, he is not able to diversify his capital in the same way that Ann can. This inability to diversify may affect his attitude toward risk and his choice of how to arrange his relationship with Ann.

3. RISK PREFERENCE

In determining the optimal allocation of risk, it also is important to take into account each party's subjective preference for risk.

An individual who is risk neutral makes decisions based solely on the expected return involved. (The "expected return" is the sum of each possible return multiplied by the probability of that return.) The magnitude of the risk is irrelevant to her decision. For example, suppose an individual is given a choice between receiving a certain payment of $140 or Coin Toss A, in which she will receive $200 if the coin comes up heads but only $100 if the coin comes up tails. A risk neutral person would prefer Coin Toss A to the certain payment of $140 because the expected return would be greater.

	return	probability	expected return
Coin Toss A:	$100	0.5	$ 50
	$200	0.5	$100
			$150
Payment:	$140	1.0	$140

In contrast, a risk averse person takes the magnitude of risk, as well as the expected return, into account when making a decision. In the previous example, a risk averse person would think: "Even though there is a 50% chance that I will get $200 if the coin comes up heads, there is also a 50% chance I will end up with only $100, if the coin comes up tails. Maybe I'm better off taking a certain $140 to risking ending up with only $100." The risk averse person then would decide whether the $10 greater expected return from Coin Toss A is enough to compensate her for the risk of receiving only $100, or $40 less than she would receive if she avoided the risks of Coin Toss A. Economists assume that people in general are risk averse and that, in this example, most people would think about their choice as described above. But economists also would acknowledge that the decision by any given person to take the certain $140 or participate in Coin Toss A would turn on how risk averse that person was.

One customary economic measure of risk aversion is the "risk premium." A risk premium is the amount of money a risk avoider would pay to obtain certainty. In Coin Toss A, a risk avoider would be prepared to pay $10 as a risk premium to obtain a certain $140.

The risk premium is one useful measure of risk aversion, but it indicates nothing about another potentially relevant factor, the expected variation of the returns. Consider Coin Toss B, described below:

	return	probability	expected return
Coin Toss B:	$ 0	0.5	$ 0
	$300	0.5	$150
			$150
Payment:	$140	1.0	$140

A risk avoider prepared to pay $10 to avoid the risk involved in Coin Toss A presumably would be prepared to pay at least the same premium to avoid the risk of Coin Toss B. Clearly though, because of the greater variation ($300 or nothing, rather than $200 or $100), Coin Toss B involves more risk than Coin Toss A. Thus, we can predict with confidence that, if the choice was between Coin Toss A and Coin Toss B, a risk averse person would select Coin Toss A.

The opposite of risk aversion is risk loving. As does a risk avoider, a risk loving person takes the magnitude of the risk, as well as the expected return, into account. But neither Coin Toss example would pose any problem for a risk loving person; she would surely choose either Coin Toss A or Coin Toss B over a certain payment of $140. The issue would become difficult only if the amount of the certain payment was increased to more than $150. Then a risk lover would focus on the comparison between the certain return and the higher return available if the coin comes up heads, rather than comparing the certain return to the lowest possible return, as would a risk averse person. But again, whether a risk lover will select the certain payment or the coin toss will depend on how large the certain payment is and how risk loving that person is. Here, too, variation may be significant. If the choice were between Coin Toss A and Coin Toss B, a risk lover would select Coin Toss B.

4. CONTROLLABLE RISKS

What do we mean by a "controllable risk?" Generally, a risk is considered controllable when one of the parties, by acting or not acting, can cause good or bad things to happen to the venture. For example, if the size of the harvest will depend in part on the willingness to get up before dawn to spray the vines with a chemical to prevent insect damage, the risk to the venture is that the employee will not expend the effort to do so.

The heart of the difficulty in distributing risk among the parties is that a party will have a greater incentive to control a risk which that party bears. Thus, in the spraying example, if the employee receives the same compensation no matter how many grapes are produced, he will have little incentive to rise early and spray the vines to prevent the insect damage. When a person does less than is optimal to control a risk, that failure is called "shirking." (More generally, the danger that a person who does not bear a risk will not take steps to control that risk is referred to as "moral hazard.") To avoid shirking, the owner (who *does* bear the risk) must monitor the employee to ensure that he takes risk reducing precautions. From a risk controlling perspective, it may be most efficient to place the risk on the employee so as to avoid the costs of monitoring.

At the same time, however, the party who is in the best position to control the risk may not (for reasons relating to risk preference) be the best person to bear it. If the owner is wealthier, less risk averse, or better able to diversify or insure against the risk, from a risk bearing perspective, she should bear the risk. Thus there is a clear tension between the risk controlling and the risk bearing perspectives.

The spraying example illustrates this general problem. We might place all the risk on the employer, thus requiring her to monitor the employee to reduce the shirking. In such case, the employer would bear the costs of monitoring and would have to come up with appropriate monitoring devices. These problems are discussed in Section B. However, because shirking *is* within the control of the employee, it may be better to have him bear the costs of his own shirking and thus avoid the necessity of monitoring. Neither of these allocations of risk is a perfect solution; each entails costs the parties would prefer to avoid and neither will eliminate completely the employee's shirking. What is required, therefore, is an arrangement that will be the best compromise between the conflicting risk controlling and risk bearing objectives of the parties. The possibilities for such an arrangement are discussed in the following sections.

B. ALLOCATING RISK TO THE OWNER

If the owner is less risk averse than the employee, the parties will not want the employee to bear the risk of the success or failure of the business. Instead, it will be preferable that the employee be paid a salary and the owner receive the profits or incur the losses. In this situation, the risk of the employee's shirking takes on greater significance for the owner who must now directly or indirectly monitor the employee. Such monitoring consists of two parts. First, the owner must decide what constitutes optimal performance by the employee. Second, having decided that, the owner must determine whether the desired level of performance is occurring or has occurred. The first part requires looking at shirking from an *ex ante* perspective, i.e., before the employee has begun to work. The second part examines the employee's conduct from an *ex post* perspective, i.e., after the employee has begun to work. In considering the costs and benefits of various monitoring devices, it is useful to keep these two perspectives in mind.

One solution would be for the owner to supervise the employee directly. This form of monitoring combines both perspectives: the owner is physically able both to prescribe optimal standards and observe whether they are being met. It also has obvious drawbacks. Deciding what the employee should do and obtaining the relatively detailed information about whether he did it would be time-consuming and costly and contrary to the principal reason the owner hired the employee, i.e., to enable the owner to spend relatively little time and effort on the business. Of course, if the owner did not want to directly supervise the employee, she could hire a supervisor. Doing that, however, would create an additional problem: Who would supervise the supervisor to ensure that she did not shirk? In a small business, the costs of such an arrangement would almost certainly outweigh the benefits, although you should keep this alternative in mind when you study publicly held corporations.

An alternative monitoring device would be an employment contract between the owner and the employee. Such a contract would contain elements of both parts of monitoring: it would specify the employee's duties and it would prescribe the sanctions to be imposed if the employee failed to perform those duties.

In deciding whether such a contract is desirable, let us examine each part separately. Some aspects of the employee's work can be satisfactorily defined in a contract; other aspects are more problematic. Consider a saleswoman for a clothing manufacturer whose job is to arrange for the clothing to be sold in stores in a given geographical area by meeting with buyers from those stores. A contract could be drafted with a provision specifying the number of hours the saleswoman was required to work and the number of stores she had to visit. Would such a provision be desirable? Where success is measured primarily by the quality of a person's effort, it is difficult to define the optimal level of that effort in a contract. The number of hours worked may not be as important as the way in which the hours were spent; the number of stores visited may not be as significant as what transpired in each store. Most important, a large number of hours spent working does not guarantee corresponding profits.

Because of the *ex ante* drafting difficulty, shirking may continue even if there is a contract. This shirking does not vitiate the desirability of a contract; it may simply cause us to bring an *ex post* perspective to bear on the drafting. In the example of the saleswoman, consider the following provision:

> Salesperson will use her best efforts in selling employer's clothes. Any dispute over this issue will be resolved by an arbitrator mutually acceptable to the parties.

The term "best efforts" prescribes the saleswoman's efforts *ex ante*. In the terms we have used, it calls upon the employee to expend the same effort she would expend if she bore the entire risk. However, it does have the advantage of being given content after the fact by reference to the actual circumstances encountered by the employee and the steps she took to accomplish the task assigned to her.

From an *ex post* perspective, the enforcement mechanism of such a clause may be a useful monitoring device. In deciding whether to enforce the clause, the employer could use easily observable measures to alert her to the possibility that the employee was shirking. For example, the employer could compare the sales of the employee with those made in the previous year or by other salespersons. If, after such comparison, the owner also found that the venture's sales were high, she could infer that the saleswoman had used her best efforts. If, however, sales were low, the owner could then invoke the judicial settling-up process to determine whether the saleswoman had, in fact, used her "best efforts." Because the saleswoman could not know *ex ante* whether her employer would try to enforce the contract, her incentive to shirk would be reduced.

From an *ex ante* perspective, another problem encountered in devising an appropriate monitoring system is that the parties may not foresee all the contingencies that might arise over the life of the contract, particularly if the contract is for a long period of time. Moreover, some contingencies which are foreseeable may be so unlikely to occur that the costs of drafting provisions to deal with them would exceed the expected benefits. If, however, such a contingency did arise, how should the contract be construed? Some economists argue that a court should decide how the parties would have provided for the contingency if they had originally thought to do so.

At first blush, such a method of analysis may seem both impossible and unrealistic. But economists who support this approach would argue that, although each party may have been concerned primarily with maximizing her own return from the venture rather than with the venture's total return, it is fair to assume each party would recognize that her share is likely to increase if the total return is greater. Therefore, a court should assume the parties would have adopted the provision maximizing the overall return.

Other analysts, including some economists, question whether the provision that would maximize overall returns easily can be identified and suggest that, in any event, reasonable persons may well be more concerned with ensuring a fair division of returns than with maximizing total returns. (These arguments will recur, in a variety of contexts, throughout this book.)

Although less expensive than direct supervision by the owner, contracting is a costly method of specifying optimal performance for both parties. Information, negotiation and drafting costs all must be incurred (lawyers' time is not cheap). Moreover, the potential cost of enforcing contracts are high and cannot be disregarded, even if they never actually materialize. Finally, students should keep in mind that the use of a contract shifts the ultimate resolution of a dispute to a third party—the court—and thereby creates uncertainty for both parties to the contract.

C. ALLOCATING RISK TO THE EMPLOYEE

As we have seen, one organizational model places the risk of the employee's shirking entirely on the owner of the business. The owner then will find it necessary to provide incentives to the employee and to incur monitoring costs, which will reduce (but not eliminate completely) the employee's shirking.

The opposite extreme would be an organizational model that places the risk of shirking entirely on the employee. For example, the owner could rent the business to the employee for a fixed fee and allow the employee to retain all the profits. Such an arrangement would create gains for the owner by eliminating her monitoring costs; almost by definition, the only monitoring would be the employee's own self-monitoring. If the employee works less hard, it will be because she values her non-work activities more than her work; her reduced profits from the business will be counterbalanced by the value she places on those activities.

A less drastic way of allocating risk is to compensate the employee so as to reward her efforts or penalize her if her efforts do not produce satisfactory results. For example, in the previous example of the saleswoman, consider the following:

> Salesperson is to be paid an annual salary of $x. However, if the net income to employer from the sale of clothing in stores for which salesperson is responsible is less than $y, her annual salary shall be reduced by z percent.

Is such a provision desirable? The relationship between the employee's effort and the owner's ultimate profit probably depends on a number of factors. Some of them probably are beyond the control of either party; some that are within their control may not relate to the specific problem of shirking. If shirking is the owner's principal concern, it may make more sense to tie the salary reduction to the gross volume of clothing that the saleswoman negotiates in each store. On the other hand, to the extent that the profits of the venture *do* depend on the saleswoman's efforts, such a clause creates incentives for the saleswoman and reduces the need to monitor her performance.

Even when the risks of the venture during the period of employment are allocated to the employee, a need for monitoring may exist because the parties have differing time horizons. An employee whose compensation is based on a measure such as gross sales for the year will necessarily want to increase current sales. The owner, in contrast, probably will have a longer time horizon; she may be willing to forego higher sales this year if her firm is likely to be able to sell the same goods, at a significantly higher price, in the following year. Or, in the vineyard problem, the employee may wish to maximize the yield so as to obtain more immediate revenue from a higher harvest while the owner might choose to crop the vines more severely so as to improve the quality of the grapes they will bear in future years. In such cases, monitoring will be necessary to protect the longer-range interests of the owner.

Finally, consider the situation of the employee after she stops working for the owner. If she shirked, she may have damaged her reputation, thus reducing her value to people who may be interested in hiring her in the future. This reduction will occur because, in making hiring decisions, employers take into account the way in which people have performed in the past. Hence, evidence that an employee has worked diligently will be valuable to the employee, because it will provide a signal to a future employer that less monitoring of the employee's shirking will be necessary. Note that the use of reputation as a self-monitoring device does not involve any reallocation of the risks or returns of the venture. Thus, reputation is a useful element in both the employment and tenancy models.

D. IN SEARCH OF THE MIDDLE GROUND

We have already seen that under one polar model, the owner will bear all the risks of the venture. Were risk the parties' only concern, this would be a desirable model, assuming, as is often the case, that the owner is the better risk bearer. But such risk allocation carries a price; the owner must incur monitoring costs and create incentives to reduce the likelihood of shirking. The profits of the venture will be reduced by these costs. Under the other polar solution, the employee bears all the risks but realizes the gains resulting from her own efforts to control those risks. Again, if controlling risk were the parties' only concern, this would be a desirable model; it has the lowest monitoring and enforcement costs and it puts the risk on the person best able to control it. But this model also carries a price: the employee must bear risks which the employer is better able to bear.

Might there be a satisfactory middle ground? Suppose that the parties agreed to divide the profits 50–50 (or some other mutually agreeable percentage). The employee would still have some incentive to shirk. This incentive would be reduced, however, because the shirking would reduce the employee's own share of the profits. The owner would still need to monitor, but because of the employee's interest in the profits of the venture, the monitoring costs would be reduced. This reduction, however, is achieved by placing part of the risk on the party less able to bear it. The parties thus have to search for that distribution of risk that is best for them, taking into account the desire both to minimize monitoring costs and to place the risk on the party better able to bear it.

As we shall see, corporations involve a complex network of arrangements between owners and employees similar to those we have been discussing. What motivates all these arrangements are the choices the shareholders and managers of a corporation make about how to distribute the risks inherent in their particular business venture.

E. AN INTEGRATED APPROACH

WILLIAM A. KLEIN AND JOHN C. COFFEE, BUSINESS ORGANIZATION AND FINANCE
5, 12–14, 21–24, 34–38 (5th Ed. 1993).

Suppose that a grocery store is owned by a person, Pamela, who devotes her full time to the management of the store. That is, she owns and operates the store. The two functions, ownership and management (operation), need not be combined in the same person. If Pamela hires a person to serve as manager in her place and delegates broad decision-making powers to that person, she is still the owner and is still called a sole proprietor. The possibility of specialization, or separation of functions, is an attribute of a sophisticated (and efficient) economic system; it also produces the kinds of problems that require the application of lawyer skills. But that gets ahead of our story.

* * *

* * * To some considerable degree, the relationships among creditors, suppliers, employees, and owners are viewed here as ones involving contributors to a *joint economic enterprise.* A more customary approach would depict the owner as the core of the enterprise and the other elements as inputs hired by the owner and having only a very narrow interest in the enterprise. On this latter view, there is less jointness, less commonality of interest. Either view is permissible and both are useful. The joint-enterprise perspective seems to offer more fresh insights and a better understanding of economic functions. If we were concerned solely with traditional, established legal doctrine, the perspective in which the owner establishes the business and then hires capital, employees, and other inputs would probably be more appropriate, though some legal institutions may be evolving in the direction of the joint-undertaking model.

Suppose that Pamela hires Chuck, whose duties will be primarily to stock the shelves and keep the store clean. In a small business it is unlikely that there will be a written contract spelling out the mutual rights and obligations of Chuck and Pamela. Even though not spelled out in writing, however, a set of rights and obligations does exist. The terms of this implicit agreement can be found in part in common-law *doctrines of agency and contract,* and in part in modern legislation affecting the employment relationship. * * *

* * *

In the common parlance, Chuck is an *"employee."* In legal terminology, Pamela is the *"principal"* and Chuck is an *"agent."* Within this category of principal and agent, the law of agency defines a subcategory that covers the Pamela–Chuck relationship, namely, *"master"* and *"servant."* Pamela is the "master" and Chuck is the "servant." These terms are used to describe a relationship in which one person (the master) "controls or has the *right to control* the physical conduct of the other" (the servant). (Restatement, Agency (2d), Sec. 2.) This means that Pamela has the right not only to expect Chuck to perform particular tasks but also to tell him how to perform them. * * * [T]he term "agent" has a broader scope in law than in common parlance; it includes any person who has agreed with another person (the "principal") to "act on his behalf and subject to his control." Restatement, Agency (2d), Sec. 1.

* * *

Suppose that Pamela decides to withdraw from the active management of the business and to hire a general manager, Morris, to run the business. To some significant degree, Pamela will need to rely on Morris's judgment about how to manage the store—about such matters as prices, subordinate personnel, merchandise quality, and so on. These decisions will be much broader in scope and greater in impact on the success or failure of the business than the decisions made by lower-level employees such as Chuck. The delegation of decision-making authority is largely unavoidable; the purpose of hiring a general manager is to shift to that person the burden of making important decisions as problems arise. Many of those problems cannot be anticipated and, even if they could, the correct solution could not be specified in advance. Pamela must of necessity rely on Morris's competence and on his good faith. * * *

As an employee of Pamela, Morris will, like Chuck, be subject to her legal right to *control*. If all goes well, Pamela will not need to exercise control, but she may consider it very important to have the right to do so. It is, after all, her money (or assets) that will be at risk. Ordinarily, a person with money invested at substantial risk will want to have the right to review and control decisions that can materially affect the value of that investment. This kind of need for control is, of course, limited. Pamela's concern will be mostly with basic policy decisions and she need not be much concerned with minor, day-to-day decisions and routine operating decisions.

Pamela's relationship with Morris, like her relationship with Chuck, will be affected significantly by the ease with which Morris can be *replaced*. This will depend in part on general economic circumstances such as the number of grocery stores in the area and the number of trained managers. It will also depend, however, on the *specific training or knowledge* that Morris acquires in managing Pamela's store. As that specific training or knowledge increases, Morris becomes more and more valuable to Pamela and more and more difficult for her to replace. To that extent, Pamela will become dependent on Morris and will find it costly to replace him. But this is a two-way street. Morris will have acquired training that is valuable to Pamela, and to Pamela alone, and to this extent he is dependent on her. This kind of symbiotic relationship can obviously lead to discord over division of the gains from the joint endeavor. Part of the job of a lawyer is to anticipate such problems and to help provide, in advance, formulas for their resolution. * * *

Pamela's relationship with Morris will also be affected by how he is compensated. In order to provide Morris with proper incentives, Pamela may insist that part of his reward be contingent on the success of the business. Morris might, in fact, demand such an arrangement. At the same time, there is likely to be a limit to the risk Morris is willing to take and he will probably insist on some assured minimal level of compensation. Thus, the compensation "package" may consist of a salary (a fixed claim) plus a bonus based on profits (a residual claim). The presence of an element of incentive compensation like a bonus based on profits shifts some of the risk of the business to Morris; that is an attribute of any residual, as opposed to fixed, claim. It aligns Morris's objectives and interests with those of Pamela, and thereby allows her to be less concerned with the need for supervision, review, and control. But as Morris's rewards become increasingly dependent on the success of the business, he will become more concerned about control. If he is paid nothing but a fixed wage, he may be willing to follow any orders that Pamela wants to give him (though he may object because of concern for his future). If, on the other hand, his rewards are heavily dependent on the profits of the business, he may want some assurance of freedom from interference by Pamela in his operation of the business. Again, there arises a conflict that can be negotiated but may be extremely difficult to resolve to the satisfaction of both Morris and Pamela. Moreover, it should be noted that the formulation of an incentive compensation formula can be a formidable task. For example, Pamela and Morris may decide that Morris is to receive some portion of the net profits of the business. But the concept of "net profits" is not self-defining; it requires a determination, for example, of the appropriate rate of depreciation of assets used in the business. Beyond that, there is the very real possibility that profits will be affected by circumstances such as the behavior of competitors, which may or may not be related to Morris's performance. There may be good reasons for making the incentive compensation contingent on profits over a fairly long period of time—for example, five years—but then what happens if Pamela wants to sell out after three years? Problems like these, again, can be difficult to resolve in advance, and are fraught with potential antagonism. One can easily appreciate why Morris and Pamela may at the outset choose to pretend that they don't exist or why they may want to assume that mutually acceptable solutions will appear as concrete issues arise.

* * *

The problems of contingent reward (risk) and control, whose interrelationship we have just seen, are in turn related to the problem of the *duration* of the relationship—in other words, to the problem of termination. Like any other employee, Morris will want as much security of employment as he can get. He will want the option of keeping his job as long as he wants it, though he will have to accept the fact that in most private employment he cannot expect too much in this regard. Pamela may want to tie up Morris's services for as long as possible, without committing herself, though again she will not have much expectation of being able to do so. Where Morris's compensation is contingent to some significant degree on the success of the business, the issue of duration of the contract will take on added importance. At the outset Morris may consider that he will need a substantial period of time to achieve his profit-making expectations. Moreover, if he is to receive a portion of the yearly profits he may want to be able to remain in command in order to protect what he has been able to create. As the length of the contract period increases, however, it becomes increasingly difficult to anticipate and deal with the problems arising from changing circumstances. To a considerable extent it will be necessary to leave problems for resolution as they arise, relying on the proposition that by and large the outcomes prescribed by law, in the absence of explicit agreement, will be consistent with what the parties would have provided had they tried to anticipate and resolve all conceivable issues. But in some circumstances, the failure to resolve issues in some detail in advance will lead to acrimony and costly litigation. That is a risk that perhaps the parties should try to take into account, however vaguely, at the beginning of their association; it is questionable whether many people do so.

* * *

* * * The duty of loyalty is, of course, a more general obligation of employees (and other agents and fiduciaries). Problems of Morris's faithfulness, loyalty, and devotion to duty are especially troublesome because they are difficult to define and even more difficult to monitor. Viewing the matter negatively, Pamela will be concerned about the possibilities of stealing, cheating, and shirking and how to prevent or limit them. For convenience, we can refer to stealing, cheating, shirking and other such volitional or controllable conduct as *self-dealing*. By a variety of techniques, an employer can control the incidence of self-dealing by employees, but not without costs in time or money. There is likely, therefore, to be a residual loss to the employer from the employee's self-dealing that it is not worthwhile to try to prevent. For example, to detect stealing by Morris (and others) Pamela probably will rely on such negative sanctions as the threat of dismissal, bad references, and even criminal action. To detect criminal behavior she will need to spend her own time in reviewing operations or hire others to do so. This is part of the cost of hiring managers. It is a cost that does not occur when Pamela manages the business herself. And no matter how great the expenditure on prevention and detection, there will remain some possibility of undetected theft.

Stealing by managers is not likely to be a central concern of many business firms. Shirking, and other forms of self-serving behavior such as lavish use of expense accounts, are more pervasive and significant problems. Control of shirking may take the form of observation (with varying degrees of care) of performance or results, followed by reward (e.g., bonus or promotion) or punishment (e.g., demotion or discharge). But observation is costly and often inaccurate and rewards and punishments are imperfect, though useful, tools for controlling self-dealing. To illustrate and expand on this observation, suppose that Pamela moves to a distant place and must, of necessity, give Morris broad discretion in the operation of the business. Now consider the question of how many hours a week he is to work. Suppose that when Pamela managed the business herself she worked 60 hours a week. Further, let's suppose that if Morris owned the business himself he would work 60 hours a week. It does not follow that Morris will work 60 hours a week as manager of Pamela's business, since the benefit to him from doing so may not be sufficient to induce that level of effort. Pamela may recognize that there is no point in trying to specify that Morris will work a set number of hours per week at some specified level of effort. Even if it were possible to prescribe unambiguously an appropriate number of hours and level of effort, it might be too difficult for Pamela to determine the number of hours actually put in by Morris, much less the level of his effort. Pamela may be better off to rely on the threat of discharge for inadequate performance (which means that she will incur costs in observing performance and in gathering information about other managers with whom she might replace Morris) and on the use of rewards based on results that tend to flow from effort.

* * *

In the Pamela–Morris kind of situation there is a form of economic specialization, with Pamela supplying risk-bearing capital and Morris supplying managerial skill. If, in the customary mode, we think of Pamela as the owner, there is a separation of ownership and control. Morris must have considerable decision-making freedom. Specification of how he should react to all possible issues is not feasible. Given the need to vest in Morris the power to exercise business judgment or discretion, self-dealing by Morris becomes possible. The duty of loyalty prescribes—in some situations with clarity and in others only with considerable ambiguity—how Morris is supposed to behave, but this code of conduct is not self-executing. Moreover, it is impossible to design a system of sharing of rewards that will make Morris's interests identical to those of Pamela. Pamela will of necessity spend some of her time or her money, or both, trying to determine how faithfully Morris is serving her interests.

Economists (and others) often seem to think of the costs of defining, detecting, and preventing self-dealing as a sort of waste. Similarly, they find waste to the extent that a benefit that Morris takes for himself, such as leisure, is worth less to him than its cost to Pamela (for example, in lost profits). (The residual loss to Pamela from self-dealing that cannot feasibly be prevented is not an economic waste since Pamela's loss is Morris's gain.) That concept of waste is, however, a peculiar one when examined closely. The possibility of self-dealing is an inevitable product of the decision to hire a manager to run a business. One can cope with this possibility in a variety of ways, like hiring monitors such as detectives or outside auditors. The cost of doing so is certainly a departure from what Pamela might hope for and from what she could achieve if she ran the business herself. But this cost is an inevitable outcome of the facts that she has chosen to retire from active management and that in our imperfect world the people on whom she must rely may not be entirely trustworthy and loyal. It is unfortunate that people are not all perfectly trustworthy and loyal; it is unfortunate that people are not all perfect in all respects. But we must learn to live with the fact of imperfection and the costs thereby imposed. A violation of the duty of loyalty may be more galling than a violation of other obligations because the violation is likely to involve a sneaky act—an act that the employee knows is wrong but expects to be able to get away with because of problems of detection. Violation of the duty of loyalty may, therefore, be seen as unethical or immoral (as contrasted, for example, with a violation of the duty of care). This might justify the imposition of punitive damages or other special remedies (though by and large the law has not proceeded in that direction) or the incurring of extraordinary costs for detection. Still, there is no more sense in bemoaning the costs of disloyalty than there is in bemoaning the costs of friction in an engine. We lubricate engines to reduce friction, but we are willing to accept some residual level of friction. We continue to use engines, despite the cost of lubrication, and despite the residual friction, because we conclude we are better off by doing so than we would be otherwise. People with capital, like Pamela, hire managers, despite the monitoring costs, because they feel they are better off than they would be with any alternative investment or venture. This observation is, of course, a tautology. It is a useful tautology in that it reminds us of the silliness of worrying about unavoidable departures from unattainable ideals. While the point may seem obvious in the present context, it is often ignored in the context of large, complex economic organizations such as publicly held corporations.

In other words, we must be careful about comparing the actual situation, with division of ownership and management, to the *mythical ideal of the owner-managed firm*. Once Pamela decides, for whatever reason, that she does not want to manage the business, the standard of an owner-managed firm is unattainable. Morris simply cannot be expected to act as he would if he were the owner. He is not an owner; and he is a human being. Pamela is not a manager any longer; she is an investor. Both think that they are better off with the other than without. If that were not so, they would not have made the deal they made. It seems more useful to compare their actual position to what they would have if they could not combine their resources (services and capital) than to what they would have in the unattainable combined-owner-manager situation. In the actual position, with separation of management from ownership of capital, both can be expected to try to bargain for as much as possible in the way of contributions by the other and returns to themselves. It is fatuous to expect that Morris will behave selflessly, as if all the returns to his efforts were his. Pamela might hope for something close to that result, but she would be silly to expect to achieve it. All of this may, again, seem obvious in the small-firm context.   For large firms it is also valid but frequently ignored both by lawyers and economists.

Suppose, however, that when Pamela hires Morris, she says, either explicitly or implicitly, that she expects him, as manager, to behave just as she would behave, or as he would behave if he were the owner.   And suppose that Morris accepts the job on those terms.   To a considerable extent the legal system seems to infer, and even to impose, such bargains.   This is what is contemplated by the law when it refers to a duty of loyalty or a *fiduciary obligation*.   That duty or obligation is like a golden rule, a broad, vague constraint applied to employment relationships (a one-way rule in favor of the employer).   It is the kind of duty associated not only with employees but with trustees, brokers, and a whole host of other kinds of people (fiduciaries) who undertake to accomplish some objective for another person.   The need to rely on a vague concept such as the duty of loyalty stems from the difficulty of specifying precisely what it is that the employer expects of the employee (on the need, that is, for discretion in the employee).   The rule of law that embodies the duty of loyalty is a useful one.   Without it, mutually advantageous economic relationships might not be feasible.   As we have seen, however, violations of the duty of loyalty may be extremely difficult to detect.   To that extent, and given the infirmities of human nature, the duty of loyalty may to a significant extent embody an unattainable ideal.   It is wholly unrealistic to expect that all employees will as a matter of conscience consistently act as faithful retainers, selflessly pursuing the interests of their employers even at their own expense, or that we can be fully effective in efforts to force them to do so.   We can publicly deplore the departures from the ideal.   It may be useful to do so—to establish ethical standards and use deprivation of respect as a tool for enforcing the loyalty aspect of the business agreement.   But we must be careful not to refuse to recognize the reality and cope with it.

Chapter 3

AN INTRODUCTION TO THE LAW OF CORPORATIONS

A. INTRODUCTION

This chapter introduces some of the basic terms and concepts of the traditional law of corporations. In approaching the problems and materials that follow, you should be particularly conscious that they intentionally cast you in the role of planner and counsellor to your client, a role to which the usual first-year law school course does not expose students more than casually. However, that is the role corporate lawyers play most of the time. These materials emphasize the use of corporate law to plan transactions.

At first, you are apt to find the role of planner somewhat uncomfortable. A real client would expect her lawyer to structure a transaction so as to maximize benefits and minimize legal and business risks. But business transactions go forward in a world fraught with uncertainty and often involve doing things that have never been done before. Such transactions raise novel and difficult legal questions. Cases, if they exist at all, are rarely on point. The client, however, wants to know more than the arguments that can be made on either side. She is paying (often at very high rates) for the benefits of her lawyer's legal expertise, experience and, most of all, judgment. Thus, in this book, we frequently ask what action you would advise a client to take. Answering this question will help you develop the intangible qualities that will allow you to make sound judgments as a business lawyer.

Creativity is another ability of the first-rate lawyer. The capacity to generate alternative approaches to surmount some legal or business obstacle marks the difference between an average counsellor and one who is outstanding. Rarely will the answer, "That is illegal," or "You cannot do it" suffice. Within the constraints of ethical conduct, lawyers are paid to figure out how *to* do something—not to explain why it *cannot* be done. The lawyer who frequently cannot find an acceptable alternative to accomplish the client's objective is likely to find herself looking for other clients.

B. SOME BASIC TERMS AND CONCEPTS

The following simplified discussion of some terms and concepts and their place in the standard corporate framework will help you understand the problems and the materials in this chapter. They all are discussed in greater detail in later chapters.

1. CORPORATE STATUTES

The statute to which we refer most often is the Revised Model Business Corporation Act (RMBCA). The RMBCA is a product of the Committee on Corporate Laws of the Section of Business Law of the American Bar Association. It was adopted in 1984 and has since been amended several times. It is not a a real statute, but it, or its predecessor, the Model Business Corporation Act, have been adopted in substance by more than 35 states It often provides the basis for states that wish to amend older corporate statutes.

A second important statute is the Delaware General Corporation Law (DGCL), which governs the many corporations organized under Delaware law. Relevant provisions of the RMBCA and the DGCL can be found in West Publishing Co., Selected Corporation and Partnership Statutes, Rules and Forms, which also includes official comments to certain sections of the RMBCA. A full discussion of the RMBCA can be found in the four-volume Model Business Corporation Act Annotated (3d ed. 1985).

2. ORGANIC DOCUMENTS

The provisions of a state's corporation statute govern all corporations organized pursuant to its terms. Every corporation statute requires that each corporation have its own *articles of incorporation* (sometimes called the *charter* or the *certificate of incorporation*), which represents, in a sense, the constitution of that corporation. The articles contain certain provisions required by statute (such as the name of the corporation) and other provisions regulating the internal affairs of the corporation. Every corporation also has *bylaws*, which usually set forth the details of the internal governance of the corporation (such as procedures for calling meetings). A corporation's articles cannot conflict with the statute under which the corporation is organized and its bylaws cannot conflict with the statute or the articles.

3. THE CORPORATE ACTORS

The traditional statutory governance model of a corporation is pyramidal. At the base are the *stockholders* (or *shareholders*), who generally are considered the "owners" of the corporation. The stockholders do not control the corporation directly. Rather, they elect a *board of directors*, which is responsible for managing or supervising the corporation's business. Beyond electing directors, stockholders do have some limited powers: they must approve certain fundamental changes such as mergers or the sale of corporate assets; they must approve amendments of the articles of incorporation; they can amend the by-laws; and they can vote on matters that corporate management presents for their approval at a shareholders meeting.

Directors can be either "outside" directors, i.e., individuals who are not corporate employees, or "inside" directors, who are employed by the corporation. Directors *qua* directors are considered to be representatives of the shareholders rather than employees of the corporation, regardless of whether they are "inside" or "outside" directors.

At the top of the metaphorical pyramid are the *officers* of the corporation, usually including a president, one or more vice-presidents, a secretary, and a treasurer. Although the corporation statute and the by-laws impose few specific duties, the officers constitute the management of the corporation and are responsible for running its business day-to-day.

This model, although accurately reflecting corporate statutes, does not always describe corporate reality. In many corporations with a relatively small number of stockholders ("close corporations"), there often is a substantial overlap among shareholders, directors and officers, and it is common for one or more people to fill all three roles. We will examine the ways in which courts and legislatures have dealt with the tensions between the model and the reality in Chapter 13.

4. CORPORATE SECURITIES

Stockholders' ownership of a corporation is represented by shares of *stock*. There is always *common stock* which represents the residual interest in the corporation after all senior claimants have been paid. There may be one or more classes of *preferred stock*, which represent ownership interests with certain priorities over the common stock. A corporation's articles of incorporation specify how many shares of common and preferred stock the corporation is *authorized* to issue without amending the articles of incorporation to authorize more. The portion of the authorized stock that has been sold and remains in the hands of the shareholders is the stock *outstanding*. *Authorized but unissued stock* generally can be sold by a corporation on whatever terms its board of directors decides are reasonable.

Stock, common or preferred, is considered an *equity security*, a term that derives from the "equity of redemption" of a mortgagor and relates to the fact that stockholders stand at the end of the line when it comes to distributions of corporate funds. The other principal class of corporate financial instruments consists of *debt securities*, which include *bonds*, *debentures* and *notes*. Debt securities represent claims on a corporation's assets that have priority over the claims represented by equity securities.

5. FIDUCIARY PRINCIPLES

The relationships among the various corporate actors are governed in part by express legal rules and in part by *fiduciary principles* drawn originally from the law of trusts. The basic fiduciary duties that officers and directors owe to the corporation are the *duty of care* and the *duty of loyalty*. Another fiduciary duty that implicates both care and loyalty is the *duty of disclosure*.

PROBLEM
CHESAPEAKE MARINE SERVICES—PART I

The Chesapeake Marine Services Company, Inc., ("Chesapeake") is incorporated in the state of Columbia * [Delaware]. Its business consists principally of the provision of barge and towing services. It also maintains a small shipyard in which it services its own vessels and does repair work for others. Its articles of incorporation and by-laws are substantially the same as those in West Publishing Co., Selected Corporation and Partnership Statutes, Rules and Forms except: (i) the articles authorize the issuance of 1,000 shares of common stock; and (ii) the articles also provide:

> Wherever a vote of the shareholders is required by statute to approve an amendment to these Articles of Incorporation or a merger or sale of all or substantially all of the assets of the corporation, such approval shall be by the holders of two-thirds of the outstanding stock.

All 1,000 shares of Chesapeake common stock are outstanding. John Apple, Chesapeake's largest shareholder, owns 350 shares. Apple is a director of Chesapeake. Apple also owns a half interest in United Harbor Services, Inc. ("United"), a somewhat smaller firm that competes with Chesapeake. Apple acquired his interest in United about three years ago, after a dispute with Chesapeake over the continuation of leases on two tugboats he owned and had leased to Chesapeake for several years. Chesapeake's board of directors refused to renew the leases and Apple conveyed the tugboats to United in exchange for half of its stock.

Apple, who has been in the marine transport business for many years, acquired his Chesapeake stock in a series of purchases over the last few years. Members of the Lambert family, the other principal shareholders of Chesapeake, expressed concern about Apple's more recent acquisitions and told Apple that they were strongly opposed to his trying to gain control of Chesapeake.

Chesapeake currently has fifteen shareholders none of whom, other than Apple, own more than 200 shares. The Chesapeake board consists of five directors: Apple, James Lambert (the president of the company),

---

* Columbia is a fictitious United States jurisdiction that has adopted the RMBCA. Alternative references to Delaware and the DCGL are provided for those who choose to deal with this and subsequent Problems as questions of Delaware law.

two other members of the Lambert family, and Nancy Carter, another substantial shareholder.

For the past few years, Chesapeake's management has been concerned about a perceived shortage of capital. The firm's business has been growing; it needs to expand the shipyard, and the board believes it could make profitable use of one or two more tugboats. Moreover, within the last year Chesapeake has experienced temporary shortages of cash. It has occasionally had to delay payments to suppliers, causing it to lose the usual trade discounts for prompt payment. A year ago Chesapeake's bank rejected Chesapeake's request for a loan because Chesapeake had already borrowed as much as the bank believed was prudent and because the bank had doubts about the future growth of Chesapeake's business.

James Lambert then decided that the best course for Chesapeake was to raise additional equity capital. At the last board meeting, he recommended an amendment to the articles of incorporation to double the number of authorized shares of common stock. Apple opposed the amendment, stating that, in his opinion, Chesapeake should not seek additional capital. Apple also indicated that he would do everything he could to block the amendment. Chesapeake's board of directors decided not to act on James Lambert's proposal, but to ask your firm for advice as to the following:

1. What risk of liability, if any, would the directors run if they recommended that the shareholders amend the articles of incorporation so as to permit Chesapeake to raise additional capital by selling new stock?

2. What actions, if any, can the board take to ensure that the proposed amendment to Chesapeake's articles of incorporation is adopted?

The partner in charge has suggested that, in developing responses to the board's questions, you consider the following:

a. What alternatives are available to a company in Chesapeake's position when it needs to raise new capital?

b. Why do the articles of incorporation contain a limit on the number of shares of common stock that can be issued? See RMBCA §§ 2.02 and 6.01(a) [DGCL § 102(a)(4)].

c. Because of the provision of the articles of incorporation, quoted above, Apple's ownership of more than one-third of the common stock puts him in a position to block any amendment to the articles. Is that provision consistent with RMBCA §§ 2.02, 7.27, 10.01, and 10.03 [DGCL §§ 102, 216, and 242]? What purpose does that provision serve?

d. RMBCA §§ 10.03, 11.03, and 12.02 [DGCL §§ 242, 251 and 271] require shareholder approval, by a majority of the shares, for certain "fundamental changes" in the corporate structure, such as amendments to the articles, sales of substantially all of a corporation's assets, and mergers. How do you reconcile these provisions with RMBCA § 8.01(b) [DGCL § 141(a)]?

e. If all the directors other than Apple believe that the proposed amendment would benefit the corporation, can Chesapeake successfully challenge Apple's opposition? Does it matter whether Apple's opposition is motivated by a good faith belief that it would not be in Chesapeake's best interest to sell more stock or whether he simply wishes to make it more difficult for Chesapeake to compete with United?

BAYER v. BERAN
49 N.Y.S.2d 2 (Sup.Ct.1944).

SHIENTAG, JUSTICE.

These derivative stockholders' suits present for review two transactions upon which plaintiffs seek to charge the individual defendants, who are directors, with liability in favor of the corporate defendant, the Celanese Corporation of America. * * * Before taking up the specific transactions complained of, I shall consider generally certain pertinent rules to be applied in determining the liability of directors of a business corporation such as is here involved. * * *

Directors of a business corporation are not trustees and are not held to strict accountability as such. Nevertheless, their obligations are analogous to those of trustees. Directors are agents; they are fiduciaries. The fiduciary has two paramount obligations: responsibility and loyalty. Those obligations apply with equal force to the humblest agent or broker and to the director of a great and powerful corporation. They lie at the very foundation of our whole system of free private enterprise and are as fresh and significant today as when they were formulated decades ago. The responsibility—that is, the care and the diligence— required of an agent or of a fiduciary, is proportioned to the occasion. It is a concept that has, and necessarily so, a wide penumbra of meaning— a concept, however, which becomes sharpened in its practical application to the given facts of a situation.

The concept of loyalty, of constant, unqualified fidelity, has a definite and precise meaning. The fiduciary must subordinate his individual and private interests to his duty to the corporation whenever the two conflict. In an address delivered in 1934, Mr. Justice, now Chief Justice, Stone declared that the fiduciary principle of undivided loyalty was, in effect, "the precept as old as Holy Writ, that "a man cannot serve two masters'. More than a century ago equity gave a hospitable reception to that principle and the common law was not slow to follow in giving it recognition. No thinking man can believe that an economy built upon a business foundation can long endure without loyalty to that principle". He went on to say that "The separation of ownership from management, the development of the corporate structure so as to vest in small groups control of resources of great numbers of small and uninformed investors, make imperative a fresh and active devotion to that principle if the modern world of business is to perform its proper function". Stone, The Public Influence of the Bar, 48 Harvard Law Review 1, 8.

A director is not an insurer. On the one hand, he is not called upon to use an extraordinary degree of care and prudence; and on the other hand it is established by the cases that it is not enough for a director to be honest, that fraud is not the orbit of his liability. The director may not act as a dummy or a figurehead. He is called upon to use care, to exercise judgment, the degree of care, the kind of judgment that one would give in similar situations to the conduct of his own affairs.

The director of a business corporation is given a wide latitude of action. The law does not seek to deprive him of initiative and daring and vision. Business has its adventures, its bold adventures; and those who in good faith, and in the interests of the corporation they serve, embark upon them, are not to be penalized if failure, rather than success, results from their efforts. The law will not permit a course of conduct by directors, which would be applauded if it succeeded, to be condemned with a riot of adjectives simply because it failed. Directors of a commercial corporation may take chances, the same kind of chances that a man would take in his own business. Because they are given this wide latitude, the law will not hold directors liable for honest errors, for mistakes of judgment. The law will not interfere with the internal affairs of a corporation so long as it is managed by its directors pursuant to a free, honest exercise of judgment uninfluenced by personal, or by any considerations other than the welfare of the corporation.

To encourage freedom of action on the part of directors, or to put it another way, to discourage interference with the exercise of their free and independent judgment, there has grown up what is known as the "business judgment rule". "Questions of policy of management, expediency of contracts or action, adequacy of consideration, lawful appropriation of corporate funds to advance corporate interests, are left solely to their honest and unselfish decision, for their powers therein are without limitation and free from restraint, and the exercise of them for the common and general interests of the corporation may not be questioned, although the results show that what they did was unwise or inexpedient." Pollitz v. Wabash R. Co., 207 N.Y. 113, 124, 100 N.E. 721, 724. Indeed, although the concept of "responsibility" is firmly fixed in the law, it is only in a most unusual and extraordinary case that directors are held liable for negligence in the absence of fraud, or improper motive, or personal interest.

The "business judgment rule", however, yields to the rule of undivided loyalty. This great rule of law is designed "to avoid the possibility of fraud and to avoid the temptation of self-interest." Conway, J., in Matter of Ryan's Will, 291 N.Y. 376, 406, 52 N.E.2d 909, 923. It is "designed to obliterate all divided loyalties which may creep into a fiduciary relation * * *." Thacher, J., in City Bank Farmers Trust Co. v. Cannon, 291 N.Y. 125, 132, 51 N.E.2d 674, 676. "Included within its scope is every situation in which a trustee chooses to deal with another in such close relation with the trustee that possible advantage to such other person might influence, consciously or unconsciously, the judgment of the trustee * * *." Lehman, Ch. J., in Albright v. Jefferson County National Bank, 292 N.Y. 31, 39, 53 N.E.2d 753, 756. The dealings of a director with the corporation for which he is the fiduciary are therefore viewed "with jealousy by the courts." Globe Woolen Co. v. Utica Gas & Electric Co., 224 N.Y. 483, 121 N.E. 378, 380. Such personal transactions of directors with their corporations, such transactions as may tend to produce a conflict between self-interest and fiduciary obligation, are, when challenged, examined with the most scrupulous care, and if there is any evidence of improvidence or oppression, any indication of unfairness or undue advantage, the transactions will be voided. "Their dealings with the corporation are subjected to rigorous scrutiny and where any of their contracts or engagements with the corporation are challenged the burden is on the director not only to prove the good faith of the transaction but also to show its inherent fairness from the viewpoint of the corporation and those interested therein." Pepper v. Litton, 308 U.S. 295, 306, 60 S.Ct. 238, 245, 84 L.Ed. 281.

While there is a high moral purpose implicit in this transcendent fiduciary principle of undivided loyalty, it has back of it a profound understanding of human nature and of its frailties. It actually accomplishes a practical, beneficent purpose. It tends to prevent a clouded conception of fidelity that blurs the vision. It preserves the free exercise of judgment uncontaminated by the dross of divided allegiance or self-interest. It prevents the operation of an influence that may be indirect but that is all the more potent for that reason. The law has set its face firmly against undermining "the rule of undivided loyalty by the "disintegrating erosion' of particular exceptions." Meinhard v. Salmon, 249 N.Y. 458, 464, 164 N.E. 545, 546.

The first, or "advertising", cause of action charges the directors with negligence, waste and improvidence in embarking the corporation upon a radio advertising program beginning in 1942 and costing about $1,000,000 a year. It is further charged that they were negligent in selecting the type of program and in renewing the radio contract for 1943. More serious than these allegations is the charge that the directors were motivated by a noncorporate purpose in causing the radio program to be undertaken and in expending large sums of money therefor. It is claimed that this radio advertising was for the benefit of Miss Jean Tennyson, one of the singers on the program, who in private life is Mrs. Camille Dreyfus, the wife of the president of the company and one of its directors; that it was undertaken to "further, foster and subsidize her career"; to "furnish a vehicle" for her talents.

Eliminating for the moment the part played by Miss Tennyson in the radio advertising campaign, it is clear that the character of the advertising, the amount to be expended therefor, and the manner in which it should be used, are all matters of business judgment and rest peculiarly within the discretion of the board of directors. Under the authorities previously cited, it is not, generally speaking, the function of a court of equity to review these matters or even to consider them. Had the wife of the president of the company not been involved, the advertising cause of action could have been disposed of summarily. Her connection with the program, however, makes it necessary to go into the facts in some detail.

[The court reviews the history of the decision to launch a program of radio advertising.]

So far, there is nothing on which to base any claim of breach of fiduciary duty. Some care, diligence and prudence were exercised by these directors before they committed the company to the radio program. It was for the directors to determine whether they would resort to radio advertising; it was for them to conclude how much to spend; it was for them to decide the kind of program they would use. It would be an unwarranted act of interference for any court to attempt to substitute its judgment on these points for that of the directors, honestly arrived at. The expenditure was not reckless or unconscionable. Indeed, it bore a fair relationship to the total amount of net sales and to the earnings of the company. The fact that the company had offers of more business than it could handle did not, in law, preclude advertising. Many corporations not now doing any business in their products because of emergency conditions advertise those products extensively in order to preserve the good will, the public interest, during the war period. The fact that the company's product may not now be identifiable did not bar advertising calculated to induce consumer demand for such identification. That a program of classical and semiclassical music was selected, rather than a variety program, or a news commentator program, furnishes no ground for legal complaint. True, variety programs have a wider popular appeal than do musicals, but it would be a very sad thing if the former were the only kind of radio programs to be used. Some of the largest industrial concerns in the country have recognized this and have maintained fine musical programs on the radio for many years.

Now we have to take up an unfortunate incident, one which cannot be viewed with the complacency displayed by some of the directors of the company. This is not a closely held family corporation. The Doctors Dreyfus and their families own about 135,000 shares of common stock, the other directors about 10,000 shares out of a total outstanding issue of 1,376,500 shares. Some of these other directors were originally employed by Dr. Camille Dreyfus, the president of the company. His wife, to whom he has been married for about twelve years, is known professionally as Miss Jean Tennyson and is a singer of wide experience.

Dr. Dreyfus, as was natural, consulted his wife about the proposed radio program; he also asked the advertising agency, that had been retained, to confer with her about it. She suggested the names of the artists, all stars of the Metropolitan Opera Company, and the name of the conductor, prominent in his field. She also offered her own services as a paid artist. All of her suggestions as to personnel were adopted by the advertising agency. While the record shows Miss Tennyson to be a competent singer, there is nothing to indicate that she was indispensable or essential to the success of the program. She received $500 an evening. It would be far-fetched to suggest that the directors caused the company to incur large expenditures for radio advertising to enable the president's wife to make $24,000 in 1942 and $20,500 in 1943.

Of course it is not improper to appoint relatives of officers or directors to responsible positions in a company. But where a close relative of the chief executive officer of a corporation, and one of its dominant directors, takes a position closely associated with a new and expensive field of activity, the motives of the directors are likely to be questioned. The board would be placed in a position where selfish, personal interests might be in conflict with the duty it owed to the corporation. That being so, the entire transaction, if challenged in the courts, must be subjected to the most rigorous scrutiny to determine whether the action of the directors was intended or calculated "to subserve some outside purpose, regardless of the consequences to the company, and in a manner inconsistent with its interests." Gamble v. Queens County Water Co., 123 N.Y. 91, 99, 25 N.E. 201, 202.

After such careful scrutiny I have concluded that, up to the present, there has been no breach of fiduciary duty on the part of the directors. The president undoubtedly knew that his wife might be one of the paid artists on the program. The other directors did not know this until they had approved the campaign of radio advertising and the general type of radio program. The evidence fails to show that the program was designed to foster or subsidize "the career of Miss Tennyson as an artist" or to "furnish a vehicle for her talents". That her participation in the program may have enhanced her prestige as a singer is no ground for subjecting the directors to liability, as long as the advertising served a legitimate and a useful corporate purpose and the company received the full benefit thereof.

The musical quality of "Celanese Hour" has not been challenged, nor does the record contain anything reflecting on Miss Tennyson's competence as an artist. There is nothing in the testimony to show that some other soprano would have enhanced the artistic quality of the program or its advertising appeal. There is no suggestion that the present program is inefficient or that its cost is disproportionate to what a program of that character reasonably entails. Miss Tennyson's contract with the advertising agency retained by the directors was on a standard form, negotiated through her professional agent. Her compensation, as well as that of the other artists, was in conformity with that paid for comparable work. She received less than any of the other artists on the program. Although she appeared with greater regularity than any other singer, she received no undue prominence, no special build-up. Indeed, all of the artists were subordinated to the advertisement of the company and of its products. The company was featured. It appears also that the popularity of the program has increased since it was inaugurated.

It is clear, therefore, that the directors have not been guilty of any breach of fiduciary duty, in embarking upon the program of radio advertising and in renewing it. It is unfortunate that they have allowed themselves to be placed in a position where their motives concerning future decisions on radio advertising may be impugned. The free mind should be ever jealous of its freedom. "Power of control carries with it a trust or duty to exercise that power faithfully to promote the corporate interests, and the courts of this State will insist upon scrupulous performance of that duty." Lehman, Ch. J., in Everett v. Phillips, 288 N.Y. 227, 232, 43 N.E.2d 18, 19. Thus far, that duty has been performed and with noteworthy success. The corporation has not, up to the present time, been wronged by the radio advertising attacked in the complaints.

[The court also found no merit in plaintiffs' second cause of action.]

GAMBLE v. QUEENS COUNTY WATER CO.
123 N.Y. 91, 25 N.E. 201 (1890).

[Mullins built a system of water pipes, known as the "Rockaway Beach Extension," at an out-of-pocket cost of about $69,000. He then contracted to sell the "Rockaway Beach Extension" to the Queens County Water Co., of which he was a shareholder, for $60,000 in bonds and $50,000 in stock. The water company's shareholders, with Mullins participating, voted to approve the transaction and a dissident shareholder then brought suit to set it aside.]

PECKHAM, J.

* * * The so-called "Rockaway Beach Extension" was not built by defendant Mullins under any contract with the defendant corporation. * * * Upon its completion, Mullins was the sole and absolute owner thereof, with power to operate it himself, or to sell it to others, or, in brief, to exercise such acts of ownership over the property as any other owner might have exercised. This is not the case of a trustee entering into a contract with himself, or purchasing from himself, where the contract is liable to be repudiated at the mere will, or even whim, of the *cestui que trust*. Having the rights of an absolute owner of this extension, Mullins was at liberty to make such contract in regard to its disposal as he should see fit, so long of course as he did not, while acting in his own interest on the one side, also act on the other in the capacity of trustee or representative, so that his interest and his duty might conflict. In this case, Mullins did not so act. He bases his right to the stock and bonds of the company defendant upon the vote of the majority of its shareholders taken at a regularly convened meeting, to purchase the property at the price named in the resolution adopted at such meeting, the price being $60,000 in bonds, and $50,000 in the stock of such company. * * * There were a majority of shareholders, and a majority of shares voted upon, in favor of such resolution, without counting the defendant Mullins or his shares, although he voted upon them in favor of such resolution. In so doing, he committed no legal

wrong. A shareholder has a legal right at a meeting of the shareholders to vote upon a measure, even though he has a personal interest therein separate from other shareholders. In such a meeting, each shareholder represents himself and his own interests solely, and he in no sense acts as a trustee or representative of others. The law of self-interest has at such time very great and proper sway. There can be little doubt, too, that at such meetings those who do vote upon their own stock vote upon it in the light solely of their own interest, or at least in what they conceive to be their own interest. Their action resulting from such votes must not be so detrimental to the interests of the corporation itself as to lead to the necessary inference that the interests of the majority of the shareholders lie wholly outside of and in opposition to the interests of the corporation, and of the minority of the shareholders, and that their action is a wanton or a fraudulent destruction of the rights of such minority. * * *

I think that where the action of the majority is plainly a fraud upon, or, in other words, is really oppressive to the minority shareholders, and the directors or trustees have acted with and formed part of the majority, an action may be sustained by one of the minority shareholders suing in his own behalf * * *. It is not, however, every question of mere administration or of policy in which there is a difference of opinion among the shareholders that enables the minority to claim that the action of the majority is oppressive, and which justifies the minority in coming to a court of equity to obtain relief. Generally the rule must be that in such cases the will of the majority shall govern. The court would not be justified in interfering, even in doubtful cases, where the action of the majority might be susceptible of different constructions. To warrant the interposition of the court in favor of the minority shareholders in a corporation or joint stock association, as against the contemplated action of the majority, where such action is within the corporate powers, a case must be made out which plainly shows that such action is so far opposed to the true interests of the corporation itself as to lead to the clear inference that no one thus acting could have been influenced by any honest desire to secure such interests, but that he must have acted with an intent to subserve some outside purpose, regardless of the consequences to the company and in a manner inconsistent with its interests. Otherwise the court might be called upon to balance probabilities of profitable results to arise from the carrying out of the one or the other of different plans proposed by or on behalf of different shareholders in a corporation, and to decree the adoption of that line of policy which seemed to it to promise the best results, or at least to enjoin the carrying out of the opposite policy. This is no business for any court to follow. * * *

[The court ruled in favor of defendants and ordered a new trial.]

C.   EQUITABLE LIMITATIONS ON LEGAL POSSIBILITIES

PROBLEM

CHESAPEAKE MARINE SERVICES—PART II

Prevented by Apple's opposition from increasing Chesapeake's stock, James Lambert came to your firm for advice about how Chesapeake might raise the additional equity capital it needs. After discussing the matter with one of the partners, he proposed the following plan. Chesapeake will organize a new corporation, CMS Shipyard, Inc. ("Shipyard"), with authorized capital of 10,000 shares of common stock, and will transfer the assets of its shipyard division to Shipyard in exchange for 2,000 shares of its common stock. Then Shipyard will sell another 1,500 shares of common stock, for $100 per share, half to members of the Lambert family and half to two or three outside investors. No Shipyard stock will be offered to Apple. Finally, Shipyard will use about $100,000 of the cash it expects to receive to expand its ship repair business and will lend the remaining $50,000 to Chesapeake.

The partner has sent you a memo describing the proposed transaction and continuing as follows:

> I don't see any problems with the mechanics of the proposed transaction. Chesapeake clearly has the power, under RMBCA § 3.02, to create Shipyard and to purchase some of its stock. Chesapeake's board does not need shareholder approval to transfer the assets of the shipyard division, because they constitute far less than "substantially all" of Chesapeake's assets. (See RMBCA § 12.-02.) In fact, the division has generated only about 15 percent of Chesapeake's profits over the past few years and the book value * of the division's assets is $200,000, or about 10 percent of the total book value of Chesapeake's assets. The fair market value of the division is more, probably about $375,000, but that still is less than 20 percent of Chesapeake's estimated total fair market value.

> On the other hand, the transaction looks like an "end run" around the two-thirds majority provision in Chesapeake's articles, and Apple probably will challenge it. Most likely, he will claim that the transaction (i) is unwise, (ii) is unfair, and, (iii) in any event, is unlawful because Chesapeake "is doing indirectly what it could not do directly." Is a court likely to view any of them as meritorious? Does Chesapeake have good responses to these claims? Is evidence relating to Lambert or Apple's motives likely to affect a court's

---

* "Book value" of an asset is the value at which it is carried on the accounts of a business. According to standard accounting practice, book value is generally equal to the cost of the asset or, in the case of a depreciable asset, cost less an allowance for depreciation arrived at by a more-or-less arbitrary formula. As a result of this practice, the "real" value of an asset may depart significantly from its book value. The book value of a corporation is the aggregate of the book value of its assets less its liabilities.

evaluation? Finally, if any of these claims appears to have merit, can Chesapeake restructure the proposed transaction to eliminate the problem and still attain most or all of its objectives? Our client wants to raise money, not get bogged down in litigation.

In answering these questions, first reconsider Bayer v. Beran. Then consider the following.

SCHNELL v. CHRIS-CRAFT INDUSTRIES, INC.
285 A.2d 437 (Del.Sup.1971).

[Plaintiffs, a group of Chris–Craft shareholders, were dissatisfied with the company's economic performance. They resolved to seek control by electing a new board of directors at Chris–Craft's next annual shareholders' meeting. On October 16, 1971, as required by federal law, they filed documents announcing their intentions with the Securities and Exchange Commission. On October 18, Chris–Craft's board met and amended the corporation's by-laws, which had previously fixed January 11 as the date of the annual meeting, to authorize the board to set an annual meeting date at any time in December or January. The board then proceeded to schedule the upcoming meeting for December 8, thereby reducing by more than a month the time available to the insurgents to solicit the support of other shareholders. The board also set the place of the meeting in Cortland, New York, a small town far from any transportation hubs. The board said it changed the meeting date because weather conditions made it difficult to get to Cortland in January and because holding the meeting well before Christmas would reduce problems with the mail. Meanwhile, however, the board took a number of other actions to impede the insurgents, including resisting providing them with the list of stockholders to which they were entitled under Delaware law. The trial court found that the defendants' actions, including the change in the date of the annual meeting, were designed to obstruct the plaintiffs' efforts to gain control. But the court declined to reschedule the meeting on its original date, holding that the plaintiffs had delayed too long in seeking judicial relief. On appeal, the Supreme Court reversed.]

HERRMANN, JUSTICE (for the majority of the Court):

* * *

It will be seen that the Chancery Court considered all of the reasons stated by management as business reasons for changing the date of the meeting; but that those reasons were rejected by the Court below in making the following findings:

I am satisfied, however, in a situation in which present management has disingenuously resisted the production of a list of its stockholders to plaintiffs or their confederates and has otherwise turned a deaf ear to plaintiffs' demands about a change in management designed to lift defendant from its present business doldrums, management has seized on a relatively new section of the Delaware Corporation Law for the purpose of cutting down on the amount of time which would otherwise have been available to plaintiffs and others for the waging of a proxy battle. Management thus enlarged the scope of its scheduled October 18 directors' meeting to include the by-law amendment in controversy after the stockholders committee had filed with the S.E.C. its intention to wage a proxy fight on October 16.

Thus plaintiffs reasonably contend that because of the tactics employed by management (which involve the hiring of two established proxy solicitors as well as a refusal to produce a list of its stockholders, coupled with its use of an amendment to the Delaware Corporation Law to limit the time for contest), they are given little chance, because of the exigencies of time, including that required to clear material at the S.E.C., to wage a successful proxy fight * between now and December 8. * * *

In our view, those conclusions amount to a finding that management has attempted to utilize the corporate machinery and the Delaware Law for the purpose of perpetuating itself in office; and, to that end, for the purpose of obstructing the legitimate efforts of dissident stockholders in the exercise of their rights to undertake a proxy contest against management. These are inequitable purposes, contrary to established principles of corporate democracy. The advancement by directors of the by-law date of a stockholders' meeting, for such purposes, may not be permitted to stand.

When the by-laws of a corporation designate the date of the annual meeting of stockholders, it is to be expected that those who intend to contest the reelection of incumbent management will gear their campaign to the by-law date. It is not to be expected that management will attempt to advance that date in order to obtain an inequitable advantage in the contest.

Management contends that it has complied strictly with the provisions of the new Delaware Corporation Law in changing the by-law date. The answer to that contention, of course, is that inequitable action does not become permissible simply because it is legally possible.

* * *

Accordingly, the judgment below must be reversed and the cause remanded, with instructions to nullify the December 8 date as a meeting date for stockholders; to reinstate January 11, 1972 as the sole date of the next annual meeting of the stockholders of the corporation; and to

---

* Shareholders in public companies rarely attend annual meetings. They vote by granting a proxy—a written authority to vote their shares—to some other person. In the event of a contest for control, both management and dissident shareholders solicit proxies from shareholders.

take such other proceedings and action as may be consistent herewith regarding the stock record closing date and any other related matters.

Note: Independent Legal Significance

A number of other cases, most of them involving mergers * or recapitalizations,** have taken what seems, on the surface at least, to be a rather different view of actions that comply with all relevant statutory provisions. In these cases, plaintiffs have argued that defendants were making use of a mechanism provided in one section of the statute to accomplish a result that they could not have accomplished had they pursued it in an arguably more straightforward fashion. In Bove v. Community Hotel Corp. of Newport, R.I., 105 R.I. 36, 249 A.2d 89 (1969), for example, holders of preferred stock had the right to receive 24 years of unpaid dividends before the corporation could pay any dividends on its common stock. Management wanted to eliminate the preferred stockholders' claim so that the corporation could sell new common stock and raise needed capital. Under Rhode Island law, the dividend claims could be eliminated by amending the charter, but such an amendment required unanimous approval of the preferred stockholders, which would not be forthcoming.

Consequently, management decided to pursue another alternative. It created a new corporation with nominal assets and proposed to merge the old corporation into it in a transaction that would eliminate the old preferred stock and the associated claims for dividends. The merger required the approval of two-thirds, rather than all, of the preferred stock. If the merger was approved, preferred stockholders who voted against it had the option of demanding to be paid a judicially determined "fair value" for their stock, rather than accepting stock in the surviving corporation. Some preferred stockholders, however, sought to enjoin the merger. Denying relief, the Rhode Island Supreme Court stated:

> Concededly, unanimity of the preferred stockholders is unobtainable in this case, and plaintiffs argue, therefore, that to permit the less restrictive provisions of the merger statute to accomplish indirectly what otherwise would be incapable of being accomplished directly by the more stringent amendment procedures of the general corporation law is tantamount to sanctioning a circumvention or perversion of that law.
>
> The question, however, is not whether recapitalization by the merger route is a subterfuge, but whether a merger which is

---

* A merger is a statutory technique for combining two or more corporations into one. The surviving corporation acquires all of the assets and assumes all of the liabilities of the merging corporations. The shareholders of the surviving corporation normally continue to hold their stock. The shareholders of the acquired corporation or corporations exchange their stock for stock of the surviving corporation or other consideration, such as debt securities or cash.

** A recapitalization involves a change in the capital structure of a corporation, usually accomplished by an amendment to the articles, as a result of which some or all of the corporation's securities are converted into securities having different characteristics.

designated for the sole purpose of cancelling the rights of preferred stockholders with the consent of less than all has been authorized by the legislature. The controlling statute is § 7–5–2. Its language is clear, all-embracing and unqualified. It authorizes any two or more business corporations *which were or might have been organized* under the general corporation law to merge into a single corporation; and it provides that the merger agreement shall prescribe " * * * the terms and conditions of consolidation or merger, the mode of carrying the same into effect * * **as well as the manner of converting the shares of each of the constituent corporations into shares or other securities of the corporation resulting from or surviving such consolidation or merger*, with such other details and provisions as are deemed necessary." (emphasis ours) Nothing in that language even suggests that the legislature intended to make *underlying purpose* a standard for determining permissibility. Indeed, the contrary is apparent since the very breadth of the language selected presupposes a complete lack of concern with whether the merger is designed to further the mutual interests of two existing and nonaffiliated corporations or whether alternatively it is purposed solely upon effecting a substantial change in an existing corporation's capital structure.

Moreover, that a possible effect of corporate action under the merger statute is not possible, or is even forbidden, under another section of the general corporation law is of no import, it being settled that the several sections of that law may have independent legal significance, and that the validity of corporate action taken pursuant to one section is not necessarily dependent upon its being valid under another. Hariton v. Arco Electronics, Inc., 40 Del.Ch. 326, 182 A.2d 22, aff'd, 41 Del.Ch. 74, 188 A.2d 123.

We hold, therefore, that nothing within the purview of our statute forbids a merger between a parent and a subsidiary corporation even under circumstances where the merger device has been resorted to solely for the purpose of obviating the necessity for the unanimous vote which would otherwise be required in order to cancel the priorities of preferred shareholders.

Notes and Questions

1. In both *Schnell* and *Bove*, plaintiffs argued that a transaction that complied with the statute should be enjoined because the transaction was improperly motivated. In the former case, the allegedly improper purpose was to obstruct a contest for control. In the latter, the motive was allegedly to circumvent a provision of the statute designed to protect the plaintiffs' claim to dividends. Why might a court grant relief in one case and not in the other?

2. There is no doubt that the by-law change in *Schnell* was authorized by the applicable statute. Indeed, although the trial court's opinion, quoted by the Supreme Court, stated that "management has seized on a relatively new section of the Delaware Corporation Law," the

change would also have complied with the old provision. What, then, is the source of the law that the Supreme Court found defendants to have violated?

3. Would the *Schnell* court have reached the same result had management made the by-law change before learning of the insurgents' plans? In other words, is a detrimental effect on plaintiffs sufficient to justify judicial relief, or is an improper purpose required as well?

4. For an analysis of the *Schnell* doctrine and the role of improper motive, see Douglas M. Branson, The Chancellor's Foot in Delaware: *Schnell* and its Progeny, 14 J. Corp. L. 515 (1989).

D. LITIGATION BY SHAREHOLDERS

A corporation's managers owe fiduciary duties to the corporation and its shareholders. Managers who breach those duties can be held liable for any losses they have caused. However, determining whether, and on what basis, shareholders can sue to enforce managers' fiduciary duties often involves conceptually difficult issues. We sketch those issues here and explore them at length in Chapter 20.

The threshold issue is whether the duty in question runs to the corporation (and only indirectly to shareholders) or to the shareholders directly. The distinction is relatively straightforward in concept. Managers owe duties to the corporation with regard to managing its business and owe duties to shareholders with regard to the exercise of their rights such as the right to vote. In some situations, it is not easy to determine whether the interests involved are those of the corporation or those of its shareholders. For example, does directors' failure to declare a dividend constitute mismanagement of the business or a violation of contractual obligations owed to shareholders? In Gordon v. Elliman, 306 N.Y. 456, 119 N.E.2d 331 (1954), the New York Court of Appeals split 4–3 on this question, holding that a suit to compel dividends involved a duty owed to the corporation, not directly to shareholders.

Whether a duty runs to the corporation or to shareholders directly has important practical consequences. Shareholders can bring a *direct suit* to remedy a breach of a duty owed to them directly. If the breach involves similar injuries to numerous shareholders, as often will be the case in a public corporation, the suit usually can be maintained as a class action.

[handwritten margin note: duty to shareholder]

If the duty runs to the corporation, a new set of conceptual problems arises. The corporation itself unquestionably has the right to sue, but more often than not, control of the corporation will lie in the hands of the managers whose conduct is at issue. They are not likely to initiate a suit against themselves. Moreover, in the ordinary course, shareholders are not authorized to act directly for the corporation, and thus could not enforce a corporate claim against the managers.

[handwritten margin note: Duty to corporation]

The *derivative suit* was developed to alleviate this problem. Originally, the derivative suit was a suit in equity brought against the corporation to compel it to bring an action against some third party, most often faithless or careless managers. The shareholder's right grew out of the alleged wrongfulness of the managers' failure to institute an action. The corporation was joined as the nominal defendant, but the plaintiff-shareholder controlled prosecution of the suit. Any recovery, however, belonged to the corporation in whose name the suit had been brought. A prevailing plaintiff-shareholder typically was awarded an attorney's fee, paid by the corporation, in consideration for the benefit she had rendered to the corporation. Today, statutory provisions supersede this combination of equity and legal actions, establish the right of shareholders to bring derivative suits, and regulate the manner in which they are prosecuted. See RMBCA §§ 7.40–7.47.

Occasionally, a shareholder's financial interest in a corporation is sufficiently large to make it attractive for her to finance, out of her own pocket, the cost of initiating and maintaining a derivative action. More commonly, the principal party in interest is not the nominal plaintiff-shareholder but her attorney. The prospect of receiving a fee from the corporation, so long as some relief is awarded or agreed to in settlement of the litigation, can make it economically attractive for an attorney to represent a shareholder on a contingent fee basis. But this prospect also raises the possibility that a derivative suit may be initiated primarily to generate an attorney's fee for plaintiff's counsel.

Chapter 4

THE CORPORATION AND
THE CONSTITUTION

A. INTRODUCTION

We now take for granted the idea that a corporation—a collective entity—can possess some of the legal attributes of a natural person. A corporation can own property, enter into contracts, and sue and be sued in its own name. Similarly, as a separate legal entity, a corporation is liable for its debts; neither its officers, directors and shareholders can be held liable for those debts. Taken together, these commonplace notions comprise one of the most powerful ideas in the history of the law of commerce.

Because a corporation is a "person" for some purposes it does not mean that whenever the law imposes a certain obligation on a "person" or establishes that a "person" has certain rights, a corporation bears those obligations or can exercise those rights. First, questions concerning the nature of the corporate "person" must be addressed.

For more than two centuries, courts and commentators have debated what constitute the essential characteristics of the corporate "person." Discussion has focused on pairs of opposing concepts: Is the corporation an entity or an aggregate of participating parties? Are corporations essentially contractual in nature, or are they products of state-granted concessions? Should corporations be viewed as strictly private in nature, or do they also serve public ends? If corporations are essentially contractual, are corporate "contracts" discrete or relational?

During most of the twentieth century, these questions received relatively little attention. There appeared to be truth to philosopher John Dewey's observation that conceptual approaches to the problem of corporate personality were useless in dealing with practical problems because "[e]ach theory has been used to serve the same ends, and each has been used to serve opposing ends." John Dewey, The Historic Background of Corporate Legal Personality, 35 Yale L.J. 655, 669 (1926). Recently, however, proponents of "the new economic theory of the firm" have revived the debate by advancing the idea that a corporation represents no more than a legal fiction that serves as a nexus for private contractual relationships among individual factors of production. Supporters of this "nexus of contracts" thesis also generally believe that, due to the power of market forces, it is almost always undesirable for the state to intervene in or attempt to modify these private contractual arrangements. See Robert Hessen, A New Concept of Corporations: A Contractual and Private Property Model, 30 Hastings L.J. 1327 (1979); Kenneth Scott, Corporation Law and the American Law Institute Corporate Governance Project, 35 Stan. L.Rev. 927 (1983); but see William W. Bratton, Jr., The New Economic Theory of the Firm: Critical Perspectives from History, 41 Stan. L.Rev. 1471 (1989).

Questions relating to the nature of the corporation have arisen with some frequency in cases involving constitutional law, which often turn on whether a corporation is entitled to the same treatment as a natural person. The Supreme Court first discussed this issue in Trustees of Dartmouth College v. Woodward, 17 U.S. (4 Wheat.) 518, 4 L.Ed. 629 (1819). In 1769, the British Crown had granted articles of incorporation to the trustees of Dartmouth College. After the American Revolution, New Hampshire, as successor to the Crown, enacted three laws amending Dartmouth's charter so as to give state officials a major role in the governance of the college. Dartmouth sued to invalidate the amendments, claiming they violated the contract clause of the U.S. Constitution (Art. I, § 10). The New Hampshire Supreme Court rejected Dartmouth's claim, and the college appealed to the Supreme Court.

The Court, in an opinion by Chief Justice Marshall, held New Hampshire's action was invalid because the charter constituted a contract between the state and the college that was "within the letter of the Constitution and within its spirit also * * *." 17 U.S. at 644. The Chief Justice described a corporation's basic attributes in terms suggesting that a corporation is both a fictional entity created by the state and the product of a contract among private parties:

> A corporation is an artificial being, invisible, intangible, and existing only in contemplation of law. Being the mere creature of law, it possesses only those properties which the charter of its creation confers upon it, either expressly, or as incidental to its very existence. These are such as are supposed best calculated to effect the object for which it was created. Among the most important are immortality, and, if the expression may be allowed, individuality; properties, by which a perpetual succession of many persons are considered as the same, and may act as a single individual. They enable a corporation to manage its own affairs, and to hold property, without the perplexing intricacies, the hazardous and endless necessity, of perpetual conveyances for the purpose of transmitting it from hand to hand. It is chiefly for the purpose of clothing bodies of men, in succession, with these qualities and capacities, that corporations were invented, and are in use. By these means, a perpetual succession of individuals are capable of acting for the promotion of the particular object, like one immortal being. But this being does

not share in the civil government of the country, unless that be the purpose for which it was created. Its immortality no more confers on it political power, or a political character, than immortality would confer such power or character on a natural person. It is no more a state instrument, than a natural person exercising the same powers would be.

Id. at 636–37.

Subsequent to *Dartmouth College*, the Court has had occasion to decide whether a corporation is entitled to various rights and privileges that the Constitution provides to natural persons. Santa Clara County v. Southern Pacific Railroad Co., 118 U.S. 394, 6 S.Ct. 1132, 30 L.Ed. 118 (1886), the most important of these cases, held that a corporation is entitled to equal protection of the law under the Fourteenth Amendment. Minneapolis & St. Louis Railway Co. v. Beckwith, 129 U.S. 26, 9 S.Ct. 207, 32 L.Ed. 585 (1888), decided two years later, extended the holding of *Santa Clara* and ruled that a corporation also is entitled to due process of law. Hale v. Henkel, 201 U.S. 43, 26 S.Ct. 370, 50 L.Ed. 652 (1906), subsequently established that a corporation is protected against unreasonable searches and seizures by the Fourth Amendment, but also held that the Fifth Amendment's protection against self-incrimination is not available to a corporation.

More recently, the Court has considered the nature of the corporation in relation to the First Amendment's protection of freedom of speech.

B. THE FIRST AMENDMENT

PROBLEM
REGULATING CORPORATE LOBBYING—PART I

You are the legislative assistant to Kathleen Bruin, who recently was elected a Columbia State Senator. In recent years, there were frequent reports that corporations exert tremendous influence on the Columbia Legislature, and Sen. Bruin campaigned heavily on the claim that, if elected, she would work to reduce corporations' political influence. Now in office, Sen. Bruin wants to propose legislation that would make it unlawful for "any business corporation, by itself or through any agent, employee or other person, to communicate, other than in a public hearing, directly with any member or employee of the Legislature of Columbia to secure or defeat the passage of any pending or proposed legislation by said Legislature."

Senator Bruin anticipates that opponents of this legislation will contend that it is both unconstitutional and unwise. As the materials that follow make clear, a court almost surely would hold the proposed legislation violated the First Amendment if it were directed at individuals. The more relevant question, on which the Senator is seeking your advice, is whether the fact the legislation regulates only business corporations would lead a court to hold it was not unconstitutional. Sen.

Bruin also has asked you to consider whether, as a matter of public policy, it makes sense to limit corporate lobbying of the Columbia Legislature.

In developing your responses to these questions, consider:

1. Is there any difference between the political activity of corporations and that of individuals?

2. What are the interests of shareholders in the political expenditures made by their corporations? By what mechanisms are those interests protected? Are those mechanisms sufficient?

3. Who actually decides what positions a corporation should take on political issues? What criteria are relevant to the decision? Does the business judgment rule protect such decisions?

4. What does it mean to say that "the corporation" supports a particular issue?

5. If there are valid reasons for concern about corporate political activities, do they arise from the size of the corporation or are the reasons more closely related to the characteristics of a corporation? Is there something about corporate status alone that makes corporate political activities more troublesome?

Regulation of Political Speech

Political speech lies at the core of the First Amendment, but the Supreme Court has not held every limitation on participation in the political process to be unconstitutional. The Corrupt Practices Act has long barred corporate and union contributions to candidates in federal elections; the Court has never ruled directly on the Act, but has treated it with considerable deference. Most notably, in United States v. United Automobile Workers, 352 U.S. 567, 588–90, 77 S.Ct. 529, 540, 1 L.Ed.2d 563 (1957), the Court reinstated an indictment of the U.A.W. under the Corrupt Practices Act for sponsoring a broadcast, directed at the general public, endorsing candidates for federal office, in the face of claims that so construing the Act would create significant First Amendment problems.

As concerns lobbying, the Court has upheld the Lobbying Act, which requires registration of lobbyists and disclosure of payments made to lobbyists. See United States v. Harriss, 347 U.S. 612, 74 S.Ct. 808, 98 L.Ed. 989 (1954). The Court first construed rather general language in the Act, describing who must register, as limited to persons who engage in "direct communication with members of Congress on pending or proposed federal legislation." Id. at 620, 74 S.Ct. at 813. It continued:

> Present-day legislative complexities are such that individual members of Congress cannot be expected to explore the myriad pressures to which they are regularly subjected. Yet full realization of the American ideal of government by elected representatives depends to no small extent on their ability to properly evaluate such pressures. Otherwise the voice of the people may all too easily be

drowned out by the voice of special interest groups seeking favored treatment while masquerading as proponents of the public weal. This is the evil which the Lobbying Act was designed to help prevent.

Toward that end, Congress has not sought to prohibit these pressures. It has merely provided for a modicum of information from those who for hire attempt to influence legislation or who collect or spend funds for that purpose. It wants only to know who is being hired, who is putting up the money, and how much. It acted in the same spirit and for a similar purpose in passing the Federal Corrupt Practices Act—to maintain the integrity of a basic governmental process.

Under these circumstances, we believe that Congress, at least within the bounds of the Act as we have construed it, is not constitutionally forbidden to require the disclosure of lobbying activities. To do so would be to deny Congress in large measure the power of self-protection. (Id. at 625, 74 S.Ct. at 816.)

Similarly, the Court has rejected challenges to legislation that denies corporations and individuals business expense deductions for lobbying activities, Cammarano v. United States, 358 U.S. 498, 79 S.Ct. 524, 3 L.Ed.2d 462 (1959), and that bars lobbying by organizations that receive tax-deductible charitable contributions, Regan v. Taxation With Representation, 461 U.S. 540, 103 S.Ct. 1997, 76 L.Ed.2d 129 (1983). In both cases, the Court reasoned that deductions and tax-exempt status are matters of grace, not of right, and that Congress has no obligation to subsidize political speech. The Court also upheld the Hatch Act, which deters federal Civil Service employees from participating in political campaigns. See United Public Workers v. Mitchell, 330 U.S. 75, 67 S.Ct. 556, 91 L.Ed. 754 (1947).

On the other hand, the Court has been considerably less tolerant of express limitations on political speech by individuals and unincorporated associations. In Buckley v. Valeo, 424 U.S. 1, 96 S.Ct. 612, 46 L.Ed.2d 659 (1976), the Court drew a fundamental distinction between campaign contributions and expenditures. Contributions are entitled to only limited First Amendment protection, because they convey undifferentiated expressions of support, not specific ideas. Thus, Congress's interest in reducing corruption and the appearance of corruption is sufficient to support a limitation on the amount any individual can contribute to a candidate for federal office.

Expenditures, in contrast, relate directly to the expression of political views and are entitled to greater protection.

A restriction on the amount of money an individual can spend on political communication during a campaign necessarily reduces the quantity of expression by restricting the number of issues discussed, the depth of their exploration, and the size of the audience reached.

This is because virtually every means of communicating in today's mass society requires the expenditure of money.

Id. at 19, 96 S.Ct. at 634.

A limit on how much an individual can spend to support a campaign for office will be subjected to "exacting scrutiny." The strict limits Congress imposed in the Federal Election Campaign Act, as amended, did not survive such scrutiny because they would have materially restricted dissemination of ideas in the political marketplace.

Relying on similar arguments, the Court subsequently held unconstitutional a local ordinance that limited individuals' expenditures of their own money on political speech, Citizens Against Rent Control/ Coalition for Fair Housing v. City of Berkeley, 454 U.S. 290, 102 S.Ct. 434, 70 L.Ed.2d 492 (1981), and a federal regulation barring independent expenditures by political action committees to support presidential candidates, Federal Election Commission v. National Conservative Political Action Committee, 470 U.S. 480, 105 S.Ct. 1459, 84 L.Ed.2d 455 (1985) (NCPAC). In the latter case, the Court explained:

> We held in *Buckley* and reaffirmed in *Citizens Against Rent Control* that preventing corruption or the appearance of corruption are the only legitimate and compelling government interests thus far identified for restricting campaign finances. * * *

> Corruption is a subversion of the political process. Elected officials are influenced to act contrary to their obligations of office by the prospect of gains to themselves or their campaigns. The hallmark of corruption is the *quid pro quo*: dollars for political favors. But here the conduct proscribed is not contributions to the candidate, but independent expenditures in support of the candidate.

Id. at 496–97, 105 S.Ct. at 1468.

In two cases, the Court has considered directly the validity of restrictions on political speech by business corporations.

FIRST NATIONAL BANK OF BOSTON v. BELLOTTI
435 U.S. 765, 98 S.Ct. 1407, 55 L.Ed.2d 707 (1978).

Mr. Justice Powell delivered the opinion of the Court.

In sustaining a state criminal statute that forbids certain expenditures by banks and business corporations for the purpose of influencing the vote on referendum proposals, the Massachusetts Supreme Judicial Court held that the First Amendment rights of a corporation are limited to issues that materially affect its business, property, or assets. The court rejected appellants' claim that the statute abridges freedom of speech in violation of the First and Fourteenth Amendments. The issue presented in this context is one of first impression in this Court. * * * We now reverse.

I

The statute at issue prohibits appellants, two national banking associations and three business corporations, from making contributions or expenditures "for the purpose of * * * influencing or affecting the vote on any question submitted to the voters, other than one materially affecting any of the property, business or assets of the corporation." The statute further specifies that "[no] question submitted to the voters solely concerning the taxation of the income, property or transactions of individuals shall be deemed materially to affect the property, business or assets of the corporation."

STATUTE @ issue

Appellants wanted to spend money to publicize their views on a proposed constitutional amendment that * * * would have permitted the legislature to impose a graduated tax on the income of individuals. * * * The parties' statement of agreed facts reflected their disagreement as to the effect that the adoption of a personal income tax would have on appellants' business; it noted that "[there] is a division of opinion among economists as to whether and to what extent a graduated income tax imposed solely on individuals would affect the business and assets of corporations." Appellee did not dispute that appellants' management believed that the tax would have a significant effect on their businesses.

Corps. wants to spend $ on disagreement on personal income tax on business

* * *

III

* * *

If the speakers here were not corporations, no one would suggest that the State could silence their proposed speech. It is the type of speech indispensable to decisionmaking in a democracy, and this is no less true because the speech comes from a corporation rather than an individual. * * *

The question in this case, simply put, is whether the corporate identity of the speaker deprives this proposed speech of what otherwise would be its clear entitlement to protection. * * *

[A]ppellee suggests that First Amendment rights generally have been afforded only to corporations engaged in the communications business or through which individuals express themselves. * * *

But the press does not have a monopoly on either the First Amendment or the ability to enlighten. Cf. Buckley v. Valeo, 424 U.S. at 51 n. 56. Similarly, the Court's decisions involving corporations in the business of communication or entertainment are based not only on the role of the First Amendment in fostering individual self-expression but also on its role in affording the public access to discussion, debate, and the dissemination of information and ideas. Even decisions seemingly based exclusively on the individual's right to express himself acknowledge that the expression may contribute to society's edification.

← Key.

* * *

We thus find no support in the First or Fourteenth Amendment, or in the decisions of this Court, for the proposition that speech that otherwise would be within the protection of the First Amendment loses that protection simply because its source is a corporation that cannot prove, to the satisfaction of a court, a material effect on its business or property. * * *

In the realm of protected speech, the legislature is constitutionally disqualified from dictating the subjects about which persons may speak and the speakers who may address a public issue. If a legislature may direct business corporations to "stick to business," it also may limit other corporations—religious, charitable, or civic—to their respective "business" when addressing the public. Such power in government to channel the expression of views is unacceptable under the First Amendment. Especially where, as here, the legislature's suppression of speech suggests an attempt to give one side of a debatable public question an advantage in expressing its views to the people,[22] the First Amendment is plainly offended. * * *

IV

The constitutionality of § 8's prohibition of the "exposition of ideas" by corporations turns on whether it can survive the exacting scrutiny necessitated by a state-imposed restriction of freedom of speech. Especially where, as here, a prohibition is directed at speech itself, and the speech is intimately related to the process of governing, "the State may prevail only upon showing a subordinating interest which is compelling," Bates v. Little Rock, 361 U.S. 516, 524 (1960), "and the burden is on the government to show the existence of such an interest." Elrod v. Burns, 427 U.S. 347, 362 (1976). * * *

Appellee nevertheless advances two principal justifications for the prohibition of corporate speech. (1) The first is the State's interest in sustaining the active role of the individual citizen in the electoral process and thereby preventing diminution of the citizen's confidence in government. (2) The second is the interest in protecting the rights of shareholders whose views differ from those expressed by management on behalf of the corporation. However weighty these interests may be in the context of partisan candidate elections, they either are not implicated in this case or are not served at all, or in other than a random manner, by the prohibition in § 8.

A

According to appellee, corporations are wealthy and powerful and their views may drown out other points of view. If appellee's arguments were supported by record or legislative findings that corporate advocacy

---

22. Our observation about the apparent purpose of the Massachusetts Legislature is not an endorsement of the legislature's factual assumptions about the views of corporations. * * * Corporations, like individuals or groups, are not homogeneous. * * *

It is arguable that small or medium-size corporations might welcome imposition of a graduated personal income tax that might shift a greater share of the tax burden onto wealthy individuals.

threatened imminently to undermine democratic processes, thereby denigrating rather than serving First Amendment interests, these arguments would merit our consideration. But there has been no showing that the relative voice of corporations has been overwhelming or even significant in influencing referenda in Massachusetts, or that there has been any threat to the confidence of the citizenry in government.

NO RECORDS or legis. findings

Nor are appellee's arguments inherently persuasive or supported by the precedents of this Court. Referenda are held on issues, not candidates for public office. The risk of corruption perceived in cases involving candidate elections, e.g., United States v. Automobile Workers, supra; simply is not present in a popular vote on a public issue. To be sure, corporate advertising may influence the outcome of the vote; this would be its purpose. But the fact that advocacy may persuade the electorate is hardly a reason to suppress it: The Constitution "protects expression which is eloquent no less than that which is unconvincing." Kingsley Int'l Pictures Corp. v. Regents, 360 U.S. at 689. We noted only recently that "the concept that government may restrict the speech of some elements of our society in order to enhance the relative voice of others is wholly foreign to the First Amendment. * * *" *Buckley*, 424 U.S. at 48–49. * * *

B

Finally, appellee argues that § 8 protects corporate shareholders, an interest that is both legitimate and traditionally within the province of state law. Cort v. Ash, 422 U.S. 66, 82–84 (1975). The statute is said to serve this interest by preventing the use of corporate resources in furtherance of views with which some shareholders may disagree. This purpose is belied, however, by the provisions of the statute, which are both underinclusive and overinclusive.

2nd arg. of Bellotti

The underinclusiveness of the statute is self-evident. Corporate expenditures with respect to a referendum are prohibited, while corporate activity with respect to the passage or defeat of legislation is permitted, even though corporations may engage in lobbying more often than they take positions on ballot questions submitted to the voters. Nor does § 8 prohibit a corporation from expressing its views, by the expenditure of corporate funds, on any public issue until it becomes the subject of a referendum, though the displeasure of disapproving shareholders is unlikely to be any less.

under inclusive

The fact that a particular kind of ballot question has been singled out for special treatment undermines the likelihood of a genuine state interest in protecting shareholders. It suggests instead that the legislature may have been concerned with silencing corporations on a particular subject. * * *

The overinclusiveness of the statute is demonstrated by the fact that § 8 would prohibit a corporation from supporting or opposing a referendum proposal even if its shareholders unanimously authorized the contribution or expenditure. Ultimately shareholders may decide, through

over inclus.

the procedures of corporate democracy, whether their corporation should engage in debate on public issues.[34] Acting through their power to elect the board of directors or to insist upon protective provisions in the corporation's charter, shareholders normally are presumed competent to protect their own interests. In addition to intracorporate remedies, minority shareholders generally have access to the judicial remedy of a derivative suit to challenge corporate disbursements alleged to have been made for improper corporate purposes or merely to further the personal interests of management.

Assuming, *arguendo*, that protection of shareholders is a "compelling" interest under the circumstances of this case, we find "no substantially relevant correlation between the governmental interest asserted and the State's effort" to prohibit appellants from speaking.

V

Because that portion of § 8 challenged by appellants prohibits protected speech in a manner unjustified by a compelling state interest, it must be invalidated. The judgment of the Supreme Judicial Court is *Reversed.*

MR. JUSTICE WHITE, with whom MR. JUSTICE BRENNAN and MR. JUSTICE MARSHALL join, dissenting.

* * *

I

There is now little doubt that corporate communications come within the scope of the First Amendment. This, however, is merely the starting point of analysis, because an examination of the First Amendment values that corporate expression furthers and the threat to the functioning of a free society it is capable of posing reveals that it is not fungible with communications emanating from individuals and is subject to restrictions which individual expression is not. Indeed, what some have considered to be the principal function of the First Amendment, the use of communication as a means of self-expression, self-realization, and self-fulfillment, is not at all furthered by corporate speech. It is clear that the communications of profitmaking corporations are not "an integral part of the development of ideas, of mental exploration and of the affirmation of self." They do not represent a manifestation of individual freedom or choice. * * * Shareholders in such entities do not share a common set of political or social views, and they certainly have not invested their money for the purpose of advancing political or social causes or in an enterprise engaged in the business of disseminating news

---

34. Appellee does not explain why the dissenting shareholder's wishes are entitled to such greater solicitude in this context than in many others where equally important and controversial corporate decisions are made by management or by a predetermined percentage of the shareholders. * * *

[Moreover,] no shareholder has been "compelled" to contribute anything. Apart from the fact, noted by the dissent, that compulsion by the State is wholly absent, the shareholder invests in a corporation of his own volition and is free to withdraw his investment at any time and for any reason. * * *

and opinion. In fact, as discussed *infra*, the government has a strong interest in assuring that investment decisions are not predicated upon agreement or disagreement with the activities of corporations in the political arena.

Of course, it may be assumed that corporate investors are united by a desire to make money, for the value of their investment to increase. Since even communications which have no purpose other than that of enriching the communicator have some First Amendment protection, activities such as advertising and other communications integrally related to the operation of the corporation's business may be viewed as a means of furthering the desires of individual shareholders. This unanimity of purpose breaks down, however, when corporations make expenditures or undertake activities designed to influence the opinion or votes of the general public on political and social issues that have no material connection with or effect upon their business, property, or assets. Although it is arguable that corporations make such expenditures because their managers believe that it is in the corporations' economic interest to do so, there is no basis whatsoever for concluding that these views are expressive of the heterogeneous beliefs of their shareholders whose convictions on many political issues are undoubtedly shaped by considerations other than a desire to endorse any electoral or ideological cause which would tend to increase the value of a particular corporate investment. * * *

The self-expression of the communicator is not the only value encompassed by the First Amendment. One of its functions, often referred to as the right to hear or receive information, is to protect the interchange of ideas. * * * This proposition does not establish, however, that the right of the general public to receive communications financed by means of corporate expenditures is of the same dimension as that to hear other forms of expression. * * * Even the complete curtailment of corporate communications concerning political or ideological questions not integral to day-to-day business functions would leave individuals, including corporate shareholders, employees, and customers, free to communicate their thoughts. Moreover, it is unlikely that any significant communication would be lost by such a prohibition. These individuals would remain perfectly free to communicate any ideas which could be conveyed by means of the corporate form. Indeed, such individuals could even form associations for the very purpose of promoting political or ideological causes.

* * *

The governmental interest in regulating corporate political communications, especially those relating to electoral matters, also raises considerations which differ significantly from those governing the regulation of individual speech. Corporations are artificial entities created by law for the purpose of furthering certain economic goals. In order to facilitate the achievement of such ends, special rules relating to such matters as limited liability, perpetual life, and the accumulation, distribution, and taxation of assets are normally applied to them. States have provided corporations with such attributes in order to increase their economic viability and thus strengthen the economy generally. It has long been recognized, however, that the special status of corporations has placed them in a position to control vast amounts of economic power which may, if not regulated, dominate not only the economy but also the very heart of our democracy, the electoral process. Although Buckley v. Valeo, 424 U.S. 1 (1976), provides support for the position that the desire to equalize the financial resources available to candidates does not justify the limitation upon the expression of support which a restriction upon individual contributions entails, the interest of Massachusetts and the many other States which have restricted corporate political activity is quite different. It is not one of equalizing the resources of opposing candidates or opposing positions, but rather of preventing institutions which have been permitted to amass wealth as a result of special advantages extended by the State for certain economic purposes from using that wealth to acquire an unfair advantage in the political process, especially where, as here, the issue involved has no material connection with the business of the corporation. The State need not permit its own creation to consume it. Massachusetts could permissibly conclude that not to impose limits upon the political activities of corporations would have placed it in a position of departing from neutrality and indirectly assisting the propagation of corporate views because of the advantages its laws give to the corporate acquisition of funds to finance such activities. Such expenditures may be viewed as seriously threatening the role of the First Amendment as a guarantor of a free marketplace of ideas. Ordinarily, the expenditure of funds to promote political causes may be assumed to bear some relation to the fervency with which they are held. Corporate political expression, however, is not only divorced from the convictions of individual corporate shareholders, but also, because of the ease with which corporations are permitted to accumulate capital, bears no relation to the conviction with which the ideas expressed are held by the communicator.

* * *

The Corrupt Practices Act.

This Nation has for many years recognized the need for measures designed to prevent corporate domination of the political process. The Corrupt Practices Act, first enacted in 1907, has consistently barred corporate contributions in connection with federal elections. This Court has repeatedly recognized that one of the principal purposes of this prohibition is "to avoid the deleterious influences on federal elections resulting from the use of money by those who exercise control over large aggregations of capital." United States v. Automobile Workers, 352 U.S. 567, 585 (1957). * * *

II

There is an additional overriding interest related to the prevention of corporate domination which is substantially advanced by Massachusetts' restrictions upon corporate contributions: assuring that shareholders are not compelled to support and financially further beliefs with which they disagree where, as is the case here, the issue involved does not materially affect the business, property, or other affairs of the corporation. The State has not interfered with the prerogatives of corporate management to communicate about matters that have material impact on the business affairs entrusted to them, however much individual stockholders may disagree on economic or ideological grounds. Nor has the State forbidden management from formulating and circulating its views at its own expense or at the expense of others, even where the subject at issue is irrelevant to corporate business affairs. But Massachusetts has chosen to forbid corporate management from spending corporate funds in referenda elections absent some demonstrable effect of the issue on the economic life of the company. In short, corporate management may not use corporate monies to promote what does not further corporate affairs but what in the last analysis are the purely personal views of the management, individually or as a group.

* * *

The Court assumes that the interest in preventing the use of corporate resources in furtherance of views which are irrelevant to the corporate business and with which some shareholders may disagree is a compelling one, but concludes that the Massachusetts statute is nevertheless invalid because the State has failed to adopt the means best suited, in its opinion, for achieving this end. It proposes that the aggrieved shareholder assert his interest in preventing the expenditure of funds for nonbusiness causes he finds unconscionable through the channels provided by "corporate democracy" and purports to be mystified as to "why the dissenting shareholder's wishes are entitled to such greater solicitude in this context than in many others where equally important and controversial corporate decisions are made by management or by a predetermined percentage of the shareholders." Ante, at 794, and n. 34. It should be obvious that the alternative means upon the adequacy of which the majority is willing to predicate a constitutional adjudication is [not] able to satisfy the State's interest * * *.

* * *

There is no apparent way of segregating one shareholder's ownership interest in a corporation from another's. It is no answer to respond, as the Court does, that the dissenting "shareholder is free to withdraw his investment at any time and for any reason." Ante, at 794 n. 34. * * * Clearly the State has a strong interest in assuring that its citizens are not forced to choose between supporting the propagation of views with which they disagree and passing up investment opportunities.

Finally, even if corporations developed an effective mechanism for rebating to shareholders that portion of their investment used to finance political activities with which they disagreed, a State may still choose to restrict corporate political activity irrelevant to business functions on the grounds that many investors would be deterred from investing in corporations because of a wish not to associate with corporations propagating certain views. The State has an interest not only in enabling individuals to exercise freedom of conscience without penalty but also in eliminating the danger that investment decisions will be significantly influenced by the ideological views of corporations. While the latter concern may not be of the same constitutional magnitude as the former, it is far from trivial. Corporations, as previously noted, are created by the State as a means of furthering the public welfare. One of their functions is to determine, by their success in obtaining funds, the uses to which society's resources are to be put. A State may legitimately conclude that corporations would not serve as economically efficient vehicles for such decisions if the investment preferences of the public were significantly affected by their ideological or political activities. It has long been recognized that such pursuits are not the proper business of corporations. The common law was generally interpreted as prohibiting corporate political participation. * * *

I would affirm the judgment of the Supreme Judicial Court for the Commonwealth of Massachusetts.

Mr. Justice Rehnquist, dissenting.

* * *

The question presented today, whether business corporations have a constitutionally protected liberty to engage in political activities, has never been squarely addressed by any previous decision of this Court. However, the General Court of the Commonwealth of Massachusetts, the Congress of the United States, and the legislatures of 30 other States of this Republic have considered the matter, and have concluded that restrictions upon the political activity of business corporations are both politically desirable and constitutionally permissible. The judgment of such a broad consensus of governmental bodies expressed over a period of many decades is entitled to considerable deference from this Court. * * *

Early in our history, Mr. Chief Justice Marshall described the status of a corporation in the eyes of federal law [in *Dartmouth College v. Woodward*].

The appellants herein either were created by the Commonwealth or were admitted into the Commonwealth only for the limited purposes described in their charters and regulated by state law. Since it cannot be disputed that the mere creation of a corporation does not invest it with all the liberties enjoyed by natural persons, our inquiry must seek to determine which constitutional protections are "incidental to its very existence." *Dartmouth College, supra,* at 636.

There can be little doubt that when a State creates a corporation with the power to acquire and utilize property, it necessarily and implicitly guarantees that the corporation will not be deprived of that property absent due process of law. Likewise, when a State charters a corporation for the purpose of publishing a newspaper, it necessarily assumes that the corporation is entitled to the liberty of the press essential to the conduct of its business. * * *

It cannot be so readily concluded that the right of political expression is equally necessary to carry out the functions of a corporation organized for commercial purposes. A State grants to a business corporation the blessings of potentially perpetual life and limited liability to enhance its efficiency as an economic entity. It might reasonably be concluded that those properties, so beneficial in the economic sphere, pose special dangers in the political sphere. Furthermore, it might be argued that liberties of political expression are not at all necessary to effectuate the purposes for which States permit commercial corporations to exist. So long as the Judicial Branches of the State and Federal Governments remain open to protect the corporation's interest in its property, it has no need, though it may have the desire, to petition the political branches for similar protection. Indeed, the States might reasonably fear that the corporation would use its economic power to obtain further benefits beyond those already bestowed. I would think that any particular form of organization upon which the State confers special privileges or immunities different from those of natural persons would be subject to like regulation, whether the organization is a labor union, a partnership, a trade association, or a corporation. * * *

It is true, as the Court points out, that recent decisions of this Court have emphasized the interest of the public in receiving the information offered by the speaker seeking protection. The free flow of information is in no way diminished by the Commonwealth's decision to permit the operation of business corporations with limited rights of political expression. All natural persons, who owe their existence to a higher sovereign than the Commonwealth, remain as free as before to engage in political activity.

I would affirm the judgment of the Supreme Judicial Court.

AUSTIN v. MICHIGAN CHAMBER OF COMMERCE

494 U.S. 652, 110 S.Ct. 1391, 108 L.Ed.2d 652 (1990).

[The Michigan Campaign Finance Act, § 54(1), prohibited corporations from using corporate funds for contributions or independent expenditures in support of or in opposition to any candidate in elections for state office. The Michigan State Chamber of Commerce, a nonprofit Michigan corporation with more than 8,000 members, three-quarters of which were for-profit corporations, alleged that the statute unconstitutionally barred it from running an advertisement in support of a candidate in a special election for the Michigan House of Representatives.

The Chamber's status as a non-profit corporation added a complicating element to the case. In Federal Election Comm'n v. Massachusetts Citizens For Life, Inc., 479 U.S. 238 (1986) (MCFL), the Court had held unconstitutional a federal regulation barring independent campaign expenditures by a non-profit membership corporation "formed for the express purpose of promoting political ideas" and supported entirely by individuals. Thus, even if the Court concluded that the Michigan statute was not unconstitutional with regard to business corporations, it had to consider whether the Chamber more closely resembled a business corporation or an advocacy group like MCFL.]

JUSTICE MARSHALL delivered the opinion of the Court.

* * *

II

To determine whether Michigan's restrictions on corporate political expenditures may constitutionally be applied to the Chamber, we must ascertain whether they burden the exercise of political speech and, if they do, whether they are narrowly tailored to serve a compelling state interest. Buckley v. Valeo, 424 U.S. 1, 44–45 (1976) (*per curiam*). Certainly, the use of funds to support a political candidate is "speech"; independent campaign expenditures constitute "political expression 'at the core of our electoral process and of the First Amendment freedoms.'" Id., at 39. The mere fact that the Chamber is a corporation does not remove its speech from the ambit of the First Amendment. See, e.g., First National Bank of Boston v. Bellotti, 435 U.S. 765, 777 (1978).

* * *

B

The State contends that the unique legal and economic characteristics of corporations necessitate some regulation of their political expenditures to avoid corruption or the appearance of corruption. State law grants corporations special advantages—such as limited liability, perpetual life, and favorable treatment of the accumulation and distribution of assets—that enhance their ability to attract capital and to deploy their resources in ways that maximize the return on their shareholders' investments. These state-created advantages not only allow corporations to play a dominant role in the nation's economy, but also permit them to use "resources amassed in the economic marketplace" to obtain "an unfair advantage in the political marketplace." MCFL, 479 U.S., at 257. As the Court explained in MCFL, the political advantage of corporations is unfair because

"[t]he resources in the treasury of a business corporation * * * are not an indication of popular support for the corporation's political ideas. They reflect instead the economically motivated decisions of investors and customers. The availability of these resources may make a corporation a formidable political presence, even though the power of the corporation may be no reflection of the power of its ideas." *Id.* at 258.

We therefore have recognized that "the compelling governmental interest in preventing corruption support[s] the restriction of the influence of political war chests funneled through the corporate form." *NCPAC, supra,* 470 U.S. at 500–501.

The Chamber argues that this concern about corporate domination of the political process is insufficient to justify restrictions on independent expenditures. Although this Court has distinguished these expenditures from direct contributions in the context of federal laws regulating individual donors, *Buckley,* 424 U.S. at 47, it has also recognized that a legislature might demonstrate a danger of real or apparent corruption posed by such expenditures when made by corporations to influence candidate elections, *Bellotti.* * * * Michigan's regulation aims at a different type of corruption in the political arena: the corrosive and distorting effects of immense aggregations of wealth that are accumulated with the help of the corporate form and that have little or no correlation to the public's support for the corporation's political ideas. * * * We emphasize that the mere fact that corporations may accumulate large amounts of wealth is not the justification for § 54; rather, the unique state-conferred corporate structure that facilitates the amassing of large treasuries warrants the limit on independent expenditures. Corporate wealth can unfairly influence elections when it is deployed in the form of independent expenditures, just as it can when it assumes the guise of political contributions. We therefore hold that the State has articulated a sufficiently compelling rationale to support its restriction on independent expenditures by corporations.

[The Court also found that the Act was "precisely targeted to eliminate the distortion caused by corporate spending while also allowing corporations to express their political views" because it permitted corporations to make independent political expenditures through separate segregated funds. The Court reasoned that "persons contributing to such funds understand that their money will be used solely for political purposes, [so] the speech generated accurately reflects contributors' support for the corporation's political views."

The Court also rejected the Chamber's claim that the Campaign Finance Act, even if constitutional with respect to for-profit corporations, could not be applied to a non-profit corporation such as the Chamber. It distinguished the Chamber from MCFL on three grounds. First, MCFL was formed solely to promote political ideas, while the Chamber had more varied purposes. Second, members of the Chamber were more like shareholders in a corporation than members of MCFL, in that they had incentives to remain involved with the Chamber even if they disagreed with its political positions. Third, "[b]ecause the Chamber accepts money from for-profit corporations, it could * * * serve as a conduit for corporate political spending."]

JUSTICE STEVENS, concurring.

In my opinion the distinction between individual expenditures and individual contributions that the Court identified in Buckley v. Valeo, 424 U.S. 1, 45–47 (1976), should have little, if any, weight in reviewing corporate participation in candidate elections. In that context, I believe the danger of either the fact, or the appearance, of quid pro quo relationships provides an adequate justification for state regulation of both expenditures and contributions. Moreover, as we recognized in First National Bank of Boston v. Bellotti, 435 U.S. 765 (1978), there is a vast difference between lobbying and debating public issues on the one hand, and political campaigns for election to public office on the other. Accordingly, I join the Court's opinion and judgment.

JUSTICE SCALIA, dissenting.

"Attention all citizens. To assure the fairness of elections by preventing disproportionate expression of the views of any single powerful group, your Government has decided that the following associations of persons shall be prohibited from speaking or writing in support of any candidate: _____" In permitting Michigan to make private corporations the first object of this Orwellian announcement, the Court today endorses the principle that too much speech is an evil that the democratic majority can proscribe. I dissent because that principle is contrary to our case law and incompatible with the absolutely central truth of the First Amendment: that government cannot be trusted to assure, through censorship, the "fairness" of political debate.

I

A

The Court's opinion says that political speech of corporations can be regulated because "[s]tate law grants [them] special advantages," and because this "unique state-conferred corporate structure * * * facilitates the amassing of large treasuries." This analysis seeks to create one good argument by combining two bad ones. Those individuals who form that type of voluntary association known as a corporation are, to be sure, given special advantages—notably, the immunization of their personal fortunes from liability for the actions of the association—that the State is under no obligation to confer. But so are other associations and private individuals given all sorts of special advantages that the State need not confer, ranging from tax breaks to contract awards to public employment to outright cash subsidies. It is rudimentary that the State cannot exact as the price of those special advantages the forfeiture of First Amendment rights. The categorical suspension of the right of any person, or of any association of persons, to speak out on political matters must be justified by a compelling state need. See Buckley v. Valeo, 424 U.S. 1, 44–45 (1976). Which is why the Court puts forward its second bad argument, the fact that corporations "amas[s] large treasuries." But that alone is also not sufficient justification for the suppression of political speech, unless one thinks it would be lawful to prohibit men and women whose net worth is above a certain figure from endorsing political candidates. Neither of these two flawed arguments is improved by combining them and saying, as the Court in effect does, that "since the State gives special advantages to these voluntary associations, and since they thereby amass vast wealth, they may be required to abandon their right of political speech."

* * *

As for the second part of the Court's argumentation, the fact that corporations (or at least some of them) possess "massive wealth": Certain uses of "massive wealth" in the electoral process—whether or not the wealth is the result of "special advantages" conferred by the State—pose a substantial risk of corruption which constitutes a compelling need for the regulation of speech. Such a risk plainly exists when the wealth is given directly to the political candidate, to be used under his direction and control. We held in Buckley v. Valeo, supra, however, that independent expenditures to express the political views of individuals and associations do not raise a sufficient threat of corruption to justify prohibition. * * *

Buckley v. Valeo should not be overruled, because it is entirely correct. The contention that prohibiting overt advocacy for or against a political candidate satisfies a "compelling need" to avoid "corruption" is easily dismissed. * * * I expect I could count on the fingers of one hand the candidates who would generally welcome, much less negotiate for, a formal endorsement by AT & T or General Motors. The advocacy of such entities that have "amassed great wealth" will be effective only to the extent that it brings to the people's attention ideas which—despite the invariably self-interested and probably uncongenial source—strike them as true.

The Court does not try to defend the proposition that independent advocacy poses a substantial risk of political "corruption," as English-speakers understand that term. * * * "Michigan's regulation," we are told, "aims at a different type of corruption in the political arena: the corrosive and distorting effects of immense aggregations of wealth that are accumulated with the help of the corporate form and that have little or no correlation to the public's support for the corporations's political ideas." Under this mode of analysis, virtually anything the Court deems politically undesirable can be turned into political corruption—by simply describing its effects as politically "corrosive," which is close enough to "corruptive" to qualify. It is sad to think that the First Amendment will ultimately be brought down not by brute force but by poetic metaphor.

* * * But it can be said that I have not accurately quoted today's decision. It does not endorse the proposition that government may ensure that expenditures "reflect actual public support for the political ideas espoused," but only the more limited proposition that government may ensure that expenditures "reflect actual public support for the political ideas espoused *by corporations*." Ante, at 1397 (emphasis added). The limitation is of course entirely irrational. Why is it perfectly all right if advocacy by an individual billionaire is out of proportion with "actual public support" for his positions? There is no explanation, except the effort I described at the outset of this discussion to make one valid proposition out of two invalid ones: When the vessel labeled "corruption" begins to founder under weight too great to be logically sustained, the argumentation jumps to the good ship "special privilege"; and when that in turn begins to go down, it returns to "corruption." Thus hopping back and forth between the two, the argumentation may survive but makes no headway towards port, where its conclusion waits in vain.

B

* * *

But even if the object of the prohibition could plausibly be portrayed as the protection of shareholders ([which Justice Brennan argued in a concurring opinion], but which the Court's opinion, at least, does not even assert), that would not suffice as a "compelling need" to support this blatant restriction upon core political speech. A person becomes a member of that form of association known as a for-profit corporation in order to pursue economic objectives, i.e., to make money. Some corporate charters may specify the line of commerce to which the company is limited, but even that can be amended by shareholder vote. Thus, in joining such an association, the shareholder knows that management may take any action that is ultimately in accord with what the majority (or a specified supermajority) of the shareholders wishes, so long as that action is designed to make a profit. That is the deal. The corporate actions to which the shareholder exposes himself, therefore, include many things that he may find politically or ideologically uncongenial: investment in South Africa, operation of an abortion clinic, publication of a pornographic magazine, or even publication of a newspaper that adopts absurd political views and makes catastrophic political endorsements. His only protections against such assaults upon his ideological commitments are (1) his ability to persuade a majority (or the requisite minority) of his fellow shareholders that the action should not be taken, and ultimately (2) his ability to sell his stock. * * * It seems to me entirely fanciful, in other words, to suggest that the Michigan statute makes any significant contribution towards insulating the exclusively profit-motivated shareholder from the rude world of politics and ideology.

* * *

II

* * *

Despite all the talk about "corruption and the appearance of corruption"—evils that are not significantly implicated and that can be avoided in many other ways—it is entirely obvious that the object of the law we have approved today is not to prevent wrongdoing but to prevent speech. Since those private associations known as corporations have so much money, they will speak so much more, and their views will be given inordinate prominence in election campaigns.   This is not an argument that our democratic traditions allow—neither with respect to individuals associated in corporations nor with respect to other categories of individuals whose speech may be "unduly" extensive (because they are rich) or "unduly" persuasive (because they are movie stars) or "unduly" respected (because they are clergymen).   The premise of our system is that there is no such thing as too much speech—that the people are not foolish but intelligent, and will separate the wheat from the chaff.   As conceded in Lincoln's aphorism about fooling "all of the people some of the time," that premise will not invariably accord with reality; but it will assuredly do so much more frequently than the premise the Court today embraces: that a healthy democratic system can survive the legislative power to prescribe how much political speech is too much, who may speak and who may not.

* * *

Because today's decision is inconsistent with unrepudiated legal judgments of our Court, but even more because it is incompatible with the unrepealable political wisdom of our First Amendment, I dissent.

JUSTICE KENNEDY, with whom JUSTICE O'CONNOR and JUSTICE SCALIA join, dissenting.

* * *

II

* * *

A

Our cases acknowledge the danger that corruption poses for the electoral process, but draw a line in permissible regulation between payments to candidates ("contributions") and payments or expenditures to express one's own views ("independent expenditures").   Today's decision abandons this distinction and threatens once protected political speech.   * * *

The majority almost admits that, in the case of independent expenditures, the danger of a political quid pro quo is insufficient to justify a restriction of this kind.   Since the specter of corruption, which had been "the only legitimate and compelling government interest[s] thus far identified for restricting campaign finances," *NCPAC*, supra, at 496–497, is missing in this case, the majority invents a new interest: combatting the "corrosive and distorting effects of immense aggregations of wealth," ante at 1397, accumulated in corporate form without shareholder or public support.   The majority styles this novel interest as simply a different kind of corruption, but has no support for its assertion.   * * *

A similar argument to that made by the majority was rejected in *Bellotti*. There, we rejected the assumption that "corporations are wealthy and powerful and their views may drown out other points of view" or "exert an undue influence" on the electorate in the absence of a showing that the relative voice of corporations was significant. 435 U.S. at 789. * * *

The speech suppressed in this case was directed to political qualifications. The fact that it was spoken by the Michigan Chamber of Commerce, and not a man or woman standing on a soapbox, detracts not a scintilla from its validity, its persuasiveness, or its contribution to the political dialogue.

* * *

B

* * *

The majority relies on the state interest in protecting members from the use of nonprofit corporate funds to support candidates whom they may oppose. We should reject this interest as insufficient to save the Act here, just as we rejected the argument in *Bellotti*, 435 U.S. at 792–793.

The Court takes refuge in the argument that some members or contributors to nonprofit corporations may find their own views distorted by the organization * * *. One need not become a member of the Michigan Chamber of Commerce or the Sierra Club in order to earn a living. To the extent that members disagree with a nonprofit corporation's policies, they can seek change from within, withhold financial support, cease to associate with the group, or form a rival group of their own. Allowing government to use the excuse of protecting shareholder rights to stifle the speech of private, voluntary organizations undermines the First Amendment.

* * *

IV

The Court's hostility to the corporate form used by the speaker in this case and its assertion that corporate wealth is the evil to be regulated is far too imprecise to justify the most severe restriction on political speech ever sanctioned by this Court. * * *

By constructing a rationale for the jurisprudence of this Court that prevents distinguished organizations in public affairs from announcing that a candidate is qualified or not qualified for public office, the Court imposes its own model of speech, one far removed from economic and political reality. It is an unhappy paradox that this Court, which has the role of protecting speech and of barring censorship from all aspects of political life, now becomes itself the censor. In the course of doing so, the Court reveals a lack of concern for speech rights that have the full protection of the First Amendment.   I would affirm the judgment.

Notes on Bellotti and Austin

1.   It is hard to dispute the *Austin* dissenters' claims that the Court's opinion cannot be reconciled with *Bellotti*.   In fact, the Court made no real effort to do so.   Perhaps that is because the six-member majority in *Austin* included the four dissenters in *Bellotti*.   A lawyer charged with interpreting the Court's opinions in these two cases must decide what weight, if any, to give to this fact.

2.   In *Bellotti* and *Austin*, different Justices describe the nature of the corporation in different terms.   How do their characterizations differ?   Which characterization seems to be the most accurate?   Why do the Justices care?   Do certain characteristics make corporations unique?   How, if at all, should those characteristics affect the permissible limits on state regulation of corporate speech?

3.   Jill Fisch suggests that the *Austin* Court's concerns about corporations' political influence derive largely from concerns about the separation of ownership and control in public corporations.   She argues that the limitations on political speech that *Austin* upholds cannot be reconciled with traditional First Amendment values.   A better policy, she suggests, would be to make managers more accountable to shareholders for political expenditures.   Jill E. Fisch, Frankenstein's Monster Hits the Campaign Trail: An Approach to Regulation of Corporate Political Expenditures, 32 Wm. & Mary L.Rev. 587 (1991).   Meir Dan–Cohen, in contrast, suggests that individual speech is valued for its expressive content, but that "a corporation's right to free speech * * * is derivative of and parasitic to the listener's interests."   Regulation of corporate speech thus may be justified because large corporations' disproportionate input might lead to "congestion that would otherwise be detrimental to listeners' interests."   Meir Dan–Cohen, Freedoms of Collective Speech: A Theory of Protected Communications by Organizations, Communities, and the State, 79 Cal. L.Rev. 1229 (1991).

C.   REGULATING CORPORATIONS' INTERNAL AFFAIRS

PROBLEM
REGULATING CORPORATE LOBBYING—PART II

Senator Bruin has reconsidered her proposed legislation because of concerns that a court might find it unconstitutional and criticism about the restrictions that it would impose on small, closely-held corporations.   She would prefer to restrict lobbying only by large, publicly-held corporations and to do so indirectly.   Accordingly, she proposes to amend the Columbia Business Corporation Law to allow any shareholder to recover from the directors of a Columbia corporation in a derivative suit "any corporate funds or other resources used, directly or indirectly, to communicate, other than in a public hearing, directly with any member or employee of the Legislature of Columbia to secure or defeat the passage of any pending or proposed legislation by said legislature, unless such use of corporate funds has been expressly authorized, after full disclosure of the position the corporation intends to advance, by a vote of the holders of 80 percent of said corporation's voting stock."

Sen. Bruin has asked for your opinion as to whether this revised legislation:

1. Is likely to limit effectively large corporations' influence on the Columbia Legislature?

2. Violates the Commerce Clause of the U.S. Constitution?

3. Raises serious First Amendment issues?

In thinking about these questions, consider how the proposed legislation differs from the legislation Sen. Bruin originally proposed and whether the courts are likely to attach significance to those differences.

––––––––

In *Dartmouth College*, supra, the Court held that a state could not unilaterally amend the provisions of a corporate charter it had granted. Justice Story, concurring, suggested that states could avoid this problem by granting charters subject to a reserved right to amend them. 17 U.S. at 712. States seized upon this suggestion and began to include in all corporate charters a clause reserving the state's power to amend or repeal any authority granted to the corporation. When general corporation laws came into vogue, states added similar reserved powers clauses to their constitutions, their general corporation laws, or both. Currently, all states reserve the power to amend the corporate charters they issue.

When states attempt to regulate foreign corporations (i.e., corporations chartered by other states), the situation becomes a bit more complex. Several provisions of the U.S. Constitution are relevant, but the obligations they impose have not all been defined precisely. A state may not impair obligations under a contract made in a sister state. (Art. I, § 10.) A state must give full faith and credit to the laws and judicial proceedings of a sister state. (Art. IV, § 1.) Under the Fourteenth Amendment, as noted previously, a state must provide all corporations with equal protection of the law and due process of law. A widely-observed conflict of laws principle, the "internal affairs doctrine," captures the principal operative thrust of these obligations: the law of the state in which a corporation is incorporated controls disputes among participants in that corporation, such as disputes between shareholders and directors and disputes between shareholder groups. See Restatement (Second) of Conflict of Laws §§ 296–310 (1971); Ralph K. Winter, Jr., State Law, Shareholder Protection, and the Theory of the Corporation, 6 J. Legal Studies 251, 252 (1977). See Chapter 8 for a more detailed discussion of the doctrine, which has profound consequences for the remainder of the materials in the book.

Two other Constitutional provisions frequently implicated by state efforts to regulate corporations are the supremacy clause (Art. VI), which nullifies state constitutions and laws that conflict with the U.S. Constitution or federal law, and the commerce clause (Art. I, § 8), which limits a state's power to regulate transactions that involve interstate commerce. Whether state antitakeover laws conflict with these constitutional provisions has been the focus of much recent litigation.

Introduction to CTS Corp. v. Dynamics Corp. of America

Responding to the takeover wave of the late 1970s and 1980s, a number of states adopted laws designed to protect local corporations from uninvited takeover bids.* During the 1980s, the Supreme Court passed on claims that two state antitakeover laws violated the Supremacy Clause and the Commerce Clause of the U.S. Constitution.

The Supremacy Clause claims were based on the Williams Act,** a measure Congress adopted in 1968 to ensure that when a public company becomes the target of a takeover bid, its shareholders will receive adequate information about the bid and have sufficient time to evaluate that information. The Williams Act imposed new costs on bidders, slowed down the timetable on which bids could be consummated, and provided target companies with opportunities to initiate litigation claiming offerors had not met their disclosure obligations. But these were side effects, not express objectives. In fact, to the extent consistent with the Act's overall goal of investor protection, Congress took "extreme care to avoid tipping the scales in favor of management or in favor of the person making the takeover bid." ***

Edgar v. MITE Corp., 457 U.S. 624, 102 S.Ct. 2629, 73 L.Ed.2d 269 (1982), involved an Illinois law regulating tender offers for any corporation 10 percent or more of whose shares were owned by Illinois residents, if the corporation also was organized under Illinois law, had its principal office in Illinois, *or* had 10 percent of its assets in Illinois.

---

* An uninvited takeover bid frequently involves an offer (called a *"tender offer"*), made directly to a corporation's shareholders, to purchase all or a large portion of that corporation's stock. If a person seeks to gain control of a corporation against the opposition of the target company's management, a tender offer often is attractive because the offer can succeed if a sufficient number of shareholders accept and tender their stock at the offered price. (See Chapter 22 for a discussion of other aspects of the law relating to takeover bids.)

** Pub. L. No. 90–439, 82 Stat. 454 (1968), codified at 15 U.S.C. §§ 78m(d)-(e), 78n(d)-(f) (1991), §§ 13(d)-(e), 14(d)-(f) of the Securities Exchange Act of 1934.

*** 113 Cong. Rec. 24664 (1967) (remarks of Senator Williams). Of course, any legislation that imposed substantial disclosure burdens on bidders and slowed down the timetable on which they could operate, as did the Williams Act, was not strictly "neutral" in its impact, even if the Act also prohibited false or misleading statements by a target company's management. On the other hand, it seems clear that Congress made an effort to limit the burdens it imposed on bidders to those necessary to implement the Act's investor protection goals.

MITE made a takeover bid for Chicago Rivet, which satisfied all three conditions.

The law required MITE to give Chicago Rivet and the Illinois Secretary of State 20 days advance notice of its bid. During that period, MITE would be barred from communicating with Chicago Rivet's shareholders. In addition, the Secretary of State could schedule a hearing on the fairness of MITE's offer, establish a timetable for that hearing, and hold MITE's offer in abeyance until the hearing was completed. If the Secretary then concluded the offer was unfair, she could block MITE from proceeding with its offer. Rather than comply with the law; MITE sued to have it declared unconstitutional.

The six Justices that considered the merits (three Justices opined only that the case was moot) all voted to hold the Illinois law unconstitutional on one or more grounds. Three concluded that the law was preempted because it conflicted with the Williams Act's "policy of neutrality," four concluded the Illinois law violated the Commerce Clause because it directly regulated interstate commerce, and five concluded the law violated the Commerce Clause because the burdens it imposed on interstate commerce were excessive in comparison to the local benefits the law produced. The Court rejected Illinois's claim that the internal affairs doctrine protected the law from constitutional attack, noting that the law was not limited to Illinois corporations but also covered foreign corporations that had the requisite proportion of Illinois shareholders and either their principal office or 10 percent of their assets in Illinois.

In an effort to avoid the impact of *MITE*, several states enacted "second generation" antitakeover laws that purported to regulate the internal affairs of corporations incorporated in that state. Indiana's statute, the Indiana Control Share Acquisitions law (ICSA), was the first to be challenged. ICSA differed from the Illinois law involved in *MITE* in that it amended to the Indiana Business Corporation Law and applied only to Indiana corporations.* ICSA provided that any person who acquired sufficient stock to pass one of three thresholds—set at 20, 33–1/3 and 50 percent of the stock of a corporation to which the Act applied and defined as "control shares"—would not be entitled to vote that stock unless a majority of that corporation's disinterested shareholders voted to approve the acquisition. An acquiror could ensure the shareholder vote would take place within 50 days by filing certain information, requesting a shareholder meeting, and agreeing to pay the meeting expenses.

ICSA thus effectively extended to 50 days the time a target company's managers had to defeat a hostile bid, since no potential acquiror would purchase stock in a target company unless it was sure it would be

---

* As an attempt to regulate only the internal affairs of Indiana corporations, ICSA was further limited to corporations that had: (1) at least 100 shareholders; (2) at least 10% of their stock owned by Indiana residents; and (3) their principal place of business or substantial assets in Indiana.

able to vote that stock. Thus the statute represented a substantial extension of the 20 business day period that the Williams Act allowed. But ICSA also made it easier for a target company's shareholders to protect themselves against certain tactics that might coerce them into accepting a bid that they preferred to reject.

Dynamics, the owner of 9.6 percent of CTS, an Indiana corporation covered by ICSA, announced a tender offer for sufficient shares to increase its ownership interest to 27.5 percent, thus potentially triggering ICSA. Dynamics simultaneously sued to enjoin enforcement of ICSA, claiming it was preempted by the Williams Act and violated the commerce clause. The Seventh Circuit, relying on *MITE*, agreed that ICSA was unconstitutional on both grounds. See Dynamics Corp. of America v. CTS Corp., 794 F.2d 250 (7th Cir.1986).

CTS CORP. v. DYNAMICS CORP. OF AMERICA
481 U.S. 69, 107 S.Ct. 1637 95 L.Ed.2d 67 (1987).

JUSTICE POWELL delivered the opinion of the Court.

[The Supreme Court first reversed the Seventh Circuit's holding that ICSA was preempted. The Court noted that it was not bound by *MITE* 's plurality holding that the Williams Act implicitly preempts state laws that conflict with a "policy of neutrality," but observed that the Indiana law "passes muster even under the broad interpretation of the Williams Act articulated * * * in *MITE*." 481 U.S. at 81. The Court then stated: (1) ICSA did not necessarily impose any delay on tender offers or preclude an offeror from purchasing shares as soon as the Williams Act permits; (2) even if ICSA did impose some delay, the delay was not unreasonable; and (3) "[t]he longstanding prevalence of state regulation in this area suggests that, if Congress intended to preempt all state laws that delay the acquisition of voting control following a tender offer, it would have said so explicitly." *Id.* at 86. It is unclear which of these statements represents the Court's holding and which are *dicta*.]

III

As an alternative basis for its decision, the Court of Appeals held that the Act violates the Commerce Clause of the Federal Constitution. We now address this holding. On its face, the Commerce Clause is nothing more than a grant to Congress of the power "[t]o regulate Commerce * * * among the several States * * *," Art. I, § 8, cl. 3. But it has been settled for more than a century that the Clause prohibits States from taking certain actions respecting interstate commerce even absent congressional action. The Court's interpretation of "these great silences of the Constitution," H.P. Hood & Sons, Inc. v. Du Mond, 336 U.S. 525, 535, 69 S.Ct. 657, 663, 93 L.Ed. 865 (1949), has not always been easy to follow. Rather, as the volume and complexity of commerce and regulation have grown in this country, the Court has articulated a variety of tests in an attempt to describe the difference between those regulations that the Commerce Clause permits and those regulations that it prohibits.

A

The principal objects of dormant Commerce Clause scrutiny are statutes that discriminate against interstate commerce. The Indiana Act is not such a statute. It has the same effects on tender offers whether or not the offeror is a domiciliary or resident of Indiana. Thus, it "visits its effects equally upon both interstate and local business," Lewis v. BT Investment Managers, Inc., [447 U.S. 27, 36, 100 S.Ct. 2009, 2015–2016, 64 L.Ed.2d 702 (1980)].

Dynamics nevertheless contends that the statute is discriminatory because it will apply most often to out-of-state entities. This argument rests on the contention that, as a practical matter, most hostile tender offers are launched by offerors outside Indiana. But this argument avails Dynamics little. "The fact that the burden of a state regulation falls on some interstate companies does not, by itself, establish a claim of discrimination against interstate commerce." Exxon Corp. v. Governor of Maryland, 437 U.S. 117, 126, 98 S.Ct. 2207, 2214, 57 L.Ed.2d 91 (1978). Because nothing in the Indiana Act imposes a greater burden on out-of-state offerors than it does on similarly situated Indiana offerors, we reject the contention that the Act discriminates against interstate commerce.

B

This Court's recent Commerce Clause cases also have invalidated statutes that may adversely affect interstate commerce by subjecting activities to inconsistent regulations. The Indiana Act poses no such problem. So long as each State regulates voting rights only in the corporations it has created, each corporation will be subject to the law of only one State. No principle of corporation law and practice is more firmly established than a State's authority to regulate domestic corporations, including the authority to define the voting rights of shareholders. See Restatement (Second) of Conflict of Laws § 304 (1971) (concluding that the law of the incorporating State generally should "determine the right of a shareholder to participate in the administration of the affairs of the corporation"). Accordingly, we conclude that the Indiana Act does not create an impermissible risk of inconsistent regulation by different States.

C

The Court of Appeals did not find the Act unconstitutional for either of these threshold reasons. Rather, its decision rested on its view of the Act's potential to hinder tender offers. We think the Court of Appeals failed to appreciate the significance for Commerce Clause analysis of the fact that state regulation of corporate governance is regulation of entities whose very existence and attributes are a product of state law. * * * See First National Bank of Boston v. Bellotti, 435 U.S. 765, 822–824, 98

S.Ct. 1407, 1439–1441 (1978) (Rehnquist, J., dissenting). Every State in this country has enacted laws regulating corporate governance. By prohibiting certain transactions, and regulating others, such laws necessarily affect certain aspects of interstate commerce. This necessarily is true with respect to corporations with shareholders in States other than the State of incorporation. Large corporations that are listed on national exchanges, or even regional exchanges, will have shareholders in many States and shares that are traded frequently. The markets that facilitate this national and international participation in ownership of corporations are essential for providing capital not only for new enterprises but also for established companies that need to expand their businesses. This beneficial free market system depends at its core upon the fact that a corporation—except in the rarest situations—is organized under, and governed by, the law of a single jurisdiction, traditionally the corporate law of the State of its incorporation.

These regulatory laws may affect directly a variety of corporate transactions. Mergers are a typical example. In view of the substantial effect that a merger may have on the shareholders' interests in a corporation, many States require supermajority votes to approve mergers. See, e.g., 2 MBCA § 73 (requiring approval of a merger by a majority of all shares, rather than simply a majority of votes cast); RMBCA § 11.03 (same). By requiring a greater vote for mergers than is required for other transactions, these laws make it more difficult for corporations to merge. State laws also may provide for "dissenters' rights" under which minority shareholders who disagree with corporate decisions to take particular actions are entitled to sell their shares to the corporation at fair market value. See, e.g., 2 MBCA §§ 80, 81; RMBCA § 13.02. By requiring the corporation to purchase the shares of dissenting shareholders, these laws may inhibit a corporation from engaging in the specified transactions.[12]

It thus is an accepted part of the business landscape in this country for States to create corporations, to prescribe their powers, and to define the rights that are acquired by purchasing their shares. A State has an interest in promoting stable relationships among parties involved in the corporations it charters, as well as in ensuring that investors in such corporations have an effective voice in corporate affairs.

---

12. Numerous other common regulations may affect both nonresident and resident shareholders of a corporation. Specified votes may be required for the sale of all of the corporation's assets. See 2 MBCA § 79; RMBCA § 12.02. The election of directors may be staggered over a period of years to prevent abrupt changes in management. See 1 MBCA § 37; RMBCA § 8.06. Various classes of stock may be created with differences in voting rights as to dividends and on liquidation. See 1 MBCA § 15; RMBCA § 6.01(c). Provisions may be made for cumulative voting. See 1 MBCA § 33, ¶ 4; RMBCA § 7.28. Corporations may adopt restrictions on payment of dividends to ensure that specified ratios of assets to liabilities are maintained for the benefit of the holders of corporate bonds or notes. See 1 MBCA § 45 (noting that a corporation's articles of incorporation can restrict payment of dividends); RMBCA § 6.40 (same). Where the shares of a corporation are held in States other than that of incorporation, actions taken pursuant to these and similar provisions of state law will affect all shareholders alike wherever they reside or are domiciled. * * *

There can be no doubt that the Act reflects these concerns. The primary purpose of the Act is to protect the shareholders of Indiana corporations. It does this by affording shareholders, when a takeover offer is made, an opportunity to decide collectively whether the resulting change in voting control of the corporation, as they perceive it, would be desirable. A change of management may have important effects on the shareholders' interests; it is well within the State's role as overseer of corporate governance to offer this opportunity. The autonomy provided by allowing shareholders collectively to determine whether the takeover is advantageous to their interests may be especially beneficial where a hostile tender offer may coerce shareholders into tendering their shares.

Appellee Dynamics responds to this concern by arguing that the prospect of coercive tender offers is illusory, and that tender offers generally should be favored because they reallocate corporate assets into the hands of management who can use them most effectively. As indicated [in our discussion of Dynamics' preemption claim,] Indiana's concern with tender offers is not groundless. Indeed, the potentially coercive aspects of tender offers have been recognized by the SEC, and by a number of scholarly commentators. The Constitution does not require the States to subscribe to any particular economic theory. We are not inclined "to second-guess the empirical judgments of lawmakers concerning the utility of legislation," Kassel v. Consolidated Freightways Corp., 450 U.S., at 679, 101 S.Ct., at 1321 (Brennan, J., concurring in judgment). In our view, the possibility of coercion in some takeover bids offers additional justification for Indiana's decision to promote the autonomy of independent shareholders.

Dynamics argues in any event that the State has " 'no legitimate interest in protecting the nonresident shareholders.' " Dynamics relies heavily on the statement by the *MITE* Court that "[i]nsofar as the * * * law burdens out-of-state transactions, there is nothing to be weighed in the balance to sustain the law." 457 U.S. at 644, 102 S.Ct. at 2641. But that comment was made in reference to an Illinois law that applied as well to out-of-state corporations as to in-state corporations. We agree that Indiana has no interest in protecting nonresident shareholders of *nonresident corporations*. But this Act applies only to corporations incorporated in Indiana. We reject the contention that Indiana has no interest in providing for the shareholders of its corporations the voting autonomy granted by the Act. Indiana has a substantial interest in preventing the corporate form from becoming a shield for unfair business dealing. * * *

D

Dynamics' argument that the Act is unconstitutional ultimately rests on its contention that the Act will limit the number of successful tender offers. There is little evidence that this will occur. But even if true, this result would not substantially affect our Commerce Clause analysis. We reiterate that this Act does not prohibit any entity— resident or nonresident—from offering to purchase, or from purchasing, shares in Indiana corporations, or from attempting thereby to gain control. It only provides regulatory procedures designed for the better protection of the corporations' shareholders. We have rejected the "notion that the Commerce Clause protects the particular structure or methods of operation in a * * * market." Exxon Corp. v. Governor of Maryland, 437 U.S. at 127, 98 S.Ct. at 2215. The very commodity that is traded in the securities market is one whose characteristics are defined by state law. Similarly, the very commodity that is traded in the "market for corporate control"—the corporation—is one that owes its existence and attributes to state law. Indiana need not define these commodities as other States do; it need only provide that residents and nonresidents have equal access to them. This Indiana has done. Accordingly, even if the Act should decrease the number of successful tender offers for Indiana corporations, this would not offend the Commerce Clause.

IV

On its face, the Indiana Control Share Acquisitions Chapter even-handedly determines the voting rights of shares of Indiana corporations. The Act does not conflict with the provisions or purposes of the Williams Act. To the limited extent that the Act affects interstate commerce, this is justified by the State's interests in defining the attributes of shares in its corporations and in protecting shareholders. Congress has never questioned the need for state regulation of these matters. Nor do we think such regulation offends the Constitution. Accordingly, we reverse the judgment of the Court of Appeals.

It is so ordered.

———

Developments Following *CTS*

Professor Roberta Romano, The Future of Hostile Takeovers: Legislation and Public Opinion, 57 U.Cin.L.Rev. 457 (1988), describes the impact of *CTS* as follows:

> Although more than twenty states enacted second generation statutes in the years between the *MITE* and *CTS* decisions, legislators and lobbyists were often reluctant to promote legislation for fear of constitutional infirmities. The most frequently adopted version of a second generation statute was therefore one with limited regulatory scope. After the *CTS* decision, however, the pace and scope of legislation changed: fourteen new statutes were adopted within approximately six months. More important, several of the new statutes strengthened less restrictive second generation statutes by using Indiana as a model, and many test *CTS* 's limits by mandating constraints on bidders that go further than the Indiana statute. * * *

Perhaps the most important reaction to *CTS* * * * is that Delaware, the leading incorporation state, enacted a [third] generation statute. * * * Part of the impetus for [Delaware's] effort stemmed from the threat of some Delaware corporations to reincorporate in states that had second generation statutes if no bill was forthcoming. Delaware feared, rightly or wrongly, that inaction would hurt its preeminence in the incorporation business.

Courts subsequently relied on *CTS* to uphold Delaware's antitakeover law and all other antitakeover laws framed as regulations of domestic corporations' internal affairs against Commerce Clause and preemption claims. Examples of such laws are control share laws and "business combination" laws, which gave a target company's incumbent directors the right for several years to block certain transactions that an aspiring acquiror was likely to want to consummate, Another example is "constituency statutes," which authorized a target company's directors to resist any takeover bid they believed would affect adversely the interests of constituencies of the corporation other than its shareholders—such as employees, customers, and communities in which the company operated. See Elliott J. Weiss, What Lawyers Do When the Emperor Has No Clothes: Evaluating CTS Corp. v. Dynamics Corp. of America and Its Progeny—Part II, 79 Geo. L.J. 211, 238–264 (1990).

On the other hand, no third generation law that regulates takeover bids for foreign corporations has survived a challenge based on the Commerce Clause, even where the law's substantive provisions closely track ICSA. Relying on *CTS*, courts have reasoned that such laws subject corporations to potentially inconsistent state regulation, i.e., between the laws of the state of incorporation and the antitakeover statute. See Id. at 218–225.

AMANDA ACQUISITION CORP. v. UNIVERSAL FOODS CORP.

877 F.2d 496 (7th Cir.1989), cert. denied, 493 U.S. 955,
110 S.Ct. 367, 107 L.Ed.2d 353 (1989).

EASTERBROOK, CIRCUIT JUDGE.

* * * Wisconsin has a third-generation takeover statute. Enacted after *CTS*, it postpones the kinds of transactions that often follow tender offers (and often are the reason for making the offers in the first place). Unless the target's board agrees to the transaction in advance, the bidder must wait three years after buying the shares to merge with the target or acquire more than 5% of its assets. We must decide whether this is consistent with the Williams Act and Commerce Clause.

I

[Amanda Acquisition Corp., a shell company formed to acquire Universal Foods Corp., a diversified firm incorporated in Wisconsin and traded on the New York Stock Exchange, made a tender offer for all outstanding shares of Universal and also brought suit claiming the

Wisconsin law, Wis. Stat. § 180.726, which covered Universal, was unconstitutional. The court described the Wisconsin law and noted that, "[a]s a practical matter, Wisconsin prohibits any offer contingent on a merger between bidder and target, a condition attached to about 90% of contemporary tender offers."]

II

* * *

A

If our views of the wisdom of state law mattered, Wisconsin's takeover statute would not survive. Like our colleagues who decided *MITE* and *CTS*, we believe that antitakeover legislation injures shareholders. Managers frequently realize gains for investors via voluntary combinations (mergers). If gains are to be had, but managers balk, tender offers are investors' way to go over managers' heads. If managers are not maximizing the firm's value—perhaps because they have missed the possibility of a synergistic combination, perhaps because they are clinging to divisions that could be better run in other hands, perhaps because they are just not the best persons for the job—a bidder that believes it can realize more of the firm's value will make investors a higher offer. Investors tender; the bidder gets control and changes things. The prospect of monitoring by would-be bidders, and an occasional bid at a premium, induces managers to run corporations more efficiently and replaces them if they will not.

Premium bids reflect the benefits for investors. * * * Only when the bid exceeds the value of the stock (however investors compute value) will it succeed. A statute that precludes investors from receiving or accepting a premium offer makes them worse off. It makes the economy worse off too, because the higher bid reflects the better use to which the bidder can put the target's assets. (If the bidder can't improve the use of the assets, it injures itself by paying a premium.)

* * *

B

Skepticism about the wisdom of a state's law does not lead to the conclusion that the law is beyond the state's power, however. We have not been elected custodians of investors' wealth. States need not treat investors' welfare as their *summum bonum*. Perhaps they choose to protect managers' welfare instead, or believe that the current economic literature reaches an incorrect conclusion and that despite appearances takeovers injure investors in the long run. Unless a federal statute or the Constitution bars the way, Wisconsin's choice must be respected.

[The Wisconsin law is not preempted by the Williams Act.]

C

The Commerce Clause grants Congress the power "[t]o regulate Commerce * * * among the several States". * * *

When state law discriminates against interstate commerce expressly—for example, when Wisconsin closes its border to butter from Minnesota—the negative Commerce Clause steps in. The law before us is not of this type: it is neutral between inter-state and intra-state commerce. Amanda therefore presses on us the broader, all-weather, be-reasonable vision of the Constitution. Wisconsin has passed a law that unreasonably injures investors, most of whom live outside of Wisconsin, and therefore it has to be unconstitutional, as Amanda sees things. * * *

Illinois's law, held invalid in *MITE*, regulated sales of stock elsewhere. Illinois tried to tell a Texas owner of stock in a Delaware corporation that he could not sell to a buyer in California. By contrast, Wisconsin's law, like the Indiana statute sustained by *CTS*, regulates the internal affairs of firms incorporated there. Investors may buy or sell stock as they please. * * *

Buyers of stock in Wisconsin firms may exercise full rights as investors, taking immediate control. No interstate transaction is regulated or forbidden. True, Wisconsin's law makes a potential buyer less willing to buy (or depresses the bid), but this is equally true of Indiana's rule. Many other rules of corporate law—supermajority voting requirements, staggered and classified boards, and so on—have similar or greater effects on some persons' willingness to purchase stock. *CTS*, 481 U.S. at 89–90, 107 S.Ct. at 1649–50. States could ban mergers outright, with even more powerful consequences. Wisconsin did not allow mergers among firms chartered there until 1947. We doubt that it was violating the Commerce Clause all those years. Every rule of corporate law affects investors who live outside the state of incorporation, yet this has never been thought sufficient to authorize a form of cost-benefit inquiry through the medium of the Commerce Clause. * * *

Wisconsin could exceed its powers by subjecting firms to inconsistent regulation. Because § 180.726 applies only to a subset of firms incorporated in Wisconsin, however, there is no possibility of inconsistent regulation. * * * This leaves only the argument that Wisconsin's law hinders the flow of interstate trade "too much". *CTS* dispatched this concern by declaring it inapplicable to laws that apply only to the internal affairs of firms incorporated in the regulating state. States may regulate corporate transactions as they choose without having to demonstrate under an unfocused balancing test that the benefits are "enough" to justify the consequences.

To say that states have the power to enact laws whose costs exceed their benefits is not to say that investors should kiss their wallets goodbye. States compete to offer corporate codes attractive to firms. Managers who want to raise money incorporate their firms in the states that offer the combination of rules investors prefer. Laws that in the short run injure investors and protect managers will in the longer run make the state less attractive to firms that need to raise new capital. If the law is "protectionist", the protected class is the existing body of managers (and other workers), suppliers, and so on, which bears no necessary relation to state boundaries. States regulating the affairs of domestic corporations cannot in the long run injure anyone but themselves. * * *

The long run takes time to arrive, and it is tempting to suppose that courts could contribute to investors' welfare by eliminating laws that impose costs in the short run. The price of such warfare, however, is a reduction in the power of competition among states. Courts seeking to impose "good" rules on the states diminish the differences among corporate codes and dampen competitive forces. Too, courts may fail in their quest. How do judges know which rules are best? Often only the slow forces of competition reveal that information. Early economic studies may mislead, or judges (not trained as social scientists) may misinterpret the available data or act precipitously. Our Constitution allows the states to act as laboratories; slow migration (or national law on the authority of the Commerce Clause) grinds the failures under. No such process weeds out judicial errors, or decisions that, although astute when rendered, have become anachronistic in light of changes in the economy. * * *

* * * A state with the power to forbid mergers has the power to defer them for three years. Investors can turn to firms incorporated in states committed to the dominance of market forces, or they can turn on legislators who enact unwise laws. The Constitution has room for many economic policies. "[A] law can be both economic folly and constitutional." *CTS*, 481 U.S. at 96–97, 107 S.Ct. at 1653–54 (Scalia, J., concurring). Wisconsin's law may well be folly; we are confident that it is constitutional.

Notes on Amanda Acquisition

1. In arguing that takeovers are beneficial, Judge Easterbrook assumes corporations should operate solely to increase shareholders' wealth. David Millon contends that this assumption, while widely accepted, is not immutable. There is an argument that corporations should operate to advance broader social purposes. Professor Millon notes that this argument has had little impact on the development of corporation law during most of the twentieth century, but suggests that concerns about the social and economic impact of hostile takeovers have reawakened interest in it. See David Millon, Theories of the Corporation, 1990 Duke L.J. 201, 227–28:

> State legislators have responded to these concerns by enacting increasingly bold legislation designed to curb hostile takeovers. Some have suggested that the legislators who pass these laws are acting as toadies to locally influential corporate managers who stand to lose their positions if their companies are taken over. The statutes themselves, however, reveal clearly that they address a quite different set of concerns. For example, a recent amendment to North Carolina's corporate statute refers expressly to a broad range of issues, including lost employment, tax revenues, and community service activities. Similarly, Wisconsin's anti-takeover statute [held constitutional in *Amanda Acquisition*] candidly declares

that Wisconsin corporations "encompass, represent and affect, through their ongoing business operations, a variety of constituencies including shareholders, employees, customers, suppliers and local communities and their economies," and the statute states further that it is intended "to promote the welfare of these constituencies" and "should allow for the stable, long-term growth of resident domestic corporations."

2. Judge Easterbrook makes a second controversial claim—that competition among states will promote development of efficient corporation laws. Some commentators who share his assumption that corporations should operate solely to increase shareholders' wealth nonetheless suggest that decisions concerning the state in which a firm should be incorporated (or reincorporated) reflect not market forces but managers' preference for laws that tolerate self-aggrandizing behavior. (These issues are considered at greater length in Chapter 8.) Lucian Bebchuk observes that the proliferation of state antitakeover laws, which clearly have the potential to benefit managers at shareholders' expense, represents strong evidence that, at least with regard to certain issues, competition among the states does not lead to laws that maximize shareholder wealth. See Lucian A. Bebchuk, Federalism and the Corporation: The Desirable Limits on State Competition in Corporate Law, 105 Harv. L. Rev. 1435, 1467–70 (1992). Judge Easterbrook seems to have accepted Bebchuck's claim insofar as it relates to antitakeover laws. See Frank H. Easterbrook & Daniel R. Fischel, The Economic Structure of Corporate Law 221–22 (1991). However, he minimizes this failure of competition as an isolated phenomenon. Other commentators suggest that if competition among the states has not produced efficient results with respect to antitakeover laws, there is little reason to believe competition is any more effective with respect to rules defining managers' fiduciary duties.

3. Professor Bebchuk also points out that to the extent one believes corporation laws should further the interests of persons other than shareholders, competition among states will not produce optimal results. "[S]hareholders, managers and entrepreneurs who seek to maximize shareholder value will ignore [the interests of non-shareholder constituencies] in evaluating corporate law rules. Consequently, if states seek to attract incorporations by offering rules that enhance shareholder value, the offered rules may well differ from the socially desirable ones. In particular, the rules produced by state competition will be systematically less favorable to non-shareholder parties than the socially desirable ones." Bebchuk, supra, at 1485.

4. Since *Amanda Acquisition* dealt with an antitakeover law, the court had no occasion to consider another issue relating to the scope of the internal affairs doctrine. Even if states are free, as *Amanda Acquisition* suggests, to adopt whatever laws they wish regulating economic relationships within domestic corporations, do they have similar freedom to adopt laws that have the effect of restricting activities that otherwise would be protected by the First Amendment if those laws are framed as regulations of corporations' internal affairs?

Chapter 5

THE CORPORATION AND SOCIETY

A. INTRODUCTION

Controversy has ebbed and flowed over the years about the role large corporations play in American society. Those corporations represent independent concentrations of economic power and, many would say, social and political power as well. Critics claim large corporations lack "legitimacy"—that their managers function as a sort of economic oligarchy making decisions that significantly affect not only shareholders but employees, consumers, suppliers, and communities, without being accountable to any of them. Edward Mason made this point cogently in his introduction to The Corporation in Modern Society:

> [W]e are all aware that we live not only in a corporate society but a society of large corporations. The management—that is, the control—of these corporations is in the hands, at most, of a few thousand men. Who selected these men, if not to rule over us, at least to exercise vast authority, and to whom are they responsible? The answer to the first question is quite clearly: they selected themselves. The answer to the second is, at best, nebulous. This, in a nutshell, constitutes the problem of legitimacy.

The Corporation in Modern Society 5 (Edward Mason, ed. 1959).

Some critics have argued that corporations should be more "responsible," that they should take account of all the constituencies their operations affect and even that they should assume responsibility for broader societal problems, such as the quality of inner city life, which they affect only tangentially. Other critics stress the need to assure that managers are "accountable" (whatever that may mean), that shareholders or others be given the authority to monitor managers' performance effectively. Defenders of existing rules, however, argue that corporations should be concerned exclusively with maximizing the profits they can earn within the law, and that market forces, government regulation and the mechanisms of the corporate governance system do constrain managers' discretion effectively.

85

This controversy raises two broad classes of questions. First, whose interests should corporations seek to serve, those of their shareholders, or those of society at large? Second, by what mechanisms should managers' discretion be harnessed? Are market forces, government regulation, and the corporate governance system sufficient, or are changes in one or another of these mechanisms necessary or desirable?

In the early 1930s, two leading corporate law scholars, Adolf A. Berle, Jr. and E. Merrick Dodd, debated the role of corporate management and of the corporation. Berle's view was that corporate powers were held in trust "at all times exercisable only for the ratable benefit of all the shareholders * * *." Adolf A. Berle, Jr., Corporate Powers as Powers in Trust, 44 Harv.L.Rev. 1049 (1931). Dodd's thesis was that the business corporation was properly seen "as an economic institution which has a social service as well as a profit making function." E. Merrick Dodd, For Whom Are Corporate Managers Trustees?, 45 Harv. L.Rev. 1145, 1148 (1932).

Twenty years later, the New Jersey Supreme Court seemed to vindicate both points of view. In A.P. Smith Manufacturing Co. v. Barlow, 13 N.J. 145, 98 A.2d 581 (1953), appeal dism'd 346 U.S. 861, 74 S.Ct. 107, 98 L.Ed. 373 (1953), it upheld the validity of a corporate gift to Princeton University. But in reaching this conclusion, the court accepted the company's argument that its gift at least arguably advanced its long-run business interests. As Professor Berle astutely observed, the effect of the decision was to recognize that "[m]odern directors are not limited to running business enterprise for maximum profit, but are in fact and recognized in law as administrators of a community system." The Corporation in Modern Society xii (E. Mason, ed. 1959).

In 1954, Professor Berle conceded that Dodd had won the argument, at least for the moment. Adolf A. Berle, Jr., The 20th Century Capitalist Revolution 169 (1954). However, he did not acknowledge that Dodd had been correct. See The Corporation in Modern Society xii (E. Mason, ed. 1959). See also, A.A. Sommer, Jr., Whom Should the Corporation Serve? The Berle–Dodd Debate Revisited Sixty Years Later, 16 Del. J. Corp. L. 33 (1991); Joseph L. Weiner, The Berle–Dodd Dialogue on the Concept of the Corporation, 64 Col. L. Rev. 1458 (1964).

Professor Dodd's thesis may be viewed as managerialism because it treats corporate managers as professionals whose duties require exercise of almost statesmanlike responsibility. Professor Berle's view became associated with notions of "corporate democracy," although he never meant to apply literally the political analogy that term suggests. Others, however, have relied on that analogy more strongly. Robert Dahl, a political scientist, described the corporation as a political entity, imposing its will on affected citizens who have no voice in its policies, unless they are stockholders. Professor Dahl's remedy was to provide representation to the affected constituencies of the corporation, perhaps by allowing them to vote or by providing representation on the board of directors for special constituencies. Robert Dahl, After the Revolution?

115 et seq. (1970). Abram Chayes urged that a "rule of law" be applied to corporations that would allow all constituencies affected by corporate activities to participate in the election of corporate directors. Abram Chayes, The Modern Corporation and the Rule of Law, in The Corporation in Modern Society 25 (E. Mason, ed. 1959). Of course, the members of these other constituencies would be considerably less concerned than a corporation's shareholders with the long-term profitability of the corporation's operations.

In the 1960s and 1970s, attention shifted to "externalities" generated by corporate activities, such as environmental pollution and workplace hazards, which market forces did not control effectively and which, at least early in that period, government did little to regulate. Concern also was aroused by reports that many large corporations had made illegal political contributions to President Nixon's 1972 reelection campaign and had paid large amounts in bribes and kickbacks to officials of foreign governments. Demands were made that the corporate governance system be strengthened to ensure, at a minimum, that corporate activities in areas of public concern were not unlawful.

At that time, boards of directors of most public companies included some "outside directors"—persons who were not full-time employees of the company. In addition, boards generally included the company's chief executive officer (CEO) and several other high-ranking officers. The outside directors were predominantly white men busily engaged in their primary occupations as senior officers of other corporations. They devoted relatively small amounts of time to the boards on which they sat as outside directors and relied principally on information furnished to them by managers. In form, they were elected by the shareholders, but in fact they were nominated by the CEO and faced no opposition for election. For the most part, it was safe to say that directors were self-selected, self-perpetuating, loyal to management, and inclined to devote little time to their directorships. They also generally were paid fairly nominal sums for their efforts, at least in comparison to their earnings from other sources.

Eventually, a consensus of sorts emerged: that the board of directors had the potential to operate as an effective disciplinary force within the corporation; that a board could ensure management was pursuing a coherent business strategy which could take account of the corporation's external and internal environment; that a board could encourage managers to take account of the social effects of business operations that pressure to meet short-run profit targets otherwise might lead managers to ignore. It also seemed clear that a board of directors would be more likely to play these roles, all of which involve monitoring managers' performance, only if a majority of directors were outsiders. What remained unclear, and still is the subject of considerable controversy, is whether a board with a clear majority of outside directors would prove to be an effective monitor, or whether directors would continue to serve largely as passive, friendly advisors to management, rarely asking penetrating questions or attempting to evaluate critically management's performance or proposals. Chapter 15 deals with these issues in more detail.

During the takeover boom of the 1980s, takeover-related litigation subjected the decisionmaking processes of many large companies' boards of directors to unprecedented scrutiny. Some boards clearly operated with considerable independence, pressuring managers to promote shareholders' interest and taking positions different from those management preferred. Other boards appeared to acquiesce uncritically in whatever management proposed, apparently unconcerned about how their decisions would affect shareholders' well-being. The takeover movement also raised the question of precisely what that well-being consisted: the ability to receive an immediate large premium for their stock, or a concern for the long-term viability of the corporation. Chapter 22 examines those issues more fully.

As noted in Chapter 4, takeovers also stimulated renewed interest in an idea that seemed to have lost currency: the notion that managers should be allowed, or even required, to take explicit account of the interests of non-shareholder constituencies when managing a corporation's business. Whether the constituency statutes that many states adopted in response to takeover pressures (see Section C.3) will lead to broader board concern for such constituencies or will have little impact on corporate operations remains to be seen.

B. CORPORATE CHARITABLE GIVING AND SOCIAL RESPONSIBILITY

It is easy to get caught up in generalizations and emotional responses when discussing "corporate responsibility." While it is important not to submerge value systems in technical legal analysis, such discussions demand careful analysis of the nature of the "responsibility," to whom it is owed, and how it should be fulfilled. To focus these issues, we examine one narrow topic, charitable giving, examining it in the context of both the older doctrine of *ultra vires* and modern limitations on such giving.

1. INTRODUCTION: CORPORATE PURPOSES AND CORPORATE POWERS: THE DOCTRINE OF ULTRA VIRES

The statutory charter that created early corporations included as one of its principal provisions a statement of the purposes for which the corporation was to be formed. According to the common law doctrine of *ultra vires* (literally, "beyond the power"), a corporation may not engage in activities outside the scope of the purposes thus defined. In a famous English case, for example, the House of Lords held that a corporation whose charter authorized it to "sell or lend all kinds of railway plant, to carry on the business of mechanical engineers and general contractors, etc." exceeded its purposes in purchasing a concession to construct and operate a railway line in Belgium. The corporation had contracted with one Riche to do the construction, but after Riche had done some of the work, the corporation repudiated the contract. The House of Lords rejected Riche's suit on the contract on the ground that the corporation lacked the power to build a railroad and thus to bind itself to the contract. Ashbury Railway Carriage & Iron Co. v. Riche, 33 N.S.Law Times Rep. 450 (1875).

The doctrine of *ultra vires* found its roots principally in a suspicion of concentrations of economic power. The historical origins of the doctrine are outlined in Justice Brandeis' dissenting opinion in Liggett v. Lee, Chapter 8. A second reason was to enable investors to limit their economic exposure to the risks of a defined business undertaking.

The legal mechanisms available to challenge an allegedly *ultra vires* act took the form of either a *quo warranto* (literally, "by what authority") proceeding instituted by the state for the forfeiture of the corporate charter or the assertion of the corporate incapacity in various forms in the context of private lawsuits. That a corporate act was unauthorized and therefore void was often asserted as a defense to an action against the corporation on a corporate obligation, as in the *Ashbury Railway Carriage* case.

The *ultra vires* doctrine also could be asserted affirmatively in a shareholder action against a corporation's managers who caused the corporation to suffer a loss by engaging in activity outside its authority. In at least one relatively modern case, the shareholders of a corporation were held personally liable as partners on a contract found to be outside the purposes specified in the articles of incorporation (although there were other factors that contributed to the result). Lurie v. Arizona Fertilizer & Chemical Co., 101 Ariz. 482, 421 P.2d 330 (1966).

In the nineteenth century, a large portion of the law of corporations was devoted to the resolution of disputes arising under the *ultra vires* doctrine; today, the issue is rarely seen in the courts. Clearly, the original purpose of the doctrine, the curbing of the powers of the large corporation, was a failure and it has been largely replaced by expanding fiduciary duties.

2. THE MODERN DOCTRINE OF ULTRA VIRES

Once states began to enact general incorporation statutes, it became a simple matter to circumvent the limitations of the *ultra vires* doctrine by drafting the articles of incorporation in as broad terms as the attorney could imagine. Purposes clauses often went on for pages, listing—or at least attempting to list—every conceivable activity in which a corporation might engage, even if the intention of the promoters was to undertake only the first activity on the list. Today, corporate statutes often provide, as does DGCL § 102(a)(3), "It shall be sufficient to state, either alone or with other businesses or purposes, that the purpose of the corporation is to engage in any lawful act or activity for which corporations may be organized under the General Corporation Law of Delaware, and by such statement all lawful acts and activities shall be within the purpose of the corporation, except for express limitations, if any." Since DGCL § 101(b) also provides that "[a] corporation may be incorporated or organized under this chapter to conduct or promote any lawful business or purposes, except as may otherwise be provided by the constitution or other law of this State" the organic documents of the corporation provide no limitation on corporate purposes. Read RMBCA § 3.04.

There is a conceptual distinction to be drawn between corporate *purposes* and corporate *powers*, although it is one that often is ignored by corporate lawyers. It would be *ultra vires* for a corporation either to engage in a business not included within the statement of purposes set forth in its charter or, in carrying on its business, to exercise a power that the charter or the statute prohibited. Articles of incorporation formerly contained a lengthy list of both "powers" and "purposes." In practice, however, it is often difficult to distinguish between the two, and in an excess of caution, attorneys often listed "powers" among what were, properly conceived, simply "purposes" of a corporation. For example the "purposes" clauses found in many form books included acquiring or dealing in real property. For most corporations this would not be a purpose but simply the "power" to acquire real estate in the normal course of affairs. But dealing in real property would clearly be a "purpose" of a corporation organized to engage in the real estate business. Today, statutes such as RMBCA § 3.02, which grants extremely broad powers to a business corporation, renders most of this learning irrelevant.

In addition to adopting a permissive approach both to the definition of corporate purposes and to the statutory grant of powers, modern corporate statutes often limit the uses to which the doctrine of *ultra vires* can be put, most importantly by precluding a corporation from using the defense of *ultra vires* against an otherwise valid obligation. See, e.g., RMBCA § 3.04. There are, however, three areas in which the doctrine continues to have some vitality, although even in those areas, both case law and statutes have narrowed their scope. First, at common law a corporation was prohibited from becoming a member of a partnership, on the theory that to do so exposed the assets of the corporation to risks created by decisions of the other partners. See Whittenton Mills v. Upton, 76 Mass. (10 Gray) 582 (1858). Most statutes today contain express authorization for corporations to become partners, and even where the statute does not so provide, a corporation can validly include such a power in its articles of incorporation.

Corporations also were not generally authorized to guarantee the obligations of others on the theory that such guarantees could not be in the interest of the shareholders. See Brinson v. Mill Supply Co., Inc., 219 N.C. 498, 14 S.E.2d 505 (1941). This limitation also has largely disappeared, as a result of case law and modern statutory provisions (although the latter are sometimes subject to qualification).

The third, and most significant, area in which the *ultra vires* doctrine was of concern, (and, indeed, remains so) relates to the "waste" of corporate assets by their use for other than corporate purposes. Although shareholders have sought to show that their corporations have "given away" or "wasted" assets in a variety of different ways, the most common charge has been that a corporate charitable donation was *ultra vires*. A simple illustration of the concept of waste in another context is that, while it is of course legal for a corporation to pay salaries to its officers, if those salaries become too high, they may become "wasteful" and therefore *ultra vires*. See, e.g., Rogers v. Hill, 289 U.S. 582, 53 S.Ct. 731, 77 L.Ed. 1385 (1933). Thus, if corporate managers overdo "their" largess, they may be guilty of wasting corporate assets.

Modern statutory provisions, such as RMBCA § 3.02(13) and DGCL § 122(9), together with a number of cases similar to those set forth below, have gone a long way toward eliminating any doubts about the power of corporations to make *some* charitable contributions. The establishment of the basic principle that corporations may use their assets for ends that are unrelated—or at least not *directly* related—to the financial well-being of the shareholders, does not put an end to the legal issues, however. It is clear that at some point, a gift that is valid in principle can become so large as to constitute a waste of corporate assets. Drawing that line, however, is another matter.

3. MODERN LIMITATIONS ON CORPORATE CHARITABLE GIVING

PROBLEM
UNION AIRLINES

You are general counsel for Union Airlines, Inc., a major U.S. domestic air carrier headquartered in Georgetown, Columbia. The company has $1 billion in assets and generates $700 million in annual revenues. Due to increased competition and higher fuel prices, Union's profits have declined steadily for the last several years, and it has posted large losses for the last three.

Wright, the company's chief executive officer just telephoned and told you that Union intends to make a corporate donation of $500,000 to the Georgetown Opera Company to help it survive a financial crisis that threatens to prevent the Opera from opening the current season.

1. Wright would like your opinion on the legality of the gift. What should you tell him? Consider RMBCA §§ 3.02 and 3.04 [DGCL §§ 122 and 124] and the materials that follow.

2. Would your advice change if you learned that Wright had been trying for years to join the board of directors of the Opera, perhaps the most socially prestigious board in Georgetown, and that the proposed gift appeared to be a *quid pro quo* for an invitation to Wright to join that board?

Note: Corporations and Charitable Contributions

While individuals tend to contribute between 2 and 3 percent of their income to charities, the average corporate gift is in the range of 1 to 2 percent of pretax income. A survey of the Fortune 500 manufacturing companies, the Fortune 500 service companies, and certain other corporations, indicated that for 1990, median contributions represented 1.2 percent of United States pretax income. Internal Revenue Service data show that contributions by all corporations represented 1.97 percent of total corporate income. The ALI, Principles of Corporate Governance: Analysis and Recommendations, § 2.01, Reporter's Note 3 (Proposed Final Draft, 1992) (citing The Conference Board, Survey of Corporate Contributions, 1990) 92. The reasons for corporate generosity are not exclusively altruistic. The Internal Revenue Code allows corporations to deduct charitable contributions up to 10 percent of their taxable income when they calculate their taxes.

Advocates of at least some corporate philanthropy, including the managements of most major corporations, typically argue that charitable giving is in the best long-run interest of the corporation. That view is not universal, however. Critics, including many shareholders, protest that such giving deprives shareholders of money they might otherwise receive as dividends. They urge that management should not give away money that properly belongs to the shareholders. If the shareholders wish to make such gifts, they should make that decision themselves.

One public corporation, Berkshire Hathaway, Inc., has attempted to bridge the gap between these competing views by allowing each shareholder to direct the corporation to donate a certain amount per share owned to a charity or charities of the shareholder's choice. See Berkshire Hathaway Inc., 1990 Annual Report, 54–55. In one of his annual letters to shareholders, Warren Buffet, Chairman of Berkshire Hathaway,* explained:

> When A takes money from B to give to C and A is a legislator, the process is called taxation. But when A is an officer or director of a corporation, it is called philanthropy. We continue to believe that contributions, aside from those with quite clear benefits to the company, should reflect the charitable preferences of owners rather than those of officers or directors.

Berkshire Hathaway Inc., 1987 Annual Report.

* Mr. Buffet is considered by many to be a unique figure in the American business community. He acquired control of Berkshire Hathaway in 1965, when it had a book value of less than $20 per share and a real value of even less, and through the acquisition of several successful businesses and investments in others, he built Berkshire into a conglomerate with a market value, at the end of 1993, of $16,025 per share.

Mr. Buffet's annual letters to shareholders "have drawn a sophisticated following" in the business and financial community. Andrew Tobias, *Letters From Chairman Buffet*, Fortune 137 (Aug. 22, 1983). They discuss, in pointed but accessible language, numerous issues relating to investing in and managing business corporations. Excerpts from Buffet's letters appear at several points in this book.

Interestingly, well over 90% of the shareholders participate annually in the program.

THEODORA HOLDING CORP. v. HENDERSON
257 A.2d 398 (Del.Ch.1969).

[For many years, Girard Henderson dominated the affairs of Alexander Dawson, Inc., through his controlling interest in that corporation. In 1955, he transferred shares to his then wife, Theodora Henderson, as part of a separation agreement. In 1967, Mrs. Henderson formed the Theodora Holding Corporation and transferred to it 27 percent of the outstanding stock of Alexander Dawson, Inc. During that year, the combined dividends paid by Alexander Dawson, Inc. to Mrs. Henderson and her corporation totalled $286,240.

From 1960 to 1966, Girard Henderson had caused Alexander Dawson, Inc. to make annual corporate contributions ranging from $60,000 to more than $70,000 to the Alexander Dawson Foundation ("the Foundation"), which Henderson had formed in 1957. All contributions were unanimously approved by the shareholders. In 1966, Alexander Dawson, Inc. donated to the Foundation a large tract of land valued at $467,750 for the purpose of establishing a camp for under-privileged boys. In April 1967, Mr. Henderson proposed that the board approve a $528,000 gift of company stock to the Foundation. One director, Theodora Ives, objected and suggested that the gift be made instead to a charitable corporation supported by her mother (Girard Henderson's ex-wife) and herself. Girard Henderson responded by causing a reduction in the Alexander Dawson, Inc. board of directors from eight members to three. The board thereafter approved the gift of stock to the Foundation.

Theodora Holding Corp. then brought suit against certain individuals, including Girard Henderson, challenging the gift and seeking an accounting and the appointment of a liquidating receiver for Alexander Dawson, Inc.]

MARVEL, VICE CHANCELLOR.

* * * Title 8 Del.C. § 122 provides as follows:

Every corporation created under this chapter shall have power to—

* * * (9) Make donations for the public welfare or for charitable, scientific or educational purposes, and in time of war or other national emergency in aid thereof.

There is no doubt but that the Alexander Dawson Foundation is recognized as a legitimate charitable trust by the Department of Internal Revenue. It is also clear that it is authorized to operate exclusively in the fields of " * * * religious, charitable, scientific, literary, or educational purposes, or for the prevention of cruelty to children or animals * * * ". Furthermore, contemporary courts recognize that unless corporations carry an increasing share of the burden of supporting charitable and educational causes that the business advantages now reposed in corporations by law may well prove to be unacceptable to the representatives of an aroused public. The recognized obligation of corporations towards philanthropic, educational and artistic causes is reflected in the statutory law of all of the states, other than the states of Arizona and Idaho.

In A.P. Smith Mfg. Co. v. Barlow, 13 N.J. 145, 98 A.2d [581], appeal dismissed, 346 U.S. 861, 74 S.Ct. 107, 98 L.Ed. 373, a case in which the corporate donor had been organized long before the adoption of a statute authorizing corporate gifts to charitable or educational institutions, the Supreme Court of New Jersey upheld a gift of $1500 by the plaintiff corporation to Princeton University, being of the opinion that the trend towards the transfer of wealth from private industrial entrepreneurs to corporate institutions, the increase of taxes on individual income, coupled with steadily increasing philanthropic needs, necessitate corporate giving for educational needs even were there no statute permitting such gifts, and this was held to be the case apart from the question of the reserved power of the state to amend corporate charters. The court also noted that the gift tended to bolster the free enterprise system and the general social climate in which plaintiff was nurtured. And while the court pointed out that there was no showing that the gift in question was made indiscriminately or to a pet charity in furtherance of personal, rather than corporate ends, the actual holding of the opinion appears to be that a corporate charitable or educational gift to be valid must merely be within reasonable limits both as to amount and purpose.   * * *

I conclude that the test to be applied in passing on the validity of a gift such as the one here in issue is that of reasonableness, a test in which the provisions of the Internal Revenue Code pertaining to charitable gifts by corporations furnish a helpful guide. The gift here under attack was made from gross income and had a value as of the time of giving of $528,000 in a year in which Alexander Dawson, Inc.'s total income was $19,144,229.06, or well within the federal tax deduction limitation of 5% of such income. The contribution under attack can be said to have ("cost") all of the stockholders of Alexander Dawson, Inc. including plaintiff, less than $80,000, or some fifteen cents per dollar of contribution, taking into consideration the federal tax provisions applicable to holding companies as well as the provisions for compulsory distribution of dividends received by such a corporation. In addition, the gift, by reducing Alexander Dawson, Inc.'s reserve for unrealized capital gains taxes by some $130,000, increased the balance sheet net worth of stockholders of the corporate defendant by such amount. It is accordingly obvious, in my opinion, that the relatively small loss of immediate income otherwise payable to plaintiff and the corporate defendant's other stockholders had it not been for the gift in question, is far out-weighed by the overall benefits flowing from the placing of such gift in channels where it serves to benefit those in need of philanthropic or educational support, thus providing justification for large private holdings, thereby benefiting plaintiff in the long run. Finally, the fact that the interests of the Alexander Dawson Foundation appear to be increasingly directed towards the rehabilitation and education of deprived but deserving young people is peculiarly appropriate in an age when a large segment of youth is alienated even from parents who are not entirely satisfied with our present social and economic system. * * *

On notice, an order in conformity with the holdings of this opinion may be presented.

KAHN v. SULLIVAN
594 A.2d 48 (Del.1991).

HOLLAND, JUSTICE:

This is an appeal from the approval of the settlement of one of three civil actions brought in the Court of Chancery by certain shareholders of Occidental Petroleum Corporation ("Occidental"). Each civil action challenged a decision by Occidental's board of directors (the "Board"), through a special committee of Occidental's outside directors ("the Special Committee"), to make a charitable donation. The purpose of the charitable donation was to construct and fund an art museum.

The shareholder plaintiffs in this litigation, Joseph Sullivan and Alan Brody, agreed to a settlement of their class and derivative actions subject to the approval of the Court of Chancery. The settlement was authorized, on behalf of Occidental, by the Special Committee. The shareholder plaintiffs in the other two civil actions, Alan R. Kahn ("Kahn") and Barnett Stepak ("Stepak"), appeared in the Sullivan action and objected to the proposed settlement. California Public Employees Retirement System ("CalPERS") was permitted to intervene as a shareholder plaintiff in the Kahn action and also appeared in opposition to the proposed settlement in the Sullivan action. * * *

FACTS

Occidental is a Delaware corporation. According to the parties, Occidental has about 290 million shares of stock outstanding which are held by approximately 495 thousand shareholders. For the year ending December 31, 1988, Occidental had assets of approximately twenty billion dollars, operating revenues of twenty billion dollars and pre-tax earnings of $574 million. Its corporate headquarters are located in Los Angeles, California.

At the time of his death on December 10, 1990, Dr. Hammer was Occidental's chief executive officer and the chairman of its board of directors. Since the early 1920's, Dr. Hammer had been a serious art collector. When Dr. Hammer died, he personally and The Armand Hammer Foundation (the "Foundation"), owned three major collections of art (referred to in their entirety as "the Art Collection"). The Art Collection, valued at $300–$400 million included: "Five Centuries of Art," more than 100 works by artists such as Rembrandt, Rubens,

Renoir and Van Gogh; the Codex Hammer, a rare manuscript by Leonardo da Vinci; and the world's most extensive private collection of paintings, lithographs and bronzes by the French satirist Honore Daumier.

For many years, the Board has determined that it is in the best interest of Occidental to support and promote the acquisition and exhibition of the Art Collection. Through Occidental's financial support and sponsorship, the Art Collection has been viewed by more than six million people in more than twenty-five American cities and at least eighteen foreign countries. The majority of those exhibitions have been in areas where Occidental has operations or was negotiating business contracts. * * *

Dr. Hammer enjoyed an ongoing relationship with the Los Angeles County Museum of Art ("LACMA") for several decades. In 1968, Dr. Hammer agreed to donate a number of paintings to LACMA, as well as funds to purchase additional art. For approximately twenty years thereafter, Dr. Hammer both publicly and privately expressed his intention to donate the Art Collection to LACMA. However, Dr. Hammer and LACMA had never entered into a binding agreement to that effect. Nevertheless, LACMA named one of its buildings the Frances and Armand Hammer Wing in recognition of Dr. Hammer's gifts.

Occidental approved of Dr. Hammer's decision to permanently display the Art Collection at LACMA. In fact, it made substantial financial contributions to facilitate that display. In 1982, for example, Occidental paid two million dollars to expand and refurbish the Hammer Wing at LACMA.

In 1987, Dr. Hammer presented Daniel N. Belin, Esquire ("Belin"), the president of LACMA's Board of Trustees, with a thirty-nine page proposed agreement which set forth the terms upon which Dr. Hammer would permanently locate the Art Collection at LACMA. LACMA and Dr. Hammer tried, but were unable to reach a binding agreement. Consequently, Dr. Hammer concluded that he would make arrangements for the permanent display of the Art Collection at a location other than at LACMA. On January 8, 1988, Dr. Hammer wrote a letter to Belin which stated that he had "decided to create my own museum to house" the Art Collection.

On January 19, 1988, at a meeting of the executive committee of Occidental's board of directors ("the Executive Committee"), Dr. Hammer proposed that Occidental, in conjunction with the Foundation, construct a museum for the Art Collection. After discussing Occidental's history of identification with the Art Collection, the Executive Committee decided that it was in Occidental's best interest to accept Dr. Hammer's proposal. * * *

The art museum concept was announced publicly on January 21, 1988. On February 11, 1988, the Board approved the Executive Committee's prior actions. * * *

On December 15, 1988, the Board was presented with a detailed plan for the Museum proposal. The Board approved the concept and authorized a complete study of the proposal. Following the December 15th Board meeting, the law firm of Dilworth, Paxson, Kalish & Kauffman ("Dilworth") was retained by the Board to examine the Museum proposal and to prepare a memorandum addressing the issues relevant to the Board's consideration of the proposal.[6] The law firm of Skadden, Arps, Slate, Meagher & Flom ("Skadden Arps") was retained to represent the new legal entity which would be necessitated by the Museum proposal. Occidental's public accountants, Arthur Andersen & Co. ("Arthur Andersen"), were also asked to examine the Museum proposal.

On or about February 6, 1989, ten days prior to the Board's prescheduled February 16 meeting, Dilworth provided each member of the Board with a ninety- six page memorandum. It contained a definition of the Museum proposal and the anticipated magnitude of the proposed charitable donation by Occidental. It reviewed the authority of the Board to approve such a donation and the reasonableness of the proposed donation. The Dilworth memorandum included an analysis of the donation's effect on Occidental's financial condition, the potential for good will and other benefits to Occidental, and a comparison of the proposed charitable contribution by Occidental to the charitable contributions of other corporations.

The advance distribution of the Dilworth memorandum was supplemented on February 10, 1989 by a tax opinion letter from Skadden Arps. * * *

During the February 16 Board meeting, a Dilworth representative personally presented the basis for that law firm's analysis of the Museum proposal, as set forth in its February 6 written memorandum. * * * Following the Dilworth presentation, the Board resolved to appoint the Special Committee, comprised of its eight independent and disinterested outside directors, to further review and to act upon the Museum proposal * * *. The Board then adjourned to allow the Special Committee to meet.

The Special Committee consisted of individuals who collectively had approximately eighty years of service on Occidental's board of directors. * * * Those Board members were not officers of Occidental, and were not associated with the Museum or the Foundation. * * *

The minutes of the February 16, 1989 meeting of the Special Committee outline its consideration of the Museum proposal. Those minutes reflect that many questions were asked by members of the Special Committee and were answered by the representatives of Dilworth, Skadden Arps, or Arthur Andersen. As a result of its own extensive discussions, and in reliance upon the experts' opinions, the Special Committee concluded that the establishment of the Museum, adjacent to Occidental's corporate offices in Los Angeles, would provide

---

6. At the time of its selection, Dilworth also represented Dr. Hammer personally.

benefits to Occidental for at least the thirty-year term of the lease. The Special Committee also concluded that the proposed museum would establish a new cultural landmark for the City of Los Angeles.

On February 16, 1989, the Special Committee unanimously approved the Museum proposal, [which committed Occidental to spend more than $85 million for a museum, to be identified as "The Armand Hammer Museum of Art and Cultural Center," to which the Art collection would be transferred. Occidental would receive public recognition for its role in establishing the Museum by the naming of the courtyard, library, *or* auditorium of the museum for Occidental.] * * *

On April 25, 1989, Occidental reported the Special Committee's approval of the Museum proposal to its shareholders in the proxy statement for its annual meeting to be held May 26, 1989. On May 2, 1989, the first shareholder action ("the Kahn action") was filed, challenging Occidental's decision to establish and fund the Museum proposal. The Sullivan action was filed on May 9, 1989. * * *

Settlement negotiations were entered into almost immediately between Occidental and the attorneys for the plaintiffs in the Sullivan action. * * *

On June 3, 1989, the parties to the Sullivan action signed a Memorandum of Understanding that set forth a proposed settlement in general terms. The proposed settlement was subject to the right of the plaintiffs to engage in additional discovery to confirm the fairness and adequacy of the proposed settlement.

On June 9, 1989, the plaintiffs in the Kahn action moved for a preliminary injunction to enjoin the proposed settlement in the Sullivan action and also for expedited discovery. * * *

In denying the motion for injunctive relief, the Court of Chancery * * * identified six issues to be addressed at any future settlement hearing:

> (1) the failure of the Special Committee appointed by the directors of Occidental to hire its own counsel and advisors or even to formally approve the challenged acts; (2) the now worthlessness of a prior donation by Occidental to the Los Angeles County Museum; (3) the huge attorney fees which the parties have apparently decided to seek or not oppose; (4) the egocentric nature of some of Armand Hammer's objections to the Los Angeles County Museum being the recipient of his donation; (5) the issue of who really owns the art; and (6) the lack of any direct substantial benefit to the stockholders.

On July 20, 1989, the Special Committee met to discuss the Museum proposal. * * *

At its July 20 meeting, the Special Committee also reviewed the July 19, 1989 decision and order of the Court of Chancery denying Kahn's request for injunctive relief in the Sullivan action. In response to one of the concerns expressed by the Court of Chancery, the Special Committee resolved to retain independent Delaware counsel with no prior connection to Occidental or its officers.   * * *

On October 6, 1989, Occidental's Board of Directors, by unanimous written consent, delegated full authority to the Special Committee to settle the shareholder litigation filed in Delaware on Occidental's behalf. * * *

The Special Committee met again on November 16, 1989.   * * * Prior to that meeting, the Special Committee received a draft of the Stipulation of Settlement of the Sullivan action, a revised Transfer Agreement in accordance with its September 20 request, and an abstract and analysis of the Transfer Agreement prepared by Morris James [the law firm the Special Committee had retained].   At the meeting on November 16, all of these documents were discussed with Brown of Morris James.   The form of a stipulation of settlement was approved unanimously by the Special Committee.

The parties to the Sullivan action presented the Court of Chancery with a fully executed Stipulation of Compromise, Settlement and Release agreement ("the Settlement") on January 24, 1990.   This agreement was only slightly changed from the June 3, 1989 Memorandum of Understanding.   The Settlement, *inter alia*, provided:

(1) The Museum building shall be named the "Occidental Petroleum Cultural Center Building" with the name displayed appropriately on the building.

(2) Occidental shall be treated as a corporate sponsor by the Museum for as long as the Museum occupies the building.

(3) Occidental's contribution of the building shall be recognized by the Museum in public references to the facility.

(4) Three of Occidental's directors shall serve on the Museum's Board (or no less than one-third of the total Museum Board) with Occidental having the option to designate a fourth director.

(5) There shall be an immediate loan of substantially all of the art collections of Dr. Hammer to the Museum and there shall be an actual transfer of ownership of the collections upon Dr. Hammer's death or the commencement of operation of the Museum—whichever later occurs.

(6) All future charitable contributions by Occidental to any Hammer-affiliated charities shall be limited by the size of the dividends paid to Occidental's common stockholders.   At current dividend levels, Occidental's annual contributions to Hammer-affiliated charities pursuant to this limitation could not exceed approximately three cents per share.

(7) Any amounts Occidental pays for construction of the Museum in excess of $50 million and any amounts paid to the Foundation upon Dr. Hammer's death must be charged against the agreed ceiling on limitations to Hammer-affiliated charities.

(8) Occidental's expenditures for the Museum construction shall not exceed $50 million, except that an additional $10 million may be expended through December 31, 1990 but only if such additional expenditures do not enlarge the scope of construction and if such expenditures are approved by the Special Committee. Amounts in excess of $50 million must be charged against the limitation on donations to Hammer-affiliated charities.

(9) Occidental shall be entitled to receive 50% of any consideration received in excess of a $55 million option price for the Museum property or 50% of any consideration the Museum receives from the assignment or transfer of its option or lease to a third party.

(10) Plaintiffs' attorneys' fees in the Sullivan action shall not exceed $1.4 million. * * *

On April 4, 1990, the settlement hearing in the Sullivan action was held.[22]

On August 7, 1990, the Court of Chancery found the Settlement to be reasonable under all of the circumstances. The Court of Chancery concluded that the claims asserted by the shareholder plaintiffs would likely be dismissed before or after trial. While noting its own displeasure with the Settlement, the Court of Chancery explained that its role in reviewing the proposed Settlement was restricted to determining in its own business judgment whether, on balance, the Settlement was reasonable.[23] The Court opined that although the benefit to be received from the Settlement was meager, it was adequate considering all the facts and circumstances.

STANDARD OF REVIEW

* * * In an appeal from the Court of Chancery, following the approval of a settlement of a class action, the function of this Court is more limited in its nature. Id.; see also Polk v. Good, 507 A.2d at 536. This Court does not review the record to determine the intrinsic fairness of the settlement in light of its own business judgment. Nottingham Partners v. Dana, 564 A.2d at 1102. This Court reviews the record

---

22. In the interim, the Special Committee met on March 29, 1990 to consider a request to approve the expenditure of an additional ten million dollars on the construction of the Museum. * * * [T]he Special Committee approved the expenditure * * *.

23. The Court of Chancery noted:

Despite this Court's expressed displeasure with the settlement efforts, as set forth in its July 19, 1989 opinion in Kahn, the settlement now before the Court is only slightly changed from the June 3, 1989 Memorandum of Understanding.

* * *

[Therefore] * * * the settlement in the Court's opinion leaves much to be desired. The Court's role in reviewing the proposed Settlement, however, is quite restricted. If the Court was a stockholder of Occidental it might vote for new directors, if it was on the Board it might vote for new management and if it was a member of the Special Committee it might vote against the Museum project. But its options are limited in reviewing a proposed settlement to applying Delaware law to the facts adduced in the record and then determining in its business judgment whether, on balance, the settlement is reasonable.

"solely for the purpose of determining whether or not the Court of Chancery abused its discretion by the exercise of its business judgment."
* * *

CLAIMS AND DEFENSES

* * * The proponents of the Settlement argued that the business judgment rule could undoubtedly have been invoked successfully by the defendants as a complete defense to the shareholder plaintiffs' claims. * * * The Objectors presented several alternative arguments in support of their contention that the shareholder plaintiffs would have been able to rebut the defense based on the protection which the presumption of the business judgment rule provides. * * *

First, the Objectors submitted that the business judgment rule would probably not protect the actions of the Special Committee because the independence of the Special Committee was questionable. In support of that argument, the Objectors assert that at least four members of the Special Committee had close ties to Dr. Hammer and personal business dealings with him. After examining the record, the Court of Chancery found that the Objectors had not established any facts that the Special Committee had any self-interest in the transaction either from a personal financial interest or from a motive for entrenchment in office. See Grobow v. Perot, Del.Supr., 539 A.2d 180, 188 (1988). The Court of Chancery also concluded that there was no evidence in the record indicating that any of the members of the Special Committee were in fact dominated by Dr. Hammer or anyone else.

Second, in a related argument, the Objectors argued that the presumption of the business judgment rule would have been overcome because the Special Committee proceeded initially without retaining independent legal counsel. * * * However, in approving the Settlement, the Court of Chancery noted that the Special Committee had retained independent counsel, and "subsequently, and for the first time, formally approved the challenged charitable contributions." Thus, the Court of Chancery specifically found that the Special Committee had the advice of independent legal counsel before it finally approved the Museum proposal. * * *

The Court of Chancery carefully considered each of the Objectors' arguments in response to the merits of the suggested business judgment rule defense. It concluded that if the Sullivan action proceeded, it was highly probable in deciding a motion to dismiss, a motion for summary judgment, or a post-trial motion, the actions of "the Special Committee would be protected by the presumption of propriety afforded by the business judgment rule." Specifically, the Court of Chancery concluded that it would have been decided that the Special Committee, comprised of Occidental's outside directors, was independent and made an informed decision to approve the charitable donation to the Museum proposal. These conclusions by the Court of Chancery are supported by the record and are the product of an orderly and logical deductive process.

Following its analysis and conclusion that the business judgment rule would have been applicable to any judicial examination of the Special Committee's actions, the Court of Chancery considered the shareholder plaintiffs' claim that the Board and the Special Committee's approval of the charitable donation to the Museum proposal constituted a waste of Occidental's corporate assets. In doing so, it recognized that charitable donations by Delaware corporations are expressly authorized by 8 Del.C. § 122(9). It also recognized that although § 122(9) places no limitations on the size of a charitable corporate gift, that section has been construed "to authorize any reasonable corporate gift of a charitable or educational nature." Theodora Holding Corp. v. Henderson, Del.Ch., 257 A.2d 398, 405 (1969). Thus, the Court of Chancery concluded that the test to be applied in examining the merits of a claim alleging corporate waste "is that of reasonableness, a test in which the provisions of the Internal Revenue Code pertaining to charitable gifts by corporations furnish a helpful guide." Id. We agree with that conclusion.

The Objectors argued that Occidental's charitable contribution to the Museum proposal was unreasonable and a waste of corporate assets because it was excessive. The Court of Chancery recognized that not every charitable gift constitutes a valid corporate action. Nevertheless, the Court of Chancery concluded, given the net worth of Occidental, its annual net income before taxes, and the tax benefits to Occidental, that the gift to the Museum was within the range of reasonableness established in Theodora Holding Corp. v. Henderson, Del.Ch., 257 A.2d 398, 405 (1969). Therefore, the Court of Chancery found that it was "reasonably probable" that plaintiffs would fail on their claim of waste. That finding is supported by the record and is the product of an orderly and logical deductive process.

Adequacy of the Settlement

In examining the Settlement, the Court of Chancery * * * evaluated not only the nature of the shareholder plaintiffs' claims but also the possible defenses to those claims. * * * After carefully evaluating the parties' respective legal positions, the Court of Chancery opined that "the [shareholder plaintiffs'] potential for ultimate success on the merits [in the Sullivan action] is, realistically, very poor."

Second, * * * after considering the legal and factual circumstances of the case *sub judice*, the Court of Chancery examined the value of the Settlement. The proponents of the Settlement argued that the monetary value of having the Museum building called the "Occidental Petroleum Cultural Center Building" was approximately ten million dollars. The Court of Chancery noted that, in support of their valuation arguments, the proponents also argued that the Settlement: (1) reinforced and assured Occidental's identification with and meaningful participation in the affairs of the Museum; (2) reinforced and protected the charitable nature and consequences of Occidental's gifts by securing the prompt delivery and irrevocable transfer of the Art Collection to the

Museum; (3) imposed meaningful controls upon the total construction costs that Occidental will pay, which had already forced the reduction of the construction budget by $19.4 million; (4) placed meaningful restrictions upon Occidental's future charitable donations to "Hammer" affiliated entities and avoided increases in posthumous payments to the Foundation or any other designated recipient after Dr. Hammer's death; (5) restored to Occidental an equitable portion of any appreciation of the properties in the event the Museum exercised its option and disposed of the properties or transferred its option for value; and (6) guaranteed that the Art Collection would continue to be located in the Los Angeles area and remain available for the enjoyment of the American public rather than dissipated into private collections or sold abroad.

The Court of Chancery characterized the proponents' efforts to quantify the monetary value of most of the Settlement benefits as "speculative." The Court of Chancery also viewed the estimate that naming the building for Occidental would have a ten million dollar value to Occidental with "a good deal of skepticism." Nevertheless, the Court of Chancery found that Occidental would, in fact, receive an economic benefit in the form of good will from the charitable donation to the Museum proposal. It also found that Occidental would derive an economic benefit from being able to utilize the Museum, adjacent to its corporate headquarters, in the promotion of its business.

Finally, the Court of Chancery applied its own independent business judgment in deciding whether the Settlement was fair and reasonable. * * * The Court of Chancery found that "the benefit [of the Settlement] to the stockholders of Occidental is sufficient to support the Settlement and is adequate, if only barely so, when compared to the weakness of the plaintiffs' claims." The Court of Chancery concluded that "although the Settlement is meager, it is adequate considering all the facts and circumstances." * * *

CONCLUSION

The reasonableness of a particular class action settlement is addressed to the discretion of the Court of Chancery, on a case by case basis, in light of all of the relevant circumstances. In this case, we find that all of the Court of Chancery's factual findings of fact are supported by the record. We also find that all of the legal conclusions reached by the Court of Chancery were based upon a proper application of well established principles of law. Consequently, we find that the Court of Chancery did not abuse its discretion in deciding to approve the Settlement in the Sullivan action. Therefore, the decision of the Court of Chancery is Affirmed.

Notes on Kahn v. Sullivan

1. Dr. Hammer's decision to renege on his oral promise to donate the Art Collection to LACMA was precipitated by LACMA's rejection of his insistence that an entire floor of LACMA's Frances and Armand Hammer Building be remodeled to house the Art Collection and that the

names of other donors, currently inscribed over galleries on that floor, be removed. Consequently, LACMA and Dr. Hammer never discussed other demands that LACMA found objectionable, such as that the main entrance to the floor be outfitted with a full length portrait of Hammer, that each work in the Collection be separately identified as donated by Hammer, that LACMA never sell any of the works in the Collection, that the collection be exhibited together on the special floor, and that no other works be exhibited with the Collection. See Robert A. Jones, Battle of the Masterpieces; The Armand Hammer–County Museum Deal: A Saga of Art, Power and Big Understandings, Los Angeles Times Magazine 8 (May 22, 1988).

2. Dr. Hammer dominated Occidental from the time he took control of the company until his death at age 92. Until 1980, when the SEC discovered the practice and objected to it, Dr. Hammer required that every person elected to Occidental's board sign and deliver to him an undated letter of resignation. At least five of the eight members of the Special Committee joined the board prior to the time he discontinued this practice. Dr. Hammer also apparently viewed himself as indispensible to Occidental's success. He dismissed four experienced executives hired by Occidental as his potential successor, concluding that none of them were up to the job.

3. While Occidental agreed to pay counsel fees to the *Sullivan* plaintiffs of up to $1.4 million, the Vice–Chancellor awarded a fee of only $800,000, reflecting, to some degree, his skepticism about the merits of the settlement. See Sullivan v. Hammer, [CCH] Fed. Sec. L. Rep. ¶ 95,415, 1990 WL 114223 (Del.Ch.1990). Counsel for the other plaintiffs, however, were awarded no fees for their efforts.

C. CORPORATE SOCIAL RESPONSIBILITY TRENDS

PROBLEMS

The three problems that follow all involve corporate actions that could have significant social consequences. You should approach them as outside counsel who the corporation in question has asked for advice. Keep in mind the distinction between legal advice, which the corporation surely wants, and policy advice, which the corporation may or may not be seeking. Also consider what your professional and ethical responsibilities are in advising your client.

In analyzing the problems, also think about the following:

1. Does the board have a fiduciary duty to choose one course of action, or might more than one course of action be consistent with those duties? To the extent that profit maximization is relevant or dispositive, is it helpful to frame the board's decisions in terms of long-term, rather than short-run, profitability?

2. What interests, if any, besides those of shareholders may or must the board consider? Is there a way in which the board can

appropriately take account of non-shareholder interests without unreasonably increasing its exposure to liability?

3. To the extent that the board may or must consider interests other than those of the shareholders, how should it determine what those interests are? Should it look to federal legislation, for example, to ascertain national public policy? To the individual consciences of board members about what is "right", "just" or "fair?"

4. How, if at all, would your advice change if the corporation was organized under a general corporation law that allowed or required boards of directors to take account of the interests of non-shareholder constituencies?

A.   MORRILL, DEW, INC.

Morrill, Dew, Inc. is a consumer products and pharmaceutical company. A researcher in Morrill, Dew's pharmaceutical laboratory realized about two years ago that MD–379, a compound Morrill, Dew had been developing as a treatment for ulcers, had considerable potential as an abortifacient (a drug that causes a woman to spontaneously abort a fetus). About a year ago, Morrill, Dew quietly began human trials of MD–379 in a government-approved program in China. The results were very positive. When taken as instructed, MD–379 caused more than 98% of the pregnant women who used it to abort. The only adverse side effects were comparable to the effects generally experienced by women experiencing spontaneous miscarriages at early stages of pregnancy.

Information about Morrill, Dew's work with MD–379 recently was leaked to the press. Pro-choice groups began to press Morrill, Dew to submit the drug for approval by the U.S. Food and Drug Administration ("FDA"), with a view to making it available for sale in the United States. Pro-life groups, on the other hand, are threatening to organize a boycott of other Morrill, Dew products if it seeks FDA approval. Management's best estimate is that, aside from the boycott threat, MD–379 could be a modestly profitable product, adding earnings of about $20 million per year to Morrill, Dew's current annual earnings of about $850 million. Management, however, fears that losses caused by a boycott of other Morrill, Dew products by pro-life groups could exceed the profits that MD–379 would generate. Of course, it also is possible that pro-choice groups will mount a boycott if Morrill, Dew does not proceed.

The board of directors is scheduled to decide at its next meeting whether to seek FDA approval or to announce that Morrill, Dew will not attempt to market the drug in the United States. Several members of the board have strong opinions, pro and con, on the morality of marketing an abortifacient. The board has asked you to make a presentation, at the start of its meeting, as to the possibility directors will be held liable should the board either seek FDA approval or abandon further work on MD–379.

B. INTERNATIONAL ELECTRONICS INC.

International Electronics Inc. ("IEI"), has a large assembly plant located in West Lyme, a small town in New Hampshire. With over 1,000 workers, IEI is the town's major employer. For the last several years, the West Lyme plant has been only marginally profitable, in part because of its size and in part because of high labor costs. IEI believes this situation is likely to continue. Its management has recommended that the plant be closed and that IEI build a new, larger plant, employing 3,000 people, in Malaysia. Because the going wage rate in Malaysia is only one-fifth that in West Lyme, management expects IEI would earn close to twenty percent per annum on its investment in the new plant, considerably in excess of IEI's average return on capital.

Closing the plant is likely to have a devastating effect on West Lyme. Building the new plant in Malaysia, on the other hand, will provide employment for a large number of people who now live in extreme poverty. To what extent can and should the board take these and other relevant "non-economic" factors into account in deciding what to do?

C. U.S. DRUGS, INC.

U.S. Drugs, Inc., produces a broad line of pharmaceutical products. It has recently developed a new drug that is extremely effective in treating certain serious liver disorders, but that, in human trials, has apparently led to heart failure in a small, but statistically significant, number of cases. As a consequence, the FDA has refused to license sale of the new drug in the United States. U.S. Drugs has invested a substantial amount of money in the development and testing of the drug, and would like to recoup that investment if possible. Its international division has developed a plan to manufacture and sell the new drug in certain Latin American countries whose drug laws are substantially more tolerant of drugs with potentially serious side effects than those of the United States, so long as adequate information is provided about those side effects to prescribing physicians and druggists. U.S. Drugs' board of directors has asked your advice on whether the company should proceed to manufacture and sell the new drug in Latin America.

1. JUDICIAL APPROACHES

DODGE v. FORD MOTOR CO.
204 Mich. 459, 170 N.W. 668 (1919).

[Although the principal issue in this famous case was whether the corporation could be compelled to pay a dividend, the case is best remembered for its discussion of the role of a corporation in society, a discussion that was elicited by Henry Ford's insistence in describing his motives for business decisions in terms of social rather than economic values.

This action was brought by the Dodge brothers, two minority shareholders, against the Ford Motor Company, Henry Ford, and other members of the board of directors, to compel the payment of a dividend, to enjoin construction of the River Rouge plant, and for other relief. The lower court granted all relief requested by plaintiffs.

Ford Motor Company was organized in 1903 with an initial capital of $150,000. Henry Ford took 225 of the 1,500 shares authorized, the Dodge brothers took 50 shares each, and several others subscribed to a few shares each. At the time the suit was brought, the company's capital was $2,000,000, the plaintiffs owned 10% of the outstanding stock, and Ford owned 58% and completely dominated the company.

The company paid regular quarterly dividends amounting to $1,200,-000 per year and, in addition, had paid during the years 1911 through 1915 a total of $41 million in "special dividends." The plaintiffs alleged that Ford had "declared it to be the settled policy of the company not to pay in the future any special dividends, but to put back into the business for the future all of the earnings of the company other than the regular dividend * * *."

The defendants appealed from a lower court order directing the corporation to pay a dividend of $19 million, enjoining it from building a smelter at the River Rouge plant and restraining it from "increasing of the fixed capital assets," or "holding of liquid assets * * * in excess of such as may be reasonably required in the proper conduct and carrying on of the business and operations" of the corporation.]

OSTRANDER, C.J.

* * * To develop the points now discussed, and to a considerable extent they may be developed together as a single point, it is necessary to refer with some particularity to the facts.

When plaintiffs made their complaint and demand for further dividends, the Ford Motor Company had concluded its most prosperous year of business. The demand for its cars at the price of the preceding year continued. It could make and could market in the year beginning August 1, 1916, more than 500,000 cars. Sales of parts and repairs would necessarily increase. The cost of materials was likely to advance, and perhaps the price of labor; but it reasonably might have expected a profit for the year of upwards of $60,000,000. * * * In justification [of their dividend policy and business plan], the defendants have offered testimony tending to prove, and which does prove, the following facts: It had been the policy of the corporation for a considerable time to annually reduce the selling price of cars, while keeping up, or improving, their quality. As early as in June, 1915, a general plan for the expansion of the productive capacity of the concern by a practical duplication of its plant had been talked over by the executive officers and directors and agreed upon; not all of the details having been settled, and no formal action of directors having been taken. The erection of a smelter was considered, and engineering and other data in connection therewith secured. In consequence, it was determined not to reduce the selling price of cars for the year beginning August 1, 1915, but to maintain the price and to accumulate a large surplus to pay for the proposed expansion of plant and equipment, and perhaps to build a plant for smelting ore. It is hoped, by Mr. Ford, that eventually 1,000,000 cars will be annually produced. The contemplated changes will permit the increased output.

The plan, as affecting the profits of the business for the year beginning August 1, 1916, and thereafter, calls for a reduction in the selling price of the cars. It is true that this price might be at any time increased, but the plan called for the reduction in price of $80 a car. The capacity of the plant, without the additions thereto voted to be made (without a part of them at least), would produce more than 600,000 cars annually. This number, and more, could have been sold for $440 instead of $360, a difference in the return for capital, labor, and materials employed of at least $48,000,000. In short, the plan does not call for and is not intended to produce immediately a more profitable business, but a less profitable one; not only less profitable than formerly, but less profitable than it is admitted it might be made. The apparent immediate effect will be to diminish the value of shares and the returns to shareholders.

It is the contention of plaintiffs that the apparent effect of the plan is intended to be the continued and continuing effect of it, and that it is deliberately proposed, not of record and not by official corporate declaration, but nevertheless proposed, to continue the corporation henceforth as a semi-eleemosynary institution and not as a business institution. In support of this contention, they point to the attitude and to the expressions of Mr. Henry Ford.

Mr. Henry Ford is the dominant force in the business of the Ford Motor Company. No plan of operations could be adopted unless he consented, and no board of directors can be elected whom he does not favor. One of the directors of the company has no stock. One share was assigned to him to qualify him for the position, but it is not claimed that he owns it. A business, one of the largest in the world, and one of the most profitable, has been built up. It employs many men, at good pay.

"My ambition," said Mr. Ford, "is to employ still more men, to spread the benefits of this industrial system to the greatest possible number, to help them build up their lives and their homes. To do this we are putting the greatest share of our profits back in the business."

"With regard to dividends, the company paid sixty per cent on its capitalization of two million dollars, or $1,200,000, leaving $58,000,000 to reinvest for the growth of the company. This is Mr. Ford's policy at present, and it is understood that the other stockholders cheerfully accede to this plan."

He had made up his mind in the summer of 1916 that no dividends other than the regular dividends should be paid, "for the present."

"Q. For how long? Had you fixed in your mind any time in the future, when you were going to pay? A. No.

"Q. That was indefinite in the future? A. That was indefinite; yes, sir."

The record, and especially the testimony of Mr. Ford, convinces that he has to some extent the attitude towards shareholders of one who has dispensed and distributed to them large gains and that they should be content to take what he chooses to give. His testimony creates the impression, also, that he thinks the Ford Motor Company has made too much money, has had too large profits, and that, although large profits might be still earned, a sharing of them with the public, by reducing the price of the output of the company, ought to be undertaken. We have no doubt that certain sentiments, philanthropic and altruistic, creditable to Mr. Ford, had large influence in determining the policy to be pursued by the Ford Motor Company—the policy which has been herein referred to.

It is said by his counsel that—

Although a manufacturing corporation cannot engage in humanitarian works as its principal business, the fact that it is organized for profit does not prevent the existence of implied powers to carry on with humanitarian motives such charitable works as are incidental to the main business of the corporation.

And again:

As the expenditures complained of are being made in an expansion of the business which the company is organized to carry on, and for purposes within the powers of the corporation as hereinbefore shown, the question is as to whether such expenditures are rendered illegal because influenced to some extent by humanitarian motives and purposes on the part of the members of the board of directors.

* * * [The cases referred to by counsel], after all, like all others in which the subject is treated, turn finally upon the point, the question, whether it appears that the directors were not acting for the best interests of the corporation. We do not draw in question, nor do counsel for the plaintiffs do so, the validity of the general proposition stated by counsel nor the soundness of the opinions delivered in the cases cited. The case presented here is not like any of them. The difference between an incidental humanitarian expenditure of corporate funds for the benefit of the employees, like the building of a hospital for their use and the employment of agencies for the betterment of their condition, and a general purpose and plan to benefit mankind at the expense of others, is obvious. There should be no confusion (of which there is evidence) of the duties which Mr. Ford conceives that he and the stockholders owe to the general public and the duties which in law he and his codirectors owe to protesting, minority stockholders. A business corporation is organized and carried on primarily for the profit of the stockholders. The powers of the directors are to be employed for that end. The discretion of directors is to be exercised in the choice of means to attain that end, and does not extend to a change in the end itself, to the reduction of profits, or to the nondistribution of profits among stockholders in order to devote them to other purposes.

There is committed to the discretion of directors, a discretion to be exercised in good faith, the infinite details of business, including the wages which shall be paid to employees, the number of hours they shall work, the conditions under which labor shall be carried on, and the price for which products shall be offered to the public.

It is said by appellants that the motives of the board members are not material and will not be inquired into by the court so long as their acts are within their lawful powers. As we have pointed out, and the proposition does not require argument to sustain it, it is not within the lawful powers of a board of directors to shape and conduct the affairs of a corporation for the merely incidental benefit of shareholders and for the primary purpose of benefiting others, and no one will contend that, if the avowed purpose of the defendant directors was to sacrifice the interests of shareholders, it would not be the duty of the courts to interfere.

We are not, however, persuaded that we should interfere with the proposed expansion of the business of the Ford Motor Company. In view of the fact that the selling price of products may be increased at any time, the ultimate results of the larger business cannot be certainly estimated. The judges are not business experts. It is recognized that plans must often be made for a long future, for expected competition, for a continuing as well as an immediately profitable venture. The experience of the Ford Motor Company is evidence of capable management of its affairs. It may be noticed, incidentally, that it took from the public the money required for the execution of its plan, and that the very considerable salaries paid to Mr. Ford and to certain executive officers and employees were not diminished. We are not satisfied that the alleged motives of the directors, in so far as they are reflected in the conduct of the business, menace the interests of shareholders. It is enough to say, perhaps, that the court of equity is at all times open to complaining shareholders having a just grievance. * * *

The decree of the court below fixing and determining the specific amount to be distributed to stockholders is affirmed. In other respect, * * * the said decree is reversed.

Note: Dodge v. Ford

Henry Ford asserted on numerous occasions that he wanted only a small profit from his venture:

> I hold this [view] because it enables a large number of people to buy and enjoy the use of a car and because it gives a larger number of men employment at good wages. Those are the two aims I have in life. But I would not be counted a success * * * if I could not accomplish that and at the same time make a fair amount of profit for myself and the men associated with me in the business.
>
> And let me say right here, that I do not believe that we should make such an awful profit on our cars. A reasonable profit is right, but not too much. So it has been my policy to force the price of the

car down as fast as production would permit, and give the benefits to users and laborers, with resulting surprisingly enormous benefits to ourselves.

Allan Nevins & Frank E. Hill, Ford: Expansion and Challenge 1915–1933, 97 (1957).

Mr. Ford was challenged on cross-examination by counsel for the Dodge brothers, Ellicott G. Stevenson, producing the following colloquy:

STEVENSON: Now, I will ask you again, do you still think that those profits were "awful profits?"

FORD: Well, I guess I do, yes.

STEVENSON: And for that reason you were not satisfied to continue to make such awful profits?

FORD: We don't seem to be able to keep the profits down.

STEVENSON: * * * Are you trying to keep them down? What is the Ford Motor Company organized for except profits, will you tell me, Mr. Ford?

FORD: Organized to do as much good as we can, everywhere, for everybody concerned.

What, demanded Stevenson, was the purpose of the company? "To do as much as possible for everybody concerned," replied Ford. " * * * To make money and use it, give employment, and send out the car where the people can use it." He added, "And incidentally to make money."

STEVENSON: Incidentally make money?

FORD: Yes, sir.

STEVENSON: But your controlling feature * * * is to employ a great army of men at high wages, to reduce the selling price of your car, so that a lot of people can buy it at a cheap price, and give everybody a car that want one.

FORD: If you give all that, the money will fall into your hands; you can't get out of it.

Id. at 99–100.

SHLENSKY v. WRIGLEY
95 Ill.App.2d 173, 237 N.E.2d 776 (1968).

SULLIVAN, JUSTICE.

This is an appeal from a dismissal of plaintiff's amended complaint on motion of the defendants. The action was a stockholders' derivative suit against the directors for negligence and mismanagement. The corporation was also made a defendant. Plaintiff sought damages and an order that defendants cause the installation of lights in Wrigley Field and the scheduling of night baseball games.

Plaintiff is a minority stockholder of defendant corporation, Chicago National League Ball Club (Inc.), a Delaware corporation with its principal place of business in Chicago, Illinois. Defendant corporation owns and operates the major league professional baseball team known as the Chicago Cubs. The corporation also engages in the operation of Wrigley Field, the Cubs' home park, the concessionaire sales during Cubs' home games, television and radio broadcasts of Cubs' home games, the leasing of the field for football games and other events and receives its share, as visiting team, of admission moneys from games played in other National League stadia. The individual defendants are directors of the Cubs and have served for varying periods of years. Defendant Philip K. Wrigley is also president of the corporation and owner of approximately 80% of the stock therein.

Plaintiff alleges that since night baseball was first played in 1935 nineteen of the twenty major league teams have scheduled night games. In 1966, out of a total of 1620 games in the major leagues, 932 were played at night. Plaintiff alleges that every member of the major leagues, other than the Cubs, scheduled substantially all of its home games in 1966 at night, exclusive of opening days, Saturdays, Sundays, holidays and days prohibited by league rules. Allegedly this has been done for the specific purpose of maximizing attendance and thereby maximizing revenue and income.

The Cubs, in the years 1961–65, sustained operating losses from its direct baseball operations. Plaintiff attributes those losses to inadequate attendance at Cubs' home games. He concludes that if the directors continue to refuse to install lights at Wrigley Field and schedule night baseball games, the Cubs will continue to sustain comparable losses and its financial condition will continue to deteriorate.

Plaintiff alleges that, except for the year 1963, attendance at Cubs' home games has been substantially below that at their road games, many of which were played at night.

Plaintiff compares attendance at Cubs' games with that of the Chicago White Sox, an American League club, whose weekday games were generally played at night. The weekend attendance figures for the two teams was similar; however, the White Sox week-night games drew many more patrons than did the Cubs' weekday games.

Plaintiff alleges that the funds for the installation of lights can be readily obtained through financing and the cost of installation would be far more than offset and recaptured by increased revenues and incomes resulting from the increased attendance.

Plaintiff further alleges that defendant Wrigley has refused to install lights, not because of interest in the welfare of the corporation but because of his personal opinions "that baseball is a 'daytime sport' and that the installation of lights and night baseball games will have a deteriorating effect upon the surrounding neighborhood." It is alleged that he has admitted that he is not interested in whether the Cubs would benefit financially from such action because of his concern for the neighborhood, and that he would be willing for the team to play night games if a new stadium were built in Chicago.

Plaintiff alleges that the other defendant directors, with full knowledge of the foregoing matters, have acquiesced in the policy laid down by Wrigley and have permitted him to dominate the board of directors in matters involving the installation of lights and scheduling of night games, even though they knew he was not motivated by a good faith concern as to the best interests of defendant corporation, but solely by his personal views set forth above. It is charged that the directors are acting for a reason or reasons contrary and wholly unrelated to the business interests of the corporation; that such arbitrary and capricious acts constitute mismanagement and waste of corporate assets, and that the directors have been negligent in failing to exercise reasonable care and prudence in the management of the corporate affairs.

The question on appeal is whether plaintiff's amended complaint states a cause of action. It is plaintiff's position that fraud, illegality and conflict of interest are not the only bases for a stockholder's derivative action against the directors. Contrariwise, defendants argue that the courts will not step in and interfere with honest business judgment of the directors unless there is a showing of fraud, illegality or conflict of interest.

The cases in this area are numerous and each differs from the others on a factual basis. However, the courts have pronounced certain ground rules which appear in all cases and which are then applied to the given factual situation. The court in Wheeler v. Pullman Iron and Steel Company, 143 Ill. 197, 207, 32 N.E. 420, 423, said:

> It is, however, fundamental in the law of corporations, that the majority of its stockholders shall control the policy of the corporation, and regulate and govern the lawful exercise of its franchise and business. * * * Every one purchasing or subscribing for stock in a corporation impliedly agrees that he will be bound by the acts and proceedings done or sanctioned by a majority of the shareholders, or by the agents of the corporation duly chosen by such majority, within the scope of the powers conferred by the charter, and courts of equity will not undertake to control the policy or business methods of a corporation, although it may be seen that a wiser policy might be adopted and the business more successful if other methods were pursued. The majority of shares of its stock, or the agents by the holders thereof lawfully chosen, must be permitted to control the business of the corporation in their discretion, when not in violation of its charter or some public law, or corruptly and fraudulently subversive of the rights and interests of the corporation or of a shareholder.

* * * Plaintiff argues that the allegations of his amended complaint are sufficient to set forth a cause of action under the principles set out in Dodge v. Ford Motor Co., 204 Mich. 459, 170 N.W. 668. * * *

From the authority relied upon in that case it is clear that the court felt that there must be fraud or a breach of that good faith which directors are bound to exercise toward the stockholders in order to justify the courts entering into the internal affairs of corporations. This is made clear when the court refused to interfere with the director[s'] decision to expand the business. * * *

Plaintiff in the instant case argues that the directors are acting for reasons unrelated to the financial interest and welfare of the Cubs. However, we are not satisfied that the motives assigned to Philip K. Wrigley, and through him to the other directors, are contrary to the best interests of the corporation and the stockholders. For example, it appears to us that the effect on the surrounding neighborhood might well be considered by a director who was considering the patrons who would or would not attend the games if the park were in a poor neighborhood. Furthermore, the long run interest of the corporation in its property value at Wrigley Field might demand all efforts to keep the neighborhood from deteriorating. By these thoughts we do not mean to say that we have decided that the decision of the directors was a correct one. That is beyond our jurisdiction and ability. We are merely saying that the decision is one properly before directors and the motives alleged in the amended complaint showed no fraud, illegality or conflict of interest in their making of that decision. * * *

Finally, we do not agree with plaintiff's contention that failure to follow the example of the other major league clubs in scheduling night games constituted negligence. Plaintiff made no allegation that these teams' night schedules were profitable or that the purpose for which night baseball had been undertaken was fulfilled. Furthermore, it cannot be said that directors, even those of corporations that are losing money, must follow the lead of the other corporations in the field. Directors are elected for their business capabilities and judgment and the courts cannot require them to forego their judgment because of the decisions of directors of other companies. Courts may not decide these questions in the absence of a clear showing of dereliction of duty on the part of the specific directors and mere failure to "follow the crowd" is not such a dereliction.

For the foregoing reasons the order of dismissal entered by the trial court is affirmed.

2. WHAT IS CORPORATE RESPONSIBILITY?: OTHER VIEWS

MILTON FRIEDMAN, CAPITALISM & FREEDOM
133–34 (1962).

The view has been gaining widespread acceptance that corporate officials * * * have a "social responsibility" that goes beyond serving the interest of their stockholders * * *. This view shows a fundamental misconception of the character and nature of a free economy. In such an economy, there is one and only one social responsibility of business— to use its resources and engage in activities designed to increase its profits so long as it stays within the rules of the game, which is to say,

engages in open and free competition, without deception or fraud. * * *
It is the responsibility of the rest of us to establish a framework of law
such that an individual in pursuing his own interest is, to quote Adam
Smith again, "led by an invisible hand to promote an end which was no
part of his intention. Nor is it always the worse for the society that it
was no part of it. By pursuing his own interest, he frequently promotes
that of the society more effectually than when he really intends to
promote it. I have never known much good done by those who affected
to trade for the public good."

Few trends could so thoroughly undermine the very foundations of
our free society as the acceptance by corporate officials of a social
responsibility other than to make as much money for their stockholders
as possible. This is a fundamentally subversive doctrine. If businessmen do have a social responsibility other than making maximum profits
for stockholders, how are they to know what it is? Can self-selected
private individuals decide what the social interest is? Can they decide
how great a burden they are justified in placing on themselves or their
stockholders to serve that social interest? Is it tolerable that these
public functions of taxation, expenditure, and control be exercised by the
people who happen at the moment to be in charge of particular enterprises, chosen for those posts by strictly private groups? If businessmen
are civil servants rather than the employees of their stockholders then in
a democracy they will, sooner or later, be chosen by the public techniques of election and appointment.

ELLIOTT J. WEISS, SOCIAL REGULATION OF BUSINESS ACTIVITY: REFORMING THE CORPORATE GOVERNANCE SYSTEM TO RESOLVE AN INSTITUTIONAL IMPASSE

28 U.C.L.A. L.Rev. 343, 418–32 (1981).

Corporations are creations of law, and have as their ultimate purpose the welfare of society. In an earlier era, when resources were
abundant, technology simple and affluence uncommon, corporations
could promote societal welfare by single-mindedly promoting their own
financial well-being. But changes in society have led to a geometric
increase in the number of situations in which corporate pursuit of
financial objectives seems inconsistent with public welfare, and to a
commensurate increase in social regulation of corporate activity. This
regulatory splurge has failed, largely because government lacks the
capacity to regulate effectively without the cooperation of the regulated.
Consequently, society now needs to reconsider the stated objective of
corporate activity. * * *

The standard that * * * can best promote social welfare is "altruistic capitalism." This standard would require corporate directors to
exercise reasonable care to ensure that management operates the business: (1) as if the firm were a pure competitor concerned with long-term
profitability; (2) as if the firm paid all the external costs and captured all

the external benefits of its operation; (3) as if the firm's customers and competitors shared all relevant information that the firm possessed; and (4) as if the firm were liable for all acts of its employees and agents.

Several aspects of this standard warrant amplification. First, the standard governs directors and contemplates that they will monitor the performance of corporate executives rather than involve themselves in the nuts and bolts of corporate decision making. * * *

Second, altruistic capitalism gives continuing prominence to corporations' financial performance; it requires that corporations temper, but not abandon, their quest for profits. A firm's compliance with this standard would not threaten its financial viability since all of its significant competitors would be operating under the same standard. * * *

Third, altruistic capitalism strikes an appropriate balance between public and private authority. * * *

Finally, substituting altruistic capitalism for the current standard of profit maximization would alter the atmosphere surrounding corporate decision making, but would not really increase corporate directors' discretionary power. Even under existing law, corporate directors have broad latitude to promote social values. * * *

Still, the existing profit maximization standard requires directors to frame and justify their decisions in financial terms. * * *

Adopting altruistic capitalism as the legal standard for corporate behavior would change the corporate decision-making environment. * * * Altruistic capitalism would not, however, be a self-executing standard. It would allow directors considerable discretion, since the business judgment rule would continue to insulate directors' reasonable decisions from judicial second-guessing. Consequently, directors governed by the standard of altruistic capitalism would be free to reach the same decisions now reached by directors pursuing traditional financial objectives, albeit after engaging in a somewhat different decision-making process.

Thus, corporate law reform should not be limited to restating the objective of corporate activity. Adoption of the suggested new legal standard is likely to have little effect on corporate behavior unless directors are committed to a policy of social responsiveness * * *.

[Professor Weiss proposes that Congress create a National Directors Corps, the members of which would be appointed by the President with the advice and consent of the Senate, and that large corporations be required to draw at least two-thirds of their directors from the National Directors Corps. He contends that "[s]election procedures, community and peer pressure, and their own views of their social roles all should lead National Directors to behave diligently and responsibly * * *." To promote accountability, he also suggests that "shareholders and outsiders affected by corporate actions * * * be allowed to sue National Directors for failure to exercise reasonable care in monitoring corporate performance. Negligent National Directors could be put on probation, or suspended or expelled from the Corps."]

ALI, PRINCIPLES OF CORPORATE GOVERNANCE: ANALYSIS AND RECOMMENDATIONS (1994)

§ 2.01 *The Objective and Conduct of the Corporation*

(a) Subject to the provisions of Subsection (b) * * *, a corporation should have as its objective the conduct of business activities with a view to enhancing corporate profit and shareholder gain.

(b) Even if corporate profit and shareholder gain are not thereby enhanced, the corporation, in the conduct of its business:

(a) Is obliged, to the same extent as a natural person, to act within the boundaries set by law;

(2) May take into account ethical considerations that are reasonably regarded as appropriate to the responsible conduct of business; and

(3) May devote a reasonable amount of resources to public welfare, humanitarian, educational, and philanthropic purposes.

Comment:

* * *

e. Corporate objective and corporate conduct. The subject matter of these Principles is the governance of business corporations. The business corporation is an instrument through which capital is assembled for the activities of producing and distributing goods and services and making investments. These Principles take as a basic proposition that a business corporation should have as its objective the conduct of such activities with a view to enhancing corporate profit and shareholder gain. This objective, which will hereafter be referred to as "the economic objective," is embodied in Subsection (a). The basic proposition is qualified in the manner stated in Subsection (b), which speaks to the conduct of the corporation. The provisions of Subsection (b) reflect a recognition that the corporation is a social as well as an economic institution, and accordingly that its pursuit of the economic objective must be constrained by social imperatives and may be qualified by social needs.

f. The economic objective. In very general terms, Subsection (a) may be thought of as a broad injunction to enhance economic returns, while Subsection (b) makes clear that certain kinds of conduct must or may be pursued whether or not they enhance such returns (that is, even if the conduct either yields no economic return or entails a net economic loss). In most cases, however, the kinds of conduct described in Subsection (b) could be pursued even under the principle embodied in Subsection (a). Such conduct will usually be consistent with economic self-interest, because the principle embodied in Subsection (a)—that the objective of the corporation is to conduct business activities with a view to enhancing corporate profit and shareholder gain—does not mean that the objective of the corporation must be to realize corporate profit and shareholder gain in the short run. Indeed, the contrary is true: long-run profitability and shareholder gain are at the core of the economic objective. Activity that entails a short-run cost to achieve an appropriately greater long-run profit is therefore not a departure from the economic objective. An orientation toward lawful, ethical, and public-spirited activity will normally fall within this description. The modern corporation by its nature creates interdependencies with a variety of groups with whom the corporation has a legitimate concern, such as employees, customers, suppliers, and members of the communities in which the corporation operates. The long-term profitability of the corporation generally depends on meeting the fair expectations of such groups. Short-term profits may properly be subordinated to recognition that responsible maintenance of these interdependencies is likely to contribute to long-term profitability and shareholder gain. The corporation's business may be conducted accordingly.

For comparable reasons, the economic objective does not imply that the corporation must extract the last penny of profit out of every transaction in which it is involved. Similarly, under normal circumstances the economic objective is met by focusing on the business in which the corporation is actually engaged.

Although a corporate decisionmaker needs to meet a standard of care in making decisions, that standard can be satisfied even when, as is often the case, a prospective profit cannot be particularized. Recurring instances of this sort include those in which the object of a corporate action is to maintain the confidence of business organizations with which the corporation deals, to foster the morale of employees, or to encourage favorable or forestall unfavorable government regulation—as by abstaining from conduct that would engender unfavorable public reaction against the corporation, providing lawful assistance in connection with lobbying or referenda activities, or voluntarily adopting a course of conduct so as to forestall legislation that would instead mandate such conduct. There is also no conflict with the economic objective when a corporation takes an action that will generate profit (or reduce the level of losses) not only for itself but also for other firms, if the corporation's benefit is likely to exceed the corporation's costs. In general, if the corporate officials who authorize a decision satisfy the test of the business judgment rule, the decision itself would satisfy § 2.01.

3. OTHER CONSTITUENCY STATUTES

a. Introduction. While corporate law traditionally has focused on the relationship between the board of directors and the shareholders, almost thirty state legislatures have adopted statutes that permit, and in one case require, a board of directors to consider the effect of any corporate action on non-shareholder interests. These interests may include the corporation's employees, customers, creditors, suppliers, the economy of the state/region/nation, community and societal interests, and the long-term and short-term interests of the corporation.

Constituency statutes were typically enacted together with anti-takeover legislation to protect corporate directors who oppose a hostile bid for control. While several of these statutes apply in the limited context of takeovers or control transactions, the majority are not so limited.

Ohio's statute, Ohio Rev. Code Ann. § 1701.59(E), which is typical, provides:

[A] director, in determining what he reasonably believes to be in the best interests of the corporation, shall consider the interests of the corporation's shareholders and, in his discretion, may consider any of the following:

(1) The interests of the corporation's employees, suppliers, creditors, and customers;

(2) The economy of the state and nation;

(3) Community and societal considerations;

(4) The long-term as well as short-term interests of the corporation and its shareholders, including the possibility that these interests may be best served by the continued independence of the corporation.

Variations abound. Some statutes impose mandatory requirements on directors. For example, insofar as a decision relates to the sale of all or substantially all of a corporation's assets, Connecticut *requires* a director of a publicly held corporation to consider the standard list of factors "in determining what he reasonably believes to be in the best interests of the corporation." Conn. Stock Corp. Act § 33–313(e). The Connecticut statute does not require that such mandatory consideration of other constituencies apply to any other decision.

The Indiana and Pennsylvania statutes do *not* require directors to consider other constituencies, but *permit* directors to subordinate share-holders' interests to those of other constituencies. Pa. Bus. Corp. L. § 1715(a) states that "directors * * * shall not be required, in consider-ing the best interests of the corporation or the effects of any action, to regard any corporate interest or the interests of any group affected by such action as a dominant or controlling interest or factor." *See also* Ind. Bus. Corp. L. § 23–1–35–1(f)). Thus, directors of Indiana and Pennsylvania corporations can claim that they acted in the best interests of a corporation even when they knowingly disregarded shareholders' economic interests.

To preclude claims by constituencies that feel their interests were not properly taken into account, the Indiana and Pennsylvania statutes also include what has been labeled a conclusive presumption of validity provision. Ind. Bus. Corp. L. § 23–1–35–1(g); Pa. Bus. Corp. L. § 1715(d). Specifically, they provide that any determination based on a disinterested board's discretionary consideration of the long-term corporate interests or the interests of "the other [enumerated] corporate constituent groups * * * shall conclusively be presumed to be valid unless it can be demonstrated that the determination was not made in good faith after reasonable investigation." Ind. Bus. Corp. L. § 23–1–35–1(g).

b. *The Future of Constituency Statutes.* In 1990, the Committee on Corporate Laws of the American Bar Association studied constituency statutes. Finding them "an inappropriate way to regulate corporate relationships or to respond to unwanted takeovers and that an expansive interpretation of the other constituencies statutes cast in the permissive mode is both unnecessary and unwise," it declined to include a constituency statute in the Revised Model Business Corporation Act. American Bar Association Committee on Corporate Laws, Other Constituencies Statutes: Potential for Confusion, 45 Bus. Law. 2253, 2270–2271 (1990). The Committee concluded that constituency statutes may be interpreted "to impose new powers and duties on directors" and "they may radically alter some of the basic premises upon which corporation law has been constructed in this country without sufficient attention having been given to all the economic, social, and legal ramifications of such a change in the law." Id. at 2253. Although the Committee believed that the statutes could create opportunities for misunderstanding and potential mischief, the debate continues; however, no serious effort has been mounted to repeal any constituency statute.

In contrast to the approach of the Committee on Corporate Laws, David Millon, Redefining Corporate Law, 24 Ind. L. Rev. 223,277 (1991) concludes:

> It is conceivable that the directors' duty [i.e., constituency] statutes herald the beginnings of a radically different understanding of corporate law and corporate purpose. If they are manifestations of a deeper design to enhance the status of nonshareholders within the corporate enterprise, several lines of development are possible. One could imagine greater nonshareholder involvement in the decision-making process, through voting rights, for example. More radically, we might revise our notion of corporate governance so as to replace the present hierarchical structure with one in which significant decision-making authority spreads downwards, from management into the hands of those most directly affected. And if nonshareholders are to have powers of control, perhaps new ownership structures should be considered as well.

––––––

For more detailed background on constituency statutes and the arguments in favor of and against them, see Symposium: Corporate Malaise—Stakeholder Statutes: Cause or Cure?, 21 Stetson L. Rev. 1 (1991); Lawrence E. Mitchell, A Theoretical and Practical Framework for Enforcing Corporate Constituency Statutes, 70 Texas L. Rev. 579

(1992); Steven M. H. Wallman, Corporate Constituency Statutes: Placing the Corporation's Interests First, 11 Bus. L. Update 1 (Nov./Dec. 1990); A.A. Sommer Jr., Whom Should the Corporation Serve? The Berle–Dodd Debate Revisited Sixty Years Later, 16 Del. J. of Corp. L. 33 (1991); Charles Hansen, Other Constituency Statutes: A Search for Perspective, 46 Bus. Law. 1355 (1991); James J. Hanks, Non–Stockholder Constituency Statutes: An Idea Whose Time Should Never Come, 3 Insights 20 (Dec. 1989); David Million, Redefining Corporate Law, 24 Ind. L. Rev. 223 (1991).

4. THE ROLE OF COUNSEL

Counseling a client who wants to take some potentially controversial action also can raise difficult issues for an attorney. Consider, by way of example, a client who wants to relocate a factory whose employees are on strike. Abrams v. Allen, 297 N.Y. 52, 74 N.E.2d 305 (1947), makes clear that a decision to relocate so as to consolidate manufacturing operations represents a presumptively valid business judgment, while a decision to relocate based solely on a desire to punish striking employees may subject directors to liability. A lawyer clearly should not advise a client to misrepresent her reasons for deciding to relocate so as to bring her decision within the protection of the business judgment rule. On the other hand, is it troublesome if the lawyer, before the client announces her decision, explains the holding of *Abrams* as to the reasons for relocating a factory that a court is and is not likely to treat as valid.

NORMAN REDLICH, LAWYERS, THE TEMPLE, AND THE MARKET PLACE
30 Bus.Lawyer 65, 65–67 (March 1975).

* * * We may sometimes resent the fact that the public is pointing to the lawyers and holding us responsible for many of the moral shortcomings of the country, but there is no way that the legal profession can avoid bearing this burden. We play too crucial a role in government and corporate life to avoid this responsibility. * * *

* * *

Let me state the problem. Lawyers, including house counsel, are both a part of, and also professionally removed from, corporate and governmental entities which have engaged, and will continue to engage, in actions which may be illegal and immoral. These entities require our advice and are entitled to our services. Moreover, society has a profound interest in having a corps of professionals giving competent legal advice to these corporate and governmental entities.

The question we face is this. How does that corps of professionals— we lawyers—so carry out our mission that we can hold our heads high and say to the public, "We have done all that we can to prevent the wrongdoings of our clients consistent with our responsibility to advise them as to the law"?   * * *

First, let us talk about our clear professional responsibility to say, "No." We all operate under a canon which commands us to "* * * exercise independent professional judgment on behalf of a client." I know how difficult it sometimes is, when an important and powerful client is embarking on some course of action which everyone is convinced is in the best interests of the company only to have the lawyer insist on some step-such as disclosure—which he feels is legally required.   * * *

A lawyer can be under enormous pressure to "go along" with a transaction when he knows that the facts are simply not as they are portrayed to a government agency or to another private party. We have all heard the seductive serpent-like song. It has many refrains: "Who will ever know?" "You're not the judge, you're only the lawyer." "I didn't hire you to tell me what I can't do." "Whose lawyer are you, anyway?" You've heard these and many more. Often nothing at all needs to be said. Everyone is going along on the basis of certain assumptions, and it is so difficult to speak up and announce, as in the famous fable, "Look, the Emperor has no clothes."

But if there is anything which is clear, it is our professional duty to refuse to approve of, or participate in, transactions which we believe to be unlawful, even if it means that we have to delay or thwart a major program of a client, or cause a considerable loss of money, or embarrass management—or even cause us to lose a major client.   * * *

Moreover, lawyers in this situation are constantly underestimating their own power. They speak not from weakness but from strength. Very often the client wants the lawyer's stamp of approval and will not proceed without it. Despite all of the pressuring, and occasional bullying, the lawyer does hold the passkey and only he can turn it. In the final analysis, we cannot expect the public to respect lawyers as independent professionals if they run for cover when a powerful client wants them to go along with a shady transaction on grounds that "everyone is doing it" or that "no one will find out."

AMERICAN BAR ASSOCIATION, MODEL RULES OF PROFESSIONAL CONDUCT (1983)

RULE 2.1   Advisor

In representing a client, a lawyer shall exercise independent professional judgment and render candid advice. In rendering advice, a lawyer may refer not only to law but to other considerations such as moral, economic, social and political factors, that may be relevant to the client's situation.

COMMENT:

Scope of Advice

A client is entitled to straightforward advice expressing the lawyer's honest assessment. Legal advice often involves unpleasant facts and alternatives that a client may be disinclined to confront. In presenting advice, a lawyer endeavors to sustain the client's morale and may put advice in as acceptable a form as honesty permits. However, a lawyer should not be deterred from giving candid advice by the prospect that the advice will be unpalatable to the client.

Advice couched in narrowly legal terms may be of little value to a client, especially where practical considerations, such as cost or effects on other people, are predominant. Purely technical legal advice, therefore, can sometimes be inadequate. It is proper for a lawyer to refer to relevant moral and ethical considerations in giving advice. Although a lawyer is not a moral advisor as such, moral and ethical considerations impinge upon most legal questions and may decisively influence how the law will be applied.

A client may expressly or impliedly ask the lawyer for purely technical advice. When such a request is made by a client experienced in legal matters, the lawyer may accept it at face value. When such a request is made by a client inexperienced in legal matters, however, the lawyer's responsibility as advisor may include indicating that more may be involved than strictly legal considerations.

* * *

Offering Advice

In general, a lawyer is not expected to give advice until asked by the client. However, when a lawyer knows that a client proposes a course of action that is likely to result in substantial adverse legal consequences to the client, duty to the client * * * may require that the lawyer act if the client's course of action is related to the representation. A lawyer ordinarily has no duty to initiate investigation of a client's affairs or to give advice that the client has indicated is unwanted, but a lawyer may initiate advice to a client when doing so appears to be in the client's interest.

Chapter 6

AN INTRODUCTION TO FINANCIAL ACCOUNTING AND VALUATION

PROBLEM
PRECISION TOOLS—PART I

Many large manufacturing companies contract with smaller firms, staffed by highly skilled machinists, to supply components that must meet demanding specifications. The large companies find contracting more efficient than setting up special, in-house departments to produce these components.

Precision Tools, Inc. ("PT") has been producing precision components for manufacturers of different kinds of communication equipment for many years. Its largest customer, from whom it derives over a third of its business, is Majestic Radio Corp., a major producer of two-way radio equipment. PT was founded by Harry Stern and John Starr, who continue to be the owners and managers. Stern and Starr are now contemplating retirement, and no member of either of their families is interested in taking over the business.

Jessica Bacon, 30, is a writer and researcher for business publications. While working on a story about the small companies that contributed to the success of IBM-compatible personal computers, she became interested in learning more about other small businesses in the country, their importance to the economy, their profitability and the kind of people who owned and operated them. Precision Tools was one of the companies she studied.

Jessica has discussed PT with Michael Lane, 32, an engineer employed by a large computer company. Michael believes rapid growth is likely in the telecommunications business, and that large companies increasingly will come to rely on dependable producers of small precision components. Michael thinks PT is well positioned to capitalize on this trend; its employees are highly skilled in fabricating a wide variety of precision components and its production machinery is state of the art.

With new and aggressive management, Michael and Jessica conclude, PT could grow rapidly.

Michael and Jessica have developed a plan to acquire PT. Michael wants to design an expanded product line that will enable PT to compete for new telecommunications business. He and Jessica also believe that he has the experience and skills to manage the operational side of the business and that Jessica, who obtained an M.B.A. before becoming a reporter, is capable of functioning as the chief financial officer.

Michael and Jessica have obtained PT's most recent financial statement, which reads as follows:

PRECISION TOOLS, INC.
BALANCE SHEET
(As of December 31)

Assets	1993	1992
Current Assets		
Cash	150,000	275,000
Accounts receivable (less allowance for doubtful accounts)	1,380,000	1,145,000
Inventories	1,310,000	1,105,000
Prepaid expenses	40,000	35,000
Total Current Assets	2,880,000	2,560,000
Fixed Assets		
Land [1]	775,000	775,000
Buildings	2,000,000	2,000,000
Machinery	1,000,000	935,000
Office equipment	225,000	205,000
Total property, plant and equipment	4,000,000	3,915,000
Less accumulated depreciation	1,620,000	1,370,000
Net Fixed Assets [2]	2,380,000	2,545,000
Total Assets	5,260,000	5,105,000
Liabilities and Equity		
Current Liabilities		
Accounts payable	900,000	825,000
Notes payable	600,000	570,000
Accrued expenses payable	250,000	235,000
Total Current Liabilities	1,750,000	1,630,000
Long Term Liabilities		
Notes payable, 12.5%, due 12/15/03	2,000,000	2,000,000
Notes payable, 11%, due 7/1/93	—	355,000
Total Liabilities	3,750,000	3,985,000
Stockholders' Equity		
Common stock (1,000 shares authorized and outstanding)		
Paid-in capital	200,000	200,000
Retained earnings	1,310,000	920,000
Total Equity	1,510,000	1,120,000
Total Liabilities and Equity	5,260,000	5,105,000

1. The land is in a modern industrial park, and was purchased for the price shown on the balance sheet fifteen years ago. Comparable nearby property recently sold for $975,000.

2. The machinery and equipment is in good repair. Depreciation is on a level (straight line) basis over the estimated life of the equipment. The building and equipment have a fair market value of approximately $200,000 in excess of the amounts shown on the balance sheet.

STATEMENT OF INCOME
(Year Ended December 31)

	1993	1992	1991
Net sales	7,500,000	7,000,000	6,800,000
Operating Expenses			
Cost of goods sold	4,980,000	4,650,000	4,607,000
Depreciation	250,000	240,000	200,000
Selling and administrative expense [1]	1,300,000	1,220,000	1,150,000
Research and development	50,000	125,000	120,000
Operating income	920,000	765,000	723,000
Interest expense	320,000	375,000	375,000
Income before taxes	600,000	390,000	348,000
Income taxes	210,000	136,000	122,000
Net Income	390,000	254,000	226,000

1. Includes salaries paid to Stern and Starr totalling $130,000 in 1993, $120,000 in 1992, and $100,000 in 1991, and bonuses totalling $120,000 in 1993, $100,000 in 1992, and $80,000 in 1991.

STATEMENT OF CASH FLOWS
(Year Ended December 31)

	1993	1992
From Operating Activities		
Net Income	390,000	254,000
Decrease (Increase) in accounts receivable	(235,000)	(34,000)
Decrease (Increase) in inventories	(205,000)	(28,000)
Decrease (Increase) in prepaid expenses	(5,000)	(3,000)
Increase (Decrease) in accounts payable	75,000	25,000
Increase (Decrease) in accrued expenses payable	15,000	7,000
Depreciation	250,000	240,000
Total from Operating Activities	285,000	461,000
From Investing Activities		
Sales (Purchases) of machinery	(65,000)	(378,000)
Sales (Purchases) of office equipment	(20,000)	(27,000)
Total from Investing Activities	(85,000)	(405,000)
From Financing Activities		
Increase (Decrease) in short-term borrowings	30,000	(40,000)
Increase (Decrease) in long-term borrowings	(355,000)	—
Total from Financing Activities	(325,000)	(40,000)
Increase (Decrease) in Cash Position	(125,000)	16,000

Jessica and Michael have asked you to review PT's financial statements. At this time, you are the only professional person advising them. Consider the following:

1.   What information do PT's financial statements provide that Jessica and Michael should consider important in deciding whether to purchase PT or how much to pay?   In particular, what do those statements tell us about the profitability of PT's operations, the value of PT's assets, and whether PT should be able to meet its financial obligations as they fall due?

2.   Based on an analysis of PT's financial statements, what further questions should Jessica and Michael ask before deciding whether to purchase PT or how much to pay for it?

A.   FINANCIAL ACCOUNTING DEMYSTIFIED

"Omigosh, accounting!   Isn't this what I went to law school to avoid?   If I wanted to learn accounting, I would have gone to B-school. Why do I have to understand this stuff?"

Don't panic!   The authors appreciate that this statement may reflect the feelings of many law students—especially those with no background in accounting or finance—when they reach this Chapter. Nonetheless, this book includes materials designed to introduce basic accounting concepts.   We believe most students will find that obtaining some grasp of basic accounting concepts will help them better understand what gives a business value.   Clients value lawyers who can read and analyze financial statements.   It is difficult for a lawyer to competently negotiate or draft documents for a transaction unless she understands both the transaction and her client's goals.   Even more valuable is the lawyer who can help her client better understand the transaction. Moreover, appreciating where value lies in any given business setting, in turn, will help students better understand what is at stake in many of the cases and problems included in this book.   In short, "[a] business client's favorite lawyer is the one about whom the client would say: 'This lawyer thinks like me!' " Robert C. Boehm, Dealing from strength: 15 winning tips for business lawyers, 2 Bus. Lawyer Today 58 (Nov./Dec. 1992).

Contrary to common belief, understanding basic accounting concepts does not require expertise in mathematics or a degree in finance.   True, as PT's financial statements evidence, accounting information is presented largely in numerical form.   But the materials that follow emphasize that, while the numbers in financial statements always appear precise, in fact (i) they are the product of a highly conceptual process that involves many subjective judgments;   (ii) they reflect that process and those judgments, not some sort of scientific truth; and (iii) they tell only part of what is important about a firm's business and finances.

This last point is significant.   The goal of financial statements is to convey information to the user, whether she be an investor, a lender, or a corporate manager.   But the information that these statements give is not the entire story of the business.   As you read the following materials, ask yourself what additional information you would want in order to understand the stories that lie behind the numbers. In so doing, you will begin to perform one of a lawyer's most important functions in a business transaction: helping the client ask the right questions.

1. INTRODUCTION TO ACCOUNTING PRINCIPLES

The two basic financial statements are the balance sheet and the income statement. The relationship of these two statements often is described using the analogy of a snapshot and a motion picture. A balance sheet—the "snapshot"—presents a picture of the firm at some given moment, listing all property it owns (its *"assets "*), all amounts it owes (its *"liabilities "*), and the value, at least conceptually, of the owners' interest in the firm (its *"equity."*). An income statement—the "motion picture"—presents a picture of the results of the firm's operations during the period between the dates of successive balance sheets.

Financial statements are produced through a three-stage process. First, a company enters on its books information concerning every transaction in which it is involved—the recording and controls stage. Next comes the audit stage; the company, sometimes with the assistance of independent public accountants, verifies the information recorded on its books. Finally, in the accounting stage, the company classifies and analyzes the audited information and presents it in a set of financial statements.

RMBCA § 16.20 requires corporations to furnish their shareholders with annual balance sheets and income statements, but allows corporations to decide what principles to use when preparing those statements. Most firms, and all public corporations, use Generally Accepted Accounting Principles, or *GAAP*, when they prepare financial statements. GAAP are promulgated—or, more accurately, legislated—by a quasi-public body, the Financial Accounting Standard Board (FASB). The rules adopted by the FASB embody not immutable scientific or mathematical truths, but the (often controversial) judgments and policy preferences of a group of highly-qualified accounting professionals. Moreover, as the perceptions, judgments and preferences of the members of the FASB change over time, so do GAAP concerning how information about various kinds of transactions should be presented. This provides our first important insight about accounting: the need to keep in mind the difference between actual events and how information about those events is presented in financial statements. Events themselves are real. How to describe them often is problematic. But if information about an event is to be included in a financial statement, GAAP control how it is presented.

A simple hypothetical illustrates this point. Assume Exco purchased land and a building for $100,000 on January 1, immediately rented the property to a tenant, who paid rent during the year in an amount exactly equal to Exco's out-of-pocket costs, and that these were the only transactions in which Exco engaged during the year. On December 31 of that year, Smith offered to purchase the land and building for $105,000, but Exco decided not to sell. Did Exco earn a profit for the year?

The answer to this question depends on what is meant by "profit." If profit means being better off at the end of the year than at the beginning, a person might argue that Exco earned a profit. It started the year with $100,000 and ended the year owning property which, assuming Smith's offer was genuine, had a fair market value of at least $105,000. In essence, Exco was at least $5,000 better off on December 31 than it had been on January 1. The $5,000 could be viewed as Exco's profit, because Exco could have realized that profit had it chosen to sell.

An economist might well respond that to determine whether Exco earned a profit depends on the rate of inflation. If inflation was less than 5 percent, Exco made a profit because on December 31 it could have exchanged the property for $105,000, which could have been used to purchase more in the way of goods and services than Exco could have purchased with $100,000 on January 1. But if inflation exceeded 5 percent, Exco should be deemed to have incurred a loss, because the $105,000 it could have received would not allow it to purchase as much in the way of goods and services as it could have purchased with $100,000 on January 1.

An accountant preparing an income statement in accordance with GAAP would report that Exco incurred a loss. GAAP require Exco to treat as an "expense" both its out-of-pocket expenditures and some portion of the cost of the building it used to generate rental income during the year. (The accountant would call this a *depreciation expense*—a charge against income not tied to any outlay of cash.) In addition, GAAP would prohibit the accountant from recording the apparent gain in the value of the property because the property had not been sold; that Smith had made a *bona fide* offer to buy the property would be deemed irrelevant.

In short, there are different meanings to "profit," of which GAAP provides but one. But it is the one that is used in preparing financial statements. Thus, unless one understands the more important assumptions and fundamental principles underlying GAAP, it is difficult to appreciate the information in those statements. The most important assumptions and principles include the following:

Separate Entity Assumption: A business enterprise is viewed as an accounting unit separate and distinct from its owners, whether or not it has a separate legal existence.

Continuity Assumption: A business enterprise is viewed as a going concern that is expected to continue in operation for the foreseeable future.

Unit of Measure Assumption: Financial statements report the results of business activity in terms of money and assume that the value of the relevant unit of money—the dollar—remains constant.

Time Period Assumption: To produce useful financial information, the results of economic activities must be allocated to discrete time periods, generally not longer than one year in duration, even though such activities often extend over or affect several time periods.

Cost Principle: Historic cost provides the best basis for recording a transaction, because it can be determined objectively and is verifiable.

Consistency Principle: A firm should consistently apply the same accounting concepts, standards and procedures from one period to the next.

Full Disclosure Principle: Financial statements should include sufficient information, in the statements or in explanatory notes, to ensure full understanding of all significant economic information about a firm.

Modifying Principles: (a) *Materiality*—Accounting only needs to be concerned with the accuracy of information that a reasonable decision-maker would consider to be important; where information is immaterial, strict adherence to GAAP is not required. (b) *Conservatism*—Accounting counteracts managers' assumed tendency to present financial information about a firm in the most favorable light possible by mandating, in general, that profits not be anticipated and that probable losses be recognized as soon as possible.

The goals of the accounting process (and of GAAP) include presenting information about a firm's financial position and the results of its operations that (i) is as accurate as possible, (ii) is as reliable as possible, and (iii) can be prepared at reasonable cost. As the Exco hypothetical makes clear, trade-offs between these goals often are required. For example, one might argue that Exco's balance sheet should report the value of its property as $105,000, because Smith offered to pay that much. But before accepting this argument, one would need to consider a host of additional questions. How can a firm determine whether an offer is *bona fide*? Assuming it is *bona fide*, should the firm be required to determine whether the property is worth more than the offer? Should a determination of current market value be required whether or not an offer to purchase has been received? How should the market value of property with unique characteristics be determined? Is market value information sufficiently important and sufficiently reliable to justify the cost of obtaining such information? Does that depend on whether the firm intends to hold the property or sell it? Should value be reported in terms of constant dollars or constant units of purchasing power? If the property is revalued, should the same thing be done for Exco's other assets and liabilities? Etc., etc., etc.

Three points emerge. First, GAAP consists of a series of conventions, none of which is immediately intuitive. These conventions are designed to resolve potential differences as to the appropriate method of presenting financial information. Second, whatever the shortcomings of

GAAP, developing better accounting rules involves complex problems to which there are no easy answers. Finally, a person who understands GAAP can better appreciate the limitations of the information presented in a firm's financial statements and the additional information that one may need to make decisions relating to that firm.

2. THE FUNDAMENTAL EQUATION

In a conceptual sense, the accounting process involves no more than elaboration of what is known as *the fundamental equation* :

$$ASSETS = LIABILITIES + EQUITY$$

Consider, first, the terms used in the fundamental equation. "Assets" refers to all property, both tangible and intangible, owned by the reporting firm. "Liabilities" refers to all amounts that firm owes to others, whether pursuant to written evidence of indebtedness or otherwise. "Equity" represents, at least in concept, the interest of the firm's owners. Equity initially includes the value of the property (including money) the owners contribute when they organize the firm. Since the owners bear the risk of the firm's operations, equity increases thereafter whenever the firm earns a profit and decreases when it incurs a loss. Equity also increases whenever the owners contribute additional property to the firm and decreases whenever they withdraw property from it. In sum, equity is the owner's residual interest, assuming (which is never the case) that all the assets and liabilities on the balance sheet could be liquidated for the amounts shown there.

The fundamental equation often is presented as a sort of magic incantation, but it is easier to understand why assets always equal liabilities plus equity (especially if one is unfamiliar with accounting) by envisioning the firm in more concrete terms. Only one abstraction is necessary: the assumption that the firm is an entity separate from its owners. Visualize the firm as an empty jar, beginning its life with no assets, no liabilities and no equity.* The firm's balance sheet, at the moment of formation, will be as follows:

$$\begin{array}{ccccc} ASSETS & = & LIABILITIES & + & EQUITY \\ \$0 & = & \$0 & + & \$0 \end{array}$$

1. Now assume that the owner of the firm invests $12 (i.e., puts $12 in the jar). The firm's balance sheet will be:

$$\begin{array}{ccccc} ASSETS & = & LIABILITIES & + & EQUITY \\ \$12 & = & \$0 & + & \$12 \end{array}$$

2. Next assume the firm borrows an additional $10 (i.e., puts $10 in the jar and records an IOU for $10). Its balance sheet will be:

---

* Students for whom the following discussion proves difficult to follow may find it helpful to begin with an empty jar or other container and physically act out each of the transactions described. When doing so, keep in mind that "equity" will be equal to the *net* value of the contents of the jar—the value, computed in accordance with GAAP, of all assets less all liabilities.

$$\text{ASSETS} = \text{LIABILITIES} + \text{EQUITY}$$
$$\$22 = \$10 + \$12$$

Note that each of these transaction had two effects on the balance sheet. The first increased assets and also increased equity; the second increased assets ($10 went into the jar) and also increased liabilities (the jar—i.e., the firm—incurred a debt in that amount). The same will be true of every transaction in which the firm is involved—it will always affect two balance sheet accounts. Moreover, because any profit or loss will always be reflected in the equity account, *the balance sheet will always remain in balance*.

3. Assume the firm buys two felt-tip pens for $2 each (i.e., the firm takes $4 in cash, an asset, out of the jar and puts $4 worth of pens—remember the cost principle—into the jar). Because one asset is exchanged for another, the balance sheet remains unchanged.

$$\text{ASSETS} = \text{LIABILITIES} + \text{EQUITY}$$
$$\$22 = \$10 + \$12$$

4. Next the firm buys a scissors on credit for $5 (i.e., it puts scissors worth $5 in the jar and incurs a liability of $5, which can be envisioned as a bill for $5 placed in the jar).

$$\text{ASSETS} = \text{LIABILITIES} + \text{EQUITY}$$
$$\$27 = \$15 + \$12$$

5. Then the firm sells one of the felt-tip pens for $3 (i.e., it exchanges a pen that cost $2 for $3 in cash. The $1 profit results in a $1 increase in equity.)

$$\text{ASSETS} = \text{LIABILITIES} + \text{EQUITY}$$
$$\$28 = \$15 + \$13$$

See if you can figure out the accounting for the following three transactions without further explanation.

6. The firm then pays the bill for the scissors.

$$\text{ASSETS} = \text{LIABILITIES} + \text{EQUITY}$$
$$\$23 = \$10 + \$13$$

7. Next the firm pays $2.00 in rent for the use of the jar.

$$\text{ASSETS} = \text{LIABILITIES} + \text{EQUITY}$$
$$\$21 = \$10 + \$11$$

8. Finally, the owner takes $5.00 out of the jar so she can go to the movies.

$$\text{ASSETS} = \text{LIABILITIES} + \text{EQUITY}$$
$$\$16 = \$10 + \$6$$

Although many business transactions are much more complex, and accounting for them is considerably more complicated, the entries made above reflect the essence of all financial accounting. Viewed conceptually, the accounting process involves no more than adjusting entries in a firm's asset, liability and equity accounts. A firm could keep an accurate set of books simply by updating, after every transaction, a balance sheet that contained only an asset, a liability and an equity account.

So proceeding, however, would not produce much *useful* financial information. Managers, investors and creditors are interested in two basic categories of financial information: (a) data about a firm's financial status at a given time, including data about the nature of its assets and liabilities; and (b) information about the results of the firm's operations (i.e., whether it has been profitable). Clearly, balance sheet # 8 does not provide this kind of information, even if we compare it with balance sheet # 1. One can tell that the firm's assets increased from $12 to $16, its liabilities increased from $0 to $10, and its equity declined from $12 to $6. But one cannot determine anything about the nature of the firm's assets (how much cash does it have? how much merchandise?), the due dates of the liabilities (must they be repaid tomorrow or in five years?), or whether the firm's operations were profitable.

GAAP address these problems by requiring that a firm's assets, liabilities and equity be assigned to a number of different sub-accounts and that an income statement be prepared reporting the results of the firm's operations. Most financial accounting problems relate to one of these processes—deciding what asset, liability and equity accounts any given transaction affects, and determining whether a transaction involves current operations, and thus should have an impact on the income statement, or whether it only affects balance sheet accounts.

3. FINANCIAL STATEMENT TERMS AND CONCEPTS

a. How Different Financial Statements Relate

As noted above, the balance sheet often is described as a "snapshot" and the income statement as a "motion picture." One also can view the income statement as a "bridge" between successive balance sheets, because it both reports on operations and records whether they resulted in a profit or a loss. The bottom line figure on the income statement— the profit or loss—then is "transferred" to the balance sheet as an increase or decrease in equity from the previous year, assuming that the time periods in both statements are the same.

The fundamental equation, and thus the balance sheet, represents the conceptual core of a firm's financial statements. Investors and creditors, however, often are more interested in a firm's income statement. They view information about the results of past operations as the best available indicator of a firm's ability to generate profits in the future.

Managers, not surprisingly, are sensitive to the importance that investors and creditors place on income statements. They not infrequently strive, where GAAP make it possible for them to do so, to "manage" their firms' income statements so as to report steady profits or, better yet, steadily rising profits. Such "management" is possible because GAAP sometimes permits the choice of accounting conventions.* An example is the valuation of inventory, discussed in the next section. The discussion of financial statement terms and concepts in the section that follows notes some aspects of GAAP that facilitate such "management" of income statement numbers.

The GAAP requirement that most firms use *accrual accounting* to prepare their financial statements is central here. In addition, the *Realization Principle* requires a firm to recognize revenue in the period that services are rendered or goods are sold, even if payment is not received in that period. Consider how these requirements would affect a lawyer who provided $1,000 in services in Year 1 and was not paid until Year 2. In which year did she "earn" the $1,000? Most individuals compute their income, at least when preparing their income tax returns, using *cash accounting*; they would report the $1,000 as earned in Year 2, when payment was received. Accrual accounting, in contrast, focuses not on the movement of cash, but on the lawyer's performance of the services. Thus, a lawyer using accrual accounting would treat the $1,000 as earned in Year 1.

The other side of the accrual accounting coin, so to speak, is the *Matching Principle*. It requires a firm to allocate to the period in which revenues are earned the expenses it incurs to generate those revenues. Thus, if the lawyer transmitted materials to her client in Year 1 via Federal Express, but did not pay the Federal Express bill until Year 2, she still would account for the Federal Express charges as an expense incurred in Year 1.

Taken together, the Realization and Matching Principles go a long way toward ensuring that an income statement prepared using accrual accounting presents a conceptually sound computation of the economic results of a firm's operations for the period it covers. Those principles also limit substantially a firm's ability to manipulate its payment and receipt of cash so as to "manage" the income it reports. But because recognition of revenues and recording of expenses are tied to events more difficult to measure than the movement of cash, the Realization and Matching Principles also increase substantially the subjectivity of information reported in income statements.

---

* Recall, from Chapter 2, that most people are risk averse. The more volatile a firm's income, the greater the risk premium investors are likely to demand before investing in that firm. This gives managers an economic incentive to "manage" the income their firm reports.

GAAP deal with this problem of subjectivity, at least in part, by requiring firms to prepare a third financial statement—a *statement of cash flows*—in addition to a balance sheet and an income statement. A firm must use cash, not "income," to pay its bills, repay its debts, and make distributions to its owners. Cash, not "income," must be on hand when the firm needs it. Over a period of many years, say 10 or 15, a firm's total income and cash flow usually will be very similar. But over shorter periods, income and cash flow often will differ substantially.

The statement of cash flows, as its name suggests, reports on the movement of cash into and out of a firm. The statement reflects all transactions that involve the receipt or disbursement of cash, whether they relate to operations or involve only balance sheet transactions such as investments in plant and equipment, new borrowings, repayment of loans, equity investments, or distributions to equity holders. It does not reflect non-cash charges such as depreciation, discussed in the next section.

b. Balance Sheet Terms and Concepts

What follows are brief descriptions of the most important balance sheet accounts. The descriptions also point out instances where the accounting treatment of certain balance sheet accounts has an impact on a firm's income statement. As you read these descriptions, consider PT's balance sheet and, where relevant, PT's income statement, both of which are set forth in the Problem at the start of this Chapter.

1. *Assets* are listed in the balance sheet in order of decreasing liquidity, i.e., their ability to be converted to cash.

(A) *Current assets* include cash and other assets which in the normal course of business will be converted into cash in the reasonably near future, generally within a year of the date of the balance sheet. More specifically:

(1) *Cash* is money in the till and money in demand deposits in the bank.

(2) *Marketable securities* are investments of cash not needed for current operations. Most firms invest surplus cash in very liquid securities, such as commercial paper and treasury bills, with a view to generating interest income.

(3) *Accounts receivable* are amounts not yet collected from customers to whom goods have been shipped or services delivered. Recognizing that some customers will not to pay their bills, GAAP require that accounts receivable be adjusted by deducting an allowance (or "reserve") for bad debts. Firms often compute this allowance on the basis of past experience. But when dramatic changes occur in the nature of a firm's customers, the nature of its business, or relevant economic conditions, past experience may not prove to be an accurate predictor of future trends.

Losses from extending credit to customers also represent a cost of doing business. Consequently, GAAP also require a firm to treat any increase in its allowance for bad debts as a charge against income, in the form of a "bad debt expense."

Most of the assets of a firm engaged in a financing business are represented by *notes or loans receivable*, which constitute a kind of account receivable. Consequently, relatively small increases or decreases in the percentage of debts the firm estimates will not be repaid are likely to have a major impact on the firm's reported earnings. Many of the banks that failed in recent years reported robust annual earnings almost up to the time they failed. Relying on past experience, they grossly underestimated the portion of outstanding loans that borrowers would not repay. Only when large numbers of borrowers began to default did it become obvious that the banks were (and for some time had been) insolvent.

(4) *Inventory* represents goods held for use in production or for sale to customers. GAAP require inventory to be valued at the lower of cost or market. Firms that hold a relatively small number of identifiable items in inventory often use the *specific identification method*. They value each inventory item at cost, unless its market value is lower than cost.

Most firms, though, find it impractical to keep track of the cost of each item in their inventory. Those firms use different methods to account for inventory. Every firm will know how much it paid for all items added to inventory during any given period, even though it often will have purchased those items at different times for different prices. By conducting a physical count at the end of the accounting period, the firm can determine the number of items remaining in inventory—known as the *closing inventory*. The accounting problem then reduces to how to value the closing inventory. This value will affect both the firm's balance sheet and its income statement. Items sold from inventory, called *cost of goods sold* ("COGS"), often represents a firm's largest single expense. To compute COGS, a firm adds its purchases to its opening inventory and then subtracts the value of its closing inventory.

Most firms use one of three accounting methods to compute the value of closing inventory (and, indirectly, COGS). GAAP allows all three. Brief descriptions of the three methods illustrate how GAAP deals with this difficult and important conceptual problem.

The *average cost method* visualizes inventory as being sold at random from a bin: a firm computes the average cost of all items purchased as inventory and values the closing inventory (i.e., the items "remaining in the bin") at that average cost.

The *first in, first out (FIFO) method* visualizes inventory as flowing through a pipeline: the items purchased first are assumed to be the first sold; the items purchased most recently are assumed to comprise the closing inventory (i.e., those items "remain in the pipeline").

3. The *last in, first out (LIFO) method* visualizes inventory as sold from the top of a stack: the items purchased most recently are assumed to be the first items sold; the items purchased first are assumed to comprise the closing inventory (i.e., those items "remain at the bottom of the stack").

In periods of changing prices, the inventory method a firm uses can have a material impact on the value of the inventory account, on COGS. and hence its reported profits. With LIFO, the inventory value will be lower, profits will be lower and, significantly, taxes will be lower than if FIFO were used. Because it gives value to the oldest inventory in stock, it is more conservative than FIFO. In an inflationary economy, because inventory replacement will cost more, the profits on each item sold will be lower; hence, LIFO more accurately reflects the economic results of the corporation. By contrast, if FIFO were used, the profit would be higher but much of that profit would be attributable to the inflationary rise in the cost of the inventory. These profits, in turn, might not be replicated when all the old inventory is sold.

(5) *Prepaid expenses* are payments a firm has made in advance for services it will receive in the coming year, such as the remaining value of a one-year insurance policy that a firm purchased and paid for two months before a year ended.

Deferred charges, such as payments made to promote the introduction of a new product, represent a type of asset similar to prepaid expenses. Deferred charges sometimes are treated as current assets because the firm expects them to produce benefits in the next year; sometimes they are treated as long-term assets because the firm will not use them up in one year. Sometimes firms inflated their reported profits by treating as deferred charges payments that they should record as current expenses. The effect of such treatment is to reduce expenses on the firm's income statement, and thus to increase net income. A large deferred charge account, and especially a large and growing deferred charge account, often should provoke further inquiry.

(B) *Fixed assets*, sometimes referred to as *property, plant and equipment*, are the assets a firm uses to conduct its operations (as opposed to those it holds for sale). Under GAAP, when a firm acquires a fixed asset, it records the asset on its balance sheet at cost. However, because the firm uses the fixed asset to generate revenue, the Matching Principle requires the firm to charge a portion of the asset's cost against that revenue.* This charge, which can be computed using one of several formulas, is recorded on the firm's income statement as a *depreciation expense*. This expense, which is not actually paid in cash, is based on the assumption that an asset ultimately will wear out. The depreciation charge is designed to match against operating income the cost of the asset over its useful life. GAAP requires a firm to add up all the

---

* No depreciation expenses are charged in connection with land a firm uses to produce revenues, because land has an unlimited life and consequently is not used up in the production process.

depreciation expenses it has charged in connection with all fixed assets it continues to own and to record the total, on the asset side of its balance sheet, as a reduction in the value of those fixed assets. This account is called the *allowance for depreciation* or *accumulated depreciation*.

The balance sheet value (or *book value*) of a firm's fixed assets—cost less the allowance for depreciation—is not intended to reflect, and usually does not reflect, either the current market value of those assets or what the firm would have to pay to replace them. In times of inflation, book value often is much lower than either current or replacement value. As technology changes, or when a company is still using a fully depreciated asset, book value may exceed market value because fixed assets have become obsolete.

(C) *Intangibles assets* have no physical existence, but often have substantial value—a cable TV franchise granting a company the exclusive right to service certain areas, for example, or a patent or trade name. GAAP require firms to carry intangible assets at cost, less an allowance for *amortization* (the equivalent of depreciation, applied to intangibles). However, GAAP do not allow a firm to record as an asset the value of an intangible asset the firm has developed or promoted, rather than purchased. Consequently, the value of many extremely well-known intangible assets, such as the brand names "Coke" and "Pepsi," does not appear on the balance sheets of the firms that own them.

Similarly, when a firm incurs expenditures for research and development (R & D), it must treat those expenditures as current expenses and match them against current revenues. It cannot record them as intangible assets or deferred charges even if a firm's R & D activities produce discoveries or lead to products that will enable the firm to generate substantial revenues in future years.

Financial statements sometimes report an intangible asset called *goodwill*. An entry for goodwill reflects the fact that the reporting company purchased another firm for a price that exceeded the fair market value of the acquired firm's tangible and identifiable intangible assets. GAAP require firms to amortize goodwill over a period of not more than 40 years.

2. *Liabilities* usually are divided into current liabilities and long-term liabilities.

(A) *Current liabilities* are the debts a firm owes that must be paid within one year of the balance sheet date. Current liabilities often are evaluated in relation to current assets which, in a sense, are the source from which current liabilities must be paid.

(B) *Long-term liabilities* are debts due more than one year from the balance sheet date. Balance sheets usually list fixed liabilities, such as mortgages and bonds, by their maturities and the interest rates they bear. Some long-term liabilities must be estimated. An insurance company, for example, can only estimate the amounts it will have to pay out on the policies it has written. Those estimates usually have a material impact on both the company's balance sheet and its income statement.

In recent years, business firms have developed a variety of techniques for engaging in *off balance sheet financing*—transactions that involve long-term financial obligations, but which, because of their form, are not recorded as liabilities on the balance sheet. GAAP require firms to report certain off balance sheet financing arrangements, such as long-term operating leases, in footnotes to their financial statements. Others, however, do not have to be disclosed. Moreover, only occasionally must a firm record contingent liabilities, such as claims by regulatory agencies or plaintiffs in civil suits, on its balance sheet. Where such claims have not yet been asserted, GAAP often does not require even footnote disclosure.

3. *Equity* represents the owners' interest in a firm. The terminology used for equity accounts will vary, depending on whether the firm is a sole proprietorship, a partnership or a corporation. Whatever the form, the amount of a firm's equity (also known as its *net worth*) will equal the difference between the book values of the firm's assets and liabilities.* If a firm's liabilities exceed its assets, equity will be a negative figure.

Corporations' books divide equity among two or three accounts. Many state laws require corporations to issue stock with some *stated* or *par value*. As explained in more detail in Chapter 9, these values are established arbitrarily, but once established, have legal and accounting significance. When a corporation issues stock with a par or stated value, its balance sheet will include a *stated capital* or *legal capital* account for each class of such stock. The amounts in those accounts is calculated by multiplying the par value of that class of stock by the number of shares issued and outstanding. In a jurisdiction that does not require stock to have par or stated value, no stated capital or legal capital account is necessary.

In economic terms, a corporation's equity can be divided between two categories. One, termed *paid-in capital*, reflects all amounts received by the corporation from purchasers of its stock.** The other, called *retained earnings* or *earned surplus*, reflects the cumulative results of the corporation's operations over the period since it was formed. Each year, this account is increased by an amount equal to net income or decreased by an amount equal to net loss. In addition, any distributions the corporation makes to its shareholders, in the form of *dividends*, are subtracted from the retained earnings account.

---

* This follows from the fundamental equation. That is, if ASSETS = LIABILITIES + EQUITY, then ASSETS – LIABILITIES = EQUITY.

** A corporation with par value stock often will divide its paid-in capital between accounts titled "stated capital" and "capital surplus." Terminology varies though, and other account titles sometimes are used.

4. INTRODUCTION TO FINANCIAL ANALYSIS

Managers, investors and creditors use the information in financial statements to engage in financial analysis of the reporting company. Such analysis involves consideration of the relationship between certain data in a firm's current and prior financial statements. It also involves comparison of data derived from a given firm's financial statements with comparable data drawn from the financial statements of other firms engaged in the same or similar businesses.

a. Liquidity Analysis

One focus of analysis is liquidity: does a firm have sufficient cash, or assets it is likely to convert into cash, to meet its financial obligations as they come due? Three commonly used indicators of a firm's liquidity are its *working capital*, defined as the difference between current assets and current liabilities; its *current ratio*, computed by dividing current assets by current liabilities; and its *liquidity ratio,* computed by dividing "quick assets" by current liabilities. Quick assets are cash, marketable securities, and accounts receivable.

As a rule of thumb, analysts prefer current assets to be at least twice as large as current liabilities. But this is a generalization. A firm with a small inventory and easily collectible accounts receivable can operate safely with a lower current ratio.

A gradual increase in a firm's current ratio, based on a comparison of successive balance sheets, is a sign of financial strength. Too large a ratio, however—4:1 or 5:1—may signal that the firm is not managing current assets efficiently.

The liquidity ratio provides a more sophisticated evaluation of liquidity than the current ratio. A company with a high current ratio nonetheless may find it difficult to meet its current obligations if most of its current assets are inventory. Quick assets can be converted into cash without selling goods from inventory.

b. Debt Coverage Analysis

Creditors, in particular, are interested in a firm's ability to pay its debts on time. They frequently will compute a firm's *debt:equity ratio*, dividing a firm's long-term debt by the book value of its equity. A ratio of more than 1:1 indicates the firm is relying principally on borrowed capital. This poses some danger for debtholders, especially where the ratio is much higher than 1:1, because if the firm's business falters, it may find itself unable to generate sufficient revenues to pay the interest due on its debt. In effect, the firm's debtholders may be bearing some of the risk ordinarily borne by equity investors.

Creditors also often are interested in the *interest coverage ratio*. They compare a firm's annual earnings to the annual interest payments due on the firm's long-term debt. Most analysts consider debt a safe investment if earnings are at least three or four times interest payments.

c. *Equity Analysis*

In valuing the firm, analysts tend to focus on its equity accounts and income statement. One common, but frequently unreliable, indicator is the firm's *net book value*. Profitable companies often show a very low net book value and very substantial earnings, especially if they generate income largely by developing or exploiting intangible assets. Examples of such companies are service businesses such as advertising agencies, whose profitability depends primarily on a continuing flow of customers rather than on their tangible assets. Companies engaged in capital-intensive businesses, such as railroads, often show a high net book value for their equity but have low or irregular earnings. The assets of insurance companies and banks are largely liquid (cash, accounts receivable, and marketable securities); the net book value of such a company often is a fair indication of its true value (so long as the company has accurately estimated its reserve for liabilities or its allowance for bad debts).

In evaluating a firm's income statement, analysts frequently look for trends in revenues and earnings. Are they increasing, decreasing, or relatively stable? Do they fluctuate dramatically or change at a relatively steady pace?

Analysts also evaluate the ratio of various expense items to revenues, both over time and in relation to the ratios of other firms in the same line of business. An income statement generally reports net sales (gross sales less returns) on the top line, and then subtracts cost of goods sold, other operating expenses, interest expenses and taxes. Operating income and income before taxes often are reported as sub-totals. Look at PT's income statement again.

One can easily calculate what percentage of net sales each category of expenses represents. These calculations often produce useful insights about trends in a company's business or additional inquiries one should make. Consider, for example, the significance of an increase in *profit margin*—the difference, stated as a percentage of net sales, between net sales and operating expense. Changes in profit margin can reflect changes in efficiency, in product line or in type of customer served. Where a company's profit margin is very low compared to other firms in the same business, profits might improve if management improves. If profit margins of all firms in a given line of business are low, competition probably is intense and increasing a firm's profit margin may well prove to be difficult.

Similar inferences can be drawn from other income statement data. What, for example, would you conclude if a firm reported an increase in *fixed costs*—depreciation and other overhead, including interest expense—as a percentage of sales? What if it reported a decrease in "discretionary" expenses, such as R & D, advertising and promotion, which a firm often can reduce without causing proportionate increases in current income?

Finally, analysts usually compute *return on equity* by dividing equity as reported on a firm's balance sheet for the previous year (*not* the current year) into the net income the firm has reported for the current year. Analysts then compare the resulting percentage to the return available on alternative investments. For example, if return on a firm's equity is less than the return available on a risk-free investment such as U.S. Treasury notes (and if reported income accurately reflects the results of the firm's operations), an analyst is likely to conclude that the firm is worth considerably less than its net book value. After all, why bear the risks of purchasing equity if one can earn a larger return on a risk-free investment?

Similarly, if a firm's return on equity greatly exceeds the returns available from risk-free investments, an analyst might conclude (subject to the *caveat* noted above and the risks associated with the firm's business) that the firm is worth considerably more than its net book value. In essence, the analyst would imply that a significant portion of the firm's earning power is attributable to the value of intangible assets that, due to GAAP, is not reflected on the firm's balance sheet.

d. Cash Flow Analysis

As should be clear by now, "income" is a concept, and computation of a firm's income generally depends on numerous subjective judgments and is heavily influenced by the assumptions underlying GAAP. Cash, on the other hand, is tangible; one can touch, smell and even taste it. Moreover, a company needs cash to pay its bills, repay its debts, and make distributions to its owners.

The sources and uses of a given firm's cash can include its operations, its purchases and sales of fixed assets, and its financing activities. The statement of cash flows reports how much cash a firm has generated and how much it has used in connection with each of these three activities. PT's statement of cash flows shows how that firm has generated and used cash during the prior two years.

Firms frequently report significantly different amounts of income and cash flow for any given year. The disparity most often is attributable, at least in part, to GAAP requirements relating to accounting for fixed assets. Recall the Exco hypothetical. GAAP require Exco to account for its purchase of the property as an exchange of one asset, $100,000 in cash, for another asset, property worth $100,000. That transaction would have no direct impact on Exco's income statement. But GAAP also would require Exco to report a depreciation expense, say $5,000 a year, in each year it used the property to generate rental income. That "expense," however, does not reflect any current disbursement of cash.

In the year Exco purchased the property, it would report cash flow much lower than its income (or, more accurately, negative cash flow much larger than the loss it would report).* In each subsequent year,

* Assuming all other expenses were paid and all rental income was received during   Year 1, Exco would report a loss of $5,000 and negative cash flow of $100,000.

Exco would report cash flow in excess of its income, because reported income would be reduced by a depreciation expense that would not involve any contemporaneous disbursement of cash. More specifically, Exco's statement of cash flows would report the amount of each year's depreciation expense as an addition to cash flow from operations. (Note the similar entry on PT's statement of cash flows.)

Changes in the amounts of cash a firm used to provide financing to customers (increases or decreases in accounts receivable), to carry inventory, and to prepay expenses, also will affect cash flow from operations, as will increases or decreases in current liabilities. The statement of cash flows also reflects investing activities: how much the firm paid for fixed assets and received from the sale of such assets. Finally, the statement reports financing activities: increases and decreases in short- and long-term borrowing, sales and repurchases of equity interests, and distributions to equity holders.

Comparison of a firm's income and cash flow statements often will provide insights into the direction of its business or suggest further inquiries that one might make. Consider the implications when cash flow from operations lags income, for example. Is the shortfall due to rapid growth in the firm's business? If so, is substantial additional financing necessary to sustain that growth? Do increases in inventory and accounts receivable reflect long-term growth in the firm's business, or a short-term effort to pump up reported earnings? If accounts receivable and inventory decreased, does that suggest the firm is managing its current assets more efficiently or that its business is declining? By asking these and similar questions, one can obtain a better understanding of a firm's business than would be the case if one analyzed that firm's income statement alone.

B. VALUING THE ENTERPRISE

PROBLEM
PRECISION TOOLS—PART II

Michael and Jessica have sought your assistance in negotiating the purchase of Precision Tools. To assist them effectively, you should consider:

(1) What techniques are the purchasers and sellers likely to use in valuing PT? What values might they place on the business?

(2) Is there a price (or range of prices) that both sides are likely to find acceptable?

1. THE OLD MAN AND THE TREE: A PARABLE OF VALUATION

Once there was a wise old man who owned an apple tree. The tree was a fine tree, and with little care it produced a crop of apples each year which he sold for $100. The man was getting old, wanted to retire to a different climate and he decided to sell the tree. He enjoyed teaching a good lesson, and he placed an advertisement in the Business Opportunities section of the Wall Street Journal in which he said he wanted to sell the tree for "the best offer."

The first person to respond to the ad offered to pay the $50 which, the offeror said, was what he would be able to get for selling the apple tree for firewood after he had cut it down. "You are a very foolish person," said the old man. "You are offering to pay only the salvage value of this tree. That might be a good price for a pine tree or perhaps even this tree if it had stopped bearing fruit or if the price of apple wood had gotten so high that the tree was more valuable as a source of wood than as a source of fruit. But my tree is worth much more than $50."

The next person to come to see the old man offered to pay $100 for the tree. "For that," said she, "is what I would be able to get for selling this year's crop of fruit which is about to mature."

"You are not quite so foolish as the first one," responded the old man. "At least you see that this tree has more value as a producer of apples than it would as a source of firewood. But $100 is not the right price. You are not considering the value of next year's crop of apples, nor that of the years after. Please take your $100 and go elsewhere."

The next person to come along was a young man who had just started business school. "I am going to major in marketing," he said. "I figure that the tree should live for at least another fifteen years. If I sell the apples for $100 a year, that will total $1,500. I offer you $1,500 for your tree."

"You, too, are foolish," said the man. "Surely the $100 you would earn by selling the apples from the tree fifteen years from now cannot be worth $100 to you today. In fact, if you placed $41.73 today in a bank account paying 6% interest, compounded annually, that small sum would grow to $100 at the end of fifteen years. Therefore the present value of $100 worth of apples fifteen years from now, assuming an interest rate of 6%, is only $41.73, not $100. Pray," said the old man, "take your $1,500 and invest it safely in high-grade corporate bonds until you have graduated from business school and know more about finance."

Before long, there came a wealthy physician, who said, "I don't know much about apple trees, but I know what I like. I'll pay the market price for it. The last fellow was willing to pay you $1,500 for the tree, and so it must be worth that."

"Doctor," advised the old man, "you should get yourself a knowledgeable investment adviser. If there were truly a market in which apple trees were traded with some regularity, the prices at which they were sold would be a good indication of their value. But there is no such market. And the isolated offer I just received tells very little about how much my tree is really worth—as you would surely realize if you had heard the other foolish offers I have heard today. Please take your money and buy a vacation home."

The next prospective purchaser to come along was an accounting student. When the old man asked "What price are you willing to give me?" the student first demanded to see the old man's books. The old man had kept careful records and gladly brought them out. After examining them the accounting student said, "Your books show that you paid $75 for this tree ten years ago. Furthermore, you have made no deductions for depreciation. I do not know if that conforms with generally accepted accounting principles, but assuming that it does, the book value of your tree is $75. I will pay that."

"Ah, you students know so much and yet so little," chided the old man. "It is true that the book value of my tree is $75, but any fool can see that it is worth far more than that. You had best go back to school and see if you can find some books that will show you how to use your numbers to better effect."

The next prospective purchaser was a young stockbroker who had recently graduated from business school. Eager to test her new skills she, too, asked to examine the books. After several hours she came back to the old man and said she was now prepared to make an offer that valued the tree on the basis of the capitalization of its earnings.

For the first time the old man's interest was piqued and he asked her to go on.

The young woman explained that while the apples were sold for $100 last year, that figure did not represent profits realized from the tree. There were expenses attendant to the tree, such as the cost of fertilizer, the expense of pruning the tree, the cost of the tools, expenses in connection with picking the apples, carting them into town and selling them. Somebody had to do these things, and a portion of the salaries paid to those persons ought to be charged against the revenues from the tree. Moreover, the purchase price, or cost, of the tree was an expense. A portion of the cost is taken into account each year of the tree's useful life. Finally, there were taxes. She concluded that the profit from the tree was $50 last year.

"Wow!" exclaimed the old man. "I thought I made $100 off that tree."

"That's because you failed to match expenses with revenues, in accordance with generally accepted accounting principles," she explained. "You don't actually have to write a check to be charged with what accountants consider to be your expenses. For example, you bought a station wagon some time ago and you used it part of the time to cart apples to market. The wagon will last a while and each year some of the original cost has to be matched against revenues. A portion of the amount has to be spread out over the next several years even though you expended it all at one time. Accountants call that depreciation. I'll bet you never figured that in your calculation of profits."

"I'll bet you're right," he replied. "Tell me more."

"I also went back into the books for a few years and I saw that in some years the tree produced fewer apples than in other years, the prices varied and the costs were not exactly the same each year. Taking an average of only the last three years, I came up with a figure of $45 as a fair sample of the tree's earnings. But that is only half of what we have to do so as to figure the value."

"What's the other half?" he asked.

"The tricky part," she told him. "We now have to figure the value to me of owning a tree that will produce average annual earnings of $45 a year. If I believed that the tree was a one year wonder, I would say 100% of its value—as a going business—was represented by one year's earnings. But if I believe, as both you and I do, that the tree is more like a corporation, in that it will continue to produce earnings year after year, then the key is to figure out an appropriate rate of return. In other words, I will be investing my capital in the tree, and I need to compute the value to me of an investment that will produce $45 a year in income. We can call that amount the capitalized value of the tree."

"Do you have something in mind?" he asked.

"I'm getting there. If this tree produced entirely steady and pre-dictable earnings each year, it would be like a U.S. Treasury bond. But its earnings are not guaranteed. So we have to take into account risk and uncertainty. If the risk of its ruin was high, I would insist that a single year's earnings represent a higher percentage of the value of the tree. After all, apples could become a glut on the market one day and you would have to cut the price and increase the costs of selling them. Or some doctor could discover a link between eating an apple a day and heart disease. A drought could cut the yield of the tree. Or, heaven forbid, the tree could become diseased and die. These are all risks. And of course we do not know what will happen to costs that we know we have to bear."

"You are a gloomy one," reflected the old man. "There are treat-ments, you know, that could be applied to increase the yield of the tree. This tree could help spawn a whole orchard."

"I am aware of that," she assured him. "We will include that in the calculus. The fact is, we are talking about risk, and investment analysis is a cold business. We don't know with certainty what's going to happen. You want your money now and I'm supposed to live with the risk. That's fine with me, but then I have to look through a cloudy crystal ball, and not with 20/20 hindsight. And my resources are limited. I have to choose between your tree and the strawberry patch down the road. I cannot do both and the purchase of your tree will deprive me of alternative investments. That means I have to compare the opportunities and the risks."

"To determine a proper rate of return," she continued, "I have looked at investment opportunities that are comparable to the apple tree, particularly in the agribusiness industry, where these factors have been taken into account. I have concluded that 20% would be an appropriate rate of return. In other words, assuming that the average earnings from the tree over the last three years (which seems to be a representative period) are indicative of the return I will receive, I am prepared to pay a price for the tree that will give me a 20% return on my investment. I am not willing to accept any lower rate of return because I don't have to; I can always buy the strawberry patch instead. Now, to figure the price, we simply divide 45 by .20."

"Long division was never my long suit. Is there a simpler way of doing the figuring?" he asked hopefully.

"There is," she assured him. "We can use an approach we Wall Street types prefer, called using a price-earnings (or P–E) ratio. To compute the ratio, we divide 100 by the rate of return we are seeking. If I was willing to settle for an 8% return, I would use a P–E ratio of 12.5 to 1. But since I want to earn 20% on my investment, I divided 100 by 20 and came up with a P–E ratio of 5:1. In other words, I am willing to pay five times the tree's estimated annual earnings. Multiplying $45 by 5, I get a value of $225. That's my offer."

The old man sat back and said he greatly appreciated the lesson. He would have to think about her offer, and he asked if she could come by the next day.

When the young woman returned she found the old man emerging from a sea of work sheets, small print columns of numbers and a calculator. "Glad to see you," he said. "I think we can do some business."

"It's easy to see how you Wall Street smarties make so much money, buying people's property for less than its true value. I think I can get you to agree that my tree is worth more than you figured."

"I'm open minded," she assured him.

"The number you worked so hard over my books to come up with was something you called profits, or earnings that I earned in the past. I'm not so sure it tells you anything that important."

"Of course it does," she protested. "Profits measure efficiency and economic utility."

"Maybe," he mused, "but it sure doesn't tell you how much money you've got. I looked in my safe yesterday after you left and I saw I had some stocks that hadn't ever paid much of a dividend to me. And I kept getting reports each year telling me how great the earnings were, but I sure couldn't spend them. It's just the opposite with the tree. You figured the earnings were lower because of some amounts I'll never have to spend. It seems to me these earnings are an idea worked up by the accountants. Now I'll grant you that ideas, or concepts as you call them, are important and give you lots of useful information, but you can't fold them up, and put them in your pocket."

Surprised, she asked, "What is important, then?"

"Cash flow," he answered. "I'm talking about dollars you can spend, or save or give to your children. This tree will go on for years yielding revenues after costs. And it is the future, not the past, that we're trying to figure out."

"Don't forget the risks," she reminded him. "And the uncertainties."

"Quite right," he observed. "I think we can deal with that. Chances are that you and I could agree, after a lot of thought, on the possible range of future revenues and costs. I suspect we would estimate that for the next five years, there is a 25% chance that the cash flow will be $40, a 50% chance it will be $50 and a 25% chance it will be $60. That makes $50 our best guess, if you average it out. Then let us figure that for ten years after that the average will be $40. And that's it. The tree doctor tells me it can't produce any longer than that. Now all we have to do is figure out what you pay today to get $50 a year from now, two years from now, and so on for the first five years until we figure what you would pay to get $40 a year for each of the ten years after that. Then, throw in the 20 bucks we can get for firewood at that time, and that's that."

"Simple," she said. "You want to discount to the present value of future receipts including salvage value. Of course you need to determine the rate at which you discount."

"Precisely," he noted. "That's what all these charts and the calculator are doing." She nodded knowingly as he showed her discount tables that revealed what a dollar received at a later time is worth today, under different assumptions of the discount rate. It showed, for example, that at an 8% discount rate, a dollar delivered a year from now is worth $.93 today, simply because $.93 today, invested at 8%, will produce $1 a year from now.

"You could put your money in a savings bank or a savings and loan association and receive 5% interest, insured. But you could also put your money into obligations of the United States Government and earn 8% interest.* That looks like the risk free rate of interest to me. Anywhere else you put your money deprives you of the opportunity to earn 8% risk free. Discounting by 8% will only compensate you for the time value of the money you invest in the tree rather than in government securities. But the cash flow from the apple tree is not riskless, sad to say, so we need to use a higher discount rate to compensate you for the risk in your investment. Let us agree that we discount the receipt of $50 a year from now by 15%, and so on with the other deferred receipts. That is about the rate that is applied to investments with this magnitude of risk. You can check that out with my cousin who just sold

---

* These numbers will vary with prevailing interest rates. The principle remains the same.

his strawberry patch yesterday. According to my figures, the present value of the anticipated annual net revenues is $268.05, and today's value of the firewood is $2.44, making a grand total of $270.49. I'll take $270 even. You can see how much I'm allowing for risk because if I discounted the stream at 8%, it would come to $388.60.

After a few minutes reflection, the young woman said to the old man, "It was a bit foxy of you yesterday to let me appear to be teaching you something. Where did you learn so much about finance as an apple grower?"

"Don't be foolish, my young friend," he counseled her. "Wisdom comes from experience in many fields. Socrates taught us how to learn. I'll tell you a little secret; I spent a year in law school."

The young woman smiled at this last confession. "I have enjoyed this little exercise but let me tell you something that some of the financial whiz kids have told me. Whether we figure value on the basis of the discounted cash flow method or the capitalization of earnings, so long as we apply both methods perfectly we should come out at exactly the same point."

"Of course!" the old man exclaimed. "Some of the wunderkinds are catching on. But the clever ones are looking not at old earnings, but doing what managers are doing and projecting earnings into the future. The question is, however, which method is more likely to be misused. I prefer to calculate by my method because I don't have to monkey around with depreciation. You have to make these arbitrary assumptions about useful life and how fast you're going to depreciate. Obviously that's where you went wrong in your figuring."

"You are a crafty old devil," she rejoined. "There are plenty of places for your calculations to go off. It's easy to discount cash flows when they are nice and steady, but that doesn't help you when you've got some lumpy expenses that do not recur. For example, several years from now that tree will require some extensive pruning and spraying operations that simply do not show up in your flow. The labor and chemicals for that once-only occasion throw off the evenness of your calculations. But I'll tell you what, I'll offer you $250. My cold analysis tells me I'm overpaying, but I really like that tree. I think the psychic rewards of sitting in its shade must be worth something."

"It's a deal," said the old man. "I never said I was looking for the highest offer, but only the *best* offer."

MORAL: There are several. Methods are useful as tools, but good judgment comes not from methods alone, but from experience. And experience comes from bad judgment.

Listen closely to the experts, and hear those things they don't tell you. Behind all the sweet sounds of their confident notes, there is a great deal of discordant uncertainty. One wrong assumption can carry you pretty far from the truth.

Finally, you are never too young to learn.

2. NOTE: OTHER THOUGHTS ON VALUING A BUSINESS

a. *Context and Valuation*

In response to the question, "How much is a business worth?", one must ask "Why do we want to know?" Valuation of a business is best viewed as a process directed to a particular end. The nature of that process, and the result it achieves, may vary according to the purpose for which a value is sought. It is one thing to negotiate the selling of a going business (or a flowering apple tree); it is quite another to appraise the business for estate tax purposes and still another matter to determine the value of a business when the owner of 80% of the business wants to buy out the other 20%.

The old man in the parable was able to sell the entire interest in the apple tree to a buyer. The buyer knew she would be able to make all decisions about the care and use of the apple tree without having to consult anybody, without having to share profits with anybody and without having to worry about any conflict of interests she might have. Suppose, however, the parable involved the old man's young partner who had a one-third interest in the apple tree. Would the value of his interest simply be one-third of the value of the tree? Or would his interest be worth a lesser percentage because he lacked the ability to convey control over the tree? That is, presumably the tree would be worth the same whether it was owned by one person or by twenty, but the value of each person's interest might not be proportionate because of the consequences of majority rule. Or, as George Orwell put it, "all animals are created equal, but some animals are more equal than others."

b. *Buying a Dream*

The decision to buy a small business often represents the embodiment of a life-long dream. Many prospective purchasers, however, tend to become preoccupied with their dreams, in the view of James E. Schrager, a businessman who also teaches entrepreneurship at the University of Chicago Graduate School of Business. They then ignore important facts relating to businesses they have become interested in purchasing. Mr. Schrager suggests that, before even discussing price, a prospective purchaser get a feel for the business by asking the current owners open-ended questions such as: "How did they start the business? What have been their most difficult hurdles? How have they kept their customers happy? Why do people buy their product? What production problems have they had? How did they locate sales and production staff? What has been their biggest success? How do they see the future?" James E. Schrager, "How Much Should You Pay for a Dream?" The Wall St. J. A6 (Aug. 17, 1992).

Mr. Schrager also advises prospective purchasers to evaluate a business's products themselves and learn how other people use them and what they think of them. A business's competition also should be assessed: Is it strong or weak? Is it well financed and profitable or struggling to remain afloat? What does the state of the competition imply about prospects that the target business can be made more profitable?

The best way to price a business often is to determine what people are paying for similar businesses. But the potential target company's financial statements are a source of important information, too. Mr. Schrager suggests that prospective purchasers look behind financial statement numbers. "Find out what makes up the cost of goods sold, investigate factory overhead charges, understand the selling and marketing expenses, and so on." Attempt to determine whether receivables really are collectible and whether inventory is obsolete. In addition, inquire into contingent liabilities, such as possibly costly environmental claims. He posits three numbers "as upper limits for the target's price: Rarely is a small business worth more than one times sales; four times book value; or eight times earnings." Of course, there are exceptions, but a price above these limits usually should be considered too rich.

Mr. Schrager concludes: "[W]hen its your net worth on the line, you need more than just dreams. You need to remember that arriving at the right price for a small business requires as much work with your head as with your heart."

c. Valuing a Business: Thoughts of Chairman Warren

[As Chairman of Berkshire Hathaway, Inc. Warren Buffet has amassed a fortune of several billion dollars over 20 years by investing in and purchasing other companies. The following excerpts from Mr. Buffet's annual letters to the shareholders of Berkshire Hathaway suggest his approach to valuing businesses.]

Appendix to the 1983 Annual Report (concerning valuing a business's "goodwill"):

When a business is purchased, accounting principles require that the purchase price first be assigned to the fair value of the identifiable assets that are acquired. Frequently, the sum of the fair values put on the assets (after the deduction of liabilities) is less than the total purchase price of the business. In that case, the difference is assigned to an asset account entitled "excess of cost over equity in net assets acquired" [i.e., "Goodwill."] * * *

When [the purchase of a business] create[s] Goodwill, it must be amortized over not more than 40 years through charges—of equal amount in every year—to the earnings account. Since 40 years is the maximum period allowed, 40 years is what managements (including us) usually elect. * * *

That's how accounting Goodwill works. To see how it differs from economic reality, let's look at an example close at hand. We'll round some figures, and greatly oversimplify, to make the example easier to follow. We'll also mention some implications for investors and managers.

Blue Chip Stamps bought See's [Candy Shops, Inc.] early in 1972 for $25 million, at which time See's had about $8 million of net tangible assets. * * * This level of tangible assets was adequate to conduct the business without use of debt, except for short periods seasonally. See's was earning about $2 million after tax at the time, and such earnings seemed conservatively representative of future earning power in constant 1972 dollars.

Thus our first lesson: businesses logically are worth far more than net tangible assets when they can be expected to produce earnings on such assets considerably in excess of market rates of return. The capitalized value of this excess return is economic Goodwill.

In 1972 (and now) relatively few businesses could be expected to consistently earn the 25% after tax on net tangible assets that was earned by See's—doing it, furthermore, with conservative accounting and no financial leverage. It was not the fair market value of the inventories, receivables or fixed assets that produced the premium rates of return. Rather it was a combination of intangible assets, particularly a pervasive favorable reputation with consumers based upon countless pleasant experiences they have had with both product and personnel.

Such a reputation creates a consumer franchise that allows the value of the product to the purchaser, rather than its production cost, to be the major determinant of selling price. Consumer franchises are a prime source of economic Goodwill. Other sources include governmental franchises not subject to profit regulation, such as television stations, and an enduring position as the low cost producer in an industry.

Let's return to the accounting in the See's example. Blue Chip's purchase of See's at $17 million over net tangible assets required that a Goodwill account of this amount be established as an asset on Blue Chip's books and that $425,000 be charged to income annually for 40 years to amortize that asset. By 1983, after 11 years of such charges, the $17 million had been reduced to about $12.5 million. * * *

But what are the economic realities? One reality is that the amortization charges that have been deducted as costs in the earnings statement each year since acquisition of See's were not true economic costs. We know that because See's last year earned $13 million after taxes on about $20 million of net tangible assets—a performance indicating the existence of economic Goodwill far larger than the total original cost of our accounting Goodwill. In other words, while accounting Goodwill regularly decreased from the moment of purchase, economic Goodwill increased in irregular but very substantial fashion.

Another reality is that annual amortization charges in the future will not correspond to economic costs. It is possible, of course, that See's economic Goodwill will disappear. But it won't shrink in even decrements or anything remotely resembling them. What is more likely is that the Goodwill will increase—in current, if not in constant, dollars—because of inflation.

That probability exists because true economic Goodwill tends to rise in nominal value proportionally with inflation. To illustrate how this works, let's contrast a See's kind of business with a more mundane business. When we purchased See's in 1972, it will be recalled, it was earning about $2 million on $8 million of net tangible assets. Let us assume that our hypothetical mundane business then had $2 million of earnings also, but needed $18 million in net tangible assets for normal operations. Earning only 11% on required tangible assets, that mundane business would possess little or no economic Goodwill.

A business like that, therefore, might well have sold for the value of its net tangible assets, or for $18 million. In contrast, we paid $25 million for See's, even though it had no more in earnings and less than half as much in "honest-to-God" assets. Could less really have been more, as our purchase price implied? The answer is yes"—even *if* both businesses were expected to have flat unit volume—as long as you anticipated, as we did in 1972, a world of continuous inflation.

To understand why, imagine the effect that a doubling of the price level would subsequently have on the two businesses. Both would need to double their nominal earnings to $4 million to keep themselves even with inflation. This would seem to be no great trick: just sell the same number of units at double earlier prices and, assuming profit margins remain unchanged, profits also must double.

But, crucially, to bring that about, both businesses probably would have to double their nominal investment in net tangible assets, since that is the kind of economic requirement that inflation usually imposes on businesses, both good and bad. A doubling of dollar sales means correspondingly more dollars must be employed immediately in receivables and inventories. Dollars employed in fixed assets will respond more slowly to inflation, but probably just as surely. And all of this inflation-required investment will produce no improvement in rate of return. The motivation for this investment is the survival of the business, not the prosperity of the owner.

Remember, however, that See's had net tangible assets of only $8 million. So it would only have had to commit an additional $8 million to finance the capital needs imposed by inflation. The mundane business, meanwhile, had a burden over twice as large—a need for $18 million of additional capital.

After the dust had settled, the mundane business, now earning $4 million annually, might still be worth the value of its tangible assets, or $36 million. That means its owners would have gained only a dollar of nominal value for every new dollar invested. (This is the same dollar-for-dollar result they would have achieved if they had added money to a savings account.)

See's, however, also earning $4 million might be worth $50 million if valued (as it logically would be) on the same basis as it was at the time of our purchase. So it would have gained $25 million in nominal value while the owners were putting up only $8 million in additional capital—over $3 of nominal value gained for each $1 invested.

Remember, even so, that the owners of the See's kind of business were forced by inflation to ante up $8 million in additional capital just to stay even in real profits. Any unleveraged business that requires some net tangible assets to operate (and almost all do) is hurt by inflation. Businesses needing little in the way of tangible assets simply are hurt the least.

And that fact, of course, has been hard for many people to grasp. For years the traditional wisdom—long on tradition, short on wisdom—held that inflation protection was best provided by businesses laden with natural resources, plants and machinery, or other tangible assets ("In Goods We Trust"). It doesn't work that way. Asset-heavy businesses generally earn low rates of return—rates that often barely provide enough capital to fund the inflationary needs *of* the existing business, with nothing left over for real growth, for distribution to owners, or for acquisition of new businesses.

In contrast, a disproportionate number of the great business fortunes built up during the inflationary years arose from ownership of operations that combined intangibles of lasting value with relatively minor requirements for tangible assets. In such cases earnings have bounded upward in nominal dollars, and these dollars have been largely available for the acquisition of additional businesses. This phenomenon has been particularly evident in the communications business. That business has required little in the way of tangible investment—yet its franchises have endured. During inflation, Goodwill is the gift that keeps giving.

But that statement applies, naturally, only to true economic Goodwill. Spurious accounting Goodwill—and there is plenty of it around—is another matter. When an overexcited management purchases a business at a silly price, the same accounting niceties described earlier are observed. Because it can't go anywhere else, the silliness ends up in the Goodwill account. Considering the lack of managerial discipline that created the account, under such circumstances it might better be labeled "No–Will." Whatever the term, the 40–year ritual typically is observed and the adrenalin so capitalized remains on the books as an "asset" just as if the acquisition had been a sensible one.

* * *

We believe managers and investors alike should view intangible assets from two perspectives:

(1) In analysis of operating results—that is, in evaluating the underlying economics of a business unit—amortization charges should be ignored. What a business can be expected to earn on unleveraged net tangible assets, excluding any charges against earnings for amortization of Goodwill, is the best guide to the economic attractiveness of the

operation. It is also the best guide to the current value of the operation's economic Goodwill.

(2) In evaluating the wisdom of business acquisitions, amortization charges should be ignored also. They should be deducted neither from earnings nor from the cost of the business. This means forever viewing purchased Goodwill at its full cost, before any amortization. Furthermore, cost should be defined as including the full intrinsic business value—not just the recorded accounting value—of all consideration given. * * *

Operations that appear to be winners based upon perspective (1) may pale when viewed from perspective (2). A good business is not always a good purchase—although it's a good place to look for one.

We will try to acquire businesses that have excellent operating economics measured by (1) and that provide reasonable returns measured by (2). Accounting consequences will be totally ignored.

From the 1978 Annual Report (concerning investment in a low-margin business):

Earnings of $1.3 million in 1978, while much improved from 1977, still represent a low return on the $17 million of capital employed in [Berkshire's textile] business. Textile plant and equipment are on the books for a very small fraction of what it would cost to replace such equipment today. And, despite the age of the equipment, much of it is functionally similar to new equipment being installed by the industry. But despite this "bargain cost" of fixed assets, capital turnover is relatively low * * *.

The textile industry illustrates in textbook style how producers of relatively undifferentiated goods in capital intensive businesses must earn inadequate returns except under conditions of tight supply or real shortage. As long as excess productive capacity exists, prices tend to reflect direct operating costs rather than capital employed. Such a supply-excess condition appears likely to prevail most of the time in the textile industry, and our expectations are for profits of relatively modest amounts in relation to capital.

We hope we don't get into too many more businesses with such tough economic characteristics.

From the 1981 Annual Report (concerning the impact of inflation):

* * * [P]unishment is inflicted by an inflationary environment upon the owners of the "bad" business [—one that produces less after-tax return for shareholders than would a tax-exempt, low-risk bond]. To continue operating in its present mode, such a low-return business usually must retain much of its earnings—no matter what penalty such a policy produces for shareholders.

Reason, of course, would prescribe just the opposite policy. An individual, stuck with a 5% bond with many years to run before maturity, does not take the coupons from that bond and pay one hundred cents on the dollar for more 5% bonds while similar bonds are available at, say, forty cents on the dollar. * * * Good money is not thrown after bad.

What makes sense for the bondholder makes sense for the shareholder. Logically, a company with historic *and prospective* high returns on equity should retain much or all of its earnings so that shareholders can earn premium returns on enhanced capital. Conversely, low returns on corporate equity would suggest a very high dividend payout so that owners could direct capital toward more attractive areas. * * *

But inflation takes us through the looking glass into the upside-down world of Alice in Wonderland. When prices continuously rise, the bad" business must retain every nickel that it can. Not because it is attractive as a repository for equity capital, but precisely because it is so unattractive, the low-return business must follow a high retention policy. If it wishes to continue operating in the future as it has in the past—and most entities, including businesses, do—it simply has no choice.

For inflation acts as a gigantic corporate tapeworm. That tapeworm preemptively consumes its requisite daily diet of investment dollars regardless of the health of the host organism. Whatever the level of reported profits (even if nil), more dollars for receivables, inventory and fixed assets are continuously required by the business in order to merely match the unit volume of the previous year. The less prosperous the enterprise, the greater the proportion of available sustenance claimed by the tapeworm.

Under present conditions, a business earning 8% or 10% on equity often has no leftovers for expansion, debt reduction or "real" dividends. The tapeworm of inflation simply cleans the plate.

From the 1986 Annual Report (concerning the value of a business to its owners):

[W]hat may be called "owner earnings" * * * represent (a) reported earnings plus (b) depreciation, depletion, amortization, and certain other non-cash charges * * * less (c) the average annual amount of capitalized expenditures for plant and equipment, etc. that the business requires to fully maintain its long-term competitive position and its unit volume. (If the business requires additional working capital to maintain its competitive position and unit volume, the increment also should be included in (c). * * *

Our owner-earnings equation does not yield the deceptively precise figures provided by GAAP, since (c) must be a guess—and one sometimes very difficult to make. Despite this problem, we consider the owner earnings figure, not the GAAP figure, to be the relevant item for valuation purposes—both for investors in buying stocks and for managers in buying entire businesses. We agree with Keynes's observation: "I would rather be vaguely right than precisely wrong." * * *

[C]alculations of this sort usually do not provide * * * pleasant news. * * * Most managers probably will acknowledge that they need to spend something more than (b) on their businesses over the longer term just to hold their ground in terms of both unit volume and competitive position. When this imperative exists—that is, when (c) exceeds (b)—GAAP earnings overstate owner earnings. Frequently this overstatement is substantial. The oil industry has in recent years provided a conspicuous example of this phenomenon. Had most major oil companies spent only (b) each year, they would have guaranteed their shrinkage in real terms.

All of this points up the absurdity of the "cash flow" numbers that are often set forth in Wall Street reports. These numbers routinely include (a) plus (b)—but do not subtract (c). Most sales brochures of investment bankers also feature deceptive presentations of this kind. These imply that the business being offered is the commercial counterpart of the Pyramids—forever state-of-the-art, never needing to be replaced, improved or refurbished. * * *

"Cash Flow," true, may serve as shorthand of some utility in descriptions of certain real estate business or other enterprises that make huge initial outlays and only tiny outlays thereafter. A company whose only holding is a bridge or an extremely long-lived gas field would be an example. But "cash flow" is meaningless in such businesses as manufacturing, retailing, extractive companies, and utilities because, for them, (c) is always significant. To be sure, businesses of this kind may in a given year be able to defer capital spending. But over a five- or ten-year period, they must make the investment—or the business decays.

Why, then, are "cash flow" numbers so popular today? In answer, we confess our cynicism: we believe these numbers are frequently used by marketers of businesses and securities in attempts to justify the unjustifiable (and thereby to sell what should be the unsalable). When (a)—that is, GAAP earnings—looks by itself inadequate to service debt of a junk bond or justify a foolish stock price, how convenient it becomes for salesmen to focus on (a) + (b). But you shouldn't add (b) without subtracting (c): though dentists correctly claim that if you ignore your teeth they'll go away, the same is not true for (c). The company or investor believing that the debt-servicing ability or the equity valuation of an enterprise can be measured by totalling (a) and (b) while ignoring (c) is headed for certain trouble. * * *

Questioning GAAP figures may seem impious to some. After all, what are we paying the accountants for if it is not to deliver us the "truth" about our business. But the accountants' job is to record, not to evaluate. The evaluation job falls to investors and managers.

Accounting numbers, of course, are the language of business and as such are of enormous help to any one evaluating the worth of a business and tracking its progress. [We] would be lost without these numbers: they invariably are the starting point for us in evaluating our own businesses and those of others. Managers and owners need to remember, however, that accounting is but an aid to business thinking, never a substitute for it.

————

For additional insightful analysis, see William A. Klein & John C. Coffee, Business Organization and Finance 303–324 (5th ed. 1993).

Chapter 7

THE CHOICE OF
ORGANIZATIONAL FORM

PROBLEM
PRECISION TOOLS—PART III

You have now turned your attention to the legal problems that must be resolved in the acquisition of Precision Tools. Initially the clients (with counsel) need to determine the legal form in which they will operate the business. In your interviews with them you have learned a number of additional facts that may be relevant to this decision.

In order to expand the business of PT as Jessica Bacon and Michael Lane contemplate, additional equipment, increased working capital and an aggressive marketing effort will require a substantial investment in the firm. Their mutual friend, Bernie Gould, has indicated that he would be willing to invest in the business if Jessica and Michael acquire PT.

Bernie is 62 years old. His insurance brokerage business is a partnership with two other individuals who are about his age. He is thinking of retiring from that business in a few years. He is married and has a son, Bill, who is presently a college junior. Bill is not sure what he wants to do when he graduates except that he has made it clear that he does not want to be an insurance broker. He is a computer buff and he is very enthusiastic about his father's involvement in the PT venture. Bernie is equally excited about the project, but he says that he is too busy with other affairs to spend much time in helping with its day-to-day management. He would like, however, to make his substantial business experience available where it can be helpful and he also insists on having some voice in the new directions PT would take.

Jessica and Michael, on the other hand, plan to spend full-time on PT. In addition to the money she plans to invest, Jessica has a stock portfolio worth about $75,000. Her retired father is relatively well-to-do and she stands to inherit several hundred thousand dollars. Michael comes from a financially modest background and has little capital aside from the money he plans to invest in the business. He is married, has two young children and owns his home.

Since they are purchasing a going concern, Jessica, Michael and Bernie think they may be able to operate it profitably during the first few years. But there is a real possibility that the company will experience losses, at least for the first few years, because they will be expanding the business by borrowing at higher than prime interest rates, and sowing some marketing seeds that will not bear fruit immediately.

When Michael first came to you about this transaction, one of the things he told you was, "We want you to incorporate the business for us." After reflecting on the matter, how should you respond? Should Jessica, Michael and Bernie take over PT in the corporate form or use another form?

A. INTRODUCTION

In planning a new business, the owners must decide which organizational form best suits their needs. This decision is by no means simple. The choice of organizational form will depend largely upon the economics of the venture, the preferences of the individual owners and tax considerations. The balance that the owners strike will dictate their choice among the three primary forms of business organization available to joint owners: the partnership, the corporation and the limited liability company.

Before the recent development of the limited liability company, the choice of organizational form was confined to a choice between the partnership and the corporation. In their default forms, i.e., the form of organization that exists by operation of law in the absence of agreement to the contrary by the owners, partnerships and corporations are polar opposites. The partnership is an entity in which all the participants have unlimited liability, an equal voice in management, and the ability to act as agents for the partnership and incur obligations that will be binding on all the partners. In contrast the corporation is based upon principles of centralized management and limited liability for the participants.

Although the major attributes of each form are antithetical, the law affords the parties considerable flexibility to agree on an organizational structure that deviates considerably from the the norms of the default models. This flexibility means that the theoretical distinctions between these two forms may not be as great as they appear. Furthermore, the limited liability company, which combines limited liability for the participants with the tax advantages of a partnership, gives owners even greater flexibility to adopt an organizational form tailored to their particular needs.

Partnerships may be either general partnerships or limited partnerships. In virtually all states, partnerships are governed by uniform statutes. General partnerships are subject to the Uniform Partnership Act ("UPA") in all states but Louisiana. Limited partnerships in virtually every jurisdiction are regulated either by the Uniform Limited Partnership Act ("ULPA") or the Revised Uniformed Limited Partnership Act ("RULPA"). These statutes allow considerable flexibility and informality in the organization and operation of partnerships.

The UPA defines a partnership as "an association of two or more persons to carry on as co-owners a business for profit." § 6(1). In a general partnership, each partner possesses an equal voice in management and the authority to act as agent for the partnership. See § 18(e) and § 9(1). Each partner is subject to unlimited liability for the debts of the partnership, as well as the torts of her partners committed within the course of the partnership's business. §§ 13–15.

UPA –
– Equal voice
– may act as a agent.

The RULPA defines a limited partnership as a "partnership formed by two or more persons * * * and having one or more general partners and one or more limited partners." § 101(7). In a limited partnership, a limited partner has no voice in the active management of the partnership, which is conducted by the general partner. ULPA § 9. Additionally, the limited partner's liability is limited to her initial contribution to the partnership, while the general partner is subject to unlimited liability. §§ 9(1), 17(1).

At the opposite end of the continuum, corporations are entities that are distinct from their owners. The principal differences between a corporation and a partnership lie in the management structure and liability provisions. In contrast to the general partnership, the management of the corporation is centralized in a board of directors, rather than the individual owners. RMBCA § 8.01. An attractive feature of the corporate form is that a shareholder of a corporation is not personally liable for the debts of the corporation. RMBCA § 6.22.

Between these two poles are hybrid forms of ownership, the most important of which is the limited liability company. Limited liability companies, the formation of which requires one or more owners, are a relatively new form of business organization. Like the corporation, a limited liability company is an entity separate from its owners, who are called "members." Members, like shareholders in a corporation, receive the benefits of limited liability. Additionally, limited liability companies may be more advantageous than limited partnerships because limited liability statutes do not require a general partner who would be subject to unlimited liability.

Limited liabil.

In this chapter, we contrast the principal non-tax features of both forms of partnership, the limited liability company, and the corporation. We discuss the primary distinctions between the default modes of operation and the principal ways in which these defaults can be varied. Finally, we consider the principal tax consequences of the choice of organizational form.

B. NON-TAX ASPECTS

1. FORMATION

The formation of a corporation requires formal action with the state. In order to incorporate, the persons creating the corporation, or incorporators, must file articles of incorporation containing certain information about the company and its incorporators, such as the corporate name, the number of authorized shares, and the name and address of each incorporator. The articles may also contain certain other information, such as corporate purpose, provisions regarding management and regulation of the corporation, and limitations on the powers of the corporation and the shareholders, officers and directors. See RMBCA § 2.02; D.G.C.L. § 102. Under the RMBCA, corporate existence begins when the articles of incorporation are filed. Failure to comply with the legal formalities of incorporation can result in the failure to recognize the existence of the corporation as a legal entity.

Forming a general partnership, on the other hand, requires no filing with the state. A partnership may arise in two ways. The most common method is consensual formation. It occurs when two or more individuals enter into a contractual relationship, usually embodied in a partnership agreement which governs the the relationship of the partners, including such matters as managerial rights, distribution rights, interests in profits and losses, and rights upon dissolution of the enterprise. Because of the definition of a partnership in UPA § 6(1), a partnership may also arise by operation of law. A non-consensual partnership often results in undesirable and unforeseen consequences to the partners, such as unlimited liability for debts of the partnership.

A limited partnership, like a corporation, requires the filing with the state of a certificate setting forth the rights and duties of the partners among themselves and identifying the general partners. RULPA § 201. Typically, the general and limited partners also execute a written partnership agreement. If new general partners are added, amended filings are necessary.

The formation of a limited liability company requires similar action with the state. One or more persons must file a certificate of formation, including the name of the limited liability company and address of its registered agent. Other information regarding the governance and operation of the limited liability company may be included in the certificate of formation. The limited liability company is recognized by law either upon the date of filing or a later date, if specified in the certificate of filing. See, e.g., 6 Del. C. Ann. § 18–201(b).

2. LIMITED LIABILITY

Limited liability is the key non-tax feature of a corporation. A corporation is a separate legal entity which is responsible for its own debts and other liabilities. A shareholder's liability is limited to her original investment in the corporation. There are three major exceptions to shareholder limited liability. Shareholders will be personally liable: 1) where the corporation is not properly formed (discussed in Chapter 8); 2) for unpaid capital contributions that they have agreed to make (considered in Chapter 9); and 3) where the veil of limited liability is pierced (examined in Chapter 11). Additionally, in many small corporations, pressing needs for capital often compel some shareholders to increase their financial exposure by personally guaranteeing loans made to the corporation.

A partnership differs from a corporation in that the general partners, in their individual capacities, are subject to unlimited liability for the obligations of the partnership. UPA § 15. Partnership liability for the torts of the partnership is joint and several. Partners are exposed only to joint liability for the partnership's contractual obligations. With respect to both contractual obligations and tort liability, each partner may bind the partnership, and thus the other partners, provided that the act giving rise to liability is performed in the ordinary course of business. UPA § 9(1); § 13.*

In a limited partnership, the general partner faces the same unlimited liability as a partner in a general partnership. A limited partner, on the other hand, is shielded by the same limited liability rule as a corporate shareholder. The limited partner's liability is limited to her investment in the enterprise, provided that she does not participate in the management of the firm. Courts have struggled to determine what constitutes "participation in management," but the cases have painted no bright lines. RULPA § 303 provides limited guidance in defining "participation." It states that certain activities, such as advising the general partner with respect to the business and voting on critical transactions, are not to be considered "participation." Thus, the statute allows a limited amount of participation in certain activities without denying limited partners the protection of limited liability.

To further insulate the participants in a limited partnership from personal liability, the law allows the general partner to be a corporation. That corporation is liable for the claims against the partnership, but its shareholders will be shielded from liability for claims arising from the corporate general partner's debts.

All limited liability company statutes provide for limited liability for the entity's members and managers. For example, Delaware's statute provides, " * * * [n]o member or manager of a limited liability company shall be obligated for any * * * liability of the limited liability company solely by reason of being a member or acting as a manager of the limited liability company." 6 Del. C. Ann. § 18–303. Unlike a limited partner-

---

* A number of states, including Delaware, have developed a registered limited liability partnership which must file an application with the Secretary of State, who registers the firm. (6 Del. C. Ann. § 1544). A partner in a registered limited liability partnership is not liable for the partnership's torts; however, the partner remains personally liable "for his own negligence, wrongful acts or misconduct or that of any person under his direct supervision and control". (6 Del. C. Ann. § 1515).

ship, all members of a limited liability company receive this protection without any restrictions on their participation in the management and control of the business. As is the case with the shareholders of a corporation, members of a limited liability corporation will be liable where the entity is not properly formed, for unpaid contributions, and where the veil of limited liability is pierced.

3. MANAGEMENT AND CONTROL

The management of a corporation is centralized in the board of directors. Under the traditional statutory model, shareholders generally elect the board of directors who oversee the day-to-day operations of the business. Absent special provisions in the articles of incorporation, RMBCA § 7.28 provides that directors are elected by a plurality of shares entitled to vote. Without specific provisions in the articles, each share is entitled to one vote. Thus, voting is done on the basis of share ownership, rather than a per-capita basis. Corporate owners often vary this model in the articles of incorporation. For example, in close corporations, because there is often a substantial overlap between owners and managers, the articles may provide for guaranteed board representation for each owner, as well as specifying the details of how the corporation is to be managed.

In a general partnership, absent contrary provisions in the partnership agreement, the management functions are vested in all the partners. Each partner has an equal voice, regardless of the amount of her capital contribution. UPA § 18(e). Decisions generally are made on the basis of a majority vote of the partners, but major changes, such as modification of a partner's decision making authority, cannot be made without the unanimous consent of the partners. UPA § 18(h).

The partners often modify these rules through the partnership agreement. Partnership agreements frequently provide that a partner's voice in management will be in proportion to her capital contribution. Thus, a partner who contributes $60,000 of a partnership's initial capital of $100,000 will be entitled to 60% of the voting power. Partners also can assign exclusive management responsibility over various functions to one or more partners.

In a limited partnership, as noted, the limited partners may not participate in the management of the business without losing the protection of limited liability. The general partners thus have responsibility for management except to a very limited degree. RULPA gives limited partners the right to vote on certain critical matters, including dissolution, changing the nature of the business, the removal of a general partner and certain other extraordinary events.

Generally, the basic document in a limited liability company is an operating agreement that controls the management of the entity. Most jurisdictions provide that absent an agreement to the contrary regarding a limited liability company's management, members have a voice in management in proportion to their capital contributions. See, e.g., 6

Del. C. Ann. § 18–402. Some jurisdictions, such as Texas, vest management responsibilities in a designated board of managers. Texas Ann. Civ. St. Art. 1528n, art. 2.12. Where the statute vests management in the firm's members, the members may appoint a manager to oversee the operation of the firm. See, e.g., Del. Code Ann. § 18–402.

4. CONTINUITY OF EXISTENCE

Generally, most states provide, either by statute or common law, that a corporation has perpetual existence. The articles of incorporation may provide for a shorter term. RMBCA § 3.02; DGCL § 102(b)(5). The parties also may agree in advance that the corporation will be dissolved in specified circumstances, such as the death or disability of one of the key participants.

In the absence of contrary provisions in the partnership agreement, a general partnership is dissolved upon the death, bankruptcy or withdrawal of a partner. UPA §§ 31–32. Most partnership agreements provide for the surviving partners to continue the business upon the death of a partner. Customarily, the remaining partners agree to pay the estate of the deceased partner the value of her partnership interest.

A partner may withdraw at any time and thereby dissolve the partnership, even if that act violates provisions in the partnership agreement. Dissolution typically exposes the partnership's assets to judicial sale and gives a minority owner the option to force the repurchase of her partnership interest. If the dissolution of the firm is caused "in contravention of the partnership agreement" (UPA § 31(d)(2)), the partner causing the dissolution is subject to various penalties, including liability to the other partners for damages resulting from her wrongful act (UPA § 38(2)(a)(II)). The other partners have the option to continue the partnership's business without the consent or participation of the partner causing the dissolution (UPA § 38(2)(b)). Additionally, the remaining partners may buy out that partner's interest, thereby avoiding sale of the assets and termination of the business.

Generally, the business of a limited partnership continues upon the death, bankruptcy or voluntary withdrawal of a limited partner. The partnership agreement contain limitations on the limited partner's right to withdraw her capital. In the absence of contrary agreement, it is only when a general partner withdraws that a limited partnership is dissolved. RULPA § 801.

Unlike a corporation, a limited liability company does not continue indefinitely. Generally, a limited liability company dissolves (1) after a fixed period provided by statute (2) by unanimous agreement of the members, or (3) on the withdrawal of a member. See, e.g., 6 Del. C. Ann. § 18–801. The operating agreement may modify these general provisions.

5. TRANSFERABILITY OF INTERESTS

One of the distinctive features of a corporation is that its stock is freely transferable without the consent of the other shareholders. This feature of ownership is often troublesome to owners of a close corporation because the success of the venture depends upon the ability of owners to work together. Therefore, the articles of incorporation of a close corporation will often contain restrictions on the transferability of stock. Even without such restrictions, free transferability may be of little practical value because of the lack of a ready market for the stock.

In a general partnership, because each partner possesses the authority to bind the partnership and subject the other partners to personal liability, it is critically important that a partner not have a new unwanted partner thrust upon her without her consent. Thus, the default rule is that the admission of a new partner requires the unanimous consent of the partners. UPA § 18(g). A partnership interest is subject to limited transferability. A partner may freely assign that interest, but the subsequent rights of her assignee are limited to the assignor's rights to share in the partnership's profits; they do not include a voice in management. UPA § 27. In order to receive a voice in management, the assignee must be admitted as a partner.

Limited partners also may freely assign their interests, but the assignee may only exercise the rights of a limited partner with the consent of all the remaining partners. Because limited partners do not participate actively in the management of the partnership, however, the restrictions on the rights of the assignee are less important.

Many limited liability company statutes allow members to assign their membership interests to other persons as provided for in the operating agreement. However, as in a partnership, the assignee may not participate in the management of the firm's business without the unanimous consent of the other members. See, e.g., 6 Del. C. Ann. §§ 18–702 and 18–704(a).

6. FINANCING MATTERS

The corporate form provides financing flexibility because there are a variety of well recognized financing devices available to a corporation, including the ability to issue stock.

Partnerships face more substantial hurdles in raising capital. Apart from injections of equity capital by existing partners, the sole method of raising equity capital in a partnership is the creation of new partnership interests. This process may be more cumbersome than the issuance of stock in a corporation because it requires the unanimous consent of the partners. While a partnership may borrow funds with the same facility as a corporation, borrowing in a partnership produces the undesirable consequence of exposing the partners to additional personal liability.

Because of the limited liability protections afforded to limited partners and the tax advantages discussed in Section D of this chapter, the limited partnership is an easier vehicle for raising capital than is the general partnership. Accordingly, it is often the form used in large enterprises organized as a partnership.

The limited liability company operating agreement may provide for various classes of members with such rights and duties as contained in the agreement. This flexibility facilitates raising capital; however, the restrictions on transfers of the right to participate in the firm's management without the unanimous consent of the other members may make attracting capital difficult.

C. PLANNING CONSIDERATIONS

1. BALANCING OWNERSHIP INTERESTS

In choosing a form of organization, the owners must consider how their choice will affect the delicate balance between majority and minority owners. This balance differs, depending upon the owners' choice between corporation and partnership. In a partnership, a dissatisfied partner or group of partners can dissolve the partnership unilaterally. Charles O'Kelley notes the advantages and counterbalancing risks associated with this dissolution mechanism:

> The at-will dissolution mechanism protects both individual and collective adaptive needs. For example, if because of changed circumstances, a partner's capital will have a higher value when invested in some other endeavor, she may simply dissolve the old partnership and reinvest her human and money capital elsewhere. Moreover, this unilateral withdrawal mechanism may be used by the majority to achieve needed team changes that, absent unanimous consent, cannot be directly accomplished within the existing partnership. Thus, if a partner's human capital has become obsolete, but the partner will not retire, the majority may simply dissolve the old partnership, purchase the firm's assets at a judicial sale, and form a new partnership that does not include the former partner. On the other hand, the dissolution process is not without cost and uncertainty, both of which operate to constrain good-faith adaptive acts, unless they are clearly necessary.

> * * *

> Partnership form thus exposes majority partners to two risks: the risk that a minority partner will extort unfair changes in team rules by opportunistically threatening to dissolve the partnership and the risk that a minority partner will shirk, content in the belief that the majority will be unwilling to expel her for fear that a court might label the resulting dissolution wrongful.

Charles R. O'Kelley, Jr., Filling Gaps in the Close Corporation Contract: A Transaction Cost Analysis, 87 Nw. U. L.Rev. 216, 238 (1992).

Consequently, in planning the partnership, the partners should consider contractual provisions focusing on wrongful dissolution to reduce the risk of opportunism. Professor O'Kelley notes:

default.

* * * For example, the risk of opportunistic dissolution by the majority and opportunistic threats of dissolution by the minority may be greatly reduced by a simple agreement among the partners that the partnership will endure for a specified term or undertaking. Any dissolution of the partnership before completion of the agreed undertaking or term would be in contravention of the partnership agreement, and therefore, an act causing wrongful dissolution.

On the other hand, if the partners' greatest concern is potential shirking by minority partners, the risk of this type of opportunism may be reduced by a contractual agreement among the partners providing that the majority may expel a partner under specified conditions. If a partner is expelled pursuant to such contractual power, then dissolution will not be considered wrongful. The expelling partners may continue the partnership's business, and need only pay to the expelled partner the "net amount due her from the partnership."

Id. at 234–35.

In contrast to the partnership default rules, which tend toward protection of the minority, corporate law provisions tend to favor the majority shareholders. In contrasting the management and continuity of existence features of a corporation with partnership default rules, Professor O'Kelley states:

Corporation

Dissolution. or withdrawal of shares.

* * * The corporation's adaptive mechanism is the board of directors acting by majority rule. Such mechanism enables the majority to insist on a change in the duties or compensation of a minority owner without incurring significant costs. If the minority shareholder is unhappy with her new status she may withdraw her human capital from the team (if not already discharged) and sell her shares. Alternatively, she may bring a petition for involuntary dissolution on the grounds that the majority's actions are oppressive or that equitable relief is necessary to protect the minority's reasonable expectations or interests. [See, e.g., RMBCA § 14.30(2)(ii).] Each of these protective devices is imperfect. If the minority shareholder sells her shares, she is likely to receive substantially less than she would if the corporation were dissolved and its assets sold as a going concern. If she seeks equitable relief, she must carry the burden of proving predicate facts entitling her to relief.

* * *

The downsides of corporate statutory governance norms, especially when compared to partnership statutory governance rules, are the relative lack of assurance that individual adaptive needs will be satisfied and the relatively greater risk of majority opportunism posed because minority shareholder[s] may not withdraw their money capital from the firm. If a partner finds it value-maximizing to withdraw her capital from the firm and invest it elsewhere, the at-will dissolution mechanism insures that she will be able to do so. In a corporation, a minority shareholder has no similar adaptive rights. On the other hand, the corporation law preference for majority adaptability combines with the lack of a unilateral minority withdrawal right to insulate the majority from the threat of minority opportunism. A minority shareholder simply has no ability to withdraw unilaterally, and thus, no ability to extort an objectively unjustifiable change in terms from the majority.

Id. at 240–41.

Of course, maintaining an optimal balance between majority and minority owners often is not be the parties' exclusive concern. The attraction of limited liability, standing alone, may be sufficient to lead prospective investors to choose the corporate form, even though they might other wise prefer a partnership governance structure. This has led some commentators to speculate that the advent of the limited liability company, which easily can be structured much like a partnership (and which is taxable as a partnership), may spell the death knell of the partnership form of organization. See Larry E. Ribstein, The Deregulation of Limited Liability and the Death of Partnership, 70 Wash U. L.Q. 417 (1992).

2. THE ECONOMICS OF THE CHOICE

RICHARD A. POSNER, ECONOMIC ANALYSIS OF LAW
392–393 (4th ed. 1992).

PROBLEMS IN FINANCING BUSINESS VENTURES

The theory of the firm tells us why so much economic activity is organized in firms but not why most of those firms are corporations. A clue is that firms in which the inputs are primarily labor rather than capital often are partnerships or individual proprietorships rather than corporations. The corporation is primarily a method of solving problems encountered in raising substantial amounts of capital.

How does the impecunious entrepreneur who has a promising idea for a new venture go about raising the necessary capital? Borrowing *all* of the needed capital is probably out of the question. If the riskless interest rate is 6 percent but the venture has a 50 percent chance of failing and having no assets out of which to repay the loan, the lender, if risk neutral, will charge an interest rate of 112 percent.[2] The high interest charge, plus amortization, will impose a heavy fixed cost on the venture from the outset. This will increase the danger of failure * * * —and in turn the interest rate.

These difficulties could in principle be overcome by careful and imaginative drafting of the loan agreement, but the transaction costs

---

2. Suppose the loan is for $100 and is to be repaid at the end of a year. The lender must charge an interest rate that will yield an expected value of $106, given a 50 percent probability of repayment. Solving the equation .5x = $106 for x yields $212–i.e., $100 in principal plus $112 in interest.

might be very high. An alternative is for the entrepreneur to admit a partner to the business who is entitled to receive a portion of the profits of the venture, if any, in exchange for contributing the necessary capital to it. The partner's compensation is determined automatically by the fortunes of the business. There is no need to compute an interest rate although this is implicit in the determination of the fraction of any future profits that he is to receive in exchange for his contribution. Most important, there are no fixed costs of debt to make the venture even riskier than it inherently is; the partner receives his profits only if earned.

But there are still problems. A partnership can be dissolved by, and is automatically dissolved on the death of, any partner. The impermanence of the arrangement may deter the commitment of large amounts of money to an enterprise in which it may be frozen for years. The partners may be able to negotiate around this hurdle but not without incurring transaction costs that may be high. Moreover, to the extent that they agree to limit the investing partner's right to dissolve the partnership and withdraw his money, the liquidity of his investment is reduced and * * * he may be placed at the mercy of the active partner. * * *

Further, since each partner is personally liable for the debts of the partnership, a prospective investor will want to figure out the likely extent of the enterprise's potential liability, or even to participate in the actual management of the firm to make sure it does not run up huge debts for which he would be liable. And still a risk of indefinite liability would remain. In principle, the enterprise could include in all of its contracts with customers and suppliers a clause limiting its liability to the assets of the enterprise * * *. But the negotiation of such waivers would be costly. And it would be utterly impracticable to limit most tort liability in this way. Nor, * * * is insurance a complete answer.

THE CORPORATION AS A STANDARD CONTRACT

The corporate form is the normal solution that the law and business practice have evolved to solve the problems discussed in the preceding section. The corporation's perpetual existence obviates the need for a special agreement limiting withdrawal or dissolution, although such an agreement may turn out to be necessary for other reasons to be discussed. The shareholder's liability for corporate debts is limited to the value of his shares (limited liability). Passive investment is further encouraged by (1) a complex of legal rights vis-à-vis management and any controlling group of shareholders, and (2) the fact that equity interests in a corporation are broken up into shares of relatively small value that can be, and in the case of the larger corporations are, traded in organized markets. The corporate form enables an investor to make small equity investments, to reduce risk through diversification * * *, and to liquidate his investment quickly and cheaply. Notice that without limited liability a shareholder would not even be allowed to sell his shares without the other shareholders' consent, since if he sold them to someone poorer than he, the risk to the other shareholders would be increased.

D. THE TAX CONSEQUENCES OF BUSINESS ORGANIZATIONS: A BRIEF EXAMINATION

Because different forms of doing business result in different tax consequences, the choice of the form of enterprise often turns on those consequences. The major tax implications of that choice are summarized below, in terms that are intended to be understandable to students who have not yet studied tax. Some of the more troublesome or complicated points are touched on only lightly or omitted altogether. Consequently, this survey should not be mistaken for a comprehensive statement of the relevant tax law.

1. PARTNERSHIP VS. CORPORATION

The principal difference in the tax treatment of business organizations is the treatment of the entity. Under the Internal Revenue Code, the corporation is a taxpayer separate from its shareholders. Corporations, and not the persons who own stock, pay taxes or deduct losses, based on the results of the corporation's operations. A partnership, by contrast, is considered an aggregate of individuals rather than a separate entity; hence, it is not a taxpayer. The partnership files an information return, but the purpose is essentially to determine how much tax the individual partners will pay on the income or loss attributable to them from the operation of the partnership. Both the income and expenses of the partnership are said to "flow-through" to the partners in proportion to their ownership interests.

This difference is significant because of the different tax rates for individuals and corporations. As of the date of this book, individual tax rates vary from 15 percent to 39.6 percent, although the effective rate may be higher because of the treatment of individual exemptions and deductions. Corporate rates are lower. Internal Revenue Code § 11 provides that the rate is 15 percent on the first $50,000 of taxable income, 25 percent on the next $25,000 of taxable income, 34 percent on taxable income from $75,000 to $10 million, and 35 percent on taxable income above $10 million.

Fluctuations in tax rates, as well as the particular circumstances of both the participants and the venture, point to the futility of generalizing about the advisability, from a tax standpoint, of choosing one form of business over another. All that can be said is that the planner should consider, among other things, the extent of non-business income and deductions, the number of dependents, the possibility of early business losses and ultimate success, the individual's needs for cash from the operations of the business, and the nature of the business itself.

The difference in tax treatment between corporations and partnerships has focused attention on what has somewhat loosely (and inaccurately) been called "double taxation." The corporation pays a tax on income it earns. When that income is distributed to shareholders as dividends, it is taxed again in the hands of the shareholders with no account taken of the tax the corporation paid earlier. In contrast, the partnership itself pays no tax. The income from the business is taxed only to the partners, regardless of whether or not the income is distributed. The following example illustrates the basic difference between taxation of partnerships and corporations.

Assume that Jessica Bacon and Michael Lane form a partnership that produces components similar to those produced by Precision Tools. At the end of each year, the partnership will compute its net income and file an information return. The partnership may pay "salaries" to Jessica and Michael and at the end of the year it will retain some of its profits in the business and distribute some portion to each partner. (There is an incongruity which must be recognized in a partnership paying a "salary" to an owner, but the Internal Revenue Code permits the payment to be deducted just as if it were paid to an employee who is not an owner.) The partnership, as noted above, will pay no tax on its net income. Jessica and Michael will pay taxes, at their respective individual tax rates, on the "salaries" which they received as well as on the amounts distributed to them. They will also be taxed on their proportionate share of the remainder of the net income that was not distributed to them. Significantly, if the partnership operates at a loss, each will be entitled to claim her proportionate share of that loss as deduction against income from other sources.

The partnership will compute its net income in much the same manner as an individual. To determine how much of the profit or the loss is attributed to each of the partners, reference is made initially to the partnership agreement. In the absence of a formal partnership agreement, or if the agreement is incomplete as to a particular point, the tax law makes certain assumptions. For example, if the partners neglect to state how much of the profits each is entitled to receive, the law presumes that they are equal partners.

If Jessica and Michael form a corporation, at the end of the year, the corporation will again pay salaries to Jessica and Michael, distribute some portion of the profits to them, and retain the balance. Unlike a partnership, the corporation will pay taxes, although, as with a partnership, the corporation also can deduct their salaries as a business expense. Jessica and Michael will pay taxes on those salaries and on any amounts that the corporation distributes to them. Unlike a partnership, they will *not* pay taxes on any profits that the corporation retains in the business, nor will they be entitled to claim a deduction if the corporation operates at a loss.

The choice of the corporate form, however, raises an additional tax question that affects the economics of the venture. When Jessica and

Michael form the corporation, they must decide what securities—stock or debt—the corporation will issue in exchange for the capital that it needs. The tax significance of this choice is significant. As noted above, when a corporation distributes dividends to its shareholders, the corporation receives no deduction for the amount distributed to its shareholder. By contrast, when the corporation pays interest on indebtedness, even if the creditor is a shareholder, the corporation receives a deduction for the interest it pays. In both cases, Jessica and Michael will be taxed on what they receive; the difference is that because interest is deductible to the corporation and dividends are not, the use of debt will reduce the corporation's taxable income and may even eliminate all so-called double taxation.

This last example illustrates what may be the most important point about the tax aspects of doing business in corporate form; namely, that individuals by forming a corporation have created a tax-paying entity. If the business earned as much money as it did when operated in a partnership form, the owners will be worse off financially if they distribute all profits to themselves as dividends. They may, of course, reduce the corporation's profits by taking personal salaries, and if their salaries are equal to the entire amount of the company's profits, the corporation ordinarily will have no profits. Under these circumstances the consequences of operating in either partnership or corporate form would produce no tax differences. The Internal Revenue Code, as noted above, permits the deduction of "ordinary and necessary" business expenses. *salaries.* The amount allowed as a deduction for salaries is limited to a reasonable amount. The salaries paid to owner-employees will be carefully scrutinized if the returns are audited. If a business grows to substantial proportions, it may become difficult to deduct as "reasonable salaries" sums which fully equal the profits of the company. Thus, if the business grows, the likelihood is that the corporation will be taxed on at least some of its income, and if that income is then distributed to the shareholders, it will be taxed again.

The difference in the personal circumstances of the partners suggests some interesting thoughts for planning a business enterprise. For example, assume that Jessica, in addition to being a participant in the business, also receives income as the beneficiary of a family trust in the amount of $25,000 a year. Michael, on the other hand, has no income. They decide that the business will pay each of them an annual salary of $50,000 per annum in the first two years during which they expect the business to operate at a loss of $120,000 each year, including the deduction for their salaries.

If the venture is a partnership, Jessica will have income of $25,000 from the trust plus $50,000 received as salary for a total of $75,000 and may claim as a deduction the $60,000 loss that constitutes her share of the partnership's loss. Thus, the total income she will report is $15,000. Michael will have income of only $50,000, against which he may deduct $60,000; hence he will pay no tax. This will leave him with $10,000 of undeducted loss which he may carry back against income reported in earlier years and obtain a refund; if some loss still remains undeducted, he may carry that loss forward and apply it against income received in subsequent years. Whether he has such prior income or subsequent income will depend upon his personal circumstances. Jessica receives immediate benefit from the fact the partnership initially operates at a loss and can enjoy a substantial income at a low tax cost. The ability to directly offset personal income with losses from a business in which the partner is active is one of the attractive tax features of the partnership form of doing business; the business functions as a tax shelter. If the parties cannot use such benefits, or if the differential in tax rates is significant, the corporate form would become more attractive than would the partnership.

The inclination of the tax advisor is therefore to seek means of avoiding double taxation. In order to do so, a tax advisor may recommend the formation of a partnership or a hybrid organization, such as a limited liability company. Within the corporate form, double taxation can be reduced by retention of earnings. In fact, if Jessica and Michael expected to reinvest all income in the business for a number of years, operating as a corporation might save them taxes. With income of $120,000, for example, the corporation would pay federal income tax of $29,050, representing less than 25% of its income. Jessica and Michael in all likelihood would have to pay considerably more in taxes if $120,000 in income were attributed to them, as would be the case if they were partners.

If earnings are to be distributed, the tax advisor will try to minimize the effect of double taxation by increasing the corporation's business deductions and reducing its taxable income. As we have noted, income is taxed both to the corporation and the shareholder when it is distributed to the shareholder as a dividend. If it is distributed to the shareholder in the form of a salary, it is still taxed to the shareholder, but it reduces the corporation's tax since it constitutes a deductible expense. The same is true of interest on a loan from shareholders. So, if the shareholder is an employee, she will have no need for dividends if the amount which would otherwise be distributed as a dividend is paid to her as a salary. Similarly, if part of her investment in the corporation is in the form of a bond or a note, the interest paid to her will be an acceptable substitute for dividends. This type of corporate structuring for tax purposes is tricky business, however. The Internal Revenue Service is alert to the possibility that a taxpayer may seek to disguise dividends as salary or interest and may challenge the corporation's asserted deductions.

2. S CORPORATIONS

An S corporation is a corporation which has elected to be taxed under the provisions of Subchapter S of the Internal Revenue Code and which pays no tax itself. Its income is taxed to the shareholders at their individual rates. While this bears resemblance to partnership taxation, there are sufficient differences to make it inaccurate to say that such corporation is taxed as a partnership. In short, an S corporation has all the corporate attributes without being subject to "double taxation" on the corporate earnings.

a. Operation of an S Corporation

To qualify for Subchapter S treatment, a corporation must be a domestic corporation and cannot have more than thirty-five shareholders. The shareholders themselves must be individuals, estates or qualified trusts. The corporation can have only one class of stock. Shares that have different voting rights may be considered as belonging to the same class as long as they are otherwise alike. Finally, the corporation must elect to be treated under Subchapter S. In order to make a Subchapter S election all of the shareholders of the corporation must consent to be taxed as an S corporation.

Generally, an S corporation is taxed in a flow-through approach based on the partnership model. Corporate income, losses and credits, flow through to shareholders on a per share basis. This means that income is allocated to a shareholder according to the number of shares held and the number of days during the year the shareholder owned her stock. In the earlier example, if the entity were an S Corporation, the tax consequences would be the same for Jessica and Michael as if it were a partnership; Jessica still would have taxable income of $15,000 and Michael would still have no taxable income and a $10,000 loss carryover to be taxed at their individual rates.

Another advantage of electing Subchapter S (assuming that the shareholders are active participants in the business so that they are not subject to the passive loss rules) is the ability to offset income from other sources by any loss generated by the corporation.

b. Termination of a Subchapter S Election

A Subchapter S election terminates if over any three year period more than 25 percent of the corporation's gross receipts constitute passive investment income. A Subchapter S election will also terminate if the number of shareholders exceeds thirty-five, or if any of the shareholders are nonresident aliens, or are not an individual, estate or qualified trust. Thus a transfer by an existing qualified shareholder to an unqualified entity or individual will automatically terminate the Subchapter S election. If a second class of stock is issued, the election will also be terminated. A Subchapter S also election can be revoked by the consent of holders of a majority of the corporation's stock.

Once the Subchapter S election is terminated or revoked, the corporation cannot make another Subchapter S election before the fifth taxable year beginning after the first year for which the termination or revocation was effective. If the IRS determines the termination was inadvertent or accidental and the disqualifying event is corrected within a reasonable time after discovery, then the corporation will not be disqualified.

3. LIMITED LIABILITY COMPANIES

Limited liability companies are becoming increasingly popular throughout the country because they represent a hybrid of the more appealing features of both the corporation and the partnership. The limited liability company affords to its members the limited liability characteristics of the corporation. From a tax standpoint, however, the limited liability company avoids the double-taxation snare of corporations. A limited liability company is taxed as a partnership. Additionally, the limited liability company is superior to the S corporation in several respects. For instance, in a limited liability company there are no limitations on the number and type of members.

Chapter 8

THE INCORPORATION PROCESS

PROBLEM
PRECISION TOOLS—PART IV

Jessica, Michael and Bernie have decided to operate Precision Tools as a corporation and have asked you to handle the incorporation process. You are now confronted with the following questions:

1. You have represented Michael in past business dealings, and it was at his suggestion that the three of them called upon you. All three have now asked you to handle the legal work in forming the corporation. Is there any reason why you should not proceed with this representation?

2. Assuming that you have selected Columbia as the place of incorporation, what are the formalities with which you must comply? Consider RMBCA §§ 2.01–2.07.

3. Assume you prepare the articles of incorporation, review them with all three parties, have them signed by the incorporator, and, since you are leaving town on vacation, you give them to Michael who agrees to file them the next day. He forgets to do so, but on that day two events occur:

    a. He places a large order for new office furniture from a local merchant for the account of the "corporation."

    b. The worker who delivers the merchandise slips on a slick surface on the "corporation's" premises which were not properly cleaned, and is injured. If the "corporation," for some reason is unable to pay for the merchandise or the injury, are Jessica, Michael, or Bernie personally liable? Consider the question under common law and RMBCA § 2.04. Read the Official Comment to RMBCA § 2.04. Contrast DGCL § 329.

4. As you are working on the incorporation papers, Michael calls to say that he has just talked with a supplier of important new equipment that the business will need and that will require special installation. The supplier can offer the company a special price on purchase and prompt installation if they sign a contract and begin work on Monday. Your clients want to go ahead. Your experience tells you

177

that it will be impossible to complete the incorporation of Precision Tools by that time, because some details need to be resolved. How should the contract be handled?

5. Should the business be incorporated in Columbia, in Delaware, or in some other jurisdiction?

6. The selection of the state of incorporation, having the consequences that it does, should cause us to reflect on the purpose of corporate law in a larger sense than the immediate impact on our clients. In that vein, consider the purposes of a corporation law:

   a. Is it designed to protect shareholders by imposing constraints on corporate managers? If so, what other constraints might achieve the same result?

   b. Is it designed to protect the best interests of the shareholders by giving maximum flexibility to corporate managers in running the business?

   c. Is it designed to allow forces of the market place to best protect the shareholders' interests? Which market places?

   d. Are there interests other than shareholders that the corporate law is intended to protect? What are those interests? How does, or how can, corporate law protect those interests?

   e. Is corporate law designed to reduce the transaction costs inherent in beginning a business venture by providing standard arrangements among the parties to the venture and facilitating private variations from those standards?

A. LAWYERS' PROFESSIONAL RESPONSIBILITIES: WHO IS THE CLIENT?

At first blush, determining who is the "client" would not seem to be a difficult task. An attorney-client relationship is either formed explicitly by a formal contractual agreement or implicitly by the client requesting, and the attorney performing, legal services for the client. In practice, however, a situation such as Precision Tools in which more than one person is requesting legal services, often arises and, when it does, the issues are more complex than might initially appear.

When Jessica, Michael and Bernie appear in the lawyer's office, why should the lawyer not incorporate their business? If all that were to be done were to comply with the simple mechanics described in Part B of this Chapter, there might be no reason why the lawyer should not perform the work. But if more is required, as it usually is, problems immediately arise. The parties often have no idea of what the legal structure of the business should consist or, indeed, whether the corporate form is most desirable for them. Issues such as the choice of securities, voting rights, and control (to name only a few) can and often should, if the parties wish, be resolved at the time of incorporation. These issues, unbeknownst to the parties, may create actual or potential conflicts between them, conflicts which will be clear to the lawyer. Moreover, when these conflicts have been identified, the parties may ask the lawyer to suggest the most desirable way of resolving them. How should the lawyer respond? To whom, if anyone, at this stage (before there even is a corporation), does the lawyer owe her loyalty?

These problems may be compounded if the enterprise is relatively small. The parties want to minimize their organizational expenses before the business has begun, and the cost of each party retaining her own lawyer at this stage may seem excessive to them. After all, the parties will say, all we want you, the lawyer, to do is to get us up and running and make sure that we won't have any major problems in the future. Why should we pay all that money to lawyers before we have even begun the business? Faced with these questions, a lawyer will have a natural tendency to proceed; whether she should is the subject of this section.

Given the frequency with which such a situation arises, it is surprising that there is relatively little guidance available to the lawyer. Consider the extent to which the following materials assist the lawyer and the unanswered questions that the lawyer must resolve for herself. Finally, bear in mind the practical consequences of the answer to the question of who is the client: only those who are clients can assert the attorney-client privilege, seek disqualification of the attorney in litigation because of the attorney's conflict of interest, or sue for malpractice.

AMERICAN BAR ASSOCIATION MODEL RULES OF PROFESSIONAL CONDUCT

(1983).

Rule 1.6 Confidentiality of Information

(a) A lawyer shall not reveal information relating to representation of a client unless the client consents after consultation, except for disclosures that are impliedly authorized in order to carry out the representation, and except as stated in paragraph (b).

(b) A lawyer may reveal such information to the extent the lawyer reasonably believes necessary:

(1) to prevent the client from committing a criminal act that the lawyer believes is likely to result in imminent death or substantial bodily harm; or

(2) to establish a claim or defense on behalf of the lawyer in a controversy between the lawyer and the client, to establish a defense to a criminal charge or civil claim against the lawyer based upon conduct in which the client was involved, or to respond to allegations in any proceeding concerning the lawyer's representation of the client.

COMMENT

The lawyer is part of a judicial system charged with upholding the law. One of the lawyer's functions is to advise clients so that they avoid any violation of the law in the proper exercise of their rights.

The observance of the ethical obligation of a lawyer to hold inviolate confidential information of the client not only facilitates the full development of facts essential to proper representation of the client but also encourages people to seek early legal assistance.

Almost without exception, clients come to lawyers in order to determine what their rights are and what is, in the maze of laws and regulations, deemed to be legal and correct. The common law recognizes that the client's confidences must be protected from disclosure. Based upon experience, lawyers know that almost all clients follow the advice given, and the law is upheld.

A fundamental principle in the client-lawyer relationship is that the lawyer maintain confidentiality of information relating to the representation. The client is thereby encouraged to communicate fully and frankly with the lawyer even as to embarrassing or legally damaging subject matter.

The principle of confidentiality is given effect in two related bodies of law, the attorney-client privilege (which includes the work product doctrine) in the law of evidence and the rule of confidentiality established in professional ethics. The attorney-client privilege applies in judicial and other proceedings in which a lawyer may be called as a witness or otherwise required to produce evidence concerning a client. The rule of client-lawyer confidentiality applies in situations other than those where evidence is sought from the lawyer through compulsion of law. The confidentiality rule applies not merely to matters communicated in confidence by the client but also to all information relating to the representation, whatever its source. A lawyer may not disclose such information except as authorized or required by the Rules of Professional Conduct or other law. See also Scope.

The requirement of maintaining confidentiality of information relating to representation applies to government lawyers who may disagree with the policy goals that their representation is designed to advance.

* * *

Disclosure Adverse to Client

The confidentiality rule is subject to limited exceptions. In becoming privy to information about a client, a lawyer may foresee that the client intends serious harm to another person. However, to the extent a lawyer is required or permitted to disclose a client's purposes, the client will be inhibited from revealing facts which would enable the lawyer to counsel against a wrongful course of action. The public is better protected if full and open communication by the client is encouraged than if it is inhibited.

Several situations must be distinguished.

First, the lawyer may not counsel or assist a client in conduct that is criminal or fraudulent. See Rule 1.2(d). Similarly, a lawyer has a duty under Rule 3.3(a)(4) not to use false evidence. This duty is essentially a special instance of the duty prescribed in Rule 1.2(d) to avoid assisting a client in criminal or fraudulent conduct.

Second, the lawyer may have been innocently involved in past conduct by the client that was criminal or fraudulent. In such a situation the lawyer has not violated Rule 1.2(d), because to "counsel or assist" criminal or fraudulent conduct requires knowing that the conduct is of that character.

Third, the lawyer may learn that a client intends prospective conduct that is criminal and likely to result in imminent death or substantial bodily harm. As stated in paragraph (b)(1), the lawyer has professional discretion to reveal information in order to prevent such consequences. The lawyer may make a disclosure in order to prevent homicide or serious bodily injury which the lawyer reasonably believes is intended by a client. It is very difficult for a lawyer to "know" when such a heinous purpose will actually be carried out, for the client may have a change of mind.

The lawyer's exercise of discretion requires consideration of such factors as the nature of the lawyer's relationship with the client and with those who might be injured by the client, the lawyer's own involvement in the transaction and factors that may extenuate the conduct in question. Where practical, the lawyer should seek to persuade the client to take suitable action. In any case, a disclosure adverse to the client's interest should be no greater than the lawyer reasonably believes necessary to the purpose. A lawyer's decision not to take preventive action permitted by paragraph (b)(1) does not violate this Rule.

* * *

Rule 1.7 Conflict of Interest: General Rule

(a) A lawyer shall not represent a client if the representation of that client will be directly adverse to another client, unless:

(1) the lawyer reasonably believes the representation will not adversely affect the relationship with the other client; and

(2) each client consents after consultation.

(b) A lawyer shall not represent a client if the representation of that client may be materially limited by the lawyer's responsibilities to another client or to a third person, or by the lawyer's own interests, unless:

(1) the lawyer reasonably believes the representation will not be adversely affected; and

(2) the client consents after consultation. ●

When representation of multiple clients in a single matter is undertaken, the consultation shall include explanation of the implications of the common representation and the advantages and risks involved.

COMMENT

Loyalty to a Client

Loyalty is an essential element in the lawyer's relationship to a client. An impermissible conflict of interest may exist before representation is undertaken, in which event the representation should be declined. If such a conflict arises after representation has been undertaken, the lawyer should withdraw from the representation. See Rule 1.16. Where more than one client is involved and the lawyer withdraws because a conflict arises after representation, whether the lawyer may continue to represent any of the clients is determined by Rule 1.9. See also Rule 2.2(c). As to whether a client-lawyer relationship exists or, having once been established, is continuing, see Comment to Rule 1.3 and Scope. * * *

Other Conflict Situations

Conflicts of interest in contexts other than litigation sometimes may be difficult to assess. Relevant factors in determining whether there is potential for adverse effect include the duration and intimacy of the lawyer's relationship with the client or clients involved, the functions being performed by the lawyer, the likelihood that actual conflict will arise and the likely prejudice to the client from the conflict if it does arise. The question is often one of proximity and degree.

For example, a lawyer may not represent multiple parties to a negotiation whose interests are fundamentally antagonistic to each other, but common representation is permissible where the clients are generally aligned in interest even though there is some difference of interest among them.

* * *

A lawyer for a corporation or other organization who is also a member of its board of directors should determine whether the responsibilities of the two roles may conflict. The lawyer may be called on to advise the corporation in matters involving actions of the directors. Consideration should be given to the frequency with which such situations may arise, the potential intensity of the conflict, the effect of the lawyer's resignation from the board and the possibility of the corporation's obtaining legal advice from another lawyer in such situations. If there is material risk that the dual role will compromise the lawyer's independence of professional judgment, the lawyer should not serve as a director.

Rule 1.13   Organization as Client

(a) A lawyer employed or retained by an organization represents the organization acting through its duly authorized constituents.

* * *

(d) In dealing with an organization's directors, officers, employees, members, shareholders or other constituents, a lawyer shall explain the identity of the client when it is apparent that the organization's interests are adverse to those of the constituents with whom the lawyer is dealing.

(e) A lawyer representing an organization may also represent any of its directors, officers, employees, members, shareholders or other constituents, subject to the provisions of rule 1.7. If the organization's consent to the dual representation is required by rule 1.7, the consent shall be given by an appropriate official of the organization other than the individual who is to be represented, or by the shareholders.

Comment
The Entity as the Client

An organizational client is a legal entity, but it cannot act except through its officers, directors, employees, shareholders and other constituents.

Officers, directors, employees and shareholders are the constituents of the corporate organizational client.   * * *

When one of the constituents of an organizational client communicates with the organization's lawyer in that person's organizational capacity, the communication is protected by Rule 1.6.   * * * This does not mean, however, that constituents of an organizational client are the clients of the lawyer. The lawyer may not disclose to such constituents information relating to the representation except for disclosures explicitly or impliedly authorized by the organizational client in order to carry out the representation or as otherwise permitted by Rule 1.6.

* * *

Clarifying the Lawyer's Role

There are times when the organization's interest may be or become adverse to those of one or more of its constituents. In such circumstances the lawyer should advise any constituent, whose interest the lawyer finds adverse to that of the organization of the conflict or potential conflict of interest, that the lawyer cannot represent such constituent, and that such person may wish to obtain independent representation. Care must be taken to assure that the individual understands that, when there is such adversity of interest, the lawyer for the organization cannot provide legal representation for that constituent individual, and that discussion between the lawyer for the organization and the individual may not be privileged.

Whether such a warning should be given by the lawyer for the organization to any constituent individual may turn on the facts of each case.

Dual Representation

Paragraph (e) recognizes that a lawyer for an organization may also represent a principal officer or major shareholder.

———

Model Rule 1.13 and EC 5–18 of the Model Code of Professional Responsibility which is followed in some jurisdictions that have not adopted some form of the Model Rules adopt the "entity theory" of the corporation. Under that theory, the lawyer represents the corporation, and not its officers, directors, employees and shareholders. The corporation is an individual, standing apart from its constituents, and hence, any attorney hired to represent the corporation represents the corporation as a distinct legal entity and not its constituents. As such, the entity theory recognizes the corporation's lawyers, along with its officers and directors, as agents of the entity. The Disciplinary Rules of the Model Code do not adopt the entity theory. They rely on the more general rules concerning confidentiality and conflicts of interest. See DR 4–101, DR 5–101, DR 5–105.

The entity theory presupposes that the constituent parts of the corporation are essentially different (and identifiable) people; it appears to adopt the paradigm of the publicly-held corporation. Where, however, the corporation is in the process of being formed, or where the same people are likely to constitute all or a majority of the stockholders, directors and officers (as in a close corporation), the theory may present serious problems.

JESSE BY REINECKE v. DANFORTH
169 Wis.2d 229, 485 N.W.2d 63 (1992).

[In 1985, Drs. Danforth and Ullrich were part of a group of twenty-three physicians who retained Douglas Flygt (Flygt), an attorney with the law firm of De Witt, Porter, Huggett, Schumacher & Morgan, S.C. (De Witt). The physicians asked De Witt to assist them in creating a corporation for the purpose of purchasing and operating a magnetic resonance imaging machine (MRI). Flygt incorporated MRIGM in 1986 and continued to serve as its corporate counsel. The twenty-three physicians became the shareholders of MRIGM, and Dr. Danforth became president of the corporation.

In May 1988, the Jesse family sued Drs. Danforth and Ullrich for medical malpractice unrelated to the activities of MRIGM. The plaintiffs retained Eric Farnsworth, also an attorney with De Witt. Farnsworth had conducted an internal conflict of interest check at De Witt, but had not found the defendants listed as clients of the firm. Drs.

Danforth and Ullrich moved to disqualify De Witt, alleging that the firm had a conflict of interest. They argued that they were clients of De Witt because of Flygt's pre-incorporation of the twenty-three physicians and because of other advice that Flygt had provided to the defendants.]

DAY, JUSTICE:

* * *

We begin with SCR 20:1.7, the conflict of interest rule [which parallels Model Rule 1.7]. Subsection (a) states: "A lawyer shall not represent a client if the representation of that client will be directly adverse to another, unless. * * *" Thus, the question is, who did or does DeWitt represent, *i.e.*, who were and are DeWitt's clients?

It is undisputed that DeWitt, through Farnsworth, represents Jean Jesse in this case. What remains disputed is whether Drs. Danforth or Ullrich were ever or are currently clients of DeWitt.

* * *

The entity rule contemplates that where a lawyer represents a corporation, the client is the corporation, not the corporation's constituents. * * *

[T]he clear purpose of the entity rule was to enhance the corporate lawyer's ability to represent the best interests of the corporation without automatically having the additional and potentially conflicting burden of representing the corporation's constituents.

If a person who retains a lawyer for the purpose of organizing an entity is considered the client, however, then any subsequent representation of the corporate entity by the very lawyer who incorporated the entity would automatically result in dual representation. This automatic dual representation, however, is the very situation the entity rule was designed to protect corporate lawyers against.

We thus provide the following guideline: where (1) a person retains a lawyer for the purpose of organizing an entity and (2) the lawyer's involvement with that person is directly related to that incorporation and (3) such entity is eventually incorporated, the entity rule applies retroactively such that the lawyer's pre-incorporation involvement with the person is deemed to be representation of the entity, not the person.

In essence, the retroactive application of the entity rule simply gives the person who retained the lawyer the status of being a corporate constituent during the period before actual incorporation, as long as actual incorporation eventually occurred.

This standard also applies to privileged communications under SCR 20:1.6. Thus, where the above standard is met, communications between the retroactive constituent and the corporation are protected under SCR 20:1.6. And, it is the corporate entity, not the retroactive constituent, that holds the privilege. This tracks the Comment to SCR 20:1.13 which states in part: "When one of the constituents of an organizational client communicates with the organization's lawyer in that person's organizational capacity, the communication is protected by Rule 1.6."

However, where the person who retained the lawyer provides information to the lawyer not directly related to the purpose of organizing an entity, then it is the person, not the corporation which holds the privilege for that communication.

Applying the above standard to the case at hand, we observe that the evidence cited and quoted by the defendants demonstrates that the above standard is met and that DeWitt represented MRIGM, not Drs. Danforth or Ullrich.

For example, defendants Drs. Danforth and Ullrich point to Flygt's affidavit wherein Flygt states that he was contacted *"to assist a group of physicians in Milwaukee in organizing an entity to own and operate one or more * * * facilities * * *."* (Emphasis added.)

Dr. Danforth points to a January 29, 1986 letter from Flygt to Dr. Danforth wherein Flygt stated:

> I would suggest that the *corporation* come to a quick resolution of the subchapter S corporation question. * * * (Emphasis added).

Drs. Danforth and Ullrich point to a May 5, 1986 letter from Flygt to Dr. Danforth which states that " to the extent that there are common expenses of the partnership, such as drafting documents, etc., *it would be appropriate to have the entity pay those fees while the attorneys fees of each individual group are its own cost."* (Emphasis added).

[Drs.] Danforth and Ullrich point to a May 13, 1987 memorandum Flygt wrote to the "Shareholders" of MRIGM. This memorandum begins, "The purpose of this letter is to advise you as to a decision *which must be made by the corporation* at this time." (Emphasis added). * * *

This evidence overwhelmingly supports the proposition that the purpose of Flygt's pre-incorporation involvement was to provide advice with respect to organizing an entity and the Flygt's involvement was directly related to the incorporation. Moreover, that MRIGM was eventually incorporated is undisputed.

In addition, with respect to Flygt's advice concerning the structure of the entity, the fact that a particular corporate structure may benefit the shareholders or the fact that there was communication between Flygt and the shareholders concerning such structuring does not mean that Drs. Danforth and Ullrich were the clients of the law firm. Again, the very purpose of the entity rule is to preclude such automatic dual representation.

* * *

Drs. Danforth and Ullrich also contend that they provided certain confidential information to attorney Flygt that should disqualify DeWitt under SCR 20:1.6, the confidential information rule. Defendants point to questionnaires Flygt provided to the physicians involved in the MRI project which inquire, in part, as to the physicians' personal finances and their involvement in pending litigation.

Because MRIGM, not the physician shareholders, was and is the client of DeWitt, and because the communications between Drs. Danforth and Ullrich were directly related to the purpose of organizing MRIGM, we conclude that Drs. Danforth or Ullrich cannot claim the privilege of confidentiality.

* * *

———

Jesse leaves open the question of whether the entity theory is retroactive if the pre-incorporation activities are not successful. Does the same rationale apply to this situation? A related issue is presented when, during the pre-incorporation stage each party retains her own lawyer, with each lawyer representing her individual client and no lawyer representing the corporation directly. If, during the initial stages of operation, after the corporation has been only formally created, a conflict arises, it would be technically correct to say that any of the lawyers represents the corporation. However, commentators argue that it may be more realistic to say that each lawyer continues to represent her individual client and that only when the corporation begins to exist in a truer sense should one say that any of the lawyers may represent the corporation. Geoffrey C. Hazard, Jr. & William Hodes, The Law of Lawyering: A Handbook on the Model Rules of Professional Conduct 398 (2d ed. 1990).

At least one court has taken a different view of the entity theory. In Opdyke v. Kent Liquor Mart, 40 Del.Ch. 316, 181 A.2d 579 (1962), the plaintiff, one of three original shareholders, asserted that the lawyer who incorporated the company breached his duty to the plaintiff by purchasing stock in the corporation from the other stockholders, a transaction adverse to the plaintiff, who had wanted to buy the stock himself. In holding that the lawyer had breached his duty to the plaintiff, the court acknowledged the entity theory, but stated:

> * * * [I]n determining the existence or non-existence of the important relationship of attorney and client a broader approach is required. The question is, What in fact was the relationship between Brown [the attorney] and the three men? * * *
>
> It is clear to us that Brown was, at the beginning of the venture, and also at its end, the attorney for the three men. The corporation was simply a form for the carrying on of a joint venture. For our present purpose Brown must be regarded as the attorney for three

joint adventurers. When they fell out he undertook to resolve their differences. He very properly told them that he could not represent any one of them against another. This was so, not because of the corporate form of the enterprise, but because of the well-settled rule that if a lawyer is retained by two clients and they get into a dispute he cannot ordinarily represent either. Indeed, Brown's justifiable insistence on this neutrality was a recognition, conscious or not, of his fiduciary duty to all three men. That he was acting in his capacity as a lawyer admits of no doubt. Why were they discussing the matter in his office if not to obtain his help and counsel in their difficulty? * * *

But by these very acts he had emphasized his role of counselor to the three men. In suggesting the settlement he was discharging a characteristic function of the legal adviser. He could not escape the fiduciary obligations of this relationship by insisting that he was acting only for a corporation.

181 A.2d at 583–4.

The modern test for determining who is or is not the client is the "reasonable expectations" test, as set forth in Westinghouse Elec. Corp. v. Kerr–McGee Corp., 580 F.2d 1311 (7th Cir.1978). Under that test, if an attorney leads an individual or entity to believe that they are a client and the belief is reasonable under the circumstances, an attorney-client relationship will be created, whether or not the client pays the attorney any money or enters into a formal retainer agreement. Because of courts' reliance on the entity theory, the reasonable expectations test is usually limited to close corporations.

Rosman v. Shapiro, 653 F.Supp. 1441 (S.D.N.Y.1987), involved the disqualification of counsel for the corporation in litigation between the corporation's two shareholders. The court noted that although normally, corporate counsel does not also become counsel for the shareholders "where, as here, the corporation is a close corporation consisting of only two shareholders with equal interests in the corporation, it is indeed reasonable for each shareholder to believe that the corporate counsel is in effect his own individual attorney." Id. at 1445. In so finding, the court relied upon evidence which established that Rosman and Shapiro jointly consulted the attorney for legal advice concerning the creation of a corporation through which they would conduct their business. Apparently relying upon the belief that both partners and their partnership are jointly represented by the partnership attorney, the court held that "it would exalt form over substance to conclude that [the attorneys] only represented [the company], solely because Rosman and Shapiro chose to deal * * * through a corporate entity." Id.

After deciding that the shareholders were both clients of the "corporation's" attorneys, the court held that the law firm would not be disqualified pursuant to Canon 4 of the former American Bar Association Code of Professional Responsibility (relating to confidential information). Canon 4 was inapplicable because, "in this case, Rosman could not reasonably have expected that any information imparted to [the law firm] would have been withheld from Shapiro during the course of that representation because [the law firm] represented Shapiro and Rosman jointly. Given the prior joint representation, [the law firm] simply could not have possessed any information which Rosman intended to be held in "confidence' or as a "secret' from Shapiro." Id. at 1446.

The court ultimately did disqualify the law firm pursuant to Canon 9 (relating to the appearance of professional impropriety). Such a decision was warranted because "the obvious appearance of impropriety stemming from [the law firm]'s representation of Shapiro against its former client, Rosman" was too great. Id. The court concluded by noting that a contrary holding "would undermine the loyalty and trust upon which the attorney-client relationship is based." Id.

Another factor which some courts consider is how closely held the corporation is and whether the corporation resembles a partnership in function. This may be an important factor because some courts have held that a lawyer representing a partnership, which in itself may not be recognized as a legal person, "represents all the partners as to matters of partnership business" as joint clients. Wortham & Van Liew v. Superior Court (Clubb), 188 Cal.App.3d 927, 932, 233 Cal.Rptr. 725, 728 (1987). If then, a court determines that a corporation functions, at its heart, as a partnership (whatever that difference may be), it may also decide that the attorney represents the corporation's constituents.

Such was the case in Hecht v. Superior Court (Ferguson), 192 Cal.App.3d 560, 237 Cal.Rptr. 528 (2d Dist.1987), involving the joint client exception to the attorney-client privilege. The court noted that prior to incorporation, the parties had run the business for many years as if it were a partnership and had viewed each other as partners. In addition, they had formed the corporation solely for tax reasons and not to change the nature of their working relationship. Indeed, as the court noted, the new corporation had been "formed as a statutory close corporation, which is akin to a partnership in its informality." 192 Cal.App.3d at 565, 237 Cal.Rptr. at 531. Under those circumstances, it was reasonable for the plaintiff to believe that she was being represented by the "corporation's" attorney. But see, Hoiles v. Superior Court (Freedom Newspapers), 157 Cal.App.3d 1192, 204 Cal.Rptr. 111 (1984) in which the court found that the existence of a close corporation did not provide a basis for an exception to the attorney-client privilege.

Courts also have considered other factors in determining the existence of the attorney-client relationship. One of these is the capacity in which the constituent acted when dealing with the attorney. If the court determines that the constituent sought legal advice on personal affairs or that the attorney represented her in a personal matter, the court may be more likely to find that a attorney-client relationship exists. See Bobbit v. Victorian House, Inc., 545 F.Supp. 1124, 1126–27 (N.D.Ill.1982). Likewise, the absence of such personal representation may indicate to the court that no attorney-client relationship exists. See e.g., Professional Serv. Industr. v. Kimbrell, 758 F.Supp. 676, 682–683 (D.Kan.1991); Wayland v. Shore Lobster & Shrimp Corp., 537 F.Supp. 1220, 1223 (S.D.N.Y.1982). Often, in examining the nature of the relationship, the courts will look to any previous association between the possible client and the attorney in order to determine whether there was any past personal representation before the lawyer became counsel for the corporation. See *Hecht,* supra.

The significance of who paid the lawyer's fees is an issue upon which the courts seem divided. Some courts have stated that the payment of the attorney's fees by the corporation and not the potential client does not disprove the existence of the attorney-client relationship. See e.g., Westinghouse Elec. Corp. v. Kerr–McGee Corp., 580 F.2d at 1317 and In re Brownstein, 288 Or. 83, 602 P.2d 655, 656 (1979). Other courts have implied that the corporation's payment is inconsistent with the conclusion that an attorney-client relationship exists between the corporate counsel and the individual. See e.g., *Wayland,* 537 F.Supp. at 1223 and Dalrymple v. National Bank & Trust Co., 615 F.Supp. 979, 983 (W.D.Mich. 1985). Still other courts have stated that the method of payment, while not dispositive of the existence of the attorney-client relationship, may be indicative of who the client is. *Hecht,* supra.

A court also may find that it was unreasonable for the constituent to believe himself to be a client if, at the time of the alleged representation, he was actually a "target" or "potential adversary" of the attorney in matters regarding the latter's representation of the entity. In *Dalrymple,* the court found that no attorney-client relationship had ever arisen between the director/defendants and the bank's attorney. There, the law firm was hired by a committee formed by the board of directors to investigate claims by a shareholder that the officers and directors were mismanaging the bank. Because the law firm was retained to represent the bank exclusively and because the directors were advised to seek their own, separate counsel, the court found that it was not reasonable for the directors to believe they were clients of the law firm. Therefore, no attorney-client relationship was formed, and the firm was not disqualified from representing a new client against the directors.

Even if no attorney-client relationship has been established between the constituents and the closely held corporation's attorney, some courts have held that the attorney may have a fiduciary duty to each of the individual shareholders. Whether such a duty exists can be either a question of law or of fact. If such a fiduciary relationship is found to exist, the corporate attorney could be responsible to a third party for a variety of duties, including negligence or fraud. See Skarbrevik v. Cohen, England & Whitfield, 231 Cal.App.3d 692, 282 Cal.Rptr. 627 (1991); Fassihi v. Sommers, Schwartz, Silver, Schwartz & Tyler, P.C., 107 Mich.App. 509, 309 N.W.2d 645, 648 (1981).

See generally, Note, An Expectations Approach to Client Identity, 106 Harv. L. Rev. 687 (1993); Peter Jarvis, Knowing Who Is and *Isn't* Your Client, The Am. Law., September 1991, at 41; Developments in the

Law—Conflicts of Interest In the Legal Profession, 94 Harv. L. Rev. 1244 (1981).

GEOFFREY C. HAZARD, JR., ETHICS IN THE PRACTICE OF LAW
58, 60–61, 63–68 (1978).

The problem of deciding who is the client arises when a lawyer supposes that a conflict of interest prevents him from acting for all the people involved in a situation. That is, if the interests of the potential clients were in harmony, or could be harmonized, no choice would have to be made between them and the lawyer could act for all. When the lawyer feels that he can act for all, it can be said simply that he has several clients at the same time. When the clients are all involved in a single transaction, however, the lawyer's responsibility is rather different from what it is when he represents several clients in transactions that have nothing to do with each other. This difference is suggested by the proposition that a lawyer serving more than one client in a single transaction represents "the situation."

The term is the invention of Louis D. Brandeis, Justice of the United States Supreme Court and before that practitioner of law in Boston. It emerged in a hearing in which Brandeis's professional ethics as a lawyer had been questioned.

* * *

The transactions complained of included the following: First, Brandeis had at one time represented one party in a transaction, later represented someone else in a way that impinged on that transaction. Second, he had acted in situations where those he served had conflicting interests, for example by putting together the bargain between parties to a business deal. Third, he had acted for a family business and continued so to act after a falling out among the family required reorganization of the business arrangement. Fourth, over a course of several years he had mediated and adjusted interests of the owners and creditors of a business in such a way as to keep the business from floundering.

The objections to Brandeis's conduct in all these situations were twofold. One was that his conduct was unethical per se because he represented conflicting interests. The other was that he had not adequately made clear to the clients that their interests were in conflict. On the second point, Brandeis acknowledged that at least in some instances he may not have adequately explained the situation to the clients and adequately defined his role as he saw it. Having acknowledged this, he defended his conduct not only on the ground of its being common practice but also on the ground that it was right. In the instances questioned, he said, he did not regard himself as being lawyer for one of the parties to the exclusion of the others, but as "lawyer for the situation." Eventually, the charge did not so much collapse as become submerged in concessions from other reputable lawyers that they had often done exactly as Brandeis.

* * *

"Situations" can arise in different ways. Two or more people who have not been clients may bring a "situation" to a lawyer. Sometimes a client who has a lawyer will become involved in a transaction with a third party who does not, and the transaction is one that ought to be handled as a "situation." Most commonly, perhaps, a lawyer may find himself in a "situation" involving clients that he has previously served in separate transactions or relationships. In this circumstances the lawyer, if he properly can, will intercede before the transaction between his clients reaches counterposed positions. Doing so is in his interests, because that way he can retain both clients.

Having a lawyer act for the situation is also in the clients' interests, if adjustment on fair terms is possible, because head-on controversy is expensive and aggravating. A lawyer who failed to avoid a head-on controversy, given reasonable opportunity to do so, will have failed in what his clients generally regard as one of his chief functions-"preventive" legal assistance.

If Brandeis was wrong, then "lawyering for the situation" is marginally illicit professional conduct because it violates the principle of unqualified loyalty to client. But if Brandeis was right, and the record of good practitioners testifies to that conclusion, then what is required is not interdiction of "lawyering for the situation" but reexamination of what is meant by loyalty to client. That is, loyalty to client, like loyalty to country, may take different forms.

It is not easy to say exactly what a "lawyer for the situation" does. Clearly, his functions vary with specific circumstances. But there are common threads. The beginning point is that no other lawyer is immediately involved. Hence, the lawyer is no one's partisan and, at least up to a point, everyone's confidant. He can be the only person who knows the whole situation. He is an analyst of the relationship between the clients, in that he undertakes to discern the needs, fears, and expectations of each and to discover the concordances among them. He is an interpreter, translating inarticulate or exaggerated claims and forewarnings into temperate and mutually intelligible terms of communication. He can contribute historical perspective, objectivity, and foresight into the parties' assessment of the situation. He can discourage escalation of conflict and recruitment of outside allies. He can articulate general principles and common custom as standards by which the parties can examine their respective claims. He is advocate, mediator, entrepreneur, and judge, all in one. He could be said to be playing God.

Playing God is a tricky business. It requires skill, nerve, detachment, compassion, ingenuity, and the capacity to sustain confidence. When mishandled, it generates the bitterness and recrimination that results when a deep trust has been betrayed. Perhaps above all, it requires good judgment as to when such intercession can be carried off without unfairly subordinating the interests of one of the parties or having later to abort the mission.

When a relationship between the clients is amenable to "situation" treatment, giving it that treatment is perhaps the best service a lawyer can render to anyone. It approximates the ideal forms of intercession suggested by the models of wise parent or village elder. It provides adjustment of difference upon a wholistic view of the situation rather than bilaterally opposing ones. It rests on implicit principles of decision that express commonly shared ideals in behavior rather than strict legal right. The basis of decision is mutual assent and not external compulsion. The orientation in time tends to be a hopeful view of the future rather than an angry view of the past. It avoids the loss of personal autonomy that results when each side commits his cause to his own advocate. It is the opposite of "going to law."

One would think that the role of "lawyer for the situation" would have been idealized by the bar in parity with the roles of partisan advocate and confidential adviser. The fact that it has not been may itself be worth exploring.

It is clear that a "lawyer for the situation" has to identify clearly his role as such, a requirement that Brandeis conceded he might not always have fulfilled. But beyond saying that he will undertake to represent the best interests of all, a lawyer cannot say specifically what he will do or what each of the clients should do in the situation. (If the outcome of the situation were clearly foreseeable, presumably the lawyer's intercession would be unnecessary.) Moreover, he cannot define his role in the terms of the direction of his effort, for his effort will not be vectored outward toward third persons but will aim at an interaction among the clients. Hence, unlike advocacy or legal counselling involving a single client, lawyering for a situation is not provided with a structure of goals and constraints imposed from outside. The lawyer and the clients must create that structure for themselves, with the lawyer being an active participant. And like the other participants he cannot reveal all that is on his mind or all that he suspects the others may have on their minds, except as doing so aids movement of the situation along lines that seem productive.

A lawyer can proceed in this role only if the clients trust him and, equally important, he trusts himself. Trust is by definition ineffable. It is an acceptance of another's act without demanding that its bona fides be objectively provable; to demand its proof is to confess it does not exist. It is a relationship that is uncomfortable for the client but perhaps even more so for the lawyer. Experienced as he is with the meanness that people can display to each other, why should the lawyer not doubt his own susceptibility to the same failing? But trust is involved also in the role of confidential adviser and advocate. Why should lawyers regard their own trustworthiness as more vulnerable in those roles than in the role of "lawyer for the situation"?

Perhaps it is because the legal profession has succeeded in defining the roles of confidential adviser and advocate in ways that substantially reduce the burden of being trustworthy in these roles. The confidential adviser is told that he may not act to disclose anything about the client, except an announced intention to commit a crime. Short of this extremity, the rules of role have it that the counsellor has no choices to make between the interests of his client and the interest of others. His commitment is to the client alone. Correlatively, the advocate is told that he may assert any claim on behalf of a client except one based on fabricated evidence or one empty of any substance at all. Short of this extremity, the advocate also has no choices to make.

The "lawyer for the situation," on the other hand, has choices to make that obviously can go against the interests of one client or another, as the latter perceives it. A lawyer who assumes to act a intercessor has to evoke complete confidence that he will act justly in the circumstances. This is to perform the role of the administered justice itself, but without the constraints inherent in that process (such as the fact that the rules are written down, that they are administered by independent judges, and that outcomes have to be justified by references to reason and precedent). The role of lawyer for the situation therefore may be too prone to abuse to be explicitly sanctioned. A person may be entrusted with it only if he knows that in the event of miscarriage he will have no protection from the law. In this respect, acting as lawyer for the situation can be thought of as similar to a doctor's "authority" to terminate the life of a hopeless patient: It can properly be undertaken only if it will not be questioned afterwards. To this extent Brandeis's critics may have been right.

Yet it seems possible to define the role of intercessor, just as it has been possible to define the role of the trustee or guardian. The role could be defined by contrast with those of confidential counsellor and advocate, perhaps to the advantage of clarity in defining all three. At minimum, a recognition of the role of lawyer for the situation could result in a clearer perception by both clients and lawyers of one very important and socially estimable function that lawyers can perform and do perform.

B. THE PROCESS OF INCORPORATION

The process of forming a corporation is simple and quick. Although the procedure differs slightly from state to state, the provisions of RMBCA §§ 2.01–2.04 illustrate the procedure generally required.

The organization is formally accomplished by an "incorporator" who, after incorporation, plays no other role in the corporation. The incorporator signs and files the articles of incorporation with the Secretary of State or another designated official, and in some cases also files with a county official in the county where the principal place of business *Filing* of the corporation in that state will be located. Sometimes the corporation will not have a place of business in the state, in which case the registered address will function as the office where service of process or other official notice is sent.

The drafting of the articles of incorporation may be a relatively complex undertaking because the promoters wish to embody some or all of the terms of a complex arrangement in the articles. On the other hand, it is possible, and probably more common, to create a corporation with a simple, one page document. The filing of the articles of incorporation is accompanied by the payment of a fee, part of which is usually calculated on the basis of the number of authorized shares or the aggregate legal capital of the company, as is more specifically described in Chapter 9. Note the minimal filing requirements contained in RMBCA § 1.20.

In Model Act jurisdictions, formal corporate existence commences with the filing of the articles of incorporation with state officials. RMBCA § 2.03. In some other states, the corporation's existence commences with the issuance of a certificate of incorporation by the Secretary of State or other official.

After the corporation has come into legal existence, the statute requires that an organizational meeting be held, either by the incorporators, who select the first members of the board of directors, or, where the initial board is named in the articles of incorporation, by the board *BD. of directors* members so named. RMBCA § 2.05. At its first meeting, the board typically accomplishes a number of standard tasks, including the election of additional members, if any, to the board, the adoption of by-laws, the appointment of officers, the adoption of a corporate seal, the designation of a bank as depository for corporate funds, and often the sale of stock to the initial shareholders. You should review the sample by-laws and sample minutes of an organizational meeting of the board of directors that are included in West Selected Corporation and Partnership Statutes, Regulations and Forms. See also, RMBCA § 2.06.

In many cases, the routine legal work associated with the incorporation process is not performed directly by the attorney but, under the attorney's instruction, by a corporation service company which performs the clerical work for a relatively modest fee. The result is a standard form of corporation, not a handcrafted one, but one that is often sufficient for ordinary situations. In addition to providing "standard" articles of incorporation, by-laws, and forms of stock certificate and handling the filing of the necessary documents with the state, service companies perform a variety of other routine tasks such as handling the qualification of the corporation to do business in other jurisdictions, acting as "registered agent" for the corporation, and assisting in the filing of annual and other reports required by the jurisdiction of incorporation and the states in which the corporation is registered as a foreign corporation. On the doors of the Wilmington, Delaware offices of the major service companies there can be found a veritable "who's who" of American industry.

C. DEFECTIVE INCORPORATION

1. AT COMMON LAW

Under modern statutes, the incorporation process is extremely simple, and there should be no reason for doing it incorrectly. Nevertheless, a slip occasionally occurs (more frequently under older statutes) and the intended corporation does not come into legal existence—at least not when the parties expected. Defects can arise from a wide variety of circumstances. The incorporators may have neglected to make any filing at all, which is the most serious omission, or they may have filed but made a relatively small error, e.g., improper notarization, shortfall on the filing fee, a neglected signature or the like. They may have failed to make a required second filing, e.g., to file with both the state and county where the principal office is to be located. Most of these defects are technical in the most Pickwickian sense; they go to the heart of nothing (which is why the RMBCA has eliminated many prior technical requirements). Does not "justice" demand that third parties be denied access to the personal resources of the shareholders should the business become unable to pay its debts, if: (1) the investors in the would-be corporation believed that they had taken all the steps necessary to create a corporation and had instructed their lawyer to file the necessary papers; (2) the lawyer thought she had filed all the necessary papers; and (3) the persons with whom the organization dealt believed they were doing business with a corporation and expected to look only to that organization for payment of any debt? Of course, there is some state interest in having parties comply with the formalities required for incorporation, but the threat to that interest seems remote when the failure of the parties to comply with some technical requirement was inadvertent. Acting on this perception, courts of equity developed the concept that the business association could, in a proper case, be a *"de facto"* corporation, even if it was not a corporation *"de jure."* Courts also developed the concept of *corporation by estoppel* to achieve results deemed "just" where the de facto corporation doctrine could not be used. Henry Winthrop Ballantine, Manual of Corporation Law and Practice 92 (1930) states:

> The so-called estoppel that arises to deny corporate capacity does not depend on the presence of the technical elements of the equitable estoppel, viz, misrepresentations and change of position in reliance thereon, but on the nature of the relations contemplated, that one who has recognized the organization as a corporation in business dealings should not be allowed to quibble or raise immaterial issues on matters which do not concern him in the slightest degree or affect his substantial rights.

CRANSON v. INTERNATIONAL BUSINESS MACHINES CORP.

234 Md. 477, 200 A.2d 33 (1964).

[handwritten: IBM is estopped to deny corp. Cranston not liable for balance]

HORNEY, JUDGE.

On the theory that the Real Estate Service Bureau was neither a *de jure* nor a *de facto* corporation and that Albion C. Cranson, Jr., was a partner in the business conducted by the Bureau and as such was personally liable for its debts, the International Business Machines Corporation brought this action against Cranson for the balance due on electric typewriters purchased by the Bureau. At the same time it moved for summary judgment and supported the motion by affidavit. In due course, Cranson filed a general issue plea and an affidavit in opposition to summary judgment in which he asserted in effect that the Bureau was a *de facto* corporation and that he was not personally liable for its debts.

The agreed statement of facts shows that in April 1961, Cranson was asked to invest in a new business corporation which was about to be created. Towards this purpose he met with other interested individuals and an attorney and agreed to purchase stock and become an officer and director. Thereafter, upon being advised by the attorney that the corporation had been formed under the laws of Maryland, he paid for and received a stock certificate evidencing ownership of shares in the corporation, and was shown the corporate seal and minute book. The business of the new venture was conducted as if it were a corporation, through corporate bank accounts, with auditors maintaining corporate books and records, and under a lease entered into by the corporation for the office from which it operated its business. Cranson was elected president and all transactions conducted by him for the corporation, including the dealings with I.B.M., were made as an officer of the corporation. At no time did he assume any personal obligation or pledge his individual credit to I.B.M. Due to an oversight on the part of the attorney, of which Cranson was not aware, the certificate of incorporation, which had been signed and acknowledged prior to May 1, 1961, was not filed until November 24, 1961. Between May 17 and November 8, the Bureau purchased eight typewriters from I.B.M., on account of which partial payments were made, leaving a balance due of $4,333.40, for which this suit was brought.

[handwritten margin note: Held as Corp.]

Although a question is raised as to the propriety of making use of a motion for summary judgment as the means of determining the issues presented by the pleadings, we think the motion was appropriate. Since there was no genuine dispute as to the material facts, the only question was whether I.B.M. was entitled to judgment as a matter of law. The trial court found that it was, but we disagree.

The fundamental question presented by the appeal is whether an officer of a defectively incorporated association may be subjected to personal liability under the circumstances of this case. We think not. *[handwritten: I]*

Traditionally, two doctrines have been used by the courts to clothe an officer of a defectively incorporated association with the corporate attribute of limited liability. The first, often referred to as the doctrine of *de facto* corporations, has been applied in those cases where there are elements showing: (1) the existence of law authorizing incorporation; (2) an effort in good faith to incorporate under the existing law; and (3) actual user or exercise of corporate powers. The second, the doctrine of estoppel to deny the corporate existence, is generally employed where the person seeking to hold the officer personally liable has contracted or otherwise dealt with the association in such a manner as to recognize and in effect admit its existence as a corporate body.

* * *

I.B.M. contends that the failure of the Bureau to file its certificate of incorporation debarred *all* corporate existence. But, in spite of the fact that the omission might have prevented the Bureau from being either a corporation *de jure* or *de facto,* we think that I.B.M. having dealt with the Bureau as if it were a corporation and relied on its credit rather than that of Cranson, is estopped to assert that the Bureau was not incorporated at the time the typewriters were purchased. In 1 Clark and Marshall, Private Corporations, § 89, it is stated:

> The doctrine in relation to estoppel is based upon the ground that it would generally be inequitable to permit the corporate existence of an association to be denied by persons who have represented it to be a corporation, or held it out as a corporation, or by any persons who have recognized it as a corporation by dealing with it as such; and by the overwhelming weight of authority, therefore, a person may be estopped to deny the legal incorporation of an association which is not even a corporation *de facto*.

In cases similar to the one at bar, involving a failure to file articles of incorporation, the courts of other jurisdictions have held that where one has recognized the corporate existence of an association, he is estopped to assert the contrary with respect to a claim arising out of such dealings.

Since I.B.M. is estopped to deny the corporate existence of the Bureau, we hold that Cranson was not liable for the balance due on account of the typewriters.

Judgment reversed; the appellee to pay the costs.

2. THE IMPACT OF THE REVISED MODEL BUSINESS CORPORATION ACT

The de facto corporation and corporation by estoppel doctrines created, in the eyes of some commentators at least, "uncertainties" about corporate existence, although it is by no means certain what harm these uncertainties did to anyone. In the typical situation, of which *Cranson* is a good example, the plaintiff must be pleasantly surprised to find that what he thought was a corporation was never validly incorporated. The de facto corporation doctrine only restores the plaintiff to the position which he originally anticipated. But the desire for predictability is strongly felt by those who plan business transactions. Sections 56 and 146 of the previous version of the Model Act reflected the legislative attempt to provide this certainty. Those sections were interpreted in Robertson v. Levy, 197 A.2d 443 (D.C.App.1964) to have abolished the de facto corporation and corporation by estoppel doctrines. Levy and Robertson had entered into a contract under which Levy was to form a corporation to purchase Robertson's business. Levy filed articles of incorporation and six days later Robertson transferred his business to the "corporation" which gave its note in exchange. In the meantime, however, the articles of incorporation had been returned as defective, and refiled, but the certificate, denoting official corporateness, was not issued until nine days after the delivery of the note. The company later failed, and Robertson sued Levy on the note, which he had signed as "president" of the "corporation."

After reviewing the historical development of de facto corporation and corporation by estoppel doctrines, the court concluded that the previously-cited sections of the Model Act, which had been adopted in the District of Columbia, were intended "to eliminate problems inherent in the de jure, de facto and, estoppel concepts." Courts were thus no longer to inquire into equities but were to recognize corporate existence only when the appropriate authorities have issued a certificate of incorporation; individuals who presume to act as a corporation are jointly and severally liable for "its" acts. That Robertson intended to look only to the "corporation" for payment of the note, and had accepted a note from the "corporation," did not, therefore, estop him from recovering from Levy personally.

RMBCA § 2.04 modifies the unequivocal prior position by imposing liability only on those persons who act "as or on behalf of a corporation" "knowing" that no corporation actually exists. See the Official Comment to § 2.04. Seemingly, RMBCA § 2.04 preserves some semblance of the de facto doctrine because knowledge encompasses "good faith." Official Comment to RMBCA § 2.04 (next to last paragraph). In other words, if some steps have been taken to bring about the corporation, liability will not be imposed on the parties who do not know that the steps to achieve corporateness were not completed.

You should consider how far does RMBCA § 2.04 go. If three individuals, who do not consult an attorney, decide to call themselves a corporation and think that is sufficient to make them so. They have a good faith belief in the existence of a corporation and do not actually know that there is no corporation. Is there "corporateness" or are they personally liable? Consider RMBCA § 2.04, the Official Comments to RMBCA § 2.04, and the common law.

One final question that you might wish to ponder, albeit with some fear in your heart, is the liability of the lawyer who fails to effect incorporation for his client and who fails to constrain the client's business dealings until full compliance with statutory requirements has been achieved.

D. PRE–INCORPORATION ACTIVITIES OF PROMOTERS

There may be occasions when it is necessary for the promoters of a corporation to execute contracts on behalf of the corporation before the formalities of incorporation are completed and the corporation has come into legal existence. This is less of a problem than it once was as the formalities of incorporation have been simplified and can now generally be completed in a few days (or upon filing, under RMBCA § 2.03(a)). Nevertheless there are still times when it is necessary to execute a contract with a third party before incorporation is completed. Since at the time of such a transaction there is no corporation capable of becoming a party to the contract, the application of traditional principles of contract and agency law presents certain conceptual questions: Can the corporation subsequently become bound by the contract, and if so, under what theory? Is the promoter who executes the contract liable on the contract if the corporation never comes into existence? Or if it fails? If the corporation does come into existence and adopts the contract as its own, can the corporation sue on the contract?

The leading English case held that a pre-incorporation contract executed by the promoters bound only the promoters and that the corporation could not subsequently become a party after it came into existence. Kelner v. Baxter, L.R. 2 P.C. 174 (1866). The underlying theory was that under traditional rules of agency law a contract could be ratified by a principal only if the principal was in existence at the time the contract was executed. The result is that, although the corporation might become liable for benefits received by it under the contract, it does not, by accepting benefits, ratify the contract and so become liable on it. Neither, in fact, can the corporation adopt the contract, even by explicit vote of its board of directors. Although a few early American decisions accepted this doctrine, e.g., Abbott v. Hapgood, 150 Mass. 248, 22 N.E. 907, 908 (1889), it has by now been almost completely repudiated in this country. It is generally accepted that a corporation may, once it comes into existence, adopt and so become liable on the contract. In McArthur v. Times Printing Co., 48 Minn. 319, 51 N.W. 216 (1892), a contract was enforced against a corporation although execution occurred prior to corporate existence. The contract sprung into being upon the formation of the corporation and adoption by the board. Ratification was impossible, since the contract could not relate back to the time prior to corporate existence, at least insofar as the corporation was affected.

Against the background of the theoretical hurdles suggested by Kelner v. Baxter, the American courts had some difficulties finding a rational basis to justify a conclusion that the corporation can become bound by a contract executed before the corporation had any life of its

4 ways.

own. There have been at least four different conceptual bases advanced to support this result: (1) ratification (however, technically a corporation cannot ratify acts that arose before its existence), (2) adoption, (3) the acceptance of a continuing offer, and (4) novation or the creation of a new contract based upon mutual agreement of the parties. See, Henry Winthrop Ballantine, Ballantine on Corporations 108 (Rev. ed. 1946). Perhaps the best explanation is that pre-incorporation agreements are *sui generis* and need not be strait-jacketed by the traditional common law principles of agency and contracts.

As a general rule, when a promoter makes a contract for the benefit of a corporation which is contemplated but has not been organized, he is personally liable on it in the absence of an agreement to the contrary. Furthermore, the promoter is not discharged from liability merely because the corporation is later organized and receives the benefits of the contract, even where the corporation adopts the contract. However, the parties may agree specifically to discharge the liability of the promoter.

Although the parties may incorporate into the contract an express agreement that the promoter would not be held personally liable, pre-incorporation contracts typically do not expressly address promoter liability. Thus, the intentions of the parties, as deduced from the contract and the facts and circumstances of the parties' dealings, determine whether the promoter is personally liable. Factors used in analyzing whether a promoter will be held liable for a pre-incorporation contract include: (1) form of signature—did the promoter sign as an agent of the corporation? (2) action of seller—did the seller intend to look only to the corporation for payment? (3) partial performance—did the promoter's partial performance of the contract indicate an intent to be held personally liable? (4) novation—did action taken by the parties discharge the promoter's liability?

The intention of the contracting parties is the principal focus of judicial opinions on the question. The promoter may claim that it was "intended" that once the contemplated corporation was brought into existence his own liability would fall by the wayside and the corporation would substitute for him. This is clear enough if the contract contains a novation provision stating that the promoter's liability terminates if the corporation is formed and manifests a willingness to become a party to the contract. As you recall from your Contracts course, a novation is a three-party arrangement in which a new corporation assumes all of a promoter's rights and liabilities under a pre-incorporation contract thereby discharging the promoter. See Restatement, Second, Contracts § 280. To be effective, the third party must assent to the substitution of the new corporation for the promoter who agrees to abandon her status as an original party to the contract.

If an express advance assent to a novation is not explicit in the pre-incorporation contract, courts utilize rules of contractual interpretation, as well as the parties' dealings, to determine the parties' intentions. For example, if the third party looked first to the promoter and then, exclusively, to the corporation, a court may infer an intent to create a novation. Thus, even without a specific novation provision, the promoter may argue that he fulfilled his promise by creating the corporation which is able to step into his shoes and giving the corporation the opportunity to pay its debt. It has been held, however, that creating the corporation is not enough, and that the corporation must adopt the contract by some affirmative act before it becomes bound and the promoter is released. RKO–Stanley Warner Theatres, Inc. v. Graziano, 467 Pa. 220, 355 A.2d 830 (1976); Herbert v. Boardman, 134 Vt. 78, 349 A.2d 710 (1975).

How is adoption accomplished? More than the creation of the corporation is needed, even though its promoter possesses knowledge of the contract. Where that promoter becomes a member of the board of directors of the corporation, at least, it is fair to impute his knowledge of the contract to the corporation, and subsequent acts by the corporation—with such knowledge—may constitute adoption. See Peters Grazing Association v. Legerski, 544 P.2d 449 (Wyo.1975). The corporation may also, of course, adopt the contract by express action of its directors.

If the corporation never comes into existence or comes into existence and subsequently becomes unable to perform its obligations under the contract, the third party may sue the individuals who signed the contract on its behalf. If the promoters do not disclose to the third party that the corporation does not exist at the time of the execution of the contract, they may be liable on a theory of breach of an implied warranty that the corporate principal exists and that the promoter has the authority to act for the corporation. When the third party relies on this implied representation to his detriment, he can sue to hold the promoter individually liable on the contract.

But what if the third party knows of the nonexistence of the corporation? How should a court construe a contract signed, to take a well known example, "D.J. Geary, for a bridge company to be organized and incorporated"? O'Rorke v. Geary, 207 Pa. 240, 56 A. 541 (1903). There are several possible interpretations: (1) The parties intend that Geary is to use his best efforts to bring a corporation into existence and to have it adopt the contract as its own. There is no intention that Geary will ever be bound personally. (2) The parties intend that Geary will be liable on the contract until such time as he successfully incorporates the corporation and has it adopt the contract. (3) The parties intend that Geary will be bound on the contract and will remain bound even if the corporation comes into existence and adopts the contract.

The rule stated in § 326 of the Restatement, Second, Agency provides: "Unless otherwise agreed, a person who, in dealing with another, purports to act as agent for a principal whom both know to be nonexistent or wholly incompetent, becomes a party to such contract." Under this rule, of course, Geary would be bound on the contract and would remain bound even if the corporation were ultimately to adopt it.

Also, the considerations of fairness may support a different result. The pre-incorporation contract may provide evidence of the parties' intentions. Thus, the to-be-formed corporation may be designated as the performing party or the promoter's signature may indicate that he did not intend to bind himself personally. While the signature format standing alone is seldom dispositive, because it applies to the whole context of the agreement, if additional contract terms indicate that the third party intended to look solely to the corporation for satisfaction, the promoter may not be held personally liable.

The third party's intentions are also a factor to be considered. In Quaker Hill, Inc. v. Parr, 148 Colo. 45, 364 P.2d 1056 (1961), for example, the plaintiff sold nursery stock to the defendants. The plaintiff's salesman insisted on executing the contract before the corporation was formed. At the suggestion of the plaintiff, the contract of sale named as purchaser a corporation that did not yet exist. The defendants did ultimately organize a corporation (using a different name than that in the contract because the original name was already in use in the state). The corporation, however, never functioned as a going concern, and the nursery stock (all of which died) remained unpaid for. The court held that the defendants were not liable for the purchase price as the evidence suggested that the plaintiffs had intended to look only to the corporation and not to the individual defendants for payment.

The third party may also argue, often successfully based on the precedents, that partial performance by the promoter during the preincorporation period gives rise to an inference that the promoter intended to be personally bound. That was, in fact, the holding of O'Rorke v. Geary. See also White & Bollard, Inc. v. Goodenow, 58 Wash.2d 180, 361 P.2d 571 (1961).

Ultimately, the problem is one of adequate drafting: there is no reason why any specific interpretation should not be spelled out explicitly in the contract and given effect by the courts. For example, the promoter may take an option, which can be assigned to the corporation after its formation. In this manner, the promoter never becomes an obligee. However, there will inevitably be cases in which the parties do not or are unable to arrange their affairs neatly, and the courts are left to struggle with the resulting problems.

E. CHOICE OF THE STATE OF INCORPORATION

1. INTRODUCTION: THE LAW APPLICABLE TO CORPORATIONS

What turns on the decision of where to incorporate? Until you know the answer to that question, you cannot intelligently choose the state of incorporation.

A corporation is a legal person, as we saw in Chapter 4, and has certain constitutional entitlements, including equal protection of the law and the right not to be deprived of property without due process of law. Under early doctrine, a state could exclude out-of-state corporations altogether from engaging in intrastate business within its borders, Bank of Augusta v. Earle, 38 U.S. (13 Pet.) 519, 10 L.Ed. 274 (1839); Paul v. Virginia, 75 U.S. (8 Wall.) 168, 19 L.Ed. 357 (1868); Railway Express Agency v. Virginia, 282 U.S. 440, 51 S.Ct. 201, 75 L.Ed. 450 (1931), and thus could subject foreign corporations to conditions on doing business within the state. Under more recent doctrine, the Court has concluded that it is "now established that whatever the extent of a state's authority to exclude foreign corporations from doing business within its boundaries, that authority does not justify imposition of more onerous taxes or other burdens on foreign corporations than those imposed on domestic corporations, unless the discrimination between foreign and domestic corporations bears a rational relation to a legitimate state purpose." Western & Southern Life Insurance Co. v. State Board of Equalization of California, 451 U.S. 648, 101 S.Ct. 2070, 68 L.Ed.2d 514 (1981). See Watson v. Employers Liability Assurance Corp., Ltd., 348 U.S. 66, 75 S.Ct. 166, 171, 99 L.Ed. 74, 83 (1954) (concurring opinion of Frankfurter, J., reviewing precedents). In practice, states do not exclude foreign corporations, but seek to assert some control, mainly for revenue raising purposes. Thus, if a company is to engage in "local" business * in a foreign state, it must register within the state so as to qualify to do business there as a foreign corporation. But if the corporation's intrastate activities are an inseparable part of an interstate transaction, it may not be required to qualify as a foreign corporation because of the constitutional prohibition against interference with interstate commerce. Eli Lilly & Co. v. Sav–On–Drugs, 366 U.S. 276, 81 S.Ct. 1316, 6 L.Ed.2d 288 (1961); Allenberg Cotton Co. v. Pittman, 419 U.S. 20, 95 S.Ct. 260, 42 L.Ed.2d 249 (1974).

Originally, the main purpose of the registration requirement was to assure that foreign corporations would be subject to the jurisdiction of the courts of the state and amenable to service of process in the state, objectives that have been largely achieved by the expansion of long-arm jurisdiction. Today, sanctions for a failure to qualify to do business are relatively mild; they generally entail little more than a temporary bar of access to local courts. This may be embarrassing when the corporation is sued and is unable to file an answer or a counterclaim; but under most statutes, registration even after the suit is filed removes this bar. RMBCA § 15.02.

Registration (also known as qualification) of a foreign corporation involves filing with a jurisdiction's secretary of state a formal application for a certificate of authority together with other requisite documents and paying a filing fee. RMBCA §§ 15.01, 15.03. Typically, a foreign

---

* What constitutes "doing business" has generated countless court opinions but remains, nevertheless, an unusually unrefined area of the law of corporations. It should be noted that "doing business" for the purpose of requiring a corporation to register as a foreign corporation is not necessarily "doing business" for the purposes of jurisdiction of the courts or amenability to service of process, and that both are different from "doing business" for the purpose of imposing state taxes.

corporation must appoint a local resident agent or designate the secretary of state to receive service of process for lawsuits brought in that state. RMBCA § 15.07. Qualification means that the foreign corporation is authorized to transact business in the state. It also becomes subject to service of process within the jurisdiction and to applicable taxes.

The principles embodied in the full faith and credit clause of the Constitution and the idea of comity require a state which hosts a foreign corporation to respect the legislative enactments and judicial decisions of the state of incorporation of the foreign corporation. When a corporation incorporated in one state does business in another it carries with it whatever rights were conferred by the act of incorporation and the applicable law of its state of incorporation.

The law of the state of incorporation also ordinarily determines the rules that govern the "internal affairs" of a corporation. Restatement, Second, Conflicts of Laws §§ 296–310. Reconsider Chapter 4, Part C. Although the term "internal affairs" has no clear definition, it generally is deemed to include matters bearing on the relationship between owners (shareholders) and managers (officers and directors). The internal affairs rule also applies to the relationships between different classes of shareholders, between shareholders and creditors, and between shareholders and employees. For example, under the internal affairs rule, the law of the state of incorporation governs the right of shareholders to vote, to receive distributions of corporate property, to receive information from the management about the affairs of the corporation, to limit the powers of the corporation to specifically chosen fields of activity, and to bring suit on behalf of the corporation when the managers refuse to do so. It also determines the procedures by which the board of directors will act, the managers' right to be indemnified by the corporation when they are sued for their conduct, and the corporation's right to issue stock and to merge with other companies. Perhaps most importantly, the internal affairs rule applies to rules defining the duties that the managers of a corporation, as fiduciaries, owe to shareholders.

This list, by no means exhaustive, suggests the impossibility of administering any other rule, at least if the corporation is a multi-state venture. How could it be decided, for example, which stockholders were entitled to vote at an annual meeting if it were necessary to refer to the potentially conflicting law of every state in which the corporation did business? Obviously with respect to such questions a choice must be made; the internal affairs rule makes it by deciding them according to the law of the state of incorporation.

Of course, the "external affairs" of a corporation are generally governed by the law of the place where the activities occur and by federal and state regulatory statutes rather than by the place of incorporation. For example, a state's labor laws govern conditions of employment and minimum wages of the operations of all businesses within the state, wherever the businesses might be incorporated. State tax laws generally apply to activities of any corporation within the state, especially those that are imposed on corporate real estate and income. (Franchise taxes, which are collected by the state of incorporation from companies incorporated there, do not depend on the situs of a corporation's activities or property.)

Some activities are governed by both internal and external rules. For example, state corporation law controls the right to merge and the procedure to be followed, but mergers are also independently subject to anti-trust laws and securities laws.

The internal affairs doctrine is a choice-of-law rule and, like other such rules is amenable to change by a particular jurisdiction (subject always to the requirements of the U.S. Constitution). Thus in an effort to protect its citizens, a state, in principle at least, is free to apply some or all of its own corporate law rules to corporations that have substantial contacts with the state even though they are incorporated elsewhere. New York and California have chosen to exercise this power over what have been called "pseudo-foreign" corporations, meaning corporations that carry on most of their activities or have a majority of their shareholders in the state but are incorporated in another state. Calif. Corp. Code. § 2115, New York B.C.L. §§ 1320.

The California statute makes certain provisions of California law governing corporate affairs applicable to a foreign corporation if (1) more than 50 percent of its property, payroll, and sales are within California and (2) more than 50 percent of its voting securities are held of record by persons with California addresses. A corporation falling within this class becomes subject to, among others, the California provisions on dividends and other distributions of corporate property, election and removal of directors, directors' standard of care, indemnification of officers and directors, and the regulation of mergers and sales of assets. One of the provisions made applicable by the statute is a requirement that "cumulative" voting (a procedure discussed in greater detail in Chapter 13) be used in the election of directors rather than "straight" voting. This provision thus makes mandatory a form of voting which is at least optional in most other states.

Suppose a corporation is incorporated in a state that allows "straight" voting for directors but it meets the California tests for pseudo-foreign corporations. How are directors elected? A California appellate court has held that the California voting provisions govern, rejecting a constitutional challenge to § 2115. Wilson v. Louisiana–Pacific Resources, Inc., 138 Cal.App.3d 216, 187 Cal.Rptr. 852 (1982). A corporation meeting all the tests of § 2115, but incorporated under Utah law, challenged the requirement that directors be elected by cumulative voting, asserting that the statute violated the full faith and credit, the commerce and contract clauses, impaired property without due process of law, and deprived the corporation of equal protection of the law. All the challenges were rejected. Among other things, the court found that a state need only have a significant contact in order to apply its law, a test that was clearly met under the legislative standard. The generally applied "internal affairs rule," the court observed, is a common law test that the legislature rejected, and it is not a constitutional requirement. The spectre of conflicting rules, which might result from differences between California and the other states was viewed as minimal. The nature of the California tests necessarily excludes claims by other states to govern the affairs of the corporation (except that the court does not mention the conflicting claim of the incorporating state which need have *no* physical contact), but in any event the burden is not so substantial.

A constitutional challenge to § 2115 could result from the Supreme Court's decision in CTS Corp. v. Dynamics Corp. of America, 481 U.S. 69, 107 S.Ct. 1637, 95 L.Ed.2d 67 (1987), discussed in detail in Chapter 4, upholding an Indiana statute dealing with corporate takeovers. The Court observed that, "No principle of corporation law and practice is more firmly established than a state's authority to regulate domestic corporations, including the authority to define voting rights of share-holders." 481 U.S. at 89, 107 S.Ct. at 1649. The Court also stated, "It is thus an accepted part of the business landscape in this country for States to create corporations, to prescribe their powers, and to define the rights that are acquired by purchasing their shares." 481 U.S. at 91, 107 S.Ct. at 1650. The context of the decision was far removed from the pseudo-foreign corporation question often associated with § 2115, so the issue is unresolved.

In McDermott Inc. v. Lewis, 531 A.2d 206 (Del.1987), the court applied Panama law to permit the shares of a Panamanian parent corporation to be voted by its subsidiary, a Delaware corporation. Under the law of Delaware (Del. Gen. Corp. L. § 160(c)), where the case was heard, the shares could not be voted. The court observed that "application of the internal affairs doctrine is not merely a principle of conflicts of law. It is also one of serious constitutional proportions—under due process, the commerce clause and the full faith and credit clause—so that the law of one state governs the relationships of a corporation to its stockholders, directors and officers in matters of internal corporate governance. The alternatives present almost intolerable consequences to the corporate enterprise and its managers. With the existence of multistate and multinational organizations, directors and officers have a significant right, under the fourteenth amendment's due process clause, to know what law will be applied to their actions. Stockholders also have a right to know by what standards of accountability they may hold those managing the corporation's business and affairs." (531 A.2d at 216–27).

For analysis of pseudo-foreign corporation statutes and the constitutional limitations on applying the law of the forum state to the internal affairs of a foreign corporation, see Norton P. Beveridge, The Internal Affairs Doctrine: The Proper Law of a Corporation, 44 Bus. Law. 693, 702–15 (1989); Deborah A. DeMott, Perspectives on Choice of Law for Corporate Internal Affairs, 48 L. & Contemp. Probs. 161 (Summer 1985).

2. PRACTICAL CONSIDERATIONS

Before making an intelligent judgment as to the state of incorporation, it is first necessary to understand the nature and scope of the business that is to be incorporated. The lawyer must know where the company intends to operate and what kinds of activity it intends to conduct in particular locations. For most businesses, particularly smaller ones, there is a strong presumption in favor of incorporating where the principal operations are to be conducted. If operations are confined to a single state, incorporating in that state will reduce filing, reporting and tax burdens. But if a company intends to operate in more than one state (which is often the case), it may be required to qualify to do business as a foreign corporation in other jurisdictions.

If the lawyer concludes that the corporation is not required to qualify as a foreign corporation in any state because all of its activities are local, local incorporation is usually most desirable. Counsel will generally recommend foreign incorporation only if particular provisions of the corporation law of the local jurisdiction are especially burdensome to the owners or managers of the corporation or the administration of the local statute is inefficient. Such a situation would be unusual for most small businesses.

Some of the other factors to be considered in deciding where to incorporate are:

1. The organization tax rates and the franchise tax rates.

2. The simplicity of operation of the corporation. For example, some jurisdictions, but not all, permit: (1) a corporation's board of directors to act by unanimous consent without a meeting or by means of a conference telephone call, and (2) a corporation to dispense with stockholder meetings and shareholders to act by the consent of the holders of a sufficient number of shares.

3. Restrictions on dividends and other distributions. These may be important for a number of reasons, and the directors may be liable personally for dividends or other distributions that are not permitted under state law.

4. Shareholder rights. Some jurisdictions severely limit the participatory rights of shareholders. It should be noted that this does not necessarily reflect an anti-shareholder attitude; simplicity in operation and restriction of the opportunity for dissidents to obstruct may be in the best interests of the majority of the shareholders (an issue we will consider in greater depth in Chapter 12).

5. Indemnification. Officers and directors are entitled to be indemnified for their expenses at the conclusion of a law suit, provided that they have not been found to have acted improperly. The scope and the procedure of indemnification provisions vary among the states (an issue we will consider again in Chapter 16). Ordinarily, this consideration is more relevant to a publicly held company than to a close corporation.

6. Provisions for close corporations. A number of states provide easier operational arrangements and a relaxing of the corporate norms to accommodate the private bargain that participants in a close corporation may want to strike, which in some cases deviates from the statutory pattern.

7. Liability for wages. Although limited liability for shareholders is the general rule, there are occasional statutory exceptions. For example, New York and Wisconsin impose some personal liability on the shareholders for unpaid wages to employees. New York B.C.L. § 630 provides that the ten largest shareholders of a company are jointly and severally liable for all "debts, wages or salaries due or owing to any of its laborers, servants or employees other than contractors, for services performed by them for such corporation." The statute does not apply to corporations whose securities are publicly traded.

Wisconsin B.C.L. § 180.0622 imposes a more limited personal liability on shareholders in by making the shareholders of every corporation, other than railroad corporations, personally liable for all debts (not to exceed six months' service in any case) owing to employees, up to the amount equal to the par value of their shares, or the consideration paid for their no par shares. As we shall soon see, this may be only a token amount. Unlike New York, however, the Wisconsin provision applies to shareholders of foreign corporations. Joncas v. Krueger, 61 Wis.2d 529, 213 N.W.2d 1 (1973).

3. POLICY CONSIDERATIONS

a. *Introduction*

The public policy issues that grow out of the selection of the state of incorporation arise as a consequence of the internal affairs rule. Should the participants in a corporation, or some group of those participants, have the freedom to select the body of law that will govern the corporation's internal affairs? Is there a danger that some states, in an effort to attract incorporations so as to generate franchise tax revenues, will adopt laws that treat certain participants unfairly? Which participants makes the decision on where to incorporate, and what factors influence their decisions?

As noted in Chapter 1, all state corporation laws now in force are essentially enabling laws. They provide for an organizational framework in which a business can operate and abjure regulatory goals. Things were not always so. The following excerpt from Mr. Justice Brandeis' famous dissenting opinion in Liggett Co. v. Lee recounts some of the historical development.

LIGGETT v. LEE
288 U.S. 517, 53 S.Ct. 481, 77 L.Ed. 929 (1933).

MR. JUSTICE BRANDEIS (dissenting in part).

* * *

[The case, itself, was a challenge to the constitutionality of a tax imposed by Florida on chain stores. The Court struck down the tax. Brandeis' dissenting view was that "Whether the corporate privilege shall be granted or withheld is always a matter of state policy * * *. If a state believes that adequate protection * * * can be secured, without revoking the corporate privilege, by imposing * * * upon corporations the handicap of higher, discriminatory license fees as compensation for the privilege, I know of nothing in the Fourteenth Amendment to prevent it from making the experiment."]

Second. The prevalence of the corporation in America has led men of this generation to act, at times, as if the privilege of doing business in corporate form were inherent in the citizen; and has led them to accept the evils attendant upon the free and unrestricted use of the corporate mechanism as if these evils were the inescapable price of civilized life, and, hence, to be borne with resignation. Throughout the greater part of our history a different view prevailed. Although the value of this instrumentality in commerce and industry was fully recognized, incorporation for business was commonly denied long after it had been freely granted for religious, educational, and charitable purposes. It was denied because of fear. Fear of encroachment upon the liberties and opportunities of the individual. Fear of the subjection of labor to capital. Fear of monopoly. Fear that the absorption of capital by corporations, and their perpetual life, might bring evils similar to those which attended mortmain. There was a sense of some insidious menace inherent in large aggregations of capital, particularly when held by corporations. So at first the corporate privilege was granted sparingly; and only when the grant seemed necessary in order to procure for the community some specific benefit otherwise unattainable. The later enactment of general incorporation laws does not signify that the apprehension of corporate domination had been overcome. The desire for business expansion created an irresistible demand for more charters; and it was believed that under general laws embodying safeguards of universal application the scandals and favoritism incident to special incorporation could be avoided. The general laws, which long embodied severe restrictions upon size and upon the scope of corporate activity, were, in part, an expression of the desire for equality of opportunity.

* * *

The removal by the leading industrial states of the limitations upon the size and powers of business corporations appears to have been due, not to their conviction that maintenance of the restrictions was undesirable in itself, but to the conviction that it was futile to insist upon them; because local restriction would be circumvented by foreign incorporation. Indeed, local restriction seemed worse than futile. Lesser states, eager for the revenue derived from the traffic in charters, had removed safeguards from their own incorporation laws. Companies were early formed to provide charters for corporations in states where the cost was lowest and the laws least restrictive. The states joined in advertising their wares. The race was one not of diligence but of laxity. Incorporation under such laws was possible; and the great industrial States yielded in order not to lose wholly the prospect of the revenue and the control incident to domestic incorporation.

b.   *History of State Competition for Corporations*

New Jersey was the first state to depart from the early philosophy of strict limitations on corporations beginning with its 1888 incorporation statute, which was followed by a revision in 1896. With its 1899 statute, Delaware entered the competition, and eventually succeeded in becoming the leading state for the incorporation of large businesses.* Charles Beard, the noted historian, described how this came about in testimony before a Senate Committee considering federal corporate legislation in 1937:

> Under the leadership of Woodrow Wilson, after he was challenged by Theodore Roosevelt to reform his own state, the legislature of New Jersey passed a series of laws doing away with corporate abuses and applying high standards to corporations. What was the result? The revenues of the State from taxes on corporations fell. Malefactors moved over into other states. In time the New Jersey Legislature repealed its strict and prudent legislation, and went back, not quite, but almost to old ways. * * * Hearings on S. 10 Before a Subcommittee of the Senate Committee on the Judiciary, 75th Cong., 1st Sess. 326 (1937).

Another commentator observed that:

> The sovereign state of Delaware is in the business of selling its corporation law. This is profitable business, for a corporation law is a good commodity to sell. The market is large, and relatively few producers compete on a national scale. The consumers of this commodity are corporations. * * * Delaware, like any other good businessman, tries to give the consumer what he wants. In fact, those who will buy the product are not only consulted about their preferences, but are also allowed to design the product and run the factory. Comment, Law for Sale: A Study of the Delaware Corporation Law of 1967, 117 U.Pa.L.Rev. 861, 861–862 (1969).

c.   *The "Race for the Bottom" Debate*

   i.   The Interventionist View: Federal Minimum Standards and Federal Chartering

Critics of Delaware suggests that it is leading a "race for the bottom" as a result of a sort of Gresham's law of corporate statutes. Their argument, in essence, is that no state can use its corporate law as

---

* New York is the leading place of incorporation, with Delaware in seventh place. However, Delaware is the state of incorporation of more than half the Fortune 500 companies and is clearly first among corporations listed on the New York Stock Exchange.

a vehicle to impose on corporations policies or governance rules that those corporations' managers dislike. Managers will respond to such efforts by reincorporating in Delaware or some other hospitable jurisdiction.

In William L. Cary, Federalism and Corporate Law: Reflections Upon Delaware, 83 Yale L.J. 663, 705 (1974), Professor Cary argued that Delaware had adopted a policy of maintaining its lead as the primary home of large corporations. This policy was reflected in legislative enactments, appointment of judges to the court of chancery and the supreme court, and the decisions of those courts. Cary observed that Delaware had eliminated what he viewed as statutory protections for shareholders, such as requiring only a majority of shareholders, rather than two-thirds, to approve a merger, and to limit managers' fiduciary obligations by, among other things, liberally interpreting the business judgment rule and permitting corporate action to thwart hostile takeover bids. To deal with this "exploitation", Cary proposed that Congress adopt a federal minimum standards law, applicable to larger public companies, that would impose federal fiduciary standards and other restrictions on corporate officers and directors.

Other proposals for federal intervention go much further. A task force under the direction of consumer activist Ralph Nader urged federal incorporation of all large corporations, not to supplement state law or be superimposed on state law as Professor Cary urged, but to replace state corporation law. Ralph Nader, Mark Green, Joel Seligman, Constitutionalizing the Corporation: The Case for Federal Chartering of Giant Corporations (1976). See also Donald E. Schwartz, A Case for Federal Chartering of Corporations, 31 Bus.Law. 1125 (1976). These proposals, unlike Professor Cary's, urged reform of corporation law not only to protect shareholder but as a means of enhancing corporate social responsibility.

ii. The Law and Economics View: The Benefits of Competition

Those who disagree with Professor Cary argue that market forces rather than legal doctrine will align the interests of shareholders and managers. They also contend that competition among states will ultimately benefit investors. The principal response to Cary came from Professor (now Judge) Ralph K. Winter, Jr.

RALPH K. WINTER, JR., STATE LAW, SHAREHOLDER PROTECTION, AND THE THEORY OF THE CORPORATION
6 J. Legal Stud. 251, 256–257, 259, 275, 276 (1977).

[Professor Cary's] claim, it is absolutely critical to note, is not that an overriding social goal is sacrificed by state law, but simply that Delaware is preventing *private* parties from optimizing their *private* arrangements. With all due respect both to Professor Cary and to the almost universal academic support for his position, it is implausible on its face. The plausible argument runs in the opposite direction: (1) If Delaware permits corporate management to profit at the expense of shareholders and other states do not, then earnings of Delaware corporations must be less than earnings of comparable corporations chartered in other states and shares in the Delaware corporations must trade at lower prices. (2) Corporations with lower earnings will be at a disadvantage in raising debt or equity capital. (3) Corporations at a disadvantage in the capital market will be at a disadvantage in the product market and their share price will decline, thereby creating a threat of a takeover which may replace management. To avoid this result, corporations must seek out legal systems more attractive to capital. (4) States seeking corporate charters will thus try to provide legal systems which optimize the shareholder-corporation relationship.

The conclusion that Delaware shares sell for less is implicit in Professor Cary's analysis, for if a "higher" legal standard for management conduct will increase investor confidence, investor confidence in Delaware stock must have been less than in stocks of other states for more than a generation. This lack of confidence would have long been reflected in the price of Delaware shares. Moreover, a reduction in the earnings of a corporation will affect its ability to raise debt capital, as well as equity, since the risk of a lender is thereby increased and a higher interest rate will be charged. Delaware corporations, therefore, not only face a lower share price but also must pay higher interest rates.

* * *

Intervention in private transactions which impose no social cost can be justified only as a means of reducing the costs to the private parties. Thus, a prime function of state corporation codes is to supply standard terms which reduce the transaction costs, and thereby increase the benefits, of investing by eliminating costly bargaining which might otherwise accompany many routine corporate dealings. But substituting a mandatory legal rule for bargaining also may impose a cost in the form of the elimination of alternatives which the parties might prefer.

Much of the legal literature calling for further federal regulation either assumes that no costs will fall upon shareholders or merely undertakes a cursory "eyeballing" of the potential costs. To be sure, self-dealing and fraud exist in corporate affairs and their elimination is desirable. But at some point the exercise of control by general rules of law may impose costs on investors which damage them in both quantity and quality quite as much as self-dealing or fraud. A paradox thus results: maximizing the yield to investors generally may, indeed almost surely will, result in a number of cases of fraud or self-dealing; and eliminating all fraud or self-dealing may decrease the yield to shareholders generally.

* * *

A state which rigs its corporation code so as to reduce the yield to shareholders will spawn corporations which are less attractive as investment opportunities than comparable corporations chartered in other states or countries, as well as bonds, savings accounts, land, etc. Investors must be attracted before they can be cheated, and except for those seeking a "one shot," "take the money and run," opportunity to raid a corporation, management has no reason to seek out such a code. * * * The chartering decision, therefore, so far as the capital market is concerned, will favor those states which offer the optimal yield to both shareholders and management.

* * *

So far as the capital market is concerned, it is not in the interest of management to seek out a corporate legal system which fails to protect investors, and the competition between states for charters is generally a competition as to which legal system provides an optimal return to both interests. Only when that competition between legal systems exists can we perceive which legal rules are most appropriate for the capital market. Once a single legal system governs that market, we can no longer compare investor reaction. Ironically, in view of the conventional wisdom, the greater danger is not that states will compete for charters but that they will not.

iii. Analysis of Interventionist and Market–Oriented Perspectives

Proponents of the view that market forces shape corporate law often point to a study by two University of Chicago economists to support their theoretical arguments. Peter Dodd and Richard Leftwich, The Market for Corporate Charters: "Unhealthy Competition" versus Federal Regulation, 55 J.Bus. 259 (1980), found no statistically significant changes in the price of the stock of companies that announced their intent to reincorporate in Delaware. However, the "events" analyzed in their study were ambiguous. Among other points, reincorporation usually is prompted by other circumstances and events, such as a proposed merger, which may have influenced the stock market's reaction more than the announced intent to reincorporate. Other commentators have pointed out that Dodd and Leftwich's results do not clearly repudiate the theory that a stockholder's position is worsened when a corporation reincorporates in Delaware.

Weiss and White examined the effect on investors, as measured by the impact on stock prices, of seemingly significant changes in corporate law doctrines by Delaware courts. They determined that investors did not react to judicial opinions that significantly changed state corporate law and suggested that their results called into question the existence of an investor-dominated market for corporate law. Elliott J. Weiss and Lawrence J. White, Of Econometrics and Indeterminacy: A Study of Investors' Reactions to "Changes" in Corporate Law, 75 Cal. L. Rev. 551 (1987).

Judge Easterbrook and Professor Fischel support the "thesis that competition creates a powerful tendency for states to enact laws that operate to the benefit of investors * * *." Frank H. Easterbrook and Daniel R. Fischel, The Economic Structure of Corporate Law 222 (1991). However, they characterize the market for state corporate law as less than efficient. Managers' opportunistic efforts to entrench themselves in their positions or to increase their compensation also impacts on the development of corporate law. Easterbrook and Fischel conclude that state competition for investors does not eliminate opportunistic behavior by managers. Similarly, competition for incorporation does not eliminate opportunistic behavior by states—even Delaware has enacted an antitakeover statute. Ultimately, though, Easterbrook and Fischel oppose a federal corporate law "because Federal laws face less competition * * *." Id. at 223.

Other commentators question whether state competition is truly effective. Lucian A. Bebchuk, Federalism and the Corporation: The Desirable Limits on State Competition in Corporate Law, 105 Harv. L. Rev. 1435 (1992) argues that managerial opportunism and externalities may lead states to undesirable corporate statutory provisions. Professor Bebchuk concludes that state competition is likely to fail to maximize shareholder value in the following three areas: 1) issues involving the potential transfer of significant value from shareholders to managers, such as self-dealing transactions; 2) issues that directly affect the strength of market discipline, such as the regulation of takeover bids; 3) issues that involve potential transfers between controlling shareholders and public shareholders, such as the regulation of parent-subsidiary transactions. According to Bebchuck: "With respect to all of these issues, state competition can be expected systematically to produce rules that favor managers and dominant shareholders more than would the value-maximizing rules. This conclusion * * * follows from a recognition of the structural forces at work in the state charter competition." Id. at 1484. One of the key premises underlying Bebchuk's analysis is his belief that market discipline (namely, the market for corporate control, the managerial labor market, the market for additional capital, and the product market) probably will not discharge managers from seeking inefficient (nonshareholder value maximizing) rules with respect to issues involving the significant redistribution of wealth from shareholders to managers.

Bebchuk also points to the presence of significant adverse impacts on parties other than managers and shareholders, so-called externalities, in areas such as the regulation of takeover bids and corporate disclosure, noting that "if the rule is designed by the states, then the competition among them will lead state officials to exclude consideration of [third party] interests." Id. at 1485.

Professor Bebchuk further elaborates his position as follows:

* * * First, with respect to issues that involve managerial opportunism, states have an incentive to make themselves attractive to

managers and dominant shareholders, and states therefore may well provide rules that benefit managers and dominant shareholders even if the rules are value-decreasing. Second, with respect to issues that involve externalities, states have an incentive to disregard the interests of parties other than managers and shareholders, and this disregard may well lead states to adopt value-decreasing rules that systematically disfavor the third parties upon whom the externalities are imposed." Id. at 1501.

Because of the failure of state competition to deal with the problem of managerial opportunism and externalities, Bebchuk advocates an expansion of federal regulation, at least in the form of federal minimum standards to govern a number of areas. These would include managers' fiduciary duties, the fiduciary duties of controlling shareholders in freezeouts, dividend restrictions, and various aspects of takeover bids now governed by state law. He concludes, "Because federal law officials would not be affected by incorporation decisions in the same way that state law officials are, the federal law process would not suffer from the above two structural biases [managerial opportunism and externalities]." Id. at 1501.

d. The Preeminence of Delaware

Stepping back from the welter of theoretical and empirical studies, the "race," whether for the bottom, as Cary described it, or the top, as portrayed by Winter may be over. History has given Delaware an insurmountable lead.

Commentators generally agree on the reasons why Delaware has become preeminent. Roberta Romano, The State Competition Debate in Corporate Law, 8 Cardozo L. Rev. 709 (1987), notes that when publicly traded firms choose to reincorporate—move from one state where they are already incorporated to another—they choose Delaware 82% of the time. Firms tend to choose Delaware because of what Romano calls "first mover advantage." Firms feel relatively confident that Delaware will respond promptly to the concerns of corporate managers in the future, because it has done so in the past.

Three factors bolster this belief. First, Delaware relies heavily on franchise taxes and therefore would have much to lose by failing to amend its statute in order to provide firms with advantages offered elsewhere. Second, the Delaware state constitution requires a two-thirds vote of both houses of the legislature to change its corporate code. The supermajority requirement makes it particularly difficult for the legislature to deprive corporations of benefits they currently enjoy. Finally, Delaware has tremendous assets in terms of "legal capital" which includes a massive body of corporate case law, judicial expertise, and an administrative body that is geared to rapidly process corporate filings.

Romano attaches particular importance to Delaware's judicial system. Courts in other jurisdictions increasingly look to and rely upon Delaware case law. Romano concludes:

> The value of a Delaware domicile to firms is more than an up-to-date code; Delaware also offers a comprehensive body of case law, which is not easily replicated by another state, and a handful of experienced judges. These factors afford firms greater predictability of the legal outcomes of their decisions, facilitating planning and reducing the costs of doing business. Indeed, the large number of corporations domiciled in Delaware contributes to the development of its case law, for the sheer numbers make it more likely that a particular issue will have been litigated. (Roberta Romano, Law as a Product: Some Pieces of the Incorporation Puzzle, 1 J. L. Econ. & Org. 225, 280 (1985).)

Professors Macey and Miller agree that Delaware is winning the race and is likely to continue to do so for reasons similar to those cited by Professor Romano. Jonathan R. Macey and Geoffrey P. Miller, Toward an Interest–Group Theory of Delaware Corporate Law, 65 Tex. L. Rev. 469 (1987). They note that Delaware corporate law provides incentives to incorporate in Delaware to all the major parties in corporate decision-making, including shareholders, managers, attorneys, and investment bankers. The Delaware code allows corporations to devise private arrangements to "contract around" its statute thereby providing for opportunities to enhance the value of the firm and thus benefit its shareholders. Managers are lured by preferential statutory provisions including those dealing with obtaining personal benefits, managerial compensation, allowing self-dealing contracts, and corporation indemnification of managers. Attorneys, especially corporate counsel, are "seduced" by Delaware corporate law, as is evidenced by the overwhelming majority of reincorporating firms who stated that their counsel suggested the move. Finally, investment bankers tend to prefer Delaware, perhaps because of case law which leads to hefty profits for its industry. Macey and Miller agree with Romano that Delaware is likely to continue winning the "race for the bottom" because it effectively guarantees corporations a continuation of favorable treatment in the future. Delaware "bonds" its promise that its corporate law will remain attractive by providing extraordinarily knowledgeable lawyers and judges and because political factors militate in favor of the continued guarantee. Various interest groups within the state, notably the bar, have a tremendous stake in preserving the primacy of Delaware.

It is easy to become simplistic in thinking about the effect of providing a legal climate managers and their lawyers find conducive. Consider the effect of a provision like DGCL § 228, which permits a majority of a corporation's shareholders to act by written consent. Professor Cary criticized this provision, because the managers of a public corporation can rely on it to avoid holding an annual meeting, at which they will be expected to respond to shareholders' questions and complaints. But does this provision clearly favor the interests of managers *as opposed to shareholders*? As we will see in Chapter 12, shareholders may benefit because the consent procedure makes it easier for shareholders to act in situations where no meeting is on the horizon and no provisions has been made to allow shareholders to call such a meeting. Thus, § 228 appears to have some benefits for shareholders as well as involving some potential costs.

e. *The ALI and the ABA*

In the 1980s, the American Law Institute (ALI) and the American Bar Association's Committee on Corporate Laws emerged as important forces in the field of corporate law. The Committee on Corporate Laws, is unique within the ABA: its membership is by invitation only and is limited to 25, and it has authority to make final decisions without reference to any higher authority within the ABA. In 1954, the Committee published the first Model Business Corporation Act, which it modelled on the Illinois corporate statute. The Committee's purpose was to produce a statute that was responsive to changing business practices and that state legislatures could use as a model when updating their corporate laws. However, when it produced and updated the Model Act and when it drafted the RMBCA in the early 1980s, the Committee largely avoided taking positions on controversial issues.

That changed in the late 1980s. The Committee proposed Subchapter F of the RMBCA, dealing with director's conflicting interest transactions, and identified its work as embodying an "entirely new approach" to that subject. Committee on Corporate Laws, Changes in the Model Business Corporation Act—Amendments Pertaining to Director's Conflicting Interest Transactions, 43 Bus. Law. 691 (1988). Similarly, in 1989 the Committee proposed new rules relating to derivative litigation that specifically addressed a number of issues that were surrounded by "[a] great deal of controversy * * *." Introductory Comment to RMBCA Subchapter D. Why the Committee adopted this new approach is unclear. One possibility is that the Committee was attempting to counter positions adopted by the ALI Corporate Governance Project with which it disagreed. Cf. Elliott Goldstein, CORPRO: A Committee That Became an Institution, 48 Bus. Law. 1333 (1993). In any event, because so many states have based their corporate statutes on the RMBCA, it seems likely the Committee's more recent innovations will receive serious attention from many state legislatures.

The ALI is an independent organization made up of prominent jurists, practitioners and academics. Its principal product has been the various Restatements of the Law. In 1978, the ALI decided to proceed with a project dealing with corporate governance issues, the premise of which was to "preserve and enhance the effectiveness of corporations as the vehicles of the free-enterprise system." Roswell B. Perkins, The Genesis and Goals of the ALI Corporate Governance Project, 8 Cardozo L.Rev. 661 (1987). The Corporate Governance Project proved to be quite controversial. Some commentators believed the reporters' recommendations largely reflected the views of academic ideologues and were at variance with corporate practice and generally accepted principles of corporate law. See, e.g., Jonathan R. Macey, The Transformation of the American law Institute, 61 Geo. Wash. L.Rev. 1212 (1993). Others defended both the work of the reporters and the scope of the Project. See Roswell B. Perkins, Thanks, Myth and Reality, 48 Bus. Law. 1313 (1993). In any event, courts began to take account of the Project's work even as it appeared in draft form. The Project's final product, ALI, Principles of Corporate Governance: Analysis and Recommendations (1994), thus seems likely to exert a major influence on developments in corporate law, even though the Principles have been heavily criticized by commentators at all points along the ideological spectrum. See Symposium, The American Law Institute's Principles of Corporate Governance, 61 Geo. Wash. L.Rev. 871 (1993).

Chapter 9

FINANCIAL STRUCTURE OF THE CORPORATION

PROBLEM
PRECISION TOOLS—PART V

Jessica Bacon, Michael Lane and Bernie Gould have agreed to organize Precision Tools Corporation ("PTC") as a Columbia corporation and to have PTC acquire all of the assets, tangible and intangible, of Precision Tools, Inc. and assume all of PT's liabilities. Stern and Starr have agreed to sell PT to them for $2 million. In addition to financing the purchase, Jessica, Michael and Bernie want to provide PTC with an additional $150,000 to finance their planned expansion of its business. Thus, they need to raise a total of $2,150,000.

Jessica and Michael each are prepared to commit $200,000 to PTC. Jessica can provide that amount in cash, but Michael cannot raise more than $100,000 at this time. However, he is prepared to give PTC a note for the additional $100,000. In exchange for their investments, Jessica and Michael each expect to receive 40% of PTC's common stock.

Bernie is prepared to invest $600,000 in PTC. In exchange for $100,000 of his investment, he will receive 20% of PTC's common stock. He is prepared to use the remaining $500,000 either to purchase preferred stock or to make a long-term loan to PTC. Whatever the form of that investment, Bernie wants to be assured that he will receive at least $50,000 in income from PTC every year before any payments (other than salary) are made to Jessica and Michael and that, if PTC is liquidated, the $500,000 will be repaid before any payments are made with respect to PTC's common stock.

In addition to the $900,000 in cash that Jessica, Michael and Bernie are prepared to invest, PTC has arranged to borrow $500,000 from Columbia National Bank ("Bank"). PTC has agreed to repay that sum in five annual installments of $100,000 each, the first of which will be due in five years, and to pay interest at 12 percent per annum on the unpaid principal. The bank will not have any right to participate in the management of PTC or any right to receive payments other than those

220

just described. However, the bank has required PTC and Bernie to agree that, whatever form Bernie's $500,000 investment takes, Bernie's funds will remain committed to PTC until the bank's loan has been repaid in full and, in the event PTC is liquidated, Bernie's claims will be subordinated to those of the bank.

Stern and Starr have agreed to provide the additional $750,000 that PTC needs by accepting a note for $750,000 of the $2 million purchase price. Consequently, PTC will be required to pay only $1.25 million in cash. The note will require PTC to make annual interest payments of $90,000 (equal to 12% of the face value of the note) and to pay the principal of $750,000 to Stern and Starr in 10 years. If PTC fails to make any interest payment when due, the $750,000 in principal will become due immediately. Stern and Starr will not have any right to participate in the management of PTC or any right to receive payments other than those just described.

In considering the following questions, you may find it helpful to recall the material you studied in Chapter 2, Introduction to the Economics of the Firm.

1. Jessica, Michael and Bernie have tentatively agreed on a capital structure that is fairly typical for a corporation like PTC. They will own 40%, 40% and 20% of PTC's common stock, respectively. Bernie also will own preferred stock or a debt security. The Bank and Stern and Starr will hold debt securities that provide them with no right to participate in the general management of PTC.

What are the interests of the parties providing funds to PTC, with regard to (a) participating in the management of PTC, (b) receiving current income with respect to their investments, and (c) recovering the capital they are committing to PTC? Consider, in this regard, the risks involved in this venture and the parties' attitudes toward bearing those risks. How does the form of the parties' proposed investments advance and protect their interests? How does it allocate risk-bearing among the parties? Consider, in particular, what Stern and Starr can do to protect their interests as creditors of PTC.

2. Would it be better for Bernie to receive preferred stock or a debt security in exchange for the $500,000 of his proposed investment that will not be allocated to common stock?

    a. What business and legal risks does the choice entail for PTC and the three investors? Keep in mind the importance of not jeopardizing the legal and tax advantages of any debt securities they may use, or the possibility that they may elect to have PTC classified as a Subchapter S corporation.

    b. What risks and benefits does the choice entail for Bernie? If Bernie elects to purchase preferred stock, how should the terms of that stock be structured to protect Bernie's interest in receiving income of $50,000 a year with respect to this portion of his investment?

3. How would you advise Jessica and Michael if they were to propose that PTC issue to each of them, in addition to equity securities, a note promising to pay $100,000 on demand of the holder, but not otherwise entitling either of them to any assured or preferred annual payment?

4. Assume Bernie is concerned that Michael and Jessica may, at some future time, seek to reduce his 20% interest in profits and control by issuing additional shares of stock to themselves or to others or to finance expansion of PTC's business.

> a. Could Bernie's concerns be met by including a preemptive rights provision in PTC's articles of incorporation? See RMBCA § 6.30 [DGCL § 1.02(b)(3)].

> b. Why might Michael and Jessica be wary of such a provision?

> c. Could Bernie's concerns be met by limiting the amount of stock PTC is authorized to issue? Would some other action be necessary to make such a limitation effective?

A. CORPORATE SECURITIES

1. INTRODUCTION

Those who finance a corporation or any other economic enterprise generally are interested in the (i) power to exercise control over the management of the enterprise; (ii) right to receive income from the firm's operations; (iii) right to share in the firm's assets if the firm becomes insolvent or liquidates voluntarily; and (iv) need to protect their investment from the inevitable risks of the business. Partnership and corporation law rely on different contractual mechanisms to allocate these interests. In a partnership, investors' interests are determined by the partnership agreement. In a corporation, the terms of investors' interests are embodied in the securities they own. That is, corporate securities are the vehicles by means of which those who provide capital to the firm specify their interests in the firm's management, income stream and assets and protect themselves against risk. The choice of securities in a corporation, therefore, reflects the trade-offs between control, profit and risk that each participant must make.

Corporate securities can be divided into two broad categories: equity securities and debt securities. In general, equity securities represent more or less permanent commitments of capital to a corporation, while debt securities represent capital invested for a limited number of years. Holders of equity securities bear more risk because their claims to income are contingent on the corporation earning a profit. In addition, their rights in the corporation's assets are subordinated to the claims of both trade creditors and holders of the corporation's debt securities.

Holders of equity securities, because they have the power to elect the corporation's board of directors, typically exert more control over the risks of the corporation's business.

Holders of debt securities bear less risk. Their claims to income are fixed, and the corporation is obligated to repay their capital at some future date certain. Moreover, debtholders' rights may be secured by a lien on some or all of the firm's assets or by contractual covenants restricting the firm's operations. Apart from such covenants, however, debtholders ordinarily play no role in the management of the firm.

The distinction between equity and debt securities is not as sharp and well defined as the foregoing summary might suggest. Corporate statutes and case law impose few limitations on planners' ability to design both types of securities with a wide variety of characteristics. In any given corporation, control, profit and risk can be allocated however the investors desire. For example, DGCL § 221 allows corporations to issue debt securities that have voting rights, while DGCL § 151 allows them to issue stock with no voting rights (so long as at least one class of stock has voting rights). See, also, RMBCA § 6.01. Nonetheless, to facilitate understanding and discussion, the following sections describe securities within the two basic categories of equity and debt. For more extended discussion of the characteristics of different securities, see William A. Klein and John C. Coffee, Jr., Business Organizations and Finance 235–298 (5th ed. 1993).

2. EQUITY SECURITIES

Although the RMBCA no longer does so, we use the terms *common stock* and *preferred stock* to describe the two basic kinds of equity securities. Corporate statutes require that at least one class of equity security must have voting rights and the right to receive the net assets of the corporation in the event the corporation is dissolved or liquidated. These rights usually are assigned to common stock.

a. Common Stock

Common stock is the most basic of all corporate securities. All corporations have common stock, and many small corporations issue no other kind of security. Common stock usually holds the exclusive power to elect a corporation's board of directors, although in a few corporations one or more classes of common stock is non-voting. In some corporations preferred stock also may have limited voting rights as described later.

All of a corporation's income that remains after the claims of holders of more senior securities (debt and preferred stock) have been satisfied "belongs," in a conceptual sense, to the holders of common stock. Whether that income should be distributed to shareholders, in the form of a *dividend*, or reinvested in the corporation's business, is largely within the discretion of the board of directors. See Section C. Boards of directors, at least in theory, reinvest income whenever they believe shareholders will benefit more from such actions than from receiving dividends.

Common stock also represents a *residual claim* on the assets of a corporation, in the sense that, if the corporation is liquidated, its assets first must be used to pay the claims of creditors and holders of preferred stock and what remains belongs to the common stock. In economic terms, the common stock bears the greatest risk of loss, if the corporation experiences economic difficulties. Similarly, it embodies the greatest potential for gain, should the corporation be successful.

As a practical matter, corporations rarely are liquidated except when they experience financial difficulty. Consequently, common stock represents a more or less permanent commitment of capital to a corporation. Holders of common stock in successful firms frequently can realize financial gains on their investments by selling their stock to other investors at prices that reflect the increased value of the firm's assets. Such gains can be realized even where a corporation is paying out none or only a small portion of its income as dividends, so long as the firm reinvests its income profitably.

The interests of common stockholders usually are protected in two ways. First, common stock generally has voting rights, and often is the only security with the right to elect the board of directors. Common stockholders also customarily have the right to remove directors; they also must approve amendments to the articles of incorporation and fundamental transactions such as mergers. Significantly, common stockholders typically have a greater right to participate in a firm's management than do the holders of any other type of corporate securities.

Second, common stock is protected by the fiduciary obligations imposed on the board of directors. As we have seen, courts defer to a considerable degree to directors' business judgments, but they do so on the assumption that directors will exercise reasonable care when making business decisions and will act in shareholders' interests. These assumptions (and obligations) extend to decisions concerning whether a corporation should reinvest its profits or distribute them as dividends. In addition, directors have a duty to refrain from engaging in transactions that will provide them with unfair profits at the corporation's expense. In short, directors have broad discretion to manage, but must bear in mind that they are managing other people's money and that they have obligations to do so carefully and loyally.

b. Preferred Stock

Absent specific provisions in a company's articles of incorporation, courts generally presume that "stock is stock"—that all equity securities have the same voting rights, right to dividends, and equity of redemption. Stock is classified as preferred stock when the articles of incorporation assign to it economic rights senior to those customarily assigned to common stock. Preferred stocks vary widely, depending on the attributes they are assigned.

Preferred stock usually has dividend rights senior to those of common stock. The seniority of preferred stock arises out of provisions limiting the payment of dividends on common stock until dividends due on preferred stock have been paid. This dividend preference often is stated as a fixed amount that must be paid annually or quarterly. Such a preference may expire if the dividend due for a given period is not paid. Alternatively, it may be *cumulative* : if a dividend is not paid when due, the right to receive it accrues and all accumulated dividend arrearages must be paid before any dividends are paid on common stock.

Preferred stock also may be made "participating." In that event, preferred stock will receive dividends whenever they are paid on common stock, either in the same amount or as a multiple of the amount paid on common stock. Indeed, operating on the principle that "stock is stock" unless a corporation's articles of incorporation specify to the contrary, some courts have interpreted preferred stock clauses to require such participation unless a contrary intent is clearly spelled out.

In addition to a dividend preference, preferred stock often is entitled to a preference on liquidation, through which the preferred stockholders have a right to receive a specified amount before any distributions are made with respect to common stock. The amount of this preference most often is the amount that the corporation received when it sold the preferred stock plus, in the case of cumulative preferred, any accumulated dividends. In some instances, a small "liquidation premium" also must be paid. However, as is the case with common stock, the preferred stock's equity of redemption is subordinate to the claims of creditors. Consequently, when a corporation does not have assets sufficient to pay its debts, the preferred stockholders receive nothing in the event of liquidation.

Preferred stock sometimes represents a permanent commitment of capital to a corporation and sometimes does not. In the latter event, the stock will be "redeemable" for some specified amount. The right to require redemption may be held by the stockholder, by the corporation, or by both. The amount for which stock is to be redeemed generally is equal to the preference to which it is entitled in the event of liquidation.

Preferred stock can have voting rights, and will be deemed to have voting rights equal to those of common stock unless the articles of incorporation provide otherwise. But the voting rights of preferred stock often are limited to specified issues and circumstances. Preferred stock usually has a statutory right to vote on changes in the corporate structure that affect adversely its rights and preferences. In addition, preferred stock often is given the right to elect some or all of a corporation's directors if dividends due on such stock are not paid for some designated period. Such provisions reflect the nature of the contract that holders of preferred stock often make with a corporation: they relinquish the right to participate in control in exchange for a priority claim to periodic dividends; only if the corporation fails to pay those dividends does the preferred stock reassert its claim to participate in (or exert) control.

The standard features of preferred stock described above may be supplemented by a variety of others, including the right to convert preferred stock into common stock at some specified ratio, the right to vote on certain transactions, or the right to require the corporation to redeem preferred stock if and when specified events should occur. All of these rights are essentially contractual in nature. That is, they must be spelled out in the articles of incorporation. Moreover, courts, influenced by the adage that "no man can serve two masters," have taken the position that, with respect to issues where the interests of preferred and common stock conflict, directors' fiduciary duties run solely to the common stock. Preferred stock is entitled only to the contractual protection spelled out in the provisions of the articles of incorporation that authorize such stock.

Corporations often sell preferred stock in lieu of debt. The two have obvious similarities. The price at which a company can sell preferred stock is influenced by factors similar to those that determine the price at which it can borrow—the dividend rate, the redemption features, whether the preferred can be converted into common stock and, if so, at what price. Consequently, the requirement that the terms of preferred stock be spelled out in the articles of incorporation can pose real timing problems, especially in the case of a publicly-held company. It usually takes a minimum of 30 days to obtain shareholder approval of an amendment to the articles of incorporation authorizing new preferred stock: during that period economic conditions are likely to change enough so that the terms of the preferred initially specified no longer reflect current market conditions.

To deal with this problem, most corporation statutes permit shareholders to authorize "blank check preferred stock," the essential characteristics of which—rights to dividends, preferences in the event of liquidation, redemption rights, voting rights, and the right to be converted into common stock—can be set by the board of directors at the time the stock is sold. See RMBCA § 6.02. While such an authorization may facilitate the sale of preferred stock, it also can enhance substantially the power of a corporation's board of directors to issue preferred stock for a variety of purposes.

3. DEBT SECURITIES

Debt securities—usually denominated as "bonds" or "debentures"—represent liabilities of a corporation. However, they differ from other liabilities, such as the claims of trade creditors, who sell goods and services with the expectation of being paid within a short period of time (30 to 90 days) or the claims of financial institutions that lend money to corporations on a short-term basis. Debt securities constitute a part of a corporation's long-term capital structure; as such, they reflect an ongoing interest in the corporation's financial fortunes.

As a matter of more precise terminology, bonds are secured by a mortgage on corporate assets, whereas debentures are backed only by the general credit of the corporation. Bonds also generally have longer maturities (20 years or more) than debentures (usually 10–20 years), although there is no rigid rule in this regard. To simplify discussion, we use the term "bond" to refer generically to both bonds and debentures.

The terms of a debt security often are fixed by a complex contract known as an "indenture." Whether or not an indenture is used, it is fundamental that the debt contract set forth a fixed obligation to repay the sum loaned to the corporation on a particular date. The instrument should also require that interest in a fixed amount be paid at periodic intervals. The interest obligation is not dependent on the corporation's having earned a profit; if a corporation fails to pay bond interest when due, it will be in default on the loan. Often, the entire principal will become due and payable immediately and the bondholders will be entitled to pursue all legal remedies to which they are entitled, including the right to initiate bankruptcy proceedings.

If a bond is secured, the terms of the security arrangement also must be specified. The debt contract also may include provisions, known as covenants or negative covenants, that require the borrower to refrain from doing certain things that might jeopardize the position of the debt holders. A corporation may agree, for example, not to pay any dividends or to repurchase any of its own shares unless it meets certain financial conditions.

Bonds may be made redeemable or "callable" at a fixed price at the option of the borrower. This right can be valuable to a corporation; if interest rates decline, it can borrow the money needed to repay outstanding high-interest bonds at a lower interest rate and then use it to finance a redemption of those high-interest bonds. To compensate bondholders for their loss of income, a bond's redemption price usually is set at something above the principal that the bondholders would be entitled to receive when the bonds mature.

Because the terms and conditions of debt securities are fixed entirely by contract and often are the result of extensive negotiations, many other provisions may be included in a debt contract. Provisions allowing bonds to be converted into stock are one example. Requirements that borrowers make payments into a "sinking fund" that will be used to repay part of the principal prior to the bond's maturity date are another.

Bonds usually do not carry the right to vote. Moreover, a borrower corporation's directors owe bondholders only such obligations as are spelled out in the debt contract. They are not fiduciaries for the bondholders. *See* Metropolitan Life Ins. Co. v. RJR Nabisco, Inc., 716 F.Supp. 1504 (S.D.N.Y.1989) (holding that RJR Nabisco did not have an implied duty to deal fairly with bondholders and could implement refinancing that greatly increased bondholders' risk, so long as bond indenture did not expressly bar such activity). See Chapter 20. Consequently, bondholders' interests are protected only to the extent that they have negotiated appropriate covenants as part of their debt contracts.

Unless the articles of incorporation provide to the contrary, a corporation's board of directors has the authority to issue debt securities without shareholder approval. The board decides whether the corporation should incur new debt, in what amount, and on what terms and conditions. It must involve shareholders only if it decides to issue debt securities that will be convertible into stock and there are not enough authorized securities available for issuance upon conversion. In such a case, the shareholders must approve an amendment to the articles of incorporation increasing the number of authorized shares. They do not, however, approve the actual issuance of the convertible debt securities.

The use of long-term debt as part of a corporation's capital structure creates a tension between debt and equity investors. Both have parallel stakes in the long term health of the corporation and both compete for the cushion of security provided by any funds that exceed the amount needed for current operations. The main difference between them is that they have made different trade-offs between risk and reward, and thus each has a different perspective on the degree of risk that the business should assume. Unless she has bargained for a right to convert her debt into stock, the debt-holder has accepted rights to fixed payments of interest and repayment of her capital in lieu of the possibly higher, but uncertain, returns available to holders of equity securities, especially common stock. The holder of common stock has assumed more risk, but also can exercise more control over the conduct of the corporation's business. Concomitantly, a debt holder is viewed as an outsider entitled only to the protection specified in her contract. The holder of common stock, on the other hand, is protected by directors' fiduciary obligations, including their obligation to deal with holders of debt securities (and preferred stock) in whatever fashion advances the interests of the common stockholders. Nevertheless, because of the potential to customize the terms of each security, it is more accurate to describe equity and debt securities as falling along a continuum, rather than presenting them as polar extremes.

4. DESIGNING A CORPORATION'S CAPITAL STRUCTURE

a. In General

As we have seen, the capital structure that any given corporation chooses—the mix of common stock, preferred stock, and long-term debt—allocates among investors rights to participate in managing the firm, claims on the firm's income, risks of insolvency, and potential financial rewards. Since investing is a voluntary act, persons organizing a corporation cannot simply select some capital structure and then impose it on potential investors. They must design the capital structure of the firm in general, and the terms of specific securities in particular, so that investors find those securities more attractive than other investments they can make.

Within the limits imposed by market forces, however, persons organizing a corporation generally have the ability to select among different capital structures that reflect differing allocations of control, risk, and claims on the corporation's income and assets. As is the case when choosing an organizational form, federal income tax considerations often will influence the organizers' choice.

b. *Tax Considerations*

The Internal Revenue Code, on its face, provides a corporation with a powerful incentive to rely as heavily as possible on debt financing. Under section 163 of the Internal Revenue Code, a corporation can deduct from its taxable income interest paid on bonds it has issued, but not dividends paid on its preferred or common stock. Consider how this affects a company whose annual income, before payment of taxes, interest or dividends, is $50,000. If the company pays a $10,000 dividend on its preferred stock, its taxable income will be $50,000. But if the company replaces the preferred stock with bonds and pays $10,000 interest on those bonds, its taxable income will be reduced to $40,000. Moreover, repayment of the principal of a bond generally will constitute a tax-free return of capital for the recipient.

While a variety of tax wrinkles may affect the use of stock and debt in particular circumstances, the fact that debt is tax-advantaged raises two questions: Why don't corporations always issue bonds rather than preferred stock? And why don't corporations raise as much of their capital as possible by selling debt to persons who might otherwise purchase common stock?

The first question is provoked by the fact that preferred stock and bonds are both senior securities and have many similar characteristics. Both entitle the holder to priority over the common stock in receiving periodic distributions (in the form of dividends or interest) and to priority claims to the corporation's assets in the event of liquidation. However, payment of preferred stock dividends rests in the discretion of the board of directors, who may choose to omit a dividend if the company is experiencing hard times. In contrast, the holder of a debt security is a creditor and is entitled to interest payments and the timely repayment of principal whether the company prospers or not. This provides one reason for a corporation to favor preferred stock over bonds. Failure to pay interest or to repay principal when due constitutes a default which can lead to bankruptcy proceedings. Failure to pay preferred stock dividends may have painful consequences, such as allowing the preferred stock to elect some portion of a corporation's board, but they are unlikely to be as drastic.

In addition, while interest payments are always deductible by the payor corporation, they also always constitute taxable income to the recipient (unless it is a tax-exempt entity). Dividends on preferred stock are not deductible by the payor, but many corporate recipients can claim a dividends-received deduction and pay tax on only 30% of the dividends they receive. Consequently, a corporation often can sell preferred stock to corporate purchasers willing to accept less in annual dividends than they would demand in interest if they were investing a comparable amount in that corporation's bonds.

c. *Leverage and the Allocation of Risk*

Both tax and business considerations limit corporations' willingness to raise capital by borrowing rather than selling common stock. The Internal Revenue Service (IRS) is keenly aware that investors, particularly in the case of a closely-held corporation, may be tempted to abuse the right to deduct interest payments. If the shareholders of a corporation attempt to treat a large portion of their investment as "debt," so as to generate large interest deductions and minimize the corporation's taxable income, the IRS may seek to characterize as equity all debt held by shareholders. If the IRS succeeds, no interest deductions will be allowed; all payments made on shareholders' "debt" will be treated as dividends.

There are also business risks involved in financing a corporation largely with borrowed money. A corporation will find it profitable to finance business activities with borrowed money whenever it can earn more income from those activities than it will pay in interest on the borrowed money. This concept is known as *"leverage."* Whatever the corporation earns in excess of its interest costs will increase the corporation's income and benefit its shareholders. In effect, the corporation is using the borrowed money as a lever to increase its (and its shareholders') income.

But leverage also increases shareholders' risk. If a corporation earns less from the activities being financed than the interest on the borrowed money, the corporation's income will decline. Interest must be paid whether or not the new investment is profitable. Consequently, corporations often are reluctant to rely on borrowed money unless they are quite confident that leverage will work to their advantage.

To illustrate, assume Ann Jones has $2 million to invest and wants to purchase a business that will cost $5 million. Ann believes she can raise the additional $3 million she needs either by selling 60% of the equity to other investors for $3 million or by borrowing $3 million from a bank. If Ann is confident the business will generate at least $1 million a year in profits, which would represent a 20% return on a $5 million investment, and Ann can borrow $3 million at less than 20% annual interest, she will prefer to borrow the money. Assuming an interest rate of 15%, her calculation will be as follows:

	Borrow $3 million	Sell equity
Income before interest	$1,000,000	$1,000,000
(Interest)	(450,000)	—
Net income	550,000	1,000,000
Income allocated to other investors	—	600,000
Income allocated to Ann	550,000	400,000

In other words, if the business performs as Ann expects, Ann will end up with $550,000 if she borrows the $3 million and with only $400,000 if she sells equity. Moreover, this calculation does not take account of taxes. Let's assume that the $1 million profit Ann expects is an after-tax figure and that Ann believes the business will generate $1.5 million in income before taxes and interest. Interest can deducted from income in calculating a business's taxable income. Consequently, if we again assume an interest rate of 15%, Ann's calculation will be as follows:

	Borrow $3 million	Sell equity
Income before interest and taxes	$1,500,000	$1,500,000
(Interest)	(450,000)	—
Pre-tax income	1,050,000	1,500,000
Taxes (@ 33%)	350,000	500,000
Net income	700,000	1,000,000
Income allocated to other investors	—	600,000
Income allocated to Ann	700,000	400,000

In other words, due to what is often described as the "tax kicker," Ann will be $300,000 better off if she borrows the $3 million she needs rather than selling additional equity, assuming, again, that the business performs as well as Ann expects.

At this point, you may well be wondering why people who own or want to buy businesses don't always borrow most of the funds they need, rather than selling equity to other investors. Leverage clearly has the potential to increase the profit that one can realize from an investment. But leverage also has a down side. Most businesses involve substantial risks. Outcomes often vary from what people expect. And, as discussed in Chapter 2, people have different attitudes towards risk. Consequently, leveraging one's investment may not work well and may not appear attractive. Consider, for example, how Ann would fare if the business she wants to buy earns only $300,000 before interest and taxes.

	Borrow $3 million	Sell equity
Income before interest and taxes	$300,000	$300,000
(Interest)	(450,000)	—
Pre-tax income	(150,000)	300,000
Taxes (@ 33%)	—	100,000
Net income	—	200,000
Income allocated to other investors	—	120,000
Income allocated to Ann	(150,000)	80,000

If Ann spreads the risk of buying the business among herself and other investors, she still ends up with $80,000. That might not seem like much of a return on a $2 million investment, but it is a lot better than the $150,000 loss Ann would have to absorb if she borrows the funds she needs.

For many years, it was conventional wisdom that, aside from situations in which the same persons held a corporation's equity and debt securities, common stock should comprise at least one-third, and more often one-half, of a corporation's long-term capital. During the 1980s, that belief was challenged, and many public corporations adopted highly-leveraged capital structures. Some had debt to equity ratios in excess of 9:1; *i.e.*, more than 90% of their long-term capital was debt. Highly-leveraged capital structures have controversial implications for corporate governance, which we discuss in Section D.

5. EXCESSIVE DEBT AND BANKRUPTCY

Another peril of a debt-heavy capital structure is that a court may treat putative debt as equity in a bankruptcy proceeding. Under the "Deep Rock Doctrine," named for a bankrupt company involved in a leading case, Taylor v. Standard Gas & Electric Co., 306 U.S. 307, 59 S.Ct. 543, 83 L.Ed. 669 (1939), bankruptcy courts have exercised their equity jurisdiction to subordinate the claims of shareholder creditors to those of other creditors when they conclude the shareholder creditors have not invested adequate equity capital in a corporation. See also Pepper v. Litton, 308 U.S. 295, 60 S.Ct. 283, 84 L.Ed. 281 (1939); Comstock v. Group of Institutional Investors, 335 U.S. 211, 68 S.Ct. 1454, 92 L.Ed. 1911 (1948). When the Deep Rock Doctrine is invoked, shareholder-creditors usually receive no repayment with respect to the "debt" they hold.

IN RE FETT ROOFING & SHEET METAL CO., INC.

438 F.Supp. 726 (E.D.Va.1977), aff'd without
opinion 605 F.2d 1201 (4th Cir.1979).

CLARKE, DISTRICT JUDGE.

This matter comes before the Court on the appeal by plaintiff from an order of United States Bankruptcy Judge Hal J. Bonney, Jr., which dismissed plaintiffs' complaint, subordinated the note claims of the plaintiff to the claims of all other creditors and set aside deeds of trust which purported to secure the note claims. Appellant contends that the Bankruptcy Judge's findings of fact and conclusions of law were completely erroneous and that appellant's claims against the bankrupt should be reinstated. Jurisdiction of this Court is based on 28 U.S.C.A. § 1334; Bankruptcy Act §§ 38, 39(c), 11 U.S.C.A. §§ 66, 67(c); and Bankruptcy Rule 801.

THE FACTS

The record below discloses that the bankrupt, Fett Roofing and Sheet Metal Co., Inc., was owned and run prior to 1965 by plaintiff herein, Donald M. Fett, Sr., as a sole proprietorship. During 1965, Mr. Fett incorporated his business, transferring to the new corporation assets worth $4,914.85 for which he received 25 shares of stock. The stated capital of the corporation was never increased during the course of the corporation's existence. Mr. Fett was the sole stockholder and also the president of the corporation. The roofing business continued to be run completely by Mr. Fett much as it had been prior to its incorporation. In short, Fett Roofing was a classic "one-man" corporation. Over the years, plaintiff advanced money to his business as the need arose. Three of these transactions made in 1974, 1975 and 1976 involved the transfer to the corporation of $7,500, $40,000 and $30,000, respectively. In each instance plaintiff borrowed from the American National Bank, made the funds available to his business and took back demand promissory notes. On April 6, 1976, at a time his business had become insolvent, plaintiff recorded three deeds of trust intended to secure these notes with the realty, inventory, equipment and receivables of Fett Roofing and Sheet Metal Co., Inc. The deeds were backdated to indicate the dates on which the money had actually been borrowed. On November 8, 1976, an involuntary petition in bankruptcy was filed.

After a trial in which both sides presented considerable evidence and the plaintiff personally testified regarding his claim, Judge Bonney made the following findings of fact.

1. The bankrupt was undercapitalized at its inception in 1965, and remained undercapitalized throughout its existence. The capital necessary for the operation and continuation of its business was provided by the complainant in the form of so-called loans on an "as-needed" basis. Promissory notes, including the three involved herein, were given to the complainant in the course of such transactions.

2. The three deeds of trust which purport to secure the said notes were all back-dated to create the impression that they were executed contemporaneously with the advance of funds and the giving of the notes; all three were in fact executed and recorded during the first week of April 1976, when the notes were, by their terms, past due.

3. The purpose of the deeds of trust was to delay, hinder, and defraud the creditors of the bankrupt, and to give the complainant a preference over them, in the event a liquidation of assets became necessary.

4. Complainant was in sole control of the affairs of the bankrupt, and was its sole stockholder. His interests were at all times identical to and indistinguishable from that of the bankrupt; he was the *alter ego* of the bankrupt.

5. At the time these three deeds of trust were executed and recorded, the bankrupt was, and for several months had been, unable to meet its obligations as they came due in the ordinary course of business. Many of the debts listed in the schedules filed by the bankrupt were incurred and delinquent prior to April 1976.

6. Complainant knew that his corporation was insolvent no later than February 1976.

Based on these findings, Judge Bonney concluded that the advances made by plaintiff to his corporation were actually contributions to capital, not loans, and that claims based on them therefore should be subordinated to those of all the other creditors of the bankrupt. The Judge further found that even if the transfers had been *bona fide* loans, the deeds of trust intended to secure them would have been null and void as having been given with actual intent to delay, hinder and defraud creditors in violation of § 67d(2)(d) of the Bankruptcy Act, 11 U.S.C.A. § 107(d)(2)(d). In addition, Judge Bonney determined that such loans were given in fraud of creditors under state law and therefore were voidable under § 70(e) of the Bankruptcy Act, 11 U.S.C.A. § 110(e).

Because we have concluded that the Bankruptcy Judge was correct in his determination that the plaintiff's transfers of money to his corporation were capital contributions and not loans we do not consider the soundness of the last two legal findings.

THE LAW

* * * A director, officer, majority shareholder, relatives thereof or any other person in a fiduciary relation with a corporation can lawfully make a secured loan to the corporate beneficiary. Faucette v. Van Dolson, 397 F.2d 287 (4th Cir.), cert. denied, 393 U.S. 938, 89 S.Ct. 301, 21 L.Ed.2d 274 (1968). However, when challenged in court a fiduciary's transaction with the corporation will be subjected to "rigorous scrutiny" and the burden will be on him " * * * not only to prove the good faith of the transaction but also to show its inherent fairness from the viewpoint of the corporation and those interested therein." Pepper v. Litton, 308 U.S. 295, 60 S.Ct. 238, 84 L.Ed. 281 (1939); Geddes v. Anaconda Copper Mining Co., 254 U.S. 590, 599, 41 S.Ct. 209, 65 L.Ed. 425 (1921).

Where a director or majority shareholder asserts a claim against his own corporation, a bankruptcy court, sitting as a court of equity, will disregard the outward appearances of the transaction and determine its actual character and effect.

Similar results have properly been reached in ordinary bankruptcy proceedings. Thus, salary claims of officers, directors and stockholders in the bankruptcy of "one-man" or family corporations have been disallowed or subordinated where the courts have been satisfied that allowance of the claims would not be fair or equitable to other creditors. And that result may be reached * * * where on the facts the bankrupt has been used merely as a corporate pocket of the dominant stockholder, who, with disregard of the substance or form of corporate management, has treated its affairs as his own. And so-called loans or advances by the dominant or controlling stockholder will be subordinated to claims of other creditors and thus treated in effect as capital contributions by the stockholder not only in the foregoing types of situations but also where the paid-in capital is purely nominal, the capital necessary for the scope and magnitude of the operation of the company being furnished by the stockholder as a loan.

Pepper v. Litton, *supra,* 308 U.S. at 308–310, 60 S.Ct. at 246.

The record on this appeal reveals the bankrupt to have been a large construction contractor requiring ample amounts of capital. As indicated above, the corporation was capitalized at slightly under $5,000 when it was created in 1965. No increment to this initial amount was ever formally made. According to the schedule filed with the Bankruptcy Judge, the bankrupt's debt to secured creditors alone stood at $413,000. This is a debt-to-equity ratio of over 80 to 1. While this fact by itself will not serve to convert what is otherwise a *bona fide* loan into a contribution to capital, it does cast serious doubt on the advances by a person in plaintiff's special situation being considered debt rather than equity. The fact that no evidence was adduced by plaintiff to show that the "borrowings" in question were formally authorized by the corporation or that interest was ever paid on them, coupled with the undisputed day-in-and-day-out control over corporate affairs wielded by plaintiff, as president and sole stockholder leave little doubt that plaintiff, ignoring corporate formalities, was infusing new capital into his business and avoiding such necessities as charter amendment or the issuance of new stock. The record discloses that the funds transferred to the corporations were used to finance the acquisition of equipment and material necessary to the functioning of the business. Although one of the advances was used to pay a *bona fide* tax liability, this does not affect its character as a capital contribution under the particular circumstances of this case. In re Trimble Co., 479 F.2d 103, 115 (3d Cir.1973). The fact that plaintiff at various times characterized these advances as "recapitalization" can only reinforce a conclusion which consideration of the entire record makes inevitable.

The Courts of this circuit have had no reluctance to pierce through surface appearances in these matters and distinguish contributions to capital from genuine loans. In Braddy v. Randolph, 352 F.2d 80 (4th Cir.1965), a case with some striking similarities to the present dispute, the plaintiff, president, director and a principal stockholder of a bankrupt corporation, filed four claims based on four notes secured by deeds of trust. In affirming the rejection of these claims, the Court of Appeals stated:

> To finance this volume and to keep the business going even though operating at a loss, the Bankrupt borrowed heavily and constantly from the four officers and the North Carolina National Bank (hereinafter Bank). The money which officers, Braddy, Zeliff, Craft and Foster, "loaned" the Bankrupt was normally acquired from the Bank by use of their personal credit and personal assets. Based on the volume of business and the fact that the Bankrupt began borrowing from the officers and the Bank at the outset of operations, we think the referee and court could reasonably conclude that these "loans" were necessitated by the initial insufficiency of the

Bankrupt's equity capital and that the "loans" made by the officers were, in effect, contributions to capital. Rather than invest more capital the officers and stockholders, by the use of the borrowed funds, substantially shifted and evaded the ordinary financial risks connected with this type of business enterprise and, at the same time, permitted the corporation to remain in a constant state of or in imminent danger of insolvency.

* * * Although the advances contested here were made well after the corporation was created, there is evidence in the record that plaintiff had "loaned" the bankrupt money over the years and that the transfers here in issue were only the latest in a series of contributions made necessary by the corporation's grossly inadequate capitalization. Since these three transactions were "part of a plan of permanent personal financing," the fact that they did not occur at the outset of corporate existence is not crucial and the claims based on them are properly subordinated to those of other creditors.

Since the transfers made by plaintiff to the bankrupt were, in contemplation of law, capital contributions the deeds of trust purporting to secure these advances were properly set aside since there was in fact "no debt to be secured." Arnold v. Phillips, 117 F.2d 497, 501 (5th Cir.1941).

As the cases make clear, no one fact will result in the determination that putative loans are actually contributions to capital. The Court is guided by equitable principles that look to the result of the transaction as well as to the formal indicia of its character. A person in the special position of the plaintiff " * * * cannot by the use of the corporate device avail himself of the privileges normally permitted outsiders in a race of creditors." Pepper v. Litton, *supra,* 308 U.S. at 311, 60 S.Ct. at 247. It is not necessary that fraud, deceit or calculated breach of trust be shown. Where, as here, a corporate insider, indeed the corporate alter ego has so arranged his dealings with his corporate principal that he achieves an unfair advantage over outside creditors dealing at arms length, the Court will subordinate his claim to theirs.

For the foregoing reasons, the Order appealed from is affirmed.

Note: *"Thin" Corporations and Bankruptcy*

Courts have employed a variety of approaches to decide whether a corporation has been adequately capitalized. In In re Mobile Steel Co., 563 F.2d 692 (5th Cir.1977), a corporation was formed to purchase the assets of an existing steel fabricating business. The organizers invested $250,000 in the corporation's common stock and purchased $250,000 in debentures. The corporation also borrowed $650,000 from a bank, secured by a pledge of realty, and more than $800,000 from a factor, secured by a pledge of accounts receivable. The court stated:

The concept of undercapitalization has never been rigorously defined. Absolute measures of capital inadequacy, such as the amount of stockholder equity or other figures and ratios drawn from the cold pages of the corporation's balance sheets and financial statements, are of little utility, for the significance of this data depends in large part upon the nature of the business and other circumstances. Nor is the fact of eventual failure an appropriate test. Cf. Automotriz Del Golfo de California S.A. (de) C.V. v. Reswick, 47 Cal.2d 792, 799, 306 P.2d 1, 6 (1957) (Carter J. dissenting) (disregard of corporate entity). This would be tantamount to ruling that an investor who takes an active role in corporate affairs must advance to his corporation all of the funds, which hindsight discloses it needed to survive. Instead, we think that for the purposes of determining whether claims against the bankrupt estate held by organizers or shareholders should be subordinated on the ground of undercapitalization, the amount of capitalization that is adequate is

> what reasonably prudent men with a general background knowledge of the particular type of business and its hazards would determine was reasonable capitalization in the light of any special circumstances which existed at the time of incorporation of the now defunct enterprise.

N. Lattin, The Law of Corporations §§ 15, 77 (2d ed. 1971); cf. H. Ballantine, Corporations 302–03 (rev. ed. 1946) (disregard of corporate entity); see generally E. Latty, Subsidiaries and Affiliated Corporations, 119–28 & 133–38 (1936). This general definition is helpful because it focuses on the culpability of the organizer-stockholders and pegs the assessment to more specific standards which do not involve open-ended quantitative questions. Foremost among the standards which the general statement suggests are the following:

> (1) Capitalization is inadequate if, in the opinion of a skilled financial analyst, it would definitely be insufficient to support a business of the size and nature of the bankrupt in light of the circumstances existing at the time the bankrupt was capitalized;

> (2) Capitalization is inadequate if, at the time when the advances were made the bankrupt could not have borrowed a similar amount of money from an informed outside source.

563 F.2d at 702–3.

What if the corporation has adequate initial capitalization, but suffers a later drain of capital? The court in In re Trimble Co., 479 F.2d 103, 116 (3d Cir.1973) stated:

> In the instant case, the corporation was adequately capitalized to begin with, but suffered overwhelming losses during the years 1958 through 1961. In such a situation, a test which may be used to decide whether a contribution by a proprietary interest is a loan or an additional injection of capital is whether the advance was made at a time when a bank or other ordinary commercial agency would be willing to lend it funds.

In In re Branding Iron Steak House, 536 F.2d 299, 301–2 (9th Cir.1976), the court stated:

> A creditor's claim cannot be subordinated to the claims of other creditors simply because the claimant is an officer, director, or controlling shareholder in a bankrupt corporation. * * * However, when it would be inequitable to permit such a creditor to share equally with other creditors, the Bankruptcy Judge may subordinate his claim. Costello v. Fazio, 256 F.2d 903 (9th Cir.1958); Anno. 51 A.L.R.2d 989, 993.

In *Costello,* supra, three individuals engaged in a partnership for the operation of a plumbing company. The partnership capital consisted of $51,620.78, of which each of the three partners had invested unequal amounts. After four years of operation the business was undergoing serious financial difficulties, and the decision was made to incorporate. In the year preceding incorporation net losses totalled $22,521.34. In anticipation of incorporation, all of the partnership capital except $6,000 was withdrawn and converted into debt evidenced by promissory notes issued to two of the partners. An expert testified that there was little hope of financial success at that time in view of the recent business reverses. The business was incorporated, and the partnership debts, including the two promissory notes issued to the former partners, were assumed by the corporation. Two years later, when the corporation filed a voluntary petition in bankruptcy, the two former partners made claims on their promissory notes. The Bankruptcy Referee refused to subordinate their claims, finding that the corporation was adequately capitalized and that the claimants had not acted for their own personal or private benefit to the detriment of the corporation. The District Court affirmed, but our Court reversed, holding that both of the critical findings of the Bankruptcy Referee were clearly erroneous.

Here, the Bankruptcy Judge concluded that the present case is controlled by *Costello.* Because of the result we reach we can assume without deciding that the Bankruptcy Judge was correct in concluding that the restaurant was undercapitalized. Nevertheless, given this assumption, undercapitalization is the only significant fact common to both our present case and *Costello.*

In *Costello,* the claimants argued that mere undercapitalization should not, in and of itself, be sufficient to require subordination of their claims. We responded that "much more" than mere undercapitalization had been shown. 256 F.2d at 910. It seems virtually undeniable that the facts in *Costello* reflect a calculated maneuver by the investors, met with consistent business reverses, to attempt to reduce their risk to the detriment of other creditors. The *Costello* court found it significant that the partners "stripped the business of 88% of its stated capital at a time when it had a minus working capital and had suffered substantial business losses." 256 F.2d at 910.

In contrast, here the bankrupt did not begin to suffer business losses until several years after its incorporation. There was thus no clear intention by Richmond and Alexander to shift their risk to other creditors in the face of business reverses. Indeed, there was no stripping away of the restaurant's capitalization at all. Richmond held promissory notes for money loaned to the restaurant from the outset. At no time was existing capital withdrawn and converted into debt.

Moreover, it is not disputed that Richmond was not at all active in the operation of the enterprise. Before the legitimate claim of an officer, director, or shareholder of a bankrupt corporation may be subordinated to the claims of other creditors, not only must that person have the ability and intent to control the corporation, but he must in fact exercise that control to the detriment of other creditors. In re Brunner Air Compressor Corp., 287 F.Supp. 256, 265 (N.D.N.Y.1968). The record is devoid of any evidence whatsoever that Richmond exercised such control.

In our view, mere undercapitalization, standing alone, is not enough to justify the subordination of the legitimate claims of officers, directors, and shareholders of a bankrupt corporation to those of other creditors. We acknowledge that a claim may be subordinated even in the absence of fraud or mismanagement, * * * Nevertheless, a Bankruptcy Court is a court of equity, and subordination requires some showing of suspicious, inequitable conduct beyond mere initial undercapitalization of the enterprise. * * *

B. AUTHORIZATION AND ISSUANCE OF EQUITY SECURITIES

First some terminology: *"Authorized"* shares are those shares of stock created by an appropriate clause in the articles of incorporation. Until shares are first sold to stockholders, they are *"authorized but unissued."* When sold, they are *"authorized and issued"* or *"authorized and outstanding."* If they are repurchased by the corporation, they become *"authorized and issued, but not outstanding."* Shares that are authorized and issued, but not outstanding are commonly referred to as *"treasury shares"* (a term not used in the RMBCA but used in other statutes).

Corporation statutes do not dictate how many or what kind of shares are authorized; the statutes do require that the articles of incorporation include the number of shares that a corporation is authorized to issue and describe certain characteristics of those shares. RMBCA §§ 2.02(a)(2), (b)(2)(iv); DGCL § 102(a)(4). See also Article Four of the Model Articles of Incorporation in West Publishing Co., Selected Corporation and Partnership Statutes, Rules and Forms.

If a corporation issues all the shares authorized in its articles of incorporation, it must amend the articles to authorize additional shares before it can issue more stock. An amendment must be recommended by the board of directors and approved by holders of at least a majority of its outstanding stock. (RMBCA § 10.03; DGCL § 242.) Recall that in the Chesapeake Marine Services Problem in Chapter 3, the corporation had sold all of its authorized stock and could not itself sell any more because a minority shareholder held sufficient stock to veto any amendment to the articles of incorporation.

1. THE SIGNIFICANCE OF AUTHORIZING STOCK

Should the organizers of a corporation authorize more shares than they initially plan to issue? The corporation may want to issue additional shares at a later date to raise new money, to use for employee benefit plans, or to acquire other companies. As a practical matter, it may seem tempting to authorize a large number of shares at first so the corporation can issue additional shares in the future without the bother of amending the articles.

However, when deciding how many shares to authorize, one should consider more than questions of convenience. A corporation's board of directors normally has sole power to decide whether additional shares should be issued. Consequently, if a corporation's original shareholders "authorize" more shares than they initially plan to purchase, they also delegate to the board of directors authority to decide if and when additional shares should be issued unless the corporation is chartered in a state whose laws require shareholder approval for the issuance of a large number of shares, see, e.g., 15 Ohio Rev.Code Ann. § 1701.83(A), or is listed on the New York Stock Exchange, whose rules require listed companies to obtain shareholder approval before they increase outstanding stock by more than 18.5%. See N.Y.S.E. Company Manual, § 312.00.

In large corporations, shareholders have relatively little influence over day-to-day management, and yielding the power to issue common stock may not constitute the surrender of much real power. Convenience usually decides the question in favor of an initial authorization of a large number of shares. However, the issue has become more complex with regard to "blank check preferred" stock described in Section A.2. Such stock was often used as consideration in corporate mergers. In the mid–1980s, however, corporations developed *"poison pill"* plans which constituted relatively powerful defenses against uninvited takeover bids. Many such plans were based on the availability of authorized but unissued blank check preferred. A corporation's board of directors first would create a new class of preferred stock with unusual features, such as a right to require the corporation to redeem the preferred at a price equal to twice its fair market value. Then the corporation would distribute to its shareholders "rights" to purchase shares of the newly-created preferred, usually by exchanging their shares of common stock for the preferred. Shareholders could exercise the rights only if some triggering event occurred, such as the announcement of an uninvited hostile takeover bid. Until such an event occurred, the corporation would have the option of redeeming the rights for a nominal payment, usually no more than $0.05 per share. But while the rights remained outstanding, they were a powerful deterrent to uninvited takeover bids because, combined with the newly-created preferred stock, they had the potential to make a takeover prohibitively expensive.*

In Moran v. Household International, Inc., 500 A.2d 1346 (Del. 1985), the court held that nothing in the Delaware statute made adoption of a poison pill plan unlawful and that a decision to adopt such a plan would be treated as a business judgment reviewable under the business judgment rule. The court added that it would review a board's decision to rely on a poison pill to deter an uninvited takeover bid under the somewhat more stringent standard applicable to defensive tactics generally. See Chapter 22. While courts in some other states declined to follow *Moran*, legislatures overrode all such decisions and authorized the creation of poison pill plans. Consequently, shareholders in publicly-held corporations now often think twice before approving proposals to authorize blank check preferred.

In a close corporation, the decision on how much stock to authorize also requires some thought. Shareholders may wish to retain control over the issuance of new shares by limiting the original authorization to the number of shares contemplated to be issued immediately. The issuance of any new shares will then require an amendment of the articles and thus a shareholder vote. Recall that it was just such a requirement that gave Apple the power to veto an increase in the authorized capital of Chesapeake Marine Services. Such a limitation can protect minority shareholders and will preserve existing control relationships. See Chapter 13.

2. PREEMPTIVE RIGHTS AND OTHER DUTIES IN THE IS-SUANCE OF SHARES

The precise number of shares that a shareholder owns in a corporation at a particular time determines her position relative to other stockholders. What is important, however, is not the absolute *number* of shares the stockholder owns, but the *percentage* of the corporation's outstanding stock those shares represent. Consider two corporations that are otherwise identical, except that A has 200 shares of common stock outstanding and B has 1,000 shares outstanding. Fifty shares of A, representing 25% of its outstanding stock, clearly will be worth more than 50 shares of B, representing 5% of its outstanding stock.

A shareholder may be concerned that if additional shares are sold to other investors, her interest in the corporation will be diminished or

---

* If the rights were triggered, and the takeover bid proceeded, the acquiror would be obliged to pay twice fair market value for all shares not tendered in response to its takeover bid, so long as the owners of those shares exercise the rights and converted their stock into the poison pill preferred.

"diluted." This concern will be valid if the shareholder is interested primarily in maintaining her proportionate ownership interest because, for example, it allows her to exercise a degree of control. (Again, recall Chesapeake Marine Services.) We will refer to this as a concern about "equity dilution."

A shareholder also may be concerned about "economic dilution"—the possibility that sales of additional shares will reduce the value of the shares she holds. This concern is most salient in two situations. First, other shareholders, particularly if they control the board of directors, may arrange to purchase additional shares at less than fair market value and thus appropriate to themselves a portion of the value of the corporation's assets. Second, the board of directors may sell shares to unrelated persons at prices that the board believes to be fair, but that the non-controlling shareholders believe is too low.

On the other hand, if a corporation sells additional shares at a price that reflects their fair market value, and if the corporation uses the funds received for those shares to produce income at a rate at least equal to the return it is generating on its existing capital, shareholders' economic interests will not be diluted. For example, if a company with 1000 shares of common stock issued and outstanding has a fair market value of $10,000, then the fair market value of each share will be $10. The sale of 500 additional shares at $10 per share will not dilute the economic value of existing shareholders' stock, if the fair market value of *all* the shares, after investing the additional $5,000, is at least $10 per share. (Of course, if the company sold new shares for less than $10, or if the company's fair value was more than $10,000, economic dilution would occur.)

The common law doctrine of *"preemptive rights"* addressed concerns about equity dilution. Courts held a shareholder had an inherent right to maintain her interest in a corporation by purchasing a proportionate share of any new stock issued for cash; i.e., a shareholder who owned 100 shares in a corporation with 1,000 shares issued and outstanding would be entitled to purchase 10% of any new issue of stock by that corporation. See Stokes v. Continental Trust Co., 186 N.Y. 285, 78 N.E. 1090 (1906). The doctrine worked reasonably well for corporations with few shareholders and simple capital structures. It became problematic where a corporation had several classes of stock outstanding, or sought to issue stock in exchange for property to be used in its business. Preemptive rights also were of questionable value in publicly-held corporations: a typical public shareholder, owning far less than 1% of the outstanding stock, presumably would care little that a new issue would reduce her proportionate interest in the firm from 0.001% to 0.0009%. Moreover, if she believed the firm was selling new stock at too low a price, she could protect herself by purchasing additional shares on the open market.

Courts and legislatures both addressed the problems posed by preemptive rights. Courts developed several exceptions to the rule that shareholders always were entitled to preemptive rights. Legislatures modified state corporate laws to provide corporations with the option of abolishing preemptive rights.

RMBCA § 6.30 adopts an "opt-in" approach. To provide shareholders with preemptive rights, a corporation must include an appropriate provision in its articles of incorporation. A simple declaration, such as "The corporation elects to have preemptive rights," will do. But absent such a declaration, no preemptive rights exist. RMBCA § 6.30(a). Delaware law no longer explicitly addresses preemptive rights. *See* DGCL § 161. However, DGCL § 157 authorizes a corporation to issue rights to purchase its stock. These could include preemptive rights, and a provision requiring such rights could be included in the articles of incorporation. *See* DGCL § 102(b)(1).

The RMBCA also addresses some of the problems associated with preemptive rights. Unless the articles provide otherwise, no preemptive rights exist with respect to shares issued to compensate executives, shares issued within six months after a company is organized, or shares sold for other than for money. RMBCA § 6.30(b). Similarly, preemptive rights are limited in corporations with multiple classes of stock. Id.

Most public corporations have abolished preemptive rights; a shareholder who wishes to maintain her proportionate interest can do so by purchasing additional shares in the market. In a closely held corporation, however, preemptive rights can provide significant protection to minority shareholders. A lawyer organizing a close corporation should consider and discuss with her clients, when preparing the articles of incorporation, whether preemptive rights should be adopted and, if so, what the terms of those rights should be. For an excellent discussion of relevant considerations, see F. Hodge O'Neal & Robert B. Thompson, O'Neal's Close Corporations § 3.39 (3d. ed. 1992).

At times, preemptive rights alone are not sufficient to protect minority shareholders' interests. In Katzowitz v. Sidler, 24 N.Y.2d 512, 301 N.Y.S.2d 470, 249 N.E.2d 359 (1969), two of the three shareholders in a corporation with preemptive rights hatched a plan to eliminate the third, who was short of funds. Although the corporation's stock was worth $1300 per share, they approved a new issue at par value of $100 a share. The cash-short shareholder, who could not afford to purchase any additional stock, sued to enjoin the offer, claiming that the new issue was designed to dilute his interest. The court granted the requested relief, stating: "The price was not so much a bargain as it was a tactic, conscious or unconscious on the part of the directors, to place Katzowitz in a compromising situation." 249 N.E.2d at 365. See, also, Bennett v. Breuil Petroleum Corp., 34 Del.Ch. 6, 99 A.2d 236 (1953) (holding shareholder with preemptive rights also had "right not to purchase" stock, which was wrongfully impaired by offering at substantially less than stock's fair value); but, see Hyman v. Velsicol Corp., 342 Ill.App. 489, 97 N.E.2d 122 (1951) (holding preemptive rights adequately protected minority shareholder's interests and declining to inquire into fairness of stock issue).

Courts also have shown a willingness to intervene, in situations where preemptive rights do not apply, to protect shareholders' proportionate interests in the control of close corporations. In Schwartz v. Marien, 37 N.Y.2d 487, 373 N.Y.S.2d 122, 335 N.E.2d 334 (1975), control of the corporation was divided between two family groups, each of which owned 50 shares of stock and had two seats on the board. When one director died, the two directors representing the other (Marien) family elected a third director to fill the vacancy on the board. The board then approved the sale of one share each to the two Marien directors and the new director and two shares to a long-time corporate employee. Schwartz, the surviving director from the other family, sought to buy five additional shares so as to maintain her family's 50% interest. The board refused.

The court held that directors of a close corporation have a fiduciary duty to protect shareholders' interests when they issue stock, whether or not shareholders have preemptive rights. Shares can be issued in a manner that treats existing shareholders differently only to advance a bona fide business purpose. Moreover, the board has the burden of proving not only that the stock issue was approved "to achieve a bona fide independent business objective, but as well that such objective could not have been accomplished substantially as effectively by other means which would not have disturbed proportionate stock of ownership." 335 N.E.2d at 338.

On the other hand, Yasik v. Wachtel, 25 Del.Ch. 247, 17 A.2d 309 (1941), denied cancellation of shares that allegedly had been issued to shift control of a close corporation. There, however, the complaining shareholder could not alone exercise control and had never combined with others to exercise control.

Shoen v. Shoen, 167 Ariz. 58, 804 P.2d 787 (App. 1990), involved a situation where control was at issue. Members of the Shoen family owned about 97% of the corporation's outstanding stock. Two factions of the family were competing for control. One controlled the board, but owned less than 50% of the outstanding stock. The remaining family members owned more than 50% and were on the verge of asserting control. The board preempted the change in control by selling about 7% of the corporation's stock—all shares not then issued and outstanding— to a group of "key employees" aligned with the family faction that controlled the board. With those shares, that faction also controlled more than 50% of the authorized stock; the other faction was reduced to potentially permanent minority status.

Because the stock sale advanced the personal interests of the directors who authorized that transaction, the court inquired into whether the stock sale was in the corporation's best interests. But the court allowed the directors to satisfy this inquiry by producing evidence that they had acted in good faith and believed the stock sale would promote loyal service by the "key employees." 804 P.2d at 795. The court also appeared to treat as legitimate and significant the board's opposition to the dissident faction's plan to sell the entire corporation if and when it gained control. For discussion of similar issues, as they relate to contests for control of public corporations, see Chapter 22.

C. REGULATION OF LEGAL CAPITAL

As we have seen, a creditor's claims against a corporation's income and assets have priority over the claims of equity securityholders. This priority is valuable, however, only if (1) the debtor corporation has received all amounts it claims to have been paid for its equity securities, and (2) the corporation is barred from jeopardizing the creditor's interests by distributing to its equity securityholders, in the form of dividends or otherwise, assets that it needs to satisfy the creditor's claims. Creditors, not surprisingly, usually seek to protect their interests by contract. But state corporation laws also provide some protection for creditors by regulating *legal capital*—the terms and conditions on which a corporation is permitted to sell stock and pay dividends.

In fact, protecting creditors was a major preoccupation of corporate law during the 19th century and most of the 20th century. However, by the 1970s, if not earlier, it became clear that the legal capital rules no longer protected creditors and probably never had. Bayless Manning's Legal Capital played a leading role in debunking these rules. California was the first state to revise its statute to take account of this new learning. Many others followed, stimulated by the revision of the legal capital provisions of the RMBCA. But in many others, including Delaware, the traditional rules remain in force.

Lawyers need to understand these rules, both the old and the new, for two reasons. First, as a condition of many financing transactions, a corporation's lawyer will be asked to opine that all of a corporation's stock is "validly issued, fully paid and nonassessable." To render such an opinion, a lawyer must review all transactions in which the corporation issued stock and to see whether they were effectuated in compliance with the governing statutory provisions.

Second, most corporation statutes explicitly provide that directors can be held liable if they approve issuance of stock or distribution of a dividend in violation of applicable statutory standards. These provisions heighten directors' concerns about their personal liability, and often lead them to seek advice of counsel in connection with decisions that might otherwise seem to involve no more than garden variety business judgments. Indeed, today the principal purpose of the legal capital rules is to provide a benchmark for the propriety of the declaration of dividends.

PROBLEM

PRECISION TOOLS—PART VI

Jessica, Michael and Bernie have agreed to pay a total of $500,000 for the common stock of PTC. In addition, Bernie will invest $500,000 in 20–year subordinated notes to be issued by PTC. They have agreed that PTC initially will issue 5,000 shares of common stock. Jessica will pay $200,000 in cash for 2,000 shares (i.e., $100 per share). Michael will pay PTC $100,000 in cash and give PTC a note for $100,000 in exchange for another 2,000 shares. Bernie will pay $100,000 in cash for the remaining 1,000 shares.

1. Prepare balance sheets for PTC reflecting its financial position after (a) the investments by Bernie, Jessica and Michael and the bank loan; and (b) the acquisition by PTC of PT's business.

2. How would you answer the following questions if PTC was organized under Delaware law. Briefly explain your answers. See DGCL §§ 102(a)(4), 152–154.

  a. Is it necessary for PTC to set a par value for its common stock?

  b. What would be the consequence of setting the par value of PTC's stock at $100 per share—the price for which the stock will be sold—or at some lower value, such as $1 per share? Does the statute limit PTC's choice? How would PTC reflect the transaction on its balance sheet if par value is $100 per share or $1 per share?

  c. If PTC decides to issue no par stock, is any further action by its board of directors either required or desirable?

  d. Can PTC accept Michael's note as payment for the 2,000 shares he will receive? Does your answer depend on whether par value is $100 per share or $1 per share? Could any problem with the note be remedied by substituting Michael's promise to serve as president of PTC for the next five years?

3. How would you answer the following questions if PTC was organized under Columbia law. Briefly explain your answers. See RMBCA §§ 6.21–6.22.

  a. Is it necessary for PTC to set a par value for its common stock?

  b. How would PTC account on its balance sheet for the proposed sale of stock?

  c. Can PTC accept Michael's note as payment for some or all of the 2,000 shares he will receive? Could PTC also issue stock in exchange for Michael's promise to serve as president of PTC for the next five years?

1. A CONCISE HISTORY OF LEGAL CAPITAL AND PAR VALUE

BAYLESS MANNING WITH JAMES J. HANKS, JR., LEGAL CAPITAL
(3d ed. 1990) pp. 5–40.

The ideal world as conceived by the creditor of the corporation is a world that is normally wholly unacceptable to the shareholder. The investor who buys shares of stock in the incorporated enterprise and the investor who lends money to the incorporated enterprise, are, as a matter of economics, engaged in the same kind of activity and are motivated by the same basic objectives. They are both making capital investment; they both expect or hope to get their money back in the long run, either by liquidating pay-out or by sale of the security; and they both expect and hope to receive income from their investment in the interim before their capital is returned to them in full. In the stereotypic model transaction, the investor who chose to take a shareholder's position rather than a creditor's position in a particular transaction, simply made a calculated economic judgment that was different from the creditor's. The shareholder estimated that he could make more money by relinquishing to creditor investors a "prior" claim for interest and a fixed principal payment on maturity, and, by opting for uncertain "dividends" and the residual claim to the assets of the enterprise that would remain after all creditors, with their fixed claims, had been paid off. The shareholder is willing to admit the "priority" of the creditor's interest claim and claim for principal payment on maturity. That does *not* imply, however, that the shareholder is willing to stand by chronologically until such time as the creditors have been paid in full. The shareholder will usually insist, that if, as he hopes, the enterprise makes money (and perhaps even if it does not), the shareholders will receive some return on (or of) their investment from time to time, regardless of the fact that there are creditor claims outstanding. Such periodic payments to shareholders are characterized as "dividends;" and, in the usual and normal case of the healthy incorporated enterprise, it is assumed that some assets will be regularly distributed out from the corporate treasury to the shareholder investors in dividend form.

Simple as this observation may be, its implications are far-reaching. If it were the case that all creditors had to be paid off before *any* payment could be made to shareholder investors, and if shareholders received nothing until ultimate liquidation of the enterprise when they would divide the residuum left after payment of all creditors—if, in other words, the terms "prior" and "before" were chronological as well as hierarchical—the creditor would not have to worry about assets being drained away into the hands of junior claimants and he would sleep better at night. But that arrangement would be wholly unacceptable to shareholders. Shareholders insist——and ultimately creditors must concede——that *during the life* of the creditor's claims, assets may be passed out to an investing group that hierarchically ranks below the creditors. The question becomes unavoidable: How much of the assets in the treasury of the incorporated enterprise may be distributed to shareholders, when and under what circumstances? * * *

Consider a newly formed corporate enterprise at the stage of its initial financing by the issue of shares; the only assets in the corporate treasury are those which the stockholders have just put in for their stock, and the enterprise has done no business. If, at that time, a prospective lender asks the question, "How much assets does the corporation have free and clear after claims of creditors" the answer will be the same as the answer to the question, "How much did the shareholders put in?" Similarly, if a loan is then made to the corporation, the question, "How much assets did the corporation have at the time of the loan" has the same answer as the question, "How much assets have the shareholders put in over all time?" On this simplistic model, the statutory stated capital scheme is based. The scheme assumes that the key to protection of the creditor lies in the answer to these two questions which, taken together, become, "How much assets have shareholders put into the corporate treasury since the formation of the corporation?" Whether or not that question is one that really interests a creditor, it is the elemental question to which the statutory legal capital scheme is addressed.

The nineteenth century pattern of corporate financing provided a ready suggestion to judges and statutory draftsmen for a way to gauge the quantity of assets that shareholders had, at some time or another, put into the corporate treasury. According to that pattern of corporate practice, an entrepreneurial organizer, the "promoter" who had conceived of an idea for a new business would make the rounds of people who had money to invest ("capitalists" all, whether little grey widows or sturdy yeomen), and seek to persuade them to invest in stock of the proposed enterprise. If the idea had appeal, and if the promoter was persuasive, * * * the subscriber, would, on call of the future board of directors of the corporation when organized, put in a set amount of money, or other assets, and would receive a set number of shares of the newly formed corporation. Given this practice, it was to be expected, and was perhaps inevitable, that in drawing up the subscription agreements for any single enterprise, a fixed mathematical relationship would be set between the amount of dollars to be invested by a subscriber and the number of shares he would receive: so many dollars to be put in for each share issued. That relationship produced the concept of the "par value" of the stock to be issued. In the normal situation, no equity investor could expect to obtain a share of stock for less than the par value of it, since presumably all other purchasers were paying that amount. Similarly, no share subscriber could be persuaded to agree to pay more than the par value for a share since other investors were receiving a similar share by paying in the par value. * * *

* * * In time, the par value of the stock was required by statute to be stated as a provision in the corporate charter.

The essentially arbitrary character of this number must be understood. If, for example, each of three investors agreed to invest $10,000 in stock of a new company, the number of shares to be issued, N, and the par value $P, could be anything—could be any number that the promoters might set so long as $N \times \$P = \$30,000$. Further, so far as the shareholders in this case were concerned, it was immaterial what "par" was so long as each one received the same number of shares for his $10,000 investment.

Against this familiar background of practice, however, it was easy for the courts—and legislatures—to take a next assumption, and it early became a matter of common understanding, that the "par value" was what the shareholder *ought* to have paid for his stock. Stock which was issued without a corresponding pay-in of assets valued at an amount equal to par was called "watered stock"—stock issued not against assets but against water. (The term also echoed an ancient sharp practice in another field, the aquatizing of livestock before weighing them in for sale.) * * *

It will be clear to the reader that the development of the "par" concept just described arose as a response to the problems of assuring equitable contribution among shareholders. But development of the shareholder's par payment obligation served, in a somewhat fortuitous and naive way, to further the corporate creditor's interest in seeing shareholder assets committed to the enterprise. One can spin at least a hypothetical argument as to why this should be and how it came to be.

The argument would go in this wise: If a creditor extends credit immediately after the incorporation of the new enterprise and if he has been informed that the par value of the shares is $P and the number of shares that have been issued is N, it is not unreasonable for him to assume that the shareholders have collectively contributed into the corporate treasury an amount of dollars equal to the par value of the shares issued multiplied by the number of shares that were issued, or $PN. In a kind of rough and ready way, assuming that there have been no other transactions, the creditor might infer that the number $PN is an approximation of the total assets of the corporation, and on that basis might conclude that he could safely lend a certain amount of funds to the enterprise.

Did any rational creditor ever in fact act that way or extend credit on such a naive basis? The answer has to be "no." But two things did occur.

First, in lawyers' discourse the number $PN came to be called the corporation's "capital."

Second, if the enterprise ultimately went broke, and the creditor did not get paid, and he found out at that later time that some shareholder had *not* in fact paid into the corporate treasury an amount of assets equal to the par value of the shares he had received, the creditor's lawyer would certainly *argue* in a suit against the shareholder that: (i) Everyone knows that shareholders should pay into the corporate treasury assets equal to the par value of the shares issued to them; (ii) the defendant shareholder did not pay in that amount; (iii) the corporation is insolvent, creditors are unpaid, and the shareholders are not liable for the corporation's debts; (iv) therefore the court should require the defendant shareholder to pay over to this energetic suing creditor, to the extent of his claim against the corporation, the amount by which the defendant shareholder failed to pay in to the corporation assets equal to the aggregate par value of the stock he received; and (v) if (iv) does not appeal to the court as the appropriate remedy, then the defendant shareholder should be required to pay into *the corporate treasury* now for the benefit of all corporate creditors, the full amount by which he failed earlier to pay into the corporate treasury assets of a value equal to the aggregate par value of the shares he received. * * *

[I]n time, this much became clear:

(1) The courts came to recognize that purchasers of shares from the corporation have some obligation to invest in the corporate enterprise;

(2) It came to be understood (perhaps "assumed" is a better word) that the measure of the investment liability of such a shareholder was the number of shares issued to him times the par value of the shares; and

(3) It came to be recognized that at least some creditors could in at least some circumstances enforce this obligation of the purchasing shareholder in some way. * * *

In the nineteenth century pattern of corporate financing, it was simply assumed that good companies—respectable companies—solid investments—would have stock with a high par value. * * * Nonetheless, eventually the practical argument prevailed and the invariable practice of using high par value common stock gradually gave way to the use of low par common stock. * * *

With this shift made, a typical transaction might see a promoter (*i.e.,* his lawyer) set a par of $10 per share and a *higher* subscription agreement, say $50 per share. What difference does it make to any shareholder that the par is lower than the purchase price, so long as each initial equity investor pays in the same amount per share? With this development, however, the prototype corporate model outlined earlier is reduced to splinters. * * * [T]he separation of par and purchase price has the effect of opening a chasm between the lawyer's perspective and economist's concept of the entrepreneur's capital investment. If there are ten subscribers in a newly incorporated enterprise each of whom buys 10 shares of stock at a price of $50 per share, the economist, or the businessman would say that the company's beginning "capital" is $5,000. But the lawyer (and later the accountant) will tell the economist or the businessman that the "capital" is determined by par, and in this case is the number of issued shares, 100, multiplied by the par value of each share, $10, for a total of $1,000; the other $4,000 is something else about which we will hear more later. With the evolution of low par stock, came the evolution of that strange lawyer's convention * * *— "legal capital"—the $1,000 in the example just given. * * *

It was not until 1912 that analysis of the matter had reached a sufficiently wide circle to produce statutory authorization of no par stock. The advent of no par stock did not, however, have the effect of eliminating the concept of legal capital. It was, and still is, statutorily necessary to designate some dollar number on the corporate balance sheet as "capital." * * * The responsibility for making that statement, and the power to make it, is placed by corporation statutes with the board of directors, and the dollar number declared by them made in the customary form of a board resolution, is the "stated capital" of the corporation. * * *

What does the law do to prevent shareholders of a distressed company from pulling assets out of the corporate treasury just when the creditor needs them? * * *

Two basic propositions slowly emerged: (1) The measuring rod for judging the propriety or impropriety of the distributions to equity holders is the corporation's "capital"; and (2) "capital" refers not to assets but to that abstract number that is obtained by multiplying the number of shares of stock outstanding by the par value assigned to each share. In due time, the emergence of low par and no par stock expanded this second proposition so that "capital" came to mean "stated capital," or "legal capital." * * *

The general idea of the legal capital scheme is that no distribution may be made to shareholders unless, after the distribution, the corporation has not only enough assets to pay its creditors but also an additional specified amount. This amount is called "stated capital". Anything over the sum of stated capital and liabilities is known as "surplus", there is a "surplus"—that is, an amount greater than the sum of (a) the amount needed to pay creditors and (b) the "stated capital". If the accounting entries representing the enterprise's assets do not total to a figure equal to the indebtedness of the enterprise plus the "capital", the capital is said to be "impaired" and the stock is said to be "under water". In the case of a corporation in a condition of "capital impairment", if the figures on the assets side of its balance sheet actually reflected their sell-off value, and if all the assets were to be sold off for cash, and if all creditors were to be paid off, the money that would be left over for the equity investors, the shareholders, would be less than the "capital" they put into the enterprise in the first place. Where that is the condition, the statutory scheme forbids the incorporated ongoing enterprise to distribute assets to shareholders by dividend or otherwise. * * *

The following statements may now be made about "legal capital."

a. Legal capital is a number expressed in dollars.

b. That number is initially the product of par value—itself an arbitrary dollar amount printed on the stock certificate and recited in the certificate of incorporation—multiplied by the number of shares "outstanding."

c. Legal capital is a number that appears on the *right-hand,* or claimant's side of the balance sheet, *not* on the left-hand asset side. "Legal capital" is *not* an asset, a fund, or a collection of assets. And it does not refer to an asset, a fund, or a collection of assets. (The same is true of "surplus.")

d. Legal capital is a number that implies that a valuation of at least that amount was placed upon some indeterminate assets that were transferred to the corporation at some indeterminate past time in exchange for shares then issued. Legal capital can at best be read to convey a message by implication—a message about a historical event.

Legal capital is entirely a legal invention, highly particularized in its meaning, historical in reference, *and not relatable in any way to the ongoing economic condition of the enterprise.* For most purposes, it is best thought of simply as a dollar number—a number having certain consequences and derived by specified statutory procedures, but just a number.

The law makes use of the concept of "legal capital" in two ways:

a. It is the maximum number of dollars up to which someone might in certain circumstances be able sometime to hold some shareholders liable if the implied statement in [a–d] above could be proved to be false.

b. It is a datum line, or water table, or bench mark, or nock on a measuring stick laid alongside the total number on the asset side of the balance sheet, on the basis of which lawyers will—or will not—sign an opinion that a proposed distribution of corporate assets to shareholders is valid, legal, and generates no liabilities either for the board of directors that declares it or the shareholders who receive it.

And here is the real bite. In the world of corporate finance, the closure of any significant transaction is utterly dependent upon opinions of legal counsel that are delivered at the closing, stating that the transaction is valid and legally enforceable. Whenever a corporate financial transaction requires the lawyers to inquire into a company's legal capital position, the impact of the statutory schemes of legal capital is enormously magnified by the Go/No-go function performed by opinions of counsel. The lawyers, in turn, are compelled to develop an understanding of the statutory scheme and of its application. From that state of affairs "legal capital" draws its perverse vitality.   * * *

2. THE ISSUANCE OF STOCK AND STOCKHOLDERS' LIABILITY

a. *Quantity of Consideration*

Under a regime of legal capital characterized by sales of stock at par, corporation law was much consumed with questions relating to "watered stock." Promoters frequently acquired stock in exchange for property worth less than the par value of the shares they received and then sought to mislead other investors about the value of their contributions. Knowing that capital must be equal to the par value of all shares issued and outstanding, promoters would report the property they contributed as an asset equal in value to the par value of the shares they received. That is, a promoter who contributed land worth $5,000 to a newly-formed corporation in exchange for 100 shares of $100 par value common stock would record the transaction as follows:

Assets		Liabilities and Equity	
Land	$10,000	Capital (100 shares common stock, $100 par value)	$10,000
Total	$10,000	Total	$10,000

Courts, operating on the flawed premise that investors and creditors deal with a corporation on the basis of its stated capital, focused their attention on the right-hand side of the balance sheet and held promoters liable for "watering" the capital account. But "capital," of course, was computed mechanically—by multiplying the number of shares issued and outstanding by the par value of those shares. The real fraud was on the left-hand side of the balance sheet in the overvaluation of the property contributed by the promoter.

Nonetheless, courts and commentators engaged in a lengthy conceptual debate concerning the basis on which promoters could be held liable for watered stock. See, e.g., Hospes v. Northwestern Manufacturing & Car Co., 48 Minn. 174, 50 N.W. 1117 (1892); Henry W. Ballantine, Stockholders' Liability in Minnesota, 7 Minn.L.Rev. 79, 90 (1922). Though important historically, that debate has little contemporary significance. States that retain traditional legal capital rules all have now adopted statutory provisions governing shareholders' liability for watered stock.

DGCL § 162 is typical. It provides that shareholders are liable for "the sum necessary to complete the amount of the unpaid balance of the consideration for which shares were issued or are to be issued by the corporation." While interesting interpretative questions relating to this section can be posed, in practice they virtually never arise. Corporate lawyers have learned they can avoid the problems associated with watered stock by setting the par value far below the price at which the corporation plans to sell its stock and by monitoring carefully transactions in which stock is issued. The most salient question today often is whether to use low-par or no-par stock. The choice usually depends on the manner in which the relevant jurisdiction calculates the tax or "franchise fee" payable on incorporation. That fee frequently is calculated on the basis of the aggregate authorized capital of the corporation, with no-par stock "deemed" to have some arbitrary par value for this purpose.

Another reason valuation problems rarely arise in this context is that most statutes now provide that the board's judgment as to the value of property exchanged for stock is conclusive, absent fraud, or, as in DGCL § 152, absent "actual fraud." This language suggests that courts should treat as determinative any good faith determination by a board of directors concerning the value of property. Here, too, interpretative questions remain, such as whether "actual fraud" differs from ordinary fraud, but again they are largely of theoretical importance. The last important case holding shareholders liable for watered stock was Bing Crosby Minute Maid Corp. v. Eaton, 46 Cal.2d 484, 297 P.2d 5 (1956).

b. *Quality of Consideration*

A question closely related to the quantity of consideration is the quality or type of consideration for which stock may validly be issued. Cash is always acceptable. Services rendered and real or personal property are also permissible because they are either convertible to cash (property) or they have already contributed to the corporation's assets (services).

Under many state statutes (e.g. DGCL § 152), however, an executory contract to render *future* services is invalid consideration. According to Professor Herwitz,

> The traditional concern about future services as consideration for stock lies chiefly in the fact that such services can prove valuable to a business only as a going concern and are totally devoid of realizable value for creditors or stockholders in the event of a liquidation of the enterprise. While of course other intangible items, notably goodwill, may prove worthless upon the failure of an enterprise, promised future services are subject to the special objection that they have no realizable value from the outset. Moreover, future services do not lend themselves readily to any objective standards for measuring the quantity of value involved. This difficulty is aggravated by the fact that such items are commonly transferred by the very people in control of the corporation, who thereby become judges of the amount of their own contributions. And in any event it has been common experience that corporate promoters are more likely to be extravagant when making payments in stock than when laying out hard cash.

David R. Herwitz, Allocation of Stock Between Services and Capital in the Organization of a Close Corporation, 75 Harv.L.Rev. 1098, 1105–6 (1962).

But a corporation certainly can pay a substantial salary advance to a person with some particular skill to induce her to come to work for the enterprise. And it also can pay her a bonus to acquire her services. If such an advance payment or bonus could be then used by the employee to purchase stock, why not just short-circuit the process and allow the corporation to issue the stock directly in exchange for the promise of future services? Petrishen v. Westmoreland Finance Corp., 394 Pa. 552, 147 A.2d 392 (1959), relied on that analogy to approve stock issued for future services under a traditional statute. A more straightforward solution would be to sell low par stock to the prospective employee at par value. Such an arrangement would raise no problems under a traditional statute, nor would it give rise to claims of unfairness so long as other shareholders purchased with knowledge of this bargain sale.

Promissory notes present another common problem; many states prohibit their use as consideration for stock, especially unsecured notes signed by a purchaser-shareholder. Suppose the note is secured? Calif.Corp.Code § 409(a)(1) provides that a promissory note "adequately secured by collateral other than the shares acquired * * *" is good consideration for the purchase of shares. Suppose the note is unsecured, but guaranteed? The court in Eastern Oklahoma Television Co., Inc. v. Ameco, Inc., 437 F.2d 138 (10th Cir.1971) held a personal guarantee of an obligation of the corporation was, in part, adequate consideration for the issuance of stock. See also Citizens Bank of Windsor v. Landers, 570 S.W.2d 756 (Mo.App. 1978).

Whether a note is given for par value, or only the excess of the purchase price over par value, may be critical. In Shoen v. Shoen, 167 Ariz. 58, 804 P.2d 787 (App. 1990), certain "key employees" of a Nevada corporation were allowed to purchase stock by making cash down payments equal to the par value of the shares they received, which amounted to less than 4% of the price for which those shares were issued, and gave the corporation non-recourse notes for the balance. The corporation's only remedy, if the purchasers defaulted, was to return their down payments and recover the stock. Other shareholders sued to have the stock issuance declared unlawful because the corporation could not recover from the key employees "the unpaid balance of the consideration for which the shares were issued." The court rejected this claim, pointing out that the notes were legally enforceable obligations and that to treat them as valid consideration for stock was not inconsistent with the Nevada statute (which is virtually identical to Delaware law in this respect).

c. *Legal Capital Under the Revised Model Act*

The RMBCA jettisons the traditional approach to legal capital in favor of a fiduciary based system. RMBCA § 6.21 abolishes the concepts of "par value" and "stated value," although a corporation may retain par value if it so elects in its articles of incorporation. RMBCA § 2.02. Shares may be issued for such consideration as the board may authorize, at a fixed price, a minimum price, a formula price or any other method of price determination. Business conditions—and not the artificial notion of par value—determine the price for which shares may be issued. According to the Official Comment to RMBCA § 6.21, "there is no minimum price at which specific shares must be issued and therefore there can be no "watered stock' liability for issuing shares below an arbitrarily fixed price." Clearly, the drafters believed that the old system of legal capital did not protect creditors' interests. What remains unclear is whether any system is needed, whether a fiduciary approach provides greater protection than the outmoded legal capital regime, or whether creditors are better protected through their own ability to contract rather than through a corporate law mechanism.

The issuance of shares still requires valid consideration, but the board of directors no longer needs to translate the consideration into dollars (for corporate law purposes, anyway) nor must it declare the consideration adequate. According to the Official Comment, shareholders' interests are protected by the business judgment of the board of directors rather than by formal statutory and accounting rules.

The RMBCA also abandons traditional restrictions on the quality of consideration. RMBCA § 6.21 permits sale of stock for future services or promissory notes. Again, the statutory scheme relies on the directors' judgment that the values exist. § 6.21(c) makes clear that shares are fully paid and non-assessable after the corporation has received the bargained-for consideration. The Official Comment notes that whether shares are validly issued depends solely on whether proper corporate procedures have been followed.

Of course, in addition to satisfying the requirements of the RMBCA, a corporation ultimately will have to prepare a financial statement. Then, if not before, it will have to place a dollar value on the property paid for stock. If those values are inflated, no liability will result under the RMBCA, but liability may exist under common law fraud or under the federal securities laws. (See Chapters 10 and 19.)

Liability of shareholders for payment of their shares is similar to that under Delaware law, except that there is no requirement that shareholders pay at least par value. RMBCA § 6.22 limits shareholders' liability to "payment of the consideration for which the shares were authorized to be issued or specified in the subscription agreement."

The Official Comments to RMBCA §§ 6.21 and 6.22, reprinted in West Publishing Co., Selected Corporation and Partnership Statutes, Rules and Forms provide a good explanation of the Model Act's approach.

3. DIVIDENDS AND OTHER DISTRIBUTIONS

PROBLEM
PRECISION TOOLS—PART VII

After three years of operations, the relevant entries on PTC's balance sheet, prior to the payment of any dividend, are as follows:

Assets		Liabilities and Equity	
Cash	$ 200,000	Current Liabilities	2,650,000
Other Current Assets	3,135,000	Long–Term Liabilities	3,750,000
Total Current Assets	3,335,000	Total Liabilities	6,400,000
Net Fixed Assets	3,475,000	Common Stock (5,000 shares	
Good Will	90,000	authorized and outstanding)	500,000
Note Receivable	100,000	Retained Earnings	100,000
		Total Equity	600,000
Total Assets	7,000,000	Total Liabilities and Equity	7,000,000

PTC earned net profits of $90,000 in its most recent year.

How would you answer the following questions under each of the following assumptions:

(a) PTC is organized under Delaware law and its common stock is $100 par value;

(b) PTC is organized under Delaware law and its common stock is $1 par value; and

(c) PTC is organized under Columbia law.

See DGCL §§ 160, 170, 172–174, 242(a)(3), 244; RMBCA §§ 6.31, 6.40 and Official Comment to § 6.40.

1. Can PTC pay a dividend to its shareholders in the amount of $200,000 at this time? What steps, if any, could it take to make lawful any dividend that otherwise would be unlawful?

2. A dispute has arisen between Bernie and the other shareholders over the continued employment of Bill Gould. The parties have decided to resolve their differences by having the company repurchase Bernie's 1,000 shares for $500,000. Assuming that the corporation can borrow sufficient money on a long term basis to finance the purchases, can it buy the stock?

3. Assume the balance sheet shown above is for a date five years after the organization of PTC and that PTC has paid no dividends and has never repurchased any of its stock. Michael, Jessica and Bernie continue to own their stock, but Michael and Jessica actually control PTC. Michael and Jessica are paid substantial salaries; Bernie receives no salary. Michael and Jessica would like to accumulate income in PTC with a view to buying the business of one of PTC's major customers. Bernie wants some dividend to be paid. Is it likely that Bernie would succeed in a suit to compel payment of a dividend?

a. The Rationale for Regulating Dividends

Investors purchase a corporation's stock in the hope that they will realize gains in the form of dividends received while they hold that stock, capital appreciation when they sell it, or some combination of the two. For various reasons shareholders may be willing, or even eager, to forego dividends and realize most of their gain in the form of capital appreciation, particularly in closely-held corporations where shareholders are employees and can take out profits in the form of salaries and other compensation. In the case of publicly-held corporations, however, many investors are reluctant to rely entirely on capital gains; changes in the fortunes of a particular company, in business conditions generally, and the tenor of the stock market make such reliance too risky. Moreover, many investors, depend on dividends from their investments for current income, and try to invest in companies with stable businesses, such as public utilities, that pay regular and substantial dividends.

When a corporation seeks to raise capital by selling stock, it must compete with alternative uses of prospective investors' funds, including consumption, the purchase of gold bars, savings accounts, money market funds, government debt obligations, real estate, and the race track, to mention just a few. Consequently, corporations try to maximize the appeal of their stock, and thus to minimize their cost of capital, by paying careful attention to their dividend policies.

Corporate law does not leave decisions concerning the payment of dividends entirely to the workings of the market place and the discretion of corporate managers. As Dean Manning points out, shareholders and creditors have sharply conflicting interests with regard to the size and frequency of dividend payments. Because directors are elected by and are accountable to shareholders, they clearly would be inclined to favor shareholders' interests if their power to declare dividends was unrestricted. To counter this tendency, corporate law traditionally has sought to protect creditors' interests with regard to dividend payments, as it has with regard to issuance of stock. Recognizing that preferred stockholders also can be jeopardized by overly-generous dividend payments, corporate law also has sought to protect their interests.

b. The Traditional Approach to Regulating Dividends

The traditional approach to restricting dividend payments relied on the concept of legal capital and the associated notion of "surplus." Some states permit dividends to be paid only to the extent that a corporation has "earned surplus." This term is generally defined to mean a surplus which arises from the accumulation of profits during the life of the enterprise.* While there are difficult interpretative questions involved in the meaning of the operative terms, the policy is plain enough. Dividends are supposed to be the fruit of the tree, and unless fruit has been borne, nothing can be picked.

More common are statutes that allow dividends to be paid out of "surplus," without regard to whether it is "earned" or not. See, e.g., DGCL § 170, N.Y.B.C.L. § 510. The theory underlying such provisions is that the only cushion on which creditors can rely is a corporation's stated capital. The rest of the shareholders' equity account is "surplus" (usually called either "earned" or "capital" surplus) and is at the disposition of the shareholders.

In addition to the payments that might be made under one of the foregoing provisions, some states also permit the payment of dividends whenever a corporation has current earnings. See DGCL § 170. Their statutes define current earnings in various ways, sometimes looking only to the most recent fiscal year, and sometimes looking to the preceding year, either alone or in combination with the current year. Such so-called "nimble dividend" provisions in effect allow the payment of dividends by currently profitable corporations even where such payments impair stated capital.

As should be clear by now, restrictions on dividends based on the concept of legal capital are unlikely to be effective. In plain fact, these limitations have proven insignificant in restricting cash payouts. The Delaware and New York statutes, which limit the protection for senior

---

* Section 2(*l*) of the Model Business Corporation Act, the predecessor to the RMBCA, provided:

"Earned surplus" means the portion of the surplus of a corporation equal to the balance of its net profits, income, gains, and losses from the date of incorporation * * *.

security holders to legal capital, can be easily manipulated. A corporation can reduce the par value of its outstanding stock by amending its articles of incorporation, thereby reducing stated capital. The amendment will not affect any asset or liability accounts. To keep the balance sheet in balance, the corporation will have to increase some other equity account, usually called "reduction surplus." Thus, by reducing par value, a corporation increases the amount of dividends it lawfully can pay. Or the corporation's managers can set the legal capital at almost any figure that they choose. Any amount paid in excess of par value constitutes "capital surplus" and can be distributed to shareholders if the corporation is not insolvent and would not be rendered insolvent. Whether such a payment is labelled a "dividend" or a "distribution," it surely reduces the assets available to pay creditors' claims.

Courts may go even further in weakening restrictions on dividend payments based on the concept of legal capital. Suppose a corporation's real estate increases in value. Can the corporation reflect the higher value on its balance sheet? If it does, the corporation will have to match the increase on the left-hand (asset) side of its balance sheet with an equivalent increase on the right-hand-side of its balance sheet. The account it will increase is shareholders' equity—more specifically, "surplus." It probably will call this increase "revaluation surplus," rather than "earned surplus." But whatever the label, surplus, and the corporation's dividend paying power, will be increased. The celebrated case of Randall v. Bailey, 23 N.Y.S.2d 173 (Sup.Ct.1940), aff'd, 288 N.Y. 280, 43 N.E.2d 43 (1942), sustained payment of a dividend based on the existence of a revaluation surplus created in this manner. Few other courts have faced this issue and none have explicitly followed Randall v. Bailey, but a decision by New York's highest court itself is significant. For a case in which Randall v. Bailey was not followed, see Woodson v. Lee, 73 N.M. 425, 389 P.2d 196 (1963).

As we saw in Chapter 6, generally accepted accounting principles stress historic cost and would not allow such an upward revaluation. But statutes based on legal capital do not require corporations to employ generally accepted accounting principles (GAAP). They can keep separate and completely legal sets of books to compute the amount available for distribution to shareholders. However, consistent with GAAP, a corporation that based its dividend payments on such books almost surely is obliged to write-down the book value of any assets worth significantly less than their cost (or cost less accumulated depreciation).

c. *Protection Against Excessive Dividends Under the Model Act*

The RMBCA abandons restrictions based on legal capital or surplus tests altogether. Instead, unless the articles provide otherwise, RMBCA § 6.40(c) simply prohibits "distributions," as defined in § 1.40(6), if after the distribution (1) "the corporation would not be able to pay its debts as they become due in the usual course of its business," or (2) "the corporation's total assets would be less than its total liabilities plus" any sum needed to satisfy the claims of preferred stockholders in the event of dissolution. The Official Comment to § 6.40 characterizes these as the "equity insolvency test" and the "balance sheet test." Neither test can be applied mechanically; both require the exercise of judgment. That judgment is exercised by a corporation's board of directors.

Dean Manning calls this provision "the big bomb" because directors face personal liability if they judge wrong. The RMBCA, and more specifically the Official Comment to § 6.40, recognizes this danger and attempts to reduce it by stating that decisions concerning distributions should be evaluated as would any other exercise of business judgment.

In evaluating the corporation's ability to meet its obligations as they come due, directors generally can assume that the company will remain a going concern. The Official Comment suggest several benchmarks directors may wish to consider, but no bright line tests. Where solvency appears to be a matter of concern, directors may find it helpful to analyze a company's liquidity and cash flows, using both reports on the results of operations and any forecasts or budgets management has prepared.

The balance sheet test is to be made on the basis of (1) specified financial statements or (2) fair valuation or other reasonable methods. The RMBCA leaves this determination to the directors and does not mandate the use of GAAP. Of course, directors can protect themselves by relying on financial reports prepared in accordance with GAAP. See RMBCA § 8.30. California law involves similar tests, but does require use of GAAP. See Calif.Corp.Code §§ 114 and 500(b).

Clearly a policy that turned on concepts of par value provided little protection to creditors because of the ease with which restrictions could be circumvented. The law as now reflected in RMBCA § 6.40 seems more realistic, but does it furnish meaningful protection to creditors? Directors cannot render the corporation insolvent by approving a distribution, but the RMBCA does not preclude them from going to the edge. No cushion is required. By contrast, consider Calif. Corp. Code § 500 which requires that a corporation's liquid and hard assets (total assets less certain intangibles) after a distribution equal at least 125% of liabilities and that directors employ GAAP in making this computation. One explanation for the different approaches is that the drafters of the RMBCA appear to have decided that corporate law is not the vehicle through which creditors should be protected. They can rely on contract, or on fraudulent conveyance law, such as the Uniform Fraudulent Conveyance Act. A similar attitude is reflected in other aspects of corporate law, which provides that managers' fiduciary duties run only to shareholders, allow only shareholders to bring derivative actions and rarely allow creditors to "pierce the corporate veil" and reach the assets of shareholders of insolvent corporations. For an excellent discussion of these issues, see Robert C. Clark, Corporate Law, Chapter 2 (1986).

d. Stock Dividends

Not all dividends involve the distribution of cash to stockholders. Corporations occasionally pay what are known as "stock dividends" in which additional shares of stock are distributed. In economic terms, such a dividend produces no meaningful change in the financial status of the corporation or its shareholders. It merely divides shareholders' ownership interests in the corporation into a greater number of shares while leaving each shareholder's proportionate interest unchanged. Indeed, the reason for paying such a "dividend" often is to produce the appearance that shareholders are receiving something when the corporation is not in a position to pay a dividend in cash.

Since a stock dividend does not result in the distribution of any of the corporation's assets, there is no need to place limitations on it for the protection of creditors. Indeed, because the par value (if any) of the shares distributed must be added to stated capital (see, e.g., DGCL § 173) a stock dividend can actually benefit creditors. RMBCA § 6.23 recognizes that a stock dividend involves the issuance of shares "without consideration." RMBCA § 1.40(6) excludes such a dividend from the definition of a "distribution."

e. Repurchase of Shares

A corporation may want to repurchase some of its outstanding stock for a variety of reasons. If the repurchase is pro rata from all shareholders, it will have almost exactly the same effect as a dividend; the only difference will be a reduction in the number of shares outstanding. But whether a repurchase is pro rata or from less than all shareholders, its impact on creditors will be the same as if the corporation paid a dividend. Consequently, corporation statutes generally impose restraints on the repurchase of stock similar to those imposed on dividends. N.Y.B.C.L. § 513 for example, generally permits repurchases only out of surplus, although it allows repurchase or redemption of redeemable shares out of capital. DGCL § 160 prohibits the repurchase of common stock if it would impair capital, which amounts to essentially the same thing. The RMBCA defines the repurchase of shares as a "distribution" in § 1.40(6) and subjects it to the limitations contained in § 6.40.

Traditional statutes classify reacquired shares as "treasury stock." Treasury stock remains "issued," but is not "outstanding." If treasury shares are resold (technically they are "sold" and not "issued" although there seems to be little or no practical distinction), the restriction imposed on surplus when they were purchased is eliminated. On the other hand, preemptive rights ordinarily do not extend to sales of treasury shares and a corporation generally may not vote treasury shares. See, e.g., DGCL § 160(c).

The RMBCA eliminates the concept of treasury shares. § 6.31 provides that reacquired shares automatically revert to the status of authorized but unissued stock, thereby avoiding the complexity of prior law.

f. Liability for Unlawful Distributions

When a corporation makes an unlawful distribution to shareholders, creditors' interests usually are placed in jeopardy. When an unlawful distribution results in actual losses to creditors, the directors who authorized that distribution can be held liable. See, e.g., RMBCA § 8.33 which imposes liability on the directors who voted for a dividend, distribution, or repurchase of stock that violates the restrictions of the Act. See also DGCL § 174; and N.Y.B.C.L. § 719.* A director held liable for an unlawful distribution has an action for contribution against shareholders who received a distribution knowing that it was improper. RMBCA § 8.33(b); DGCL § 174(c). While shareholders of a Delaware corporation can exculpate directors from liability for many breaches of the duty of due care, they cannot provide such exculpation for unlawful distributions. DGCL § 102(b)(7).

D. CORPORATE DIVIDEND POLICY: LEGAL AND ECONOMIC ISSUES

Decisions as to whether dividends lawfully can be paid arise only when corporations are in financial difficulty. In solvent corporations, decisions relating to dividends involve a basic financial policy issue: should cash not needed for current operations be reinvested in the business or distributed to shareholders? Professors Klein and Coffee observe that, apart from changing the corporation's capital structure,

> there is no necessary connection between the dividend decision and the investment decision. If a corporation lacks spare cash, because it has paid dividends or for any other reason, it can still take advantages of investment opportunities as long as it is able to finance those investments by selling new securities.

William A. Klein & John C. Coffee, Jr., Business Organization and Finance 377 (5th ed. 1993). Nonetheless, courts traditionally have examined the investment opportunities available to a corporation when evaluating a challenge to its dividend policy.

1. CLOSE CORPORATIONS

DODGE v. FORD MOTOR CO.
204 Mich. 459, 170 N.W. 668 (1919).

[The factual background of this famous action is set forth in Chapter 5, as is the portion of the court's decision refusing to enjoin Ford's plans to expand production and lower the price of its cars, even though

---

* New York also makes the violation of the restrictions on distributions a criminal offense under some circumstances. See N.Y.Penal Law § 190.35.

demand at current prices exceeded Ford's production capacity. The following portion of the opinion deals with the Dodge brothers request, which the trial court granted, for an order compelling Ford to pay a special dividend of $19 million, equal to one-half of its cash surplus, in addition to the $1.2 million regular dividend it had declared.]

* * * [T]he case for plaintiffs must rest upon the claim * * * that in any event the withholding of the special dividend asked for by plaintiffs is arbitrary action of the directors requiring judicial interference.

The rule which will govern courts in deciding these questions is not in dispute. It is, of course, differently phrased by judges and by authors, and, as the phrasing in a particular instance may seem to lean for or against the exercise of the right of judicial interference with the actions of corporate directors, the context, or the facts before the court, must be considered. This court, in Hunter v. Roberts, Throp & Co., 83 Mich. 63, 71, 47 N.W. 131, 134, recognized the rule in the following language:

> It is a well-recognized principle of law that the directors of a corporation, and they alone, have the power to declare a dividend of the earnings of the corporation, and to determine its amount. Courts of equity will not interfere in the management of the directors unless it is clearly made to appear that they are guilty of fraud or misappropriation of the corporate funds, or refuse to declare a dividend when the corporation has a surplus of net profits which it can, without detriment to its business, divide among its stockholders, and when a refusal to do so would amount to such an abuse of discretion as would constitute a fraud, or breach of that good faith which they are bound to exercise towards the stockholders.

In Cook on Corporations (7th Ed.) § 545, it is expressed as follows:

> The board of directors declare the dividends, and it is for the directors, and not the stockholders, to determine whether or not a dividend shall be declared.

> When, therefore, the directors have exercised this discretion and refused to declare a dividend, there will be no interference by the courts with their decision, unless they are guilty of a willful abuse of their discretionary powers, or of bad faith or of a neglect of duty. It requires a very strong case to induce a court of equity to order the directors to declare a dividend, inasmuch as equity has no jurisdiction, unless fraud or a breach of trust is involved. There have been many attempts to sustain such a suit, yet, although the courts do not disclaim jurisdiction, they have quite uniformly refused to interfere. The discretion of the directors will not be interfered with by the courts, unless there has been bad faith, willful neglect, or abuse of discretion.

> Accordingly, the directors may, in the fair exercise of their discretion, invest profits to extend and develop the business, and a

reasonable use of the profits to provide additional facilities for the business cannot be objected to or enjoined by the stockholders.

* * *

When plaintiffs made their complaint and demand for further dividends, The Ford Motor company had completed its most prosperous year of business [and had earned a profit of almost $60 million]. * * * It had assets of more than $132,000,000, a surplus of almost $112,000,000, and its cash on hand and municipal bonds were nearly $54,000,000. Its total liabilities, including capital stock, was a little over $20,000,000. * * * Considering only these facts, a refusal to declare and pay further dividends appears to be not an exercise in discretion on the part of the directors but an arbitrary refusal to do what the circumstances required to be done. * * *

[The court reviewed Ford's plans to finance an major expansion of its business.]

Assuming the general plan and policy of expansion and the details of it * * * were for the best ultimate interest of the company and therefore of its shareholders, what does it amount to in justification of a refusal to declare and pay a special dividend or dividends? The Ford Motor Company was able to estimate with nicety its income and profit. It could sell more cars than it could make. Having ascertained what it would cost to produce a car and to sell it, the profit upon each car depended upon the selling price. That being fixed, the yearly income and profit was determinable, and, within slight variations, was certain.

There was appropriated—voted—for the smelter $11,325,000. * * * [A]ssuming that the plans required an expenditure sooner or later of $9,895,000 for duplication of the plant, and for land and other expenditures $3,000,000, the total is $24,220,000. The company was continuing business, at a profit—a cash business. If the total cost of proposed expenditures had been immediately withdrawn in cash from the cash surplus (money and bonds) on hand August 1, 1916, there would have remained nearly $30,000,000.

Defendants say, and it is true, that a considerable cash balance must be at all times carried by such a concern. But, as has been stated, there was a large daily, weekly, monthly, receipt of cash. The output was practically continuous and was continuously, and within a few days, turned into cash. Moreover, the contemplated expenditures were not to be immediately made. The large sum appropriated for the smelter plant was payable over a considerable period of time. So that, without going further, it would appear that, accepting and approving the plan of the directors, it was their duty to distribute on or near the 1st of August, 1916, a very large sum of money to stockholders. * * *

The decree of the court below fixing and determining the specific amount to be distributed to stockholders is affirmed. In other respects, * * * the said decree is reversed.

Note: Dividend Decisions in Close Corporations

As the authorities cited in Dodge v. Ford suggest, shareholders face an uphill battle when they bring an action to compel a corporation's board of directors to declare a dividend. Rare indeed is the corporation that is so flush with cash and so clearly profitable that a court will find a board's refusal to declare a dividend reflects "bad faith" or "an abuse of discretion." In assessing the precedential force of Dodge v. Ford, one also should keep in mind the business struggle in which that case played a part. Ford's business then principally involved assembling cars using parts supplied by others. The Dodge brothers, in addition to owning 22% of Ford's stock, were among Ford's largest suppliers. In addition, the Dodge brothers had begun manufacturing cars in competition with Ford. Ford's decision to withhold dividends deprived the Dodge brothers of cash they needed to finance the expansion of their manufacturing operations, and Ford's plan to reduce the selling price of its cars placed additional competitive pressure on those operations.

At the time of the case, Ford Motor Company was a closely-held corporation. Most other attempts by shareholders to compel boards of directors to declare dividends also have involved closely-held companies. Gottfried v. Gottfried, 73 N.Y.S.2d 692 (Sup.Ct.1947), is typical. The plaintiff-shareholders alleged that (1) there was bitter animosity between the directors (who were the majority shareholders) and the plaintiffs (the minority shareholders); (2) the majority shareholders sought to coerce the minority shareholders to sell their stock to them at a grossly inadequate price; (3) the majority shareholders wanted to avoid heavy personal income taxes on any dividends that might be declared; (4) the majority shareholders, who were on the corporation's payroll, paid themselves excessive salaries and bonuses and borrowed money from the corporation; and (5) the nonpayment of dividends was designed to compel the minority shareholders, who were not on the corporation's payroll, to sell their stock to the majority shareholders.

Although the court expressed sympathy for the minority shareholders, who had been discharged from the corporate payroll, it did not find that the hostility and dissension among shareholders provided a sufficient basis on which to conclude that the refusal to pay dividends was due to the directors' "bad faith." According to the court "The essential test of bad faith is to determine whether the policy of the directors is dictated by their personal interests rather than corporate welfare. Directors are fiduciaries. Their [beneficiaries] are the corporation and the stockholders as a body. Circumstances appraised in the light of the financial condition and requirements of the corporation, will determine the conclusion as to whether the directors have or have not been animated by personal, as distinct from corporate considerations." Id. at 695.

The court found that bonuses and corporate loans to the majority shareholders were a long-standing company practice. In addition, the remuneration to one defendant could not be considered excessive because he had played an important role in the "tremendous expansion" of the company's subsidiary, Hanscom Baking Corporation, between 1933 and 1946. In dismissing the complaint and directing judgment for the defendants, the court concluded:

The testimony discloses that many general considerations affected the policy of the Board of Directors in connection with dividend payments. Some of the major factors were as follows: The recognition that earnings during the war years might be abnormal and not representative of normal earning capacity; the pressing need for heavy expenditures for new equipment and machinery, replacement of which had been impossible during the war years; heavy expenditures required to finance the acquisition and equipment of new Hanscom stores in harmony with the steady growth of the business; the increased initial cost of opening new stores because, under present conditions, it has become difficult to lease appropriate sites necessitating actual acquisition by ownership of locations; the erection of a new bakery for Hanscom at a cost of approximately $1,000,000 inasmuch as the existing plant is incapable of producing the requirements of Hanscom sales which are running at the rate of approximately $6,000,000 per annum; unstable labor conditions with actual and threatened strikes; several pending actions involving large sums of money under the Federal Fair Labor Standards Act; a general policy of financing expansion through earnings requiring long-term debt.

The plaintiffs oppose many of these policies of expansion. There is no evidence of any weight to the effect that these policies of the Board of Directors are actuated by any motives other than their best business judgment. If they are mistaken, their own stock holdings will suffer proportionately to those of the plaintiffs. With the wisdom of that policy the court has no concern. It is this court's conclusion that these policies and the expenditures which they entail are undertaken in good faith and without relation to any conspiracy, scheme and plan to withhold dividends for the purpose of compelling the plaintiffs to sell their stock or pursuant to any other sinister design. 72 N.Y.S.2d at 700–01.

Zidell v. Zidell, Inc., 277 Or. 413, 560 P.2d 1086 (1977), further exemplifies courts' reluctance to compel the declaration of a dividend. Corporations owned mainly by two brothers paid no dividends while both brothers were employees. After the plaintiff resigned his position because of an internal dispute about compensation, small dividends were declared. Plaintiff protested that they were unreasonably small. The court noted:

Plaintiff had the burden of proving bad faith on the part of the directors in determining the amount of corporate dividends. In the present case, plaintiff has shown that the corporations could afford to pay additional dividends, that he has left the corporate payroll, that those stockholders who are working for the corporations are receiving generous salaries and bonuses, and that there is hostility between him and the other major stockholders.

560 P.2d at 1089.

Nonetheless, because the defendants were able to point to credible explanations for a conservative dividend policy—future needs for expensive improvements, accumulating large inventory, renovation of the plant—the court refused to find that the low dividends were due to bad faith.

Only occasionally have courts been prepared to intervene. In Miller v. Magline, Inc., 76 Mich.App. 284, 256 N.W.2d 761 (1977), the corporation's board of directors had adopted a management compensation scheme providing for a low base salary plus a generous incentive bonus program, with any remaining profits to be retained by the corporation as working capital. The court ruled that defendant directors had breached their fiduciary duty to plaintiffs by not declaring a dividend:

> It is our opinion that under all of the circumstances of the case, that the directors of the management group were placed in the impossible situation of trying to give an impartial answer to the determination as to whether dividends should be granted. They already were taking a profit distribution via a percentile of profits before taxes. Therefore, we deem it an untenable position to argue that nonpayment of dividends is justified on the basis that such a concept of profit distribution would imperil the continued well being of the corporation. If such retention of profits were indicated they should have been more diligent in seeing that distributions based upon percentage of profits also should be curtailed.

256 N.W.2d at 770.

As these cases suggest, a shareholder in a close corporation often is well advised to enter into an agreement requiring dividends be paid under appropriately defined circumstances. A shareholder in a close corporation generally cannot easily sell her stock; if she is not employed by the company and receives no dividends (whether labelled as such or disguised as salary or bonus payments), she receives no meaningful economic return from her investment. As we shall see in Chapter 13, courts have become increasingly sensitive to such situations. They tend to uphold agreements relating to the payment of dividends and otherwise extend protections to a minority shareholders who they conclude have been exploited.

2. PUBLIC CORPORATIONS

KAMIN v. AMERICAN EXPRESS CO.
86 Misc.2d 809, 383 N.Y.S.2d 807 (1976), aff'd on opinion below
54 A.D.2d 654, 387 N.Y.S.2d 993 (1st Dept.1976).

[In 1972, American Express purchased almost 2 million shares of stock in Donaldson, Lufkin & Jenrette, Inc. (DLJ), for $29.9 million. By

1975, the stock had declined in value to approximately $4 million. American Express announced that it would distribute the DLJ stock as a dividend. Two shareholders sued to enjoin distribution of the dividend. They argued that American Express would be better off selling the DLJ stock.

The shareholders pointed out that a distribution of the DLJ stock would not have any impact on American Express's liability for income taxes. On the other hand, if American Express sold the DLJ stock, it could reduce otherwise taxable capital gains by an amount equal to its roughly $26 million loss on the DLJ stock and thus save approximately $8 million in taxes. In effect, the shareholders' argument was that rather than distribute $4 million in DLJ stock as a dividend, American Express could sell the stock, save $8 million in taxes, and then (if it wished) distribute $12 million (the sale price plus the tax savings) as a dividend.

The American Express board of directors considered the shareholders' argument at a meeting on October 17, 1975, and decided to proceed with the dividend. The board had previously been advised by its accountants that if the DLJ stock was distributed as a dividend, rather than sold, American Express would not have to reduce its reported income for 1975 to reflect its loss on its investment. Rather, it could bypass its income statement and simply reduce retained earnings by $29.9 million—the book value of the stock it would be distributing.]

EDWARD J. GREENFIELD, JUSTICE.

Examination of the complaint reveals that there is no claim of fraud or self-dealing, and no contention that there was any bad faith or oppressive conduct. The law is quite clear as to what is necessary to ground a claim for actionable wrongdoing. * * *

More specifically, the question of whether or not a dividend is to be declared or a distribution of some kind should be made is exclusively a matter of business judgment for the Board of Directors.

> * * * Courts will not interfere with such discretion unless it be first made to appear that the directors have acted or are about to act in bad faith and for a dishonest purpose. It is for the directors to say, acting in good faith of course, when and to what extent dividends shall be declared * * * The statute confers upon the directors this power, and the minority stockholders are not in a position to question this right, so long as the directors are acting in good faith * * *.

Thus, a complaint must be dismissed if all that is presented is a decision to pay dividends rather than pursuing some other course of conduct. * * * The directors' room rather than the courtroom is the appropriate forum for thrashing out purely business questions which will have an impact on profits, market prices, competitive situations, or tax advantages. * * *

* * * The affidavits of the defendants and the exhibits annexed thereto demonstrate that the objections raised by the plaintiffs to the proposed dividend action were carefully considered and unanimously rejected by the Board at a special meeting called precisely for that purpose at the plaintiffs' request. The minutes of the special meeting indicate that the defendants were fully aware that a sale rather than a distribution of the DLJ shares might result in the realization of a substantial income tax saving. Nevertheless, they concluded that there were countervailing considerations primarily with respect to the adverse effect such a sale, realizing a loss of $25 million, would have on the net income figures in the American Express financial statement. Such a reduction of net income would have a serious effect on the market value of the publicly traded American Express stock. This was not a situation in which the defendant directors totally overlooked facts called to their attention. They gave them consideration, and attempted to view the total picture in arriving at their decision. While plaintiffs contend that according to their accounting consultants the loss on the DLJ stock would still have to be charged against current earnings even if the stock were distributed, the defendants' accounting experts assert that the loss would be a charge against earnings only in the event of a sale, whereas in the event of distribution of the stock as a dividend, the proper accounting treatment would be to charge the loss only against surplus. While the chief accountant for the SEC raised some question as to the appropriate accounting treatment of this transaction, there was no basis for any action to be taken by the SEC with respect to the American Express financial statement.

The only hint of self-interest which is raised, not in the complaint but in the papers on the motion, is that four of the twenty directors were officers and employees of American Express and members of its Executive Incentive Compensation Plan. Hence, it is suggested, by virtue of the action taken earnings may have been overstated and their compensation affected thereby. Such a claim is highly speculative and standing alone can hardly be regarded as sufficient to support an inference of self-dealing. There is no claim or showing that the four company directors dominated and controlled the sixteen outside members of the Board. * * *

Note: Dividend Decisions in Public Corporations

To assess the merits of the American Express board's decision to distribute the DLJ stock as a dividend requires consideration of two questions. First, was the board correct in its belief that stock market investors are more interested in the accounting treatment of American Express's divestiture of its interest in DLJ than in that transaction's financial impact on American Express? Second, even if the board's assessment was correct, was it appropriate for the board to seek to increase the market price of American Express stock by abjuring a transaction (selling the DLJ stock and recording the loss) that would have produced greater economic benefits for the company. In this regard, see Henry T.C. Hu, Risk, Time and Fiduciary Principles in Corporate Investment, 38 U.C.L.A. L.Rev. 277, 281 (1990), arguing that managers' fiduciary duty should be reformulated to require maximization of the "intrinsic value" (i.e., the discounted cash flow value) of a corporations' stock, and that managers should disregard "evidence that stock market pricing of shares is, to a disturbing extent, ill-informed and irrational."

The result in *Kamin* in any event underlines courts' propensity to extend to dividend decisions by public corporations, even more so than closely-held firms, the protection of the business judgment rule. Note the *Kamin* court's pithy observation that the appropriate battleground for such decisions is the boardroom, not the courtroom.

Economists traditionally have found the payment of dividends mysterious. Merton Miller and Franco Modigliani, two Nobel laureates, have pointed out that shareholders effectively can declare their own dividends by selling stock or borrowing money collateralized by their stock, while allowing the company to accumulate capital. Dividends seem especially puzzling when a firm simultaneously goes into the market to raise fresh capital. Merton Miller & France Modigliani, Dividend Policy, Growth and the Valuation of Shares, 34 J. Business 411 (1961). Other economists have found that "changes in dividends have an effect upon share prices, apparently because the changes communicate unique information to investors about management's perception of the corporation's future profitability." Richard O. Kummert, State Statutory Restrictions on Financial Distributions by Corporations to Shareholders, Part I, 55 Wash.L.Rev. 359, 366 (1980). Professor Kummert believes that empirical evidence shows that corporate boards also believe that dividend policy affects share prices.

Other commentators suggest a tie between dividends and agency costs. Frank Easterbrook, Two Agency–Cost Explanations of Dividends, 74 Amer.Econ.Rev. 650 (1984) argues that shareholders may prefer dividends because when they are paid, managers must resort more frequently to the market place for new capital. Thus managers subject themselves to closer monitoring by investment bankers and new investors, who will demand both fidelity and the proper adjustment between risk and prudence. Warren Buffet offers the following observations about corporations' dividend policies:

WARREN BUFFET, LETTER TO SHAREHOLDERS, BERKSHIRE HATHAWAY INC.
1984 Annual Report.

[A]llocation of capital is crucial to business and investment management. Because it is, we believe managers and owners should think hard about the circumstances under which earnings should be retained and under which they should be distributed.

The first point to understand is that all earnings are not created equal. In many businesses—particularly those that have high asset/profit ratios—inflation causes some or all of the reported earnings to become ersatz.   The ersatz portion—let's call these earnings "restricted"—cannot, if the business is to retain its economic position, be distributed as dividends.   Were these earnings to be paid out, the business would lose ground in one or more of the following areas: its ability to maintain its unit volume of sales, its long-term competitive positions, its financial strength.   No matter how conservative its payout ratio, a company that consistently distributes restricted earnings is destined for oblivion unless equity capital is otherwise infused.

Restricted earnings are seldom valueless to owners, but they often must be discounted heavily.   In effect, they are conscripted by the business, no matter how poor its economic potential.   * * *

Let's turn to the much-more-valued unrestricted variety.   These earnings may, with equal feasibility, be retained or distributed.   In our opinion, management should choose whichever course makes greater sense for the owners of the business.

This principle is not universally accepted.   For a number of reasons managers like to withhold unrestricted, readily distributable earnings from shareholders—to expand the corporate empire over which the managers rule, to operate from a position of exceptional financial comfort, etc.   But we believe there is only one valid reason for retention. Unrestricted earnings should be retained only when there is a reasonable prospect—backed preferably by historical evidence or, when appropriate, by a thoughtful analysis of the future—that *for every dollar retained by the corporation, at least one dollar of market value will be created for owners.*   This will happen only if the capital retained produces incremental earnings equal to, or above, those generally available to investors.

To illustrate, let's assume that an investor owns a risk-free 10% perpetual bond with one very unusual feature.   Each year the investor can elect either to take his 10% coupon in cash, or to reinvest the coupon in more 10% bonds with identical terms; i.e., a perpetual life and coupons offering the same cash-or-reinvest option.   If, in any given year, the prevailing interest rate on long-term, risk-free bonds is 5%, it would be foolish for the investor to take his coupon in cash since the 10% bonds he could instead choose would be worth considerably more than 100¢ on the dollar.   Under these circumstances, the investor wanting to get his hands on cash should take his coupon in additional bonds and then immediately sell them.   By doing that, he would realize more cash than if he had taken his coupon directly in cash.   Assuming all bonds were held by rational investor, no one would opt for cash in an era of 5% interest rates, not even those bondholders needing cash for living purposes.

If, however, interest rates were 15%, no rational investor would want his money invested for him at 10%. Instead, the investor would choose to take his coupon in cash, even if his personal cash need were nil.   The opposite course—reinvestment of the coupon—would give an investor additional bonds with market value far less than the cash he could have elected. If he should want 10% bonds, he can simply take the cash received and buy them in the market, where they will be available at a large discount.

An analysis similar to that made by our hypothetical bondholder is appropriate for owners in thinking about whether a company's unrestricted earnings should be retained or paid out. Of course, the analysis is much more difficult and subject to error because the rate earned on reinvested earnings is not a contractual figure, as in our bond case, but rather a fluctuating figure. Owners must guess as to what the rate will average over the intermediate future. However, once an informed guess is made, the rest of the analysis is simple: you should wish your earnings to be reinvested if they can be expected to earn high returns, and you should wish them paid to you if low returns are the likely outcome of reinvestment.

* * *

In judging whether managers should retain earnings, shareholders should not simply compare total incremental earnings in recent years to total incremental capital because that relationship may be distorted by what is going on in a core business. During an inflationary period, companies with a core business characterized by extraordinary economics can use small amounts of incremental capital in that business at very high rates of return * * *. But, unless they are experiencing tremendous unit growth, outstanding businesses by definition generate large amounts of excess cash. If a company sinks most of this money in other businesses that earn low returns, the company's overall return on retained capital may nevertheless appear excellent because of the extraordinary returns being earned by the portion of earnings incrementally invested in the core business. The situation is analogous to a Pro–Am golf event: even if all of the amateurs are hopeless duffers, the team's best-ball score will be respectable because of the dominating skills of the professional.

Many corporations that consistently show good returns both on equity and on overall incremental capital have, indeed, employed a large portion of their retained earnings on an economically unattractive, even disastrous, basis. Their marvelous core businesses, however, whose earnings grow year after year, camouflage repeated failure in capital allocation elsewhere (usually involving high-priced acquisitions of businesses that have inherently mediocre economics). The managers at fault periodically report on the lessons they have learned from the latest disappointment. They then usually seek out future lessons. (Failure seems to go to their heads.)

In such cases, shareholders would be far better off if earnings were retained only to expand the high-return business, with the balance paid in dividends or used to repurchase stock (an action that increases the owners' interest in the exceptional business while sparing them participation in subpar businesses). Managers of high-return businesses who consistently employ much of the cash thrown off by those businesses in other ventures with low returns should be held to account for those allocation decisions, regardless of how profitable the overall enterprise is.

Nothing in this discussion is intended to argue for dividends that bounce around from quarter to quarter with each wiggle in earnings or in investment opportunities. Shareholders of public corporations understandably prefer that dividends be consistently predictable. Payments, therefore, should reflect long-term expectations for both earnings and returns on incremental capital. Since the long-term corporate outlook changes only infrequently, dividend patterns should change no more often. But over time distributable earnings that have been withheld by managers should earn their keep. If earnings have been unwisely retained, it is likely that managers, too, have unwisely retained.

————

In recent years, there has been considerable debate about the relationship between public corporations' dividend policies and their capital structure. Saul Levmore, Monitors and Freeriders in Commercial and Corporate Settings, 92 Yale L.J. 49 (1982), noted that a corporation's capital structure provides a device for monitoring management. Professor Levmore argues that debt holders, in pursuing their need to guard the security of their capital, provide signals to shareholders about the financial stability of the firm and about managerial performance and misconduct. As Professor Levmore notes, this early warning system enables a firm to reduce its agency costs and thereby lower its capital costs. Thus, while too much debt in the capital structure crowds the safety of the equity holders, and reduces shareholder values, the presence of some permanent debt benefits the stockholders and enhances share values.

The debate about public corporations' capital structure became quite heated by the end of the 1980s, following a decade in which many public corporations became the targets of hostile takeovers financed by high-yield debt and many others, perhaps to fend off takeover bids, adopted highly leveraged capital structures. Discussion of these issues also demonstrated that the debate has a political as well as an economic dimension.

MICHAEL JENSEN, ECLIPSE OF THE PUBLIC CORPORATION
Harv. Bus. Rev. 61 (Sept–Oct 1989).

The publicly held corporation, the main engine of economic progress in the United States for a century, has outlived its usefulness in many sectors of the economy and is being eclipsed. New organizations are emerging in its place—organizations that are corporate in form but have no public shareholders and are not listed or traded on organized exchanges. These organizations use public and private debt, rather than public equity, as their major source of capital. Their primary owners are not households but large institutions and entrepreneurs that designate agents to manage and monitor on their behalf and bind those agents with large equity interests and contracts governing the use and distribution of cash.

* * * [T]his organizational innovation should be encouraged. By resolving the central weakness of the public corporation—the conflict between owners and managers over the control and use of corporate resources—these new organizations are making remarkable gains in operating efficiency, employee productivity, and shareholder value. Over the long term, they will enhance U.S. economic performance relative to our most formidable international competitor, Japan, whose companies are moving in the opposite direction. * * * [C]ompanies increasingly resemble U.S. companies of the mid–1960s and early 1970s—an era of gross corporate waste and mismanagement that triggered the organizational transformation now under way in the United States.

* * * The forces behind the decline of the public corporation differ from industry to industry. But its decline is real, enduring, and highly productive. It is not merely a function of the tax deductibility of interest. Nor does it reflect a transitory LBO phase through which companies pass before investment bankers and managers cash out by taking them public again. Nor, finally, is it premised on a systematic fleecing of shareholders and bondholders by managers and other insiders with superior information about the true value of corporate assets.

The current trends do not imply that the public corporation has no future. The conventional twentieth-century model of corporate governance—dispersed public ownership, professional managers without substantial equity holdings, a board of directors dominated by management-appointed outsiders—remains a viable option in some areas of the economy, particularly for growth companies whose profitable investment opportunities exceed the cash they generate internally. * * * Companies choosing among a surplus of profitable projects are unlikely to invest systematically in unprofitable ones, especially when they must regularly turn to the capital markets to raise investment funds.

The public corporation is not suitable in industries where long-term growth is slow, where internally generated funds outstrip the opportunities to invest them profitably, or where downsizing is the most productive long-term strategy. In the tire industry, the shift to radials, which last three times longer than bias-ply tires, meant that manufacturers needed less capacity to meet world demand. Overcapacity inevitably forced a restructuring. The tenfold increase in oil prices from 1973 to 1981, which triggered worldwide conservation measures, forced oil producers into a similar retrenchment.

Industries under similar pressure today include steel, chemicals, brewing, tobacco, television and radio broadcasting, wood and paper products. In these and other cash-rich, low-growth or declining sectors, the pressures on management to waste cash flow through organizational slack or investments in unsound projects is often irresistible. It is in precisely these sectors that the publicly held corporation has declined most rapidly. Barring regulatory interference, the public corporation is also likely to decline in industries such as aerospace, automobiles and auto parts, banking, electric power generation, food processing, industrial and farm implements, and transportation equipment.

The public corporation is a social invention of vast historical importance. Its genius is rooted in its capacity to spread financial risk over the diversified portfolios of millions of individuals and institutions and to allow investors to customize risk to their unique circumstances and predilections. By diversifying risks that would otherwise be borne by owner-entrepreneurs and by facilitating the creation of a liquid market for exchanging risk, the public corporation lowered the cost of capital. These tradable claims on corporate ownership (common stock) also allowed risk to be borne by investors best able to bear it, without requiring them to manage the corporations they owned.

From the beginning, though, these risk-bearing benefits came at a cost. Tradable ownership claims create fundamental conflicts of interest between those who bear risk (the shareholders) and those who manage risk (the executives.) The genius of the new organizations is that they eliminate much of the loss created by conflicts between owners and managers, without eliminating the vital functions of risk diversification and liquidity once performed exclusively by the public equity markets. * * *

A central weakness and source of waste in the public corporation is the conflict between shareholders and managers over the payout of free cash flow — that is, cash flow in excess of that required to fund all investment projects with positive net present values when discounted at the relevant cost of capital. For a company to operate efficiently and maximize value, free cash flow must be distributed to shareholders rather than retained. But this happens infrequently; senior management has few incentives to distribute the funds, and there exist few mechanisms to compel distribution. * * *

Managers have incentives to retain cash in part because cash reserves increase their autonomy vis-à-vis the capital markets. Large cash balances (and independence from the capital markets) can serve a competitive purpose, but they often lead to waste and inefficiency. Consider a hypothetical world in which companies distribute excess cash to shareholders and then must convince the capital markets to supply funds as sound economic projects arise. Shareholders are at a great advantage in this world, where management's plans are subject to enhanced monitoring by the capital markets. Wall Street's analytical, due diligence, and pricing disciplines give shareholders more power to quash wasteful projects.

Managers also resist distributing cash to shareholders because retaining cash increases the size of the companies they run—and managers have many incentives to expand company size beyond that which maximizes shareholder wealth. Compensation is one of the most important incentives. Many studies document that increases in executive pay are strongly related to increases in corporate size rather than value.

The tendency of companies to reward middle managers through promotions rather than annual performance bonuses also creates a cultural bias toward growth. Organizations must grow in order to generate new positions to feed their promotion-based reward systems.

Finally corporate growth enhances the social prominence, public prestige, and political power of senior executives. Rare is the CEO who wants to be remembered as presiding over an enterprise that makes fewer products in fewer plants in fewer countries than when he or she took office—even when such a course increases productivity and adds hundreds of millions of dollars of shareholder value. The perquisites of the executive suite can be substantial, and they usually increase with company size.

The struggle over free cash flow is at the heart of the role of debt in the decline of the public corporation. Bank loans, mezzanine securities, and high-yield bonds have fueled the wave of takeovers, restructurings, and going-private transactions. The combined borrowings of all nonfinancial corporations in the United States approached $2 trillion in 1988, up from $835 billion in 1979. The interest charges on these borrowings represent more than 20% of corporate cash flows, high by historical standards.

This perceived "leveraging of corporate America" is perhaps the central source of anxiety among defenders of the public corporation and critics of the new organizational forms. But most critics miss three important points. First, the trebling of the market value of public-company equity over the last decade means that corporate borrowing had to increase to avoid a major *deleveraging*.

Second, debt creation *without retention of the proceeds of the issue* helps limit the waste of free cash flow by compelling managers to pay out funds they would otherwise retain. Debt is in effect a substitute for dividends—a mechanism to force managers to disgorge cash rather than spend it on empire-building projects with low or negative returns, bloated staffs, indulgent perquisites, and organizational inefficiencies.
* * *

Borrowing allows for no such managerial discretion. Companies whose managers fail to make promised interest and principal payments can be declared insolvent and possibly hauled into bankruptcy court. In the imagery of G. Bennett Stewart and David M. Glassman, "Equity is soft, debt hard. Equity is forgiving, debt insistent. Equity is a pillow, debt a sword." Some may find it curious that a company's creditors wield far more power over managers than its public shareholders, but it is also undeniable.

Third, debt is a powerful agent for change. For all the deeply felt anxiety about excessive borrowing, "overleveraging" can be desirable and effective when it makes economic sense to break up a company, sell off parts of the business, and refocus its energies on a few core operations. Companies that assume so much debt they cannot meet the debt service payments out of operating cash flow force themselves to rethink their entire strategy and structure. Overleveraging creates the crisis atmosphere managers require to slash unsound investment programs, shrink overhead, and dispose of assets that are more valuable outside the company. The proceeds generated by these overdue restructurings can then be used to reduce debt to more sustainable levels, creating a leaner, more efficient and competitive organization. * * *

Critics of leverage also fail to appreciate that insolvency in and of itself is not always something to avoid—and that the costs of becoming insolvent are likely to be much smaller in the new world of high leverage than in the old world of equity-dominated balance sheets. * * *

How can insolvency be less costly in a world of high leverage? Consider an oversimplified example. Companies A and B are identical in every respect except for their financial structures. Each has a going-concern value of $100 million (the discounted value of its expected future cash flows) and a liquidation or salvage value of $10 million. Company A has an equity-dominated balance sheet with a debt ratio of 20%, common for large public companies. Highly leveraged Company B has a debt ratio of 85%, common for LBOs.

Now both companies experience business reversals. What happens? Company B will get in trouble with its creditors much sooner than Company A. After all, Company B's going-concern value doesn't have to shrink very much for it to be unable to meet its payments on $85 million of debt. But when it does run into trouble, its going-concern value will be nowhere near its liquidation value. If the going-concern value shrinks to $80 million, there remains $70 million of value to preserve by avoiding liquidation. So Company B's creditors have strong incentives to preserve the remaining value by quickly and efficiently reorganizing their claims outside the courtroom.

No such incentives operate on Company A. Its going-concern value can fall dramatically before creditors worry about their $20 million of debt. By the time creditors do intervene, Company A's going-concern value will have plummeted. And if Company A's value falls to under $20 million, it is much more likely than Company B to be worth less than its $10 million salvage value. Liquidation in this situation is the likely and rational outcome, with all its attendant conflicts, dislocations, and costs.

ALFRED RAPPAPORT, THE STAYING POWER OF THE PUBLIC CORPORATION
Harv. Bus. Rev. 96 (Jan–Feb 1990).

Reports of the "eclipse of the public corporation" underestimate its institutional staying power and unique capacity for renewal. In his recent HBR article, Michael C. Jensen, a distinguished scholar of corporate finance and governance, argues for a revolution in the structure of ownership and control in the U.S. economy.

I share many of his criticisms of large public companies, especially their dismal performance over the past 20 years. But I disagree profoundly with his advocacy of the "LBO Association" as a superior organizational form. A program of radical and comprehensive reform of the public company—a program based on new approaches to how executives are paid, companies governed, business strategies evaluated, and excess resources distributed to shareholders—can inspire an unprecedented rejuvenation of this vital institution. Indeed, the renewal process is already under way.

Let's be clear: The publicly held corporation is worth saving. As an organizational form, it is inherently flexible and capable of renewal—properties that are crucial to stability and progress in a market-driven economy and that transitory organizations like LBOs cannot replicate. A company's institutional permanence is essential to customers expecting long-term satisfaction on service and product upgrades, suppliers making investment decisions about next-generation components, and employees whose planning horizons and commitments extend for decades. This is not to argue blindly in favor of the organizational status quo or against hardheaded and continual evaluations of business units. But public companies are more than collections of assets to be traded or taken private for one-time gain. They are vibrant, dynamic institutions—capable of long periods of underperformance, to be sure, but also fully capable of self-correction.

Moreover, the driving force behind efficiency and value creation in LBOs—taking on a mountain of debt that rewards shareholders and disciplines management—can impose real costs on business strategy and flexibility. As Jensen readily acknowledges, buyout companies do get in financial trouble more frequently than public companies do. He assures us that troubled private companies are reorganized quickly and efficiently, often under new management, and without entering formal court proceedings—an innovation he calls the "privatization of bankruptcy."

Jensen may be right that leverage in and of itself is not an invitation to Chapter 11 or liquidation. But the prospect of frequent voluntary reorganizations among buyout companies should not be dismissed lightly. In a world of fierce global competition, distinctions between reorganization and liquidation are not particularly meaningful. Either way, the weakened company has almost surely lost the competitive battle.

Today's environment puts a premium on rapid response to change—the capacity to adapt quickly to new technologies in production or distribution, unanticipated shifts in consumer tastes, or major economic dislocations. That requires the financial flexibility of a public company not burdened with extraordinary debt.

Finally, and rather ironically, the very act of going private in the interest of shareholders abolishes the single best source of information about corporate value: the daily stock price. Managers of public companies receive continuous feedback on their performance from the collective judgment of objective investors who have a compelling interest to be accurate in their assessments of the future. Imperfect as it may be (and as unwilling as some public company managers may be to concede the point), there is no better barometer of a company's long-term prospects than how much investors are willing to pay for its shares. Incorporating the stock market's signals into strategic deliberations is an advantage enjoyed only in the public company structure.

LETTERS TO THE EDITOR OF THE
HARVARD BUSINESS REVIEW
Harv. Bus. Rev. 182 et seq. (Nov–Dec 1989).

[*From William C. Norris, former Chairman and CEO of Control Data Corp.*:] An American business system driven by hostile takeovers and the threat of takeovers, featuring highly efficient allocation of assets among LBO companies, won't be competitive in the long run. Even if it were, I believe that it would not be acceptable to most Americans because it fails to provide the degree of social justice that we want. * * *

[*From Ira Millstein, private attorney and counsel to The Business Roundtable* :] We don't need to eclipse public corporations by relying on LBO Associations to achieve the management excellence and congruity of interests between management and owners sought by Mr. Jensen. Such excellence can be achieved by relying on the factors he writes off as lost causes—boards of directors and competitive product markets—both of which are alive and getting well. * * *

Jensen seeks managers who will operate their corporations as world-class competitors, slim and trim, and who are ready to pay out free cash flow or excess assets value to the shareholders * * *. Wall Street can do the job, he notes, that markets and boards have failed to do, by substituting a few owners, like institutions, who will work with astute deal makers, like the LBO boutiques. Together they can "actively" manage, using high-yield junk bonds for financing.

But what happens if there is no public market to reliquify the frozen investment? Are the institutions and the deal makers forever investors? If so, they may not be too astute. We have no significant evidence that most LBO Associations will not go public again. Only time will tell.

How many corporations can be managed by Wall Street, by truly astute managers and earnest institutions? Haven't the transaction costs begun to outweigh the asserted benefits? These problems and flaws in and of themselves make panacean enthusiasm for reliance on Jensen's model highly questionable. * * *

[*From Roberto C. Goizueta, Chairman and CEO, Coca–Cola Company* :] "Eclipse of the Public Corporation" is a good academic exercise and thought provoking, but that is all.

Corporate legitimacy * * * derives from the fact that in the context of our democratic and capitalistic system the publicly held company, its faults notwithstanding, *has proven to be* the most effective instrument for creating the products, services, jobs, and earnings by which the members of society can improve their lives. These corporations will remain large and successful only to the extent that they continue to serve the public well. * * *

Corporations' profitability cannot become secondary without endangering our national economic well-being. But this is not the same as requiring maximum profits and cash flows to the disregard of public-interest issues that government regulations do not mandate.

The current climate that engenders larger and larger LBOs runs contrary to everything I have said. When a corporation gets "mortgaged," the interests of lenders takes precedence over everything else, paying down debt become the number one goal. In such circumstances, it is nearly impossible to serve the public interest well, to be socially, as well as fiscally, responsible. Furthermore, the need to service the huge debt load virtually eliminates any margin for error in management's decision-making process. Risk taking and the entrepreneurial spirit, therefore, as well as investments for the long term, * * * get wiped out rather than enhanced.

[*Professor Jensen's response* :] * * * A shareholder-driven company doesn't ignore its stakeholders. What it does is to invest resources to benefit each of these constituencies to the point where the additional benefits to the company (measured in terms of real cash flows in the short and long term) exceed the additional cost. * * *

If the champions of stakeholders mean something else, if they argue for spending corporate funds on constituencies without any expectation of long-term benefit to the company, then they're advocating the waste of corporate resources. In some cases, the expenditures might generate social benefits that exceed their cost, even if the private benefits to the corporation are less than their cost. In these cases, the corporation would be subsidizing others, but the expenditure would be socially desirable.

There are, however, no forces in such a system to ensure that resources are spent where the social benefits exceed the costs. Resources are spent in ways that reflect the preferences of top management * * *. This means that to the extent we have CEOs who run their companies without regard for shareholders and efficiency, we are likely to cripple the economy. The solution to social problems emanating from the presence of externalities such as air or water pollution, poor education, crime or poverty is to establish proper rules of the game through the political and legal systems * * *. The advocates of stakeholder theory would have us depend on the beneficence of self-appointed corporate top management spending someone else's money—a solution that history reveals will not work.

Chapter 10

THE REGULATION OF SECURITIES ISSUANCE

A. INTRODUCTION

1. WHY SECURITIES REGULATION?

The purchasers of securities—from the largest banks, insurance companies, and other "institutional investors" to the most modest householder looking for a more profitable place than a savings account to invest a small nest egg—are, in a sense, consumers. In that respect the securities laws, state and federal, constitute an enormously complex and comprehensive consumer protection scheme—one of the earliest such schemes to find its way into the American legal system. Why, it might be asked, was it that laws designed to protect purchasers of securities came so long before any similar effort was made to protect purchasers of consumer products; and why do those laws remain, for the most part, more far-reaching and often better enforced?

There is, to be sure, more than one reason. But certainly the most important is to be found in the central role played by the market for securities in a capitalist economy. Since the early part of the century it has been the perception of lawmakers (a perception to which some critics now take exception) that without the kind of protection furnished investors by the securities laws, the capital markets and ultimately the economy—would be far less healthy. It is hardly any surprise that the two most important federal statutes, the Securities Act of 1933 and the Securities Exchange Act of 1934, were passed in the depths of the Great Depression.

In addition to the '33 Act and the '34 Act, and the major amendments in 1954, 1964 and 1975, there are four other principal pieces of securities legislation: the Public Utilities Holding Company Act of 1935, the Trust Indenture Act of 1939, the Investment Company Act of 1940, and the Investment Advisers Act of 1940. None of these four, however, is as significant to the average corporate practitioner as the '33 and the '34 Acts, and we will not consider them further in these materials.

Throughout all of these statutes, as Professors Loss and Seligman put it in the leading treatise on securities law, "there is the recurrent theme * * * of disclosure, again disclosure, and still more disclosure." 1 Louis Loss and Joel Seligman, Securities Regulation 27 (3d ed. 1989). In none of them is this as true as it is in the Securities Act of 1933. Taking its cue from Justice Brandeis's famous dictum that "sunlight is the best disinfectant, electric light the best policeman," * the Congress responded to the crisis of confidence that then beset the securities markets with a statute that depends almost exclusively on disclosure. Its central instrument is the registration statement that must be filed with the Securities and Exchange Commission prior to the offer or sale of any security sold through the use of the mails or the facilities of interstate commerce unless one of the numerous rather complex exemptions to this basic requirement is available.

2. THE UNDERWRITING PROCESS

In order to understand the manner in which the '33 Act functions, it is first necessary to understand a little of the manner in which new securities are typically sold in this country.** The entire process is usually called "underwriting," a term that stems from the "old-fashioned," or "strict," or "standby" system of underwriting that originated in England. Underwriting of this sort amounts to an insurance scheme. An investment banker (or "underwriter" in securities jargon) assists the company that issues the securities (the "issuer") in selling its securities to the public and agrees, for a fee, to insure the success of the offering from the issuer's point of view by purchasing any part of the new issue not taken up by the public within a certain time. This method is seldom used today in the United States except for certain types of offerings to existing shareholders by means of warrants or rights.

"Firm commitment" underwriting is the form of most ordinary securities offerings. It can be analogized to the merchandising of radios, or writing paper, or any consumer good sold at retail. There is a "manufacturer," the issuer; there are "wholesalers," the underwriters; and there are "retailers," the securities dealers who sell to members of the public who become the ultimate investors. In a firm commitment underwriting the members of the underwriting group do not insure the offering in the usual sense, but actually purchase the securities, reselling them at a markup (the "spread") to a larger group of firms that compose the "selling group" of dealers. They in turn resell, again at a differential, to the investing public.

A third type of underwriting, most prevalent in relatively small offerings by companies "going public" for the first time, is known as "best efforts" underwriting. It is not an underwriting at all since it does not guarantee the success of the offering, but rather entails a

---

* Louis Dembitz Brandeis, Other People's Money and How the Bankers Use It 92 (1914).

** The following discussion is largely drawn from 1 Louis Loss and Joel Seligman, Securities Regulation, at 317–342 (3d ed. 1989).

commitment by the underwriters only to use their best efforts to market the securities, as agent for the issuer. The underwriters, and the selling group where the size of the offering calls for one, still play an important role in this variety of offering; without their contacts with potential investors and their selling effort, few issuers would be able to place any substantial amount of securities with the public. In this as in other types of underwriting, moreover, the investment banking houses that act as "lead underwriters" often perform a valuable financial consulting service—advising the issuer on the form of the offering, its timing, the amount of securities that can be expected to be sold, and the price. With respect to this last item, of course, the underwriter occupies a role in all but best-efforts underwritings that is at least partially adversarial to the issuer; the lower the price at which the offering is made, the lower the risk assumed by the underwriter.

3. THE SECURITIES ACT OF 1933

The dominant feature of the '33 Act is Section 5, which, to oversimplify a bit, makes it unlawful, unless there is an exemption, to sell any security * by use of the mails or the facilities of interstate commerce unless a registration statement regarding the security is in effect. In order to get the desired information about the security into the hands of investors without requiring them to go to the SEC to read the registration statement, Congress also requires that a "statutory prospectus" (in the jargon of the profession), including the most important portions of the registration statement, be delivered to the buyer prior to or at the same time as the security.**

The information that must be included in the registration statement is set forth in "Schedule A" to the Act *** as amplified and interpreted by SEC regulations.

* A discussion of the term "security" contained in Section 2(1) of the '33 Act, a central question in the application of federal securities law, is beyond the scope of this casebook.

** The form of this requirement gave rise to the criticism that the purchaser received in most cases only a "retrospectus," the effective decision to purchase having been made prior to the receipt of any form of prospectus. Congress responded to this objection in 1954 by amending the Act to permit the delivery of a "preliminary prospectus"—also called a "red herring" because of the legend announcing its preliminary character required to be printed on its cover in red—which is in effect the final draft of the prospectus as it is first filed by the issuer with the SEC for its review. It is permitted to omit certain pieces of information that will be eventually added to the final prospectus, including the price of the securities, which has typically not been firmly settled between the issuer and the underwriters at the time the preliminary prospectus is filed.

The Commission has taken further steps by regulation to encourage the dissemination of preliminary prospectuses to potential purchasers of the security prior to the time the registration statement becomes effective and final sales may take place.

*** The following is a summary listing of the 32 items included in the schedule. (Only Items 1–27 must be included in "Part I" of the registration statement, which is the prospectus.):

1. Business name of issuer

2. State of incorporation of organization

3. Business address

4. Names and addresses of officers, directors, and promoters

5. Underwriters' names and addresses

6. Owners of securities

By this time, you may have been struck by the broad sweep of Section 5, which, without any exemptions from its operation, would encompass virtually every sale of a security anywhere within the United States (the courts having given an extremely broad reading to what constitutes the use of the facilities of interstate commerce). This apparent breadth is the consequence of the approach of the drafters of the statute to defining the area of applicability of Section 5, which was to lay down an all-encompassing prohibition and then to exclude by various exemptions virtually all transactions other than a new public offering of securities. As a consequence, the true scope of the statute cannot be understood without at least a general idea of the nature of the exemptions from its registration requirements which we will examine later in this chapter.

4. THE SECURITIES EXCHANGE ACT OF 1934

Because of the impact of integrated disclosure system for the registration of security (which is discussed in this section), an overview on the Securities Exchange Act of 1934 is in order. Unlike the '33 Act, which is a relatively narrow statute focused almost entirely on the offer and sale of new issues of securities to the public by a company or a controlling person, the '34 Act has a much broader range. The '34 Act is an amalgamation of provisions touching nearly every aspect of securities trading and the regulation of securities exchanges and securities professionals.

The '34 Act requires that issuers having a class of security traded on a national securities exchange, or those having assets of $5 million or more and a class of equity security held of record by five hundred or more persons, must register the security with the SEC. This registration is to be distinguished from registration under the '33 Act, although the

7. Amount of securities held or subscribed for

8. Description of issuer's business

9. Issuer's capitalization

10. Options in connection with securities to be offered

11. Amount of stock issued or to be offered

12. Amount and nature of funded debt

13. Use of proceeds from securities

14. Executive salaries

15. Estimated amount of proceeds from securities

16. Offering price to public

17. Underwriters' commissions

18. Offering expenses of issuer

19. Information concerning prior offerings

20. Payments to promoters

21. Information concerning property acquired or to be acquired with proceeds from securities

22. Officers', stockholders', or directors' interests in the property acquired

23. Names and addresses of counsel passing on legality of issue

24. Information concerning material contracts

25. Balance sheets

26. Profit and loss statements

27. Profit and loss statements for acquired business

28. Copies of underwriting contracts

29. Copies of opinions of counsel

30. Copies of contracts

31. Copies of organization papers

32. Copies of underlying securities agreements or indentures

registration form calls for much of the same information contained in a '33 Act registration statement.

Companies that have so registered ("reporting companies") are required to file various periodic and other reports with the Commission designed to keep the information in its files reasonably current. The most important of these is the annual report filed on Form 10–K. This is supplemented by a quarterly report on Form 10–Q and occasional reports that must be filed upon the occurrence of significant events in a company's business (Form 8–K). These reports are publicly available either from the Commission itself or from one of a large number of libraries and information services that maintain copies, or digest and reproduce the information contained in the reports. They are an important source of information for investment analysts and investors that follow the securities of reporting companies closely. Together with the annual report to shareholders (which is somewhat different from the 10–K report) and the material usually included in management proxy solicitations, these reports put a good deal of information in the hands of shareholders, investors, and investment analysts that contributes, in theory at least, substantially to the efficient functioning of the securities markets and the effective performance of their role as allocators of capital resources.

The SEC has adopted an integrated disclosure system for the registration of securities. The integrated disclosure system integrates the disclosure requirements under the '33 and '34 Securities Acts. In adopting the new system, the SEC explained its goals were "to reverse or eliminate overlapping or unnecessary disclosure and dissemination requirements whenever possible, thereby reducing burdens on registrants while at the same time ensuring that security holders, investors and the marketplace have been provided with meaningful, nonduplicative information upon which to base investment decisions." SEC, Special Report, 1982 Integrated Disclosure Adoptions (March 11, 1982).

The SEC established a three-tier system of registration statement and prospectus disclosure based on the registrant's reporting history under the '34 Act. The framework for the three level system is provided by three registration forms: S–1; S–2; and S–3. Form S–1 remains the long-form registration statement generally available to issuers. Form S–2, which involves less detailed disclosure, may be used by issuers having reported for three or more years under the '34 Act. Issuers incorporate certain '34 Act information into the prospectus. Form S–3 requires the least detailed level of disclosure and provides for the fullest degree of incorporation by reference from '34 Act reporting.

In an effort to further simplify some issuers' reporting requirements, the SEC adopted the Small Business Initiatives (57 Fed. Reg. 36,442 (1992)). The initiatives created a new integrated registration and reporting system for issuers to comply with the '33 Act and the '34 Act. Those businesses which satisfy the definition of a "small business issuer" are eligible to use the simplified reporting system, which consists of the newly created Form SB–2 for registration under the '33 Act, Form 10–SB for registration under the '34 Act, Form 10–KSB for annual reports, and Form 10–QSB for quarterly reports. A "small business issuer" is one which meets the following criteria: (1) annual revenues of less than $25,000,000; (2) a U.S. or Canadian issuer; (3) not an investment company; and (4) does not have a public float (the aggregate market value of the issuer's outstanding securities held by non-affiliates) of $25,000,000 or more.

Additionally, the '34 Act requires special disclosure of certain kinds of transactions. Thus, the solicitation of proxies may be made only subject to the rules, and specified information must be provided (Section 14(a)). If a bidder seeks to buy a large number of shares in a special transaction, and invites shareholders to "tender" their shares, that "tender offer" is also subject to special rules (Section 14(d)).

The proxy rules, in particular, supplement the periodic reporting requirements. Proxy solicitations occur at regular intervals, on the occasion of annual meetings. The Commission has prescribed rules designed to produce meaningful disclosure to investors as well as to facilitate the conduct of the meeting. Not only must the proxy statement contain pertinent information about directors who are candidates for election, but the company must also send an annual report with detailed financial and other information to its shareholders.

Officers and directors and 10% shareholders of companies that are subject to the reporting requirements must report their stock holdings to the SEC, and any changes in their ownership (Section 16(a)). More than that, if they derive any profit from purchases and sales occurring within six months of each other ("short swing profits") they must surrender those profits on demand to their company (Section 16(b)). The idea behind this seemingly Draconian provision is to prevent so called "insider trading" based on undisclosed information.

The '34 Act creates both civil liabilities that may be privately enforced and various enforcement tools that the SEC may use. Thus, there may be civil recovery if false or misleading information is filed with the Commission (subject to numerous technical limits) (Section 18) or if defined insiders derive short swing profits. Any contractual provisions made in violation of the statute is void as between the parties (Section 29). This provision, and the anti-fraud rules adopted by the SEC, have given rise to implied private rights of action in favor of the persons they were intended to benefit.

After first creating the SEC, and endowing it with power to define improper conduct, prescribe disclosure requirements, and go to court and function quasi-judicially, the '34 Act also regulates the trading markets. The securities exchanges, such as the New York Stock Exchange, the American Stock Exchange, the Midwest Stock Exchange, the Pacific Coast Stock Exchange, must register with the SEC and adopt satisfactory rules designed to promote just and equitable principles of trade and to prevent manipulation and fraud. The stock exchanges limit trading on their "floors" to companies whose securities are listed, and each exchange has its own standards for listing securities, based on the size of the company, its performance and the number of shareholders. Some brokerage firms are members of exchanges; it is said they own "seats" on an exchange. The SEC has supervisory power over the exchanges and the administration of their rules.

However, not all trading occurs on stock exchanges; indeed most of it takes place in the "over the counter" market. An organization known as the National Association of Securities Dealers, Inc. ("NASD") functions as a self-regulatory rulemaking body for activity in that arena, and its existence and functions are recognized in the statute. Most stockbrokers belong to the NASD, and find it commercially necessary to maintain their membership in good order. Again, the SEC has supervisory power over this private regulatory body.

The Commission also has power to regulate extensions of credit (so-called "margin") in the securities business; it can suspend trading of securities; and it may define manipulation and deception. The most famous rule ever adopted by the SEC is Rule 10b–5, which was adopted in 1942 pursuant to the Commission's power under Section 10(b) to define conduct which constitutes manipulation or deception.

In addition to regulation of the market place, the '34 Act requires brokers and dealers who engage in the interstate commerce of securities (a defined term) to register with the SEC, and comply with rules governing their conduct, or else face suspension or revocation of their licenses. The NASD and the stock exchanges may discipline their members under the statutory scheme of self regulation. There are other self-regulatory groups, dealing with municipal securities and clearing agencies as well, but these are more specialized activities.

B. PREPARATION OF THE REGISTRATION STATEMENT: AN OVERVIEW

The following excerpt presents an overview of general principles involved with the preparation of a registration statement. Do not be concerned with specific references to dates, timing, and expenses which may be out of date.

CARL W. SCHNEIDER, JOSEPH M. MANKO AND ROBERT S. KANT, GOING PUBLIC—PRACTICE, PROCEDURES AND CONSEQUENCES
27 Vill.L.Rev. 1, 10–17, 19–20, 25–31, 33 (1981).

The Registration Statement

The registration statement is the disclosure document required to be filed with the SEC in connection with a registered offering. It consists physically of two principal parts. Part I of the registration statement is the prospectus, which is the only part that normally goes to the public offerees of the securities. It is the legal offering document. Part II of the registration statement contains supplemental information which is available for public inspection at the office of the SEC.

The registration forms contain a series of detailed "items" and instructions, in response to which disclosures must be made. But they are not forms in the sense that they have blanks to be completed like a tax return. Traditionally, the prospectus describes the company's business and responds to all the disclosures required in narrative rather than item-and-answer form. It is prepared as a brochure describing the company and the securities to be offered. The usual prospectus is a fairly stylized document, and there is a customary sequence for organizing the material.

* * *

In the typical first public offering, the items to which it is most difficult to respond, and which require the most creative effort in preparation, deal with the description of the company's business, properties, material transactions with insiders, and use of proceeds. Other matters required to be disclosed in the prospectus deal with the details of the underwriting, the plan for distributing the securities, capitalization, pending legal proceedings, competition, description of securities being registered, identification of directors and officers and their remuneration, options to purchase securities, and principal holders of securities. There are also detailed requirements concerning financial statements and financial information concerning the company's business segments.

* * *

The Commission has also evolved certain principles of emphasis in highlighting disclosures of adverse facts. It cannot prohibit an offering from being made if disclosure is adequate, but its policies on disclosure can make the offering look highly unattractive. In particular, if there are sufficient adverse factors in an offering, these are required to be set forth in detail in the very beginning of the prospectus under a caption such as "Introductory Statement" or "Risk Factors of the Offering."

To the same end, the SEC has required that boldface reference be made to certain adverse factors on the prospectus cover page. The cover page statements must cross reference disclosures within the prospectus on such matters as high risk factors, immediate equity dilution of the public's investment, and various forms of underwriting compensation beyond the normal spread. To add to the brew, the Commission sometimes insists that certain factors be emphasized beyond what the attorneys working on the matter consider to be their true importance. A usual example is that prominent attention must be called to transactions between the company and its management. Often, matters of relative insignificance, in terms of amounts involved, are made to appear very important by the amount of space given and placement in the prospectus.

The SEC, which reviews the registration statement, has no authority to pass on the merits of a particular offering. The SEC has no general power to prohibit an offering because it considers the investment opportunity to be a poor risk. The sole thrust of the federal statute is disclosure of relevant information. No matter how speculative the investment, no matter how poor the risk, the offering will comply with federal law if all the required facts are disclosed. By contrast, some state securities or "blue sky" laws, which are applicable in the jurisdictions where the distribution takes place, do regulate the merits of the securities. * * *

The prospectus is a somewhat schizophrenic document, having two purposes which often present conflicting pulls. On the one hand, it is a selling document. It is used by the principal underwriters to form the underwriting syndicate and a dealer group, and by the underwriters and dealers to sell the securities to the public. From this point of view, it is desirable to present the best possible image. On the other hand, the prospectus is a disclosure document, an insurance policy against liability. With the view toward protection against liability, there is a tendency to resolve all doubts against the company and to make things look as bleak as possible. In balancing the purposes, established underwriters and experienced counsel, guided at least in part by their knowledge of the SEC staff attitudes, traditionally lean to a very conservative presentation, avoiding glowing adjectives and predictions. The layman frequently complains that all the glamour and romance has been lost. "Why can't you tell them," he says, "that we have the most aggressive and imaginative management in the industry?" It takes considerable client education before an attorney can answer this question to the client's satisfaction.

Until relatively recently, it was traditional to confine prospectuses principally to objectively verifiable statements of historic fact. It is now considered proper, and in some instances essential, to include some information in a prospectus, either favorable or adverse to the company, which is predictive or based upon opinions or subjective evaluations. However, no such "soft information" should be included in the prospectus unless it has a reasonable basis in fact and represents management's good faith judgment.

PREPARING THE REGISTRATION STATEMENT

The "quarterback" in preparing the registration statement is normally the attorney for the company. Company counsel is principally responsible for preparing the non-financial parts of the registration statement. Drafts are circulated to all concerned. There are normally several major revisions before sending the job to the printer, and at least a few more printed drafts before the final filing. Close cooperation is required among counsel for the company, the underwriters' counsel, the accountants, and the printer. Unless each knows exactly what the others expect, additional delay, expense, and irritation are predictable.

* * *

Review by the SEC

After the registration statement is filed initially, the Commission's Division of Corporation Finance reviews it to see that it responds appropriately to the applicable form. The Division's staff almost always finds some deficiencies, which are communicated either by telephone, usually to company counsel, or through the "letter of comments" or "deficiency letter." Amendments to the registration statement are then filed in response to the comments. When the comments are reflected to the satisfaction of the SEC staff, the SEC issues an order allowing the registration statement to become effective. Only after the registration statement is effective may sales to the public take place.

* * *

If counsel, or the accountants with respect to financial comments, believe that the staff's comments are inappropriate or should not be met for some other reason, the comments will be discussed with the examiner, usually by telephone but in person if the matter is sufficiently serious. If a point cannot be resolved to counsel's satisfaction through discussions with the examiner, it is considered appropriate to request that the matter be submitted to the Branch Chief who supervises the examiner. When a significant issue is involved, higher levels of staff review may be requested if counsel remains unsatisfied. However, review should be sought at successive levels, and counsel should not leapfrog to a senior official before the subordinates have been consulted. The Commission's staff is generally reasonable in dealing with counsel's objections. However, as a practical matter, an offering cannot usually come to market unless an accommodation has been reached on all comments. Therefore, the staff usually has the last word on whether the company has adequately responded to the comments, even if the comments are not legally binding in the formal sense.

* * *

Preliminary Preparation

For the average first offering, a very substantial amount of preliminary work is required which does not relate directly to preparing the registration statement as such. To have a vehicle for the offering, the business going public normally must be conducted by a single corporation or a parent corporation with subsidiaries. In most cases, the business is not already in such a neat package when the offering project commences. It is often conducted by a number of corporations under common ownership, by partnerships, or by combinations of business entities. Considerable work must be done in order to reorganize the various entities by mergers, liquidations and capital contributions. Even when there is a single corporation, a recapitalization is almost always required so that the company will have an appropriate capital structure for the public offering. To mention a few other common projects in preparing to go public, it is often necessary to enter into, revise, or terminate employment agreements, adopt stock option plans and grant options thereunder, transfer real estate, revise leases, rewrite the corporate charter and by-laws, prepare new stock certificates, engage a transfer agent and registrar, rearrange stockholdings of insiders, draw, revise or cancel agreements among shareholders, and revamp financing arrangements.

* * *

TIMETABLE

Although laymen find it difficult to believe, the average first public offering normally requires two to three months of intensive work before the registration statement can be filed. One reason so much time is required is the need to accomplish the preparatory steps just referred to at the same time the registration statement is being prepared. There are many important and often interrelated business decisions to be made and implemented, and rarely are all of these questions decided definitively at the outset. Some answers must await final figures, or negotiations with underwriters, and must be held open until the last minute. Inevitably, a businessman first exposed to these considerations will change his mind several times in the interim. Furthermore, drafting of the prospectus normally begins before the financial statements are available. Almost inevitably, some rewriting must be done in the non-financial parts after the financial statements are distributed in order to blend the financial and non-financial sections together. Laymen frequently have the frustrating feeling as the deadline approaches that everything is hopelessly confused. They are quite surprised to see that everything falls into place at the eleventh hour.

After the registration statement is filed with the Commission, the waiting period begins. It is during this interval that red herrings are distributed. The Commission reviews the registration statement and finally issues its letter of comments. There is a wide variation in the time required for the SEC to process a registration statement. Relevant factors include the level of the Commission's backlog of filings and the time of the year. There is normally a considerable rush of filings at the end of each calendar quarter, and particularly at the end of March for filings with financial statements as of December 31.

The SEC's current policy calls for the issuance of an initial letter of comments within thirty days of the filing of a registration statement, but the delay is often longer and at times has exceeded one hundred days. The increased number of first-time registration statements and other filings * * *, coupled with reductions in the number of the SEC's review personnel, raised the possibility of long delays in issuing comment letters. This occurred despite various initiatives by the SEC during the past several years including the adoption of various "short-form" registration statements for certain types of companies and transactions, increases in the dollar amount of securities which could be sold without registration and the processing of certain offerings in regional offices of the SEC.

As a result, the SEC in late 1980 announced a new procedure designed to reduce delays in the review and processing of registration statements and other documents filed with it. Under the new procedure, the SEC will review offerings by public companies on a selective basis and certain registration statements of established public companies will no longer be reviewed at all. It is hoped that the new procedure will enable the SEC to reduce time delays by concentrating its resources on certain areas, including first time public offerings which will continue to receive thorough review.

The overall time lapse between the beginning of preparation of a company's first registration statement and the final effective date may well exceed six months. It rarely will be less than three months.

* * *

EXPENSES

A major expense in going public is usually the underwriters' compensation. The underwriting cash discount or cash commission on a new issue generally ranges from 7% to 10% of the public offering price. The maximum amount of direct and indirect underwriting compensation is regulated by the National Association of Securities Dealers, Inc. (NASD), a self-regulatory agency which regulates broker-dealers. Normally, the three largest additional expenses are legal fees, accounting fees, and printing costs.

Legal fees for a first offering of at least $5,000,000 generally would be between $55,000 and $115,000, with $75,000 to $100,000 being typical. This amount includes not only the preparation of the registration statement itself, but also all of the corporate work, house cleaning and other detail which is occasioned by the public offering process. Fees for smaller offerings tend to be somewhat lower. In part, this may reflect the fact that offerings for start-up companies, which tend to be smaller in size, typically require less legal work in investigating business operations, since there are none. However, start-up offerings can be more difficult in other respects—for example, risk factors are more prevalent and minor matters may require disclosure on points which would be immaterial to an established company with a history of operations. Therefore, start-up offerings occasionally are even more demanding than offerings of larger seasoned companies.

* * *

For each registration statement, there is a filing fee * * * which fee is non-refundable.

Among the other expenses to be borne are original issue and transfer taxes, if applicable, transfer agent and registrar fees, printing of stock certificates and "blue sky" expenses. The company is generally required to reimburse the underwriter for the NASD filing fee * * *. Occasionally the company must pay an expense allowance (sometimes on an accountable basis and sometimes on a non-accountable basis) to the underwriters. This is a negotiated figure which can range from several thousand dollars to $100,000 or more in some cases. The company frequently pays the underwriters' counsel a special fee for compliance with applicable state securities laws (so-called "blue sky" work), which can range up to many thousand dollars, depending on the number and identity of the jurisdictions involved.

* * *

For a normal first public stock offering of several million dollars, total expenses in the [$225,000] to [$500,000] range would be typical, exclusive of the underwriting discount or commission but inclusive of any expense allowance (whether or not accountable) payable to the underwriter. However, it should be emphasized that there are wide variations among offerings. The estimates for aggregate as well as individual expenses given above can be too low if unusual problems or complications develop in a particular offering. Average costs have increased substantially in recent years, due to a number of factors including general inflation, the added scope and content of certain disclosure items in the forms, and ever expanding notions of due diligence obligations.**

Another cost of going public arises out of the heavy burden and time demand it may impose on the company's administrative and executive personnel. Throughout the period of selecting the underwriters and preparing the registration statement, these activities can, and often do, absorb a significant amount of executive time.

* * *

C. CIVIL LIABILITIES UNDER THE SECURITIES ACT

A noninitiate observing a securities offering for the first time would be impressed with the care taken by participants in drafting the registration statement. It might be noted that this care is reflected in the cost of the process. Although it varies widely from one offering to another, the average cost of first public offerings of several million dollars, exclusive of the underwriting commissions, is in the $225,000 to $500,000 range. The seriousness with which the underwriters and represen-

---

** According to the SEC, issuers who made offerings by means of Form S-1 in 1991 averaged expenses of $617,000 of which an average of $300,000 went to legal and accounting expenses.—Eds.

tatives of the issuer and their lawyers, accountants, and other experts treat a public offering is due in no small part to the Draconian liability provisions of the '33 Act.

The most significant of these provisions for a registered offering is found in Section 11, which was specifically intended to remove the common law obstacles to an action by a defrauded purchaser of securities, such as the requirement that the plaintiff plead and prove privity, scienter, reliance and causation.* Under Section 11 the plaintiff need only show that he or she purchased a security covered by a registration statement (not necessarily from the issuer, an underwriter, or a participating dealer), that there was a material misstatement or omission in the registration statement, and that the plaintiff lost money on the purchase. The plaintiff may sue a variety of persons including:

1. the signers of the registration statement, including the issuer;

2. the directors and those who have been named with their consent as prospective directors;

3. the accountants, engineers, appraisers and other experts named as having prepared or certified some portion of the registration statement; and

4. the underwriters.

Several of the other elements of a common law action for deceit may become issues in a Section 11 action, but they take the form of defenses as to which the burden of proof is on the defendants. They can, for example, escape liability for all or part of the plaintiff's losses if they can show that the fall in the price of the security was due to causes other than the misleading portions of the registration statement. Section 11(e). The most important defense, one that permeates the entire process of the preparation of a registration statement, is the so called "due diligence defense."

With respect to those portions of the statement prepared or certified by experts (in the jargon of the profession the "expertised" portions), such as the financial statements, the non-expert defendants are not liable if they can show that they had no reasonable ground to believe and did not believe that the portion in question was materially false. Section 11(b)(3)(C). With respect to the "unexpertised" portions of the registration statement (or the liability of the expert for the portion he "expertised"), a defendant must show that he "had, after reasonable investigation, reasonable ground to believe and did believe" that there was no material misstatement or omission. Section 11(b)(3)(A) and (B).

Section 11(c) provides that "[i]n determining * * * what constitutes reasonable investigation and reasonable ground for belief, the standard of reasonableness shall be that required of a prudent man in the management of his own property." The due diligence defense is ex-

* For a discussion of the elements of an   Section C.
action for fraud or deceit, see Chapter 19,

plored in the *BarChris* case, excerpts from which are set forth below. In practice it is interpreted as requiring all those who might be liable under Section 11 to review the registration statement and conduct a reasonable investigation in order to satisfy themselves of its accuracy.

The other principal liability provisions of the '33 Act are found in Section 12. Its first paragraph furnishes the principal "teeth" against violations of the registration requirements of Section 5. In effect it allows anyone who has purchased an illegally unregistered security from the issuer or an underwriter to rescind the transaction at any time within one year after the sale. This is true regardless of whether the buyer knew that the security was being sold in violation of Section 5. The operation of Section 12(1) is illustrated by Henderson v. Hayden, Stone, Inc., 461 F.2d 1069 (5th Cir.1972) in which the court allowed the plaintiff, whom it said "can only be described as a sophisticated investor," to rescind a purchase of $180,000 worth of stock of a total offering of $300,000 for which the seller believed (wrongly as it turned out) that an exemption from the registration requirement was available.

Section 12(2), like Section 11, provides a basis of liability for a materially false or misleading statements on an omission to state material facts made in connection with the sale of a security through the use of the mails or the facilities of interstate commerce. It is broader than Section 11 or 12(1) in some respects, particularly in that it does not require that the security in question be registered or that the misstatement or omission have appeared in a registration statement. It applies to oral communications. Strict privity is not required. Section 12(2) renders the seller liable if he did not exercise "reasonable care." The requirement of "reasonable care" imparts a negligence, not an intent or scienter, standard. The plaintiff-purchaser need not show that she relied on the misstatement; however, the defendants can assert a reliance defense if the plaintiff knew of the untruths or omissions.

Courts are divided with respect to whether Section 12(2) is limited to public offerings. Compare Farley v. Baird, Patrick & Co., Inc., 750 F.Supp. 1209 (S.D.N.Y.1990) (the language of Section 12(2), which prohibits false and misleading statements in oral communication or a prospectus, is broad enough to reach post-distribution trading) and Pacific Dunlop Holdings Inc. v. Allen & Co., 993 F.2d 578 (7th Cir.1993) (Section 12(2) applies to secondary market transactions with Ballay v. Legg Mason Wood Walker, Inc., 925 F.2d 682 (3d Cir.1991), cert. denied ___ U.S. ___, 112 S.Ct. 79, 116 L.Ed.2d 52 (1991) (the object and structure of the 1933 Act support a narrow interpretation of Section 12(2). The section follows Sections 11 and 12(1) of 1933 Act which govern the registration of securities. The placement of Section 12(2) among the 1933 Act provisions concerned with the initial distribution of securities indicates that Congress designed Section 12(2) to protect purchasers in initial public offerings) and Bank of Denver v. Southeastern Capital Group, Inc., 763 F.Supp. 1552 (D.Colo.1991).

Professor Louis Loss leads a number of commentators who believe that Section 12(2) should apply to both public and private offerings. His main argument centers on the statutory provision which states that Section 12(2) covers any person who offers or sells a security "by means of a prospectus or oral communication." Loss argues that this language means that Section 12(2) covers any offer or sale of a security, since the term "prospectus" is defined in Section 2(10) as including any written communication offering any security for sale. He does not believe the legislative history can be read to exclude the coverage of private offerings by Section 12(2), because to do so would go too far. Louis Loss, Securities Act Section 12(2): A Rebuttal, 48 Bus. Law. 47 (1992).

However, Elliot J. Weiss, The Courts Have It Right: Securities Act Section 12(2) Applies Only to Public Offerings, 48 Bus. Law. 1 (1992), concludes the Third Circuit interpreted Section 12(2) correctly in Ballay v. Legg Mason Wood Walker, Inc. Weiss contends that the term "by means of a prospectus or oral communication" was included in the Section 12(2) as a limiting term, or else it would have been omitted. According to Weiss it becomes clear that this section was only intended to cover public offerings, in light of the placement of Section 12(2) within the '33 Act and the legislative history surrounding the section.

At the time the '33 Act was passed its liability provisions were considered by many participants in the securities industry to be so onerous that fear was expressed in many quarters that the financing of new ventures would cease altogether and "grass would grow in Wall Street." That has not, of course, proved to be the case. But securities professionals and their lawyers have continued to treat Section 11 with a great deal of respect. So great, indeed, that the first lawsuit brought under Section 11 to run its full course to a district court decision was not decided until 1968. The case, Escott v. BarChris Construction Corp., sent tremors throughout the financial community—not so much because of its strict application of the provisions of Section 11, which, after all was not more rigorous than the interpretation given to the section by most observers all along, but because the opinion was the first authoritative holding that Section 11 did indeed mean what it seemed to say. The case shocked issuers, directors, investment bankers, accountants, and their counsel into awareness that perhaps their practices had become a little sloppy during the "Go–Go Years" of the sixties and stimulated a searching re-examination of those practices by those involved.

ESCOTT v. BARCHRIS CONSTRUCTION CORP.

283 F.Supp. 643 (S.D.N.Y.1968).

McLean, District Judge.

This is an action by purchasers of 5½ per cent convertible subordinated fifteen year debentures of BarChris Construction Corporation (BarChris). Plaintiffs purport to sue on their own behalf and "on behalf of all other and present and former holders" of the debentures. When the action was begun on October 25, 1962, there were nine plaintiffs. Others were subsequently permitted to intervene. At the time of the trial, there were over sixty.

The action is brought under Section 11 of the Securities Act of 1933 (15 U.S.C.A. § 77k). Plaintiffs allege that the registration statement with respect to these debentures filed with the Securities and Exchange Commission, which became effective on May 16, 1961, contained material false statements and material omissions.

Defendants fall into three categories: (1) the persons who signed the registration statement; (2) the underwriters, consisting of eight investment banking firms, led by Drexel & Co. (Drexel); and (3) BarChris's auditors, Peat, Marwick, Mitchell & Co. (Peat, Marwick).

The signers, in addition to BarChris itself, were the nine directors of BarChris, plus its controller, defendant Trilling, who was not a director. Of the nine directors, five were officers of BarChris, *i.e.*, defendants Vitolo, president; Russo, executive vice president; Pugliese, vice president; Kircher, treasurer; and Birnbaum, secretary. Of the remaining four, defendant Grant was a member of the firm of Perkins, Daniels, McCormack & Collins, BarChris's attorneys. He became a director in October 1960. Defendant Coleman, a partner in Drexel, became a director on April 17, 1961, as did the other two, Auslander and Rose, who were not otherwise connected with BarChris.

[The BarChris Construction Corp. was in the business of building bowling alleys. It had begun in 1946 as a partnership organized by Vitolo and Pugliese, which was incorporated in 1955. The advent of automatic pin setting machines in 1952 provided a powerful stimulus to the industry, from which BarChris benefitted handsomely. In 1960 it built some three percent of all of the bowling lanes constructed in the United States. Between 1956 and 1960 the company's sales leaped from $800,000 to over $9 million.]

* * *

In general, BarChris's method of operation was to enter into a contract with a customer, receive from him at that time a comparatively small down payment on the purchase price, and proceed to construct and equip the bowling alley. When the work was finished and the building delivered, the customer paid the balance of the contract price in notes, payable in installments over a period of years. BarChris discounted these notes with a factor and received part of their face amount in cash. The factor held back part as a reserve.

In 1960 BarChris began a practice which has been referred to throughout this case as the "alternative method of financing." In substance this was a sale and leaseback arrangement. * * * In instances in which this method applied, BarChris would build and install what it referred to as the "interior package." * * * When it was completed, it would sell the interior to a factor, James Talcott Inc. (Talcott), who would pay BarChris the full contract price therefor. The factor then proceeded to lease the interior either directly to BarChris's customer or back to a subsidiary of BarChris. In the latter case, the subsidiary in turn would lease it to the customer.

Under either financing method, BarChris was compelled to expend considerable sums in defraying the cost of construction before it received reimbursement. As a consequence, BarChris was in constant need of cash to finance its operations, a need which grew more pressing as operations expanded.

In December 1959, BarChris sold 560,000 shares of common stock to the public at $3.00 per share. * * *

By early 1961, BarChris needed additional working capital. The proceeds of the sale of the debentures involved in this action were to be devoted, in part at least, to fill that need.

The registration statement of the debentures, in preliminary form, was filed with the Securities and Exchange Commission on March 30, 1961. A first amendment was filed on May 11 and a second on May 16. The registration statement became effective on May 16. The closing of the financing took place on May 24. On that day BarChris received the net proceeds of the financing.

By that time BarChris was experiencing difficulties in collecting amounts due from some of its customers. Some of them were in arrears in payments due to factors on their discounted notes. As time went on those difficulties increased. Although BarChris continued to build alleys in 1961 and 1962, it became increasingly apparent that the industry was overbuilt. Operators of alleys, often inadequately financed, began to fail. Precisely when the tide turned is a matter of dispute, but at any rate, it was painfully apparent in 1962.

In May of that year BarChris made an abortive attempt to raise more money by the sale of common stock. It filed with the Securities and Exchange Commission a registration statement for the stock issue which it later withdrew. In October 1962 BarChris came to the end of the road. On October 29, 1962, it filed in this court a petition for an arrangement under Chapter XI of the Bankruptcy Act. BarChris defaulted in the payment of the interest due on November 1, 1962 on the debentures.

[The court here launches on a twenty-five page exposition of the facts. It finds that the prospectus contained a number of errors:

1. The earnings for 1960 were overstated as a result of inaccurate estimates of the percentage completion of some alleys under construction and treating as income certain amounts that should not have been so treated.

2. Because of the accounting treatment of several items of current assets, net current assets were overstated by a relatively small amount.

3.   Under the "alternative method of financing" described by the court above, BarChris remained liable as guarantor of 100 percent of its subsidiary's obligations on leases of the bowling alleys that BarChris had constructed. The prospectus falsely stated that the contingent liabilities as of Dec. 31, 1960, to which the company was subject as a consequence amounted to only 25 percent of the unexpired lease payments.

4.   For similar reasons, the contingent liabilities as of April 30, 1961 were also understated.

5.   BarChris had acquired all of the stock of two customers with which it had contracts to build alleys. Payments on those contracts by the customers were improperly included in BarChris's income for the three months ended March 31, 1961 even though the payments were merely transfers from one segment of the company to another.

6.   The prospectus gave a figure for a backlog of unfilled orders as of March 31, 1961 that was substantially overstated.

7.   The statements in the prospectus regarding advances made by certain officers to the company were misleading and substantially understated the amount of those loans outstanding as of the date of the prospectus.

8.   The "Use of Proceeds" section of the prospectus indicated that a substantial portion of the proceeds of the offering would be used for working capital. In fact, at the time of the offering the company's cash resources were already severely strained, and it used over $1 million of the proceeds to pay off outstanding obligations.

9.   The prospectus stated that, "Since 1955, the Company has been required to repurchase less than ½ of 1% of [the promissory notes discounted to factors and guaranteed by BarChris." The truth was that by May, 1961 several of its customers were seriously delinquent in the payment of their notes, the situation was getting rapidly worse, and the factor had indicated that it might require BarChris to repurchase over $1,350,000 worth of notes.]

* * *

SUMMARY

For convenience, the various falsities and omissions which I have discussed in the preceding pages are recapitulated here. They were as follows:

1.   1960 Earnings
     (a) Sales

As per prospectus	$9,165,320
Correct figure	8,511,420
Overstatement	$ 653,900

    (b) Net Operating Income

As per prospectus	$1,742,801
Correct figure	1,496,196
Overstatement	$ 246,605

      (c) Earnings per Share

As per prospectus	$.75
Correct figure	.65
Overstatement	$.10

2. 1960 Balance Sheet
     Current Assets

As per prospectus	$4,524,021
Correct figure	3,914,332
Overstatement	$ 609,689

3. Contingent Liabilities as of December 31, 1960 on
     Alternative Method of Financing

As per prospectus	$ 750,000
Correct figure	1,125,795
Understatement	$ 375,795
Capitol Lanes should have been shown as a direct liability	$ 325,000

4. Contingent Liabilities as of April 30, 1961

As per prospectus	$ 825,000
Correct figure	1,443,853
Understatement	$ 618,853
Capitol Lanes should have been shown as a direct liability	$ 314,166

5. Earnings Figures for Quarter ending March 31, 1961
     (a) Sales

As per prospectus	$2,138,455
Correct figure	1,618,645
Overstatement	$ 519,810

     (b) Gross Profit

As per prospectus	$ 483,121
Correct figure	252,366
Overstatement	$ 230,755

6. Backlog as of March 31, 1961

As per prospectus	$6,905,000
Correct figure	2,415,000
Overstatement	$4,490,000

7. Failure to Disclose Officers' Loans Outstanding and
     Unpaid on May 16, 1961 $ 386,615

8. Failure to Disclose Use of Proceeds in Manner not
     Revealed in Prospectus
     Approximately $1,160,000

9. Failure to Disclose Customers' Delinquencies in May
     1961 and BarChris's Potential Liability with Re-
     spect Thereto

                                                  Over $1,350,000

10. Failure to Disclose the Fact that BarChris was Al-
      ready Engaged, and was about to be More Heavily
      Engaged, in the Operation of Bowling Alleys

MATERIALITY

It is a prerequisite to liability under Section 11 of the Act that the fact which is falsely stated in a registration statement, or the fact that is omitted when it should have been stated to avoid misleading, be "material." The regulations of the Securities and Exchange Commission pertaining to the registration of securities define the word as follows (17 C.F.R. § 230.405(*l*)):

The term "material", when used to qualify a requirement for the furnishing of information as to any subject, limits the information required to those matters as to which an average prudent investor ought reasonably to be informed before purchasing the security registered.

What are "matters as to which an average prudent investor ought reasonably to be informed"? It seems obvious that they are matters which such an investor needs to know before he can make an intelligent, informed decision whether or not to buy the security.

Early in the history of the Act, a definition of materiality was given in Matter of Charles A. Howard, 1 S.E.C. 6, 8 (1934), which is still valid today. A material fact was there defined as:

> * * * a fact which if it had been correctly stated or disclosed would have deterred or tended to deter the average prudent investor from purchasing the securities in question.

The average prudent investor is not concerned with minor inaccuracies or with errors as to matters which are of no interest to him. The facts which tend to deter him from purchasing a security are facts which have an important bearing upon the nature or condition of the issuing corporation or its business.

Judged by this test, there is no doubt that many of the misstatements and omissions in this prospectus were material. * * *

* * *

THE "DUE DILIGENCE" DEFENSES

[The court here quotes the provisions of Section 11 that set forth the defenses of due diligence and reliance on experts.]

Every defendant, except BarChris itself, to whom, as the issuer, these defenses are not available, and except Peat, Marwick, whose position rests on a different statutory provision, has pleaded these affirmative defenses. Each claims that (1) as to the part of the registration statement purporting to be made on the authority of an expert (which, for convenience, I shall refer to as the "expertised portion"), he had no reasonable ground to believe and did not believe that there were any untrue statements or material omissions, and (2) as to the other parts of the registration statement, he made a reasonable investigation, as a result of which he had reasonable ground to believe and did believe that the registration statement was true and that no material fact was omitted. * * *

Before considering the evidence, a preliminary matter should be disposed of. The defendants do not agree among themselves as to who the "experts" were or as to the parts of the registration statement which were expertised. Some defendants say that Peat, Marwick was the expert, others say that BarChris's attorneys, Perkins, Daniels, McCormack & Collins, and the underwriters' attorneys, Drinker, Biddle & Reath, were also the experts. On the first view, only those portions of the registration statement purporting to be made on Peat, Marwick's authority were expertised portions. On the other view, everything in the registration statement was within this category, because the two law firms were responsible for the entire document.

The first view is the correct one. To say that the entire registration statement is expertised because some lawyer prepared it would be an unreasonable construction of the statute. Neither the lawyer for the company nor the lawyer for the underwriters is an expert within the meaning of Section 11. The only expert, in the statutory sense, was Peat, Marwick, and the only parts of the registration statement which purported to be made upon the authority of an expert were the portions which purported to be made on Peat, Marwick's authority.

The parties also disagree as to what those portions were. Some defendants say that it was only the 1960 figures (and the figures for prior years, which are not in controversy here). Others say in substance that it was every figure in the prospectus. The plaintiffs take a somewhat intermediate view. They do not claim that Peat, Marwick expertised every figure, but they do maintain that Peat, Marwick is responsible for a portion of the text of the prospectus, i.e., that pertaining to "Methods of Operation," because a reference to it was made in footnote 9 to the balance sheet.

Here again, the more narrow view is the correct one. The registration statement contains a report of Peat, Marwick as independent public accountants dated February 23, 1961. This relates only to the consolidated balance sheet of BarChris and consolidated subsidiaries as of December 31, 1960, and the related statement of earnings and retained earnings for the five years then ended. This is all that Peat, Marwick purported to certify. It is perfectly clear that it did not purport to certify the 1961 figures, some of which are expressly stated in the prospectus to have been unaudited.

Moreover, plaintiffs' intermediate view is also incorrect. The cross reference in footnote 9 to the "Methods of Operation" passage in the prospectus was inserted merely for the convenience of the reader. It is not a fair construction to say that it thereby imported into the balance sheet everything in that portion of the text, much of which had nothing to do with the figures in the balance sheet.

I turn now to the question of whether defendants have proved their due diligence defenses. The position of each defendant will be separately considered.

* * *

[Only representative portions of the court's discussion are included.]

KIRCHER

Kircher was treasurer of BarChris and its chief financial officer. He is a certified public accountant and an intelligent man. He was thoroughly familiar with BarChris's financial affairs. He knew the terms of BarChris's agreements with Talcott. He knew of the customers' delinquency problem. He participated actively with Russo in May 1961 in the successful effort to hold Talcott off until the financing proceeds came in. He knew how the financing proceeds were to be applied and he saw to it that they were so applied. He arranged the officers' loans and he knew all the facts concerning them.

Moreover, as a member of the executive committee, Kircher was kept informed as to those branches of the business of which he did not have direct charge. He knew about the operation of alleys, present and prospective. * * * In brief, Kircher knew all the relevant facts.

Kircher worked on the preparation of the registration statement. He conferred with Grant and on occasion with Ballard. He supplied information to them about the company's business. He read the prospectus and understood it. He knew what it said and what it did not say.

Kircher's contention is that he had never before dealt with a registration statement, that he did not know what it should contain, and that he relied wholly on Grant, Ballard and Peat, Marwick to guide him. He claims that it was their fault, not his, if there was anything wrong with it. He says that all the facts were recorded in BarChris's books where these "experts" could have seen them if they had looked. He says that he truthfully answered all their questions. In effect, he says that if they did not know enough to ask the right questions and to give him the proper instructions, that is not his responsibility.

There is an issue of credibility here. In fact, Kircher was not frank in dealing with Grant and Ballard. He withheld information from them. But even if he had told them all the facts, this would not have constituted the due diligence contemplated by the statute. Knowing the facts, Kircher had reason to believe that the expertised portion of the prospectus, i.e., the 1960 figures, was in part incorrect. He could not shut his eyes to the facts and rely on Peat, Marwick for that portion.

As to the rest of the prospectus, knowing the facts, he did not have a reasonable ground to believe it to be true. On the contrary, he must have known that in part it was untrue. Under these circumstances, he was not entitled to sit back and place the blame on the lawyers for not advising him about it.

Kircher has not proved his due diligence defenses.

* * *

AUSLANDER

Auslander was an "outside" director, i.e., one who was not an officer of BarChris. He was chairman of the board of Valley Stream National Bank in Valley Stream, Long Island. In February 1961 Vitolo asked him to become a director of BarChris. Vitolo gave him an enthusiastic account of BarChris's progress and prospects. As an inducement, Vitolo said that when BarChris received the proceeds of a forthcoming issue of securities, it would deposit $1,000,000 in Auslander's bank.

In February and early March 1961, before accepting Vitolo's invitation, Auslander made some investigation of BarChris. He obtained Dun & Bradstreet reports which contained sales and earnings figures for periods earlier than December 31, 1960. He caused inquiry to be made of certain of BarChris's banks and was advised that they regarded BarChris favorably. He was informed that inquiry of Talcott had also produced a favorable response.

On March 3, 1961, Auslander indicated his willingness to accept a place on the board. Shortly thereafter, on March 14, Kircher sent him a copy of BarChris's annual report for 1960. Auslander observed that BarChris's auditors were Peat, Marwick. They were also the auditors for the Valley Stream National Bank. He thought well of them.

Auslander was elected a director on April 17, 1961. The registration statement in its original form had already been filed, of course, without his signature. On May 10, 1961, he signed a signature page for the first amendment to the registration statement which was filed on May 11, 1961. This was a separate sheet without any document attached. Auslander did not know that it was a signature page for a registration statement. He vaguely understood that it was something "for the SEC."

Auslander attended a meeting of BarChris's directors on May 15, 1961. At that meeting he, along with the other directors, signed the signature sheet for the second amendment which constituted the registration statement in its final form. Again, this was only a separate sheet without any document attached. Auslander never saw a copy of the registration statement in its final form.

At the May 15 directors' meeting, however, Auslander did realize that what he was signing was a signature sheet to a registration statement. This was the first time that he had appreciated that fact. A copy of the registration statement in its earlier form as amended on May 11, 1961 was passed around at the meeting. Auslander glanced at it briefly. He did not read it thoroughly.

At the May 15 meeting, Russo and Vitolo stated that everything was in order and that the prospectus was correct. Auslander believed this statement.

In considering Auslander's due diligence defenses, a distinction is to be drawn between the expertised and non-expertised portions of the prospectus. As to the former, Auslander knew that Peat, Marwick had audited the 1960 figures. He believed them to be correct because he had confidence in Peat, Marwick. He had no reasonable ground to believe otherwise.

As to the non-expertised portions, however, Auslander is in a different position. He seems to have been under the impression that Peat, Marwick was responsible for all the figures. This impression was not correct, as he would have realized if he had read the prospectus carefully. Auslander made no investigation of the accuracy of the prospectus. He relied on the assurance of Vitolo and Russo, and upon the information he had received in answer to his inquiries back in February and early March. These inquiries were general ones, in the nature of a credit check. The information which he received in answer to them was also general, without specific reference to the statements in the prospectus, which was not prepared until some time thereafter.

It is true that Auslander became a director on the eve of the financing. He had little opportunity to familiarize himself with the company's affairs. The question is whether, under such circumstances, Auslander did enough to establish his due diligence defense with respect to the non-expertised portions of the prospectus.

Although there is a dearth of authority under Section 11 on this point, an English case under the analogous Companies Act is of some value. In Adams v. Thrift, [1915] 1 Ch. 557, aff'd, [1915] 2 Ch. 21, it was held that a director who knew nothing about the prospectus and did not even read it, but who relied on the statement of the company's managing director that it was "all right," was liable for its untrue statements.

Section 11 imposes liability in the first instance upon a director, no matter how new he is. He is presumed to know his responsibility when he becomes a director. He can escape liability only by using that reasonable care to investigate the facts which a prudent man would employ in the management of his own property. In my opinion, a prudent man would not act in an important matter without knowledge of the relevant facts, in sole reliance upon representations of persons who are comparative strangers and upon general information which does not purport to cover the particular case. To say that such minimal conduct measures up to the statutory standard would, to all intents and purposes, absolve new directors from responsibility merely because they are new. This is not a sensible construction of Section 11, when one bears in mind its fundamental purpose of requiring full and truthful disclosure for the protection of investors.

I find and conclude that Auslander has not established his due diligence defense with respect to the misstatements and omissions in those portions of the prospectus other than the audited 1960 figures.

* * *

GRANT

Grant became a director of BarChris in October 1960. His law firm was counsel to BarChris in matters pertaining to the registration of securities. Grant drafted the registration statement for the stock issue in 1959 and for the warrants in January 1961. He also drafted the registration statement for the debentures. In the preliminary division of work between him and Ballard, the underwriters' counsel, Grant took initial responsibility for preparing the registration statement, while

Ballard devoted his efforts in the first instance to preparing the indenture.

Grant is sued as a director and as a signer of the registration statement. This is not an action against him for malpractice in his capacity as a lawyer. Nevertheless, in considering Grant's due diligence defenses, the unique position which he occupied cannot be disregarded. As the director most directly concerned with writing the registration statement and assuring its accuracy, more was required of him in the way of reasonable investigation than could fairly be expected of a director who had no connection with this work.

There is no valid basis for plaintiffs' accusation that Grant knew that the prospectus was false in some respects and incomplete and misleading in others. Having seen him testify at length, I am satisfied as to his integrity. I find that Grant honestly believed that the registration statement was true and that no material facts had been omitted from it.

In this belief he was mistaken, and the fact is that for all his work, he never discovered any of the errors or omissions which have been recounted at length in this opinion, with the single exception of Capitol Lanes. He knew that BarChris had not sold this alley and intended to operate it, but he appears to have been under the erroneous impression that Peat, Marwick had knowingly sanctioned its inclusion in sales because of the allegedly temporary nature of the operation.

Grant contends that a finding that he did not make a reasonable investigation would be equivalent to a holding that a lawyer for an issuing company, in order to show due diligence, must make an independent audit of the figures supplied to him by his client. I do not consider this to be a realistic statement of the issue. There were errors and omissions here which could have been detected without an audit. The question is whether, despite his failure to detect them, Grant made a reasonable effort to that end.

Much of this registration statement is a scissors and paste-pot job. Grant lifted large portions from the earlier prospectuses, modifying them in some instances to the extent that he considered necessary. But BarChris's affairs had changed for the worse by May 1961. Statements that were accurate in January were no longer accurate in May. Grant never discovered this. He accepted the assurances of Kircher and Russo that any change which might have occurred had been for the better, rather than the contrary.

It is claimed that a lawyer is entitled to rely on the statements of his client and that to require him to verify their accuracy would set an unreasonably high standard. This is too broad a generalization. It is all a matter of degree. To require an audit would obviously be unreasonable. On the other hand, to require a check of matters easily verifiable is not unreasonable. Even honest clients can make mistakes. The statute imposes liability for untrue statements regardless of whether they are intentionally untrue. The way to prevent mistakes is to test oral information by examining the original written record.

There were things which Grant could readily have checked which he did not check. For example, he was unaware of the provisions of the agreements between BarChris and Talcott. He never read them. Thus, he did not know, although he readily could have ascertained, that BarChris's contingent liability on Type B leaseback arrangements was 100 per cent, not 25 per cent. He did not appreciate that if BarChris defaulted in repurchasing delinquent customers' notes upon Talcott's demand, Talcott could accelerate all the customer paper in its hands, which amounted to over $3,000,000.

As to the backlog figure, Grant appreciated that scheduled unfilled orders on the company's books meant firm commitments, but he never asked to see the contracts which, according to the prospectus, added up to $6,905,000. Thus, he did not know that this figure was overstated by some $4,490,000.

Grant was unaware of the fact that BarChris was about to operate Bridge and Yonkers. He did not read the minutes of those subsidiaries which would have revealed that fact to him. On the subject of minutes, Grant knew that minutes of certain meetings of the BarChris executive committee held in 1961 had not been written up. Kircher, who had acted as secretary at those meetings, had complete notes of them. Kircher told Grant that there was no point in writing up the minutes because the matters discussed at those meetings were purely routine. Grant did not insist that the minutes be written up, nor did he look at Kircher's notes. If he had, he would have learned that on February 27, 1961 there was an extended discussion in the executive committee meeting about customers' delinquencies, that on March 8, 1961 the committee had discussed the pros and cons of alley operation by Bar-Chris, that on March 18, 1961 the committee was informed that Bar-Chris was constructing or about to begin constructing twelve alleys for which it had no contracts, and that on May 13, 1961 Dreyfuss, one of the worst delinquents, had filed a petition in Chapter X.

Grant knew that there had been loans from officers to BarChris in the past because that subject had been mentioned in the 1959 and January 1961 prospectuses. In March Grant prepared a questionnaire to be answered by officers and directors for the purpose of obtaining information to be used in the prospectus. The questionnaire did not inquire expressly about the existence of officers' loans. At approximately the same time, Grant prepared another questionnaire in order to obtain information on proxy statements for the annual stockholders' meeting. This questionnaire asked each officer to state whether he was indebted to BarChris, but it did not ask whether BarChris was indebted to him.

* * *

The application of proceeds language in the prospectus was drafted by Kircher back in January. It may well have expressed his intent at that time, but his intent, and that of the other principal officers of BarChris, was very different in May. Grant did not appreciate that the earlier language was no longer appropriate. He never learned of the situation which the company faced in May. He knew that BarChris was short of cash, but he had no idea how short. He did not know that BarChris was withholding delivery of checks already drawn and signed because there was not enough money in the bank to pay them. He did not know that the officers of the company intended to use immediately approximately one-third of the financing proceeds in a manner not disclosed in the prospectus, including approximately $1,000,000 in paying old debts.

* * *

As far as customers' delinquencies is concerned, although Grant discussed this with Kircher, he again accepted the assurances of Kircher and Russo that no serious problem existed. He did not examine the records as to delinquencies, although BarChris maintained such a record. Any inquiry on his part of Talcott or an examination of BarChris's correspondence with Talcott in April and May 1961 would have apprised him of the true facts. It would have led him to appreciate that the statement in this prospectus, carried over from earlier prospectuses, to the effect that since 1955 BarChris had been required to repurchase less than one-half of one per cent of discounted customers' notes could no longer properly be made without further explanation.

Grant was entitled to rely on Peat, Marwick for the 1960 figures. He had no reasonable ground to believe them to be inaccurate. But the matters which I have mentioned were not within the expertised portion of the prospectus. As to this, Grant was obliged to make a reasonable investigation. I am forced to find that he did not make one. After making all due allowances for the fact that BarChris's officers misled him, there are too many instances in which Grant failed to make an inquiry which he could easily have made which, if pursued, would have put him on his guard. In my opinion, this finding on the evidence in this case does not establish an unreasonably high standard in other cases for company counsel who are also directors. Each case must rest on its own facts. I conclude that Grant has not established his due diligence defenses except as to the audited 1960 figures.

* * *

Note: "Materiality"

"Materiality" is a concept that is central to the securities laws. The term was originally drawn from the common law of fraud, which gives the plaintiff a cause of action only if the defendant has made a "material" misstatement. It appears throughout the securities statutes, both in the context of required disclosure and in the provision of rights of action to investors who have been misled by material misstatements or omissions. Nowhere in the statutes, however, is there a definition of the word "material." The Securities and Exchange Commission has sought to define it when used to qualify a requirement for disclosure under the '33 Act by saying that it "limits the information required to those matters as to which an average prudent investor ought reasonably to be informed before purchasing the security registered." Rule 405. The federal courts have wrestled with the definition of materiality for years.

In SEC v. Texas Gulf Sulphur Co., 401 F.2d 833 (2d Cir.1968), cert. denied 394 U.S. 976, 89 S.Ct. 1454, 22 L.Ed.2d 756 (1969), the court created a problem that would plague judges and commentators for years. The court emphasized that a material fact is one

> " 'which in reasonable and objective contemplation *might* affect the value of the corporation's stocks or securities * * *.' " Thus was born a dispute over whether a fact was material only if a reasonable person "would" consider it important or whether it is enough that this hypothetical individual "might" consider it important. The Supreme Court exacerbated the problem in Mills v. Electric Auto–Lite Co., 396 U.S. 375, 384, 90 S.Ct. 616, 621, 24 L.Ed.2d 593, 602 (1970), in which it was claimed that shareholders had been misled in the exercise of their voting rights. The Court said that the alleged misstatement was material if "it might have been considered important by a reasonable shareholder," but went on to elaborate by indicating that this meant that such a misstatement must "have a significant *propensity* to affect the voting process * * *."

When the Court finally focussed on the "would-might" controversy, however, it decided not to choose at all but to lay down a somewhat different standard. In TSC Indus., Inc. v. Northway, 426 U.S. 438, 449, 96 S.Ct. 2126, 2132, 48 L.Ed.2d 757, 766 (1976), the Court, in what appears to be the last word on the matter, ruled that, "An omitted fact is material if there is a substantial likelihood that a reasonable shareholder would consider it important on deciding how to vote." Although *Northway* also involved shareholder voting rather than a decision to buy or sell a security, its standard presumably applies in the latter context as well.

Developing a (more or less) refined verbal formulation of the standard of materiality, however, is only half the battle—if indeed it is that. For, as reading the opinion in *Escott* should bring home, it is still necessary to apply the standard to a particular set of facts. As with any other standard that calls on a court or jury to determine what some hypothetical and presumably objective reasonable person would or would not do, that is often a difficult task.

D. EXEMPTIONS FROM THE '33 ACT REGISTRATION REQUIREMENTS

PROBLEMS

PISCES TACKLE

Pisces Tackle Corp. has been in business for five years and has firmly established its reputation as a quality fishing rod manufacturer. Phil Flyer, Les Leader, and Harriet Hooks, its principals, would now like to expand into the production of a line of less expensive rods and also to begin to manufacture a new type of reel that Flyer has developed. To accomplish both of these ends they need to raise about $2,000,000. They could probably manage the first objective with only $1,000,000. This latter sum they believe they could raise from a group of about fifteen friends and relatives including four physicians and two dentists, all of whom have previously invested in similar speculative ventures; three trial lawyers; a securities lawyer; Hooks' Aunt Minnie, a wealthy widow with no business experience; three business executives; and a stockbroker.

1. Flyer, Leader, and Hooks are anxious to avoid the expense and delay of registration. They have asked you to review for them the methods they might use to raise either $1,000,000 or $2,000,000 without registering. What should you tell them? Consider §§ 3(a)(11), 3(b), 4(2) and 4(6) and Rules 147 and 501–506.

2. After discussing the various alternatives, your clients have decided to raise the full $2,000,000. They do not feel that among the three of them they know enough potential investors to raise that entire amount. They have discussed their plans with Sarah Sinker, a young stockbroker, and she has expressed an interest in assisting them. She has been involved in several small public offerings, but has never done a private placement before. In preparation for a meeting with Sarah and a vice president of her firm, you are asked to respond to the following questions:

a. Assuming that Sarah's firm is retained, can she place an advertisement in the local newspaper describing briefly the nature of the offering and soliciting expressions of interest? Can she place a similar notice in the monthly newsletter her firm sends to its customers? Can she mention the offering in speeches she gives occasionally to private groups? Can she send a letter to investors on a list maintained by her firm of customers the firm knows to be interested in small, speculative offerings of this sort? Can she send a letter to other brokers in the community asking for similar lists they may maintain and circularize investors on those lists? What can be said in any such communications? See Rule 502(c).

b. Is there any limit to the number or qualifications of persons that may be approached about the stock? Are there any limits on the number or qualifications of purchasers? If so, what must Sinker do to ascertain whether particular prospects meet the qualifications? Can all of the prospects on the list prepared by Flyer, Leader and Hooks buy stock? See Rules 505(b)(2), 506(b)(2), and 501(a), (e), and (h).

c. What information must the company furnish prospective purchasers of stock? In what form should it be furnished? See Rule 502(b).

d. Are there any other precautions the company must take to comply with the exemption? See Rules 502(d) and 503.

The '33 Act provides for two types of exemptions: exempt *securities* and exempt *transactions*. The broadest of the exemptions is found in Section 4(1), which exempts "[t]ransactions by any person other than the issuer, underwriter, or dealer." In this one simple clause the statute eliminates from its coverage the great bulk of ordinary trading by investors on the securities exchanges or the over-the-counter market after the initial issuance of a security.

The second class of exempt transactions, those "by an issuer not involving any public offering" (Section 4(2)), is also of substantial importance. Without this so-called "private offering exemption" the smallest closely held corporation would be required to go through the costly and time consuming process of filing a registration statement under the '33 Act when it first issues stock to its shareholders.* While the issuance of new shares of stock to the two or three shareholders of a closely held corporation, all of whom will participate actively in the business, would clearly fall within the exemption, describing the limits of a private offering when larger numbers of investors not all of whom are directly connected with the business are involved has proved a difficult task for the courts and the SEC. We shall examine below how they have dealt with that task.

Another transaction exemption is contained in Section 4(6), which exempts "transactions involving offers or sales * * * solely to one or more accredited investors" so long as the aggregate offering price does not exceed $5 million. The term "accredited investors" is defined in Section 2(15) of the Act to include certain institutional investors such as banks, insurance companies, and investment companies, as well as other persons who, on the basis of such factors as wealth and financial sophistication, qualify under rules to be promulgated by the SEC.

The remaining classes of exempt transactions are relatively technical and need not concern us here.

Section 3 of the Act defines the types of securities that are exempt from the operation of Section 5. It begins with a lengthy list—including securities of banks, governments, and charitable organizations, as well as

---

* It is possible that one of the other exemptions, in particular the intrastate offering exemption of Section 3(11), discussed in greater detail below, might also apply.

certain kinds of commercial paper, insurance contracts, and securities issued in recapitalization or reorganization transactions—that is of little general importance.

Section 3(a)(11) establishes the so-called "intrastate offering exemption," which, like the private offering exemption, may prove useful to the small company seeking to avoid the burdens of registering an offering of new securities. The exemption is available only for an issue *offered and sold* exclusively to "persons resident within" one state.*

The SEC interprets "residence" in the domiciliary sense (See SEC, Securities Act Release No. 4434 (Dec. 6, 1961)), and this creates some uncertainty in efforts to comply with the terms of the exemption. It is quite possible that a potential offeree reasonably believed by the issuer on the basis of objective appearance to have her principal residence in the state, may, in fact, be domiciled elsewhere. (This is often true, for example of persons in the military service.) The risk is more substantial than it might first appear, because the exemption is unavailable for not only that offer but also for the entire issue, thereby opening the seller to liability to every person who has purchased securities sold in the offering.

Until the promulgation of Rule 147, the lack of a clear definition of certain other key parts of the exemption also gave pause to careful lawyers considering the possibility of using it. The '33 Act requires, for example, that the issuer be "doing business within" the state in which the offer is made, but it gives no indication of how much business is required. There is also often considerable difficulty in determining what is "an issue." When the issuer has sold securities to nonresidents of the state previously, are those sales to be "integrated" into a subsequent offering made entirely within the state? In 1974 the SEC alleviated some of the problems faced by the lawyer trying to comply with the exemption by adopting Rule 147, which provides a set of more or less objective conditions within which an offer can be guaranteed exempt treatment.

In practice the utility of the exemption seems to depend largely on local conditions. It is obviously riskier to attempt such an offering in a metropolitan area that encompasses more than one state. Moreover in some states the failure to register an offering under the '33 Act increases the burden of complying with the local blue sky law (discussed more fully below), with the result that there is little or no net saving in time and expense. Finally, use of the intrastate offering exemption simply seems to have met with greater acceptance in some areas than in others, with some practitioners still deeming it too risky and others having found they could use it successfully.

The remaining statutory exemption of particular interest to counsel to a small corporation is Section 3(b), which empowers the SEC to

---

* The District of Columbia is not a "state" for the purposes of the exemption.   1 Louis Loss, Securities Regulation 602 (2d ed. 1961).

exempt, according to such conditions as it sees fit to establish, other issues of up to $5 million.

The judicial and administrative exemptions for smaller issuers from the 1933 Act's registration provisions previously was characterized by a lack of clarity. This confusion stemmed in large part to the lack of adequate definitions for key terms contained in the statute. One unclear provision was the "private placement" exemption found in Section 4(2) which exempts from the registration requirements contained in Section 5 "transactions by an issuer not involving any public offering". The issuers (and their counsel) faced the problem of deciding whether a transaction did not involve any public offering, because "a public offering" was not defined by the statute. Issuers making "private placements" to large institutional investors used this exemption in a safe manner. The SEC generally had no objection to these transactions because it was comfortable with the idea that these large investors were in a position to demand material information as needed. However, the SEC and the courts became concerned with the use of the private placement exemption for "non-public" offerings to investors (and prospective investors) who might not have had the ability to secure the type of information that would be available if the issuer went through the registration process.

For example, in SEC v. Ralston Purina Corp., 346 U.S. 119, 73 S.Ct. 981, 97 L.Ed. 1494 (1953), the Supreme Court held that the applicability of Section 4(2) depends on whether the class of persons to whom the securities are offered "need the protection of the ['33] Act." The Court held that the private placement exemption applies to investors who are "able to fend for themselves," regardless of how many there are. Because many of the employees in their corporate positions lacked access to the kind of information that would have been available in a prospectus, the Court held that registration under the '33 Act was required. Later cases raised doubts whether the private placement exemption would be available to raise start-up capital for new ventures, unless the offerees were insiders or sophisticated investors with access to all material information about the issuer. Hill York Corp. v. American Intern. Franchises, 448 F.2d 680 (5th Cir.1971); SEC v. Continental Tobacco Co. of S.C., 463 F.2d 137 (5th Cir.1972). Beginning in 1974, the SEC and Congress took a number of steps intended to alleviate the burdens imposed by the securities laws on small issuers. Those efforts culminated in 1982 with the promulgation of Regulation D, which attempts to coordinate the various exemptions in a coherent scheme.

The SEC promulgated Regulation D to correct what it considered were disproportionate restraints imposed on small issuers by the registration requirements of '33 Act. These restraints, the SEC perceived, made it difficult for small issuers to raise capital, because they had to comply with the costly registration requirements contained in Section 5. Regulation D consists of eight rules, designated as Rules 501–508. Rules 501–503 include definitions and conditions used in applying the exemptions. It is in Rules 504–506 that three exemptions from the registration requirements are found.

Rule 504 provides an exemption for "small" offerings. Pursuant to Rule 504(b)(2), any non-public company can sell up to $1,000,000 in securities during a 12–month period without having to comply with any federal registration requirements; however, state securities provisions (which are discussed in Section E of this chapter) remain applicable. In addition, there is no limit on the number of investors to whom the securities can be sold, unlike Rules 505 and 506. Rule 504 also allows for the general solicitation of investors and generally provides for the free transferability of securities acquired under the rule. Rule 504(b)(1) and Rule 502(c) and (d).

Rule 505 exempts certain medium sized offerings which meet the following conditions. First, Rule 505(b)(2)(i) provides that the offering must be less than $5,000,000 in a 12–month period. Second, under Rule 505(b)(2)(ii) sales of securities can not be made to more than 35 non-accredited purchasers, although sales to accredited investors are unlimited. Rule 501(a) defines various types of investors considered to be accredited, such as institutional investors, key insiders, and wealthy individuals. Third, the offering must not utilize any general advertising or solicitation (Rule 502(c)). Fourth, the information requirements are set forth in Rule 502(b)(2). Note the application of the concept of integrated disclosure in Rule 502(b)(2)(ii).

Rule 506 exempts certain private offerings which meet similar conditions as in Rule 505, except there is no dollar limit, with one additional consideration. As in Rule 505, the offering can be made to an unlimited number of accredited purchasers, but to not more than 35 non-accredited investors. Also there must be no general advertising or solicitation and certain disclosure requirements must be met. However, Rule 506(b)(2)(ii) creates the additional requirement that for each purchaser who is not an accredited investor, the issuer must make a reasonably believe that the purchaser has "such knowledge and experience in financial and business matters that he is capable of evaluating the merits and risks of the prospective investment." Unsophisticated purchasers may participate in an offering if a purchaser representative, as defined in Rule 501(h), is present.

Note the leeway provided by Rule 508. It is also worth noting that Preliminary Note 3 to Regulation D provides that the regulation is not exclusive and "the issuer can claim the availability of any other applicable exemption."

Finally, the anti-fraud provisions of the securities laws, particularly Sections 12(2) and 17(a) of the 1933 Act and Section 10(b) and Rule 10b–5 of the 1934 Act, still apply, and that to avoid liability under those provisions, it may be necessary to make some affirmative disclosures. See Preliminary Note 1 to Regulation D.

E. STATE BLUE SKY LAWS

From 1870 to 1930, the public sale of corporate stocks and bonds increased dramatically, and so did the incidence of securities fraud. To counter the predation practiced by peddlers of securities on innocent investors, state legislatures began enacting securities laws. Better known as "blue sky" laws after an early judicial opinion condemning "speculator schemes which have no more basis than so many feet of "blue sky,' " these statutes regulate the sales of securities to purchasers within the jurisdiction.

The first such law, enacted in Kansas in 1911, provided for the registration of securities and securities salespeople. A security covered by the Act could not be sold until a state agency issued a permit. The Kansas statute governing the denial of permits provided:

> But, if said bank commissioner finds that such articles of incorporation or association, charter, constitution and by-laws, plan of business or proposed contract, contain any provision that is unfair, unjust, inequitable or oppressive to any class of contributors, or if he decides from his examination of its affairs that said investment company is not solvent and does not intend to do a fair and honest business, and in his judgment does not provide a fair return on the stocks, bonds, or other securities by it offered for sale, then he shall notify such investment company in writing of his findings, and it shall be unlawful for such company to do any further business in this state * * *. (Kan.L.1911, c. 133, § 5).

State regulation of securities spread rapidly. By 1933 all states, except Nevada, had enacted blue sky laws.

Generally speaking these laws contain some form of one or more of three basic regulatory devices: (1) anti-fraud provisions which made it unlawful to make a false or misleading statement or to omit a material fact in connection with the sale of a security; (2) registration or licensing of certain persons engaged in the securities business prior to their trading in securities within a state; (3) registration or licensing of securities prior to any dealing in the securities, which frequently involves procedures and standards for an affirmative administrative approval of the merits of a particular issue. "Each of the three regulatory devices represents a somewhat different philosophical approach toward the same end of protecting the investing public. Antifraud provisions are intended to enable the administrator to issue public warnings, to investigate suspected fraudulent activities, to take injunctive or other steps to stop them, and as a last resort to punish them. Registration of brokers, dealers, agents and investment advisers is intended to prevent dishonest or unqualified persons from entering the securities business, to supervise their activities within the state once registration has been achieved, and to remove them from registration if they fall below any of the statutory standards. Registration of securities is intended to give the investor 'a run for his money' by excluding from the state those securities which do not satisfy the statutory standards." * The Securities Act of 1933, Section 18, and the Securities Exchange Act of 1934, Section 28(a), expressly preserve the effect of the state securities laws.

Although there is not space here to discuss them further, the impact of blue sky laws on the selling of securities is often quite important. In a large public offering in which securities will be sold in many states, it is necessary for someone, usually counsel for the underwriters, to "blue sky" the issue, assuring compliance with the requirements of the laws of every state in which it is to be offered. As these laws vary considerably from one state to another, this is a substantial task.

Blue sky laws also complicate the administration of the exemptions to the registration requirements of the 1933 Act. Even before the actions taken by Congress and the SEC to expand the availability of exemptions under federal law, the exemptions under the various state laws that required registration were not always coordinated with the federal exemptions. Under the impetus of the Small Business Investment Incentive Act, the SEC has actively encouraged state legislatures and state securities administrators to develop exemptions that better harmonize with the federal system. Regulation D, the product of a cooperative effort between the Commission and the North American Securities Administrators Association (NASAA), was the principal result.

In September 1983, NASAA adopted the Uniform Limited Offering Exemption (ULOE) as an official policy guideline. ULOE, where adopted by a state legislature, grants a state securities administrator the authority to create by rule a limited offering exemption, following Rules 505 and 506 with certain conditions and limitations, to further the objectives of compatibility with Regulation D and uniformity among the states.

More recently, the Small Corporate Offering Registration Form (SCOR) was developed by a study group of the subcommittee on Private Offering Exemption and Simplification of Capital Formation of the State Regulation of Securities Committee of the American Bar Association Business Law Section, working closely with various committees of the NASAA. This cooperative effort lead to the approval in April 1989 of SCOR as a uniform form for adoption. SCOR is available in about thirty states.

The creation of SCOR will make the use of Rule 504 a more viable possibility for small firms seeking to raise capital. SCOR meets the needs of small business through a simplified question and answer disclosure document that serves as a uniform registration form for purposes of state registration. After an issuer completes the answers to the SCOR Form and attaches the required financial statement (which an independent accountant reviews, but does not audit, thereby substantially reducing the cost), the issuer files the form with the securities

* 1 Louis Loss and Joel Seligman, Securities Regulation 61 (3d ed. 1989).

administrators for those states in which the issuer seeks registration. After the issuer completes the registration process in the various states, the issuer distributes to the public copies of the completed SCOR form as the disclosure document in the offering.

F. DISCLOSURE POLICY

PROBLEM
A DINNER CONVERSATION

At a dinner party you fall into a conversation about the securities laws with an economics professor at a local university. He argues that the disclosure requirements of the '33 Act provide little or no social benefit, or at least that the substantial costs of registration under the Act are not nearly justified by any reductions in fraud or improvements in the efficiency of the capital markets. He further asserts that the disclosure requirements are unnecessary because corporate managers possess sufficient incentives to disclose voluntarily all (or virtually all) information material to investors. Voluntary disclosure is likely, he maintains, because the alternative is to forego access to the capital markets, because of the competition among issuers for investors' funds, the likelihood that full disclosure will reduce a corporation's cost of raising capital, and the ability of some investors to negotiate for information they consider material. He is willing to admit that perhaps a federal statute simply prohibiting fraud in the sale of securities and establishing a civil action for damages (similar to Section 12(2) of the '33 Act) may serve some useful purpose, but he vigorously maintains that were it not for the entrenched interests of the securities bar and the accounting profession, whose members profit handsomely from the '33 Act, its registration requirements would long ago have been abolished.

Rising to the defense of your profession, you present a strong, lawyerlike argument to the contrary. What is it? Do you believe it? Consider the following:

DAVID J. SCHULTE, THE DEBATABLE CASE FOR SECURITIES DISCLOSURE REGULATION

13 Journal of Corporation Law 535, 537–547 (1988).

III. PUBLIC INTEREST JUSTIFICATIONS FOR FEDERAL MANDATORY DISCLOSURE

The classical justification for market regulation is that it serves the public interest of wealth maximization in response to market failure. Wealth can be maximized if markets efficiently perform their resource allocation function. Socially optimal disclosure leads to allocatively efficient markets, which ultimately benefit all members of society. This section discusses the social goal of optimal disclosure and the means for achieving that goal.

A.   The Public Interest Goals of Mandatory Disclosure
1.   Correction of Market Failure

In a competitive market, the pricing system usually can be relied upon to achieve an efficient (optimal) allocation of resources.   Information has its own market, because it has value to decision makers. Information, however, is a "public good," and like other public goods, tends to be underproduced because of the ability of some users to "free-ride" from others' efforts at producing it.

The key characteristics of a public good are that it is difficult to exclude others from using it and its consumption by one user does not diminish its availability to others.   Public parks are examples of public goods.   People can enjoy them without paying for their production. Those with an economic interest in ensuring access to the good will pay for it, regardless of the marginal indirect benefit to free riders.   However, because free riders pay nothing for goods they nevertheless value, there is no market signal to produce socially optimal quantities of the good, and the good tends to be underprovided.

a.   Inefficient Research

Information about securities is difficult to keep from two groups of free riders: investors and competitors.   First, news from securities analysts tends to leak out quickly.   Many ultimate users of the information do not have to compensate the analyst because of the incentive for those investors who do pay the analyst to "tip" nonpaying investors. The payor has an incentive to tip in order to create excitement and induce the analyst's predicted market activity.   The consequence is undercompensated, and therefore, underprovided, securities research, because the analyst is unable to capture the full value that investors would pay for the research.   If the socially optimal level of research will not be performed, the information market has "failed."

Another problem is redundant production of information.   Securities analysts may be duplicating others' efforts wastefully.   Too much of some bits of information will be produced resulting in another market failure.

b.   Insufficient Production

(1)   Conflicts of Interest

While the individual investors or securities analyst may not be able to "appropriate the full value" of his research, a corporation "can appropriate the full value" that investors place on information by selling its stock for more money.   The corporation is the only information-producing entity that is in privity with all investors.   Agency theory suggests that if disclosure is worthwhile to investors, the firm will have sufficient incentive to provide it.   The assumption underlying agency theory, however, that management is a "repeat player" that can maximize its long run interests only by maintaining the market's confidence, may not be true in a market characterized by hostile takeovers and management led leveraged buy outs (LBOs).   These transactions undermine agency theory because management's interest sometimes conflicts with that of the shareholders.   A conflict of interests could result in management withholding information which investors would consider material.

(2) Competitors

The ability of the agency relationship to provide managerial incentives to produce socially optimal levels of disclosure also is undermined by the second group of free riders: competitors. Competitors may benefit from the disclosure by one firm to potential investors of information relevant to the industry in which they operate. Yet, these competitors cannot be charged for the information and, therefore, it will be underproduced. Each firm may be willing to disclose information which could be relevant to investors if all other firms in the industry follow suit, but there is no assurance that this will occur.

There is some support for the conclusion that free riders cause underproduction of information. Securities analysts have complained about their difficulties in obtaining information important for investment decisions but not required for disclosure. * * * Nonetheless, in an unregulated information market, there will be strong incentives for each firm to hold out and not disclose in order to prevent giving other firms a competitive advantage.

Because securities markets are the principal allocative mechanism for investment capital, the behavior of securities prices is important because of their effect on allocative efficiency. If securities prices are distorted because of the failures of the information market discussed above then, some form of regulation is justified as being in the "public interest." [32] The following more controversial "public interest" arguments also are used to justify regulation.

2. Increase Public Confidence in the Market

The justification most commonly offered for mandatory disclosure regulation is that it is necessary to preserve public confidence in the capital markets. Mandatory disclosure regulation reduces the fear of exploitation [33] and, accordingly, ensures that investors will not withdraw their capital to the detriment of society as a whole. An investor who believes that the market is a "fair game" invests more resources in equity securities and spends less time investigating thereby causing economic gains. This is a controversial justification for regulation, however, because the costs of enforcing the disclosure may outweigh any confidence gains. There is no good evidence that the incidence of investor exploitation has dropped under regulation. Thus, there may be a greater social cost than benefit.

32. The information market failures can be overcome by standardization of disclosure formats [Frank H.] Easterbrook and [Daniel R.] Fischel, Mandatory Disclosure and the Protection of Investors, 70 Va. L. Rev. 669, 686–87 (1984). This standardization may occur privately or through regulation. *Id.* at 687. A governmental imposed disclosure format would be preferable if it is less costly than privately developed formats. *Id.*

33. * * * An Interview with John C. Burton, Mgmt. Acct. 21 (May 1975) (mandatory disclosure gives investors more confidence that they are getting the whole story) * * *.

In addition, average investors actually are not exploited, because so long as professional traders engage in research and trading, market prices will reflect fully all publicly available information. Thus, the uninformed trader can take a free ride on professional traders' work, confident that he will not be exploited since the professional investors will not be. Moreover, mandatory disclosure does not serve egalitarian goals, because the average investor who obtains disclosure statements will be unable to take advantage of available bargains regardless of the quantity of disclosures forced on him. Last, these "paranoid traders" easily can protect themselves by investing their capital in mutual funds, securing whatever real or imagined advantage these professionals have. Because data strongly suggests that most professional traders and money managers do not outperform the market consistently, this advantage is more imagined than real. Thus, the existence of information asymmetry is at best a controversial basis for regulation.

3. Reduce Fund

Like deficiencies of information, fraud reduces allocative efficiency. Therefore, the rules against fraud compliment the disclosure rules by imposing a cost on firms that engage in fraudulent behavior. Reduction of fraud is a controversial justification for federal regulation, because fraud was illegal in every state when the federal rules were passed. The supporters of the Securities Act of 1933 and the Securities Exchange Act of 1934, however, justify the national rules because the state laws were ineffective against interstate frauds. The passage of the federal securities laws in 1933 and 1934 occurred after the third major securities fraud wave of the century. There is evidence that information deemed material by the SEC would not have been disseminated absent regulation. After the establishment of the SEC, data concerning stop orders, letters of deficiency, and the withdrawal of registration statements indicated that a larger percentage of securities would have been sold which omitted or misrepresented information which the SEC defines as "material."

The foregoing rationale has been criticized by Professors Easterbrook and Fischel. They have argued that the incidence of fraud is just as high today as before the 1933 Act. While they provided only three anecdotes of modern fraud for support, their point is that fraud still can and does occur, despite the existence of disclosure regulation. Furthermore, they argued that, consistent with the "reduce fraud" justification, the increased reports of fraud do not prove that the state laws were "ineffective" anymore than the existence of murder proves that state criminal laws similarly are "ineffective," and should be replaced with a national murder statute enforced by a Federal Homicide Commission.

The Chicago professors' rebuttal of the state ineffectiveness argument circumvents the true cause of the state's failure to prevent fraud. Professor Seligman's extensive historical research documented the frustration of state securities commissioners in attempting to prevent interstate fraud. For example, the Iowa Secretary of State reported that he was "powerless to stop fraudulent securities sales through the mails." Further support for Seligman's "fraud prevention" justification for mandatory federal regulation of securities is demonstrated by observation of the current incidence of securities fraud actions among firms too small to be subject to the SEC's mandatory disclosure system, or exempt from the system. With respect to firms not subject to mandatory disclosure, Seligman observed that "omission or misrepresentation of material investment persisted as a common phenomena."

While Professors Easterbrook and Fischel have not agreed with the "reduce fraud" rationale for regulation, they have agreed with the type of information regulated by the SEC, and have offered their own rationale for a rule against fraud. They again take a cost-benefit position in suggesting that "[t]he rule against fraud, [whatever its source], is most beneficial when enforcement costs are low and when it is possible to separate untruths from statements that, [albeit] are low and when it is possible to separate untruths from statements that, [albeit] true, do not accurately predict the future." Thus, SEC enforcement should, and does, concentrate on verifiable statements of fact, not predictions. The usual criticisms leveled against the SEC for its emphasis on historical fact fail to consider that both the chance of enforcement error and the cost of enforcement are lowest for these representations.

Easterbrook and Fischel also advanced their own justification for federal rules against fraud: "[T]he [resulting] efficiency of enforcing in one case all claims arising out of a single transaction." First, almost all large corporations' securities sell in interstate markets. If claims arising from these securities were litigated in multiple forums, there could be inconsistent judgments and legal standards. Second, since claims of fraud usually involve numerous written documents, litigating these claims in one forum would maximize efficiency. Last, federal securities laws' nationwide service of process and liberal venue rules permit low costs consolidation of claims in a single forum.

B.   Novel Public Interest Theories Supporting Federal Mandatory Disclosure

1.   Control of Interstate Disclosure

Easterbrook and Fischel contended that a federal rule of disclosure which determines the disclosures required for securities sold within the state, is necessary to prevent states from exploiting investors in other states. For example, a group of IBM investors living in Missouri could bring litigation there, contending that under Missouri securities laws, IBM failed to make certain disclosures which are not required by any other state. It would be in Missouri's interest to sustain the claim and order IBM to pay damages. The money to pay the Missouri investors will come primarily from residents of the states. Other states may retaliate, resulting in an environment in which states call for too much disclosure by firms incorporated in other states. Only federal regulation, concluded Easterbrook and Fischel, may be able to prevent states from interstate exploitation in securities transactions.

* * *

2.　Controlling the Costs of the Common–Law Process

State common-law fraud actions are a costly form of forcing disclosure of material information: an offending party does not know until long after the fact whether his disclosures or omissions will be found to violate the law. The mere risk of violation increases the firm's cost of capital by increasing the risk of a judgment against the firm and a consequent loss of productive assets. Investors would be willing to pay to reduce that risk, because it does not affect the prospects of the projects the firm undertakes. The cost to firms of compliance ex ante with mandatory disclosure regulation may be less than the cost of the risk of being found in violation of the law ex post.

Additionally, society would benefit if firms and investors could merely reduce the aggregate amount of litigation. The resources invested in litigation are socially wasteful: they merely divide up an existing pile of money. A system that reduces the volume of litigation by determination in advance whether disclosures are adequate would make society better off, even if "too much disclosure" is required.

These justifications for mandatory disclosure may not be supported by evidence. It is unlikely that federal securities laws have reduced socially undesirable litigation. Casual observation of rule 10b–5 litigation does not support the argument that litigation has been reduced. Nonetheless, the existence of a federal forum with liberal joinder rules creates more efficient litigation of securities claims.

3.　Average Investors Need Disclosure

The average investor's claim to extensive disclosure has been reduced in importance because of the investor's demonstrated inability to take advantage of it. Investors merely should diversify their securities portfolios by purchasing "index funds," obviating the need for disclosures.

This argument against mandatory disclosure is valid, as far as it goes. For many investors, Professor Coffee argued, it may be rational to fail to diversify their securities portfolios in order to diversify their entire investment portfolio. For example, an executive is likely to have a substantial investment in his business, real estate, and insurance. These investments all have different degrees of nonmarket, or investment-specific risk. The executive desiring to diversify this nonmarket risk can counterbalance these investments against securities investments. Modern portfolio theory dictates that this investors should find securities that react countercyclically with present "locked-in" investments. By including countercyclic investments, the investor reduces the overall risk of his investment portfolio. Thus, ordinary investors need basic financial disclosure in order to diversity their total investment portfolio around existing assets.

* * *

C. The Failure of Nonfederal Means of Disclosures Regulation

The need for federal regulation of disclosure is founded on the failure of the following nonfederal means of enforcement to produce socially optimal levels of disclosure.

1. The New York Stock Exchange

Chicago School Scholars have argued that organized exchanges produce socially optimal disclosure. They argue that organized exchanges have incentives to adopt rules that benefit investors. Organized exchanges reduce the costs of trading, both by increasing liquidity and by lowering transaction costs. Exchanges can attract more trades, as well as increase profits, by adopting rules governing listed firms that inure to the benefit of traders. Thus, Exchanges have an incentive to adopt disclosure rules that satisfy investor demand, much like a manufacturing company selects inputs that are most likely to satisfy consumer demand.

Firms have incentives to list their securities with exchanges that attract the most capital from investors. Competition among exchanges for investors' capital and for the listing of firms increases the exchange's incentive to adopt socially optimal disclosure rules. Consistent with this expectation, the Chicago professors have argued, firms listed on national exchanges do in fact disclose more information than unlisted firms.

With all these incentives to the contrary, why was an exchange like the New York Stock Exchange (NYSE) unable to satisfy the perceived social need for disclosure regulation? Professor Seligman agreed with the Chicago School view that the NYSE's goal of retention of membership and listings provides a strong incentive to adopt rules reflecting the member's economic interests. His quarrel with the Chicago School was over the definition of those economic interests. Seligman described the pre–1933 NYSE as understaffed and impotent, unable to enforce periodic disclosure requirements. He observed that self-regulatory organizations with voluntary membership have well known inherent limitations, such as a mutual lack of enthusiasm for regulation, "and a resistance to changes in the regulatory pattern because of vested economic interests." He noted that prior to the adoption of the 1933 and 1934 federal securities laws the NYSE disclosure requirements easily could be evaded by corporations, simply by choosing to be traded as an "unlisted" [81] security on any one of eighteen other exchanges. The existence of these alternatives gave the NYSE an incentive not to enforce its listing requirements. Thus, the economic interests of corporations in Seligman's view was nondisclosure, and the NYSE catered to that interest.

---

81. An "unlisted" security made no corporate disclosure. * * *

Which view of NYSE disclosure efficacy is more correct? Neither of the cited articles contained empirical support for its conclusion. Seligman even noted an increase in NYSE listing applications, despite his argument that firms would "delist" in order to avoid disclosure. Easterbrook and Fischel did not provide evidence that firms seeking financing on the NYSE paid a lower price for their capital, even though such evidence would have been probative of the firms' economic interests in disclosure. The NYSE was characterized by Easterbrook and Fischel as a product market with knowledgeable investors dictating corporate behavior by voting with their investment dollars. Seligman viewed the NYSE as a weak check on demonic corporations. The truth probably lay somewhere in between. Easterbrook and Fischel's theory does not explain the anecdotal evidence of nondisclosure detailed by Professor Seligman. Seligman, however, did not address the observation of Easterbrook and Fischel that firms that bind themselves to follow an exchange's rules will have a competitive advantage in attracting capital.

2. States

Theoretically, states could enforce a mandatory disclosure system. The Chicago School views competition among states for corporate charters as analogous to competition among exchanges or listed firms: both are primarily influenced to set rules that will benefit investors. Like easily shifting investment out of the NYSE, for example, an investor can shift investment among firms chartered in different states. Firms then have the incentive to incorporate in and, thus, abide by the rules of the state which is most likely to attract investment dollars because of investor-favorable rules. If compulsory disclosure is optimal, state law would require disclosure to make the state more attractive to investors— and thus firms. If this competition does work to produce optimal levels of enforced disclosure, federally enforced disclosure laws would interfere with the system.

Professor Seligman sharply disagreed, labeling the history of state corporate law as "chartermongering." The states are unable to enforce restrictive corporation statutes, he argues, much like the NYSE was unable to promulgate and enforce effective disclosure rules. The firms have "economic interests" in nondisclosure. Additionally, as noted above, state blue sky law failed miserably to either prevent fraud or enforce disclosure rules. State blue sky officials supported federal regulation because they were powerless to prevent fraudulent securities sales made across state lines.

Easterbrook and Fischel agree with Seligman to a certain extent. They admitted that legal requirements to disclose information may be necessary if "multi-state third party effects" (market failure) prevent interstate competition from arriving at the optimal level of disclosure. If interstate fraud is an externality that state law is unable to prevent, federal rules will be beneficial.

3. *Private Citizens*

Both schools of thought agree that private actions alone would not ensure optimal levels of corporate disclosure. Professors Seligman, Easterbrook, and Fischel have argued that civil suits cannot protect investors because of the high costs of litigation. In addition, there also is the likelihood of corporate insolvency by the time the fraud is discovered. Furthermore, the potential for overenforcement because of excessive penalties available to private plaintiffs may deter truthful disclosure. For these reasons, federal disclosure regulation may be a less costly and more efficacious means of encouraging optimal disclosure than either federal or state antifraud rules alone.

IV. EVALUATION OF FEDERAL MANDATORY DISCLOSURE
A. *The Paradox of Regulation*

Federal regulation of the information market through mandatory disclosure rules is justifiable if there is market-failure—as is the case with public goods. Yet, once the free market pricing rule is replaced with regulation, it becomes impossible to determine whether resources are expended optimally on information disclosure. The reason is that there is no way for regulators to measure demand for the good regulated—in this case the good regulated being information. The pricing system is the only reliable method of measuring social preferences through supply and demand equilibrium. A "Catch–22" occurs because market failure also renders the pricing system unreliable. The tendency in regulation, however, is to oversupply the public good, because the perceived demand is for a good with no cost. Thus, users of information will overstate their demand. The users of free disclosures (investors) arguably would not demand the same quantity or quality of information if it had to be purchased based on its economic value. The information market failures discussed above, however, would occur in the absence of regulation.

B. *Some Empirical Evidence*

Reconsider the hypothesis that securities markets are the principal mechanism for allocation of investment capital. The bulk of regulated disclosures today are from secondary markets. The secondary market for securities will have allocative efficiency consequences because it determines the firm's cost of obtaining additional capital. The critical empirical question to test the ability of mandatory disclosure regulation to direct investment capital accurately is whether the dispersion of actual returns on new issues is lower after the disclosure laws were enacted. Professor Coffee argued that if the federal securities laws reduced the dispersion of investment returns on new issues, it reasonably can be inferred that allocative efficiency has been enhanced. The greater the variance associated with securities returns, "the greater the uncertainty * * * of investor expectations, and the less the likelihood that our capital allocation mechanism is working efficiently." Professor Coffee also borrowed Professor Stigler's conclusion in another context that price dispersion did decline after the passage of the Securities Act of 1933. If the significance of this decline is that the capital market is more efficient allocatively, then society does benefit from federal mandatory disclosure.

————

For contrasting viewpoints on the mandatory disclosure system, see Frank H. Easterbrook and Daniel R. Fischel, Mandatory Disclosure and The Protection of Investors, 70 Va.L.Rev. 669 (1984), Frank H. Easterbrook and Daniel R. Fischel, The Economic Structure of Corporate Law Chapter 11 (1991), Joel Seligman, The Historical Need For A Mandatory Corporate Disclosure System, 9 J. of Corp. L. 1 (1983), and John C. Coffee, Jr., Market Failure and The Economic Case For a Mandatory Disclosure System, 70 Va.L.Rev. 717 (1984).

Chapter 11

PROTECTION OF CREDITORS:
LIMITATIONS ON LIMITED
LIABILITY

A. THE FUNCTION OF LIMITED LIABILITY

As we have seen, one principal advantage of the corporate form of business is that a shareholder's potential loss is limited to the amount that she has invested in the enterprise. Many states provide, directly or indirectly, for limited liability, and there is a strong presumption in favor of such limitations when a creditor seeks to hold the shareholders liable for the corporation's debts. The general rule is that the corporation is liable for its own obligations, and a creditor of the corporation may look only to the corporate assets for recovery.

Like most other rules, however, limited liability has its exceptions. Where justice requires, courts disregard the corporate entity and allow the plaintiffs to reach the assets of the shareholders. This result is metaphorically described as "piercing the corporate veil." Particularly where the corporation is a wholly owned subsidiary of another corporation, courts use colorful phrases to justify disregarding the corporate fiction. They do so when they find the subsidiary to be the "agent," "alias," "alter ego," "corporate double," "dummy," or "instrumentality" of the parent. None of these terms is particularly instructive in describing when a court will "pierce the corporate veil." As Justice Cardozo observed, "the whole problem of the relation between [shareholder and corporation] is one that is still enveloped in a mist of metaphor. Metaphors in law are to be narrowly watched, for starting as devices to liberate thought, they end often by enslaving it." Berkey v. Third Avenue Railway Co., 244 N.Y. 84, 94, 155 N.E. 58, 61 (1926).

This chapter deals with those relatively rare instances in which courts disregard the general principle of limited liability. A useful perspective on this question is to see it as a matter of allocation of losses. When the assets of a corporation are inadequate to fulfill its obligations to the plaintiff, under what circumstances should the court shift the burden of those losses from the plaintiff to the shareholders of the corporation? A number of factors may lead a court to do so: (1) insufficient attention to corporate formalities; (2) "abuse" of the corporate entity by pushing its advantages to extremes; and (3) whether the corporation is "undercapitalized."

The legal rules imposing liability on shareholders for corporate obligations can be evaluated by considering the economic consequences of the legal norm of limited liability: a substantial portion of the risk of business failure shifts to creditors and away from shareholders. There are two principal types of creditors: voluntary creditors who contract with the corporation, and involuntary creditors—mainly tort victims. The difference between them appears to be their ability to bargain with the corporation. Yet even this distinction may become blurred; the contract creditor who sells merchandise or services over the telephone to a corporation generally does not engage in more investigation or bargaining than does the tort victim. What then is an appropriate standard for determining when the risk should be shifted from the shareholders to the creditors?

As the following materials indicate, there is considerable indeterminacy in the existing case law. Consequently, from a planning perspective, it is often difficult to know in advance what steps the participants in a new venture must take in order to ensure the benefits of limited liability or whether those steps will prove adequate if the corporation is unable to pay its debts.

B. CRITIQUES OF LIMITED LIABILITY

This section examines various critiques of the theory of limited liability and the application of that doctrine within various contexts. It begins with a discussion of the general theory and then considers that theory as applied to close corporations. It then analyzes the applicability of a limited liability regime to voluntary creditors, a context in which the doctrine is at its apogee. Finally it looks at the treatment of tort claimants, where the attack on limited liability is strongest.

Forms of business organization that provide for limited liability appear in virtually every developed legal system. We have become so accustomed to them that we tend to ignore the significant public policy issues they present. What public purpose is served by allowing a few individuals, perhaps even one person, to create an enterprise and limit their liabilities growing out of that business? Does any public policy support such a regime? If so, what conditions or qualifications should be placed on the privilege?

1. THE ECONOMIC JUSTIFICATION FOR LIMITED LIABILITY

FRANK H. EASTERBROOK AND DANIEL R. FISCHEL, THE ECONOMIC STRUCTURE OF CORPORATE LAW
41–44 (1991).

Publicly held corporations dominate other organizational forms when the technology of production requires firms to combine both the specialized skills of multiple agents and large amounts of capital. Limited liability reduces the costs of this separation and specialization of functions in a number of respects.

First, limited liability decreases the need to monitor agents. To protect themselves, investors could monitor their agents more closely. The more risk they bear, the more they will monitor. But beyond a point extra monitoring is not worth the cost. * * * Limited liability makes * * * passivity a more rational strategy and so potentially reduces the cost of operating the corporation.

Second, limited liability reduces the costs of monitoring other shareholders. Under a rule exposing equity investors to unlimited liability, the greater the wealth of other shareholders, the lower the probability that any one shareholder's assets will be needed to pay a judgment. Thus existing shareholders would have incentives to engage in costly monitoring of other shareholders to ensure that they do not transfer assets to others or sell to others with less wealth. Limited liability makes the identity of other shareholders irrelevant and thus avoids these costs.

Third, by promoting free transfer of shares, limited liability gives managers incentives to act efficiently. Although individual shareholders lack the expertise and incentive to monitor the actions of specialized agents, the ability of investors to sell creates opportunities for investors as a group to and constrains agents' actions. * * * [The] potential for displacement gives existing managers incentives to operate efficiently in order to keep share prices high.

With limited liability, the value of shares is set by the present value of the income stream generated by a firm's assets. The identity and wealth of other investors is irrelevant. Shares are fungible; they trade at one price in liquid markets. Under a rule of unlimited liability shares would not be fungible. Their value would be a function of the present value of future cash flows and the wealth of shareholders. Their lack of fungibility would impede their acquisition. * * * Limited liability allows a person to buy a large bloc without any risk of being surcharged, and thus it facilitates beneficial control transactions. A rule that facilitates transfers of control also induces managers to work more effectively to stave off such transfers, and so it reduces the costs of specialization whether or not a firm is acquired.

Fourth, limited liability makes it possible for market prices to reflect additional information about the value of firms. With unlimited liability, shares would not be homogeneous commodities and would no longer have one market price. Investors would be required to expend greater resources analyzing the prospects of the firm to know whether "the price is right." When all can trade on the same terms, though, investors trade until the price of shares reflect the available information about a firm's prospects. Most investors need not expend resources searching for additional information.

Fifth, * * * limited liability allows more efficient diversification. Investors can cut risk by owning a diversified portfolio of assets. Firms can raise capital at lower costs because investors need not bear the special risk associated with nondiversified holdings. This applies only under a rule of limited liability or some good substitute. * * *

Sixth, limited liability facilitates optimal investment decisions. When investors hold diversified portfolios, managers maximize investors' welfare by investing in any project with a positive net present value. * * * In a world of unlimited liability managers * * * would reject as "too risky" some projects with positive net present values. Investors would want them to do this because it would be the best way to reduce risks. By definition this would be a social loss, because projects with net present value are beneficial uses of capital. * * * The increased availability of funds for projects with positive net values is the real benefit of limited liability.

––––––

Do economic efficiency considerations adequately explain the doctrine of limited liability? Stephen Presser asserts that, while Easterbrook and Fischel's six factors were important in the evolution of the doctrine, they do not provide a full explanation. Stephen B. Presser, Thwarting the Killing of the Corporation: Limited Liability, Democracy, and Economics, 87 Nw. U. L.Rev. 148, 155–156 (1992).

Presser attacks Easterbrook and Fischel's theory on three grounds. First, he disagrees with their assertion that unlimited liability produces high monitoring costs that discourage investment. He contends that even in an unlimited liability regime, shareholders would still invest if the return on their investment were high enough; they would simply base their investment on the corporation's proven business strategies or the self-monitoring abilities of management. Id. at 158–59.

Presser's second objection arises from Easterbrook and Fischel's contention that unlimited liability would lead to increased costs arising from the need to monitor other investors. He notes that monitoring would be required only where unlimited liability was joint and several. He believes that it is likely, however, that an unlimited liability regime would involve pro rata liability for shareholders so that any individual shareholder would be liable only in the proportion that her investment bore to the total investment in the firm. Under such a system, the need for monitoring other shareholders disappears because the wealth of other shareholders is irrelevant. The only important criteria is investment in the firm. Id. at 160–61.

Finally, Presser notes that the benefits of diversified investments, such as the increased incentives for managers to invest in risky projects and a concomitant decrease in investment costs, could be obtained in other ways apart from limited liability. For example, diversification could be achieved at the firm level, if firms had sufficient capital to invest in a wide range of opportunities. Id. at 162.

Presser looks to the historical justification for limiting liability and concludes that "the imposition of limited liability was perceived as a means of encouraging the small-scale entrepreneur, and of keeping entry into business markets competitive and democratic." Coupled with economic efficiency, business democracy explains the continuing appeal of limited liability.

2. CLOSE CORPORATIONS

Easterbrook and Fischel note that the economic efficiency rationales for limited liability begin to break down when applied to close corporations. Because these are companies owned by a small number of investors who often are also managers, there is much less separation of management and risk bearing than there is in public corporations. Limited liability becomes unnecessary to reduce monitoring costs because the managers who would need to be monitored are also those who supply the capital. Moreover, the lack of liquidity in a close corporation makes irrelevant the need for limited liability to create an efficient market for the corporation's stock. There is also no threat of new investors replacing the existing management in close corporations because the management and risk-bearing functions are united. Finally, limited liability is more likely to encourage risk taking by close corporations because the decisionmakers in a close corporation have more to gain personally by shifting losses to creditors than do managers of a public company. Thus, limiting shareholders' liability for close corporations is likely to generate external costs. Easterbrook and Fischel conclude that a court can reduce the extent to which third parties bear these costs by disregarding limited liability in close corporations when there has been an abuse of the privilege.

Professor Presser does not agree that the argument for piercing the corporate veil is stronger for close corporations than publicly held corporations. He contends that Easterbrook and Fischel ignore the principal historical justification for limited liability—promoting individual investment in smaller firms. Thus, it is precisely in the context of such firms that limited liability should be most protected. Presser, supra, at 164, 171–72. David Leebron takes a middle position. He suggests that limited liability should exist for close corporation shareholders subject to two conditions: (1) shareholders should not be allowed to reduce capital available for involuntary creditors by using personally guaranteed debt rather than equity to finance the corporation and (2) shareholder-managers should be required to carry adequate insurance for foreseeable tort liabilities. Leebron asserts that these conditions would protect against the major abuses that typically concern the advocates of unlimited liability for close corporation shareholders. David W. Leebron, Limited Liability, Tort Victims, and Creditors, 91 Col. L. Rev. 1565, 1636 (1991).

3. VOLUNTARY CREDITORS

The justifications for limited liability are strongest when considering voluntary creditors such as employees, consumers, trade creditors and commercial lenders. Easterbrook and Fischel argue that limited liability is appropriate with respect to contract creditors because they can bargain for a risk premium to protect themselves. The authors discuss the purported infirmities in a limited liability system as they affect contract creditors:

> Limited liability's greatest effect is on the probability that any given creditor will be paid *ex post*. Even if firms pay for engaging in risky activities, and thus take the right precautions, creditors of failed businesses are less likely to receive full compensation under a rule of limited liability. This is not an "argument" against limited liability, however, unless distributional concerns dominate. There is little role for distributional arguments when all of the parties are in privity, for they can strike their own bargains and are apt to contract around any unwelcome rule purportedly designed for their benefit. More to the point, they can choose to hold, under any rule, a different proportion of debt and equity which alters the risk. At all events * * * insurance makes distributional concerns much less serious than they might at first appear. The ability of potential victims to protect themselves against loss through insurance is a strong reason for disregarding distributional concerns in choosing among liability rules.

Id. at 52. See also Robert W. Hamilton, The Corporate Entity, 49 Tex.L.Rev. 979, 984–89 (1971); David C. Cummins, Comment, Disregard of the Corporate Entity: Contract Claims, 28 Ohio St.L.J. 441, 442, 468 (1968); Robert Charles Clark, The Duties of the Corporate Debtor to its Creditors, 90 Harv.L.Rev. 505, 543 (1977).

Is Easterbrook and Fischel's argument persuasive with respect to all voluntary creditors? What about trade creditors who have much less ability to obtain important information relevant to the determination of risk?

4. TORT CLAIMANTS

Another area of critical inquiry focuses on the treatment of involuntary tort claimants. Is there any reason why the courts should treat tort claimants differently from contract creditors? In a contractual arrangement, a creditor can adjust her return so as to account for the perceived risks of lending to the corporation. This means of self-protection is not available to the tort claimant who is an involuntary creditor of the corporation. Thus it might be expected that courts would protect tort victims more than contract creditors when considering whether to disregard limited liability.

A recent comprehensive study casts considerable doubt on that expectation. Robert Thompson analyzed 1600 cases through 1985 and, counterintuitively, found that courts pierced the corporate veil more often in contract cases (about 42% of the cases) than in a tort actions (about 31% of the cases). Robert B. Thompson, Piercing the Corporate Veil: An Empirical Study, 76 Cornell L. Rev. 1036 (1991). Professor Thompson concluded that his results depart from traditional expectations primarily because many contract cases involve alleged misrepresentations that would effectively obviate the basis for the parties' contract. However, even without the misrepresentation cases, Thompson found that courts pierce in 34% of the nonmisrepresentation contract cases and only 27% of the nonmisrepresentation tort cases. Id. at 1069.

Thompson's findings may provide support for Professors Hansmann and Kraakman who are the strongest advocates of disregarding limited liability in cases involving involuntary tort creditors. Henry Hansmann and Reinier Kraakman, Toward Unlimited Shareholder Liability for Corporate Torts, 100 Yale L.J. 1879 (1991). Hansmann and Kraakman advocate eliminating limited liability in tort cases because it gives the managers of a corporation incentives to incur too much risk, knowing that some of the costs of the corporation's activities will be externalized. With limited liability, the corporation can disregard the expected tort costs of a project and thus will invest in projects whose total social costs exceed total social benefits.

Hansmann and Kraakman would replace limited liability with a rule that subjects shareholders to pro-rata liability for tort damages in excess of the firm's resources. If shareholders faced full liability for such damages, share prices would decline to reflect the potential additional personal liability. Managers would then have a greater incentive to consider the full expected social costs of the firm's torts and adjust the company's behavior accordingly.

Hansmann and Kraakman contend that a pro-rata rule overcomes the major objections to unlimited liability in the tort context. They note that in a true unlimited liability system, liability would be joint and several, making the expected value of a corporation's stock dependent on the wealth of each individual shareholder. A shareholder with a net worth of $1 million would value her stock differently than would a shareholder with a net worth of $100,000 because she would be exposed to greater potential tort liability. As a result, it would be difficult to establish an efficient stock price. Moreover, because a large tort judgment against any individual corporation could wipe out a shareholder's wealth, she could not diversify her risk by holding a broad portfolio of stocks.

With pro-rata liability, they argue, the expected value of the stock is not a function of the wealth of the individual shareholder. Rather, such value would be a function of the anticipated future earnings of the corporation, discounted by the potential tort liability. And, with pro-rata liability, shareholders could, in fact, diversify their risk of unlimited tort liability, by holding a broader portfolio of stocks, and market pricing would be efficient.

If the efficiency of the capital markets would not be impaired by an unlimited tort liability rule, Hansmann and Kraakman continue, shareholder liability should be viewed as a question of tort, not corporate, law. Thus, the important question becomes: "When are a corporation's shareholders cheaper cost avoiders and/or cheaper insurers than persons who may be injured by the corporation's activities?" Id. at 1916. In an unlimited liability system, courts will determine which costs are more efficiently borne by a corporation's shareholders and which should lie where they fall. Thus, corporations will be forced to take into account those costs which otherwise would be borne by innocent third parties under a regime of limited liability. The result will be more efficient corporate behavior.

Hansmann and Kraakman's argument is not universally accepted, even by those who criticize a limited liability regime. Professor Leebron, supra, agrees that investors would tolerate unlimited pro rata liability in tort, and that such liability would lead to greater efficiency. However, he asserts that the argument that shareholders are necessarily better loss bearers than tort victims only applies in the absence of insurance markets. If, for instance, there are few shareholders and the injuries to tort victims are not severe, shareholders will be comparably inefficient risk bearers. Similarly, if insurance is available to tort victims, but not to shareholders, tort victims may be in a better position to bear the risk. Because the availability of shareholder liability insurance would be a function of both expected tort liability and business risks, it would be difficult to obtain. Leebron suggests that this problem would be mitigated by obtaining liability insurance at the enterprise level. He concludes that limited liability should be allowed only where the company obtains reasonable insurance. For an attempt to apply capital market theory to limited liability, see Joseph A. Grundfest, The Limited Future of Unlimited Liability: A Capital Markets Perspective, 102 Yale L.J. 387 (1992).

PROBLEM
PRECISION TOOLS—PART VIII

PTC was a supplier of tools and components to Higgins Corporation, a manufacturer of smoke alarm systems for industrial use. Although these systems were generally considered high quality, Higgins found itself in great difficulty because it was inefficiently managed. Higgins was heavily indebted to PTC for merchandise purchased. In order to protect both its investment in Higgins, and its market, PTC made every effort to keep Higgins afloat, by extending payment terms and waiving interest costs. It even offered consulting services.

Ultimately, all efforts failed and Higgins went into bankruptcy. In the subsequent auction, Michael, Jessica and Bernie purchased the assets for $100,000—a price well below market value. They formed a new Columbia corporation called New Higgins Corporation to continue Higgins' existing business and for $25,000 purchased all the stock in proportion to their stock ownership of PTC. Counsel advised them that the separate corporate structure would be desirable so as to avoid jeopardizing PTC's assets by the added risks of a new venture.

As part of its initial financing, in addition to selling its stock, New Higgins borrowed $75,000 from PTC's regular bank; the loan was guaranteed by the three stockholders and PTC. Jessica arranged the loan in her capacity as chief financial officer of New Higgins, the same position she holds at PTC. Finally, Michael, Jessica and Bernie loaned New Higgins $50,000 as working capital and took back a three-year note, bearing an annual interest rate of 2% over the prime rate.

Michael and Jessica, who are directors of PTC, became the directors and, together with Shawn Nelson, who they hired to manage the company, were the officers of New Higgins. Shawn is the only salaried officer of New Higgins.

At counsel's insistence, after the annual shareholders' meeting to elect directors, New Higgins holds a formal board meeting to elect officers and ratify prior decisions. In order to reduce overhead, New Higgins consolidated its office with PTC's, and they now share bookkeeping and accounting personnel. New Higgins maintains its own bank account and pays PTC $300 per month for rent and "administrative services" that are performed by PTC employees.

One of the cost advantages that Michael, Jessica and Bernie anticipated in owning New Higgins was that PTC could share a common sales force with the new corporation since there was a big overlap in their customer base. As a consequence, the New Higgins sales force has been pared substantially.

In its first two years of existence, New Higgins lost money and, to provide working capital, PTC loaned New Higgins $25,000 after the first year and an additional $50,000 after the second year. These loans were two-year notes at prevailing interest rates. In the third and fourth years, the business prospered and, because of prior losses, New Higgins paid no taxes. After paying interest on its various notes, New Higgins then distributed all of its profits as a dividend to Michael, Jessica and Bernie.

Six months ago a factory that had purchased a New Higgins system burned down in a tragic fire in which three people were killed. The alarm system proved to be defective, resulting in a crucial delay in calling the firefighters. The families of the victims and the owner of the factory brought suit against New Higgins, alleging gross negligence in the manufacture and installation of the equipment, Because it was clear that the assets of the company and its insurance would not be sufficient to cover the losses, plaintiffs also sought recovery from PTC, Michael, Jessica and Bernie, asserting various theories that disregard the separate incorporation of New Higgins.

Prior to the fire, as part of its expanding business, New Higgins purchased the principal components for its systems from Acme Electronics, generally paying within 60 days of receiving Acme's invoice. At the time of the fire, New Higgins had unpaid invoices of $500,000 and subsequently received invoices for an additional $250,000. None of those invoices had been paid. Acme seeks to hold PTC, Michael, Jessica and Bernie liable for the entire $750,000.

Plaintiffs' counsel in both suits have approached you, as counsel for all the defendants, about a settlement of the claims. The plaintiffs' lawyers say they are confident that the court will pierce the corporate veil and hold your clients liable. Advise PTC, Michael, Jessica and Bernie as to the likelihood that a court will impose liability on any or all of them for each of the claims against New Higgins.

A PLANNING PROBLEM
MASON AND BILDER

Your clients, Melissa Mason and Don Bilder were classmates in architecture school. Melissa now has her own small architecture practice. Don recently left a large firm to become a contractor specializing in remodelling urban residential real estate. They have decided to go into the real estate development business together. They want to begin by purchasing and rehabilitating six contiguous townhouses on a block on the fringes of an area that had previously been run down but is in the process of renovation. The houses were acquired by the city for back taxes several years ago and are all vacant and in various states of disrepair. Melissa and Don believe they can purchase the shells for an average of about $50,000 each. They estimate that the renovation work will cost between $50,000 and $80,000 for each house, assuming that there are no serious structural defects. Melissa's and Don's respective capital contributions to the venture will consist of another $10,000 per house representing the difference between what a bank will lend for construction and the expected cost of the renovation. They will thus each invest $60,000 in the venture.

Don's assets consist of his contracting business having a net worth of about $100,000 in a corporation, Don's, Inc., of which he is the sole shareholder. He is presently working on three other jobs, but as soon as they are finished he plans to devote full time to the project with Melissa. If these six renovations are successful, both expect to devote all their energies to similar development undertakings.

Melissa and Don have come to you for advice on how best to structure their undertaking. They have discussed several possible alternatives including:

1. Creating a new corporation in which they will invest equal amounts, that will buy the houses.

2. Setting up six separate corporations, in which they will each invest $10,000, that will own one house apiece.

3. Having the stock of the six corporations owned by a single corporation (a holding company), all of whose stock will be owned by Don and Melissa.

They would like you to advise them not only as to the corporate structure but also as to the form in which their investment should be made. Your clients would like to minimize the risks for the overall venture, and protect their own investment to the extent possible. Which one of the above three alternatives would you recommend? Do you have any better suggestions?

C. TORT CREDITORS

WALKOVSZKY v. CARLTON

18 N.Y.2d 414, 276 N.Y.S.2d 585, 223 N.E.2d 6 (1966).

FULD, JUDGE.

This case involves what appears to be a rather common practice in the taxicab industry of vesting the ownership of a taxi fleet in many corporations, each owning only one or two cabs.

The complaint alleges that the plaintiff was severely injured four years ago in New York City when he was run down by a taxicab owned by the defendant Seon Cab Corporation and negligently operated at the time by the defendant Marchese. The individual defendant, Carlton, is claimed to be a stockholder of 10 corporations, including Seon, each of which has but two cabs registered in its name, and it is implied that only the minimum automobile liability insurance required by law (in the amount of $10,000) is carried on any one cab. Although seemingly independent of one another, these corporations are alleged to be 'operated * * * as a single entity, unit and enterprise' with regard to financing, supplies, repairs, employees and garaging, and all are named as defendants. The plaintiff asserts that he is also entitled to hold their stockholders personally liable for the damages sought because the multiple corporate structure constitutes an unlawful attempt 'to defraud members of the general public' who might be injured by the cabs.

The defendant Carlton has moved * * * to dismiss the complaint on the ground that as to him it 'fails to state a cause of action'. The court at Special Term granted the motion but the Appellate Division, by a divided vote, reversed, holding that a valid cause of action was sufficiently stated. * * * The law permits the incorporation of a business for the very purpose of enabling its proprietors to escape personal liability (see, e.g., Bartle v. Home Owners Co-op., 309 N.Y. 103, 106, 127 N.E.2d 832, 833) but, manifestly, the privilege is not without its limits. Broadly speaking, the courts will disregard the corporate form, or, to use accepted terminology, 'pierce the corporate veil', whenever necessary 'to prevent fraud or to achieve equity'. (International Aircraft Trading Co. v. Manufacturers Trust Co., 297 N.Y. 285, 292, 79 N.E.2d 249, 252.) In determining whether liability should be extended to reach assets beyond those belonging to the corporation, we are guided, as Judge Cardozo noted, by 'general rules of agency'. (Berkey v. Third Ave. Ry. Co., 244 N.Y. 84, 95, 155 N.E. 58, 61, 50 A.L.R. 599.) In other words, whenever anyone uses control of the corporation to further his own rather than the corporation's business, he will be liable for the corporation's acts 'upon the principle of respondeat superior applicable even where the agent is a natural person'. (Rapid Tr. Subway Constr. Co. v. City of New York, 259 N.Y. 472, 488, 182 N.E. 145, 150.) Such liability, moreover, extends not only to the corporation's commercial dealings * * * but to its negligent acts as well. * * *

* * *

In the case before us, the plaintiff has explicitly alleged that none of the corporations "had a separate existence of their own" and, as indicated above, all are named as defendants. However, it is one thing to assert that a corporation is a fragment of a larger corporate combine which actually conducts the business. (See Berle, The Theory of Enterprise Entity, 47 Col.L.Rev. 343, 348—350.) It is quite another to claim that the corporation is a "dummy" for its individual stockholders who are in reality carrying on the business in their personal capacities for purely personal rather than corporate ends. Either circumstance would justify treating the corporation as an agent and piercing the corporate veil to reach the principal but a different result would follow in each case. In the first, only a larger corporate entity would be held financially responsible * * * while, in the other, the stockholder would be personally liable. * * * Either the stockholder is conducting the business in his individual capacity or he is not. If he is, he will be liable; if he is not, then it does not matter—insofar as his personal liability is concerned—that the enterprise is actually being carried on by a larger "enterprise entity". (See Berle, The Theory of Enterprise Entity, 47 Col.L.Rev. 343.)

* * *

The individual defendant is charged with having "organized, managed, dominated and controlled" a fragmented corporate entity but there are no allegations that he was conducting business in his individual capacity. Had the taxicab fleet been owned by a single corporation, it would be readily apparent that the plaintiff would face formidable barriers in attempting to establish personal liability on the part of the corporation's stockholders. The fact that the fleet ownership has been deliberately split up among many corporations does not ease the plaintiff's burden in that respect. The corporate form may not be disregarded merely because the assets of the corporation, together with the mandatory insurance coverage of the vehicle which struck the plaintiff, are insufficient to assure him the recovery sought. If Carlton were to be held individually liable on those facts alone, the decision would apply equally to the thousands of cabs which are owned by their individual drivers who conduct their businesses through corporations organized pursuant to section 401 of the Business Corporation Law, * * * and carry the minimum insurance required by [the Vehicle and Traffic Law]. These taxi owner-operators are entitled to form such corporations, and we agree with the court at Special Term that, if the insurance coverage required by statute "is inadequate for the protection of the public, the remedy lies not with the courts but with the Legislature." It may very well be sound policy to require that certain corporations must take out liability insurance which will afford adequate compensation to their potential tort victims. However, the responsibility for imposing conditions on the privilege of incorporation has been committed by the Constitution to the Legislature * * * and it may not be fairly implied, from any statute, that the Legislature intended, without the slightest discussion or debate, to require of taxi corporations that they carry automobile liability insurance over and above that mandated by the Vehicle and Traffic Law.

This is not to say that it is impossible for the plaintiff to state a valid cause of action against the defendant Carlton. However, the simple fact is that the plaintiff has just not done so here. While the complaint alleges that the separate corporations were undercapitalized and that their assets have been intermingled, it is barren of any "sufficiently particular(ized) statements" * * * that the defendant Carlton and his associates are actually doing business in their individual capacities, shuttling their personal funds in and out of the corporations "without regard to formality and to suit their immediate convenience." (Weisser v. Mursam Shoe Corp., 2 Cir., 127 F.2d 344, 345) Such a "perversion of the privilege to do business in a corporate form" (Berkey v. Third Ave. Ry. Co., 244 N.Y. 84, 95, 155 N.E. 58, 61, supra) would justify imposing personal liability on the individual stockholders. Nothing of the sort has in fact been charged, and it cannot reasonably or logically be inferred from the happenstance that the business of Seon Cab Corporation may actually be carried on by a larger corporate entity composed of many corporations which, under general principles of agency, would be liable to each other's creditors in contract and in tort.[3]

---

3. In his affidavit in opposition to the motion to dismiss, the plaintiff's counsel claimed that corporate assets had been 'milked out' of, and 'siphoned off' from the enterprise. Quite apart from the fact that these allegations are far too vague and conclusory, the charge is premature. If the plaintiff succeeds in his action and becomes a judgment creditor of the corporation, he may then sue and attempt to hold the individual defendants accountable for any dividends and property that were wrongfully distributed * * *.

In point of fact, the principle relied upon in the complaint to sustain the imposition of personal liability is not agency but fraud. Such a cause of action cannot withstand analysis. If it is not fraudulent for the owner- operator of a single cab corporation to take out only the minimum required liability insurance, the enterprise does not become either illicit or fraudulent merely because it consists of many such corporations. The plaintiff's injuries are the same regardless of whether the cab which strikes him is owned by a single corporation or part of a fleet with ownership fragmented among many corporations. Whatever rights he may be able to assert against parties other than the registered owner of the vehicle come into being not because he has been defrauded but because, under the principle of respondeat superior, he is entitled to hold the whole enterprise responsible for the acts of its agents.

In sum, then, the complaint falls short of adequately stating a cause of action against the defendant Carlton in his individual capacity.

The order of the Appellate Division should be reversed * * *.

KEATING, JUDGE (dissenting).

The defendant Carlton, the shareholder here sought to be held for the negligence of the driver of a taxicab, was a principal shareholder and organizer of the defendant corporation which owned the taxicab. The corporation was one of 10 organized by the defendant * * *. The sole assets of these operating corporations are the vehicles themselves and they are apparently subject to mortgages.*

From their inception these corporations were intentionally undercapitalized for the purpose of avoiding responsibility for acts which were bound to arise as a result of the operation of a large taxi fleet having cars out on the street 24 hours a day and engaged in public transportation. And during the course of the corporations' existence all income was continually drained out of the corporations for the same purpose.

The issue presented by this action is whether the policy of this State, which affords those desiring to engage in a business enterprise the privilege of limited liability through the use of the corporate device, is so strong that it will permit that privilege to continue no matter how much it is abused, no matter how irresponsibly the corporation is operated, no matter what the cost to the public. I do not believe that it is.

Under the circumstances of this case the shareholders should all be held individually liable to this plaintiff for the injuries he suffered. * * * At least, the matter should not be disposed of on the pleadings by a dismissal of the complaint. "If a corporation is organized and carries on business without substantial capital in such a way that the corporation is likely to have no sufficient assets available to meet its debts, it is inequitable that shareholders should set up such a flimsy organization to escape personal liability. The attempt to do corporate business without providing any sufficient basis of financial responsibility to creditors is an

_____

* It appears that the medallions, which are of considerable value, are judgement proof. (Administrative Code of City of New York § 436–2.0.)

abuse of the separate entity and will be ineffectual to exempt the shareholders from corporate debts. It is coming to be recognized as the policy of law that shareholders should in good faith put at the risk of the business unincumbered capital reasonably adequate for its prospective liabilities. If capital is illusory or trifling compared with the business to be done and the risks of loss, this is a ground for denying the separate entity privilege." (Ballantine, Corporations (rev.ed., 1946), s 129, pp. 302–303.)

In Minton v. Cavaney, 56 Cal.2d 576, 15 Cal.Rptr. 641, 364 P.2d 473, the Supreme Court of California had occasion to discuss this problem in a negligence case. The corporation of which the defendant was an organizer, director and officer operated a public swimming pool. One afternoon the plaintiffs' daughter drowned in the pool as a result of the alleged negligence of the corporation.

Justice Roger Traynor, speaking for the court, outlined the applicable law in this area. "The figurative terminology 'alter ego' and 'disregard of the corporate entity'", he wrote, 'is generally used to refer to the various situations that are an abuse of the corporate privilege. * * * The equitable owners of a corporation, for example, are personally liable when they treat the assets of the corporation as their own and add or withdraw capital from the corporation at will * * *; when they hold themselves out as being personally liable for the debts of the corporation * * *; Or *when they provide inadequate capitalization and actively participate in the conduct of corporate affairs*". (56 Cal.2d, p. 579, 15 Cal.Rptr., p. 643, 364 P.2d p. 475; italics supplied.)

Examining the facts of the case in light of the legal principles just enumerated, he found that "(it was) undisputed that there was no attempt to provide adequate capitalization. (The corporation) never had any substantial assets. It leased the pool that it operated, and the lease was forfeited for failure to pay the rent. Its capital was 'trifling compared with the business to be done and the risks of loss'". (56 Cal.2d, p. 580, 15 Cal.Rptr., p. 643, 364 P.2d p. 475.)

It seems obvious that one of 'the risks of loss' referred to was the possibility of drownings due to the negligence of the corporation. And the defendant's failure to provide such assets or any fund for recovery resulted in his being held personally liable.

* * *

The defendant Carlton claims that, because the minimum amount of insurance required by the statute was obtained, the corporate veil cannot and should not be pierced despite the fact that the assets of the corporation which owned the cab were "trifling compared with the business to be done and the risks of loss" which were certain to be encountered. I do not agree.

The Legislature in requiring minimum liability insurance of $10,-000, no doubt, intended to provide at least some small fund for recovery against those individuals and corporations who just did not have and were not able to raise or accumulate assets sufficient to satisfy the claims of those who were injured as a result of their negligence. It certainly could not have intended to shield those individuals who organized corporations, with the specific intent of avoiding responsibility to the public, where the operation of the corporate enterprise yielded profits sufficient to purchase additional insurance. Moreover, it is reasonable to assume that the Legislature believed that those individuals and corporations having substantial assets would take out insurance far in excess of the minimum in order to protect those assets from depletion. Given the costs of hospital care and treatment and the nature of injuries sustained in auto collisions, it would be unreasonable to assume that the Legislature believed that the minimum provided in the statute would in and of itself be sufficient to recompense "innocent victims of motor vehicle accidents * * * for the injury and financial loss inflicted upon them".

The defendant, however, argues that the failure of the Legislature to increase the minimum insurance requirements indicates legislative acquiescence in this scheme to avoid liability and responsibility to the public. In the absence of a clear legislative statement, approval of a scheme having such serious consequences is not to be so lightly inferred.

The defendant contends that the court will be encroaching upon the legislative domain by ignoring the corporate veil and holding the individual shareholder. This argument was answered by Mr. Justice Douglas in Anderson v. Abbott, supra, [321 U.S.] 366–367, 64 S.Ct. p. 540, where he wrote that: "In the field in which we are presently concerned, judicial power hardly oversteps the bounds when it refuses to lend its aid to a promotional project which would circumvent or undermine a legislative policy. To deny it that function would be to make it impotent in situations where historically it has made some of its most notable contributions. If the judicial power is helpless to protect a legislative program from schemes for easy avoidance, then indeed it has become a handy implement of high finance. *Judicial interference to cripple or defeat a legislative policy is one thing; judicial interference with the plans of those whose corporate or other devices would circumvent that policy is quite another.* Once the purpose or effect of the scheme is clear, once the legislative policy is plain, we would indeed forsake a great tradition to say we were helpless to fashion the instruments for appropriate relief.' (Emphasis added.)

The defendant contends that a decision holding him personally liable would discourage people from engaging in corporate enterprise.

What I would merely hold is that a participating shareholder of a corporation vested with a public interest, organized with capital insufficient to meet liabilities which are certain to arise in the ordinary course of the corporation's business, may be held personally responsible for such liabilities. Where corporate income is not sufficient to cover the cost of insurance premiums above the statutory minimum or where initially adequate finances dwindle under the pressure of competition, bad times or extraordinary and unexpected liability, obviously the shareholder will not be held liable * * *.

The only types of corporate enterprises that will be discouraged as a result of a decision allowing the individual shareholder to be sued will be those such as the one in question, designed solely to abuse the corporate privilege at the expense of the public interest.

For these reasons I would vote to affirm the order of the Appellate Division.

DESMOND, C.J., and VAN VOORHIS, BURKE and SCILEPPI, JJ., concur with FULD, J.

KEATING, J., dissents and votes to affirm in an opinion in which BERGAN, J., concurs.

––––––––

On remand, the court upheld an amended complaint against the shareholder as sufficiently alleging that the defendants conducted business in their individual capacities. 29 A.D.2d 763, 287 N.Y.S.2d 546 (2d Dept.1968), aff'd mem. 23 N.Y.2d 714, 296 N.Y.S.2d 362, 244 N.E.2d 55 (1968). The case later settled.

Notes and Questions

1. *Walkovsky* suggests that a shareholder such as Carlton may be held liable, on an "agency" theory, if she failed to observe the formalities of corporate existence. Why should that be significant? How does observance of corporate formalities relate to the risks involved in running a taxi business, or to the question of who should bear the loss if a taxi inflicts injuries in excess of available insurance coverage?

2. Judge Keating argues in dissent that Seon's capital was inadequate. Do you think he would make the same argument if Seon had had $10,000 in capital and no liability insurance? Would the argument appear equally powerful?

3. More generally, consider how a wealthy person and a person with few assets would analyze the risks involved in operating a taxi business. To which of them would limited liability be more important? Absent any regulatory requirement, which of them is more likely to purchase a substantial amount of liability insurance? What do the answers to these questions suggest as to who is subsidized and who is burdened by limited liability rules and mandatory insurance requirements?

D. CONTRACT CREDITORS

BRUNSWICK CORP. v. WAXMAN
459 F.Supp. 1222 (E.D.N.Y.1978), aff'd 599 F.2d 34 (2d Cir.1979).

[The following statement of facts is based on the opinion by the Court of Appeals.

Brunswick Corporation (Brunswick) brought this diversity action against the individual defendants seeking over a million dollars in damages. This amount represented the deficiency due under conditional sales contracts between Brunswick and the Waxman Construction Corporation (Construction Corp.) whereby the latter entity purchased bowling lanes and pinsetters. The individual defendants, Harry Waxman and the late Sydney Waxman, signed the contracts as president and secretary of the Construction Corp. Plaintiff urged that the Waxmans should be held personally liable for the deficiency.

In August 1960, the Waxmans formed Construction Corp. as a no-asset New York corporation to act as signatory and obligor on a series of conditional sales agreements for the purchase of bowling equipment to be operated in five new bowling alleys. The five alleys and the Brunswick equipment were operated by the Waxmans through five separate partnerships. These partnerships owned or leased the real property on which the bowling alleys were located, but charged Construction Corp. no rent for the use of the premises. Nor did the Waxmans pay rent to Construction Corp. for the use of the bowling equipment. In addition, in their individual or partnership capacities, the Waxmans owned all the licenses and permits necessary to operate the alleys. Proceeds from the daily operation of the businesses were deposited in individual bowling alley accounts and later transferred into a central Waxman enterprises bank account from which funds were withdrawn to meet the necessary operating expenses of the alleys. It was from this central bank account that amounts due on the sales contracts with Brunswick were withdrawn and deposited in Construction Corp. account. The court below found that Construction Corp.'s sole corporate activity was the transfer of funds into and out of its bank account for the purpose of meeting the installment payments under the Brunswick contracts. Construction Corp. held no stockholders' or directors' meetings, adopted no bylaws, and issued no stock. While it filed federal and New York State income tax returns, none of these returns showed any income, nor did they report the Brunswick equipment as corporate assets.

Due to a general decline in the bowling industry, Construction Corp. was unable to meet its payment obligations under the sales contracts. Pursuant to a 1963 extension agreement, title to the Brunswick equipment was transferred from Construction Corp. to five new corporations, which were also to receive from the Waxmans an additional $375,000 in non-Brunswick assets. However, the Waxmans never transferred the additional assets to the five corporations. In addition, these newly formed corporations were as inactive as Construction Corp. had been. By late 1965, two of the five corporations, Bruckner Lanes, Inc. and Pike Lanes, Inc., were in default. In 1966, Brunswick repossessed its equipment held by Bruckner Lanes and sold it at a substantial deficiency. Although an extension agreement was reached with Pike Lanes in 1966, that corporation continued in substantial default and its equipment was also repossessed and sold by Brunswick at a substantial deficiency.]

BARTELS, DISTRICT JUDGE.

DISCUSSION

Brunswick's basic claim in this action is that the Waxmans operated Brunswick's equipment in their individual capacities and in complete disregard of the corporations they had formed. Accordingly, Brunswick contends, the Waxmans have abandoned the protection of limited liability those corporations would have otherwise provided, and have, as a matter of law, rendered themselves personally liable for their corporations' obligations.

Historically the corporate form has for centuries been used for various diverse governmental and private purposes, and today it has become a key institution in the American free enterprise system. *See* H. Henn, Law of Corporations, 11–25 (2d ed. 1970). This concept has, among others, three basic objectives, to provide (1) limited liability, (2) perpetual existence, and (3) transferability of shares. As stated in Bartle v. Home Owners Co-operative, Inc., 309 N.Y. 103, 127 N.E.2d 832 (1955), "the law permits the incorporation of a business for the very purpose of escaping personal liability." However, when the privilege of incorporation has been abused, it is necessary to "pierce the corporate veil" to "prevent fraud or to achieve equity." International Aircraft Trading Co. v. Manufacturers Trust Co., 297 N.Y. 285, 79 N.E.2d 249 (1948). As early as 1905 Judge Sanborn in United States v. Milwaukee Refrigerator Transit Co., 142 F. 247, 255 (C.C.E.D.Wis.1905), observed: "when the notion of legal entity is used to defeat public convenience, justify wrong, protect fraud, or defend crime, the law will regard the corporation as an association of persons."

The circumstances under which the court should disregard the corporate fiction are not always clear and it is difficult, if not impossible, to formulate a precise and categorical definition applicable to all situations, *see* Berkey v. Third Ave. Ry. Co., 244 N.Y. 84, 155 N.E. 58, 61 (1926), each case being *sui generis*. The burden, however, in each case rests upon the plaintiff to establish that there is a basis which serves for disregard of the corporate form.

The Instrumentality Rule

New York courts, whose rules we must follow, have advanced a variety of theories to define the particular circumstances and factors which justify disregard of the corporate entity. Some have applied the theory of agency, holding that a corporation may be so dominated and controlled by its stockholders as to become a mere agent, acting for the stockholders as principals. *See e.g.* Berkey v. Third Ave. Ry. Co., *supra;* Majestic Factors Corp. v. Latino, 15 Misc.2d 329, 184 N.Y.S.2d 658 (1959). "No conceptual problems are involved where liability is imposed upon shareholders under conventional theories of agency or tort law— independently of any theory of corporation law or of the corporate entity." 2 G. Hornstein, Corporation Law and Practice, 263 (1959). But the agency theory is not always available and as Mr. Justice Dore explained in Lowendahl v. Baltimore & O.R. Co., 247 App.Div. 144, 287 N.Y.S. 62, aff'd, 272 N.Y. 360, 6 N.E.2d 56 (1936), "any severely logical application of agency rules would destroy the protection afforded stock-holders by incorporation." For if all systems of control exercised over a corporation by those who own it are illegal, then "the rule of the separate entity and responsibility of corporations for their own acts and contracts is swallowed up in the exception." *Id.* This is particularly true when the corporation is owned and controlled by one or two persons. Thus, except in case of express agency, estoppel, or tort, *Lowendahl* advanced the so-called "instrumentality" rule as a practical and effective "theory for breaking down corporate immunity when equity so re-quires." 287 N.Y.S. at 75.

Under the "instrumentality" rule, the factors which determine whether the corporate veil should be withdrawn are (1) domination and control over the corporation by those who are to be held liable which is so complete that the corporation has no separate mind, will, or existence of its own; (2) the use of this domination and control to commit fraud or wrong or any other dishonest or unjust act; and (3) injury or unjust loss resulting to the plaintiff from said control and wrong. 287 N.Y.S. at 76. While this rule emerged in the parent-subsidiary context, some of the same criteria have been carried over in determining whether to pierce the corporate veil in other contexts. For instance, in this case the Waxmans disregarded their corporations after the signing of the con-tracts so that thereafter they did not function as active corporations. The corporations were acting for themselves and not as agents for the Waxmans in acquiring title to the property and in incurring liability for the purchase price. Subsequently, the corporations did receive moneys from the Waxmans in order to meet their payments to Brunswick. Since, however, we find that there was no misappropriation of corporate assets or profits, and consequently no fraud or wrong to Brunswick, we do not find that all the criteria of the instrumentality rule for imposing personal liability are present. We must therefore invoke some different criteria if we are to disregard the corporate form. Under such circum-stances, the overwhelming weight of authority requires at least some type of abuse of the corporate concept which is the cause of the injury to third parties.

Personal Conduct of Corporate Business

Absent special circumstances, limited personal liability cannot be effectuated simply by the act of incorporation. The protection extends only to those transactions which are engaged in by a corporation, for its own purposes, in fact as well as in name. If, as Judge Fuld observed in Walkovszky v. Carlton, 18 N.Y.2d 414, 418, 276 N.Y.S.2d 585, 588, 223 N.E.2d 6, 8 (1966), "the corporation is a "dummy' for its individual stockholders who are in reality carrying on the business in their personal capacities for purely personal rather than corporate ends" then stockholders must be personally liable and financially responsible as well. *See,* African Metals Corp. v. Bullowa, 288 N.Y. 78, 41 N.E.2d 466 (1942). Fraud or other wrongful purpose is not a necessary element. For example, a failure to observe corporate formalities coupled with inadequate capitalization has frequently been cited as a basis for disregarding the corporate entity and imposing individual liability where such facts are causally connected with the injury. *See, e.g.* Anderson v. Abbott, 321 U.S. 349, 64 S.Ct. 531, 88 L.Ed. 793 (1944); DeWitt Truck Brokers v. W. Ray Flemming Fruit Co., 540 F.2d 681 (4th Cir.1976); Francis O. Day v. Shapiro, 105 U.S.App.D.C. 392, 267 F.2d 669 (1959).

Some courts have held that unjust enrichment alone may justify imposition of personal liability on those who have conducted ostensibly corporate business in their individual capacities. However, we have been unable to find any New York authority to this effect. *But cf.* Bartle v. Home Owners Co-operative, Inc., *supra.* Another example of disregarding corporate formalities is where stockholders have represented that they would be liable for their corporations' obligations, and are therefore estopped from denying liability. *See, e.g.* Weisser v. Mursam Shoe Corp., 127 F.2d 344 (2d Cir.1942). Likewise stockholders will be liable if they deprived their corporation of the income and profits required to meet its obligations. As the Court of Appeals observed in Natelson v. A.B.L. Holding Co., *supra,* 260 N.Y. at 238, 183 N.E. at 375, the business of a corporation must be carried on by the corporation "and its profits must be available to meet liabilities, before the individuals may share." It is not merely the disregard of corporate formalities which justifies piercing, but the fact that the stockholders' conduct has caused the creditors' losses which justifies the imposition of personal liability.

Parties' Contentions

Brunswick asserts that the Waxmans are liable personally and that the language of *Walkovszky, supra,* and *African Metals, supra,* in effect, establishes a *per se* rule which imposes liability simply on the basis of a failure to observe the corporate formalities. We find no support for this broad assertion. Actually, *Walkovszky* is not applicable. There the plaintiff was injured when he was run down by a taxicab owned by the defendant-corporation which in turn was wholly owned by the individual defendant as a stockholder. The complaint alleged fraud and that the corporation did not have a separate existence, and charged that its assets were insufficient. The complaint was dismissed because, as Judge Fuld observed, the plaintiff had failed to make any

"sufficiently particularized statements" * * * that the defendant
* * * and his associates are actually doing business in their individ-

ual capacities, shuttling their personal funds in and out of the corporations "without regard to formality and to suit their immediate convenience."

18 N.Y.2d 420, 276 N.Y.S.2d 590, 223 N.E.2d 10.

African Metals, supra, is also inapposite because there the action was for rescission predicated upon fraud. To accomplish the fraud, the individual defendants organized a corporation with very limited assets and no credit facilities. A sale of nickel cathodes was negotiated in the name of the corporation by the defendants who individually and fraudulently manipulated the sale and retained the purchase money. The court observed that where there is fraud

> Incorporation does not exempt the individuals from liability for an enterprise which they themselves choose to carry on as individuals independently of the corporation. It cannot be said, as a matter of law, upon this record, that there is no evidence or inferences from evidence that these defendants were not joint venturers dealing personally in this enterprise.

288 N.Y. at 85, 41 N.E.2d at 470.

The Waxmans in defending their actions, insist that they are exempt from personal liability because they do not satisfy all the criteria of the instrumentality rule. We do not believe that this rule is completely applicable to the present circumstances. Although we conclude that the Waxmans' corporations had no separate mind or existence, we also find that these corporations were never sufficiently functional to justify describing them as an instrumentality which committed wrongs causing plaintiff's injury.

No-Asset Corporations

The transactions between Brunswick and the Waxmans' corporations were much like a common form of real estate transaction in which a "dummy" corporation is established for the sole purpose of taking title and assuming mortgage obligations and thus exempting the sole stockholder from liability. There is no question that the Waxmans employed a no-asset or "straw" corporation to purchase the bowling alleys from Brunswick. Straw corporations have been used for many purposes, such as compliance with state usury or investment laws and insulation of principals from liability.

When Brunswick made its initial sale to the Waxman Construction Corp. for the Bruckner and Turnpike Lanes it knew that the land and buildings upon which the lanes and pinsetters were to be erected, were owned by the Waxmans and that the Construction Corp. was a no-asset corporation. Brunswick was under no illusion that the Construction Corp. was an agent for the Waxmans.[4] Although under-capitalization of

---

4. In fact, P.L. Fulvio, Brunswick's major accounts manager, stated in a memorandum to Brunswick's credit committee dated December 2, 1964 that "I reminded Barell [the Waxmans' attorney] and [Sydney] Waxman that I was not doing business with Waxman but with his corporation. * * *"

the bowling operation might under other circumstances indicate that the corporate form was being used to mislead creditors and should be pierced, Brunswick had full knowledge of the lack of capitalization, and consented to it. Brunswick was not misled into doing business with a no-asset corporation and is hardly in a position now to complain that in the absence of any additional assets in that corporation its liability should be shifted to the Waxmans. As the court said in Hanson v. Bradley, 298 Mass. 371, 10 N.E.2d 259, 264 (S.J.C.1937):

> The plaintiff was not wronged by the fact that the corporation was organized with a trifling capital and could not live except upon borrowed money; nor by the fact that the lenders insisted upon security. He knew the essential facts and accepted the situation.

The result is that the complaint should be and hereby is dismissed and judgment entered for the defendants.

So ordered.

KINNEY SHOE CORP. v. POLAN
939 F.2d 209 (4th Cir.1991).

CHAPMAN, SENIOR CIRCUIT JUDGE:

Plaintiff-appellant Kinney Shoe Corporation ("Kinney") brought this action * * * against Lincoln M. Polan ("Polan") seeking to recover money owed on a sublease between Kinney and Industrial Realty Company ("Industrial"). Polan is the sole shareholder of Industrial. The district court found that Polan was not personally liable on the lease between Kinney and Industrial. Kinney appeals asserting that the corporate veil should be pierced, and we agree.

I.

The district court based its order on facts which were stipulated by the parties. In 1984 Polan formed two corporations, Industrial and Polan Industries, Inc., for the purpose of re-establishing an industrial manufacturing business. The certificate of incorporation for Polan Industries, Inc. was issued by the West Virginia Secretary of State in November 1984. The following month the certificate of incorporation for Industrial was issued. Polan was the owner of both corporations. Although certificates of incorporation were issued, no organizational meetings were held, and no officers were elected.

In November 1984 Polan and Kinney began negotiating the sublease of a building in which Kinney held a leasehold interest. The building was owned by the Cabell County Commission and financed by industrial revenue bonds issued in 1968 to induce Kinney to locate a manufacturing plant in Huntington, West Virginia. Under the terms of the lease, Kinney was legally obligated to make payments on the bonds on a semi-annual basis through January 1, 1993, at which time it had the right to purchase the property. Kinney had ceased using the building as a manufacturing plant in June 1983.

The term of the sublease from Kinney to Industrial commenced in December 1984, even though the written lease was not signed by the parties until April 5, 1985. On April 15, 1985, Industrial subleased part of the building to Polan Industries for fifty percent of the rental amount due Kinney. Polan signed both subleases on behalf of the respective companies.

Other than the sublease with Kinney, Industrial had no assets, no income and no bank account. Industrial issued no stock certificates because nothing was ever paid in to this corporation. Industrial's only income was from its sublease to Polan Industries, Inc. The first rental payment to Kinney was made out of Polan's personal funds, and no further payments were made by Polan or by Polan Industries, Inc. to either Industrial or to Kinney.

Kinney filed suit against Industrial for unpaid rent and obtained a judgment in the amount of $166,400.00 on June 19, 1987. A writ of possession was issued, but because Polan Industries, Inc. had filed for bankruptcy, Kinney did not gain possession for six months. Kinney leased the building until it was sold on September 1, 1988. Kinney then filed this action against Polan individually to collect the amount owed by Industrial to Kinney. Since the amount to which Kinney is entitled is undisputed, the only issue is whether Kinney can pierce the corporate veil and hold Polan personally liable.

The district court held that Kinney had assumed the risk of Industrial's undercapitalization and was not entitled to pierce the corporate veil. Kinney appeals, and we reverse.

II.

We have long recognized that a corporation is an entity, separate and distinct from its officers and stockholders, and the individual stockholders are not responsible for the debts of the corporation. See, e.g., DeWitt Truck Brokers, Inc. v. W. Ray Flemming Fruit Co., 540 F.2d 681, 683 (4th Cir.1976). This concept, however, is a fiction of the law " 'and it is now well settled, as a general principle, that the fiction should be disregarded when it is urged with an intent not within its reason and purpose, and in such a way that its retention would produce injustices or inequitable consequences.' " Laya v. Erin Homes, Inc., 352 S.E.2d 93, 97–98 (W.Va.1986) (quoting Sanders v. Roselawn Memorial Gardens, Inc., 152 W.Va. 91, 159 S.E.2d 784, 786 (1968).

Piercing the corporate veil is an equitable remedy, and the burden rests with the party asserting such claim. DeWitt Truck Brokers, 540 F.2d at 683. A totality of the circumstances test is used in determining whether to pierce the corporate veil, and each case must be decided on its own facts. The district court's findings of facts may be overturned only if clearly erroneous. Id.

Kinney seeks to pierce the corporate veil of Industrial so as to hold Polan personally liable on the sublease debt. The Supreme Court of Appeals of West Virginia has set forth a two prong test to be used in determining whether to pierce a corporate veil in a breach of contract case. This test raises two issues: first, is the unity of interest and ownership such that the separate personalities of the corporation and the individual shareholder no longer exist; and second, would an equitable result occur if the acts are treated as those of the corporation alone. *Laya*, 352 S.E.2d at 99. Numerous factors have been identified as relevant in making this determination.

The district court found that the two prong test of *Laya* had been satisfied. The court concluded that Polan's failure to carry out the corporate formalities with respect to Industrial, coupled with Industrial's gross undercapitalization, resulted in damage to Kinney. We agree.

It is undisputed that Industrial was not adequately capitalized. Actually, it had no paid in capital. Polan had put nothing into this corporation, and it did not observe any corporate formalities. As the West Virginia court stated in Laya, " '[i]ndividuals who wish to enjoy limited personal liability for business activities under a corporate umbrella should be expected to adhere to the relatively simple formalities of creating and maintaining a corporate entity.' " *Laya*, 352 S.E.2d at 100 n. 6 (quoting Labadie Coal Co. v. Black, 672 F.2d 92, 96–97 (D.C.Cir. 1982)). This, the court stated, is " 'a relatively small price to pay for limited liability.' " Id. Another important factor is adequate capitalization. "[G]rossly inadequate capitalization combined with disregard of corporate formalities, causing basic unfairness, are sufficient to pierce the corporate veil in order to hold the shareholder(s) actively participating in the operation of the business personally liable for a breach of contract to the party who entered into the contract with the corporation." *Laya*, 352 S.E.2d at 101–02.

In this case, Polan bought no stock, made no capital contribution, kept no minutes, and elected no officers for Industrial. In addition, Polan attempted to protect his assets by placing them in Polan Industries, Inc. and interposing Industrial between Polan Industries, Inc. and Kinney so as to prevent Kinney from going against the corporation with assets. Polan gave no explanation or justification for the existence of Industrial as the intermediary between Polan Industries, Inc. and Kinney. Polan was obviously trying to limit his liability and the liability of Polan Industries, Inc. by setting up a paper curtain constructed of nothing more than Industrial's certificate of incorporation. These facts present the classic scenario for an action to pierce the corporate veil so as to reach the responsible party and produce an equitable result. Accordingly, we hold that the district court correctly found that the two prong test in *Laya* had been satisfied.

In *Laya*, the court also noted that when determining whether to pierce a corporate veil a third prong may apply in certain cases. The court stated: "When, under the circumstances, it would be reasonable for that particular type of a party [those contract creditors capable of protecting themselves] entering into a contract with the corporation, for example, a bank or other lending institution, to conduct an investigation of the credit of the corporation prior to entering into the contract, such party will be charged with the knowledge that a reasonable credit investigation would disclose. If such an investigation would disclose that the corporation is grossly undercapitalized, based upon the nature and the magnitude of the corporate undertaking, such party will be deemed to have assumed the risk of the gross undercapitalization and will not be permitted to pierce the corporate veil." *Laya*, 352 S.E.2d at 100. The district court applied this third prong and concluded that Kinney "assumed the risk of Industrial's defaulting" and that "the application of the doctrine of 'piercing the corporate veil' ought not and does not [apply]." While we agree that the two prong test of Laya was satisfied, we hold that the district court's conclusion that Kinney had assumed the risk is clearly erroneous.

Without deciding whether the third prong should be extended beyond the context of the financial institution lender mentioned in *Laya*, we hold that, even if it applies to creditors such as Kinney, it does not prevent Kinney from piercing the corporate veil in this case. The third prong is permissive and not mandatory. This is not a factual situation that calls for the third prong, if we are to seek an equitable result. Polan set up Industrial to limit his liability and the liability of Polan Industries, Inc. in their dealings with Kinney. A stockholder's liability is limited to the amount he has invested in the corporation, but Polan invested nothing in Industrial. This corporation was no more than a shell—a transparent shell. When nothing is invested in the corporation, the corporation provides no protection to its owner; nothing in, nothing out, no protection. If Polan wishes the protection of a corporation to limit his liability, he must follow the simple formalities of maintaining the corporation. This he failed to do, and he may not relieve his circumstances by saying Kinney should have known better.

III.

For the foregoing reasons, we hold that Polan is personally liable for the debt of Industrial, and the decision of the district court is reversed and this case is remanded with instructions to enter judgment for the plaintiff.

Reversed and Remanded With Instructions.

E. UNDERCAPITALIZATION

Courts using undercapitalization as a test for veil-piercing focus on the initial relationship between the corporation's assets and the risks associated with its business activities. The undercapitalization doctrine requires that a corporation begin its activities with sufficient financial resources so that it can satisfy any losses likely to be generated by its ventures. The first question is what, precisely, is "capital?" Typically, capital consists of shareholder equity, although, in a tort context, it also may include insurance coverage. Moreover, it is often not uncommon for one or more of the principal shareholders to lend the corporation substantial amounts of money; whether such loans will be considered capital depends on the totality of the circumstances, including the risks of the new venture and the proportion that the loans bear to the total capital of the corporation.

In O'Hazza v. Executive Credit Corp., 246 Va. 111, 431 S.E.2d 318 (1993), the O'Hazza family contributed $10,000 in initial equity capital to the corporation and subsequently lent it approximately $140,000 over a two-year period. In reversing the trial court's decision to hold the individual shareholders personally liable for an unpaid corporate loan, the Virginia Supreme Court stated:

> Initial capitalization of a corporation can be an indicator of whether a corporation was created and operated as a sham or as the alter ego for another corporation or person. If, from its inception, a corporation is unable to pay its costs of doing business because of grossly inadequate capitalization, its legitimacy is suspect. Under such circumstances, stock holders may not be entitled to the corporate shield. Thus, the court in re County Green Ltd. Partnership, 438 F.Supp. 701 (W.D.Va.1977), held that initial capitalization of $100, accompanied by a situation in which the controlling shareholder drained the corporation's earnings and increased the corporation's financial dependency, were factors used to justify a decision to pierce the corporate veil.

> In the instant case, the creditor produced no evidence to show what an appropriate level of capitalization would have been for a business that installed sound equipment. Consequently, a determination that $10,000 was insufficient initial capitalization is questionable, particularly in light of the $9,412 profit shown on the corporation's federal tax return for 1987, its first year of operation.

> We note also that, to gain certain tax advantages, small corporations increasingly, and legitimately, choose to initially capitalize the entity with a small portion of the investment represented by stock and with the larger portion of capital set up as loans to the corporation. If the corporation fails, these loans are subordinated to those of other creditors. And, as pointed out by the O'Hazzas, federal courts, in distinguishing between corporate debt and risk capital, have considered a loan made to a corporation by stockholders without expectation of repayment as an indication that the transaction involved venture capital, not a true loan.

431 S.E.2d at 321.

The question of undercapitalization involves the adequacy of the capital when the corporation is formed. The logic of the doctrine suggests that capital should be increased as the risk of the corporation's business also grows, but the logic does not appear to have been widely accepted. Courts have concentrated generally on initial capitalization, although they may consider a corporation undercapitalized if it grows substantially without enjoying a corresponding increase in its capital. However, a corporation is not required to increase its capital base simply because it loses money. William P. Hackney and Tracey G. Benson, Shareholder Liability for Inadequate Capital, 43 U. Pitt. L. Rev. 837, 898–99 (1982).

Professor Thompson, supra, argues that undercapitalization is not a significant factor in veil-piercing cases. He finds that undercapitalization was present in only 19% of the contract cases and 13% of the tort cases in which the corporate veil was pierced. This data suggests that when considering undercapitalization, context does not matter greatly. Nevertheless, undercapitalization may affect the outcome when it is present; in the cases in which undercapitalization was found, the corporate veil was pierced almost three-quarters of the time. The Ninth Circuit, interpreting California law, has stated that "undercapitalization alone will justify piercing the corporate veil." Nilsson, et al. v. Louisiana Hydrolec, 854 F.2d 1538, 1544 (9th Cir.1988), but it is not clear that this statement is accurate. See Stephen B. Presser, Piercing the Corporate Veil §§ 1.05[2] n.16, 2.05 (1993).

What should be the significance of a corporation's capital in determining whether to pierce the corporate veil? Would an insistence on adequate capital unduly deter high-risk, high-profit ventures? How much deterrence is "too much?" To what extent does insurance provide a solution? Recall Judge Keating's dissent in *Walkovszky*. Are courts or legislatures better equipped to answer these questions? Reconsider Note: "Thin" Corporations in Chapter 9, Section A.

F. PARENT–SUBSIDIARY AND AFFILIATE CORPORATIONS

The division of a business enterprise into multiple corporations is done for the convenience and profit maximization of the owners. Sometimes the relationship is that of parent and subsidiary: one corporation owns the stock of another. Sometimes one corporation owns the stock of many corporations, all of whom are subsidiaries of the parent and affiliates of each other. In the first case, a plaintiff who asserts an injury caused by a corporate subsidiary will seek to reach the assets of the parent to satisfy the judgment. In the second instance, the plaintiff will attempt to recover from the affiliates if neither the corporation that caused the injury or the parent corporation have sufficient assets. While it may be appropriate to respect the limited liability of the shareholders of the *parent* corporation, it can be argued that all the related corporations should be treated as a single entity. The courts have not adopted such a universal rule.

1. PARENT–SUBSIDIARY CORPORATIONS   *Can't sue parent because subsidiary was not a mere instrumentality*

AMERICAN TRADING AND PRODUCTION CORP. v. FISCHBACH & MOORE

311 F.Supp. 412 (N.D.Ill.1970).

McCormick Place, an exposition hall in Chicago, Illinois, was destroyed by fire on January 16, 1967. Also destroyed were exhibits scheduled to be displayed at the Semi–Annual National Housewares Show, which was to begin that day. The plaintiffs in these consolidated cases are these exhibitors and their subrogees, and insurance company subrogees of the Metropolitan Fair and Exposition Authority, which owned and operated McCormick Place. Defendants are Fischbach and Moore, Incorporated ["Parent"] and its wholly owned subsidiary, Fischbach and Moore Electrical Contracting, Inc. ["Subsidiary"]. The complaints sound in tort and allege that faulty electrical wiring installed by defendants in McCormick Place for the Housewares Show was the cause of the fire.

Defendant Fischbach and Moore, Incorporated has moved for summary judgment pursuant to Rule 56 of the Federal Rules of Civil Procedure, contending that it has neither performed electrical work in McCormick Place nor acted in a manner making it liable for the alleged torts of its Subsidiary. Because the pleadings, affidavits, depositions, answers to interrogatories and exhibits on file demonstrate that no genuine issue of material fact exists, and because the undisputed evidence clearly shows that the Parent did not itself furnish the allegedly defective electrical work, nor operate the Subsidiary as its "mere instrumentality," the motion for summary judgment is granted.

Fischbach and Moore, Incorporated is a publicly held New York corporation with its principal place of business in New York City. Active primarily in the business of electrical contracting and related endeavors, it has divisions and approximately 20 subsidiaries throughout the United States and Canada which are similarly engaged. Among the latter is defendant Fischbach and Moore Electrical Contracting, Inc., a Delaware corporation with its principal place of business in Chicago, Illinois.

It is undisputed that the Parent corporation has never been a party to a contract with the management of McCormick Place, and that none of its employees has provided electrical installation or supervisory services for McCormick Place. Its asserted liability for damages must rest, therefore, not on its own performance of electrical work but on such performance by the Subsidiary.

For a corporation to be held liable for the torts of a subsidiary, it must appear that the subsidiary was operated as a "mere instrumentality" of the parent. This rule is rarely applied, and only under special circumstances, for it runs contrary to the established principle of corporate limited liability. "The instrumentality rule should only be invoked after mature consideration and caution. Indiscriminate application would destroy the purpose of the corporate law." Brown v. Margrande Compania Naviera, 281 F.Supp. 1004, 1006 (E.D.Va.1968).

The tests to be applied were set out in Steven v. Roscoe Turner Aeronautical Corporation, 324 F.2d 157 (7th Cir.1963), at 160:

> "In order to establish that a subsidiary is the mere instrumentality of its parent, three elements must be proved: control by the parent to such a degree that the subsidiary has become its mere instrumentality; fraud or wrong by the parent through its subsidiary, e.g. torts, violation of a statute or stripping the subsidiary of its assets; and unjust loss or injury to the claimant, such as insolvency of the subsidiary."

Application of these principles to this case requires a narration of the facts relating to the interrelationship of the two defendant corporations. The pertinent factual details, which are undisputed, follow.

At the time of the fire, all four of the Subsidiary's directors were also directors of the Parent, and four of the Subsidiary's eight officers were also officers of the Parent. However, the corporations maintain separate offices and conduct separate directors' meetings. The financial books and records of the Subsidiary are maintained by its employees in Chicago, and contain only entries related to its own operations. The Subsidiary has its own bank accounts and negotiates its own loans from third parties; however, these loans are reviewed and guaranteed by the Parent. On occasion, the Subsidiary has borrowed money from the Parent; these loans are evidenced by notes and call for interest at the prime rate.

The Subsidiary and Parent file separate tax returns. However, financial statements of the Parent and all subsidiaries are consolidated. The payroll of the Subsidiary is paid by the Subsidiary rather than the Parent, and salary levels are determined by the Subsidiary subject to review by the Parent. The Subsidiary has never purchased goods or services from the Parent, nor has the Parent purchased goods and services from the Subsidiary. Purchasing is independently handled by each corporation, as are labor-union relations.

The Subsidiary notifies the Parent of bids made on contracting jobs and of contracts awarded. However, neither bids nor contracts are reviewed by the Parent, nor are matters relating to the manner of performance and the materials to be used subject to review. On contracts exceeding $5,000,000 the profit "mark up" to be charged may be determined after consultation with the Parent. The Subsidiary forwards schedules to the Parent regarding new jobs acquired and contracts on hand for each three month period, and submits reports on material purchases, estimates, salary changes and financial data on a more frequent basis.

On one occasion the Subsidiary sought review by the Parent of a lease it had negotiated for additional yard space for its equipment. On other occasions, the Parent has determined which of its subsidiaries should bid on a particular project. There is evidence that the Parent's management considered it and the subsidiaries to be one "family." This is reflected in some annual reports and in advertising in Fortune magazine, wherein the Parent claimed the credit in its own name for projects (including McCormick Place) in fact performed by the Subsidiary.

Financial data of record reveals that the Subsidiary's net worth was $511,503 in 1966 and $684,574 in 1967. It paid dividends of $100,000 in 1966 and $369,000 in 1967, which amounts represented substantially all of its after tax earnings. The corresponding gross income figures for those years, $6,128,000 and $12,798,000 represent 4.42% and 8.07%, respectively, of the consolidated gross income of the Parent and its subsidiaries. The Parent's gross income, apart from the income from subsidiaries, approximated $77,000,000 in each of these two years.

The Parent and all subsidiaries are participants in a group liability insurance policy. The subsidiary pays its own share of the premium, and has $15,000,000 worth of coverage applicable to liability arising out of the McCormick Place fire.

These facts, even when viewed in the light most favorable to the plaintiffs, conclusively show that the Subsidiary is not the mere instrumentality of the parent, as that concept has been defined in the case law. Neither ownership of all of the stock of a subsidiary, nor identity of officers and directors, nor both combined are sufficient to justify "piercing the corporate veil." "While stock control and common directors and officers are generally prerequisites for application of the instrumentality rule, yet, they are not sufficient by themselves to bring the rule into operation. * * * Such factors are common business practice and exist in most parent and subsidiary relationships." Steven v. Roscoe Turner Aeronautical Corp., 324 F.2d at 161.

The additional factors which must be present have been variously described as "direct intervention" in the subsidiary's affairs, Kingston Dry Dock Co. v. Lake Champlain Transportation Co., 31 F.2d 265, 267 (2d Cir.1929), the "act of operation" of the subsidiary's business, Berkey v. Third Avenue Ry. Co., 244 N.Y. 84, 155 N.E. 58 (1926), or "the exercise of control, not the opportunity to exercise control." Brown v. Margrande Compania Naviera, 281 F.Supp. at 1006.

The facts of record here show at most that the Parent exercises supervision and guidance of the general performance of the Subsidiary. Thus it requires various financial reports and is consulted as to mark ups on large jobs. It is clear, however, that the Parent does not "operate" the business. It does not compute bids, negotiate contracts or purchase goods and services for the Subsidiary. It does not supervise the manner in which the Subsidiary's contracting jobs are performed, and it does not use its own goods, equipment or employees in the Subsidiary's business operations.

Exercise of some degree of supervision by a 100% stockholder is not sufficient to render the subsidiary its instrumentality or alter ego.

"That a stockholder should show concern about the company's affairs, ask for reports, sometimes consult with its officers, give advice, and even object to proposed action is but the natural outcome of a relationship * * *." United States v. Elgin, J. & E. Ry., 298 U.S. 492, 503–04, 56 S.Ct. 841, 844, 80 L.Ed. 1300 (1936). In Steven v. Roscoe Turner Aeronautical Corp., 324 F.2d at 162, similar supervisory concern was held to be "sound business practice" which did not raise "a genuine factual issue under the instrumentality rule." Such participation in a subsidiary's affairs does not amount to the domination of day to day business decisions and disregard of the corporate entity necessary to impose liability on a parent.

Another factor deemed significant in applying the instrumentality test is the extent to which corporate formalities are observed. In the instant case, separate corporate identities are scrupulously maintained. The physical locations of the corporations are different; the records of each are separately maintained; there is no commingling of funds; payrolls are separately administered; contracts are independently negotiated and signed; assets are not transferred back and forth; and purchasing, hiring and firing are independently conducted. The fact that the Parent considers its subsidiaries to be members of a "family" does not destroy the separate existence of each member. Nor does the Parent's boastful advertising show in any way that corporate identities were otherwise ignored by the participants in the conduct of their enterprises.

Moreover, even if it could be said that the Subsidiary [was] the mere instrumentality of the parent, that circumstance by itself would not justify imposition of liability. For it has long been the law that the corporate entity is only ignored when the ends of justice require it. Some element of unfairness, something akin to fraud or deception, or the existence of a compelling public interest must be present in order to disregard the corporate fiction.

None of the elements of injustice relied on in earlier cases exist here. It has not been shown or even suggested that the operators of McCormick Place, or the exhibitors, believed they were dealing with the Parent rather than the Subsidiary, or were misled as to the financial strength of the Subsidiary. On the contrary, it is clear that the Parent played no part in the electrical installation in McCormick Place and that the Subsidiary conducted its affairs in its own name. The record is barren of any evidence of misrepresentation, deception or mistake.

Nor has the Parent stripped the Subsidiary of its assets or otherwise operated it as an undercapitalized "sham" or "dummy." The Subsidiary is an independent and self sufficient operating entity, with ample net worth and income to meet the needs of its operations. Furthermore, it carries liability insurance in excess of the extraordinary damages allegedly suffered by these complainants. There is no evidence here "of such complete control of the subsidiary by the parent as to render the former a mere tool of the latter, and to compel the conclusion that the corporate identity of the subsidiary is a mere fiction." National Lead Co. v. Federal Trade Commission, 227 F.2d 825, 829 (7th Cir.1955).

Thus no fraud, injustice or unfairness has been suggested or disclosed which would justify ignoring the separate identities of these two corporations. To impose liability in such circumstances would be an unwarranted invasion of the established principle of limited liability, which was properly and understandably relied upon by these defendants in the conduct of their separate affairs.

Because defendant Fischbach and Moore, Incorporated neither participated in the acts allegedly causing plaintiffs' damages, nor treated its subsidiary codefendant as its mere instrumentality, an order will enter granting its motion for summary judgment and dismissing it from this consolidated case.

2. AFFILIATE CORPORATIONS

MY BREAD BAKING CO. v. CUMBERLAND FARMS, INC.

353 Mass. 614, 233 N.E.2d 748 (1968).

CUTTER, JUSTICE.

The remaining count in this action alleges conversion of certain property by Cumberland Farms, Inc. (C. F. Inc.). There was a substantial verdict for the plaintiff (My Bread) against C. F. Inc. and also a verdict for each codefendant.[1] The case is before us on C. F. Inc.'s exception to the judge's refusal to direct a verdict for it. The facts are stated in their aspect most favorable to My Bread.

In August, 1960, Byron Haseotes discussed with Joseph Duchaine, "the sole proprietor" of My Bread, the sale of the latter's bakery products in "Cumberland Farms" retail dairy stores. Haseotes was the secretary and treasurer and a stockholder of C. F. Inc., of each codefendant, and of fifteen other corporations.

After August, 1960, My Bread began selling its bakery products in the retail dairy stores, and provided bakery racks for use in this operation. The racks were delivered by My Bread directly to the local store in which they were used. In September, 1963, when the business arrangement with My Bread was terminated, My Bread sought the return of the racks. It was prevented by the local store managers, acting on the instructions of Haseotes, from recovering them from all but a few of the "Cumberland Farm" stores. Title to the racks remained in My Bread at all times.

In August, 1960, the capital stock of C. F. Inc. and of each codefendant was owned by Haseotes, his parents, his brothers, and his sisters. There was no joint financing of these corporations. The officers and directors of each corporation were the same. The sole business of

---

1. Cumberland Farms Dairy Stores, Inc., Cape Cod Farms, Inc., Narragansett Food Stores, Inc., Central Food Stores, Inc., and Commonwealth Dairy Stores, Inc. are the codefendants.

codefendants "was the operation of chains of [small] retail dairy stores
* * *." C. F. Inc. did not operate retail stores. It conducted "a bottling
* * * plant which processed and packages milk and other dairy products
and * * * [sold] its dairy products at * * * wholesale * * * to the * * *
five" codefendants. Haseotes testified that in August, 1960, C. F. Inc.
did not sell dairy products to all of the "Cumberland Farms" stores in
which My Bread was to sell its bakery products. In 1962 or 1963,
however, it began to do so. All of the defendants used the trade name
"Cumberland Farms." Persons dealing with all of these corporations
treated them as "Cumberland Farms."

C. F. Inc. never owned any stock interest in the five codefendants,
nor did those corporations own any stock in it. The advertising of all six
corporations was purchased in separate transactions and always used the
trade name "Cumberland Farms." In August, 1960, the Haseotes
family dairy businesses were operated out of headquarters in Woonsocket. Processing and bottling were then done in two plants, one in
Woonsocket and the other in Boston. Prior to the alleged conversion,
the Woonsocket and Boston plants were consolidated in a new plant in
Canton, and each defendant corporation moved its principal office to that
plant. Thereafter the "same business manager operated all the businesses from the Canton address." Haseotes "participated in the operation of all the corporations and it was his decision where money was to
go in the various corporations."

In August, 1963, Haseotes as sales manager of C. F. Inc., signed and
sent out circular memoranda concerning the sale of bread (including My
Bread products) in "Cumberland Farms" stores. These were on C. F.
Inc. letterhead and were addressed to a large number of retail stores or
store managers in mandatory language, using such terms as "must" and
stating policies "to be strictly adhered to." There was in evidence a loaf
which had on its wrapper the name "Cumberland Farms" and a notation
that it was distributed by "Cumberland Farms, Inc. of Boston."

Haseotes testified that, in his dealings with My Bread, he never
acted on behalf of C. F. Inc. because that corporation did not operate
retail stores, nor did it have any control over the store operating
corporations. One of My Bread's officers, however, testified that he
"always dealt with * * * Haseotes as 'Cumberland Farms'," although he
did on occasion on Haseotes's request make out checks to other corporations. He also obtained certificates of insurance which included the
names of several of the Haseotes corporations.

1. C. F. Inc. contends that the conversions of the bakery racks
were "committed by the local store managers, employed by the [code-
fendant] store-operating corporations," that there was no evidence that
these managers were agents for C. F. Inc. so as to make that corporation
liable for their acts, and that the codefendant corporations must each be
treated as distinct and separate from C. F. Inc. and each other. The
issue, of course, is whether there was evidence which, on any theory of

law, would warrant the jury in finding C. F. Inc. liable for the conversion.

C. F. Inc. thus seeks to have us apply the principle that corporations are generally to be regarded as separate from each other and from their respective stockholders where there is no occasion "to look beyond the corporate form for the purpose of defeating fraud or wrong, or for the remedying of injuries." See e.g. M. McDonough Corp. v. Connolly, 313 Mass. 62, 65–66, 46 N.E.2d 576, 579. The general principle is not of unlimited application. A corporation or other person controlling a corporation and directing, or participating actively, its operations may become subject to civil or criminal liability on principles of agency or of causation. This may sometimes occur where corporations are formed, or availed of, to carry out the objectives and purposes of the corporations or persons controlling them. The circumstances in which one corporation, or a person controlling it, may become liable for the acts or torts of an affiliate or a subsidiary under common control have been frequently discussed. Although common ownership of the stock of two or more corporations together with common management, standing alone, will not give rise to liability on the part of one corporation for the acts of another corporation or its employees, additional facts may be such as to permit the conclusion that an agency or similar relationship exists between the entities. Particularly is this true (a) when there is active and direct participation by the representatives of one corporation, apparently exercising some form of pervasive control, in the activities of another and there is some fraudulent or injurious consequence of the intercorporate relationship, or (b) when there is a confused intermingling of activity of two or more corporations engaged in a common enterprise with substantial disregard of the separate nature of the corporate entities, or serious ambiguity about the manner and capacity in which the various corporations and their respective representatives are acting. In such circumstances, in imposing liability upon one or more of a group of "closely identified" corporations, a court "need not consider with nicety which of them" ought to be held liable for the act of one corporation "for which the plaintiff deserves payment." See W.W. Britton, Inc. v. S. M. Mill Co., 327 Mass. 335, 338–39, 98 N.E.2d 637, 639.

It may be, as one commentator suggests (see Peairs, Business Corporations §§ 8–10, 33) that Massachusetts has been somewhat more "strict" than other jurisdictions in respecting the separate entities of different corporations. Nevertheless, our law concerning disregarding the corporate fiction has been stated * * * essentially in the same general terms employed in decisions elsewhere. Where there is common control of a group of separate corporations engaged in a single enterprise, failure (a) to make clear which corporation is taking action in a particular situation and the nature and extent of that action, or (b) to observe with care the formal barriers between the corporations with a proper segregation of their separate businesses, records, and finances, may warrant some disregard of the separate entities in rare particular situations in order to prevent gross inequity.

On the evidence the jury could have reached the following conclusions. (a) Haseotes was responsible by an order to the local stores for a high-handed, inexcusable refusal by employees of the various retail stores to return My Bread's racks to it at the termination of the bread sale arrangement. (b) Although no one of the codefendant operating store corporations was a subsidiary of C. F. Inc. (in the sense that C. F. Inc. owned the whole or a part of its stock), all the defendant corporations (including C. F. Inc.) were under the full stock control of the Haseotes family and were operated as a closely coordinated single enterprise. Haseotes himself could be found to have been a dominant figure in the whole "Cumberland Farms" enterprise. (c) The basic common enterprise was the processing, distribution, and sale of milk and dairy products. C. F. Inc., on the evidence, could be reasonably regarded as the principal corporation of the enterprise and the codefendants as its affiliates or satellites so that, when one thought of "Cumberland Farms," one would naturally think of C. F. Inc. (d) Because all the corporations were operated ambiguously from the same headquarters as part of a single enterprise, the jury could reasonably infer that Haseotes, in furtherance of the interests of C. F. Inc. in the distribution of its products, was intervening actively in the conduct of the satellite corporations. (e) Haseotes without (so far as this record shows) clear indication of the capacity in which (and the corporations for which) he was acting, dealt in 1960 with Duchaine of My Bread for "Cumberland Farms" in a very confused manner. Although My Bread's representatives probably knew of the existence of the separate corporations, they might reasonably think (absent a clear indication by Haseotes that he was acting for the retail store corporations and not for C. F. Inc.) that My Bread, with respect to the general wholesale distribution of bread, was dealing with C. F. Inc. That was the corporation which was engaged, for the whole "Cumberland Farms" enterprise, in the general wholesale distribution of milk and other dairy products. It would have been the logical corporation to arrange to purchase bread at wholesale for distribution through the "Cumberland Farms" stores. (f) The bill of exceptions reveals no basis for an inference that any of the codefendants was inadequately capitalized, a ground frequently relied upon, when taken with other factors, as permitting disregard of a corporate entity.

The jury could properly infer (because of Haseotes's actions, the general corporate situation, and Haseotes's failure to dispel ambiguities) that Haseotes in all matters connected with the My Bread arrangement was acting for C. F. Inc. and that the satellite companies in following Haseotes's orders concerning the bread racks were caused to act by C. F. Inc. and were acting as its agents.

The jury could reasonably decide that C. F. Inc., through Haseotes, brought about and was liable for the conversions. A directed verdict was properly refused.

Exceptions overruled.

Note: *Mangan v. Terminal Transportation System*

In Mangan v. Terminal Transportation System, 157 Misc. 627, 284 N.Y.S. 183 (1935), aff'd, per curiam 247 App.Div. 853, 286 N.Y.S. 666 (3d Dept.1936), the plaintiffs were struck by a cab owned by one of four cab operating companies, all of which were 60% owned by Yellow Truck & Coach Manufacturing Company. Yellow Truck was a holding company that also owned all the stock in the defendant, Terminal Transportation Company. Presumably because Yellow Truck had no assets and Yellow Truck's own parent company, General Motors, was too hard to reach, the plaintiffs sued Terminal, alleging that it controlled the four cab operating companies as mere agents and instrumentalities. Terminal was actively involved in the operating companies' businesses, having contracted to service all the operating companies' cabs and hiring and firing their drivers. Additionally, Terminal was completely owned by the same holding company, Yellow Truck, that owned a majority share in the four operating companies. The holding company also elected the same directors for Terminal and the operating companies. These factors led the court to disregard the corporate entity and hold Yellow Truck liable for the plaintiffs' injuries.

G. CRITIQUE OF LIMITED LIABILITY IN THE INTRA–ENTERPRISE CONTEXT

Economic growth in the nineteenth and twentieth centuries led ever-larger corporations to divide their operations among wholly or partly owned subsidiaries. The original conception of a corporation, however, was that of a fictional entity in which the entity's assets, liabilities and operations—the entire "enterprise"—was presumed to be its own, not those of another corporation or personality. Adolf A. Berle, Jr., The Theory of Enterprise Entity, 47 Col. L. Rev. 343 (1947). Instead of treating their subsidiaries as separate entities, the parent corporations "handled them [so] that they [] ceased to represent a separate enterprise and [became], as a business matter, more or less indistinguishable parts of a larger enterprise." *Id.* at 348. Faced with this situation, courts developed an often ad hoc approach to hold parent corporations responsible for the liabilities of their subsidiaries, using terms like "agency" and "mere instrumentality" to justify their decisions. As Berle described this judicial development,

> The courts disregard the corporate fiction specifically because it has parted company with the enterprise-fact, for whose furtherance the corporation was created; and having got that far, they then take the further step of ascertaining what is the actual enterprise-fact and attach the consequences of the acts of the component individuals or corporations to the enterprise entity, to the extent that the economic outlines of the situation warrant or require * * *. [These cases] suggest that to preserve the independence of an enterprise

which is needed to support the continuance of separate legal personality, the stockholders must provide the entity with separate assets sufficient to give it at least a reasonable business chance to carry out its asserted functions.

Id. at 348–49. Courts were particularly likely to disregard a separate corporate entity when the company's liabilities arose from criminal, fraudulent or other objectionable activities.

As the following materials suggest, Berle's theory of enterprise entity continues to provide the theoretical framework for the issue of intra-enterprise liability.

RICHARD A. POSNER, AN ECONOMIC ANALYSIS OF LAW
4th ed. 1992.

§ 14.5 PIERCING THE CORPORATE VEIL

Although limited liability serves an important function in making equity investments attractive to individuals, disregarding it—piercing the corporate veil, in the jargon of corporation law—may promote efficiency in two situations.

1. Consider the taxi enterprise whose owners incorporate each taxicab separately in order to limit tort liability to accident victims. If such liability were a negotiated obligation, the creditor-victim would charge a higher interest rate to reflect the increased risk of a default; but it is not and cannot be. The result of separate incorporation is therefore to externalize a cost of taxi service.

Yet piercing the veil may not be optimal even in this situation. Permitting tort victims to reach the shareholders' assets would be a source of additional risk to the shareholders—and an increase in risk is a real cost to people who are risk averse. Although the company could insure itself against its torts, this would not be a completely satisfactory alternative. The managers might fail to take out adequate insurance; the insurance company might for a variety of reasons refuse or be unable to pay a tort judgment against the insured (the insurance company might, for example, become insolvent); the particular tort might be excluded from the coverage of the insurance policy. All this may sound pretty remote—until one replaces taxicab collisions by nuclear reactor accidents or asbestos-caused lung disease. * * *

A simple alternative to piercing the corporate veil is to require any corporation engaged in dangerous activity to post a bond equal to the highest reasonable estimate of the probable extent of its tort liability. Shareholders would be protected (in what sense?) and accident costs internalized.

2. A stronger case for piercing the corporate veil is warranted where separate incorporation misleads creditors. Corporations permitted to represent that they have greater assets to pay creditors than they

actually have increase the costs that creditors must incur to ascertain the true credit worthiness of the corporations with which they deal.

* * *

Often a shareholder is a corporation rather than an individual, and it might seem that the policy of risk shifting that underlies the principle of limited liability would not apply in that case. If a parent corporation is made liable for its subsidiary's debts, the exposure of the parent's shareholders to liability, although greater than if the subsidiary enjoyed limited liability, is limited to their investment in the parent and can be further reduced by their holding a diversified portfolio of equities.

It may be necessary to distinguish in this regard, however, between the publicly held corporation (many shareholders, regularly traded stock) and the close corporation (few shareholders, no market in the stock). Suppose that Mr. A. Smith wants to invest in a mining venture but the entire Smith fortune (other than that which Smith plans to commit to the mining venture) is invested in a radio station owned by a corporation of which Smith is the sole stockholder. If he forms a new corporation to conduct the mining venture, and if the assets of affiliated corporations can be pooled to satisfy the claims of creditors of one of the affiliates, then Smith has hazarded his entire fortune on the outcome of the mining venture. In this case there is no difference between piercing the corporate veil to reach the assets of an affiliated corporation and piercing it to reach an individual shareholder's assets.

But where a large, publicly held corporation operates through wholly owned subsidiaries, it may seem artificial in the extreme to treat these as separate entities for purposes of deciding what assets shall be available to satisfy creditors' claims. The question can be evaluated by dividing affiliated firms into two groups: firms in unrelated businesses and firms in closely related businesses. In the first group, maximization of the parent corporation's profits will require that the profits of each subsidiary be maximized separately; so the assets, costs, etc. of each subsidiary should be the same as they would be if they were separate firms. True, the common owner could take measures that concealed or distorted the relative profitability of his different enterprises, as by allocating capital among them at arbitrary interest rates. But such measures are costly; they reduce the information available to the common owner about the efficiency with which his various corporations are being managed. * * *

Even when the activities of affiliated corporations are closely related—when for example they produce complementary goods—each corporation normally will be operated as a separate profit center in order to assure that the profits of the group will be maximized. It is true that if there are substantial cost savings from common ownership, as in some cases where the affiliated corporations operate at successive stages in the production of a good, the two corporations will be managed differently from separately owned corporations in the same line of business; their operations will be more closely integrated than would be those of independent corporations. But it would be perverse to penalize such a corporation for its superior efficiency by withdrawing from it the privilege of limited liability that its nonintegrated competitors enjoy. Moreover, in this case as well, the common owner has a strong incentive to avoid intercorporate transfers that, by distorting the profitability of each corporation, make it more difficult for the common owner to evaluate their performance. That is why the price at which one division of a vertically integrated firm will "sell" its output to another division is normally the market price for the good in question (less any savings in cost attributable to making an intrafirm transfer compared to a market transaction) rather than an arbitrary transfer price designed to increase the profits of one division at the expense of the other.

The important difference between a group of affiliates engaged in related businesses and one engaged in a number of unrelated businesses is not that the conduct of the corporations in the first group will differ from that of nonaffiliated corporations in the same business but that the creditor dealing with a group of affiliates in related businesses is more likely to be misled into thinking that he is dealing with a single corporation. * * * The misrepresentation principle, however, seems adequate to deal with these cases. Indeed, where there is no misrepresentation, a rule abrogating the limited liability of affiliated corporations would not reduce the risks of any class of creditors but would increase their information costs. Although the creditor of A Corporation would know that if A defaulted he could reach the assets of its affiliate B, he would also know that if B defaulted, B's creditors might have a claim on the assets of A that might cause A to default on the debt to him. So to know how high an interest rate to charge, he would have to investigate B's financial situation as well as A. And B might be in a completely unrelated business.

The primary rationale for limited liability—investors are more willing to fund new business ventures when their liability is limited to the amount they invest—has been criticized as not applying fully when the investor is a parent corporation. See Phillip I. Blumberg, Limited Liability and Corporate Groups, 11 J. of Corp. Law 573 (1986). Limited liability originally protected the ultimate investors in an enterprise, the shareholders. Blumberg argues that the advantages of limited liability disappear when extended to the parent or affiliate of a subsidiary. For example, while it may seem unjust to hold shareholders liable for corporate actions ordered by the directors and managers, this unfairness argument does not apply to a parent that most likely controls and directs its subsidiary. Additionally, the need to attract thousands of investors to fund a large corporate enterprise by assuring them that their liability is limited is not a factor when one corporation provides most or all the capital for a subsidiary. As a result, eliminating limited liability for corporate groups will not affect the capital markets.

Corporations maintain subsidiaries presumably for the increased efficiencies that the subsidiaries provide. One such efficiency is the ability for a corporation to engage in a high-risk activity through a subsidiary. The parent obtains the opportunity for a high return on its investment while simultaneously being shielded from any liability the subsidiary may incur. Eliminating limited liability in the parent-subsidiary context would require companies to consider whether the benefits received from this increased efficiency outweigh the increased liability costs associated with its expansion into risky ventures. David Leebron, Limited Liability, Tort Victims, and Creditors, 91 Col. L. Rev. 1565, 1613–23 (1991). Leebron would impose unlimited liability on any parent that owned a majority of the subsidiary's shares, partly because majority ownership ensures that the parent actually controlled the subsidiary. Under this system, corporations would be unable to externalize their costs through subsidiaries. As noted in Section B, although Leebron agrees with Posner that there is no need to abandon limited liability regarding contractual creditors, Leebron argues that unlimited liability is warranted in the case of tort creditors. Unlike contractual creditors, tort claimants cannot monitor the corporation, do not choose to enter into a relationship with it and cannot negotiate better terms for themselves before finalizing the relationship.

Christopher Stone agrees that corporations should not be able to escape unlimited liability by establishing small, thinly capitalized subsidiaries to handle a potentially lucrative but high-risk business such as toxic chemicals. Christopher D. Stone, The Place of Enterprise Liability in the Control of Corporate Conduct, 90 Yale L.J. 1 (1980). He observes that restrictions on investor liability, whatever their justifications regarding contract creditors, conflict with at least two legal ideals when applied to involuntary creditors. First, tort claimants may not receive adequate compensation for their injuries. Second, deterrence is undermined because the corporation discounts the costs of its activities to those who may be harmed. Stone argues that the law has determined that capital markets and their participants are favored over other social actors, such as innocent tort victims. As a solution, Stone proposes that the presumption against piercing the corporate veil be reversed, particularly when hazardous activities caused the injury sought to be satisfied.

The virtues of limited liability as applied to corporate groups, particularly in the bankruptcy context, are sharply debated between Posner and Professor Jonathan Landers. See Jonathan M. Landers, A Unified Approach to Parent, Subsidiary and Affiliated Questions in Bankruptcy, 42 U. Chi. L. Rev. 589 (1975). Professor Landers argues that the structuring of a complex business enterprise into several corporations is undertaken for the convenience of the organizers, who believe that such a structure will maximize their returns from the enterprise as a whole. To them, it is irrelevant from which segment of the business the profits derive. Commingling of funds and loose organization is of no consequence to the people who form and operate the business in this manner. Landers favors allowing persons who do business with any part of the corporate structure to satisfy their claims from the entire enterprise. Landers would generally allow the loans from a parent to a subsidiary to be subordinated to the subsidiary's other creditors the consolidation of the parent's and subsidiary's estates if both companies enter bankruptcy. Additionally, Landers believes that Posner's consent and contract analysis neglects the plight of the tort claimant who is conscripted into doing business with the company. For a further discussion of these issues, see Richard A. Posner, The Rights of Affiliated Creditors of Affiliated Corporations, 43 U. Chi. L. Rev. 499 (1976), Jonathan M. Landers, Another Word on Parents, Subsidiaries and Affiliates in Bankruptcy, 43 U. Chi. L. Rev. 527 (1976).

Professor Thompson, supra, concludes that there is a relationship between the number of shareholders and the courts' willingness to pierce the corporate veil. He finds that in almost 50% of the cases in which there was only one shareholder, the court pierced the corporate veil, but that this percentage decreased to about 35% where the corporation had more than three shareholders.

H. ALTERNATIVES TO LIMITED LIABILITY

1. IMPOSING SHAREHOLDER LIABILITY UNDER FEDERAL LAW

Although state law generally governs corporate issues, a growing body of federal law allows federal courts to find shareholders personally liable for corporate activities that violate federal mandates. While this body of law is becoming more well defined, one comprehensive study found that federal courts pierced the veil inconsistently within various statutory areas. Note, Piercing the Corporate Law Veil: The Alter Ego Doctrine Under Federal Common Law, 95 Harv. L. Rev. 853 (1982). The author found that federal courts would more frequently veil pierce to give force to federal policies.

Perhaps the leading expression of veil piercing by a federal court to effectuate federal statutory guidelines is Anderson v. Abbott, 321 U.S. 349, 64 S.Ct. 531, 88 L.Ed. 793 (1944). In that case, the Supreme Court refused to apply a state limited liability law that would have protected the shareholders. Instead, it followed federal statutory provisions, since repealed, and disregarded the corporate entity to hold the shareholders liable. The court noted that while a state may adopt its own limited liability laws, a state may not endow its "corporate creatures with the power to place themselves above the Congress of the United States and defeat the federal policy * * * which Congress has announced." 321 U.S. at 365, 64 S.Ct. at 539.

Since *Anderson* the federal courts have developed a flexible body of federal case law to pierce the veil even when the applicable federal statute does not specifically so direct. The federal courts may veil pierce to insure that the corporate entity does not interfere with federal policy. Chicago v. Matchmaker Real Estate Sales Center, Inc., 982 F.2d 1086

(7th Cir.1992) exemplifies this approach. In this case, the corporation's chief executive officer, who was also the corporation's sole shareholder, was held liable for compensatory damages resulting from "racial steering" by corporate employees when showing houses for sale in the Chicago area in violation of two federal statutes, the Civil Rights Act of 1866 and the Fair Housing Act of 1968. The court noted that "where common ownership and management exists, corporate formalities must not be rigidly adhered to when inquiry is made of civil rights violations." Presumably, courts would impose personal liability to further federal anti-discrimination policies in other areas by encouraging corporate control persons to make certain discrimination does not occur. Note, however, that the court in *Matchmaker* stressed the common ownership and management of the corporation before holding the sole shareholder liable. Thus, it is unclear to what extent courts will hold shareholders liable to further federal policy in the absence of common ownership and management. The result may also be different if a controlling person is merely a shareholder and not also the corporate chief executive officer.

The most important federal statute that can lead to shareholder liability, at least in financial terms, is the Comprehensive Environmental Response, Compensation and Liability Act (CERCLA), 42 U.S.C. § 9601 *et seq*. This law places financial responsibility for cleaning up hazardous waste sites on, among others, any person who owned or operated such a site at the time of disposal of such wastes. In Lansford–Coaldale Joint Water Auth. v. Tonolli Corp., 4 F.3d 1209, 1222 (3d Cir.1993), the court observed that:

> "[t]o be an operator requires more than merely complete ownership and the concomitant general control that comes with ownership. At a minimum it requires active involvement in the activities of the subsidiary." [United States v. Kayser–Roth Corp., 910 F.2d 24, 27 (1st Cir.1990), cert. denied, 1084 U.S. 498, 111 S.Ct. 957, 112 L.Ed. 1045 (1991)]. Whereas a corporation's "mere oversight" of the subsidiary * * * corporation's business in a "manner consistent with the investment relationship" does not ordinarily result in operator liability, a corporation's "actual participation and control" over the other corporation's decision-making does.

Other courts have held shareholders liable as operators without any evidence that they were actively involved in management, reasoning that CERCLA's remedial and cost-sharing objectives require imposition of liability on every person who has the authority to prevent a corporation from contaminating a site. See, e.g., Donahey v. Bogle, 987 F.2d 1250 (6th Cir.1993).

2. FRAUDULENT CONVEYANCE AND EQUITABLE SUBORDINATION CONCEPTS

Apart from veil piercing, courts use other methods to protect creditors' interests. One such method is to set aside certain conveyances that are fraudulent to creditors under the Uniform Fraudulent Conveyance

Act (UFCA), codified in the U.S. Bankruptcy Code and many state statutes. The UFCA protects creditors from two general types of transfers: (1) transfers with the intent to defraud creditors, and (2) transfers that constructively defraud creditors. In order to support a finding of intentional fraud, the court must usually find an actual intent by the debtor to "hinder, delay or defraud." A finding of constructive fraud generally involves a transfer by the debtor while insolvent or near insolvency that is not made for fair consideration.

In the bankruptcy context, the UFCA could be utilized in place of veil piercing to set aside a fraudulent transfer that the corporation has made to its shareholders when it has outstanding debts to creditors. Thus, a court could set aside the transfer and apply it against the corporation's debts to its creditors. For example, the UFCA could be used to set aside an "excess" salary payment from a corporation to its sole shareholder that far exceeds the value of the shareholder's services to the corporation.

The UFCA background may illuminate the attention courts pay to the observance of corporate formalities and the intermingling of corporate and personal assets in deciding veil piercing cases. A disregard of corporate formalities often provides indirect evidence of a fraudulent conveyance. The intermingling of corporate and personal assets may provide direct evidence of a fraudulent conveyance.

Limits exist on the use of the UFCA in lieu of veil piercing. First, the UFCA requires a specific finding of a fraudulent transaction, which may be difficult to establish. Second, unlike veil piercing, which may impose unlimited liability on shareholders, the UFCA allows a court to set aside only the amount of the fraudulent conveyance, which may not satisfy a creditor's entire claim. Third, the fraudulent conveyance may be unrelated to a creditor's claim.

The doctrine of equitable subordination (discussed in Chapter 9) represents a second method to protect the interests of creditors. This doctrine is applicable only in federal bankruptcy proceedings. Under equitable subordination, certain creditors' claims, particularly those of corporate insiders, are subordinated to other creditors to reach an equitable result. Subordination thus allows outside creditors to receive payment before insiders. The result achieved by the equitable subordination doctrine is significant because priority in a federal bankruptcy proceeding often determines which creditors will get paid.

However, in contrast to veil piercing and application of fraudulent conveyance principles, equitable subordination does not increase the resources from which a creditor may satisfy her claim. It does not disregard the corporate form or hold a shareholder personally liable for the corporation's obligations. The doctrine only alters the normal priority of certain creditors' claims against the corporation's available resources. Nevertheless, it improves the chances that the corporation will be able to satisfy the creditors' debts. If a corporation is insolvent, the claims of outside creditors will likely exhaust the corporation's assets and the shareholder-officer probably will receive nothing.

Before the court will invoke the equitable subordination doctrine, there must be a showing of fraudulent conduct, mismanagement, or inadequate capitalization. Some cases explicitly reject inadequate capitalization as the sole basis for subordination. See, e.g., In re Branding Iron Steak House, 536 F.2d 299 (9th Cir.1976). As a baseline, courts generally look to whether a claimant engaged in some form of "inequitable conduct" and whether the misconduct resulted in injury to the bankrupt's creditor or conferred an unfair advantage on the claimant. In re Mobile Steel Co., 563 F.2d 692, 699–700 (5th Cir.1977). Some courts have abandoned the insider misconduct standard. See, e.g., Burden v. United States, 917 F.2d 115, 119–20 (3d Cir.1990).

Chapter 12

MANAGEMENT AND CONTROL
OF THE CORPORATION

A. THE CORPORATE ACTORS:
SHAREHOLDERS, DIRECTORS,
AND OFFICERS

Three sets of actors—shareholders, directors, and officers—play important roles in the corporate governance system. Statutes generally stipulate the same basic governance structure for all corporations, regardless of their size or number of shareholders, although many statutes now also allow closely-held corporations to adopt governance structures that deviate from this statutory norm.

In the standard governance system, the board of directors has the central role and bears ultimate responsibility for the conduct of the corporation's business. RMBCA § 8.01(b), for example, provides: "All corporate powers shall be exercised by or under authority of, and the business and affairs of a corporation shall be managed under the direction of its board of directors * * *."

This statutory mandate does not mean the board of directors, acting as such, must manage a corporation's day-to-day business. Rather, the board may, and often does, delegate responsibility for day-to-day operations to the corporation's officers and employees. Some statutes, in fact, require corporations to have certain officers, usually a president, one or more vice presidents, a secretary, and a treasurer. See, e.g., N.Y.B.C.L. § 715. Most modern statutes, though, allow a corporation to designate the officers it will have, either in its bylaws or by action of its board of directors. See, e.g. RMBCA § 8.40. The Official Comment to RMBCA § 8.40 explains: "Experience has shown * * * that little purpose is served by a statutory requirement that there be certain officers, and statutory requirements may sometimes create problems of implied or apparent authority or confusion with nonstatutory offices the corporation desires to create."

Modern statutes generally say little about officers' duties and powers. See e.g., RMBCA § 8.41. Implicit in the statutory scheme, howev-

Bd. delegates to officers

er, is the notion that all power exercised by a corporation's officers derive from the power assigned by statute to the board of directors and, consequently, must be delegated by the board to the officers.

Even though shareholders are a corporation's ultimate owners, corporate statutes do not authorize shareholders to manage the corporation's business directly. Rather, statutes make shareholders responsible for electing the corporation's directors. "Directors are elected at the first annual shareholders meeting and at each annual meeting thereafter * * *." RMBCA § 8.03(d). Shareholder meetings are to be held annually. RMBCA § 7.01. If an annual meeting has not been held in the previous 15 months, any holder of voting stock can require the corporation to convene an annual meeting, at which new directors can be elected. RMBCA § 7.03(a). Statutes also generally authorize shareholders to remove directors with or without cause, unless a corporation's articles of incorporation provide that directors can be removed only for cause. RMBCA § 8.08. Shareholders' power to remove directors for cause cannot be restricted.

In sum, corporate statutes establish a basic governance structure in which shareholders elect (and have the power to remove) a corporation's directors; directors are charged with managing the corporation's business; and officers and employees carry on day-to-day operations using powers that the board of directors has delegated to them. But this structure is subject to two important caveats. First, before effectuating certain *fundamental transactions* such as mergers or sale of substantially all of a corporation's assets (or amending the articles of incorporation in some significant fashion), the board must secure the approval of a majority of the corporation's shareholders. Put differently, one could say that shareholders have the power to veto such fundamental transactions and amendments. Second, shareholders also generally can amend a corporation's bylaws and may be able to make recommendations to the board concerning some matters within the board's sphere of responsibility.

This chapter focuses on the issues that arise as a consequence of the division of authority among a corporation's officers, directors, and shareholders. The chapter also reviews briefly the procedures that boards of directors and shareholders must follow when exercising their powers. The first section considers questions relating to the authority of a corporation's officers and employees, questions that turn largely on principles of agency law. The next section addresses the procedures a board of directors must follow in order to exercise its authority. Issues relating to the substance of directors' responsibilities are the focus of several subsequent chapters.

The largest part of the chapter deals with shareholders' rights with respect to the governance of the corporation that they "own." Issues involving shareholders' rights arise most frequently when some or most of a corporation's shareholders disagree with a policy or decision that the board supports. In such a situation, the board may seek to implement the policy or decision it favors without triggering shareholders' veto rights, while shareholders may attempt to participate in or otherwise influence the board or try to alter its membership. This chapter's discussion of shareholder rights addresses several issues relating to these conflicts. First, it outlines how statutes and courts have defined shareholders' rights with regard to corporate combinations, perhaps the most important class of fundamental transactions. Next, it addresses shareholders' rights with respect to sales of a substantial portion of a corporation's assets. Then it considers shareholders' rights to influence the decisions of, or alter the membership of, a corporation's board of directors, and how courts limit boards of directors' ability to avoid or frustrate shareholders' exercise of those rights. Finally, it reviews the procedures shareholders must follow to exercise their voting rights and related issues involving shareholders' rights to inspect corporate books and records.

B.   ACTION BY EXECUTIVES: AGENCY PRINCIPLES AND THE AUTHORITY OF CORPORATE OFFICERS

1.   INTRODUCTION TO SOME BASIC AGENCY CONCEPTS

The corporation, an incorporeal entity, can act only through the agency of flesh and blood human beings. An understanding of the law of corporations, therefore, requires some knowledge of the law of agency. If you have not already had a formal course in agency law, you have by now at least been exposed to some agency principles in other basic courses. We review those principles here before examining their operation in the corporate context.

An agency is a consensual relationship between two parties, the *principal* and the *agent*. The principal selects the agent, who then must agree to act on the principal's behalf. The principal has the power to terminate the agency relationship unilaterally and can dictate to the agent how the agent will perform her duties. The relationship between principal and agent is of a *fiduciary* character which, oversimplifying a bit, means that the agent owes to the principal a duty of loyalty and obedience. The agent is bound not to act contrary to a reasonable order of the principal given within the scope of the agent's employment. Also, within the scope of the employment, the agent must always put the interests of the principal above her own. Perhaps of greatest relevance to the material in this chapter, the existence of an agency relationship confers on the agent a legal *power* to create rights in the principal's favor and, correlatively, to subject the principal to liability to third parties.

There are several possible sources of an agent's power to bind her principal in a legal relationship with a third party. First, the agent may have been granted *actual authority* to bind the principal. According to the Restatement, Second, Agency, § 7, this authority "is the power of the agent to affect the legal relations of the principal by acts done in accordance with the principal's manifestations of consent to [her]." "Actual authority" describes what the principal causes the agent to believe is the scope of her authority. Actual authority may be *express*, growing out of explicit words or conduct granting the agent power to do the act, or may be *implied* from words or conduct taken in the context of the relations between the principal and the agent. In either case, the authority "can be created by written or spoken words or other conduct of the principal which, reasonably interpreted, causes the agent to believe that the principal desires [her] so to act on the principal's account." Restatement, Second, Agency § 26.

Although it sounds paradoxical, an agent also may bind her principal even though she lacks the actual authority to do so. A principal, for example, may create *apparent authority* "by written or spoken words or any other conduct * * * which, reasonably interpreted, causes the third person to believe that the principal consents to have the act done on [her] behalf by the person purporting to act for [her]." Restatement, Second, Agency § 27. Note that the existence of *actual* authority depends upon communications between the principal and the agent, whereas the existence of *apparent* authority depends on communications between the principal and the third party.* In other words, to create apparent authority the principal must do or say something that induces the third party to believe that the agent has authority.

An agent also may bind her principal by what the Restatement calls *"inherent agency power."* (Restatement, Second, Agency § 8A). The clearest example of such power (which, using the terminology of the Restatement, is not "authority") is the rule that a principal is liable for the *torts* of her servant under the doctrine of *respondeat superior*. Since a principal normally would not authorize an agent to commit a tort, it is clear that this rule cannot be based on any theory of delegation of power. Instead, the rule embodies the concept that it is fair to charge the principal with the costs of a tort committed by an agent who was acting on behalf of the principal.

Finally, a principal may become obligated to a third party by *ratifying* the act of another who, at the time of the act, lacked the power to bind the principal. Ratification is defined by the Restatement, Second, Agency § 8 as "the affirmance by a person of a prior act which did not bind [her] but which was done or professedly done on [her] account, whereby the act, as to some or all persons, is given effect as if originally authorized by [her]." When someone ratifies an unauthorized act done by another in her name, it is said that the ratification "relates back" so as to leave the resulting state of affairs precisely as it would have been had the authority been conferred before the act. The ratification creates an agency relationship regardless of whether such a relationship existed at the time of the act in question.

* The principle of *estoppel* is often used to impose liability on the principal in situations in which apparent authority might have been used. The technical distinction is that for the principal to be estopped from denying the agent's authority, the third party must have changed position in reliance on some representation by the principal. *See* Restatement, Second, Agency § 31.

Ratification may be inferred from "any act, words or conduct which reasonably tend to show intention to ratify." Meyers v. Cook, 87 W.Va. 265, 104 S.E. 593 (1920). It is probably enough in many instances that the incipient principal acquiesces in the transaction without raising objection to it. The ratifier's decision to accept the act need not be communicated. According to Professor Seavey, "Affirmance does not require a manifestation of consent to the agent, to the other party or any one." William Seavey, Handbook of the Law of Agency 67 (1964).

A hypothetical may help illustrate these concepts. Suppose that Priscilla Principal, a horse breeder, says to her employee, Andrew Agent, "Andy, please go down to the stables, put up a sign, "HORSES FOR SALE," and sell all of my horses for $500 apiece." Andrew has *express authority* to sell the horses. He also probably has *implied authority* to accept an apparently valid check in payment since, as long as Priscilla had not previously demanded cash in such transactions, it is reasonable to assume that she intended that Andrew accept checks. He may or may not have implied authority to accept a used car or a hogshead of tobacco worth $500, depending on what would be reasonably understood from the circumstances (such as the normal practices in the trade or in the locality) and from the prior dealings between him and Priscilla.

Suppose, now that Priscilla gives him the same instructions but adds, "except Secretariat. Whatever you do, don't sell Secretariat." She also sends out letters to prospective buyers saying, "I am selling off my horses. If you are interested, please see Andrew Agent at the stables. He is authorized to act for me." If Andrew sells Secretariat to a recipient of the letter, Priscilla may not recover the horse. By communicating what would appear to a reasonable person to be an intention to give Andrew the authority to sell Secretariat, she has clothed him with *apparent authority* and is bound by his act, even though it was directly contrary to her instructions.

Now suppose that Priscilla has delegated the management of her horse farm to Andrew, who regularly buys and sells horses according to his own judgment. Under these circumstances, if he sells Secretariat to a stranger who has not received Priscilla's letter (and who thus has no basis for believing in Andrew's apparent authority), the sale is binding on Priscilla by virtue of Andrew's *inherent agency power*.

Another view of this situation is that Andrew has apparent authority by virtue of his position. If it is assumed that Andrew is a general agent with broad customary authority to sell any horse on the farm, the third person has a basis for believing in Andrew's authority and the letter does not add anything.

Finally, suppose that Andrew has never before sold any horses for Priscilla (and thus has no inherent power), but he nevertheless purports to sell Secretariat to the stranger. When Priscilla learns of the sale, she declares, "Well I guess that's okay. Five hundred dollars is a pretty good price for that nag anyway." She has *ratified* the transaction and becomes bound as if Andrew had been authorized to accomplish it in the first place. Indeed, she ratifies the transaction even if she says nothing but takes no steps to rescind it.

2. SPECIAL PROBLEMS OF AGENCY IN A CORPORATE CONTEXT: THE INHERENT AUTHORITY OF OFFICERS

PROBLEM
AGENCY RELATIONS—PART I

In order to test your understanding of agency concepts, consider on what basis, if any, the principal would be bound if the parties executed a contract in the following circumstances:

1. The board of directors of Precision Tools Corporation passes a resolution directing Michael Lane, the president of the corporation, to contract for the construction of a new building.

2. Jessica Green, the vice president of PTC, purchases $1000 worth of equipment. She frequently purchases materials used in PTC's operations, but the board has never explicitly authorized her to do so.

3. Will Wright is a foreman in the plant. He has been instructed not to purchase any machinery or equipment without first asking Michael or Jessica, and he has never done so. One day while Michael and Jessica are away at a business conference, a representative of a wholesale machinery dealer visits the plant and tells Wright that he has a temporary oversupply which he is willing to sell at a substantial discount. Wright signs a purchase order for $1000 of equipment.

4. Wright goes to an auto dealer (who has never seen him before) and signs a contract to purchase a new pickup truck for Precision Tools. He signs, "Precision Tools Corp., by Will Wright." When he tells Michael what he has done, Michael responds, "You shouldn't really have done that without asking us, Will. But I guess you're right, we do need the truck." They accept delivery without protest.

AGENCY RELATIONS—PART II

Harold Hawks entered into a contract a little over a year ago with Acoustics Incorporated, a small manufacturer of high fidelity speakers, under the terms of which he was to become the exclusive regional distributor for Acoustics' products for a period of three years. The contract provided that Hawks was to purchase speakers from the corporation at its listed wholesale prices and resell them to his customers at a 15% markup. It also contained the somewhat unusual provision that if Hawks' purchases in any given year exceeded $500,000, he would be paid a "commission" at the end of the year of 2% of *all* his purchases.

Hawks negotiated the contract with Acoustics' president, James Huston, whose signature appeared at the bottom of the document thus:

Acoustics, Incorporated

By /s/ James Huston

James Huston, President

A few months after the contract was signed there was a management shakeup at Acoustics and Huston was dismissed.

During the first year of the contract, Hawks purchased $650,000 worth of speakers from the firm. He wrote the new president, Margo Pickford, asking for his 2% commission. Her letter of response said that she knew nothing of the contract and denied any liability under it. Furthermore, she said, while Acoustics would be happy to continue with Hawks as a distributor, it did not consider the arrangement exclusive, and was in fact in the process of working out an arrangement with another distributor in the same region.

There was a second exchange of correspondence, in which Hawks sent Pickford a copy of the contract, and she wrote back that even if Huston had signed it, he had not been authorized to do so.

1. You have been retained to advise Hawks as to his legal rights. You are considering whether to file a breach of contract action. On what theories might you proceed? What additional information would you like to have? How would you get it?

2. You represent the corporation in an action brought by Hawks. Would you advise settling the claim?

AGENCY RELATIONS—PART III

You represent the Third National Bank and Trust Company which is about to loan a substantial amount of money to Universal Widgets, Inc., a wholly owned subsidiary of Universal Inc. The loan is to be secured by a mortgage on Universal Widgets' plant, and, because Universal Widgets is a relatively new company with a short operating history, the bank has also insisted on a guarantee executed by the parent corporation. You have been asked by the bank to handle the closing of the deal, at which you will be asked to provide an opinion that the mortgage, note, and guarantees are "valid, binding, and enforceable in accordance with their terms."

What documents must Universal and Universal Widgets present at the closing in order for you to opine that each will be bound by the mortgage, note and guarantee?

———

Some uncertainty exists as to the nature and extent of the authority possessed by corporate officers. The officer with the greatest authority—the senior officer in any given corporation—generally is designated the chief executive officer or *CEO*. At one time, a corporation's president usually was the CEO. More recently, though, titles have become less uniform. In some companies, the president still is the CEO. In others, especially large corporations, the CEO is likely to hold no other title beside chair of the board (unless someone other than the CEO chairs board meetings). In many smaller companies, the CEO has the title of general manager.

In addition to the CEO, corporations generally have a chief financial officer, or *CFO*, who sometimes holds the title of treasurer. The same person can be the CEO and the CFO and, in the case of small companies, often is. A corporation also usually is required to charge one officer with responsibility for preparing minutes of directors' and shareholders' meetings and authenticating the corporation's books and records. See RMBCA § 8.40(c). That person often has the title of secretary.

Corporations, especially large firms, usually have a number of other officers. In recent years, titles have proliferated, although not to the same extent as in government. We are not aware of any corporate official holding a title equivalent to Deputy Assistant to the Special Assistant to the Deputy Assistant Undersecretary for [Whatever]. However, corporate titles such as "Senior Executive Vice–President" or "Chief Operating Officer and Member of the Office of the President" are far from uncommon.

Courts often have been less than meticulous in specifying the agency theory on which they were relying to hold a corporation liable as a consequence of the act of some officer holding one of these or some other title. In some given situation, an officer might be held to possess express authority as a consequence of the board of directors having appointed that person to a particular corporate office. Alternatively, a court could find the officer to have apparent authority, i.e., the power that a reasonable person dealing with the corporation would believe that officer to possess. Or, authority could be held to arise by implication, as a consequence of prior dealings between an officer and a third party that the board never sought to challenge.

Driven by pragmatic concerns, courts have developed rules of thumb designed to facilitate dealings between third parties and corporations. The court observed in Moyse Real Estate Co. v. First National Bank of Commerce, 110 Miss. 620, 70 So. 821 (1916):

> Nearly all of the big business and a large part of the small business is now conducted by corporations, and if it be the law that persons dealing with the president of a corporation about matters of business clearly within the powers of the corporation to transact must deal at arm's length, and demand that the president exhibit his credentials before entering into contracts with him, it seems to us that not only the corporation, but also those dealing with corporations, will be seriously hampered. * * *

> If it be true that the president did not possess the authority assumed by him in the present case, the proof of his lack of authority was in the possession of the corporation, and there would have been no difficulty in the way of its production. On the other hand, it might be very difficult and expensive for the plaintiff to have secured the evidence to show his authority.

Since some corporeal person must carry on the corporation's business, courts assume that the CEO, whether known as the president or by some other title, has authority to bind the corporation in transactions entered into in the ordinary course of business. However, that authority does not extend to "extraordinary" transactions, which must be approved by the board of directors. *See* Lee v. Jenkins Brothers, infra.

Generalization is more difficult with respect to subordinate officers. Their authority depends on the how a board or CEO has elected to delegate responsibility within the company's management structure; it cannot be inferred from some inherent characteristic of the corporate governance system. Thus, any given case is likely to turn on a court's assessment of the facts and circumstances of the transaction at issue. A third party who deals with a corporation's subordinate officers generally bears the burden of demonstrating that an act was within the officer's authority. Moreover, courts require a third party who knows that a given transaction will benefit some officer personally to inquire in greater depth as to whether the officer has valid authority to enter into the transaction at issue. In Branding Iron Motel, Inc. v. Sandlian Equity, Inc., 798 F.2d 396 (10th Cir.1986), the court held that a lender could not rely on what would otherwise be adequate evidence that a motel president had apparent authority to enter into a mortgage, where the lender knew the president was the ultimate beneficiary of the mortgage. In Schmidt v. Farm Credit Services, 977 F.2d 511 (10th Cir.1992), the court held that a lender could not rely on a board resolution authorizing the president to sign a loan agreement, but had to make further inquiries, where the lender knew the president would benefit personally from the loan. See, also, Squaw Mountain Cattle Co. v. Bowen, 804 P.2d 1292 (Wyo.1991) (president held not to have authority to agree to settlement that provided him with large personal monetary benefit.)

LEE v. JENKINS BROTHERS
268 F.2d 357 (2d Cir.1959), cert. denied 361 U.S. 913, 80 S.Ct. 257, 4 L.Ed.2d 183 (1959).

[Lee sued Jenkins Brothers, a corporation, to recover pension payments allegedly due him under an oral contract made in 1920 on behalf of the corporation by Yardley. The Court of Appeals affirmed the District Court's dismissal of the case, ruling that Lee had not produced sufficient evidence of the alleged agreement to present a jury question. The court went on to discuss whether there was evidence sufficient to present a jury question as to whether Yardley had apparent authority to bind the corporation to the alleged agreement assuming, *arguendo*, a finding that there was an agreement.]

MEDINA, J.:

Our question on this phase of the case then boils itself down to the following: can it be said as a matter of law that Yardley as president, chairman of the board, substantial stockholder and trustee and son-in-law of the estate of the major stockholder, had no power in the presence of the company's most interested vice president to secure for a "reasonable" length of time badly needed key personnel by promising an experienced local executive a life pension to commence in 30 years at the age of 60, even if Lee were not then working for the corporation, when the maximum liability to Jenkins under such a pension was $1500 per year.

A survey of the law on the authority of corporate officers does not reveal a completely consistent pattern. For the most part the courts perhaps have taken a rather restrictive view on the extent of powers of corporate officials, but the dissatisfaction with such an approach has been manifested in a variety of exceptions such as ratification, estoppel, and promissory estoppel. For the most part also there has been limited discussion of the problem of apparent authority, perhaps on the assumption that if authority could not be implied from a continuing course of action between the corporation and the officer, it could not have been apparent to third parties either.

Such an assumption is ill-founded. The circumstances and facts known to exist between officer and corporation, from which actual authority may be implied, may be entirely different from those circumstances known to exist as between the third party and the corporation. The two concepts are separate and distinct even though the state of the proofs in a given case may cause considerable overlap.

The rule most widely cited is that the president only has authority to bind his company by acts arising in the usual and regular course of business but not for contracts of an "extraordinary" nature. The substance of such a rule lies in the content of the term "extraordinary" which is subject to a broad range of interpretation.

The growth and development of this rule occurred during the late nineteenth and early twentieth centuries when the potentialities of the corporate form of enterprise were just being realized. As the corporation became a more common vehicle for the conduct of business it became increasingly evident that many corporations, particularly small closely held ones, did not normally function in the formal ritualistic manner hitherto envisaged. While the boards of directors still nominally controlled corporate affairs, in reality officers and managers frequently ran the business with little, if any, board supervision. The natural consequence of such a development was that third parties commonly relied on the authority of such officials in almost all the multifarious transactions in which corporations engaged. The pace of modern business life was too swift to insist on the approval by the board of directors of every transaction that was in any way "unusual."

The judicial recognition given to these developments has varied considerably. Whether termed "apparent authority" or an "estoppel" to deny authority, many courts have noted the injustice caused by the practice of permitting corporations to act commonly through their executives and then allowing them to disclaim an agreement as beyond the authority of the contracting officer, when the contract no longer suited its convenience. Other courts, however, continued to cling to the past with little attempt to discuss the unconscionable results obtained or the doctrine of apparent authority. Such restrictive views have been generally condemned by the commentators.

The summary of holdings pro and con in general on the subject of what are and what are not "extraordinary" agreements is inconclusive at best * * *. But the pattern becomes more distinct when we turn to the more limited area of employment contracts.

It is generally settled that the president as part of the regular course of business has authority to hire and discharge employees and fix their compensation. In so doing he may agree to hire them for a specific number of years if the term selected is deemed reasonable. But employment contracts for life or on a "permanent" basis are generally regarded as "extraordinary" and beyond the authority of any corporate executive if the only consideration for the promise is the employee's promise to work for that period. Jenkins would have us analogize the pension agreement involved herein to these generally condemned lifetime employment contracts because it extends over a long period of time, is of indefinite duration, and involves an indefinite liability on the part of the corporation.

It is not surprising that lifetime employment contracts have met with substantial hostility in the courts, for these contracts are often oral, uncorroborated, vague in important details and highly improbable. * * *

However, at times such contracts have been enforced where the circumstances tended to support the plausibility of plaintiff's testimony. Thus when the plaintiff was injured in the course of employment and he agreed to settle his claim of negligence against the company for a lifetime job, authority has been generally found and the barrage of other objections adequately disposed of. And where additional consideration was given such as quitting other employment, giving up a competing business, or where the services were "peculiarly necessary" to the corporation, the courts have divided on the enforceability of the contract.

What makes the point now under discussion particularly interesting is the failure of the courts denying authority to make lifetime contracts to evolve any guiding principle. More often than not we find a mere statement that the contract is "extraordinary" with a citation of cases which say the same thing, without giving reasons. * * *

Where reasons have been given to support the conclusion that lifetime employments are "extraordinary," and hence made without authority, a scrutiny of these reasons may be helpful for their bearing on the analogous field of pension agreements. It is said that: they unduly restrict the power of the shareholders and future boards of directors on questions of managerial policy; they subject the corporation to an inordinately substantial amount of liability; they run for long and indefinite periods of time. Of these reasons the only one applicable to pension agreements is that they run for long and indefinite periods of time. There the likeness stops. Future director or shareholder control is in no way impeded; the amount of liability is not disproportionate; the agreement was not only not unreasonable but beneficial and necessary to the corporation; and pension contracts are commonly used fringe benefits in employment contracts. Moreover, unlike the case with life employment contracts, courts have often gone out of their way to find pension promises binding and definite even when labeled gratuitous by the employer. The consideration given to the employee involved is not at all dependent on profits or sales, nor does it involve some other variable suggesting director discretion.

Apparent authority is essentially a question of fact. It depends not only on the nature of the contract involved, but the officer negotiating it, the corporation's usual manner of conducting business, the size of the corporation and the number of its stockholders, the circumstances that give rise to the contract, the reasonableness of the contract, the amounts involved, and who the contracting third party is, to list a few but not all of the relevant factors. In certain instances a given contract may be so important to the welfare of the corporation that outsiders would naturally suppose that only the board of directors (or even the shareholders) could properly handle it. It is in this light that the "ordinary course of business" rule should be given its content. Beyond such "extraordinary" acts, whether or not apparent authority exists is simply a matter of fact.

Accordingly, we hold that, assuming there was sufficient proof of the making of the pension agreement, Connecticut, in the particular circumstances of this case, would probably take the view that reasonable men could differ on the subject of whether or not Yardley had apparent authority to make the contract, and that the trial court erred in deciding the question as a matter of law. We do not think Connecticut would adopt any hard and fast rule against apparent authority to make pension agreements generally, on the theory that they were in the same category as lifetime employment contracts. * * *

In Joseph Greenspon's Sons Iron & Steel Co. v. Pecos Valley Gas Co., 34 Del. 567, 156 A. 350 (1931), the president of a gas company signed a contract to purchase 45 miles of gas pipe for approximately $145,000 without having obtained express authority from the gas company's board of directors. The court charged the jury that the president had implied authority to enter into contracts in the usual course of the corporation's business and stated that it was for the jury to decide whether the pipe order was such a contract.

The court also noted that a corporation's president could have the power to enter into a contract not in the ordinary course of business as a consequence of (1) some provision of statutory law, (2) the articles of incorporation, (3) a bylaw of the company, (4) a resolution of the board of directors, or (5) evidence that the corporation had allowed the president to act in similar matters and had recognized, approved and ratified the president's actions.

In Scientific Holding Co., Ltd. v. Plessey Inc., 510 F.2d 15 (2d Cir.1974), a contract for Plessey to purchase International Scientific Ltd. (ISL), a predecessor to Scientific, was amended at the closing, when it became clear that ISL could not to satisfy a financial condition to the purchase agreement. Kovar, ISL's president and chief operating officer, expressed concern about whether he was authorized to sign the amendment, but eventually agreed to do so. Several months later, Plessey sought to enforce the amendment. Scientific then attempted to repudiate it.

The court said that whether Kovar had authority to sign to the amendment was unclear. However, it ruled, even assuming Kovar lacked such authority, "Scientific's failure to repudiate the amendment for lack of authorization [from March] until mid-July estopped it from doing so later." Plessey prevailed.

FIRST INTERSTATE BANK OF TEXAS v. FIRST NATIONAL BANK OF JEFFERSON
928 F.2d 153 (5th Cir.1991).

[In February 1982, New Orleans Property Development (NOPD) asked First National Bank of Jefferson (FNJ) to purchase $3 million in industrial revenue bonds. FNJ obtained a commitment from First Interstate to purchase $1 million of the bonds, then agreed to buy the entire $3 million. First Interstate and FNJ subsequently reached an oral agreement that First Interstate would purchase $2 million of the bonds if FNJ committed to repurchase those bonds on demand. Attorneys for the banks then prepared a draft Bond Purchase Agreement (BPA) and sent a copy to FNJ Senior Vice President John Boyd. Boyd discussed the BPA with FNJ President Arceneaux, who left Boyd with the impression that execution of the BPA was an "acceptable approach."

On July 29, 1982, First Interstate and FNJ purchased the NOPD bonds and executed the BPA. Boyd signed the BPA for FNJ.

In August 1988, First Interstate asked FNJ to repurchase its NOPD bonds pursuant to the BPA. FNJ refused, asserting that Boyd had not been authorized to sign the BPA. At the trial of First Interstate's suit to enforce the BPA, the district court held that First Interstate had not produced sufficient evidence to present a jury question as to whether Boyd had authority to sign the BPA and directed a verdict in favor of FNJ.]

W. Eugene Davis, Circuit Judge:

First Interstate argues that the district court erroneously directed a verdict for FNJ on the issue of Boyd's authority. * * * Our review of the record persuades us that reasonable, fair-minded jurors could reach different conclusions about whether Boyd had actual or apparent authority to bind FNJ.

The parties agree that Louisiana law governs our analysis. Louisiana agency law recognizes two types of authority, actual and apparent. We begin with a discussion of actual authority.

A.

Actual authority can be express or implied. The district court held that a jury was not entitled to find that Boyd had express actual authority to execute the BPA because no corporate resolution or by-law specifically authorized the transaction. A principal, however, can confer actual authority orally. The following testimony could convince a jury that FNJ likely gave Boyd express actual authority to sign the BPA.

Boyd testified that FNJ authorized him to sign the BPA. Boyd said that he discussed the NOPD transaction, including the BPA, with Arceneaux and other FNJ officers. Arceneaux denied having such discussions. The district court weighed Boyd's testimony, but "considered [it] very weak." Given the corroborating evidence, we are persuaded that it was sufficiently strong for a reasonable jury to credit it.

Boyd's position in the FNJ hierarchy lends credence to his assertion that the bank authorized him to sign the BPA. Boyd was one of only four FNJ senior vice presidents, an office of considerable responsibility. He was hired by and reported directly to President Arceneaux. Not only did Boyd handle loans himself, [including the NOPD loan,] he also supervised several FNJ vice presidents. * * * A juror could surmise that a person who held the position of senior vice president, who was responsible for handling the NOPD loan account, and who supervised other loan officers was the type officer FNJ would have authorized to sign the inter-bank agreement at issue here. * * *

The record demonstrates that the BPA did not obligate FNJ any further than its March 12 commitment letter to NOPD. On that date, FNJ committed to buy the entire $3 million bond issue. President Arceneaux conceded that the letter bound FNJ to take the entire issue. The commitment letter does not condition the bond purchase on FNJ's ability to find a co-lender. Thus, the July 29 BPA did not extend FNJ's obligation on the bonds beyond its March 12 commitment. Both agreements made FNJ the principal lender on a $3 million loan. The fact that the BPA did not expand FNJ's exposure supports Boyd's assertion that FNJ authorized him to sign the BPA.

In sum, we conclude that the evidence presented a jury question whether FNJ gave Boyd express actual authority to execute the BPA.

B.

We now turn briefly to the issue of implied actual authority. " 'Implied authority' is actual authority which is inferred from the circumstances and nature of the agency. An agent is vested with the implied authority to do all of those things necessary or incidental to the agency assignment." Demolle v. Horace Mann Ins. Co., 491 So.2d 695, 698 (La.Ct.App. 5th Cir.), writ denied, 496 So.2d 1041 (La.1986). "Implied authority connotes permission from the principal for the agent to act, though that permission is not expressly set forth orally or in writing." AAA Tire & Export, Inc. v. Big Chief Truck Lines, 385 So.2d 426, 429 (La.Ct.App. 1st Cir.1980).

First Interstate argues that a juror might infer from the nature of the bank's business and Boyd's position in that business that Boyd had implied actual authority to sign the BPA. [However, Article 2997 of the Louisiana Civil Code, which provides that the power of an agent to sell, to buy, to contract a loan or to acknowledge a debt must be express, defeats this argument.] * * * The district court correctly declined to submit this theory to the jury. We turn finally to First Interstate's apparent authority argument.

C.

A corporation will be liable to a third party even for the unauthorized acts of its agent under the doctrine of apparent authority if (1) the corporation manifests the agent's authority to the third party, and (2) the third party reasonably relies on the agent's purported authority as a result of the manifestation. We conclude that First Interstate also introduced sufficient evidence to create a jury question on Boyd's apparent authority to bind FNJ.

When FNJ hired Boyd as a senior vice president, it manifested to the public that Boyd had the authority to bind the bank in agreements necessary to conduct the bank's business. See Cook v. Ruston Oil Mills & Fertilizer, 170 La. 10, 127 So. 347, 353 (1930) ("[T]he corporation, by the very fact of the appointment of such manager, holds him out to the public as the person authorized to bind it by contracts necessary in the prosecution of its business."). On the day of the NOPD closing, FNJ specifically manifested to First Interstate that Boyd was authorized to execute the necessary closing papers on behalf of FNJ. FNJ sent Boyd and one of its trust officers to the closing with a certification that Boyd was its senior vice-president and that he was acting on behalf of FNJ's Board of Directors. The BPA was signed by the parties at the closing. The jury was entitled to conclude that when FNJ sent Boyd to the closing with a certificate of his authority, the bank was also manifesting Boyd's authority to sign the BPA, without which First Interstate would not have agreed to buy the NOPD bonds.

FNJ also implicitly manifested Boyd's authority when its president, Arceneaux, sent Boyd to consummate a deal that Arceneaux himself helped negotiate. LaRue, the loan officer representing First Interstate in the NOPD transaction, testified that he spoke to Arceneaux about the deal. LaRue said that he and Ken Anderson, First Interstate's executive vice president, agreed with Arceneaux in a telephone conversation that First Interstate would buy $2 million in bonds if FNJ acquiesced in a buy-out provision. If a jury accepts this testimony, it could conclude that Arceneaux's conversation with Anderson and LaRue was a specific manifestation of FNJ's willingness to commit to the BPA. The jury could also view this evidence as a manifestation by FNJ that Boyd, the

FNJ senior vice president in charge of this transaction, was authorized to sign the BPA. * * *

FNJ argues that the doctrine of apparent authority does not apply in this case because First Interstate did not inquire into the extent of Boyd's authority. * * * We disagree. A third party can rely on the apparent authority of an agent until something occurs that would cause a reasonable person to inquire further into the circumstances. The cases cited by FNJ in which courts found a duty to inquire are distinguishable. In those cases, the agent was either not an officer or even an employee of the purported principal; thus, a reasonable person would have inquired about the agent's authority.

A jury could conclude that First Interstate need not have made further inquiry. * * * Because a reasonable jury could conclude that Boyd had apparent authority to bind FNJ on the BPA, a directed verdict was inappropriate. * * *

Affirmed in part, Reversed in part, and Remanded.

3. THE CREATION OF EXPRESS AUTHORITY

Given the existence of questions as to the authority of corporate officers, including the CEO, careful counsel representing a party involved in a major transaction with a corporation usually will insist on receiving adequate evidence that the individuals who purport to act for the corporation are authorized to do so.

In essence, what is required is evidence that the board of directors has delegated authority to the officer to act on behalf of the corporation. The best evidence of a board decision is a copy of the minutes of the board of directors' meeting at which the resolution formalizing the decision was adopted. The resolution, in addition to approving the transaction in question, should designate the CEO or some other officer to execute the documents and do the other acts necessary to consummate the transaction. In the case of a particularly significant transaction, the minutes might include, as an attachment, a copy of the contract that the board has authorized the officer to sign.

Somewhat less important transactions may be covered by more general delegations of authority. For example, a board might authorize the CEO or some other officer to enter into contracts of a certain type or up to a certain value. If a party to a transaction with the corporation has doubts as to the authority of the official with whom she is dealing, she can request a copy of the resolution delegating such authority and the minutes of the board meeting at which the resolution was adopted.

But a question remains: how can a third party be sure the minutes and resolution are genuine? Customary practice is to have the secretary of the corporation (or other officer charged with maintaining the corporation's books and records) certify the minutes and resolution. The secretary has been held to have express authority to certify such documents, so that a corporation is bound by the secretary's certification.

This allows inquiry into an officer's authority to enter into a contract to stop short of requiring a majority of the directors to swear in person that, yes, they did vote to authorize the officer to act. See In the Matter of Drive–In Development Corp., 371 F.2d 215 (7th Cir.1966), cert. denied 387 U.S. 909, 87 S.Ct. 1691, 18 L.Ed.2d 626 (1967). It is also why some statutes do not permit the same person to be both president and secretary.

C. FORMALITIES OF ACTION BY THE BOARD OF DIRECTORS

PROBLEM
WIDGET CORPORATION

You are counsel to the Widget Corporation, which is incorporated in a jurisdiction that has adopted the RMBCA, and which has articles and bylaws similar to the Model Articles of Incorporation and Model Bylaws in West Publishing Company's Selected Corporation and Partnership Statutes, Rules and Forms. Article III, Section 2 of Widget's bylaws provides for an eight-member board of directors. Widget's president advises you that she has just negotiated a sale of one of the corporation's plants on advantageous terms that will provide desperately needed working capital for the corporation. The sale agreement requires board authorization; the president hopes to close the sale and receive the proceeds within 36 hours. One of Widget's directors is in a local hospital for minor surgery, one is in London on business, one is mountain climbing in Nepal, and one is sailing in the Caribbean.

1. Would a unanimous vote by the four available directors at a special meeting of the board be effective? Consider RMBCA §§ 8.20, 8.22, 8.23, and 8.24 [DGCL § 141] and Article III of the Model Bylaws.

2. Suppose the president visits the ailing board member in the hospital, explains the sale fully, and has him execute a proxy authorizing the president to cast the director's vote in favor of the sale at the board meeting. The transaction subsequently receives the unanimous vote of the four available directors at a special meeting. Is this valid board action?

3. What other alternatives are available for the board to authorize the sale? Consider RMBCA §§ 8.20, 8.21 and 8.23 [DGCL § 141] and Article III of the Model By-laws.

4. How could the articles of incorporation and by-laws be modified to deal with some future crisis where it is not possible to assemble a majority of directors at a board meeting? Consider RMBCA §§ 8.22, 8.24 and 8.25 [DGCL § 141].

1. ACTION BY THE BOARD AT A MEETING

The board of directors traditionally takes formal action by vote at a meeting. Each director has one vote and may not vote by proxy.

Lippman v. Kehoe Stenograph Co., 11 Del.Ch. 80, 95 A. 895 (1915). Unless the articles or by-laws provide otherwise, the vote of a majority of the directors present at a board meeting at which there is a quorum is necessary to pass a resolution. See RMBCA § 8.24(c).

One reason for the requirement that the board come together at a meeting to act is the view that the board is a collegial body. By consulting together, board members may draw on each other's knowledge and experience. More ideas and points of view are likely to be considered in the formulation of decisions, which may produce better results than if the directors act without consultation.

On a less pragmatic level, the directors have authority to act only as a body, not as individuals. In Baldwin v. Canfield, 26 Minn. 43, 1 N.W. 261 (1879), which involved the validity of a deed that all of a corporation's directors signed but that the board never approved at a meeting, the court stated:

> As we have already seen, the court below finds that, by its articles of incorporation, the government of the [corporation], and the management of its affairs, was vested in the board of directors. The legal effect of this was to invest the directors with such government and management *as a board,* and not otherwise. This is in accordance with the general rule that the governing body of a corporation, as such, are agents of the corporation only as a board, and not individually. Hence it follows that they have no authority to act, save when assembled at a board meeting. The separate action, individually, of the persons comprising such governing body, is not the action of the constituted body of men clothed with the corporate powers.

Courts have refused to uphold informal action by directors without a meeting when the board's alleged authority to bind the corporation was challenged by the corporation (Peirce v. Morse–Oliver Bldg. Co., 94 Me. 406, 47 A. 914 (1900)), the directors of the corporation (Schuckman v. Rubenstein, 164 F.2d 952 (6th Cir.1947), cert. denied 333 U.S. 875, 68 S.Ct. 905, 92 L.Ed. 1151 (1948)), the corporation's trustee in bankruptcy (Hurley v. Ornsteen, 311 Mass. 477, 42 N.E.2d 273 (1942)), or pledgees of the corporation's stock (Baldwin v. Canfield, 26 Minn. 43, 1 N.W. 261 (1879)). Although courts frequently fail to articulate their reasons for requiring formal board action, "underlying most all of the decisions * * * is a single policy: to protect shareholders and their investment from arbitrary, irresponsible or unwise acts on the part of the directors. When presented with informal director action, the courts will decline to apply the general rule when the shareholders, by their actions, indicate that they do not wish the protection or when such application will not afford them any greater protection." Note, Corporations: When Informal Action by Corporate Directors Will Be Permitted to Bind the Corporation, 53 Boston U.L.Rev. 101 (1973).

Courts nonetheless are not blind to the fact that informal board action, particularly in close corporations, is extremely common. This reality has led courts to seek to protect innocent third parties from the strict application of the traditional rule permitting board action only at a meeting. Thus, courts have relied on numerous justifications to hold corporations liable on agreements never approved at formal board meetings.

a. *Unanimous Informal Agreement by the Directors.* In Gerard v. Empire Square Realty Co., 195 App.Div. 244, 249, 187 N.Y.S. 306, 310 (1921) the court noted, "if all the directors are of one mind * * * discussion is futile * * *." In all probability there will be no discussion at all; the directors, being in agreement, will simply act, and, as a result, there will be no opportunity to further the corporate purpose.

b. *Emergency.* Situations arise where the board must make very quick decisions to prevent great harm or to take advantage of great opportunity. In such a situation, it may be impossible to assemble the board at a meeting. The corporation must proceed on the opinions of those directors who can be contacted in whatever manner contact may be made.

c. *Representation of the Interests of All Shareholders.* A conclusion reached at a meeting at which all the shareholders of the corporation are present will likely bind the corporation. See e.g., Brainard v. De La Montanya, 18 Cal.2d 502, 116 P.2d 66 (1941); In re Kartub, 7 Misc.2d 72, 152 N.Y.S.2d 34 (1956), aff'd 3 A.D.2d 896, 163 N.Y.S.2d 938 (1957). Courts have also held the corporation bound if the directors who participate in the informal action constitute a majority of the board and own a majority of the corporation's issued and outstanding shares. See e.g., Air Technical Development Co. v. Arizona Bank, 101 Ariz. 70, 416 P.2d 183 (1966); Phillips Petroleum Co. v. Rock Creek Mining Co., 449 F.2d 664 (9th Cir.1971).

To buttress these common law exceptions to the general rule, a majority of states have enacted statutory provisions allowing informal director action under some conditions. RMBCA § 8.21, for example, allows action to be taken without a meeting on the unanimous written consent of the directors. The Official Comment notes, "Under section 8.21 the requirement of unanimous consent precludes the possibility of stifling or ignoring opposing argument. A director opposed to an action that is proposed to be taken by unanimous consent, or uncertain about the desirability of that action, may compel the holding of a directors' meeting to discuss the matter simply by withholding his consent." RMBCA § 8.20(b) permits board action to be taken by a conference telephone call. The Official Comment to RMBCA § 8.20 notes: "The advantage of the traditional meeting is the opportunity for interchange that is permitted by a meeting in a single room at which members are physically present. If this opportunity for interchange is thought to be available by the board of directors, a meeting may be conducted by electronic means although no two directors are physically present at the same place * * *."

However, modern statutes also have led some courts to take a harder line towards corporations that disregard statutory requirements governing board actions. These courts reason that the more liberal statutory approaches to informal director action should pre-empt the common law doctrines described above. Village of Brown Deer v. Milwaukee, 16 Wis.2d 206, 114 N.W.2d 493 (1962), cert. denied 371 U.S. 902, 83 S.Ct. 205, 9 L.Ed.2d 164 (1962), involved a corporation whose president and majority shareholder had customarily made decisions without involving the board. The president signed a petition on behalf of the corporation for municipal annexation of land. The Wisconsin statute permitted a board to act by unanimous written consent without a meeting, but the president had not obtained the directors' consent. The court reasoned:

> * * * Corporations owe their existence to the statutes. Those who would enjoy the benefits that attend the corporate form of operation are obliged to conduct their affairs in accordance with the laws which authorized them. * * *

> The legislature having specified the means whereby corporations could function informally, it becomes incumbent upon the courts to enforce such legislative pronouncements. The legislature has said that the corporation could act informally, without a meeting, by obtaining the consent in writing of all of the Directors. In our opinion, this pronouncement has preempted the field and prohibits corporations from acting informally without complying with [the statute].

114 N.W.2d at 497.

2. NOTICE AND QUORUM

Notice and quorum requirements apply to board meetings. The notice requirement makes personal attendance at a meeting reasonably possible. Directors know when regularly scheduled board meetings will be held. RMBCA § 8.22(a) acknowledges this fact by permitting directors to waive notice of regular meetings unless a company's articles of incorporation or bylaws require that notice be given. For special meetings, RMBCA § 8.22(b) requires that two days' notice be given of the date, time and place of meeting, unless the articles of incorporation or bylaws impose different requirements. Many companies provide directors with notice of the purpose of all meetings, so that directors will be better prepared to discuss the matters that will be on the agenda. RMBCA § 8.22 does not require such notice, but permits it to be included in the articles of incorporation or bylaws. Action taken at a board meeting held without the required notice is invalid. See Schmidt v. Farm Credit Services, 977 F.2d 511 (10th Cir.1992).

Any director who does not receive proper notice may waive notice by signing a waiver before or after the meeting, RMBCA § 8.23(a), or by attending or participating in the meeting and not protesting the absence of notice. RMBCA § 8.23(b). However, a director who attends a meeting solely to protest the manner in which it was convened is not deemed to have waived notice. RMBCA § 8.23(b).

The quorum requirement helps preclude action by a minority of the directors. The statutory norm for a quorum is a majority of the total number of directors, although the articles of incorporation or bylaws may increase the quorum requirement or reduce it to no less than one-third of the board. RMBCA § 8.24. Action taken in the absence of a quorum is invalid. See Schoen v. Consumers United Group, 670 F.Supp. 367 (D.D.C. 1986).

3. COMMITTEES OF THE BOARD

Boards that have large numbers of members, such as the boards of many large, publicly-held companies, are unwieldy and often find it difficult, when acting as a whole, effectively to discharge all of their responsibilities. The trend in recent years toward increasing the proportion of outside directors has exacerbated this problem. Many companies have responded by delegating responsibility for many board functions to committees empowered to exercise, in defined areas, the authority of the board. See generally John A. McMullen, Committees of the Board of Directors, 29 Bus.Law. 755 (1974). This practice now is authorized explicitly in nearly every state. See RMBCA § 8.25.

The executive committee is a common board committee because it can have the full authority of the board in all but a few essential transactions such as the declaration of a dividend or approval of a merger. See RMBCA § 8.25 (e). Thus the executive committee often is the vehicle through which the board acts between meetings on less important matters of corporate housekeeping which, for technical reasons, require board approval.

The audit committee is another common board committee, particularly in publicly-held corporations. Its functions usually include selection of the company's auditors, specification of the scope of the audit, review of audit results, and oversight of internal accounting procedures. The "improper payments" scandals of the mid-'70s increased the visibility of audit committees. Following disclosure that many large companies had used millions of dollars to pay bribes and make unlawful political contributions, the New York Stock Exchange began to require publicly-held companies to have audit committees.

Other relatively common committees include finance (usually responsible for giving advice on financial structure, the issuance of new securities, and the management of the corporation's investments), nomination (responsible for nominating new directors and officers), and compensation (responsible for fixing the salaries and other compensation of executives). Boards often create specialized committees to deal with specific problems. See Chapter 20 for a discussion of special litigation committees in connection with derivative suits.

A board committee can be permanent or temporary. Its functions can be active—making decisions on behalf of the board—or passive—

doing research and presenting information so the full board can make more informed decisions. Case law and statutes increasingly reflect the view that committees are desirable because directors who are committee members have more incentive to develop expertise in the area of the committee's responsibility. RMBCA § 8.30(b) recognizes the expanding use of committees and permits a director to rely on the reports or actions of a committee on which she does not serve, so long as the committee reasonably merits her confidence.

D. ACTION BY SHAREHOLDERS

1. INTRODUCTION

Shareholders meet at a regularly-scheduled annual meeting, and also may meet at special meetings convened for particular purposes. Unless a corporation's articles of incorporation provide otherwise, each share is entitled to one vote.

Election of directors is the most important item of business at the annual meeting. Shareholders elect directors annually unless the articles of incorporation provide for staggered terms, in which event shareholders elect directors for terms of two or three years. RMBCA §§ 8.05, 8.06. The shareholders' power to elect directors is exclusive, except when a board seat is vacant in which case, unless the articles provide otherwise, either shareholders or the remaining directors can fill the vacancy. RMBCA § 8.10.

No matter other than the election of directors is required to be considered at an annual meeting. However, boards of directors often seek shareholder approval of other matters, such as the appointment of auditors, the adoption of management compensation plans, or the ratification of decisions that a board has made.

Most modern statutes also permit shareholders to act by means of written consent in lieu of a meeting. Under RMBCA § 7.04, action by written consent requires the approval of *all* the shareholders. This requirement effectively limits use of the consent procedure to closely held corporations. DGCL § 228 differs significantly; it allows holders of a *majority* of a company's voting stock to act by means of written consent. Consequently, shareholders holding a majority of the stock in a Delaware corporation can act without providing advance notice to the company's management or to other shareholders. As with most such statutory provisions, a company can include a provision in its articles of incorporation eliminating or restricting this power.

The general principle governing shareholder voting is that action taken by the "affirmative vote of the majority of shares present in person or represented by proxy at the meeting and entitled to vote on the subject matter shall be the act of the stockholders * * *." DGCL § 216. Most statutes require more than simple majority approval of certain transactions. See e.g. RMBCA § 11.03(e) (requiring majority of all shares entitled to vote to approve a merger). Statutes also generally allow a corporation to include in its articles of incorporation a provision requiring that a greater number of shares approve all shareholder actions or some particular actions.

Unlike directors, shareholders may vote by proxy. RMBCA § 7.22. A proxy is simply a limited form of agency power by which a shareholder authorizes another, who will be present at the meeting, to exercise the shareholder's voting rights. A proxy may give the proxy holder discretion to vote as she pleases or may direct her to vote in a particular way. In public corporations, management typically solicits from shareholders proxies authorizing one or more members of management to vote the shareholder's stock at the meeting. This proxy solicitation process is regulated primarily by the federal securities laws, a subject we consider in detail in Chapter 14.

2. SHAREHOLDERS' VETO AND EXIT RIGHTS

PROBLEM
LAFRANCE COSMETICS—PART I

LaFrance Cosmetics, Inc., a Columbia corporation, manufactures a line of cosmetics. Its articles of incorporation authorize two million shares of common stock, of which one million shares are issued and outstanding. Mimi LaFrance, who founded LaFrance and continues to chair the board, owns 400,000 shares. Her son, Pierre, the president and CEO, owns 100,000 shares, as does her daughter, Margaret, who is not otherwise involved in the business. The remaining 400,000 shares were bequeathed by Mimi's late husband, Maurice, to the Columbia Museum of Modern Art and are held in trust by the Third National Bank. The board of LaFrance consists of Mimi, Pierre, Margaret, Victor Gauguin, a retired businessman, and Lauren Miller, the senior vice-president responsible for the bank's trust department.

Pierre, with Mimi's support, has been seeking to expand LaFrance's business into related lines. He recently approached Sweet Violet, Inc. another Columbia corporation, about a business combination. Sweet Violet, which manufactures perfume and related toiletries, has about 250 shareholders, none of whom owns more than 10% of the 100,000 shares of Sweet Violet common stock currently outstanding. After extensive negotiations, Pierre and Sweet Violet's management agreed in principle on a transaction in which LaFrance would acquire Sweet Violet for 400,000 shares of LaFrance common stock.

Pierre then sought the LaFrance board of directors' approval of the proposed acquisition. Margaret objected strongly. In recent years, LaFrance has reinvested most of its income in an effort to become a more effective competitor of the large, publicly-held companies that dominate the cosmetics business. Margaret, dissatisfied with the relatively modest dividends LaFrance has been paying, has urged Pierre and Mimi to abandon this effort and sell LaFrance to one of those companies. She argued that the acquisition of Sweet Violet was inconsistent with her preferred strategy. LaFrance's other two directors, however, supported the proposed acquisition, Victor Gauguin strongly and Lauren Miller more moderately. Lauren also remarked that, while she favored the move, some other members of the Bank's investment committee had questioned whether this was a good time for LaFrance to expand. The LaFrance board then voted 4–1 to approve the proposed acquisition of Sweeet Violet for 400,000 shares of LaFrance stock.

As counsel to LaFrance, Pierre has asked you to advise him on how to structure the proposed acquisition of Sweet Violet. Pierre is concerned about the possibility that Margaret, and perhaps the Bank, will vote against the transaction and seek to obtain the fair value of their shares by exercising dissenters' rights. The latter possibility would be particularly troublesome, because LaFrance already is strapped for cash. Pierre's preference is to avoid a vote by LaFrance's shareholders and, in all events, to avoid giving those shareholders dissenters' rights. Pierre also has advised you that Sweet Violet's management is indifferent as to how the proposed transaction is structured, so long as Sweet Violet's shareholders end up with 400,000 shares of LaFrance stock.

The proposed acquisition could be structured as either (1) a statutory merger of Sweet Violet into LaFrance, (2) a "triangular" merger of Sweet Violet into a subsidiary of LaFrance, (3) a statutory share exchange, or (4) an exchange of LaFrance stock for Sweet Violet's assets, followed by the dissolution of Sweet Violet.

1. For each of these alternatives, determine:

(a) The applicable statutory requirements, including whether a vote by LaFrance's shareholders would be required (consider RMBCA §§ 11.01, 11.02, 11.03, 12.02, and 10.03);

(b) Whether LaFrance's shareholders would be entitled to dissenters' rights (consider RMBCA § 13.02);

(c) Whether Margaret is likely to succeed in a suit to block the transaction if LaFrance's shareholders are not given the right to vote or to assert dissenter's rights.

2. Would your answers to these questions differ if LaFrance was a Delaware corporation.

a. Background

As noted above, corporate statutes condition a board of directors' power to effectuate certain fundamental changes in a firm's form, scope or continuity of existence on the board's first obtaining shareholders' approval. Transactions subject to this requirement vary from state to state, but generally include most amendments to the articles of incorporation, significant mergers, the sale of all or substantially all of a corporation's assets, and dissolution. Shareholders' rights with respect to these matters can most accurately be described as *veto rights*, in that shareholders' authority is limited to blocking such changes by withholding their approval. Put differently, shareholders have no power to initiate fundamental changes.

It is important to note that the shareholders' veto power is limited to those fundamental changes prescribed in the statute. Many transaction which could be viewed as involving a fundamental change in the corporation's business, such as the acquisition of a new division for cash, do not require shareholder approval, notwithstanding the impact of such a transaction on the shareholders' investment.

At common law, one shareholder in a corporation could block all others from making any fundamental change in the corporation's business or charter, even a change as simple as extending the life of a corporation beyond its expiration date. See William J. Carney, Fundamental Corporate Changes, Minority Shareholders, and Business Purposes, 1980 Am. Bar. Foundation Rsch. J. 69, 77–82. This rule was based on the idea that the charter was was a contract, both among the corporations's shareholders and between the corporation and the state, in which every shareholder had vested rights. Id. at 78 & n. 32. Majority shareholders were powerless to overcome a dissenter's opposition, except by buying her out.

State legislatures began to recognize that the unanimous consent requirement created the potential for tyranny by the minority. Situations arose in which an entrepreneurial investor apparently purchased stock in a company after some fundamental change had been proposed in order to veto that change and thus force the majority to repurchase her shares at a premium. See, e.g., Windhurst v. Central Leather Co., 101 N.J.Eq. 543, 551–52, 138 A. 772, 776 (Ch. 1927), aff'd per curiam 107 N.J.Eq. 528, 153 A. 402 (1931) ("while I cannot say that Windhurst is a *professional* privateer,' * * * it would seem * * * that his venture was not entirely free of a piratical character.") Legislatures responded by amending corporation statutes to allow fundamental changes that were approved by a corporation's board of directors and a majority or supramajority of its shareholders. See, e.g., Act of May 27, 1896, ch. 932, §§ 57, 58, 1896 N.Y. Laws 994 (voluntary dissolution and merger).

Concurrent with this weakening of minority shareholders' voice, legislatures granted shareholders a right, in effect, to "opt out" of a transaction involving a fundamental change in which their vote was required. A shareholder can dissent from the transaction and require the corporation to pay her in cash the value of her shares as determined by a court in an appraisal proceeding, if the transaction nonetheless is supported by the requisite majority of the corporation's shareholders. See, e.g., RMBCA § 13.02. In Chicago Corp. v. Munds, 20 Del.Ch. 142, 149, 172 A. 452, 455 (1934), a Delaware court described this development as follows:

> At common law it was in the power of any single stockholder to prevent a merger. When the idea became generally accepted that, in the interest of adjusting corporate mechanisms to the requirements of business and commercial growth, mergers should be permitted in spite of the opposition of minorities, statutes were enacted in state after state which took from the individual stockholder the

right theretofore existing to defeat the welding of his corporation with another. In compensation for the lost right a provision was written into the modern statutes giving the dissenting stockholder the option completely to retire from the enterprise and receive the value of his stock in money.

Some scholars rely on such explanations to argue that appraisal statutes were enacted to substitute an exit right for the veto rights that individual shareholders previously possessed. See Carney, *supra*. Others point out that this account fails to explain differences between appraisal statutes or certain significant features of appraisal statutes. See Hideki Kanda & Saul Levmore, The Appraisal Remedy and the Goals of Corporate Law, 32 UCLA L.Rev. 429, 434 (1985).

Whatever the rationale underlying appraisal statutes, three points remain clear. First, different states' corporation statutes provide shareholders with veto rights and dissenter's rights with regard to different sets of transactions. Second, shareholders are not entitled to assert dissenters' rights with respect to every transaction on which they are entitled to vote. Third, every corporation statute authorizes shareholders to dissent from certain transactions involving fundamental changes and to require the corporation to repurchase their stock for its fair value.

b. The Mechanics of Corporate Combinations

Questions relating to voting and appraisal rights arise most often in connection with corporate combinations—transactions that place the business operations of two or more companies under the control of one management. Corporate combinations raise numerous legal issues and are the basis of a great deal of corporate litigation. In subsequent chapters, we consider many of those issues, including whether the boards of directors of constituent corporations exercised reasonable care in approving a combination (see Chapter 16), whether constituent corporations made adequate disclosure of relevant facts to their shareholders (see Chapter 18), what tactics the board of directors of a target company can employ to resist an uninvited takeover bid (see Chapter 22), and what constitutes fair dealing in a combination involving a parent corporation and a controlled subsidiary and whether appraisal is the exclusive remedy available to shareholders in connection with such a transaction (see Chapter 23). Our concern in this chapter is limited to two narrower issues. This section discusses how corporate statutes define the availability of voting and appraisal rights in connection with different forms of corporate combinations. The next section considers whether the form or the substance of a combination should determine the availability of voting and appraisal rights.

Corporations can use a number of different transactional techniques to combine the operations of two or more companies in one firm. Business and tax considerations often dominate the choice of which technique to use. If selling rights in certain property would trigger significant financial or tax obligations, for example, the firms involved probably will try to structure the combination so that the entity holding title to those rights either survives the transaction or is extinguished by operation of law. Similarly, if the management of the post-combination firm would prefer to operate acquired firms as divisions, so as to avoid the administrative burden of maintaining subsidiary corporations, those planning the combination will liquidate or otherwise eliminate all but one of the corporations that survive the combination. But whatever transactional technique is used, and whatever the structure of the resulting business enterprise, the functional result largely will be the same: what were two or more separate business enterprises now will operate as parts of the same business entity, under the control of one board of directors and one management team.

The transactional technique used to effectuate a corporate combination can have dramatically different effects, though, on the voting and appraisal rights of the shareholders of the corporate parties to the combination. To illustrate, we will consider the transactional dynamics and impact on voting and appraisal rights of four basic techniques for bringing two (or more) corporations under the control of one management: (1) a statutory merger, (2) a triangular merger, (3) a statutory share exchange, and (4) an acquisition by one corporation of the assets of another. In the discussion that follows, we designate the principal corporation surviving the combination—the parent corporation—as P, any subsidiary of P as S, and the corporation to be acquired—the target corporation—as T. To illustrate the differences between different states' laws, we outline the statutory requirements applicable to each of these transactions under the RMBCA and the DGCL. For a full treatment, see 5 Martin D. Ginsburg & Jack S. Levin, Mergers, Acquisitions and Leveraged Buyouts ¶ 1502 (CCH Tax Trans. Lib. 1993).

i. Statutory Merger

In a statutory merger,* as in all the other forms of corporate combination, P and T begin as separate legal entities. To effectuate a statutory merger, the boards of directors of P and T first adopt a plan of merger that (a) designates which corporation (here P) is to survive the merger, (b) describes the terms and conditions of the merger, (c) describes the basis on which shares of T will be converted into shares of P (or other property, such as cash or bonds), and (d) sets forth any amendments to P's articles of incorporation necessary to effectuate the plan of merger. RMBCA § 11.01; DGCL § 251(a). The plan of merger then is submitted to the shareholders of both P and T. A majority of the shares of both P and T entitled to vote on the merger must vote in favor. RMBCA § 11.03; DGCL § 251(b).

However, if the transaction qualifies as a so-called *"small scale merger "*—one that does not increase by more than 20 percent P's

---

* Statutory merger means a combination effected pursuant to a corporate statute's merger provision and to distinguish it from

outstanding voting stock—no vote by P's shareholders is required.* RMBCA § 11.03(g); DGCL § 251(f). According to the Official Comment to RMBCA § 11.03(g), "The theory behind this subsection is that shareholders' votes should be required only if the transaction fundamentally alters the character of the enterprise or substantially reduces the shareholders' participation in voting or profit distribution." Similarly, if P owned at least 90 percent of the stock of T prior to the merger, the transaction can proceed as a "*short form*" merger and no vote by the shareholders of P or T is required. RMBCA § 11.04; DGCL § 253.

After any required shareholder approval is secured, the plan of merger is filed with an appropriate state office and the merger becomes effective. By operation of law, T immediately ceases to exist, the assets of T become the assets of P, and the liabilities of T become the liabilities of P. No formal conveyances or assignments need to be executed. All shares of T are converted into shares of P (unless the plan of merger provides for use of cash or other property). Former shareholders of T automatically become shareholders of P; they also lose all rights they had as shareholders of T, unless they dissent and seek appraisal of their shares. RMBCA § 11.06; DGCL § 259. Shareholders of P retain their rights as shareholders of the surviving corporation, but they, too, are entitled to exercise dissenter's rights. RMBCA § 13.02; DGCL § 262.** However, if the transaction qualifies as a small scale or short form merger, dissenter's rights are not available to shareholders of P. RMBCA § 13.02, DGCL § 262(b)(1).

ii. Triangular Merger

Sometimes an acquiring corporation will want to use the statutory merger technique because of the relative ease with which assets can be transferred and liabilities assumed, but will seek to avoid certain legal or business consequences of a statutory merger. For example, P may be concerned about subjecting its own assets to unknown or contingent liabilities associated with T's business. Corporation lawyers often employ a "triangular merger" to deal with such a situation.

A triangular merger is a variant form of statutory merger. The principal difference is that, after negotiating the terms of the combination with T, P creates a subsidiary corporation, S, and transfers to S, in

---

other forms of business combinations often described by the generic term "merger".

* We assume, wherever relevant, that P has authorized sufficient shares to effectuate the transaction in question. If sufficient shares of stock are not authorized, P's articles of incorporation will have to be amended, and P's shareholders will be entitled to vote on that amendment. In addition, if P is publicly held, as a practical matter the rules of the New York Stock Exchange (NYSE) or the National Association of Securities Dealers (NASD) may require a shareholder vote even though no vote is required by state law. NYSE and NASD rules require shareholder approval of any transaction in which a corporation will issue additional shares that exceed by more than 18.5 percent the number of shares outstanding before the transaction. Absent such a vote, the new shares will not be listed on the Exchange or traded through the NASD's automated quotation (NASDAQ) system.

** However, if the constituent corporations in a merger are widely held public corporations and the merger consideration is stock, dissenter's rights are not available to shareholders of P or T. See DGCL § 262 (b)(1)–(2).

exchange for 100% of its stock, the consideration that T's shareholders are to receive. (In the case of LaFrance's proposed acquisition of Sweet Violet, that would be 400,000 shares of LaFrance common stock.) Then, S and T follow the steps necessary to effectuate a statutory merger: the boards of S and T adopt the plan of merger; the shareholders of S and T vote to approve the merger; and T then is merged into S by operation of law. The only differences are that, rather than having S distribute its own shares to the shareholders of T, S distributes shares of P (or other property) to the shareholders of T,* and S, rather than P, becomes the owner of T's property and assumes T's liabilities.**

From the point of view of T's shareholders, it makes little difference whether a combination is structured as a statutory merger or a triangular merger. In either case, they vote on the transaction and, if they wish to exit, they can exercise dissenter's rights. Structuring a combination as a triangular merger, however, has a major impact on the rights of P's shareholders. In both cases they end up as shareholders of a corporation that controls the businesses formerly operated by P and T. But in the case of a triangular merger, it is the shareholders of *S*, not the shareholders of *P*, who vote on the merger and who can exercise dissenter's rights. S, of course, has only one shareholder—P. And P's board of directors, not P's shareholders, has the power to exercise P's rights as a shareholder of S. In short, if one looks no further than the four corners of the relevant statutes, by using the triangular merger technique, P's board can eliminate P's shareholders' right to vote on a corporate combination and to seek appraisal of their shares. RMBCA § 13.02.

iii. Exchange of Shares

Results that are functionally identical to those achieved by a statutory merger or a triangular merger can be achieved using a third form of combination—a statutory share exchange. As with a statutory merger, the boards of P and T first must approve an agreement, here called a plan of exchange, that spells out the terms on which shares of T will be exchanged for shares of P (or cash or other property). *See* RMBCA § 11.02.*** Shareholders of T, but not those of P, then must approve the plan of exchange. RMBCA § 11.03.

Once approved, the plan of exchange is filed and shares of P are issued to the shareholders of T (unless the plan calls for use of cash or other property). T's former shareholders thereby become shareholders of P; they have no further rights as shareholders of T, unless they dissent and seek appraisal of their stock. RMBCA § 11.06. The status of P's shareholders is unchanged. Upon the effectuation of the exchange, T becomes a subsidiary of P, creating a corporate structure

---

* RMBCA § 11.01(b)(3) explicitly authorizes use of stock of a non-party corporation as consideration in a merger, as does DGCL § 251(b).

** The transaction could also be structured as a reverse triangular merger in which S is merged into T.

*** Delaware law contains no provision for a statutory share exchange.

identical to that which would result from a triangular merger. If P does not want to operate T as a subsidiary, but wishes to end with precisely the same structure as would result from merging T into P, it can follow the exchange of shares by 1) dissolving T, distributing all of its assets to P and having P assume all of its liabilities, or 2) merging T into P in a "short form" merger.

iv. *Exchange of Stock for Assets*

In the fourth type of combination, P uses its stock (or some combination of stock, cash and other securities) to buy the assets of T. As with all the other forms of combination (except the tender offer), the first step in such a transaction is approval of an agreement of sale by the boards of directors of P and T. See RMBCA § 12.02; DGCL § 271. The shareholders of T, the selling corporation, but not the shareholders of P, the acquiring corporation, then must approve the terms of the sale agreement. Under RMBCA § 13.02(a)(3), T's shareholders will have dissenter's rights if they vote against the transaction. If T is a Delaware corporation, though, dissenter's rights will not be available. See DGCL § 262.

If a combination is structured as an exchange of stock for assets, T's assets will have to be transferred by deed or other form of conveyance, a process that can generate a good deal of paperwork. P may, but need not, also assume some or all of T's liabilities. Alternatively, T may retain sufficient liquid assets to pay off its liabilities. In a few jurisdictions (notably California and Pennsylvania), statutory requirements or common law principles relating to transferee liability may result in P being held responsible for certain of T's obligations.

If T is dissolved following sale of its assets (and assumption or payment of its liabilities), a stock for asset exchange will result in a corporate structure functionally identical to that produced by a statutory merger. P will own all of the assets of T, and usually will be responsible for all of T's liabilities. P, in turn, will be owned by its shareholders and the former shareholders of T.

v. *Tender Offers*

P can also seek to acquire T by offering to purchase T's shares directly from the T shareholders, either for P stock or for cash or other property. Through such a *tender offer*, P can acquire control of T without a vote of the T board of directors. Unlike the other forms of acquisition, T shareholders "approve" the transaction by accepting P's offer rather than through a formal vote. Similarly, there are no dissenters' rights; T shareholders who wish to disapprove do so by refusing to tender their shares. If holders of a majority of T's shares tender their stock (and no state antitakeover law or provision of T's articles of incorporation prevents P from voting the shares it acquires), P will control T after the exchange of shares is completed. P then often will seek to acquire the remaining shares of T in some form of "second-step" transaction so as to avoid problems in managing the businesses of P and T as part of an integrated whole that may arise due to the presence of a minority interest in T.

P can make a tender offer without any vote by its shareholders, unless P does not have sufficient stock authorized to effectuate a proposed share exchange. P's shareholders also will not have dissenters' rights in the tender offer. Whether either company's shareholders have dissenter's rights in connection with the second step will depend on the form of that transaction.

vi. Summary

In short, four basic techniques, and numerous combinations and permutations of those techniques, are available to effectuate a transaction that will combine the business operations of two or more corporations under the control of one management group. If stock of P, the surviving corporation, is the only consideration to be paid to the shareholders of T, the acquired corporation, each technique will result in the former shareholders of P and T emerging as the shareholders of P, and in P emerging as the owner, directly or through a wholly owned subsidiary, of its assets and the assets of T. As suggested by the following charts summarizing the statutory rules, the RMBCA and the Delaware statute provide that, despite this near identity of result, whether the shareholders of P and T are entitled to vote on or dissent from a corporate combination will turn on the technique used to effectuate that combination.

RMBCA

	P (Surviving corporation)		T (Acquired corporation)	
	Vote	Dissent	Vote	Dissent
Statutory Merger	Yes § 11.03	Yes § 13.02	Yes § 11.03	Yes § 13.02
Triangular Merger	No	No	Yes § 11.03	Yes § 13.02
Statutory Share Exchange	No § 11.03	No § 13.02	Yes § 11.03	Yes § 13.02
Stock for Assets	No	No	Yes § 12.02	Yes § 13.02

Del.Gen.Corp.L.

	P (Surviving corporation)		T (Acquired corporation)	
	Vote	Dissent	Vote	Dissent
Statutory Merger	Yes § 251	Yes § 262*	Yes § 251	Yes § 262*
Triangular Merger	No	No	Yes § 251	Yes § 262*
Statutory Share Exchange	N.A.	N.A.	N.A.	N.A.
Stock for Assets	No	No	Yes § 271	No

* Unless DGCL § 262(b)(1) applies.

c. De Facto and De Jure Approaches

Where the structure of a corporate combination is such that the applicable statute does not provide for voting or appraisal rights, a shareholder seeking to veto the combination or to assert dissenter's rights often will ask a court to treat the combination as if it were a merger, i.e., a *de facto merger*, even though it is cast in some other form. In Irving Bank Corp. v. Bank of New York Co., Inc., 140 Misc.2d 363, 530 N.Y.S.2d 757 (1988), the court observed that "A study of those cases in which courts have found de facto merger demonstrates that the factual situation of each case must be independently studied, without 'slavish adherence to determinations made in other cases, where there are similarities and also degrees of difference.'" Id. at 760 (citing Applestein v. United Board & Carton Corp., 60 N.J.Super. 333, 351, 159 A.2d 146, 156 (1960), aff'd 33 N.J. 72, 161 A.2d 474 (1960)). The court summarized cases finding de facto mergers as follows:

> In Lirosi v. Elkins, 89 A.D.2d 903, 453 N.Y.S.2d 718 (2d Dep't 1982), the court held that a transfer of assets from one corporation to another, and the subsequent dissolution of the former corporation, constituted a de facto merger. In Gilbert v. Burnside, 197 N.Y.S.2d 623 (1959), rev'd 13 A.D.2d 982, 216 N.Y.S.2d 430 (2d Dep't 1961) aff'd 11 N.Y.2d 960, 229 N.Y.S.2d 10, 183 N.E.2d 325 (1962), the court held a "reorganization agreement" to be a de facto merger where the agreement provided for the sale of all of the assets of a corporation and its subsequent dissolution. In both cases, the Court found that the dissolution of the acquired corporation was an imminently expected occurrence.
>
> There have been decisions in other jurisdictions finding de facto mergers in situations similar to those above. See, e.g., Applestein v. United Board & Carton Corp., 60 N.J.Super. 333, 159 A.2d 146 (1960), aff'd 33 N.J. 72, 161 A.2d 474 (1960) (where the agreement provided for a sale of assets, the dissolution of the seller and for the acquirer to assume all the debts of the acquired corporation, a de facto merger existed); Rath v. Rath Packing Company, 257 Iowa 1277, 136 N.W.2d 410 (1965) ("Plan of Reorganization" agreement held de facto merger where agreement provided for sale of all assets, assumption of all debts and liabilities, cessation of business of acquired corporation under its name; and acquiring company to change name to "Rath–Needham"); Farris v. Glen Alden Corporation, 393 Pa. 427, 143 A.2d 25 (1958) ("Reorganization Agreement" held de facto merger, where agreement provided for acquirer to immediately acquire all the assets of the target; acquirer to assume all of target's liabilities; target is to be dissolved).

Most recent decisions, however, have adopted a de jure approach to evaluating corporate combinations.

Our concern here is with shareholders' voting and appraisal rights. Persons with claims against corporations that have sold their assets and dissolved also often urge courts to apply the de facto merger doctrine, especially when their claims arise after the period in which claims can be asserted against former shareholders of those corporations. Some courts have been receptive to these claims, see, e.g., Ray v. Alad Corp., 19 Cal.3d 22, 136 Cal.Rptr. 574, 560 P.2d 3 (1977), but "most * * * state courts, and federal courts interpreting state law, have declined to adopt the 'product line' theory when faced with the issue." Giraldi v. Sears, Roebuck & Co., 687 F.Supp. 987 (D.Md.1988).

HARITON v. ARCO ELECTRONICS, INC.
40 Del.Ch. 326, 182 A.2d 22 (1962), aff'd 41 Del.Ch. 74, 188 A.2d 123 (1963).

SHORT, VICE CHANCELLOR.

Plaintiff is a stockholder of defendant Arco Electronics, Inc., a Delaware corporation. The complaint challenges the validity of the purchase by Loral Electronics Corporation, a New York corporation, of all the assets of Arco. Two causes of action are asserted, namely (1) that the transaction is unfair to Arco stockholders, and (2) that the transaction constituted a de facto merger and is unlawful since the merger provisions of the Delaware law were not complied with. * * *

Plaintiff now concedes that he is unable to sustain the charge of unfairness. The only issue before the court, therefore, is whether the transaction was by its nature a de facto merger with a consequent right of appraisal in plaintiff.

Prior to the transaction of which plaintiff complains Arco was principally engaged in the business of the wholesale distribution of components or parts for electronics and electrical equipment. * * *

Loral was engaged, primarily, in the research, development and production of electronic equipment. * * *

In the summer of 1961 Arco commenced negotiations with Loral with a view to the purchase by Loral of all of the assets of Arco in exchange for shares of Loral common stock. * * * [A]n agreement for the purchase was entered into between Loral and Arco on October 27, 1961. This agreement provides, among other things, as follows:

1. Arco will convey and transfer to Loral all of its assets and property of every kind, tangible and intangible; and will grant to Loral the use of its name and slogans.

2. Loral will assume and pay all of Arco's debts and liabilities.

3. Loral will issue to Arco 283,000 shares of its common stock.

4. Upon the closing of the transaction Arco will dissolve and distribute to its shareholders, pro rata, the shares of the common stock of Loral.

5. Arco will call a meeting of its stockholders to be held December 21, 1961 to authorize and approve the conveyance and delivery of all the assets of Arco to Loral.

6. After the closing date Arco will not engage in any business or activity except as may be required to complete the liquidation and dissolution of Arco.

Pursuant to its undertaking in the agreement for purchase and sale Arco caused a special meeting of its stockholders to be called for December 27, 1961. * * * At the meeting 652,050 shares were voted in favor of the sale and none against. The proposals to change the name of the corporation and to dissolve it and distribute the Loral stock were also approved. The transaction was thereafter consummated.

Plaintiff contends that the transaction, though in form a sale of assets of Arco, is in substance and effect a merger, and that it is unlawful because the merger statute has not been complied with, thereby depriving plaintiff of his right of appraisal.

Defendant contends that since all the formalities of a sale of assets pursuant to 8 Del.C. § 271 have been complied with the transaction is in fact a sale of assets and not a merger. In this connection it is to be noted that plaintiffs nowhere allege or claim that defendant has not complied to the letter with the provisions of said section.

The question here presented is one which has not been heretofore passed upon by any court in this state. In Heilbrunn v. Sun Chemical Corporation, Del., 150 A.2d 755, the Supreme Court was called upon to determine whether or not a stockholder of the *purchasing* corporation could, in circumstances like those here presented, obtain relief on the theory of a de facto merger. The court held that relief was not available to such a stockholder. It expressly observed that the question here presented was not before the court for determination. It pointed out also that while Delaware does not grant appraisal rights to a stockholder dissenting from a sale, citing Argenbright v. Phoenix Finance Co., 21 Del.Ch. 288, 187 A. 124, and Finch v. Warrior Cement Corp., 16 Del.Ch. 44, 141 A. 54, those cases are distinguishable from the facts here presented, "because dissolution of the seller and distribution of the stock of the purchaser were not required as a part of the sale in either case." In speaking of the form of the transaction the Supreme Court observes:

> The argument that the result of this transaction is substantially the same as the result that would have followed a merger may be readily accepted. As plaintiffs correctly say, the Ansbacher enterprise [seller] is continued in altered form as a part of Sun [purchaser]. This is ordinarily a typical characteristic of a merger. Sterling v. Mayflower Hotel Corp., 33 Del. 293, 303, 93 A.2d 107, 38 A.L.R.2d 425. Moreover the plan of reorganization *requires* the dissolution of

Ansbacher and the distribution to its stockholders of the Sun stock received by it for the assets. As a part of the plan, the Ansbacher stockholders are compelled to receive Sun stock. From the viewpoint of Ansbacher, the result is the same as if Ansbacher had formally merged into Sun.

This result is made possible, of course, by the overlapping scope of the merger statute and the statute authorizing the sale of all the corporate assets. This possibility of overlapping was noticed in our opinion in the *Mayflower* case.

There is nothing new about such a result. For many years drafters of plans of corporate reorganization have increasingly resorted to the use of the sale-of-assets method in preference to the method by merger. Historically at least, there were reasons for this quite apart from the avoidance of the appraisal right given to stockholders dissenting from a merger.

* * * The doctrine of de facto merger in comparable circumstances has been recognized and applied by the Pennsylvania courts, both state and federal, Lauman v. Lebanon Valley Railroad Co., 30 Pa. 42; Marks v. Autocar Co., D.C., 153 F.Supp. 768; Farris v. Glen Alden Corporation, 393 Pa. 427, 143 A.2d 25. * * * The *Farris* case demonstrates the length to which the Pennsylvania courts have gone in applying this principle. It was there applied in favor of a stockholder of the purchasing corporation, an application which our Supreme Court expressly rejected in *Heilbrunn*.

The right of appraisal accorded to a dissenting stockholder by the merger statutes is in compensation for the right which he had at common law to prevent a merger. Chicago Corporation v. Munds, 20 Del.Ch. 142, 172 A. 452. * * *

While plaintiff's contention that the doctrine of de facto merger should be applied in the present circumstances is not without appeal, the subject is one which, in my opinion, is within the legislative domain. * * * The argument underlying the applicability of the doctrine of de facto merger, namely, that the stockholder is forced against his will to accept a new investment in an enterprise foreign to that of which he was a part has little pertinency. The right of the corporation to sell all of its assets for stock in another corporation was expressly accorded to Arco by § 271 of Title 8, Del.C. The stockholder was, in contemplation of law, aware of this right when he acquired his stock. He was also aware of the fact that the situation might develop whereby he would be ultimately forced to accept a new investment, as would have been the case here had the resolution authorizing dissolution followed consummation of the sale. * * *

There is authority in decisions of courts of this state for the proposition that the various sections of the Delaware Corporation Law conferring authority for corporate action are independent of each other and that a given result may be accomplished by proceeding under one section which is not possible, or is even forbidden under another. * * *

In a footnote to Judge Leahy's opinion [in Langfelder v. Universal Laboratories, 68 F.Supp. 209, 211 n. 5 (D.Del.1946), aff'd 163 F.2d 804 (3d Cir.1947)] the following comment appears:

> The text is but a particularization of the general theory of the Delaware Corporation Law that action taken pursuant to the authority of the various sections of that law constitute acts of independent legal significance and their validity is not dependent on other sections of the Act. * * *

* * *

I conclude that the transaction complained of was not a de facto merger, either in the sense that there was a failure to comply with one or more of the requirements of § 271 of the Delaware Corporation Law, or that the result accomplished was in effect a merger entitling plaintiff to a right of appraisal.

Defendant's motion for summary judgment is granted. Order on notice.

Note

One commentator offers the following perspective on *Hariton* :

> The basic premise implicitly adopted in *Hariton* may perhaps be stated more affirmatively. One does not invest in a unique corporate entity or even a particular business operation, but rather in a continuous course of business which changes over a long period of time. Certainly the best investments are growth investments—investments in enterprises which change with time, technology, business opportunities, and altered demand; and the worst investments are those which diminish in value because the type of business has lost importance and the corporation has been unable to adapt to the changed conditions. Although a shareholder's enthusiasm dwindles when an enterprise changes internally for the worst, no one suggests that he should have an option to compel the return of his investment. Viewed this way, the fact that the change—for better or for worse—comes through marriage, whether by merger or assets sale, seems purely incidental. The fact that the corporate entity in which one invested disappears as a result of a merger or of a sale of assets coupled with dissolution is also beside the point. One's investment may gain immortality when it takes a new form, i.e., a share in a successor enterprise.

Ernest Folk, De Facto Mergers in Delaware: Hariton v. Arco Electronics, Inc., 49 Va.L.Rev. 1261, 1280–81 (1963).

TERRY v. PENN CENTRAL CORP.
668 F.2d 188 (3d Cir.1981).

ADAMS, CIRCUIT JUDGE.

[Penn Central Corporation ("Penn Central") sought to acquire Colt Industries Inc. ("Colt"), by merging Colt with PCC Holdings, Inc.

("Holdings"), a wholly-owned subsidiary of Penn Central. Howard L. Terry and W.H. Hunt, shareholders of Penn Central, sought to enjoin the transaction on the ground that they were entitled to dissenter's rights.]

Terry and Hunt contend that * * * the proposed merger between Holdings and Colt constitutes a *de facto* merger between Colt and Penn Central, and that the Penn Central shareholders are therefore entitled to the protections for dissenting shareholders that Pennsylvania corporate law provides for shareholders of parties to a merger. Although this reasoning, with its emphasis on the substance of the transaction rather than its formal trappings, may be attractive as a matter of policy, it contravenes the language employed by the Pennsylvania legislature in setting out the rights of shareholders.

Section 908 of the Pennsylvania Business Corporation Law (PBCL), 15 P.S. § 1908, provides that shareholders of corporations that are parties to a plan of merger are entitled to dissent and appraisal rights, but adds that for an acquisition other than such a merger, the only rights are those provided for in Section 311 of the PBCL, 15 P.S. § 1311 (Purdon 1967 & Supp.1981–82). Section 311, in turn, provides for dissent and appraisal rights only when an acquisition has been accomplished by "the issuance of voting shares of such corporation to be outstanding immediately after the acquisition sufficient to elect a majority of the directors of the corporation." In this case the shares of Penn Central stock to be issued in the Colt transaction do not exceed the number of shares already existing, and thus the transaction is not covered by Section 311. Any statutory dissent and appraisal rights for Penn Central shareholders are therefore contingent upon Penn Central's status as a party to the merger within the meaning of Section 908. And as the district court points out, the PBCL describes the parties to a merger as those entities that are *actually* combined into a single corporation. * * * At the consummation of the proposed merger plan here, both Holdings and Penn Central would survive as separate entities, and it would therefore appear that Penn Central * * * is not a party to the merger.

Appellants argue that Penn Central is nevertheless brought into the amalgamation by the *de facto* merger doctrine as set out in Pennsylvania law in Farris v. Glen Alden Corp., 393 Pa. 427, 143 A.2d 25 (1958). * * *

None of these cases persuades us that a Pennsylvania court would apply the *de facto* merger doctrine to the situation before us. Although [In re Jones & Laughlin Steel Corp., 488 Pa. 524, 412 A.2d 1099 (1980)] suggests that dissent and appraisal rights might be available if fraud or fundamental unfairness were shown, we are not faced with such a situation. No allegation of fraud has been advanced, and the only allegation of fundamental unfairness is that the appellants will, if the merger is consummated, be forced into what they consider a poor investment on the part of Penn Central without the opportunity to receive an appraised value for their stock. Even if appellants' evaluation of the merits of the proposed merger is accurate, poor business judgment on the part of management would not be enough to constitute unfairness cognizable by a court. And the denial of appraisal rights to dissenters cannot constitute fundamental unfairness, or the *de facto* merger doctrine would apply in every instance in which dissenters' rights were sought and the 1959 amendments by the legislature would be rendered nugatory.[7] * * *

In the absence of any explicit guidance to the contrary by the Pennsylvania courts, we conclude that the language of the legislature in 1959 precludes a decision that the transaction in this case constitutes a *de facto* merger sufficient to entitle Penn Central shareholders to dissent and appraisal rights. We therefore hold that appellants do not possess such rights if a transaction such as the one involved here is consummated. * * *

The American Law Institute has adopted a functional approach to determining a shareholder's right to vote on or dissent from a corporate combination modelled largely on Chapter 12 of the California Corporations Code. A shareholder is entitled to vote on any transaction that qualifies as a "Transaction in Control," see ALI, Principles of Corporate Governance § 6.01(b) (1994), and is entitled to appraisal rights in connection with any business combination, whatever its form, "unless those persons who were shareholders of the corporation immediately before the combination own 60 percent or more of the total voting power of the surviving * * * corporation immediately thereafter * * *." Id., § 7.21(a).

ALI, PRINCIPLES OF CORPORATE GOVERNANCE (1994)

§ 1.38. Transaction in Control

(a) Subject to Subsection (b), a "transaction in control" with respect to a corporation means:

(1) A business combination effected through (i) a merger, (ii) a consolidation, (iii) an issuance of voting equity securities to effect an acquisition of the assets of another corporation which acquisition would constitute a transaction in control under Subsection (a)(2) with respect to the other corporation, or (iv) an issuance of voting equity securities in exchange for at least a majority of the voting equity securities of another corporation, in each case whether effected directly or by means of a subsidiary;

---

7. A different result might be reached if here, as in *Farris,* the acquiring corporation were significantly smaller than the acquired corporation such that the acquisition greatly transformed the nature of the successor corporation. But in this situation we do not have such a case: after the merger Penn Central would remain a major, diversified corporation, and would continue on the course of acquiring other corporations.

(2) A sale of assets that would leave the corporation without a significant continuing business; or

(3) An issuance of securities or any other transaction by the corporation (other than pursuant to a transaction described in Subsection (a)(1)) that, alone or in conjunction with other transactions or circumstances, would cause a change in control of the corporation;

(b) A transaction is not a transaction in control within § 1.38(a) if the transaction consists of:

* * *

(3) A transaction described in Subsection (a)(1) if those persons who were the holders of voting equity securities in the corporation immediately before the transaction would own immediately after the transaction at least 75 percent of the surviving corporation's voting equity securities, in substantially the same proportions in relation to other preexisting shareholders of the corporation.

Comment:

a. Comparison with existing law. * * *

A central theme of § 1.38 is that the mere form in which a transaction is cast should not determine the manner in which the transaction is characterized. A continuing problem in corporation law is to identify those transactions that are so different from the day-to-day operation of the corporation's business that a different decisionmaking process, appraisal rights for shareholders who disapprove, or both, are appropriate. The traditional approach to this problem has been to specify the covered transactions by reference to the form in which those planning the transactions have cast them. * * *

This approach has resulted in an important problem. From the perspective of the managers who plan commercial transactions, the transaction often can be cast in a variety of forms without altering its economic substance. Thus, * * * the assertion of something akin to what has become to be called the de facto merger doctrine was inevitable. * * *

There are substantial difficulties associated with each of the four approaches to the de facto merger problem. The provision of different shareholder approval and appraisal procedures for substantially identical transactions is difficult to justify, whether accomplished by statute or through judicial deference to the equal dignity the legislature may have accorded different transactional forms. Judicial efforts to identify the essential characteristics of a merger may result in the imposition of the most restrictive procedures on all transactions because sales of assets and triangular mergers are substantially identical to two-party mergers. Finally, legislative efforts to incorporate the de facto merger doctrine into the corporate statute have reduced the problem, but not eliminated it. Although the net is cast more broadly, its reach is still determined by transaction form, leaving planners room to recast transactions to avoid shareholder approval and appraisal procedures.   * * *

[Section 6.01] follows the approach of * * * treating all transactions in control alike, regardless of the form in which they are cast, and also follows the approach of those states that do not require approval of a merger agreement by shareholders of a corporation that is party thereto whose rights are not diluted by more than 25 percent.   Section 1.38 seeks to avoid the difficulties encountered by courts and legislatures in dealing with the de facto merger problem by defining the range of transactions of concern by reference to their substance rather than their form.

3. TRANSACTION SIZE AND SHAREHOLDERS' RIGHTS
PROBLEM
LAFRANCE COSMETICS—PART II

5 directors

Five years have passed since LaFrance acquired Sweet Violet.   La-France's board of directors is unchanged; its stock is held as follows:

Mimi LaFrance	400,000 shares
Pierre LaFrance	100,000 shares
Margaret LaFrance	100,000 shares
Third National Bank, Trustee	400,000 shares
Former shareholders of Sweet Violet and others	400,000 shares
Total	1,400,000 shares

66% of assets

LaFrance has invested heavily in the perfume business; the Sweet Violet division now accounts for nearly two-thirds of the book value of LaFrance's assets.   LaFrance's investment produced a sharp increase in perfume sales; they have accounted for about 70% of LaFrance's total sales last year.   But this investment has not produced the profits Mimi and Pierre anticipated.   The perfume business has become more competitive, profit margins have declined, and LaFrance has had difficulty integrating perfume into its cosmetics business.   Despite increased sales, the Sweet Violet division produced only 20% of LaFrance's net income last year.   These disappointing results have depressed the price of LaFrance stock, for which a limited trading market has developed.   Most recent sales have been at about $40 per share.

70% sales

20% NET

LaBelle, S.A., a large French perfume manufacturer, recently approached LaFrance with an offer to buy the Sweet Violet division for $50 million in cash, which is slightly more than the division's book value. Mimi and Pierre are anxious to accept the offer.   Margaret continues to believe the entire company should be sold.   She opposes the sale of Sweet Violet alone, fearing that Mimi and Pierre will use the proceeds to finance another ill-advised expansion effort.   Lauren Miller now supports Margaret's position, but Victor Gauguin continues to side with Mimi and Pierre.

2 - Marg + Laud

is on BD NOT sharehold

While a majority of LaFrance's directors thus will vote to accept LaBelle's offer, it is unclear whether a majority of LaFrance's shareholders would concur. Margaret and the bank almost certainly would oppose selling Sweet Violet to LaBelle. The views of the remaining shareholders are unknown, but many of them no doubt have been disappointed with LaFrance's results in recent years. Consequently, they might well be inclined to support Margaret's proposal that the entire company, not merely Sweet Violet, be sold.

Pierre has asked for your advice in connection with two conditions of LaBelle's offer. The first is that, at the closing, LaFrance deliver an unqualified opinion of counsel to the effect that LaFrance has complied with all applicable provisions of Columbia law in effectuating the sale of Sweet Violet. The other is that the closing occur within 120 days of today.

Pierre has asked what procedures LaFrance must follow to effectuate the sale of the Sweet Violet division. He wants to know, in particular, (i) if you are prepared to opine that shareholder approval is not required and (ii) assuming you reach that conclusion, how likely is it that Margaret or some other shareholder nonetheless could assert a claim that would survive a motion to dismiss for failure to state a claim and/or a motion for summary judgment, thus preventing the sale from closing within 120 days. In developing your response, consider RMBCA §§ 12.01 and 12.02, and the Official Comment to RMBCA § 12.01.

GIMBEL v. SIGNAL COMPANIES, INC.

316 A.2d 599 (Del.Ch.1974), aff'd per curiam 316 A.2d 619 (Del. 1974).

[On December 21, 1973, at a special meeting, the board of directors of Signal Companies, Inc. ("Signal") approved a proposal to sell its wholly owned subsidiary Signal Gas & Oil Co. ("Signal Oil") to Burmah Oil Inc. ("Burmah") for a price of $480 million. Based on Signal's books, Signal Oil represented 26% of Signal's total assets, 41% of its net worth, and produced 15% of Signal's revenues and earnings. The contract provided that the sale would take place on January 15, 1974 or upon obtaining the necessary governmental consents, whichever was later, but, in no event, after February 15, 1974, unless mutually agreed.

On December 24, 1973, plaintiff, a Signal shareholder, sued for a preliminary injunction to prevent consummation of the sale. The plaintiff, among other contentions, alleged that approval only by Signal's board was insufficient and that a favorable vote from a majority of the outstanding shares of Signal was necessary to authorize the sale].

QUILLEN, CHANCELLOR.

* * *

I turn first to the question of 8 Del.C. § 271(a) which requires majority stockholder approval for the sale of "all or substantially all" of the assets of a Delaware corporation. A sale of less than all or substantially all assets is not covered by negative implication from the statute.

Folk, The Delaware General Corporation Law, Section 271, p. 400, ftnt. 3; 8 Del.C. § 141(a).

It is important to note in the first instance that the statute does not speak of a requirement of shareholder approval simply because an independent, important branch of a corporate business is being sold. The plaintiff cites several non-Delaware cases for the proposition that shareholder approval of such a sale is required. But that is not the language of our statute. Similarly, it is not our law that shareholder approval is required upon every "major" restructuring of the corporation. Again, it is not necessary to go beyond the statute. The statute requires shareholder approval upon the sale of "all or substantially all" of the corporation's assets. That is the sole test to be applied. While it is true that test does not lend itself to a strict mathematical standard to be applied in every case, the qualitative factor can be defined to some degree notwithstanding the limited Delaware authority. But the definition must begin with and ultimately necessarily relate to our statutory language.

In interpreting the statute the plaintiff relies on Philadelphia National Bank v. B.S.F. Co., 41 Del.Ch. 509, 199 A.2d 557 (Ch.1964), rev'd on other grounds, 42 Del.Ch. 106, 204 A.2d 746 (Supr.Ct.1964). In that case, B.S.F. Company owned stock in two corporations. It sold its stock in one of the corporations, and retained the stock in the other corporation. The Court found that the stock sold was the principal asset B.S.F. Company had available for sale and that the value of the stock retained was declining. The Court rejected the defendant's contention that the stock sold represented only 47.4% of consolidated assets, and looked to the actual value of the stock sold. On this basis, the Court held that the stock constituted at least 75% of the total assets and the sale of the stock was a sale of substantially all assets. * * *

The key language in the Court of Chancery opinion in *Philadelphia National Bank* is the suggestion that "the critical factor in determining the character of a sale of assets is generally considered not the amount of property sold but whether the sale is in fact an unusual transaction or one made in the regular course of business of the seller." (41 Del.Ch. at 515, 199 A.2d at 561). Professor Folk suggests from the opinion that "the statute would be inapplicable if the assets sale is "one made in furtherance of express corporate objects in the ordinary and regular course of the business' " (referring to language in 41 Del.Ch. at 516, 199 A.2d at 561). Folk, *supra*, Section 271, p. 401.

But any "ordinary and regular course of the business" test in this context obviously is not intended to limit the directors to customary daily business activities. Indeed, a question concerning the statute would not arise unless the transaction was somewhat out of the ordinary. While it is true that a transaction in the ordinary course of business does not require shareholder approval, the converse is not true. Every transaction out of normal routine does not necessarily require shareholder approval. The unusual nature of the transaction must strike at the heart of the corporate existence and purpose. As it is written at 6A Fletcher, Cyclopedia Corporations (Perm.Ed.1968 Rev.) § 2949.2, p. 648:

> The purpose of the consent statutes is to protect the shareholders from fundamental change, or more specifically to protect the shareholder from the destruction of the means to accomplish the purposes or objects for which the corporation was incorporated and actually performs.

It is in this sense that the "unusual transaction" judgment is to be made and the statute's applicability determined. If the sale is of assets quantitatively vital to the operation of the corporation and is out of the ordinary and substantially affects the existence and purpose of the corporation, then it is beyond the power of the Board of Directors. With these guidelines, I turn to Signal and the transaction in this case.

Signal or its predecessor was incorporated in the oil business in 1922. But, beginning in 1952 Signal diversified its interests. In 1952, Signal acquired a substantial stock interest in American President lines. From 1957 to 1962 Signal was the sole owner of Laura Scudders, a nationwide snack food business. In 1964, Signal acquired Garrett Corporation which is engaged in the aircraft, aerospace, and uranium enrichment business. In 1967, Signal acquired Mack Trucks, Inc., which is engaged in the manufacture and sale of trucks and related equipment. Also in 1968, the oil and gas business was transferred to a separate division and later in 1970 to the Signal Oil subsidiary. Since 1967, Signal has made acquisition of or formed substantial companies none of which are involved or related with the oil and gas industry. As indicated previously, the oil and gas production development of Signal's business is now carried on by Signal Oil, the sale of the stock of which is an issue in this lawsuit. * * *

Based on the company's figures, Signal Oil represents only about 26% of the total assets of Signal. While Signal Oil represents 41% of the Signal's total net worth, it produces only about 15% of Signal's revenues and earnings. * * *

While it is true, based on the experience of the Signal–Burmah transaction and the record in this lawsuit, that Signal Oil is more valuable than shown by the company's books, even if, as plaintiff suggests in his brief, the $761,000,000 value attached to Signal Oil's properties by the plaintiff's expert Paul V. Keyser, Jr., were substituted [for $376.2 million] as the asset figure, the oil and gas properties would still constitute less than half the value of Signal's total assets. Thus, from a straight quantitative approach, I agree with Signal's position that the sale to Burmah does not constitute a sale of "all or substantially all" of Signal's assets.

In addition, if the character of the transaction is examined, the plaintiff's position is also weak. While it is true that Signal's original purpose was oil and gas and while oil and gas is still listed first in the certificate of incorporation, the simple fact is that Signal is now a conglomerate engaged in the aircraft and aerospace business, the manufacture and sale of trucks and related equipment, and other businesses besides oil and gas. The very nature of its business, as it now in fact exists, contemplates the acquisition and disposal of independent branches of its corporate business. Indeed, given the operations since 1952, it can be said that such acquisitions and dispositions have become part of the ordinary course of business. The facts that the oil and gas business was historically first and that authorization for such operations are listed first in the certificate do not prohibit disposal of such interest. As Director Harold M. Williams testified, business history is not "compelling" and "many companies go down the drain because they try to be historic."

It is perhaps true, as plaintiff has argued, that the advent of multibusiness corporations has in one sense emasculated § 271 since one business may be sold without shareholder approval when other substantial businesses are retained. But it is one thing for a corporation to evolve over a period of years into a multi-business corporation, the operations of which include the purchase and sale of whole businesses, and another for a single business corporation by a one transaction revolution to sell the entire means of operating its business in exchange for money or a separate business. In the former situation, the processes of corporate democracy customarily have had the opportunity to restrain or otherwise control over a period of years. Thus, there is a chance for some shareholder participation. The Signal development illustrates the difference. For example, when Signal, itself formerly called Signal Oil and Gas Company, changed its name in 1968, it was for the announced "need for a new name appropriate to the broadly diversified activities of Signal's multi-industry complex." * * *

I conclude that measured (quantatively and qualitatively) the sale of the stock of Signal Oil by Signal to Burmah does not constitute a sale of "all or substantially all" of Signal's assets. * * * Accordingly, insofar as the complaint rests on 8 Del.C. § 271(a), in my judgment, it has no reasonable probability of ultimate success. * * *

In Katz v. Bregman, 431 A.2d 1274 (Del.Ch.1981), the court held that a corporation's sale of assets that constituted more than 51 percent of its total assets and generated approximately 45 percent of its net sales in the previous year, and that would cause the corporation to de[part radically from its historically successful line of business, constituted a sale of substantially all of the corporation's assets.

The Official Comment to RMBCA § 12.01 also contains an extensive discussion of what constitutes "all or substantially all."

4. SHAREHOLDERS' POWER TO INITIATE ACTION

PROBLEM
LAFRANCE COSMETICS—PART III

The sale of the Sweet Violet Division still is pending. LaBelle is prepared to accept your opinion that shareholder approval is not required. However, Margaret, who seems to have the support of the Third National Bank, is investigating what actions she might take, as a shareholder, to block the sale. Pierre has asked you to prepare an analysis of the actions LaFrance's shareholders have the power to initiate; the procedures they would need to follow; and what LaFrance's board of directors might do to counter any such initiatives. More specifically, Pierre has asked you to respond to the following questions:

1. Do LaFrance's shareholders have a right to have a special meeting of shareholders called to adopt a resolution compelling the board to abandon the sale of Sweet Violet? Alternatively, can the shareholders adopt a resolution recommending that the board abandon the sale of Sweet Violet? What would be the probable effect of such a resolution? Consider *Auer v. Dressel*.

2. Can LaFrance's shareholders act other than at a properly called meeting?

3. Could the shareholders remove the directors who support the sale and replace them with new directors who oppose the sale? Consider RMBCA §§ 7.02, 7.04, 7.05, 7.25, 8.05, 8.08, and 8.10, and Model By-laws, Article III § 9 and Article II §§ 2, 4, 7, and 11. Would your answer be different if the articles contained the a provision stating: "A director may be removed only for cause." Consider *Auer v. Dressel* and *Campbell v. Loew's*.

4. Could those shareholders "pack" the board by amending the articles of incorporation or the by-laws (or both) and adding new directors who would vote against the sale? Assume that the by-laws of LaFrance are similar to the Model By-laws but provide for a board of five directors. Assume further that the articles of incorporation of LaFrance contain no provisions regarding the number of directors. Alternatively, assume that in the alternative, the articles provide for a five member board. Consider RMBCA §§ 10.20, 10.02, 10.03, 8.03, and 8.10, and Model By-laws, Article III §§ 2 and 9, and Article XI. Reconsider *Auer v. Dressel* and *Campbell v. Loew's*.

5. If LaFrance's shareholders request that a shareholders' meeting be called to consider proposals that would alter the membership of the LaFrance board, what discretion, if any, could LaFrance's board or management exercise in responding to that demand? What other tactics might the board employ to counter the shareholders' initiative? Reconsider *Schnell v. Chris–Craft Indus., Inc.* (Chapter 3); consider *Blasius Industries, Inc. v. Atlas Corp. and Stahl v. Apple Bancorp, Inc.*

6. To what extent would your answers to the foregoing questions change if LaFrance were a Delaware corporation? Consider DGCL §§ 141 and 228.

a. Shareholder Meetings; Procedural Concerns

As in the case of action by directors, certain procedural requirements must be satisfied for shareholders to act, whether at an annual meeting, a special meeting, or by means of written consents.

i. The Call

[handwritten margin note: Call a meeting]

A corporation's bylaws usually fix the date of the annual meeting. See RMBCA § 7.01(a); Model By-laws, Article II § 1. Most corporation statutes provide that the board of directors, owners of 10 percent of the shares, or any person so authorized by the articles of incorporation or bylaws may call a special meeting of shareholders. See RMBCA § 7.02(a); Model By-laws, Article II § 2. DGCL § 211(d) excludes stock ownership as a qualification for calling such a meeting.

[handwritten margin note: under DELAWARE]

The Delaware courts have never addressed the question of whether a given percentage of a corporation's shareholders have inherent power to call a special meeting. One could argue that shareholders have such power, at least if the purpose of the meeting is to take some action, such as removal of a director for cause, that itself is within shareholders' inherent power. *See Auer* v. *Dressel,* infra. On the other hand, shareholders' statutory power to act by written consent pursuant to DGCL § 228 may provide an effective mechanism for the exercise of shareholders' power, and therefore shareholders may have no inherent power to call a special meeting.

ii. Notice

[handwritten margin note: written notice]

A corporation must give written notice of an annual or special meeting to all shareholders entitled to vote at the meeting. See RMBCA § 7.05; Model By-laws, Article II § 4. Only matters "within the purpose or purposes described in the meeting notice" may be considered at a special meeting. See RMBCA § 7.02(c). However, shareholders can waive notice, either in writing or by attending the meeting and not objecting to the absence of notice. See RMBCA § 7.06.

[handwritten margin notes: 1) NOTICE w PURPOSE 2) MAY WAIVE 3) set Date]

[handwritten margin note: Bd. sets Record Date]

To satisfy the notice requirement, a board must set a "record date" prior to the meeting and provide that only shareholders "of record" as of that date will be entitled to vote at the meeting. See RMBCA § 7.07; Model Bylaws, Article II § 5. The board, not the shareholders who called the meeting, has the exclusive power to set the record date and send out notices, unless the articles provide otherwise. See Young v. Janas, 103 A.2d 299 (Del.Ch.1954). This power can have tactical significance, because a meeting generally can be set for anywhere between 10 and 60 days after notice is sent. See RMBCA § 7.05(a).

On occasion, timing requirements relating to shareholder action take on great significance. That was the case when Bendix, a Delaware corporation, attempted to take over Martin Marietta, which was incorporated in Maryland. Bendix made a cash tender offer that, if successful, would have allowed it to purchase a majority of Martin Marietta's stock on September 17, 1982. Martin Marietta responded by offering to purchase a majority of Bendix stock (a tactic known as the "Pac–Man Defense.") However, because its offer was made six days later, federal law prevented Martin Marietta from purchasing Bendix stock until September 23.

Differences between Delaware and Maryland law nonetheless seemed to give Martin Marietta the upper hand. Using Delaware's consent procedure, Martin Marietta could remove a majority of the Bendix board and replace it with new directors as soon as it acquired a majority of Bendix' shares—i.e., on September 23. Bendix, on the other hand, was powerless to compel a special meeting of Martin Marietta shareholders any earlier than 10 days after it became a 10 percent shareholder and filed a call—i.e., September 27. By that date, assuming no judicial intervention, Martin Marietta would already control Bendix and would cause Bendix to desist from all actions directed at changing the make-up of the Martin Marietta board.

In the event, both Bendix and Martin Marietta succeeded in acquiring a majority of the other's stock, Bendix on September 17 and Martin Marietta on September 23. Before the courts could resolve the welter of litigation that surrounded their competing takeover bids, though, Allied Corporation appeared on the scene. It reached an agreement to purchase all of Bendix and to sell back to Martin Marietta most of the shares that Bendix had purchased. Thus Bendix, the original bidder, ended up as a subsidiary of Allied, and Martin Marietta, the original target, succeeded in remaining an independent (but much more heavily leveraged) company.

iii. Quorum

A quorum must be represented at a shareholders meeting, either in person or by proxy, for an action taken at the meeting to be effective. A quorum usually consists of a majority of the shares entitled to vote, unless the articles of incorporation provide otherwise. See RMBCA § 7.25(a). The RMBCA sets no minimum or maximum quorum but requires an amendment establishing (or reducing) a supermajority quorum requirement to meet that same requirement. RMBCA §§ 7.25(a), 7.27. DGCL § 216 allows a majority of shares to amend a corporation's articles of incorporation or bylaws to increase the quorum requirement *DEI.* or to reduce it to as little as one-third of the shares entitled to vote, unless the articles or bylaws require some greater vote.

iv. Action by Written Consent

As discussed above, both the RMBCA and DGCL allow shareholders to act by written consent rather than at a meeting. However, the two statutes vary considerably.

RMBCA § 7.04(a) requires the consent in writing of all shareholders entitled to vote on an action. Consequently, all voting shareholders also must receive advance notice of the action to be taken. Unless the bylaws provide otherwise, the record date for determining which shareholders must consent to an action is the date the first shareholder consents in writing to that action. RMBCA § 7.04(b).

DGCL § 228 allows a majority of the shareholders entitled to vote on an action to act by means of written consent. Prompt notice that action has been taken by consent must be given to nonconsenting shareholders, but no advance notice is required. DGCL § 228(c). Every consent must be dated when signed, and the period during which consents can be signed is effectively limited to 60 days from the date the first consent delivered to the corporation was signed. See DGCL § 228(c). That date also serves as the record date for a consent solicitation initiated by shareholders; if the board is soliciting consents, it may set a record date. DGCL § 213(b).

b. What Actions Can Shareholders Initiate?

Gimbel is noteworthy not merely for its discussion of what constitutes "all or substantially all" of a corporation's assets, but for what it says about board and shareholder power. The court implicitly held that, absent some statutory requirement for shareholder approval, a board is authorized to take all actions it deems necessary in managing a corporation's business. By construing the Signal shareholders' reelection of the directors who converted Signal into a multi-business corporation as a tacit ratification of that strategy, the court also implied that the shareholders' most appropriate vehicle for expressing disapproval of directors' business judgments is the election of new directors. That philosophy also underlies RMBCA §§ 12.01 and 12.02 and the Official Comment to § 12.01.

In re Time Inc. Shareholder Litigation, Fed.Sec.L. Rep. ¶ 94,514 (Del.Ch.1989), aff'd Paramount Communications Inc. v. Time, Inc. (Chapter 22), reflects a similar point of view. The boards of Time and Warner Communications Inc. (WCI) had approved a plan for a triangular, stock-for-stock merger of WCI into a Time subsidiary. To comply with New York Stock Exchange rules, the plan provided for a vote of approval by Time's shareholders, as well as those of WCI. Before the shareholder meetings could be held, Paramount made a cash tender offer, at a substantial premium over the market price, for all outstanding shares of Time, subject to the condition that Time abandon its merger with WCI. Time's board responded by restructuring the WCI transaction as a cash tender offer by Time for 51% of WCI's stock, to be followed by a merger of WCI into a Time subsidiary. The first stage of this plan did not call for any vote by Time's shareholders.

Time shareholders sued to enjoin Time's cash tender offer. The court held that, under Delaware law, Time's shareholders had no right to vote on either the proposed cash tender offer or the proposed triangular merger. Chancellor Allen then observed:

The value of a shareholder's investment, over time, rises or falls chiefly because of the skill, judgment and perhaps luck—for it is present in all human affairs—of the management and directors of the enterprise. When they exercise sound or brilliant judgment, shareholders are likely to profit; when they fail to do so, share values likely will fail to appreciate. In either event, the financial vitality of the corporation and the value of the company's shares is in the hands of the directors and managers of the firm. The corporation law does not operate on the theory that directors, in exercising their powers to manage the firm, are obligated to follow the wishes of a majority of shares. In fact, directors, not shareholders, are charged with the duty to manage the firm.

In the decision they have reached here, the Time board may be proven in time to have been brilliantly prescient or dismayingly wrong. In this decision, as in other decisions affecting the financial value of their investment, the shareholders will bear the effects for good or ill. That many, presumably most, shareholders would prefer the board to do otherwise than it has done does not * * * in my opinion, afford a basis to interfere with the effectuation of the board's business judgment.

AUER v. DRESSEL

306 N.Y. 427, 118 N.E.2d 590 (1954).

[The plaintiffs, who owned a majority of the Class A stock of R. Hoe & Co., Inc., brought an action for an order to compel the president of the corporation to call a special shareholders' meeting pursuant to a by-law provision requiring such a meeting when requested by holders of a majority of the stock. The articles of incorporation provided for an eleven-member board, nine of whom were to be elected by the Class A stockholders and two of whom were to be elected by the Common stockholders. The purposes of the special meeting were:

A. to vote on a resolution endorsing the administration of Joseph L. Auer, the former President and demanding his reinstatement;

B. to amend the articles of incorporation and by-laws to provide that vacancies on the board of directors arising from the removal of a director by the shareholders be filled only by the shareholders;

C. to consider and vote on charges to remove four Class A directors for cause and to elect their successors;

D. to amend the by-laws to reduce the quorum requirement for board action.

The president refused to call the meeting on the ground, among others, that the foregoing purposes were not proper subjects for a Class A shareholder meeting.]

DESMOND, JUDGE.

* * * The obvious purpose of the meeting here sought to be called (aside from the indorsement and reinstatement of former president Auer) is to hear charges against four of the class A directors, to remove them if the charges be proven, to amend the by-laws so that the successor directors be elected by the class A stockholders, and further to amend the by-laws so that an effective quorum of directors will be made up of no fewer than half of the directors in office and no fewer than one third of the whole authorized number of directors. No reason appears why the class A stockholders should not be allowed to vote on any or all of those proposals.

The stockholders, by expressing their approval of Mr. Auer's conduct as president and their demand that he be put back in that office, will not be able, directly, to effect that change in officers, but there is nothing invalid in their so expressing themselves and thus putting on notice the directors who will stand for election at the annual meeting. As to purpose (B), that is, amending the charter and by-laws to authorize the stockholders to fill vacancies as to class A directors who have been removed on charges or who have resigned, it seems to be settled law that the stockholders who are empowered to elect directors have the inherent power to remove them for cause, In re Koch, 257 N.Y. 318, 321, 322, 178 N.E. 545, 546 * * *. Of course, as the Koch case points out, there must be the service of specific charges, adequate notice and full opportunity of meeting the accusations, but there is no present showing of any lack of any of those in this instance. Since these particular stockholders have the right to elect nine directors and to remove them on proven charges, it is not inappropriate that they should use their further power to amend the by-laws to elect the successors of such directors as shall be removed after hearing, or who shall resign pending hearing. Quite pertinent at this point is Rogers v. Hill, 289 U.S. 582, 589, 53 S.Ct. 731, 734, 77 L.Ed. 1385, which made light of an argument that stockholders, by giving power to the directors to make by-laws, had lost their own power to make them; quoting a New Jersey case, In re Griffing Iron Co., 63 N.J.L. 168, 41 A. 931, the United States Supreme Court said: " "It would be preposterous to leave the real owners of the corporate property at the mercy of their agents, and the law has not done so' ". Such a change in the by-laws, dealing with the class A directors only, has no effect on the voting rights of the common stockholders, which rights have to do with the selection of the remaining two directors only. True, the certificate of incorporation authorizes the board of directors to remove any director on charges, but we do not consider that provision as an abdication by the stockholders of their own traditional, inherent power to remove their own directors. Rather, it provides an additional method. Were that not so, the stockholders might find themselves without effective remedy in a case where a majority of the directors were accused of wrongdoing and, obviously, would be unwilling to remove themselves from office.

We fail to see, in the proposal to allow class A stockholders to fill vacancies as to class A directors, any impairment or any violation of paragraph (h) of article Third of the certificate of incorporation, which says that class A stock has exclusive voting rights with respect to all matters "other than the election of directors". That negative language should not be taken to mean that class A stockholders, who have an absolute right to elect nine of these eleven directors, cannot amend their by-laws to guarantee a similar right, in the class A stockholders and to the exclusion of common stockholders, to fill vacancies in the class A group of directors.

* * * Any director illegally removed can have his remedy in the courts, see People ex rel. Manice v. Powell, 201 N.Y. 194, 94 N.E. 634.

The order should be affirmed, with costs, and the Special Term directed forthwith to make an order in the same form as the Appellate Division order with appropriate changes of dates.

[VAN VOORHIS, J., dissented on the grounds that none of the cited purposes were appropriate subjects for action by shareholders at the requested meeting. Proposal A, the indorsement of Auer's tenure as president, was only "an idle gesture." The dissent argued that the second proposal was improper because the articles of incorporation authorized the directors to fill vacancies on the board, and the change sought would have denied the common stockholders their rights to a say in the replacement of directors through their two representatives on the board. Such a change, it was argued could be made only through special voting procedures. Proposal C, the removal of directors, was improper because a shareholders meeting was "altogether unsuited to the performance of duties which partake of the nature of the judicial function." Since most shareholders would vote by proxy, their decision would have to be made before the meeting at which the charges against the directors would be made and discussed. The fourth proposal was treated as irrelevant without action on the other three.]

CAMPBELL v. LOEW'S, INC.
36 Del.Ch. 563, 134 A.2d 852 (1957).

[This case involved a battle for control of Loew's Inc., by two factions, one headed by its President, Vogel, and the other by Tomlinson. At the February, 1957 shareholders' meeting the two factions effected a compromise; each faction was to have 6 directors and a neutral director would complete the 13 member board. In July, 1957, two of the Vogel directors, one Tomlinson director and the neutral director resigned. On July 30, 1957 there was a board meeting attended only by the five Tomlinson directors, who attempted to fill two vacancies. These elections were ruled invalid for lack of a quorum. Tomlinson v. Loew's Inc., 36 Del.Ch. 516, 134 A.2d 518 (1957) aff'd, 37 Del.Ch. 8, 135 A.2d 136 (Del.Supr.1957). Meanwhile, on July 29, 1957, Vogel, as president, sent out a notice calling a special shareholders' meeting for September 12, 1957 for the following purposes:

   1. to fill director vacancies;

2. to amend the by-laws to increase the number of board members from 13 to 19; to increase the quorum from 7 to 10; and to elect six additional directors;

3. to remove Tomlinson and Stanley Meyer as directors and to fill the vacancies thus created.

The plaintiff brought an action to enjoin this special shareholder's meeting and for other relief. The court first considered plaintiff's claim that the Vogel, as president, lacked the power to call a stockholders' meeting to amend the bylaws and fill vacancies on the board. Relying on a bylaw explicitly granting the president power to call special meetings of stockholders "for any purpose," the court rejected this claim.]

SEITZ, CHANCELLOR.

* * *

Plaintiff next argues that the stockholders have no power between annual meetings to elect directors to fill newly created directorships.

Plaintiff argues in effect that since the Loew's by-laws provide that the stockholders may fill "vacancies", and since our Courts have construed "vacancy" not to embrace "newly created directorships" (Automatic Steel Products v. Johnston, 31 Del.Ch. 469, 64 A.2d 416, 6 A.L.R.2d 170), the attempted call by the president for the purpose of filling newly created directorships was invalid.

Conceding that "vacancy" as used in the by-laws does not embrace "newly created directorships", that does not resolve this problem. I say this because in Moon v. Moon Motor Car Co., 17 Del.Ch. 176, 151 A. 298, it was held that the stockholders had the inherent right between annual meetings to fill newly created directorships. See also Automatic Steel Products v. Johnston, above. There is no basis to distinguish the Moon case unless it be because the statute has since been amended to provide that not only vacancies but newly created directorships "may be filled by a majority of the directors then in office * * * unless it is otherwise provided in the certificate of incorporation or the by-laws * * *". 8 Del.C. § 223. Obviously, the amendment to include new directors is not worded so as to make the statute exclusive. It does not prevent the stockholders from filling the new directorships. * * *

I therefore conclude that the stockholders of Loew's do have the right between annual meetings to elect directors to fill newly created directorships.

Plaintiff next argues that the shareholders of a Delaware corporation have no power to remove directors from office even for cause and thus the call for that purpose is invalid. The defendant naturally takes a contrary position.

While there are some cases suggesting the contrary, I believe that the stockholders have the power to remove a director for cause. This power must be implied when we consider that otherwise a director who is guilty of the worst sort of violation of his duty could nevertheless remain on the board. It is hardly to be believed that a director who is disclosing the corporation's trade secrets to a competitor would be immune from removal by the stockholders. Other examples, such as embezzlement of corporate funds, etc., come readily to mind.

But plaintiff correctly states that there is no provision in our statutory law providing for the removal of directors by stockholder action. In contrast he calls attention to § 142 of 8 Del.C., dealing with officers, which specifically refers to the possibility of a vacancy in an office by removal. He also notes that the Loew's by-laws provide for the removal of officers and employees but not directors. From these facts he argues that it was intended that directors not be removed even for cause. I believe the statute and by-law are of course some evidence to support plaintiff's contention. But when we seek to exclude the existence of a power by implication, I think it is pertinent to consider whether the absence of the power can be said to subject the corporation to the possibility of real damage. I say this because we seek intention and such a factor would be relevant to that issue. Considering the damage a director might be able to inflict upon his corporation, I believe the doubt must be resolved by construing the statutes and by-laws as leaving untouched the question of director removal for cause. This being so, the Court is free to conclude on reason that the stockholders have such inherent power.

I therefore conclude that as a matter of Delaware corporation law the stockholders do have the power to remove directors for cause. I need not and do not decide whether the stockholders can by appropriate charter or by-law provision deprive themselves of this right.   * * *

I turn next to plaintiff's charges relating to procedural defects and to irregularities in proxy solicitation by the Vogel group.

Plaintiff's first point is that the stockholders can vote to remove a director for cause only after such director has been given adequate notice of charges of grave impropriety and afforded an opportunity to be heard. * * *

I am inclined to agree that if the proceedings preliminary to submitting the matter of removal for cause to the stockholders appear to be legal and if the charges are legally sufficient on their face, the Court should ordinarily not intervene. The sufficiency of the evidence would be a matter for evaluation in later proceedings. But where the procedure adopted to remove a director for cause is invalid on its face, a stockholder can attack such matters before the meeting. This conclusion is dictated both by the desirability of avoiding unnecessary and expensive action and by the importance of settling internal disputes, where reasonably possible, at the earliest moment. Otherwise a director could be removed and his successor could be appointed and participate in important board action before the illegality of the removal was judicially established. This seems undesirable where the illegality is clear on the face of the proceedings.   * * *

Turning now to plaintiff's contentions, it is certainly true that when the shareholders attempt to remove a director for cause, " * * * there must be the service of specific charges, adequate notice and full opportunity of meeting the accusation * * * ". See Auer v. Dressel, * * * above. While it involved an invalid attempt by directors to remove a fellow director for cause, nevertheless, this same general standard was recognized in Bruch v. National Guarantee Credit Corp. [13 Del.Ch. 180, 116 A. 738], above. The Chancellor said that the power of removal could not "be exercised in an arbitrary manner. The accused director would be entitled to be heard in his own defense".

Plaintiff asserts that no specific charges have been served upon the two directors sought to be ousted; that the notice of the special meeting fails to contain a specific statement of the charges; that the proxy statement which accompanied the notice also failed to notify the stockholders of the specific charges; and that it does not inform the stockholders that the accused must be afforded an opportunity to meet the accusations before a vote is taken.

Matters for stockholder consideration need not be conducted with the same formality as judicial proceedings. The proxy statement specifically recites that the two directors are sought to be removed for the reasons stated in the president's accompanying letter. Both directors involved received copies of the letter. Under the circumstances I think it must be said that the two directors involved were served with notice of the charges against them. * * *

I next consider plaintiff's contention that the charges against the two directors do not constitute "cause" as a matter of law. It would take too much space to narrate in detail the contents of the president's letter. I must therefore give my summary of its charges. First of all, it charges that the two directors (Tomlinson and Meyer) failed to cooperate with Vogel in his announced program for rebuilding the company; that their purpose has been to put themselves in control; that they made baseless accusations against him and other management personnel and attempted to divert him from his normal duties as president by bombarding him with correspondence containing unfounded charges and other similar acts; that they moved into the company's building, accompanied by lawyers and accountants, and immediately proceeded upon a planned scheme of harassment. They called for many records, some going back twenty years, and were rude to the personnel. Tomlinson sent daily letters to the directors making serious charges directly and by means of innuendos and misinterpretations.

Are the foregoing charges, if proved, legally sufficient to justify the ouster of the two directors by the stockholders? I am satisfied that a charge that the directors desired to take over control of the corporation is not a reason for their ouster. Standing alone, it is a perfectly legitimate objective which is a part of the very fabric of corporate existence. Nor is a charge of lack of cooperation a legally sufficient basis for removal for cause.

The next charge is that these directors, in effect, engaged in a calculated plan of harassment to the detriment of the corporation. Certainly a director may examine books, ask questions, etc., in the discharge of his duty, but a point can be reached when his actions exceed the call of duty and become deliberately obstructive. In such a situation, if his actions constitute a real burden on the corporation then the stockholders are entitled to relief. The charges in this area made by the Vogel letter are legally sufficient to justify the stockholders in voting to remove such directors. In so concluding I of course express no opinion as to the truth of the charges.

I therefore conclude that the charge of "a planned scheme of harassment" as detailed in the letter constitutes a justifiable legal basis for removing a director.

I next consider whether the directors sought to be removed have been given a reasonable opportunity to be heard by the stockholders on the charges made. * * *

There seems to be an absence of cases detailing the appropriate procedure for submitting a question of director removal for cause for stockholder consideration. I am satisfied, however, that to the extent the matter is to be voted upon by the use of proxies, such proxies may be solicited only after the accused directors are afforded an opportunity to present their case to the stockholders. This means, in my opinion, that an opportunity must be provided such directors to present their defense to the stockholders by a statement which must accompany or precede the initial solicitation of proxies seeking authority to vote for the removal of such director for cause. If not provided then such proxies may not be voted for removal. And the corporation has a duty to see that this opportunity is given the directors at its expense. Admittedly, no such opportunity was given the two directors involved. * * *

I therefore conclude that the procedural sequence here adopted for soliciting proxies seeking authority to vote on the removal of the two directors is contrary to law. The result is that the proxy solicited by the Vogel group, which is based upon unilateral presentation of the facts by those in control of the corporate facilities, must be declared invalid insofar as they purport to give authority to vote for the removal of the directors for cause.

A preliminary injunction will issue restraining the corporation from recognizing or counting any proxies held by the Vogel group and others insofar as such proxies purport to grant authority to vote for the removal of Tomlinson and Meyer as directors of the corporation. * * *

[Chancellor Seitz went on to deal with a number of other questions relating to the use by the Vogel faction of corporate funds and facilities in the solicitation of proxies. He ruled, among other things, that the Vogel faction, which stood for existing policy, was justified in using corporate funds for the solicitation of proxies. He did not rule on whether the Tomlinson faction would also have access to the corporate treasury for that purpose. Finally, the Chancellor declined to issue an injunction ordering the four Vogel directors to attend board meetings so as to constitute a quorum. He held that, under the circumstances, at least, it was not a breach of their fiduciary duty to engage in a concerted plan to prevent the board from acting by refusing to attend meetings.]

––––––––

Chancellor Seitz' ruling that the Vogel faction could use corporate funds to solicit proxies to remove directors who opposed its business policies had substantial precedential support. In Hall v. Trans–Lux Daylight Picture Screen Corp., 20 Del.Ch. 78, 171 A. 226 (Del.Ch.1934), the court reasoned that because directors properly can use corporate funds to inform shareholders about transactions for which their approval is sought, directors also should be able to use corporate funds in a contest for control "in the interest of an intelligent exercise of judgment on the part of the stockholders upon policies to be pursued * * *." However, where no question of policy is involved, "where the expenditures [to solicit proxies] are solely in the personal interest of the directors to maintain themselves in office, [they] are not proper." Id. at 228. See, also, Empire Southern Gas Co. v. Gray, 29 Del.Ch. 95, 102, 46 A.2d 741, 744 (1946).

Of course, as the court pointed out in Steinberg v. Adams, 90 F.Supp. 604, 608 (S.D.N.Y.1950), "generally policy and personnel do not exist in separate compartments. A change in personnel is sometimes indispensible to a change in policy. A new board may be the symbol of the shift in policy, as well as the means of obtaining it." Consequently, almost every time a proxy contest arises, incumbent directors will be able to justify use of corporate funds on the grounds that the insurgents' challenge, in essence, is motivated by disagreement about policies the incumbents have pursued.

Incumbents thus have a tremendous advantage in a proxy contest. They have access to the corporate treasury. Insurgents must use their own funds to finance a proxy solicitations, and can recover their costs only if they prevail. See Steinberg v. Adams, supra; Rosenfeld v. Fairchild Engine & Airplane Corp., 309 N.Y. 168, 128 N.E.2d 291 (1955).

Incumbent directors, however, may want more than a financial advantage. They may attempt to use their control over the corporation's business and affairs to impede the insurgents' efforts. Schnell v. Chris–Craft Industries (Chapter 3) makes clear that such tactics are subject to equitable limitations. More recent cases elaborate that principle.

5. BOARD RESPONSES TO SHAREHOLDER INITIATIVES

BLASIUS INDUSTRIES, INC. v. ATLAS CORP.
564 A.2d 651 (Del.Ch.1988).

[Blasius began to accumulate Atlas shares for the first time in July, 1987. On October 29, 1987, Blasius disclosed that it owned 9.1% of

Atlas' common stock and stated in that it intended to encourage Atlas' management to consider a restructuring of the company. Blasius also disclosed that it was exploring the feasibility of obtaining control of Atlas.

Atlas' management did not welcome the prospect of Blasius' controlling shareholders involving themselves in Atlas' affairs. Atlas' new CEO, Weaver, had overseen a business restructuring of a sort and thought it should be given a chance to produce benefit before another restructuring was attempted.

Early in December, 1987, Blasius suggested that Atlas engage in a leveraged restructuring and distribute to its shareholders a one-time dividend of $35 million in cash and $125 million in subordinated debentures. Atlas's management responded coolly to this proposal. Mr. Weaver expressed surprise that Blasius would suggest using debt to accomplish a substantial liquidation of Atlas at a time when Atlas' future prospects were promising.

On December 30, 1987, Blasius delivered to Atlas a signed written consent (1) adopting a precatory resolution recommending that the board develop and implement a restructuring proposal, (2) amending the Atlas bylaws to, among other things, expand the size of the board from seven to fifteen members—the maximum number under Atlas' charter, and (3) electing eight named persons to fill the new directorships. Blasius also informed Atlas of its intent to solicit consents from other Atlas shareholders pursuant to Del.Gen.Corp.L. § 228.

Mr. Weaver immediately conferred with Mr. Masinter, Atlas' outside counsel and a director, who viewed the consent as an attempt to take control of Atlas. They decided to call an emergency meeting of the board, even though a regularly scheduled meeting was to occur only one week hence, on January 6, 1988. In a telephone meeting held the next day, the board voted to amend Atlas' bylaws to increase the size of the board from seven to nine and then appointed John M. Devaney and Harry J. Winters, Jr. to fill the two newly created positions.]

ALLEN, CHANCELLOR.

Plaintiff attacks the December 31 board action as a selfishly motivated effort to protect the incumbent board from a perceived threat to its control of Atlas. * * *

Defendants, of course, contest every aspect of plaintiffs' claims. They claim the formidable protections of the business judgment rule. * * *

III.

* * *

While I am satisfied that the evidence is powerful, indeed compelling, that the board was chiefly motivated on December 31 to forestall or preclude the possibility that a majority of shareholders might place on the Atlas board eight new members sympathetic to the Blasius proposal, it is less clear with respect to the more subtle motivational question: whether the existing members of the board did so because they held a good faith belief that such shareholder action would be self-injurious and shareholders needed to be protected from their own judgment.

On balance, I cannot conclude that the board was acting out of a self-interested motive in any important respect on December 31. I conclude rather that the board saw the "threat" of the Blasius recapitalization proposal as posing vital policy differences between itself and Blasius. It acted, I conclude, in a good faith effort to protect its incumbency, not selfishly, but in order to thwart implementation of the recapitalization that it feared, reasonably, would cause great injury to the Company.

The real question the case presents, to my mind, is whether, in these circumstances, the board, even if it *is* acting with subjective good faith * * *, may validly act for the principal purpose of preventing the shareholders from electing a majority of new directors. The question thus posed is not one of intentional wrong (or even negligence), but one of authority *as between the fiduciary and the beneficiary* * * *.

IV.

* * *

The shareholder franchise is the ideological underpinning upon which the legitimacy of directorial power rests. Generally, shareholders have only two protections against perceived inadequate business performance. They may sell their stock (which, if done in sufficient numbers, may so affect security prices as to create an incentive for altered managerial performance), or they may vote to replace incumbent board members.

It has, for a long time, been conventional to dismiss the stockholder vote as a vestige or ritual of little practical importance. It may be that we are now witnessing the emergence of new institutional voices and arrangements that will make the stockholder vote a less predictable affair than it has been. Be that as it may, however, whether the vote is seen functionally as an unimportant formalism, or as an important tool of discipline, it is clear that it is critical to the theory that legitimates the exercise of power by some (directors and officers) over vast aggregations of property that they do not own. Thus, when viewed from a broad, institutional perspective, it can be seen that matters involving the integrity of the shareholder voting process involve consideration not present in any other context in which directors exercise delegated power. * * *

The distinctive nature of the shareholder franchise context also appears when the matter is viewed from a less generalized, doctrinal point of view. From this point of view, as well, it appears that the ordinary considerations to which the business judgment rule originally responded are simply not present in the shareholder voting context. That is, a decision by the board to act for the primary purpose of preventing the effectiveness of a shareholder vote inevitably involves the question who, as between the principal and the agent, has authority with respect to a matter of internal corporate governance. That, of course, is true in a very specific way in this case which deals with the question who should constitute the board of directors of the corporation, but it will be true in every instance in which an incumbent board seeks to thwart a shareholder majority. A board's decision to act to prevent the shareholders from creating a majority of new board positions and filling them does not involve the exercise of *the corporation's power* over its property, or with respect to *its* rights or obligations; rather, it involves allocation, between shareholders as a class and the board, of effective power with respect to governance of the corporation. * * * Action designed principally to interfere with the effectiveness of a vote inevitably involves a conflict between the board and a shareholder majority. Judicial review of such action involves a determination of the legal and equitable obligations of an agent towards his principal. This is not, in my opinion, a question that a court may leave to the agent finally to decide so long as he does so honestly and competently; that is, it may not be left to the agent's business judgment. * * *

Plaintiff argues for a rule of *per se* invalidity once a plaintiff has established that a board has acted for the primary purpose of thwarting the exercise of a shareholder vote. * * *

A *per se* rule that would strike down, in equity, any board action taken for the primary purpose of interfering with the effectiveness of a corporate vote would have the advantage of relative clarity and predictability. It also has the advantage of most vigorously enforcing the concept of corporate democracy. The disadvantage it brings along is, of course, the disadvantage a *per se* rule always has: it may sweep too broadly.

In two recent cases dealing with shareholder votes, this court struck down board acts done for the primary purpose of impeding the exercise of stockholder voting power. In doing so, a *per se* rule was not applied. Rather, it was said that, in such a case, the board bears the heavy burden of demonstrating a compelling justification for such action. * * *

In my view, our inability to foresee now all of the future settings in which a board might, in good faith, paternalistically seek to thwart a shareholder vote, counsels against the adoption of a *per se* rule invalidating, in equity, every board action taken for the sole or primary purpose of thwarting a shareholder vote, even though I recognize the transcending significance of the franchise to the claims to legitimacy of our scheme of corporate governance. It may be that some set of facts would justify such extreme action. This, however, is not such a case. * * *

[In this case], [t]he board was not faced with a coercive action taken by a powerful shareholder against the interests of a distinct shareholder constituency (such as a public minority). It was presented with a consent solicitation by a 9% shareholder. Moreover, here it had time (and understood that it had time) to inform the shareholders of its views on the merits of the proposal subject to stockholder vote. The only justification that can, in such a situation, be offered for the action taken is that the board knows better than do the shareholders what is in the corporation's best interest. While that premise is no doubt true for any number of matters, it is irrelevant (except insofar as the shareholders wish to be guided by the board's recommendation) when the question is who should comprise the board of directors. The theory of our corporation law confers power upon directors as the agents of the shareholders; it does not create Platonic masters. It may be that the Blasius restructuring proposal was or is unrealistic and would lead to injury to the corporation and its shareholders if pursued. * * * The board certainly viewed it that way, and that view, held in good faith, entitled the board to take certain steps to evade the risk it perceived. It could, for example, expend corporate funds to inform shareholders and seek to bring them to a similar point of view. But there is a vast difference between expending corporate funds to inform the electorate and exercising power for the primary purpose of foreclosing effective shareholder action. A majority of the shareholders, who were not dominated in any respect, could view the matter differently than did the board. If they do, or did, they are entitled to employ the mechanisms provided by the corporation law and the Atlas certificate of incorporation to advance that view. They are also entitled, in my opinion, to restrain their agents, the board, from acting for the principal purpose of thwarting that action.

I therefore conclude that, even finding the action taken was taken in good faith, it constituted an unintended violation of the duty of loyalty that the board owed to the shareholders. I note parenthetically that the concept of an unintended breach of the duty of loyalty is unusual but not novel. That action will, therefore, be set aside by order of this court. * * *

Blasius applied the principle, announced in *Schnell*, that "inequitable action does not become permissible simply because it is legally possible." But while *Blasius* discussed at greater length than did *Schnell* why an otherwise legal action relating to the corporate electoral process was deemed inequitable, it left unresolved, as did *Schnell*, *what* makes such an action inequitable. In Stahl v. Apple Bancorp, Inc., 579 A.2d 1115 (Del.Ch.1990), Chancellor Allen attempted to place in context *Schnell*, *Blasius* and several other Delaware decisions that have involved this issue.

Apple Bancorp's board had chosen a record date for its annual meeting, but had not formally announced that date. Stahl, who owned 30 percent of Apple's stock, informed the board he intended to conduct a proxy contest to gain control, and subsequently made a cash tender offer for all the bank's stock. The board deferred the record date and the annual meeting. Stahl, relying on *Schnell* and *Blasius*, sued to require the board to set a record date and a date for the annual meeting.

Chancellor Allen denied Stahl's request for relief and offered the following explanation of how his decision related to *Schnell* and its progeny:

> [I]t is well established * * * that where corporate directors exercise their legal powers for an inequitable purpose their action may be rescinded or nullified by a court at the instance of an aggrieved shareholder. The leading Delaware case of Schnell v. Chris–Craft Industries, Inc. announced this principle and applied it in a setting in which directors advanced the date of an annual meeting in order to impede an announced proxy contest.

> Under this test the court asks the question whether the directors' purpose is "inequitable." An inequitable purpose is not necessarily synonymous with a dishonest motive. Fiduciaries who are subjectively operating selflessly might be pursuing a purpose that a court will rule is inequitable. Thus, for example, there was no inquiry concerning the board's subjective good faith in *Condec Corporation v. Lunkenheimer Company*, where this court held that the issuance of stock for the principal purpose of eliminating the ability of a large stockholder to determine the outcome of a vote was invalid as a breach of loyalty. * * *

> *Lerman v. Diagnostic Data, Inc.* * * * explicitly expresses the view that inequitable conduct does not necessarily require an evil or selfish motive. There the court held a bylaw invalid in the situation before it where that bylaw would have precluded a shareholder from mounting a proxy contest. The court referred to the fact that the bylaw "whether designedly inequitable or not, has had a terminal effect on the aspirations of Lerman and his group."

> Each of these cases dealt with board action with a principal purpose of impeding the exercise of stockholder power through the vote. They could be read as approximating a *per se* rule that board action taken for the principal purpose of impeding the effective exercise of the stockholder franchise is inequitable and will be restrained or set aside in proper circumstances.

> Consistent with these authorities, in *Blasius* and in *Aprahamian* [v. HBO & Co., 531 A.2d 1204 (Del.Ch.1987)], this court held that action designed primarily to impede the effective exercise of the franchise is not evaluated under the business judgment form of review * * *. These statements are simply restatements of the principle applied in *Schnell*. *Blasius* did, however, go on to reject the notion of *per se* invalidity of action taken to interfere with the effective exercise of the corporate franchise; it admitted the possibility that in some circumstances such action might be consistent with the directors equitable obligations. It was suggested, however, that

such circumstances would have to constitute "compelling justification," given the central role of the stockholder franchise.

Thus, *Blasius'* reference to "compelling justification" reflects only the high value that the prior cases had placed upon the exercise of voting rights and the inherently particularized and contextual nature of any inquiry concerning fiduciary duties. Neither it nor *Aprahamian* represent new law. * * *

In no sense can the decision not to call a meeting be likened to kinds of board action found to have constituted inequitable conduct relating to the vote. In each of these franchise cases the effect of the board action—to advance (*Schnell*) or defer (*Aprahamian*) a meeting; to adopt a bylaw (*Lerman*); or to fill board vacancies (*Blasius*)—was practically to preclude effective stockholder action (*Schnell, Blasius, Lerman*) or to snatch victory from an insurgent slate on the eve of the noticed meeting (*Aprahamian*). Here the election process will go forward at a time consistent with the company's bylaws and with Section 211 of our corporation law. Defendant's decision does not preclude plaintiff or any other Bancorp shareholder from effectively exercising his vote, nor have proxies been collected that only await imminent counting. Plaintiff has no legal right to compel the holding of the company's annual meeting under Section 211(c) of the Delaware General Corporation Law, nor does he, in my opinion, have a right in equity to require the board to call a meeting now.

579 A.2d at 1121–23.

6. SHAREHOLDERS' RIGHT OF INSPECTION

To exercise fully their right to vote, and especially their right to initiate action, shareholders may need access to a corporation's books and records. At common law, a shareholder was deemed to have a right to inspect corporate books and records deriving from her equitable ownership of the corporation's assets. The right extended beyond the formal minutes of official actions "to include the documents, contracts, and papers of the corporation." Otis–Hidden Co. v. Scheirich, 187 Ky. 423, 219 S.W. 191, 194 (1920). But, to avoid disruption of the corporation's business, a shareholder was restricted to exercising her right to inspection at reasonable times and places and, more importantly, only when inspection was for a "proper purpose." See, e.g., In re Steinway, 159 N.Y. 250, 53 N.E. 1103 (1899); State ex rel. Rogers v. Sherman Oil Co., 31 Del. 570, 117 A. 122 (Del.Supr.1922).

Every state corporate statute now provides for a right of inspection, but statutory provisions vary considerably. Some have been construed to merely codify the common law right. See, e.g., State ex rel. O'Hara v. National Biscuit Co., 69 N.J.L. 198, 54 A. 241 (1903); Dines v. Harris, 88 Colo. 22, 291 P. 1024 (1930). Others impose limits on which shareholders are eligible to assert the right and which records are subject to inspection. DGCL § 220 (a) limits inspection to stockholders of record, thus making it difficult for investors who hold their shares in nominee accounts to exercise the right. Many states limit inspection rights to shareholders who own a certain percentage of a corporation's shares or who have held their shares for some minimum period. N.Y.B.C.L. § 624(b), which is typical, allows inspection by a shareholder who owns 5 percent of any class of stock or who has held her stock for at least six months. RMBCA § 16.02 grants inspection rights to beneficial owners as well as shareholders of record, but divides corporate records into two categories. Shareholders can readily inspect the articles of incorporation, by-laws, minutes of shareholder meetings and like documents. See RMBCA §§ 16.01(e), 16.02(a). But to inspect minutes of board meetings, accounting records, or the shareholder list, a shareholder must have a proper purpose and describe "with reasonable particularity" that purpose and the records to be inspected, which records must be "directly connected" with that purpose. RMBCA § 16.02(b).

The traditional remedy of a shareholder seeking inspection is a writ of mandamus. To prevent obstruction of a shareholder's right to inspect, many statutes make a corporation that refuses to grant inspection liable for the shareholder's costs, including reasonable attorney's fees, on the corporation, unless the corporation can establish that it acted reasonably. See, e.g., RMBCA § 16.04(c).

a. Proper Purpose

Probably the most difficult hurdle faced by a shareholder seeking inspection of corporate books and records is the establishment of a proper purpose. Statutes usually do not define proper purpose or define it using vague terms such as "a purpose reasonably related to such person's interest as a stockholder." DGCL § 220(b); see also Official Comment to RMBCA § 16.02. A shareholder has no right to inspection "if his purpose be to satisfy his curiosity, to annoy or harass the corporation, or to accomplish some object hostile to the corporation or detrimental to its interests." Albee v. Lamson & Hubbard Corp., 320 Mass. 421, 69 N.E.2d 811, 813 (1946). Inspection will be denied where the object is to sell information for personal profit, see, e.g., State ex rel. Theile v. Cities Service Co., 31 Del. 514, 115 A. 773 (1922), or to aid a competing business, see, e.g., Slay v. Polonia Publishing Co., 249 Mich. 609, 229 N.W. 434 (1930). Conversely, determination of the value of shares, see, e.g., Bankers Trust Co. v. H. Rosenhirsch Co., 20 Misc.2d 792, 190 N.Y.S.2d 957 (1959), communication with other shareholders (including solicitation of proxies, solicitation of shareholders to join in a derivative suit and offers to purchase stock), see, e.g., Weber v. Continental Motors Corp., 305 F.Supp. 404 (S.D.N.Y.1969), and ascertainment of possible corporate mismanagement, see e.g., Briskin v. Briskin Manufacturing Co., 6 Ill.App.3d 740, 286 N.E.2d 571 (1972) have been held to constitute proper purposes. Once a proper purpose has been established, the fact that a shareholder may have other, improper purposes for seeking inspection generally does not constitute a valid reason to refuse inspection. See, e.g., General Time Corp. v. Talley Industries, Inc., 43 Del.Ch. 531, 240 A.2d 755 (Del.1968).

In determining whether the shareholder has alleged or proved a proper purpose for inspection, courts usually have focused on whether the asserted purpose is germane to the shareholder's economic interest in the corporation. Some courts, however, also have had occasion to consider whether inspection is available to a shareholder primarily concerned with a corporation's social or political policies.

STATE EX REL. PILLSBURY v. HONEYWELL, INC.
291 Minn. 322, 191 N.W.2d 406 (1971).

[Petitioner, a member of a prominent and wealthy Minneapolis family, wanted to stop production by Honeywell Inc. (Honeywell) of anti-personnel fragmentation bombs used in Vietnam. He purchased 100 shares for the "sole purpose" of gaining a voice in Honeywell's affairs and then requested a shareholders list in order to solicit proxies for the election of new directors. When Honeywell refused his request, he filed for a writ of mandamus. After discovery, the court denied relief, holding that the same result would pertain whether it applied Minnesota law or the law of Delaware, Honeywell's state of incorporation.]

KELLY, JUSTICE.

* * *

The trial court ordered judgment for Honeywell, ruling that petitioner had not demonstrated a proper purpose germane to his interest as a stockholder. Petitioner contends that a stockholder who disagrees with management has an absolute right to inspect corporate records for purposes of soliciting proxies. He would have this court rule that such solicitation is per se a "proper purpose." Honeywell argues that a "proper purpose" contemplates concern with investment return. We agree with Honeywell.

This court has had several occasions to rule on the propriety of shareholders' demands for inspection of corporate books and records. Minn.St. 300.32, not applicable here, has been held to be declaratory of the common-law principle that a stockholder is entitled to inspection for a proper purpose germane to his business interests. While inspection will not be permitted for purposes of curiosity, speculation, or vexation, adverseness to management and a desire to gain control of the corporation for economic benefit does not indicate an improper purpose.

Several courts agree with petitioner's contention that a mere desire to communicate with other shareholders is, per se, a proper purpose. This would seem to confer an almost absolute right to inspection. We believe that a better rule would allow inspections only if the shareholder has a proper purpose for such communication. * * *

The act of inspecting a corporation's shareholder ledger and business records must be viewed in its proper perspective. In terms of the corporate norm, inspection is merely the act of the concerned owner checking on what is in part his property. In the context of the large firm, inspection can be more akin to a weapon in corporate warfare. * * * Because the power to inspect may be the power to destroy, it is important that only those with a bona fide interest in the corporation enjoy that power.

That one must have proper standing to demand inspection has been recognized by statutes in several jurisdictions. Courts have also balked at compelling inspection by a shareholder holding an insignificant amount of stock in the corporation.

Petitioner's standing as a shareholder is quite tenuous. He only owns one share in his own name, bought for the purposes of this suit. He had previously ordered his agent to buy 100 shares, but there is no showing of investment intent. While his agent had a cash balance in the $400,000 portfolio, petitioner made no attempt to determine whether Honeywell was a good investment or whether more profitable shares would have to be sold to finance the Honeywell purchase. Furthermore, petitioner's agent had the power to sell the Honeywell shares without his consent. Petitioner also had a contingent beneficial interest in 242 shares. Courts are split on the question of whether an equitable interest entitles one to inspection. See 5 Fletcher, Private Corporations, § 2230 at 862 (Perm. ed. rev. vol. 1967). Indicative of petitioner's concern regarding his equitable holdings is the fact that he was unaware of them until he had decided to bring this suit.

Petitioner had utterly no interest in the affairs of Honeywell before he learned of Honeywell's production of fragmentation bombs. Immediately after obtaining this knowledge, he purchased stock in Honeywell for the sole purpose of asserting ownership privileges in an effort to force Honeywell to cease such production. * * * But for his opposition to Honeywell's policy, petitioner probably would not have bought Honeywell stock, would not be interested in Honeywell's profits and would not desire to communicate with Honeywell's shareholders. His avowed purpose in buying Honeywell stock was to place himself in a position to try to impress his opinions favoring a reordering of priorities upon Honeywell management and its other shareholders. Such a motivation can hardly be deemed a proper purpose germane to his economic interest as a shareholder.[5]

5. We do not question petitioner's good faith incident to his political and social philosophy; nor did the trial court. In a well-prepared memorandum, the lower court stated: "By enumerating the foregoing this Court does not mean to belittle or to be derisive of Petitioner's motivation and intentions because this Court cannot but draw the conclusion that the Petitioner is sincere in his political and social philoso-phy, but this Court does not feel that this is a proper forum for the advancement of these political-social views by way of direct contact with the stockholders of Honeywell Company or any other company. If the courts were to grant these rights on the basis of the foregoing, anyone who has a political-social philosophy which differs with that of a company in which he becomes a shareholder can secure a writ and

* * * From the deposition, the trial court concluded that petitioner had already formed strong opinions on the immorality and the social and economic wastefulness of war long before he bought stock in Honeywell. His sole motivation was to change Honeywell's course of business because that course was incompatible with his political views. If unsuccessful, petitioner indicated that he would sell the Honeywell stock.

We do not mean to imply that a shareholder with a bona fide investment interest could not bring this suit if motivated by concern with the long- or short-term economic effects on Honeywell resulting from the production of war munitions. Similarly, this suit might be appropriate when a shareholder has a bona fide concern about the adverse effects of abstention from profitable war contracts on his investment in Honeywell.

In the instant case, however, the trial court, in effect, has found from all the facts that petitioner was not interested in even the long-term well-being of Honeywell or the enhancement of the value of his shares. His sole purpose was to persuade the company to adopt his social and political concerns, irrespective of any economic benefit to himself or Honeywell. This purpose on the part of one buying into the corporation does not entitle the petitioner to inspect Honeywell's books and records.

Petitioner argues that he wishes to inspect the stockholder ledger in order that he may correspond with other shareholders with the hope of electing to the board one or more directors who represent his particular viewpoint. * * * While a plan to elect one or more directors is specific and the election of directors normally would be a proper purpose, here the purpose was not germane to petitioner's or Honeywell's economic interest. Instead, the plan was designed to further petitioner's political and social beliefs. Since the requisite propriety of purpose germane to his or Honeywell's economic interest is not present, the allegation that petitioner seeks to elect a new board of directors is insufficient to compel inspection. * * *

The order of the trial court denying the writ of mandamus is affirmed.

Pillsbury probably marks the low tide in the stockholder's right to inspect. The tenor of the times may explain both the result and the court's remark that "the power to inspect may be the power to destroy." While Mr. Pillsbury was launching his campaign against Honeywell, other protestors against the Vietnam war were engaged in more violent activities, including pouring blood on draft board files and even bombing government-supported research facilities.

any company can be faced with a rash and multitude of these types of actions which are not bona fide efforts to engage in a proxy fight for the purpose of taking over the company or electing directors, which the courts have recognized as being perfectly legitimate and acceptable."

Pillsbury has not been followed by the Delaware courts. Credit Bureau of St. Paul, Inc. v. Credit Bureau Reports, Inc., 290 A.2d 689 (Del.Ch.1972), aff'd 290 A.2d 691 (Del.1972), criticized the decision. In Conservative Caucus v. Chevron Corp., 525 A.2d 569 (Del.Ch.1987), the court upheld a request for a stockholder list by a shareholder seeking to solicit the support of fellow shareholders for a resolution directed at discouraging the corporation from doing business with Angola. The court stated:

> [The *Pillsbury*] holding is, of course, not binding on this court and it was criticized by the Delaware Supreme Court in *Credit Bureau Reports, Inc. v. Credit Bureau of St. Paul, Inc.*
>
> The facts are also different here. Plaintiff has testified that it seeks the stock list to warn the stockholders about the allegedly dire economic consequences which will fall upon Chevron if it continues to do business in Angola. Some of these possible economic consequences, according to plaintiff, are: sanctions by the U.S. Government; adverse consequences imposed by the Export–Import Bank; an embargo by the U.S. Defense Department on purchases of oil which has its source in Angola; a denial of certain federal tax credits; the risk to personnel and facilities of an unstable government; and, the risk of war in Angola. These are surely matters which might have an adverse affect on the value of the stock of Chevron. I, therefore, find that the holding in *Pillsbury* is not persuasive.

Id. at 572

b. *What Comprises a "Stockholder List?"*

New issues have arisen as a consequence of changes in corporations' record-keeping practices and investors' patterns of stock ownership. A corporation's records must list only the names of *"stockholders of record "*—persons holding legal title to outstanding shares of stock. See, e.g. RMBCA § 16.01(c). Today, however, most investors hold stock in public corporations in nominee accounts in *"street name."* Consequently, one cannot determine from those corporations' stockholder lists who beneficially owns most of their stock. In fact, one cannot even determine much about the nominee owners of record.

Most stock brokerage firms and financial institutions—which might be called "first tier" nominees—are members of Depositary Trust Company, an entity formed to hold their and their customers' stock. Depositary Trust registers all of its members' stock in one name, "CEDE & Co.," which allows it to simplify stock transfers among its members. But this practice results in many corporations' stockholder lists showing only that CEDE & Co. owns a large portion of their stock. The lists contain no indication either of which brokerage houses and institutions hold that stock or the beneficial owners are.

Depositary Trust has eliminated the first of these problems. At the request of any corporation, it will prepare in minutes a "CEDE breakdown"—a list of all firms holding stock in the name of CEDE & Co. The corporation then can contact those firms to determine the number of beneficial owners each represents, so as to facilitate distribution through those firms of annual reports, notices of shareholder meetings, and other data. The brokerage firms and institutions generally will not volunteer the names of the customers for whom they hold stock, though; they consider that information confidential.

Brokerage firms, however, must comply with a Securities and Exchange Commission requirement that they ask each customer who holds stock in street name whether she objects to disclosure to her name to corporations in which she has invested. See SEC Rel. No. 34–22533, 50 F.R. 204 (1985). Brokerage firms also must deliver within seven business days a list of non-objecting beneficial owners (a *"NOBO list "*) to any corporation that requests such a list .

Delaware courts require corporations to deliver to shareholders entitled to inspect stockholder lists both CEDE breakdowns and NOBO lists already within those corporations' possession. See Hatleigh Corp. v. Lane Bryant, Inc. 428 A.2d 350 (Del.Ch.1981) (CEDE breakdown); Shamrock Assoc. v. Texas Am. Energy Corp., 517 A.2d 658 (Del.Ch.1986) (NOBO list).* They also require a corporation to have a CEDE breakdown produced if it has not already done so. See Tactron, Inc. v. KDI Corp., 1985 WL 44699 (Del.Ch. 1985). However, in RB Assoc. of N.J., L.P. v. Gillette Co., 1988 WL 27731 (Del.Ch. Mar. 22, 1988), the court declined to compel Gillette, which had not requested and had no intention of requesting production of a NOBO list, to request that such a list be produced. After explaining that a CEDE breakdown can be obtained almost instantaneously, which makes production of one necessary in order to put "contesting parties * * * on substantially the same footing, the court continued:

> A NOBO list is different in two material respects. First, the evidence demonstrates that such a list takes approximately ten days to produce. It is not immediately available to the issuer. Second, a modern proxy solicitation can hardly be conducted at all without the benefit of a breakdown of the persons for whom a depository company holds its shares. * * *

> A NOBO list plays no central role in a proxy contest. While the information it discloses (i.e., the identity of the ultimate owners) may, of course, be of use in telephone solicitations, that information is not necessary for the effective working of the written proxy solicitation process. * * *

> * * * Neither broad concepts of fairness, nor the words of Section 220, in my opinion, require that a corporation be forced * * * to exercise the option created by the applicable SEC Rules at the behest of a shareholder. What fairness does require [is that

---

* Delaware courts also require production of stock transfer sheets and computer tapes listing a corporation's stockholders. See   Tannetics, Inc. v. A.J. Indus., Inc., 1974 WL 2038 (Del.Ch.1974).

Gillette be ordered to produce a NOBO list if it chooses to request that one be prepared].

Id. at * 6– * 7.

SADLER v. NCR CORPORATION

928 F.2d 48 (2d Cir.1991).

[NCR, a Maryland corporation, was resisting a takeover bid by AT&T, in part by refusing to redeem a "poison pill" that presented a substantial obstacle to AT&T. AT&T sought to eliminate that obstacle by soliciting proxies to remove NCR's incumbent directors and to elect new directors prepared to redeem the poison pill. NCR's articles of incorporation provided that directors could be removed only by the affirmative vote of 80 percent of all outstanding shares.

In connection with its proxy solicitation, AT&T arranged for the Sadlers, New York resident shareholders of NCR, to seek to inspect NCR's shareholder list pursuant to N.Y. BCL § 1315 and compel NCR to request and provide a NOBO list. § 1315 grants inspection rights to New York residents who have held stock in a foreign corporation for more than six months.

The district court held that the Sadlers were qualified to seek inspection pursuant to § 1315, even though they were acting on behalf of AT&T, and also ordered NCR to provide a NOBO list.]

Jon O. Newman, Circuit Judge.

[The court affirmed that the Sadlers were eligible to request inspection, and then turned to their attempt to compel production of a NOBO list.]

The matter was given extended consideration by Chancellor Allen in *RB Associates*. In declining to order compilation of a NOBO list, he distinguished it in two respects from CEDE lists, which Delaware and New York require a corporation to compile upon request of a qualified shareholder. * * *

We do not find either distinction compelling. Since compilation of a NOBO list is a relatively simple mechanical task, the fact that compilation takes longer than for a CEDE list is an insubstantial basis for distinction. As to both sets of information, the underlying data exist in discrete records readily available to be compiled into an aggregate list. Nor are the functions of the lists significantly dissimilar. Both facilitate direct communication with stockholders, in the case of a NOBO list, at least with those beneficial owners who have indicated no objection to disclosure of their names and addresses.

Though Delaware chooses to construe the reach of its requirements on stockholder list disclosure narrowly in this respect, * * * we think New York would apply section 1315 to permit a qualifying shareholder to require the compilation and production of such a list.

Even if the statute might not require compilation of NOBO lists routinely, we agree * * * that compilation was properly ordered in this case. The effect of NCR's 80 percent rule is to count as a "no" vote on the replacement of directors every share that is not voted at the special meeting. Thus, the shares of non-voting beneficial owners who might oppose management if solicited by management opponents armed with a NOBO list are counted in favor of management. Denying such opponents an opportunity to contact the NOBOs is inconsistent with the statute's objective of seeking "to the extent possible, to place shareholders on an equal footing with management in obtaining access to shareholders." *Bohrer* [*v. International Banknote Co.*], 150 A.D.2d [196,] 196–97, 540 N.Y.S.2d [445,] 446 [(1st Dept. 1989)]. In effect, NCR already has the votes of those NOBOs who, for lack of solicitation, decline to vote. As to them, NCR has all the access it needs.

* * *

The order of the District Court is affirmed.

Chapter 13

CONTROL PROBLEMS IN THE CLOSELY HELD CORPORATION

A. INTRODUCTION

1. OVERVIEW

One of the difficulties of the American law of corporations is that on its face, it attempts to fit small, closely held, or "close," corporations, which characteristically have few shareholders, into the same legal structure as publicly held giants of the size and character of General Motors and AT&T. Although the corporation statutes of some other industrialized countries make special provision for the close corporation, often treating it in an entirely separate statute and endowing it with a name distinct from that applied to its larger cousin *, until recently most American statutes applied identical rules to all corporations regardless of how big they were or how many shareholders they had.

The principal difficulty with the failure to differentiate between close and public corporations grows out of the fact that the shareholders of a close corporation are likely to think of themselves as partners who have elected to incorporate their business for tax reasons or to take advantage of limited liability. They may want the flexibility to design their own control arrangements, but they often will find that such arrangements conflict with the legal norms that govern corporations,

---

* France, for example, distinguishes between a *societé anonyme* ("S.A."), which is public and generally large, and a *societé a responsabilité limité* ("S.A.R.L."), a small to medium size company with 50 or fewer shareholders. In Germany the equivalent distinction is drawn between the Aktiengesellschaft ("A.G.") and the Gesellschaft mit beschrankte Haftung ("G.m.b.H."). In England there is separate statutory treatment of the private company and the public company. Scholars in the Continental countries draw a conceptual distinction between "associations of persons," which encompass their equivalents of our partnerships, and "associations of capital," the S.A. and the A.G. The S.A.R.L. and the G.m.b.H. are considered hybrids that fall in between the two extremes. As you read the following materials you might ask yourself whether a similar conceptual distinction could play a useful role in American law. See Henry G. Manne, Our Two Corporate Systems: Law and Economics, 53 Va.L.Rev. 259 (1967).

such as the principle that the board of directors is responsible for managing the corporation's business. Shareholders in a close corporation may well think it strange that they should be required to act as "directors," especially since they own the business and have the power to elect the directors. What is wrong with their simply agreeing among themselves how the business should be managed?

The tension between the legally-sanctioned model (recall Chapter 7 and our discussion of default models) and the needs and desires of the participants in the business venture creates a challenge for the attorney. It is a challenge, however, that an attorney usually can meet by careful planning and drafting. In this chapter we will examine the devices, some within the corporate framework and some extrinsic to it, that are available to the corporate planner. As planners, you should be aware of two significant trends: (1) the increased emphasis on dispute resolution and (2) the increased recognition of private ordering devices rather than the reliance on judicial intervention.

For many years the major hurdle that the planner of the close corporation faced was the reluctance of the courts to give effect to arrangements—whether embodied in the articles, by-laws, or a separate instrument—that departed too far from the traditional statutory model. Two parallel developments, starting primarily in the 1960's, have substantially loosened the bonds of this judicial straitjacket. First, the courts have taken a more realistic view of the practical demands of operating a business as a close corporation and have become far more tolerant of departures from the norm. Second, and perhaps more important, legislatures have recognized the unnecessary rigidity of the traditional structure and the problems that frequently arose out of the strict application of this structure to close corporations.

A growing number of states have amended their corporation statutes to allow more flexibility to close corporation planners. The most common statutory approach is to presume all corporations are alike but expressly to authorize close corporations to adopt governance structures that vary from the traditional model. See e.g., RMBCA §§ 7.32, 8.01(b). See also F. Hodge O'Neal & Robert B. Thompson, O'Neal's Close Corp. § 1.14 (3rd ed.) A second approach is the "comprehensive" close corporation statute, which allows the corporation to elect treatment under a special statutory regime. DGCL §§ 341–356 provides a good example of such a statute. Only a corporation that meets certain tests and elects close corporation status can make use of those sections of the Delaware statute.

Still, in some jurisdictions more modern statutes have not been adopted and the relevant case law may raise doubts as to the validity of particular governance arrangements or may make clear that certain departures from the traditional model—such as the management of a corporation by its shareholders without the intervention of a board of directors—are altogether unavailable. In such circumstances, counsel organizing a close corporation may find it advisable to consider incorporating in a jurisdiction that has adopted a more modern approach. Doing so, of course, will entail the additional expense and inconvenience associated with foreign incorporation, discussed in Chapter 8.

Notwithstanding the modern trend toward accepting departures from the norm, the student should be familiar with the older rules, not only because they are still operative in some jurisdictions, but because such familiarity is indispensable to a full appreciation of the significance of more modern statutory provisions and judicial thinking. Consequently, we have included in the following materials some cases that reflect traditional modes of judicial thinking, even though some of the rules they enunciate no longer have much operational significance. In addition, the policy questions these cases raise retain much of their importance.

We note at the outset that there is no generally agreed-upon definition of a "close corporation." In Donahue v. Rodd Electrotype Co. of New England, Inc., 367 Mass. 578, 328 N.E.2d 505 (1975), the court analyzed the characteristics of a close corporation as follows:

> There is no single, generally accepted definition. Some commentators emphasize an "integration of ownership and management," in which the stockholders occupy most management positions. Others focus on the number of stockholders and the nature of the market for the stock. In this view, close corporations have few stockholders; there is little market for corporate stock. The Supreme Court of Illinois adopted this latter view in Galler v. Galler, 32 Ill.2d 16, 203 N.E.2d 577 (1965): "For our purposes, a close corporation is one in which the stock is held in a few hands, or in a few families, and wherein it is not at all, or only rarely, dealt in by buying or selling." We accept aspects of both definitions. We deem a close corporation to be typified by: (1) a small number of stockholders; (2) no ready market for the corporate stock; and (3) substantial majority stockholder participation in the management, direction and operations of the corporation.

> As thus defined, the close corporation bears striking resemblance to a partnership. Commentators and courts have noted that the close corporation is often little more than an "incorporated" or "chartered" partnership. The stockholders "clothe" their partnership "with the benefits peculiar to a corporation, limited liability, perpetuity and the like." In the Matter of Surchin v. Approved Business Machine Co., Inc., 55 Misc.2d 888, 889, 286 N.Y.S.2d 580, 581 (Sup.Ct.1967). In essence, though, the enterprise remains one in which ownership is limited to the original parties or transferees of their stock to whom the other stockholders have agreed, in which ownership and management are in the same hands, and in which the owners are quite dependent on one another for the success of the enterprise. Many close corporations are "really partnerships, between two or three people who contribute their capital, skills, experience and labor." Kruger v. Gerth, 16 N.Y.2d 802, 805, 263

N.Y.S.2d 1, 3, 210 N.E.2d 355, 356 (1965) (Desmond, C.J., dissenting).

Frank Easterbrook and Daniel Fischel question the court's analogy and suggest that participants in a close corporation may not want to be governed by partnership law. As discussed in Chapter 7, corporate "default" rules differ from partnership "default" provisions in many respects. The tax consequences of operating as a corporation rather than a partnership also are strikingly different. Noting these differences, Easterbrook and Fischel conclude:

> Proponents of the partnership analogy assume that participants in closely held corporations are knowledgeable enough to incorporate to obtain the benefits of favorable tax treatment but ignorant of all other differences between corporate and partnership law. There is no support for this assumption once you recognize that people have to jump through a lot of formal hoops (assisted by counsel) to incorporate but can become partners by accident. * * *

> * * * A claim that people alert to the tax effects of incorporation were unaware of other effects is hard to take seriously, and when such people do not contract for the use of partnership-like rules, it is appropriate to apply corporate rules.

Frank Easterbrook and Daniel Fischel, The Economic Structure of Corporate Law 250–251 (1991).

2. PREINCORPORATION AGREEMENTS: AN INTRODUCTION TO PLANNING AND DISPUTE RESOLUTION

It is possible to organize a corporation without giving much thought at all to governance arrangements. Commercial services offer to do so for less than $50, plus filing fees. Many people no doubt create corporations in this fashion and agree informally on whatever financial and control arrangements they believe are necessary.

However, working out these arrangements more formally prior to incorporation and memorializing them in a preincorporation agreement. has a number of advantages.* It may be desirable to bind the promoters in advance of securing financial commitments from investors. Moreover, as we shall see, some of the more useful control devices must be set forth in the articles (see, e.g., RMBCA § 8.01(b)), while others may be included in a separate agreement. If such an agreement is needed, it often makes sense to write it before any money changes hands. Moreover, from a practical point of view, the discipline of spelling out the details of financial and control arrangements can prove useful. All the parties' arrangements can be taken into account. Misunderstandings

---

* Professor O'Neal distinguishes between a "promoters' contract," which merely binds the parties to proceeding with the organization of a corporation with a defined configuration, and a "shareholders' agreement," which consists of arrangements intended to bind the shareholders in various ways (to be discussed below) that will survive long after the corporation has been formally organized. He suggests that where both ends are sought, it may be best to use two different documents. F. Hodge O'Neal & Robert E. Thompson, O'Neal's Close Corp. § 2.29 (3rd ed.).

can be identified and resolved. Gaps in the structure are more likely to be noticed than if the parties give just casual attention to such matters.

However, limits exist on the utility of contracting as a means of avoiding future disputes. Contracting can be expensive and time consuming. Even where shareholders are prepared to incur the expense, anticipating the problems that actually will arise often is difficult. There is also a danger that dissension will develop relating to hypothetical problems that may well not arise. Some amount of planning usually is better than none, but judgment must be exercised as to how detailed the parties' contractual arrangements should be.

3. LAW AND ECONOMICS PERSPECTIVE ON CLOSE CORPORATIONS

In The Economic Structure of Corporate Law, Easterbrook and Fischel address the problems associated with closely held corporations from a law and economics perspective. Id. at 228–232. They focus on that fact that in closely held corporations, risk-bearing and management often are in the same hands.

This feature of closely held corporations has both advantages and disadvantages. Because managers also bear the cost of their actions, there is no specialization of functions. In addition, if managers also must invest in the firm, there are a limited number of qualified managers among whom to choose. Investors are less efficient risk bearers because they commit a greater percentage of their wealth to the firm. In public corporations, investors have greater latitude to diversify their investment portfolios.

In most closely held corporations, fewer conflicts of interest exist between management and the firm because what is good for the manager is good for the firm. Because many closely held corporations are based on familial or other personal relationships, agency costs and conflicts of interest are even further limited. Accordingly, there is less need for monitoring because managers are less likely to engage in self-dealing.

The lack of a public market for corporate shares is a significant detriment to the investors in a closely held corporation. Without a market for shares, investors encounter difficulty in valuing their share holdings. Simply put, there is no market price and shares are difficult to transfer. Moreover, investors do not have the protection offered by a market determined price. The illiquidity of the shares raises the possibility of conflicts over dividend policy. In a public corporation, investors can easily sell their shares if the corporate dividend policy is unacceptable. However, if a closely held corporation does not declare dividends, an investor who needs money is not able to sell her shares.

Easterbrook and Fischel identify another problem which stems from the lack of a public market: close corporation shareholders cannot rely on the market for corporate control to monitor managers' performance. In publicly held corporations, the market for corporate control constrains managers' conduct and facilitates the transfer of assets to higher valued uses. Because restrictions exist on an outsider's ability to acquire shares in a closely-held enterprise, the constraint on the conduct of management provided by the market for corporate control generally does not exist. Due to these potential problems, closely held firms "must promise to outsiders, and on average deliver, at least the competitive risk-adjusted rate of return available from other sorts of ventures." Id. at 232.

B. CONTROL DEVICES RELATING TO SHAREHOLDER VOTING

The most basic control devices are those designed to assure that all or certain shareholders are represented on a corporation's board. Three basic choices are available: An arrangement that merely ensures representation on the board; one that gives some or all shareholders the ability to veto board decisions with which they disagree; or one that contains some dispute resolution device. We begin with cumulative voting, a device designed to assure board representation for minority shareholders. Some states require both close and publicly-held corporations to use cumulative voting.

1. CUMULATIVE VOTING

PROBLEM
PRODUCTION CORPORATION

Production Corporation has an 8 member board of directors and 1500 shares of voting stock issued and outstanding. Assume that George, a Production shareholder, wants to evaluate the possibility of i) getting himself elected to the board, or ii) winning control of a majority of the board (5 positions). At the upcoming shareholders' meeting, George expects that 900 shares will be voted.

1. How many shares must George assemble to elect himself or a majority of the board under a straight voting system? How many shares are necessary under a cumulative voting system?

2. Assume cumulative voting is mandated by statute and that you represent the management of Production Corporation, which wishes to frustrate cumulative voting. What actions would you recommend?

There are two principal methods for conducting an election of directors. In straight voting each share is entitled to one vote for each director to be elected, but a shareholder is limited in the number of votes she may cast for any given director to the number of shares she owns. This means that any shareholder or group of shareholders controlling 51% of the shares may elect all of the members of the board.

Cumulative voting, the alternative method, is designed to allow shareholder groups to elect directors in rough proportion to the shares held by each group and thus to guarantee minority representation on the board. Under cumulative voting, each share again carries a number of votes equal to the number of directors to be elected, but a shareholder may "cumulate" her votes. Cumulating simply means multiplying the number of votes a shareholder is entitled to cast by the number of directors for whom she is entitled to vote. If there is cumulative voting, the shareholder may cast them all for one candidate or allocate them in any manner among a number of candidates.

The number of shares required to elect a given number of directors under a cumulative voting regime may be calculated by the following formula:

$$x = \frac{s \times d}{D + 1} + 1$$

Where:

x = Number of shares required to elect directors;
s = Number of shares represented at the meeting;
d = Number of directors it is desired to elect; and
D = Total number of directors to be elected.

To understand this formula, it is helpful to work through a simple example. Suppose that four directors are to be elected at a meeting at which 1000 shares are represented and will vote. In order to elect one director a minority group would have to control 201 shares. With that number, the minority group would have 804 votes (201 × 4), which would all be cast for one candidate. The majority would have 799 × 4 or 3196 votes. If the majority distributed these equally among four candidates, each would receive 799 votes, and the one candidate receiving the minority's 804 votes would be guaranteed a seat. In other words, just over 20% of the shares guarantees the election of one of four directors. If only three directors were to be elected, it would require just over 25% to elect one director. What percentage is necessary to elect one member to a five member board? (Note that the reason for the " + 1" at the end of the formula is the avoidance of the tie that would occur if, in this example, the minority controlled only 200 votes. Then it would be possible for five candidates each to receive 800 votes.) A little further consideration will easily show how the formula would work if it were desired to elect more than one director.

Some states require mandatory cumulative voting in implementing a policy favoring minority representation. Some jurisdictions, including California (Calif. Corp. Code § 708), provide for mandatory cumulative voting by statute. A few states, such as Arizona, Kentucky, and Missouri, provide for mandatory cumulative voting in their state constitutions. Most states do not require that cumulative voting be mandatory. In "opt out" states, such as Illinois, Minnesota, Pennsylvania, and Texas, cumulative voting exists unless there is a provision in the corporation's articles to the contrary. In "opt in" states, such as

Delaware (DGCL § 214) and New York (N.Y.B.C.L. § 618), cumulative voting only exists to the extent it is provided for in the corporation's articles. See also RMBCA § 7.28(d).

If the applicable statute gives the planner the opportunity to choose whether or not to implement a cumulative voting system, the corporation's CEO, as well as its counsel, must face the desirability of providing for minority representation on the board when a shareholder (or a group of shareholders) holds sufficient shares to make minority directors a realistic possibility. If the factions are badly split, the result of placing minority representatives on the board may simply remove critical decisions from the board room, with the effect that most are made by management, perhaps in informal consultation with the majority directors, and brought to board meetings only to be ratified. Critics of cumulative voting insist that to serve its intended function the board must function as a team, and that injecting factionalism into its operations merely reduces its effectiveness. On the other hand, cumulative voting is more equitable in that: it allows a voice to stockholders with large, but not controlling interests; it promotes the representation of divergent points of view, which will often result in superior decision-making; and it may discourage self-dealing and other improper conduct by a dominant faction because of the increased flow of information to and monitoring by representatives of minority interests.

A corporation's management occasionally seeks to undermine the effectiveness of cumulative voting to prevent the election of what management usually characterizes as "disruptive" or "divisive" representatives of minority interests. One popular method is to classify the board of directors, and stagger the election of directors so each class will be elected in different years. By staggering the elections, there will be fewer vacancies to be filled each year, thereby lowering the total number of votes for each shareholder. As the total number of votes is lowered, the majority has the advantage, as the process moves back toward straight voting. However, statutory limitations exist on how a corporation can classify its board. See, e.g., RMBCA § 8.06 and DGCL § 141(d).

Another method of diluting the effect of cumulative voting focuses on decreasing the total number of the corporation's directors. By reducing the size of the board, the corporation is again frustrating the intent of cumulative voting by decreasing the total number of votes a shareholder may cast and thereby increasing the percentage of stock necessary for a minority shareholder to elect one director. The courts have generally upheld this technique, even though it undermines cumulative voting. A planner may guard against the implementation of this technique by inserting provisions in the corporation's articles requiring a supermajority of votes in order to reduce the number of directors.

2. OTHER DEVICES WITHIN THE CORPORATE MACHINERY

Parts I–VII of Precision Tools in Chapters 6–9 and 11 were designed to introduce you to some of the basic concepts of corporate law and corporate finance. Although each section built on previous units, each was designed to be self-contained, with the answers to the questions often not being dependent on the answers to questions in other parts of the problem. This chapter is intended to integrate the previous materials and to deal with governance arrangements that are peculiar to the closely-held corporation.

The study of such arrangements focuses on the bargaining and contracting which will permit the parties to determine an appropriate structure for their own venture. The challenge a lawyer faces is how best to take advantage of the flexibility the law now allows, to anticipate the future needs and potential problems of the parties, and to create solutions at the outset which will either reduce the likelihood of problems occurring or provide acceptable dispute resolution mechanisms should problems arise. Such planning requires the lawyer to view the transaction as a whole rather than as a series of disconnected parts. In so doing, the parties can determine better their true *interests* rather than their bargaining *positions* (see Roger Fisher & William Ury, *Getting to Yes* (1981)) and thus better negotiate workable compromises. These planning skills are among the most important for a business lawyer to possess, regardless of the size of the transaction. They are particularly necessary when, as in Precision Tools, there are relatively few parties and the legal questions are comparatively simple. The emphasis in this chapter, then, is as much on planning and dispute resolution mechanisms as it is on legal doctrine.

PROBLEM
PRECISION TOOLS REVISITED—PART I

Review Parts III and V of Precision Tools (Chapters 7 and 9, respectively) and assume that the facts in those parts were developed in a series of meetings in your office. Assume further that during those meetings, Bernie made clear that by "having some voice" in the business, he means the ability to elect one-half of the directors. The parties have tentatively agreed on a four-member board of directors consisting of the three of them and an additional director chosen by Bernie.

1) What advice would you give to the parties as to the desirability of a four-person board? *

2) How can the capital structure be used to achieve the board representation which the parties desire? Would it matter if Bernie received 40 percent of the common stock of Precision Tools rather than any senior securities and Jessica and Michael each received 30 percent of the common stock?

3) If the parties decided not to use the capital structure as a vehicle for achieving their goal, what other alternatives do they have? Specifically:

---

* Recall the materials in Chapter 8, Section A, dealing with the lawyer's professional responsibility. The conflict issue has now become more pointed and troublesome.

a) What types of voting agreements might they enter into? What should be the basic provisions of each of them?

b) What enforcement mechanisms, if any, should each contain?

c) What legal restrictions affect the validity of each?

d) What are the advantages and disadvantages of each?

In answering Question 3, assume that the applicable law is:

a) non-statutory law;

b) Columbia.   Consider RMBCA §§ 2.02, 7.22, 7.30, 7.31, 7.32;

c) Delaware.   Consider DGCL § 218;

d) New York.   Consider N.Y.B.C.L. §§ 609(f), (g), 620(a);

e) California.   Consider Calif. Corp. Code § 706.

———

One simple technique for ensuring shareholder representation on the board, which is somewhat more flexible than cumulative voting, is class voting for directors.   This entails dividing the voting stock into two or more classes, each of which is entitled to elect one or more directors. RMBCA § 6.01(c); DGCL § 102(a)(4).   In the simple case of a corporation with three shareholders, each of whom wishes to be assured of electing one director, three classes of shares would be created (usually denominated, somewhat prosaically, classes "A", "B", and "C").   Each class would have the right to elect one director.   Since it is not necessary to issue (or authorize) the same number of shares for each class, class voting can be used to guarantee board representation to a shareholder who owns too few shares to be able to elect a director through cumulative voting.   The rights of the different classes may be adjusted in other ways as well.   For example, each class might be required to approve all or certain actions that require shareholder approval.   In fact, the number and variety of changes that can be rung on this basic device are limited only by the imagination of the drafter.   Classes can be created that have differing numbers of shares, different rights in the event of liquidation, or different dividend or preemptive rights.

Class voting has its pitfalls.   The principal problem is who fills the vacancy in a class when the director dies and is the sole holder of the stock.   There are a number of possible answers to that question, but they all affect the future political balance within the company and introduce the possibility of an unwanted person being introduced into the corporate structure.   The planner therefore must focus on the future implications of what appears to be a simple present situation.

3.   DEVICES OUTSIDE THE CORPORATE MACHINERY

Shareholders typically use one of three classes of devices to limit or control the manner in which stock will be voted: (1) voting trusts, (2) irrevocable proxies, and (3) vote pooling agreements.

Shareholders create a *voting trust* by conveying legal title to their stock to a voting trustee or a group of trustees pursuant to the terms of a trust agreement. This transfer is normally registered on the corporation's stock transfer ledger, which shows the trustees as legal owners of the shares. The former shareholders—now beneficiaries of the trust— receive voting trust certificates in exchange for their shares; these evidence their equitable ownership of their stock. Voting trust certificates usually are transferable and entitle the owner to receive whatever dividends are paid on the underlying stock. They are, in effect, shares of stock shorn of their voting power and, in some jurisdictions, certain other rights normally appurtenant to the ownership of stock, such as the right to inspect the corporate books or to institute a derivative suit. See Henry W. Ballantine, Ballantine on Corporations § 184(b) (Rev. ed. 1946). But see, RMBCA § 16.02 and N.Y.B.C.L. § 624(b) which give inspection rights to voting trust certificate holders. Since the terms of the trust agreement are a matter of contract, the trustees may be given full discretion to vote the shares in the trust for the election of directors and for any other matter to come before the shareholders, or may be limited to voting on only certain matters.

At an earlier stage in the development of corporation law, courts tended to view voting trusts with suspicion, in many cases holding them void as against public policy because they separated shareholders' voting power and economic ownership. State legislatures responded by passing statutes permitting voting trusts but subjecting them to certain regulations, usually a limitation on their effective life and a requirement that their terms be made a matter of public record so that other shareholders would know, or could learn, that a voting trust exists. See RMBCA § 7.30 and DGCL § 218. Today virtually all jurisdictions have such legislation.

Some of the judicial dislike for the voting trust has survived, however, in the doctrine that an arrangement that amounts to a voting trust in operation but does not comply with the terms of a voting trust statute is invalid. The attempted application of this doctrine is illustrated in the *Ringling Brothers* litigation summarized below and in the *Lehrman* case set out following the discussion of *Ringling*.

Many of the same concerns that led to judicial invalidation of voting trusts are equally applicable to the *irrevocable proxy*. It is quite common for a shareholder to give a proxy to vote her shares to someone else, and even to give that person entire discretion to decide how they should be voted. But the ordinary proxy, like any agency power, may be revoked at the will of the principal, and the proxy holder remains subject to the control of the principal. See Restatement, Second, Agency § 118.

Sometimes, however, the parties want to make the grant of the proxy irrevocable, subject perhaps to some contingency or to the passage of a specified time. In such a case, the shareholder loses control of the exercise of the franchise for the period of the proxy, and it can be said that "the vote is separated from the stock," the very problem that lay at the heart of courts' objections to voting trusts. Thus, whether because they find them to violate basic principles of agency law, or to be against public policy, courts previously evidenced reluctance to enforce an irrevocable proxy.

Agency law does recognize as valid an agency power "coupled with an interest." See Restatement, Second, Agency §§ 138–139. The modern trend is to recognize this principle in the corporate context and to uphold irrevocable proxies that are "coupled with an interest." The difficulty is to determine what sort of "interest" will support an irrevocable proxy. The more conservative view is that the interest must be in (or pertain to) the stock itself, such as that created by a pledge of the equitable interest by one who has contracted or who has an option to purchase the shares. In re Chilson, 19 Del.Ch. 398, 168 A. 82 (Ch. 1933). Other courts have rejected a formalistic application of agency principles and approached the problem with a greater appreciation of the practical realities of arranging the affairs of a close corporation. Irrevocable proxies have been upheld, for example, where the proxy has been given as an inducement to the holder to furnish money to the corporation. Hey v. Dolphin, 92 Hun. 230, 36 N.Y.S. 627 (1895); Chapman v. Bates, 61 N.J.Eq. 658, 47 A. 638 (Err. & App. 1900).

As the problem presents itself most often to the close corporation planner, the putative proxy holder seldom has a direct interest in the stock. Commonly, two or more shareholders seek to enter into a contractual arrangement involving the grant of irrevocable proxies, the consideration for which is merely the mutual promises of the parties to the agreement. In this situation it is hard to find an "interest" sufficient to support the proxy. Faced with this problem some courts have found that where the proxy holder was induced to purchase stock in reliance on the agreement, her interest in the corporation as shareholder is enough. A few other courts have been willing to go even farther than this already strained interpretation and, though nominally adhering to the doctrine, have broadened it "to such an extent that it is hardly recognizable." F. Hodge O'Neal & Robert B. Thompson, O'Neal's Close Corp. § 5.13 (3rd ed.). Although not always admitting it, these courts have enforced irrevocable proxies supported by only the mutual promises contained in a shareholders' agreement simply because the business realities of the close corporation seemed to demand it. As one court put it, "The power to vote the stock was necessary in order to make * * * control of the corporation secure." State ex rel. Everett Trust & Savings Bank v. Pacific Waxed Paper Co., 22 Wash.2d 844, 852, 157 P.2d 707, 711 (1945).

Recognizing that the artificial requirement that a proxy must be coupled with an interest in order to be irrevocable makes little sense in the close corporation context, some state legislatures have effectively eliminated it by statute. See, e.g. N.Y.B.C.L. §§ 609(f), (g), 620(a). Absent such a statute or a clear holding by the state courts upholding irrevocable proxies in shareholder agreements, the planner is probably well-advised not to rely too heavily on an irrevocable proxy, simpliciter.

See William H. Painter, Painter on Close Corporations § 3:66 (3d ed. 1991) and L. Proctor Thomas, Comment, Irrevocable Proxies, 43 Tex. L.Rev. 733 (1965).

The third technique often found in close corporation control arrangements is the so-called *vote pooling agreement*. As is the case with voting trusts and irrevocable proxies, the basic purpose of such an agreement is to bind some (or occasionally all) of the shareholders to vote together—either in a particular way or pursuant to some specified procedure—on designated questions or on all questions that come before the shareholders. It is generally accepted that such agreements are valid. See, e.g., RMBCA § 7.32 and New York B.C.L. § 620(a). The difficulty they pose is the manner in which they are to be enforced. The Official Comment to RMBCA § 7.31 states:

> Section 7.31(b) provides that voting agreements may be specifically enforceable. A voting agreement may provide its own enforcement mechanism, as by the appointment of a proxy to vote all shares subject to the agreement; the appointment may be made irrevocable under section 7.22. If no enforcement mechanism is provided, a court may order specific enforcement of the agreement and order the votes cast as the agreement contemplates. This section recognizes that damages are not likely to be an appropriate remedy for breach of a voting agreement, and also avoids the result reached in Ringling Bros.-Barnum & Bailey Combined Shows v. Ringling, 29 Del.Ch. 610, 53 A.2d 441 (1947) * * *.

Note: *Ringling Brothers Litigation*

Ringling Bros.-Barnum & Bailey Combined Shows, Inc. v. Ringling, 29 Del.Ch. 610, 53 A.2d 441 (1947), involved a corporation that had seven directors had 1000 shares of common stock issued and outstanding. Edith Ringling and Aubrey Haley each owned 315 shares and John Ringling North owned 370. The corporation had cumulative voting. If all shares were represented at a meeting, 126 were needed to elect one director, 251 to elect two directors, and 376 to elect three directors. Acting alone, Ringling, Haley, and North each could be sure of electing two directors. The seventh director would be determined by whether Ringling and Haley pooled their votes. If they did, they could select the seventh director. If they acted alone, North could elect that director.

Ringling and Haley, who were sisters, executed a ten year "Memorandum of Agreement" in 1941. The Agreement was intended to allow them to use their majority shareholdings, and the corporation's cumulative voting structure, to control the corporation. After providing that if either party wished to sell any shares in the corporation she would offer them for sale to the other party on the same term as those at which she proposed to sell to the outsider, the Agreement provided:

> 2. In exercising any voting rights to which either party may be entitled by virtue of ownership of stock or voting trust certificates held by them in either of said corporations each party will consult

and confer with the other and the parties will act jointly in exercising such voting rights in accordance with such agreement as they may reach with respect to any matter calling for the exercise of such voting rights.

    3. In the event the parties fail to agree with respect to any matter covered by paragraph 2 above, the question in disagreement shall be submitted for arbitration to Karl D. Loos, of Washington, D.C., as arbitrator and his decision thereon shall be binding upon the parties thereto. Such arbitration shall be exercised to the end of assuring for the respective corporations good management and such participation therein by the members of the Ringling family as the experience, capacity and ability of each may warrant. The parties may at any time by written agreement designate any other individual to act as arbitrator in lieu of said Loos.

At the annual shareholders' meeting in 1946, Haley was ill and her husband refused to coordinate his votes with Ringling. Loos, the arbitrator, determined that Ringling and Haley should vote their stock so as to elect five directors. Mr. Haley refused to abide by Loos's decision and cast all his wife's votes for his wife and himself. As a consequence, a third candidate favored by North was elected to the board. Ringling then brought suit to enforce the voting agreement. Haley argued that the arbitration procedure operated as a voting trust, separated voting from ownership, and was void because it did not comply with Delaware's the voting trust provisions of Delaware law.

The Court of Chancery, 29 Del.Ch. 318, 49 A.2d 603 (1946) noted "The stockholders under the present Agreement vote their own stock at all times which is the antithesis of a voting trust because the latter has for its chief characteristic the severance of the voting rights from the other attributes of ownership." 49 A.2d at 608. It held the agreement to be a valid shareholder voting agreement, not an illegal voting trust.

Turning to how the agreement should be enforced, the court concluded that "the stock held under the Agreement should have been voted pursuant to the direction of the arbitrator Loos to the parties or their representatives. When a party or her representative refuses to comply with the direction of the arbitrator, while he is properly acting under its provisions (as did Aubrey B. Haley's proxy here), then I believe the Agreement constitutes the willing party to the Agreement an implied agent possessing the irrevocable proxy of the recalcitrant party for the purpose of casting the particular vote. Here an implied agency based on an irrevocable proxy is fully justified to implement the Agreement without doing violence to its terms. Moreover, the provisions of the Agreement make it clear that the proxy may be treated as one coupled with an interest so as to render it irrevocable under the circumstances." 49 A.2d at 611.

On appeal, the Delaware Supreme Court upheld the voting agreement but rejected the Court of Chancery's decision as to how the agreement should be enforced. Ringling Bros.-Barnum & Bailey Combined Shows, Inc. v. Ringling, 29 Del.Ch. 610, 53 A.2d 441 (1947). The appellate court sidestepped the noncomplying shareholder's argument that the arbitration procedure operated as a voting trust by holding that the agreement had not transferred any voting rights to the arbitrator, because he lacked formal power to vote the stock.

> Should the agreement be interpreted as attempting to empower the arbitrator to carry his directions into effect? Certainly there is no express delegation or grant of power to do so, either by authorizing him to vote the shares or to compel either party to vote them in accordance with his directions. The agreement expresses no other function of the arbitrator than that of deciding questions in disagreement which prevent the effectuation of the purpose "to act jointly." The power to enforce a decision does not seem a necessary or usual incident of such a function. Mr. Loos is not a party to the agreement. It does not contemplate the transfer of any shares or interest in shares to him, or that he should undertake any duties which the parties might compel him to perform. They provided that they might designate any other individual to act instead of Mr. Loos. The agreement does not attempt to make the arbitrator a trustee of an express trust. What the arbitrator is to do is for the benefit of the parties, not for his own benefit. Whether the parties accept or reject his decision is no concern of his, so far as the agreement or the surrounding circumstances reveal. We think the parties sought to bind each other, but to be bound only to each other, and not to empower the arbitrator to enforce decisions he might make.

> From this conclusion, it follows necessarily that no decision of the arbitrator could ever be enforced if both parties to the agreement were unwilling that it be enforced, for the obvious reason that there would be no one to enforce it. Under the agreement, something more is required after the arbitrator has given his decision in order that it should become compulsory: at least one of the parties must determine that such decision shall be carried into effect. Thus, any "control" of the voting of the shares, which is reposed in the arbitrator, is substantially limited in action under the agreement in that it is subject to the overriding power of the parties themselves. (53 A.2d at 445).

As concerned the appropriate remedy, the court held that since Haley had voted her stock in breach of the agreement, her votes should not be counted. The only effective votes were those cast by Ringling and North.

Question

What would be the result in *Ringling* under RMBCA § 7.31(b)?

LEHRMAN v. COHEN
42 Del. 222, 222 A.2d 800 (1966).

HERRMANN, JUSTICE.

The primary problem presented on this appeal involves the applicability of the Delaware Voting Trust Statute. Other questions involve the legality of stock having voting power but no dividend or liquidation rights except repayment of par value, and an alleged unlawful delegation of directorial duties and powers.

[Giant Food, Inc., a Delaware corporation that runs a chain of supermarkets, was organized in 1935 by N.M. Cohen and Samuel Lehrman. Initially its voting stock consisted of Class AC shares, all of which were owned by members of the Cohen family, and Class AL shares, all of which were owned by members of the Lehrman family. Each class was entitled to elect two members of a four member board. A settlement of a family dispute that arose after Samuel Lehrman's death in 1949 left his son, Jacob, owning all of the AL shares. The number of AL shares owned by Jacob Lehrman equalled the number of AC shares held by the Cohen family. In order to prevent a deadlock, one share of a third class of stock, AD, was created, which was entitled to elect a fifth director. The AD stock had no right to dividends or distributions in liquidation beyond its $10 value. The one AD share was immediately issued to Joseph B. Danzansky, who had served as the company's counsel since 1944. Danzansky voted to elect himself the fifth director, and remained in that post until the events that gave rise to the suit. The court's statement of the facts continues:]

From the outset and until October 1, 1964, the defendant N.M. Cohen was president of the Company. On that date, a resolution was adopted at the Company's annual stockholders' meeting to give Danzansky a fifteen year executive employment contract at an annual salary of $67,600, and options for 25,000 shares of the non-voting common stock of the Company. The AC and AD stock were voted in favor and the AL stock was voted against the resolution. At a directors meeting held the same day, Danzansky was elected president of the Company by a 3–2 vote, the two AL directors voting in opposition. On December 11, 1964, Danzansky resigned as director and voted his share of AD stock to elect as the fifth director, Millard F. West, Jr., a former AL director and investment banker whose firm was one of the underwriters of the public issue of the Company's stock. The newly constituted board ratified the election of Danzansky as president; and, on January 27, 1965, after the commencement of this action and after a review and report by a committee consisting of the new AD director and one AL director, Danzansky's employment contract was approved and adopted with certain modifications.

The plaintiff brought this action on December 11, 1964, basing it upon two claims: The First Claim charges that the creation, issuance, and voting of the one share of Class AD stock resulted in an arrangement illegal under the law of this State for the reasons hereinafter set forth. The Second Claim, addressed to the events of October 1, 1964, charges that the election of Danzansky as president of the Company and his employment contract violated the terms of the [1949] deadlock-breaking arrangement, as made between the holders of the AC and AL stock, and constituted breaches of contract and fiduciary duty. The plaintiff and the defendants filed cross-motions for summary judgment as to the First Claim. The Court of Chancery, after considering the contentions now before us and discussed *infra,* granted summary judgment in favor of the defendants and denied the plaintiff's motion for summary judgment. The plaintiff appeals.

I.

The plaintiff's primary contention is that the Class AD stock arrangement is, in substance and effect, a voting trust; that, as such, it is illegal because not limited to a ten year period as required by the Voting Trust Statute. The defendants deny that the AD stock arrangement constitutes a disguised voting trust; but they concede that if it is, the arrangement is illegal for violation of the Statute. Thus, issue is clearly joined on the point.

The criteria of a voting trust under our decisions have been summarized by this Court in Abercrombie v. Davies, 36 Del.Ch. 371, 130 A.2d 338 (1957). The tests there set forth, accepted by both sides of this cause as being applicable, are as follows: (1) the voting rights of the stock are separated from the other attributes of ownership; (2) the voting rights granted are intended to be irrevocable for a definite period of time; and (3) the principal purpose of the grant of voting rights is to acquire voting control of the corporation.

Adopting and applying these tests, the plaintiff says, as to the first element, that the AD arrangement provides for a divorcement of voting rights from beneficial ownership of the AC and AL stock; that the creation and issuance of the share of AD stock is tantamount to a pooling by the AC and AL stockholders of a portion of their voting stock and giving it to a trustee, in the person of the AD stockholder, to vote for the election of the fifth director; that after the creation of the AD stock, the AC and AL stockholders each hold but 40% of the voting power, and the AD stockholder holds the controlling balance of 20%; that the AD stock has no property rights except the right to a return of the $10. paid as the par value; and that, therefore, there has been a transfer of the voting rights devoid of any participating property rights. So runs the argument of the plaintiff in support of his contention that the first of the *Abercrombie* criteria for a voting trust is met.

The contention is unacceptable. The AD arrangement did not separate the voting rights of the AC or the AL stock from the other attributes of ownership of those classes of stock. Each AC and AL stockholder retains complete control over the voting of his stock; each can vote his stock directly; no AL or AC stockholder is divested of his right to vote his stock as he sees fit; no AL or AC stock can be voted against the shareholder's wishes; and the AL and AC stock continue to elect two directors each.

The AD stock arrangement, as we view it, became a part of the capitalization of the Company. The fact that there is but a single share, or that the par value is nominal, is of no legal significance; the one share and the $10. par value might have been multiplied many times over, with the same consequence. It is true that the creation of the separate class of AD stock may have diluted the voting *power* which had previously existed in the AC and AL stock—the usual consequence when additional voting stock is created—but the creation of the new class did not divest and separate the voting *rights* which remain vested in each AC and AL shareholder, together with the other attributes of the ownership of that stock. The fallacy of the plaintiff's position lies in his premise that since the voting power of the AC and AL stock was reduced by the creation of the AD stock, the percentage of reduction became the *res* of a voting trust. In any recapitalization involving the creation of additional voting stock, the voting power of the previously existing stock is diminished; but a voting trust is not necessarily the result.

Since the holders of the Class AC and Class AL stock of the Company did not separate the voting rights from the other attributes of ownership of those classes when they created the Class AD stock, the first *Abercrombie* test of a voting trust is not met.

This conclusion disposes of the second and third *Abercrombie* tests, i.e., that the voting rights granted are irrevocable for a definite period of time, and that the principal object of the grant of voting rights is voting control of the corporation. Having held that the AC and AL stockholders have not divested themselves of their voting rights, although they may have diluted their voting powers, we do not reach the remaining *Abercrombie* tests, both of which assume the divestiture of voting rights.

In the final analysis, the essence of the question raised by the plaintiff in this connection is this: Is the substance and purpose of the AD stock arrangement sufficiently close to the substance and purpose of § 218 to warrant its being subjected to the restrictions and conditions imposed by that Statute? The answer is negative not only for the reasons above stated, but also because § 218 regulates trusts and pooling agreements amounting to trusts, not other and different types of arrangements and undertakings possible among stockholders. The AD stock arrangement is neither a trust nor a pooling agreement.

We hold, therefore, that the Class AD stock arrangement is not controlled by the Voting Trust Statute.

II.

The plaintiff's second point is that even if the Class AD stock arrangement is not a voting trust in substance and effect, the AD stock is illegal, nevertheless, because the creation of a class of stock having voting rights only, and lacking any substantial participating proprietary interest in the corporation, violates the public policy of this State as declared in § 218.

The fallacy of this argument is twofold: First, it is more accurate to say that what the law has disfavored, and what the public policy underlying the Voting Trust Statute means to control, is the separation of the vote from the stock—not from the stock ownership. 5 Fletcher Cyclopedia Corporations, § 2080, pp. 363–369; compare Abercrombie v. Davies, supra. Clearly, the AD stock arrangement is not violative of that public policy. Secondly, there is nothing in § 218, either expressed or implied, which requires that all stock of a Delaware corporation must have both voting rights and proprietary interests. Indeed, public policy to the contrary seems clearly expressed by 8 Del.C. § 151(a) which authorizes, in very broad terms, such voting powers and participating rights as may be stated in the certificate of incorporation. Non-voting stock is specifically authorized by § 151(a); and in the light thereof, consistency does not permit the conclusion, urged by the plaintiff, that the present public policy of this State condemns the separation of voting rights from beneficial stock ownership.

We conclude that the plaintiff's contention in this regard cannot withstand the force and effect of § 151(a). In our view, that Statute permits the creation of stock having voting rights only, as well as stock having property rights only. The voting powers and the participating rights of the Class AD stock being specified in the Company's certificate of incorporation, we are of the opinion that the Class AD stock is legal by virtue of § 151(a).

* * *

We are told that if the AD stock arrangement is allowed thus to stand, our Voting Trust Statute will become a "dead letter" because it will be possible to evade and circumvent its purpose simply by issuing a class of non-participating voting stock, as was done here. We have three negative reactions to this argument:

First, it presupposes a divestiture of the voting rights of the AC and AL stock—an untenable supposition as has been stated. Secondly, it fails to take into account the main purpose of a Voting Trust Statute: to avoid secret, uncontrolled combinations of stockholders formed to acquire voting control of the corporation to the possible detriment of non-participating shareholders. It may not be said that the AD stock arrangement contravenes that purpose. Finally on this point, if we misconceive the legislative intent, and if the AD stock arrangement in this case reveals a loophole in § 218 which should be plugged, it is for the General Assembly to accomplish—not for us to attempt by interstitial judicial legislation.

III.

The plaintiff advances yet another reason for invalidating the AD stock. The essence of this argument is that the only function of that class of stock is to break directorial deadlocks; that the issuance of the AD stock is merely a technical device to permit that result; that, as such, it is illegal because it permits the AC and AL directors of the Company to delegate their statutory duties to the AD director as an arbitrator.

As to the means adopted for the accomplishment of that purpose, we find the AD stock arrangement valid by virtue of § 141(a) of the Delaware Corporation Law which provides:

> The business of every corporation organized under the provisions of this chapter shall be managed by a board of directors, except as hereinafter or in its certificate of incorporation otherwise provided.

The AD stock arrangement was created by the unanimous action of the stockholders of the Company by amendment to the certificate of incorporation. The stockholders thereby provided how the business of the corporation is to be managed, as is their privilege and right under § 141(a). It was this stockholder action which delegated to the AD director whatever powers and duties he possesses; they were not delegated to him by his fellow directors, either out of their own powers and duties, or otherwise.

It is settled, of course, as a general principle, that directors may not delegate their duty to manage the corporate enterprise. But there is no conflict with that principle where, as here, the delegation of duty, if any, is made not by the directors but by stockholder action under § 141(a), via the certificate of incorporation.

* * *

Finding no error in the judgment below, it is affirmed.

————

Oceanic Exploration Co. v. Grynberg, 428 A.2d 1 (Del.1981), upheld a contract labelled a "voting trust agreement" that was extended under circumstances that did not comply with DGCL § 218. The court recognized that the "agreement" did not fit into the situation contemplated by the language of the statute. Even though the agreement gave voting rights to a trustee, the overall agreement was so multifaceted and extensive that the court held it to be antithetical to the type of agreement to which the voting trust statute was directed and beyond the scope of the statute. The court found that the main purpose of § 218 was " 'to avoid secret, uncontrolled combinations formed to acquire control of the corporation to the possible detriment of non-participating shareholders.' " The contract in question was so far divorced from that purpose that it made the contemplated regulation unnecessary. Finally, the "agreement" violated no current public policy. The court stated that the trend is "not to extend the voting trust restrictions beyond the class of trust being regulated and beyond the reasons for statutory regulation."

C. RESTRICTIONS ON THE DISCRETION OF THE BOARD

PROBLEM

PRECISION TOOLS REVISITED—PART II

The parties have agreed that Michael will be the president and chief executive officer of the new company; Jessica will be vice-president and chief financial officer; and Bernie will be secretary. Michael will have control over the operational part of the business and Jessica will run its financial end. Because both Michael and Jessica will derive most of their income from the business, each will be paid a reasonable salary. At this time, Bernie will not be paid a salary for his more limited participation.

Jessica and Michael would like to guarantee their officerships; without such a guarantee, they are concerned that future events may permit the other directors to remove them. They would also like to ensure the amount of compensation they are to draw from the corporation for the first few years. Bernie understands their concerns and is willing to enter into some arrangement that would fulfill these objectives, provided that, since he will not draw money in the form of a salary, he has some assurance that their salaries will not be increased above the agreed-upon amount, and that he will receive dividends should the corporation show a profit. The three have asked about the validity of an agreement by which they would bind themselves "to use their best efforts" to elect each other to their respective officerships, to have Michael and Jessica each paid salaries of $75,000 per year, and to have the corporation pay a dividend annually equal to one-third of its net profits. They also want to know whether it is possible to fix the amount of money which can be spent on research and development in the next few years.

1. Advise Michael and Jessica how to implement their understanding. In this connection, consider:

(a) Whether the agreement can be between only Michael and Jessica or whether it must be unanimous.

(b) Whether the provisions of the agreement can or must be put in the corporation's articles of incorporation or by-laws.

In each case, assume that the applicable law is:

(a) non-statutory law;

(b) RMBCA §§ 2.02 and 7.32;

(c) N.Y.B.C.L. §§ 620 and 715(b);

(d) Calif.Corp.Code §§ 204 and 300;

(e) DGCL §§ 350, 351 and 354.

2.   What are the advantages and disadvantages of requiring a high vote and/or high quorum (e.g., 80 percent) in order to amend the articles of incorporation and/or the by-laws with respect to the issues of concern to the parties? Which specific issues? If such requirements are desirable, should they relate to actions by the shareholders, the directors, or both?

In each case, assume that the applicable law is:

(a) non-statutory law;

(b) RMBCA §§ 2.02, 7.25, 7.27, 7.32, 8.24 and 10.21;

(c) N.Y.B.C.L. §§ 616 and 709; and

(d) Calif.Corp.Code § 204.

You may wish to reconsider the Chesapeake Marine Problem, Chapter 3.

3.   In addition to using an agreement or provisions in the articles of incorporation should Michael and Jessica execute employment contracts with the corporation? What benefits are there for them and the corporation? Consider RMBCA §§ 8.43 and 8.44.

1. RESTRICTIONS IN SHAREHOLDER VOTING AGREEMENTS

Haenel v. Epstein, N.Y.L.J., June 10, 1980 (Sup.Ct.) at 13 summarized as follows New York common law governing shareholder voting agreements that purport to restrict the discretion of the board of directors:

The New York Court of Appeals, prior to the enactment of Business Corporation Law section 620(a) and 620(b) set forth, in four cases, dubbed "the big four" the law with regard to shareholder agreements.

Manson v. Curtis (223 N.Y. 313, 119 N.E. 559 [1918]) involved an agreement between the holders of a majority, but not all, of the shares of a corporation. The agreement provided that each party was to name three directors, with a seventh director to be elected as mutually agreed upon. One of the parties, the plaintiff, was to be continued in his position of General Manager for a year and, as such, was to manage the business of the corporation and shape its policy. The court, finding, in effect, the provision concerning election of directors, to be, standing alone, innocent and legal, determined that the agreement as a whole was invalid as its fundamental and dominant purpose was to vest management authority solely in plaintiff. So construed, the latter provisions were found to deprive the directors of their statutory duty to manage the corporation. The agreement was found totally illegal and not capable of "severability."

Stated simply, the Court of Appeals in Manson decided that while it was not illegal for two or more stockholders owning the majority of stock to agree upon the directors whom they would elect, the powers delegated to the non-directors were too broad. (See 50 Columbia Law Review No.

1, January, 1950, "The Corporate Director: Can his hands be tied in advance," Edmund T. Delaney).

Manson recited the law as to the interaction of majority stockholders; dominant managers; and the statutory authority of a board of directors. Employing the often used terminology "a sterilized board of directors," the case set forth the law as follows:

> The affairs of every corporation shall be managed by its board of directors * * *.

> The corporation is the owner of the property but the directors in the performance of their duty possess it, and act in every way as if they owned it.

> Directors are the exclusive executive representatives of the corporation and are charged with the administration of its internal affairs and the management and use of its assets * * *. Clearly the law does not permit the stockholders to create a sterilized board of directors * * *. We conclude that the agreement here is illegal and void and its violation is not a basis for a cause of action. (223 N.Y. at pp. 319–324) (Compare Business Corporation Law section 701).

Manson, significant not only for its holding, but for its dictum on the permissible scope of shareholder agreements, stated in that regard as follows:

> An ordinary agreement, among a minority in number, but a majority in shares, for the purpose of obtaining control of the corporation by the election of particular persons as directors is not illegal. Shareholders have the right to combine their interests and voting powers to secure such control of the corporation and the adoption of an adhesion by it to a specific policy and course of business. Agreements upon a sufficient consideration between them, of such intendment and effect, are valid and binding, if they do not contravene any express charter or statutory provision or contemplate any fraud, oppression or wrong against other stockholders or other illegal object.

This concept, expressed in dictum, later formed the basis of the legislature's enactment of Business Corporation Law 620(a).

Finally, the court in Manson indicated that if all stockholders agreed, they "may do as they choose with the corporate concerns and assets, provided the interests of creditors are not affected, because they are the complete owners of the corporation."

* * *

In McQuade v. Stoneham (263 N.Y. 323, 189 N.E. 234 [1934]), the agreement was not between all shareholders, but between the holder of the majority of the shares and two other shareholders. By the agreement's terms, the parties were to use their best efforts to keep one another in office as directors and officers; and salaries, amount of capital, number of shares, by-laws and policy were not to be changed except by unanimous consent. Holding the agreement invalid, the court stated:

> Stockholders may, of course, combine to elect directors. That rule is well settled. As Holmes, Ch.J., pointedly said (Brightman v. Bates, 175 Mass. 105, 111): "If stockholders want to make their power felt, they must unite. There is no reason why a majority should not agree to keep together." The power to unite is, however, limited to the election of directors and is not extended to contracts whereby limitations are placed on the power of directors to manage the business of the corporation by the selection of agents at defined salaries.

The agreement restricted the powers of the board of directors. It did not condition such intrusion by use of such terms as "subject to the discretion of the Board of Directors" or "so long as they remain faithful, efficient and competent." As such, there was an impermissible usurpation of function.

Clark v. Dodge (269 N.Y. 410, 199 N.E. 641 [1936]) followed. It represented an apparent change in the thinking of the court. Here, the agreement was signed by all shareholders. Dodge was to vote for Clark as director and General Manager so long as Clark proved faithful, efficient and competent. The court sustained a cause of action for specific enforcement of the agreement. In distinguishing McQuade, the court held that here the impairment of the directors' powers was slight. The court held as follows:

> There was no attempt to sterilize the board of directors, as in the Manson and McQuade cases. The only restrictions on Dodge were (a) that as a stockholder he should vote for Clark as a director—a perfectly legal contract; (b) that as a director he should continue Clark as general manager, so long as he proved faithful, efficient and competent—an agreement which could harm nobody; (c) that Clark should always receive as salary or dividends one-fourth of the "net income." For the purposes of this motion, it is only just to construe that phrase as meaning whatever was left for distribution after the directors had in good faith set aside whatever they deemed wise; (d) that no salaries to other officers should be paid, unreasonable in amount or incommensurate with services rendered—a beneficial and not a harmful agreement.

The court's thinking in Clark was influenced by the fact that all stockholders signed the agreement. This is evidenced as follows:

> As the parties to the action are the complete owners of the corporation, there is no reason why the exercise of the power and discretion of the directors cannot be controlled by valid agreement between themselves, provided that the interest of creditors is not affected (269 N.Y. at p. 410).

Thus, following Clark, the state of the law was and is that all stockholders can agree to infringe "slightly" upon the statutory authority of the board of directors. So, too, it was and still is the law that a majority, but less than all the stockholders, can agree to vote for certain persons as directors (see also "Shareholder Agreements and the Statutory Norm," 43 Cornell L.Q. 68, 72–73 [1957]) * * *.

Long Park, Inc. v. Trenton–New Brunswick Theaters Co. (297 N.Y. 174, 77 N.E.2d 633 [1948]) is the fourth in the line of the "big four." As in Clark, the agreement involved all shareholders. By its terms, one of the shareholders was to be "manager," and was to be given full authority to supervise the operation of the corporation. The court held the agreement sterilized the board of directors, was a complete surrender of the directors' powers, and, therefore, was invalid as a violation of the statute giving management powers to the directors. Apparently, the court determined that the agreement had exceeded the permissible limits of infringement construed in Clark.

TRIGGS v. TRIGGS

46 N.Y.2d 305, 413 N.Y.S.2d 325, 385 N.E.2d 1254 (1978).

[The following statement of facts is taken from the dissenting opinion of GABRIELLI, J.]

The bone of contention in this case is control of Triggs Color Printing Corporation, a small firm founded by decedent in 1925. The firm appears to have prospered for some years and, with the passage of time, decedent's three sons became involved in the business to varying degrees. As of 1963, the corporation had issued some 254 shares of voting stock. Of these, decedent personally owned 149 shares and the remainder were distributed equally between his three sons, with each son owning 35 shares. At that time, decedent apparently selected his son Ransford, the plaintiff in this action, as the one he deemed best suited to control the business following decedent's death. To that end, decedent transferred 36 of his shares to plaintiff. Thus, out of the 254 voting shares, decedent owned 113 shares, plaintiff owned 71 shares, and each of the other two sons owned 35 shares.

Shortly thereafter, plaintiff and decedent entered into the written agreement at issue in this case. The two agreed to vote their shares together so as not only to elect both of them as directors, but also to elect decedent chairman of the board at a guaranteed annual salary and to appoint plaintiff president of the corporation at a guaranteed annual salary. Additionally, the agreement contained the following provision: "It is the present contemplation of Frederick Triggs, Sr. to execute an agreement with the Corporation for the Corporation to repurchase his stock in the event of his death. In the event for any reason that such agreement has not been executed between the said Frederick Triggs, Sr. and the Corporation, then, in that event, the remaining Stockholder, to wit: Ransford D. Triggs, shall have the right and option to purchase the said stock of Frederick Triggs, Sr. for a period of sixty (60) days following the death of Frederick Triggs, Sr."

A few months later, decedent did enter into a repurchase agreement with the corporation. One year later, in 1964, the repurchase agreement with the corporation was canceled by consent of both decedent and the corporation. During the next few years, plaintiff gradually assumed an ever greater role in corporate affairs, and decedent's influence waned. Eventually the two had a falling out, and decedent appears to have begun to regret his choice of plaintiff as his successor. The corporation experienced some financial difficulties under plaintiff's management, and the salary paid to decedent was decreased, at first with his consent and later over his objections. Finally, in February, 1970, decedent executed a codicil to his will by which he bequeathed his 113 shares of voting stock to his other two sons, and declared the 1963 agreement with plaintiff to be null and void. In April, 1970, decedent died.

Following decedent's death, plaintiff sought to exercise the option to purchase the 113 shares from the estate, but the estate refused to transfer the stock. Some four years later, in September, 1974, plaintiff commenced this action seeking to compel the estate to honor the option. * * * Following service of an answer, but some time prior to trial, defendant moved to dismiss the complaint for failure to state a cause of action, alleging for the first time that the agreement was illegal.

OPINION OF THE COURT

JONES, JUDGE.

* * *

After a trial without a jury the court granted respondent specific performance of the stock purchase option. A majority at the Appellate Division agreed, and we now affirm. The pertinent facts are recited in the dissenting opinion.

* * *

Appellant contends that because the March 19, 1963 agreement was not executed or approved by all of the corporate shareholders, its provisions requiring the election of respondent and his father as officers and fixing their compensation constituted an impermissible restriction of the rights and obligations of the board of directors to manage the business of the corporation under the doctrine of Manson v. Curtis, 223 N.Y. 313, 119 N.E. 559 and related cases (see 3 White, New York Corporations [13th ed.], par. 620.03, subd. [2]). No argument is made that the stock purchase option, standing alone would be invalid; the assertion is that the agreement must be read as a whole and that it must be invalidated in its entirety. The critical issue is whether, because of the initial inclusion of provisions which could have been said to fetter the authority of the board to select corporate officers and to fix their compensation, the stock purchase provision is now unenforceable.

The uncontroverted evidence is that in the years following the signing of the agreement, the assertedly illegal provisions of the agreement were ignored; no attempt was made to observe or enforce them and the management of corporate affairs was in no way restricted in consequence of the 1963 agreement. The evil to which the cited rule of law is addressed was never sought to be achieved nor was it realized. Although Triggs, Sr., and Ransford continued to serve as directors, the record discloses there were also three or four other, independent directors. That Triggs, Sr., continued to be elected chairman of the board (he was also elected corporate treasurer) and Ransford, corporate president and that for several years their salaries were fixed by the board at the figures stated in the March 19, 1963 agreement was in consequence of action freely taken by the entire board of directors and cannot be attributed to the sanction of the March 19, 1963 agreement of which the other directors, constituting a majority of the board, were wholly unaware. Indeed Triggs, Sr., took no exception when, on May 11, 1965, the board reduced his salary from $20,000 (the agreement figure) to $10,800, and when the board later entirely eliminated his salary his complaint in April of 1969 was predicated on the departure from the board's action of May 11, 1965 rather than on any asserted violation of the provisions of the March 19, 1963 agreement. *Father didn't argue.*

The legal issue here, too, depends on what is now an affirmed factual determination. The claim of illegality, raised for the first time some 13 years after the agreement had been signed, must fail because, as the trial court concluded, the March 19, 1963 agreement "did not in any way sufficiently stultify the Board of Directors in the operations of this business" within the doctrine on which appellant would rely.

Analytically we are presented with an agreement which in a single document deals with two different sets of obligations. On the one hand, *2 obligations* the agreement contains the stock purchase option exercisable on the *(1)* death of the father as to which, standing alone, there is no claim of *or* illegality. On the other, there are the provisions with respect to the election of corporate officers and the fixation of their salaries, which are *2* of questionable legality. Any illegality exists, however, only to the extent that the agreement operated to restrict the freedom of the board of directors to manage corporate affairs. * * * The fact is that the courts below have enforced only the stock option provisions of the March 19, 1963 agreement.

* * *

Accordingly, the order of the Appellate Division should be affirmed, with costs.

GABRIELLI, JUDGE (dissenting).

I respectfully dissent. Defendant executor appeals from an order of the Appellate Division which affirmed a judgment of Supreme Court, following a nonjury trial, which granted plaintiff specific performance of an option to purchase certain stock from the estate of his deceased father. The order appealed from should be reversed since the underlying agreement is unenforceable in that it improperly sought to limit the *it is invalid* powers of the board of directors to manage the corporation. Moreover, even were the agreement itself valid, the option was terminated in accord with its own provisions some time prior to decedent's death.

* * *

It has long been the law in this State that a corporation must be managed by the board of directors (Business Corporation Law, § 701) who serve as trustees for the benefit of the corporation and all its shareholders. To prevent control of the corporation from being diverted into the hands of individuals or groups who in some cases might not be subject to quite the same fiduciary obligations as are imposed upon directors as a matter of course, the courts have always looked unfavorably towards attempts to circumvent the discretionary authority given the board of directors by law. Such matters normally arise in the context of an agreement between shareholders to utilize their shares so as to force the board of directors to take certain actions. Unless in accord with some statutorily approved mechanism for shifting power *620(b)* from the board of directors to other parties (e.g., Business Corporation Law, § 620, subd. [b]), such agreements have been found valid only where the proponent of the agreement can prove that the violation of the statutory mandate is minimal and, more importantly that there is no danger of harm either to the general public or to other shareholders (see Clark v. Dodge, 269 N.Y. 410, 199 N.E. 641).

It is, of course, proper for shareholders to combine in order to elect directors whom they believe will manage the corporation in accord with what those shareholders perceive to be the best interests of the corporation. Thus, an agreement between two shareholders to vote for a particular director or directors is not illegal and may be enforceable in *620(a)* an appropriate case (Business Corporation Law, § 620, subd. [a]). If some shareholders seek to go beyond this, however, if they agree to vote their shares so as to impose their decisions upon the board of directors, such an agreement will normally be unenforceable. The agreement sought to be enforced in this case is just such an agreement.

In essence, the agreement between decedent and plaintiff consisted *3 provisions of agreement* of three fundamental provisions: first, decedent promised to vote his shares so as to ensure the election of plaintiff as a director and his appointment as president for a 10–year period at a given salary; second, plaintiff promised to vote his shares so as to ensure the continuation of decedent as chairman of the board at a given salary for at least 10 years; and, third, decedent gave plaintiff a conditional option to purchase decedent's voting shares after his death. It is beyond dispute that the promises to secure the appointment of each party at a specific position other than director at a guaranteed annual salary are illegal. Plaintiff contends that the agreement is nonetheless enforceable by analogy to our decision in Clark v. Dodge, 269 N.Y. 410, 199 N.E. 641, *supra,* in which we sustained an agreement between two shareholders who together owned all of the shares in the corporation. This argument is based on a fundamental misinterpretation of the significance of our decision in that case. Rather than illustrating any divergence from the great body of other cases which have found such agreements to be illegal and unenforceable, the *Clark* decision reflects a reasoned and flexible application of the principles which are in fact common to all such cases.

The dispositive consideration must always be the possibility of harm to either the other shareholders or to the general public either prospectively at the time the agreement was entered into or at the time it is sought to be enforced. In those cases in which the agreement is made by less than all the shareholders, almost any attempt to reduce the authority granted to the board by law will create a significant potential for harm to other shareholders even if the potential for harm to the general public is minimal. This is so because the effect of such an agreement is to deprive the other shareholders of the benefits and protections which the law perceives to exist when the corporation is managed by an independent board of directors, free to use its own business judgment in the best interest of the corporation.

In *Clark,* the possibility of harm to other shareholders was nonexistent, for in fact there were no other shareholders. In the instant case, in contradistinction, there were and are two other shareholders, not privy to the agreement between plaintiff and decedent. Moreover, the instant agreement for the continuation of plaintiff and decedent in their respective positions is in no way dependent on their performances in those positions, whereas the agreement in *Clark* provided that Clark was to be continued as manager "so long as he proved faithful, efficient and competent" (Clark v. Dodge, 269 N.Y. 410, 417, 199 N.E. 641, 643, *supra*).

It has been suggested that even if the agreement is indeed illegal on its face, the defendant, in order to successfully assert the defense of illegality, must prove that the other shareholders did not know of and acquiesce in the agreement. This contention is illogical, and is at any rate inapplicable to the instant case. In this as in all actions the burden of proof is in the first instance always on the plaintiff who must prove his cause of action. * * * [E]ven were the burden with respect to this issue to be improperly placed upon defendant, that burden has been met.

It has also been suggested that the option should be severed from the other provisions of the agreement and separately enforced since it alone would not be illegal. The flaw in this argument is that it improperly assumes that decedent would have given plaintiff this option by itself, without the other parts of their agreement. This assumption is one in which we may not indulge. Indeed, it appears that the illegal parts of the agreement were an intrinsic part of the covenant between these parties. * * *

In sum, law and logic both compel the conclusion that the option which plaintiff seeks to enforce was an inseverable part of a basically illegal agreement. As such, it may not be enforced.

* * *

Accordingly, I vote to reverse the order appealed from and to dismiss the complaint.

FUCHSBERG, JUDGE (dissenting). *The agree., per its terms, was even forceable After Ikeds Death*

My vote too is for reversal. However, the decisional path that I would take differs appreciably not only from that of the majority but from that of my fellow dissenters as well.

Specifically, unlike the other dissenters, I am of the opinion that the parties entered into an enforceable agreement. But, for the reasons well stated both in Judge Gabrielli's alternative rationale and in Mr. Justice Lupiano's dissenting memorandum at the Appellate Division (61 A.D.2d 911, 402 N.Y.S.2d 820), I conclude that we are required to find that the agreement was not ambiguous and that, as a matter of law, it terminated in accordance with its terms during the father's lifetime.

I also take issue with the majority's reasoning that the option was enforceable only because it was separable from an otherwise illegal contract. In my view, the entire agreement is lawful qua agreement, and since it is one entered into between the controlling stockholders of a small, nonpublic corporation, it is not to be scrutinized by a rigid, hypertechnical reading of section 27 of the General Corporation Law, now part of section 701 of the Business Corporation Law.

Small, closely held corporations whose operation is dominated, as its stockholders and creditors usually are aware, by a particular individual or small group of individuals, must be distinguished, legally and pragmatically, from large corporations whose stock is traded on a public securities exchange and where the normal stockholders' relationship to those managing the corporation is bound to be impersonal and remote. Obviously, the latter's operations are rarely, if ever, covered by stockholders' agreements, and the Business Corporation Law itself is the sole restriction on their management.

In the close corporation, investors who themselves are not part of the dominant group commonly rely on the identities of the individuals who run the business and on the likelihood of their continuance in power. As a practical matter, these individuals will be expected to exercise a broad discretion and considerable informality in carrying out their management functions; this flexibility may be regarded as one of the strengths of a smaller organization. Indeed, faith in the integrity and ability of the managers is what usually motivates the investment. Looked at realistically, such corporations, often organized solely to obtain the advantage of limited personal liability for their principals, to qualify for a particular tax classification, or for some similar reason, are frequently "little more * * * than chartered partnerships" (Ripin v. United States Woven Label Co., 205 N.Y. 442, 447, 98 N.E. 855, 856). Control of such matters as choice of officers and directors, amounts of executive salaries, and options to buy or sell each other's stock—exactly the sort of things with which the agreement before us dealt—is usually mapped out by agreements among stockholders.

In short, so long as an agreement between stockholders relating to the management of the corporation bears no evidence of an intent to defraud other stockholders or creditors, deviations from precise formalities should not automatically call for a slavish enforcement of the statute. For this is the "governing criteri[on]" by which to test "the validity of a stockholders' agreement" (Delaney, The Corporate Director: Can His Hands Be Tied in Advance, 50 Colum.L.Rev. 52, 61; see, also, 1 O'Neal, Close Corporations, § 5.08). This would not leave without remedy those minority stockholders in close corporations whose interests may be abused. Available to them and at least equally effective are the equitable remedies by which officers and directors can be made to respond for violations of their trust obligations (Meinhard v. Salmon, 249 N.Y. 458, 164 N.E. 545).

Analysis of the agreement and its surrounding circumstances here illustrates the wisdom of this approach. The corporation had for a long time been a one-man business in every sense, the man being Triggs, the father. Until he gave a minority interest to each of his sons, he was the owner of all the voting stock; afterwards, it was all owned by the father and his sons, who were preparing to succeed him. At the time of the agreement, the father, together with the son who was the other party to the disputed writing, held the majority of this stock. Given their service in the business, their stockholding, and their relationship to each other and to the history of the corporation, it was to be expected—and not at all extraordinary—that an arrangement for their continuance in office and their compensation would be executed. There is not the slightest indication that, had the parties gone through the routine of presenting the contract to duly called stockholders' and directors' meetings, it would not have been rubber-stamped as a matter of course. It is significant that no other stockholder challenged the agreement during the father's lifetime and that the dispute since then has gravitated only around the son's insistence that the option to purchase his father's shares had not expired, a term which in any event, though it found its way into the stockholders' agreement, related to an essentially personal matter distinct from any corporate management obligations as such.

In sum, given that no other shareholder or member of the general public has been harmed, there is no good reason to measure the agreement by the less sophisticated standards of yesteryear. Tellingly, the often conflicting and unpatterned holdings that characterized our varied decisions on this point in the past have been overshadowed by the enactment of subdivision (b) of section 620 of the Business Corporation

Law. At that time, the Legislature expressly indicated that it intended to overrule, at least in part, many of those decisions that struck down shareholders' agreements. In doing so, it made clear its purpose to approve and expand the ruling in Clark v. Dodge, 269 N.Y. 410, 199 N.E. 641, *supra*, which upheld a controverted stockholders' agreement in a close corporation context.

———

In Galler v. Galler, 32 Ill. 2d 16, 203 N.E.2d 577 (1964), two brothers, who together owned in equal parts nearly all the shares of a family corporation, entered into an extensive agreement designed to provide financial protection to each of their families and to assure that their families would retain equal control of the corporation following the death of either brother. The matters covered by the agreement included the number of directors, a supermajority quorum requirement, notice of meetings, voting for named persons as directors, declaration of dividends, and salary continuation arrangements. After the death of one brother, the other refused to abide by the agreement. The widow of the brother who had died then sued for specific performance. An intermediate appellate court that the agreement was void as against public policy because it restricted the discretion of the board of directors. The Illinois Supreme Court reversed.

The court acknowledged that shareholders in close corporations have special needs: there is no ready market for their stock, a large minority shareholder may find himself at the mercy of an oppressive majority, and, because each director has a substantial share interest, it often is not possible to secure "independent board judgment free from personal motivations concerning corporate policy." Id. at 27, 203 N.E.2d at 584. The court found that despite its breadth and duration (the agreement was intended to govern as long as one of the parties to it was alive), the agreement offended no public policy because it inflicted no harm on the corporation or any other person. Rather, the agreement served the legitimate purpose of providing support and maintenance for the shareholders' immediate families. Consequently, specific performance was ordered.

Subsequent cases have moved in the direction foreshadowed by *Galler* and Judge Fuchsberg's dissent in *Triggs*. Legislatures have moved in the same direction. The RMBCA was amended in 1991 to be more hospitable to contractual arrangements governing close corporations. RMBCA § 7.32 expressly validates seven specific categories of shareholder agreements that modify traditional corporate law norms and contains a catchall authorization of other variations not contrary to public policy. See also DGCL § 350, 351, 354, Calif. Corp. Code § 300, and N.Y.B.C.L. § 620(b). RMBCA § 7.32(b) spells out the requisite procedural formalities. RMBCA § 7.32(c) provides an express statutory rescission remedy to a purchaser of shares who did not know of the existence of the shareholder agreement. RMBCA § 7.32(d) ties the applicability of the new provisions to the absence of a public market for the corporation's shares. Compare DGCL § 342 and Calif. Corp. Code § 158.

However, even under modern statutes interpretative problems arise, particularly with respect to compliance with statutory procedures. Zion v. Kurtz, 50 N.Y.2d 92, 428 N.Y.S.2d 199, 405 N.E.2d 681 (1980), involved an agreement between the two stockholders of a Delaware corporation which specified that no "business or activities" shall be conducted without the consent of the minority shareholder. The agreement was not incorporated in the articles, of incorporation and thus did not comply fully with DGCL § 351. In a 4 to 3 decision, the court nevertheless held that the agreement was enforceable.

The majority observed that it was "[c]lear from those provisions [of the close corporation statute] that the public policy of Delaware does not proscribe a provision such as that contained in the shareholders' agreement here in issue even though it takes all management functions away from the directors." Moreover, referring to N.Y.B.C.L. § 620(b), the court stated that it was also "clear that no New York public policy stands in the way of our application of the Delaware statute and decisional law above referred to."

Gabrielli, J., dissented, arguing that the effect of the agreement was to "sterilize" the board of directors, and that the courts of neither Delaware nor New York had shown tolerance for those arrangements in close corporations that deviated from the statutory norm as to accept such an extreme. Although he admitted that the agreement might have been enforced in Delaware had it been made part of the articles of incorporation, he viewed its inclusion there as a mandatory requirement of the statute. He also disagreed with the majority's view that "Since there are no intervening rights of third persons, the agreement requires nothing that is not permitted by statute, and all of the stockholders of the corporation assented to it, the certificate of incorporation may be ordered reformed, by requiring Kurtz to file the appropriate amendments, or more directly he may be held estopped to rely upon the absence of those amendments from the corporate charter." The dissent concluded that the Delaware and New York statutes require that the close corporation "give notice of its unorthodox management structure through its filed certificate of incorporation. The obvious purpose of such a requirement is to prevent harm to the public before it occurs. If, as the majority's holding suggests, this requirement of notice to the public through the certificate of incorporation is without legal effect unless and until a third party's interests have actually been impaired, then the prophylactic purposes of the statutes governing 'close corporations' would effectively be defeated."

2. HIGH VOTING OR QUORUM REQUIREMENTS

Control devices designed to provide for minority shareholder representation on the board of directors or otherwise to protect minority shareholders' interests may be worth very little if holders of a majority of a corporation's stock retain the power to expand the board or to amend protective provisions in the corporation's articles or bylaws. Consequently, at least in those situations where participants in a close corporation wish to operate more or less as would partners, such control devices often are supplemented by provisions designed to allow each participant or some number of participants to veto all board decisions or certain significant decisions, such as those to appoint or remove officers, set salaries, fix dividends, or issue new stock.

The most straightforward way to create veto rights is to require that an extraordinary majority of directors or shareholders must approve all or certain specified actions. One approach is to require unanimous approval. However, many lawyers follow the practice of setting the supermajority requirement sufficiently high to make opposition of one shareholder or one director sufficient to block board or shareholder action. A requirement that a board action be approved of 80% of the directors, for example, effectively requires unanimity if the board has four or fewer members.

The reason for the caution in this area is that a few courts have struck down extraordinary majority voting requirements for one reason or another. The New York Court of Appeals, for example, held in Benintendi v. Kenton Hotel, 294 N.Y. 112, 60 N.E.2d 829 (1945), that by-law provisions requiring unanimity for any action by either the board or the shareholders were invalid as against public policy because they made it difficult for the corporation to conduct its business and created a substantial risk of deadlock. See also Kaplan v. Block, 183 Va. 327, 31 S.E.2d 893 (1944). Although this ruling was subsequently reversed by the legislature (N.Y.B.C.L. §§ 616 and 709), similar cases in other jurisdictions together with a number of decisions invalidating extraordinary majority requirements on statutory grounds created the small, but ever-nagging possibility that the courts might invalidate such provisions. That possibility seems, however, to be fading. Courts have come more and more to accept the fact that departures by close corporations from the traditional corporate model do not inevitably entail untoward results. Moreover, a great many legislatures have enacted statutory provisions that authorize, specifically or by implication, high vote requirements in the articles or by-laws. See, e.g., RMBCA §§ 2.02, 7.25(c), and 8.24(c) and N.Y.B.C.L. §§ 616 and 709.

A high quorum requirement for either shareholder meetings or board meetings, see, e.g., RMBCA §§ 7.27 and 8.24(a), can serve many of the same functions as a supermajority voting requirement or can supplement such a requirement by preventing a board or the shareholders from acting in the absence of one director or shareholder. At least one court has held, however, that where directors deliberately stay away from board meetings in order to prevent some action from being taken, they cannot, as shareholders, "complain of an irregularity which they themselves have caused." Gearing v. Kelly, 11 N.Y.2d 201, 203, 227 N.Y.S.2d

897, 182 N.E.2d 391 (1962). But see Campbell v. Loew's, Inc. (Chapter 12).

Jones v. Wallace, 291 Or. 11, 628 P.2d 388 (1981), involved a by-law which provided that a quorum at a shareholders' meeting consisted of all the corporation's outstanding shares entitled to vote. Based on this by-law, two minority shareholders sought to set aside an action at a meeting at which one shareholder was not present. The court held the by-law invalid because the Oregon statute provided that a provision increasing the quorum requirements for a shareholders' meeting must appear in the articles and this, according to the Court, was "not an unimportant technicality."

3. EMPLOYMENT CONTRACTS FOR EXECUTIVES

Contracts of employment normally are not specifically enforceable, even if one of the parties to the contract is a corporation. There have been exceptions, however. In Jones v. Williams, 139 Mo. 1, 39 S.W. 486 (1897), for example, the court granted specific performance of a contract employing the plaintiff as editor of a newspaper for five years. It relied in part on the fact that editorial control of a newspaper is a unique sort of power whose loss could not easily be compensated in damages and in part on the fact that the plaintiff had been induced by the contract to leave another position and to invest a substantial sum of money in the stock of the paper.

Specific performance may have much to recommend it in the circumstances that often surround internecine disputes in close corporations. See, e.g., Collins v. Collins Fruit Co., 189 So.2d 262 (Fla.App.1966). Nevertheless, most courts seem unwilling to depart from the standard rule, allowing only an action for damages for breach of contract when an officer is fired before the expiration of her contract. See F. Hodge O'Neal and Robert B. Thompson, O'Neal's Close Corp. § 6.05 (3rd ed.).

Where the contract is for the employment of an officer of a corporation, a more troublesome problem exists. On occasion, courts have held such contracts invalid, not merely unenforceable, because the term of the contract extended beyond that of the board of directors. The theory of most of such holdings is that it is against public policy to allow one board to bind its successors in a matter as important as the appointment of officers. See, e.g., Edwards v. Keller, 133 S.W.2d 823 (Tex.Civ.App. 1939), but note that Texas subsequently amended its corporation statute to change the result. In other cases, whose results perhaps are more defensible, courts have held merely that contracts of employment for an unusually long duration, particularly for the lifetime of the person employed, are invalid. See F. Hodge O'Neal and Robert B. Thompson, O'Neal's Close Corp. § 6.06 (3rd ed.).

A partial answer to the difficulties this may pose is to have the agreement provide that the party is to be employed not as an officer but in some non-elected capacity, such as general manager, sales manager, or operations supervisor. As artificial as this distinction may appear, it seems to have overcome the reluctance of some courts to uphold long-term employment contracts. E.g., Streett v. Laclede–Christy Co., 409 S.W.2d 691 (Mo.1966). See F. Hodge O'Neal & Robert B. Thompson, O'Neal's Close Corp. § 6.10 (3rd ed.).

D. RESTRICTIONS ON THE TRANSFER OF SHARES

PROBLEMS
PRECISION TOOLS REVISITED—PART IV

In the course of your discussions with Jessica, Michael and Bernie, they expressed concern about what would happen to their interests in the corporation should one of them die, withdraw, or have their employment involuntarily terminated. You advised them that it is standard practice for shareholders in close corporations to enter into an agreement by which they restrict the transfer of their stock. Bearing in mind the details of their personal situations set out in Parts I and II of Precision Tools, they have asked you draft such an agreement for them.

Because there are so many approaches to a stock transfer agreement, you have decided to prepare an outline of the major issues which should be addressed in drafting any agreement. Draft the outline, considering the following questions:

(1) What events trigger the applicability of the restrictions? The death of one of the parties? The termination of employment (should it make a difference if the termination is voluntary or involuntary)? Should the parties be allowed to make a gift of their stock (to family? third parties?)? Pledge the stock as collateral for a loan?

(2) Who should have the option (or be required) to purchase the shares subject to the restrictions? In what circumstances should the transfer of the shares be mandatory, i.e., the agreement require that upon the triggering event, the shareholder is obligated to sell and the prospective purchaser to buy? Alternatively, when should the transfer be subject to the option of one or more of the parties?

(3) Assuming that more than one person has an interest in purchasing the shares, in what order should there be a right of refusal? If no one exercises the right to purchase the shares under the agreement, is the seller free to sell to a third party without restriction?

(4) How is the price at which any transfers take place to be determined? Will it vary depending upon the occasion for the transfer? Will the agreement specify a price or will it set forth a formula pursuant to which the price will be determined? How often will such a determination be made? Whether or not there is a formula, what happens if the parties fail to agree upon the price?

(5) How will any purchase options be funded?

(6) In what instrument(s) should the restrictions be included? Consider RMBCA § 2.02 and DGCL § 202.

1. INTRODUCTION

Were the closely held enterprise operated as a partnership, the partners would have the right of *delectus personae,* the power of each partner to veto the admission into the partnership of a new member. Uniform Partnership Act, § 18(g). The owners of a small business who have chosen to incorporate also want to have this power. It is appropriate, therefore, that in most closely-held corporations the shareholders include some arrangement in their organizational scheme which approximates the right of *delectus personae.* Such arrangements usually take the form of transfer restriction agreements whereby the ability of the shareholders to alienate their stock is limited in some fashion.

In planning the affairs of the close corporation, there is a practical problem that complicates the drafting, as well as the interpretation, of transfer restriction agreements. It is evident that however carefully the owners of a close corporation and their counsel design machinery to insure the desired balance of control, that machinery can run amok or cease functioning altogether should one of the shareholders sell, give, or bequeath his stock. The second aim of a transfer restriction agreement, then, is to provide for the continuation of a workable control scheme when one of the shareholders dies or decides to sell or give away his interest.

Stock transfer agreements are also extremely important in creating a market for otherwise illiquid shares and planning the estates of the shareholders. Any sound estate plan provides some measure of liquidity to the estate in order to pay the decedent's personal debts, the expenses of administering the estate, and federal and state estate taxes. Where the estate consists in significant part of stock in a closely held corporation, for which shares there is by definition no ready market, the desired liquidity can often be furnished by some sort of stock purchase agreement combined with adequate planning for its funding. In addition, the buy-sell agreement at the time of death of a stockholder assists in establishing a value for the stock at that time. This is important for the purpose of determining the amount of estate taxes that are due; it reduces the risk that the taxing authorities will claim that the stock is worth substantially more than its value as established by the agreement. Finally, a buy-out provision may meet the desire of shareholders to diversify the assets of their estates to be passed on to their heirs. This diversification is particularly desirable in a close corporation whose success may depend in large measure on the abilities and efforts of one or two shareholders, whose deaths may make it imprudent for the estate to continue to hold the stock.

It is well to keep in mind that there are a variety of ways in which a shareholder may dispose of stock. The most common ones are by sale or bequest. But the planner should also consider the prospect of inter vivos transfers by way of gifts, creation of trusts, pledges, or other means by which the right to vote the stock and receive dividends might pass to the hands of someone other than the original, and perhaps key, shareholder.

Given the sound reasons underlying transfer restrictions, it is curious that their validity and enforceability have been the subject of a great deal of controversy and uncertainty.

The general American rule has been that unreasonable restraints on the alienation of personal property are void. Litigation seeking to soften that rule has often foundered on the poor drafting of the restraints in question. The result has been a number of decisions which have questioned the validity of many transfer restrictions. Recently, however, courts have recognized the need for such restrictions and have become more tolerant in their approach. See, e.g., Allen v. Biltmore Tissue Corp., 2 N.Y.2d 534, 161 N.Y.S.2d 418, 141 N.E.2d 812 (1957). In addition, some statutes expressly authorize transfer restrictions (RMBCA § 6.27 and DGCL § 202) or, indeed, require them for close corporations (DGCL § 342(a)(2)). See, also, Model Close Corporation Supplement, §§ 10–17.

There are two basic approaches to drafting buy-sell agreements. The designated purchaser may be the corporation that issues the stock, a technique known as an "entity purchase" agreement or "redemption agreement." Alternatively, the purchase option (or occasionally obligation) may be given to the other shareholders, in which case the agreement is known as a "cross-purchase" arrangement. Fairly frequently the two approaches are combined.

2. TYPES OF TRANSFER RESTRICTIONS

Transfer restrictions may take three basic forms, two or more of which are often found combined in the same agreement. First, the restriction may impose limitations on the freedom of a shareholder to transfer stock. Second, the corporation or the remaining shareholders may be given an option to purchase the shares of another shareholder upon the occurrence of certain events, such as the death of a shareholder or the termination of his or her employment with the corporation. Third, what is often called a "buy-sell agreement" may require the corporation or the remaining shareholders to purchase the stock of another shareholder upon the occurrence of similar triggering events. This requirement is often coupled with a coordinate obligation of the shareholder or her estate to sell the stock.

Although transfer restriction agreements are generally a matter of contract and may therefore be cast in whatever form is appropriate for the circumstances of the particular corporation and its shareholders, restrictions on the freedom of shareholder to transfer his or her shares commonly take one of three forms:

(1) Under a "right of first refusal," before a shareholder is free to sell his or her stock to a third person it first must be offered to the corporation or to the remaining shareholders (or both) at the same price

and on the same terms and conditions offered by the outsider. Typically the right, if extended to the other shareholders, is given in proportion to their respective holdings. If any shareholder is unable to purchase or declines to do so, his or her allocation may be taken up proportionately by the remaining shareholders.

(2) Another common form of restriction is the first option provision. RMBCA § 6.27(d)(1) and DGCL § 202(c)(1). The principal distinction between a first option provision and a right of first refusal is that the offer to the corporation or the remaining shareholders is made at a price and on terms fixed by the arrangement rather than by an offer made by an outside purchaser. Even if the basic restriction is cast in the form of a right of first refusal, it may be desirable to include a first option provision to deal with transfers of stock other than by sale to third parties. Obviously, a right of first refusal would not serve to deal with transfers by gift or devise.

(3) Finally, a shareholder's disposition of stock may be conditioned upon the consent of the corporation's board of directors or of the other shareholders. Modern statutes allow the parties to provide for a consent restriction if such "prohibition is not manifestly unreasonable." RMBCA § 6.27(d)(3) and DGCL § 202(c)(3). See also, Colbert v. Hennessey, 351 Mass. 131, 217 N.E.2d 914 (1966) (shareholders' agreement requiring consent of shareholders held binding on heirs of parties to the agreement).

Since one of the major purposes of transfer restriction agreements is to give shareholders some degree of control over the identity of co-owners of the business, such agreements often entitle the corporation or its remaining shareholders to purchase the stock of any shareholders who withdraw from the business. Such options may be activated upon the death of a shareholder, the termination of his or her employment, the pledging of his or her shares to another, or any other action that threatens to replace the shareholder by another. These options typically confer an absolute right to purchase the stock even though the shareholder or his or her estate may wish to retain the shares.

Where a right of first refusal gives the corporation or the remaining shareholders the option to purchase the shares of a deceased or withdrawing stockholder, a "buy-sell agreement" imposes an obligation to purchase. Usually used to provide liquidity to the estate of a deceased stockholder, these agreements are frequently funded by insurance policies taken out on the lives of the principal stockholders.

Transfer restrictions are most commonly adopted at the time a close corporation is formed; the restriction is a matter of negotiation among the initial shareholders. What is the status of a shareholder who purchases stock, either from the corporation or from one of the initial shareholders, after the transfer restriction becomes effective? The applicability of the agreement to a newcomer may depend on the document in which the agreement is inserted in the first instance: the articles of incorporation, a by-law provision, or a separate contract among the shareholders. A purchasing shareholder may not be bound if the restriction is in an agreement among shareholders to which he is not a party. It is customary, therefore, to make transfer restrictions a part of the by-laws or the articles. As between these two instruments, should there be any difference with respect to the enforceability of the restriction? Consider carefully the language of RMBCA § 2.02. See F. Hodge O'Neal & Robert B. Thompson, O'Neal's Close Corp. § 7.13 (3rd ed.).

In order to be valid against a purchaser of the stock without notice, a transfer restriction must be "noted conspicuously" on the stock certificate itself. RMBCA § 6.27(b) and Uniform Commercial Code § 8–204. The term "conspicuous" is defined in RMBCA § 1.40(3). For a judicial interpretation of what is "conspicuous" see Ling & Co. v. Trinity Savings & Loan Ass'n, 482 S.W.2d 841 (Tex.1972). Even if not conspicuous, a transfer restriction is enforceable against a transferee with knowledge. RMBCA § 6.27(b).

A related question is whether the shareholders of the corporation may adopt a by-law containing transfer restrictions that is valid against a shareholder who does not consent to the by-law. In Tu–Vu Drive–In Corp. v. Ashkins, 61 Cal.2d 283, 38 Cal.Rptr. 348, 391 P.2d 828 (1964), the court gave an affirmative answer to that question. Three years after the corporation in *Tu–Vu* was organized, the board of directors adopted a by-law provision giving a right of first refusal to the other shareholders and then to the corporation, before any shareholder could sell to an outsider. The by-law was approved by the plaintiff, who owned 54% of the stock. Subsequently, one of the minority shareholders granted to an outsider an option to purchase her stock, although it was never exercised. The plaintiff brought an action for a declaratory judgment that the by-law was enforceable over the minority stockholder's asserted right to choose to whom she wished to sell her stock. The question, according to the court, was whether the restriction was an unreasonable restraint on alienation. Holding that it was not, the court said, "In the light of the legitimate interests to be furthered by the by-law [the defendant's] asserted right becomes 'innocuous and insubstantial.' The by-law merely proscribes [the defendant's] choice of transferees while insuring to her the price and terms equal to those offered by the outsider."

3. THE VALUATION PROCESS

The valuation provisions of a share transfer restriction agreement are among the most important—and difficult—to draft. There are a variety of techniques available, of which it is only possible here to suggest a few of the more important. Reconsider Chapter 6, Part B. See generally, F. Hodge O'Neal, Restrictions on Transfer of Stock in Closely Held Corporations: Planning and Drafting, 65 Harv.L.Rev. 773 (1952). They include:

1. *Book Value.* This is a popular method but one that may lead to inequitable results. The book value of a company may bear little relationship to its value as an ongoing concern. Moreover, despite its

apparent simplicity, book value turns out in application often to be remarkably ambiguous. Does it, for example, include intangible assets, especially "goodwill"? What about income taxes that are accrued but unpaid, and may not appear on the books? If the corporation carries insurance on life of the shareholder whose death is the occasion for the exercise of a buy-sell provision, are the proceeds of the insurance to be included? Should assets that have appreciated substantially be written up before book value is calculated? If this technique is used, it is desirable that these and other questions be anticipated and dealt with in the agreement; and doing so turns what starts out to be a simple approach into one full of complexity.

2. *Capitalized Earnings.* An agreement may attempt to reach an objective appraisal of the fair value of the stock which is more sophisticated than that provided by book value by establishing a formula according to which the earnings of the business may be capitalized. Like book value, however, this technique presents certain difficulties of drafting. It is especially critical that the earnings of the business be carefully defined.

3. *Right of First Refusal.* Where the principal concern is that one of the parties may sell his interest to an outsider, providing that a shareholder must, before selling, offer his shares to the corporation (or the other shareholders) at the same price, and on the same terms and conditions offered by the outsider, has great appeal. This approach may, however, substantially increase the already great difficulties a shareholder in a close corporation faces in selling his stock, because a prospective buyer may well be put off by the prospect of spending considerable effort in negotiating a sale only to have the shares bought out from under him pursuant to a right of first refusal. Moreover, this approach is obviously useful only for prospective sales to third parties and is of no utility in providing for the transfer of shares by gift, devise, or inheritance.

4. *Appraisal.* It is possible to avoid some of the pitfalls of the preceding methods by simply leaving the valuation of the shares to appraisal by a neutral third party according to some predetermined procedure. One of the most convenient techniques of doing so is to provide for arbitration according to the rules of the American Arbitration Association or some other recognized arbitral organization.

5. *Mutual Agreement.* Another relatively popular technique is for the parties to the agreement to set a value for the shares and to revise it at stated intervals, usually annually. While this may lead to a fairer price, it is subject to the significant drawback that for psychological reasons, the parties often neglect to conduct the revaluations; focusing implicitly on the possibility that one of them might soon die or that they may have a falling out is not a particularly pleasant undertaking.

CONCORD AUTO AUCTION, INC. v. RUSTIN

627 F.Supp. 1526 (D.Mass.1986).

MEMORANDUM AND ORDER

YOUNG, DISTRICT JUDGE.

Close corporations, Concord Auto Auction, Inc. ("Concord") and E.L. Cox Associates, Inc. ("Associates") brought this action for the specific performance of a stock purchase and restriction agreement (the "Agreement"). Concord and Associates allege that Lawrence H. Rustin ("Rustin") as the administrator of E.L. Cox's estate ("Cox") failed to effect the repurchase of Cox's stock holdings as provided by the Agreement. * * *

* * *

I. Background

Both Concord and Associates are Massachusetts Corporations. Concord operates a used car auction for car dealers, fleet operators, and manufacturers. Associates operates as an adjunct to Concord's auction business by guaranteeing checks and automobile titles. Both are close corporations with the same shareholders, all siblings: Cox (now his estate), Powell, and Thomas. At all times relevant to this action, each sibling owned one-third of the issued and outstanding stock in both Concord and Associates.

To protect "their best interests" and the best interests of the two corporations, the three shareholders entered into a stock purchase and restriction agreement on February 1, 1983. The Agreement provides that all shares owned by a shareholder at the time of his or her death be acquired by the two corporations, respectively, through life insurance policies specifically established to fund this transaction. This procedure contemplates the "orderly transfer of the stock owned by each deceased Shareholder." At issue in the instant action are the prerequisites for and effect of the repurchase requirements as set forth in the Agreement.

This dispute arises because Rustin failed to tender Cox's shares as required by Paragraph 2, *Death of Shareholder*. Rustin admits this but alleges a condition precedent: that Powell, specifically, and Thomas failed to effect both the annual meeting and the annual review of the stock price set in the Agreement as required by Paragraph 6, *Purchase Price:* "Each price shall be reviewed at least annually no later than the annual meeting of the stockholders * * * (commencing with the annual meetings for the year 1984) * * *," here February 21, 1984. Rustin implies that, had the required meeting been held, revaluation would or should have occurred and that, after Cox's accidental death in a fire on March 14, 1984, Powell in particular as well as Thomas were obligated to revalue the stock prior to tendering the repurchase price.

There is no dispute that the By-Laws call for an annual meeting on the third Tuesday of February, here February 21, 1984. There is no dispute that none took place or that, when Cox died, the stocks of each corporation had not been formally revalued. No one disputes that Paragraph 6 of the Agreement provides for a price of $672.00 per share of Concord and a price of $744.00 per share for Associates. This totals $374,976 which is covered by insurance on Cox's life of $375,000. There is no substantial dispute that the stock is worth a great deal more, perhaps even twice as much. No one seriously disputes that Paragraph 6 further provides that:

> * * * all parties may, as a result of such review, agree to a new price by a written instrument executed by all the parties and appended to an original of this instrument, and that any such new price shall thereupon become the basis for determining the purchase price for all purposes hereof unless subsequently superceded pursuant to the same procedure. The purchase price shall remain in full force and effect and until so changed.

Rustin asserts that the explicit requirement of a yearly price review "clashes" with the provision that the price shall remain in effect until changed. He argues a trial is required to determine the intent of the parties:

> The question then arises, presenting this Court with a material issue of fact not susceptible to determination on a motion for summary judgment: Did the parties intend, either to reset, or at least to monitor, yearly, the correspondence between the Paragraph 6 price and the current value of the companies? If so, who, if anyone, was principally responsible for effecting the yearly review required by the Agreement, and for insuring an informed review?

In answering these questions the Court first outlines its proper role in the interpretation of this contract.

II. Discussion

A Court sitting in diversity will apply the substantive law of the forum state, here Massachusetts. In Massachusetts as elsewhere, absent ambiguity, contracts must be interpreted and enforced exactly as written. Where the language is unambiguous, the interpretation of a contract is a question of law for the court. Further, contracts must be construed in accordance with their ordinary and usual sense.

Contrary to Rustin's assertion, the Court in applying these standards holds that there is no ambiguity and certainly no "clash" between the dual requirements of Paragraph 6 that there be an annual review of share price and that, absent such review, the existing price prevails. When, as here, the Court searches for the meaning of a document containing two unconditional provisions, one immediately following the other, the Court favors a reading that reconciles them. The Court rules that the Agreement covers precisely the situation before it: no revaluation occurred, therefore the price remains as set forth in the Agreement. This conclusion is reasonable, for the Agreement is not a casual memorialization but a formal contract carefully drafted by attorneys and signed by all parties.

Moreover, the Court interprets Paragraph 2 to provide, in unambiguous terms:

> "In the event of the death of any Shareholder subject to this agreement, his respective * * * administrator * * * *shall*, within sixty (60) days after the date of death * * * give written notice thereof to each Company which notice *shall* specify a purchase date not later than sixty (60) days thereafter, *offering to each Company for purchase* as hereinafter provided, and *at the purchase price set forth in Paragraph 6*, all of the Shares owned on said date by said deceased Shareholder. * * *" [Emphasis by the Court].

Rustin, therefore, was unambiguously obligated as administrator of Cox's estate to tender Cox's shares for repurchase by Concord and Associates. His failure to do so is inexcusable unless he raises cognizable defenses.

All of Rustin's defenses turn on two allegations: that his performance is excused because the surviving parties failed to review and to adjust upward the $374,976 purchase price. Rustin contends that the parties meant to review the price per share on an annual basis. No affidavit supports this assertion, nor does any exhibit. In fact, absent any evidence for this proposition, Rustin's assertion is no more than speculation and conjecture. While Rustin contends that the failure to review and revalue constitutes "unclean hands" and a breach of fiduciary duty which excuses his nonperformance, he places before the Court only argument not facts.

It simply does not follow that because a meeting was not held and the prices were not reviewed that a trial of the parties' intentions is required. The Agreement is the best evidence of the parties' intent. Although the text of the Agreement provides that share price "shall" be reviewed "at least annually," the Agreement also states that "The purchase price shall remain in full force and effect unless and until so changed."

* * *

Even if competent evidence adduced at trial would support Rustin's allegations, his proposition would of necessity require judicial intervention, a course this Court does not favor. Rustin produces not a shred of evidence that the parties intended that a court should intercede to set the share price in the event the parties failed to do so themselves. Every first year law student learns that although the courts can lead an opera singer to the concert hall, they cannot make her sing. Lumley v. Guy, 118 Eng.Rep. 749 (1853). While this Court will specifically enforce a consensual bargain, memorialized in an unambiguous written document, it will not order the revision of the share price. Such intrusion into the private ordering of commercial affairs offends both good judgment and good jurisprudence. Moreover, the record before the Court indicates that the parties fully intended what their competent counsel drafted and they signed.

Moreover, the nucleus of Rustin's premise is that somehow Powell should have guaranteed the review and revision of the share prices. On the contrary, nothing in the record indicates that a reasonable trier of fact could find that Powell's duties and responsibilities included such omnipotence. More to the point, the By–Laws suggest that several individuals shared the responsibility for calling the required annual meeting: "In case the annual meeting for any year shall not be duly called or held, the Board of Directors or the President shall cuase (sic) a special meeting to be held. * * *" Pursuant to the By–Laws, Cox himself had the power, right, and authority to call a meeting of the stockholders of both companies, in order to review the price per share— or for any other purpose for that matter.

Furthermore, nothing in the record indicates that somehow Powell, Thomas, Concord, or Associates was charged with the duty of raising the share price. In fact, this is discretionary and consensual: "all parties *may*, as a result of such review, *agree* to a new price by a written instrument *executed by all parties*. * * *" Nowhere can the Court find any affirmative duty to guarantee either an annual meeting or a share price revision. To fault Powell for not doing by fiat what must be done by consensus credits Powell with powers she simply does not have. The mere fact that, as a shareholder of Concord and Associates, Powell benefits from the enforcement of the Agreement at the $374,976 purchase price does not, as matter of law, create an obligation on her part to effect a review or revision of the purchase price. One cannot breach a duty where no duty exists, and Rustin cannot manufacture by allegation a duty where neither the Agreement nor the By–Laws lends any support.

Applying the above analysis, the Court discounts three of Rustin's defenses as meritless: that specific performance is not warranted because Concord and Associates breached the Agreement they seek to enforce; that they have unclean hands because they failed to effect a review and revaluation of the shares; and that specific performance is conditional upon an annual review of share value to be held no later than the third Tuesday of February. The record demonstrates no evidence that share transfer is conditional, rather it appears absolute and automatic. Absent a duty to "guarantee" the occurrence of the annual meeting or the "review," the Court cannot find that Powell's failure, if any, to upgrade the share price constitutes a fiduciary breach.

Of Rustin's fourth defense, that the value of the stock increased so substantially that specific enforcement would be unfair and unjust to Cox's estate, little need be said. This defense as well as Rustin's counterclaims rest on the allegation that Powell, in particular, and Thomas "knew" that a revaluation would result in a higher price and "failed to effect an annual review." Of Powell, Rustin argues that she had a "special responsibility" to effect a review of the purchase price because her siblings looked to her for financial expertise and to call a meeting. Nowhere is this "special responsibility" supported by the Agreement or the By–Laws. Rustin also implies that the sisters "knew" that failure to revalue would inure to their benefit. This presumes they knew that Cox would die in an accidental fire three weeks after the deadline for the annual meeting. To call this preposterous understates it, for nothing immunized the sisters from an equally unforeseeable accident. Rustin's argument withers in the light of objectivity to a heap of conclusory straws.

Rustin goes on to argue that the sisters had a fiduciary duty to revalue the shares *after Cox's death* and *before tender*. Nowhere in the Agreement is there the slightest indication they were so obligated. Nowhere is there evidence of willfulness, intent to deceive, or knowing manipulation. * * *

Agreements, such as those before the Court, "among shareholders of closely held corporations are common and the purpose of such contracts are clear." * * *

Moreover, specific performance of an agreement to convey will not be refused merely because the price is inadequate or excessive. New England Trust Co. v. Abbott, 162 Mass. 148, 155, 38 N.E. 432 (1894); see Lee v. Kirby, 104 Mass. 420, 430 (1870); Allen v. Biltmore Tissue Corp., 2 N.Y.2d 534, 543, 161 N.Y.S.2d 418, 141 N.E.2d 812 (1957) ("The validity of the restriction on transfer does not rest on any abstract notion of intrinsic fairness of price. To be invalid, more than mere disparity between option price and current value of the stock must be shown"); Renberg v. Zarrow, 667 P.2d 465, 470 (Okla.1983)("In the absence of fraud, overreaching, or bad faith, an agreement between the stockholders that upon the death of any of them, the stock may be acquired by the corporation is binding. Even great disparity between the price specified in a buy-sell agreement and the actual value of the stock is not sufficient to invalidate the agreement.") The fact that surviving shareholders were allowed to purchase Cox' shares on stated terms and conditions which resulted in the purchase for less than actual value of the stock does not subject the agreement to attack as a breach of the relation of trust and confidence, there being no breach of fiduciary duty.

Rather than evidence of any impropriety, the Court rules that the purchase prices were carefully set, fair when established, evidenced by an Agreement binding all parties equally to the same terms without any indication that any one sibling would reap a windfall. The courts may not rewrite a shareholder's agreement under the guise of relieving one of the parties from the hardship of an improvident bargain. *Id.* at 471 (citations omitted). The Court cannot protect the parties from a bad bargain and it will not protect them from bad luck. Cox, the party whose estate is aggrieved, had while alive every opportunity to call the annual meeting and persuade his sisters to revalue their stock. Sad though the situation be, sadness is not the touchstone of contract interpretation.

* * *

III. Conclusion

* * * The Agreement shall be specifically enforced. Rustin's counterclaims are dismissed and, for the reasons set forth above, the Court ALLOWS Concord's and Associates' motions for summary judgment on all matters. Rustin must sell the Cox shares for the $374,976 purchase price to which all parties agreed. Rustin is hereby ORDERED to:

(1) Deliver the certificates for the Cox shares fully endorsed for purchases pursuant to paragraphs 2 and 6 of the February 1, 1983 Agreement no later than thirty days after the date of this order.

(2) Accept a purchase price of $672.00 per share of Auction and $744.00 per share of Associates as set forth in paragraph 6 of the Agreement.

* * *

SO ORDERED.

The extent to which courts will use fiduciary duties as well as other concepts to protect minority shareholders from oppressive conduct by majority shareholders is discussed later in this chapter.

4. ADDITIONAL DRAFTING PROBLEMS

Vogel v. Melish, 46 Ill.App.2d 465, 196 N.E.2d 402 (1964) provides a lesson to the drafter. Two equal shareholders entered into an agreement which provided that "if either party desired to sell, transfer, assign or convey or otherwise dispose of any shares, an offer must be transmitted to the other party who then had the right to accept such offer in full or in part in the manner set forth * * *" in the agreement. The agreement contained no specific provisions with respect to the shares in the event of the death of one of the parties. Strictly construing the agreement, the court concluded that the arrangement "terminated the restriction on alienation at the death of one of the parties." Thus, on the death of one of the shareholders, the transfer of his shares to his executor did not give the surviving shareholder the option to purchase the decedent's shares and all shares were free of any restraint. Perhaps because transfer restrictions are restraints on alienation and therefore disfavored at common law, courts may tend to ignore the intent of the parties and limit the scope of such restrictions.

As we have seen, the parties, in formulating transfer restrictions, may be motivated by a variety of considerations, including the desire to exercise something like the right of *delectus personae*, the maintenance of a control balance within the corporate structure so that no one shareholder becomes dominant, and the provision of liquidity for the estate of a deceased stockholder. Unfortunately, these aims may occasionally conflict. Helmly v. Schultz, 219 Ga. 201, 131 S.E.2d 924 (1963) provides an interesting illustration. The transfer restriction agreement there was included in a by-law which provided as follows:

> No stockholder shall sell or give away his stock in the corporation without first offering to sell the same to the remaining stockholders substantially in proportion to the stock already owned by them. Such remaining stockholders shall have fifteen (15) days from the date such offer is made to them in which to purchase said stock before the same may be given or sold to any other person. The price to be paid by such remaining stockholders for such stock shall be the book value of the stock on the first day of the month in which said offer is made. A reference to this bylaw shall appear on each stock certificate issued by the corporation.

When Mrs. Schultz decided to sell her shares, to comply with the by-law, she offered them first to the stockholders adding the condition that all her stock be purchased at the same time and paid for in cash. Only one of the shareholders sought to accept the offer. When Mrs. Schultz refused to sell to him alone, he brought an action for specific performance of the contract he alleged had been formed by his acceptance. The court refused to grant relief, holding that the offer, made "according to the by-laws," was "to *all the stockholders*—each in his proportionate share * * *." Thus the court found that the purpose of the by-law was "to keep the stock ownership in equal proportion among the original stockholders." Had their principal intention been to prevent outsiders from acquiring stock, they could have provided in the transfer restriction for a disproportionate purchase by one or more shareholders.

5. FUNDING

A buy-sell arrangement is of little practical utility unless the person or persons who have the option (or obligation) to purchase have the financial ability to do so. Unless some means of funding is provided, both the shareholders and the corporation may find themselves without the wherewithal to purchase the shares, and the corporation may even be prevented by statutory restrictions from making the purchase if it lacks the necessary surplus. Reconsider Chapter 9, Part C(e).

Where the putative purchaser is the corporation, one means of funding the purchase is the establishment of a sinking fund in which the corporation regularly sets aside money to be saved for that purpose. A second, and more common, technique is for the corporation to purchase and maintain life insurance on the lives of the shareholders in an amount adequate to fund all or a substantial part of any repurchase for which the corporation may become obligated on their death. Where this is the case it is important that the effect of the receipt of insurance proceeds on the value of the corporation be taken into account when drafting the valuation section of the agreement. A third method of funding is to defer payment by the use of promissory notes or installment obligations.

E. OPPRESSION OF MINORITY SHAREHOLDERS: DISSENSION, DEADLOCK, AND DISSOLUTION

PROBLEM
PRECISION TOOLS REVISITED—PART V

A.

When Michael, Jessica and Bernie formed Precision Tools, they entered into a shareholder voting agreement providing that each would vote for a board of directors made up of the three of them and a fourth person to be designated by Bernie. Pursuant to their mutual understanding, which they did not reduce to writing, Michael was elected president and CEO and Jessica was elected vice-president and chief financial officer.

After operating under this agreement for three years, Jessica and Bernie became increasingly dissatisfied with Michael's performance as president. They decided that he was not an effective executive, that he was indecisive, and that he had allowed PTC's overhead expenses to grow excessively. They also were upset that serious personality clashes had developed between Michael and with them and several key employees. Jessica and Bernie were particularly distressed by the fact that, for the first time, PTC had operated at a loss. They concluded that unless steps were taken to remove Michael, PTC's decline would continue.

At the next board of directors meeting, Jessica, Bernie and Bernie's designee voted to remove Michael as an officer and employee. Over Michael's objection, they also appointed Jessica president and CEO at a salary substantially higher than Michael had been paid. Finally, they voted to terminate payment of dividends for the foreseeable future and to conserve all available funds for future business development.

1. Is it likely that Michael would succeed in a suit to restore him to his position as president and/or compel the payment of dividends if a Columbia court were to follow *Wilkes?*.

2. In determining whether Michael has a valid claim, should a Columbia court use the *Wilkes'* analysis? Should it adopt the approach of the Delaware Supreme Court in *Nixon*? Is there some other methodology that might be more appropriate?

B.

Assume that only Bernie and his designee become dissatisfied with Michael. Jessica continues to support him as CEO. Bernie and his designee then begin to vote against most of the resolutions that Jessica and Michael bring to the board for approval, including all proposals to fund expansion of PTC's business. One such proposal is to buy one of PTC's principal suppliers from the estate of its founder at a very attractive price. Bernie explains that he intends to continue to block all major new investments because he has no confidence in Michael's ability to manage PTC. Michael and Jessica, concerned that PTC's competitive position is in jeopardy, offer to buy Bernie's stock, but Bernie demands a price that they believe is unreasonably high.

What is the likelihood that Michael and Jessica would succeed in a suit to hold Bernie liable for the losses PTC has incurred as a consequence of his negative votes, assuming that they can prove PTC has in fact been damaged?

C.

1. If the facts were as stated in "A" above, would Michael succeed in a suit to compel the dissolution of PTC? Would your answer differ if PTC were incorporated in:

> (a) New York (consider N.Y.B.C.L. §§ 1104–a, 1118, and Matter of Kemp & Beatley, Inc.).

> (b) Columbia (consider RMBCA §§ 14.30, 14.32, 14.34).

> (c) Delaware (consider DGCL §§ 226, 352, 353, 355).

2. If the facts were as stated in "B" above, would Michael and Jessica succeed in a suit to compel the dissolution of PTC? Would dissolution or a mandatory buy-out represent attractive remedies from their point of view?

Consider how your answers to all the above questions would influence your recommendations concerning the provisions that Michael, Jessica and Bernie should include in a shareholders' agreement, the articles of incorporation and/or by-laws, before making their initial investments in PTC. For example, should they adopt a contractual buyout arrangement or required the use of a mediator to deal with freeze-outs and deadlocks? How might each of the parties have reacted to suggestions made by the others?

1. INTRODUCTION

Perhaps the most difficult planning problem facing the participants in a close corporation is how to deal with the day, which comes all too frequently in the life of closely held businesses, when the owners cease to get along with each other. Conflict may manifest itself in a variety of ways. There are recorded cases in which shareholders have ceased speaking to each other, yet have managed to continue their business for years. In at least a few instances intracorporate disputes have ended in violence. See Nashville Packet Co. v. Neville, 144 Tenn. 698, 235 S.W. 64 (1921). One principal source of difficulty is that differences over matters of business policy or practice frequently are aggravated by differences of a more personal nature, which may become still more intense because participants are related to each other or have been close friends. *See* Ronald J. Watkins, Birthright: Murder, Greed and Power in the U–Haul Family Dynasty (1993).   One can even think of this aspect of close corporation practice as "corporate domestic relations" law.

How courts deal with breakdowns in the relationship among participants in close corporations is largely a function of judicial attitudes. If a court conceives of the relationship among participants in a close corporation as little different from the relationship among partners, as did the court in Donahue v. Rodd Electrotype Co. of New England, Inc., 367 Mass. 578, 328 N.E.2d 505 (1975), it is likely to hold that the participants are obliged to deal with each other much as partners do, as did the *Donahue* court.   On the other hand, a court that conceives of the parties' relationship as essentially contractual, will be more inclined to hold the parties to the terms of their corporate "contract."   See Frank H. Easterbrook and Daniel R. Fischel, The Economic Structure of Corporate Law 228–252 (1991),

2. JUDICIAL PROTECTION OF MINORITY INTERESTS IN THE CLOSE CORPORATION

When relations among shareholders in a close corporation break down, those who hold a majority of the stock often seek to "oppress" or "freeze out" the minority interest.   Numerous techniques can be used to accomplish this end, and new ones continue to be created by enterprising shareholders and their attorneys.   See, generally, F. Hodge O'Neal & Robert B. Thompson, O'Neal's Oppression of Minority Shareholders (2nd ed., 1986).

Of course, the possibility that the parties may one day come to a parting of ways is seldom entirely absent from the thoughts of the individuals who embark on a corporate venture.   In fact, that possibility provides one of the principal stimuli for the planning exercise;   so long as relations among the parties remain good, they are not likely to have to resort to contractual provisions or formal governance arrangements to work out any differences of opinion that may arise.   The difficulty for the planner is to walk the narrow line between protecting minority shareholders against oppression and designing control mechanisms that are so veto prone or cumbersome that they make it difficult to manage the corporation's business.   Consequently, before deciding what control mechanisms to recommend, a planner must understand what devices are available to minimize the likelihood of oppression and what attitude a court is likely to adopt when confronted with allegations that a majority has treated a minority unfairly.

WILKES v. SPRINGSIDE NURSING HOME, INC.
370 Mass. 842, 353 N.E.2d 657 (1976).

HENNESSEY, CHIEF JUSTICE.

On August 5, 1971, the plaintiff (Wilkes) filed a bill in equity for declaratory judgment in the Probate Court for Berkshire County, naming as defendants T. Edward Quinn (Quinn), Leon L. Riche (Riche), the First Agricultural National Bank of Berkshire County and Frank Sutherland MacShane as executors under the will of Lawrence R. Connor (Connor), and the Springside Nursing Home, Inc. (Springside or the corporation). Wilkes alleged that he, Quinn, Riche and Dr. Hubert A. Pipkin (Pipkin) entered into a partnership agreement in 1951, prior to the incorporation of Springside, which agreement was breached in 1967 when Wilkes's salary was terminated and he was voted out as an officer and director of the corporation. Wilkes sought, among other forms of relief, damages in the amount of the salary he would have received had he continued as a director and officer of Springside subsequent to March, 1967.

* * * A judgment was entered dismissing Wilkes's action on the merits. We granted direct appellate review. On appeal, Wilkes argued in the alternative that (1) he should recover damages for breach of the alleged partnership agreement; and (2) he should recover damages because the defendants, as majority stockholders in Springside, breached their fiduciary duty to him as a minority stockholder by their action in February and March, 1967.

* * * [W]e reverse so much of the judgment as dismisses Wilkes's complaint and order the entry of a judgment substantially granting the relief sought by Wilkes under the second alternative set forth above.

* * *

[In 1951, Wilkes, Riche, Quinn, and Pipkin purchased a building lot to use as a nursing home.]

* * * [O]wnership of the property was vested in Springside, a corporation organized under Massachusetts law.

Each of the four men invested $1,000 and subscribed to ten shares of $100 par value stock in Springside.[6] At the time of incorporation, it was understood by all of the parties that each would be a director of Springside and each would participate actively in the management and decision making involved in operating the corporation.[7] It was, further, the understanding and intention of all the parties that, corporate resources permitting, each would receive money from the corporation in equal amounts as long as each assumed an active and ongoing responsibility for carrying a portion of the burdens necessary to operate the business.

6. On May 2, 1955, and again on December 23, 1958, each of the four original investors paid for and was issued additional shares of $100 par value stock, eventually bringing the total number of shares owned by each to 115.

7. Wilkes testified before the master that, when the corporate officers were elected, all four men "were * * * guaranteed directorships." Riche's understanding of the parties' intentions was that they all wanted to play a part in the management of the corporation and wanted to have some "say" in the risks involved; that, to this end, they all would be directors; and that "unless you [were] a director and officer you could not participate in the decisions of [the] enterprise."

The work involved in establishing and operating a nursing home was roughly apportioned, and each of the four men undertook his respective tasks. * * *

At some time in 1952, it became apparent that the operational income and cash flow from the business were sufficient to permit the four stockholders to draw money from the corporation on a regular basis. Each of the four original parties initially received $35 a week from the corporation. As time went on the weekly return to each was increased until, in 1955, it totalled $100.

In 1959, after a long illness, Pipkin sold his shares in the corporation to Connor, who was known to Wilkes, Riche and Quinn through past transactions with Springside in his capacity as president of the First Agricultural National Bank of Berkshire County. Connor received a weekly stipend from the corporation equal to that received by Wilkes, Riche and Quinn. He was elected a director of the corporation but never held any other office. He was assigned no specific area of responsibility in the operation of the nursing home but did participate in business discussions and decisions as a director and served additionally as financial adviser to the corporation.

* * *

[Beginning in 1965, personal relationships between Wilkes and the other shareholders began to deteriorate.] As a consequence of the strained relations among the parties, Wilkes, in January of 1967, gave notice of his intention to sell his shares for an amount based on an appraisal of their value. In February of 1967 a directors' meeting was held and the board exercised its right to establish the salaries of its officers and employees.[10] A schedule of payments was established whereby Quinn was to receive a substantial weekly increase and Riche and Connor were to continue receiving $100 a week. Wilkes, however, was left off the list of those to whom a salary was to be paid. The directors also set the annual meeting of the stockholders for March, 1967.

At the annual meeting in March, Wilkes was not reelected as a director, nor was he reelected as an officer of the corporation. He was further informed that neither his services nor his presence at the nursing home was wanted by his associates.

The meetings of the directors and stockholders in early 1967, the master found, were used as a vehicle to force Wilkes out of active participation in the management and operation of the corporation and to cut off all corporate payments to him. Though the board of directors had the power to dismiss any officers or employees for misconduct or neglect of duties, there was no indication in the minutes of the board of

10. The by-laws of the corporation provided that the directors, subject to the approval of the stockholders, had the power to fix the salaries of all officers and employees. This power, however, up until February, 1967, had not been exercised formally; all payments made to the four participants in the venture had resulted from the informal but unanimous approval of all the parties concerned.

directors' meeting of February, 1967, that the failure to establish a salary for Wilkes was based on either ground. The severance of Wilkes from the payroll resulted not from misconduct or neglect of duties, but because of the personal desire of Quinn, Riche and Connor to prevent him from continuing to receive money from the corporation. Despite a continuing deterioration in his personal relationship with his associates, Wilkes had consistently endeavored to carry on his responsibilities to the corporation in the same satisfactory manner and with the same degree of competence he had previously shown. Wilkes was at all times willing to carry on his responsibilities and participation if permitted so to do and provided that he receive his weekly stipend.

1. We turn to Wilkes's claim for damages based on a breach of the fiduciary duty owed to him by the other participants in this venture. In light of the theory underlying this claim, we do not consider it vital to our approach to this case whether the claim is governed by partnership law or the law applicable to business corporations. This is so because, as all the parties agree, Springside was at all times relevant to this action, a close corporation as we have recently defined such an entity in Donahue v. Rodd Electrotype Co. of New England, Inc. [367 Mass. 578], 328 N.E.2d 505 (1975).

In *Donahue*, we held that "stockholders in the close corporation owe one another substantially the same fiduciary duty in the operation of the enterprise that partners owe to one another." [*Id.* at 593 (footnotes omitted)], 328 N.E.2d at 515. As determined in previous decisions of this court, the standard of duty owed by partners to one another is one of "utmost good faith and loyalty." Cardullo v. Landau, 329 Mass. 5, 8, 105 N.E.2d 843 (1952). Thus, we concluded in *Donahue,* with regard to "their actions relative to the operations of the enterprise and the effects of that operation on the rights and investments of other stockholders," "[s]tockholders in close corporations must discharge their management and stockholder responsibilities in conformity with this strict good faith standard. They may not act out of avarice, expediency or self-interest in derogation of their duty of loyalty to the other stockholders and to the corporation." [367 Mass. at 593 n. 18], 328 N.E.2d at 515.

In the *Donahue* case we recognized that one peculiar aspect of close corporations was the opportunity afforded to majority stockholders to oppress, disadvantage or "freeze out" minority stockholders. In *Donahue* itself, for example, the majority refused the minority an equal opportunity to sell a ratable number of shares to the corporation at the same price available to the majority. The net result of this refusal, we said, was that the minority could be forced to "sell out at less than fair value," [367 Mass. at 592], 328 N.E.2d at 515, since there is by definition no ready market for minority stock in a close corporation.

"Freeze outs," however, may be accomplished by the use of other devices. One such device which has proved to be particularly effective in accomplishing the purpose of the majority is to deprive minority stockholders of corporate offices and of employment with the corporation.

F.H. O'Neal, "Squeeze–Outs" of Minority Shareholders 59, 78–79 (1975). See [367 Mass. 589], 328 N.E.2d 505. This "freeze-out" technique has been successful because courts fairly consistently have been disinclined to interfere in those facets of internal corporate operations, such as the selection and retention or dismissal of officers, directors and employees, which essentially involve management decisions subject to the principle of majority control. As one authoritative source has said, "[M]any courts apparently feel that there is a legitimate sphere in which the controlling directors or shareholders can act in their own interest even if the minority suffers." F.H. O'Neal, *supra* at 59 (footnote omitted).

The denial of employment to the minority at the hands of the majority is especially pernicious in some instances. A guaranty of employment with the corporation may have been one of the "basic reason[s] why a minority owner has invested capital in the firm." Symposium—The Close Corporation, 52 Nw.U.L.Rev. 345, 392 (1957). See F.H. O'Neal, *supra* at 78–79. The minority stockholder typically depends on his salary as the principal return on his investment, since the "earnings of a close corporation * * * are distributed in major part in salaries, bonuses and retirement benefits." 1 F.H. O'Neal, Close Corporations § 1.07 (1971).[13] Other noneconomic interests of the minority stockholder are likewise injuriously affected by barring him from corporate office. See F.H. O'Neal, "Squeeze–Outs" of Minority Shareholders 79 (1975). Such action severely restricts his participation in the management of the enterprise, and he is relegated to enjoying those benefits incident to his status as a stockholder. See Symposium—The Close Corporation, 52 Nw.U.L.Rev. 345, 386 (1957). In sum, by terminating a minority stockholder's employment or by severing him from a position as an officer or director, the majority effectively frustrate the minority stockholder's purposes in entering on the corporate venture and also deny him an equal return on his investment.

* * * The distinction between the majority action in *Donahue* and the majority action in this case is more one of form than of substance. Nevertheless, we are concerned that untempered application of the strict good faith standard enunciated in *Donahue* to cases such as the one before us will result in the imposition of limitations on legitimate action by the controlling group in a close corporation which will unduly hamper its effectiveness in managing the corporation in the best interests of all concerned. The majority, concededly, have certain rights to what has been termed "selfish ownership" in the corporation which should be balanced against the concept of their fiduciary obligation to the minority.

Therefore, when minority stockholders in a close corporation bring suit against the majority alleging a breach of the strict good faith duty owed to them by the majority, we must carefully analyze the action

---

13. We note here that the master found that Springside never declared or paid a dividend to its stockholders.

taken by the controlling stockholders in the individual case. It must be asked whether the controlling group can demonstrate a legitimate business purpose for its action. See Bryan v. Brock & Blevins Co., 343 F.Supp. 1062, 1068 (N.D.Ga.1972), aff'd, 490 F.2d 563, 570–571 (5th Cir.1974); Schwartz v. Marien, 37 N.Y.2d 487, 492, 373 N.Y.S.2d 122, 335 N.E.2d 334 (1975). In asking this question, we acknowledge the fact that the controlling group in a close corporation must have some room to maneuver in establishing the business policy of the corporation. It must have a large measure of discretion, for example, in declaring or withholding dividends, deciding whether to merge or consolidate, establishing the salaries of corporate officers, dismissing directors with or without cause, and hiring and firing corporate employees.

When an asserted business purpose for their action is advanced by the majority, however, we think it is open to minority stockholders to demonstrate that the same legitimate objective could have been achieved through an alternative course of action less harmful to the minority's interest. See Schwartz v. Marien, *supra*. If called on to settle a dispute, our courts must weigh the legitimate business purpose, if any, against the practicability of a less harmful alternative.

Applying this approach to the instant case it is apparent that the majority stockholders in Springside have not shown a legitimate business purpose for severing Wilkes from the payroll of the corporation or for refusing to reelect him as a salaried officer and director. The master's subsidiary findings relating to the purpose of the meetings of the directors and stockholders in February and March, 1967, are supported by the evidence. There was no showing of misconduct on Wilkes's part as a director, officer or employee of the corporation which would lead us to approve the majority action as a legitimate response to the disruptive nature of an undesirable individual bent on injuring or destroying the corporation. On the contrary, it appears that Wilkes had always accomplished his assigned share of the duties competently, and that he had never indicated an unwillingness to continue to do so.

It is an inescapable conclusion from all the evidence that the action of the majority stockholders here was a designed "freeze out" for which no legitimate business purpose has been suggested. Furthermore, we may infer that a design to pressure Wilkes into selling his shares to the corporation at a price below their value well may have been at the heart of the majority's plan.[14]

In the context of this case, several factors bear directly on the duty owed to Wilkes by his associates. At a minimum, the duty of utmost good faith and loyalty would demand that the majority consider that their action was in disregard of a long-standing policy of the stockholders that each would be a director of the corporation and that employment with the corporation would go hand in hand with stock ownership; that

---

14. This inference arises from the fact that Connor, acting on behalf of the three controlling stockholders, offered to purchase Wilkes's shares for a price Connor admittedly would not have accepted for his own shares.

Wilkes was one of the four originators of the nursing home venture; and that Wilkes, like the others, had invested his capital and time for more than fifteen years with the expectation that he would continue to participate in corporate decisions. Most important is the plain fact that the cutting off of Wilkes's salary, together with the fact that the corporation never declared a dividend, assured that Wilkes would receive no return at all from the corporation.

2. The question of Wilkes's damages at the hands of the majority has not been thoroughly explored on the record before us. Wilkes, in his original complaint, sought damages in the amount of the $100 a week he believed he was entitled to from the time his salary was terminated up until the time this action was commenced. However, the record shows that, after Wilkes was severed from the corporate payroll, the schedule of salaries and payments made to the other stockholders varied from time to time. In addition, the duties assumed by the other stockholders after Wilkes was deprived of his share of the corporate earnings appear to have changed in significant respects. Any resolution of this question must take into account whether the corporation was dissolved during the pendency of this litigation.

Therefore our order is as follows: So much of the judgment as dismisses Wilkes's complaint and awards costs to the defendants is reversed. * * *

————

Courts have demonstrated varying degrees of sensitivity to the problems of minority shareholders. Few have embraced fully *Donahue*'s "utmost good faith and loyalty" test. Indeed, the *Wilkes* court found it necessary to adopt a mode of analysis that allows a majority more flexibility to manage the corporation's business as it sees fit, and subsequent decisions adopting a "partnership" approach, in Massachusetts and elsewhere, have tended to follow *Wilkes*, not *Donahue*.

Daniels v. Thomas, Dean & Hoskins, Inc., 246 Mont. 125, 804 P.2d 359 (1990), employed an approach that allows majority interests even more flexibility. Daniels, an employee and minority shareholder of Thomas, Dean & Hoskins, Inc. (TD&H), purchased stock through an employee stock purchase plan which required employees to also purchase stock in Thomas & Dean Properties, Inc. (T&D Properties). The employee also entered into a buy-sell agreement which established a formula for determining the repurchase price for TD&H stock, but not for T&D Properties stock.

Several years later, Daniels sought to terminate his employment with TD&H. He met with Thomas, the president and a director of both TD&H and T&D Properties, to negotiate his termination agreement but they were unable to agree upon a price for the T&D Properties stock. Thomas tied the valuation of the stock to the shareholder agreement and refused to waive its anti-competition clause. Moreover, Thomas indicated that if Daniels did not sell his T&D Properties stock, Thomas would bleed the assets from T&D Properties. Daniels sued, alleging breach of fiduciary duty based upon Thomas' oppressive negotiation tactics. The trial court found that Thomas had breached his fiduciary duty and thereafter determined the value of the T&D Properties stock.

The Supreme Court of Montana reversed. The court first held that Thomas, the majority shareholder, owed a duty to all TD&H shareholders, not just to Daniels. Consequently, "[w]hen applying the [*Wilkes*] balancing test, we hold that Thomas successfully demonstrated that his duty to these other shareholders was not to pay Daniels a price for Daniels' * * * shares that the corporation could not afford so as not to harm the other shareholders or the corporation. Daniels, however, failed to demonstrate the practicability of a less harmful alternative, he merely insisted that the corporation buy his shares at the price he named." Id., at 367. Moreover, the court used an approach similar to that applied to business judgments to evaluate Thomas's actions as a director of T&D Properties. It focused on whether a "reasonable basis exists to indicate that the directors of the corporation acted in good faith," not whether the director acted in utmost good faith and loyalty. Id. at 367. Where the trial court found that Thomas's actions were oppressive, the appellate court determined that those actions were "consistent with negotiation tactics * * *." Id. at 368.

The dissent argued that "[t]he 'business judgment' rule applies to officers and directors acting in a corporate capacity, when no fiduciary relationship is involved. When a fiduciary status is established, the actions of officers and directors are examined, not under the 'business judgment rule' but rather whether the fiduciary exercised the utmost good faith and loyalty, in this case towards all of the shareholders of T&D Properties." 804 P.2d at 373.

Easterbrook and Fischel contend that the analytic approach employed in *Wilkes* "is in all likelihood closer to the bargain the parties would have reached themselves if transactions costs were zero" and that *Wilkes* is consistent with contractual analysis. Frank H. Easterbrook and Daniel R. Fischel, The Economic Structures of Corporate Law 247 (1991). Other commentators and courts disagree. Consider the following:

> In close corporations, freezeouts generally arise in the context of a dispute over the disentanglement of what are essentially partnership arrangements among more or less active participants for whose securities there is no market. The parties are visibly at loggerheads over division of the business's prosperity or over the conduct of its business; their disagreements are of a continuing kind, likely both not to be resolved until the business terminates and to plague the parties as they remain unable to disentangle satisfactorily. There is, therefore, reason to facilitate or encourage the departure of one group or the other from the enterprise—both in terms of the personal well-being of the participants, and because of the impact of

continuing disagreements on their conduct of the enterprise. It does not follow that corporate law should permit the controlling group to have an advantage in bargaining over the terms of the break-up. Still, the difficulty with flatly forbidding freezeouts is that, if the majority does not have the power to force the minority out, the majority may be forced to accede to the demands of the minority because of the threat of deadlock. Moreover, unlike the investors in a public corporation, the parties in a close corporation can contract in advance about their arrangements; any skew in the corporate law that permits majority power to displace the minority can thus be offset by contract. Modern statutes purport to offer special solutions for the problem of disentangling the essentially personal relationships of parties in conflict in close corporations. See, e.g., Del.Code tit. 8, §§ 352, 355 (1975); N.Y.—McKinney's Bus.Corp.Law § 1104 (1963); id. § 1111(b)(3), (c). If, notwithstanding such legislation, freezeouts are permitted by statute, any judicially imposed solution will require compliance with some conception of "fairness," however crude it may be. But it is hard to see any role for "business purpose" as a doctrine in filtering permissible from impermissible freezeouts in close corporations, even as that conception is rigorously confined in cases like Schwartz v. Marien, 37 N.Y.2d 487, 492, 373 N.Y.S.2d 122, 127, 335 N.E.2d 334, 338 (1975), or Wilkes v. Springside Nursing Home, Inc., 370 Mass. 842, 353 N.E.2d 657, 663 (1976).

Victor Brudney & Marvin A. Chirelstein, A Restatement of Corporate Freezeouts, 87 Yale L.J. 1354, 1356–57 n. 9 (1977).

In Nixon v. Blackwell, 626 A.2d 1366 (Del.1993), the Delaware Supreme Court went out of its way to address the question of whether minority shareholders in close corporations are entitled to special protections. After holding that it was not unfair for a corporation that had repurchased stock from certain employee-shareholders to refuse to purchase stock owned by non-employee minority shareholders, the court added the following coda to its opinion:

> We wish to address one further matter which was raised at oral argument before this Court: Whether there should be any special, judicially-created rules to "protect" minority stockholders of closely-held Delaware corporations.

> The case at bar points up the basic dilemma of minority stockholders in receiving fair value for their stock as to which there is no market and no market valuation. It is not difficult to be sympathetic, in the abstract, to a stockholder who finds himself or herself in that position. A stockholder who bargains for stock in a closely-held corporation and who pays for those shares * * * can make a business judgment whether to buy into such a minority position, and if so on what terms. One could bargain for definitive provisions of self-ordering permitted to a Delaware corporation through the certificate of incorporation or by-laws by reason of the

provisions in 8 Del.C. §§ 102, 109, and 141(a). Moreover, in addition to such mechanisms, a stockholder intending to buy into a minority position in a Delaware corporation may enter into definitive stockholder agreements, and such agreements may provide for elaborate earnings tests, buy-out provisions, voting trusts, or other voting agreements. See, e.g., 8 Del.C. § 218.

The tools of good corporate practice are designed to give a purchasing minority stockholder the opportunity to bargain for protection before parting with consideration. It would do violence to normal corporate practice and our corporation law to fashion an ad hoc ruling which would result in a court-imposed stockholder buy-out for which the parties had not contracted.

In 1967, when the Delaware General Corporation Law was significantly revised, a new Subchapter XIV entitled "Close Corporations; Special Provisions," became a part of that law for the first time. While these provisions were patterned in theory after close corporation statutes in Florida and Maryland, "the Delaware provisions were unique and influenced the development of similar legislation in a number of other states. * * *" See Ernest L. Folk, III, Rodman Ward, Jr., and Edward P. Welch, 2 Folk on the Delaware General Corporation Law 404 (1988). Subchapter XIV is a narrowly constructed statute which applies only to a corporation which is designated as a "close corporation" in its certificate of incorporation, and which fulfills other requirements, including a limitation to 30 on the number of stockholders, that all classes of stock have to have at least one restriction on transfer, and that there be no "public offering." 8 Del.C. § 342. Accordingly, subchapter XIV applies only to "close corporations," as defined in section 342. "Unless a corporation elects to become a close corporation under this subchapter in the manner prescribed in this subchapter, it shall be subject in all respects to this chapter, except this subchapter." 8 Del.C. § 341. The corporation before the Court in this matter, is not a "close corporation." Therefore it is not governed by the provisions of Subchapter XIV.[19]

One cannot read into the situation presented in the case at bar any special relief for the minority stockholders in this closely-held, but not statutory "close corporation" because the provisions of

---

19. We do not intend to imply that, if the Corporation had been a close corporation under Subchapter XIV, the result in this case would have been different. "[S]tatutory close corporations have not found particular favor with practitioners. Practitioners have for the most part viewed the complex statutory provisions underlying the purportedly simplified operational procedures for close corporations as legal quicksand of uncertain depth and have adopted the view that the objectives sought by the subchapter are achievable for their clients with considerably less uncertainty by cloaking a conventionally created corporation with the panoply of charter provisions, transfer restrictions, by-laws, stockholders' agreements, buy-sell arrangements, irrevocable proxies, voting trusts or other contractual mechanisms which were and remain the traditional method for accomplishing the goals sought by the close corporation provisions." David A. Drexler, Lewis S. Black, Jr., and A. Gilchrist Sparks, III, Delaware Corporation Law and Practice § 43.01 (1993).

Subchapter XIV relating to close corporations and other statutory schemes [20] preempt the field in their respective areas. It would run counter to the spirit of the doctrine of independent legal significance, and would be inappropriate judicial legislation for this Court to fashion a special judicially-created rule for minority investors when the entity does not fall within those statutes, or when there are no negotiated special provisions in the certificate of incorporation, by-laws, or stockholder agreements.

Id. at 1379–81.

Note: *Alternative Contractual Approaches*

Sometimes it is assumed that once a court has held that the relationship among participants in a close corporation is essentially contractual, it will be clear what duties those participants owe each other. Jordan v. Duff and Phelps, Inc., 815 F.2d 429 (7th Cir.1987), makes clear that that is not necessarily the case. Jordan, a securities analyst, was employed by Duff & Phelps, Inc., although he had no written employment contract. He was eligible to purchase 250 shares pursuant to Duff & Phelps' employee stock purchase plan. Before buying stock, Jordan was required to sign a "Stock Restriction and Purchase Agreement" requiring him to sell his stock back to Duff & Phelps, at its adjusted book value as of the end of the preceding year, if his employment terminated for any reason. By 1983, Jordan had purchased 188 shares and was making installment payments on another 62 shares.

To resolve certain family problems, Jordan decided to accept an offer of employment from another firm located in a different city. On November 16, 1983, Jordan tendered his resignation to the CEO of Duff & Phelps. After being advised that if he made his resignation effective as of December 31, 1983, he would receive the increase in the book value of his shares through the end of 1983, Jordan resigned effective as of that date. The CEO accepted Jordan's his resignation without informing him of pending negotiations to sell Duff & Phelps to a public corporation. At the end of 1983, Jordan delivered his 188 shares to Duff & Phelps, received a check for $23,225, and gave up his right to purchase the remaining 62 shares.

On January 10, 1984, Duff & Phelps announced that it had agreed to be acquired by the company with which it had been negotiating. Had Jordan remained an employee and exercised his right to purchase the additional 62 shares, he would have been entitled to receive about $452,000.* Jordan reacted to this announcement by attempting to

---

20. It is to be noted that Delaware statutory law provides for many forms of business enterprise: partnerships pursuant to 6 Del.C. §§ 1501–43; limited partnerships pursuant to 6 Del.C. § 17–101–1109; limited liability companies pursuant to 6 Del.C. §§ 18–101–1106; business trusts pursuant to Title 12, §§ 3801–20.

* The Federal Reserve Board ultimately disapproved that merger, but Duff & Phelps then arranged to be acquired in a leveraged buy out by an employee stock ownership trust. Had Jordan held 250 shares at the time of that transaction, he would have received almost $500,000 for his stock.

return the check he had received and demanding that Duff & Phelps pay him what he would have received had he known of the merger negotiations and decided not to sell. When Duff & Phelps rejected his demand, Jordan brought suit, alleging that Duff & Phelps had breached its duty to disclose about the merger negotiations before accepting his resignation.

One aspect of Jordan's claim required the court to balance the protections owed to individual shareholders against the interests of the corporation as a whole. In a public corporation, disclosure is apt to jeopardize the consummation of transactions that are being negotiated; consequently, disclosure may not be required so long as the corporation chooses not to speak. (See Basic Inc. v. Levinson, Chapter 19). In a close corporation, disclosure of confidential information to one or a few shareholders is practicable without substantial risk to the interests of the corporation as a whole. Consequently, the CEO's silence was not justified on utilitarian grounds.

That holding set the stage for a debate between Judges Easterbrook and Posner, two titans of the law and economics movement, as to the nature of the obligations Duff & Phelps owed to Jordan. Easterbrook, writing for the court, began by setting forth the notion that although the fiduciary duties owed by a majority shareholder reflect "a standby or off-the-rack guess about what the parties would agree to if they dickered about the subject explicitly, parties may contract with greater specificity for other arrangements." Id. at 436. Easterbrook then explained his off-the-rack guess that Duff & Phelps and Jordan, *as a consequence of their employment "contract,"* would have agreed that Duff & Phelps owed Jordan a duty to disclose the merger negotiations:

> * * * [A] person's status as an employee "at will" does not imply that the employer may discharge him for every reason. Illinois, where Jordan was employed, has placed some limits on the discharge of at-will employees. * * * We do not disparage the utility of at-will contracts; this very panel recently recognized the value of informal (meaning not legally binding) employment relations. * * * But employment at will is still a contractual relation, one in which a particular duration ("at will") is implied in the absence of a contrary expression. The silence of the parties may make it necessary to imply other terms—those we are confident the parties would have bargained for if they had signed a written agreement. One term implied in every written contract and therefore, we suppose, every unwritten one, is that neither party will try to take opportunistic advantage of the other. "[T]he fundamental function of contract law (and recognized as such at least since Hobbes's day) is to deter people from behaving opportunistically toward their contracting parties, in order to encourage the optimal timing of economic activity and to make costly self-protective mea-

sures unnecessary." Richard A. Posner, *Economic Analysis of Law* 81 (3d ed. 1986).

815 F.2d at 438.

Judge Posner dissented. He also approached the issue principally as a matter of contract law, but disagreed with the majority's conclusion that Duff & Phelps owed Jordan any duties other than to repurchase his stock at adjusted book value. Posner focused on the fact that Jordan's status as a shareholder was tied to his remaining an employee. Posner reasoned that because Jordan was an "at will" employee who Duff & Phelps could discharge at any time, his status as a shareholder also was entirely contingent. That negated the existence of a right to be informed; hence, Duff & Phelps had no duty to disclose. Posner also argued that Duff & Phelps' conduct was not opportunistic. He claimed that shareholders such as Jordan are adequately protected by market constraints, such as the firm's desire to protect its reputation. Consequently, no occasion for opportunism should be deemed to exist.

In Ingle v. Glamore Motor Sales Co., 73 N.Y.2d 183, 538 N.Y.S.2d 771, 535 N.E.2d 1311 (1989), a key employee of a closely-held corporation had purchased stock subject to an agreement to resell it to the corporation if his employment was terminated for any reason. When the corporation terminated his employment without cause, the shareholder-employee argued that the termination violated a fiduciary duty owed to him as a shareholder. The New York Court of Appeals disagreed. The court said that whatever duties of good faith and fair dealing might arise in dealing with a minority shareholder as a shareholder, New York law provides no authority for a similar duty in the at-will employment context. In seeking to impose such a duty, the plaintiff was attempting "to award the sequential relationship of his employment status to his shareholders' agreement by extracting an obligation from the agreement to manufacture a legally unrecognized employment security. Divestiture of his status as a shareholder, by operation of the repurchase provision, is a contractually agreed to consequence flowing directly from the firing, not vice versa." 538 N.Y.S.2d at 1314, 535 N.E.2d at 744. The court interpreted the agreement governing the plaintiff's purchase of stock as expressly confirming that the parties did not intend to protect him against discharge at will.

Arguing against the majority's approach, the dissent noted, "What is remarkable about the majority opinion is that it appears to treat the employment at-will rule as a sort of categorical imperative which necessarily dictates the result in this case." The dissent viewed the case as one where an individual who was an officer, director, part owner, and active manager of a close corporation would be entitled to equitable remedies applied outside the realm of ordinary legal rules governing master and servant. The dissent considered the plaintiff the type of person whose minority interest needed the special protection that courts of equity have imposed on majority shareholders in a close corporation. The plaintiff was not a typical salaried employee; he purchased a minority interest to participate in the growth and increased value of the business and to receive the intangible benefits, such as independence, prestige, and feeling of achievement, of being part of the management of a successful, small business. The loss of these intangibles in a squeeze-out by the majority shareholders called for equitable relief.

The issue underlying the debate between Judges Easterbrook and Posner in *Jordan* and between the majority and dissent in *Ingle*—how a court should go about filling in the terms of an incomplete or implicit corporate "contract"—has been the subject of considerable academic commentary. In *Jordan*, Judge Easterbrook side-stepped that issue by basing his decision on Jordan's implicit employment contract. Easterbrook's reluctance to impute broader notions of fiduciary duty to the controlling shareholders of Duff & Phelps may have reflected a view that he has elsewhere expressed—that the choice of the corporate form itself is evidence that the parties intend to be governed by the norms generally applicable to corporate managers and shareholders. See Frank H. Easterbrook & Daniel R. Fischel, The Economic Structure of Corporate Law 228–252 (1991). The majority in *Ingle* more or less adopted that point of view, as did the Delaware Supreme Court in *Nixon*.

David Charny also uses contractual analysis as his framework for analyzing the duties owed to minority shareholders in close corporations. In contrast to Easterbrook and Fischel, however, he suggests that in filling in the terms of the corporate "contract," courts should consider not only the express terms of the agreements between the parties, but also informal discussions, past practices, and the participants' reasonable income expectations. David Charny, Hypothetical Bargains: The Normative Structure of Contract Interpretations, 89 Mich. L. Rev. 1815, 1870–72 (1991). More significantly, where Easterbrook and Fischel generally conclude that shareholders would have bargained for a weak set of fiduciary duties, Professor Charny argues that courts should presume that the parties intended to accord considerable protection to minority shareholders' interests and imply a strong set of fiduciary duties. He points out that if that is not the parties' intent, the parties can simply opt out out of these implied obligations. Approaching the issue in this fashion, Charny adds, will allow courts to more efficiently resolve intra-corporate disputes. Id. at 1872.

Jason Johnston comes at the issue from a slightly different angle. He contends that Easterbrook and Fischel's contractual arguments disregard the power disparity between minority and majority shareholders. He claims that their error is to assume that the weaker party, the minority shareholder, typically would prefer to rely on market forces, such as a majority shareholder's interest in preserving her reputation, for protection from opportunistic behavior. In contrast, Professor Johnston suggests that most minority shareholders would prefer to rely on an imperfect legal system, even if it tends to interpret fiduciary duties too broadly. Jason Scott Johnston, Opting In and Opting Out: Bargaining for Fiduciary Duties in Cooperative Ventures, 70 Wash. U. L. Q. 291, 297 (1992). Johnston also questions claims that imposing broad fiduciary duties would be economically inefficient. Id. at 295–98. He argues that if courts can enhance efficiency by implying expansive fiduciary duties as part of the corporate "contract," in many circumstances, minority shareholders will be prepared to make larger firm-specific investments. Id. at 333–337.

John Hetherington, who also favors a contract-oriented approach, advances still another argument:

> Bargaining is costly, and the parties may be expected to engage in it only when the prospective benefits exceed the costs. In resolving disputes ex post, the efficiency and productivity of exchange transactions would be enhanced if the courts sought the allocation which the parties would have made ex ante had they then considered that the gains of bargaining exceeded the costs.

John A.C. Hetherington, Defining the Scope of Controlling Shareholders' Fiduciary Responsibilities, 22 Wake Forest L.Rev. 9, 20 (1987). Commenting that the traditional law and economics analysis seems compulsively "committed to preserving the prerogatives of majorities and the vulnerability of at-will employees and close corporation minorities as essential to the maintenance and enhancement of the productivity of business enterprises," Professor Hetherington also notes:

> One is struck in this area by what seems to be the obsessive concern of policymakers, commentators, and, on occasion, judges over the perceived risk that persons in relatively disadvantaged positions—employees at will and small minorities in close corporations—will behave strategically when dealing with those who occupy dominant and controlling positions. Preserving the vulnerability of the disadvantaged in these business relationships becomes a policy goal. The point here is not, of course, that there is no risk of such behavior: it is the implicit normative judgment that the allocation of rights (and wealth) produced by past business arrangements is "right" and that any movement toward reallocation is presumptively undesirable.

John A. C. Hetherington, Bargaining For Fiduciary Duties: Preserving the Vulnerability of the Disadvantaged?, 70 Wash. U. L. Q. 341, 351 (1992).

Note: Tort Approach to Oppression

Courts have recently developed the tort of freeze-out which requires a pattern of oppressive conduct. Specifically, majority shareholders utilize various means to deprive the minority shareholders of financial benefits from the corporation. Sugarman v. Sugarman, 797 F.2d 3 (1st Cir.1986), involved a family corporation controlled by Leonard Sugarman, the son of one of the founders and the holder of a majority of the corporation's stock. The plaintiffs, grandchildren of another founder, owned the remainder of the firm's shares. The plaintiffs pleaded "the theory of 'freeze-out' of minority shareholders." 797 F.2d at 6. They alleged that Leonard had deprived them of desired corporate employment, paid himself "excessive" compensation thereby draining off the firm's earnings, and refused to pay dividends. The court held that neither the payment of excessive salaries nor an offer to repurchase shares at an inadequate price constituted *per se* oppressive conduct. Rather, the court emphasized that such activities must be tied to a course of conduct that freezes-out a minority interest from all financial benefits provided by the corporation. The court concluded that Leonard's conduct involved all the necessary ingredients. Pointing out how the *Sugarman* court's approach differs from that in *Wilkes*, one commentator notes, "The activity is tortious, the tort must be intentional, and the deprivation must be purposeful. This, of course, is quite different from the traditional twin duties of a fiduciary to act in the beneficiary's best interests and to avoid self-dealing." Lawrence E. Mitchell, The Death of Fiduciary Duty in Close Corporations, 138 U. Pa. L. Rev. 1675, 1720 (1990).

Note: Corporate Repurchase of Minority Shareholder's Stock

One context in which the question of "freeze-out" often occurs is when the corporation refuses to repurchase the complaining minority shareholder's stock after having made such a repurchase from one or more other stockholders—the situation that gave rise to liability in *Donahue*. Notwithstanding the decision in *Donahue,* courts are reluctant to adopt a *per se* requirement that the minority shareholder be bought out upon demand if the corporation has made a previous repurchase from another shareholder.

In Goode v. Ryan, 397 Mass. 85, 489 N.E.2d 1001 (1986), the executor of a deceased stockholder sought to have the corporation repurchase the estate's stock shortly after the stockholder's death but declined the corporation's offer. Thereafter, the corporation liquidated and the estate received its proportionate share of the liquidating distributions. The executor sued to recover the value of the stock at the time of the original offer. The court noted that there had been no other evidence of oppressive conduct toward the deceased shareholder who had never been an officer or director and had not received any salary. The court also found no evidence that the majority had enriched itself at the expense of the minority shareholder. In holding that the corporation had been under no obligation to purchase the shares after death, the court stated,

> * * * In the absence of any agreement among shareholders or between the corporation and the shareholder, or a provision in the corporation's articles of organization or by-laws, neither the corporation nor a majority of shareholders is under any obligation to purchase the shares of minority shareholders when minority shareholders wish to dispose of their interest in the corporation. * * *

> "While the plaintiff's predicament * * * is unfortunate, the situation was not caused by the defendants but is merely one of the risks of ownership of stock in a close corporation. * * * It is not the proper function of this court to reallocate the risks inherent in

the ownership of corporate stock in the absence of corporate or majority shareholder misconduct." (489 N.E.2d at 1004–5.)

Toner v. Baltimore Envelope Co., 304 Md. 256, 498 A.2d 642 (1985), reached the same result. In that case, the company's stock was divided among two voting groups which were deadlocked as to whether to sell the company to a third party. To break the deadlock, one group purchased all the voting and non-voting stock of one stockholder and caused the corporation to repurchase the non-voting stock from other holders. The plaintiff, a holder of non-voting stock whose shares had not been purchased, sued to compel the corporation to repurchase her shares on the ground that she had been denied an equal opportunity to participate in the repurchase. The court held that absent a showing that the discriminatory repurchase was itself a breach of duty, as had been true in *Donahue,* the stockholder had no right to have her shares repurchased.

Other jurisdictions have been more sympathetic to the minority shareholder in such cases, although the facts of those cases indicate an independent breach of duty arising from the refusal to repurchase. See Estate of Schroer v. Stamco Supply, Inc., 19 Ohio App.3d 34, 482 N.E.2d 975 (1984); Comolli v. Comolli, 241 Ga. 471, 246 S.E.2d 278 (1978); Tillis v. United Parts, Inc., 395 So.2d 618 (Fla.App.1981).

Some commentators have expressed concern that a *per se* equal opportunity rule will hinder the ability of a close corporation to function effectively. Easterbrook and Fischel argue that the *Donahue* court, in fashioning the equal opportunity rule, "missed the boat." They express the fear that "[M]ost firms could not survive if the purchase of the interest of a retiring member required that everyone else be given the opportunity to sell out at the same price." Frank H. Easterbrook and Daniel R. Fischel, The Economic Structure of Corporate Law 250–251 (1991). They also note, "It is hard to imagine, for example, how closely held corporations could function under a requirement that all shareholders have an 'equal opportunity' to receive salary increases and continue in office regardless of their conduct. Yet this is the logical implication of *Donahue,* which holds that the business justifications for unequal treatment are irrelevant." Id. at 247.

3. DEADLOCK, ARBITRATION AND OTHER ALTERNATIVE DISPUTE RESOLUTION TECHNIQUES

Minority shareholders frequently attempt to protect their interests by conditioning their investments in close corporations on adoption of a governance structure that will allow one or more minority shareholders to veto some or all decisions of the majority. As we have seen, various combinations of governance devices can readily be used to create such a structure. For example, cumulative voting or a shareholder voting agreement can be used to assure minority representation on the board of directors, and when combined with a supermajority voting or quorum requirement will allow the minority to block board actions to which it objects.

Minority shareholders can use veto powers selectively, or can elect to create a deadlock. It is not difficult to misunderstand the meaning of the term "deadlock." It does not signify simply that a sufficient number of directors or shareholders are not prepared to support a particular decision. For example, if the directors are evenly split on an issue, or if they are divided 3–1 when an 80% vote is required, there is no deadlock; the motion simply fails for want of the needed vote. If such occurrences happen only occasionally, the corporation can continue to function normally. A true deadlock exists when relations among the shareholders or directors have deteriorated to the point that whenever one faction says something is red, the other says it is green, with the result that virtually no resolution can be approved. At the point of real deadlock, the corporation may become nearly paralyzed. It might continue to operate after a fashion, but trying to do business in such circumstances usually is neither comfortable nor convenient.

Adopting a governance structure that gives each significant shareholder veto rights may appear an attractive alternative to more elaborate pre-incorporation planning. Even if the parties subsequently disagree about particular decisions, their shared interest in enhancing the profitability of the corporation provides a substantial incentive for them to accommodate their differences. As Hirschman might put it, the unavailability of exit, and a shared sense of loyalty, will lead them to lower their voices.

Nonetheless, deadlock remains a possibility. Consequently, before deciding to rely primarily on veto rights to protect their interests, prospective investors in a close corporation should consider what limits exist on shareholders' exercise of veto rights, whether they would be better off relying on some alternative dispute resolution mechanism, and what remedies are available if a deadlock is created.

a. Limitations on the Exercise of Veto Rights

SMITH v. ATLANTIC PROPERTIES, INC.

12 Mass.App.Ct. 201, 422 N.E.2d 798 (1981).

CUTTER, JUSTICE.

In December, 1951, Dr. Louis E. Wolfson agreed to purchase land in Norwood for $350,000, with an initial cash payment of $50,000 and a mortgage note of $300,000 payable in thirty-three months. Dr. Wolfson offered a quarter interest each in the land to Mr. Paul T. Smith, Mr. Abraham Zimble, and William H. Burke. Each paid to Dr. Wolfson $12,500, one quarter of the initial payment. Mr. Smith, an attorney, organized the defendant corporation (Atlantic) in 1951 to operate the real estate. Each of the four subscribers received twenty-five shares of stock. Mr. Smith included, both in the corporation's articles of organization and in its by-laws, a provision reading, "No election, appointment or resolution by the Stockholders and no election, appointment, resolution, purchase, sale, lease, contract, contribution, compensation, proceeding or act by the Board of Directors or by any officer or officers shall be valid or binding upon the corporation until effected, passed, approved or ratified by an affirmative vote of eighty (80%) per cent of the capital stock issued outstanding and entitled to vote." This provision (hereafter referred to as the 80% provision) was included at Dr. Wolfson's request and had the effect of giving to any one of the four original shareholders a veto in corporate decisions.

Atlantic purchased the Norwood land. Some of the land and other assets were sold for about $220,000. Atlantic retained twenty-eight acres on which stood about twenty old brick or wood mill-type structures, which required expensive and constant repairs. After the first year, Atlantic became profitable and showed a profit every year prior to 1969, ranging from a low of $7,683 in 1953 to a high of $44,358 in 1954. The mortgage was paid by 1958 and Atlantic has incurred no long-term debt thereafter. Salaries of about $25,000 were paid only in 1959 and 1960. Dividends in the total amount of $10,000 each were paid in 1964 and 1970. By 1961, Atlantic had about $172,000 in retained earnings, more than half in cash.

For various reasons, which need not be stated in detail, disagreements and ill will soon arose between Dr. Wolfson, on the one hand, and the other stockholders as a group.[3] Dr. Wolfson wished to see Atlantic's earnings devoted to repairs and possibly some improvements in its existing buildings and adjacent facilities. The other stockholders desired the declaration of dividends. Dr. Wolfson fairly steadily refused to vote for any dividends. Although it was pointed out to him that failure to declare dividends might result in the imposition by the Internal Revenue Service of a penalty under the Internal Revenue Code, I.R.C. § 531 et seq. (relating to unreasonable accumulation of corporate earnings and profits), Dr. Wolfson persisted in his refusal to declare dividends. The other shareholders did agree over the years to making at least the most urgent repairs to Atlantic's buildings, but did not agree to make all repairs and improvements which were recommended in a 1962 report by an engineering firm retained by Atlantic to make a complete estimate of all repairs and improvements which might be beneficial.

The fears of an Internal Revenue Service assessment of a penalty tax were soon realized. Penalty assessments were made in 1962, 1963, and 1964. These were settled by Dr. Wolfson for $11,767.71 in taxes and interest. Despite this settlement, Dr. Wolfson continued his opposition to declaring dividends. The record does not indicate that he developed any specific and definitive schedule or plan for a series of necessary or desirable repairs and improvements to Atlantic's properties. At least none was proposed which would have had a reasonable chance of

---

3. At least one cause of ill will on Dr. Wolfson's part may have been the refusal of the other shareholders to consent to his transferring his shares in Atlantic to the Louis E. Wolfson Foundation, a charitable foundation created by Dr. Wolfson.

satisfying the Internal Revenue Service that expenditures for such repairs and improvements constituted "reasonable needs of the business," I.R.C. § 534(c), a term which includes (see I.R.C. § 537) "the reasonably anticipated needs of the business." Predictably, despite further warnings by Dr. Wolfson's shareholder colleagues, the Internal Revenue Service assessed further penalty taxes for the years 1965, 1966, 1967, and 1968. These taxes were upheld by the United States Tax Court in Atlantic Properties, Inc. v. Commissioner of Int. Rev., 62 T.C. 644 (1974), and on appeal in 519 F.2d 1233 (1st Cir.1975). See the discussion of these opinions in Cathcart, Accumulated Earnings Tax: A Trap for the Wary, 62 A.B.A.J. 1197–1199 (1976). An examination of these decisions makes it apparent that Atlantic has incurred substantial penalty taxes and legal expense largely because of Dr. Wolfson's refusal to vote for the declaration of sufficient dividends to avoid the penalty, a refusal which was (in the Tax Court and upon appeal) attributed in some measure to a tax avoidance purpose on Dr. Wolfson's part.

On January 30, 1967, the shareholders, other than Dr. Wolfson, initiated this proceeding in the Superior Court, later supplemented to reflect developments after the original complaint. The plaintiffs sought a court determination of the dividends to be paid by Atlantic, the removal of Dr. Wolfson as a director, and an order that Atlantic be reimbursed by him for the penalty taxes assessed against it and related expenses. The case was tried before a justice of the Superior Court (jury waived) in September and October, 1979.

The trial judge made findings (but in more detail) of essentially the facts outlined above and concluded that Dr. "Wolfson's obstinate refusal to vote in favor of * * * dividends was * * * caused more by his dislike for other stockholders and his desire to avoid additional tax payments than * * * by any genuine desire to undertake a program for improving * * * [Atlantic] property." She also determined that Dr. Wolfson was liable to Atlantic for taxes and interest amounting to "$11,767.11 plus interest from the commencement of this action, plus $35,646.14 plus interest from August 11, 1975," the date of the First Circuit decision affirming the second penalty tax assessment. The latter amount includes an attorney's fee of $7,500 in the Federal tax cases. She also ordered the directors of Atlantic to declare "a reasonable dividend at the earliest practical date and reasonable dividends annually thereafter consistent with good business practice." In addition, the trial judge directed that jurisdiction of the case be retained in the Superior Court "for a period of five years to [e]nsure compliance." Judgment was entered pursuant to the trial judge's order. After the entry of judgment, Dr. Wolfson and Atlantic filed a motion for a new trial and to amend the judge's findings. This motion, after hearing, was denied, and Dr. Wolfson and Atlantic claimed an appeal from the judgment and the former from the denial of the motion. The plaintiffs * * * requested payment of their attorneys' fees in this proceeding and filed supporting affidavits. The motion was denied, and the plaintiffs appealed.

1. The trial judge, in deciding that Dr. Wolfson had committed a breach of his fiduciary duty to other stockholders, relied greatly on broad language in Donahue v. Rodd Electrotype Co., 367 Mass. 578, 586–597, 328 N.E.2d 505 (1975), in which the Supreme Judicial Court afforded to a minority stockholder in a close corporation equality of treatment (with members of a controlling group of shareholders) in the matter of the redemption of shares. The court (at 592–593, 328 N.E.2d 505) relied on the resemblance of a close corporation to a partnership and held that "stockholders in the close corporation owe one another substantially the same fiduciary duty in the operation of the enterprise that partners owe to one another" (footnotes omitted). That standard of duty, the court said, was the "utmost good faith and loyalty." The court went on to say that such stockholders "may not act out of avarice, expediency or self-interest in derogation of their duty of loyalty to the other stockholders and to the corporation." Similar principles were stated in Wilkes v. Springside Nursing Home, Inc., 370 Mass. 842, 848–852, 353 N.E.2d 657 (1976), but with some modifications, mentioned in the margin, of the sweeping language of the *Donahue* case. * * *

In the *Donahue* case, 367 Mass. at 593 n. 17, 328 N.E.2d 505, the court recognized that cases may arise in which, in a close corporation, majority stockholders may ask protection from a minority stockholder. Such an instance arises in the present case because Dr. Wolfson has been able to exercise a veto concerning corporate action on dividends by the 80% provision (in Atlantic's articles [of] organization and by-laws) already quoted. The 80% provision may have substantially the effect of reversing the usual roles of the majority and the minority shareholder. The minority, under that provision, becomes an ad hoc controlling interest.

* * *

Dr. Wolfson testified that he requested the inclusion of the 80% provision "in case the people [the other shareholders] whom I knew, but not very well, ganged up on me." The possibilities of shareholder disagreement on policy made the provision seem a sensible precaution. A question is presented, however, concerning the extent to which such a veto power possessed by a minority stockholder may be exercised as its holder may wish, without a violation of the "fiduciary duty" referred to in the *Donahue* case, 367 Mass. at 593, 328 N.E.2d 505, as modified in the *Wilkes* case. * * *

The decided cases in Massachusetts do little to answer this question. The most pertinent guidance is probably found in the *Wilkes* case, 370 Mass. at 849–852, 353 N.E.2d 657, * * * essentially to the effect that in any judicial intervention in such a situation there must be a weighing of the business interests advanced as reasons for their action (a) by the majority or controlling group and (b) by the rival persons or group. It would obviously be appropriate, before a court-ordered solution is sought or imposed, for both sides to attempt to reach a sensible solution of any incipient impasse in the interest of all concerned after consideration of all relevant circumstances. See Helms v. Duckworth, 249 F.2d 482, 485–488 (D.C.Cir.1957).

2. With respect to the past damage to Atlantic caused by Dr. Wolfson's refusal to vote in favor of any dividends, the trial judge was justified in finding that his conduct went beyond what was reasonable. The other stockholders shared to some extent responsibility for what occurred by failing to accept Dr. Wolfson's proposals with much sympathy, but the inaction on dividends seems the principal cause of the tax penalties. Dr. Wolfson had been warned of the dangers of an assessment under the Internal Revenue Code, I.R.C. § 531 et seq. He had refused to vote dividends in any amount adequate to minimize that danger and had failed to bring forward, within the relevant taxable years, a convincing, definitive program of appropriate improvements which could withstand scrutiny by the Internal Revenue Service. Whatever may have been the reason for Dr. Wolfson's refusal to declare dividends (and even if in any particular year he may have gained slight, if any, tax advantage from withholding dividends) we think that he recklessly ran serious and unjustified risks of precisely the penalty taxes eventually assessed, risks which were inconsistent with any reasonable interpretation of a duty of "utmost good faith and loyalty." The trial judge (despite the fact that the other shareholders helped to create the voting deadlock and despite the novelty of the situation) was justified in charging Dr. Wolfson with the out-of-pocket expenditure incurred by Atlantic for the penalty taxes and related counsel fees of the tax cases.[10]

3. The trial judge's order to the directors of Atlantic, "to declare a reasonable dividend at the earliest practical date and reasonable dividends annually thereafter," presents difficulties. It may well not be a precise, clear, and unequivocal command which (without further explanation) would justify enforcement by civil contempt proceedings * * *. It also fails to order the directors to exercise similar business judgment with respect to Dr. Wolfson's desire to make all appropriate repairs and improvements to Atlantic's factory properties. See the language of the Supreme Judicial Court in the *Wilkes* case, 370 Mass. at 850–852, 353 N.E.2d 657, see note 5, *supra.*

The somewhat ambiguous injunctive relief is made less significant by the trial judge's reservation of jurisdiction in the Superior Court, a provision which contemplates later judicial supervision. We think that such supervision should be provided now upon an expanded record. The present record does not disclose Atlantic's present financial condition or what, if anything, it has done (since the judgment under review) by way of expenditures for repairs and improvements of its properties and in respect of dividends and salaries. The judgment, of course, necessarily

---

10. We do not now suggest that the standard of "utmost good faith and loyalty" may require some relaxation when applied to a minority ad hoc controlling interest, created by some device, similar to the 80% provision, designed in part to protect the selfish interests of a minority shareholder. This seems to us a difficult area of the law best developed on a case by case basis.

disregards the general judicial reluctance to interfere with a corporation's dividend policy ordinarily based upon the business judgment of its directors. See Crocker v. Waltham Watch Co., 315 Mass. 397, 402, 53 N.E.2d 230 (1944); Donahue v. Rodd Electrotype Co., 367 Mass. at 590, 328 N.E.2d 505, and authorities cited; 1 O'Neal, Close Corporations § 3.63a and 2 O'Neal § 8.08; Forced Dividends, 1 J.Corp.L. 420 (1976).

Although the reservation of jurisdiction is appropriate in this case (see Nassif v. Boston & Maine R.R., 340 Mass. 557, 566–567, 165 N.E.2d 397 [1960]; Department of Pub. Health v. Cumberland Cattle Co., 361 Mass. 817, 834, 282 N.E.2d 895 [1972]), its purpose should be stated more affirmatively. Paragraph 2 of the judgment should be revised to provide: (a) a direction that Atlantic's directors prepare promptly financial statements and copies of State and Federal income and excise tax returns for the five most recent calendar or fiscal years, and a balance sheet as of as current a date as is possible; (b) an instruction that they confer with one another with a view to stipulating a general dividend and capital improvements policy for the next ensuing three fiscal years; (c) an order that, if such a stipulation is not filed with the clerk of the Superior Court within sixty days after the receipt of the rescript in the Superior Court, a further hearing shall be held promptly (either before the court or before a special master with substantial experience in business affairs), at which there shall be received in evidence at least the financial statements and tax returns above mentioned, as well as other relevant evidence. Thereafter, the court, after due consideration of the circumstances then existing, may direct the adoption (and carrying out), if it be then deemed appropriate, of a specific dividend and capital improvements policy adequate to minimize the risk of further penalty tax assessments for the then current fiscal year of Atlantic. The court also may reserve jurisdiction to take essentially the same action for each subsequent fiscal year until the parties are able to reach for themselves an agreed program.

* * *

b. Alternative Dispute Resolution Techniques

Rather than run the risk that a deadlock will develop, the parties may wish to make provision for resolving any differences that might arise. If minority interests are protected by equal representation on the board of directors, the solution may be as simple as providing for an uneven number of directors. However, the selection of the "neutral" director itself may pose a problem and shareholders also may wish to consider how they will fill a vacancy if the "neutral" director dies or resigns (perhaps in disgust). In evaluating these possibilities, recall the deadlock-breaking mechanisms employed in *Ringling* and in *Lehrman v. Cohen*.

The arrangements in both *Lehrman* and *Ringling* partook of many of the characteristics of a simple arbitration agreement. But it is significant that in neither case did the parties characterize the arrangement as a conventional arbitration scheme (although Loos was designated as "arbitrator" in *Ringling*). It is apparent from the opinions, moreover, that the Delaware courts were reluctant to say straightforwardly that they were enforcing an arbitration agreement. Underlying this apparent aversion to applying the law of arbitration to the sort of dispute that often arises in close corporations may be a judicial reservation about the practical limitations of the use of arbitration to resolve disputes over the management of corporations.

To begin with, it is obvious, that the directors or shareholders cannot run to an arbitrator every time they disagree over some business decision. Moreover, following a pattern consecrated by long historical precedent, the courts have tended to be jealous of incursions by arbitration into their jurisdiction, and have managed to establish a variety of obstacles to the enforcement of arbitration agreements. While in most jurisdictions nearly all of those obstacles have been removed by legislation providing that agreements to arbitrate future disputes are to be given specific performance, the use of arbitration in the corporate context continues to raise special problems related to some of the same doctrines you have come across in the previous material on the validity of other control arrangements.

Although modern courts willingly accept arbitration as an effective means of resolving disputes among shareholders, many advantages exist in having a shareholders' agreement provide for arbitration when the shareholders or directors are deadlocked on a particular action. First, arbitration is generally cheaper and quicker than court proceedings. A speedy resolution of a problem is especially important in the context of a close corporation. Often a prompt decision may be able to quell a specific dispute before it grows into a larger, more personal problem. Second, arbitration is less formal and less intimidating then litigation. Rather than having to wait for a court date, arbitration can be begun when both sides are prepared. Furthermore, with relaxed rules of evidence and procedure, the parties can work towards a resolution that is more tailored to their situation than litigation might produce. One specific advantage in this regard is the ability of the parties to choose the arbitrator, particularly someone who is an expert in the area of the dispute or deadlock. As a result of this procedural flexibility, the decision can be rendered with an eye towards resolving potential disputes or deadlocks. Finally, today arbitration is easily enforceable.

As arbitration has become more popular, and has become a more formal tool for dispute resolution, some of its purported advantages are less significant. While arbitration is for the most part still less costly than litigation, the potential savings resulting from the use of arbitration tend to disappear as the formality of the process increases. Furthermore, delays are not foreign to arbitration, and can occur when parties cannot agree on an arbitrator or a hearing date. Finally, like adjudication, arbitration is ultimately an adversarial process, which may solve a particular dispute or deadlock, but may not reach the root of a problem.

Unlike arbitration and adjudication, another alternative dispute resolution mechanism, mediation, does not function on the premise that the problem will be solved by the binding decision of some third party after an adversarial proceeding. Rather, mediation envisions the parties working together, with the help of a neutral mediator, to craft a mutually satisfying solution by which each party will agree to abide.

The role of the mediator is very important if the parties are going to resolve a dispute. A good mediator should remain impartial and be skilled in facilitating communication between the parties. It is important for the mediator to be able to get the parties to see the underlying causes for the dispute or deadlock, and for each to understand the basis for the other's position. No rules exist as to who may serve as mediator. Therefore, the parties can choose any respected neutral third party, even the corporation's attorney where appropriate.

Distinct advantages exist in choosing mediation as a method of dispute resolution. First, in using mediation, the parties retain the greatest amount of control over the procedural format for resolving the dispute or deadlock. The sessions occur outside hearing of other parties which encourages parties to open up regarding their underlying concerns. In addition, the flexibility of the process allows for the parties to work towards an agreement that satisfies both, rather than the more traditional "win-lose" situation fostered by litigation or arbitration. Second, the process will hopefully leave each party with a genuine understanding of the other's position. This may pave the way to rebuilding a working relationship, so the parties may avoid the need for such assistance in the future when problems inevitably arise. Finally, the informality of the process allows for even more savings than arbitration does, because attorneys are not required.

Mediation, however, also has its disadvantages. As a result of the non-binding nature of the process, the mediator cannot compel the resolution of a dispute or deadlock. If the mediator cannot induce a settlement between the parties, the process may ultimately resolve nothing. When the parties cannot agree, legal proceedings will likely result, and the entire mediation process ironically will be an extra cost, rather than leading to a cost savings. However, on an ex ante basis, the overall benefits outweigh the overall costs.

In order to protect against the breakdown of the mediation process and resolution of a dispute or deadlock by litigation, the shareholders and their attorney may implement a procedure made up of mediation and arbitration. Such a procedure calls first for the use of mediation to resolve the dispute. The parties hopefully will realize that mediation constitutes their last opportunity to have considerable control over the resolution of their problems. By providing for arbitration in the event of a failed mediation, the parties may be able to avoid litigation, which was their goal as evidenced by using alternative dispute resolution mechanisms. Thus, a combination of mediation and arbitration may provide a method for attempting to resolve the parties' underlying grievances, rather than merely solving the current specific problem.

For an analysis of alternative dispute resolution techniques, see Lewis D. Solomon and Janet Stern Solomon, Using Alternative Dispute Resolution Techniques To Settle Disputes Among Shareholders of Closely Held Corporations, 22 Wake Forest L.R. 105 (1987).

4. DISSOLUTION

Corporate statutes require a corporation's board of directors and shareholders to vote to dissolve the corporation. See RMBCA §§ 14.02– 14.07. If that occurs, the corporation will terminate its existence in an orderly fashion; it will sell off its assets, pay off its creditors, and distribute whatever remains to its shareholders. Shareholders, too, can agree in advance that they will cause the corporation to be dissolved on the occurrence of certain events, such as the death of a shareholder, or at the request of some given portion of the shareholders.

Many statutes also allow a minority of a corporation's shareholders to petition a court to dissolve because directors or shareholders are deadlocked or because those in control of the corporation are abusing their power or otherwise oppressing minority shareholders. See RMBCA § 14.30(2). Granting this relief is within the court's discretion, and the Official Comment to RMBCA § 14.30 advises courts to be "cautious" when considering the abuse of power "so as to limit [such cases] to genuine abuse rather than instances of acceptable tactics in a power struggle for control of a corporation." Delaware, however, has no provision for involuntary dissolution in its general corporation law. DGCL § 355 does provides shareholder with the option of dissolving a corporation that has elected close corporation status, but, as previously noted, few corporations have elected such treatment.

Involuntary dissolution, or the threat thereof, usually enters the picture only when the participants in a close corporation have ceased to get along with one another. At that point, the absence of a ready market for stock can prove burdensome. If one of the shareholders wants to extricate herself by selling out, the only persons interested in purchasing her stock are likely to be the other shareholders. But, if they are in conflict with the would-be seller, seldom will they be in the mood to offer a generous price. More often, they will try to freeze out the dissident, who then is likely to seek dissolution so as to recover her investment. Frequently, the dissident shareholder will be less interested in terminating the corporation's legal existence than she will be in using the threat of liquidation as leverage to bargain for a better price for her stock. See generally, John A. C. Hetherington and Michael P. Dooley, Illiquidity and Exploitation: A Proposed Statutory Solution to the Remaining Close Corporation Problem, 63 Va.L.Rev. 1 (1977).

While at first glance dissolution may appear a sensible solution when a close corporation is paralyzed because of shareholder dissension or an attempt to freeze out one of the shareholders, on closer examination it becomes evident that the problem is more complex. First, there is the question of whether dissolution will be in the best interest of the community of interests known as "the corporation." Are the difficulties so severe that attempts at continued operation would lead only to deterioration of the business and a wasting of assets, or could the corporation continue to operate profitably? Second, there is the problem of finding an equitable resolution among the shareholders. If involuntary dissolution is sought, there must be at least one shareholder who finds that alternative worse for his interests than an attempt to continue the battle. In many instances, the result of dissolution would be that one shareholder or group of shareholders would be able to take over the business for themselves, perhaps at a price unfair to the others. While the facts of every case will differ, the court faced with a petition for dissolution almost inevitably will find itself trying to find the most equitable solution without much in the way of useful statutory guidance.

MATTER OF KEMP & BEATLEY, INC.
64 N.Y.2d 63, 484 N.Y.S.2d 799, 473 N.E.2d 1173 (1984).

COOKE, CHIEF JUDGE.

When the majority shareholders of a close corporation award *de facto* dividends to all shareholders except a class of minority shareholders, such a policy may constitute "oppressive actions" and serve as a basis for an order made pursuant to section 1104–a of the Business Corporation Law dissolving the corporation. In the instant matter, there is sufficient evidence to support the lower courts' conclusion that the majority shareholders had altered a long-standing policy to distribute corporate earnings on the basis of stock ownership, as against petitioners only. Moreover, the courts did not abuse their discretion by concluding that dissolution was the only means by which petitioners could gain a fair return on their investment.

I

The business concern of Kemp & Beatley, incorporated under the laws of New York, designs and manufactures table linens and sundry tabletop items. The company's stock consists of 1,500 outstanding shares held by eight shareholders. Petitioner Dissin had been employed by the company for 42 years when, in June 1979, he resigned. Prior to resignation, Dissin served as vice-president and a director of Kemp & Beatley. Over the course of his employment, Dissin had acquired stock in the company and currently owns 200 shares.

Petitioner Gardstein, like Dissin, had been a long-time employee of the company. Hired in 1944, Gardstein was for the next 35 years involved in various aspects of the business including material procurement, product design, and plant management. His employment was terminated by the company in December 1980. He currently owns 105 shares of Kemp & Beatley stock.

Apparent unhappiness surrounded petitioners' leaving the employ of the company. Of particular concern was that they no longer received any distribution of the company's earnings. Petitioners considered themselves to be "frozen out" of the company; whereas it had been their experience when with the company to receive a distribution of the company's earnings according to their stockholdings, in the form of either dividends or extra compensation, that distribution was no longer forthcoming.

Gardstein and Dissin, together holding 20.33% of the company's outstanding stock, commenced the instant proceeding in June 1981, seeking dissolution of Kemp & Beatley pursuant to section 1104–a of the Business Corporation Law. Their petition alleged "fraudulent and oppressive" conduct by the company's board of directors such as to render petitioners' stock "a virtually worthless asset." Supreme Court referred the matter for a hearing, which was held in March 1982.

Upon considering the testimony of petitioners and the principals of Kemp & Beatley, the referee concluded that "the corporate management has by its policies effectively rendered petitioners' shares worthless, and * * * the only way petitioners can expect any return is by dissolution". Petitioners were found to have invested capital in the company expecting, among other things, to receive dividends or "bonuses" based upon their stock holdings. Also found was the company's "established buyout policy" by which it would purchase the stock of employee shareholders upon their leaving its employ.

The involuntary-dissolution statute (Business Corporation Law, § 1104–a) permits dissolution when a corporation's controlling faction is found guilty of "oppressive action" toward the complaining shareholders. The referee considered oppression to arise when "those in control" of the corporation "have acted in such a manner as to defeat those expectations of the minority stockholders which formed the basis of [their] participation in the venture." The expectations of petitioners that they would not be arbitrarily excluded from gaining a return on their investment and that their stock would be purchased by the corporation upon termination of employment, were deemed defeated by prevailing corporate policies. Dissolution was recommended in the referee's report, subject to giving respondent corporation an opportunity to purchase petitioners' stock.

Supreme Court confirmed the referee's report. It, too, concluded that due to the corporation's new dividend policy petitioners had been prevented from receiving any return on their investments. Liquidation of the corporate assets was found the only means by which petitioners would receive a fair return. The court considered judicial dissolution of a corporation to be "a serious and severe remedy." Consequently, the order of dissolution was conditioned upon the corporation's being permitted to purchase petitioners' stock. The Appellate Division affirmed, without opinion. 99 A.D.2d 445, 471 N.Y.S.2d 245.

At issue in this appeal is the scope of section 1104–a of the Business Corporation Law. Specifically, this court must determine whether the provision for involuntary dissolution when the "directors or those in control of the corporation have been guilty of * * * oppressive actions toward the complaining shareholders" was properly applied in the circumstances of this case. We hold that it was, and therefore affirm.

II

Judicially ordered dissolution of a corporation at the behest of minority interests is a remedy of relatively recent vintage in New York. Historically, this State's courts were considered divested of equity jurisdiction to order dissolution, as statutory prescriptions were deemed exclusive. Statutes permitting judicial dissolution of corporations either limited the types of corporations under their purview or restricted the parties who could petition for dissolution to the Attorney–General, or the directors, trustees, or majority shareholders of the corporation (*see, generally,* Business Corporation Law, §§ 1101–1104).

Minority shareholders were granted standing in the absence of statutory authority to seek dissolution of corporations when controlling shareholders engaged in certain egregious conduct. Predicated on the majority shareholders' fiduciary obligation to treat all shareholders fairly and equally, to preserve corporate assets, and to fulfill their responsibilities of corporate management with "scrupulous good faith," the courts' equitable power can be invoked when "it appears that the directors and majority shareholders 'have so palpably breached the fiduciary duty they owe to the minority shareholders that they are disqualified from exercising the exclusive discretion and the dissolution power given to them by statute.' " (Leibert v. Clapp, 13 N.Y.2d, at p. 317, 247 N.Y.S.2d 102, 196 N.E.2d 540, *supra,* quoting Hoffman, New Horizons for the Close Corporation, 28 Brooklyn L.Rev. 1, 14.) True to the ancient principle that equity jurisdiction will not lie when there exists a remedy at law the courts have not entertained a minority's petition in equity when their rights and interests could be adequately protected in a legal action, such as by a shareholder's derivative suit.

Supplementing this principle of judicially ordered equitable dissolution of a corporation, the Legislature has shown a special solicitude toward the rights of minority shareholders of closely held corporations by enacting section 1104–a of the Business Corporation Law. That statute provides a mechanism for the holders of at least 20% of the outstanding shares of a corporation whose stock is not traded on a securities market to petition for its dissolution "under special circumstances" (*see* Business Corporation Law, § 1104–a, subd. [a]). The circumstances that give rise to dissolution fall into two general classifications: mistreatment of complaining shareholders (subd. [a], par. [1]), or misappropriation of corporate assets (subd. [a], par. [2]) by controlling shareholders, directors or officers.

Section 1104–a (subd. [a], par. [1]) describes three types of proscribed activity: "illegal", "fraudulent", and "oppressive" conduct. The first two terms are familiar words that are commonly understood at law. The last, however, does not enjoy the same certainty gained through long usage. As no definition is provided by the statute, it falls upon the courts to provide guidance.

The statutory concept of "oppressive actions" can, perhaps, best be understood by examining the characteristics of close corporations and the Legislature's general purpose in creating this involuntary-dissolution statute. It is widely understood that, in addition to supplying capital to a contemplated or ongoing enterprise and expecting a fair and equal return, parties comprising the ownership of a close corporation may expect to be actively involved in its management and operation. The small ownership cluster seeks to "contribute their capital, skills, experience and labor" toward the corporate enterprise (Kruger v. Gerth, 16 N.Y.2d 802, 805, 263 N.Y.S.2d 1, 210 N.E.2d 355 [Desmond, Ch. J., dissenting].

As a leading commentator in the field has observed: "Unlike the typical shareholder in the publicly held corporation, who may be simply an investor or a speculator and cares nothing for the responsibilities of management, the shareholder in a close corporation is a co-owner of the business and wants the privileges and powers that go with ownership. His participation in that particular corporation is often his principal or sole source of income. As a matter of fact, providing employment for himself may have been the principal reason why he participated in organizing the corporation. He may or may not anticipate an ultimate profit from the sale of his interest, but he normally draws very little from the corporation as dividends. In his capacity as an officer or employee of the corporation, he looks to his salary for the principal return on his capital investment, because earnings of a close corporation, as is well known, are distributed in major part in salaries, bonuses and retirement benefits." (O'Neal, Close Corporations [2d ed.], § 1.07, at pp. 21–22 [n. omitted].)

Shareholders enjoy flexibility in memorializing these expectations through agreements setting forth each party's rights and obligations in corporate governance. In the absence of such an agreement, however, ultimate decision-making power respecting corporate policy will be reposed in the holders of a majority interest in the corporation (*see, e.g.,* Business Corporation Law, §§ 614, 708). A wielding of this power by any group controlling a corporation may serve to destroy a stockholder's vital interests and expectations.

As the stock of closely held corporations generally is not readily salable, a minority shareholder at odds with management policies may be without either a voice in protecting his or her interests or any reasonable means of withdrawing his or her investment. This predicament may fairly be considered the legislative concern underlying the provision at issue in this case; inclusion of the criteria that the corporation's stock not be traded on securities markets and that the complaining shareholder be subject to oppressive actions supports this conclusion.

Defining oppressive conduct as distinct from illegality in the present context has been considered in other forums. The question has been resolved by considering oppressive actions to refer to conduct that substantially defeats the "reasonable expectations" held by minority shareholders in committing their capital to the particular enterprise (*see, e.g.,* Exadaktilos v. Cinnaminson Realty Co., 167 N.J.Super. 141, 153–156, 400 A.2d 554, affd. 173 N.J.Super. 559, 414 A.2d 994; Masinter v. Webco Co., 262 S.E.2d 433 [West Va.]; but *cf.* Polikoff v. Dole & Clark Bldg. Corp., 37 Ill.App.2d 29, 36, 184 N.E.2d 792; Baker v. Commercial Body Bldrs., 264 Or. 614, 630, 507 P.2d 387).* This concept is consistent with the apparent purpose underlying the provision under review. A shareholder who reasonably expected that ownership in the corporation would entitle him or her to a job, a share of corporate earnings, a place in corporate management, or some other form of security, would be oppressed in a very real sense when others in the corporation seek to defeat those expectations and there exists no effective means of salvaging the investment.

Given the nature of close corporations and the remedial purpose of the statute, this court holds that utilizing a complaining shareholder's "reasonable expectations" as a means of identifying and measuring conduct alleged to be oppressive is appropriate. A court considering a petition alleging oppressive conduct must investigate what the majority shareholders knew, or should have known, to be the petitioner's expectations in entering the particular enterprise. Majority conduct should not be deemed oppressive simply because the petitioner's subjective hopes and desires in joining the venture are not fulfilled. Disappointment alone should not necessarily be equated with oppression.

Rather, oppression should be deemed to arise only when the majority conduct substantially defeats expectations that, objectively viewed, were both reasonable under the circumstances and were central to the petitioner's decision to join the venture. It would be inappropriate, however, for us in this case to delineate the contours of the courts' consideration in determining whether directors have been guilty of oppressive conduct. As in other areas of the law, much will depend on the circumstances in the individual case.

The appropriateness of an order of dissolution is in every case vested in the sound discretion of the court considering the application (*see* Business Corporation Law, § 1111, subd. [a]). Under the terms of this statute, courts are instructed to consider both whether "liquidation of the corporation is the only feasible means" to protect the complaining shareholder's expectation of a fair return on his or her investment and whether dissolution "is reasonably necessary" to protect "the rights or

---

* In Baker v. Commercial Body Builders, Inc., 264 Or. 614, 507 P.2d 387, 393 ((1973), the court described "oppressive conduct" as follows:

"burdensome, harsh and wrongful conduct; a lack of probity and fair dealing in the affairs of a company to the prejudice of some of its members, or a visible departure from the standards of fair play on which every shareholder who entrusts his money to a company is entitled to rely."

interests of any substantial number of shareholders" not limited to those complaining (Business Corporation Law, § 1104–a, subd. [b], pars. [1], [2]). Implicit in this direction is that once oppressive conduct is found, consideration must be given to the totality of circumstances surrounding the current state of corporate affairs and relations to determine whether some remedy short of or other than dissolution constitutes a feasible means of satisfying both the petitioner's expectations and the rights and interests of any other substantial group of shareholders (*see, also,* Business Corporation Law, § 1111, subd. [b], par. [1]).

By invoking the statute, a petitioner has manifested his or her belief that dissolution may be the only appropriate remedy. Assuming the petitioner has set forth a prima facie case of oppressive conduct, it should be incumbent upon the parties seeking to forestall dissolution to demonstrate to the court the existence of an adequate, alternative remedy (*cf.* Baker v. Commercial Body Bldrs., 264 Or. 614, 507 P.2d 387, *supra;* White v. Perkins, 213 Va. 129, 189 S.E.2d 315). A court has broad latitude in fashioning alternative relief, but when fulfillment of the oppressed petitioner's expectations by these means is doubtful, such as when there has been a complete deterioration of relations between the parties, a court should not hesitate to order dissolution. Every order of dissolution, however, must be conditioned upon permitting any shareholder of the corporation to elect to purchase the complaining shareholder's stock at fair value (*see* Business Corporation Law, § 1118).

One further observation is in order. The purpose of this involuntary dissolution statute is to provide protection to the minority shareholder whose reasonable expectations in undertaking the venture have been frustrated and who has no adequate means of recovering his or her investment. It would be contrary to this remedial purpose to permit its use by minority shareholders as merely a coercive tool * * *. Therefore, the minority shareholder whose own acts, made in bad faith and undertaken with a view toward forcing an involuntary dissolution, give rise to the complained-of oppression should be given no quarter in the statutory protection.

III

There was sufficient evidence presented at the hearing to support the conclusion that Kemp & Beatley had a long-standing policy of awarding *de facto* dividends based on stock ownership in the form of "extra compensation bonuses." Petitioners, both of whom had extensive experience in the management of the company, testified to this effect. Moreover, both related that receipt of this compensation, whether as true dividends or disguised as "extra compensation", was a known incident to ownership of the company's stock understood by all of the company's principals. Finally, there was uncontroverted proof that this policy was changed either shortly before or shortly after petitioners' employment ended. Extra compensation was still awarded by the company. The only difference was that stock ownership was no longer a basis for the payments; it was asserted that the basis became services rendered to the corporation. It was not unreasonable for the fact finder to have determined that this change in policy amounted to nothing less than an attempt to exclude petitioners from gaining any return on their investment through the mere recharacterization of distributions of corporate income. Under the circumstances of this case, there was no error in determining that this conduct constituted oppressive action within the meaning of section 1104–a of the Business Corporation Law.

Nor may it be said that Supreme Court abused its discretion in ordering Kemp & Beatley's dissolution, subject to an opportunity for a buy-out of petitioners' shares. After the referee had found that the controlling faction of the company was, in effect, attempting to "squeeze-out" petitioners by offering them no return on their investment and increasing other executive compensation, respondents, in opposing the report's confirmation, attempted only to controvert the factual basis of the report. They suggested no feasible, alternative remedy to the forced dissolution. In light of an apparent deterioration in relations between petitioners and the governing shareholders of Kemp & Beatley, it was not unreasonable for the court to have determined that a forced buy-out of petitioners' shares or liquidation of the corporation's assets was the only means by which petitioners could be guaranteed a fair return on their investments.

Accordingly, the order of the Appellate Division should be modified, with costs to petitioners-respondents, by affirming the substantive determination of that court but extending the time for exercising the option to purchase petitioners-respondents' shares to 30 days following this court's determination.

Note: Reasonable Expectations and Dissolution

A number of other courts have adopted the "reasonable expectations" test to determine whether dissolution is an appropriate remedy. See Robert B. Thompson, The Shareholder's Cause of Action for Oppression, 48 Bus. L. 699, 715–16 (1993). In Exadaktilos v. Cinnaminson Realty Co., 167 N.J.Super. 141, 400 A.2d 554, 561 (1979), the court explained the "reasonable expectations" test as follows:

"The special circumstances, arrangements and personal relationships that frequently underlie the formation of close corporations generate certain expectations among the shareholders concerning their respective roles in corporate affairs, including management and earnings. These expectations preclude the drawing of any conclusions about the impact of a particular course of corporate conduct on a shareholder without taking into consideration the role that he is expected to play. Accordingly, a court must determine initially the understanding of the parties in this regard."

Minnesota has gone even further, It has embodied in the involuntary dissolution section of its corporations statute, Minn.Stat.Ann. § 302A.751, a test that also incorporates the fiduciary concepts developed in *Doanhue* and *Wilkes*.

Subd. 3a. Considerations in Granting Relief Involving Closely Held Corporations. In determining whether to order equitable relief, dissolution, or a buy-out, the court shall take into consideration the duty which all shareholders in a closely held corporation owe one another to act in an honest, fair, and reasonable manner in the operation of the corporation and the reasonable expectations of the shareholders as they exist at the inception and develop during the course of the shareholders' relationship with the corporation and with each other.

Professor Thompson notes: "The increasing use of the reasonable expectations standard reflects a move away from an exclusive search for egregious conduct by those in control of the enterprise and toward greater consideration of the effect of conduct on the complaining shareholder, even if no egregious conduct by controllers can be shown." Robert B. Thompson, Corporate Dissolution and Shareholders' Reasonable Expectations, 66 Wash. U. L. Q. 193, 219–220 (1988). See, also, Robert W. Hillman, The Dissatisfied Participant in the Solvent Business Venture: A Consideration of the Relative Permanence of Partnerships and Close Corporations, 67 Minn.L.Rev. 1 (1982). Easterbrook and Fischel, on the other hand, oppose judicial decisions and state statutes that provide for dissolution if the majority shareholders frustrate a minority shareholder's "reasonable expectations." They argue that this vague and open-ended standard provides disgruntled minority shareholders with an opportunity to coerce majority shareholders by threatening in bad faith to initiate lawsuits seeking dissolution. Frank H. Easterbrook and Daniel R. Fischel, Close Corporations and Agency Costs, 38 Stan. L. Rev. 271, 288 (1986).

Note: Is Dissolution the Only Appropriate Remedy?

In *Kemp and Beatley*, the court relied on N.Y.B.C.L. § 1118 to held that dissolution should be ordered only if the corporation declined to purchase petitioners' stock. Professors Hetherington and Dooley point out that rarely is a shareholder seeking dissolution primarily interested in terminating the corporation's existence.

> * * * [A] partnership is "dissolved" whenever one of the general partners withdraws from the firm, and dissolution requires only such a settling of accounts as will be sufficient to allow the departing partner to withdraw his interest. It does not mean the end of the business. The remaining partners are free to continue the enterprise, and only if they choose not to do so will the firm's assets be liquidated.

> In corporate involuntary dissolution cases, the courts appear to assume that a decree will result in the termination of the business. Perceiving a public interest in the continuation of profitable firms, courts understandably grant dissolution reluctantly and only after considering competing interests in preserving the firm. The concern is misplaced in this instance, and both the courts and the legislatures have misperceived the effect of a dissolution decree. In

practical effect a decree is no different than the dissolution of a partnership. The entry of a decree results in the termination of the business only if both the majority and the minority shareholders desire that result. Each faction has the ability at any stage of the proceeding to insure the continued existence of the firm by buying out, or selling out to, the other faction. The business will cease only if continuing it is not in the interest of any of its shareholders.

The point becomes clearer if one focuses on the motives for bringing a dissolution proceeding. Except for the rare case where the petition is prompted by pique, a shareholder suing for dissolution is trying to accomplish one of three things: (1) to withdraw his investment from the firm; (2) to induce the other shareholders to sell out to him; or (3) to use the threat of dissolution to induce the other shareholders to agree to a change in the balance of power or in the policies of the firm. All of these objectives can be accomplished without dissolution. If the petitioner wants to sell out, he is interested in receiving the highest possible price and is indifferent whether the purchase funds are raised by the other shareholders individually or by a sale of the firm's assets. If the second or third objectives motivate the suit, it is plain that the petitioner does not want dissolution at all. In all three situations, a dissolution petition is a means to another end.

Since the petitioner can always achieve his purposes without dissolution, and since the defendant will always oppose it, the dispute is very likely to be settled without liquidating the firm's assets and terminating its business. The court's decision to grant or to deny dissolution is significant only as it affects the relative bargaining strength of the parties; negotiations will go forward in any event.

John A. C. Hetherington and Michael P. Dooley, Illiquidity and Exploitation: A Proposed Statutory Solution to the Remaining Close Corporation Problem, 63 Va.L.Rev. 1, 26–27 (1977). In a survey of reported cases from 1960 through 1976 in which dissolution was sought, Professors Hetherington and Dooley found that rarely did the court order dissolution. Even more striking, where a decree of dissolution was entered most of the disputes were settled before the firm's assets were liquidated. In the few instances in which the decree ultimately was carried out, either the corporation was in marginal financial condition or the business was continued in some other form. Id. at 32–33.

Even where statutes do not provide for alternative remedies, as the New York statute did in *Kemp and Beatley*, courts have relied on their inherent equity authority to devise other remedies where they have found minority shareholders have been oppressed or a deadlock exists. In Baker v. Commercial Body Builders, Inc., 264 Or. 614, 507 P.2d 387 (1973), the court listed ten possible forms of relief that it could order short of outright dissolution:

(a) The entry of an order requiring dissolution of the corporation at a specified future date, to become effective only in the event that the stockholders fail to resolve their differences prior to that date.

(b) The appointment of a receiver, not for the purposes of dissolution, but to continue the operation of the corporation for the benefit of all of the stockholders, both majority and minority, until differences are resolved or "oppressive' conduct ceases.

(c) The appointment of a "special fiscal agent' to report to the court relating to the continued operation of the corporation, as a protection to its minority stockholders, and the retention of jurisdiction of the case by the court for that purpose.

(d) The retention of jurisdiction of the case by the court for the protection of the minority stockholders without appointment of a receiver or "special fiscal agent.'

(e) The ordering of an accounting by the majority in control of the corporation for funds alleged to have been misappropriated.

(f) The issuance of an injunction to prohibit continuing acts of "oppressive' conduct and which may include the reduction of salaries or bonus payments found to be unjustified or excessive.

(g) The ordering of affirmative relief by the required declaration of a dividend or a reduction and distribution of capital.

(h) The ordering of affirmative relief by the entry of an order requiring the corporation or a majority of its stockholders to purchase the stock of the minority stockholders at a price to be determined according to a specified formula or at a price determined by the court to be a fair and reasonable price.

(i) The ordering of affirmative relief by the entry of an order permitting minority stockholders to purchase additional stock under conditions specified by the court.

(j) An award of damages to minority stockholders as compensation for any injury suffered by them as the result of "oppressive' conduct by the majority in control of the corporation.

507 P.2d at 395–6. See also, Masinter v. WEBCO Co., 164 W.Va. 241, 262 S.E.2d 433 (1980); New Jersey Bus. Corp. Act § 14A:12–7. In Hendley v. Lee, 676 F.Supp. 1317 (D.S.C 1987), which involved a petition for dissolution, the court found that a deadlock existed but rejected both dissolution and a division of the assets of the corporation as remedies. It ordered a buyout. When neither party elected to sell, the court determined who should be required to sell by looking at the financial condition of the parties, their ability to engage in other activities and the tax consequences to each party.

In Jordan v. Bowman Apple Products Co., Inc., 728 F.Supp. 409 (D. W.Va. 1990), the court held that Virginia's adoption of a statute authorizing dissolution or the appointment of a custodian in cases where minority shareholders were oppressed supersedes shareholders' common law right of action for oppression and limited plaintiff's remedies to those available under the statute. One could read the New York Court of Appeals decision in *Ingle* as implicitly expressing the same point of view.

Professors Hetherington and Dooley argue that a better approach to remedying abuse of a minority shareholder may be to mandate by statute a buy out right at an agreed on price or, in the absence of an agreement, at a judicially determined price. Dissolution then would be ordered only if the defendants do not purchase the stock at the agreed upon price or the price fixed by the court. Hetherington and Dooley, *supra, at* 45. They maintain that their proposal would provide a "low-cost convenient remedy making exploitative behavior costly to the majority and giving the majority an incentive to conduct the affairs of the firm in a manner that retains the support and confidence of the minority." Id. at 47–48.

Easterbrook and Fischel disagree with Hetherington and Dooley's buyout proposal. Easterbrook and Fischel argue that minority shareholders currently have a number of remedies, such as involuntary dissolution in egregious situations, damages for breach of fiduciary duty, or the appointment of a custodian or provisional director. Mandatory buy-out provisions would arguably permit minority shareholders to impose costs on other investors and may encourage these shareholders to act in an opportunistic manner resulting in attempts "to extract a disproportionate share of benefits from other investors." Frank H. Easterbrook and Daniel R. Fischel, The Economic Structure of Corporate Law 242 (1991). A right to bail out would give a minority shareholder greater protection against opportunistic behavior by majority shareholders, "but at the cost of greater transaction costs as deadlocks multiply, an increase in the price of equity and debt capital [as creditors demand compensation for the new risk that a shareholder could withdraw assets from the corporation], and perhaps the denial of any opportunity to invest." Id. at 243. Finally, Easterbrook and Fischel note that minority shareholders have the opportunity to negotiate buy-out rights for a broad range of freeze-out transactions. In the absence of negotiated rights, they argue that "it would be inefficient to impose [a buy-out] provision on shareholders in closely held corporations * * *. It vindicates the current corporate law, which * * * follows the contractual path of wealth maximization despite the cries of 'unfairness.'" Id. at 243.

RMBCA § 14.34, which was added in 1991, provides a buyout option somewhat similar to that suggested by Hetherington and Dooley and provided for by N.Y.B.C.L. § 1118. RMBCA § 14.34 operates in conjunction with RMBCA § 14.30, which establishes the grounds for judicial dissolution. If a shareholder of a closely-held corporation petitions for dissolution under RMBCA § 14.30, the corporation can short circuit the dissolution proceeding by electing to purchase the petitioning shareholder's stock, as can any other shareholder(s) if the corporation decides not to act. The petitioning shareholder and the corporation or purchasing shareholder(s) than have 60 days to agree on price and terms. If they do not, either party can petition to stay the dissolution proceeding. The court then will determine the "fair value" of the stock and require that it be transferred at that price.

One question that arises both under statutes providing for a buy-out and when a court finds oppression and allows a corporation to purchase a minority shareholder's stock in lieu of dissolution, is what weight should be given to a shareholder agreement regulating transfers of stock. Matter of Pace Photographers, Ltd., 71 N.Y.2d 737, 530 N.Y.S.2d 67, 525 N.E.2d 713 (1988), involved a shareholder agreement fixing the price at which stock could be purchased if any shareholder decided to "sell, hypothecate, transfer, encumber or otherwise dispose of" his stock * * *." The court held that the agreement did not control the price at which the stock should be transferred when the corporation elected to buy a petitioning shareholder's stock pursuant to N.Y.B.C.L. § 1118, because the agreement did not include a dissolution proceeding under N.Y.B.C.L. § 1104–a in its list of voluntary transactions that would trigger the pricing provision.

Chapter 14

THE ROLE OF THE SHAREHOLDER IN THE GOVERNANCE OF THE PUBLIC CORPORATION

In Chapter 12, we saw that the statutory corporate governance structure is one in which shareholders elect the directors who then supervise the corporation's business and select the officers who run that business on a daily basis. Statutes remove most decisions about the direction of corporate policy and operation of the corporations' business from the shareholders' power. The statutory model thus largely divorces ownership from control. In practice, in most publicly-held corporations, the separation is greater than the theory might suggest. Shareholders, to be sure, always formally *elect* the directors, but rarely do they play any meaningful role in *selecting* them. The rules governing access to public corporations' proxy statements make it impractical for most shareholders to nominate or solicit support for candidates for election to the board. Incumbent directors, who govern access to the corporation's proxy statement and can tap the corporate treasury to fund proxy solicitations, effectively determine who is nominated and who is elected. The corporation's chief executive officer is far more likely to influence these decisions than is any shareholder or shareholder group. In short, subject to the often important influence of market forces, most public corporations are firmly controlled by self-perpetuating boards of directors or by the senior corporate officers that those boards ostensibly have elected.

Dean Robert Clark notes that because directors and officers can use the powers that the law delegates to them to advance their personal goals "in ways that hurt other persons having claims on the organization," the central major problem in corporate law "is how to keep managers accountable to their other-directed duties while nonetheless allowing them great discretionary power over appropriate matters." Robert Charles Clark, Corporate Law § 1.5 (1986). The chapters that follow deal with issues that arise largely as a consequence of the separation of ownership and control in public corporations and the possibility that directors or officers will use their powers in ways that are

531

inconsistent with shareholders' interests.   This chapter begins with a discussion of theories of the firm—of the nature and character of the public corporation—because those theories provide the backdrop against which doctrinal and policy decisions are debated.   The chapter then shifts its focus to shareholders and the extent to which, as "owners," they are (or should be) able to influence decision making in public corporations.

Questions as to the proper role of shareholders in a corporate governance system have been complicated by the major shift in share ownership in recent years.   Institutional investors (e.g., pension funds, insurance companies, mutual funds, etc.) now own a large portion of the stock of many corporations—in some, more than half the outstanding stock.   Consequently, when discussing shareholders' involvement in corporate decision making, it is important to specify with which "shareholders" one is concerned—individuals, who generally hold relatively small amounts of stock, or institutions, which typically hold, and have the resources to acquire, much larger stock positions.

A.   THEORIES OF THE FIRM

1.   THE BERLE-MEANS CORPORATION

The nature of the public corporation—the "theory of the firm"—has been the subject of debate at least since the 19th century.   See William W. Bratton, Jr., The New Economic Theory of the Firm, 41 Stan. L. Rev. 1471 (1989).   The modern debate, however, dates from 1932, when Professors Adolf Berle and Gardiner Means published The Modern Corporation and Private Property, a study of the characteristics of the two hundred largest corporations listed on the New York Stock Exchange that highlighted the development of a separation between ownership and control.

ADOLF A. BERLE AND GARDINER C. MEANS,
THE MODERN CORPORATION AND
PRIVATE PROPERTY 5
66, 84, 86–88 (1932).

[A] large body of security holders has been created who exercise virtually no control over the wealth which they or their predecessors in interest have contributed to the enterprise.   In case of management control, the ownership interest held by the controlling group amounts to but a very small fraction of the total ownership.

* * *

* * * [T]he position of ownership has changed from that of an active to that of a passive agent.   In place of actual physical properties over which the owner could exercise direction and for which he was responsi-

ble, the owner now holds a piece of paper representing a set of rights and expectations with respect to an enterprise. But over the enterprise and over the physical property—the instruments of production—in which he has an interest, the owner has little control. At the same time he bears no responsibility with respect to the enterprise or its physical property.

* * *

[O]wnership is so widely distributed that no individual or small group has even a minority interest large enough to dominate the affairs of the company. When the largest single interest amounts to but a fraction of one per cent—the case in several of the largest American corporations—no stockholder is in the position through his holdings alone to place important pressure upon the management or to use his holdings as a considerable nucleus for the accumulation of the majority of votes necessary to control.

* * *

In such companies where does control lie? To answer this question, it is necessary to examine in greater detail the conditions surrounding the electing of the board of directors. In the election of the board the stockholder ordinarily has three alternatives. He can refrain from voting, he can attend the annual meeting and personally vote his stock, or he can sign a proxy transferring his voting power to certain individuals selected by the management of the corporation, the proxy committee. As his personal vote will count for little or nothing at the meeting unless he has a very large block of stock, the stockholder is practically reduced to the alternative of not voting at all or else of *handing over his vote to individuals over whom he has no control and in whose selection he did not participate.* In neither case will he be able to exercise any measure of control. Rather, control will tend to be in the hands of those who select the proxy committee by whom, in turn, the election of directors for the ensuing period may be made. Since the proxy committee is appointed by the existing management, the latter can virtually dictate their own successors. Where ownership is sufficiently sub-divided, the management can thus become a self-perpetuating body even though its share in the ownership is negligible. This form of control can properly be called "management control." (emphasis in original)

2. THE CONTRACTUAL THEORY OF THE CORPORATION

For almost fifty years, most discussions of corporate governance issues focused on problems relating to the accountability of corporate managers that appeared to arise from the separation of ownership from control in public corporations. Beginning in the late 1970s, though, a number of economists and lawyers began to advance a contractual theory of the corporation. They accepted the Berle–Means conclusion that ownership was divorced from control in most public corporations, but saw that as a strength, not a weakness, of the corporate form. The central thrust of their argument was that investment is a voluntary activity, that investors understand what Justice Scalia called "the deal" when they purchase corporate stock. Consequently, these commentators reasoned, the relationships among shareholders and between shareholders and managers are essentially contractual in nature.

HENRY N. BUTLER, THE CONTRACTUAL THEORY OF THE CORPORATION

11 George Mason U. L.Rev., Summer 1989, at 99.

INTRODUCTION

The modern corporation is one of the most successful inventions in history, as evidenced by its widespread adoption and survival as a primary vehicle of capitalism over the past century. Economists, however, have only recently begun * * * to view the firm as a "nexus of contracts" among participants in the organization. When applied to the corporate form of organization, the theory of the firm is often referred to as the contractual theory of the corporation.

* * * The contractual theory views the corporation as founded in private contract, where the role of the state is limited to enforcing contracts. In this regard, a state charter merely recognizes the existence of a "nexus of contracts" called a corporation. Each contract in the "nexus of contracts" warrants the same legal and constitutional protections as other legally enforceable contracts. Moreover, freedom of contract requires that parties to the "nexus of contracts" must be allowed to structure their relations as they desire.

* * *

I. Background: The Berle–Means Approach to Corporate Governance

* * *

Over the years, the Berle and Means thesis has provided the basis for many calls for more stringent legal controls on managerial behavior. This area of corporate policy is called "corporate governance," which refers to the manner in which the relations between the parties to the corporate contract are restrained by government regulation or private ordering. * * *

Much of the Berle and Means analysis is based on their belief that shareholders should, but do not, play a major, direct role in monitoring corporate managers. * * * [H]owever, the reality of the large corporation is far from democratic because shareholders rarely have the incentive to exercise their legal rights. * * * The so-called "Wall Street Rule" is that "rationally ignorant" shareholders sell their stock rather than become involved in the internal affairs of the corporation. Because of the seeming indifference of shareholders, Berle and Means and their progeny have assumed that directors and managers are free to operate the corporation in a manner not necessarily in the shareholders' best interest.

The Berle and Means perspective on the corporation has fostered the view among some legal commentators that corporation law is the only meaningful constraint on managerial behavior. This has led to public policy arguments that place great emphasis on the role of laws in governing the relationship between shareholders and managers. In essence, some commentators have assumed that managers, freed from legal constraints, can abuse shareholders' interests without cost. Corporation law, according to this view, plays a pre-eminent role in maintaining balance in the large corporation characterized by a separation of ownership and control. These critics of corporation law often assume that the law is not fulfilling that role and that states or even the federal government must take a more active role in regulating the internal affairs of the corporations they create. A more cynical view of their motivations is that some lawyers are attempting to increase the demand for their legal services at the expense of lower-cost, market-oriented governance mechanisms.

* * *

II.   The Theory of the Firm and the Nature of the Corporation

* * *

C.   The Corporate Firm: Residual Claimants, Shareholders, and Monitors

* * * The attractiveness of the corporation relative to other forms of business associations is due in large part to the economic benefits of issuing shares of stock that limit after shareholders liability to the initial investment in the firm. The issuing of stock facilitates the productive specialization of activities. The publicly traded corporation allows individuals with no managerial expertise to participate in corporations as owners by purchasing shares of stock. The corporate form also allows specialization, or centralization, of management functions through the hiring of professional managers. Specifically, the corporation allows individuals with little financial capital, but considerable managerial talents, to specialize as professional managers of corporations. * * *

The presence of "rationally ignorant" shareholders, however, presents managers of corporations with opportunities to engage in activities that are not necessarily in the shareholders' best interests. These so-called "agency costs" are discussed below.

D.   Agency Theory and the Corporation

* * *

In general, agency theory suggests that unity of ownership and control is not a necessary condition of efficient performance of a firm. This perspective stresses the voluntary, contractual nature of the corporation. A first step in understanding this market-oriented approach is to recognize that it is based in part on the assumption that the shareholders' primary interest is in the maximization of the value of their investments and that the contractual relations among participants in the firm must convince shareholders that managers will not abuse the shareholders' interests. A corporation's managers, which are defined to include its officers and directors, are agents of the shareholders. In this view, the so-called separation of ownership and control in the large corporation is an agency relationship, which exists because the benefits of the relationship exceed the agency costs associated with it. * * *

* * *

Agency theory and transaction costs economics attempt to explain the development of institutional arrangements that convince shareholders voluntarily to allow managers to control their resources. The resources devoted to controlling agency costs are properly identified as agency costs. Thus, agency costs include not only the direct costs associated with agents acting in their own interest at the expense of shareholders, but also the costs of controlling managerial agents through legal or market governance arrangements. * * *

III. Corporate Governance Mechanisms and the Contractual Theory of the Corporation

Much of the economic literature on the governance of the modern corporation reflects an evolutionary view of the development and use of certain governance mechanisms. This view is clearly reflected in Professors Fama's and Jensen's statement: "Absent fiat, the form of organization that survives in an activity is the one that delivers the product demanded by customers at the lowest price while covering costs." The modern corporation is passing the test of time. This section offers a summary of the governance mechanisms that are believed to explain the phenomenal success of the modern corporation.

The discussion focuses on powerful market forces that encourage managers to act in shareholders' interests. * * * In order to raise capital at the lowest possible price, managers must offer contract terms—including evidence of the existence of intra-firm incentive structures—that convince investors that agency costs will be minimized. This section identifies and discusses those contractual terms.

A. The Market for Corporate Control

A potential concern of investors is that intra-firm corporate governance devices such as managerial incentive contracts designed by entrenched managers, although clearly more useful than monitoring by diffuse shareholders, may not always be effective in controlling managerial agency costs. An alternative control mechanism, beyond the direct control of entrenched managers, is found in the stock market. The stock market discipline of managers is manifest in the threat of tender offer, takeovers, or other forms of changes in corporate control whenever entrenched managers adopt strategies and behavior that fail to maximize the value of the corporation's shares. The so-called market for corporate control provides an external monitoring mechanism that forces managers to be concerned about their shareholders. * * *

If a firm is not performing up to its financial potential under current and expected market conditions, regardless of the reason, then it is an attractive target for a change in corporate control. According to the theory, the acquiring firm purchases the stock of the target company, replaces the inefficient managers with efficient managers, and then reaps a large profit as the stock price rises to reflect the increased earning potential under the more efficient managerial team. In basic terms, the firm's assets are worth more in the hands of the new managers. In many instances, the source of the premium for the replacement of managers is the reduction of agency costs. But a more general view of the role of the market for corporate control is that it is the *threat* of takeover, not the actual occurrence of a takeover, which serves to align managers' interests with shareholders' interests.

* * *

Exclusive reliance on the market for corporate control to solve all of the potential conflicts of interest associated with the separation of ownership and control is neither justified nor necessary. Managerial discretion is constrained by other market and legal mechanisms. For example, in some large corporations, agency costs are reduced by the corporation being owned by large owners who have the incentive to closely monitor managerial behavior. Nevertheless, the market for corporate control * * * provides the glue that holds together the nexus of contracts.

* * *

H. Corporate Law and Fiduciary Duties

Emphasis on the interaction of market forces under the contractual theory of the corporation has led some scholars to argue that markets will lead managers to adopt optimal governance structures and that corporate law is irrelevant. However, the market mechanisms may be inadequate to deal with last-period, or one-time, divergences when the agent rationally concludes that the benefits of the one-time use of discretion is worth whatever penalties may be forthcoming in the employment market for the agent's services. In this regard, corporate law of fiduciary duties serves as a legal constraint on managerial opportunism.

Moreover, because markets do not operate without cost, it appears that corporate law plays a productive role in the contractual theory of the corporation by providing a standard form contract that reduces the transaction and negotiating costs of reaching and adhering to optimal contracts. * * * The terms of corporate law is one of the governance mechanisms that can be selected by the contracting parties to minimize corporate agency costs.

I. Evaluation of the Contractual Theory

The managers of firms select the mix of legal and market governance mechanisms that is optimal given the particular circumstances of the firm. The "nexus of contracts" specifies the extent of reliance upon differing mechanisms. Managers substitute among the various governance mechanisms until the marginal net productivity of each mechanism is equal. The corporate governance mechanisms, when combined in the manner most appropriate for the particular circumstances of each firm, resolve most of the conflicts between shareholders and managers identified at the end of Section II.

The contractual theory of the corporation does not assert that agency costs are reduced to zero, rather it asserts that agency costs are minimized by the contractual terms agreed upon in the face of market and legal constraints. The contractual theory of the corporation provides theoretical and empirical bases for understanding not only the organization and success of the large corporation, but also the appropriate role of privately negotiated contracts and mandatory legal rules.

———

As the following materials illustrate, some commentators have accepted the contractarians' thesis that the purpose of corporate activity is to maximize shareholder gain, but have questioned whether it is accurate to view the corporation as no more than a "nexus of contracts." They also have suggested that the contractarians' market-based approach reflects a normative bias against governmental (including judicial) intervention in corporate affairs.

ROBERT CHARLES CLARK, AGENCY COSTS VERSUS FIDUCIARY DUTIES, IN PRATT AND ZECKHAUSER, PRINCIPALS AND AGENTS: THE STRUCTURE OF BUSINESS

55–64, 66–69 (1985).

PITFALLS OF THE AGENCY COSTS APPROACH

Lawyers and economists often study the same phenomena but approach them in different ways. In some contexts their awareness of these differences can be mutually enlightening. The received agency costs literature describes managers as "agents" of stockholders and the corporation as a "nexus of contracts." But the important relationships and real problems that engage the "agency costs" commentators are conceived by legal authorities in a subtly different way, because the legal system has evolved its own unique strategy for dealing with them. The precise characteristics of the legal strategy, I believe, are often unknown or misunderstood, and could usefully be subjected to a close economic analysis.

Much of the economic literature talks about "firms" rather than "corporations," and does not distinguish sharply between closely held business organizations (whatever their legal form) and publicly held corporations. For a number of reasons, failure to make this distinction clearly can be a source of almost fatal confusion. Throughout this paper, I will be referring only to publicly held (or "public") business corporations, which of course account for the great bulk of business revenues in the United States. * * *

Managers Are Not Agents of Stockholders

To an experienced corporate lawyer who has studied primary legal materials, the assertion that corporate managers are agents of investors, whether debtholders or stockholders, will seem odd or loose. The lawyer would make the following points: (1) corporate officers like the president and treasurer are agents of the corporation itself; (2) the board of directors is the ultimate decision-making body of the corporation (and in a sense is the group most appropriately identified with "the corporation"); (3) directors are not agents of the corporation but are sui generis; (4) neither officers nor directors are agents of the stockholders; but (5) both officers and directors are "fiduciaries" with respect to the corporation and its stockholders.

These legal characterizations are not just semantic differences from the usual terminology of the agency costs literature. To see the distinction, let us first contrast the legal conception of the agent with that of the corporate director and then examine the more general legal concept of the fiduciary.

Though lawyers use the concept of agency in a variety of senses, the core legal concept implies a relationship in which the principal retains the power to control and direct the activities of the agent. Typically, the principal sets the ultimate objective and general strategy for the agent to pursue, occasionally specifies details of the agent's behavior, and stands ready to countermand specific acts of the agent.

A review of elementary corporate law shows that this power of the principal to direct the activities of the agent does not apply to the stockholders as against the directors or officers of their corporation. By statute in every state, the board of directors of a corporation has the power and duty to manage or supervise its business. The stockholders do not. To appreciate the point fully, consider the following activities: setting the ultimate goal of the corporation—for example, whether its legal purpose will be to maximize profits; choosing the corporation's lines of business—hiring and firing the full-time executives who will actually run the company; and exercising supervisory power with respect to the day-to-day operations of the business. Stockholders of a large publicly held corporation *do not* do these things; as a matter of efficient operation of a large firm with numerous residual claimants they *should not* do them; and under the typical corporate statute and case law they *cannot* do them.

* * *

The legal relationship between the stockholder and the manager is very different from the legal relationship between the ordinary principal and agent. So what? the reader might ask. Do these differences have any bearing on the kinds of problems that have been at the heart of the agency costs literature? To some degree, yes. Ignoring the legal restrictions on stockholders' decision-making power makes it easier to talk as if stockholders and managers "bargain" over and "contract" about the terms of their relationship, or "implicitly" or "virtually" do so—and this is the next, more serious pitfall of the agency costs literature.

* * *

A Corporation Is Not a Nexus of Actual Contracts

* * *

[I]s it realistic or useful to view the modern public corporation as consisting only, or even principally, of a set of contracts? I think not. This extreme contractualist viewpoint is almost perverse. It is likely to blind us to most of the features of the modern public corporation that are distinctive, puzzling, and worth exploring. To see this, we must first consider the notion of contract, and then note the extent to which the corporation, considered as a multitude of legal relationships, consists of noncontractual legal relationships.

* * * [T]he core notion of contract, and the most relevant for theorizing about the optimality of commercial relationships, is that the rights and duties between the two parties are specified and fixed by their own voluntary and actual agreement. Let me refer to a set of legal relationships determined solely in this way as constituting an "actual contract."

Most of the particular rules that make up the legal relationships among corporate officers, directors, and stockholders—that is, the relationships that constitute corporate law and give operational meaning to the legal concept of the corporation—are not the product of actual contracts made by the persons subject to them. Furthermore, they are often not the product of "implicit" contracts between these people, if by that term we mean that the individuals actually understood the governing rules but simply did not advert to them when entering their roles as officers, directors, or stockholders.

But some will insist that contracts may be implicit in a more remote but meaningful sense: Such as a contract exists if the parties, assuming they are rational and reasonable, would have agreed to the rules in question, if they had thought and bargained about them beforehand. Moreover, the whole set of legal relationships that make up corporate law may well be seen as a large-scale "standardized contract" or "form contract"—a miniature version of the libertarian philosophers' social contract—to which various people "consent" when they voluntarily step into the standardized roles of the officer, director, or stockholder. But I would insist that the use of the term contract in connection with "implicit contracts" and "standardized contracts" is metaphorical, and that the metaphor is seriously misleading.

Most corporate case law deals with alleged breaches of fiduciary duties by managers, though a given opinion might focus as readily on a question of procedure or process as on a question of definition or application of the duty. Fiduciary duties are sometimes waivable by stockholders and sometimes not waivable. But in either event the duties are highly unlikely to have been the result of any actual compact or understanding between manager and investor.

Since actual voluntary consent to the governing rules of a relationship is the essence of my notion of actual contracts, let me restate my view in terms of three grades of consent that might be given to corporate law by participants in the modern public corporation. The first level is consent to the *role* of officer, director, or stockholder. Many millions of people in the United States have voluntarily entered these roles, often with some vague awareness of, and lack of objection to, the fact that they thereby become subject to an unspecified, large, and perhaps arcane assortment of legal rights and duties. This acceptance of the legal rules, however, does not explain their origins. Most of these millions of people play no direct part in articulating, justifying, criticizing, changing, getting established as law, or enforcing the myriad particular rules that govern and define the roles they play.

The second level is consent to particular deviations from the otherwise governing rules in particular situations. * * *

* * * [L]awyers, courts, and commentators often argue over the extent to which such expressions of consent are informed, uncoerced, and untainted by conflicts of interest, and thus whether they should be declared legally valid.

The third level of consent is bargaining about and creation of the particular terms of a particular relationship among participants in a public corporation. A chief executive officer, for example, may bargain with a board of directors about compensation and terms of employment. Other important examples are hard to come by.

With these qualifications and understandings, I suggest again that the legal relationships among participants in the modern public corporation are not primarily the product of actual contracts.

Why It Matters Whether Contracts Are Actual Rather Than Implicit or Standardized

At this point some readers may be ready to concede that a large firm is not a nexus of actual contracts in a strict sense, but would argue that the distinction does not matter much. The important point is that firms can be usefully understood as if they were sets of contracts. One can still maintain that firms are virtually contractual in all essential aspects.

But this response, which resembles a lawyer's defense strategy of confession and avoidance, is not adequate. Viewing corporations as essentially contractual may have [several] troublesome consequences.

* * *

It may be objected that some corporate law rules seem to fit the model of "standard presumptions" adopted because they fit the normal case, and that it is intuitively plausible that the relevant participants would actually agree to them, if the issue were put to them for explicit consideration and bargaining. This group of rules is likely to include the more elementary structural features of the corporate form of organization, such as limited liability of stockholders and free transferability of shares, which are often embodied in statutes. I agree that there are such rules, and they constitute an important class. In my view, they result from (fairly slow, crude) processes of legal evolution that favor rules that reduce transaction costs. But I would note that with many other rules, it is not at all obvious that they can be analyzed this way; the analysis has to be made in detail before it becomes convincing.

Another objection might be that while most rules of corporate law are imposed on the parties subject to it, they are usually free to "bargain around" them. A stockholder, for example, can bargain around limited liability by expressly guaranteeing specific corporate debts. *Failure* to bargain around a rule then amounts to accepting it, and one might even argue that the nonbargainers "contract" to obey the rule. (Similarly, one can argue that failure to reincorporate in another state implies real consent to those rules that could be changed by reincorporation.)

But some important corporate law rules cannot be bargained around (unless, perhaps, one is willing to depart from the manager or stockholder roles or to modify their parameters drastically). Basic fiduciary duties fall in this category, along with insider trading rules and the norm that directors rather than stockholders manage public corporations. * * *

Moreover, bargaining around is costly. If the cost of bargaining is expected to exceed the benefits, the standard legal rule is simply tolerated—but this does not mean that it is the best available rule to govern the behavior in question. An alternative rule might make some people better off and no one worse off. Yet the substitution need not occur. For example, bargaining around a waivable fiduciary duty * * * might require the preparation and distribution of a special proxy statement and the collection of a stockholder vote. The associated expense may deter many such bargains with investors. A different version of the legal doctrine might eliminate the transaction costs and deterrent effects of the need to seek shareholder consent. Thus, at any given time, it is an open question whether the standard legal rule is better than some imagined or proposed one. The interested commentator will have to make an independent assessment of the costs and benefits of the opposing rules, rather than simply assuming that the existing rule must be fit because it has survived (so far) without provoking much bargaining around.

* * *

Indeterminacy of Results. The basic pitfall with implicit-contracts reasoning is that it is frequently indeterminate and therefore manipulable. This is true whether the purpose of the reasoning is to advance positive or normative theory. It is especially true of complex, multi-faceted relationships, such as those among directors, officers, stockholders, and the large bureaucratic organizations with which they are associated.

In arguments about which rules rational managers and investors would have agreed to, much depends on what one assumes about the characteristics of the bargaining parties, their knowledge, the bargaining process, and the state of the financial and business world. The implicit-contracts form of reasoning is often indeterminate precisely because there is no consensus about which assumptions to use.

———

Professor Victor Brudney, Corporate Governance, Agency Costs and the Rhetoric of Contract, 85 Col.L.Rev. 1403 (1985), agrees with much of Dean Clark's analysis. Brudney also rejects the idea that the markets can effectively constrain managerial discretion. He notes that because there is no pressure to disclose the magnitude of managerial discretion or the uncertainty of the connection between managerial inputs and rewards, investors have difficulty in assessing the quality of management before investing. Brudney argues that existing studies fail to demonstrate that an efficient market can be said to exist for managers services or managerial arrangements. Further, Brudney questions whether the market for a corporation's stock can adequately check managers' discretion. He contends that the stock price reflects an investor's lump choice as to the future prospects of the firm rather than a choice made by separating the quality of management from other factors which are, at best, only indirectly related to such quality. For Brudney, evidence that the market responds efficiently to new information does not change the analysis. "At best, the market price correctly reflects the existence of managerial discretion and the concomitant potential for diversion of assets and for operating inefficiency * * *. [It] does not of its own force drive management to compete in limiting its rewards or its power to divert assets, or even to be more effective managers." Id. at 1425.

Brudney also is disturbed by the ideology implicit in the contractual theory. As he states:

> The current "nexus-of-contracts" rhetoric * * * offers the added fillip of freeing managers from the constraints which even the "private" conception of the corporation imposed on management for the benefit of stockholders by way of judicially fashioned fiduciary

principles. * * * [D]uring the twentieth century, courts have substantially eroded the restraints of those principles in applying them to corporate management of investor-owned firms—both in terms of substantive rules and in terms of the procedure for enforcing them. But the rhetoric of contract serves to obscure that erosion, and to complete the process of legitimating the substantial discretion which corporate management has, both to shirk in its performance and to divert corporate assets to its own benefit at investors' expense. Id. at 1409–10.

———

The contractarians have not taken these criticisms lying down. The following excerpt illustrates their response.

HENRY N. BUTLER & LARRY E. RIBSTEIN, OPTING OUT OF FIDUCIARY DUTIES: A RESPONSE TO THE ANTI–CONTRACTARIANS
65 Wash. L. Rev. 1, 12–18 (1990).

C.   ADHESION AND FREEDOM OF CHOICE: THE FORMATION OF THE CORPORATE CONTRACT

* * *

1.   *The "Adhesion" Analysis*

According to [Professor Victor] Brudney, shareholders do not freely consent to corporate arrangements as in "conventional" contracts. Rather, dispersed shareholders must accept, without any direct bargaining over details or alternatives, package deals crafted by managers. In this respect, Brudney greatly overstates the shareholders' plight. In fact, investors are offered a formidable array of investment alternatives—including corporations with different capital and ownership structures, and such diverse investments as limited partnerships, mutual funds, money market accounts, real estate, and simple savings accounts. Clearly investors are not *forced* to accept any particular investment. If contractual volition is lacking—if, as Brudney argues, these are "adhesion" contracts—it is only in the sense that investors do not dicker over individual terms, but accept contractual packages. * * *

* * *

[T]he contract advocated by Brudney is not even a superior product. For many reasons, a contracting party does not usually want to "have it my way," but is often willing to accept the * * * corporation's package. In fact, because sellers often offer the terms they believe buyers want, it may be impossible to determine who is dictating the terms of a contract by merely identifying the printer of the contract. Although there is always the chance that the terms could be improved through dickering, this is a costly process in terms of time, attorneys' fees, and other transaction costs.

Not only is the extra cost of a customized contract usually not worth the benefit of dickering, but in many situations a standardized contract is a better one: there is more information available concerning a standardized form; important terms have been clarified by interpretation; and error costs and information costs are less than in individually negotiated deals. * * *

2. *The Information Problem*

Professor Brudney's second concern about using the "rhetoric of contract" in the corporate context is that the average investor lacks sufficient information about the package he is buying. * * *

* * *

In general, the issue here should not be what is, and what is not, a "contract" in some abstract sense. Concerns about information and adhesion problems in the corporation amount to a conclusion that voluntary arrangements in the corporation are not, like other voluntary arrangements, presumptively efficient. This conclusion depends on the viability of markets in this setting, and is therefore the subject of economic analysis. The issue cannot be resolved by labels.

D. THE CORPORATION AS "IMPLICIT" CONTRACT

Professor Melvin A. Eisenberg argues that the corporation should not be regarded as fundamentally contractual because many of the terms governing the corporate relationship are merely "implicit bargains" and not real contracts. An implicit bargain is a term used by labor economics to refer to terms that, like real bargains, involve an economic quid pro quo. They are not "real" contracts because they are enforced by market, rather than legal, mechanisms. * * *

The fact that many of the parties to a corporation are governed largely by implicit terms *supports* rather than undermines the contract theory of the corporation. The choice of implicit and explicit terms is one of many examples of how the parties, if unhindered by legal rules, choose the combination of legal and extra-legal devices appropriate to their relationship. It is a clear nonsequitur to say that because the parties to firms sometimes choose implicit instead of legally enforceable terms they should be forced to submit to mandatory legal rules. More specifically, the parties' choice of market mechanisms to support an implicit promise by managers not to behave opportunistically should not be trumped by mandatory fiduciary duties.

———

A few commentators have faulted the contractual theory of the corporation on the more fundamental ground that it fails to take account of interests other than the financial claims of shareholders and managers. The following excerpt reflects this point of view.

LYMAN P. Q. JOHNSON, THE DELAWARE JUDICIARY AND THE MEANING OF CORPORATE LIFE AND CORPORATE LAW
68 Tex. L.Rev. 865, 892–96 (1990).

Two aspects of the contractual model warrant mention here. First, shareholder welfare remains central to the model because shareholder contractual rights are chiefly and most riskily at stake. Furthermore, the singular focus on shareholder welfare severely curtails both managerial and judicial discretion. Management's charge is simply to fulfill "the implicit terms of their employment agreement with shareholders." Judges are not free to roam the social landscape, but are to confine themselves to figuring out what the bargain is and then enforcing it or penalizing its breach. Corporate law is regarded as private law *par excellence*, and any sense of corporate law as public law is completely absent. In this way, the model allegedly achieves its own esteemed virtue—commercial and juridical accountability. * * *

The contractual model also supposedly fulfills the norms of judicial modesty, determinacy, and economic self-reliance. Persons are economic actors who, as contracting parties, are exhorted to protect themselves by shrewd bargaining, not by expecting managers or judges to look after them. * * * Firms are a convenient meeting place for wary actors to negotiate to their own advantage. Enduring relationships are not valued in their own right, but will be attended to out of enlightened self-interest and dropped just as fast when better opportunities arise. * * * Furthermore, this restless dynamic allows rapid redeployment of assets, and thereby the social good of ever greater efficiency in the use of resources can be achieved.

This vision of commercial activity, stark and mechanistic as it is, may well be a largely accurate description of human affairs. It might even be proffered with a tinge of regret. Certainly, the belief that the world really works this way will shape one's understanding of law. The vision relies on certain base unchanging principles of human behavior drawn from economics, which, as a social science, is naively believed to be immune from deeper critiques of law. The law's function, then, is fatalistically to accept and conform to perceived reality.

Obvious problems with the contractual model are that, as an ontological matter, the world of social action might not work quite the way it is thought, and that, as an epistemological matter, relying on the insights of economics alone may preclude us from completely knowing whether it does. Moreover, the model ignores the way in which the very practice of contracting is grounded on noncontractual social and legal values. Finally, the stoic way in which this viewpoint chooses to respond to its own existential analytic is laden with normative preference. It espouses crafty resignation and wariness over other equally available stances toward economic acquaintances, such as "foolish" sacrifice, commitment, and preservation of trust. It also fails to acknowledge the richness of human motivation and the deeper affection felt for those who are closer rather than more distant in the economic sphere. The result is to ignore the important tasks of explaining why people should (or should not) consider the effects of their actions on others and of analyzing the respective roles of markets and state intervention (whether legislative or judicial) for inducing that behavior.

Thus, while the notion of accountability and efficiency serve as this model's apparent lifelines to more widely shared social norms, the dreary egoistic underpinnings make it clear that those notions are only enticing window dressing; they are not essential. The contractual model subscribes to the root norm that, in a pinch, people do—therefore they should—act to save their own skin. If that is one's sense of life, why should the ethos in work and business or corporate law be different? Inevitably, the model shifts from description to prescription—we should be what we are—and the normative cards are played. In this case, the hand reminds one of B. F. Skinner's work with pigeons. No doubt, people, like pigeons, often respond with distressing predictability to given stimuli. The difference is that people can choose to respond otherwise.

3. BEYOND CONTRACTUAL THEORY

Professor (later Judge) Frank Easterbrook and Professor Daniel Fischel have been the most prominent proponents of the contractual theory of the corporation, at least within the field of corporate law. During the 1980s, they addressed almost every major issue in corporate law in a series of articles that reflected the contractual point of view. In 1991, their work culminated in The Economic Structure of Corporate Law (1991). This book drew heavily on their earlier articles and also took account of certain developments of the late 1980s, particularly the proliferation of takeover defenses and state antitakeover laws, that could not easily be reconciled with their earlier writings. Publication of the book provided an occasion for commentators to review both Easterbrook and Fischel's theoretical contributions and the manner in which they have attempted to take account of these newer developments.

WILLIAM W. BRATTON, THE ECONOMIC STRUCTURE OF THE POST–CONTRACTUAL CORPORATION
87 Nw. U. L.Rev. 180, 180–197 (1992).

I. INTRODUCTION

The political economics of corporate law changed abruptly during the 1980s. At the decade's start, the prevailing economics counseled that excess management power needed to be curbed for productivity's sake. Law reform was assumed to be an appropriate means to this end. But this antimanagerial paradigm fell from favor, and by the time the takeover market became white-hot in 1984 and 1985, a "contract paradigm" had taken its place. The large American corporations reemerged as a nexus for a set of contracts among individual factors of production. Corporate governance followed suit, and reappeared as a field well suited to microeconomic modeling. By the time the stock market crashed in 1987, academic corporate law's determinant presumptions had been reversed. Credit for this change goes in the first instance to Professor (later Judge) Frank Easterbrook and Professor Daniel Fischel, the leading exponents of the new "contractarian" view.

Easterbrook and Fischel led corporate legal theory up the mountain of contract. They restated every topic of consequence in the terms of financial economics. In so doing, they captured the rhetoric of academic corporate law, rewriting the story of shareholder-management relations to accord with a theme of self-protection through contract. Where once we had shareholder dependence, they substituted cheap opportunities to diversify firm-specific risk. Where once we had unfair wealth transfers, they substituted market pricing that accounted for the risks of misallocated gains. Where we once had excess management power, they substituted market constraints. Where we once had "needs" that called for reform, they substituted "costs" that blocked reform.

Now Easterbrook and Fischel summarize their enterprise with *The Economic Structure of Corporate Law.* * * * It may be that no comparable integration of corporate law and economics has appeared since 1934, when Berle and Means published *The Modern Corporation and Private Property.*

* * *

II.   THE GOING CONCERN
A.   Components of the Economic Model

1. *Mythic Origins.*—Easterbrook and Fischel bring a familiar bundle of assumptions to bear in their model of corporate law. Here free choice, intense competition, rational self-interest, and contractual risk-allocation determine the life of the large corporation.

It all begins with a creation story in which corporate governance provisions originate at the transactional margin. In the beginning, owner-managers go public selling equity securities to outsiders. The selling managers make determinant choices of jurisdiction and governing terms. But, because this generative public offering occurs in a competitive market, they have an incentive to choose terms that meet the expectations of the security-holding public. If they offer the wrong terms, they get paid less for their securities.

The story denudes management of significant power to engage in suboptimal self-serving behavior. The purchasing shareholders, being rational economic actors, assume that the selling managers will engage in self-serving behavior at holders' expense. They accordingly bid down the stock. This gives the selling managers an incentive to build in governance devices that control their own misbehavior.

After the moment of creation, market controls take over. Competition in markets for employment, products, and corporate control keeps managers in line. At the same time, stock market prices, which take governance problematics into account, effectively protect new investors by bringing them in at a risk-adjusted rate of return and providing them a low-cost means of evaluating management's performance. Over time, competition in the marketplace favors the survival of maximizing governance terms.

2. *The Presumption Against Regulation.*—The creation story opens the door for one of Easterbrook and Fischel's main points about corporate law: that there should be a presumption against having any more of it than already exists. The actors create governance terms, and the market prices them. Therefore, terms mandated by law are justifiable only if "the terms chosen by firms are *both* unpriced and systematically perverse from investor's standpoints."

Easterbrook and Fischel make their market governance case with care. Their system is substantially—not absolutely—effective. * * * They assume the real world market prices do not perfectly reflect all risks all the time. Even so, Easterbrook and Fischel make a strong claim for institutional primacy for the market price. The market, they say, does the best available evaluative job. The evaluation is thoroughgoing, even extending to governance terms.

Easterbrook and Fischel also stop short of claiming that market forces build an absolute barrier to inefficient managerial self-service. Here the law assists the market, fleshing out voluntary governance terms with gap-filling fiduciary duties. Easterbrook and Fischel's managers also make questionable allocative decisions. But, as to these, Easterbrook and Fischel take a deregulatory position. They make a strong claim respecting investor expectations, asserting that investors do not require legal protection. Risk-averse equity investors protect themselves from this conduct through portfolio diversification. Those who do not diversify fully are not risk averse.

What investors expect, say Easterbrook and Fischel, is whatever maximizes firm value, and, as between longstanding voluntary relations and regulation, the former are entitled to the presumption of efficiency. A showing of wrongdoing does not, in and of itself, justify regulation. Those who argue to the contrary subscribe to the "Nirvana fallacy"—the incorrect assumption that everything can be made perfect. Easterbrook and Fischel counsel against regulation even where a plausible, but arguable, case for a mandated governance improvement has been made. Under the creation story, corporations can always opt-in to the rule in their certificates of incorporation. And, on the rare occasion when the case for intervention is clear cut, deterrent liability rules fare better than regulatory supervision.

* * *

B.   The Disappearing Nexus of Contracts

The foregoing describes Easterbrook and Fischel's going concern without mentioning the nexus-of-contracts corporation. In making this omission, the description follows the lead of the book.

* * *

2.   The Containment [of the Nexus of Contracts Corporation] Explained

Easterbrook and Fischel have stepped back from the nexus-of-contracts corporation because developments in both theory and practice made manifest its inadequacy as a foundation for any plausible legal theory. The theoretical development was the "mandatory/enabling" discussion of the late 1980s. This showed that shareholder-manager relationships did not, in the main, lie within the zone of free contract. The practical development was the failure of crucial subject matter—the law addressed to takeovers—to develop in conformity to the model's predictions. This showed emphatically that corporate law does not always instantiate contractual norms. The fact that these two topics had been the principal focus of corporate legal scholarship for a number of years made these developments doubly debilitating for the proposition that corporations are comprised of a nexus of contracts.

(a) Mandatory corporate law affirmed.—The mandatory/enabling discussion was an extended consideration of the implications of the nexus-of-contract proposition. The proposition on the table was this: If the firm is contract, then the parties in interest should be able to "opt-out" of the terms provided by state law and substitute their own terms. Discussion of this proposition iterated contract law's "overreaching" analysis. It turned out that process defects make the corporate charter amendment an inappropriate context for complete freedom of contract, even when viewed through the lens of an economic model. Shareholders have a collective action problem when managers propose charter amendments. Small stakes make it irrational for individual holders to invest in information acquisition. Moreover, managers, by virtue of their control of the structure and timing of the amendment process, can easily turn the shareholders' disadvantaged negotiating position to their own advantage. The upshot is a contract failure: the shareholders rationally vote to approve an amendment that decreases value to them.

A consensus of sorts emerged from the discussion. The amendment process is deemed reliable as to amendments such as poison pills or stock option plans that are company-specific and transaction-specific. But, as to general, open-ended proposals such as broad-brush abolition of director and officer fiduciary duties, contract failure is probable. Therefore, according to the consensus, charter amendments sometimes should be subject to mandatory regulation even under a contract paradigm.

* * * The consensus confirmed the legitimacy of legal intervention in corporate affairs from an economic perspective. * * * Although no one mentioned it at the time, this also began a process of disassociation between corporate law and economics and the nexus-of-contracts concept of the corporation. The process continues today.

Easterbrook and Fischel joined the mandatory/enabling consensus, albeit with qualifications. * * * In taking this position they do not, of course, expunge contract from their theory of the firm. They still tell a creation story in which free contract reigns. But, since contract turns out to be a matter of degree, the issue goes to the dimensions of the zone of contract freedom provided for by a particular model. Easterbrook and Fischel's zone is rhetorically expansive, but more compact as a practical matter of degree. A blank contracting slate occurs only in respect to recent and prospective initial public offerings. Since most Fortune 500 companies went public long ago, the critical questions respecting most corporations remain legitimate subject matter for legal mandates.

(b) Takeovers reversed.—Takeovers made a contractual picture of the public corporation plausible in the first place. Under the managerialist paradigm of the corporation, managers had unassailable and excessive power. As hostile tender offers proliferated, market actors broke the power of target managers through the simple expedient of purchasing shares. In effect, what was thought unassailable was assailed successfully through the medium of the discrete contract. As discrete contracts came to alter the flow of corporate power, the nexus-of-contracts corporation came into economic and legal theory.

Fittingly, developments begun in the late 1980s in response to takeovers are prompting the nexus-of-contracts corporation's subsequent departure. Shark repellant charter amendments and poison pill plans—"contractual" modifications that entrench management and devalue the shareholders' investment—retained the support of the courts even as they became more widespread and effective. In addition, state legislatures came down emphatically on the side of defending managers. Their antitakeover statutes imposed significant costs on hostile control transfers. Viewed cumulatively, these changes open up a rift between the contract paradigm's implicit normative structure, on the one hand, and that of actual corporate contracts and state corporate law, on the other.

To their credit, Easterbrook and Fischel not only admit, but explore the negative implications of these developments for the contractual corporation. They conclude that takeover law has developed in an inefficient direction. Managers exploit the collective action problem in getting shareholders to assent to shark repellant provisions. And, in the "last period," when managers defend their jobs from attack, the ordinary controls of the capital and labor markets do not operate. Judicial intervention become the only available means to the end of inefficient deployment of assets.

Furthermore, Easterbrook and Fischel abandon the "race to the top" story of state corporate law. * * *

Today, Easterbrook and Fischel speak of the performance of state corporate law with less confidence. In their opinion, while survival still is the best measure of success, state corporate law is a process of satisfying rather than optimizing. No one, moreover, knows what the market wants. Easterbrook and Fischel do find a contractual term to describe the proliferation of antitakeover statutes. * * * They ascribe the legislation to management "opportunism." But this is bravado. Their model no longer fuses state law together with contract so as to make economics the sole determinant of the law's evolution.

————

Developments in the late 1980s, including the increased prominence of institutional investors and growing disenchantment with hostile takeovers as a central component of the corporate governance system, also led scholars to reexamine Berle and Means' assumptions as to the causes of the divorce of ownership from control in American corporations. Mark Roe, in particular, has argued effectively that patterns of corporate ownership and control in the United States are in large part a product of political rather than economic forces.

MARK J. ROE, STRONG MANAGERS AND WEAK OWNERS: THE POLITICAL ROOTS OF THE SEPARATION OF OWNERSHIP FROM CONTROL
(forthcoming, 1994).

The public corporation—with its fragmented shareholders buying and selling on the stock exchange—is the dominant form of enterprise in the United States. Why? The conventional paradigm accepted by most corporate law academics is economic. Technology dictated large enterprises as an engineering matter. The large through-put technologies that developed at the end of the 19th century—double the diameter of the pipe and the engineer quadrupled the pipe's through-put—meant cheaper production accrued to the firm with the largest scale. Only America had a continent-wide economy with low internal trade barriers, providing a market to those who could achieve the technologically feasible large-scale efficiencies. But to get the tremendous outputs from the new scale economies required tremendous capital inputs to build (via construction and merger) the facilities and distribution system.

Individuals, even a handful of individuals, lacked sufficient capital. * * * Even John Rockefeller in his heyday—the richest man in America—held only a fraction of Standard Oil. The new large-scale enterprises eventually had to draw capital from many dispersed shareholders, who demanded diversification. And when the founders passed from the scene, salaried managers, not investors, took day-to-day control of the operations. This combination of a huge enterprise, concentrated management, and dispersed diversified stockholders shifted corporate control from shareholders to managers. Without their own money on the line, these managers could pursue their own agenda, sometimes to the detriment of the enterprise. Dispersed shareholders and concentrated management became the quintessential characteristics of the large American firm.

* * *

Separation of ownership and control was functional, allowing skilled managers without capital to run the firm and separating unskilled descendants from control of a firm they could not run well. Dispersed individuals would hold the stock, frequently in 100–share lots. Institutions would neither hold nor vote big blocks of stock. Banks held none .or their own account. Insurers rarely held stock for most of the twentieth century. Mutual funds and pensions have only recently become an important economic phenomenon. They hold stock in small parcels, usually too small to have much influence.

* * *

The control and play of capital is likely to attract more than a little political attention; how a nation regulates capital's deployment will affect how large firms are organized. The history of American financial fragmentation, the existence for decades of different governance systems abroad, and the modest contemporary concentration of institutional ownership in America all suggest that there is more than one way to move capital to large firms, and that the American-style public corporation is more a local custom than the universal highest evolutionary form.

America's path to the large firm with fragmented ownership might not have been the inevitable result of the marketplace, but of the political economy of American financial history. Quite a bit of evidence indicates that American politics deliberately fragmented financial institutions, their portfolios, and their ability to network stock into influential blocks. If so, one could hypothesize that had American political history taken a different path, American financial intermediaries would be different, and the structure of authority in the American large public firm might also be different.

Contractarian thought is one key branch of the economic model. It comes in two forms: The descriptive forms says most corporate law in fact is contractarian; corporate law is a standard contract that shareholders and managers can vary at will. That is, a demystified contractarian corporation is a set of contracts among shareholders and managers. * * * But contractarians (and I am not wholly excluding myself here), who tend to look at state corporate law—particularly Delaware corporate law—to find how law governs the relationship between shareholders and managers, may have misidentified the key arenas for corporate contract-making. True, the state law legal framework roughly corresponds with what contractarian thought would prescribe. But what if it turns out that the key relationships between shareholders and managers are found neither in state corporate law, nor in federal securities law, but in the deep historical regulations governing financial institutions? What if the law prohibited key aggregations of stockholding, that which would occur through financial institutions? What if law did this deliberately for political reasons, not primarily to foster financial safety?

If these financial rules were critical, then the contractarian branch of the economic model would have to be rethought. The prescriptive form could survive; contractarians would want to examine financial rules to see whether they reflect a standard-form contract. The descriptive form would be weakened; it could survive, but only if seriously down-sized. Contractarians would concede that financial rules shaped the division of authority inside the large public firm, and that only when those financial rules are assumed as exogenous, given, and immutable, does the contractarian framework come into play. Contract-making between shareholders and managers would not occur just to resolve economic problems, principally of agency cost, but to resolve those economic problems in a manner restricted by American law and politics.

The prevailing paradigm is that the modern corporation survived because it was the fittest means of dealing with large-scale organization. But if politics cut off lines of development, as I shall argue, then whether it is the inevitable form for large-scale firms becomes doubtful. Politics and the organization of financial intermediaries cannot be left out of the equation. Although I am less hawkish on whether a serious economic cost results from the different form, it's plausible that at least some costs are incurred and whether there are big efficiency costs becomes a serious question for inquiry.

Today, the costs of the Berle–Means corporation are seen as necessary. To make an omelet one must crack eggs; to light your room one must waste energy via the lightbulb's heat. Package deal. In the standard paradigm, the costs are a necessary trade-off, part of the price paid to get the productive benefits of the large firm. But if we could create large firms through other means of getting capital from households to large firms, then whether these costs are truly necessary becomes an open question.

My thesis in this book is not to displace that part of the current paradigm that reflects the historical emergence of technology, scale economies, and far-flung investors. Rather, the point is to displace the paradigm's next analytical step, that these developments necessarily had to yield fragmented firm ownership, with distant shareholders and all-powerful management (or, more accurately, my goal is to insert an excluded step, that these technological developments could have led to powerful shareholding institutions). The classical theory can survive as an explanation for the American corporation—and it does explain a lot of the firm's features—but only after financial institutions are assumed to be fragmented. If a nation does not fragment its financial system, or if a nation builds other means of corporate governance—by privileging labor or managers or financiers, for example—then different organizations emerge.

* * *

Another paradigm, a political paradigm, better explains the modern American corporation than the prevailing paradigm does alone. * * * The size and technology story fails to fully explain ownership patterns. There are organizational alternatives to fragmented ownership; the most prominent concentrated institutional ownership, a result prevalent in other countries. Enterprises could have obtained economies of scale and investors could have obtained diversification through large financial intermediaries that brought small investors and large firms together. These institutions could have shared power in the enterprise with the new managers. But American law and politics deliberately diminished the power of financial institutions to hold the large equity blocks that would foster serious oversight of managers, including the adaptations I've noted in prior sections. The origin of the modern corporation lies in technology, economics, and politics.

Think about it. Fragmented securities markets are not the only way to move savings from households to the large firm. One could move savings from people to firms directly through securities markets, or indirectly through large financial intermediaries, which could then take big blocks of stock, sit in boardrooms, and balance power with the CEO. The increasing institutionalization of American securities markets and the concentrated ownership abroad mean this was economically viable. As I've said, I am less hawkish on the prescriptive form of the thesis— that an important efficiency has been lost—than I am on the historical form of the thesis. The institutional alternatives would raise a distinctive set of problems: bad management in the intermediary, instability of the intermediary, and political discomfort with concentrated private accumulations of power. All these are possible, but do not refute the proposition that there is more than one way to organize large scale enterprise, and that the short list of alternatives has at least one clear contender with the securities markets, namely the powerful financial intermediary.

* * *

B. HOW SHAREHOLDERS ACT

PROBLEM
UNIVERSAL MOTORS CORPORATION—PART I

Universal Motors Corporation (UMC) is a Delaware corporation whose common stock is traded on the NASDAQ system. It presently has 100 million shares of common stock outstanding. The officers and directors of the company own approximately 20 percent of the stock and financial institutions own another 55 percent. In recent months its stock price has been about $20 per share which is close to its all-time low. As a consequence, UMC's management is afraid of a possible takeover.

At the December meeting of the UMC board, management raised its concerns and presented a list of alternative defensive tactics that UMC's general counsel had suggested the board might adopt. Redd, an outside director who is the CEO of a large corporation in which his family owns 40% of the stock, said his board had concluded that the most effective takeover defense was a dual-class recapitalization plan. Accordingly, he proposed that UMC adopt a plan under which the articles of incorporation would be amended to create two classes of common stock, Class A and Class B. Each share of Class A stock would have one vote and would be entitled to such dividends as the board declared. By contrast, each share of Class B stock would have ten votes and be entitled, on a per share basis, to 90 percent of any dividend paid to the holders of the Class A stock. If the arrangement were approved by the shareholders, all outstanding common stock would become Class A stock unless, within 30 days, the shareholder elected to receive Class B stock. Class A stock would not be convertible into Class B stock at any subsequent date.

If all officers and directors of UMC were to convert their stock into Class B stock, they would have more than 50% of the total voting power unless the public holders of more than 13 million shares also converted their common stock into Class B stock.* Redd said that based on what had happened at his company, such conversion by the public holders was unlikely because most of them seemed more interested in larger dividends than in greater voting rights. And if management ended with more than 50% of UMC's voting power, it would have the ability to elect the entire board of UMC and to adopt any measures of which it approved, including those designed to further deter all uninvited takeover bids.

Management agreed to review Redd's proposal and to present a firm recommendation to the board for discussion at its February meeting.

A

You are a lawyer in UMC's outside law firm. Shortly after the board meeting, the president of UMC sought your advice about the proposed dual-class recapitalization plan.

1) She pointed out that management's stockholdings in UMC represent only about half of the interest that Redd's family owns in their corporation. Moreover, UMC has far more institutional shareholders. "Is it likely," she asked, "that UMC's shareholders will approve a dual-class recapitalization plan, assuming that there is no organized opposition to such a plan? Where might the opposition come from?

2) The CEO also asked you whether UMC can lawfully adopt a dual-class recapitalization plan, or whether such a plan could be found to violate either Delaware or federal law. The CEO also is concerned about

---

* That is, if management acquires 20 million Class B shares, it will have 200 million votes. If public shareholders convert 13 million shares, those shareholders will have 130 million votes. The remaining public shareholders will hold 67 million Class A shares and will have 67 million votes. The total voting power of the public shares, 197 million votes, will then be less than the voting power of the management group. Conversion by public shareholders of less than 13 million shares will, of course, increase the disparity in the voting power of public shareholders and the management group.

whether, assuming such plans are not now invalid, it seems likely that the Delaware legislature or the U.S. Congress will act to outlaw such plans because they seem to conflict with widely held notions of corporate democracy.

How do you respond to her questions?

B

At its February meeting, the UMC board adopted a resolution recommending that UMC's shareholders approve an amendment to the articles of incorporation implementing a dual-class recapitalization plan essentially in the form outlined above. UMC's general counsel has advised you that both she and the board believe that it would be a good idea for UMC to issue a press release announcing the board's action. She is aware that if the press release violated any S.E.C. rules, that might complicate the plan to have the amendments considered at the upcoming annual meeting of UMC shareholders. In particular, she is concerned about whether the proxy rules, especially Rules 14a–1 and 14a–3 would be violated if the release:

a) Announced the board's decision; contained a brief description of the plan; said that it would be put to a shareholder vote in June; and stated that the board had adopted a resolution recommending that the shareholders adopt the plan.

b) In addition to the above, explained that management and the board believe that the plan is in the best interests of UMC's shareholders because it ensures the continuity of UMC's management, removes concern about uninvited takeover bids, and thus enhances management's ability to promote the long-term interests of UMC and its shareholders.

How do you respond to her questions?

C

Assume that UMC issued an appropriate press release. Herbert Rogers, an investor with a large and diversified stock portfolio that includes 1,000 shares of UMC common stock, read about the plan and reacted indignantly to it as an effort by UMC's management to entrench itself in office. Rogers would like to mobilize other UMC shareholders to vote against the proposed plan, but has no interest in attempting to oust the incumbent board or seek control of UMC.

You are a lawyer experienced in advising participants in proxy contests. Rogers has asked you what procedures he would have to follow, and what costs he is likely to incur if he were to (1) publicize his views against the plan and/or (2) encourage other shareholders to vote against the plan. Rogers is concerned, among other things, about the possibility that UMC will attempt to embroil him in costly litigation. Rogers also is interested in your view as to the likelihood of successfully defeating the adoption of the plan.

How do you respond to Rogers' questions?

D

The Columbia Employees Retirement Fund (CERF) is one of UMC's largest institutional shareholders, owning approximately 1 percent of UMC's stock. Elaine Meadows, the state treasurer is in charge of CERF's investment and voting decisions. Meadows, an elected official, is seriously considering running for governor next year. Like Rogers, Meadows is offended by dual-class recapitalization plans. Based on informal talks at meetings of pension fund managers, she is confident that some other funds could be convinced to vote against UMC's proposal, but she is not sure how widespread this opposition might be.

You are a lawyer in the law firm that advises CERF on issues relating to its investments, including voting decisions. Meadows has asked you the following questions:

1) If CERF seeks to convince other shareholders to vote against the plan, what requirements under the proxy rules would apply to its activities?

2) How likely is it that other institutions can be convinced to vote against the plan? Are all of UMC's institutional shareholders likely to adopt the same position, or is CERF likely to need the support of individual shareholders for the campaign to succeed?

3) Can Meadows carry on a campaign to defeat the plan consistent with her fiduciary responsibilities to CERF's beneficiaries? Alternatively, could such a campaign trigger any other potential liabilities under the federal securities laws?

4) What criticisms might Meadows face if CERF chose to actively oppose the plan? How might she respond to those criticisms?

How do you respond to Meadows' questions?

1. INTRODUCTION

We have already seen that most corporation statutes require that a corporation hold an annual meeting of stockholders to elect the board of directors. There is also a requirement that the stockholders approve certain transactions that affect the structure of a corporation, such as amendments to the articles of incorporation, mergers, and sales of assets. Finally, most corporation statutes permit stockholders to amend corporate by-laws.

In the largest corporations, many thousands of stockholders are scattered throughout the country, each holding a relatively small number of shares. It is simply impossible to convene the stockholders at one time and place to consider and act upon the matters that require their approval. The substitute process that permits effective stockholder action is proxy voting.

The authorization for stockholders to vote by proxy is found in state corporation statutes, of which RMBCA § 7.22 is typical. First, the statute permits shareholders to vote in person or by proxy. Second, it limits the validity of the proxy to a period of 11 months from the date of its execution unless the appointment form specifies a longer period. Under certain circumstances, not relevant in the public corporation, the shareholder can make her appointment of a proxy irrevocable.

As we saw in Chapter 12, "proxy" is simply another word for agent. Ordinarily, one thinks of a principal conferring power upon an agent to accomplish the principal's business. The shareholder's appointment of a proxy, or agent, to act on her behalf at the shareholder meeting is quite different. Most striking is the fact that in connection with voting at the meeting, it is the agents (who are usually members of the management) rather than the principal who solicit the agency relationship. Because the stockholders who grant the proxy (the principals) are scattered throughout the country, there is arguably a federal interest in the proxy solicitation process.

The body of law that regulates this process marks one of the great intersections of federal and state law. State law validates the process of proxy voting, and federal law prescribes the conditions on which it may proceed. Congress delegated the specifics of federal proxy regulation to the Securities and Exchange Commission, whose rules are described later in this section.

The main emphasis of the federal securities laws is disclosure. The legislative history of SEC proxy regulation indicates that the Congressional concern was to provide "fair corporate suffrage." H.R.Rep. No. 1383, 73d Cong., 2d Sess. 2, 13–14 (1934). The SEC's operating theory is that fairness is achieved by adequately informing investors so that they can make an informed choice. The SEC also has tried to neutralize, to a limited extent, the effect of management's control of the proxy soliciting process. Its rules prescribe the form of the proxy document creating the formal agency power, define the scope of the agent's power, and require management to provide an opportunity to shareholders to vote on matters that other shareholders intend to bring before the meeting.

On closer examination, "fair suffrage" often is closely related to the substantive fairness of the corporate transaction on which the shareholders are voting. Thus the extent of the federal involvement in corporate law through its regulation of proxies is more substantial than appears at first. Although state law may require a shareholder vote on a particular transaction, it rarely prescribes the specific information that must be furnished to shareholders before they vote; those requirements are determined primarily by federal law. For example, a merger requires shareholder approval under state law. State law does not require the solicitation of proxies to obtain that approval, but if, as is customary in large corporations, a solicitation is undertaken, it is largely regulated by federal law. If the terms of the merger are unfair, shareholders may seek their remedies under state law. If the terms of the merger are not correctly or fairly described in the proxy solicitation (a failing that often accompanies unfairness in the deal), that failure creates a federal claim giving rise to federal remedies. A federal court would have to ponder whether certain aspects of the deal were so significant to an investor's decision that disclosure was required. The answer to that question may entail a federal inquiry into whether the terms of the merger were substantively fair—a question one would have thought to be solely one of state law. For reasons which will become clearer, shareholders often prefer to argue over disclosure rather than substantive fairness, but the underlying issues often are the same. Framing the issue as one of full disclosure federalizes the controversy. The question of the federalization of state corporation law will be considered in greater detail in Chapter 18.

Another important path that crosses the federal-state intersection is the role of self-regulatory organizations. While state law authorizes voting by proxies, and federal law conditions the solicitation of proxies upon compliance with federal law, nothing in either federal or state law requires management to solicit proxies. Yet the proxy solicitation process both informs investors and allows them a degree of participation in the decision. Both the New York Stock Exchange and the American Stock Exchange, in their general rules, policies, and procedures relating to listed companies, state that companies whose securities are listed on those exchanges are required to solicit proxies for all meetings of stockholders.

2. THE COLLECTIVE ACTION PROBLEM

As the materials in Section A suggest, one way by which shareholders can voice their disapproval of corporate management is to vote against proposals with which they do not agree. Yet shareholders only infrequently use their franchise as an effective monitoring device.

ROBERT CHARLES CLARK, CORPORATE LAW
pp. 389–394 (1986).

From an economic point of view, there is a strong argument that the power to control a business firm's activities should reside in those who have the right to the firm's residual earnings, that is, those earnings that are left over when all fixed and definite obligations of the firm have been provided for. The intuition behind this argument is that giving control to the residual claimants will place the power to monitor the performance of participants in the firm and the power to control shirking, waste, and so forth in the hands of those who have the best incentive to use the power.

To be sure, the nature of the modern firm complicates this argument, since the benefits of managerial expertise and the need to prevent wasteful duplication of decision making have led to a professional class of managers distinct from public shareholders. Managers have control over ordinary business operations, even though they do not have full ownership rights to their firm's residual earnings. (Of course, they usually own substantial residual claims because of stock option programs and similar arrangements.) Yet it can still be argued that ultimate control ought to reside in the ultimate claimants on the residual earnings.

This viewpoint supports the conclusion that common shareholders should possess voting rights that, at a minimum, give them the power to select or remove the directors and, therefore, the indirect power to control the identity of top management. We could argue further that voting rights should be proportional to one's share of the residual interest in the firm. Otherwise, there would be some misalignment between the power and the incentive to monitor and enforce company performance.

* * *

Whenever shareholders of a publicly held company vote upon matters affecting the corporation, they engage in collective action that suffers from many systemic difficulties. Such difficulties include "rational apathy" of shareholders, the temptation of individual shareholders to take a "free ride," and unfairness to certain shareholders even where collective action is successful.

Often the aggregate cost to shareholders of informing themselves of potential corporate actions, independently assessing the wisdom of such actions, and casting their votes will greatly exceed the expected or actual benefits garnered from informed voting. Recognition of this phenomenon accounts for the usual rules that entrust corporate management with all ordinary business decisions. But the same problem still exists with respect to the major subjects of shareholder voting: the election of directors and the approval or rejection of major organic changes such as mergers.

Consider a simplified case. Outta Control Corp., with 1 million voting common shares outstanding, has 10,000 shareholders, each of whom owns 1 block of 100 shares. The directors propose a plan to merge Outta Control into Purchaser Corp., which would result in the acquisition by the former Outta Control shareholders, in exchange for their old shares, of voting common shares in Purchaser with a total market value of $50 million. In fact, Purchaser would have been willing to exchange $60 million worth of its shares if it had not agreed, under prodding by Outta Control's managers and in return for their cooperation in recommending the merger, to give extraordinary salary increases to those officers of Outta Control who would continue their employment after the merger. Payments would also be made to departing officers under so-called consulting and noncompetition agreements. Moreover, a majority of Outta Control's directors are not officers and would seek a new merger agreement at a much higher price if the current proposal were not approved by the shareholders.

Assume that all of this information is contained in a 240 page proxy statements that is sent to Outta Control's shareholders and that any rational shareholder who reads it would decide to vote against the merger. Assume further that if the merger proposal were disapproved, a new one would be adopted that would yield these shareholders the additional $10 million gain which Purchaser Corp. was prepared to pay. Thus, the actual benefit to be derived from collective shareholder action against the merger plan would be $1000 per shareholder.

Shareholders do not expect, however, to discover a reason for concluding that disapproval will avert a corporate harm or open the door to a larger corporate gain every time they read a proxy statement. To make our problem complete, assume that the shareholders in it make a rational assessment of the probabilities of such an occurrence. Because of their assessment, they assign an expected benefit of $50 per shareholder to collective action of the sort described, that is, action based on each shareholder's reading the proxy statement, making up his mind, and voting.

Now suppose the average cost of informed shareholder action is simply the opportunity cost[4] of reading the proxy statement before sending in the proxy card and that this amount is $120 per shareholder (three hours of reading at $40 per hour—a rather low estimate). Thus the total cost of collective action would be $1.2 million. This cost would still be less than the actual benefit to be gained in this case, from collective action by informed voters. But the cost of such collective action greatly exceeds the expected benefit—$120 versus $50 per shareholder—so sensible shareholders will not read the proxy statement. They will be rationally apathetic. At the same time, management will be shielded from shareholder policing of their fiduciary duties, thereby allowing them to receive compensation that is unnecessary to induce their services.

One legal approach toward improving the efficiency of collective action is to make it cheaper for each shareholder to act in an informed way. Suppose that in our example the opportunity cost of reading the proxy statement concerning the proposed merger were only $10 per shareholder, because the SEC had devised a system of proxy rules that produced extremely concise, quickly understandable proxy statements that emphasize crucial data. Suppose that the SEC also monitors the statement and requires that the crucial information appear in bold face type. The expected benefit of collective action by informed voting is still $50 per shareholder, but the cost of such action is now only $10 per shareholder. The net expected benefit is therefore $40 per shareholder.

Yet the desired collective action still may not occur. Any one shareholder may realize that only 50 percent of the shareholders are needed to block the merger. If the shareholder believes that enough

---

4. The cost attributable to doing one thing to the exclusion of another stems from opportunity sacrificed to pursue the chosen course. This sacrifice is called "opportunity cost."

other shareholders will respond to the incentive of the $40 net expected benefit and will act accordingly to produce the desirable collective result, he might decide to save himself the cost of reading the streamlined proxy statement. He can still participate in any benefits of collective action that arise through the work of the other shareholders. He will be a free rider on their efforts. The net expected benefit of his action as a free rider would be $50 rather than $40.

Of course, it may also occur to him that if all the other shareholders thought similarly, no collective action would be taken, and everyone would lose the chance of reaping the benefits. He might realize that giving in to the temptation to achieve an individual gain superior to everyone else's would jeopardize the attainment of collective benefits. Conceivably this realization might prompt him to read the proxy statement. But it is doubtful whether this would happen in practice and, as a matter of theory (game theory, that is), a rational, self-interested shareholder would not do so.[5] The situation is like the prisoner's dilemma of game theory and may call for solutions similar in strategy to those that would solve that dilemma.*

* * *

Let us again alter the hypothetical so that the free rider problem, like the rational apathy problem, effectively disappears. Suppose that one shareholder, Ajax, owns 200,000 shares, while every other shareholder owns only one block of 100 shares. The other facts remain the same. The expected benefit to Ajax is now $100,000, which is, let us assume, more than the expected cost of reading the proxy statement and convincing the holders of 300,100 others shares also to vote against the merger. (He would do this by waging a proxy contest—a technique discussed in the next subsection.) Unless it deeply galls Ajax to think that he will be treated unfairly, he will take action to achieve the collective benefit even if he cannot be reimbursed for the costs and risks of such action.[7] Acting strictly for his own benefit, he will nevertheless have created a collective good for all the other shareholders in the company. The smaller shareholders will get the benefit of his concern without bearing a

---

5. Why not? Because, whether he assumes the other shareholders will read or will not read, he will expect to be better off if he doesn't. Assume the others will read: His own expected benefit is $50 if he doesn't read, and $40 if he does. Assume the others will not read (so the original merger plan goes through): His own expected benefit is $0 if he doesn't read, but minus $10 if he does.

* Two persons have been arrested for bank robbery and each is interrogated by the police in separate rooms. Each is told that if she alone confesses, she will receive a sentence of two years, but that if her companion confesses while she refuses, then she will receive a ten year sentence. Each is also told that a confession from both will produce a six year sentence. Of course, each one understands that silence from both will produce no sentence. The six year term is the predicted result, since neither can risk silence and the ten year sentence.—Eds.

7. We can assume that Ajax will not try to be a free rider because his particular expected benefit is so high that he would not risk depending on action by other shareholders.

pro rata share of cost. This phenomenon is an example of what one economist calls the systematic exploitation of the large by the small.

The obvious problem here is one of fairness to the guardian shareholder. Less obviously, problems of allocative efficiency may also arise. The prospect of being taken advantage of by the smaller shareholders may deter investors from becoming dominant shareholders in the first place. The problem once again resembles the prisoner's dilemma, but in this situation the players are all investors as they contemplate buying into any publicly held corporation. But in the real world there are many factors that tempt investors to obtain large percentage interests in companies, not the least of which is the chance of acquiring the various special benefits of controlling the corporation on an ongoing basis. Any force toward misallocation created by the phenomenon of exploitation of the large by the small is likely to be more than offset by these factors. Thus, the only remaining problem will be unfair treatment of the large, but not controlling, shareholder who undertakes a proxy contest or similar action for the corporation's benefit.

3. DUAL CLASS VOTING: CORPORATE GOVERNANCE AND FEDERAL REGULATION

In most public corporations, each share of common stock is entitled to cast one vote. This "one share, one vote" norm is not the product of state law. Most state statutes require only that some voting rights be assigned to one class of common stock and otherwise authorize both nonvoting common stock and common stock with multiple votes per share. See RMBCA § 6.01; DGCL § 151.

A one share, one vote capital structure is consistent with the theoretical view that holders of common stock, because they bear the residual risk of profit and loss, are the persons most likely to exercise responsible control over a company's managers. Such a structure, however, is not inevitable; indeed, until the end of the nineteenth century, there were efforts made to restrict the voting power of large shareholders. And in some countries with civil law systems, the corporate law either restricts the number of votes that a shareholder may cast or authorizes such restrictions if placed in the articles of incorporation. See David L. Ratner, The Government of Business Corporations: Critical Reflections on the Rule of "One Share, One Vote," 56 Corn. L. Rev. 1 (1970).

Why, then, have shareholder voting and the one share, one vote capital structure endured in the United States? Not because shareholder votes frequently are important, but because, when contests for control arise, what might best be described as the shareholders' residual voting power becomes critically important. A person outside a company's management can purchase a majority of the company's stock, or otherwise mobilize the support of the owners of a majority of the stock, and then use the voting rights she has acquired or mobilized to replace the incumbent directors with directors she has chosen. It is this potential, not the shareholders' annual endorsement of management's nominees and proposals, that makes shareholder voting important in the operation of the corporate governance system.

From the late 1970s through the 1980s, there was an active market for corporate control. Both entrepreneurial investors and established companies sought control of public corporations over the opposition of the targets' managers. Most bidders made cash tender offers for all or a majority of their target's stock. A few sought control through proxy solicitations directed at the target's existing shareholders.

Managers of many companies reacted by taking steps to reduce the possibility that they would become the targets of uninvited takeover bids. Frequently, they proposed changes in the governance structure of their firm, dubbed "shark repellents" that were designed to impede or defeat uninvited takeover bids. Although almost all shark repellents put to a shareholder vote were approved, they failed to deter determined acquirors. Successful bidders then usually found that incumbent directors bowed to the inevitable and resigned, even where shark repellents would have allowed them to remain in office until their terms expired.

The failure of these devices led to the development of a second generation of takeover defenses. Two of these seemed to have the potential to be "showstoppers"—defenses no hostile acquiror would attempt to overcome. One, the "poison pill," a term used to describe the right to purchase stock or debt structured so as to make an uninvited takeover bid prohibitively expensive, is discussed in Chapter 22. The other was dual-class common stock, a capital structure in which one class of common stock had one vote per share and a second class of common stock had multiple votes per share.

Dual-class common stock was particularly attractive to managers or a family group who already controlled a substantial block of a corporation's stock. If the control group could acquire high-vote common stock, say with 10 votes per share, while the remaining stockholders held ordinary common stock, with one vote per share, the control group could control the election of the company's directors by holding as little as 10 percent of the company's total common stock. For example, assume a company with 100 shares. If the control group holds 10 high-vote shares, it will cast 100 votes (10 times 10 votes per share). Public shareholders, holding the remaining 90 ordinary shares, will be able to cast only 90 votes.

To implement a dual-class common stock plan, two steps were required. First, shareholders had to approve a charter amendment that authorized the issuance of high-vote common stock. Then, some arrangement had to be made to distribute the high-vote stock to the control group and, more importantly, to ensure that a potential acquiror could not buy high-vote stock.

Corporations commonly employed two mechanisms to this end. Some distributed high-vote stock to all shareholders, subject to prohibitions on the transfer of such stock except to family members of a beneficial owner or to trusts for the benefit of family members. Any transfer in violation of this prohibition, including transfer to a potential acquiror, would result in automatic conversion of the high-vote stock into ordinary common stock.

Other corporations sought to make the high-vote stock unattractive to ordinary shareholders by limiting the dividends payable on that stock to 90 percent of the dividends payable on ordinary common stock. Then, they gave all shareholders a one-time option to convert their ordinary common stock into high-vote common stock, with the expectation that few shareholders outside the control group would decide to convert. Alternatively, they distributed high-vote (but lower dividend) common stock to all shareholders and gave them the option of converting it into ordinary common stock. In many instances, companies also restricted the transferability of the high-vote common stock. See, generally, Jeffrey N. Gordon, Ties That Bond: Dual Class Common Stock and the Problem of Shareholder Choice, 76 Calif.L.Rev. 1, 39–42 (1988).

State law, although not appearing to call into question the validity of such plans, precluded the use of strong-arm tactics to secure shareholder approval of dual-class common stock plans, see Lacos Land Co. v. Arden Group, Inc., 517 A.2d 271 (Del.Ch.1986) (enjoining dual-class plan where CEO had threatened to act in violation of his fiduciary duties if shareholders did not approve plan). A New York Stock Exchange (NYSE) rule posed a more severe obstacle. For more than 60 years, the NYSE had required that all the common stock of every company listed on the exchange had to have one vote per share. See New York Stock Exchange Listed Company Manual, § 313.00. This requirement made implementing a dual-class common stock plan problematic, at least for listed companies.

There was, however, competitive pressure on the NYSE to modify its one share, one vote rule. In 1984, General Motors had issued a new class of common stock, with only one-half vote per share, to finance its acquisition of Electronic Data Systems. The NYSE, reluctant to delist General Motors, declared a moratorium on enforcement of the rule. Within two years, 46 NYSE-listed companies issued stock that violated the rule, most of it in connection with dual-class common stock plans, and well over 100 non-NYSE companies also implemented such plans. If the NYSE insisted on enforcing its rule, corporations could simply list their stock on the American Stock Exchange or have it traded through the NASDAQ system.

In 1985, the NYSE proposed to amend its rule to allow common stock with disparate voting rights to be listed, provided that shareholders had approved the disparate voting rights plan. The NYSE then sought SEC approval of the proposed amendment, as it was required to do by Section 19(c) of the Securities Exchange Act of 1934. The SEC held public hearings and solicited comments on whether it should (1) require the NYSE to retain its one share, one vote rule; (2) require additional safeguards before allowing listed companies to adopt dual class common stock plans; or (3) adopt a uniform one share, one vote rule applicable to all exchanges and NASDAQ. The last option would effectively impose a one share, one vote rule on all publicly-traded corporations.

Commentators supporting the NYSE proposal emphasized three lines of argument: "(1) sound economic and policy reasons exist for permitting companies to adopt disparate voting rights plans; (2) there is no empirical evidence that the adoption of disparate voting rights plans affects share prices adversely; and (3) corporate governance matters, such as shareholder voting rights, fall within the realm of state rather than federal control. * * *" Securities Exchange Act Release No. 34–34263 (June 22, 1987).

Other commentators "offered several reasons why they believed disparate voting rights plans should be prohibited. First, they believed that the shareholder vote is an essential element in corporate accountability." Id. Second, they questioned whether a shareholder vote to ratify a disparate voting rights plan effectively protects against management abuse or provides a legitimate means to protect shareholders' rights. Some disputed the significance of studies that concluded that disparate voting rights plans did not reduce significantly shareholder wealth. One suggested that the best measure of the diminution of shareholder wealth such plans produce is the premiums that public shareholders typically receive when managers obtain control by purchasing such shareholders' stock in leveraged buy-out transactions.

Following these hearings, the SEC adopted Rule 19c–4, effectively barring trading in the stock of any domestic corporation that issued securities or took other corporate actions that nullified, restricted, or disparately reduced the per share voting rights of outstanding common stock. Id. However, the Commission did not seek to restrict sale of low-vote or non-voting common stock in initial public offerings. The following excerpt explains the Commission's reasoning.

SECURITIES AND EXCHANGE COMMISSION
Voting Rights Listing Standards; Disenfranchisement Rule.
Release No. 34–25891; 53 FR 26376 July 12, 1988.

III. DISCUSSION

* * * In proposing Rule 19c–4, the Commission recognized that regulation of shareholder voting rights under the Federal securities laws raises difficult and complex issues. The Commission noted that the initial NYSE proposal to abandon its one share, one vote standard had important ramifications for management accountability, tender offers and changes in corporate control, the rights of majority and minority shareholders, competition among SROs, and the integrity of the nation's securities markets. The Commission continues to believe that the issue of shareholder voting rights has far-reaching implications, and that a

rule ensuring a minimum level of shareholder protection from disenfranchising actions is appropriate and consistent with the purposes of the Act. Further, the Rule, which will operate through the listing standards of SROs, has been crafted to be consistent with federalism objectives by seeking to minimize intrusion into traditional state regulation. * * *

While certain disparate voting rights plans serve to disenfranchise existing shareholders, the Commission * * * agrees that there may be valid business or economic reasons for issuing disparate voting rights stock. * * * The Commission believes, however, that disparate voting rights plans that disenfranchise existing shareholders are inconsistent with the requirements of the Act. Shareholders who purchase voting shares in a company do so with the understanding that the shares will be accompanied by the voting rights attendant to the stock at the time of purchase. The diminution or limitation of these rights is inconsistent with the investor protection and fair corporate suffrage policies embodied in * * * the Act. * * *

The Commission recognizes that under state law, disparate voting rights plans generally are permitted subject to shareholder approval. The Commission also recognizes, however, that collective action problems may make defeating an issuer recapitalization proposal extremely difficult. * * * Frequently, a disparate voting rights plan is presented to shareholders in a form, such as an offer to exchange higher vote stock for lower vote stock with a dividend sweetener, that provides shareholders with an incentive to accept less than full voting rights stock rather than oppose the recapitalization, although, acting collectively, shareholders as a group might prefer to retain their voting rights and reject the sweetener offered by management. The coercive nature of some disparate voting rights plans may also be exacerbated by management's ability to set the proxy agenda and use corporate funds to lobby shareholders in favor of its proposal. The Commission also has heard testimony from institutional investors describing the pressure placed on managers of corporate pension plans during the shareholder voting process.

Although the Commission does not believe that shareholders invariably are powerless to defeat an issuer-sponsored proposal to recapitalize, the Commission does believe that, because of the forces cited above, the shareholder voting process is not fully effective in preventing the adoption of disparate voting rights plans that disenfranchise shareholders. The Commission believes that it is preferable for a company's insiders wishing to gain voting control to do so through a repurchase of shares in which such repurchase is subject to market discipline and judicial review regarding state corporate fiduciary requirements. * * *

The Commission has reviewed the empirical evidence regarding the wealth impact of disparate voting rights plans on common stock price. * * * [T]he measurement of immediate change in securities price is not a complete indicator of the negative effects of disenfranchising actions. As several commentators have suggested, the negative effects of a permanent deprivation of shareholder voting rights may not appear until some time after the disenfranchising action is announced or occurs, and may be impossible to measure precisely at the time of enactment. For example, loss of independent shareholder control in a company may not manifest itself until sometime in the future through a lower takeover premium offered for the company's shares, or through management actions undertaken without the discipline of accountability to shareholders.[81]

* * *

Finally, in adopting Rule 19c–4, * * * the Commission does not seek to prohibit issuers from issuing stock with restricted or no voting rights, as those restrictions are a consideration the investor will take into account when deciding to purchase a security. Rather, the Commission seeks to prevent the deprivation of voting rights that occurs after a security has been purchased. * * * We believe this approach is consistent with the role of the Commission in regulating the public securities markets for the protection of investors. Rule 19c–4 identifies those situations in which shareholders are disenfranchised and prohibits companies from continued access to the national securities marketplace if they take such action. In doing so, Rule 19c–4 is consistent with the federalism objective of minimal intrusion into areas of traditional state regulation.

BUSINESS ROUNDTABLE v. SECURITIES AND EXCHANGE COMMISSION
905 F.2d 406 (D.C.Cir.1990).

STEPHEN F. WILLIAMS, CIRCUIT JUDGE:

In 1984 General Motors announced a plan to issue a second class of common stock with one-half vote per share. The proposal collided with a longstanding rule of the New York Stock Exchange that required listed companies to provide one vote per share of common stock. The NYSE balked at enforcement, and after two years filed a proposal with the Securities and Exchange Commission to relax its own rule. The SEC did not approve the rule change but responded with one of its own. On July

---

81. Recent transactions involving Resorts International illustrate this point. In 1986, there were 5.7 million shares of Class A stock outstanding, having one vote each, and 750,000 shares of Class B stock outstanding with 100 votes each. The Class B stock represented less than 12% of the outstanding shares but had 93% of the voting power. In early 1986, the Class B stock generally traded at a 2–3 point premium (5–7.5%) above the Class A stock, within the 50 dollar range. After the death of Resorts' Chairman in April 1986, negotiations for the Class B holdings of the estate, which constituted approximately 72% of the outstanding shares of the class, culminated with the sale of the Class B stock to Donald Trump at $135 per share in July 1987. Although the price of the Class A rose to the $60 range during July and August 1987, following the purchase of the Class B block it declined steadily to the point where it was trading at the $20 level during February 1988 and currently trades in the $30 range.

7, 1988, it adopted Rule 19c–4, barring national securities exchanges and national securities associations, together known as self-regulatory organizations (SROs), from listing stock of a corporation that takes any corporate action "with the effect of nullifying, restricting or disparately reducing the per share voting rights of [existing common stockholders]." The rule prohibits such "disenfranchisement" even where approved by a shareholder vote conducted on one share/one vote principles.   Because the rule directly controls the substantive allocation of powers among classes of shareholders, we find it in excess of the Commission's authority under § 19 of the Securities Exchange Act of 1934, as amended (the "Exchange Act").   Neither the wisdom of the requirement, nor of its being imposed at the federal level, is here in question.

* * * As we shall develop below, we find that the Exchange Act cannot be understood to include regulation of an issue that is so far beyond matters of disclosure (such as are regulated under § 14 of the Act), and of the management and practices of self-regulatory organizations, and that is concededly a part of corporate governance traditionally left to the states.

* * *

As mentioned above, the Commission does not suggest that it might support Rule 19c–4 by reference to the first two of the possible heads of jurisdiction in § 19(c)—assurance of fair administration of the self-regulatory organization itself and conformity to the requirements of the Exchange Act or rules thereunder applicable to the organization.   Thus it is driven to the third—"otherwise in furtherance of the purposes" of the Exchange Act.

What then are the "purposes" of the Exchange Act?   The Commission supports Rule 19c–4 as advancing the purposes of a variety of sections, but we first take its strongest—§ 14's grant of power to regulate the proxy process.   The Commission finds a purpose "to ensure fair shareholder suffrage."   * * * Indeed, it points to the House Report's declarations that "[f]air corporate suffrage is an important right," and that "use of the exchanges should involve a corresponding duty of according to shareholders fair suffrage."   The formulation is true in the sense that Congress's decision can be located under that broad umbrella.

But unless the legislative purpose is defined by reference to the means Congress selected, it can be framed at any level of generality—to improve the operation of capital markets, for instance.   In fact, although § 14(a) broadly bars use of the mails (and other means) "to solicit * * * any proxy" in contravention of Commission rules and regulations, it is not seriously disputed that Congress's central concern was with disclosure.   See *J.I. Case Co. v. Borak*, ("The purpose of § 14(a) is to prevent management or others from obtaining authorization for corporate action by means of deceptive or inadequate disclosure in proxy solicitation."); see also *Santa Fe Industries, Inc. v. Green*, (emphasizing Exchange Act's philosophy of full disclosure and dismissing the fairness of the terms of the transaction as "at most a tangential concern of the statute" once full and fair disclosure has occurred).

While the House Report indeed speaks of fair corporate suffrage, it also plainly identifies Congress's target—the solicitation of proxies by well informed insiders "without fairly informing the stockholders of the purposes for which the proxies are to be used." The Senate Report contains no vague language about "corporate suffrage," but rather explains the purpose of the proxy protections as ensuring that stockholders have "adequate knowledge" about the "financial condition of the corporation * * * [and] the major questions of policy, which are decided at stockholders' meetings." Finally, both reports agree on the power that the proxy sections gave the Commission—"power to control the conditions under which proxies may be solicited."

That proxy regulation bears almost exclusively on disclosure stems as a matter of necessity from the nature of proxies. Proxy solicitations are, after all, only communications with potential absentee voters. The goal of federal proxy regulation was to improve those communications and thereby to enable proxy voters to control the corporation as effectively as they might have by attending a shareholder meeting.

We do not mean to be taken as saying that disclosure is necessarily the sole subject of § 14. For example, the Commission's Rule 14a–4(b)(2) requires a proxy to provide some mechanism for a security holder to withhold authority to vote for each nominee individually. It thus bars a kind of electoral tying arrangement, and may be supportable as a control over management's power to set the voting agenda, or, slightly more broadly, voting procedures. But while Rule 14a–4(b)(2) may lie in a murky area between substance and procedure, Rule 19c–4 much more directly interferes with the substance of what the shareholders may enact. It prohibits certain reallocations of voting power and certain capital structures, even if approved by a shareholder vote subject to full disclosure and the most exacting procedural rules.

The Commission noted in the preamble to the Proposed Rule its conviction that collective action problems could cause even a properly conducted shareholder vote (with ample disclosure and sound procedures) to bring about results injurious to the shareholders. We do not question these findings. But we think the Commission's reliance on them is a clue to its stretch of the congressional purposes. As the Commission itself observed, "[s]ection 14(a) contains an implicit assumption that shareholders will be able to make use of the information provided in proxy solicitations in order to vote in corporate elections." In 1934 Congress acted on the premise that shareholder voting could work, so long as investors secured enough information and, perhaps, the benefit of other procedural protections. It did not seek to regulate the stockholders' choices. If the Commission believes that premise misguided, it must turn to Congress.

With its step beyond control of voting procedure and into the distribution of voting power, the Commission would assume an authority that the Exchange Act's proponents disclaimed any intent to grant. Noting that opponents expressed alarm that the bill would give the Commission "power to interfere in the management of corporations," the Senate Committee on Banking and Currency said it had "no such intention" and that the bill "furnish[ed] no justification for such an interpretation."

There are, of course, shadings within the notion of "management." With the present rule the Commission does not tell any corporation where to locate its next plant. But neither does state corporate law; it regulates the distribution of powers among the various players in the process of corporate governance, and the Commission's present leap beyond disclosure is just that sort of regulation. The potpourri of listing standards previously submitted to the Commission under § 19(b) suggests the sweep of its current claim. These govern requirements for independent directors, independent audit committees, shareholder quorums, shareholder approval for certain major corporate transactions, and other major issues traditionally governed by state law. If Rule 19c–4 is closely enough related to the proxy regulation purpose of § 14, then all these issues appear equally subject to the Commission's discretionary control.

Surprisingly, the Commission does not concede a lack of jurisdiction over such issues. When questioned at oral argument as to what state corporation rules are not related to "fair corporate suffrage," SEC counsel conceded only that further intrusions into state corporate governance "would present more difficult situations." In fact the Commission's apparent perception of its § 19 powers has been immensely broad, unbounded even by any pretense of a connection to § 14. In reviewing the previous SRO rule changes on issues of independent directors and independent audit committees, it grounded its review in a supposed mandate to "protect investors and the public interest." The Commission made no attempt to limit the concept by reference to the concrete purposes of any section. Rather, it reasoned that the rule changes protected investors by "creat[ing] uniformity that helps to assure investors that all the companies traded in those markets have the fundamental safeguards they have come to expect of major companies." If Rule 19c–4 were validated on such broad grounds, the Commission would be able to establish a federal corporate law by using access to national capital markets as its enforcement mechanism. This would resolve a longstanding controversy over the wisdom of such a move [7]in the face of disclaimers from Congress and with no substantive restraints on the power. It would, moreover, overturn or at least impinge severely on the tradition of state regulation of corporate law.   * * * We read the Act as

7.   * * * In 1934, ironically, the President of the New York Stock Exchange actually favored federalization of the corporate law in an attempt to derail the momentum for federal regulation of the securities markets * * *. Rule 19c–4 presents the worst of all worlds from that perspective, turning regulation of securities markets into the vehicle for federalizing corporate law.

reflecting a clear congressional determination not to make any such broad delegation of power to the Commission.

If the Commission's one share/one vote rule is to survive, then, some kind of firebreak is needed to separate it from corporate governance as a whole. But the Commission's sole suggestion of such a firebreak is a reference to "the unique historical background of the NYSE's one share, one vote rule." It is true that in the Senate hearings leading to enactment of the Exchange Act there were a few favorable references to that rule. But these few references are culled from 9500 pages of testimony in the Senate hearings. No legislator directly discussed the NYSE's rule and no references were made to it in any of the Committee Reports. The most these references show is that legislators were aware of the rule and that it was an important part of the background. Even if we imputed the statements to a member of Congress, none comes near to saying, "The purposes of this act, although they generally will not involve the Commission in corporate governance, do include preservation of the one share/one vote principle." And even then we doubt that such a statement in the legislative history could support a special and anomalous exception to the Act's otherwise intelligible conceptual line excluding the Commission from corporate governance.

[The court also rejected the Commission's arguments that §§ 6(b), 15A or 11A of the Securities and Exchange Act authorized it to issue Rule 19c–4.]

* * *

We do not decide whether the Commission could invoke other statutory provisions to provide the legal authority for promulgating these or similar regulations. The sections relied on here are insufficient. Even if other statutory provisions could support the Commission's asserted authority, we cannot supply grounds to sustain the regulations that were not invoked by the Commission below. In any case, a change in the jurisdictional basis would almost certainly alter the substantive content of the final regulations.

The petition for review is granted and Rule 19c–4 is vacated.

4. HOW THE PROXY PROCESS WORKS: LAW AND PRACTICE

a. *The Annual Meeting*

Annual stockholder meetings have become a rite of spring, since most corporations hold their annual meetings shortly after they have distributed their annual financial statements for the previous year. At that time the stockholders are barraged with documents from their companies—the notice of the annual meeting, a proxy statement, a proxy and an annual report. How does the entire process work?

The board of directors selects the date of the annual meeting which usually is fixed in the by-laws. Because the shareholder body changes daily, it is necessary to fix a record date to determine which shareholders are entitled to receive notice and to vote at the meeting. The corporation maintains a record of its stockholders, and when ownership of stock changes, the transfer agent, customarily a bank, records the change. Since the procedure usually requires several days to take effect, a small number of persons who have sold their stock and no longer consider themselves as stockholders actually appear as stockholders of record on the record date and will be entitled to vote.

b. Shareholder Voting

The board of directors must select the nominees for election as directors on whose behalf proxies will be solicited. That is, the material sent to the stockholders solicits authorization for the proxy holder to vote in favor of specified persons who will be placed in nomination at the annual meeting. No one is actually nominated until the meeting has convened, but by that time the stockholder voters will have already instructed their proxy for whom to vote. SEC rules require those soliciting a proxy to disclose for whom they intend to vote, and not deviate from that choice except under unusual circumstances. Other candidates may be nominated at the meeting, but in effect, the votes have been cast and the election decided before the candidates have been nominated. The reason for this result is that the proxy on which the shareholders confer the authority to vote is not a formal ballot on which they make choices but rather, as we have seen, is a power of attorney.

The board of directors must also decide what other matters will be submitted for action at the meeting. Authority and instructions as to how to vote on those matters will have to be solicited, and disclosure must be made in the proxy material. The directors usually recommend how to vote, and the proxy gives authority to vote in accordance with the board's recommendations unless instructions are given to the contrary. Some of the matters on which directions are sought will be initiated by the board or by management, such as ratification of the board's choice of independent auditors who will examine and certify the financial statements, proposed amendments to the articles of incorporation which have been approved by the board of directors, or approval of management compensation plans. Other items might be matters that stockholders have told management they intend to present at the meeting.

c. Filing Proxy Material

After these decisions have been made, the proxy materials, consisting of the proxy statement and the form of proxy, must be prepared for filing with the SEC. To some extent the preparation of the proxy materials constitutes a markup of the previous year's materials, but the rules and the matters on the agenda change from year to year and a substantial effort will be required to prepare the filings. Ordinarily the proxy materials are reviewed by the board of directors but most of the work must be performed by management, which has the data, and by counsel who understands the legal requirements.

After the materials have been filed they are reviewed by the staff of the Division of Corporation Finance. It is customary for the company to wait until it has received comments before sending anything to the stockholders. Otherwise, if the staff has strong objections to material already sent to stockholders, it may recommend that the SEC bring a lawsuit to enjoin the meeting until corrective action is taken. Such an action, needless to say, would be embarrassing and costly to the company, and management considers it prudent to allow the Commission staff full opportunity to comment.

A sample proxy statement and form of proxy appears in West Publishing Co., Selected Corporation and Partnership Statutes, Rules and Forms.

d. Identifying the Shareholders: Street Names

Who are the stockholders and how does one discover their identity in order to communicate with them? In Chapter 12, we saw that the corporation's stockholder list shows the stockholders of record but does not identify the beneficial owners. Today, largely for reasons of convenience, many stockholders choose to have their shares registered in the name of their broker where the shares are kept on deposit. When shares are transferred from one brokerage firm to another on behalf of a customer the change may be reflected only on the records of a central clearing house depository, which is used to minimize the danger of losing stock certificates by eliminating their physical movement. In addition, many shares are owned in trust or custodial accounts under the supervision of a bank. As a consequence of these practices, much of the ownership of securities is recorded in what is known as "street name." The corporation is unaware of who are the beneficial owners of the stock; all it knows is the name of the record holder and at least the number of beneficial owners. If an issuer requests, brokers and banks will furnish the names and addresses of non-objecting or consenting beneficial owners with whom the issuer may communicate directly. In many cases, issuers will not request these lists because they will be required to give them to a plaintiff seeking a stockholder list in litigation. See Chapter 12. Without such lists, the issuer can communicate only with the record holder.

Because of widespread beneficial ownership, it has become necessary to devise a mechanism for corporations to communicate with beneficial owners so they may direct the voting of their shares. SEC Rules 14a–13, 14b–1 and 14b–2 under the Securities Exchange Act of 1934 require corporations to attempt to communicate with the beneficial owners through the record owners, and establish procedures for doing so. In addition, the rules of self-regulatory organizations provide that a broker may either request voting instructions from the beneficial owners or forward signed proxies to them. These rules also permit the broker to vote the proxy in certain uncontested matters if the beneficial owner does not give instructions to the broker in a timely fashion. See New York Stock Exchange Rule 451 and 452; American Stock Exchange

Rules 575 and 577; National Association of Securities Dealers Rules of Fair Practice, Article III Section 1 (providing only for forwarding signed proxies).

e. Control of the Machinery

From the foregoing description, it should be obvious that the solicitation of proxies, which is necessary if shareholders are to act as a body, requires an elaborate machinery. Detailed records of stockholders must be maintained, material must be prepared, reviewed, filed and mailed, and counsel must play a significant role. All of this is expensive. The expenses are borne by the company since they relate to a necessary function that management must discharge. If a shareholder seeks to oppose management's proposals, or if she wishes to offer a candidate in opposition to those nominated by the board of directors, she must duplicate the entire process and bear the expense on her own, subject to obtaining reimbursement of expenses in limited circumstances. Can the federal law attain its objective of "fair corporate suffrage" if state law gives management effective control over the solicitation process? On the other hand, is there a practical alternative?

f. Counting the Proxies

The final aspect of the proxy machinery involves counting the votes. The proxy holders present their proxies at the meeting and then, having established that they are the agent for the number of shares so evidenced, they cast their ballot. In an uncontested election, no one has any interest in challenging their count. However, if a contested election of directors is involved or if there has been opposition to a proposed transaction, or if approval of a transaction requires more than a majority vote, then the count of the proxies becomes crucial. There are several wrinkles that can make the count contentious. For one thing, proxies are revocable and they may be revoked either by notice to the company or by a later designation of someone else as a proxy to vote in a different way. In the latter case, the later dated proxy constitutes the valid designation of an agent and automatically cancels the earlier designation. But which one is the later proxy? How does one tell? Or, suppose one of the contestants argues that the proxy held by the other side is invalid because the proxy was not signed properly or because some other defect appears. Who settles this question?

Ordinarily, the board of directors designates inspectors of election, and, in some cases, state law requires the appointment of inspectors of election. Generally, these people are not members of management, but are professionals hired to do the job. What law applies? Until recently, the practical answer has been found in the practices of corporate lawyers who have developed such rules as those dealing with proper signatures, fiduciary voting, dating of proxies and the like. If there is an election campaign with two sides actively seeking proxies, the lawyers for each side customarily agree on a set of rules in advance of the meeting to serve as the ground rules applicable to that election. These unofficial documents have guided courts in those instances where the issues are litigated.

There has been a recent increase in the number of cases in which the courts have intervened in the practices of those who act as inspectors of election at shareholder meetings. In many of those cases, the courts have not hesitated to set aside some or all of the disputed proxies because they have disagreed with the way in which the inspectors have resolved the disputes. Some of these cases have resulted from modern technology, i.e., the validity of "proxygrams" (proxies sent by telegrams) or proxies sent by fax machines. For the courts, the analytic conflict is between the need for certainty and a quick resolution of an election on the one hand and the need to protect the shareholder franchise on the other. In Delaware, the legislature has acted to remove whatever ambiguities may have been created by the recent cases. DGCL § 231, added in 1990, addresses voting procedures and requires that public corporations (as defined in the statute), in advance of any stockholder meeting, appoint one or more inspectors to act at the meeting and make a written report thereof. The inspectors may be independent third parties or employees of the corporation. Their duties include ascertaining the number of shares outstanding and the voting power of each, determining the shares represented at a meeting and the validity of proxies and ballots cast, counting all votes and ballots and certifying their result. New subsections 212(c) and (d), also added in 1990, authorize the use of datagram and telecopied proxies and deal with their validity.

Delaware cases which preceded the legislation include Concord Financial Group, Inc. v. Tri–State Motor Transit Co., 567 A.2d 1 (Del.Ch. 1989) and Parshalle v. Roy, 567 A.2d 19 (Del.Ch.1989). Cases from other jurisdictions include Carey v. Pennsylvania Enterprises, Inc., 876 F.2d 333 (3d Cir.1989) and Pena v. Westland Development Co., Inc., 107 N.M. 560, 761 P.2d 438 (App.1988).

C. FEDERAL REGULATION OF PROXY SOLICITATIONS

Section 14 of the Securities Exchange Act of 1934 and the SEC's rules adopted under that section regulate many aspects of the proxy solicitation process. Section 14 applies to every company that has a class of securities listed on a stock exchange or has a class of securities owned by 500 or more holders of record and assets of at least $5,000,000. Securities Exchange Act §§ 12(b),(g). The rules refer to all such companies as "registrants."

For many years, the proxy rules applied to all solicitations of proxies in much the same fashion, whether conducted by a company's management, a dissident shareholder, or some other person. Both the SEC and the courts interpreted the term "solicitation" to include every communication likely to influence a shareholder's decision to grant a proxy. The proxy rules made it unlawful to solicit a shareholder unless the solicitation was accompanied or preceded by a full proxy statement that the SEC staff had reviewed. This requirement significantly impeded non-management shareholders' participation in the corporate electoral process; the proxy rules, in effect, served to stifle "shareholder democracy."

In 1992, following an extensive review, the SEC revised its rules to deregulate substantially the proxy solicitation process. The focus of the deregulation was on communications by minority shareholders and other persons not affiliated with the management of a company with respect to which proxies were being solicited. As a consequence, the rules governing proxy solicitations by a company's management now differ substantially from the rules applicable to solicitations by others.

1. THE PROXY RULES AS THEY APPLY TO MANAGEMENT

Management's request that a shareholder grant it a proxy to vote her shares at an upcoming shareholders meeting clearly falls within Rule 14a–1's definition of a solicitation. The Rule's definition of both "proxy" and "solicitation" also may encompass other communications not generally thought of as constituting proxy solicitations.

When management plans to solicit proxies, it must first prepare a proxy statement and a form of proxy. Schedule 14A specifies in considerable detail certain information that management must include in its proxy statement, including information about candidates for election as director and about management's compensation arrangements. In addition, Rule 14a–9 prohibits inclusion of materially false or misleading statements in a proxy solicitation—a prohibition that the SEC interprets as requiring disclosure of both the negative and the positive aspects of any proposal for which management is seeking shareholder approval. Thus, for example, if management is seeking shareholder authorization of an amendment to the articles that will divide the board of directors into classes, the SEC will require management to explain in its proxy statement that classifying the board may serve to discourage uninvited takeover bids, as well as setting forth management's reasons for recommending that shareholders authorize a classified board.

Subject to the exception discussed below, Rule 14a–3 requires that every solicitation be accompanied or preceded by the definitive proxy statement. In addition, if management is soliciting proxies for an annual meeting or a special meeting at which directors are to be elected, each proxy statement must be accompanied or preceded by an annual report containing information which in part is specified by the Rule and in part is left to the discretion of management. This requirement applies not only to ordinary proxy solicitations but to any other communication by management that is deemed to constitute the solicitation of a proxy.

Rule 14a–4 regulates the form of proxy. Management must give shareholders an opportunity to vote either for or against each matter to be acted upon other than elections to office. If directors are to be elected, the proxy form must provide a means by which shareholders may withhold their votes on directors as a group or on individual candidates. A proxy may confer discretionary authority on matters where the shareholder does not specify a choice if the form of proxy states in boldface type how the proxy will be voted on each matter. The shares represented by the proxy must be voted at the meeting in accordance with the shareholder's instructions.

Rule 14a–6 requires management to file preliminary copies of its proxy statement and form of proxy with the Commission at least 10 days prior to disseminating those materials to shareholders. However, if the solicitation involves nothing more than an unopposed election of directors, ratification of selection of auditors and shareholder proposals, no preliminary material need be filed. The SEC staff endeavors to review and comment on the proxy materials within this 10–day period.

Prior to the 1992 amendments, the SEC treated preliminary proxy material as confidential and barred management from soliciting proxies until those materials were cleared by the SEC staff and distributed to shareholders. Now, the SEC places preliminary proxy materials in a public file when they are received, unless they relate to a business combination or other extraordinary transaction, in which event the Commission automatically treats the materials as confidential. In addition, the SEC now allows management to begin soliciting proxies using the preliminary proxy materials it has filed, so long as management does not provide a form of proxy to any shareholders it solicits. This change in the rules is designed to permit management to seek shareholders' reactions to proposals or transactions for which management plans to seek shareholder approval, prior to the filing of definitive proxy materials, and to modify those proposals or transactions if shareholders' initial reactions are negative.

Rule 14a–7 provides that a shareholder who wants to solicit proxies may require the company to mail her proxy soliciting material provided that she bear the cost of the mailing. Alternatively, the company can furnish the shareholder with a list of names and addresses for such categories of shareholders as she may specify.

As discussed in greater detail in Section E, Rule 14a–8 permits a shareholder who has owned 1% or $1,000 of the company's stock for at least one year to submit to the company a proposed resolution that she will introduce at the shareholders meeting and have that resolution included in the proxy statement. The submission must be made within the time period specified in the rule. The shareholder is also entitled to have a supporting statement included with the proposal, but the resolution and the statement may not exceed 500 words.

2. COMMUNICATIONS REASONABLY CALCULATED TO PROCURE A PROXY

Rule 14a–1 defines "solicitation" to include: (1) any request for a proxy whether or not accompanied by or included in a form of proxy; (2)

any request to execute or not to execute, or to revoke, a proxy; or (3) the furnishing of a form of proxy *or other communication* to security holders under circumstances reasonably *calculated* to result in the procurement, withholding or revocation of a proxy. In addition to the traditional proxy, the definition of "proxy" includes a consent or authorization. In the definition of "solicitation," the most important interpretive question concerns the meaning of "calculated." Does it mean "intended" or "likely?" How do the different meanings affect the determination of whether there was a solicitation? Which is more consistent with the purposes of the proxy rules?

Studebaker Corp. v. Gittlin, 360 F.2d 692 (2d Cir.1966), illustrates the broad interpretation the SEC and the courts have given the term "solicitation." Gittlin, a shareholder in Studebaker, sought inspection of the company's shareholder list in preparation for an effort to gain control of the board of directors. New York law required that, since he had not been a shareholder for six months, he own or have the support of holders of 5% of Studebaker's stock in order to obtain the list. Gittlin met this requirement by obtaining authorization from 42 other shareholders, and a state court ordered Studebaker to allow inspection. The company then asked a federal court to enjoin enforcement of the state court order because Gittlin had obtained the authorizations in violation of the federal proxy rules.

The SEC, appearing *amicus curiae*, argued that soliciting authorization to inspect the shareholder list was subject to the proxy rules even if the request was not part of a planned proxy solicitation. The Second Circuit responded:

> We need not go that far to uphold the order of the district court. In SEC v. Okin, 132 F.2d 784 (2d Cir.1943), this court ruled that a letter which did not request the giving of any authorization was subject to the Proxy Rules if it was part of "a continuous plan" intended to end in solicitation and to prepare the way for success. This was the avowed purpose of Gittlin's demand for inspection of the stockholders list and, necessarily, for his soliciting authorizations sufficient to aggregate the 5% of the stock required by § 1315 of New York's Business Corporation Law. Presumably the stockholders who gave authorizations were told something and, as Judge L. Hand said in Okin, "one need only spread the misinformation adequately before beginning to solicit, and the Commission would be powerless to protect shareholders." 132 F.2d at 786. Moreover, the very fact that a copy of the stockholders list is a valuable instrument to a person seeking to gain control, * * * is a good reason for insuring that shareholders have full information before they aid its procurement.

360 F.2d at 696.

A controversy relating to a proposed merger of the Rock Island Railroad with the Union Pacific Railroad in 1963 led to two decisions that illustrate the factors courts consider when deciding whether to subject a communication to the requirements of the proxy rules. On May 13, 1963, the Rock Island and Union Pacific announced an agreement to merge. On June 24, 1963, Chicago and Northwestern Railway unveiled a competing offer for the Rock Island. For Northwestern's offer to succeed, the Rock Island's shareholders would have to vote down the merger with Union Pacific, which the boards of the Rock Island and Union Pacific formally approved on June 27, 1963. Northwestern also needed Interstate Commerce Commission approval of its offer, and applied for that approval on July 3, 1963.

On July 26, 1963, Union Pacific published a newspaper advertisement explaining that it opposed Northwestern's offer because it would affect railroad service adversely. The advertisements appeared in cities served by the Rock Island and in Washington and New York, which the Rock Island did not serve.

A Rock Island shareholder filed suit, claiming that the advertisement was a communication reasonably calculated to procure a proxy and thus constituted an unlawful solicitation. The court disagreed, noting that the ad informed the public about an issue pending before a government agency and thus served a public interest independent of the decision the Rock Island's shareholders would have to make. The court also considered it significant that the Rock Island shareholders' meeting had not been called at the time the ad was published. In fact, the meeting, scheduled for November 15, 1963, was not called until October 1. Brown v. Chicago, R.I. & P.R.R. Co., 328 F.2d 122, 124–5 (7th Cir.1964).

In contrast, once the contestants began to formally solicit proxies, a different court held that another communication not specifically directed at the Rock Island's shareholders nonetheless constituted a solicitation. A brokerage firm prepared a report concluding that the Rock Island's shareholders would benefit more from Northwestern's offer than from Union Pacific's and distributed the report to its customers. Northwestern, which had assisted the brokerage firm in preparing the report, distributed additional copies of the report to Rock Island shareholders. The court held that the report was reasonably calculated to influence a Rock Island shareholder's decision on whether to grant a proxy and therefore was a solicitation. Union Pacific R.R. Co. v. Chicago & N.W. Ry. Co., 226 F.Supp. 400 (N.D.Ill.1964).

Smallwood v. Pearl Brewing Company, 489 F.2d 579 (5th Cir.1974), involved a somewhat different issue. Approximately two months prior to mailing its proxy statement soliciting shareholder approval of a merger, a company advised its shareholders by letter of the proposed merger. The company also indicated that the board believed that the merger would be beneficial to shareholders. The court held that the letter was not a communication reasonably calculated to result in the procurement of a proxy. No proxies were actually mentioned and the correspondence "if not totally innocuous was not overwhelmingly prejudicial either." Id. at 601. The court also noted that requiring compliance with the proxy rules would impede prompt disclosure to investors of a major, pending corporate transaction.

This last point has great significance. A constant tension exists between the timing requirements of the proxy rules and the SEC's policy urging prompt disclosure of significant corporate information. Both the courts and the SEC recognize that labeling a communication a "solicitation" stifles some communication; it often will be impractical promptly to prepare and circulate material that meets all requirements of the proxy rules. Consequently, the courts strive to maintain a reasonable balance between serving the needs of the marketplace and protecting the integrity of the proxy solicitation process.

LONG ISLAND LIGHTING COMPANY v. BARBASH
779 F.2d 793 (2d Cir.1985).

[The Long Island Lighting Company (LILCO) was the focus of a local political campaign, in which candidate Matthews urged public ownership of the utility. Matthews acquired sufficient shares to demand a special shareholders' meeting to consider his proposal. A group favorable to Matthews' proposal, Citizens to Replace LILCO, published a newspaper advertisement accusing LILCO of mismanagement and attempting to pass through to ratepayers needless costs relating to construction of the Seabrook nuclear power plant and urging support for a campaign to have the public power authority acquire LILCO.

LILCO complained that the ad was unlawful because it constituted an unfiled proxy solicitation and because it was false and misleading. The district court declined to hold that the ad represented a solicitation because it appeared in a general publication and could only indirectly affect the proxy contest at LILCO.]

CARDAMONE, CIRCUIT JUDGE:

II

* * *

In our view the district court erred in holding that the proxy rules cannot cover communications appearing in publications of general circulation and that are indirectly addressed to shareholders.

* * *

These rules apply not only to direct requests to furnish, revoke or withhold proxies, but also to communications which may indirectly accomplish such a result or constitute a step in a chain of communications designed ultimately to accomplish such a result. * * *

The question in every case is whether the challenged communication, seen in the totality of circumstances, is "reasonably calculated" to influence the shareholders' votes. Determination of the purpose of the communication depends upon the nature of the communication and the circumstances under which it was distributed.

* * *

Deciding whether a communication is a proxy solicitation does not depend upon whether it is "targeted directly" at shareholders. See Rule 14a–6(g), (requiring that solicitations in the form of "speeches, press releases, and television scripts" be filed with the SEC). As the SEC correctly notes in its amicus brief, it would "permit easy evasion of the proxy rules" to exempt all general and indirect communications to shareholders, and this is true whether or not the communication purports to address matters of "public interest." The SEC's authority to regulate proxy solicitations has traditionally extended into matters of public interest.

* * *

WINTER, CIRCUIT JUDGE, dissenting:

In order to avoid a serious first amendment issue, I would construe the federal regulations governing the solicitation of proxies as inapplicable to the newspaper advertisement in question. * * *

II

The content of the Committee's advertisement is of critical importance. First, it is on its face addressed solely to the public. Second, it makes no mention either of proxies or of the shareholders' meeting demanded by Matthews. Third, the issues the ad addresses are quintessentially matters of public political debate, namely, whether a public power authority would provide cheaper electricity than LILCO. Claims of LILCO mismanagement are discussed solely in the context of their effect on its customers. Finally, the ad was published in the middle of an election campaign in which LILCO's future was an issue.

On these facts, therefore, LILCO's claim raises a constitutional issue of the first magnitude. It asks nothing less than that a federal court act as a censor, empowered to determine the truth or falsity of the ad's claims about the merits of public power and to enjoin further advocacy containing false claims. We need not resolve this constitutional issue, however.

Where advertisements are critical of corporate conduct but are facially directed solely to the public, in no way mention the exercise of proxies, and debate only matters of conceded public concern, I would construe federal proxy regulation as inapplicable, whatever the motive of those who purchase them. This position, which is strongly suggested by relevant case law, *see infra,* maximizes public debate, avoids embroiling the federal judiciary in determining the rightness or wrongness of conflicting positions on public policy, and does not significantly impede achievement of Congress' goal that shareholders exercise proxy rights on the basis of accurate information.

It is of course true that LILCO shareholders may be concerned about public allegations of mismanagement on LILCO's part. However, shareholders are most unlikely to be misled into thinking that advertisements of this kind, particularly when purchased in the name of a committee so obviously disinterested in the return on investment to LILCO's shareholders, are either necessarily accurate or authoritative sources of information about LILCO's management. Such advertisements, which in no way suggest internal reforms shareholders might bring about through the exercise of their proxies, are sheer political advocacy and would be so recognized by any reasonable shareholder.

To be sure, the fact that a corporation has become a target of political advocacy might well justify unease among shareholders. No one seriously asserts, however, that the right to criticize corporate behavior as a matter of public concern diminishes as shareholders' meetings become imminent.

3. SOLICITATIONS BY SHAREHOLDERS AND OTHERS

At the time *Barbash* was decided, the proxy rules required every person who solicited a proxy to deliver to every solicitee a proxy statement containing detailed information about the solicitor and various other matters. A communication in the mass media, such as the advertisement at issue in *Barbash*, was deemed to be directed at all of a company's shareholders. Consequently, it could not lawfully be published unless the solicitor had first filed a proxy statement with the SEC, received staff clearance, and circulated copies of that statement to all of the company's shareholders—i.e., all of the persons who would be "solicited" by the newspaper ad. In addition, the ad itself would have to be filed in advance with the SEC and cleared by the staff. The only exception to these requirements was for a non-management solicitation directed to not more than 10 persons. Concern about the impact of these and related requirements led the Commission to review and modify its proxy rules.

REGULATION OF COMMUNICATIONS AMONG SHAREHOLDERS
SEC Rel. No. 34–31326, pp. 7–17 (Oct. 22, 1992).

The amendments to the proxy rules and other disclosure provisions adopted today follow upon an extensive three-year examination by the Commission of the effectiveness of the proxy voting process and its effect on the corporate governance system in this country. * * *

Within the overall scope of this broad examination, the Commission has focused particularly on the role of its proxy and disclosure rules in impeding shareholder communication and participation in the corporate governance process. This demonstrated effect of the current rules is contrary to Congress's intent that the rules assure fair and effective shareholder suffrage. Apart from attempts to obtain proxy voting authority, to the degree the current rules inhibit the ability of shareholders not seeking proxy authority to analyze and discuss issues pertaining to the operation of a company and its performance, these rules may in fact run exactly contrary to the best interests of shareholders.

The amendments adopted today reflect a Commission determination that the federal proxy rules have created unnecessary regulatory impediments to communication among shareholders and others and to the effective use of shareholder voting rights. The Commission has also determined that modifications in the current rules are desirable to reduce these burdens and to achieve the purposes set forth in the Exchange Act.

* * *

In 1956, the Commission significantly expanded the definition of "solicitation" of a proxy to embrace "any communication" which could be viewed as being "reasonably calculated" to influence a shareholder to give, deny or revoke a proxy. In adopting the sweeping 1956 definition, the Commission sought to address abuses by persons who were actually engaging in solicitations of proxy authority in connection with election contests. The Commission does not seem to have been aware, or to have intended, that the new definition might also sweep within all the regulatory requirements persons who did not "request" a shareholder to grant or to revoke or deny a proxy, but whose expressed opinions might be found to have been reasonably calculated to affect the views of other shareholders positively or negatively toward a particular company and its management or directors. Since any such persuasion—even if unintended—could affect the decision of shareholders even many months later to give or withhold a proxy, such communications at least literally could fall within the new definition.

The literal breadth of the new definition of solicitation was so great as potentially to turn almost every expression of opinion concerning a publicly-traded corporation into a regulated proxy solicitation. Thus, newspaper op-ed articles, public speeches or television commentary on a specific company could all later be alleged to have been proxy solicitations in connection with the election of directors, as could private conversations among more than 10 shareholders. This created a basis upon which claims that the proxy rules, including the mandatory disclosure, filing and dissemination provisions of those rules, could be brought to bear not only on persons seeking authority to vote another's shares, but also on those persons merely expressing a view or opinion on management performance or on initiatives presented by management and others for a shareholder vote.

If the current proxy rules apply to a communication, the effect can be very costly. Among other things, the person making the communication would be required to prepare a proxy statement and mail it to every shareholder of the company who is deemed to have been solicited. Where a communication appears in the public media, the Commission has taken the position that all shareholders have been solicited. In such a case, the cost of the mailing requirement alone could run into hundreds of thousands of dollars, and the decision on whether a solicitation occurred will be judged purely in hindsight. Thus, shareholders can be deterred from discussing management and corporate performance by the prospect of being found after the fact to have engaged in a proxy solicitation. The costs of complying with those rules also has meant that, unless they have substantial financial backing, shareholders and other interested persons may effectively be cut out of the debate regarding proposals presented by management or shareholders for a vote.

While voting rights are valuable assets and an uninformed exercise of those rights could represent a wasted opportunity for the voting shareholder, that concern does not justify the government's requiring that all private conversations on matters subject to a shareholder vote be reported to the government. In the Commission's view, the antifraud provisions provide adequate protection against fraudulent and deceptive communications to shareholders on matters presented for a vote by persons not seeking proxy authority and not in the classes of persons ineligible for the exemption.

A regulatory scheme that inserted the Commission staff and corporate management into every exchange and conversation among shareholders, their advisors and other parties on matters subject to a vote certainly would raise serious questions under the free speech clause of the First Amendment, particularly where no proxy authority is being solicited by such persons. This is especially true where such intrusion is not necessary to achieve the goals of the federal securities laws.

The purposes of the proxy rules themselves are better served by promoting free discussion, debate and learning among shareholders and interested persons, than by placing restraints on that process to ensure that management has the ability to address every point raised in the exchange of views. Indeed, the Commission has not perceived, and the comments have not demonstrated, shareholder abuses where proxy authority is not being sought by the person engaged in the communications. However, there have been situations in which discontented shareholders have been subjected to legal threats based on the possibility the shareholder might have triggered proxy filing requirements by expressing disagreement to other shareholders.

---

a. Exempt Solicitations

The Commission concluded that "the best protection for shareholders and the marketplace is to identify those classes of solicitations that warrant application of the proxy statement disclosure requirement, and to foster the free and unrestrained expression of views by all other parties by the removal of any regulatory cost, burden or uncertainty that could have the effect of deterring the free expression of views by disinterested shareholders who do not seek authority for themselves." Id. at 23–24. Consequently, it amended Rule 14a–2 to exempt from the filing requirement of Rule 14a–6 and the proxy statement delivery requirement of Rule 14a–3 any solicitation by a person, whether or not a shareholder, who does not seek proxy voting authority and does not furnish shareholders with a form of proxy. Thus a person soliciting in support of a shareholder proposal can rely on the exemption, so long as she is not seeking proxy voting authority and is not otherwise ineligible. Moreover, if a solicitation is oral or is by a person who owns securities of the registrant worth less than $5 million, no notice relating to the solicitation need be filed with the SEC. A solicitor who owns more than $5 million in securities and conducts a written solicitation must file a notice, within three days *following* the first dissemination of those materials, listing only her name and address and attaching the soliciting materials.

This exemption is not available to (i) the registrant, (ii) a person acting on behalf of or financed by the registrant, (iii) a person soliciting in opposition to a merger or other extraordinary transaction where that person has proposed or plans to propose an alternative transaction to which it will be a party, (iv) certain large shareholders interested in seeking control of the registrant, or (v) a person who would receive a benefit from a successful solicitation that she would not share *pro rata* with other shareholders.

As a result of these amendments, the SEC staff will no longer review proxy soliciting material disseminated by persons not seeking authority to vote other shareholders' stock. The only significant regulatory constraint on such solicitations (as well as regulated solicitations) will be Rule 14a–9's prohibition of materially false and misleading proxy solicitations.

b. Shareholder Announcements of Voting Decisions

The SEC also amended Rule 14a–1 to exclude from the definition of solicitation an announcement by a shareholder of how she intends to vote, whether or not coupled with an explanation of the shareholder's decision. Such an announcement can, without limitation, be published, broadcast, or disseminated to the media. Because it is deemed not to constitute a solicitation, none of the proxy rules apply.

c. Regulated Solicitations

The SEC also substantially eliminated staff review of soliciting materials other than management's initial proxy statement. Most such materials now can be filed with the Commission in definitive form at the time they are disseminated. The Commission explained that it "believes that the most cost-effective means to address hyperbole and other claims and opinions viewed as objectionable is not government screening of the contentions or resort to the courts. Rather, the parties should be free to reply to the statements in a timely and cost- effective manner, challenging the basis for the claims and countering with their own views on the subject matter through the dissemination of additional soliciting material." Id. at 43.

d. *The Impact of the Revised Proxy Rules*

According to the Investor Responsibility Research Center, an organization that monitors the activities of institutional investors and shareholder activists, during the 1993 proxy season, the first in which the new SEC rules governing shareholder communications were in effect, the new rules "energized long-time activists and brought some investors, such as labor unions and money managers, into the process for the first time." Patrick S. McGurn, Shareholder Activism Continues to Thrive, IRRC Corporate Governance Bulletin 7 (May–June 1993). A number of shareholder proponents took advantage of the new rules to actively solicit support for their proposals from institutional investors. Shareholder proposals on governance issues garnered record support, including a majority of the votes cast in several instances. But, in the view of some analysts, the most significant development was corporate managers' increased willingness to meet with activist shareholders and discuss their concerns. This receptivity was stimulated by managers' awareness that shareholders otherwise would find it easier to mobilize support for shareholder proposals or opposition to proposals or candidates that management was supporting.

The impact of the new rules was evident in connection with voting by shareholders of Centel Corp. on a proposed merger with Sprint. In January 1992, Centel's management had announced that they were seeking a buyer for the company and estimated that shareholders would realize $45 to $65 per share. In July, after no better offers were received (and at a time when Centel was trading at $46 per share), Centel's board recommended a stock-for-stock merger with Sprint worth about $33.50 per Centel share. A shareholder rebellion ensued. Within a month after the new SEC rules went into effect, Eagle Asset Management, an institutional investor holding 5.4 percent of Centel's stock, mailed a twenty-page booklet arguing against the merger to Centel's 200 largest shareholders. When management responded, Eagle fired off a rejoinder via Federal Express. Even though Eagle's effort failed—the merger ultimately was supported by holders of 50.5 percent of Centel's stock—the new rules appeared to have a major impact. David Shell, an Eagle vice-president, estimated that the merger would have been opposed by only 20 to 30 percent of Centel's shareholders had the old rules been in effect, rather than almost half. See Fran Hawthorne, What the New SEC Rules Do For Activism, Institutional Investor 47 (April 1993).

e. *Disclosure of Plans and Proposals by Significant Shareholders*

In rejecting claims that the new rules went too far in deregulating the proxy solicitation process, the SEC observed that the circumstances under which a large shareholder, or a group of shareholders acting together, must disclose to the SEC, the company, other shareholders and the market its plans regarding a given company are adequately addressed by Section 13(d) of the 1934 Act and the rules adopted thereunder. Section 13(d) requires any "person" who becomes the owner of 5 percent of the stock of a registrant to file a Schedule 13D within 10 business days of the acquisition. "Person" is defined to include a "group" and Rule 13(d)–5(b)(1) states that a "group" will be deemed to have "acquired" the shares of its members when two or more persons "agree to act together for the purpose of acquiring, holding, voting or disposing of equity securities."

Schedule 13D requires detailed information about the person filing the Schedule (or each member of the filing group), how that person financed the acquisition of the corporation's securities, the purpose of acquiring those securities, and all "contracts, arrangements, understandings or relationships (legal or otherwise)" relating to the corporation among the members of a group or between the person (or group members) filing the form and any other persons.

GAF Corp. v. Milstein, 453 F.2d 709 (2d Cir.1971), upheld a claim that a group made up of four members of the Milstein family, who together owned in excess of 10 percent of a class of GAF stock, "acquired" the stock that those family members owned at the moment they agreed to work together to seek control of GAF and violated § 13(d) by failing to timely file a Schedule 13D. The court noted that § 13(d) was adopted to alert the marketplace to rapid accumulations of stock that might signal a pending shift in control, and stated that the alleged conspiracy among the Milsteins represented the kind of conduct at which the section was directed.

Professor Bernard Black argues that, with the amendment of the proxy rules, § 13(d), the SEC's expansive interpretation of that section and the rules issued thereunder constitute a very substantial regulatory impediment to increased activism by institutional investors. Bernard S. Black, Next Steps in Corporate Governance Reform: 13(d) Rules and Control Person Liability, in Kenneth Lehn & Robert Kamphuis, eds., Modernizing Securities Regulation: Economic and Legal Perspectives 197–209 (1992). Black observes:

> The 13D filing isn't complex, but it involves substantial litigation risk, which means heavy legal bills, win or lose. Proponents are commonly sued by the SEC or the company's managers for various real or imagined misdisclosures. * * *

> The 13(d) rules thus create a double bind for shareholders who own modest individual stakes. If they don't organize, collective action problems are severe. If they do organize, they've formed a group, with attendant reporting requirements and litigation risk. The larger and thus potentially more effective the group is, the more burdensome the reporting requirements will be. Each member can file its own 13D, but each filing must identify all other group

members and disclose all information about other filers which "the filing person knows or has reason to know."

Professor Black suggests that the SEC act to reduce the obstacles caused by § 13(d) by redefining "group" to exclude agreements to vote a company's stock and by revising the "expansive and litigation-prone disclosure requirements of Schedule 13D." Other commentators have made similar suggestions.

D. INSTITUTIONAL INVESTORS AND CORPORATE GOVERNANCE

The portion of corporate stock held by institutional investors—private and public pension funds, investment companies, insurance companies, bank non-pension trusts, foundations and endowments—has increased rapidly in recent years. According to a Securities and Exchange Commission estimate, institutional investors held 23 percent of public corporations' outstanding stock in 1955. That percentage increased gradually over the next 25 years, to 33.1 percent in 1980, then increased much much more rapidly in the next 10 years. By 1990, institutional investors owned approximately 53 percent of public corporations' outstanding stock. Carolyn K. Brancato and Patrick A. Gaughan, Institutional Investors and Capital Markets. 1991 Update 8.

These statistics tell only part of the story. Brancato and Gaughan found that institutions owned more than 80 percent of the stock in 3 percent of all public companies that had institutional shareholders, more than 70 percent of the stock in 15.9 percent of those companies, and more than 50 percent of the stock in 50.4 percent of those companies. Id. at 16. But studies by Brancato and others also demonstrate that American financial institutions generally hold very diversified investment portfolios, comprised of stock in hundreds and even thousands of companies. Very rarely does an American financial institution acquire a large stock position in one or a few portfolio companies with a view to exercising control or influencing that company's business. The situations at Exxon, IBM and General Electric are typical. In 1990, the top five shareholders in Exxon held 4.76 percent of its outstanding stock and the top 25 shareholders held 11.47 percent. The comparable figures at IBM and GE, respectively, were 4.70 percent and 13.54 percent and 4.89 percent and 12.89 percent. Carolyn K. Brancato, et al., Institutional Investor Concentration of Economic Power: A Study of Institutional Holdings and Voting Authority in U.S. Publicly Held Corporations App. 2 (Mimeo 1991). These data suggest both that corporate ownership now is less fragmented than was the case when Berle and Means first highlighted the divorce of ownership from control and that ownership still is divorced from control.

Two British professors describe the corporate system in the United States as "characterized by: [a] large number of listed companies; [a] liquid capital market where ownership and control rights are frequently traded; [and] [f]ew intercorporate equity holdings." Julian Franks & Colin Mayer, Corporate Control: A Synthesis of the International Evidence 2 (Mimeo. 1992). In contrast, they state, "Continental European and Japanese corporate systems typically have: [f]ew listed companies; [a]n illiquid capital market where ownership and control is infrequently traded; [and] [c]omplex systems of intercorporate holdings." Id. at 2–3.

1. THE COLLECTIVE ACTION PROBLEM AND INSTITUTIONAL INVESTORS

Recall Dean Clark's analysis of the collective action problem in Section B of this chapter. In the first part of that analysis, Dean Clark assumes that the shareholder is an individual investor for whom "rational apathy" may be the most efficient course of action. What happens to the problem if the shareholder (Ajax, in the second part of Dean Clark's discussion) is a financial institution? Professor Bernard Black responds as follows:

> A shareholder who owns a large percentage stake is more likely to engage in monitoring than a shareholder who owns a smaller stake. Thus legal rules that prevent shareholders from owning large stakes or acting jointly increase incentives to remain passive. Moreover, the higher the cost of making a shareholder proposal, the greater the incentive to remain silent. Thus, rules that increase the cost of a proxy campaign or prevent cost-sharing among shareholders discourage shareholder action. Conversely, rules that shift costs to the company encourage shareholder action.

> Moreover, the standard model overstates the case for passivity. When the voting outcome is in doubt, apathy becomes much less rational as shareholdings grow. Both a shareholder's gains from the voting outcome she favors and the likelihood that her vote will be decisive increase with the number of shares owned. A shareholder who owns 1,000 shares is 1,000 times more likely to cast a decisive vote than a shareholder who owns a single share, and realizes 1,000 times the net gain if her vote is decisive. Thus, the incentive to cast an informed vote increases *exponentially* as shareholdings grow. A 1,000 share holder has 1,000,000 times more incentive to become informed than someone who owns a single share!

> Diversification also enhances incentives to monitor by creating the potential for economies of scale in monitoring. Many process and structural issues arise in similar form at many companies. A shareholder who offers the same proposal at a number of companies can reduce her per-company solicitation cost, while preserving the per-company benefit from success. Similarly, a shareholder who votes on the same proposal many times has reason to invest more time and attention in casting an informed vote.

Bernard Black, Agents Watching Agents: The Promise Of Institutional Investor Voice, 39 UCLA L. Rev. 811, 821–822 (1992).

2. INSTITUTIONAL INVESTORS AND MONITORING

The ability of institutional investors to reduce collective action problems suggests that they may be able to exercise monitoring functions in ways that individual investors cannot. Whether they should, however, is a separate question, and one which has provoked considerable controversy. The traditional view has been that there is no reason to believe that institutions can or will monitor corporate management effectively. Professor Black is one of the principal advocates of an increased role for institutional investors as monitors of corporate management.

BERNARD BLACK, AGENTS WATCHING AGENTS: THE PROMISE OF INSTITUTIONAL INVESTOR VOICE
39 UCLA L. Rev. 811, 815–819 (1992).

The case for institutional oversight, broadly speaking, is that product, capital, labor, and corporate control market constraints on managerial discretion are imperfect, corporate managers need to be watched by someone, and the institutions are the only watchers available. The concerns about institutional oversight arise for two main reasons. First, controlling shareholders may divert funds to themselves at the expense of noncontrolling shareholders. Second, the institutions are themselves managed by money managers who need (and often don't get) watching and appropriate incentives. Mutual fund investors, for example, have little information about the corporate governance actions of mutual funds managers, little reason to care, and no power to do anything except sell their shares and invest in another fund. Public pension fund managers are watched as much by state politicians and the press as by fund beneficiaries.

Pure theory can't tell us whether we'd be better off if imperfectly watched money managers did more watching of corporate managers. Institutional detail matters. A complicating factor is that there are many different types of institutions: corporate pension plans; public pension plans; mutual funds; commercial banks; insurers; investment banks; foundations and endowments. Each has its own incentives, conflicts of interests, culture, history, and regulatory scheme. Some can take the lead in corporate governance initiatives. Conflicts of interest make others likely to be only followers.

Regulation is pervasive. It governs what the institutions, as currently constituted, can do. But it also determines, in substantial part, what the institutions are. Banks, mutual funds, insurers, and pension funds are in significant part defined by a web of regulation. Each could be defined differently, if we so choose. Regulatory detail matters.

The benefits and costs of institutional oversight defy easy summary. Taking them as a whole, I believe that there is a strong case for measured reform that will facilitate joint shareholder action not directed at control, and reduce obstacles to particular institutions owning stakes not large enough to confer working control. Such reform will let six or ten institutions collectively have a significant say in corporate affairs, while limiting the power of any one institution to act on its own. I will call this limited role institutional voice. Institutional voice means a world in which particular institutions can easily own a 5–10% stake in particular companies, but can't easily own much more than 10%; in which institutions can readily talk to each other and select a minority of a company's board of directors, but can't easily exercise day-to-day control or select a majority of the board.

Institutional voice should be distinguished from institutional control, from a world where Citibank or Prudential could control General Motors in the way that Deutsche Bank controls Daimler–Benz. The far-reaching reform needed for concentrated control has large potential benefits, because with control can come strong oversight. But strong oversight is inevitably accompanied by strong potential for abuse of control. Moreover, the extensive legal reform needed for institutional control involves redefining our institutions, at least in part. It's hard to predict how the newly recreated institutions would behave. Thus, the relative costs and benefits of institutional control are unclear.

The line that divides voice from control is admittedly fuzzy. We can see institutional power as lying along a rough continuum, with passivity at one end, voice in the middle, and control at the other end. Today, legal rules, agenda control, conflicts of interests, cultural factors, and historical accident combine to keep financial institutions far over toward the passivity end of the continuum. I believe that legal reform should allow—and where necessary encourage—the institutions to move toward the middle of the continuum. Such reform has little downside risk and holds substantial promise of improved corporate performance. We can't know today how much of that promise will be realized. But as long as the costs are small, institutional voice is worth a try. In economic terms, the expected benefit outweighs the expected cost.

The necessary reform will be partly deregulatory. We need to reduce the legal barriers that discourage institutions from offering shareholder voting proposals, * * * owning large stakes in particular companies, and exercising the influence that stakes could convey. But deregulation is not enough. We also need rules that encourage monitoring. We could, for example, spread some monitoring costs over all shareholders by expanding the range of proposals that shareholders can include in company proxy statements. We may also need new conflict-of-interest rules, plus more aggressive enforcement of the existing rules, to ensure that money managers act in their beneficiaries' interest; agenda rules that increase shareholder influence over the shareholder voting agenda; and rules that limit manager ability to manipulate election outcomes.

The central theme of this Article—Agents Watching Agents—affects institutional monitoring in several ways. First, and most obviously, institutional voice means asking one set of agents (money managers) to watch another set of agents (corporate managers). Money managers have limited incentives to monitor because they keep only a fraction of the portfolio gains. But money managers also won't take the legal chances that an individual shareholder might because they face personal risk if they breach their fiduciary duty or break other legal rules. The institution, however, realizes most of the gains from such misdeeds. That limits the downside risk from institutional voice.

Second, institutional voice requires a number of institutions, including different types of institutions, to join forces to exercise influence. That furthers limits the downside risk from institutional power, because money managers can monitor each others' actions to some extent. Reputation is a central element in this second form of watching. Diversified institutions interact over and over, at many different companies, over a span of years. Institutions that earn good reputations will elicit cooperation from other institutions; institutions that cheat will invite retaliation.

Third, corporate managers can watch their watchers. Corporate managers indirectly control the largest category of institutional investor, the corporate pension fund. Also, if other institutions abuse their power, corporate managers can complain—loudly and often—to state and federal lawmakers. If the costs to other shareholders, including smaller institutions, of abuse of power by the largest institutions exceed the other shareholders' gains from better monitoring, those shareholders will support corporate managers' efforts to clip the large institutions' wings. Political outcomes are hard to predict, but financial institutions have lost political battles before. Money managers know that, which limits their incentive to misbehave in the first place.

Moreover, much of the promise of shareholder monitoring lies in informal shareholder efforts to monitor corporate managers or to express a desire for change in a company's management or policies. That enhances corporate managers' ability to police money manager behavior. Corporate managers can cooperate only with those money managers who earn a reputation for promoting long-term company value.

A second central theme of this Article is diversification. Diversification creates the opportunity for economies of scale in monitoring. Scale economies, in turn, affect the issues that the institutions will care about. Institutions are likely to devote more attention to process and structure issues, which promise scale economies, than to company-specific concerns. Process and structure issues include the value of confidential voting, the desirability of poison pills and other antitakeover devices, the composition and structure of the board of directors, the process by which directors are nominated, whether a company should have a nonexecutive chairman, and the form of management compensation.

Diversification also means that money managers interact repeatedly at different companies. That makes it easier for money managers to watch each other and makes reputation an important constraint on money manager behavior. Diversification also limits the risk that money managers will divert funds to themselves. Insider trading, for example, won't materially affect portfolio performance if done only occasionally, and a money manager who frequently trades on inside information runs a high risk of being caught.

Partly because institutional incentives push against direct, company-specific monitoring, a central reform goal should be to facilitate indirect monitoring through the board of directors. If the institutions can more easily select directors, at least for a minority of board seats, they can hire directors to watch companies on their behalf. Currently, directors are often more loyal to corporate officers than to the shareholders whom the directors nominally serve. Shareholder-nominated directors will owe more loyalty to shareholders and may be more willing to ask tough questions when a company's performance lags, or when its CEO has dreams of grandeur.

Reform should focus on the process of voting, rather than substantive governance rules. For example, corporate boards may perform better if they include some directors who are nominated by large institutions. But we shouldn't legislate that result. Instead, we should empower the institutions to make their own decisions about optimal governance structures. They have incentives to make good choices—or at least better choices than lawmakers would make. Moreover, procedural reform won't force oversight or impose large regulatory costs on companies or shareholders. Oversight will take place only where the institutions conclude that the benefits of monitoring outweigh the cost.

Critics worry that the institutions will botch the job of monitoring corporate managers. There will undoubtedly be mistakes and false starts. Institutional shareholders won't develop monitoring skills overnight. But we should let them learn from their mistakes, like other actors in our market economy. In practice, legal change will occur gradually. That will make the inevitable mistakes less costly, and allow time to adjust the reforms if the initial efforts have unforeseen consequences. Given the level of congressional inertia, reform should, where possible rely on federal agency action rather than legislative command.

The promise of institutional voice is substantial. In a companion article, I collect evidence of a number of systematic shortfalls in corporate performance. * * * Unshackled institutions could take steps to remedy these shortfalls. There is also limited direct evidence that some institutions already do valuable monitoring. The direct evidence isn't conclusive, but that isn't surprising, since the institutions don't currently do much monitoring. Importantly, there is little evidence that greater shareholder oversight will be harmful.

––––––––

Other writers are more skeptical. Their doubts are of two types. First, institutional investors are not managing their own money; they are fiduciaries for other people and have the same agency cost problems that we have seen in the traditional corporate governance structure. Second, institutional investors still face considerable legal and political obstacles that hinder their power to play a more active role in monitoring. The following materials analyze both sets of problems.

MELVIN EISENBERG, THE STRUCTURE OF THE CORPORATION: A LEGAL ANALYSIS
56–58 (1976).

The appropriate relation between institutional shareholders and their portfolio corporations has prompted considerable debate. Managers and their allies seek to constrain the discretion of such shareholders; shareholder democrats seek to expand it. One issue in the debate has been whether, considering their power and sophistication, institutional investors owe an obligation to their fellow shareholders to oversee corporate managers and to effect management changes when necessary. Generally speaking, the institutional investors have taken the position that their primary obligation is to their own beneficiaries, not to their fellow shareholders in portfolio companies; that they have neither the time nor the skills to exercise an oversight function; and that a company whose management should be changed is normally an unsound investment, so that an investor which does not like incumbent management should switch out of the investment as quickly as possible, rather than stay in and try to accomplish a change. Some of these arguments appear overstated. There are undoubtedly many cases in which a corporation's assets outshine its management and an institution's position is too large to be liquidated except at a substantial loss, so that it would do better to try to change management than to sell the stock. It seems likely that there have been additional, unstated, reasons for the institutions' promanagement position, including obedience to the mores of the financial community, a desire to stay on good terms with management in order to promote a free flow of inside information, and in the case of certain institutions, particularly banks, a desire to obtain or retain business in their noninvestor capacities. Nevertheless, the position that the primary duty of a financial institution is to protect the interests of its own beneficiaries, and that such institutions are in any event not equipped to oversee management, seems essentially sound.

JOHN C. COFFEE, JR., LIQUIDITY VERSUS CONTROL: THE INSTITUTIONAL INVESTOR AS CORPORATE MONITOR
91 Col. L. Rev. 1277, 1281–1289 (1991).

* * * Put simply, the agents controlling institutional investors have considerable reason to remain "rationally apathetic" about corporate governance and little reason to become active participants. Why? Various reasons will be advanced, but one stands out: * * * a trade-off exists and must be recognized between liquidity and control. Investors that want liquidity may hesitate to accept control.

This assertion—that a preference for liquidity chills the willingness of institutional investors to participate in the control of major corporations—may sound heretical. With only a few exceptions, both practitioners and academics have shared the assumption that institutions are on the verge of becoming active monitors. * * *

* * * [T]wo polar views of the institutional investor compete for supremacy today: (1) the academic view of financial institutions as Prometheus chained to the rock by outmoded regulations that serve only to entrench and insulate incumbent managements, and (2) corporate management's image of these same institutions as frenzied gamblers in a financial casino, each competing to outdo the other in short-term performance. Both sides in this debate share the common assumption that, for better or worse, institutional investors would soon dominate corporate managements in the absence of political constraints.

This Article disagrees with that assumption. It will argue that the primary explanation for institutional passivity is not overregulation, but the insufficiency of existing incentives to motivate institutional money managers to monitor. Although proponents of institutional activism have analyzed at length the potential ability of institutional investors to hold corporate managers accountable, they have largely ignored the question of who holds institutional money managers accountable. The problem of who will guard the guardian is a timeless one, but it is particularly complicated when the proposed guardian is the institutional investor. Not only do the same problems of agency cost arise at the institutional investor level, but there are persuasive reasons for believing that some institutional investors are less accountable to their "owners" than are corporate managements to their shareholders. Put simply, the usual mechanisms of corporate accountability are either unavailable or largely compromised at the institutional level. This conclusion does not deny that there has been overregulation of institutional investors, but it suggests its impact may have been overstated by the new critics. More importantly, this perspective implies that deregulation alone is an inadequate policy response. If the diagnosis that rational apathy will continue to prevail at the institutional level is accurate, then the law must intervene to correct the market's failure by creating adequate incentives for institutional managers to monitor.

* * * [I]s such a union of liquidity and control desirable? Do we want the institutional monitor to have the same ability to exit the firm costlessly as does the individual shareholder? Would the institutional monitor who possessed such liquidity undertake the often costly burden of monitoring? These are difficult questions, but the choices are not limited to a simple yes or no. Rather, public policy could choose any of a number of possible positions along a continuum that runs from allowing investors to combine liquidity and control to requiring an election between them. * * *

At present, any attempt by institutional investors in the United States to exercise control over corporate managements will entail a probable sacrifice of this liquidity, which may be an unacceptable cost to them. Put more generally, when faced with the choice, U.S. institutional investors have traditionally preferred liquidity to control. This empirical observation leads in turn to a broader, normative contention; liquidity and control are antithetical. American law has said clearly and consistently since at least the 1930's that those who exercise control should not enjoy liquidity and vice versa. Ultimately, this Article will defend the proposition that the separation of liquidity and control is not only a cause of institutional passivity, but to some degree should be. In short, those institutions that most desire liquidity would make poor monitors.

Nor should this contention seem surprising: most other industrial societies seems to have reached a similar resolution (either by legal rule or by business adaptation). From a comparative perspective, advanced industrial economies can be classified along a continuum ranging from those, such as Japan and Germany, that permit financial institutions to control corporate managements, but effectively deny them liquidity, to those that inhibit institutional control, but maximize their liquidity. On such a continuum, the dominant American organizational form—the Berle/Means public corporation—represents the latter pole: investors have only limited ability to control management, but near-perfect liquidity in deep and relatively stable financial markets. The oft-repeated "Wall Street Rule" expressed the basic equilibrium that until recently prevailed: dissatisfied investors could sell, but they could not effectively challenge management.

The tension between liquidity and control can also explain why the historic passivity of the institutional investor is declining. Today, the press reports on an almost daily basis that institutional investors are displaying a new activism. Clearly, some institutions—most typically, public pension funds—sponsor shareholder proposals, lobby state legislatures, and, in a few cases, support insurgents in proxy contests. What explains this new activism? On a theoretical level, the trade-off between liquidity and control is simply a context-specific application of Albert O. Hirschman's famous generalization that the members of any organization face a choice between "exit" and "voice." If an easy, low-cost "exit" is possible (such as that provided by securities markets), the members will rationally have little interest in exercising a more costly "voice." But if "exit" is blocked, the members will become more interested in exercising a "voice" in governance decisions. From this perspective, the new activism of American institutional investors can be explained as the product of "voice" becoming less costly, because of the growth in institutional ownership of securities and the resulting increased capacity for collective action, while "exit" has become more difficult, because institutional investors, who increasingly own large unmarketable blocks, must accept substantial price discounts in order to liquidate theses blocks. These trends toward greater "voice" and lesser "exit" seem likely to continue for institutional investors. As a result, greater institutional activism is predictable, even in the face of a static legal environment.

The trade-off between "exit" and "voice" also suggest a regulatory strategy: restrict "exit" to encourage "voice." Undoubtedly, such a policy could be carried too far and might at some point induce institutional investors to prefer alternative investments to equity securities. Still, the new critics of regulation have not recognized the reverse side of this coin: simplified "exit" may mean less "voice." At a minimum then, a strategy for deregulation should accord a priority to relaxing those rules that inhibit "voice," while exercising considerable caution before making "exit" easier. In other words, rather than "unleashing" institutional investors en masse, the more sensible policy may be a selective one: deregulate first those institutions most likely to exercise "voice" rather than seek "exit."

EDWARD B. ROCK, THE LOGIC AND (UNCERTAIN) SIGNIFICANCE OF INSTITUTIONAL SHAREHOLDER ACTIVISM
79 Georgetown L.J. 445, 469–476 (1991).

Optimists assume that an institutional investor with a two percent stake in a company will behave like an individual investor with a comparable stake. But one cannot assume that agents will act like principals.

1. CONFLICTS OF INTERESTS

Institutional investors are intermediaries: the investment and voting decisions are made by someone other than the beneficiaries. The central problem is whether those managing the assets, whether in-house or outside managers, can be relied upon to act to maximize the value of the assets under their management.

A number of factors may interfere, including widely recognized conflicts of interest. The in-house plan administrator, an executive of the plan sponsor charged with the responsibility of managing the corporation's pension plan, will inevitably face a conflict, implicit or explicit, between managing the pension plan "for the exclusive purpose of providing benefits to participants and their beneficiaries," as required by the Employee Retirement Income Security Act (ERISA), and managing the fund for the benefit of the corporation or management.

Outside money managers likewise face severe conflicts of interest. Corporate managers can and do pressure outside money managers to vote for management's proposals and to help further management's interests. For example, management may threaten to change banks unless the bank votes the shares it holds in a fiduciary capacity for management. Management may similarly threaten the corporation's insurance company. The pressure may be very crude or more subtle.

* * *

Structurally, the choice facing any money manager, public or private, in house or outside, is the same as the choice facing the entrepreneurs discussed earlier: the money manager must consider the benefits of acting in the interests of the beneficiaries and the costs of doing so. These costs include both the direct costs of providing the collective good (the cost of monitoring and organizing other shareholders) and the indirect costs of alienating corporate management, the people who allocate funds among outside managers. Whether it is rational for the money manager to provide the collective good will depend on the relative costs and benefits, including the benefits from alternative courses of action. Given the pressures from corporate managers, the question becomes whether money managers have sufficient positive incentives to act in shareholder's interest.

2. THE COLLECTIVE ACTION PROBLEM REPEATED?

a. Economic Incentives

In addition to conflicts of interests, other factors interfere with alignment of the interest of money managers and beneficiaries. The easiest problem to solve may be the collective action problem. If one assumes that money managers or a subset of money managers are collectively better off when corporate management is disciplined, but that, because of the costs and alternatives outlined above, it is not rational for any individual money manager to assume the burden of disciplining, then the collective action problem reemerges and surmounting the problem will become easier as concentration of shareholding increases.

But this assumes that discipline will be in the collective interest of money managers. Under what circumstance will that be true? When does rational apathy among money managers lead to a collective action problem, that is, a situation where, although it is irrational for any individual money manager to provide the collective good, the money managers as a group would be better off if the good were provided?

The short answer is that there are precious few incentives for money managers to act in the interests of their principals. Because of this divergence between the interests of money managers and the interest of their principals, one cannot assume that because improving corporate governance may increase the value of the managed portfolios, improving corporate governance will be in the interests of the money managers. Consider widely diversified and passive (indexed) money managers as paradigm cases. Such money managers are critically important for several reasons. First, most institutional investors are widely diversified. Second, the enormous and increasing evidence that portfolio managers rarely outperform the market has driven more and more assets into passive (indexed) portfolios. Finally, the large public funds that have been particularly prominent in corporate governance matters are largely indexed.

While an increase in discipline may increase the value of the widely diversified and indexed portfolio, and thus benefit the money managers' principals, it is not at all clear that discipline is a collective good for the managers of such a portfolio. To the extent that money managers are evaluated in comparison to other managers and to market indices, such money managers will have no selective incentives to engage in actions that improve the performance of widely diversified funds across the board. A change that benefits all will benefit none.

The potential divergence of the interests of money managers and their principles—a new version of the classic agency problem—is crucial to understanding the potential for institutional shareholder activism. In a provocative article advocating that institutional investors identify and elect professional directors [discussed in Chapter 15], Ronald Gilson and Reinier Kraakman argue that it is in the interest of the passive (indexed) portfolio manager to adopt an active corporate governance strategy. The premise of their argument is that diversified institutional shareholders will benefit from an across the board improvement in the quality of corporate governance because it will increase the value of their portfolios as a whole. But in making that assertion, Gilson and Kraakman ignore the potential divergence of interest between passive portfolio managers and the beneficiaries of the funds they manage. Although adopting a corporate governance strategy may be in the interest of the beneficiaries, Gilson and Kraakman provide no argument for concluding that adopting such a policy will be in the interests of the money managers themselves (on whom they depend). In fact, such a strategy seems unlikely to help passive (indexed) portfolio managers improve their standing in comparison to peers.

Indeed, passive portfolio managers have significant incentives *not* to adopt such a strategy. Not only do they face the conflicts of interest discussed above, they also confront a second, less obvious disincentive. In the competition among passive (indexed) portfolio managers, the principal way to improve performance is to cut costs. The key to competition among indexed fund managers is to be the lowest cost producer because, by hypothesis, everyone produces the same gross gain or loss. But corporate governance activities, to be effective, are costly.

Discipline will be a collective good for money managers when there are selective incentives. For managers who are not widely diversified, typically outside money managers, improved discipline and performance of the firms in their portfolios may selectively improve their performance, relative to competitors who do not hold the stock. This account would suggest that such money managers may face a collective action problem analogous to that faced by shareholders, a problem that might be surmounted if the concentration of shareholdings increases. But several problems confront this account of shareholder activism. First, such money managers are subject to the greatest amount of pressure from client corporations and prospective clients to vote with management. Second, the selective incentive for money widely held by money managers, namely in the large, publicly traded firms in which institutional activism has been greatest. Finally, the leading institutional activists are largely indexed. For these reasons, this account cannot provide the full story.

If the collective benefit from improved corporate performance is unlikely to explain the distribution of shareholder activism across firms, then what does? It may be that the private benefits from shareholder activism, benefits that may be unrelated to improved corporate performance but that may increase as the prominence of the target increases, better explain the focus of shareholder activism. That is, the actual pattern of shareholder activism may be more consistent with the political entrepreneur account.

In addition, certain forms of discipline may be considered tests of a money manager's loyalty, and therefore passing such tests will be in the manager's individual interests. Certain choices may be so clearly in the interests of beneficiaries that a failure to act by money managers would be viewed as shirking, incompetence, or betrayal. But note that in this situation discipline is not in the collective interests of money managers, but is simply a result of competition among money managers. Indeed, not disciplining is the collective good that cannot always be achieved.

ROBERTA ROMANO, PUBLIC PENSION FUND ACTIVISM IN CORPORATE GOVERNANCE RECONSIDERED
93 Col. L. Rev. 795, 796–852 (1993).

This Article seeks to add a dose of realism to the debate over shareholder activism in corporate governance by underscoring what was once widely recognized in the literature but of late has been overlooked: public pension funds face distinctive investment conflicts that limit the benefits of their activism. Public fund managers must navigate carefully around the shoals of considerable political pressure to temper investment policies with local considerations, such as fostering in-state employment, which are not aimed at maximizing the value of their portfolios' assets. This tension is not an isolated phenomenon. Much of the activity of states in what is referred to as economic development— providing tax concessions or direct payments to in-state businesses—is in response to similar concerns. * * *

The hypothesized conflict that prevents private funds from opposing incumbent management is consequently not unique to that sector: corporate managers who threaten private fund managers or their employers with loss of business as the price of opposition can just as effectively threaten public funds with economic loss through, for example, local plant closings. Such pressure is, however, likely to be geographically constrained compared to that created by private sector financial relationships, because state officials are most concerned with effects on local labor markets. * * *

Public funds have, in fact, been more active than other institutional investors in corporate governance over the past few years. * * * But as public funds increase their activism and that activism affects the interests of politically organized groups, such as unions and corporate managers, political pressure on these funds will increase significantly. For instance, after it was disclosed that a New York state pension fund had invested in a leveraged buyout fund that financed contested tender offers, including the RJR/Nabisco buyout, the governor created a task force to investigate pension fund investment policy. The task force recommended restricting public pension funds' involvement in hostile takeovers and instructing them to take local concerns, such as the state economy and in-state employment, into account when acquiring or voting shares. If activist public funds are required to embrace such an investment agenda, then their investment objective will diverge from that of other equity holders, who desire to maximize share value and will therefore not benefit from public funds' increased role in corporate governance.

* * *

* * * [S]tate statutes fix the composition of public pension fund boards. Designated board members typically fall into one of three categories: gubernatorial appointees; representatives elected by fund beneficiaries; and individuals named by virtue of their office. The designation of employer executives (state officials) as fund trustees is not unique to public pension plans—trustees of private plans are typically officers of the employer-sponsor. It does, however, raise potentially serious conflict of interest problems, as trustees have dual roles, representing employers as well as employees. The political affiliation of a significant number of fund trustees render public pension funds especially vulnerable to pressure by other state officials. This vulnerability is exacerbated by the magnitude of fund holdings. Particularly in times of fiscal difficulty, fund assets are an inviting target for state officials seeking new sources of financing for local projects. There are numerous examples of governors pressuring public pension funds to use their assets to assist distressed local entities, both public and private.

* * *

In the 1990s, states experiencing fiscal difficulty have taken unilateral action against fund assets rather than employed the earlier New York approach of "requesting" their use in public debt purchases. Among the tactics employed are reducing contributions and retirement funds, altering actuarial and income assumptions in order to decrease contribution levels, and transferring assets from pension fund to general state accounts. These policies are particularly troubling because many state pension funds are in weak financial condition: in 1991, twenty state funds were less than seventy-five percent funded. However, the most widespread type of political pressure on public funds investment policies today involves demands to stimulate local economic activity directly by financing development projects that over-extended states cannot fund rather than by bailing out government entities. Most such investments are "social investments"—investments whose return is not commensurate with their risk. Such investments use pensions assets for broader social purposes at the expense of fund beneficiaries or a subset of beneficiaries.

* * *

[C]ontroversies over the organization of the California and New York pension fund board suggest that board composition makes a difference for fund investment and voting policies. Given that many public fund board members are politicians or political appointees, investment and voting decisions may well be imbued with non-portfolio value-maximizing considerations even when there is no observable political pressure from other state officials. In order to determine whether this is so one must examine whether fund performance varies significantly with board composition. In particular, do funds with a higher proportion of appointed and ex officio board members perform more poorly than those with less politicized board structures?

Board members who are elected by plan participants and are themselves fund beneficiaries are likely to be less susceptible to political influence or pressure because their personal retirement funds are at stake and their positions do not depend on the good graces of state officials. This hypothesis draws support from research on the incentive alignment problems caused by the separation of ownership and control in the modern corporation. Studies have found that corporate performance is positively correlated with the proportion of equity owned by management. Elected board members, as participants in a fund's retirement plan, have a strong interest in plan performance, as do corporate managers who hold stock in their firms. In addition, in some states, pension fund earnings in excess of actuarial requirements can be used to provide cost-of-living adjustments to retirees. The incentives of elected members to ensure that the board follows value-maximizing investment strategies are even greater in such states.

Appointed and ex officio members do not have similar financial incentives, and, although their reputations will be harmed if a plan experiences financial difficulty on their watch, the effect of social investments on plan performance may not be observed until several years later, when board membership has turned over. Unlike publicly traded corporations, for which low stock prices signal poor management decisions, there is no capital market monitoring public pension plan boards' decisions that could inform fund beneficiaries of poor investments and thereby mitigate the intertemporal mismatching of board members' incentives.

There is an important caveat to applying the corporate manager-owner analogy to public pension fund board members. Public employee pensions are government liabilities set by employment contract, and are independent of plan assets. If a plan's assets are insufficient to meet retiree claims, the state's annual contributions will be used entirely to pay current expenses rather than to increase plan assets through investment. Accordingly, even the more political board members have some interest in the growth of fund assets through investments because increased portfolio earnings will reduce required annual contributions. But again, the mismatching of the timing of investment returns and board tenure weakens these members' incentives.

The composition of public fund boards may also explain why public funds are more active in corporate governance than private funds even if private fund managers lack conflicts of interest involving other business relations with issuers. Public funds are frequently managed by individuals with aspirations to higher political office whose reputations can be enhanced by populist crusading against corporate management. For example, Elizabeth Holtzman, New York City comptroller and a trustee for the city's pension funds, publicized her active approach to corporate governance while campaigning for the Democratic party's nomination for U.S. Senator. Private fund managers do not obtain such personal professional benefits from corporate governance activism. In addition, on-the-job consumption benefits figure more importantly for financial managers in the public sector, where financial compensation is lower than in the private sector. The prototypical free rider problem of corporate governance activities—that only the activist bears the costs of activism while all of the firm's investors receive the benefits—could therefore be mitigated for public funds more readily than for private funds because public funds are more likely to be managed by political entrepreneurs, who benefit personally from such visible activity.

* * *

Proponents of public pension fund activism in corporate governance believe that such activities benefit investors. This position implies that there is a positive relation between activism and fund performance. But the relation between activism and performance is surely more complex than this simple hypothesis. For example, poor financial results could spur a fund to be active in corporate governance in order to increase future returns by improving the performance of companies in the funds' stock portfolio. Such a strategy would make fund performance appear to be inversely related to activism. Hence, if, as is likely, there is a lag between the fruits of activism and performance, then a negative relation between activism and performance should not automatically be interpreted as evidence that institutional activism hurts fund beneficiaries, while a finding of positive relation between activism and performance might actually be a spurious result.

* * *

The data bolster the Article's thesis that public funds face political pressure on their decision-making. Funds with more politicized board structures perform significantly more poorly than those with more independent boards. Policies favoring social investments also appear to affect performance negatively, although the relationship is statistically significant only at ten percent. Restrictions on South Africa investments adversely affect fund performance, most probably because of their impact on asset allocation—portfolios weighted toward small firm stocks performed poorly over the sample period. A fund's activism in corporate governance does not appear to affect its performance.

There is little evidence that public and private fund managers differentially support corporate management in proxy voting. In the vast majority of cases, especially matters touching upon corporate control, both groups of investors appear to follow the same voting strategy. Of course, these data do not address recent gubernatorial efforts to interfere in the internal organization of the New York and California state pension funds. These events indicate that, as public funds become increasingly active in corporate governance, they will experience increased political pressure on both voting and investment decisions. This pressure will produce non-value-maximizing decisions at odds with the interest of other investors. This tendency suggests that shareholder activism by public pension funds will not be able to replace an active market in corporate control as the most potent disciplining force for aligning managers' incentives with shareholders' interests.

BERNARD BLACK, AGENTS WATCHING AGENTS: THE PROMISE OF INSTITUTIONAL INVESTOR VOICE
39 UCLA L. Rev. 811, 822–824 (1992).

A broad array of state and federal rules makes it hard for a single shareholder to own a large percentage stake in a single company. Other rules encumber joint action by a number of shareholders and increase the cost of a proxy campaign. * * *

For an active shareholder or a shareholder group, owning a 5% stake triggers filing requirements under section 13(d) of the Securities Exchange Act and related S.E.C. rules. Owning a 10% stake can trigger short-swing profit forfeiture under Exchange Act section 16(b) and related S.E.C. rules. A large shareholder or group also risks being considered a control person, with adverse consequences under securities, bankruptcy, and other laws. And a shareholder or group can't cross the trigger percentage for the company's poison pill, often 10 to 15%, without manager approval. Banks, insurers, and mutual funds face additional legal limits on their ability to hold large stakes. Corporate crossholdings are discouraged by an extra layer of taxation, and by unfavorable accounting treatment for stakes under 20%.

The obstacles to owning a large stake are greater for an active shareholder than for a passive shareholder. For example, an active shareholder must report its holdings and plans on Schedule 13D; a passive shareholder can file a shorter Schedule 13G. An active shareholder may have to make a costly filing under the Hart–Scott–Rodino premerger notification rules; a passive shareholder is exempt. Depending on the company's takeover defenses and state of incorporation, a successful proponent could lose voting power under a control share antitakeover statute; incur an obligation to buy everyone else's stock at a premium to market under a cashout law; trigger change-of-control provisions in various debt instruments, employment agreements or employee benefit plans; or even trigger a poison pill. Catch–22 indeed!

Legal obstacles are especially great if shareholders want to choose some directors instead of rubberstamping the incumbents' choices. The S.E.C.'s proxy rules help shareholders on some matters, but mostly create obstacles for director elections. The sponsoring institution(s) risk being deemed to be a control person, or to have "deputized" the director (which would create short-swing profit forfeiture liability under section 16(b)). Choosing directors also creates a risk of insider trading liability under Exchange Act section 10(b), because the director will have access to insider information.

Legal rules also raise the costs of a proxy campaign or other shareholder action. The S.E.C.'s shareholder proposal rule, Rule 14a–8, allows some proposals to be included in company proxy statements, but excludes several key areas, including director nominations and solicitations in opposition to manager proposals. * * * Obstacles to forming shareholder groups discourage cost-sharing that might otherwise reduce these cost barriers.

Often the law is uncertain. This creates legal risk, which is especially troublesome for institutional fiduciaries. They face personal risk on the downside, while their beneficiaries get most of the upside. For many money managers, the adverse publicity from a lawsuit is a major deterrent without more. Legal uncertainty also encourages company managers to sue shareholders, because the managers can impose costs on shareholders even if they lose the suit.

Moreover, corporate managers begin a proxy contest with various advantages. They can spend the shareholders' money to support their own proposals or fight a shareholder proposal. They can issue large blocks of stock to employees (who will predictably vote promanager) through a leveraged employee stock ownership plan. Managers can also control, in various ways, the voting of some shares that they don't own.

No single legal rule forecloses shareholder action. But the obstacles are many, and their cumulative effect is large. A shareholder who remains quiet is safe. A shareholder who buys a large stake, especially a shareholder who becomes active on governance issues, pays a price. That price, for a shareholder whose stake is kept small by legal rules, is often enough to make passivity the preferred choice.

————

In addition to the restrictions which Professor Black analyzes, there are numerous other obstacles to free institutional investor action arising from the diverse nature of the institutional universe.

Private pension funds, established by employers to provide retirement income for their employees, have a number of provisions relating to the acquisition and disposition of assets and voting decisions. The employer, as sponsor of the plan, usually delegates this decision-making power to one or more fiduciaries who administer the plan. In large corporations, these fiduciaries are often employees of the sponsoring employer, thereby creating an immediate conflict of interest on the part of the fiduciary. Whoever the fiduciaries, however, they are subject to state and federal restrictions on their freedom to act. At common law, a fiduciary must act "with strict honesty and candor and solely in the interest of the beneficiary." And the federal Employee Retirement Income Security Act of 1974 (ERISA) imposes the same duties on fiduciaries of plans subject to the Act.

Fiduciaries of public pension plans (the most active institutions in the corporate governance movement), while not subject to ERISA, are nevertheless governed by state fiduciary law and state statutory law constraining their discretion. They must also comply with the requirements of the Internal Revenue Code which seem to impose obligations similar to those of ERISA.

The same analysis applies to other types of institutions. Investment companies and investment advisers are subject to state fiduciary requirements as well as the obligations under the Investment Company Act of 1940 and the Investment Advisers Act of 1940. They are also subject to the pressure to produce superior investment performance. And insurance companies, depending on whether they are stock or mutual companies, and the nature of the plans they administer, may be subject to ERISA and are, in any event, subject to the traditional corporate duties of care and loyalty. With respect to these latter duties, of course, the same difficulties faced by any shareholder in a derivative suit against a corporate manager would obtain in an action challenging a voting decision as a breach of fiduciary duty. For a fuller discussion of these issues, see A.A. Sommer, Jr., Corporate Governance in the Nineties: Managers Vs. Institutions, 59 U. Cin. L. Rev. 357, 362–367 (1990).

E.   SHAREHOLDER PROPOSALS

PROBLEMS
UNIVERSAL MOTORS CORPORATION—PART II
A

UMC maintains plants around the country, a number of which are old and inefficient. Recently, rumors have circulated that the company intends to close several factories in Ohio, including one in Lima, Ohio, that employs 5,000 people and accounts for a substantial portion of that community's payroll. The output of that plant accounts for less than 1% of UMC's revenues and profits. UMC's policy, whenever it closes a plant, is to give severance pay equal to three month's wages or salary and, if possible, to offer employment at another UMC facility.

Prior to last year's annual shareholder meeting, Students For Social Justice (SFSJ), a student organization at nearby State University, purchased 100 shares of UMC stock. That stock now is trading at $20 per share. SFSJ now wants to submit a shareholder proposal for inclusion in UMC's proxy statement for its upcoming annual meeting. It has prepared a draft resolution reading as follows:

RESOLVED, that the by-laws be amended to add the following provision: The corporation shall not substantially discontinue the use of any significant business or plant facility unless (1) the company gives one year's notice in writing to the affected employees and community representatives of the extent of the proposed closing or reduction, (2) a hearing is conducted at which an opportunity is provided to employees and citizens of the affected communities to express their views on any aspect of the proposed closing or reduction and (3) the Board of Directors is furnished with a written report of a detailed study on the economic, environmental and social consequences of the proposed action upon the affected community. Such report shall become a record of the Corporation and copies shall be made available to shareholders upon payment of reasonable costs.

SFSJ also has prepared the following draft supporting statement:

The power to discontinue a plant or other facility carries with it the power to visit major economic, environmental and social consequences upon a particular community—consequences that may be calamitous. The proposed new by-law simply requires the Board of Directors to be aware of these consequences before the Corporation acts on such matters, which are neither routine nor trivial, and enables the owners of the Corporation to acquire, in addition to already available financial information, some knowledge concerning the social impact of their company's activities. The Company's disregard for the welfare of its workers necessitates revised procedures in making these far-reaching decisions.

The by-law would impose requirements upon the Corporation that are similar to but far less extensive than those calling upon federal agencies to furnish environmental impact statements before undertaking certain projects, and for much the same reasons. Application of the by-law is limited to actions upon "significant" facilities so as to avoid harassment of the company. Implementation and interpretation will devolve upon the Board, which must decide the issue in good faith.

SFSJ has asked the University Board of Trustees to support the resolution, and has obtained editorial support from the student newspaper. In addition, SFSJ has written letters to alumni and community leaders in Lima and the vicinity to seek their support. The University owns a large bloc of UMC stock; it also receives large annual gifts from UMC. Local politicians have taken up the plant closing issue, and a bill has been introduced in the state legislature to require all employers in Ohio to follow procedures similar to those proposed by SFSJ.

SFSJ has asked your advice as to whether the SEC is likely to require UMC management to include the proposal in its proxy statement. SFSJ also has asked you if there are any changes it should make in its proposal or supporting statement to improve the prospects that UMC will be required to include the proposal in its proxy statement.

How do you respond to these questions?

B

The Columbia Employees Retirement Fund has decided not to solicit proxies in opposition to the UMC dual-class voting plan (see Part I). Instead, CERF is considering submitting the following proposal to UMC for inclusion in the UMC proxy statement for the meeting at which the voting plan will be considered:

RESOLVED, that the shareholders of the Universal Motors Corporation recommend that the Board of Directors, in accordance with the laws of the State of Delaware, and the Certificate of Incorporation of the Universal Motors Corporation, adopt a resolution setting forth an amendment to the Certificate of Incorporation of the Universal Motors Corporation that the directors of the Corporation be elected by the holders of Class A and Class B stock in direct proportion that each Class bears to the total outstanding stock of the Corporation.

[Supporting statement omitted]

May UMC management exclude the proposal from the proxy statement?

1. EVOLUTION OF THE SHAREHOLDER PROPOSAL RULE

The power that shareholders of a publicly-held corporation theoretically possess to secure corporate action by adopting a resolution at the annual meeting of shareholders is, by itself, illusory. A tiny fraction of the shareholders actually attend the meeting. Practically all the shares are represented by proxy, and state law and the SEC proxy rules either bind the proxy holders to vote in a prescribed way, or give the proxy holders complete discretion. Because of collective action problems, management can turn away almost any shareholder resolution it opposes or secure the approval of almost any resolution it supports, including those it presents to the shareholders.

What has happened, as we have already noted, is that the proxy soliciting process has become the surrogate for the meeting. The shareholder who wants her resolution to succeed at the meeting must solicit proxies in advance and comply with the requirements described earlier. If the shareholder wants to take control of the company, this effort can be cost justified. But suppose she simply wants to amend the by-laws to require that the board of directors consist of a majority of independent directors. Or that she wants the company to cease doing business with a country that she believes oppresses human rights. In the latter case, she may really seek to focus public attention on an issue, spark some debate and thereby force the corporation to change its way of doing business. She will derive no personal benefit from passage of the resolution, and the expense of her own solicitation of proxies cannot be cost justified. Nevertheless, as we saw in Chapter 12, if the matter is appropriate for shareholder action, the shareholder has a right to present the proposal at the meeting. She also may have the right to have the resolution appear in the proxy statement.

In 1938, the SEC took the position that the shareholder had such a right under Section 14(a) of the Securities Exchange Act of 1934, and in 1942 it formalized its views by adopting the first version of the shareholder proposal rule which is now Rule 14a–8. As originally adopted, the rule required management to include in its proxy statement a shareholder proposal that was going to be introduced at the meeting, so long as the proposal was a "proper subject for action by security holders." The SEC considered proposals that dealt with general political, social or economic matters as not proper subjects for action by shareholders.

The legal basis for the SEC's position is Rule 14a–9, the anti-fraud provision of the proxy rules, which the SEC has interpreted to ensure that the proxy statement accurately reflects all the issues that will properly arise at the meeting. As one court stated:

> [S]ince a shareholder may present a proposal at the annual meeting regardless of whether the proposal is included in a proxy solicitation, the corporate circulation of proxy materials which fail to make reference to a shareholder's intention to present a proper proposal at the annual meeting renders the solicitation inherently misleading.

New York City Employees' Retirement System v. American Brands, Inc., 634 F.Supp. 1382, 1386 (S.D.N.Y.1986).

An early case, S.E.C. v. Transamerica Corp., 163 F.2d 511 (3d Cir.1947), provided the standard by which the propriety of the subject matter is to be determined. In *Transamerica*, a shareholder submitted several proposals for inclusion in the company's proxy statement. One proposal would have resulted in shareholder election of the independent public auditors of the company's financial statements; another would have amended the by-laws with respect to the procedure for by-law amendment. A third resolution would have required the corporation to send a report of the annual meeting to the shareholders. The company excluded all the proposals on the ground that the rule did not require their inclusion; the SEC then sought to enjoin the company's proxy solicitation.

The court agreed with the SEC that a "proper subject" is one in which the shareholders may properly be interested under the law of the state of incorporation. Applying that test, all of the proposals were properly includible in Transamerica's proxy materials. The election of auditors was clearly within the stockholders' concern since the corporation is run for their benefit, and the financial condition (as shown in the financial statements) is critical to the corporation. The amendment to the by-laws was proper because Delaware law specifically allows shareholders to amend the by-laws. The only basis for exclusion was the company's own by-law provision that required advance notice to be contained in the notice of the annual meeting, which was not done in this case. However, that self-imposed restriction could not diminish the power given by the state to the shareholders. The report of the meeting was proper because, the court said, "we can perceive no logical basis for concluding that it is not a proper subject for action by the security holders." Id. at 517. In the view of both the court and the SEC, the shareholder proposal rule is a federal mechanism to enhance a state created right of the shareholder.

The stockholder movement began in the 1930's with an emphasis on shareholder democracy. Proposals often related to voting and the conduct of annual shareholder meetings and would have required corporations to institute mandatory cumulative voting or send post-meeting reports to all shareholders. In 1970, the focus of the proposals changed dramatically. The new proponents were shareholders with few shares who were more concerned with issues of corporate social responsibility than with shareholder democracy. These shareholders offered proposals relating to the environmental impact of corporate activity, race and sex discrimination, and the conduct of business in parts of the world where human rights had not been respected. The first major effort in this respect was by a group called the Project on Corporate Responsibility, which created Campaign GM in 1970.

Campaign GM sought approval by General Motors (GM) shareholders of several resolutions, the most important of which would have created a Shareholder Committee for Corporate Responsibility to examine GM's social performance and its impact in several designated areas of conduct. The Project also urged GM to elect its first black and first woman to the board of directors. The proposal for a shareholder committee was supported by 2.73% of the votes cast at the meeting. Despite the low vote, within months after the annual meeting, GM's board of directors created a Public Policy Committee and elected its first black member, Rev. Leon Sullivan. About a year later, it elected its first woman member. See Donald E. Schwartz, The Public–Interest Proxy Contest: Reflections on Campaign GM, 69 Mich.L.Rev. 419 (1971).

Shareholder activists viewed Campaign GM as a success because it demonstrated that a skillful use of publicity could lead to substantive changes in the corporate system even though the proposals themselves were defeated. As a result, many other groups began using shareholder proposals to advance their programs. Church groups, for example, became the most active shareholder proponents and launched a campaign to eliminate or alter corporate presence in South Africa. The so-called Sullivan Principles, developed by Rev. Leon Sullivan, received considerable impetus from shareholder resolutions offered at scores of meetings. Other proponents raised numerous public policy issues, including opposition to the Arab boycott of Israel, national defense, foreign policy, religious discrimination in Northern Ireland and nuclear power. See Donald E. Schwartz, Toward New Corporate Goals: Co–Existence with Society, 60 Geo.L.J. 57 (1971). For an attack on the use of shareholder proposals to advance social causes, see Henry G. Manne, Shareholder Social Proposals Viewed by an Opponent, 24 Stan. L.Rev. 481 (1972).

2. THE RULE IN OPERATION

Paragraph 14a–8(c) contains 13 grounds for excluding a shareholder proposal. These may be classified into eight reasons for omission based upon the proposal itself and five reasons designed to prevent abuse of the shareholder proposal process. See Donald E. Schwartz and Elliott J. Weiss, An Assessment of the SEC Shareholder Proposal Rule, 65 Geo. L.J. 635, 658 (1977). The most important grounds for exclusion are those in subparagraphs (c)(1), (5) and (7), relating to the propriety of the proposal under state law, and the economic significance of the proposal. The SEC has amended the rule on several occasions, and the SEC releases in connection with these amendments constitute their principal legislative history. See e.g., Securities Exchange Act Release 12999 (November 22, 1976), Securities Exchange Act Release 19135 (October 14, 1982) (proposing amendments) and Securities Exchange Act Release 20091 (August 16, 1983).

a. *The Interpretative Process*

The flesh on the bones of Rule 14a–8 is provided primarily through interpretations by the staff of the Division of Corporation Finance of the SEC. The staff furnishes these interpretations in response to company inquiries asking whether it will recommend that the Commission take any enforcement action if the company omits a shareholder proposal from its proxy statement. Because the inquiries deal with possible Commission enforcement action, the staff responses are known as "no-action" letters.

Each year, the staff issues more than 300 no-action letters relating to Rule 14a–8. On rare occasions, the Commission itself makes the substantive interpretation, but the vast majority of interpretations are issued by the staff with no formal Commission review. The letters are available at the SEC's offices in Washington or through computer or other research services. Selected letters are also identified or printed in looseleaf services. The entire body of no-action letters has become the common law of Rule 14a–8.

The process by which a no-action letter is issued most closely resembles a ritual dance in which each party's steps can be clearly predicted. The shareholder sends a letter to the company which may be anything from a simple request that a proposal be included to an elaborate presentation with a legal opinion in support of inclusion, depending upon the sophistication and experience of the proponent. The company then sends a letter to the SEC advising of its intent to omit the proposal, accompanied either by an opinion of outside counsel or the company's own legal staff stating the grounds on which the proposal can be excluded. This opinion is often based on a detailed analysis of past staff no-action letters on the same or related issues; it strongly resembles a traditional brief in litigation in which counsel analyzes and distinguishes existing case law. In some cases, the proponent will submit a reply which may or may not include a contrary legal opinion. When all the papers have been submitted, the staff issues its letter.

The form of that letter has varied over time. In simpler days when shareholder proposals were less concerned with social issues, the staff's response spelled out its reasons for concurring or disagreeing with the company. In Medical Committee on Human Rights v. Securities and Exchange Commission, 432 F.2d 659 (D.C.Cir.1970), vacated as moot 404 U.S. 403, 92 S.Ct. 577, 30 L.Ed.2d 560 (1972), the court held that such a letter was a reviewable order. In an effort to avoid becoming embroiled in litigation about subsequent no-action letters, the staff stopped giving its reasons and simply stated whether or not it would recommend enforcement action if the proposal were omitted. Recently, the pendulum has begun to swing back toward giving a fuller explanation of the staff's reasons, although it is doubtful that the swing will ever be complete. In today's terminology, if the staff concludes that the proposal can be omitted, it advises the company that "[T]here appears to be some basis for your view that the proposal may be excluded pursuant to Rule 14a–8(c) [appropriate subparagraph number]," although the staff does not state what that basis is. If the staff concludes that the proposal cannot be omitted, it states that "the Division is unable to concur in your view that the proposal may be excluded." In such a case, the staff now briefly explains the basis for its position.

Sometimes the staff will find a middle ground which has the effect of helping shareholders who may not be skilled in the arcane art of drafting proposals. This middle ground arises most often when the substance of the proposal may be proper but the form in which it is drafted may render it excludable. For example, if the proposal is in the form of a mandatory resolution which is not proper under state law, but if made precatory, would be proper, the staff will concur that there is "some basis" for exclusion because of the form of the proposal but will note that the defect could be cured. The staff will also advise that if the proponent submits a revised proposal, the staff will not concur in the omission of the proposal from the proxy statement.

b. Application of the Rule

Under subsections (c)(1) and (c)(7), a corporation may exclude a proposal if the proposal is either not a "proper subject for action by security holders" or it involves "ordinary business operations." Both of these questions are decided under the law of the issuer's state of incorporation. Under subsection (c)(5), a proposal may be omitted if it relates to operations that do not meet a minimum economic test *and* are "not otherwise significantly related" to the company's business.

The analytic framework under (c)(1) and (c)(7) involves the application of state law and the governance system that we studied in Chapter 12. As we saw there, state law provides that the business and affairs of a corporation are to be managed by, or under the direction of, the board of directors. The role of shareholders is limited to those matters on which the statute requires that they vote, issues on which management solicits their vote, or those matters that they can properly raise at a shareholders' meeting.

When looked at in the language of Rule 14a–8, the governance system is easy to state and difficult to apply. The question of what is a "proper subject" is to be decided under state law; the problem is that there is very little state law on which to base a decision. The principal case on this subject is Auer v. Dressel in which the issue was whether the president of the company was required to call a shareholders' meeting that had been demanded by a shareholder who held sufficient stock to satisfy the statutory requirement. The corporation claimed that it was not obligated to call the meeting to consider a resolution that made a recommendation to the board concerning a matter within its authority—rehiring the president. The court held that the meeting had to be called even if the shareholders' vote did not bind the board of directors to act because the matters to be voted on were sufficiently significant. Even a recommendation would put the directors on notice that they might be removed if they did not act in accordance with the shareholders' wishes.

Auer provides the conceptual underpinning for determinations under both (c)(1) and (c)(7). Under (c)(1), as it has been interpreted in recent years, the form of the resolution is significant. If a resolution is mandatory and addresses a matter concerning which shareholders do not have authority to bind the directors or the corporation, it can be omitted as inconsistent with state law. If the resolution is cast as a recommendation, the Note to (c)(1) makes clear that it may be a "proper subject" under state law. In such a case, the question of excludability will turn on the subject matter of the proposal. State law contemplates that "ordinary business" decisions will be made by the company's management. Thus a resolution that deals with "ordinary business" can be excluded under subsection (c)(7) and, inferentially, under the broader rubric of (c)(1). If, on the other hand, the resolution does not deal with "ordinary business," a shareholder has the right to present it at the meeting and the company cannot omit it under either subsection. The antithesis of "ordinary business" appears to be "public policy;" if a proposal that otherwise might be considered to involve "ordinary business" *also* implicates questions of public policy, it cannot be excluded under (c)(7).

A similar methodology is used in determining whether a proposal can be omitted under (c)(5). The principal purpose of (c)(5) is to exclude proposals whose economic significance to the corporation would be de minimis; the measuring rod is 5% of sales, assets or earnings. Some proposals, however, may be significant even though they do not meet the statistical test, either because they relate to corporate structure (e.g., cumulative voting) or because they raise public policy issues that relate directly to the corporation's business. Such proposals cannot be excluded under (c)(5). It seems clear that the "significantly related" test of (c)(5) is analytically very close to the "ordinary business" standard of (c)(7). Indeed, the SEC staff has stated that there may be other grounds for excluding a proposal even if it cannot be omitted under (c)(5). In recent years, the staff's interpretations have focused more on (c)(7) and less on (c)(5).

c. Judicial Enforcement of Rule 14a–8

The SEC, of course, has the power to seek an injunction to compel a company to include a shareholder proposal in its proxy statement. See *Transamerica*, supra. Private enforcement of Rule 14a–8 also is available to shareholders who wish to challenge the omission of a proposal. In Roosevelt v. E.I. Du Pont de Nemours & Co., 958 F.2d 416 (D.C.Cir. 1992), the court held that a shareholder had an implied private right of action under Rule 14a–8 to maintain her suit against the company for injunctive relief. The court reasoned that Section 14(a) supports such a right of action no less than it supports an action for damages (see J.I. Case Co. v. Borak, Chapter 18). Moreover, the court found that it would be demonstrably inequitable to deny the right to sue, and that such a denial "would upset longstanding administrative arrangements and shareholder expectations." Id. at 421.

AMALGAMATED CLOTHING AND TEXTILE WORKERS UNION v. WAL-MART STORES, INC.

821 F.Supp. 877 (S.D.N.Y.1993).

Wood, District Judge.

Plaintiffs, Wal–Mart shareholders, sought to enjoin the company from omitting their Proposal from proxy solicitation material the company plans to distribute in advance of Wal–Mart's June 4, 1993 annual meeting. Plaintiffs seek to submit to a shareholder vote a request for Wal–Mart's directors to prepare and distribute reports about Wal–Mart's equal employment opportunity ("EEO") and affirmative action policies, programs and data, along with a description of Wal–Mart's efforts to 1) publicize its EEO policies to suppliers, and 2) purchase goods and services from minority- and female-owned suppliers. Plaintiffs allege that Wal–Mart's omission of their proposal violates Securities and Exchange Commission ("SEC" or "Commission") Rule 14a–8.

Wal–Mart moves to dismiss the Amended Complaint. Wal–Mart asserts that it may exclude the proposal because it "deals with a matter relating to the conduct of [Wal–Mart's] ordinary business operations," an excludable category under Rule 14a–8(c)(7). Plaintiffs cross-move for summary judgment. The court treats the motions as cross-motions for summary judgment. The court denies Wal–Mart's motion and grants plaintiffs' motion for the reasons, and to the extent, set forth below.

I. BACKGROUND

Plaintiffs Amalgamated Clothing and Textile Workers Union ("ACTWU") is a labor union representing approximately 250,000 workers internationally. Plaintiffs National Council of Churches of Christ in the U.S.A., Unitarian Universalist Association and Literary Society of Saint Catherine of Sienna are religious organizations, which invest in socially responsible corporations as part of their religious missions. Each plaintiff believes that "issues concerning equal employment opportunity and affirmative action are important to shareholder value." Plaintiffs' stated ultimate goal is to improve Wal–Mart's EEO record and that of the discount retail store industry; to that end, they submit proposals, such as this one, to foster dialogue between plaintiffs and Wal–Mart and between plaintiffs and other shareholders. Under SEC Rule 14a–8(a)(1), plaintiffs, as owners of at least $1,000 worth of Wal–Mart stock, are eligible to submit proposals for inclusion in Wal–Mart's proxy material.

Wal–Mart operates a chain of retail stores throughout the Untied States. Wal–Mart is a Delaware corporation with its principal place of business in Bentonville, Arkansas. As a Delaware corporation, Wal–Mart is subject to Delaware corporate law pertaining to the use of shareholder proxies at annual meetings and is concurrently subject to the rules adopted by the SEC, which regulate the content and solicitation of proxies.

* * * [Plaintiffs'] Proposal requests Wal–Mart's board of directors to prepare the following reports by September 1993:

1. A chart identifying employees according to their sex and race in each of the nine major EEOC defined job categories for 1990, 1991, 1992 listing either numbers or percentages in each category.

2. A summary description of Affirmative Action Programs to improve performance especially in job categories where women and minorities are under utilized and a description of major problems in meeting the company's goals and objectives in this area.

3. A description of steps taken to increase the number of managers who are qualified females and ethnic minorities.

4. A description of ways in which Wal–Mart publicizes our company's policies to merchandise suppliers and service providers to encourage forward action on their part as well.

5. A description of Wal–Mart's efforts to purchase goods and services from minority and female owned business enterprises.

Plaintiffs envision a brief report, that could, in their view, range from the one page analysis produced by J.C. Penney as part of its annual report to a five page internal memorandum made available to shareholders of CIGNA Corporation.

II. DISCUSSION

A. Regulatory Framework

1. The Importance of Proxies

A proxy is a means by which a shareholder authorizes another person to represent her and vote her shares at a shareholders' meeting in accordance with the shareholder's instructions on the proxy card. Proxies have become an indispensable part of corporate governance because the "[r]ealities of modern corporate life have all but gutted the myth that the shareholders in large publicly held companies personally attend annual meetings." Stroud v. Grace, 606 A.2d 75, 86 (Del.1992). As one leading commentator explained, the "widespread distribution of corporate securities, with the concomitant separation of ownership and management, puts the entire concept of the stockholders' meeting at the mercy of the proxy instrument." Louis Loss, Fundamentals of Securities Regulation 449 (2d ed. 1988). This is because under state law— Delaware law, in Wal–Mart's case—a quorum of the shares eligible to vote must be represented at an annual meeting either in person or by proxy in order to elect directors and transact "any other proper business" that may be conducted. Thus, the failure of the vast majority of shareholders to attend annual meetings means that without the proxy mechanism for representing shares eligible to vote, corporations effectively would be unable to elect directors and take other required actions.

2. Shareholder Proposals

Under Delaware law, a shareholder in attendance at the annual meeting may offer a proposal for shareholder approval, as long as the proposal involves a proper subject on which shareholders may vote. * * * Unless the shareholders' proposed resolution is included in the proxy material, however, other shareholders would not have advance notice of the intention to make the proposal or have the ability to vote on the proposal via the proxy. See Stroud, 606 A.2d at 87 (Delaware law "does not require the board to disclose * * * matters to be discussed at regularly scheduled annual meetings").

3. Proxy Solicitations

* * *

Rule 14a–8(a) requires a company to include a shareholder's proposal in the company's proxy statement and provide shareholders with the opportunity to vote on the proposal by executing the proxy card. This ostensibly broad directive is limited by thirteen content-based exceptions. Most relevant to this case is Rule 14–8(c)(7), which permits a company to omit a shareholder proposal if "the proposal deals with a matter relating to the conduct of the ordinary business operations of the registrant." A shareholder proposal pertaining to "ordinary business operations" would be improper if raised at an annual meeting, because the law of most states (including Delaware) leaves the conduct of ordinary business operations to corporate directors and officers rather than the shareholders. See e.g., Del. Code Ann. tit. 8 § 141(a). As one court explained, "management cannot exercise its specialized talents effectively if corporate investors assert the power to dictate the minutiae of daily business decisions." Medical Committee for Human Rights v. SEC, 432 F.2d 659, 679 (D.C.Cir.1970), vacated as moot, 404 U.S. 403, 92 S.Ct. 577, 30 L.Ed.2d 560 (1972). The SEC adopted this exception to save management the cost and burden of including a proposal in proxy material that would be improper if raised by a shareholder at the annual meeting.

* * *

B. Standard for Court's Determination Whether a Proposal May Be Excluded as Pertaining to "Ordinary Business Operations"

Determining whether Wal–Mart may exclude plaintiffs' Proposal under the "ordinary business operations" exception requires the court to construe the meaning of the SEC's own rules. When a court interprets an administrative regulation, "the ultimate criterion" is the agency's interpretation of the regulation, which becomes of controlling weight unless that interpretation is "plainly erroneous or inconsistent with the regulations." Thus before deciding whether Wal–Mart may omit the Proposal on the basis of the"ordinary business operations" exception, I must first examine how the SEC interprets Rule 14a–8(c)(7).

1. The SEC's Interpretive Release Standard

Both the present form of Rule 14a–8, which contains the phrase "ordinary business operations," and the SEC Interpretive Release that accompanied it, were adopted after a formal notice and comment rule-making period in 1976. The 1976 Release "established the principles by which [the Commission] intended the 'ordinary business' provision of Rule 14a–8 to be interpreted." Writing in January 1992, the SEC stated that "[t]hese principles are no less applicable today than when the Commission adopted them" in 1976.

The SEC issued the 1976 Interpretive Release to resolve previous interpretive difficulties over Rule 14a–8(c)(7)'s intended meaning. The Release states in pertinent part that

> the term "ordinary business operations" has been deemed on occasion to include certain matters which have significant policy, economic or other implications inherent in them. For instance, a proposal that a utility company not construct a proposed nuclear power plant has in the past been considered excludable * * *. In retrospect, however, it seems apparent that the economic and safety considerations attendant to nuclear power plants are of such magnitude that a determination whether to construct one is not an "ordinary" business matter. Accordingly, proposals of that nature as well as others having major implications be considered beyond the

realm of an issuer's ordinary business operations, and future interpretive letters of the Commission's staff will reflect that view.

* * * Thus, *where proposals involve business matters that are mundane in nature and do not involve any substantial policy or other
considerations, the subparagraph may be relied upon to omit them.*

Adoption of Amendments Relating to Proposals by Security Holders,
Exchange Act Release No. 12999, (Dec. 3, 1976) ("1976 Interpretive
Release") (emphasis added).[7]

2. *Development of SEC Interpretation Through No–Action Letter Review Process*

The general guidance provided to parties and the court by the 1976
Interpretive Release and state corporate law has been supplemented by
the no-action letters issued by the SEC staff and the rare discretionary
review of no-action letters provided by the full Commission.[8] No-action
letters can provide insight into the meaning of the term "ordinary
business operations," because, unlike general interpretive releases, no-
action letters address specific issues and build upon the SEC's "vast
experience of daily contact with the practical workings of this rule."
Peck v. Greyhound Corp., 97 F.Supp. 679, 681 (S.D.N.Y.1951). However, as the SEC itself maintains, the ad hoc nature of these letters means
that courts cannot place them on a precedential par with formal rule-
making or adjudication. Before turning to how the SEC has applied
Rule 14a–8(c)(7) to similar proposals through numerous no-action letters, the court will, therefore, address the extent to which it must defer
to positions taken in no-action letters.

a. *Deference Owed to No–Action Position*

An individual no-action letter by itself is not an expression of agency
interpretation to which the court must defer. See Roosevelt at 427 n.
19. By responding to a company's request for a no-action letter, the
"Commission and its staff do not purport in any way to issue 'rulings' or
'decisions' on shareholder proposals management indicates it intends to
omit, and they do not adjudicate the merits of a management's posture
concerning such a proposal."

---

7. The law of the company's state of
incorporation is also a source of authority
as to which proposals relate to "ordinary
business operations" under Rule 14a–
8(c)(7) and which proposals are "proper
subject for action by shareholders" under
rule 14a–8(c)(1). However,, most states, including Delaware, have not developed the
law on this issue beyond the statement that
the directors and officers shall mange the
business affairs of the corporation. In
practice over the last half century the SEC
rather than state courts have been determining whether proposals may be excluded
on these bases. See Louis Loss & Joel

Seligman, 4 Securities Regulation 2012 (3rd
ed. 1990) (SEC staff develops a "common
law" of includable proposals).

8. Shareholders and management have
no right to appeal staff advice to the Commission, although the commission may, in
its discretion, grant a party's request for
review. The position of the full Commission in affirming or reversing a staff determination is also informal, and does not "affect[]the right of * * * a shareholder * * *
to institute a private action with respect to
the management's intention to omit the
proposal from its proxy materials."

The SEC staff reviews annually approximately 350 requests for no-action letters regarding shareholder proposals and over 6,700 proxy statements, and itself acknowledges that its staff "necessarily cannot do more in each case than make a quick analysis of the material submitted that, perforce, lacks the kind of in-depth study that would be essential to a definitive determination ...." * * * The administrative constraints on the SEC staff led the agency to express concern at its inability to enforce § 14(a) on its own through the informal no-action letter process, and it has acknowledged a need for its efforts to be supplemented by private enforcement in the courts. See Roosevelt, 958 F.2d at 424.

However, although the court need not defer to an individual no-action position, courts have relied on the consistency of the SEC staff's position and reasoning on a given issue, or the lack of consistency, in determining whether a proposal that was deemed excludable by the SEC staff can in fact be omitted under Rule 14a–8(c)(7). * * *

In determining whether to defer to a position drawn from a series of no-action letters, courts must recognize that a change in SEC position does not necessarily reveal capricious action by the agency; changes in conditions and public perceptions justify changes in the SEC's construction of the "ordinary business operations" exception. The nature of the exceptions permits, if not requires, the SEC to reevaluate earlier positions "in light of new considerations, or changing conditions which indicate that its earlier views are no longer in keeping with the objectives of Rule 14a–8." The SEC has revised its position with respect to the inclusion of proposals on a number of issues formerly excludable under Rule 14a–8(c)(7) such as plant closings, tobacco production, cigarette advertising and all forms of senior executive and director compensation. * * * Thus, an SEC departure from a prior position must be considered in light of changing public and shareholder concerns. Having addressed the various considerations that help to determine the level of deference owed to no-action letters, the court now examines the SEC's interpretation of the "ordinary business operations" exception in its no-action letters dealing with similar EEO and affirmative action proposals.

b. SEC's No–Action Letter Position on Ordinary Business Operations

Although the SEC has been dealing with proposals like plaintiffs' since the mid–1970s, its treatment of these proposals has changed over time. Prior to 1983, the SEC took the position that proposals requesting reports on EEO data and policies could not be excluded, because the determination whether a report should be issued was a matter of policy rather than ordinary business operations. In 1983, the SEC changed its interpretation of the exception and determined that the subject of the report requested, rather than the fact that the information requested was in the form of a report, would determine the proposal's excludability under the "ordinary business operations" exception.

Since 1983, the SEC has determined whether employment policy proposals must be included in proxy materials by examining whether the proposals relate to "day-to-day" employment matters and, therefore, are excludable as relating to "ordinary business operations," or whether the proposals relate to significant policy considerations and, therefore are not excludable. Day-to-day employment matters have been interpreted as including matters concerning: employee health benefits, general compensation issues not focused on senior executives, management of the workplace, employee supervision, labor-management relations, employee hiring and firing, conditions of employment and employee training and motivation. The SEC has also viewed a proposal requesting a company to hire contractors from within its service area as excludable under Rule 14a–8(c)(7).

Despite the SEC's general view that employee hiring and firing and supplier decisions are related to a company's ordinary business operations, the SEC has until recently recognized that the issues of EEO and affirmative action raise policy considerations elevating them above the excludable day-to-day issues. Thus, in 1988, the SEC staff stated, and the full Commission affirmed, that AT&T may not exclude a shareholder proposal to phase out those aspects of AT&T's affirmative action program directed toward recruiting, employing or promoting individuals from any particular racial or ethnic group. The staff stated that AT&T could not rely on the exception for "ordinary business operations" because the proposal involved "policy issues," described by the SEC staff as "the Company's affirmative action program, designed to assure equal employment opportunities for minority group members * * *."

Similarly, on February 14, 1991, the SEC took the position that a proposal requesting the publication of EEO data and the adoption of an affirmative action program and a program for purchasing from vendors controlled by women and minorities was not excludable, because it related to "general policy decisions which are beyond the conduct of the Company's day-to-day operations."

In the same vein, on March 8, 1991 the SEC reviewed a proposal that was identical to a proposal plaintiff ACTWU submitted to Wal–Mart in 1991, and contained four of the five requests included in the 1993 Proposal at issue here. The SEC took the position that although the proposal "concerns employment and other matters that involve the Company's ordinary business operations, * * * questions with respect to equal employment opportunity and affirmative action involve policy decisions beyond those personnel matters that constitute the Company's ordinary course of business."

Thus, through March 1991, the SEC's no-action letters determined that companies could not exclude proposals requesting the information requested in plaintiffs' Proposal here. On April 4, 1991, however, the full Commission appeared to shift position, and voted 3–2 to reverse the staff position stated in a no-action letter issued to Capital Cities/ABC. The proposal there requested information quite similar to that requested here in plaintiffs' 1993 Proposal, although a notable difference is that Capital Cities/ABC, the proposal requested a summary of timetables to implement affirmative action programs. The divided Commission determined that the proposal was excludable because it "involves a request for detailed information on the composition of the company's work force, employment practices and policies, and the selection of program content."

After the Commission's decision in Capital Cities/ABC, the parties there reached a settlement whereby the shareholder proponents withdrew their petition for review of the Commission's action in the Court of Appeals for the District of Columbia Circuit. In exchange, Capital Cities/ABC agreed not to object to the shareholder proponent's request to vacate the Commission's April 4, 1991 letter. By letter dated July 15, 1991, the Commission agreed to vacate its earlier action rendering the decision of no precedential value, according to Richard Y. Roberts, one of the SEC Commissioners.

On April 10, 1992, the staff issued Wal–Mart a no-action letter with respect to plaintiffs' 1992 proposal, also relying on the rationale of Capital Cities/ABC, notwithstanding that the Commission had earlier vacated its decision in Capital Cities/ABC. * * * Wal–Mart, thereafter, omitted plaintiffs' proposal from its 1992 proxy materials.

In October 1992 the SEC staff expressed in more sweeping terms the view that companies could exclude EEO proposals, reversing the position it took in AT&T in 1988 and Dayton Hudson in 1991. See Cracker Barrel Old Country Stores, Inc., No–Action Letter, 1992 WL 289095, 1992 SEC No–Act. LEXIS 984 * 43 (Oct. 13, 1992). The articulated reason for that decision was that the SEC found distinctions between policies implicating broad social issues and the conduct of day-to-day business simply too hard to draw as regards the employment of the general workforce. The shareholder proposal in Cracker Barrel was prompted by that company's announcement of a policy to discriminate against gay men and lesbians. The proposal asked the corporation (1) to include sexual orientation in its anti-discriminatory policy, and (2) to enforce its amended policy. The SEC staff and later the Commission characterized the proposal as requesting that the directors "Implement hiring policies relating to sexual orientation and incorporate such policies into the corporate employment policy statement." Based on this characterization of the proposal, the SEC staff explained:

> Notwithstanding the general view that employment matters concerning the workforce of the company are excludable as matters involving the conduct of day-to-day business, exceptions have been made in some cases where a proponent based an employment-related proposal on "social policy" concerns. In recent years, however, *the line between includable and excludable employment-related proposals based on social policy considerations has become increasingly difficult to draw.* The distinctions recognized by the staff are characterized by many as tenuous, without substance and effectively nullifying the application of the ordinary business exclusion to employment-related proposals.

The Division has reconsidered the application of Rule 14a–8(c)(7) to employment-related proposals in light of these concerns and the staff's experience with these proposals in recent years. As a result, the Division has determined that *the fact that a shareholder proposal concerning a company's employment policies and practices for the general workforce is tied to a social issue will no longer be viewed as removing the proposal from the realm of ordinary business operations* of the registrant. Rather, determinations with respect to any such proposals are properly governed by the employment-based nature of the proposal.

Id. at * 2– * 3 (emphasis added). On January 15, 1993, the Commission affirmed the Division's position that the proposal was excludable from the Company's proxy material, relying on Rule 14a–8(c)(7), without any further elaboration on the staff's rationale for its determination.

During 1993 the SEC staff issued several no-action letters on shareholder proposals involving employment-related matters. In each case, including those raising EEO issues, the staff decided that the proposal was excludable based on its view that the proposal was "principally directed at the Company's employment policies and practices which are matters relating to the conduct of ordinary business operations."

Thus, the SEC's current no-action position is that it can no longer continue to draw the lines between includable and excludable proposals * * * As a result, shareholder proposals involving EEO and affirmative action policies are now deemed excludable by the SEC because they relate to employment policies, and employment policies are viewed as ordinary business matters.

C. Whether Wal–Mart May Exclude Plaintiffs' Proposal

Having considered the SEC's formal interpretive guidelines for Rule 14a–8 and the SEC's application of those guidelines through the no-action letter process, the court turns to whether Wal–Mart carries its burden of showing that the Proposal may be excluded from management's proxy material because it falls within the "ordinary business operations" exception. Wal–Mart first contends that the court should defer to Cracker Barrel and the 1993 Wal–Mart no-action letter, which categorically reject the SEC's prior position on EEO and affirmative action proposals. It alternatively contends that the Proposal's request for "detailed" information about Wal–Mart's employee and supplier relations involves shareholders in the details of implementing rather than adopting corporate policy, and that the Proposal is thus excludable because the choice between ways to implement corporate policy is mundane in nature and does not involve substantial policy considerations.

1. Whether the Court Should Defer to the SEC's Cracker Barrel Position

The court does not defer to the SEC's position in Cracker Barrel and is not persuaded by its reasoning, because the reasoning in Cracker

Barrel sharply deviates from the standard articulated in the 1976 Interpretive Release. The parties, the SEC and courts all agree that courts must defer to the 1976 Interpretive Release. As discussed above, that Release interpreted Rule 14a–8(c) (7) as permitting the exclusion of "proposals that are mundane in nature and do not involve any substantial policy or other considerations."

Cracker Barrel fails to apply both parts of the Release's conjunctive standard. In Cracker Barrel, the Commission explicitly acknowledged that proposals in favor of or against the adoption of an EEO program continue to raise "social policy" issues, and it did not suggest any diminished public or shareholder interest in these social issues. It nonetheless took the position that the SEC's inability to continue to draw lines warranted an across the board rule that any proposal relating to employment matters is excludable because it relates to day-to-day business affairs, regardless of whether the proposal also involves a substantial policy consideration. This interpretation contravenes the 1976 Interpretive Release's explicit recognition that all proposals could be seen as involving some aspect of day-to-day business operations. That recognition underlay the Release's statement that the SEC's determination of whether a company may exclude a proposal should not depend on whether the proposal could be characterized as involving some day-to-day business matter. Rather, the proposal may be excluded only after the proposal is also found to raise no substantial policy consideration. The SEC did not follow the 1976 Interpretive Release standard in Cracker Barrel or in the 1993 no-action letter issued to Wal–Mart, in that the SEC focused only on whether employment policies generally involve day-to-day business matters.[13]

2. Whether Application of the 1976 Interpretive Release Standard Independently Permits Wal–Mart to Exclude the Proposal

Having concluded that deference is not owed to Cracker Barrel and the 1993 Wal–Mart no action letter, the court considers whether Wal–Mart has carried its burden for excluding the Proposal under the standard articulated by the 1976 Interpretive Release and the corpus of SEC no-action letters that properly applied that standard.   * * *

Wal–Mart itself does not deny that equality and diversity in the workplace involve substantial policy considerations. Indeed, it would be difficult to sustain such a position in light of, among other things, the continued interest of Congress in employment discrimination since 1964,

---

13. This is not say that the SEC cannot change its views with regard to what issues involve substantial policy considerations. If the SEC finds that the issues of EEO and affirmative action programs no longer implicate significant policy considerations, the 1976 Interpretive Release permits exclusion of proposals relating to them. No such change of view exists at Cracker Barrel.

Nor does the court suggest that the SEC may not abandon the 1976 Interpretive Release altogether, so long as, in doing so, it complies with appropriate procedures, which procedures need not be addressed here. The court's holding today is limited to the proposition that a court should not defer to a position taken by the SEC in a no-action letter that is inconsistent with an SEC interpretation offered in the context of formal notice and comment rulemaking.

which was most recently underscored in the Civil Rights and Glass Ceiling Acts of 1991.

Rather, Wal–Mart argues that the Proposal would involve shareholders in dictating the implementation of a policy, albeit one of social import. Plaintiffs challenge that characterization of their Proposal. Regardless of whether the court characterizes the Proposal as seeking to adopt a policy or as seeking to implement a policy, the same inquiry guides the court: Does the proposal involve shareholders in dictating mundane matters that involve no substantial policy considerations?

The Proposal seeks to identify general corporate policy regarding equal employment opportunities and efforts, if any, to promote those policies among its suppliers, on whom Wal–Mart may have some influence. As plaintiffs argue the Proposal does not involve shareholders in demanding, or monitoring compliances with, a specific timetable to accomplish plaintiff's ultimate goal of improving Wal–Mart's EEO record. This aspect of the Proposal notably distinguishes it from the proposal considered in Capital Cities/ABC that the Commission found excludable. Plaintiff's Proposal does not require Wal–Mart to gather any employee-related information that it does not already gather for the purpose of complying with government regulations. The Proposal states that the report should be prepared "at reasonable cost, omitting confidential information," and may be comparable to the one or two page reports produced by other companies in Wal–Mart's industry. * * * The Proposal thus generally involves a significant policy consideration and does not otherwise fall within the exception for proposals relating to the conduct of Wal–Mart's "ordinary business operations."

However, the court finds that a literal reading of the Proposal suggests that the requested report must contain every "step" Wal–Mart management has taken to increase the number of female and minority managers and state all the "ways" Wal–Mart publicizes its EEO and affirmative action policies. Such "steps" could range from formal policies announced by the board of directors and officers, to the individual acts of each supervisor who implements these policies, and to other personnel and purchasing actions that occur hundreds of times each business day. A request for this latter information is excludable because it involves the mundane matters of Wal–Mart's day-to-day business affairs that involve no substantial policy consideration. The court, therefore, finds that the Proposal may be omitted from Wal–Mart's 1993 proxy material to the extent that plaintiffs agree [14] to the inclusion of the following proposal as an alternative to paragraphs 1–5 of the Proposal they submitted to Wal–Mart:

1. A chart identifying employees according to their sex and race in each of the nine major EEOC defined job categories for 1990, 1991, and 1992, listing either numbers or percentages in each category.

---

14. Plaintiffs consented to this change in language in an April 19, 1993 telephone conference with the court.

2. A summary description of any Affirmative Action policies and programs to improve performances, including job categories where women and minorities are underutilized.

3. A description of any policies and programs oriented specifically toward increasing the number of managers who are qualified and/or females and/or belong to ethnic minorities.

4. A general description of how Wal–Mart publicizes our company's Affirmative Action policies and programs to merchandise suppliers and service providers.

5. A description of any policies and programs favoring the purchase of goods and services from minority- and/or female owned business enterprises.

In modifying the Proposal, the court notes the practice of the SEC staff to revise a proposal submitted to it to correct minor defects. These changes to the Proposal reflect a balance of the rights of shareholders to obtain information on an issue raising significant policy considerations and the right of management to run the day-to-day affairs of the corporation free from shareholder supervision.

III.   Conclusion

* * *

For all the reasons discussed above, the court concludes that Wal–Mart has not sustained its burden of establishing that it may omit plaintiffs' Proposal, as modified, from Wal–Mart's 1993 proxy solicitation material. The court, therefore, denies Wal–Mart's motion and grants plaintiff's motion for summary judgment. As stated in the court's Order dated April 19, 1993, Wal–Mart is enjoined from omitting plaintiff's Proposal, as amended, from Wal–Mart's 1993 proxy material.

LOVENHEIM v. IROQUOIS BRANDS, LTD.

618 F.Supp. 554 (D.D.C.1985).

GASCH, DISTRICT JUDGE.

I.   BACKGROUND

This matter is now before the Court on plaintiff's motion for preliminary injunction.

Plaintiff Peter C. Lovenheim, owner of two hundred shares of common stock in Iroquois Brands, Ltd. (hereinafter "Iroquois/Delaware"), seeks to bar Iroquois/Delaware from excluding from the proxy materials being sent to all shareholders in preparation for an upcoming shareholder meeting information concerning a proposed resolution he intends to offer at the meeting. Mr. Lovenheim's proposed resolution relates to the procedure used to force-feed geese for production of paté de foie gras in France,[2] a type of paté imported by Iroquois/Delaware. Specifically, his resolution calls upon the Directors of Iroquois/Delaware to:

> [F]orm a committee to study the methods by which its French supplier produces paté de foie gras, and report to the shareholders its findings and opinions, based on expert consultation, on whether this production method causes undue distress, pain or suffering to the animals involved and, if so, whether further distribution of this product should be discontinued until a more humane production method is developed.

Mr. Lovenheim's right to compel Iroquois/Delaware to insert information concerning his proposal in the proxy materials turns on the applicability of section 14(a) of the Securities Exchange Act of 1934, and the shareholder proposal rule promulgated by the Securities and Exchange Commission ("SEC"), Rule 14a–8.

* * *

Iroquois/Delaware has refused to allow information concerning Mr. Lovenheim's proposal to be included in proxy materials being sent in connection with the next annual shareholders meeting. In doing so, Iroquois/Delaware relies on an exception to the general requirement of Rule 14a–8, Rule 14a–8(c)(5). That exception provides that an issuer of securities "may omit a proposal and any statement in support thereof" from its proxy statement and form of proxy:

> if the proposal relates to operations which account for less than 5 percent of the issuer's total assets at the end of its most recent fiscal year, and for less than 5 percent of its net earnings and gross sales for its most recent fiscal year, and is not otherwise significantly related to the issuer's business.

Rule 14a–8(c)(5), 17 C.F.R. § 240.14a–8(c)(5).

* * *

2. Paté de foie gras is made from the liver of geese. According to Mr. Lovenheim's affidavit, force-feeding is frequently used in order to expand the liver and thereby produce a larger quantity of paté. Mr. Lovenheim's affidavit also contains a description of the force-feeding process:

> Force-feeding usually begins when the geese are four months old. On some farms where feeding is mechanized, the bird's body and wings are placed in a metal brace and its neck is stretched. Through a funnel inserted 10–12 inches down the throat of the goose, a machine pumps up to 400 grams of corn-based

mash into its stomach. An elastic band around the goose's throat prevents regurgitation. When feeding is manual, a handler uses a funnel and stick to force the mash down.

Affidavit of Peter C. Lovenheim at ¶ 7. Plaintiff contends that such force-feeding is a form of cruelty to animals. *Id.*

Plaintiff has offered no evidence that force-feeding is used by Iroquois/Delaware's supplier in producing the paté imported by Iroquois/Delaware. However his proposal calls upon the committee he seeks to create to investigate this question.

C.   *Applicability of Rule 14a–8(c)(5) exception*

* * *

Iroquois/Delaware's reliance on the argument that this exception applies is based on the following information contained in the affidavit of its president: Iroquois/Delaware has annual revenues of $141 million with $6 million in annual profits and $78 million in assets. In contrast, its paté de foie gras sales were just $79,000 last year, representing a net loss on paté sales of $3,121. Iroquois/Delaware has only $34,000 in assets related to paté. Thus none of the company's net earnings and less than .05 percent of its assets are implicated by plaintiff's proposal. These levels are obviously far below the five percent threshold set forth in the first portion of the exception claimed by Iroquois/Delaware.

Plaintiff does not contest that his proposed resolution relates to a matter of little economic significance to Iroquois/Delaware. Nevertheless he contends that the Rule 14a–8(c)(5) exception is not applicable as it cannot be said that his proposal "is not otherwise significantly related to the issuer's business" as is required by the final portion of that exception. In other words, plaintiff's argument that Rule 14a–8 does not permit omission of his proposal rests on the assertion that the rule and statute on which it is based do not permit omission merely because a proposal is not economically significant where a proposal has "ethical or social significance."[8]

Iroquois/Delaware challenges plaintiff's view that ethical and social proposals cannot be excluded even if they do meet the economic or five percent test. Instead, Iroquois/Delaware views the exception solely in economic terms as permitting omission for any proposals relating to a de minimis share of assets and profits. Iroquois/Delaware asserts that since corporations are economic entities, only an economic test is appropriate.

The Court would note that the applicability of the Rule 14a–8(c)(5) exception to Mr. Lovenheim's proposal represents a close question given the lack of clarity in the exception itself. In effect, plaintiff relies on the word "otherwise," suggesting that it indicates the drafters of the rule intended that other noneconomic tests of significance be used. Iroquois/Delaware relies on the fact that the rule examines other significance in relation to the issuer's business. Because of the apparent

---

8. The assertion that the proposal is significant in an ethical and social sense relies on plaintiff's argument that "the very availability of a market for products that may be obtained through the inhumane force-feeding of geese cannot help but contribute to the continuation of such treatment." Plaintiff's brief characterizes the humane treatment of animals as among the foundations of western culture and cites in support of this view the Seven Laws of Noah, an animal protection statute enacted by the Massachusetts Bay Colony in 1641, numerous federal statutes enacted since 1877, and animal protection laws existing in all fifty states and the District of Columbia. An additional indication of the significance of plaintiff's proposal is the support of such leading organizations in the field of animal care as the American Society for the Prevention of Cruelty to Animals and The Humane Society of the United States for measures aimed at discontinuing use of force-feeding.

ambiguity of the rule, the Court considers the history of the shareholder proposal rule in determining the proper interpretation of the most recent version of that rule.

Prior to 1983, paragraph 14a–8(c)(5) excluded proposals "not significantly related to the issuer's business" but did not contain an objective economic significance test such as the five percent of sales, assets, and earnings specified in the first part of the current version. Although a series of SEC decisions through 1976 allowing issuers to exclude proposals challenging compliance with the Arab economic boycott of Israel allowed exclusion if the issuer did less than one percent of their business with Arab countries or Israel, the Commission stated later in 1976 that it did "not believe that subparagraph (c)(5) should be hinged solely on the economic relativity of a proposal." Securities Exchange Act Release No. 12,999, 41 Fed.Reg. 52,994, 52,997 (1976). Thus the Commission required inclusion "in many situations in which the related business comprised less than one percent" of the company's revenues, profits or assets "where the proposal has raised *policy questions* important enough to be considered "significantly related' to the issuer's business."

As indicated above, the 1983 revision adopted the five percent test of economic significance in an effort to create a more objective standard. Nevertheless, in adopting this standard, the Commission stated that proposals will be includable notwithstanding their "failure to reach the specified economic thresholds if a significant relationship to the issuer's business is demonstrated on the face of the resolution or supporting statement." Securities Exchange Act Release No. 19,135, 47 Fed.Reg. 47,420, 47,428 (1982). Thus it seems clear based on the history of the rule that "the meaning of "significantly related' is not *limited* to economic significance."

[The court granted plaintiff's motion for a preliminary injunction.]

Note: Ordinary Business, Public Policy and Management Accountability

It appears that the question of whether a proposal constitutes ordinary business or is a matter of public policy relates directly to the issues of management accountability raised in Chapters 4 and 5. The reason is that if a proposal relates to ordinary business, management can deprive the shareholders of their "voice" by excluding the proposal from the proxy statement. If management, which controls the proxy machinery can also control access to the proxy statement, its own accountability to the shareholders is diminished. Thus the question of who decides whether the proposal is ordinary business becomes extremely significant.

Almost from the outset, both the courts and the SEC have recognized (implicitly or explicitly) this significance and the need to impose limits on management. That is why *Auer* is important, and it explains why the court in *Roosevelt* stressed the existence of a private right of action under Rule 14a–8. It also explains why courts which normally would not intervene in business decisions (which is what (c)(7) concerns) do, in fact, exercise their own judgment when faced with a shareholder proposal. Put differently, although "ordinary business" is related to the principles underlying the business judgment rule, it also is directly tied to the "internal affairs" of the corporation. And, when dealing with the latter, courts feel less compelled to defer to corporate management.

These issues arose most directly in Medical Committee for Human Rights v. Securities and Exchange Commission, 432 F.2d 659 (D.C.Cir. 1970), vacated as moot 404 U.S. 403, 92 S.Ct. 577, 30 L.Ed.2d 560 (1972). The Medical Committee, a public interest group, opposed the Vietnam War and, particularly, the manufacture by Dow Chemical Company (Dow) of napalm for use in the war. Although napalm constituted a very small part of Dow's business, it was important to the government's war effort, and Dow strongly defended its manufacture on patriotic grounds.

The Medical Committee submitted a proposal to Dow requesting the Dow board to adopt an amendment to Dow's certificate of incorporation that would have barred the sale of napalm to any buyer unless the buyer gave reasonable assurance that the napalm would not be used on or against human beings. Dow refused to include the proposal on the grounds that it was submitted to promote a general political cause (no longer a ground for exclusion under the Rule) and that it related to the ordinary business of the company. The SEC staff agreed with Dow and the SEC approved the staff's determination.

In a strongly-worded opinion, the Court of Appeals for the District of Columbia Circuit reversed the SEC's decision. The core of the court's analysis is as follows:

> As our earlier discussion indicates, the clear import of the language, legislative history, and record of administration of section 14(a) is that its overriding purpose is to assure to corporate shareholders the ability to exercise their right—some would say their duty—to control the important decisions which affect them in their capacity as stockholders and owners of the corporation. * * * Here, in contrast to the situations detailed above which led to the promulgation of Rule 14a–8(c)(2), the proposal relates solely to a matter that is completely within the accepted sphere of corporate activity and control. No reason has been advanced in the present proceedings which leads to the conclusion that management may properly place obstacles in the path of shareholders who wish to present to their co-owners, in accord with applicable state law, the question of whether they wish to have their assets used in a manner which they believe to be more socially responsible but possibly less profitable than that which is dictated by present company policy. Thus, even accepting Dow's characterization of the purpose and intent of the Medical Committee's proposal, there is a strong argument that permitting the company to exclude it would contravene the purpose of section 14(a).

However, the record in this case contains indications that we are confronted with quite a different situation. The management of Dow Chemical Company is repeatedly quoted in sources which include the company's own publications as proclaiming that the decision to continue manufacturing and marketing napalm was made not *because* of business considerations, but *in spite of* them; that management in essence decided to pursue a course of activity which generated little profit for the shareholders and actively impaired the company's public relations and recruitment activities because management considered this action morally and politically desirable. The proper political and social role of modern corporations is, of course, a matter of philosophical argument extending far beyond the scope of our present concern; the substantive wisdom or propriety of particular corporate political decisions is also completely irrelevant to the resolution of the present controversy. What *is* of immediate concern, however, is the question of whether the corporate proxy rules can be employed as a shield to isolate such managerial decisions from shareholder control. * * * We think that there is a clear and compelling distinction between management's legitimate need for freedom to apply its expertise in matters of day-to-day business judgment, and management's patently illegitimate claim of power to treat modern corporations with their vast resources as personal satrapies implementing personal political or moral predilections. It could scarcely be argued that management is more qualified or more entitled to make these kinds of decisions than the shareholders who are the true beneficial owners of the corporation; and it seems equally implausible that an application of the proxy rules which permitted such a result could be harmonized with the philosophy of corporate democracy which Congress embodied in section 14(a) of the Securities Exchange Act of 1934.

432 F.2d at 681.

A narrower view of the shareholder's right is found in Carter v. Portland General Electric Co., 227 Or. 401, 362 P.2d 766 (1961) where the court, applying Oregon law, affirmed management's refusal to include in the proxy statement a shareholder statement in opposition to management plans for the construction of a dam. A motion on the floor of the meeting was also ruled out of order, and the court refused to overturn any of management's actions. In holding that the shareholder request was not a "proper subject" for stockholder consideration, the court observed:

> * * * Granted, that the proposed dam project would commit a large part of the corporate defendant's assets and credit. By the same token, it also involved extensive engineering, economic, financial and even political considerations. It is impossible to believe that the obviously voluminous character of such data could have been abbreviated to the point that any communication with the stockholders or debate at the annual meeting could have resulted in any knowing or sensible vote by the stockholders.

362 P.2d at 769.

What, then, is "ordinary business"? As the court noted in *Wal–Mart*, the SEC stated in its 1976 amendments to the proxy rules that ordinary business matters are those "that are mundane in nature and do not involve any substantial policy considerations." At first blush, such matters would seem to be relatively simple to identify: the selection of products to be manufactured; the location of a factory; the terms of a labor contract; the compensation package for employees. The problem is that some issues which seem to fall within these examples also raise public policy questions. In *Medical Committee,* the decision to manufacture napalm could be viewed as ordinary business because it is simply the choice of product mix. But because of the context in which the question arose—-the Vietnam War—-the decision clearly had broad public policy implications which made it proper for shareholders to express their views. The fact that Dow's own management chose to manufacture napalm in spite of, rather than because of, business reasons reinforced the court's decision. In many cases, therefore, the SEC staff or the courts base their analysis on whether the issue raises a sufficiently strong public policy question so as to take it outside the realm of "ordinary business." See, e.g., Grimes v. Ohio Edison Co., 992 F.2d 455 (2d Cir.1993); Grimes v. Centerior Energy Corp., 909 F.2d 529 ((D.C.Cir. 1990); New York City Employees' Retirement System v. Brunswick Corp., 789 F.Supp. 144 (S.D.N.Y.1992); New York City Employees' Retirement System v. Dole Food Co., 795 F.Supp. 95 (S.D.N.Y.1992), appeal dismissed 969 F.2d 1430 (2d Cir.1992).

Perhaps the most controversial example of the tension between ordinary business and public policy is the series of recent proposals concerning the creation of shareholder advisory committees (SACs). Apart from their substance, these proposals are significant because the proponents attempted to cast their resolutions as mandatory by-law amendments. Thus the resolutions raise the question of whether shareholders can assert an absolute right to amend the by-laws under state law as a means of obtaining inclusion of the proposal in the proxy statement.

In 1992, Robert Monks, a shareholder activist, submitted a proposal to Exxon to establish an SAC to review and evaluate the performance of the board. The committee of shareholder representatives was to advise the board on matters related to the "enhancement of shareholder value." The SAC would have had the power to engage experts and incur other expenses (estimated at $12.5 million in the first year) to be paid by Exxon. The members of the SAC were to receive a fee for their services, be reimbursed for their expenses, and indemnified in connection with their work on the committee. Finally, the SAC could include a statement of not more than 2,500 words in Exxon's proxy statement concerning its activities and its evaluation of management.

Exxon opposed inclusion, among other reasons, on the grounds that it was not a proper subject for shareholder action under (c)(1) and that it constituted ordinary business under (c)(7). With respect to the former, the company contended that state law prohibited a by-law establishing an advisory committee to the board. With respect to the latter, the company argued that the management of the business and affairs of the company, to which the proposal related, was specifically delegated to the board by New Jersey law under which Exxon was incorporated. Thus, the decision as to whether to create any committees in furtherance of the management of the company constituted "ordinary business."

The SEC staff rejected these arguments. It disagreed with the conclusion that state law prohibited a by-law creating such a committee. More significantly, the staff stated that "although the purpose of the shareholders' committee is to provide a means of communication with management, the nature and scope of that communication would appear as not involving matters concerning the conduct of the Company's ordinary business operations." Thus the staff concluded that the proposal could not be omitted.

Later that year, the California Public Employees' Retirement System (CalPERS) submitted a similar proposal to Pennzoil, a Delaware corporation. Like Exxon, Pennzoil resisted the proposal. Unlike Exxon, Pennzoil succeeded. Pennzoil argued that the proposal was inconsistent with Delaware law in several respects. First, Pennzoil contended that having elected the directors, the shareholders had "exhausted their ability to dictate the direction of the business and affairs of the corporation by vesting that power in their elected board members." Opinion Letter of Richards, Layton & Finger to Pennzoil Company (January 7, 1993). As to the expenditure of corporate funds for the committee's activities, Pennzoil asserted that the proposal would "abrogate the duty of the Board of Directors to exercise its informed business judgment concerning expenditures by the Company." Id. Finally, Pennzoil argued that the SAC went beyond the use of committees contemplated by DGCL § 141(c) because there was no statutory authorization for a shareholder committee, nor would such a committee be subject to any kind of oversight.

The SEC staff essentially accepted these arguments, finding some basis for exclusion under (c)(1). Significantly, when CalPERS requested reconsideration of the proposal if redrafted in precatory language, the staff declined to reverse its position on the ground that there was still "a substantial question as to whether, under Delaware law, the directors may adopt a by-law provision that specifies that it may be amended only by shareholders."

The full significance of these letters is not yet clear. It is likely that those who believe in more active shareholder monitoring will continue to present resolutions creating SACs, notwithstanding the result in Pennzoil. At the same time, as two members of the law firm that rendered the opinion in support of Pennzoil have observed, "a corporation might successfully oppose inclusion of such a SAC proposal * * * if it articulates specifically the manner in which the power of its board of directors would be abrogated * * * and it is able to marshal authority for its position." Charles F. Richards, Jr. and Anne C. Foster, Exxon Revisited: The SEC Allows Pennzoil to Exclude Both Mandatory and Precatory Proposals Seeking to Create a Shareholder Advisory Committee, 48 Bus. Law. 1509, 1519 (1993).

The staff's decision in Pennzoil restricting the use of the mandatory by-law as a device to ensure inclusion of a shareholder proposal is consistent with its 1983 determination that the subject matter of a report requested, rather than the fact that the information requested was in the form of a report, would determine the proposal's excludability under the "ordinary business" test of (c)(7). Such an approach seems sensible; were it otherwise, there would be no limitations on the scope of a shareholder proposal provided that it was cast in the form of a by-law amendment.

Chapter 15

THE ROLE OF OUTSIDE DIRECTORS IN THE GOVERNANCE OF THE PUBLIC CORPORATION

PROBLEM
WHAT CAN OUTSIDE DIRECTORS CONTRIBUTE?

You are the principal outside counsel to the Columbia Employees Retirement Fund (CERF), which manages an $8 billion investment portfolio, about 40% of which is invested in corporate equities. The trustees of CERF recently have been discussing with CERF's general manager whether, in light of recent changes in the SEC proxy rules, CERF should become more active in trying to influence the governance of corporations whose stock it holds. Several trustees have been intrigued by the observation that "all arguments about corporate governance ultimately converge on the role of outside directors." They have asked the general manager to prepare an assessment of what impact improved performance by boards comprised primarily of outside directors is likely to have on the financial performance of portfolio companies. The general manager, in turn, has asked you to prepare a memorandum addressing the following questions.

1. How can CERF "become more active in trying to influence the governance of corporations whose stock it holds?"

2. What potential roles can outside directors play in the corporate governance system?

3. What are the strengths and weaknesses of a system that relies on outside directors as a principal governance device? Consider:

    a. What duties or tasks can outside directors reasonably be expected to perform?

    b. What kinds of people typically serve as outside directors? How are they selected?

636

c.　What input do shareholders and other corporate constituencies have in the selection process?

4.　What are the principal weaknesses of boards of directors as they currently operate?　What changes might be made to remedy these weaknesses?

4.　Should these changes be made through state law?　Through federal law?　By corporations themselves?　Is one or another of these groups more likely to act?

A.　INTRODUCTION

Apart from specifying a few decisions that a board of directors cannot delegate, such as the declaration of a dividend, corporate statutes describe directors' duties in very general terms.　RMBCA § 8.01, for example, states only that "All corporate powers shall be exercised by or under the authority of, and the business and affairs of the corporation managed under the direction of, its board of directors."　DGCL § 141(a) provides simply that "The business and affairs of every corporation * * * shall be managed by or under the direction of a board of directors."

A board of directors consisting of all of a company's senior officers could comply with these statutory mandates, in that it would possess the capability to manage the company's business.　But such a board would constitute no more than a committee of senior officers, all wearing hats labelled "Director."　Presumably, the decisions it made would not differ from the decisions its members otherwise would make when wearing their "Officer" hats.　As a consequence, an all insider board would add little of value to a company's governance structure.

Much discussion in recent years has focused on how boards of directors can improve the performance of public corporations.　An apparent consensus has developed that boards of directors should consist primarily of outside directors—people who are not part of, and have no strong ties to, a company's management.　Such directors at least have the potential to reduce agency costs associated with the separation of ownership from control by "monitoring" managers' performance.　See, e.g., Statement of the Business Roundtable, Corporate Governance and American Competitiveness, 46 Bus. Law. 241 (1990); Statement of the Business Roundtable, The Role and Composition of the Board of Directors of the Large Publicly–Owned Corporation, 33 Bus. Law. 2083 (1978); American Bar Association Committee on Corporate Laws, Corporate Director's Guidebook, 33 Bus. Law. 1595 (1978).

Once one inquires into what is meant by "monitoring," though, the appearance of consensus evaporates.　Some commentators define monitoring narrowly, suggesting that boards should limit themselves to establishing financial goals for the corporation and evaluating senior executives' success in meeting those goals.　In this view, a board's principal functions are to discharge top managers whose performance is unsatisfactory and to ensure that management succession arrangements are in place.

Other commentators take a more expansive approach. They would have boards of directors review and approve major corporate actions and become more involved in establishing corporate priorities and long-term objectives. Still other commentators would have the board assume major responsibility for fixing the annual budget and allocating funds among a corporation's operating divisions, as well as reviewing regularly the extent to which the corporation was meeting the goals the board had set. Such a board might be pro-active, initiating some proposals on its own, rather than simply reacting to management's proposals. It also would be more inclined to openly question the latter.

The American Law Institute, which devoted more than ten years to a study of corporate governance issues, suggests that directors' functions and powers be defined as follows.

ALI, PRINCIPLES OF CORPORATE GOVERNANCE (1994)

§ 3.02. FUNCTIONS AND POWERS OF THE BOARD OF DIRECTORS

Except as otherwise provided by statute:

(a) The board of directors of a publicly held corporation should perform the following functions:

(1) Select, regularly evaluate, fix the compensation of, and, where appropriate, replace the principal senior executives.

(2) Oversee the conduct of the corporation's business to evaluate whether the business is being properly managed.

(3) Review and, where appropriate, approve the corporation's financial objectives and major corporate plans and actions.

(4) Review and, where appropriate, approve major changes in, and determinations of other major questions of choice respecting, the appropriate auditing and accounting principles and practices to be used in the preparation of the corporation's financial statements.

(5) Perform such other functions as are prescribed by law, or assigned to the board under a standard of the corporation.

(b) A board of directors also has power to:

(1) Initiate and adopt corporate plans, commitments, and actions.

(2) Initiate and adopt changes in accounting principles and practices.

(3) Provide advice and counsel to the principal senior executives.

(4) Instruct any committee, principal senior executive, or other officer and review the actions of any committee, principal senior executive, or other officer.

(5) Make recommendations to shareholders.

(6) Manage the business of the corporation.

(7) Act as to all other corporate matters not requiring shareholder approval.

(c) Subject to the board's ultimate responsibility for oversight under Subsection (a)(2), the board may delegate to its committees authority to perform any of its functions and exercise any of its powers.

B. THE FUNCTIONS OF THE BOARD

1. HOW BOARDS OF DIRECTORS OPERATE

ELLIOTT J. WEISS, THE BOARD OF DIRECTORS, MANAGEMENT, AND CORPORATE TAKEOVERS: OPPORTUNITIES AND PITFALLS, IN ARNOLD W. SAMETZ (ed.),THE BATTLE FOR CORPORATE CONTROL: SHAREHOLDER RIGHTS, STAKEHOLDER INTERESTS AND MANAGERIAL RESPONSIBILITIES
36–38 (1991)

When we speak of boards of directors, we have in mind the nonmanagement, or outside, members of corporate boards. To be sure, virtually all boards include some of the company's senior executives and some boards include a majority of these inside directors. But nobody takes very seriously the notion that inside directors behave very differently when they are functioning as directors than they do when they are functioning as managers. * * * Thus, when we speak about the relationship between corporate boards and management, we are referring to the relationship between outside directors and senior executives.

* * * The universally held, modern view is that a company's senior executives, not its directors, have primary responsibility for the success or failure of the company's business. The board, in general, is expected only to oversee senior executives and to evaluate their performance.

Most commentators agree that four factors constrain outside directors' ability to perform effectively even these oversight and evaluation functions. First, most directors hold very demanding, full-time jobs as senior officials of other organizations. Consequently, they have limited time available to devote to their secondary jobs as directors of other organizations. * * *

Second, outside directors usually lack expertise in the business of the companies on whose boards they sit. Antitrust laws effectively prohibit companies from having on their boards directors employed by their competitors and, even absent legal prohibitions, few companies would want to invite into their boardrooms people whose primary loyalties ran to one of their competitors. But directors' awareness that they lack relevant expertise is an intimidating factor, making directors understandably reluctant to speak out at board meetings for fear that they will be perceived as naive or uninformed.

Third, directors depend upon a company's executives to supply them with information about the issues the board is to consider and about corporate performance in general; rarely do directors have access to reliable, independent sources of information about corporate activities or management's performance. Executives, of course, generally want the board to approve the proposals they make and to think well of their performance. Consequently, executives rarely are inclined to provide the board with information likely to lead it to reject their proposals or to focus on the negative aspects of their performance. But without such information—or sources from which it might readily be obtained—directors find it difficult to question meaningfully what executives propose to do or how well they have performed.

Finally, directors have little in the way of financial incentives and face little in the way of legal pressures to perform effectively. The fees most directors receive, while substantial if viewed in relation to average workers' salaries, usually represent only a minor portion of directors' income. Few directors own large enough stock positions in the firms on whose boards they sit to motivate them to work hard to ensure that those firms prosper.

* * *

Many commentators believe these constraints limit the contribution directors can make, or can be expected to make, to a company's business success. They also are skeptical about whether directors can deal effectively with situations where managers' and shareholders' interests conflict. They point out that directors' concern about the former, promoting business success, often further impedes their inclination to deal with the latter, since directors, with considerable justification, believe that any effort on their part to limit managers' self-dealing is likely to jeopardize their ability to work effectively with those same managers on solving a company's business problems. * * *

BAYLESS MANNING, THE BUSINESS JUDGMENT RULE AND THE DIRECTOR'S DUTY OF ATTENTION: TIME FOR REALITY

39 Bus.Law. 1477, 1481–1492 (1984).

REAL-WORLD CONDUCT OF DIRECTORS

* * * In the real world, what do such directors—"good" directors— actually do in the discharge of their responsibilities? What is generally expected of them in the market place.[6]

Time Devoted

The outside directors of a corporation are part-time people with respect to the amount of working time that is allocated to the affairs of the company. The most recent survey (1982) shows that the average director of a publicly held company devotes a total of about 123 hours per year to his board and committee work, including travel. That averages less than 3 hours a week, or about 1.5 working days a month.

Directors of companies in crisis conditions often find themselves compelled to devote much greater amounts of time. Also, in some companies, special agreements (with or without special compensation) between the company and a particular director may obligate him to devote more time to his directorship than the rest of the members of the board.

Complexity of Enterprise

Many of today's corporations are not only large, they have usually become highly diversified in their business operations—even those that are not conglomerates. They often operate on a worldwide basis, and their products and services have in many cases become highly technical. This diversification and complexity of operations have been overlaid upon the ordinary problems of all businesses: accounting control, personnel succession, labor relations, financial vitality, competition, governmental regulations, profitability, product development, marketing, and the like.

No human being can stay on top of all this in a major company on a one-and-a-half-day-a-month basis.

Pace and Deliberation

Much of the routine housekeeping work of a board of directors does not demand or warrant significant deliberation. Some important matters that come to the board can be and are dealt with in a deliberate manner over several meetings. A few matters, like the choice of a new CEO from among several in-house candidates, can often be pondered and observed carefully over a period of years, but most significant matters cannot be dealt with in that way by a board. The pace of commercial events often demands quick response or even, as in takeover situations, almost instant response. Even issues that are fully recognized to be vitally important can often not be considered extensively by a board because its agenda is at the time crammed with other exigent items or with matters which, though less significant, are mandated as compulsory agenda items under applicable laws or regulations.

Uncertainty and risk-Taking

Businessmen make business decisions. They are not courts, able and willing to pursue a matter to the last argument in the search of the

---

6. While an effort will be made here to keep in mind the great diversity of the nation's tens of thousands of corporations, most of our available data relates to larger companies, and the descriptions offered here may be correspondingly skewed.

"right" answer. They are not researchers meticulously seeking truth. They are not scientists striving for ever more refined solutions in a field of narrow specialization. And when an issue comes to a board of directors, the process of discussion and decision is nothing like the lawyer's world of briefs and adversary argumentation. The decisions the businessman must make are fraught with risk, and he is quite accustomed to making these decisions in a hurry on the basis of hunch and manifestly sparse data. The businessman and the board of directors thrive or die in a sea of uncertainty. The chairman of a major bank recently made the point well when he said, "If I'm right three times out of ten, I am doing very well, and if I'm right four times out of ten, I'll do better than anybody else."

* * *

Decisional Process

To judge by their statements, many lawyers without personal boardroom experience have a total misconception of the decisional process as it actually functions in the boardroom. The lawyer's professional experience in courts, legislatures, and semi-political bodies tends to lead him to assume that all decisional process is inevitably made up of a series of discrete, separate issues presented one at a time, debated by both or all sides, and voted on. In fact boards of directors typically do not operate that way at all, except, perhaps, in conditions of internal warfare or mortal crisis. Actions are usually by consensus. If a significant sentiment of disagreement is sensed by the chairman, the matter is usually put over for later action, and sources of compromise and persuasion are pursued in the interim. Advice from individual directors is most often volunteered to, or solicited by, the CEO informally on a one-on-one basis, rather than pursued in group debate at a board meeting.

Character of the Agenda

A transcript of a typical board meeting will reflect four kinds of items on the agenda. Fully three quarters of the board's time will be devoted to reports by the management and board committees, routine housekeeping resolutions passed unanimously with little or no discussion, and information responding to specific questions that had earlier been put to the management by directors about a wide range of topics sometimes accompanied by suggestions from the board members, usually procedural in character. Perhaps the remaining one quarter of the meeting time will be addressed to a decision, typically unanimous, on one or two specific different business items, such as the sale of a subsidiary or the establishment of a compensation plan. If, as is the average, a board meets eight times a year, the arithmetic would indicate that a full year of the board's work would contain only ten or fifteen discrete transactional decisions of the type that are generally assumed to make up the main work of the board; and of those discrete transactional matters, many will be neither very important nor controversial, such as a decision to terminate a long-standing banking relationship in favor of a new one that provides better service.

Contrariwise, some issues that have little economic significance may, because of their delicacy, consume great amounts of the board's time—such as the awkward matter of imposing mandatory retirement on the aging founder, builder, and principal owner of the company.

Agenda-Setting—Initiatives by the Board

Agenda-setting and the scope of board initiative together comprise the single most important, and least understood, aspect of the board's work life.

With the two very important exceptions noted below, the question of what the board will discuss and act on is typically determined by the management or by the corporation's automatic built-in secular equivalent of an ecclesiastical calendar, that is, shareholders' meeting date, fiscal year, cycle of audit committee meetings, and similar matters. The board can, and a good board will, from time to time suggest topics for exploration or discussion, or request the management to report in the near future on this or that matter of interest to the board. The board can press management to get on with a necessary undertaking or desired program, such as the establishment of a job classification system, and to report back to the board about the action taken. But the board itself has little capacity to generate significant proposals, other than generalized suggestions looking toward the establishment of procedures or systems. Almost all of what a board does is made up of matters that are brought to it; matters generated by the board itself are very rare. Typically, boards cannot take, and are not expected to take, initiatives.

There are two major exceptions to this generalization about agenda-setting. Both are of extreme importance, and both are fully understood by normal, healthily functioning boards and managements.

First, no board can deny the existence of a built-in paramount responsibility with regard to what may be called the organic or structural integrity of the company. This organic integrity is essentially made up of two elements. A company must have a *functioning management* in place and operating at all times. A board can itself see that this is done. And a company must have an *internal information system* in place that is generally suitable for an enterprise of the company's character to keep the management informed about what is going on and particularly to provide the accounting data on which to base financial statements. The board cannot design, install, operate, or monitor the operation of such systems; but the board can press for the installation and call for periodic assurances that they are in place. As to these two organic elements of the enterprise, the directors may not wait for the management to bring issues to their attention. The responsibility of the board in these two key regards is inherent and ongoing; it is up to the board to take the initiative to keep itself informed about them and to take such periodic action as its business judgment dictates.

Second, no director or group of directors may choose to ignore credible signals of serious trouble in the company. If a director is informed through a credible source that there is reason to believe that the chief financial officer is a compulsive gambler, the director must take an initiative; he may not sit back and wait for the management to bring the matter to the board's attention. There will usually be a wide range of possible actions which a director could reasonably take to pursue such a matter and thereby fulfill his obligation as a director; but he cannot simply do nothing. Execution of this responsibility of a director will be episodic and, typically, infrequent, but the responsibility itself is ongoing and present every day.

Actions Not Taken

All these realities of directional life add up to a deeper one. From among an infinite number of useful things that a board of directors *might* reasonably have done or looked into in a given time period, the number that will *not* have been done by the most qualified, best-run, and most diligent board in the world will always be far greater than the number that *were* done. If a corporate transaction goes sour, or a company fails, any plaintiff's lawyer of even the most modest talent and imagination will always be able to find a subject matter X as to which he can denounce its directors, declaiming: "Surely any reasonable prudent person in these circumstances would have explored subject X, but this board sat back, did nothing, and did not even inquire into it." That argument in hindsight will always sound plausible. It may appeal to some juries, or even some courts, inexperienced in the reality of business life. But it is most often just hokum and rhetoric.

No court confronted with this retrospective argument about directional delinquency should ever allow itself to forget the reality that at any given time the roster of possible candidates for a place on the agenda of the board is infinite and that agenda items are mutually exclusive, that is, hours spent on one agenda item are hours not spent on an infinity of other possible agenda items. The number of items considered will always be vastly exceeded by the number not considered. And the plaintiff's retrospective indictment, though apparently plausible, is in fact hollow, because it can be as easily designed to hurl against the best-performing board as against the worst.

* * *

Homework and Scope of Inquiry

Assume that a particular item has in ordinary course come onto the board's agenda and that it is one of that limited number that specifically calls for affirmative decisional action. No one disputes that the board should look into the matter before acting, but in a particular situation, what does that mean? How much time should be devoted to the item (to the exclusion of others)? Is it enough for the directors to read the papers sent by the management? The appendices? A summary cover letter? With what degree of concentration? And what degree of comprehension by the individual director? Regardless of the topic's technical character, what of the director's specialized experience or absence of qualification in the subject? In what degree, if any, should the director carry out research going beyond the documentation provided to him by the company or draw on recollection of data (or rumors) acquired elsewhere? Should the director insist that he be provided an opinion of outside consultants in support of the information and recommendations made by the management?

One does not have to reflect very long about such questions to come to two realizations. The first is that there is no conceivable way to lay down *a priori* answers to such questions. The second is that the point made earlier about agenda-setting in general context has even greater application in the specific. At all times and in all circumstances, the scope of investigation actually undertaken on a matter, whatever it is, will always be less than the possible scope and depth of investigation that could have been undertaken. In every instance of corporate misfortune, it will therefore be an easy cheap shot to fling at the director on the witness stand, "You mean you voted to proceed with this birdcage transaction without even consulting the definitive manual on birdcages put out by the U.S. Department of Commerce?"

No one believes that a director should be able with impunity simply to ignore the work of the board, never doing his homework; but the director's judgment as to the scope of inquiry called for in the circumstances is itself a business judgment of the most basic character.

Attendance

Apparently the simplest aspect of the topic of directional attention relates to his attending meetings of the board. But consider four instances. Able director W, whose technical experience on one topic is critically valuable to the board, is always well prepared, but he is heavily committed in many activities and able to attend only half the board meetings; X, also a director of broadly experienced competence and helpful when present, is senior and semiretired and he misses half the meetings because he lives abroad half of the year; Y, a director of no special competence, attends all the meetings to no visible good effect; Z, a director of average capacity is lazy and seldom shows up, but he owns sixty percent of the stock of the company. How should the law react to such circumstances?

What of the director who missed the meeting where particular action was taken; as a nonactor, should he be more exposed or less exposed to later attack?

How important is attendance, taken alone? In the real world, the answer will depend on the decisional process actually utilized by the CEO and his board. If the CEO is in continuous consultation with his directors, and if decisions of substance are worked out through prior soundings so that the meeting is only a formality (a very common pattern), or if the CEO arranges the agenda so that big issues do not come up unless his key qualified directors are present to participate, then the whole issue of frequency of attendance may be peripheral at best. A judge who does not regularly show up in his courtroom can be safely concluded not to be doing his job and to be either ill or delinquent, but that image cannot be automatically transferred to the wholly different processes of boards of directors. In most circumstances it will be very hard for a plaintiff to demonstrate that a director's sporadic attendance was causally linked to later difficulties of the company.

Reliance

* * *

[D]irectors may safely rely upon officers and employees of the corporation, accountants, engineers, lawyers, and other expert consultants who they have reason to believe are competent. Expert consultation inspired by a perceived need to know on the part of the board is obviously constructive and indispensable. An inoculation of expert outside opinion is also of help in preventing an epidemic of liability in the board room. The law has also become more realistic in recognizing that much of a board's work is, and must be, done in committee, and in according to the board the privilege of reliance upon the work product of its committees.

It is less widely understood, and not explicitly recognized in the law, that the dynamics of the boardroom are also deeply dependent upon a matrix of other reliances among individual officers and directors. Director X, at a meeting asks in respect of particular transaction A, "Will we have any trouble with our auditors if we do A?" Director Y, who is recognized by his colleagues to be the board's most knowledgeable member in matters of accounting (who may, or may not, be a member of the audit committee) says, "Don't worry, X, I don't think we'll have any problem there." Thereupon the conversation moves on to another topic, the group deferring in an informal way to the expertise and judgment of one of its members in whom it has confidence. (The same interchange could, of course, have involved the company's chief financial officer rather than Y.) Does this kind of interchange among businessmen comply with legally articulated standards like "duty to inquire," or "duty to inform itself"? If the answer is "no" (as at least some commentators would undoubtedly say), then the tension between the law and reality is in a crisis condition. To operate at all, any group decisional process must be built on a substrate of such interconnected informal delegation and deference. A board is free to ask any question, but a board that does not have confidence in and rejects the answer it receives is at a point of pathological collapse as a decisional apparatus.

A correlative of the board's reliance must be a special informal obligation on the part of the person or committee relied upon to do his or its homework well or to be willing to answer to a board member's question, "I do not know." The expectations of the rest of the board are that they will receive a specially informed opinion, and they are entitled to get it.

So, once again, the normal decisional process in the boardroom is quite different from the piece-by-piece, person-by-person, issue-by-issue, question-by-question, adversary interrogational and debate process which a lawyer or judge tends to perceive as the normal way to arrive at professional conclusions. (That is one of the major reasons why businessmen think lawyers make poor directors until they learn, if they learn, that corporate decision-making requires other ways of doing.)

Depth of Inquiry

The point about deference and reliance as an element of "inquiry" has another aspect with which the lawyer will more readily empathize because it matches part of his own working experience. Assuming that the director specifically undertakes to "inquire" into a matter, how deeply should he go? Wherever the questioning stops, it would always be possible to question still further, as every lawyer knows.

In the boardroom context, there is no inherent limit to the possible circumstances and conditions that are relevant to a business decision. When and where to stop is always a matter of sophisticated judgment in the immediate circumstances involving the importance of the decision (as then perceived), the costs of further pursuit, the board's confidence in the answers so far received, the confidence in the persons who purport to have explored the matter and are reporting to the board, the special intensity of the directors' concern about the particular matter, competing demands for attention to other important matters, the rate at which, and the matter on which, the inquirer decides to ration out his always-finite supply of political capital within the board, and so forth. The *gestalt* at the instant that a director decides not to pursue his questions further cannot be faithfully recaptured later in a courtroom setting.

On this topic, it is always easy for a courtroom advocate, a judge, a law review commentator, a journalist, or a politician to write sentences like, "The director cannot just be dumb. He cannot just accept any answer, however preposterous, to his question." But that is only an old rhetorical trick that can be called argument by negative hyperbole. Negative hyperbole may sometimes be good advocacy, but it is never good law-making. The egregious behavior which the advocate conjures up in such sentences is indeed egregious and is condemnable as such; but such bizarre behavior virtually never occurs in real life, and the tub-thumping sentence stated in the negative provides no future affirmative guidance whatever to counsel, judges, or directors concerning what a well-intentioned director should do.

Setting aside outlandish situations in which the negative hyperbole is not hyperbole but a description of what actually happened, ultimately the law must allow the director to exercise his judgment about the scope and depth of his inquiry, exactly as it must realistically allow the board to exercise its judgment about its agenda.

Judgment

Finally, we come to the matter of judgment itself. Assume, again, that a board is going through one of those episodes of discrete transactional decision which lawyers' discourse assumes to be normal but is in fact rare. Assume that questions have been asked and inquiry made to a satisfactory extent, whatever that may mean. Now, as perceived by the legal writing, the board weighs the matter and makes a judgment, and it is that judgment that is protected by the business judgment rule.

Boardroom reality is far different from this lawyer-oriented model, not only in the respects discussed earlier but usually in the character of "judgment" itself. The differences are fundamental and warrant comment.

* * *

* * * [O]ne can observe that the work of corporate management and directors has the same general characteristics as that of the high political official or general. Actions are most often multiple. The company's course of conduct is a resultant of countless tradeoffs. Resources are never sufficient. Competitors and others are devoted to obstruction. Occasionally one can discern a clean go or no-go issue that will be decided by a board of directors—whether to shut down all foreign operations and take a big current write-off, for example—but such instances are not frequent, and even when they appear to arise they are nearly always linked to other decisional implications, as when, for example, a board decides not to fire the chief executive today but at the same time takes other moves to pre-position possible successors for tomorrow. As a result, seeking in retrospect to revisit and evaluate a single "judgment on an issue" by a board of directors will almost always be a distortion of reality, because no such free-standing single judgment ever happened.

* * * [J]udgments of boards of directors are mainly in the nature of decisions whether to hurl a veto. A chief executive who generally enjoys the confidence of his board will usually be able to carry any proposal he makes if he does his homework, prepares his supporting arguments, is backed up by his other officers, and—of key importance—personally throws his full weight behind the proposal. Courts and the public must understand that quite commonly a director will go along with a business proposal that he does not really like. He may well think, and will sometimes say aloud in the board meeting, "I do not like this proposal. It seems risky and I believe other uses for the same resources would be more promising. But I may be wrong; I respect the contrary views of my colleagues; and I have to accord great weight to the CEO's strong support for this project. *After all, he is the one who will have the primary responsibility for seeing to it that it works out successfully.* So I will not vote no." When that happens, everyone in the corporate world knows the meaning of the italicized words. The director is saying that he will go along this time, but the CEO is on notice that if he proves to be wrong and the project fails, he may well have lost that director's confidence.

To cite another illustration. Even if a director is strongly opposed to a project, he may still go along because the CEO is determined to proceed and, in the director's best judgment, the disruption that would be caused by firing the CEO at this time would be more injurious to the interests of the company and its shareholders than the negative risks of the project proposed. In such a case, the real business judgment the director makes is not to throw his javelin today. That kind of aggregative judgment is not, in the lawyer's sense, "on the merits" of the narrow particular issue at hand, but it is very much on the issue of the director's perception of the best interests of the company. How can a court later evaluate such a nonjudgment judgment?

Thus, the decisional process of a board of directors only occasionally involves a go or no-go issue at all; often involves a cost-benefit mix of tradeoffs on multiple issues, in search of the least bad result; and is continuously obscured by the weight given by directors to the injury that will likely be visited upon the interests of the company and shareholders if the board splinters or if it suddenly dumps its CEO.

* * *

Diversity of Enterprise and Style

* * *

At any one moment in time each company occupies some position on a spectrum that ranges from the wholly owned, one-man business, through the enterprise that is predominantly owned and wholly controlled by one man or one family, through the enterprise that is similarly controlled but has hundreds of shareholders who have no personal interaction with the company's management, and so on up to a great, faceless, meritocratic corporate bureaucracy.

Companies also differ from each other markedly in personality and in operating style. Contemporary literature has hit upon the term "corporate culture" to refer to the evident fact that each company is a distinctive social organization with its own viewpoints, management style, attitudes, self-image, and ways of doing. Every board of directors also has its own personality and manner of working with the management.

* * *

Spasmodic Intensity of Attention

Not only is company A different from company B. An additional clearly observable phenomenon in the sociology of boardroom life is that the board of company A behaves differently at different times. The intensity and quantity of all forms of the board's attention rises and falls as the company passes through calm or stormy seas. When matters are going well, the board tends to settle into watchful but quiet routine, confident in the management's performance and willing to be led. If the wind begins to rise, the board will stir and come to life, ask many questions, occasionally exercise its veto, and perhaps oust the CEO. If the hurricane comes, the board members will typically respond energetically out of their sense of responsibility, pouring time, energy, study, attention, and initiative into the company's affairs, sometimes to the point of temporarily assuming full executive control. When the storm is weathered, perhaps with a new captain installed, the board will resume a less active but watchful mode. Thus, a degree of attention that would be normal in usual circumstances could be considered as insufficient when the going gets rough.

2. EMPIRICAL STUDIES OF BOARDS OF DIRECTORS

The first major empirical study of what directors actually do concluded that they largely failed to fulfill their primary theoretical functions. Myles Mace, Directors: Myth and Reality (1971). Mace found that directors rarely challenged a CEO or initiated debate on an issue. Directors also generally did not effectively monitor management's performance because CEOs typically provided them with limited information; they devoted little time to reviewing and discussing that information; and boardroom culture emphasized collegiality and the avoidance of controversy. Sometimes, however, directors brought useful expertise to bear on boardroom discussions.

Mace concluded that most outside directors were reluctant to replace an incumbent CEO, no matter how poor the corporation's performance, and that directors usually relied on the CEO to nominate her successor. Only when a vacancy developed suddenly—for example, if a CEO died unexpectedly—did boards generally take the initiative to select a CEO. Finally, Mace found that most boards in fact did not establish basic corporate objectives, strategies and policies. All too often, directors served as little more than "attractive ornaments on the corporate Christmas tree." Id. at 107. Mace reaffirmed these conclusions in a subsequent study. Myles L. Mace, Directors: Myth and Reality—Ten Years Later, 32 Rutg. L. Rev. 293 (1979).

Mace's work was a powerful indictment of most corporate boards. A more recent study suggests directors have become increasingly involved in corporate affairs. Jay W. Lorsch and Elizabeth MacIver, Pawns or Potentates: The Reality of America's Corporate Boards (1989). Scandals involving bribery of foreign officials in the 1970's, economic challenges and the fear of personal liability have combined to make directors take their duties more seriously and to expect the same from their colleagues. Directors today regularly receive and review more information from management prior to the board's regular meeting, including the minutes of prior meetings, the agenda for the next meeting, the corporation's financial statements, management proposals, and committee reports. This information has increased in both quantity and quality, and the outside directors review it more carefully.

Directors still view their primary duties to be selecting a good CEO and replacing a bad one. But most believe that boards have, and should, become more active in planning the corporation's strategy in areas such as expansion into new products and markets and selling or purchasing major assets. The reaction of CEOs to this development has been mixed. Some CEOs resent the board's intrusion into what has traditionally been their domain; others welcome the advice of other experienced executives.

Of lesser importance, but shared by nearly all directors, is a belief that directors should assure that corporations act both legally and ethically. This development has been attributed to both the growing presence of previously unrepresented groups on boards and the increasing public pressure being placed on corporations in areas of public concern. Nearly all directors still believe that management should remain firmly in the hands of the CEO and other senior executives, but directors are more willing to question and even challenge decisions and policies they think are unwise. Most directors, though, prefer to express their concerns privately to the CEO rather than "publicly" in a board meeting. Directors also usually do not respond effectively to what Lorsch and MacIver term "gradual crises"—those that reflect a decline in a corporation's long-term viability.

Other factors continue to deter directors from becoming more involved in corporate affairs. Directors differ as to whom they are accountable. A minority believe that when a decision is made, only the concerns of current shareholders should be considered. Others believe they should focus more on the corporation's long-term prospects. A growing number of directors try to balance the interests of shareholders, employees, customers and other constituencies, but most directors are reluctant to admit that at times they do not treat the interests of shareholders as paramount.

Lorsch and MacIver also discuss what motivates a person to serve as an outside director. The opportunity to learn and gain business experience is critical, particularly where the knowledge obtained may help a director manage her own company. Social and professional prestige also are cited frequently. But directors appear less willing than in the past to serve on multiple boards, despite the greater prestige that this greater number of positions might bring, because of a desire to serve more effectively. Other explanations offered for declining invitations to serve include lack of time, conflicts of meeting times and conflicts of interest with some other corporation.

Lorsch and MacIver completed their study before the outside directors of General Motors, American Express, Westinghouse, Kodak, and IBM, to name but a few, ousted the CEOs of those companies in 1992 and 1993. Causation is always difficult to identify, but these changes appear to reflect the confluence of rising pressure from institutional investors, a stubbornly recessionary economy, and the culmination of a long series of bad business decisions by the ousted CEOs. Whether they also augur a paradigm shift in corporate governance is less clear. For a suggestion that such a shift is occurring, made by an attorney who was active in many of the events referred to in this paragraph, see Ira M. Millstein, The Evolution of the Certifying Board, 48 Bus. Law. 1485 (1993). Notwithstanding this suggestion, as of the writing of this book, there is much speculation but not enough evidence to support any definitive conclusions.

3. THE INCREASING IMPORTANCE OF BOARD COMMITTEES

One change in board structure that has been widely accepted, both in theory and in practice, is the division of the board into committees with different areas of responsibility. By operating through, and dividing the work of the board among, committees, outside directors can more easily increase their oversight of and involvement in corporate affairs.

Reliance on board committees, particularly the audit committee, has increased dramatically, in part as a consequence of SEC proxy disclosure and stock exchange requirements. See Item 6(d)(1) of Schedule 14A; New York Stock Exchange Company Manual § 303.00. One study reported that 98.7 percent of the corporations surveyed had audit committees and 95 percent and 60 percent of the corporations, respectively, had compensation and nominating committees. Korn/Ferry International, Board of Directors: Twentieth Annual Study 14 (June 1993). All members of the audit and compensation committees and 80 percent of the members of the nominating committees studied, on average, were outside directors. Id. at 15 (Table 4B).

The audit committee monitors and investigates a corporation's financial transactions and financial reports. One of its functions is to prevent financial improprieties. The audit committee also is a direct link between the corporation's independent accounting firm and the board of directors. It can perform a wide range of tasks: recommending independent auditors to the full board; conferring with the auditors before, during, and after their audit about its scope, procedures, problems, and results; and discussing with the corporation's internal auditors the nature and effectiveness of their work. Audit committees have also frequently investigated suspect payments and other financial irregularities.

Through its independent access to financial information and its contact with the independent auditors, the audit committee can better inform the board of the company's financial activities and improve the board's monitoring of management. The committee offers management an opportunity to review the company's financial reporting and controls. It also can give a company's internal auditors direct access to the board. Finally, it can shield the external auditors from undue management influence by providing a forum in which the auditors can confer directly with board members about accounting practices, the quality of internal controls, and other potentially troublesome issues.

The ALI proposes that every large public corporation (a corporation with at least 2,000 shareholders and $100 million in assets) have an audit committee. See ALI, Principles of Corporate Governance (1994), § 3A.05 (Comment c). As a matter of corporate practice, the ALI recommends that smaller public corporations have audit committees as well. Id., § 3A.02. No audit committee member should be an executive or an employee of the corporation or a relatively recent employee, and at least a majority of the committee members should have no significant relationship to the senior executives whose performance is covered by the financial statements the auditors are charged with reviewing.

The ALI also recommends that large public corporations have two other committees whose members should be as independent of management as are the members of the audit committee. A nominating committee should be given primary responsibility for identifying candidates for election to the board. The CEO and senior executives also should be allowed to play a role in proposing nominees. Id., § 3A.04. A compensation committee should be charged with overseeing the manner in which senior executives are paid. Id., § 3A.05. It should be alert both to overly generous compensation arrangements and to ensuring that compensation arrangements provide managers with appropriate incentives.

A 1993 change in the federal tax law gives the compensation committee added importance. The law limits a corporation's ability to deduct compensation in excess of $1 million per year paid to its five highest-paid officers. This cap, however, will not apply to incentive compensation tied to performance goals that have been established by a compensation committee made up of "outside" directors and approved by shareholders. Under this provision, a director must not be (i) an employee, (ii) a former employee who continues to receive compensation (other than a qualified pension) from the corporation, (iii) a former officer, or (iv) a person receiving compensation from the corporation (other than directors' fees) for consulting or other personal services.

C. WHO THE OUTSIDE DIRECTORS ARE

How a board performs clearly will be influenced by who the directors are. Studies show that an increasing percentage of corporations prefer that outside directors constitute a majority of the board. One survey found that corporations reported an average of three inside directors and nine outside directors. Korn/Ferry International, Board of Directors Twentieth Annual Survey 13 (June 1993). Another survey found that 63% of outside directors of large corporations were CEOs of other companies, and most of them were white males more than 55 years old. Jay Lorsch and Elizabeth MacIver, Directors: Pawns or Potentates: The Reality of America's Corporate Boards 18 (1989). Although these numbers may shift somewhat in coming years, the pool from which outside directors are drawn seems likely to remain both small and rather homogenous.

The trend toward boards comprised primarily of outside directors has been widely endorsed. The ALI recommends that the boards of large public corporations should have a majority of directors who have no significant relationships with the corporation's senior executives. ALI, Principles of Corporate Governance, (1994), § 3A.01. For large corporations, a board having a majority of independent directors "is conducive to objective analysis of managerial performance [while] [p]ermitting senior executives to serve on the board ensures knowledgeable and detailed board discussion about the business, and encourages management to take important issues to the board." Id., § 3A.01, Comment *c.* The boards of other public corporations should have at least three independent directors, "in the belief that [three] is the number of directors necessary to attain a critical mass on the board." Id. See also, American Bar Association Committee on Corporate Laws, The Corporate Director's Guidebook, 33 Bus. Law. 1591, 1625 (1978); New York Stock Exchange Company Manual § 303.

1. THE MEANING OF "INDEPENDENT"

The monitoring model discussed in Section A is premised on the assumption that directors who are independent of management can act to reduce agency costs within the large corporation by checking management overreaching and vetoing unwise management proposals. But what is meant by "independent" and how much is reliance on independent directors is justified? Board members must develop a working relationship among themselves; the board must also work with management. These two goals may be in conflict and a balance must be struck between them. Directors also must be willing to offer constructive criticism of corporate management. A danger exists, however, that outside directors will hesitate to rock the boat, even if they feel strongly that management is wrong in its strategy or decisions. As Mace, Manning and Lorsch and MacIver all point out, even outside directors who take their positions seriously and conscientiously usually defer to a CEO who stands behind her proposals. Outside directors generally prefer to resign quietly rather than challenge publicly the CEO or other board members.

Recognizing this need for balance, it would be possible to have a limited definition of "independent" that would exclude only people who are presently employed directly by the corporation. Under this definition, directors who are former employees and those who have current business or professional relationships with the corporation, such as the corporation's outside lawyers or investment bankers, would be "independent."

However, independence may vary with the context. Thus, when evaluating questions relating to directors' fiduciary duties, the ALI uses the term "interested" and counts as interested a director who has a significant financial interest in a particular transaction and a director whose judgment may be influenced by a relationship she has with someone who has such a financial interest. ALI, Principles of Corporate

Governance (1994), § 1.23. We consider this definition further in Chapter 17.

On the other hand, when considering a director's qualification to serve on committees of the board, such as the audit committee, the ALI looks at whether the director has a "significant relationship" with a senior executive. Such a relationship includes employment with the firm within the past two years; being an immediate family member of a senior executive; engaging in transactions with the corporation, directly or indirectly, in an amount exceeding $200,000; or working for a law firm or investment bank that the corporation employs. ALI, Principles of Corporate Governance (1994), § 1.34.

Michigan has adopted a more innovative approach, allowing corporations to have a special "independent" director who then can exercise certain powers not available to other directors. Mich. Comp. Laws Ann. § 450.1107(3) (West 1990). The independent director must be elected by the shareholders, not appointed by the board. Either the board or the shareholders must designate the director as independent, and either group can later revoke this designation if it concludes the director is not sufficiently independent. To ensure competence, the director must have at least five years of business, legal or financial experience. The director cannot be, nor have been within the past three years: (i) an officer or employee of the corporation or its affiliates; (ii) engaged in any business transactions with the corporation for more than $100,000; or (iii) an officer, partner, or immediate family member of anybody in these categories, or enter into a relationship or transaction with them. Finally, the director must not have more than three years of aggregate experience with the corporation as a director, whether independent or not. This last requirement is designed to counteract the erosion of independence that many directors experience as a consequence of working collaboratively with a corporation's managers. An independent director who has served three years can remain on the board but loses her "independent" status.

Michigan law also requires a court to scrutinize less closely a self-dealing transaction that an independent director has approved. Similar deference is to be given to an independent director's approval of indemnification of expenses incurred by a director who has been sued for acts committed in an official capacity. (See Chapter 16). An independent director also is granted the power to dismiss a derivative suit brought by a shareholder on the corporation's behalf. (See Chapter 20). A corporation can pay an independent director extra compensation and can reimburse her expenses. The statute also authorizes an independent director to communicate directly with shareholders at the company's expense, which could increase her influence by making it possible for her to threaten public disclosure if she disagrees with a majority of the board. However, the overall thrust of the new independent director position is not to alter radically the way a corporation behaves, but to add a truly outside view and voice to corporate boards. See Cyril

Moscow, Margo Rogers Lesser & Stephen H. Schulman, Michigan's Independent Director, 46 Bus. Law. 57 (Nov. 1990).

2. IS FORMAL "INDEPENDENCE" SIGNIFICANT?

Some commentators question whether outside directors, even if they satisfy one or another of the above criteria of "independence," will safeguard the interest of shareholders and others. They suggest that outside directors have a "structural bias" against taking actions that conflict with the interests or preferences of a corporation's managers—a "mind set" that prevents them from acting independently.

Outside directors who are or have been corporate CEOs, as well as professionals who deal principally with corporate clients, often are almost instinctively pro-management; they are members of the "corporate club." * They tend to sympathize with the pressures and uncertainties that confront CEOs and to empathize with the difficulties that CEOs face. Moreover, directors who are also CEOs avoid actions that they would not want the outside directors on their boards to take. They abide by what one commentator calls the Golden Rule of The Boardroom: "Do unto the managers of a company on whose board you sit only what you would have the directors of your company do unto you." Weiss, supra, at 40.

The question of structural bias is complex. Two other commentators have concluded:

> The process by which board members are selected, the criteria by which their candidacy and continued service are evaluated, and the motives and rewards that impel nominees and directors to serve on the board all interact to form a highly cohesive group of mutually attractive individuals. All available evidence suggests that the strength of this attraction among the directors and the value they each place upon their membership in the group are extremely high. For example, the selection criteria generate boards of directors who have highly similar backgrounds, goals, talents, and work experience: a highly cohesive, cooperative set of directors who share corporate attitudes and loyalties. In addition, the shared perception of mutual agreeableness enhances the interpersonal attraction among ingroup members and this enhanced mutual attraction creates even more conformity. The very high nonmonetary personal value that directors place on continued membership on these highly prestigious boards tend to multiply the overall cohesion of the group

---

* According to one survey, corporations most often have directors who are senior executives of other corporations (80 percent of corporations surveyed), retired executives of other companies (68 percent), and academicians (52 percent). Korn/Ferry International, Board of Directors Twentieth Annual Study 4 (June 1993). From 1988 to 1992, the number of corporations with ethnic minority directors increased from 33 to 46 percent, the number with female directors increased from 58 to 60 percent, and the number with directors representing a major shareholder increased from 26 to 28 percent. The largest declines were in corporations with former government officials as directors (30 percent to 23 percent) and with "professional" directors (26 percent to 18 percent.)

even more. Finally, enhanced self-esteem derived from being singled out for membership in the select group and the increased attention associated with continued group membership contribute importantly to ingroup cohesion within the boardroom.

James D. Cox and Harry L. Munsinger, Bias in the Boardroom: Psychological Foundations and Legal Implications of Corporate Cohesion, Law & Contemp. Probs., Summer 1985, at 83, 98–99.

On the other hand, a former SEC Commissioner, corporate executive and experienced practitioner, while noting concern about structural bias, states:

> Is the system malfunctioning to the extent that we must look to alternative sources for corporate monitoring? The system of independent directors works reasonably well and has improved considerably over time. Moreover, we may be expecting too much from directors, both because of a failure to understand the nature of the board's relationship to the management and because of a failure to define clearly the board's responsibility in some crucial areas. While the board's basic function is to monitor the management and to hire and fire the CEO, that function cannot be successfully performed in an adversarial environment. Success in business requires risk-taking and risk-taking requires a united team of board and management. Thus, whether the directors are chosen by management, by an independent nominating committee or by an independent chairman, in most companies they will inevitably be identified with the management's strategic policies, which they have approved. The board's identification with the management's goals is a major element in creating the "slowness to act" that some observers find to be a defect in the current system. In my view, it is simply the natural consequence of a strength—the unity of the board and management on strategic corporate issues. Of course, some boards are shamelessly derelict, but there is not a systemic problem unless there is a wide pattern of dereliction; unsatisfactory individual conduct calls for policing, either through the courts or through shareholder action, not a structural solution.

Stephen J. Friedman, Corporate Governance in the Nineties——Institutional Investors and the Evolution of the Law, The Business Lawyer Update (Jan./Feb. 1992) 6.

Despite the problems created by depending on independent directors to oversee corporations, the empirical evidence supports their use. One pioneering study, based on the board structure and performance of 266 corporations in 1970, 1976 and 1980, concludes, "As corporate board independence increases, corporate financial performance tends to increase." Barry D. Baysinger & Henry N. Butler, Revolution Versus Evolution in Corporation Law: The ALI's Project and the Independent Director, 52 Geo. Wash. L. Rev. 557, 572 (1984). The improvement in financial performance does not occur contemporaneously but over the long run. See also, Barry D. Baysinger & Henry N. Butler, Corporate

Governance and the Board of Directors: Performance Effects of Changes in Board Composition, 1 J. Law, Econ. & Org. 101, 116 (1983), which qualifies these findings as follows:

> The better performing firms—that is, those firms that either started with above average performance and remained above average or those that started below average and rose to the ranks of above average—have boards that began the period with far fewer than a majority of independent directors and ended the period with fewer than a majority as well. * * * At the least, it is not necessary to have a majority of independent directors (to say nothing of having all monitors on the board) to achieve superior relative financial performance.

Id. at 119.

3. CONSTITUENCY DIRECTORS

In searching for "independent" directors, it has been suggested that directors be chosen from constituencies that represent interests other than those of the shareholders, such as employees. Alternatively, directors could be selected from groups whose members are less likely to be a part of the traditional corporate establishment, such as women, representatives of minority groups, environmentalists, or consumer advocates. The argument in support of this suggestion is that directors drawn from these groups will not share the club mentality of current outside directors and will be less likely to be co-opted into deferring automatically to the CEO. Moreover, they could broaden the board's decision-making perspective by providing a better understanding of the feelings and attitudes of the corporation's various constituencies. For a discussion of an early attempt to broaden the composition of the General Motors board, see Donald E. Schwartz, The Public–Interest Proxy Contest: Reflections on Campaign GM, 69 Mich. L. Rev. 419 (1971).

However appealing the rhetoric of this suggestion, mandating its implementation raises serious difficulties. What groups should be represented? If the constituencies can be designated, how many representatives on the board will each constituency have and how will the constituencies select their representatives? What weight will be given to the interests of the various constituencies when they conflict with each other or with the interests of the shareholders? Will directors responsible to different interests create a divisive, adversary atmosphere? Will the board become a political organ working out conflicts through shifting alliances among directors representing different interests? The tug-of-war among competing groups may damage the board's collegiality and result in a board's inability to reach timely decisions.

Well-meaning individuals also may lack the requisite expertise and experience to make corporate decisions. They may be unaware of a corporation's problems and the dynamics of board meetings. These individuals may offer little constructive input or may be co-opted into the existing corporate apparatus, its goals and functions. Non-establishment directors may be perceived of as an obstructive, disruptive force among board members and between the board and management. Will the interests of these individuals conflict with those of the corporation? Suspicions exist that non-club members would use information acquired through service on a board in a manner hostile to the best interest of the corporation, for example, by channelling information for litigation purposes to public agencies, public interest groups, or corporate shareholders. Even if guidelines could be established for secrecy and the release of information by directors, an adverse relationship among board members would likely reduce board effectiveness. The board's monitoring function would likely be short-circuited and management might be freer from evaluation by the board, even with respect to the traditional corporate goals of long-term profit maximization shareholders' interest. Moreover, there is the issue of whether a privately owned corporation should perform quasi-governmental functions; reformers might look instead to the political process. See Daniel R. Fischel, The Corporate Governance Movement, 35 Vand. L. Rev. 1259 (1982).

BAYLESS MANNING, A TAXONOMY OF CORPORATE LAW REFORM, IN COMMENTARIES ON CORPORATE STRUCTURE AND GOVERNANCE
120–22 (Donald E. Schwartz, ed., 1979).

A small group of critics of the American corporation * * * takes as an immutable axiom that for all institutions and for all time, the only institutional decisions that are legitimate are those that are arrived at on the basis of a consensus of all persons who have an interest in, or are affected by, the outcome. Thus, in their view, a board of directors of a corporation should not be allowed to decide to close a plant, since many other people will be affected by that decision. The solution * * * under the bland name "co-determination" is that boards of directors should be required by law to include representatives of labor unions. It is pointed out that a variant of this feature has been introduced in Germany * * *.

One immediate question raised by this proposal relates to its internal philosophic consistency. If one were truly serious about including on a board of directors representatives of the various parties who have an economic interest in the enterprise, then it would include not only representatives of shareholders and employees but also representatives of lenders, suppliers, customers, contractors, lessors (and lessees), municipalities, states, school districts, charities, the U.S. Treasury, etc., all of which have a stake in the enterprise's income stream. Would all these groups be enthusiastic to see their interests guarded by labor union representatives?

* * *

But the split-board concept is faulty at a more fundamental level. Must special-interest participationism be accepted as a universal axiom to be applied unthinkingly to every form of organized human behavior? Aside from the question of its wide application to other institutions (armies, churches, schools, ship crews, courts, etc.), the core of the question as addressed to commercial enterprises is whether one recognizes and accepts that the commercial corporation—whether small or large—should be first and foremost an organization designed to operate efficiently to produce goods and services for the society, rather than a political organization designed to maximize political expression. To the degree that the managerial and decisionmaking structure of the incorporated enterprise is altered to resemble a New England town meeting, a Quaker consensus session, an Italian Parliament, or a two-party power negotiation, the capacity of the enterprise to carry out its basic economic function cannot fail to be impeded.

* * *

Seen from [the perspective of economic efficiency], the role of common shareholders as the ultimate constituency of the corporation makes a great deal of sense. Unlike any of the other constituents who tap the income stream of the enterprise-workers, creditors, tax collectors, suppliers, etc., the common shareholder is playing for the entrepreneurial margin and only the entrepreneurial margin. Nothing so clears the mind and sharpens his taste for efficiency as the recognition that everyone else gets paid ahead of him and that he gets nothing unless there is something left over. No other constituency of the enterprise has the same incentive to achieve a high level of efficiency for the enterprise as a whole, since the economic interest of each other constituency is narrower or has a limiting cap on it or runs directly counter to the interest of the aggregate enterprise's cost control. Shareholders—particularly the professional sharp-eyed investors with a nervous focus on the bottom line—perform a vital function for the enterprise and for the efficiency of the economy as a whole.

It is the responsibility of the board of directors and management of an enterprise, and it is to the special economic interest of the common shareholders, to attend to the operating efficiency of the enterprise as a whole. No other group has that perspective of the aggregate. To lodge within the board of directors a cell whose commitment is to a single constituency of the enterprise—whether to employees, lenders, consumers, or any other group—rather than to the interest of the aggregate enterprise is a certain way to dilute and in time to destroy the feature of the corporate form that, more than any other, has accounted for its extraordinary economic success.

––––––

Dean Manning is correct in questioning whether a variety of constituencies would be "enthusiastic" about having their interests protected by a union representative on the board. But his analysis is incomplete;

presumably each of the groups he names could also want board representation. In fact, the focus has been on employee representation because employees are the easiest constituency to identify rather than because they are the constituency best able to protect non-shareholder interests.

Not all commentators are as negative toward constituency directors. Professor Alfred F. Conard professes some skepticism but suggests that customers and employees could practicably be represented on boards. However, he questions whether environmentalists will make positive contributions and more generally argues that the interests of corporate constituencies can be served more efficiently by means other than board membership. Alfred F. Conard, Reflections on Public Interest Directors, 75 Mich. L. Rev. 941 (1977).

Professor Brudney, on the other hand, argues: "[N]either theory nor practice permits the conclusion that the independent director can be as successful a monitor of social responsibility as it is claimed he is, or even as he may be, as a monitor of integrity. And in the context of social responsibility, even more than self-dealing, there is reason to believe that the losses from using him as a substitute for regulation will exceed the gains." Victor Brudney, The Independent Director–Heavenly City or Potemkin Village?, 95 Harv.L.Rev. 597, 658 (1981). For a view endorsing the inclusion of constituency representatives on boards and in board decision making, see Lawrence E. Mitchell, A Critical Look at Corporate Governance, 45 Vand. L. Rev. 1263 (1992).

One form of constituency director is the "public director" whose function is to represent the interests of society at large. Christopher Stone has argued that the appointment of such a director would lead to enhanced corporate social responsibility. Christopher D. Stone, Where the Law Ends: The Social Control of Corporate Behavior 158–173 (1975). Recall that Professor Weiss has advanced a similar proposal. (Chapter 5). For a more skeptical view, see Phillip I. Blumberg, The Role of the Corporation In Society Today, 31 Bus. Law. 1403, 1406 (1976).

D.   PROPOSALS TO ENHANCE BOARD PERFORMANCE

Corporations and boards of directors have been subject to criticism for many years, going back at least as far as Berle and Means. Some of this criticism is based on a perceived lack of accountability to the shareholders and the problems of the separation of ownership and control that are inherent in the fundamental structure of the large public corporation. More recently, however, the focus of the criticism has changed. Today, there is a perception that some correlation exists between corporate performance and corporate governance, and a fear that the prevailing corporate governance system makes American corporations less competitive in a global economy. Current suggestions for reform, therefore, focus relatively more on the goal of enhancing corporate (and thus shareholder) value through improved performance and less on questions of the harm to shareholders from management over-reaching and self-dealing.

As you read the following proposals for change, consider these questions: To what extent are the problems being experienced by American companies attributable to the existing corporate governance system? Can reforming the governance system improve corporations' productivity and competitiveness? Do these reform proposals amount to no more than platitudes that have little potential to enhance "cooperation" among officers, directors and shareholders? Should outside directors be "professionals" who devote all their time to service on boards or would full-time directors lack the insights, obtainable only from experience, that represent the principal contribution of current, part-time directors? Additionally, what reason is there to think that professional directors will be any more effective in enhancing shareholder value than the managers who devote all their time and expertise to a particular company? Are outside directors and institutional investors likely to become more actively involved in corporate management, given the obstacles and incentives? Are directors and shareholders likely to change the current system? Should change come instead from legislatures or, rather, from courts who can more stringently enforce directors' obligations to monitor management's performance? Should CEOs play no role in the nomination of directors, or is such a prohibition unnecessary or unwise? Is it true that whatever benefits corporations helps society as a whole?

In 1990, a group of lawyers representing large public companies and leading institutional investors held a series of meetings whose goal was to reach agreement on a set of principles designed to reconcile the tensions between the owners and managers of public corporations. Their statement marked a new effort to reach consensus on the framework of a corporate governance system. See The Working Group On Corporate Governance, A New Compact For Owners And Directors, Harvard Bus.Rev. (July/August 1991) 41. In 1993, the California Governance Group (CGG), an ad-hoc seven-member team composed of executive officers of, and legal advisers to, some of California's largest corporations and investment funds met to reconsider the matters addressed in the Compact. The product of the CGG's efforts to date, the eleven principles set forth below, reflect both the CGG's new perspective and consideration of the most recent developments in corporate governance.

CALIFORNIA GOVERNANCE GROUP, SECOND COMPACT FOR OWNERS AND DIRECTORS
Corporate Governance Advisor 4–7 (August–September 1993).

THE ELEVEN PRINCIPLES

The CGG has adopted the following eleven principles of corporate governance, which comprise the Second Compact. The principles mainly relate to issues concerning board and committee composition, boardroom practices and communications between shareholders and management. These principles are not necessarily endorsed by the CGG's employers or clients, nor are they intended to reflect a comprehensive or exclusive list or principles of good corporate governance. Indeed, the first tenet set forth below holds that there is no one ideal corporate governance blueprint; nonetheless, the CGG recommends that managers and boards consider the implementation of these preferred practices on an orderly basis and over a reasonable period of time.

1. **The corporate governance structure of each corporation should be specifically tailored to the nature and characteristics of that corporation. There is no one "model" corporate governance structure which best serves the needs of every corporation.**

No single corporate governance model is appropriate for all corporations, because they vary widely in size, complexity, structure and culture. For example, an appropriate board makeup for a small start-up corporation usually would prove inadequate for a Fortune 500 corporation. Therefore, each corporation's governance structure should be arranged to suit its particular needs (within the broad constraints of current state corporations codes and common law).

2. **The Chairman and the board of directors together should establish and articulate a set of guidelines for the selection and retention of directors.**

The CGG recognizes that a single formal set of criteria for board membership will not work for every corporation; however, its members believe that adopting some set of flexible guidelines for the selection and retention of prospective directors for any particular corporation is appropriate. The ideal board of directors reflects a healthy mix of varying expertise and experiences. To that end, boards should consider undertaking efforts to expand their search for qualified directors in innovative ways.

Every director must advance shareholder interests first and foremost; however, in doing so, an effective director must also be willing and able to reconcile various and sometimes conflicting interests, e.g., the needs of employees, lenders, customers, suppliers, local communities and the environment. Certain other specific traits regarded as generally desirable for all directors are identified below:

● Regular attendance and informed participation at board and committee meetings;

● Considered judgment coupled with the ability to make decisions unaffected by personal or other narrow interests;

● Broad business perspective; and

● Ability to deal with complex issues and rapid change.

In implementing any established guidelines, the board should seek recommendations from current directors and from management, and the whole board should discuss the application of any guidelines to particular candidates. The board should also give due consideration to shareholder suggestions and reactions.

The CGG is aware that some commentators believe that every director should own a significant number of shares in the corporation. Because the ability to invest in the corporation may depend on the candidate's personal means, the CGG believes it is inappropriate to mandate acquisition and ownership of an arbitrary number of shares. However, a candidate's willingness to invest in a number of shares of the corporation's stock which is economically meaningful to the candidate is relevant to the candidate's identification with a commitment to advance shareholder interests. It may be appropriate to permit directors to elect to receive all or part of their directorship fees in the form of shares in the corporation.

Due to the heavy time commitments required of directors of large corporations, the intense media scrutiny, and the ever-increasing exposure to litigation, securing and retaining first-rate directors is becoming more and more difficult. Accordingly, the CGG believes that existing regulatory restrictions on board membership in certain industries should be re-evaluated and possibly eliminated in order to allow for a larger pool of capable prospects for board service.

3. Board seats should not be allocated to specific constituency directors.

Perhaps one of the most important principles of corporate governance holds that each director must represent the interests of all shareholders. Although it is appropriate in specific instances for board representation to be concentrated in areas associated with the corporation's special interests, no seats should be mandated by charter or custom to any particular constituency. Indeed, in the case of major corporations, the prolificacy of actual or potential constituency relationships renders the specific allocation of seats to particular special interests impractical, if not impossible.

4. Boards of large, publicly-traded corporations should be composed of a majority of directors who are "independent" of management."

Adequately defining "independent director" is an arduous task. The definition set forth in Section 303 of the New York Stock Exchange Listed Company Manual provides a minimum standard. Under that definition, no affiliate, officer or employee of a corporation qualifies as being independent of management, nor does any person who has a relationship that, in the opinion of the board of directors of the corporation, "would interfere with the exercise of independent judgment."

The CGG rejects the proposition put forth by some commentators that the existence of any economic relationship—regardless of its materiality—between a director and a corporation should void the director's status as "independent." Accordingly, a representative of, an advisor to, or customer or supplier of, a corporation generally should be "disqualified" from independent status on that basis only when the relationship is financially significant to the representative or to the corporation.

The somewhat controversial question of whether former officers or employees should be categorically disqualified as independent directors is currently under study by the New York Stock Exchange. The CGG is inclined to believe that such Exchange review of the standard set forth in Section 303 is warranted as such person may, in certain specific instances, find it difficult to exercise truly independent judgment.

In any event, the CGG is convinced that a mechanical application of a definition of "independent director" to every situation is counterproductive. In particular, any attempt to define "independent" through the legislative or regulatory process should be discouraged, as the outcome of such an undertaking would inevitably prove to be too restrictive for some situations and too permissive for others.

5. **Certain committees of boards of large publicly traded corporations should consist exclusively of independent directors, and certain other committees should have at least a majority of independent directors.**

The compensation committee should be composed exclusively of independent directors so that it may conduct an objective review of base salaries, bonuses and incentive plans for senior officers and other key employees. The compensation committee should take executive responsibility for evaluating the performance of senior management and overseeing the development of a senior management succession plan (except where the latter task is assumed by another board committee).

The audit committee should also be composed exclusively of independent directors. Certain other important committees, e.g., the nominating committee, should be composed of at least a majority of independent directors and, in most cases, exclusively independent directors.

Senior corporate officers must have meaningful input into the committee process. The CGG believes it to be particularly important that both the compensation committee and the nominating committee be fully informed by, and have the benefit of, their recommendations. Further, the input of important senior corporate officers, such as the chief financial officer, comptroller, general auditor and the general counsel, will be necessary for other committees, such as the audit committee, to properly carry out their responsibilities.

6. **Corporations should implement procedures, if such are not already in place, to facilitate and promote meaningful communication among independent directors.**

The CGG believes it is important to provide opportunities for free and effective communication among independent directors before crises arise. Independent directors typically communicate informally at luncheon or dinner meetings or at informal discussions before or after meetings of the full board. Where such ad-hoc meetings are not adequate to promote effective communication, a more formal forum may be appropriate. For example, independent directors could meet annually at the corporate headquarters to discuss the performance of the corporation's most senior officers. A leader of the independent directors would thereafter meet with the CEO to communicate the results of the meeting. Likewise, the CEO would at that time be afforded an opportunity to present a "review" of the board's performance.

Although perhaps controversial to some, such a separate annual meeting of the independent directors, coordinated by a leader, is not at odds with traditional corporate governance practice. For example, it is already customary to exclude executive officers of large corporations from the boardroom while their compensation is considered and while members of the audit committee consult with independent auditors.

Such a meeting, and, indeed, communication and relations among independent directors in general, may be more productive where the independent directors have selected a leader. The CGG recognizes the need to promote effective leadership while ensuring that good working relationships and a collegial, team approach are maintained, and believes selecting a leader among the independent directors may promote both of these goals.

7. **Frivolous litigation involving corporations, directors and officers, and discovery attendant to such litigation, should be limited and subject to sanctions.**

While litigation may sometimes be an appropriate means of ensuring that board members perform their fiduciary duties, frivolous proceedings are widespread and must be curbed. Such litigation is not only wasteful, but may "chill" the free flow of verbal and written information and dialogue among directors both inside and outside the boardroom. It also discourages talented prospects from serving on boards. Some limitations on such litigation, including the imposition of appropriate sanctions, costs and disqualification of counsel, merit consideration.

8. **While meaningful communication between senior corporate officers and investors is essential and should be promoted, investors must acknowledge that shareholder participation in day-to-day management is inappropriate.**

The CGG encourages investors to take an interest in the business and long-term performance of the corporation. Managers should be forthcoming in responding to those concerns except as they may be restricted by laws relating to disclosure and "inside" information. Management/investor dialogue is usually most effective where it is regular and ongoing, but remains informal. Accordingly, formal shareholder "advisory committees" are, in the CGG's view, not constructive, and should generally be discouraged.

9. **So long as effective channels of direct communication are open, major investors should minimize public criticism of management.**

Public conflict between shareholders and management can prove harmful to the corporation. In particular, it may weaken management's position in dealing with third parties. It should be avoided, except as a last resort when direct communication is unavailable or ineffective.

Executive compensation is currently the focus of public comment and media scrutiny as well as SEC attention. The CGG believes such external pressures may be sufficient to thwart excessive compensation in most instances. Further, the compensation process is now subject to full disclosure with the introduction of compensation committee reports in proxy statements.

Accordingly, criticism of executive compensation should be limited to exceptional circumstances and should not concentrate on the absolute amount of compensation. Rather, shareholders should properly focus their attention on the structure and the process of determining compensation, which should take account of the corporation's goals and its performance in light of those goals. Total shareholder return, including market price performance, may be an important consideration. However, because market price (whether above or below expectations) is not an infallible yardstick, other more qualitative or subjective factors are legitimate, including, for example, creativity, leadership and the ability to meet or avoid a crisis.

10. **Boards should institute procedures to measure individuals director performance.**

Shareholders can and should exercise their informed judgment in evaluating the performance of the board as a whole. However, shareholders are generally not sufficiently well-informed to accurately assess the performance of individual directors. As a result, they may be tempted to judge directors on criteria or agendas other than achievements in advancing the welfare of the corporation and its shareholders (e.g., based on controversial political or social beliefs which are not directly related to the corporation's operations). The board itself therefore should evaluate individual directors and be sure to focus on criteria which are properly related to the subject corporation's prosperity. The nominating committee might best perform this function. If a director is determined by the board to be performing his or her corporate duties unsatisfactorily, then the nominating committee or its chairperson should take appropriate action.

11. **Management's primary responsibility is to achieve long-term prosperity of the corporation for the benefit of *all* shareholders. Shareholders, similarly, should endeavor to act for the common benefit.**

As the original Compact recognized, excessive shareholder pressure relating to short-term results or the specific goals of particular shareholders is inappropriate. Different owners may have different specific goals and investment expectations; nevertheless, all shareholders benefit from the ongoing long-term prosperity of the corporation. At the same time, corporate officers should remain accountable for satisfactory operating results in both the intermediate and long-term in order that U.S. securities markets may remain relatively vigorous, liquid and viable in the global marketplace.

Note: Other Proposals for Reform

1. The California Governance Group's proposal is deliberately general; it recognizes the diverse nature of the corporate universe and does not attempt to impose a specific structure on all corporations. Others have not been so reluctant. Martin Lipton and Jay Lorsch, for example, argue that corporate boards must undertake their own reform rather than depending on legislation, judicial decisions or active institutional investors. Like many others, Lipton and Lorsch assert that a board's ability to perform is limited by many factors, including lack of time, the amount and complexity of information to be processed in decision-making, a lack of cohesion among board members, deference to the CEO or chairman, and uncertainty regarding their role as directors.

Recognizing that any changes in corporate governance must still leave the day-to-day management of a corporation with its officers, Lipton and Lorsch argue that these obstacles can be reduced in several ways. First, boards should be limited to ten directors, with a ratio of at least two independent directors for each inside director. This composition will allow directors to know each other better and work more closely as a team, while allowing greater discussion among those with differing views. To avoid the potential entrenchment of incompetent directors, terms should be limited to ten or twelve years and a mandatory retirement age imposed. To ensure that directors are able to spend enough time on their duties, no person should serve on more than three boards. Additionally, both the frequency and length of board meetings should be increased, and all meetings should have specific agendas established in advance to address the corporation's most pressing concerns. Directors should elect their own leader, a person who will coordinate discussions with and, if necessary, challenge the CEO. Boards should also become more involved than they presently are in establishing and reviewing long-term corporate performance, as well as regularly evaluating the CEO. The directors should meet regularly with the corporation's largest shareholders to hear the latter group's concerns. Such meetings will, according to Lipton and Lorsch, help reduce the growing tension between large shareholders and corporate boards. Martin Lipton and Jay W. Lorsch, A Modest Proposal for Improved Corporate Governance, 48 Bus. Law. 59 (1992).

2. Ronald Gilson and Reinier Kraakman propose a different alternative: the creation of a class of professional directors. Ronald J. Gilson & Reinier Kraakman, Reinventing the Outside Director: An Agenda for Institutional Investors, 43 Stan. L. Rev. 863 (1991). Gilson and Kraak-

man argue that relying on part-time directors does not adequately protect shareholders' interests. They assert that even if traditional outside directors, drawn from top management of other corporations, are technically independent, they are tied too closely to the management of the corporations on whose boards they serve.

Gilson and Kraakman do not believe professional directors will supplant the traditional board. Rather, they will form a group within the board large enough to demand information otherwise not forthcoming from management and to have its voice heard in boardroom discussions. The lure of high compensation, professional interest and prestige will be enough to attract highly skilled people, such as professors at graduate business schools and partners from major accounting firms. These directors will possess both the skills and, most important, the time to become familiar with the corporations on whose boards they sit. They will serve on the boards of no more than six corporations. They will be able to conduct independent research if needed, and focus on a particular corporation if a crisis arises. The problem of managerial accountability will not arise because these professional directors will depend on their positions for their livelihoods. If their performance is inadequate, the shareholders will replace them. Moreover, if these directors fail they will have forsaken both their earlier successful careers and their reputations.

Gilson and Kraakman suggest that institutional investors provide the impetus for this reform. Only such large shareholders have the voting power to elect professional directors, but all shareholders would benefit from their efforts. Gilson and Kraakman also argue that current regulatory obstacles to their proposal, particularly those under the federal securities laws, should be easy to overcome. Recall Professor Rock's critique of Gilson and Kraakman in Chapter 14. And see Martin Lipton & Steven A. Rosenblum, A New System of Corporate Governance: The Quinquennial Election of Directors, 58 U. Chi. L. R. 187 (1991) (arguing that Gilson and Kraakman's proposal will increase confrontation between directors and institutional shareholders and suggesting that directors be elected every five years, instead of annually, to encourage them to focus on the corporation's long-term health rather than on immediate profits).

3. One former executive and member of the General Motors board has offered several more specific proposals for improving corporate governance. Elmer W. Johnson, An Insider's Call for Outside Direction, Harv. Bus. Rev. 46 (March–April 1990). Johnson believes that such improvement is necessary in order to make American companies more productive. He contends that a CEO should not remain on a board after retirement, so as to avoid stifling the succeeding CEO in undertaking innovative projects. Like Lipton and Lorsch, Johnson believes that the size of the board should be limited; for him, seven, or at most nine, should be the maximum. Such a number would improve group dynamics and make the board less susceptible to domination by the CEO. One of the outside directors should be selected to be ombudsman to receive

the company's reports and lead any investigation that might be required. All or most of the directors should be required to own a significant number of the corporation's stock, in order to align the director's interest with the company's and limit the number of board memberships any one person could hold.

4. In Pawns or Potentates: The Reality of America's Corporate Boards (1989) Jay W. Lorsch and Elizabeth MacIver propose several changes in corporate governance to make the system serve companies and society better. They advocate a lesser role for CEO's in the selection of outside directors and a widening of the pool from which such directors are chosen. They strongly believe that management compensation should be linked to corporate performance. Directors should use their time more effectively and devote more of that time to evaluating the CEO. Boards should select a presiding director, who would lead them in times of crisis. The CEO position should be separated from the chairmanship, as is done in British companies. The chairman would assure that the board functions smoothly, and the CEO would continue to manage the corporation's operations. Interestingly, Lorsch and MacIver believe that state law should require boards to consider constituencies such as employees when they make decisions. They dismiss the idea, however, that there be mandatory constituency representation on boards.

E. COMPARATIVE PERSPECTIVES

In a period of international competitiveness and concern about America's decline in the world marketplace, whether real or perceived, it is useful to consider what lessons might be drawn from abroad. Perhaps the most prominent experiment in overhauling corporate governance is Germany's policy of codetermination, under which workers share power by electing directors. Codetermination has existed in Germany since 1870, and was adopted in its current form after World War II. Today, the German corporate legal system is based on a two-tier board structure. An executive board, composed of the firm's top executives, manages the corporation, and a supervisory board, from which members of the executive board are excluded, selects corporate managers. In industrial companies with 2,000 or more employees, the employees and shareholders each elect one-half of the members of the supervisory board. The executive board and the supervisory board meet separately. The supervisory board can discuss the performance of the corporate managers without the embarrassing presence of corporate management.

The inclusion of workers on corporate boards has not resulted in either greater productivity or increased employee control of companies; investors and their representatives have retained decision-making power. The main benefit of codetermination seems to be that workers obtain greater information about a corporation, information that management might otherwise prefer to not share with employees. This increased sharing of information decreases the need for strategic bargaining behavior, such as during salary negotiations, and the resultant costs of this behavior. Despite its costs and limited benefits, other European countries and some American companies are adopting forms of codetermination. See Henry Hansmann, When Does Worker Ownership Work? ESOPs, Law Firms, Codetermination, and Economic Democracy, 99 Yale L. J. 1749, 1803–05 (1990); Christian J. Meier–Schatz, Corporate Governance and Legal Rules: A Transnational Look at Concepts and Problems of Internal Management Control, J. Corp. L. 431 (Winter 1988).

Like Germany, Japan maintains a quite different system of corporate governance than does the United States. Japanese firms engage in cross-ownership with one another in a keiretsu, characterized by bank ownership of large blocks of shares in a corporation and companies owning shares of their customer and supplier firms. In spite of the great concentration of ownership of Japanese companies by banks and other firms, the actual management is left to inside directors appointed by the CEO with shareholders' approval. Stockholders apparently do exercise some influence on management through informal, monthly meetings among keiretsu members. No single member dominates at these meetings, and it is unclear whether actual business occurs, or whether these meetings perform a social function that facilitates later decision making. Management attempts to reach consensus on major decisions, like the appointment of a CEO, with the keiretsu members. Mark J. Roe, Some Differences in Corporate Structure in Germany, Japan, and the United States, 102 Yale L. J. 1927 (1993). Roe hypothesizes that German and Japanese CEOs and directors are more accountable and better able to personify shareholders than American CEOs through the regular interaction and shared authority, factors absent in most American boardrooms. He is reluctant to argue, however, that American corporations can or should attempt to follow the example set by their German and Japanese counterparts. See also Ronald J. Gilson and Mark J. Roe, Understanding the Japanese Keiretsu: Overlaps Between Corporate Governance and Industrial Organization, 102 Yale L. J. 871 (1993).

Chapter 16

THE DUTY OF CARE
OF CORPORATE
DIRECTORS

Fiduciary duty is perhaps the most important concept in the Anglo–American law of corporations. The word "fiduciary" comes from the Latin *fides,* meaning faith or confidence, and was originally used in the common law to describe the nature of the duties imposed on a trustee. Perhaps because many of the earliest corporations cases involved charitable corporations, courts began to analogize the duties of a director in managing corporate property to the duties of a trustee in managing trust property.

The original analogy between a trustee and those who control a corporation was a close one. But as corporations began to play a role of increasing importance in an increasingly complex commercial world, the strictures based on the law of trusts gradually eroded. Today, the basic notion survives that officers, directors and controlling shareholders owe some sort of enforceable duty to the corporation, and, through the corporation, to the shareholders. The term "fiduciary duty," however, has no fixed meaning; its parameters are continually evolving. Justice Frankfurter recognized the complexities inherent in the concept when he noted in SEC v. Chenery Corp., 318 U.S. 80, 85, 63 S.Ct. 454, 458, 87 L.Ed. 626, 632 (1943):

> But to say that a man is a fiduciary only begins analysis; it gives direction to further inquiry. To whom is he a fiduciary? What obligations does he owe as a fiduciary? In what respect has he failed to discharge these obligations? And what are the consequences of his deviation from duty?

A. INTRODUCTION

Directors are not insurers. Business is inherently risky. Directors, particularly when first elected to a board, may be concerned about the possibility that they will be held liable for losses the corporation suffers as a consequence of the board's decisions. They often ask what they must do to avoid such liability.

The answer to that question often begins with the duty of care. The premises underlying the duty of care are deceptively easy to state but have proved unusually difficult to translate into workable normative or positive statements. No one seriously disagrees with the proposition that directors should perform their duties with reasonable care. And no one seriously disagrees with the proposition that directors who do not benefit from a particular decision should not be held personally liable for good faith errors of judgments if that decision results in losses to the corporation. Yet, as we will see in this chapter, translating those beliefs into legal principles gives rise to many extremely difficult issues.

One can begin analyzing these issues by considering the context in which they arise. Lawyers often are trained to think in a litigation context: what are the liability consequences of some particular conduct after the conduct has occurred? But corporate lawyers much more frequently advise clients in a counselling or preventive context: what should (or must) the client do when faced with the responsibility of exercising oversight over the corporation's business? The contextual difference is particularly significant when the director does not benefit from her decision *and* there is a large differential between her compensation and the amount of the corporation's assets. Viewed in this light, the question of what should (or must) be done may be viewed as aspirational. Additionally, as a normative matter, how do we want directors to behave, even in a world in which there is no danger of personal liability?

RMBCA § 8.30(a), which is representative of most state statutes that prescribe a standard of care, answers the aspirational question by stating that "[a] director shall discharge his duties * * * in good faith, with the care an ordinarily prudent person in a like position would exercise under similar circumstances and in a manner he reasonably believes to be in the best interest of the corporation." This standard, as the Official Comment explains, focuses on "the manner in which the director performs his duties, not the correctness of his decision." Moreover, " 'skill,' in the sense of technical competence in a particular field, should not be a qualification for the office of director." Official Comment to Section 8.30(a).

The question of a director's duty of care is closely related to what, precisely, directors do in their capacity as directors. Although the cases and commentary (with the notable exception of Dean Manning's article) do not always recognize it, directors' conduct may be viewed along a continuum. At one end, directors perform their monitoring function; they exercise oversight of the firm's on-going business operations which are under the direct control and supervision of the management. When monitoring, directors may or may not be making discrete decisions; their focus is generally on the continuing operation of the business. At the other end of the spectrum, directors clearly engage in specific decision-making: to build a new plant, raise capital for a new project, acquire another corporation.

At the monitoring end of the continuum, directors' conduct is subject to the test of reasonableness. When specific decision-making is involved, however, the business judgment rule generally protects directors against liability for unwise substantive decisions; if liability is threatened, it is because the directors' decision-making process was faulty. However, there is no clear line between process and substance. When called into question in a particular case, how should the directors' conduct be judged? Should it be by the "reasonable care" standard of RMBCA § 8.30 or by the less stringent business judgment rule? And, in turn, what is the relationship between the duty of care and the business judgment rule? This chapter provides an initial exploration into these issues.

PROBLEM

FASHION, INC.—PART I

Loren Peters, age 55, is a wealthy retired businesswoman. She began her career as a model, moved into fashion design, and built a very successful women's clothing company. Because her talents were primarily as a designer, she left most of the details of the business and finance operations to the vice-president of the company, Amy Fine. When her company recently needed to raise substantial additional capital, Loren elected to sell the company to Fashion, Inc. (Fashion), a Columbia corporation primarily engaged in the manufacture and sale of women and children's clothing. Loren received $25 million in Fashion stock in exchange for the stock of her company; Amy, who had also been a stockholder, received $5 million in Fashion stock and chose to retire from the fashion business. At the time of the sale, Lane Brown, the chairman of the board and CEO of Fashion invited Loren to join Fashion's board of directors. He said that the company would value her input and advice, and particularly her expertise in women's fashions.

Fashion has annual sales of more than $2 billion. Its stock is traded on the New York Stock Exchange and has a total market value of about $800 million. No single shareholder owns more than 5% of Fashion's stock.

The Fashion board of directors now has eleven members. In addition to Brown, there are two inside directors: the chief financial officer and the senior vice-president for marketing. The other directors are a partner in Fashion's investment banking firm, a partner in Fashion's regular outside law firm, the retired former CEO of Fashion, the dean of Columbia State University business school, the president of an international children's rights organization, and three CEO's of large publicly-held corporations.

Loren is very interested in becoming a director of Fashion and has come to you to discuss the legal ramifications of doing so. She is concerned about her potential liability for failing to meet her fiduciary duties. She is not concerned about her knowledge of the fashion industry or her basic understanding of finance. She does want to know, however, in how much depth she needs to understand the company's financial statements. She is also aware that, like most large public corporations, Fashion is subject to a wide range of regulatory statutes, both federal and state, with which, in her own company, she had little experience. Accordingly, she wants to know what, if anything, she must do as a director in connection with the company's compliance with these statutes. She also is curious about what protection the company can give her if she should be sued for breach of fiduciary duties. Finally, as she put it, "what are my duties as a director and how am I supposed to fulfill them?"

B. THE GENERAL STANDARD OF CARE

FRANCIS v. UNITED JERSEY BANK

87 N.J. 15, 432 A.2d 814 (1981).

POLLOCK, J.

[Pritchard & Baird, Inc., was a reinsurance broker, a firm that arranged contracts between insurance companies by means of which companies that wrote large policies sold participations in those policies to other companies in order to share the risks. According to the custom in the industry, the selling company pays the applicable portion of the premium to the broker, which deducts its commission and forwards the balance to the reinsuring company. The broker thus handles large amounts of money as a fiduciary for its clients.

As of 1964, all the stock of Pritchard & Baird was owned by Charles Pritchard, Sr., one of the firm's founders, and his wife and two sons, Charles, Jr. and William. They were also the four directors. Charles, Sr., dominated the corporation until 1971, when he became ill and the two sons took over management of the business. Charles, Sr. died in 1973, leaving Mrs. Pritchard and the sons the only remaining directors.

Contrary to the industry practice, Pritchard & Baird did not segregate its operating funds from those of its clients; instead, it deposited all funds in the same account. From this account Charles, Sr. had drawn "loans," that correlated with corporate profits and were repaid at the end of each year. After his death, Charles, Jr. and William began to draw ever larger sums (still characterizing them as "loans") that greatly exceeded profits. They were able to do so by taking advantage of the "float" available to them during the period between the time they received a premium and the time they had to forward it (less commission) to the reinsurer.

By 1975 the corporation was bankrupt. This action was brought by the trustees in bankruptcy against Mrs. Pritchard and the bank as administrator of her husband's estate. Mrs. Pritchard died during the pendency of the proceedings, and her executrix was substituted as defendant. As to Mrs. Pritchard, the principal claim was that she had been negligent in the conduct of her duties as a director of the corporation.]

The "loans" were reflected on financial statements that were prepared annually as of January 31, the end of the corporate fiscal year. Although an outside certified public accountant prepared the 1970 financial statement, the corporation prepared only internal financial statements from 1971–1975. In all instances, the statements were simple documents, consisting of three or four 8 1/2 x 11 inch sheets.

The statements of financial condition from 1970 forward demonstrated:

	WORKING CAPITAL DEFICIT	**SHAREHOLDERS' LOANS**	**NET BROKERAGE INCOME**
1970	$ 389,022	$ 509,941	$ 807,229
1971	not available	not available	not available
1972	$ 1,684,289	$ 1,825,911	$1,546,263
1973	$ 3,506,460	$ 3,700,542	$1,736,349
1974	$ 6,939,007	$ 7,080,629	$ 876,182
1975	$10,176,419	$ 10,298,039	$ 551,598.

Mrs. Pritchard was not active in the business of Pritchard & Baird and knew virtually nothing of its corporate affairs. She briefly visited the corporate offices in Morristown on only one occasion, and she never read or obtained the annual financial statements. She was unfamiliar with the rudiments of reinsurance and made no effort to assure that the policies and practices of the corporation, particularly pertaining to the withdrawal of funds, complied with industry custom or relevant law. Although her husband had warned her that Charles, Jr. would "take the shirt off my back," Mrs. Pritchard did not pay any attention to her duties as a director or to the affairs of the corporation. 162 N.J.Super. at 370, 392 A.2d 1233.

After her husband died in December 1973, Mrs. Pritchard became incapacitated and was bedridden for a six-month period. She became listless at this time and started to drink rather heavily. Her physical condition deteriorated, and in 1978 she died. The trial court rejected testimony seeking to exonerate her because she "was old, was grief-stricken at the loss of her husband, sometimes consumed too much alcohol and was psychologically overborne by her sons." 162 N.J.Super. at 371, 392 A.2d 1233. That court found that she was competent to act and that the reason Mrs. Pritchard never knew what her sons "were doing was because she never made the slightest effort to discharge any of her responsibilities as a director of Pritchard & Baird." 162 N.J.Super. at 372, 392 A.2d 1233.

* * *

III.

Individual liability of a corporate director for acts of the corporation is a prickly problem. Generally directors are accorded broad immunity and are not insurers of corporate activities. The problem is particularly nettlesome when a third party asserts that a director, because of nonfeasance, is liable for losses caused by acts of insiders, who in this case were officers, directors and shareholders. Determination of the liability of Mrs. Pritchard requires findings that she had a duty to the clients of Pritchard & Baird, that she breached that duty and that her breach was a proximate cause of their losses.

* * *

As a general rule, a director should acquire at least a rudimentary understanding of the business of the corporation. Accordingly, a director should become familiar with the fundamentals of the business in which the corporation is engaged. [Campbell v. Watson, 62 N.J.Eq. 395, 416, 50 A. 120 (Ch. 1901)]Because directors are bound to exercise ordinary care, they cannot set up as a defense lack of the knowledge needed to exercise the requisite degree of care. If one "feels that he has not had sufficient business experience to qualify him to perform the duties of a director, he should either acquire the knowledge by inquiry, or refuse to act." *Ibid.*

Directors are under a continuing obligation to keep informed about the activities of the corporation. Otherwise, they may not be able to participate in the overall management of corporate affairs. * * * Directors may not shut their eyes to corporate misconduct and then claim that because they did not see the misconduct, they did not have a duty to look. The sentinel asleep at his post contributes nothing to the enterprise he is charged to protect.

Directorial management does not require a detailed inspection of day-to-day activities, but rather a general monitoring of corporate affairs and policies. Accordingly, a director is well advised to attend board meetings regularly. * * * Regular attendance does not mean that directors must attend every meeting, but that directors should attend meetings as a matter of practice. A director of a publicly held corporation might be expected to attend regular monthly meetings, but a director of a small, family corporation might be asked to attend only an annual meeting. The point is that one of the responsibilities of a director is to attend meetings of the board of which he or she is a member. * * *

While directors are not required to audit corporate books, they should maintain familiarity with the financial status of the corporation by a regular review of financial statements. In some circumstances, directors may be charged with assuring that bookkeeping methods conform to industry custom and usage. The extent of review, as well as the nature and frequency of financial statements, depends not only on the customs of the industry, but also on the nature of the corporation and the business in which it is engaged. Financial statements of some small corporations may be prepared internally and only on an annual basis; in a large publicly held corporation, the statements may be produced monthly or at some other regular interval. Adequate financial review normally would be more informal in a private corporation than in a publicly held corporation. * * *

The review of financial statements, however, may give rise to a duty to inquire further into matters revealed by those statements. Upon discovery of an illegal course of action, a director has a duty to object and, if the corporation does not correct the conduct, to resign.

In certain circumstances, the fulfillment of the duty of a director may call for more than mere objection and resignation. Sometimes a director may be required to seek the advice of counsel * * * concerning the propriety of his or her own conduct, the conduct of other officers and directors or the conduct of the corporation * * * Sometimes the duty of a director may require more than consulting with outside counsel. A director may have a duty to take reasonable means to prevent illegal conduct by co-directors; in any appropriate case, this may include threat of suit. * * *

A director is not an ornament, but an essential component of corporate governance. Consequently, a director cannot protect himself behind a paper shield bearing the motto, "dummy director." * * * The New Jersey Business Corporation Act, in imposing a standard of ordinary care on all directors, confirms that dummy, figurehead and accommodation directors are anachronisms with no place in New Jersey law. * * *

The factors that impel expanded responsibility in the large, publicly held corporation may not be present in a small, close corporation. Nonetheless, a close corporation may, because of the nature of its business, be affected with a public interest. For example, the stock of a bank may be closely held, but because of the nature of banking the directors would be subject to greater liability than those of another close corporation. Even in a small corporation, a director is held to the standard of that degree of care that an ordinarily prudent director would use under the circumstances.

A director's duty of care does not exist in the abstract, but must be considered in relation to specific obligees. In general, the relationship of a corporate director to the corporation and its stockholders is that of a fiduciary. Shareholders have a right to expect that directors will exercise reasonable supervision and control over the policies and practices of a corporation. The institutional integrity of a corporation depends upon the proper discharge by directors of those duties.

While directors may owe a fiduciary duty to creditors also, that obligation generally has not been recognized in the absence of insolvency. With certain corporations, however, directors are deemed to owe a duty to creditors and other third parties even when the corporation is solvent. Although depositors of a bank are considered in some respects to be creditors, courts have recognized that directors may owe them a fiduciary duty. Directors of nonbanking corporations may owe a similar duty when the corporation holds funds of others in trust. * * *

* * *

As a reinsurance broker, Pritchard & Baird received annually as a fiduciary millions of dollars of clients' money which it was under a duty to segregate. To this extent, it resembled a bank rather than a small family business. Accordingly, Mrs. Pritchard's relationship to the clientele of Pritchard & Baird was akin to that of a director of a bank to its depositors. * * *

As a director of a substantial reinsurance brokerage corporation, she should have known that it received annually millions of dollars of loss and premium funds which it held in trust for ceding and reinsurance companies. Mrs. Pritchard should have obtained and read the annual statements of financial condition of Pritchard & Baird. Although she had a right to rely upon financial statements prepared in accordance with N.J.S.A. 14A:6–14, such reliance would not excuse her conduct. * * *

From those statements, she should have realized that, as of January 31, 1970, her sons were withdrawing substantial trust funds under the guise of "Shareholders' Loans." The financial statements for each fiscal year commencing with that of January 31, 1970, disclosed that the working capital deficits and the "loans" were escalating in tandem. Detecting a misappropriation of funds would not have required special expertise or extraordinary diligence; a cursory reading of the financial statements would have revealed the pillage.

* * *

The judgment of the Appellate Division is affirmed.

Note: A Unitary Standard?

RMBCA § 8.30(a) refers to the care "an ordinarily prudent person in a like position would exercise." Is that a unitary standard, or is the director's background and experience relevant in determining the appropriate standard of care? Should it matter, for example, if the director is the chief financial officer? A representative of a labor union who has been elected because of a collective bargaining agreement? A person without a general business background who has been elected to express the interests of a minority group? An investment banker whose only contribution at board meetings is in connection with proposed financings? Because of the relative scarcity of cases, the issue has not arisen often and, as in *Francis*, where it has, the director's conduct has verged on total nonfeasance. See e.g. Barnes v. Andrews, 298 Fed. 614 (S.D.N.Y.1924) (an inactive director must "inform himself of what was going on with some particularity"): Gamble v. Brown, 29 F.2d 366 (4th Cir.1928) (aged and infirm director held liable); McDonnell v. American Leduc Petroleums, Limited, 491 F.2d 380 (2d Cir.1974) (president and director who "had little business experience" and maintained "passive role" held liable to the extent that the corporation was damaged by conduct of others about which she knew or should have known by examining the corporation's books). Compare Anderson v. Akers, 7 F.Supp. 924 (W.D.Ky.1934) (director of "unsound mind" held not liable) aff'd in part and rev'd in part 86 F.2d 518 (6th Cir.1936), rev'd in part per curiam 302 U.S. 643, 58 S.Ct. 53, 82 L.Ed. 500 (1937); Harman v. Willbern, 374 F.Supp. 1149 (D.Kan.1974) (director, who sold his shares and remained on the board "in name only" and who relied on the corporation's officers while the corporation was looted, held not liable).

The trial court's opinion in Francis v. United Jersey Bank, 162 N.J.Super. 355, 392 A.2d 1233 (1978) contains the following passage:

> It has been urged in this case that Mrs. Pritchard should not be held responsible for what happened while she was a director of Pritchard & Baird because she was a simple housewife who served as a director as an accommodation to her husband and sons. Let me start by saying that I reject the sexism which is unintended but which is implicit in such an argument. There is no reason why the average housewife could not adequately discharge the functions of a director of a corporation such as Pritchard & Baird, despite a lack of business career experience, if she gave some reasonable attention to what she was supposed to be doing. The problem is not that Mrs. Pritchard was a simple housewife. The problem is that she was a person who took a job which necessarily entailed certain responsibilities and she then failed to make any effort whatever to discharge those responsibilities. The ultimate insult to the fundamental dignity and equality of women would be to treat a grown woman as though she were a child not responsible for her acts and omissions.

> It has been argued that allowance should be made for the fact that during the last years in question Mrs. Pritchard was old, was grief-stricken at the loss of her husband, sometimes consumed too much alcohol and was psychologically overborne by her sons. I was not impressed by the testimony supporting that argument. There is no proof whatever that Mrs. Pritchard ever ceased to be fully competent. There is no proof that she ever made any effort as a director to question or stop the unlawful activities of Charles, Jr. and William. The actions of the sons were so blatantly wrongful that it is hard to see how they could have resisted any moderately firm objection to what they were doing. The fact is that Mrs. Pritchard never knew what they were doing because she never made the slightest effort to discharge any of her responsibilities as a director of Pritchard & Baird.

392 A.2d at 1241.

At the very least, there appears to be some minimum standard to which all directors will be held. The Official Comment to RMBCA § 8.30(a) states that "[t]he combined phrase 'in a like position * * * under similar circumstances' is intended to recognize that (a) the nature and extent of responsibilities will vary, depending upon such factors as the size, complexity, urgency, and location of activities carried on by the particular corporation, (b) decisions must be made on the basis of the information known to the directors without the benefit of hindsight, and (c) the special background, qualifications, and management responsibilities of a particular director may be relevant in evaluating his compliance with the standard of care. Even though the quoted phrase takes into account the special background, qualifications and management responsibilities of a particular director, it does not excuse a director lacking business experience or particular expertise from exercising the common sense, practical wisdom, and informed judgment of an 'ordinarily prudent person.' " Clear?

1. DUTY OF INQUIRY

In a large corporation where directors delegate the on-going operation of the business to management, part of the directors' monitoring function involves the subsequent oversight to those to whom the delegation has been made. How much, and under what circumstances, such oversight is required is a question which directors confront on a continuing basis. To what extent, for example, must the directors inquire into the details of the corporation's financial statements which have been reviewed and certified by the corporation's independent public accountants? Absent some reason to be suspicious, can directors rely on management to bring problems to them? The issue arises most frequently today in the area of law compliance as corporations become subject to an increasing amount of regulation, both statutory and administrative. Many commentators believe that directors *should* institute law compliance programs to avoid future problems. But are directors *required* to do so, particularly when there is no evidence that the corporation may not be in compliance? Must there be a "triggering event" before such a requirement arises, or is the establishment of such programs now a part of a director's legal duty of care?

As you read the following materials, think about the following questions: Should directors be held personally liable for damages suffered by a corporation due to legal violations by subordinates? How closely related to the essential nature of the corporation's business must the violations be? What if the director did not know the illegal conduct was taking place? Is it possible that a corporate officer would not know that the corporation's employees were engaging in illegal activities during the course of their employment? Given that directors have the ability to delegate many of their managerial duties to others, should they be held liable for conduct which was hidden from them? What if the director should have known about the illegal activities but purposefully did not investigate? Finally, what if the director knew of prior violations and implemented a compliance program designed to stop the conduct, but the conduct nevertheless continued?

GRAHAM v. ALLIS-CHALMERS MANUFACTURING CO.

41 Del.Ch. 78, 188 A.2d 125 (1963).

WOLCOTT, JUSTICE.

This is a derivative action on behalf of Allis–Chalmers against its directors and four of its non-director employees. The complaint is based upon indictments of Allis–Chalmers and the four non-director employees named as defendants herein who, with the corporation, entered pleas of guilty to the indictments. The indictments, eight in number, charged violations of the Federal anti-trust laws. The suit seeks to recover damages which Allis–Chalmers is claimed to have suffered by reason of these violations.

The directors of Allis–Chalmers appeared in the cause voluntarily. The non-director defendants have neither appeared in the cause nor been served with process. Three of the non-director defendants are still employed by Allis–Chalmers. The fourth is under contract with it as a consultant.

The complaint alleges actual knowledge on the part of the director defendants of the anti-trust conduct upon which the indictments were based or, in the alternative, knowledge of facts which should have put them on notice of such conduct.

However, the hearing and depositions produced no evidence that any director had any actual knowledge of the anti-trust activity, or had actual knowledge of any facts which should have put them on notice that anti-trust activity was being carried on by some of their company's employees. The plaintiffs, appellants here, thereupon shifted the theory of the case to the proposition that the directors are liable as a matter of law by reason of their failure to take action designed to learn of and prevent anti-trust activity on the part of any employees of Allis–Chalmers.

By this appeal the plaintiffs seek to have us reverse the Vice Chancellor's ruling of non-liability of the defendant directors upon this theory, and also seek reversal of certain interlocutory rulings of the Vice Chancellor refusing to compel pre-trial production of documents, and refusing to compel the four non-director defendants to testify on oral depositions. We will in this opinion pass upon all the questions raised, but, as a preliminary, a summarized statement of the facts of the cause is required in order to fully understand the issues.

Allis–Chalmers is a manufacturer of a variety of electrical equipment. It employs in excess of 31,000 people, has a total of 24 plants, 145 sales offices, 5000 dealers and distributors, and its sales volume is in excess of $500,000,000 annually. The operations of the company are conducted by two groups, each of which is under the direction of a senior vice president. One of these groups is the Industries Group under the direction of Singleton, director defendant. This group is divided into five divisions. One of these, the Power Equipment Division, produced the products, the sale of which involved the anti-trust activities referred to in the indictments. The Power Equipment Division, presided over by McMullen, non-director defendant, contains ten departments, each of which is presided over by a manager or general manager.

The operating policy of Allis–Chalmers is to decentralize by the delegation of authority to the lowest possible management level capable of fulfilling the delegated responsibility. Thus, prices of products are ordinarily set by the particular department manager, except that if the product being priced is large and special, the department manager might confer with the general manager of the division. Products of a standard character involving repetitive manufacturing processes are sold out of a price list which is established by a price leader for the electrical equipment industry as a whole.

Annually, the Board of Directors reviews group and departmental profit goal budgets. On occasion, the Board considers general questions concerning price levels, but because of the complexity of the company's operations the Board does not participate in decisions fixing the prices of specific products.

The Board of Directors of fourteen members, four of whom are officers, meets once a month, October excepted, and considers a previously prepared agenda for the meeting. Supplied to the Directors at the meetings are financial and operating data relating to all phases of the company's activities. The Board meetings are customarily of several hours duration in which all the Directors participate actively. Apparently, the Board considers and decides matters concerning the general business policy of the company. By reason of the extent and complexity of the company's operations, it is not practicable for the Board to consider in detail specific problems of the various divisions.

The indictments to which Allis–Chalmers and the four non-director defendants pled guilty charge that the company and individual non-director defendants, commencing in 1956, conspired with other manufacturers and their employees to fix prices and to rig bids to private electric utilities and governmental agencies in violation of the anti-trust laws of the United States. None of the director defendants in this cause were named as defendants in the indictments. Indeed, the Federal Government acknowledged that it had uncovered no probative evidence which could lead to the conviction of the defendant directors.

The first actual knowledge the directors had of anti-trust violations by some of the company's employees was in the summer of 1959 from newspaper stories that TVA proposed an investigation of identical bids. Singleton, in charge of the Industries Group of the company, investigated but unearthed nothing. Thereafter, in November of 1959, some of the company's employees were subpoenaed before the Grand Jury. Further investigation by the company's Legal Division gave reason to suspect the illegal activity and all of the subpoenaed employees were instructed to tell the whole truth.

Thereafter, on February 8, 1960, at the direction of the Board, a policy statement relating to anti-trust problems was issued, and the Legal Division commenced a series of meetings with all employees of the company in possible areas of anti-trust activity. The purpose and effect of these steps was to eliminate any possibility of further and future violations of the anti-trust laws.

As we have pointed out, there is no evidence in the record that the defendant directors had actual knowledge of the illegal anti-trust actions of the company's employees. Plaintiffs, however, point to two FTC decrees of 1937 as warning to the directors that anti-trust activity by the company's employees had taken place in the past. It is argued that they were thus put on notice of their duty to ferret out such activity and to take active steps to insure that it would not be repeated.

The decrees in question were consent decrees entered in 1937 against Allis–Chalmers and nine others enjoining agreements to fix uniform prices on condensors and turbine generators. The decrees recited that they were consented to for the sole purpose of avoiding the trouble and expense of the proceeding.

None of the director defendants were directors or officers of Allis–Chalmers in 1937. The director defendants and now officers of the company either were employed in very subordinate capacities or had no connection with the company in 1937. At the time, copies of the decrees were circulated to the heads of concerned departments and were explained to the Managers Committee.

In 1943, Singleton, officer and director defendant, first learned of the decrees upon becoming Assistant Manager of the Steam Turbine Department, and consulted the company's General Counsel as to them. He investigated his department and learned the decrees were being complied with and, in any event, he concluded that the company had not in the first place been guilty of the practice enjoined.

Stevenson, officer and director defendant, first learned of the decrees in 1951 in a conversation with Singleton about their respective areas of the company's operations. He satisfied himself that the company was not then and in fact had not been guilty of quoting uniform prices and had consented to the decrees in order to avoid the expense and vexation of the proceeding.

Scholl, officer and director defendant, learned of the decrees in 1956 in a discussion with Singleton on matters affecting the Industries Group. He was informed that no similar problem was then in existence in the company.

Plaintiffs argue that because of the 1937 consent decrees, the directors were put on notice that they should take steps to ensure that no employee of Allis–Chalmers would violate the anti-trust laws. The difficulty the argument has is that only three of the present directors knew of the decrees, and all three of them satisfied themselves that Allis–Chalmers had not engaged in the practice enjoined and had consented to the decrees merely to avoid expense and the necessity of defending the company's position. Under the circumstances, we think knowledge by three of the directors that in 1937 the company had consented to the entry of decrees enjoining it from doing something they had satisfied themselves it had never done, did not put the Board on notice of the possibility of future illegal price fixing.

Plaintiffs have wholly failed to establish either actual notice or imputed notice to the Board of Directors of facts which should have put them on guard, and have caused them to take steps to prevent the future possibility of illegal price fixing and bid rigging. Plaintiffs say that as a minimum in this respect the Board should have taken the steps it took in 1960 when knowledge of the facts first actually came to their attention as a result of the Grand Jury investigation. Whatever duty, however, there was upon the Board to take such steps, the fact of the 1937 decrees has no bearing upon the question, for under the circumstances they were [put on] notice of nothing.

Plaintiffs are thus forced to rely solely upon the legal proposition advanced by them that directors of a corporation, as a matter of law, are liable for losses suffered by their corporations by reason of their gross inattention to the common law duty of actively supervising and managing the corporate affairs. Plaintiffs rely mainly upon Briggs v. Spaulding, 141 U.S. 132, 11 S.Ct. 924, 35 L.Ed. 662.

From the Briggs case and others * * * it appears that directors of a corporation in managing the corporate affairs are bound to use that amount of care which ordinarily careful and prudent men would use in similar circumstances. Their duties are those of control, and whether or not by neglect they have made themselves liable for failure to exercise proper control depends on the circumstances and facts of the particular case.

The precise charge made against these director defendants is that, even though they had no knowledge of any suspicion of wrongdoing on the part of the company's employees, they still should have put into effect a system of watchfulness which would have brought such misconduct to their attention in ample time to have brought it to an end. However, the Briggs case expressly rejects such an idea. On the contrary, it appears that directors are entitled to rely on the honesty and integrity of their subordinates until something occurs to put them on suspicion that something is wrong. If such occurs and goes unheeded, then liability of the directors might well follow, but absent cause for suspicion there is no duty upon the directors to install and operate a corporate system of espionage to ferret out wrongdoing which they have no reason to suspect exists.

The duties of the Allis–Chalmers Directors were fixed by the nature of the enterprise which employed in excess of 30,000 persons, and extended over a large geographical area. By force of necessity, the company's Directors could not know personally all the company's employees. The very magnitude of the enterprise required them to confine their control to the broad policy decisions. That they did this is clear from the record. At the meetings of the Board in which all Directors participated, these questions were considered and decided on the basis of summaries, reports and corporate records. These they were entitled to rely on, not only, we think, under general principles of the common law, but by reason of 8 Del.C. § 141(f) as well, which in terms fully protects a director who relies on such in the performance of his duties.

In the last analysis, the question of whether a corporate director has become liable for losses to the corporation through neglect of duty is determined by the circumstances. If he has recklessly reposed confidence in an obviously untrustworthy employee, has refused or neglected cavalierly to perform his duty as a director, or has ignored either willfully or through inattention obvious danger signs of employee wrongdoing, the law will cast the burden of liability upon him. This is not the case at bar, however, for as soon as it became evident that there were grounds for suspicion, the Board acted promptly to end it and prevent its recurrence.

Plaintiffs say these steps should have been taken long before, even in the absence of suspicion, but we think not, for we know of no rule of law which requires a corporate director to assume, with no justification whatsoever, that all corporate employees are incipient law violators who, but for a tight checkrein, will give free vent to their unlawful propensities.

We therefore affirm the Vice Chancellor's ruling that the individual director defendants are not liable as a matter of law merely because, unknown to them, some employees of Allis–Chalmers violated the antitrust laws thus subjecting the corporation to loss.

* * *

The judgment of the court below is affirmed.

———

Graham grew out of the heavy electrical equipment price fixing conspiracy, one of the first instances in which executives of major corporations received jail terms for violations of the antitrust laws. For a discussion of those events see John Brooks, Business Adventures, ch. 7 (1969). Notwithstanding the evidence in the criminal cases and similar evidence in *Graham* that subordinate employees had concealed their illegal behavior from their supervisors, there was skepticism in the press and in Congress that senior executives were, in fact, innocent of all knowledge of what was going on.

There was some indication that the decentralization of Allis–Chalmers discussed by the courts was accompanied by severe pressures on the heads of the various organizational units to show steadily increasing profits for the segment of the organization for which they were responsible. These pressures were apparently independent of the conditions in the particular markets in which the organizational unit operated; it is obviously quite difficult to increase profits at a time of stagnant or declining demand. If this description of the mode of management in use at Allis–Chalmers is correct, was the court too quick to say that it is not necessary for a board of directors to establish "a corporate system of espionage"?

ALI, PRINCIPLES OF CORPORATE GOVERNANCE (1994)

§ 4.01. Duty of Care of Directors and Officers; The Business Judgment Rule

(a) A director or officer has a duty to the corporation to perform the director's or officer's functions in good faith, in a manner he or she reasonably believes to be in the best interests of the corporation, and with the care that an ordinarily prudent person would reasonably be expected to exercise in a like position and under similar circumstances * * *

(1) The duty in Subsection (a) includes the obligation to make, or cause to be made, an inquiry when, but only when, the circumstances would alert a reasonable director or officer to the need therefor. The extent of such inquiry shall be such as the director or officer reasonably believes to be necessary.

(2) In performing any of his or her functions (including his oversight functions), a director or officer is entitled to rely on materials and persons in accordance with §§ 4.02 and 4.03.

Comment to § 4.01(a)(1)-(a)(2):

a. *Comparison with present law.*

* * *

Since the "inquiry" obligation in Subsection (a)(1) is a fundamental part of the duty of care obligations established in the first paragraph of § 4.01(a), Subsection (a)(1) merely provides clarity and emphasis. Subsection (a)(1) adds no substantive principles to the first paragraph of Subsection (a) and does not expand the obligation that already exists under present law * * *

b. *The circumstances under which the duty of inquiry arises and the extent of such inquiry.* A duty to inquire only arises if it is reasonably called for by specific facts and circumstances. The thrust of the first sentence of Subsection (a)(1) is that a "triggering" circumstance is needed which would "alert a reasonable director or officer" to the need for inquiry.

In the typical large corporation, for example, the board of directors will receive periodic financial statements and written and oral reports from officers. This is consistent with the directors' continuing obligation to keep informed and to oversee the conduct of the corporation's business. There is, however, no need for a director to "go behind" these reports unless a warning or alerting signal of some type appears. The alerting circumstances can take many forms. The nature of the circumstances must be such that they would alert a reasonable director or officer. If such circumstances exist, and a director or officer fails to make inquiry, a breach of the duty of care has occurred.

Once a director or officer is put on the alert, the extent of the inquiry required must again be considered in the context of specific facts and circumstances. A director or officer need only make "such inquiry" as he or she "reasonably believes to be necessary." The phrase "reasonably believes," as used in § 4.01(a)(1) and other subsections of Part IV, has both a subjective and an objective content. A director or officer will fail to comply with the second sentence of § 4.01(a)(1) if he or she does not believe an inquiry is adequate or if he or she is unreasonable in believing the director or officer has made all the inquiry that is necessary. The phrase "reasonably believes" is thus intended to have a meaning that is generally consistent with the way it has been used in analogous areas of the law. * * *

c. Procedures, programs, and other techniques to assist the board. One aspect of the board's general duty of care obligation in the oversight and inquiry areas is an affirmative obligation of directors to be reasonably concerned with the existence and effectiveness of procedures, programs, and other techniques (which may involve appropriate delegations in accordance with § 4.01(b)) to assist the board in overseeing the corporation's business. Although almost no case law exists on this subject, there is general acceptance of the idea that in a corporation of any significant scale or complexity such techniques represent a basic mechanism to assist the board in properly fulfilling its oversight role.

It is true that in Graham v. Allis–Chalmers Manufacturing Co., the Delaware Supreme Court seemed to envision a passive role for the board, at least with respect to one kind of oversight technique, a law compliance program. * * *

The *Allis–Chalmers* case was decided nearly 30 years ago, and a basic theme of the commentaries in Part IV has been that the "obligation" component of duty of care provisions is a flexible and dynamic concept. Today, an ordinarily prudent person serving as the director of a corporation of any significant scale or complexity should recognize the need to be reasonably concerned with the existence and effectiveness of procedures, programs, and other techniques to assist the board in its oversight role.

In contrast to the passive implications of the *Allis–Chalmers* reasoning (e.g., "no duty * * * to install and operate a corporate system * * * to ferret out wrongdoing"), the *Corporate Director's Guidebook* (p. 1610) states:

> "The corporate director should be concerned that the corporation has programs looking toward compliance with applicable laws and regulations, both foreign and domestic, that it circulates (as appropriate) policy statements to this effect to its employees, and that it maintains procedures for monitoring such compliance."

See *Business Roundtable Statement* (p. 101) (identifying law compliance as a "core function" of the board and emphasizing "the need for policies and implementing procedures on corporate law compliance. These * * * should be designed to promote such compliance on a sustained and systematic basis by all levels of operating management").

The *Corporate Director's Guidebook* and the *Business Roundtable Statement* were intended as corporate practice recommendations rather than as rules of law. Nevertheless, they reflect the fact that the affirmative establishment and maintenance of law compliance programs is widely accepted business practice today. See, e.g., Small, The Evolving Role of the Director in Corporate Governance, 30 Hastings L.J. 1353, 1360–61 n. 35 (1979); Veasey & Manning, Codified Standard—Safe Harbor or Uncharted Reef?, 35 Bus. Law. 919, 930 (1980).

The terms "procedures," "programs," and "other techniques" are used very broadly. They include, for example, internal reporting processes for checking compliance, information programs, appropriate delegations in accordance with § 4.01(b), and the use of auditors, attorneys, and committees of the board. Very often the effective development and implementation of such oversight techniques will require individual directors or committees to rely heavily on other directors or committees, officers, employees, experts, or other persons. * * *

Note: State Law Duty of Inquiry

1. RMBCA § 8.30 does not address the duty to inquire or the duty to implement law compliance programs. However, the Official Comment to § 8.30(a) implies that there is no affirmative duty to institute such programs or inquire behind statements of others absent knowledge or notice which would suggest a particular problem requiring investigation.

2. It is difficult to find cases in which the issue of the duty to inquire has arisen. Thus it is unclear whether the "red flag" test of *Graham* remains good law, at least with respect to the responsibility to institute law compliance programs. However, as two commentators have argued, "[i]f the expected role of a director has grown to include the installation of legal compliance systems, good counselling suggests that it be done. Nevertheless, despite advances in recommended corporate practices, heightened sensitivity, better supervision and advanced technology, it does not follow that failure to install a surveillance system results in liability." R. Franklin Balotti & Jesse A. Finkelstein, Del. Law of Corps & Bus. Orgs., 2d Ed. § 4.08 (1990).

3. Although the Delaware Supreme Court has not explicitly overruled *Graham*, it has indicated that there are problems with applying its logic in the contemporary corporate world. Thus in Aronson v. Lewis, 473 A.2d 805, 813 n.7 (Del.1984), the court noted that "[a]lthough questions of director liability in * * * cases [such as *Graham*] have been adjudicated upon concepts of business judgment, they do not actually present issues of business judgment." And in Mills Acquisition Co. v. Macmillan, Inc., 559 A.2d 1261, 1284 n.32 (Del.1988), when considering a lack of board oversight in connection with a tender offer, the court observed that "a board can take little comfort in what was said under far different circumstances in [*Graham*]. Nor can decisions reached under such circumstances be sustained."

4. Some commentators disagree with the ALI's suggestion that *Graham* would be decided differently today. One writer argues that "*Allis–Chalmers*, rather than being one of the weaker legs in our law, is one of the stronger and one of the more practical applications of reality to the management of corporations and criticism can be seen as largely, or to a large degree, ivory tower." Rodman Ward, Fiduciary Standards Applicable to Officers and Directors and the Business Judgment Rule Under Delaware Law, 3 Del. J. Corp. L., 244, 247 (1978). For the contrary view, see E. Norman Veasey & Bayless Manning, Codified Standard—Safe Harbor or Uncharted Reef?, 35 Bus. Law. 919, 930 (1980). For a discussion of the ALI's change of position on the duty of inquiry and the considerable criticism and pressure from the business community and segments of the organized bar, see Joel Seligman, A Sheep in Wolf's Clothing: The American Law Institute Principles of Corporate Governance Project, 55 Geo. Wash. L. Rev. 325, 360–366 (1987).

5. Although the comment to ALI § 4.01(a)(1)-(a)(2) states that the Subsection specifically is not intended to expand directors' existing obligations, the ALI cites only four states which have specific statutory provisions requiring inquiry, and it is not clear that these statutes support the ALI's position. One of the states, Washington, has subsequently amended its statute to eliminate the duty to inquire. See Wash. Bus. Corp. Act § 23B.08.300 (effective July 1, 1990). The language of the three remaining statutes (Alaska, Pennsylvania and California) parallel the language in California, which provides:

> A director shall perform the duties of a director, including duties as a member of any committee of the board upon which the director may serve, in good faith, in a manner such director believes to be in the best interests of the corporation and its shareholders and with such care, *including reasonable inquiry,* as an ordinarily prudent person in a like position would use under similar circumstances.

Cal. Corp. Code § 309 (a) (emphasis added).

The commentary to this section explains the scope of "reasonable inquiry" as follows:

* * * reasonable care under some circumstances could include a duty of inquiry. In other words, a director may not close his eyes to what is going on about him in the conduct of the corporate business and, *if he is put on notice by the presence of suspicious circumstances,* he may be required to make such "reasonable inquiry" as an ordinarily prudent person in his position would make under similar circumstances. There was no intention of imposing upon any director a duty to make an inquiry regardless of the circumstances * * * or to add a separate requirement of inquiry apart from a director's general duty of care. * * *

Cal. Corp. Code Ann. § 309(a) (emphasis added).

6. Professor Michael P. Dooley disagrees with the ALI's conclusion that corporate directors should know that they will be held personally liable for their failure to implement law compliance programs. He argues that directors should be held secondarily liable for another person's violation of regulatory statutes only if Congress specifically imposes such liability. Dooley also believes that law compliance programs present implementation problems different from those associated with implementation of other corporate programs, such as accounting systems. "Determining which corporate assets need to be secured is relatively easy, but deciding which laws directors should be most concerned about is not." Michael P. Dooley, Two Models of Corporate Governance, 47 Bus. Law. 461, 486 (1992).

2. DUE CARE AND CRIMINAL LIABILITY

What should be the relationship between the duty of care under state corporate law and the standard for a director's individual criminal liability that results from a failure to supervise subordinates' activities? This question has arisen most often in areas which have an impact on public health and welfare, such as food and drug contamination and hazardous dumping into the environment.

As early as 1943 the United States Supreme Court held corporate managers liable for criminal acts committed by their subordinates. In United States v. Dotterweich, 320 U.S. 277, 64 S.Ct. 134, 88 L.Ed. 48 (1943), the Court found that the corporation's president was subject to criminal prosecution for "introducing or delivering adulterated or misbranded drugs into interstate commerce" in violation of the Food and Drug Act. 320 U.S. at 278, 64 S.Ct. at 135. The court held that because the Food and Drug Act contained no criminal mens rea, or guilty mind, requirement, the prosecution did not have to prove criminal knowledge on the part of the corporate officer. This lack of criminal mens rea "puts the burden of acting at hazard upon a person otherwise innocent but standing in a responsible relation to a public danger." 320 U.S. at 281, 64 S.Ct. at 136.

In United States v. Park, 421 U.S. 658, 95 S.Ct. 1903, 44 L.Ed.2d 489 (1975), the president of Acme Markets, Inc. was charged, along with his company, with five violations of the Federal Food, Drug, and Cosmetics Act in allowing food to be held in a company warehouse where it was exposed to contamination by rodents. The company pleaded guilty, but Park pleaded innocent and was tried before a jury which convicted him. He was fined $50 on each of the five counts.

Park's conviction was ultimately affirmed by the Supreme Court in an opinion by Chief Justice Burger, who observed:

> [In] providing sanctions which reach and touch the individuals who execute the corporate mission—and this is by no means necessarily confined to a single corporate agent or employee—the Act imposes not only a positive duty to seek out and remedy violations when they occur but also, and primarily, a duty to implement measures that will insure that violations will not occur. The requirements of foresight and vigilance imposed on responsible corporate agents are beyond question demanding, and perhaps onerous, but they are no more stringent than the public has a right to expect of those who voluntarily assume positions of authority in business enterprises whose services and products affect the health and wellbeing of the public that supports them.

421 U.S at 672, 95 S.Ct. at 1911, 44 L.Ed.2d at 501.

The Court defined "responsible corporate agent" so as to preclude the jury from convicting an officer on the basis of his corporate position alone. Rather, liability attached only if the jury could find that Park "had a responsible relation to the situation, and by virtue of his position * * * had * * * authority and responsibility to deal with the situation." Id. at 674, 95 S.Ct. at 1912. The Court found significant Park's awareness that Acme's internal system for ensuring its Philadelphia and Baltimore warehouses' sanitary conditions was not working, and his failure to restructure that system once notified that similar sanitary problems had arisen at two of Acme's warehouses. However, the Court recognized that even the implementation of a new internal system might fail to prevent all violations. The Court indicated that Park could have raised an affirmative defense that he was powerless to prevent the violation, and sought a jury instruction requiring the government to prove beyond a reasonable doubt that he was capable of preventing the violation. See Joseph G. Block and Nancy A. Voisin, Criminal Enforcement of Environmental Laws: The Responsible Corporate Officer Doctrine—Can You Go to Jail for What You Don't Know?, 22 Envtl. L. 1347, 1354–55 (1992).

Personal liability of directors for actions of subordinates has also been strenuously debated in the area of environmental violations. Criminal liability is most easily found where the director was aware of the environmental violation, whether she actually instructed her subordinates to perform the illegal acts or simply acquiesced in the performance of such acts by others. Where the director charged with environmental liability did not participate in the illegal acts, imposition of liability is more difficult. It is important to note that the Food and Drug Act, at issue in *Dotterweich* and *Park*, imposes strict criminal liability.

Thus, an individual can be found liable under the statute even if she did not participate in, or have actual knowledge of, the criminal acts. Conversely, most modern environmental laws do not impose strict criminal liability, but require the government to prove the violator's criminal knowledge. See e.g., Clean Water Act, 3 U.S.C. § 1319(c)(2)(A), (B) (CWA); Clean Air Act, 42 U.S.C. § 7413(c)(1), (2), (3), (5) (CAA); Resource Conservation and Recovery Act, 42 U.S.C. § 6928(d) (RCRA). One court struck the inclusion of the responsible corporate officer doctrine in a charge under RCRA against a supervisor who did not participate in the alleged violation because it "would allow a conviction without the requisite specific intent." United States v. White, 766 F.Supp. 873, 895 (E.D.Wash.1991).

In contrast to RCRA, which does not mention responsible corporate actors, CWA and CAA expressly include the term "responsible corporate officer" in their definition of who can be found liable. One court has construed this inclusion to show that Congress intended the preservation of water and air resources to outweigh:

> [H]ardships suffered by "responsible corporate officers" who are held criminally liable in spite of their lack of "consciousness of wrongdoing." * * * Under this interpretation a "responsible corporate officer," to be held criminally liable, would not have to "willfully or negligently" cause a permit violation. Instead, the willfulness or negligence of the actor would be imputed to him by virtue of his position of responsibility.

United States v. Brittain, 931 F.2d 1413, 1419 (10th Cir.1991).

Thus, it seems that where a criminal statute either calls for strict liability for corporate defendants or includes "responsible corporate officers" in its definition of who can be held liable, a corporate director who fails to supervise subordinates adequately is likely to be held liable for corporate criminal violations.

The question of whether directors are required to institute law compliance programs has been made more complex by the recent adoption of the Federal Sentencing Guidelines for Organizations which make the adoption of such programs extremely beneficial to a corporation. The Guidelines, which provide substantial fines for any corporation convicted of a federal crime, are designed to provide "incentives for organizations to maintain internal mechanisms for deterring, detecting, and reporting criminal conduct." 18 U.S.C. App., § 8, Introductory Commentary. Under the Guidelines, a corporation's culpability, and therefore its sanction, can be reduced by the existence of an "effective program to prevent and detect violations of law." 18 U.S.C. § 8C2.5(f). Federal criminal laws which are likely to be violated by corporations include those relating to foods and drugs, the environment, employment practices, antitrust and worker safety.

The Guidelines do not address the question of the personal liability for directors where the corporation has committed a crime. The presumption behind the Guidelines is that corporate sanctions will be sufficient to motivate directors and officers to implement law compliance programs because such programs are in the best interests of the corporation. The practical effect of the Guidelines is that law compliance programs which are insufficient to mitigate a corporation's criminal liability are likely to be used as evidence in a derivative suit to show that a director did not act reasonably in carrying out her oversight duties.

It is important to note that a compliance program will not reduce culpability if "high-level personnel" of the organization or anyone in charge of the compliance program participated in, condoned, or was willfully ignorant of the offense. Thus, in order to take advantage of the reduction in culpability offered by the Guidelines' "safe harbor," the corporation's program must be detailed and must comply with all industry standards and government regulations, and any offense charged to the corporation must be committed by low-level, non-supervisory personnel. And, apparently, ineffective law compliance programs will be no more helpful in mitigating corporate liability than the failure to implement any program at all.

C. THE BUSINESS JUDGMENT RULE

PROBLEM
FASHION, INC.—PART II

You have again heard from Loren Peters, who has been a director of Fashion for the past three years, during which time Fashion's business has continued to thrive. She has just received notice of an emergency meeting of Fashion's board of directors, to be held tomorrow. She telephoned Lane Brown to ask what the meeting was about. He responded that the meeting was to consider a potential acquisition of United Stores, Inc. (United), a large department store chain that is one of Fashion's major customers. From recent newspaper stories, Loren is aware that United is in serious financial difficulty and will require a capital infusion of more than $500 million to avoid bankruptcy. In addition, some major reorganization of United's business probably will be required to enable it to reverse the series of losses that have created the current crisis.

Lane told Loren that he would present the board with a complete report at the meeting, including financial statements prepared by United's accountants, a detailed study of United and the benefits of the acquisition prepared by Linda Jordan, Fashion's chief financial officer, and Lane's own recommendation. He also said that a vote at the meeting was essential because the agreement he had negotiated with United would expire before the transaction could receive shareholder approval unless the steps necessary for such approval were commenced immediately.

Loren knows that Lane is a close personal friend of United's CEO. She is apprehensive about whether Fashion's management has the skills and experience necessary to turn around United's business, especially because neither Lane nor the other top management in Fashion have any substantial experience managing retail operations. She also suspects that, if the terms of the deal seem reasonable, most, if not all, of the other directors will be inclined to go along with Lane's proposal because of the success he has achieved in managing Fashion's business. As before, Loren has asked for your advice as to how to proceed at the upcoming board meeting.

1. THE SCOPE OF THE BUSINESS JUDGMENT RULE

The business judgment rule traditionally protects directors from liability for specific business decisions that result in losses to the corporation. In Gries Sports Enterprises, Inc. v. Cleveland Browns Football Co., Inc., 26 Ohio St.3d 15, 496 N.E.2d 959 (1986), the court observed:

> The business judgment rule is a principle of corporate governance that has been part of the common law for at least one hundred fifty years. It has traditionally operated as a shield to protect directors from liability for their decisions. If the directors are entitled to the protection of the rule, then the courts should not interfere with or second-guess their decisions. If the directors are not entitled to the protection of the rule, then the courts scrutinize the decision as to its intrinsic fairness to the corporation and the corporation's minority shareholders. The rule is a rebuttable presumption that directors are better equipped than the courts to make business judgments and that the directors acted without self-dealing or personal interest and exercised reasonable diligence and acted with good faith. A party challenging a board of directors' decision bears the burden of rebutting the presumption that the decision was a proper exercise of the business judgment of the board.

> * * *

> While the business judgment rule protects directors from personal liability in damages, it also applies to cases of "transactional justification," where an injunction is sought against board action, or against a decision itself, in which case the focus is on the decision as contrasted with the liability of the decision maker. There is a distinction between a "transactional justification" case involving or affecting the decision itself and the protection from personal liability of the decision maker. The former is sometimes referred to as involving the business judgment "doctrine," and the latter the business judgment "rule."

496 N.E.2d at 963–964.

Similarly, in Aronson v. Lewis, 473 A.2d 805, 812 (Del.1984), the Delaware Supreme Court stated:

> The business judgment rule is an acknowledgment of the managerial prerogatives of Delaware directors under Section 141(a). * * * It is

a presumption that in making a business decision the directors of a corporation acted on an informed basis, in good faith and in the honest belief that the action taken was in the best interests of the company. * * * Absent an abuse of discretion, that judgment will be respected by the courts. The burden is on the party challenging the decision to establish facts rebutting the presumption. * * *

The Delaware Supreme Court has suggested that the business judgment rule involves both procedural and substantive due care. Grobow v. Perot, 539 A.2d 180, 189 (Del.1988) Procedural due care implicates the process used in reaching a decision. Substantive due care raises the question of "whether the complaints state a claim of waste of assets, i.e., whether 'what the corporation has received is so inadequate in value that no person of ordinary, sound business judgment would deem it worth that which the corporation has paid. [Saxe v. Brady, 40 Del.Ch. 474, 184 A.2d 602, 610 (1962)].' " *Grobow*, supra at 184. See also, Litwin v. Allen, 25 N.Y.S.2d 667 (Sup.Ct. 1940).

The business judgment rule is essentially a creature of the courts, and statutory treatment is ambiguous at best. DGCL § 141 contains no statement of the required standard of care or of the business judgment rule. RMBCA § 8.30(d), although it relieves directors of liability if they have complied with the balance of the section, does not codify the business judgment rule, and the Official Comment is equally unhelpful. As the Reporter to the ABA Committee on Corporate Laws for the RMBCA has explained, the

> somewhat ambiguous formulation [in the Official Comment] of very basic concepts about directorial liability was a compromise position taken by the Committee on Corporate Laws only after extended and extremely time-consuming efforts to codify the business judgment rule within the context of § 8.30; these efforts did not lead to anything nearly approaching consensus. The compromise * * * was informally capsulated by one committee member who commented in effect, "we are saying that there is a business judgment rule, that we know what it is and when it should be applied, but we can't define it.

Robert W. Hamilton, Cases and Materials on Corporations—Including Partnerships and Limited Partnerships (4th ed. 1990), 702–703.

For the ALI's formulation of the business judgment rule, see ALI, Principles of Corporate Governance, § 4.01(c) (1994).

JOY v. NORTH

692 F.2d 880 (2d Cir.1982).

Winter, Judge:

While it is often stated that corporate directors and officers will be liable for negligence in carrying out their corporate duties, all seem agreed that such a statement is misleading. Whereas an automobile driver who makes a mistake in judgement as to speed or distance injuring a pedestrian will likely be called upon to respond in damages, a corporate officer who makes a mistake in judgment as to economic conditions, consumer tastes or production line efficiency will rarely, if ever, be found liable for damages suffered by the corporation. Whatever the terminology, the fact is that liability is rarely imposed upon corporate directors or officers simply for bad judgment and this reluctance to impose liability for unsuccessful business decisions has been doctrinally labelled the business judgment rule. Although the rule has suffered under academic criticism, see, e.g., Cary, Standards of Conduct Under Common Law, Present Day Statutes and the Model Act, 27 Bus.Lawyer 61 (1972), it is not without rational basis.

First, shareholders to a very real degree voluntarily undertake the risk of bad business judgment. Investors need not buy stock, for investment markets offer an array of opportunities less vulnerable to mistakes in judgment by corporate officers. Nor need investors buy stock in particular corporations. In the exercise of what is genuinely a free choice, the quality of a firm's management is often decisive and information is available from professional advisors. Since shareholders can and do select among investments partly on the basis of management, the business judgment rule merely recognizes a certain voluntariness in undertaking the risk of bad business decisions.

Second, courts recognize that after-the-fact litigation is a most imperfect device to evaluate corporate business decisions. The circumstances surrounding a corporate decision are not easily reconstructed in a courtroom years later, since business imperatives often call for quick decisions, inevitably based on less than perfect information. The entrepreneur's function is to encounter risks and to confront uncertainty, and a reasoned decision at the time made may seem a wild hunch viewed years later against a background of perfect knowledge.

Third, because potential profit often corresponds to the potential risk, it is very much in the interest of shareholders that the law not create incentives for overly cautious corporate decisions. Some opportunities offer great profits at the risk of very substantial losses, while the alternatives offer less risk of loss but also less potential profit. Shareholders can reduce the volatility [5] of risk by diversifying their holdings. In the case of the diversified shareholder, the seemingly more risky alternatives may well be the best choice since great losses in some stocks will over time be offset by even greater gains in others.[6] Given mutual

---

5. For purposes of this opinion, volatility" is "the degree of dispersion or variation of possible outcomes." Klein, Business Organization and Finance 147 (1980).

6. Consider the choice between two investments in an example adapted from Klein, Business Organization and Finance 147–49 (1980):

	Investment A	
Estimated Probability of Outcome	Outcome Profit or Loss	Value
.4	+15	6.0
.4	+1	.4
.2	−13	−2.6
		3.8

funds and similar forms of diversified investment, courts need not bend over backwards to give special protection to shareholders who refuse to reduce the volatility of risk by not diversifying. A rule which penalizes the choice of seemingly riskier alternatives thus may not be in the interest of shareholders generally.

Whatever its merit, however, the business judgment rule extends only as far as the reasons which justify its existence. Thus, it does not apply in cases, e.g., in which the corporate decision lacks a business purpose, is tainted by a conflict of interest, is so egregious as to amount to a no-win decision, Litwin v. Allen, 25 N.Y.S.2d 667 (N.Y. Co. Sup. Ct. 1940), or results from an obvious and prolonged failure to exercise oversight or supervision. * * *

SMITH v. VAN GORKOM

488 A.2d 858 (Del.1985).

[Trans Union Corporation was a publicly traded, diversified holding company. Its chairman and chief executive officer was Jerome W. Van Gorkom who was then nearing retirement age. Its Board of Directors consisted of five company officers and five outside directors.) Four of the latter were chief executive officers of large public corporations; the fifth was the former Dean of the University of Chicago Business School.

At the time of the events in the case, Trans Union faced a major business problem relating to investment tax credits (ITCs). Its competitors generated sufficient taxable income to allow them to make use of all ITCs they generated and took these tax benefits into account in setting the terms of lease notes. Trans Union did not have sufficient income to take advantage of all of its ITCs, but nevertheless had to match its competitors' prices. In July 1980, Trans Union management submitted its annual revision of the company's five year forecast to the board. That report discussed alternative solutions to the ITC problem and concluded that the company had sufficient time to develop its course of action. The report did not mention the possible sale of the company.

On August 27, Van Gorkom met with senior management to consider the ITC problem. Among the ideas mentioned were the sale of Trans Union to a company with a large amount of taxable income, or a

| | Investment B | |
Estimated Probability of Outcome	Outcome Profit or Loss	Value
.4	+6	2.4
.4	+2	.8
.2	+1	.2
		3.4

Although A is clearly "worth" more than B, it is riskier because it is more volatile. Diversification lessens the volatility by allow-

ing investors to invest in 20 or 200 A's which will tend to guarantee a total result near the value. Shareholders are thus better off with the various firms selecting A over B, although after the fact they will complain in each case of the 2.6 loss. If the courts did not abide by the business judgment rule, they might well penalize the choice of A in each such case and thereby unknowingly injure shareholders generally by creating incentives for management always to choose B.

leveraged buyout.* This latter alternative was discussed again at a meeting on September 5. At that meeting, the chief financial officer, Donald Romans, presented preliminary calculations based on a price between $50 and $60 per share but did not state that these calculations established a fair price for the company. While Van Gorkom rejected the leveraged buy out idea, he stated that he would be willing to sell his own shares at $55 per share.

Without consulting the board of directors or any officers, Van Gorkom decided to meet with Jay A. Pritzker, a corporate takeover specialist whom he knew socially. Prior to that meeting, Van Gorkom instructed Trans Union's controller, Carl Peterson, to prepare a confidential calculation of the feasibility of a leveraged buy out at $55 per share. On September 13, Van Gorkom proposed a sale of Trans Union to Pritzker at $55 per share. Two days later, Pritzker advised Van Gorkom that he was interested in a purchase at that price. By September 18, after two more meetings that included two Trans Union officers and an outside consultant, Van Gorkom knew that Pritzker was ready to propose a cash-out merger ** at $55 per share if Pritzker could also have the option to buy one million shares of Trans Union treasury stock at $38 per share (a price which was 75 cents above the current market price). Pritzker also insisted that the Trans Union board act on his proposal within three days, *i.e.,* by Sunday, September 21 and instructed his attorney to draft the merger documents.

On September 19, without consulting Trans Union's legal department, Van Gorkom engaged outside counsel as merger specialists. He called for meetings of senior management and the board of directors for the next day, but only those officers who had met with Pritzker knew the subject of the meetings.

Senior management's reaction to Pritzker's proposal was completely negative. Romans objected both to the price and to the sale of treasury shares as a "lock-up". Immediately after this meeting, Van Gorkom met with the board. He made an oral presentation outlining the Pritzker offer but did not furnish copies of the proposed merger agreement. Neither did he tell the board that he had approached Pritzker. He stated that Pritzker would purchase all outstanding Trans Union shares for $55 each and Trans Union would be merged into a wholly owned entity Pritzker formed for this purpose; for 90 days Trans Union would be free to receive but not to solicit competing offers; only published, rather than proprietary information could be furnished to other bidders; the Trans Union board had to act by Sunday evening,

* A leveraged buyout is a purchase of the shares owned by the public shareholders of a company whereby the buyers, often the company's management, borrow the money from financial institutions that rely on the assets of the company for their security. Thus, the company, in effect, finances its own purchase. In Trans Union's case, a leveraged buyout would have increased the company's interest expense, thus reducing taxable income and exacerbating the ITC problem.—Eds.

** A cash-out merger is a merger in which the shareholders of the acquired company receive cash for the shares. Thus they have no continuing economic interest either in the old company or the new company that succeeds it.—Eds.

September 21; the offer was subject to Pritzker obtaining financing by October 10, 1980; and that if Pritzker met or waived the financing contingency, Trans Union was obliged to sell him one million newly issued shares at $38 per share. According to Van Gorkom, the issue for the board was whether $55 was a fair price rather than the best price. He said that putting Trans Union "up for auction" through a 90 day "market test" would allow the free market an opportunity to judge whether $55 was fair. Outside counsel advised the board that they might be sued if they did not accept the offer, and that a fairness opinion from an investment banker was not legally required.

At the board meeting, Romans stated that his prior studies in connection with a possible leveraged buy out did not indicate a fair price for the stock. However, it was his opinion that $55 was "at the beginning of the range" of a fair price.

The board meeting lasted two hours, at the end of which the board approved the merger, with two conditions:

(1) Trans Union reserved the right to accept any better offer during the 90 day market test period.

(2) Trans Union could share its proprietary information with other potential bidders.

At that time, however, the board did not reserve the right actively to solicit other bids.

Van Gorkom signed the as yet unamended merger agreement, still unread either by himself or the other board members, that evening "in the midst of a formal party which he hosted for the opening of the Chicago Lyric Opera."

On September 22, Trans Union issued a press release announcing a "definitive" merger agreement with Marmon Group, Inc., an affiliate of a Pritzker holding company. Within ten days, rebellious key officers threatened to resign. Van Gorkom met with Pritzker who agreed to modify the agreement provided that the "dissident" officers agreed to stay with Trans Union for at least six months following the merger.

The board reconvened on October 8 and, without seeing their text, approved the proposed amendments regarding the 90 day market test and solicitation of other bids. The board also authorized the company to employ its investment banker to solicit other offers.

Although the amendments had not yet been prepared, Trans Union issued a press release on the following day stating that it could actively seek other offers and had retained an investment banker for that purpose. The release also said that Pritzker had obtained the necessary financing commitments and had acquired one million shares of Trans Union at $38 per share and that if Trans Union had not received a more favorable offer by February 1, 1981, its shareholders would meet to vote on the Pritzker bid. Van Gorkom executed the amendments to the merger agreement on October 10, without consulting the board and apparently without fully understanding that the amendments significantly constrained Trans Union's ability to negotiate a better deal.

Trans Union received only two serious offers during the market test period. One, from General Electric Credit Corporation, fell through when Trans Union would not rescind its agreement with Pritzker to give GE Credit extra time. The other offer, a leveraged buyout by management (except Van Gorkom) arranged through Kohlberg, Kravis, Roberts & Co. ("KKR") was made in early December at $60 per share. It was contingent upon completing equity and bank financing, which KKR said was 80% complete, with terms and conditions substantially the same as the Pritzker deal. Van Gorkom, however, did not view the KKR deal as "firm" because of the financing contingency (even though the Pritzker offer had been similarly conditioned) and he refused to issue a press release about it. KKR planned to present its offer to the Trans Union board, but withdrew shortly before the scheduled meeting, noting that a senior Trans Union officer had withdrawn from the purchasing KKR group after Van Gorkom spoke to him. Van Gorkom denied influencing the officer's decision, and he made no mention of it to the board at the meeting later that day.

The shareholders commenced their lawsuit on December 19, 1980. Management's proxy statement was mailed on January 21 for a meeting scheduled for February 10, 1981. The Trans Union board met on January 26 and gave final approval to both the Pritzker merger and a supplement to its proxy statement which was mailed the next day. On February 10, 1981, the shareholders approved the Pritzker merger by a large majority.]

HORSEY, JUSTICE (for the majority):

* * *

II.

We turn to the issue of the application of the business judgment rule to the September 20 meeting of the Board.

The Court of Chancery concluded from the evidence that the Board of Directors' approval of the Pritzker merger proposal fell within the protection of the business judgment rule. The Court found that the Board had given sufficient time and attention to the transaction, since the directors had considered the Pritzker proposal on three different occasions, on September 20, and on October 8, 1980 and finally on January 26, 1981. On that basis, the Court reasoned that the Board had acquired, over the four-month period, sufficient information to reach an informed business judgment on the cash-out merger proposal. The Court ruled:

> * * * that given the market value of Trans Union's stock, the business acumen of the members of the board of Trans Union, the substantial premium over market offered by the Pritzkers and the ultimate effect on the merger price provided by the prospect of other

bids for the stock in question, that the board of directors of Trans Union did not act recklessly or improvidently in determining on a course of action which they believed to be in the best interest of the stockholders of Trans Union.

The Court of Chancery made but one finding; *i.e.,* that the Board's conduct over the entire period from September 20 through January 26, 1981 was not reckless or improvident, but informed. This ultimate conclusion was premised upon three subordinate findings, one explicit and two implied. The Court's explicit finding was that Trans Union's Board was "free to turn down the Pritzker proposal" not only on September 20 but also on October 8, 1980 and on January 26, 1981. The Court's implied, subordinate findings were: (1) that no legally binding agreement was reached by the parties until January 26; and (2) that if a higher offer were to be forthcoming, the market test would have produced it, and Trans Union would have been contractually free to accept such higher offer. However, the Court offered no factual basis or legal support for any of these findings; and the record compels contrary conclusions.

* * *

Under Delaware law, the business judgment rule is the offspring of the fundamental principle, codified in 8 Del.C. § 141(a), that the business and affairs of a Delaware corporation are managed by or under its board of directors. In carrying out their managerial roles, directors are charged with an unyielding fiduciary duty to the corporation and its shareholders. The business judgment rule exists to protect and promote the full and free exercise of the managerial power granted to Delaware directors. The rule itself "is a presumption that in making a business decision, the directors of a corporation acted on an informed basis, in good faith and in the honest belief that the action taken was in the best interests of the company." [Aronson v. Lewis, 473 A.2d 805, 812 (Del.1984)] Thus, the party attacking a board decision as uninformed must rebut the presumption that its business judgment was an informed one. *Id.*

The determination of whether a business judgment is an informed one turns on whether the directors have informed themselves "prior to making a business decision, of all material information reasonably available to them." *Id.*

Under the business judgment rule there is no protection for directors who have made "an unintelligent or unadvised judgment." Mitchell v. Highland–Western Glass, Del.Ch., 167 A. 831, 833 (1933). A director's duty to inform himself in preparation for a decision derives from the fiduciary capacity in which he serves the corporation and its stockholders. Since a director is vested with the responsibility for the management of the affairs of the corporation, he must execute that duty with the recognition that he acts on behalf of others. Such obligation does not tolerate faithlessness or self-dealing. But fulfillment of the fiduciary function requires more than the mere absence of bad faith or fraud. Representation of the financial interests of others imposes on a director an affirmative duty to protect those interests and to proceed with a critical eye in assessing information of the type and under the circumstances present here.

Thus, a director's duty to exercise an informed business judgment is in the nature of a duty of care, as distinguished from a duty of loyalty. Here, there were no allegations of fraud, bad faith, or self-dealing, or proof thereof. Hence, it is presumed that the directors reached their business judgment in good faith, and considerations of motive are irrelevant to the issue before us.

The standard of care applicable to a director's duty of care has also been recently restated by this Court. In Aronson, *supra*, we stated:

> While the Delaware cases use a variety of terms to describe the applicable standard of care, our analysis satisfies us that under the business judgment rule director liability is predicated upon concepts of gross negligence. (footnote omitted)

473 A.2d at 812.

We again confirm that view. We think the concept of gross negligence is also the proper standard for determining whether a business judgment reached by a board of directors was an informed one.

In the specific context of a proposed merger of domestic corporations, a director has a duty under 8 Del.C. § 251(b), along with his fellow directors, to act in an informed and deliberate manner in determining whether to approve an agreement of merger before submitting the proposal to the stockholders. Certainly in the merger context, a director may not abdicate that duty by leaving to the shareholders alone the decision to approve or disapprove the agreement. Only an agreement of merger satisfying the requirements of 8 Del.C. § 251(b) may be submitted to the shareholders under § 251(c).

It is against those standards that the conduct of the directors of Trans Union must be tested, as a matter of law and as a matter of fact, regarding their exercise of an informed business judgment in voting to approve the Pritzker merger proposal.

III.

The issue of whether the directors reached an informed decision to "sell" the Company on September 20, 1980 must be determined only upon the basis of the information then reasonably available to the directors and relevant to their decision to accept the Pritzker merger proposal. This is not to say that the directors were precluded from altering their original plan of action, had they done so in an informed manner. What we do say is that the question of whether the directors reached an informed business judgment in agreeing to sell the Company, pursuant to the terms of the September 20 Agreement presents, in reality, two questions: (A) whether the directors reached an informed business judgment on September 20, 1980; and (B) if they did not, whether the directors' actions taken subsequent to September 20 were adequate to cure any infirmity in their action taken on September 20. We first consider the directors' September 20 action in terms of their reaching an informed business judgment.

-A-

On the record before us, we must conclude that the Board of Directors did not reach an informed business judgment on September 20, 1980 in voting to "sell" the Company for $55 per share pursuant to the Pritzker cash-out merger proposal. Our reasons, in summary, are as follows:

The directors (1) did not adequately inform themselves as to Van Gorkom's role in forcing the "sale" of the Company and in establishing the per share purchase price; (2) were uninformed as to the intrinsic value of the Company; and (3) given these circumstances, at a minimum, were grossly negligent in approving the "sale" of the Company upon two hours' consideration, without prior notice, and without the exigency of a crisis or emergency.

As has been noted, the Board based its September 20 decision to approve the cash-out merger primarily on Van Gorkom's representations. None of the directors, other than Van Gorkom and Chelberg, had any prior knowledge that the purpose of the meeting was to propose a cash-out merger of Trans Union. No members of Senior Management were present, other than Chelberg, Romans and Peterson; and the latter two had only learned of the proposed sale an hour earlier. Both general counsel Moore and former general counsel Browder attended the meeting, but were equally uninformed as to the purpose of the meeting and the documents to be acted upon.

Without any documents before them concerning the proposed transaction, the members of the Board were required to rely entirely upon Van Gorkom's 20–minute oral presentation of the proposal. No written summary of the terms of the merger was presented; the directors were given no documentation to support the adequacy of $55 price per share for sale of the Company; and the Board had before it nothing more than Van Gorkom's statement of his understanding of the substance of an agreement which he admittedly had never read, nor which any member of the Board had ever seen.

Under 8 Del.C. § 141(e) "directors are fully protected in relying in good faith on reports made by officers." The term "report" has been liberally construed to include reports of informal personal investigations by corporate officers, Cheff v. Mathes, Del.Supr., 199 A.2d 548, 556 (1964). However, there is no evidence that any "report," as defined under § 141(e), concerning the Pritzker proposal, was presented to the Board on September 20. Van Gorkom's oral presentation of his understanding of the terms of the proposed Merger Agreement, which he had not seen, and Romans' brief oral statement of his preliminary study regarding the feasibility of a leveraged buy-out of Trans Union do not qualify as § 141(e) "reports" for these reasons: The former lacked substance because Van Gorkom was basically uninformed as to the essential provisions of the very document about which he was talking. Romans' statement was irrelevant to the issues before the Board since it did not purport to be a valuation study. At a minimum for a report to enjoy the status conferred by § 141(e), it must be pertinent to the subject matter upon which a board is called to act, and otherwise be entitled to good faith, not blind, reliance. Considering all of the surrounding circumstances—hastily calling the meeting without prior notice of its subject matter, the proposed sale of the Company without any prior consideration of the issue or necessity therefor, the urgent time constraints imposed by Pritzker, and the total absence of any documentation whatsoever—the directors were duty bound to make reasonable inquiry of Van Gorkom and Romans, and if they had done so, the inadequacy of that upon which they now claim to have relied would have been apparent.

The defendants rely on the following factors to sustain the Trial Court's finding that the Board's decision was an informed one: (1) the magnitude of the premium or spread between the $55 Pritzker offering price and Trans Union's current market price of $38 per share; (2) the amendment of the Agreement as submitted on September 20 to permit the Board to accept any better offer during the "market test" period; (3) the collective experience and expertise of the Board's "inside" and "outside" directors; and (4) their reliance on Brennan's legal advice that the directors might be sued if they rejected the Pritzker proposal. We discuss each of these grounds *seriatim:*

(1)

A substantial premium may provide one reason to recommend a merger, but in the absence of other sound valuation information, the fact of a premium alone does not provide an adequate basis upon which to assess the fairness of an offering price. Here, the judgment reached as to the adequacy of the premium was based on a comparison between the historically depressed Trans Union market price and the amount of the Pritzker offer. Using market price as a basis for concluding that the premium adequately reflected the true value of the Company was a clearly faulty, indeed fallacious, premise, as the defendants' own evidence demonstrates.

The record is clear that before September 20, Van Gorkom and other members of Trans Union's Board knew that the market had consistently undervalued the worth of Trans Union's stock, despite steady increases in the Company's operating income in the seven years preceding the merger. The Board related this occurrence in large part to Trans Union's inability to use its ITCs as previously noted. Van Gorkom testified that he did not believe the market price accurately reflected Trans Union's true worth; and several of the directors testified that, as a general rule, most chief executives think that the market undervalues their companies' stock. Yet, on September 20, Trans Union's Board apparently believed that the market stock price accurately reflected the value of the Company for the purpose of determining the adequacy of the premium for its sale.

* * *

The parties do not dispute that a publicly-traded stock price is solely a measure of the value of a minority position and, thus, market price represents only the value of a single share. Nevertheless, on September 20, the Board assessed the adequacy of the premium over market, offered by Pritzker, solely by comparing it with Trans Union's current and historical stock price.

Indeed, as of September 20, the Board had no other information on which to base a determination of the intrinsic value of Trans Union as a going concern. As of September 20, the Board had made no evaluation of the Company designed to value the entire enterprise, nor had the Board ever previously considered selling the Company or consenting to a buy-out merger. Thus, the adequacy of a premium is indeterminate unless it is assessed in terms of other competent and sound valuation information that reflects the value of the particular business.

Despite the foregoing facts and circumstances, there was no call by the Board, either on September 20 or thereafter, for any valuation study or documentation of the $55 price per share as a measure of the fair value of the Company in a cash-out context. It is undisputed that the major asset of Trans Union was its cash flow. Yet, at no time did the Board call for a valuation study taking into account that highly significant element of the Company's assets.

We do not imply that an outside valuation study is essential to support an informed business judgment; nor do we state that fairness opinions by independent investment bankers are required as a matter of law. Often insiders familiar with the business of a going concern are in a better position than are outsiders to gather relevant information; and under appropriate circumstances, such directors may be fully protected in relying in good faith upon the valuation reports of their management.

Here, the record establishes that the Board did not request its Chief Financial Officer, Romans, to make any valuation study or review of the proposal to determine the adequacy of $55 per share for sale of the Company. The Board rested on Romans' elicited response that the $55 figure was within a "fair price range" within the context of a leveraged buy-out. No director sought any further information from Romans. No director asked him why he put $55 at the bottom of his range. No director asked Romans for any details as to his study, the reason why it had been undertaken or its depth. No director asked to see the study; and no director asked Romans whether Trans Union's finance department could do a fairness study within the remaining 36–hour period available under the Pritzker offer.

Had the Board, or any member, made an inquiry of Romans, he presumably would have responded as he testified: that his calculations were rough and preliminary; and, that the study was not designed to determine the fair value of the Company, but rather to assess the feasibility of a leveraged buy-out financed by the Company's projected cash flow, making certain assumptions as to the purchaser's borrowing needs. Romans would have presumably also informed the Board of his view, and the widespread view of Senior Management, that the timing of the offer was wrong and the offer inadequate.

The record also establishes that the Board accepted without scrutiny Van Gorkom's representation as to the fairness of the $55 price per share for sale of the Company—a subject that the Board had never previously considered. The Board thereby failed to discover that Van Gorkom had suggested the $55 price to Pritzker and, most crucially, that Van Gorkom had arrived at the $55 figure based on calculations designed solely to determine the feasibility of a leveraged buy-out.[19] No questions were raised either as to the tax implications of a cash-out merger or how the price for the one million share option granted Pritzker was calculated.

We do not say that the Board of Directors was not entitled to give some credence to Van Gorkom's representation that $55 was an adequate or fair price. Under § 141(e), the directors were entitled to rely upon their chairman's opinion of value and adequacy, provided that such opinion was reached on a sound basis. Here, the issue is whether the directors informed themselves as to all information that was reasonably available to them. Had they done so, they would have learned of the source and derivation of the $55 price and could not reasonably have relied thereupon in good faith.

None of the directors, Management or outside, were investment bankers or financial analysts. Yet the Board did not consider recessing the meeting until a later hour that day (or requesting an extension of Pritzker's Sunday evening deadline) to give it time to elicit more information as to the sufficiency of the offer, either from inside Management (in particular Romans) or from Trans Union's own investment banker, Salomon Brothers, whose Chicago specialist in merger and acquisitions was known to the Board and familiar with Trans Union's affairs.

19. As of September 20 the directors did not know: that Van Gorkom had arrived at the $55 figure alone, and subjectively, as the figure to be used by Controller Peterson in creating a feasible structure for a leveraged buy-out by a prospective purchaser; that Van Gorkom had not sought advice, information or assistance from either inside or outside Trans Union directors as to the value of the Company as an entity or the fair price per share for 100% of its stock; that Van Gorkom had not consulted with the Company's investment bankers or other financial analysts; that Van Gorkom had not consulted with or confided in any officer or director of the Company except Chelberg; and that Van Gorkom had deliberately chosen to ignore the advice and opinion of the members of his Senior Management group regarding the adequacy of the $55 price.

Thus, the record compels the conclusion that on September 20 the Board lacked valuation information adequate to reach an informed business judgment as to the fairness of $55 per share for sale of the Company.

(2)

This brings us to the post-September 20 "market test" upon which the defendants ultimately rely to confirm the reasonableness of their September 20 decision to accept the Pritzker proposal. In this connection, the directors present a two-part argument: (a) that by making a "market test" of Pritzker's $55 per share offer a condition of their September 20 decision to accept his offer, they cannot be found to have acted impulsively or in an uninformed manner on September 20; and (b) that the adequacy of the $17 premium for sale of the Company was conclusively established over the following 90 to 120 days by the most reliable evidence available—the marketplace. Thus, the defendants impliedly contend that the "market test" eliminated the need for the Board to perform any other form of fairness test either on September 20, or thereafter.

Again, the facts of record do not support the defendants' argument. There is no evidence: (a) that the Merger Agreement was effectively amended to give the Board freedom to put Trans Union up for auction sale to the highest bidder; or (b) that a public auction was in fact permitted to occur.

* * *

(3)

The directors' unfounded reliance on both the premium and the market test as the basis for accepting the Pritzker proposal undermines the defendants' remaining contention that the Board's collective experience and sophistication was a sufficient basis for finding that it reached its September 20 decision with informed, reasonable deliberation.[21] *Compare* Gimbel v. Signal Companies, Inc., Del.Ch., 316 A.2d 599 (1974), aff'd per curiam, Del.Supr., 316 A.2d 619 (1974). There, the Court of Chancery [preliminarily] enjoined a board's sale of stock of its wholly-owned subsidiary for an alleged grossly inadequate price. It did so based on a finding that the business judgment rule had been pierced for failure of management to give its board "the opportunity to make a reasonable and reasoned decision." 316 A.2d at 615. The Court there reached this

---

21. Trans Union's five "inside" directors had backgrounds in law and accounting, 116 years of collective employment by the Company and 68 years of combined experience on its Board. Trans Union's five "outside" directors included four chief executives of major corporations and an economist who was a former dean of a major school of business and chancellor of a university. The "outside" directors had 78 years of combined experience as chief executive officers of major corporations and 50 years of cumulative experience as directors of Trans Union. Thus, defendants argue that the Board was eminently qualified to reach an informed judgment on the proposed "sale" of Trans Union notwithstanding their lack of any advance notice of the proposal, the shortness of their deliberation, and their determination not to consult with their investment banker or to obtain a fairness opinion.

result notwithstanding the board's sophistication and experience; the company's need of immediate cash; and the board's need to act promptly due to the impact of an energy crisis on the value of the underlying assets being sold—all of its subsidiary's oil and gas interests. The Court found those factors denoting competence to be outweighed by evidence of gross negligence; that management in effect sprang the deal on the board by negotiating the asset sale without informing the board; that the buyer intended to "force a quick decision" by the board; that the board meeting was called on only one-and-a-half days' notice; that its outside directors were not notified of the meeting's purpose; that during a meeting spanning "a couple of hours" a sale of assets worth $480 million was approved; and that the Board failed to obtain a *current* appraisal of its oil and gas interests. The analogy of *Signal* to the case at bar is significant.

(4)

Part of the defense is based on a claim that the directors relied on legal advice rendered at the September 20 meeting by James Brennan, Esquire, who was present at Van Gorkom's request. Unfortunately, Brennan did not appear and testify at trial even though his firm participated in the defense of this action.

Several defendants testified that Brennan advised them that Delaware law did not require a fairness opinion or an outside valuation of the Company before the Board could act on the Pritzker proposal. If given, the advice was correct. However, that did not end the matter. Unless the directors had before them adequate information regarding the intrinsic value of the Company, upon which a proper exercise of business judgment could be made, mere advice of this type is meaningless; and, given this record of the defendants' failures, it constitutes no defense here.[22]

* * *

A second claim is that counsel advised the Board it would be subject to lawsuits if it rejected the $55 per share offer. It is, of course, a fact of corporate life that today when faced with difficult or sensitive issues, directors often are subject to suit, irrespective of the decisions they make. However, counsel's mere acknowledgement of this circumstance cannot be rationally translated into a justification for a board permitting itself to be stampeded into a patently unadvised act. While suit might result from the rejection of a merger or tender offer, Delaware law makes clear that a board acting within the ambit of the business judgment rule faces no ultimate liability. Thus, we cannot conclude that the mere threat of litigation, acknowledged by counsel, constitutes either

---

22. Nonetheless, we are satisfied that in an appropriate factual context a proper exercise of business judgment may include, as one of its aspects, reasonable reliance upon the advice of counsel. This is wholly out- side the statutory protections of 8 Del.C. § 141(e) involving reliance upon reports of officers, certain experts and books and records of the company.

legal advice or any valid basis upon which to pursue an uninformed course.

* * *

-B-

[The court examined the board's post-September 20 conduct and determined that the board had been grossly negligent and that its conduct did not cure the deficiencies in its September 20 actions.]

IV.

[As to] questions which were not originally addressed by the parties in their briefing of this case * * * [t]he parties' response, including reargument, has led the majority of the Court to conclude: (1) that since all of the defendant directors, outside as well as inside, take a unified position, we are required to treat all of the directors as one as to whether they are entitled to the protection of the business judgment rule; and (2) that considerations of good faith, including the presumption that the directors acted in good faith, are irrelevant in determining the threshold issue of whether the directors as a Board exercised an informed business judgment. For the same reason, we must reject defense counsel's *ad hominem* argument for affirmance: that reversal may result in a multi-million dollar class award against the defendants for having made an allegedly uninformed business judgment in a transaction not involving any personal gain, self-dealing or claim of bad faith. * * *

[P]laintiffs have not claimed, nor did the Trial Court decide, that $55 was a grossly inadequate price per share for sale of the Company. That being so, the presumption that a board's judgment as to adequacy of price represents an honest exercise of business judgment (absent proof that the sale price was grossly inadequate) is irrelevant to the threshold question of whether an informed judgment was reached.

V.

The defendants ultimately rely on the stockholder vote of February 10 for exoneration. The defendants contend that the stockholders' "overwhelming" vote approving the Pritzker Merger Agreement had the legal effect of curing any failure of the Board to reach an informed business judgment in its approval of the merger.

The parties tacitly agree that a discovered failure of the Board to reach an informed business judgment in approving the merger constitutes a voidable, rather than a void, act. Hence, the merger can be sustained, notwithstanding the infirmity of the Board's action, if its approval by majority vote of the shareholders is found to have been based on an informed electorate. *Cf.* Michelson v. Duncan, Del.Supr., 407 A.2d 211 (1979), aff'g in part and rev'g in part, Del.Ch. 386 A.2d 1144 (1978). The disagreement between the parties arises over: (1) the Board's burden of disclosing to the shareholders all relevant and material information; and (2) the sufficiency of the evidence as to whether the Board satisfied that burden.

* * *

The burden must fall on defendants who claim ratification based on shareholder vote to establish that the shareholder approval resulted from a fully informed electorate. On the record before us, it is clear that the Board failed to meet that burden.

* * *

VI.

To summarize: we hold that the directors of Trans Union breached their fiduciary duty to their stockholders (1) by their failure to inform themselves of all information reasonably available to them and relevant to their decision to recommend the Pritzker merger; and (2) by their failure to disclose all material information such as a reasonable stockholder would consider important in deciding whether to approve the Pritzker offer.

We hold, therefore, that the Trial Court committed reversible error in applying the business judgment rule in favor of the director defendants in this case.

On remand, the Court of Chancery shall conduct an evidentiary hearing to determine the fair value of the shares represented by the plaintiffs' class, based on the intrinsic value of Trans Union on September 20, 1980. * * * Thereafter, an award of damages may be entered to the extent that the fair value of Trans Union exceeds $55 per share.

* * *

Reversed and Remanded for proceedings consistent herewith.

McNEILLY, JUSTICE, dissenting:

The majority opinion reads like an advocate's closing address to a hostile jury. And I say that not lightly. Throughout the opinion great emphasis is directed only to the negative, with nothing more than lip service granted the positive aspects of this case. In my opinion Chancellor Marvel (retired) should have been affirmed. The Chancellor's opinion was the product of well reasoned conclusions, based upon a sound deductive process, clearly supported by the evidence and entitled to deference in this appeal. Because of my diametrical opposition to all evidentiary conclusions of the majority, I respectfully dissent.

It would serve no useful purpose, particularly at this late date, for me to dissent at great length. I restrain myself from doing so, but feel compelled to at least point out what I consider to be the most glaring deficiencies in the majority opinion. The majority has spoken and has effectively said that Trans Union's Directors have been the victims of a "fast shuffle" by Van Gorkom and Pritzker. That is the beginning of the majority's comedy of errors. The first and most important error made is the majority's assessment of the directors' knowledge of the affairs of Trans Union and their combined ability to act in this situation under the protection of the business judgment rule.

Trans Union's Board of Directors consisted of ten men, five of whom were "inside" directors and five of whom were "outside" directors. The "inside" directors were Van Gorkom, Chelberg, Bonser, William B. Browder, Senior Vice–President–Law, and Thomas P. O'Boyle, Senior Vice–President–Administration. At the time the merger was proposed the inside five directors had collectively been employed by the Company for 116 years and had 68 years of combined experience as directors. The "outside" directors were A.W. Wallis, William B. Johnson, Joseph B. Lanterman, Graham J. Morgan and Robert W. Reneker. With the exception of Wallis, these were all chief executive officers of Chicago based corporations that were at least as large as Trans Union. The five "outside" directors had 78 years of combined experience as chief executive officers, and 53 years cumulative service as Trans Union directors.

The inside directors wear their badge of expertise in the corporate affairs of Trans Union on their sleeves. But what about the outsiders? Dr. Wallis is or was an economist and math statistician, a professor of economics at Yale University, dean of the graduate school of business at the University of Chicago, and Chancellor of the University of Rochester. Dr. Wallis had been on the Board of Trans Union since 1962. He also was on the Board of Bausch & Lomb, Kodak, Metropolitan Life Insurance Company, Standard Oil and others.

William B. Johnson is a University of Pennsylvania law graduate, President of Railway Express until 1966, Chairman and Chief Executive of I.C. Industries Holding Company, and member of Trans Union's Board since 1968.

Joseph Lanterman, a Certified Public Accountant, is or was President and Chief Executive of American Steel, on the Board of International Harvester, Peoples Energy, Illinois Bell Telephone, Harris Bank and Trust Company, Kemper Insurance Company and a director of Trans Union for four years.

Graham Morgan is a chemist, was Chairman and Chief Executive Officer of U.S. Gypsum, and in the 17 and 18 years prior to the Trans Union transaction had been involved in 31 or 32 corporate takeovers.

Robert Reneker attended University of Chicago and Harvard Business Schools. He was President and Chief Executive of Swift and Company, director of Trans Union since 1971, and member of the Boards of seven other corporations including U.S. Gypsum and the Chicago Tribune.

Directors of this caliber are not ordinarily taken in by a "fast shuffle". I submit they were not taken into this multi-million dollar corporate transaction without being fully informed and aware of the state of the art as it pertained to the entire corporate panorama of Trans Union. True, even directors such as these, with their business acumen, interest and expertise, can go astray. I do not believe that to be the case here. These men knew Trans Union like the back of their hands and were more than well qualified to make on the spot informed business judgments concerning the affairs of Trans Union including a 100% sale of the corporation. Lest we forget, the corporate world of then and now operates on what is so aptly referred to as "the fast track". These men were at the time an integral part of that world, all professional business men, not intellectual figureheads.

The majority of this Court holds that the Board's decision, reached on September 20, 1980, to approve the merger was not the product of an *informed* business judgment, that the Board's subsequent efforts to amend the Merger Agreement and take other curative action were *legally and factually* ineffectual, and that the Board did *not deal with complete candor* with the stockholders by failing to disclose all material facts, which they knew or should have known, before securing the stockholders' approval of the merger. I disagree.

* * *

ON MOTIONS FOR REARGUMENT

Following this Court's decision, Thomas P. O'Boyle, one of the director defendants, sought, and was granted, leave for change of counsel. Thereafter, the individual director defendants, other than O'Boyle, filed a motion for reargument and director O'Boyle, through newly-appearing counsel, then filed a separate motion for reargument. Plaintiffs have responded to the several motions and this matter has now been duly considered.

* * * Although O'Boyle continues to adopt his fellow directors' arguments, O'Boyle now asserts in the alternative that he has standing to take a position different from that of his fellow directors and that legal grounds exist for finding him not liable for the acts or omissions of his fellow directors. * * *

We reject defendant O'Boyle's new argument as to standing because not timely asserted. Our reasons are several. *One,* in connection with the supplemental briefing of this case in March, 1984, a special opportunity was afforded the individual defendants, including O'Boyle, to present any factual or legal reasons why each or any of them should be individually treated. Thereafter, at argument before the Court on June 11, 1984, the following colloquy took place between this Court and counsel for the individual defendants at the outset of counsel's argument:

Counsel: I'll make the argument on behalf of the nine individual defendants against whom the plaintiffs seek more than $100,000,000 in damages. That is the ultimate issue in this case, whether or not nine honest, experienced businessmen should be subject to damages in a case where—

Justice Moore: Is there a distinction between Chelberg and Van Gorkom vis-a-vis the other defendants?

Counsel: No, sir.

Justice Moore: None whatsoever?

Counsel: I think not.

Two, in this Court's Opinion dated January 29, 1985, the Court relied on the individual defendants as having presented a unified defense. We stated:

> The parties' response, including reargument, has led the majority of the Court to conclude: (1) that since all of the defendant directors, outside as well as inside, take a unified position, we are required to treat all of the directors as one as to whether they are entitled to the protection of the business judgment rule. * * *

Note: Commentary on Van Gorkom

Van Gorkom created a firestorm in much of the corporate community. Few had believed that the Delaware Supreme Court would hold experienced directors liable in a case in which the shareholders received a 50% premium over the existing market price for their stock, notwithstanding Justice Moore's colloquy with counsel in the final reargument. Consider the following analyses of the case.

ANDREW G.T. MOORE II, THE 1980s—DID WE SAVE THE STOCKHOLDERS WHILE THE CORPORATION BURNED?
70 Wash. Univ. L.Q. 277, 281–282 (1992).

In large part * * * *Van Gorkom* is one of the most misunderstood cases in corporate law. *Van Gorkom* was not new law. It was the application of well-established legal principles to egregious facts. It is said that the case pushed aside the business judgment rule and a court substituted its own business judgment for that of the corporation's directors. That is incorrect. *Van Gorkom* was much more a case about process in the takeover environment than anything else. The Court said to directors that the protection of the business judgment rule is not a birthright of directors but, rather, is given in return for care, loyalty, and unyielding good faith to the corporation.

There was one aspect of *Van Gorkom* that the Court found especially troublesome. Trans Union's directors were stalwart in their unified defense of what occurred. This position was taken even though it was obvious that certain directors were more culpable than others, and in the face of the Court's invitation that they take separate positions with a clear hint of exoneration for all but the most culpable insiders. Indeed, one of the directors was ill and did not even attend the meeting at which the merger was approved. In a way, they were "daring" us to find them all liable in a strategic maneuver to save certain insiders. In light of our decision finding all the directors liable, the strategic maneuver to cast down the gauntlet before the Delaware Supreme Court hardly appears to have been among the wisest decisions in the annals of corporate America.

The Trans Union case, however, was not the harbinger of director upheaval many predicted. Indeed, *Van Gorkom* provided valuable guidance to directors at a most opportune time—just before the takeover winds of the 1980s gained hurricane force. If anything, it became the beacon by which directors, faced with the inherent conflicts imposed by hostile tender offers, steered their companies through the shoals of either defensive tactics or auctions intended to maximize shareholder values. The club-like attitude in the board room gave way, without becoming unsupportive, to a searching questioning concern for the merits of corporate action.

LEO HERZEL & LEO KATZ, SMITH v. VAN GORKOM: THE BUSINESS OF JUDGING BUSINESS JUDGMENT
41 Bus. Law. 1187, 1188–1191 (1986).

To most (including the authors) the court's decision seems misguided and Trans Union's actions entirely proper. Van Gorkom was a seasoned chief executive officer and substantial stockholder. He was well placed and motivated to strike a good deal, even when acting by himself. The other directors were also experienced and sophisticated. There was no reason why they shouldn't have been able to recognize and approve a good deal at the drop of a hat. Investment bankers are expensive and surely not indispensable. When a good offer is in hand, they may well be superfluous. Merger documents are written by lawyers for lawyers, and typically no one else scrutinizes them. Admittedly, the board was a bit slapdash in its compliance with corporate formalities— did Van Gorkom really have to sign at a social affair for the opera? But that's not a breach of the duty of care.

In small part, the court's decision may rest on a simple misunderstanding of how the world works: how business decisions are made, how bargains are struck. But the court's decision rests on more than misunderstanding; it rests on widespread fallacy. Unless identified and undermined, it may in turn undermine the entire business judgment rule.

To begin with, the court failed to appreciate that courts are not very good at evaluating a director's business acumen and disciplining his or her lapses. That job is accomplished much more efficiently by the market for directors. Courts can only review a single transaction at a time. That makes it very difficult for them to tell whether the litigated misfortune is due to bad luck or bad decision making. The market, on the other hand, evaluates directors on the basis of a long record of transactions. Because over time good luck and bad luck cancel out, the long-term record is the best available indicator of a director's shortcomings. Put differently, the court has to judge a director by a single swing of the bat; the market can look at the batting average. Besides, the court can only award damages, which frequently come out of the pockets of insurance companies anyway. The market, on the other hand, can deny the incompetent director future employment.   * * *

One important effect of *Smith v. Van Gorkom* is likely to be much greater randomness and unpredictability on the part of future courts passing on future board decisions. One can't judge board performance by a single transaction, but that's what courts will be doing * * * Courts will try to do so by devising rules about how long the board should meet, what documents it should read, which outside experts it should consult. The rules are bound to be very complex and context sensitive—more randomness, more unpredictability. Finally, courts will have to decide in every case whether the matter in issue is the "product" of a board decision and hence entitled to a lot of respect, or an aspect of its decision-making procedure entitled to no respect. And who's to know how the court will draw that distinction in a given case?   * * *

The other effect of *Smith v. Van Gorkom* will be greater formalism on the part of the board, as it goes about the business of cultivating an aura of care, diligence, thoroughness, and circumspection (As one director put it: "Prudence and diligence are no longer assumed but require a certain amount of posturing.")

Such formalism has a lot of costs. Most obviously, it will mean more reliance on and more fees for lawyers, investment banker, accountants, management consultants, and economists, and who knows, maybe sociologists, statisticians, psychologists, demographers, and population geneticists. In short, experts of every stripe, whose advice might shed some light on some aspect of the board's decision. After all, every decision has untold consequences and ramifications.

DIEDRE A. BURGMAN AND PAUL N. COX. CORPORATE DIRECTORS, CORPORATE REALITIES AND DELIBERATIVE PROCESS: AN ANALYSIS OF THE TRANS UNION CASE

11 J.Corp.L. 311, 359–65 (1986).

The costs imposed by *Trans Union* are excessive only by reference to an underlying definition of unacceptable cost, just as they are justified only by reference to a competing definition of justifiable cost. The neoclassical model's extreme position, that a legal requirement compelling process expenditures imposes, per se, excessive costs, is a judgment grounded upon two underlying propositions. First, managers and directors are in the best position to assess the need for these expenditures. Second, managers and directors, by virtue of market constraints, necessarily will undertake this assessment in the best interests of shareholders. *Trans Union* recognizes these underlying propositions to a degree, because substantial director discretion remains after the decision. The case, however, effectively rejects the per se approach, implicitly because the Delaware court's judgment rests on a set of values distinct from and alien to those of the neoclassical model.

The Delaware court's values are examined best by imagining the world contemplated by a no-duty (or no enforceable duty) proposal. In such a world, no possibility of resorting to a forum for particularized review of claimed mismanagement exists. Only the device of "exit" (disposing of one's shares) is available, even in a case presenting egregious facts. Particularized review is not possible in such a world because egregious facts cannot exist; the possibility of egregious facts exists only by reference to some criterion, and the no-duty world repeals authoritative criteria. The notion that directors and managers must exercise care in the service of shareholders, even if that notion is conceived as merely a (generally unenforced) term in a standard form contract, is deprived of its status as a controlling conception of manager and director role. This result must occur because the extent to which managers or directors behave compatibly with shareholder interests becomes merely an effect, even if a probable effect, of market constraints on manager and director behavior. The adequacy or inadequacy of market constraints is not a meaningful inquiry in the no-duty world because the reference point remaining in such a world is the observed effect of market constraints on managerial behavior. Market constraints necessarily are "adequate" because in a no-duty world they define adequacy. * * *

This explanation * * * independent of the functions served by market mechanisms assumes a value premise alien to the neoclassical model. Under the model, the sole criterion for assessing a legal rule, in the absence of third party effects, is whether the rule facilitates or impedes private exchange. If shareholders would not pay or contract for a legal role definition, the definition is not worthwhile.

It is by no means indisputable that shareholders would not pay for the law's definition. However, the more fundamental argument supporting the definitional function of the duty of care is that there is a value to retaining and enforcing an authoritative definition of standards of conduct for persons who are not merely "private parties," but within the Delaware court's model of the corporation, fiduciaries acting on behalf of and for the benefit of the complex of interests that is the corporation. This value exists not merely because such a definition tends to reduce "agency costs," but because a felt need exists for an authoritative concept of the relationship that risks such costs. Perhaps the value is best understood if stated negatively, as a rejection of the notion that the board is or ought to be its own judge of the standard of conduct that will be demanded of it, even if its actual behavior is constrained by forces that tend to move it (or senior management) in desirable directions. If this value requires a label, the concession theory of corporate law, with its emphasis upon governmental consent to private economic activity, is a convenient possibility. The Delaware court's insistence upon its role as an ultimate monitor, however, can be explained without going this far. Even within a conception of the corporation that treats the law as providing a standard form contract to facilitate private exchange, there is value in both definition and insistence on compliance with that definition, even if the conclusion is drawn that the definition adopted should provide the board with wide discretion. An expectation of rational investors that provides a good candidate for a standard term in the corporate contract (apart from, but quite as plausible as, a preference for legal schemes that promise net gains from monitoring) is that managers and directors will be informed adequately and will deliberate before making their judgments. A value implicit in a contract incorporating such an expectation is the availability of a judicial forum for enforcing it.

2. RELIANCE

In *Van Gorkom*, the court rejected the directors' argument that they were protected from liability because they relied on the information that Van Gorkom presented to them. Such reliance is not unusual. Indeed, directors—in particular outside directors, who are necessarily less involved in the everyday affairs of a corporation—routinely rely on the chief executive officer and other top management for information and recommendations in connection with their decision-making. Such reliance is clearly efficient, and it is sound policy that directors should generally be entitled to rely on that information when the care with which they have acted is challenged. See Bates v. Dresser, 251 U.S. 524, 40 S.Ct. 247, 64 L.Ed. 388 (1920). There may be limits, however, on the extent to which reliance may be justified. Reports to the board may contain on their face sufficient warning of their own inadequacy to put a reasonable director on notice that better information should be demanded. And reports prepared by or under the supervision of corporate employees who have a personal interest in the outcome of the decision on which they bear may require closer than usual scrutiny. See Gallin v. National City Bank, 155 Misc. 880, 281 N.Y.S. 795 (1935) (directors liable for excess payments made pursuant to bonus plan after relying on false figures prepared under supervision of beneficiaries of plan).

Directors also frequently rely on opinions provided by attorneys, accountants, engineers, financial specialists, and other expert professional advisors. Here again the general rule is that such reliance is justified and protects directors who relied in good faith on such advice against liability if the advice turns out to be poor. In Gilbert v. Burnside, 13 A.D.2d 982, 216 N.Y.S.2d 430 (1961), aff'd 11 N.Y.2d 960, 229 N.Y.S.2d 10, 183 N.E.2d 325 (1962), a shareholder brought a derivative suit seeking reimbursement from the directors for money expended by the corporation preparatory to an acquisition that was ultimately declared illegal. Significantly, the directors had relied upon the advice of counsel that the proposed acquisition was legal. The trial court held for the plaintiff. In reversing that decision the Appellate Division said, "The judgment below determines, in effect, that these financiers (the Glen Alden directors) knew, or should have known, more Pennsylvania law than eminent Pennsylvania counsel." 13 A.D.2d at 983, 216 N.Y.S.2d at 432. The case law pertaining to reliance on counsel in duty of care cases is summarized in Douglas W. Hawes and Thomas J. Sherrard, Reliance on Advice of Counsel As Defense in Corporate and Securities Cases, 62 Va.L.R. 1, 42–49 (1976).

Reliance imposes certain duties on directors. Under RMBCA § 8.30(b), a director must make "a judgment as to the reliability and competence of the source of information upon which he proposes to rely." Official Comment to RMBCA § 8.30(b). Furthermore, "[i]nherent in the concept of good faith is the requirement that, in order to rely on a report, statement, opinion, or other matter, the director must have read the report or statement in question, or have been present at a meeting at which it was orally presented, or have taken other steps to become generally familiar with its contents." Id.

If the purpose of permitting reliance is to facilitate efficient decision-making, what does that last statement mean? Does it literally mean that a director who does not read a lengthy and highly technical report that she would not understand if she did read it cannot rely on its contents and conclusions? Or does it mean that such a report, in order to be the basis for reliance, must contain at least a summary which *is* understandable to a lay reader, even if the body of the report is not? What "other steps" might a director take?

As discussed in Chapter 15, in recent years, committees have assumed much greater significance in the operation of the board. RMBCA § 8.30 (b)(3) permits directors to rely on a committee if the director "reasonably believes the committee merits confidence." The section recognizes the difference between reliance on an expert and reliance on a committee. Thus "in Section 8.30(b)(3), the concept of 'confidence' is substituted for 'competence' in order to avoid any inference that technical skills are a prerequisite." Official Comment to Section 8.30(b). See Arthur W. Hahn and Carol B. Manzoni, The Monitoring Committee and Outside Directors' Evolving Duty of Care, 9 Loyola University L.J. 585 (1978).

3. DUE CARE AND THE BUSINESS JUDGMENT RULE

Although the business judgment rule can be stated without much difficulty, its meaning is much harder to express. One scholar defined the problem as follows:

> In the eyes of most commentators, [the statutory standard of due care] is aspirational and does not provide the test for directorial liability. Rather, the liability standard is the so-called business judgment rule, which shields even negligent directors from liability in many circumstances * * *. Other interpretations of the relationship between the duty of care and the business judgment rule are possible. Section 4.01 of the Principles of Corporate Governance

views the business judgment rule as a 'safe harbor': A director who fails to meet the standards of the business judgment rule may nevertheless avoid liability by establishing that he or she met the due care standards of good faith and the ordinary prudence of persons in a like situation. Yet a third interpretation of the relationship between the principle of due care and the business judgment rule is that the latter is simply an articulation of what the basic due care standard means. Despite these different approaches to what appears to be a fundamental issue relating to directorial liability, it appears unlikely that in practical application these formulations will bring different results.

Robert W. Hamilton, Reliance and Liability Standards for Outside Directors, 24 Wake Forest L. Rev. 5, 22–23 (1989).

BAYLESS MANNING, THE BUSINESS JUDGMENT RULE AND THE DIRECTOR'S DUTY OF ATTENTION: TIME FOR REALITY.
39 Bus.Law. 1477, 1492–1495 (1984).

The center of the analytic difficulty is this. In the general field of negligence law we are all able to talk of the "reasonable man" and of the prudent standard of performance because we have from our daily experience a clear conception of what the actor is doing and a fairly clear conception of the way in which people normally do it. We know what an automobile driver is doing; he is driving a car. We all know from general experience how one would normally do that in the circumstances—and therefore how he should do it.

The situation with regard to the directors of corporations is totally different. There is no agreed upon roster of functions of a director, analogous to driving the car. We do not have any common standard or experience as to what directors do; and what they do varies from company to company, from situation to situation, and from time to time.

Abandoning all effort to state what directors do, the present law simply announces that they must do it "carefully," like a prudent person. But, once again, we have no external measuring rod for assessing how the directors should do it (whatever "it" is). There is no common experience among courts or juries as to how "it" is normally done, and therefore should be done.

However abstract these statements may sound, the point is not abstract at all. A negligent transgression presupposes a departure from normal behavior. The whole concept of negligence and of "reasonable man" presupposes as a predicate a clear conception of *what* the person is doing, and a community understanding of a standard of normalcy about *how* he should do it. *Both those pieces are missing in the case of the work of corporate directors.*

Next, the cases that have been litigated have concerned discrete judgments by boards, and the courts' responses drawing on standard tort language have been addressed to individual discrete events. But the heart of the director's true responsibility is attention to his ongoing multiple functions: a process, a flow of events, a continuum of the company's current history. Analogies to driving automobiles just do not fit, because the law of negligence tort is aimed not at a flow of generalized performances, but at a discrete incident in which someone was hurt. To use technical language, the referent of the automobile driver's legal duty is the isolated event of the accident, not his general performance as a driver. In the case of a director, the proper referent for his legal duty should be the *flow* of his performance of his directorial functions, not the individual incident.

The analytic legal problem is still more acute. Most negligence torts are acts of commission as where the driver negligently runs over the pedestrian. The legal articulations of the business judgment rule have, on this analogy, always presupposed that the directors took a particular action; the law then addressed the question whether they had exercised due care in doing so. The traditional formulation of the business judgment rule explicitly assumes that it is available to protect the director if, but only if, some specific transactional act was taken. As has been stated here in several forms, however, in major part the life and activity of the boardroom does not consist of taking affirmative action on individual matters; it is instead a continuing flow of supervisory process, punctuated only occasionally by a discrete transactional decision. In corporate litigation tomorrow, arising out of the debris of a company that has failed, the charge that will be leveled at the directors is that they were "negligent" in the they passively stood by without taking affirmative action about this or that. If that is the charge, then by existing definitions the business judgment rule would not be available to protect the director. That would mean, astonishingly, that, given the realities of the way boards operate, the business judgment rule would not operate at all in respect of fully ninety percent of what directors are actually engaged in.

––––––––––

The relationship between the duty of care and the business judgment rule is complex; as Professor Hamilton indicates, both courts and commentators have struggled to arrive at a coherent formulation that links the two. A part of the problem is that although both the duty of care and the business judgment rule require the director to be informed, the standard for measuring a director's conduct may differ, depending on whether the court is invoking the duty of care or the business judgment rule. On the one hand, the tort-like standard applicable to the duty of care suggests that directors will be held to an ordinary negligence standard. On the other hand, as the Delaware Supreme Court stated in *Aronson*, "[U]nder the business judgment rule director liability is predicated upon concepts of gross negligence." 473 A.2d 805, 812 (Del.1984). Whether that statement also means that, under Delaware law, the standard for the duty of care outside the business judgment rule is also gross negligence is not clear.

Another part of the problem is that courts often confuse the decision-making process with the substantive outcome when determining director liability. The business judgment rule, of course, is intended to remove courts from scrutinizing the substance of specific decisions, but both the business judgment rule and the duty of care can involve judicial examination of the director's process. This confusion is what is troubling Manning in the foregoing excerpt. But, as one commentator has noted:

> [T]he argument that courts should not try to improve upon the performance of managers addresses a false issue. The issue in duty of care litigation is the process, not the merits, of decisionmaking. Courts do not make business decisions. They evaluate board procedure, a matter well within judicial competence. * * * Only two elements appear fundamental to a realistic standard of care, and these two elements alone ought to define the limits of due care. The first is an alertness to potentially significant corporate problems. The second is an obligation of deliberative decisionmaking on issues of fundamental corporate concern.

Stuart R. Cohn, Demise of the Director's Duty of Care: Judicial Avoidance of Standards and Sanctions Through the Business Judgment Rule, 62 Texas L. Rev. 591, 607, 613 (1983).

Two recent cases illustrate the difficulty which courts sometimes have in distinguishing between the duty of care and business judgment rule. In Brane v. Roth, 590 N.E.2d 587 (Ind.App.1992), the directors of a rural grain elevator cooperative authorized the co-op's manager to engage in hedging transactions for the co-op to protect against losses from changes in grain prices. The manager did not hedge sufficiently and the co-op suffered substantial losses. In a derivative suit by the stockholders against the directors, the trial court found that "the directors breached their duties by retaining a manager inexperienced in hedging; failing to maintain reasonable supervision over him; and failing to attain knowledge of the basic fundamentals of hedging to be able to direct the hedging activities and supervise the manager properly." Id. at 589–90.

The Indiana Court of Appeals affirmed the trial court's judgment for the plaintiffs. On appeal the directors argued that they should have been protected by the business judgment rule because they had relied appropriately on the manager. In rejecting this argument, the court noted that the business judgment rule does not protect directors who "failed to inform themselves of all material information reasonably available to make their decision." That conclusion, of course, is consistent with the business judgment rule: as we have seen, "judgment" implies an informed judgment.

But at this point, the court switched analytic gears, finding that the directors' "failure to provide adequate supervision of the manager's actions was a *breach of their duty of care* to protect Co-op's interests in a reasonable manner." (emphasis added). Then, returning to its earlier analysis, the court found that the business judgment rule did not shield the directors from liability. Id. at 592. Thereafter, the court rejected a gross negligence standard for the directors' conduct (which arguably would have been required in a business judgment rule case) and held, instead, that ordinary negligence (the standard under the then-existing Indiana statute) was all that was required.

The implications of *Brane* are substantial. At one level, the case can be read to require directors who are responsible for managing financial risk (not simply directors of farm co-ops) to inform themselves about techniques available to reduce that risk or face liability for their failure to do so. See "Future Shock," The Economist, March 13, 1993, p. 94; Andrew J. Kreiger, "Who's Minding the Store?", Forbes, June 21, 1993, p. 250. At a deeper level, the opinion implies that directors may lose the protection of the business judgment rule with respect to activities that are *both* part of on-going monitoring and a specific business decision if, after the decision, the directors do not exercise reasonable care in supervising the effects of the decision. Although *Brane* can be read as consistent with the ALI's formulation in § 4.01(a)(1)—the circumstances should have alerted a reasonable director to make inquiry—an equally persuasive reading is that the decision imposes a greater duty than would the ALI, which allows such inquiry "as the director * * * reasonably believes to be necessary." And, of course, unlike Mrs. Pritchard in *Francis*, the directors in *Brane* did not totally abdicate their duties as directors. Rather, in one specific area, they failed to exercise reasonable care.

Hoye v. Meek, 795 F.2d 893 (10th Cir.1986) also illustrates the difficulty that courts have in distinguishing between the duty of care and the business judgment rule. In *Hoye*, the Guaranty Trust Company, of which Meek was a director and president, suffered large losses from some of its investments. In a suit by the trustee in bankruptcy, the trial court held that Meek had breached his duty of care by failing to curb the extent of the investment and to monitor the company's investment decisions and results, and by delegating excessive authority to his son. On appeal, the Tenth Circuit rejected Meek's argument that he was entitled to the protection of the business judgment rule and stated:

> * * * We are not persuaded by appellant's argument that, because Maxwell had operated the company at a profit for seven years, the directors' and president's duty to monitor activities was dissipated. * * * [D]irectors and officers are charged with knowledge of those things which it is their duty to know and ignorance is not a basis for escaping liability. Where suspicions are aroused, or should be aroused, it is the directors' duty to make necessary inquiries. We hold that appellant failed to make the necessary inquiries. He had a

duty to keep abreast of Guaranty's investments, particularly investments that posed a double risk of decrease in market price and an increase in transactional costs.

Appellant of course would not be required to have the ability to predict increasing interest rates during the two-year period here involved. A decision made in good faith, based on sound business judgment, would not alone subject appellant to liability. * * * But in order to come within the ambit of the business judgment rule, a director must be diligent and careful in performing the duties he has undertaken. In the instant case, appellant's breach of duty resulted from both his delegation of authority to Maxwell without adequate supervision and his failure to avert Guaranty's continued exposure to increasing indebtedness. At each monthly board meeting during this two-year period, the directors could have decided to halt this increasing exposure to risk.

Assuming appellant's good faith, that alone was not sufficient to shield him from liability. It is undisputed that, as Guaranty was on the verge of filing for bankruptcy, appellant attempted to find other sources of capital for the company. This eleventh hour effort, however, was not sufficient to fulfill his duty of care as a director and president. The Oklahoma statute requires good faith *and* the diligence, care and skill of a prudent man.

795 F.2d at 896 (emphasis in original).

4. THE BUSINESS JUDGMENT RULE AND ILLEGAL CONDUCT

Although the business judgment rule will act as a shield from liability for the director who makes business decisions which he believes in good faith are in the best interests of the company, the presumption will be lost if it can be shown that the director acted fraudulently, illegally or with a conflict of interest. The latter will be treated in the next chapter. The following case shows how a court deals with directors who involve the corporation in illegal acts.

MILLER v. AMERICAN TELEPHONE & TELEGRAPH CO.
507 F.2d 759 (3d Cir.1974).

Seitz, Chief Judge.

Plaintiffs, stockholders in American Telephone and Telegraph Company ("AT & T"), brought a stockholders' derivative action in the Eastern District of Pennsylvania against AT & T and all but one of its directors. The suit centered upon the failure of AT & T to collect an outstanding debt of some $1.5 million owed to the company by the Democratic National Committee ("DNC") for communications services provided by AT & T during the 1968 Democratic national convention. Federal diversity jurisdiction was invoked under 28 U.S.C.A. § 1332.

Plaintiffs' complaint alleged that "neither the officers or directors of AT & T have taken any action to recover the amount owed" from on or about August 20, 1968, when the debt was incurred, until May 31, 1972, the date plaintiffs' amended complaint was filed. The failure to collect was alleged to have involved a breach of the defendant directors' duty to exercise diligence in handling the affairs of the corporation, to have resulted in affording a preference to the DNC in collection procedures in violation of § 202(a) of the Communications Act of 1934, 47 U.S.C.A. § 202(a) (1970), and to have amounted to AT & T's making a "contribution" to the DNC in violation of a federal prohibition on corporate campaign spending, 18 U.S.C.A. § 610 (1970).

* * *

On motion of the defendants, the district court dismissed the complaint for failure to state a claim upon which relief could be granted. 364 F.Supp. 648 (E.D.Pa.1973). The court stated that collection procedures were properly within the discretion of the directors whose determination would not be overturned by the court in the absence of an allegation that the conduct of the directors was "plainly illegal, unreasonable, or in breach of a fiduciary duty * * *." Id. at 651. Plaintiffs appeal from dismissal of their complaint.

* * *

I.

The pertinent law on the question of the defendant directors' fiduciary duties in this diversity action is that of New York, the state of AT & T's incorporation. The sound business judgment rule, the basis of the district court's dismissal of plaintiffs' complaint, expresses the unanimous decision of American courts to eschew intervention in corporate decision-making if the judgment of directors and officers is uninfluenced by personal considerations and is exercised in good faith. Pollitz v. Wabash Railroad Co., 207 N.Y. 113, 100 N.E. 721 (1912); Bayer v. Beran, 49 N.Y.S.2d 2, 4–7 (Sup.Ct.1944); 3 Fletcher, Private Corporations § 1039 (perm. ed. rev. vol. 1965). Underlying the rule is the assumption that reasonable diligence has been used in reaching the decision which the rule is invoked to justify. Casey v. Woodruff, 49 N.Y.S.2d 625, 643 (Sup.Ct.1944).

Had plaintiffs' complaint alleged only failure to pursue a corporate claim, application of the sound business judgment rule would support the district court's ruling that a shareholder could not attack the directors' decision. Where, however, the decision not to collect a debt owed the corporation is itself alleged to have been an illegal act, different rules apply. When New York law regarding such acts by directors is considered in conjunction with the underlying purposes of the particular statute involved here, we are convinced that the business judgment rule cannot insulate the defendant directors from liability if they did in fact breach 18 U.S.C.A. § 610, as plaintiffs have charged.

Roth v. Robertson, 64 Misc. 343, 118 N.Y.S. 351 (Sup.Ct.1909), illustrates the proposition that even though committed to benefit the corporation, illegal acts may amount to a breach of fiduciary duty in New York. In *Roth,* the managing director of an amusement park company had allegedly used corporate funds to purchase the silence of persons who threatened to complain about unlawful Sunday operation of the park. Recovery from the defendant director was sustained on the ground that the money was an illegal payment:

> For reasons of public policy, we are clearly of the opinion that payments of corporate funds for such purposes as those disclosed in this case must be condemned, and officers of a corporation making them held to a strict accountability, and be compelled to refund the amounts so wasted for the benefit of stockholders.   * * * To hold any other rule would be establishing a dangerous precedent, tacitly countenancing the wasting of corporate funds for purposes of corrupting public morals. Id. at 346, 118 N.Y.S. at 353.

The plaintiffs' complaint in the instant case alleges a similar "waste" of $1.5 million through an illegal campaign contribution.

Abrams v. Allen, 297 N.Y. 52, 74 N.E.2d 305 (1947), reflects an affirmation by the New York Court of Appeals of the principle of *Roth* that directors must be restrained from engaging in activities which are against public policy. In *Abrams* the court held that a cause of action was stated by an allegation in a derivative complaint that the directors of Remington Rand, Inc., had relocated corporate plants and curtailed production solely for the purpose of intimidating and punishing employees for their involvement in a labor dispute. The Court of Appeals acknowledged that, "depending on the circumstances," proof of the allegations in the complaint might sustain recovery, *inter alia,* under the rule that directors are liable for corporate loss caused by the commission of an "unlawful or immoral act." Id. at 55, 74 N.E.2d at 306. In support of its holding, the court noted that the closing of factories for the purpose alleged was opposed to the public policy of the state and nation as embodied in the New York Labor Law and the National Labor Relations Act. Id. at 56, 74 N.E.2d at 307.

The alleged violation of the federal prohibition against corporate political contributions not only involves the corporation in criminal activity but similarly contravenes a policy of Congress clearly enunciated in 18 U.S.C.A. § 610. That statute and its predecessor reflect congressional efforts: (1) to destroy the influence of corporations over elections through financial contributions and (2) to check the practice of using corporate funds to benefit political parties without the consent of the stockholders. United States v. CIO, 335 U.S. 106, 113, 68 S.Ct. 1349, 92 L.Ed. 1849 (1948).

The fact that shareholders are within the class for whose protection the statute was enacted gives force to the argument that the alleged breach of that statute should give rise to a cause of action in those shareholders to force the return to the corporation of illegally contributed funds. Since political contributions by corporations can be checked and shareholder control over the political use of general corporate funds effectuated only if directors are restrained from causing the corporation to violate the statute, such a violation seems a particularly appropriate basis for finding breach of the defendant directors' fiduciary duty to the corporation. Under such circumstances, the directors cannot be insulated from liability on the ground that the contribution was made in the exercise of sound business judgment.

Since plaintiffs have alleged actual damage to the corporation from the transaction in the form of the loss of a $1.5 million increment to AT & T's treasury, we conclude that the complaint does state a claim upon which relief can be granted sufficient to withstand a motion to dismiss.

II.

We have accepted plaintiffs' allegation of a violation of 18 U.S.C.A. § 610 as a shorthand designation of the elements necessary to establish a breach of that statute. This is consonant with the federal practice of notice pleading. That such a designation is sufficient for pleading purposes does not, however, relieve plaintiffs of their ultimate obligation to prove the elements of the statutory violation as part of their proof of breach of fiduciary duty. At the appropriate time, plaintiffs will be required to produce evidence sufficient to establish three distinct elements comprising a violation of 18 U.S.C.A. § 610: that AT & T (1) made a contribution of money or anything of value to the DNC (2) in connection with a federal election (3) for the purpose of influencing the outcome of that election. The first two of these elements are obvious from the face of the statute; the third was supplied by legislative history prior to being made explicit by 1972 amendments to definitions applicable to § 610.

* * *

The order of the district court will be reversed and the case remanded for further proceedings consistent with this opinion.

5. CAUSATION

Claims that directors failed to exercise reasonable care or that directors' decisions are not protected by the business judgment rule generally fall into one of two categories. In nonfeasance cases, such as *Francis* and *Graham,* the plaintiff's charge is that if directors had carried out their responsibilities with more diligence, they would have prevented some series of events that caused the corporation a loss. In transactional cases, such as *Van Gorkom,* the plaintiff's charge is that if the directors had not approved of some specific, identifiable transaction, a loss that the corporation or its shareholders incurred as a consequence of that transaction would have been avoided.

It would seem to follow that an essential element of plaintiffs' case, in both nonfeasance and transactional situations, is proof that the defendant directors' negligence, and not some other factor, caused the loss in question. Moreover, in *Francis, Van Gorkom,* and numerous other cases, courts have held that plaintiffs who establish that directors breached their duty of care also must prove that the directors' breach was the proximate cause of their loss.

This principle traces to Judge Learned Hand's decision in Barnes v. Andrews, 298 Fed. 614 (S.D.N.Y.1924). There Judge Hand found that Andrews, a director of a corporation that had become bankrupt, had been inexcusably inattentive in carrying out his directorial responsibilities. Nonetheless, Judge Hand declined to hold Andrews liable because plaintiff had not proven that Andrews' negligence had caused the corporation to fail:

> * * * This cause of action rests upon a tort, as much though it be a tort of omission as though it had rested upon a positive act. The plaintiff must accept the burden of showing that the performance of the defendant's duties would have avoided loss, and what loss it would have avoided. * * *

> When the corporate funds have been illegally lent, it is a fair inference that a protest would have stopped the loan, and that the director's neglect caused the loss, but when a business fails from general mismanagement, business incapacity, or bad judgment, how is it possible to say that a single director could have made the company successful, or how much in dollars he could have saved? Before this cause can go to a master, the plaintiff must show that, had Andrews done his full duty, he could have made the company prosper, or at least could have broken its fall. He must show what sum he could have saved the company. Neither of these has he made any effort to do.

> The defendant is not subject to the burden of proving that the loss would have happened, whether he had done his duty or not. If he were, it would come to this: That, if a director were once shown slack in his duties, he would stand charged prima facie with the difference between the corporate treasury as it was, and as it would be, judged by a hypothetical standard of success. How could such a standard be determined? How could any one guess how far a director's skill and judgment would have prevailed upon his fellows, and what would have been the ultimate fate of the business, if they had? How is it possible to set any measure of liability, or to tell what he would have contributed to the event? Men's fortunes may not be subjected to such uncertain and speculative conjectures. It is hard to see how there can be any remedy, except one can put one's finger on a definite loss and say with reasonable assurance that protest would have deterred, or counsel persuaded, the managers who caused it. No men of sense would take the office, if the law imposed upon them a guaranty of the general success of their companies as a penalty for any negligence.

298 Fed. at 616–617.

As is evidenced by *Barnes,* requiring proof that a director caused a given loss reduces considerably the likelihood that inattentive directors will be held liable in cases of general business failure. Even with the benefit of 20/20 hindsight, plaintiffs often will find it difficult to prove that had the directors been more diligent, the business would have flourished. However, as *Francis* demonstrates, that burden is not insurmountable. The court there defined Mrs. Pritchard's duties in a fashion that allowed it to conclude her failure to perform was in fact the proximate cause of the corporation's losses:

> In this case, the scope of Mrs. Pritchard's duties was deter-mined by the precarious financial condition of Pritchard & Baird, its fiduciary relationship to its clients and the implied trust in which it held their funds. Thus viewed, the scope of her duties encompassed all reasonable action to stop the continuing conversion. Her duties extended beyond mere objection and resignation to reasonable at-tempts to prevent the misappropriation of the trust funds. * * *

> Within Pritchard & Baird, several factors contributed to the loss of the funds: commingling of corporate and client monies, conver-sion of funds by Charles, Jr. and William and dereliction of her duties by Mrs. Pritchard. The wrongdoing of her sons, although the immediate cause of the loss, should not excuse Mrs. Pritchard from her negligence which also was a substantial factor contributing to the loss. Her sons knew that she, the only other director, was not reviewing their conduct; they spawned their fraud in the backwater of her neglect. Her neglect of duty contributed to the climate of corruption; her failure to act contributed to the continuation of that corruption. Consequently, her conduct was a substantial factor contributing to the loss.

> Analysis of proximate cause is especially difficult in a corporate context where the allegation is that nonfeasance of a director is a proximate cause of damage to a third party. * * * Nonetheless, where it is reasonable to conclude that the failure to act would produce a particular result and that result has followed, causation may be inferred. We conclude that even if Mrs. Pritchard's mere objection had not stopped the depredations of her sons, her consulta-tion with an attorney and the threat of suit would have deterred them. That conclusion flows as a matter of common sense and logic from the record. Whether in other situations a director has a duty to do more than protest and resign is best left to case-by-case determinations. In this case, we are satisfied that there was a duty to do more than object and resign. Consequently, we find that Mrs. Pritchard's negligence was a proximate cause of the misappropria-tions.

> To conclude, by virtue of her office, Mrs. Pritchard had the power to prevent the losses sustained by the clients of Pritchard & Baird. With power comes responsibility. She had a duty to deter

the depredation of the other insiders, her sons. She breached that duty and caused plaintiffs to sustain damages.

432 A.2d at 827–829.

Nonetheless, proof that directors' breach of their duty of care caused a given loss is much easier in a transactional setting. Where directors have been shown to have wrongfully approved some given transaction, a plaintiff usually can plausibly contend that had the directors been more diligent, the transaction would not have occurred and the resulting loss would have been avoided. In *Van Gorkom,* for example, plaintiffs established that Trans Union's directors had been grossly negligent in agreeing to sell the company for $55 per share. That, however, did not necessarily mean the directors were liable. Indeed, the Delaware Supreme Court remanded the case with instructions that the Court of Chancery "conduct an evidentiary hearing to determine the fair value of [Trans Union's stock as of the date of the board's decision]. * * * Thereafter, an award of damages *may be entered* to the extent that the fair value of Trans Union exceeds $55 per share." 488 A.2d at 893 (emphasis added). The clear implication of the court's instruction, consistent with *Barnes'* causation requirement, was that if the Court of Chancery determined Trans Union had been worth less than $55 per share, no damages should be awarded. Because the case was settled, the question was never decided.

Cede & Co. v. Technicolor, Inc., 634 A.2d 345 (Del.1993), involved similar issues. A former shareholder claimed that Technicolor's directors had negligently agreed to sell the company at the inadequate price of $23 per share. After a trial on the merits, the Chancellor, relying on *Barnes,* dismissed the shareholder's claim on the ground that even if the directors had been negligent, the shareholder had suffered no loss because Technicolor's fair value at the time it was sold was only $21.60 per share.

The Delaware Supreme Court reversed. Reviewing the Chancellor's factual findings, the court found that Technicolor's directors had improperly approved the sale because they had failed to inform themselves "of all material information that [was] reasonably available to them." Id. at 367. The court then characterized the Chancellor's reliance on *Barnes* as "misguided," reasoning that "*Barnes,* a tort action, does not control a claim for breach of fiduciary duty." Id. at 371. Continuing, the court held that: "A breach of either the duty of loyalty or the duty of care rebuts the presumption that the directors have acted in the best interests of the shareholders, and requires the directors to prove that the transaction was entirely fair." *Id.*

Turning to the question of appropriate relief, the court

emphasize[d] that the measure of any recoverable loss by [the plaintiff shareholder] under an entire fairness standard of review is not necessarily limited to the difference between the price offered and the "true" value as determined under appraisal proceedings. * * * The Chancellor may incorporate elements of rescissory damages into his determination of fair price, if he considers such elements: (1) susceptible to proof; and (2) appropriate under the circumstances.

Id. at 371. The latter holding was potentially quite significant, in the context of the Technicolor litigation, because the company that had purchased Technicolor resold it a short time later at a much higher price. The import of *Technicolor* in situations where similar facts are not present is less clear. Of possible relevance is In re Tri–Star Pictures, Inc. Litigation, 634 A.2d 319 (Del.1993), handed down a month after *Technicolor*. There the court cites with apparent favor cases in which breaches of fiduciary duty have been found and relatively nominal damages have been awarded, absent evidence of loss based on stock values, "because equity will not suffer a wrong without a remedy." Id. at 333.

For the more traditional view of the need to prove causation in an action for breach of fiduciary duty, see F.D.I.C. v. Bierman, 2 F.3d 1424, 1434 (7th Cir.1993) ("It is well established that a director will not be liable for losses to the corporation absent a showing that his act or omission proximately caused the subsequent losses").

D. LIMITATION OF DIRECTORS' LIABILITY

PROBLEM
FASHION, INC.—PART III

Two years have passed since the events in Part II. At the board meeting to approve the merger with United, Wendy Andrews, one of the outside directors, raised a number of questions about United and complained that, notwithstanding the reports at the meeting, she had not had sufficient time to study the transaction. The final vote on the merger was 10 in favor and none against. Andrews abstained and Donald Coleman, another outside director, was absent. Thereafter, the merger received shareholder approval.

Subsequent events have proved disastrous to Fashion. The acquisition necessitated additional capital of $750 million, adversely affecting Fashion's financial position and causing it to incur substantial losses. In the past two years, the price of Fashion's stock has declined more than 50%. Last year, a shareholder of Fashion brought a derivative suit against the entire Fashion board, alleging gross negligence in connection with the merger.

1. After the complaint was filed, the defendants requested the corporation to advance $100,000 to them in order to pay a retainer to their counsel in the lawsuit. May the board authorize this payment? If not, what procedures must the defendants follow to obtain the advance? Must any conditions be imposed on this payment?

2. In the course of the litigation, defendants incurred expenses of $1,000,000, consisting of legal, accounting and experts' fees, court costs, and other administrative costs. Assume that the case was settled with the directors agreeing to pay $15 million to the corporation. Of that amount, $10 million was to be paid under Fashion's D & O liability policy. Thereafter, defendants requested the corporation to indemnify them for all their expenses.

(a) May the corporation make the requested payment?

(b) What procedures must be followed?

(c) Are there any limits on the payment?

(d) If the corporation refuses to indemnify, do the defendants have any other means to recover their expenses?

1. INTRODUCTION

In the 1980s, for reasons that will be discussed later, corporate directors' fear of liability increased dramatically. Indeed, some outside directors withdrew from board membership altogether or declined to stand for re-election. To allay these fears, many states enacted legislation to reduce the risk of directors' personal liability for monetary damages. The statutory responses took three different forms: the adoption of a charter provision eliminating or reducing the personal liability of directors for monetary damages, primarily in due care cases; a change in the standard of liability to require a higher degree of fault than ordinary negligence; and a limit on the monetary amount for which a director could be held personally liable.

These statutes are designed to shield officers and directors of large, publicly-held corporations from the wide variety of potential liabilities and expenses that they face. Corporate executives may be actual or potential defendants in derivative suits or direct actions by shareholders, or in civil actions brought by third parties. They may also be the subject of civil actions, criminal actions or administrative proceedings instituted by the government. They are occasionally required to pay substantial damages, penalties or fines, and, more frequently, must incur large expenses for legal counsel in the defense of actual or threatened actions.

In addition to statutory exculpation provisions, most directors and officers are protected against some of those costs by indemnification and insurance. These are contractual arrangements between directors and corporations that shift all or a part of the risk of liability for wrongdoing from the individual to the corporate entity. The fear of being subject to personal liability is a real barrier to corporations' ability to attract and retain competent executives. This fear especially affects less wealthy officers and directors. Until recently, corporate law itself gave added protection to executives in the performance of their duties through application of the business judgment rule, which acted as an almost impenetrable shield. In recent years, however, that shield has shown signs of erosion. As *Van Gorkom* illustrates, the amount of potential damages can be very great.

Some critics recognize the need to reduce the risks and costs of frivolous litigation but argue that the risk shifting created by indemnification and insurance reduces management's incentive to act responsibly and thus impedes an effective system of management accountability. See Joseph W. Bishop, Sitting Ducks and Decoy Ducks: New Trends in the Indemnification of Corporate Directors and Officers, 77 Yale L.J. 1078 (1968).

Other scholars defend the efficiency of the existing system. Professor Reinier Kraakman argues that while it would appear that imposing personal liability would lead to the maximum control over organizational conduct, risk shifting is generally a more efficient way of achieving the desired behavior. He notes that stockholders are efficient risk-bearers because of their ability to diversify their investments. By contrast, corporate managers are undiversified risk bearers who are not able to work for more than one firm at a time. Hence, unless they are paid to do otherwise, they will tend to evaluate business decisions with a risk-averse bias that may be detrimental to the best interests of the stockholders. Reinier Kraakman, Corporate Liability Strategies and the Cost of Legal Controls, 93 Yale L.J. 857 (1984).

Kraakman contends that the inefficiency of managers as risk-bearers extends to their inability to bear the inevitable legal risks which any business must face, no matter how well it is managed. If personal liability attaches to those risks, then "competent corporate decisionmakers will either demand insulation from them or require compensation for bearing them." Id. at 865. He concludes that because enterprise liability works with little personal risk to the managers, it should be the norm, with managerial liability being imposed only when enterprise liability is likely to fail.

2. STATUTORY EXCULPATION OF DIRECTORS

DGCL § 102(b)(7) and RMBCA § 2.02(b)(4) exemplify statutes that permit a charter provision to reduce directors' personal liability for violations of the duty of due care. These sections are not self-executing; they require the stockholders affirmatively to adopt any exculpatory provision in the articles of incorporation. The Delaware statute limits exculpation by excluding from its coverage a breach of the director's duty of loyalty to the corporation or its shareholders, acts or omissions not in good faith, intentional misconduct, knowing violations of law, and transactions in which the director has obtained an improper personal benefit, such as from insider trading.

Similarly, the RMBCA excludes from its coverage liability for improperly received financial benefits, intentional infliction of harm on the corporation or the shareholders, and intentional violations of criminal law. In addition, RMBCA § 2.02(b)(4) does not exculpate a director for making unlawful distributions. Both statutes apply only to liability for monetary damages and have no effect on the availability of equitable relief for a breach of fiduciary duty. Like DGCL § 102(b)(7), RMBCA § 2.02(b)(4) requires shareholder approval of exculpatory provisions. Unlike Delaware, however, the RMBCA contains no exceptions for the duty of loyalty or for "acts or omissions not in good faith." In rejecting these exclusions, the ABA Committee on Corporate Laws noted that the phrase "duty of loyalty" appeared nowhere else in the Delaware statute and that the "acts or omissions" standard was potentially too vague. See Committee on Corporate Laws, Changes in the Revised Model Business Corporation Act—Amendment Pertaining to the Liability of Directors, 45 Bus. Law. 695, 697 (1990).

Over two-thirds of state corporate laws now allow some form of charter provision to limit director liability. The exceptions provided by other states that differ from those allowed by DGCL § 102(b)(7) and RMBCA § 2.02(b)(4) include actions that create liability to a third party and improper appropriations of business opportunities of the corporation. At least eleven states have followed RMBCA § 2.02(b)(4) in omitting a "duty of loyalty" exception.

A few states have changed statutorily the standard of conduct giving rise to personal liability. For example, under Indiana law, a director who has breached or failed to perform her duties in accordance with the statutory standard of care will not be liable for the breach or failure unless it constituted "willful misconduct or recklessness." Ind.Code Ann. § 23–1–35(1)(e)(2). This limitation applies to actions for equitable relief as well as damages, and includes suits by both third parties and stockholders. Unlike the charter option provisions, these statutes are self-executing. They do not require shareholder approval to become effective nor do they permit the corporation to opt out of the liability limitation provisions, even if the stockholders wish to do so.

Virginia is the only state whose statute allows a limit to be placed on the amount of damages for which a director or officer can be held liable. Except where the director or officer has engaged in willful misconduct or a knowing violation of criminal law or federal or state securities law, Va.Code Ann. § 13.1–692.1 limits personal liability to the amount that is the lesser of: 1) the monetary limit specified in the corporation's articles of incorporation or, if approved by the shareholders, the by-laws; or 2) the greater of $100,000 or the compensation received from the corporation during the preceding twelve months. Like the statutes that change the standard of conduct, the Virginia provision does not require shareholder approval to become effective. Thus, absent a contrary provision in the articles of incorporation or by-laws, the liability of a director or officer will be limited to the greater of $100,000 or her cash compensation for the past year. In the decision on the remand of Sandberg v. Virginia Bankshares, Inc. (discussed in Chapter 18), 979 F.2d 332 (4th Cir.1992), the Court of Appeals concluded that a jury's finding that directors had acted in conscious disregard of whether a proxy statement contained material misrepresentations was sufficient to satisfy the "knowing violation" provision of the Virginia statute. Accordingly, the court held that the liability cap was inapplicable. Id. at 343.

The Virginia statute has the seeming virtue of certainty; directors will know *ex ante* the maximum extent of their liability for a breach of the duty of due care. At the same time, as one commentator has pointed out, perhaps the reason why no other state has adopted such a cap is that "no specific dollar limit can ever be appropriate for the thousands of corporations typically chartered under the law of any state. While $100,000 may be the right limit for some corporations, it will be too high or too low for others." James J. Hanks, Jr., Evaluating Recent State Legislation on Director and Officer Liability Limitation and Indemnification, 43 Bus. Law. 1207, 1236 (1988).

The ALI takes a still different and quite unique approach. Its goal is to adopt "a concept of mitigation of disproportionate liability, not abrogation of the duty of care." Thus the ALI goes beyond the existing statutory scheme to recommend that, even absent an enabling statute, courts uphold a corporate charter provision limiting directors' and officers' liability for certain breaches of their duty of care. ALI Principles of Corporate Governance, (1994) § 7.19. The ALI does not permit complete exculpation of directors; the corporation can never reduce the amount for which directors can be held liable to less than the director's annual compensation. If damages are less than the compensation, the director is responsible for the full amount. If damages exceed the director's annual salary, the director is liable for an amount at least equal to the compensation. The board retains the right to set the exculpation level at any amount higher than the director's annual salary. The ALI explicitly rejects exculpation for breaches of directors' duty of loyalty, partly because investors would not be able to estimate the cost to them of such a provision.

The ALI explains that:

> The rationale for such a limitation rests on a variety of considerations, of which five stand out: First and most fundamentally, it is justified on grounds of fairness, because the potential liability in cases where it applies would otherwise be excessive in relation to the nature of the defendant's culpability and the economic benefits expected from serving the corporation. Second, such a limitation should reduce the pressures on directors to act in an unduly risk-averse manner. Realistically, the risk of liability for due care violations tends to be one-sided: directors can be held liable for excessively risky acts or decisions, but not, as practical matter, for excessively cautious ones. Given the frequently nominal investment of directors in their corporation's stock, a substantial risk of liability for negligence might lead risk-averse directors to opt for more hesitant policies than shareholders desire (particularly to the extent that shareholders hold reasonably diversified portfolios and so are substantially protected against any firm-specific risk). Third, it is likely that the duty of care will be implemented by courts more

evenly and appropriately when the potential penalties that may result are not perceived as Draconian. Fourth, such a limitation may serve to reduce the cost of insurance (often borne by the corporation) because the likely exposure of the insurer is reduced. Although the threat of derivative litigation is only one of the determinants of the cost of D & O insurance, a limitation on due care liability at least contributes to cost reduction and also protects defendants from the danger that their insurance coverage may be inadequate or that an exception to their coverage may be applicable to this case.

Finally, a limitation on liability also reduces the economic incentives for the plaintiff's attorney to sue, at least in those circumstances where the ceiling would be applicable, because under § 7.17 a plaintiff's attorney's fees are limited to a reasonable percentage of the total recovery.

Id. Comment *c*.

Perhaps the most extreme position is that of Professor Kenneth Scott who has argued that "very little of any value would be lost by outright abolition of the legal duty of care and its accompanying threat of a lawsuit." He contends that "[O]ther pressures and incentives bear on management's performance—competition in the product and capital markets, the managerial labor market, and executive incentive compensation arrangements. And, even without any threat of negligence liability, the board members, to protect their own reputation as directors, managers, or professionals and to maximize the value of their own stock holdings or those they represent, have reason to monitor and, if necessary, oust top management." Furthermore, "[t]he objective of promoting careful decisions by the board is also not much enhanced by the duty of care action. * * * If subsequently-determined personal liability ever became a significant factor, the board members would be biased towards taking fewer business risks and following more costly and time-consuming decisionmaking procedures. It is most doubtful whether that would be in the best interest of shareholders." Kenneth E. Scott, Corporation Law and the American Law Institute Corporate Governance Project, 35 Stan.L.Rev. 927, 935–37 (1983).

Any attempt to exculpate directors from liability raises serious public policy questions. Should there ever be a limit on a director's liability for a breach of the duty of due care? If so, is not the issue so fundamental that shareholders should always decide whether, and to what extent, to exculpate directors? However, in a large, publicly-held corporation, where the role of the shareholder is likely to be limited to approving management's proposals as set forth in the proxy material, can a shareholder vote on this question ever be meaningful?

JAMES J. HANKS, JR., EVALUATING RECENT STATE LEGISLATION ON DIRECTOR AND OFFICER LIABILITY LIMITATION AND INDEMNIFICATION
43 Bus. Law. 1207, 1231–1236 (1988).

The principal public policy issue in director and officer liability legislation is the allocation of the economic cost of the directors' exculpated conduct. * * *

Charter option statutes simply permit the stockholders to decide for themselves whether to assume this risk or to leave it with the directors. By contrast, the other director liability statutes enacted to date are direct or indirect determinations by the legislatures to shift the risk from the directors to the stockholders. Self-executing statutes are a direct legislative determination that this risk should be borne by the stockholders. * * *

In considering this type of legislation from a policy viewpoint, it is not only appropriate but necessary to consider the role of the director in corporate governance and in the larger society. Supporters of legislatively shifting the costs of directors' misconduct from the directors to the stockholders argue that the role of directors is different from that of other purveyors of personal services. * * * Directors * * * act for the owners, [and] they make the decisions that the owners would otherwise have to make. Unless they engage in conduct in which no reasonable owner would be likely to engaged, directors should not expect to be monetarily liable. * * * Except for * * * egregious situations, it is difficult to justify imposing monetary liability on a director for the result of his decisions.

Nothing in the history of the development of corporations or corporation law suggests that the personal assets of directors were intended to constitute a financial safety net for stockholders or others willing to second-guess directors' decisions. In any event, the damage claims in stockholder derivative suits against directors and officers typically far exceed the aggregate net worth of the individual defendants. As a practical matter, dollar-for-dollar recovery by the corporation from its directors of officers for their wrongful conduct is (and probably always has been) a myth. In addition, this type of exposure for directors and officers may be viewed as inconsistent with the principle of limited liability for investors that has been the foundation of corporation law and finance for generations. * * *

In the end, sounder policy reasons permit the stockholders to decide whether to limit the liability of their directors, at least as to suits by the corporation or the stockholders. After all, it is the stockholders' money at stake. As long as the right of the stockholders to exculpate their directors is limited to liability to the corporation or to the stockholders themselves (in either derivative or direct suits), the state's regulatory interests should be minimal.

3. INDEMNIFICATION

The right of a corporate officer or director to be indemnified and the power of the corporation to indemnify her voluntarily against damages, fines, or penalties growing out of the performance of corporate duties are governed by both corporate statutes and the articles of incorporation, by-laws or private contracts of the corporation.

The common law concerning the *right* of a corporate officer or director to indemnification was long confused. Little precedent guided corporations as to the limitations on their *power* to indemnify directors and officers. Dissatisfaction with the judicial handling of indemnification eventually led New York to enact the first indemnification statute in 1941. Today every jurisdiction has adopted legislation dealing with the matter, and most have enacted comprehensive indemnification statutes.

Indemnification provisions are of two types, permissive and mandatory; comprehensive statutes include both. A permissive, or enabling, provision gives a corporation the power to indemnify its corporate managers under certain circumstances. Mandatory statutes accord a director or officer who meets the statutory standards a right to indemnification.

E. NORMAN VEASEY, JESSE A. FINKELSTEIN & C. STEPHEN BIGLER, DELAWARE SUPPORTS DIRECTORS WITH A THREE-LEGGED STOOL OF LIMITED LIABILITY, INDEMNIFICATION AND INSURANCE
42 Bus.Law 401, 404–412 (1987).

Section 145 of the Delaware General Corporation Law is the statutory authority for indemnification. It combines specific statutory rights and limitations on indemnification. It applies to any person involved (as a plaintiff or defendant) in actual or threatened litigation or an investigation by reason of the status of such person as an officer, director, employee, or agent of the corporation or of another corporation, trust, partnership, joint venture, or other enterprise he served at the request of the indemnifying corporation.

* * *

The general statutory framework of the entitlement to ultimate indemnification is found in subsections (a) and (b) of section 145. Section 145(a) permits indemnification of officers, directors, employees, and agents for attorneys' fees and other expenses as well as judgments or amounts paid in settlement in civil cases. This subsection applies only to third-party actions, not to actions brought by or in the right of the corporation. The person seeking indemnification must have acted in good faith and in a manner he reasonably believed to be in or not opposed to the best interests of the corporation in respect of the claim made against him. In criminal cases the indemnitee may be indemnified for fines and costs provided that, in addition to the foregoing standard of conduct, he did not have reasonable cause to believe his conduct was unlawful.

Section 145(b) pertains to actions brought by or in the right of the corporation. Most frequently, of course, it applies to derivative suits. This subsection permits indemnification only for attorneys' fees and other expenses. It does not permit indemnification of judgments or amounts paid in settlement. The principal difference between section 145(a) and section 145(b), aside from the fact that the latter permits indemnification only for expenses and attorneys' fees, is that section 145(b) does not permit any indemnification "in respect of any claim, issue or matter as to which such person shall have been adjudged to be liable to the corporation," although it does permit some limited court relief "to the extent that the Court of Chancery or the court in which such action or suit was brought shall determine upon application that, despite the adjudication of liability but in view of all the circumstances of the case, such person is fairly and reasonably entitled to indemnity for such expenses [as the] court shall deem proper." There are no definitive criteria in the statute or the case law articulating the showing that must be made to satisfy the court that indemnification is proper.

* * * [Under section 145(b)] it seems that indemnification may not be made (absent court relief provided in the statute) if the director has been adjudged liable to the corporation on any recognized basis of personal liability such as self-dealing, statutory violations, or gross negligence. This provision must be harmonized with the contemporaneously adopted section 102(b)(7) authorizing the limitation on or elimination of liability of directors in certain cases.

It is important to keep in mind the distinctions between indemnification in respect of third-party actions and that applicable to derivative actions. Section 145(b) permits indemnification only of expenses in derivative suits and does not authorize indemnification of judgments or amounts paid in settlement in derivative suits. On the other hand, such broader indemnification power is expressly authorized for third-party actions by section 145(a). It can be argued that since section 145(b) does not expressly prohibit indemnification of judgments or amounts paid in settlement in derivative suits, such indemnification may be provided under the "nonexclusive" provision of section 145(f). It would seem that since subsections (a) and (b) should be read in *pari materia,* the express inclusion of the broader indemnification power in (a) and its exclusion in (b) demonstrates a legislative intent to prohibit indemnification of judgments or amounts paid in settlement in derivative suits. The policy behind this distinction is based on the fact that in a derivative action the ultimate plaintiff is the corporation on whose behalf the suit is brought. Consequently, any resulting money judgment against, or settlement funds provided by, the defendant is paid to the corporation in order to make it whole. The corporation would not receive that benefit if it were to reimburse a defendant for the amount of the judgment or settlement funds that the defendant is required to pay the corporation.

As mentioned above, section 145(a) authorizes indemnification for various classes of indemnitees in third-party actions, while section 145(b) does so for actions brought by or in the right of the corporation. Although the scope of the permitted indemnification differs, these statutes are permissive. Implementation of the authority granted requires action by the corporation. Indemnification may, therefore, be denied unless it is made mandatory by statute or otherwise.

Mandatory indemnification by statute is provided in section 145(c). * * *

The phrase found in section 145(c), "on the merits or otherwise," permits the indemnitee to be indemnified as a matter of right in the event he wins a judgment on the merits in his favor or if he successfully asserts a "technical" defense, such as a defense based upon a statute of limitations. The same statutory language contemplates the dismissal of the suit in conjunction with a negotiated settlement where the dismissal is with prejudice and without any payment or assumption of liability. A dismissal without prejudice, however, is insufficient to invoke mandatory indemnification under the statute.

Until 1984, the indemnification provisions of the Model Business Corporation Act (now the RMBCA) were "substantially identical" to those of Delaware because the drafting committees for the two statutes worked together to produce a joint document. See John F. Olson and Josiah O. Hatch III, Director and Officer Liability: Indemnification and Insurance § 4.09 (1992). Unhappiness with certain features of the indemnification statutes and the construction given them by Delaware courts in particular led the drafters of the Model Act to amend it in 1980. The differences between the two statutes are reflected in the current RMBCA which is generally more conservative than Delaware in the extent to which indemnification is available.

RMBCA § 8.58(a) is an exclusive statute in that it allows indemnification only to the extent prescribed by the statute. Corporations can narrow, but not expand, the types of indemnification permitted by the statute. Private indemnification agreements are valid only if they are consistent with the statute. In contrast to the RMBCA, Delaware is non-exclusive and allows indemnification to be broadened by charter, by-law or contract. See DGCL § 145(f).

Both statutes establish similar standards of conduct that directors must meet to be allowed indemnification. RMBCA § 8.51 requires that the person acted in good faith; that her conduct, if done in her official capacity, was in the best interests of the corporation, and any other conduct was "at least not opposed to its best interest"; and, if the proceeding was criminal, that there was no reasonable cause to believe that the conduct was unlawful. DGCL § 145(a) permits indemnification if the defendant acted in good faith and in a manner "reasonably believed to be in or not opposed to the best interests of the corporation." If the action is criminal, the Delaware standard is the same as the RMBCA.

Both the RMBCA and DGCL require the defendant to be successful "on the merits or otherwise". For indemnification to be required under the RMBCA, however, success must be "*wholly* on the merits or otherwise*," meaning that the defendant must be found not liable on all counts. This requirement was a reaction against the decision in Merritt–Chapman & Scott Corp. v. Wolfson, 321 A.2d 138 (Del.Super.1974), in which the court required partial indemnification of defendants who had been successful on several, but not all, of the criminal counts against them. See Official Comment to RMBCA § 8.52.

RMBCA § 8.53 allows expenses to be advanced to defendants unless it is obvious that § 8.51 would preclude indemnification. DGCL § 145(e) also allows advances for expenses but does not limit the board's authority to make the advances. Both statutes require an "undertaking" by the defendant to repay any advances made if the indemnitee is found ultimately not entitled to indemnification. However, RMBCA § 8.53(a)(1), unlike DGCL § 145(e), also requires that the director furnish a written statement of a "good faith belief" that the director has met the standard of conduct set forth in RMBCA § 8.51.

Note: Interpreting Indemnification Statutes

Every indemnification statute raises a number of interpretive questions, including:

(1) Who is covered by the statute?

(2) What kind of actions are covered?

(3) What types of expenses can be indemnified?

(4) To what standard of conduct is an indemnitee to be held before being indemnified, and who should determine whether the appropriate standard of conduct has been met?

(5) Should indemnification payments be required to be disclosed to shareholders?

Curiously, there is little case law addressing these questions.

1. *Persons Covered.* The question of who is covered is not as simple as might first appear. Present officers and directors certainly are covered. How about former officers and directors who are sued because of their conduct when they held their positions? Officers and directors of a subsidiary? Does it matter if the subsidiary is wholly or partially owned? After the heyday of mergers, what about predecessor corporations? In addition to officers and directors, are other employees and agents covered by the statute?

In People v. Uran Mining Corp., 13 A.D.2d 419, 216 N.Y.S.2d 985 (1961), the court held that a director was not entitled to reimbursement for his expenses in defending an injunction action brought by the state in connection with the fraudulent sale of securities. The court examined the extent of the director's participation in the sale and concluded that he lacked the good faith required by the New York indemnification statute. A former director, discharged for allegedly accepting kickbacks, was allowed to recover attorneys' fees spent defending himself in the corporation's suit against him for fraud and breach of fiduciary duty. MCI Telecommunications Corp. v. Wanzer, 1990 WL 91100 (Del.Super.1990).

In Hibbert v. Hollywood Park, Inc., 457 A.2d 339 (Del.1983), a group of directors sued the corporation and another faction of directors, alleging that the latter used false and misleading proxy soliciting materials and had otherwise breached their fiduciary duties. The suit was dismissed and the plaintiff directors sought indemnification under a by-law requiring indemnification for reasonable expenses in any action in which they were involved as a party or otherwise. The Delaware Supreme Court held that indemnification was not limited to persons who are defendants. The court also found that plaintiffs' litigation was consistent with their duties as directors.

2. *Actions Covered*. A more subtle issue is the type of action to be covered. Derivative suits and third party actions for damages or an injunction are clearly within the statute. Other exposures to liability include criminal prosecutions (and investigations, even if there is no prosecution); administrative proceedings, both state and federal; and arbitrations. If the principal justification for indemnification is to protect directors and officers from personal liability for having caused the corporation to take legitimate business risks, does that justification apply equally to all of these actions?

3. *Expenses Covered*. Litigation creates a number of different expenses, including court costs, attorneys' fees, fines, judgments and amounts paid in settlement. Clear public policy reasons require differentiating among them, and the statutes do so. For example, if a corporation could indemnify a director for amounts paid in settlement of a derivative suit, it would be taking from the director with one hand while giving the same amount with the other, a situation that would not be true in a third-party action.

Notwithstanding this problem, New York amended its statute in 1986 to permit indemnification for settlements in a derivative suit if a court finds that the director or officer is fairly and reasonably entitled to indemnity in view of all of the circumstances of the case. N.Y. B.C.L. § 722(c). In approving the bill, the Governor of New York stated that the change was designed to help the state attract competent directors and officers and thus to "enhanc[e] the business climate in New York State for the continuing success of New York corporations". Executive Memorandum, July 24, 1986, 1986 N.Y. Laws 209th Session. The RMBCA also permits indemnification for payments made by a director in settlement of a derivative suit, if a court finds "the director is fairly and reasonably entitled to indemnification in view of all the relevant circumstances."   RMBCA § 8.54(2).   If the director was found liable, however, indemnification is limited to reasonable expenses.   Id.   Neither New York law nor the RMBCA addresses the circularity problem that these sections create.

One of the biggest problems facing a potential indemnitee is that she will be required to incur immediate expenses such as legal fees long before a final determination is made as to the propriety of her conduct. Can the corporation make advance payments to her to meet these ongoing costs?   If so, must someone make a determination as to the probable outcome of the litigation and whether she is likely to satisfy the standard of conduct after the dust settles?   Must an advance for litigation expenses be secured?   If so, then a dichotomy is created between rich directors who can afford to pay litigation expenses, regardless of whether the corporation advances these expenses, and poorer directors, who might be unable to afford either litigation or the security for any bond that might be required to secure the advances.

Recent statutes have eliminated the statutory requirement for such a bond and have permitted advances upon the giving of an undertaking to repay and the satisfaction of other conditions.   See RMBCA § 8.53; DGCL § 145(e).   In Swenson v. Thibaut, 39 N.C.App. 77, 250 S.E.2d 279 (1978), the court took a similar approach.   The plaintiff-shareholder in a derivative suit sought to enjoin the advancing of legal fees to the defendant directors.   The court construed a section of the North Carolina statute that was similar to RMBCA § 8.53 in requiring the director to give an "undertaking" to repay the advances if she was unsuccessful in her defense.   The court rejected the argument that the term "undertaking" meant the posting of full security for all advances and defined it to be a written promise not made under seal given as security for the performance of an act.   The court also rejected the argument that the advance was prohibited by the North Carolina equivalent of RMBCA § 8.31, noting that, in any event, the advances had been approved by disinterested directors.

In Citadel Holding Corporation v. Roven, 603 A.2d 818 (Del.1992), the Delaware Supreme Court interpreted the terms of an indemnity agreement that promised to indemnify a director for claims arising "by reason of his service as a director."   Id. at 820.   Despite a specific provision in the agreement that excluded any obligation on the corporation to indemnify the director for liability under Section 16(b) of the Securities Exchange Act of 1934 (relating to short-swing profits) the court held that the only limit on advancement of litigation expenses was "reasonableness."   Reasonable expenses included the defendant's attorneys' fees, although these expenses were limited to actions related to the corporation's business.

In Advanced Mining Systems, Inc. v. Fricke, 623 A.2d 82 (Del.Ch. 1992), the Delaware Court of Chancery interpreted DGCL § 145(e) to hold that the advancement of legal expenses and ultimate indemnification are two distinct acts.   If a board approves advancing expenses, it is making "essentially * * * a decision to advance credit." Although the board may decide that it is in the best interests of the corporation to advance these expenses, the statute does not require it to do so. Only a specific provision in the articles of incorporation, by-laws or private agreement between the director and corporation can mandate an advance.

Advanced Mining Systems was followed in Heffernan v. Pacific Dunlop GNB Corp., 965 F.2d 369 (7th Cir.1992), a case decided under Delaware law. Heffernan was a former director of GNB Holdings, Inc., who sold his substantial stockholding in the company to Pacific Dunlop. Thereafter, Pacific Dunlop sued Heffernan for failure to disclose large liabilities of GNB when it was sold. Heffernan demanded an advance of his litigation expenses from GNB under its by-laws. GNB refused, arguing that Heffernan was not being sued "by reason of the fact" that he was a director, a requirement of the by-laws and the statute. The Seventh Circuit, reversing the lower court and remanding the case, held that the advance was required because, "Delaware's 'by reason of the fact' phrase is broad enough to encompass suits against a director in his official capacity as well as suits against a director that arise more tangentially from his role, position or status as a director." Id. at 375. On remand, the district court emphasized the importance of the actual terms of the articles of incorporation, by-laws or contract in deciding whether the parties intended to make the advancing of expenses mandatory.

Citadel, Advanced Mining Systems and *Heffernan* demonstrate that the drafters of by-laws and indemnification agreements must state quite explicitly the conditions for indemnification that the provisions will cover. They also show that a corporation may be held responsible for advancement of expenses under conditions that the corporation neither intended nor foresaw. See Lewis S. Black, Jr. and Frederick H. Alexander, Advancing Litigation Expenses Under Mandatory Indemnification Provisions, 26 Regulation 65 (1993).

4. *Standard of Conduct.* Perhaps the hardest questions are those connected with the required standard of conduct for indemnification. If after trial, a court determines that an indemnitee is innocent of the charges leveled against her, that determination is sufficient to warrant indemnification. But suppose the indemnitee wins on a technical defense such as the statute of limitations? What about a nolo contendere plea? And suppose the case is settled rather than going to trial so that the court never passes on the merits of the plaintiff's claim concerning the indemnitee's conduct? In B & B Investment Club v. Kleinert's, Inc., 472 F.Supp. 787 (E.D.Pa.1979), a securities fraud action, the defendant treasurer negotiated a settlement that involved a dismissal with prejudice but no monetary payment; the defendant president settled by paying $35,000. The court held that the treasurer's settlement constituted success on the merits even though the plaintiffs contended that they had settled for no money from the treasurer only because of the president's payment. In Dornan v. Humphrey, 278 A.D. 1010, 106

N.Y.S.2d 142 (1951), the directors were determined to have been success-ful "on the merits or otherwise" when a derivative suit was dismissed because of the statute of limitations. In Galdi v. Berg, 359 F.Supp. 698 (D.Del.1973), however, the defendant-director was unable to obtain mandatory indemnification when a derivative suit alleging negligence was dismissed without prejudice because the same issue was being litigated in another pending case. The court concluded that the dismiss-al did not constitute "success on the merits or otherwise" under the Delaware statute.

The issue is equally complex when criminal actions are involved. In Merritt–Chapman & Scott Corp. v. Wolfson, 264 A.2d 358 (Del.Su-per.1970), the defendants were convicted of various counts of a criminal indictment. One charge in one of the counts was dismissed; the defendants were found guilty of the balance of the count. The court held that the dismissal of the charge did not constitute "success on the merits or otherwise" and denied indemnification. Thereafter the convic-tions were reversed and, after two retrials, the case was settled by the entry of various pleas in exchange for the dismissal of the balance of the counts. In a second suit seeking indemnification, the court held that any result in a criminal action other than conviction constituted "suc-cess" warranting indemnification and rejected the argument that indem-nification could be granted only when there had been a finding of innocence. The court held also that success need not be complete and granted indemnification for the expenses with respect to the counts which had been dismissed pursuant to the plea bargain. Merritt–Chapman & Scott Corp. v. Wolfson, 321 A.2d 138 (Del.Super.1974).

The standard of conduct required to indemnify a director should be related to the standard of care required of her in performing her duties, but should they be the same? RMBCA § 8.51 varies the standard from that found in § 8.30 by permitting indemnification if the director acts in a manner which she reasonably believed was "not opposed to" the best interests of the corporation. What does that phrase mean? Is it a device for lowering the standard of care in the indemnification context? Or is it designed to deal with specific types of cases in which there are valid policy reasons to permit indemnification even if the standard of care has not been satisfied? See the Official Comment to RMBCA § 8.51(a) for an explanation of why the two standards should *not* be the same.

Closely related to the standard of conduct is the question of who determines whether it has been met. The statutes suggest four possibil-ities: the board of directors, the stockholders, independent legal counsel, or a court. Consider the pros and cons of each. In connection with a determination by the board, be aware of a potential trap. Suppose that the board is hostile to the indemnitee and refuses to indemnify her, notwithstanding the statute. Should she have an alternate route to secure the indemnification which the statute contemplates? What about the expenses which she incurs in enforcing her statutory rights? See RMBCA § 8.54.

As lawyers, you should be concerned whether there can be such an animal as an "independent" legal counsel when the issue is whether management is entitled to indemnification. The by-laws of some corporations contain a definition of independent legal counsel similar to the following: "A law firm, or a member of a law firm that is experienced in matters of corporation law and neither presently is, nor in the past five years has been, retained to represent: (1) the company or indemnitee in any matter material to either such party, or (2) any other party to the proceeding giving rise to a claim for indemnification hereunder." The by-law also includes any person who would be considered to have a conflict of interest under the applicable standards of professional conduct. See Ohio Gen.Corp.L. § 1701.13(E)(4)(a).

5. *Disclosure*. Critics argue that the problems of indemnification are exacerbated because no state or federal law requires the corporation to disclose indemnification payments to the stockholders. They contend that a corporation which must disclose such payments will be more careful in making them; presumably, the payments themselves might be the subject of a further derivative suit by a stockholder alleging a waste of corporate assets. Because such payments are not considered to be compensation, they do not come within the SEC's proxy rules. A new provision in the RMBCA, § 16.21(a), now requires disclosure in the corporation's annual report to stockholders but most state statutes, including Delaware, do not have a similar requirement.

Note: Charter, by-Law and Contract Provisions

Whether because of uncertainty as to the scope of indemnification allowed or required under the applicable statutory and case law or because of a desire to amplify or clarify the various rights and obligations of the corporation and its executives, many corporations include in their articles of incorporation or by-laws some provision relating to indemnification. In addition, in recent years, directors' increasing fear of liability and the higher cost or actual unavailability of liability insurance has led many corporations to enter into indemnification agreements with their management that are separate from the indemnification provided for in corporate articles of incorporation and by-laws.

In many cases, the corporate by-law will do nothing more than track the statute while the indemnification agreement will contain provisions that go beyond the express indemnification sections of the statute. Are such provisions valid simply because they are in a contract rather than in a by-law? RMBCA § 8.58(a) restricts these provisions to those consistent with the statute. By contrast, DGCL § 145(f) provides specifically that statutory rights and procedures concerning indemnification are not exclusive. Thus, a corporation may indemnify a director through its own policies under circumstances not prescribed in the statute. It is doubtful, however, that a corporation could agree to indemnify a director for *any* action undertaken. As one article noted:

> Some commentators have criticized section 145(f) as too liberal and have expressed concern that public policy could be subverted if,

for instance, a director is indemnified according to a by-law in spite of a finding in a derivative suit that he had breached his fiduciary duty to the corporation. Although there is no case law on point, it is probable that a Delaware court would not allow indemnification under a by-law or pursuant to a contract when the proposed indemnification is prohibited by law or public policy. To the extent the statute can be read to embody the public policy limitations of indemnification, a by-law or agreement purporting to expand these limits would likely be void as violative of public policy.

E. Norman Veasey, Jesse A. Finkelstein & C. Stephen Bigler, Delaware Supports Directors With a Three–Legged Stool of Limited Liability, Indemnification and Insurance, 42 Bus.Law. 401, 413 (1987).

4. INSURANCE

Directors' and officers' liability insurance ("D & O insurance") is a relatively recent development. It was not until the mid–1960s, when an increasing number of lawsuits began to generate fears of liability, that these policies began to find favor among large numbers of corporations. Various factors, both legal and social, combined in the 1980s to lead insurance companies to increase their premiums and either reduce the coverage of, or cancel completely, liability insurance. These factors included greater numbers of initial stock offerings, bankruptcies, and corporate mergers and acquisitions, all of which increased the number of claims against directors. See Roberta Romano, What Went Wrong With Directors' and Officers' Liability Insurance?, 14 Del.J.Corp.L. 1 (1989). Additionally, the size of claims paid increased dramatically, especially to shareholders bringing derivative suits. Courts tended to place the risk burden on the insurers by interpreting policies in favor of the insured even when the claim would appear to not be covered by the policy. Romano discounts the impact that *Van Gorkom* had in causing the insurance crisis, noting that it was already underway when that case was decided. By the end of the decade, the insurance crisis seems to have peaked. Romano suggests that the crisis perhaps reflected partly the apex of a normal business cycle and that corrections made in the insurance market structure itself relieved the pressure on D & O insurance policies. Nevertheless, the concerns that initially gave rise to D & O insurance remain valid today, and the policy issues that liability insurance raises are particularly significant in creating an adequate system of management accountability.

Most state statutes contain express authorization for corporations to purchase D & O insurance. See RMBCA § 8.57; DGCL § 145(g). New York's statute, which differs slightly from the RMBCA and·Delaware provisions, states that "it is the public policy of this state to spread the risk of corporate management, notwithstanding any other general or special law of this state or of any other jurisdiction including the federal government." N.Y. B.C.L. § 727(e).

A D & O policy consists of two separate but integral parts. See Joseph Hinsey IV, The New Lloyd's Policy Form for Directors and

Officers Liability Insurance—An Analysis, 33 Bus.Law. 1961 (1978); Joseph F. Johnston, Jr., Corporate Indemnification and Liability Insurance for Directors and Officers, 33 Bus.Law. 1993 (1978). The first part is designed to reimburse the corporation for its lawful expenses in connection with indemnifying its directors and officers. This part of a D & O policy reduces the amounts that corporate directors or officers would otherwise be required to pay in those instances where the corporation is unable or, less likely, unwilling to indemnify. It thus encourages and facilitates corporate indemnification of directors and officers. The second part insures individuals, acting in their capacity as officers or directors of the insured corporation, against losses, including judgments and settlements. Their coverage under D & O policies is limited in a number of ways. A deductible amount for each director and officer and for the corporation serves as a deterrent to carelessness or misconduct. Directors and officers also usually bear a certain percentage, typically 5%, of the loss above the deductible amount. The payment of fines and penalties imposed in a criminal suit or action are excluded from the definition of "loss," as are other fines, penalties, and punitive damages imposed by a final adjudication that are uninsurable under the law pursuant to which the policy is construed. D & O policies generally do not provide coverage for costs that may be protected against through other types of insurance. Additionally, many policies contain "laser" exclusions, tailored to eliminate coverage for risks inherent in a specific corporation.

The premiums for a D & O policy are costly and are set on a case-by-case basis taking into account the size of the corporation, its type of business, financial condition and merger and acquisition history, the number of directors and officers, the corporation's past litigation history, and special circumstances, such as governmental investigations, adverse publicity potential and political activity. Small corporations have experienced difficulty in obtaining D & O policies because fewer checks and balances are built into their corporate structures. The premiums for a D & O policy are generally split between the corporation and the individual on a ninety-ten basis, with the corporation bearing the larger share.

D & O insurance provides protection beyond that which indemnification can afford in several important areas. First, amounts paid in judgment or settlement in a derivative suit can be recovered under the standard D & O policy, assuming that none of the limitations described above are applicable. Second, such insurance covers conduct that does not satisfy the statutory standard but which does not constitute "active and deliberate dishonesty." For example, in *Van Gorkom*, given the finding that the directors were grossly negligent in not informing themselves sufficiently prior to approving the merger, statutory indemnification would have been unlikely. However, the corporation's insurance carrier paid $10,000,000—the full policy limit—as part of the $23,000,-000 settlement of the case. Thus, even a finding of gross negligence will not necessarily preclude payment under a D & O policy where the wrongs committed were not wilful or dishonest. Finally, a D & O policy provides protection if the corporation becomes insolvent or is otherwise unable to pay indemnification or if the corporation refuses to do so, assuming that the other requirements of the policy are satisfied.

To some, there is something troubling about a statute that allows a corporation to insure its executives for conduct sufficiently egregious to be outside the scope of indemnification. For such critics, this trouble is exacerbated by the fact that insurance is expensive and is paid for almost entirely by the corporation. As one group of writers has argued, "the question is * * * whether wrongful acts should be indemnified at all. Why should an executive of a drug company be indemnified for the costs of a criminal fine if he is convicted of allowing a harmful drug to injure several thousand people when the same act as a private individual would send him to jail? An untenable double standard has been created. The more powerful an executive becomes, the less likely he is to pay for an abuse of power." Ralph Nader, Mark Green & Joel Seligman, Taming the Giant Corporation, 108 (1976).

Those who defend the existing statutory scheme do so with a very simple argument: the public policy question of the scope of insurance coverage is a question of insurance law rather than corporate law. The statute only authorizes the purchase of insurance and leaves the determination of the limits on that insurance to insurance companies and state insurance commissioners. See S. Samuel Arsht, The Business Judgment Rule Revisited, 8 Hofstra L.Rev. 93 (1979).

The question of the scope of insurance has another aspect which we have seen before in other contexts: who should bear the risks of malfeasance? Those who support the present system would argue that this is a question to be decided by the insurance companies through their exclusions and pricing policies. If those companies reach conclusions that are harmful from a corporate perspective, stockholders are free to change their investment to a company which does not insure or whose management is less likely to engage in litigation-provoking activities. To be valid, this argument must assume that stockholders have information about the existence and coverage of D & O insurance and the payments under the policy, an assumption that is not generally true. Thus, if we are talking about the market setting the limits on corporate behavior, it is a market with limited information.

Chapter 17

DUTY OF LOYALTY

A. INTRODUCTION: ON CONFLICTS OF INTEREST AND THE DUTY OF LOYALTY

In Chapter 16, we saw how the duty of care attempts to solve the problems that arise when a director does not act in the best interests of the shareholders in her decision-making, even if she does not benefit personally from her decision. In this chapter, we will examine how the duty of loyalty (or fair dealing, as some commentators call it) deals with agency costs in situations in which a director's decision may not be in the best interests of the shareholders precisely because she *does* benefit from that decision. Simply put, the duty of loyalty requires a manager to place the corporation's best interests (and thus those of the stockholders) above her own.

Consider a transaction in which a director proposes to sell property to her corporation. As a director, she has a duty to maximize the value of the transaction to the corporation by having the corporation pay the lowest possible price. As the owner of the property, her own best interest is to receive the highest possible price. The economic imperatives of the two positions are in clear conflict. The transaction involves "self-dealing;" the director has a "conflict of interest" when she votes on the transaction.

Even though the director is subject to competing demands because of her financial stake in the transaction, the existence of a conflict does not mean that the consummated transaction will be unfair to the corporation.

> [I]t is important to keep firmly in mind that it is a contingent risk we are dealing with—that an interest conflict is not in itself a crime or a tort or necessarily injurious to others. Contrary to much popular usage, having a "conflict of interest" is not something one is "guilty of"; it is simply a state of affairs. Indeed, in many situations, the corporation and the shareholders may secure major benefits from a transaction despite the presence of a director's conflicting

interest. Further, while history is replete with selfish acts, it is also oddly counterpointed by numberless acts taken contrary to self interest.

RMBCA Subchapter F, Introductory Comment.

Self-dealing transactions can be both fair and beneficial to a corporation. Were it not so, it would be very easy to formulate a rule proscribing directors from engaging in transactions with their corporations. An "interested" director, however, will frequently be uniquely situated to help the corporation. She may have knowledge about how the corporation will benefit from the transaction and the ability to effectuate the transaction at minimal cost. It has long been recognized that a prohibition against directors engaging in transactions with their corporations,

> [W]hile it would afford little protection to the corporation against actual fraud or oppression, would deprive it of the aid of those most interested in giving aid judiciously, and best qualified to judge of the necessity of that aid, and of the extent to which it may safely be given.

Twin Lick Oil v. Marbury, 91 U.S. (1 Otto) 587, 589, 23 L.Ed. 328 (1875).

Some self-dealing transactions *are* unfair to the corporation; the interested director is appropriating the difference between the fair market value of the transaction to the corporation and the payment actually made. Thus, the effect of an unfair self-dealing transaction is no different from the direct diversion of corporate funds or assets. However, self-dealing is apt to be more common than flagrant diversion because the interested director

> [M]ay more easily rationalize an inflated purchase price than outright stealing. It is frequently possible to identify and exaggerate some reasons why [a corporation] should pay dearly for some particular piece of land or property. That having been done, [the director] may continue to think of himself as a just and honorable man.

Robert Charles Clark, Corporate Law 143 (1986).

The principal difficulty in this area of the law is establishing appropriate criteria for measuring the validity of the transaction. The business judgment rule, which is premised on the director's independent judgment, does not provide an appropriate standard because in a conflict transaction, by definition, the director's judgment cannot be independent. A substitute test, however, has proved difficult to articulate. A director who engages in a transaction with the corporation may well be acting in good faith, but how is that to be tested? The law requires that the transaction be "fair" to the corporation, but fairness itself can be difficult to determine. The difficulty reflects the common wisdom that when one tries to serve two masters, necessarily there are questions about which is being served.

The issue of divided loyalty is not limited to situations in which a director engages, directly or indirectly, in a transaction with the corporation, although that is the focus of this chapter. Subsequent chapters will consider conflicting loyalties in different contexts: insider trading (Chapter 19), sale of control (Chapter 21), protection of control (Chapter 22), and parent-subsidiary mergers (Chapter 23). The methodology may differ with the context, but the question remains the same: how should a court evaluate the conduct of a director who is faced with what, put broadly, is a conflict of interest?

PROBLEM

MILTON CORPORATION—PART I.

Milton Corporation, (the "Corporation") constructs, owns and operates hotels and restaurants throughout the United States. It is a public company, whose common stock is listed on the New York Stock Exchange, and was founded by by the Milton family in 1935. For the first twenty years of the company's existence, its stock was owned entirely by members of that family.

Following the public offering of stock in 1955, and at the present time, public investors own 60% of the Corporation's stock; the Milton family owns the remaining 40%. The board of directors of the Corporation consists of James Milton, the president and chief executive; Samuel Milton (James' brother); Janet Milton Hayes (their sister), the chief financial officer; John Quincy, the general counsel of the Corporation; and Michael Brown, Ruth Grey and Robert White, each of whom is a prominent business executive having no other connections with the Corporation.

The Milton family owns all the stock of Realty Investors Corporation ("RIC") which was formed in 1940. The three directors of RIC are: James Milton, Samuel Milton, and Janet Milton Hayes. RIC, from the beginning of its operations, has purchased the land on which the Corporation's hotels and restaurants are situated, and thereafter leased the land on a long term basis to the Corporation. RIC also buys and sells real estate to other real estate developers. Although some of the sites selected by the Corporation for construction are on property previously acquired by RIC in independent transactions, the Corporation initiates most transactions. RIC enters the picture to acquire the land and work out the rental terms with the Corporation. The rental arrangements between RIC and the Corporation have provided for approximately the same rents that generally prevailed in the local area, as a fixed fee. They also provided for a fixed percentage of the Corporation's revenues from operations. From time to time, these arrangements have resulted in RIC's deriving far greater profits from some units than did the Corporation. The board of directors of the Corporation has approved each transaction between RIC and the Corporation at a meeting at which all directors were present, but at which the Miltons did not vote. When the Corporation sold its shares to the public the transactions between RIC and the Corporation were fully disclosed in the prospectus.

The Corporation is considering leasing property from RIC on which it plans to build a new hotel. The terms of this proposed transaction are the same as the earlier deals, except that RIC will also receive a percentage of the profits from the concessionaires who will operate in the hotel. Accordingly, the Corporation will receive that much less from the operation of those concessions. RIC requires this added compensation because RIC bought the parcel of land in question for speculation, and not in connection with a transaction initiated by the Corporation. RIC has received lucrative offers from unrelated parties to lease or sell the property. The arrangement RIC proposes to enter into with the Corporation will provide RIC with a smaller profit than it would have made from at least two of the other offers.

A special meeting of the board of directors of the Corporation will consider the proposed transaction. The board has asked you to analyze the situation and make your recommendations.

In answering the following questions, assume that the applicable law is:

    a) Common law.

    b) DGCL § 144.

    c) A statute based on former RMBCA § 8.31.

    d) RMBCA Subchapter F.

1. Who may be counted for a quorum of the board of directors at the meeting to consider the transaction? How many votes will be required to approve the transaction?

2. Assume that the transaction is approved by a unanimous vote of Quincy, Brown, Gray and White, meeting in the absence of the Milton family directors.

    a) What standard will a court use in determining whether to enjoin the transaction or impose personal liability on the Milton family? The board of directors?

    b) Will the business judgment rule apply to the transaction under the facts of this problem?

    c) Who will have the burden of proof in litigation?

    d) How will the party with the burden of proof establish the fairness or unfairness of the transaction?

3. Assume that the Corporation informs its shareholders of the facts as set forth above and seeks ratification of the transaction at a special meeting of shareholders. Can the shares of the Milton family be counted in determining whether a quorum is present or whether the

transaction has been ratified? What effect does shareholder ratification have on any claim for liability?

4. What role does the duty of loyalty play in monitoring directors' performances? To the extent that market mechanisms may be available to reduce the likelihood that directors will engage in self-dealing to the detriment of the corporation, how effective are those mechanisms likely to be?

B. THE COMMON LAW STANDARD

1. ORIGINS AND EVOLUTION

HAROLD MARSH, ARE DIRECTORS TRUSTEES?, CONFLICT OF INTEREST AND CORPORATE MORALITY
22 Bus.Law 35, 36–44 (1966).

* * *

There have been several different rules adopted by courts and legislatures to deal with this problem of conflict of interest, which correspond roughly with successive periods in the legal history of this country. Therefore in the discussion immediately following, I propose to consider the principles which have been advanced at one time or another, in more or less chronological order, even though the earlier ones have been largely if not completely abandoned.

I. Types of Legal Regulations
a. *Prohibition*

In 1880 it could have been stated with confidence that in the United States the general rule was that any contract between a director and his corporation was voidable at the instance of the corporation or its shareholders, without regard to the fairness or unfairness of the transaction. This rule was stated in powerful terms by a number of highly regarded courts and judges in cases which arose generally out of the railroad frauds of the 1860's and 1870's.

* * *

Under this rule it mattered not the slightest that there was a majority of so-called disinterested directors who approved the contract. The courts stated that the corporation was entitled to the unprejudiced judgment and advice of all of its directors and therefore it did no good to say that the interested director did not participate in the making of the contract on behalf of the corporation. " * * * the very words in which he asserts his right declare his wrong; he ought to have participated." * * * Furthermore, the courts said that it was impossible to measure the influence which one director might have over his associates, even though ostensibly abstaining from participation in the discussion or vote. "* * * a corporation, in order to defeat a contract entered into by directors, in which one or more of them had a private interest, is not bound to show that the influence of the director or directors having the private interest determined the action of the board. The law cannot accurately measure the influence of a trustee with his associates, nor will it enter into the inquiry." * * *

Perhaps the strongest reason for this inflexibility of the law was given by the Maryland Supreme Court which stated that, when a contract is made with even one of the directors, "the remaining directors are placed in the embarrassing and invidious position of having to pass upon, scrutinize and check the transactions and accounts of one of their own body, with whom they are associated on terms of equality in the general management of all the affairs of the corporation." Or, as Justice Davies of the New York Supreme Court expressed the same thought: "The moment the directors permit one or more of their number to deal with the property of the stockholders, they surrender their own independence and self control."

This rule applied not only to individual contracts with directors, but also to the situation of interlocking directorates where even a minority of the boards were common to the two contracting corporations. Not only that, it was also applied to the situation where one corporation owned a majority of the stock of another and appointed its directors, even though they might not be the same men as sat on the board of the parent corporation. It is interesting to note that the courts during this era had no difficulty in identifying so-called dummy directors, even though their inability to do so was later given as one of the reasons why this rule of law had to be abandoned. * * *

This principle, absolutely inhibiting contracts between a corporation and its directors or any of them, appeared to be impregnable in 1880. It was stated in ringing terms by virtually every decided case, with arguments which seemed irrefutable, and it was sanctioned by age. * * *

* * *

Thirty years later this principle was dead.

b. Approval by a Disinterested Majority of the Board

It could have been stated with reasonable confidence in 1910 that the general rule was that a contract between a director and his corporation was valid if it was approved by a disinterested majority of his fellow directors and was not found to be unfair or fraudulent by the court if challenged; but that a contract in which a majority of the board was interested was voidable at the instance of the corporation or its shareholders without regard to any question of fairness.

One searches in vain in the decided cases for a reasoned defense of this change in legal philosophy, or for the slightest attempt to refute the powerful arguments which had been made in support of the previous rule. Did the courts discover in the last quarter of the Nineteenth Century that greed was no longer a factor in human conduct? If so, they did not share the basis of this discovery with the public; nor did they humbly admit their error when confronted with the next wave of corporate frauds arising out of the era of the formation of the "trusts" during the 1890's and early 1900's.

The only explanation which seems to have been given for this change in position was the technical one that a trustee, while forbidden to deal with himself in connection with the trust property, could deal directly with the cestui que trust if he made full disclosure and took no unfair advantage; and that the case of a director who abstained from representing the corporation but dealt in his personal capacity with a majority of disinterested directors was properly analogized to a trustee dealing with the cestui que trust. * * *

But in no case is there any discussion or attempted refutation of the reasons previously given by the courts as to why it is impossible, in such a situation, for any director to be disinterested. Some courts seem simply to admit that the practice has grown too widespread for them to cope with. * * *

As the New York Supreme Court stated in Genesee & W.V. Ry. Co. v. Retsof Min. Co.:

> The rule contended for by the learned counsel for the defendant has been considerably relaxed of late years. Indeed, it would be difficult to conduct the affairs of the multifarious corporations of the country, many of which, although apparently sustaining the relations of rivals in business, are nevertheless practically controlled by the same directors, if the element of good faith, instead of individual interests, were not established as the basis of intercorporate action.

* * *

However, this apparent survival of the older rule was nothing but a meaningless facade. As early as 1903 the New Jersey courts decided that the strict rule did not apply to a case of "interlocking directorates." Since the case of a contract between two corporations with common directors was thought to present an entirely different problem than a contract with a director individually, without any inquiry into the question whether the common director or directors owned more stock in one of the two corporations than the other, all that a director had to do in order to avoid the older rule was to incorporate the business in which he expected to have dealings with the corporation on whose board he sat. Since most such businesses would be incorporated anyway for other reasons, this meant that the older rule was virtually abrogated except with respect to approval of salaries.

* * *

Under the rule that a disinterested majority of the directors must approve a transaction with one of their number, the question arose whether this meant a disinterested quorum (i.e., normally a majority of the whole board) or merely a disinterested majority of a quorum, so that the interested director or directors could be counted to make up the quorum. Virtually all of the cases held that the interested director could not be counted for quorum purposes. * * *

c. *Judicial Review of the Fairness of the Transaction*

By 1960 it could be said with some assurance that the general rule was that no transaction of a corporation with any or all of its directors was automatically voidable at the suit of a shareholder, whether there was a disinterested majority of the board or not; but that the courts would review such a contract and subject it to rigid and careful scrutiny, and would invalidate the contract if it was found to be unfair to the corporation.

It is difficult in most States to determine with exactness the point of time at which the rule changed again, or indeed to prove beyond a reasonable doubt that it has in fact changed in a particular State. There are a large number of cases which deal with situations where a majority of the board were interested and which discuss them solely in terms of a review of the fairness of the transaction, without bothering to cite or discuss any of the previous decisions, perhaps in the same State, enunciating the rule that there must be approval by a disinterested majority of the board. Some of these cases could be distinguished from the previous holdings on the basis that they deal with interlocking directorates rather than contracts with interested directors, if one wishes to take any stock in that distinction. There is another large group of cases which deal with situations where it does not appear that a majority of the board were interested in the transaction, but the opinions of the courts deal with the problem solely in terms of fairness, without mentioning any requirement of a disinterested majority. These cases are not necessarily inconsistent with such a requirement, but they in all probability indicate that these courts have gone over to the modern rule.

NORWOOD P. BEVERIDGE, JR., THE CORPORATE DIRECTOR'S FIDUCIARY DUTY OF LOYALTY: UNDERSTANDING THE SELF-INTERESTED DIRECTOR TRANSACTION
41 DePaul L.Rev. 655, 659–62 (1992).

All current thinking on the corporate director's duty of loyalty appears to start with the proposition, which seems now to be universally accepted, that transactions between a director and his corporation at common law were generally voidable without regard to fairness. It is submitted that this proposition is completely erroneous.

Professor Marsh appears to have been the first to make the claim that self-interested contracts were voidable regardless of the fairness of the transactions. * * *

However, the general rule in 1880 was actually the opposite of that described. Interested director contracts were not always voidable. One of the leading treatises stated:

> But the weight of authority and of reason appears to indicate that such a contract would be valid * * *. There is no necessary impropriety in a contract between a director and the corporation, if the latter is represented by other agents. On the contrary, such contracts are, in many instances, the natural result of circumstances, and are justified by the approved usages of businessmen.

An earlier treatise of the time held to the same effect: "The managers or directors of a corporation are not trustees of its property in such a sense, as to disenable them from purchasing the property or stock belonging to it, with the same effect as though they were not managers or directors."

* * *

Once we accept the fact that, according to the great weight of authority, interested director transactions were never thought to be voidable without regard to fairness, we are freed from the necessity of answering Professor Marsh's perplexing question of why there was an unexplained change in legal philosophy. If we review the early cases in light of agency and trust law principles, we can also stop wondering why corporate law, as some critics would have it, does not follow the strict prohibitions of trust and agency law.

In fact, the nineteenth-century cases did make the analogy to trust and agency law, but there never was, and there is not now, any doctrine in either agency or trust law that categorically prohibits transactions between the fiduciary and the person represented; it is a matter of prohibiting the fiduciary from standing on both sides of the transaction. The fiduciary cannot represent both himself and his principal or beneficiary. Validation of the transaction then requires (1) a full disclosure by the fiduciary of his conflict of interest and any material information he may have about the transaction, and (2) informed consent by or on behalf of the principal or beneficiary.

* * *

As applied to the corporation, the question of consent initially turned on whether the consent of the board was sufficient or whether the consent of all or some of the shareholders would be required. There was some conflict in the early cases, but the general answer was that the consent of an informed board would suffice. This raised the additional questions of what should be done if a majority of the directors were interested, so that a disinterested quorum could not be assembled, and what should be done if the interested director participated in the giving of consent by the board, whether or not his vote was needed or his presence was needed to constitute a quorum.

If we examine the cases cited by Professor Marsh in support of his assertion that interested director contracts were voidable in spite of fairness, we will see that the cases were actually concerned with transactions in which the interested director was active in representing both sides of the deal.   * * *

2.   THE MODERN STANDARD

The requirements for the validity of an interested director transaction are now governed by statutes in most states. Common law jurisprudence on the duty of loyalty is of continuing vitality, however, because many of these statutes have been held to have codified common law standards.

SHLENSKY v. SOUTH PARKWAY BUILDING CORP.
19 Ill.2d 268, 166 N.E.2d 793 (1960).

[The plaintiffs, minority shareholders of South Parkway Building Corporation (Building Corporation), sued to require defendant directors to personally account for damages suffered by the corporation in the various transactions. The trial court held that defendants breached their fiduciary duties in all of the challenged transactions and ordered an accounting for the benefit of the shareholders. The appellate court reversed on the ground that, under Illinois law, the plaintiffs had failed to sustain the burden of establishing that the transactions were fraudulent.

The main operating asset of the Building Corporation was a 3–story commercial building on a city lot in Chicago. Since the inception of Building Corporation, defendant Englestein was a director and majority shareholder of the corporation. In each of the challenged transactions the second party was a corporation owned by Englestein in which he acted as either an officer or director or both. In each case, the court found that the transactions were approved by an interested majority of the Building Corporation's board of directors.]

Bristow, J.

In [Dixmoor Golf Club, Inc. v. Evans, 325 Ill. 612, 156 N.E. 785 (1927)] this court stated at page 616 of 325 Ill., at page 787 of 156 N.E.: "The directors of a corporation are trustees of its business and property for the collective body of stockholders in respect to such business. They are subject to the general rule, in regard to trusts and trustees, that they cannot, in their dealings with the business or property of the trust, use their relation to it for their own personal gain. It is their duty to administer the corporate affairs for the common benefit of all the stockholders, and exercise their best care, skill, and judgment in the management of the corporate business *solely in the interest of the corporation.*   * * * It is a breach of duty for the directors to place themselves in a position where their personal interests would prevent them from acting for the best interests of those they represent." (Italics ours.)

The court expounded that while a director is not disqualified from dealing with the corporation and buying its property, or selling property to it, the transaction will be subject to the closest scrutiny, and if not conducted with the utmost fairness, "to the end that the corporation shall have received full value," it will be set aside. The court then held that since the board of directors therein was dominated by one member, and had purchased land from him for the corporation at a price that was 2½ times more than required by his option, the transaction would be set aside, even though the corporation had use for the land, and had received some benefit from the transaction.

The same year, this court in White v. Stevens, 326 Ill. 528, 158 N.E. 101, 103, without referring to the Dixmoor case, reiterated that a director may deal with the corporation of which he is a member, provided he acts fairly and for the interest of the company. The court also recognized that corporations having directors in common may contract with each other "if the contracts are fair and reasonable," but emphasized that such transactions would be carefully scrutinized by equity. In the case before it, where the allegedly offending corporation had "procured the furniture for the hotel company at prices charged by manufacturers and wholesalers and furnished it to the hotel company at the same price," the court found that "the most careful scrutiny fails to disclose any unfairness to or overreaching of the hotel company in the entire transaction."

* * *

* * * [I]n Winger v. Chicago City Bank & Trust Co., 394 Ill. 94, 67 N.E.2d 265, * * * [a]fter reviewing the English and American authorities on the fiduciary status of corporate directors, the court * * * reaffirmed the rule in the Dixmoor case, and noted further that the fact that directors do not deal directly with themselves, but deal with another corporation which they own or control, will not change the effect of the transaction. In fact, the court pointed out that it is practically the unanimous opinion of courts that, even if only one of the directors voting for the transaction profited thereby, and his vote was necessary, the transaction would be tainted with the same illegality and fraud as though they were all interested. Under those circumstances, the directors have the burden of overcoming the presumption against the validity of the transaction, by showing its fairness and propriety.

* * * [W]e find that the Winger case, construed in its entirety, holds that transactions between corporations with common directors may be avoided only *if unfair,* and that the directors who would sustain the challenged transaction have the burden of overcoming the presumption against the validity of the transaction by showing its fairness.

While the acts of the directors in the Winger case may have been a more flagrant breach of fiduciary duty, as defendants contend, than those involved in the instant case—depending upon one's view point—those circumstances do not change the rule of law applied by the court. Moreover, we agree with the court that no distinction should be made, as defendants suggest, between transactions of a director with his corporation and those in which he hides behind the corporate veil and deals through another corporation which he owns or controls.

* * *

In the leading case of Geddes v. Anaconda Copper Mining Co., 254 U.S. 590, 41 S.Ct. 209, 65 L.Ed. 425, followed by an imposing body of authority, the operative facts were somewhat analogous to those in the case at bar in that they involved transactions between corporations with common directors and allegedly inadequate consideration. The challenged transaction there, however, involved a sale of all the corporate property, whereas the transactions in the instant case involve agreements allegedly siphoning a substantial portion of the corporate assets. The United States Supreme Court, after noting that the record showed beyond controversy that Ryan was an officer and director and dominated the affairs of the buying and selling companies, as well as their boards of directors, set aside the transaction. In so doing, the court promulgated the oft quoted rule at page 599 of 254 U.S., at page 212 of 41 S.Ct.: "The relation of directors to corporations is of such a fiduciary nature that transactions between boards having common members are regarded as jealously by the law as are personal dealings between a director and his corporation, and where the fairness of such transactions is challenged the burden is upon those who would maintain them to show their entire fairness and where a sale is involved the full adequacy of the consideration. Especially is this true where a common director is dominating in influence or in character. This court has been consistently emphatic in the application of this rule, which, it has declared, is founded in soundest morality, and we now add in the soundest business policy."

In our judgment, the Geddes rule, which is essentially the same as that applied in the Winger case, is not only legally cogent, but is consistent with the entire concept of the fiduciary relation in the fabric of our commercial law. The contrary rule, urged by defendants, whereby those attacking the transactions of fiduciaries would have the burden of establishing its unfairness or fraudulency is not only without substantial support in the case law, but would put a premium on sharp practices by directors by putting the onus of proof on their victims, and would also tend to further separate corporate management from ownership.

In contrast, the rule of the Geddes and Winger cases, insofar as it provides that the directors shall have the burden of establishing the fairness and propriety of the transactions, not only protects shareholders from exploitation, but permits flexibility in corporate dealings. While the concept of "fairness" is incapable of precise definition, courts have stressed such factors as whether the corporation received in the transaction full value in all the commodities purchased; the corporation's need for the property; its ability to finance the purchase; whether the transaction was at the market price, or below, or constituted a better bargain than the corporation could have otherwise obtained in dealings with others; whether there was a detriment to the corporation as a result of the transaction; whether there was a possibility of corporate gain siphoned off by the directors directly or through corporations they controlled; and whether there was full disclosure—although neither disclosure nor shareholder assent can convert a dishonest transaction into a fair one.

Moreover, where the corporate directors fail to establish the fairness of the challenged transaction, it may either be set aside, or affirmed and damages recovered for the losses sustained by the corporation.

In the light of this analysis of the appropriate rules and guiding considerations, we shall determine the propriety of the five challenged transactions of the board of the Building Corporation herein.

Inasmuch as the authorization of the payment of $100,000 to the Store [one of the three tenants in the building owned by the Building Corporation] for its fixtures was conditioned on the subsequent modification of its lease, we shall consider these transactions together. It is undisputed that at the time of these transactions the board of the Building Corporation consisted of seven members, and that director Sturm resigned in protest of the payment of $100,000 to the Store. The remaining six directors present and voting for that purchase included Englestein, the owner and president of the Store; Mackie, a Store director; and Bernstein, who was the lawyer for Englestein and for the Store, as well as for Englestein's other business enterprises. We cannot, under the circumstances, perceive just how defendants can seriously characterize Bernstein as an independent and disinterested director representing only the Building Corporation.

It is therefore apparent that the fixture purchase authorized on March 18, 1948, could not conceivably be deemed to have been approved by an independent and disinterested majority of directors of the Building Corporation. Furthermore, as pointed out in the Geddes case, it is not the mere number of common directors which determines whether approval has been given by an independent and disinterested majority of directors, but rather whether a majority of the directors are dominated by an individual or a group.

Nor was the modification of the Store lease on May 4, 1948, effected by an independent and disinterested majority. At that time only five members of the board were present, Townsend being out of town and apparently informed by telephone, and the votes of approval included Englestein, Mackie and Bernstein, along with Teter, and Peyla, who thought that the Store rent was being increased. Therefore, in view of the lack of approval by a disinterested majority, it was incumbent upon defendants to sustain the burden of establishing the fairness of these transactions.

It is uncontroverted that the Building Corporation had no commercial use for the fixtures, which even included the asphalt tile and built-in partitions, all of which were continued to be used by the Store. Moreover, since the used fixtures had limited intrinsic value, as compared with their cost of $100,000, the only consideration which the corporation could realize from this substantial outlay would be through its rental charges. While the directors on May 4, 1948, increased the minimum rent payable by the Store by some $5,000, they eliminated practically all of the percentage rents, except the 1½ per cent on sales over $1,100,000, which was tantamount to a 40% reduction in future rents, and also waived some $24,316 of accrued rent owed by the Store.

In defense of this transaction, defendants and the Appellate Court stress that the economic health of the Store was of great value to the Building Corporation, since it meant the retention of a tenant and benefited all the other tenants, which were economically interdependent, and therefore justified pouring money into the Store. In our judgment, however, the economic interdependence of the tenancies (Neisner's, Walgreen's, and the Store) hardly justifies giving one of them—the Store owned by Englestein—all of the financial benefits, and requiring the other tenants to pay rents which were 10 to 20 times higher per square foot than the rent paid by Englestein's Store. In this connection, the evidence showed that the rent paid by the Store, even in 1948, was $20,737, or $.24 per square foot, as compared with rentals of $42,875 or $2.00 per square foot paid by Neisner's for similar space, and $30,708 or $5.44 per square foot paid by Walgreen's. It is also difficult for us to comprehend just why the Store was such a valuable tenant when other tenants paid much higher rentals, and when the record shows that the subsequent tenant of the premises willingly paid a rental over 2½ times as much as that paid by the Store.

It is therefore patent from the evidence that defendants not merely failed to establish the fairness of this $100,000 used fixture purchase and rent reduction scheme, but that it was tantamount to a deliberate depletion of corporate assets, for the benefit of another corporation in which 3 of the 6 directors had adverse interests. Under those circumstances, the findings and orders of the master and chancellor that defendants' conduct constituted a breach of their fiduciary duty, for which they must account to the Building Corporation, were neither contrary to the manifest weight of the evidence, nor predicated on a conclusive presumption, as defendants argue. It was therefore error for the Appellate Court to have set aside those findings.

C. THE STATUTORY APPROACH

Most contemporary statutes provide that an interested director transaction will not automatically be void or voidable *either* because there has been disclosure to, and approval by, a disinterested decision-maker (directors or shareholders) *or* because the transaction is fair to the corporation. Under such a provision, what role does a court have in determining the fairness of the transaction to the corporation? Because the statute is written in the disjunctive, one possible answer is that there will be judicial consideration of fairness only if there has been no prior approval by a disinterested decision-maker. If this interpretation is correct, it would represent a major reduction in judicial scrutiny (and, hence, potentially less protection for minority shareholders), particularly from the early days of the common law. It could, however, be viewed as economically efficient and less costly because it would give prospective certainty to a transaction in which the decisional process has been good, presumably on the theory that good process will lead to substantively fair decisions in most instances.

Alternatively, the statute can be read as removing the absolute bar against interested director transactions but leaving no clear standard in its stead. Support for this reading comes from the language in many statutes that a transaction that satisfies one or more of the tests will not be void or voidable *solely* because of the director's interest. See, e.g., DGCL § 144. Under this construction, the statute relates primarily to the burden of proof in litigation challenging a conflict of interest transaction rather than to the validity of the transaction itself. Thus, the burden of establishing validity initially would be on the interested director but would shift to the shareholder challenging the transaction if there had been approval by a disinterested decision-maker. This interpretation always leaves the question of the transaction's fairness for the court to determine; the only question (although it often may be outcome-determinative) is who must establish fairness or unfairness. While this interpretation can be supported as a means of deterring management self-dealing, it also flies in the teeth of the statute's literal language.

The problem of interpretation stems from the differing stages of development of the case law at the time the statutes were enacted. Many jurisdictions had adopted a general rule that contracts between interested directors would not automatically be invalidated, but had not expressly overruled earlier cases applying an automatic voidability rule. Some jurisdictions retained vestiges of the automatic voidability rule in specific situations, e.g., where the interested director represented both parties to the transaction in the bargaining process, where the interested director was counted for purposes of determining the presence of a quorum, or where the interested director's vote was necessary for approval of the transaction. Thus, if the statute was designed to reverse the case law, the question remains: what case law?

Unfortunately legislative history and official commentaries (where they are available) are of little help. See, e.g., the discussion of the legislative history of the New York statute in Note, The Status of the Fairness Test Under Section 713 of the New York Business Corporation Law, 76 Colum.L.Rev. 1156, 1166–74, 1179–82 (1976). Given the longstanding disfavor with which director conflict of interest transactions have been viewed, however, it might be thought that a legislative enactment purporting to shield them completely from judicial scrutiny would have done so explicitly. Indeed, one court, in interpreting the New Jersey statute, stated that "notwithstanding the use of 'or' to connect the subdivisions of the statute, the preferable construction is to require that a particular transaction pass muster under each subdivision." Scott v. Multi–Amp Corp., 386 F.Supp. 44, 67 (D.N.J.1977).

Recent amendments to the RMBCA further complicate the analysis of the statutory treatment of interested director transactions. As discussed in greater detail in Section E, in 1989, the Corporate Laws Committee of the American Bar Association amended the RMBCA to replace the existing § 8.31 with Subchapter F. The purpose of the amendment was to substitute a bright line test for the uncertainty of the existing statutory regime and to reduce judicial intervention in self-dealing transactions. In many cases, Subchapter F will not change the result, but the analytic methodology differs substantially. Only a few states have adopted Subchapter F, and it is not clear what the future will hold. For the moment, former § 8.31 is representative of most statutes and will be considered as such in this Section.

In reading the following cases, consider the interplay between the statute and the common law standards and the extent to which the courts apply those standards when interpreting the statute.

REMILLARD BRICK CO. v. REMILLARD-DANDINI CO.

109 Cal.App.2d 405, 241 P.2d 66, 73–77 (1952).

[Stanley and Sturgis controlled a majority of the shares of Remillard–Dandini Co. Remillard–Dandini Co. owned all the shares of San Jose Brick & Tile, Ltd. Stanley and Sturgis controlled the boards of directors of Remillard–Dandini Co. and San Jose Brick & Tile, Ltd. and were executive officers of both corporations and drew salaries from them. The court refers to Remillard–Dandini Co. and San Jose Brick & Tile, Ltd. as the "manufacturing companies." Stanley and Sturgis owned, controlled and operated Remillard–Dandini Sales Corp. which the court refers to as the "sales corporation."

Plaintiff, a minority shareholder of Remillard–Dandini Co., alleged that the majority directors of the manufacturing companies used their power to have the manufacturing companies enter into contracts with the sales corporation, so that the manufacturing companies were stripped of their sales function, and that through the sales corporation, Stanley and Sturgis realized profits which would have gone to the manufacturing companies. Stanley and Sturgis maintained that the minority shareholder and the minority directors of the manufacturing companies were informed of their interests in the contracts. The court invalidated the contracts.]

PETERS, PRESIDING JUSTICE.

It is argued that, since the fact of common directorship was fully known to the boards of the contracting corporations, and because the * * * majority stockholders consented to the transaction, the minority stockholder and directors of the manufacturing companies have no legal cause to complain. In other words, it is argued that if the majority directors and stockholders inform the minority that they are going to mulct the corporation, section 820 of the Corporations Code * constitutes an impervious armor against any attack on the transaction short of actual fraud. If this interpretation of the section were sound, it would be a shocking reflection on the law of California. It would completely disregard the first sentence of section 820 setting forth the elementary rule that "Directors and officers shall exercise their powers in good faith, and with a view to the interests of the corporation", and would mean that if conniving directors simply disclose their dereliction to the powerless minority, any transaction by which the majority desire to mulct the minority is immune from attack. That is not and cannot be the law.

Section 820 of the Corporations Code is based on former section 311 of the Civil Code, first added to our law in 1931. Stats. of 1931, Chap. 862, p. 1777. Before the adoption of that section it was the law that the mere existence of a common directorate, at least where the vote of the common director was essential to consummate the transaction, invalidated the contract. Caminetti v. Prudence etc. Ins. Ass'n, 62 Cal.App.2d 945, 950, 146 P.2d 15. That rule was changed in 1931 when section 311 was added to the Civil Code, and limited to a greater extent by the adoption of section 820 of the Corporations Code. If the conditions provided for in the section appear, the transaction cannot be set aside simply because there is a common directorate. Here, undoubtedly, there was a literal compliance with subdivision b of the section. The fact of

---

* Section 820 of the Corporations Code, enacted in 1947 and based on former section 311 of the Civil Code, provided:

Directors and officers shall exercise their powers in good faith, and with a view to the interests of the corporation. No contract or other transaction between a corporation and one or more of its directors, or between a corporation and any corporation, firm, or association in which one or more of its directors are directors or are financially interested, is either void or voidable because such director or directors are present at the meeting of the board of directors or a committee thereof which authorizes or approves the contract or transaction, or because his or their votes are counted for such purpose, if the circumstances specified in any of the following subdivisions exist:

(a) The fact of the common directorship or financial interest is disclosed or known to the board of directors or committee and noted in the minutes, and the board or committee authorizes, approves, or ratifies the contract or transaction in good faith by a vote sufficient for the purpose without counting the vote or votes of such director or directors.

(b) The fact of the common directorship or financial interest is disclosed or known to the shareholders, and they approve or ratify the contract or transaction in good faith by a majority vote or written consent of shareholders entitled to vote.

(c) The contract or transaction is just and reasonable as to the corporation at the time it is authorized or approved.

Common or interested directors may be counted in determining the presence of a quorum at a meeting of the board of directors or a committee thereof which authorizes, approves, or ratifies a contract or transaction.—Eds.

the common directorship was disclosed to the stockholders, and the * * * majority stockholders, did approve the contracts.

But neither section 820 of the Corporations Code nor any other provision of the law automatically validates such transactions simply because there has been a disclosure and approval by the majority of the stockholders. That section does not operate to limit the fiduciary duties owed by a director to all the stockholders, nor does it operate to condone acts which, without the existence of a common directorate, would not be countenanced. That section does not permit an officer or director, by an abuse of his power, to obtain an unfair advantage or profit for himself at the expense of the corporation. The director cannot, by reason of his position, drive a harsh and unfair bargain with the corporation he is supposed to represent. If he does so, he may be compelled to account for unfair profits made in disregard of his duty. Even though the requirements of section 820 are technically met, transactions that are unfair and unreasonable to the corporation may be avoided. California Corporation Laws by Ballantine and Sterling (1949 ed.), p. 102, § 84. It would be a shocking concept of corporate morality to hold that because the majority directors or stockholders disclose their purpose and interest, they may strip a corporation of its assets to their own financial advantage, and that the minority is without legal redress. Here the unchallenged findings demonstrate that Stanley and Sturgis used their majority power for their own personal advantage and to the detriment of the minority stockholder. They used it to strip the manufacturing companies of their sales functions—functions which it was their duty to carry out as officers and directors of those companies. There was not one thing done by them acting as the sales corporation that they could not and should not have done as officers and directors and in control of the stock of the manufacturing companies. It is no answer to say that the manufacturing companies made a profit on the deal, or that Stanley and Sturgis did a good job. The point is that those large profits that should have gone to the manufacturing companies were diverted to the sales corporation. The good job done by Stanley and Sturgis should and could have been done for the manufacturing companies. If Stanley and Sturgis, with control of the board of directors and the majority stock of the manufacturing companies, could thus lawfully, to their own advantage, strip the manufacturing companies of their sales functions, they could just as well strip them of their other functions. If the sales functions could be stripped from the companies in this fashion to the personal advantage of Stanley and Sturgis, there would be nothing to prevent them from next organizing a manufacturing company, and transferring to it the manufacturing functions of these companies, thus leaving the manufacturing companies but hollow shells. This should not, is not, and cannot be the law.

It is hornbook law that directors, while not strictly trustees, are fiduciaries, and bear a fiduciary relationship to the corporation, and to all the stockholders. They owe a duty to all stockholders, including the minority stockholders, and must administer their duties for the common benefit. The concept that a corporation is an entity cannot operate so as to lessen the duties owed to all of the stockholders. Directors owe a duty of highest good faith to the corporation and its stockholders. It is a cardinal principle of corporate law that a director cannot, at the expense of the corporation, make an unfair profit from his position. He is precluded from receiving any personal advantage without fullest disclosure to and consent of *all* those affected. The law zealously regards contracts between corporations with interlocking directorates, will carefully scrutinize all such transactions, and in case of unfair dealing to the detriment of minority stockholders, will grant appropriate relief. Where the transaction greatly benefits one corporation at the expense of another, and especially if it personally benefits the majority directors, it will and should be set aside. In other words, while the transaction is not voidable simply because an interested director participated, it will not be upheld if it is unfair to the minority stockholders. These principles are the law in practically all jurisdictions.

MARCIANO v. NAKASH
535 A.2d 400 (Del.1987).

WALSH, JUSTICE.

This is an appeal from a decision of the Court of Chancery which validated a claim in liquidation of Gasoline, Ltd. ("Gasoline"), a Delaware corporation, placed in custodial status pursuant to 8 Del.C. § 226 by reason of a deadlock among its board of directors. Fifty percent of Gasoline is owned by Ari, Joe, and Ralph Nakash (the "Nakashes") and fifty percent by Georges, Maurice, Armand and Paul Marciano (the "Marcianos"). The Vice Chancellor ruled that $2.5 million in loans made by the Nakashes faction to Gasoline were valid and enforceable debts of the corporation, notwithstanding their origin in self-dealing transactions. The Marcianos argue that the disputed debt is voidable as a matter of law but, in any event, the Nakashes failed to meet their burden of establishing full fairness. We conclude that the Vice Chancellor applied the proper standard for review of self-dealing transactions and the finding of full fairness is supported by the record. Accordingly, we affirm.

I

The factual basis underlying the contested loans was fully developed in the Court of Chancery. The liquidation proceeding marked the end of a joint venture launched in 1984 by the Marcianos and the Nakashes to market designer jeans and sportswear. Through a solely owned corporation called Guess? Inc. ("Guess"), the California based Marcianos had been engaged in the design and distribution of stylized jeans for several years. In 1983 they decided to form a separate division to market copies of Guess creations in a broader retail market. In order to secure financing and broaden market exposure the Marcianos entered into negotiations with the New York based Nakash brothers, the owners of

Jordache Enterprises, Inc. a leading manufacturer of jeans. Ultimately, it was agreed that the Nakashes would receive fifty percent of the stock of Guess for a consideration of $4.7 million. As a result, the three Nakash brothers joined three of the Marcianos on the Guess board of directors.

Similarly, when Gasoline was formed, stock ownership and board composition was shared equally by the two families. Although corporate control and direction were equally divided, from an operational standpoint Gasoline functioned in New York under the Nakashes' operational guidance while the parent, Guess, continued under the primary attention of the Marcianos. Differences between the two factions quickly surfaced with resulting deadlocks at the director level of both Guess and Gasoline. The Marcianos filed an action, partly derivative, against Guess and the Nakashes in California followed by the Delaware proceeding in which the Marcianos sought the appointment of a custodian for Gasoline in addition to asserting derivative claims for diversion of corporate opportunities and assets arising out of the Nakashes' operation of Gasoline. Ultimately, the derivative aspect of the Delaware action was stayed in favor of the California proceedings and the Court of Chancery, after a court-ordered shareholder's meeting failed to resolve the director deadlock, appointed a custodian whose power was limited to resolving deadlocks on the Gasoline board.

The custodial arrangement failed to resolve the underlying policy differences between the two factions and neither group appeared willing to invest additional funds or provide guarantees to permit Gasoline to function as a viable commercial enterprise. In early 1987 the custodian advised the Court of Chancery that because of a lack of financing Gasoline had no prospects of continuation and recommended liquidation. A court-approved plan of liquidation authorized the custodian to sell the assets of Gasoline (with both the Marcianos and the Nakashes permitted to bid), pay all valid debts of the corporation and distribute the net proceeds to the shareholders. The determination of those debts, in particular the loan claims asserted by the Nakashes, was sharply disputed in the Court of Chancery and is the focus of this appeal.

The circumstances underlying the Nakashes' claim were determined by the Vice Chancellor following an evidentiary hearing. Prior to March, 1986, Gasoline had secured the necessary financing to support its inventory purchases from the Israel Discount Bank in New York. The bank advanced funds at one percent above prime rate secured by Gasoline's accounts receivable and the Nakashes' personal guarantee. Although requested to do so, the Marcianos were unwilling to participate in loan guarantees because of their dissatisfaction with the Nakashes' management. In response, the Nakashes withdrew their guarantees causing the Israel Discount Bank to terminate its outstanding loan of $1.6 million.

Without consulting the Marcianos, the Nakashes advanced approximately $2.3 million of their personal funds to Gasoline to enable the corporation to pay outstanding bills and acquire inventory. In June, 1986, the Nakashes arranged for U.F. Factors, an entity owned by them, to assume their personal loans and become Gasoline's lender. U.F. Factors charged interest at one percent over prime to which the Nakashes added one percent for their personal guarantees of the U.F. Factors loan. As of April 24, 1987, Gasoline's debt to U.F. Factors amounted to $2,575,000 of which $25,000 represented the Nakashes' guarantee fee. Another Nakash entity, Jordache Enterprises, also sought payment from Gasoline of two percent of the company's gross sales, or $30,000 for warehousing and invoicing services.

In November, 1986, the Nakashes had replaced the U.F. Factors loan, secured by a series of promissory notes executed by Gasoline, with a line of credit collateralized by Gasoline's assets including trademarks and copyrights. This action took place without the knowledge or consent of the custodian and was subsequently rescinded by the Nakashes. At the time of the court-ordered sale of assets, the Nakashes and their entities were general creditors of Gasoline. If allowed in full the Nakashes' claim will exhaust Gasoline's assets, leaving nothing for its shareholders.

The parties agree that the loans made by the Nakashes to Gasoline were interested transactions. The Nakashes as officers of Gasoline executed the various documents which supported the loans and at the same time guaranteed those loans extended through their wholly owned entities. It is also not disputed that, given the control deadlock, the questioned transactions did not receive majority approval of Gasoline's directors or shareholders. The Marcianos argue that the loan transaction is voidable at the option of the corporation notwithstanding its fairness or the good faith of its participants. A review of this contention, rejected by the Court of Chancery, requires analysis of the concept of director self-dealing under Delaware law.

II

It is a long-established principle of Delaware corporate law that the fiduciary relationship between directors and the corporation imposes fundamental limitations on the extent to which a director may benefit from dealings with the corporation he serves. Guth v. Loft, Inc., Del. Supr., 5 A.2d 503 (1939). Thus, the "voting [for] and taking" of compensation may be deemed "constructively fraudulent" in the absence of shareholder ratification, or statutory or bylaw authorization. Cahall v. Lofland, Del.Ch., 114 A. 224, 232 (1921). Perhaps the strongest condemnation of interested director conduct appears in Potter v. Sanitary Co. of America, Del.Ch., 194 A. 87 (1937), a decision which the Marcianos advance as definitive of the rule of per se voidability. In Potter the Court of Chancery characterized transactions between corporations having common directors and officers "constructively fraudulent," absent shareholder ratification.

Support can also be found for the per se rule of voidability in this Court's decision in Kerbs v. California Eastern Airways Inc., Del.Supr.,

90 A.2d 652 (1952). The Kerbs court, in considering the validity of a profit sharing plan, ruled that the self-interest of the directors who voted on the plan caused the transaction to be voidable. The court concluded that the profit sharing plan was voidable based on the common law rule that the vote of an interested director will not be counted in determining whether the challenged action received the affirmative vote of a majority of the board of directors. Id. at 658 (citing Bovay v. H.M. Byllesby & Co., Del.Supr., 38 A.2d 808 (1944)).

The principle of per se voidability for interested transactions, which is sometimes characterized as the common law rule, was significantly ameliorated by the 1967 enactment of section 144 of the Delaware General Corporation Law. The Marcianos argue that section 144(a) provides the only basis for immunizing self-interested transactions and since none of the statute's component tests are satisfied the stricture of the common law per se rule applies. The Vice Chancellor agreed that the disputed loans did not withstand a section 144(a) analysis but ruled that the common law rule did not invalidate transactions determined to be intrinsically fair. We agree that section 144(a) does not provide the only validation standard for interested transactions.

It overstates the common law rule to conclude that relationship, alone, is the controlling factor in interested transactions. Although the application of the per se voidability rule in early Delaware cases resulted in the invalidation of interested transactions, the result was not dictated simply by a tainted relationship. Thus in *Potter*, the Court, while adopting the rule of voidability, emphasized that interested transactions should be subject to close scrutiny. Where the undisputed evidence tended to show that the transaction would advance the personal interests of the directors at the expense of stockholders, the stockholders, upon discovery, are entitled to disavow the transaction. *Potter*, 194 A. at 91. Further, the court examined the motives of the defendant directors and the effect the transaction had on the corporation and its shareholders. Id.

In other Delaware cases, decided before the enactment of section 144, interested director transactions were deemed voidable only after an examination of the fairness of a particular transaction vis-a-vis the nonparticipating shareholders and a determination of whether the disputed conduct received the approval of a noninterested majority of directors or shareholders. The latter test is now crystallized in the ratification criteria of section 144(a), although the non-quorum restriction of *Kerbs* has been superceded by the language of subparagraph (b) of section 144.

The Marcianos view compliance with section 144 as the sole basis for avoiding the per se rule of voidability. The Court of Chancery rejected this contention and we agree that it is not consonant with Delaware corporate law. This Court in Fliegler v. Lawrence, Del.Supr., 361 A.2d 218 (1976), a post-section 144 decision, refused to view section 144 as either completely preemptive of the common law duty of director fidelity or as constituting a grant of broad immunity. As we stated in *Fliegler*: "It merely removes an 'interested director' cloud when its terms are met and provides against invalidation of an agreement 'solely' because such a director or officer is involved." Id. at 222. In *Fliegler* this Court applied a two-tiered analysis: application of section 144 coupled with an intrinsic fairness test.

If section 144 validation of interested director transactions is not deemed exclusive, as Fliegler clearly holds, the continued viability of the intrinsic fairness test is mandated not only by fact situations, such as here present, where shareholder deadlock prevents ratification but also where shareholder control by interested directors precludes independent review. Indeed, if an independent committee of the board, contemplated by section 144(a)(1) is unavailable, the sole forum for demonstrating intrinsic fairness may be a judicial one. In such situations the intrinsic fairness test furnishes the substantive standard against which the evidential burden of the interested directors is applied. It is this burden which was addressed by this Court in Weinberger v. UOP, Inc., Del. Supr., 457 A.2d 701 (1983):

> When directors of a Delaware corporation are on both sides of a transaction, they are required to demonstrate their utmost good faith and the most scrupulous inherent fairness of the bargain.
>
> * * *
>
> The requirement of fairness is unflinching in its demand that where one stands on both sides of a transaction, he has the burden of establishing its entire fairness, sufficient to pass the test of careful scrutiny by the courts.

Id. at 710.

This case illustrates the limitation inherent in viewing section 144 as the touchstone for testing interested director transactions. Because of the shareholder deadlock, even if the Nakashes had attempted to invoke section 144, it was realistically unavailable. The ratification process contemplated by section 144 presupposes the functioning of corporate constituencies capable of providing assents. Just as the statute cannot "sanction unfairness" neither can it invalidate fairness if, upon judicial review, the transaction withstands close scrutiny of its intrinsic elements.[3]

3. Although in this case none of the curative steps afforded under section 144(a) were available because of the director-shareholder deadlock, a non-disclosing director seeking to remove the cloud of interestedness would appear to have the same burden under section 144(a)(3), as under prior case law, of proving the intrinsic fairness of a questioned transaction which had been approved or ratified by the directors or shareholders. Folk, The Delaware General Corp. Law: A Commentary and Analysis, 86 (1972). On the other hand, approval by fully-informed disinterested directors under section 144(a)(1), or disinterested stockholders under section 144(a)(2), permits invocation of the business judgment rule and limits judicial review to issues of gift or waste with the burden of proof upon the party attacking the transaction.

III

On the issue of intrinsic fairness, the Court of Chancery concluded that the "U.F. Factors loans compared favorably with the terms available from unrelated lenders" and that the need for external financing had been clearly demonstrated. The Marcianos attack this ruling as factually and legally erroneous. Since the Vice Chancellor's factual findings were arrived at after an evidentiary hearing we are not free to reject them unless they are without record support or not the product of a logical deductive process. We find this standard to have been fully satisfied here.

Apart from the initial investment of $300,000 contributed equally by the Marcianos and the Nakashes, Gasoline's financial needs had been met through external borrowings. It is unnecessary to lay blame for the impasse which resulted in the Marcianos refusal to supply additional equity funding. It suffices to note that throughout 1985 and 1986, Gasoline was able to function only through cash advances from, and loans obtained by, the Nakashes, first through the Israel Discount Bank and later through U.F. Factors. During this period the evidence reflects the continued threat of bank overdrafts and inability to pay for purchases, particularly imported finished goods.

A finding of fairness is particularly appropriate in this case because the evidence indicates that the loans were made by the Nakashes with the bona fide intention of assisting Gasoline's efforts to remain in business. Directors who advance funds to a corporation in such circumstances do not forfeit their claims as creditors merely because of relationship. Further, in arranging for the loan, the interested directors were not depriving the corporation of a business opportunity but were instead providing a benefit for the corporation which was unavailable elsewhere.

The Marcianos argue that the Nakashes failed to demonstrate the full fairness of the loan transactions in two fundamental respects: the cost of the borrowings and the use of the funds. It is not disputed, however, that the direct financing by the Nakashes was essentially duplicative of the terms imposed by the Israel Discount Bank in an apparent arms-length transaction. We agree therefore with the Vice Chancellor that, on a comparative basis, the direct loans were favorable to Gasoline.

* * *

We hold, therefore, that the Court of Chancery properly applied the intrinsic fairness test in determining the validity of the interested director transactions and its finding of full fairness is clearly supported by the record. Accordingly, the decision is AFFIRMED.

Note: *Marciano v. Nakash*

The Delaware Supreme Court's opinion in *Marciano* is the source of some uncertainty about the proper interpretation of DGCL § 144. On the one hand, the text of the opinion appears to confirm the language in *Fliegler* that, regardless of § 144, interested director transactions are always subject to an intrinsic fairness test. On the other hand, footnote 3 seems to move away from such a test by referring to the use of the business judgment rule after there has been disinterested approval under § 144 (a)(1) or (a)(2).

Some of the ambiguity may stem from the decision in *Fliegler* itself. There, a shareholder brought a derivative suit on behalf of Agau Mines against its officers and directors (including the named defendant Lawrence), and another corporation, United States Antimony Corp. (USAC), which was owned primarily by Lawrence and the other defendants. Lawrence had acquired, in his individual capacity, certain mining properties which he transferred to USAC. Agau later acquired USAC in exchange for 800,000 shares of Agau stock. Fliegler, believing the self-interested transaction to be unfair, challenged the transaction. The defendants claimed that they had been relieved of the burden of proving the transaction's fairness because it had been ratified by Agau's shareholders pursuant to § 144(a)(2). The court, however, held that the purported ratification did not affect the burden of proof because the majority of shares voted in favor of the acquisition were cast by the defendants in their capacity as Agau stockholders. Only one-third of the disinterested shareholders cast votes. Thus, the *Fliegler* court determined that despite the absence of any provision in § 144(a)(2) requiring *disinterested* shareholder approval of an interested director transaction, as a condition of shifting the burden of proof from the interested director to the challenging shareholder, it would impose such a requirement.

Having decided the burden of proof question, the court then addressed the proper interpretation of the disjunctive language of § 144. The court rejected the argument that compliance with § 144(a)(2) automatically validated the transaction and concluded that the statute "merely removes an 'interested director' cloud when its terms are met and provides against invalidation of an agreement 'solely' because such a director or officer is involved. Nothing in the statute sanctions unfairness to Agau or removes the transaction from judicial scrutiny." 361 A.2d at 222. It is this last language that appears to be in conflict with footnote 3 in *Marciano*.

At least one recent decision has cited *Marciano* with no apparent recognition of the potential ambiguity in the opinion. See Citron v. E.I. Du Pont de Nemours & Co., 584 A.2d 490, 500–01 (Del.Ch.1990). The disjunctive reading in footnote 3 of *Marciano* would, however, be consistent with other holdings of the Delaware Supreme Court. See, e.g., Puma v. Marriott, 283 A.2d 693 (Del.Ch.1971) (not decided under § 144 but applying business judgment standard of review where disinterested directors approved purchase of corporations owned by family group including inside directors, according to terms not dictated by inside directors). For competing views on the proper interpretation of *Fliegler* and *Marciano*, see Melvin A. Eisenberg, Self–Interested Transactions in Corporate Law, 13 J. Corp. L. 997 (1988), and E. Norman Veasey, et al.,

Counseling Directors on the Business Judgment Rule and the Duty of Loyalty, 731 PLI/Corp. 475 (Westlaw 1991) and Charles Hansen, John F. Johnson & Frederick H. Alexander, The Role of Disinterested Directors in "Conflict" Transactions: The ALI Corporate Governance Project and Existing Law, 45 Bus.Law. 2083 (1990).

D. FAIRNESS: PROCEDURAL AND SUBSTANTIVE

Although the validity of an interested director transaction may be subject to review under the business judgment rule in some circumstances, that is not the general rule. Rather, at both common law and under existing statutes, the test is whether the transaction was "fair" to the corporation at the time it was entered into. Fairness has procedural and substantive elements, both of which must be satisfied before the transaction will be validated. *Shlensky* and the cases it cites refer to the test as one of "entire fairness." Who has the ultimate burden of proving substantive fairness (or the lack of it) may depend on how the issue of procedural fairness is resolved.

1. PROCEDURAL FAIRNESS

a. *Disinterested Director Approval*

One test for procedural fairness is whether the transaction was approved by disinterested directors. Under this test, a director is "disinterested" if neither she nor her family nor any entity in which she has a financial interest have a financial interest in the transaction, and if her judgment is not adversely affected by her relationship with the interested director. At common law, many cases held that a transaction between an interested director and her corporation was voidable without regard to its substantive fairness if the director's vote was needed to make up the majority to approve it or even if the director's presence was necessary to constitute a quorum to bring the matter to a vote.

ALI, PRINCIPLES OF CORPORATE GOVERNANCE (1994)

§ 1.23. INTERESTED

(a) A director or officer is "interested" in a transaction if:

(1) The director or officer, or an associate of the director or officer, is a party to the transaction;

(2) The director or officer has a business, financial, or familial relationship with a party to the transaction, and that relationship would reasonably be expected to affect the director's or officer's judgment with respect to the transaction in a manner adverse to the corporation;

(3) The director or officer, an associate of the director or officer, or a person with whom the director or officer has a business,

financial, or familial relationship, has a material pecuniary interest in the transaction (other than usual and customary directors' fees and benefits) and that interest would reasonably be expected to affect the directors's or officer's judgment in a manner adverse to the corporation; or

(4) The director or officer is subject to a controlling influence by a party to the transaction or a person who has a material pecuniary interest in the transaction, and that controlling influence could reasonably be expected to affect the director's or officer's judgment with respect to the transaction in a manner adverse to the corporation.

* * *

Comment to § 1.23:

* * * An officer who is a director is presumed to be interested when passing on a transaction entered into by a senior executive to whom the officer is subordinate. * * * Normally, however, the burden of coming forward with evidence and the burden of proof will be on the party attacking a transaction or conduct of a director, senior executive, or dominating shareholder to show specifically that the transaction or conduct was not authorized by disinterested directors or authorized or ratified by disinterested shareholders.

A person who neither is an associate of, nor has a pecuniary interest in or financial relationship to, a party to the transaction will normally not be interested within the meaning of § 1.23. However, § 1.23 permits a court to conclude that a "familial relationship" may cause a person to be considered an interested director or officer. On the facts of a particular case, and particularly where a corporation is not a publicly held corporation, a court may conclude that a familial relationship more remote than one which would constitute the person an associate, but which involves the same degree of intimacy as a relationship with a family member who is an associate, may be sufficiently significant as to cause the person to be an interested director or officer. Furthermore, a court may determine that what is in effect a "familial relationship" exists for purposes of § 1.23 even though the relationship is not a legally established matrimonial relationship. * * *

What appears to be disinterested board approval may be disregarded by a court where the board is in fact subject to a controlling influence by a director who is interested in the transaction. Such an influence is most likely to occur in the case of a board that is dominated by a controlling shareholder.

It is not intended that a person would be treated as subject to a controlling influence, and therefore interested, because of a long-time friendship or other social relationship, or solely because of a long-time business association through service on the same board of directors or other relationship not involving direct pecuniary dealing. However, where senior executives of two corporations sit on each other's board of directors, and each senior executive is in a position to review the other's compensation or other transactions in which the senior executive is pecuniarily interested, a court could consider that fact in determining whether in the circumstances of a particular case each of the senior executives is interested when reviewing such transactions.

A director is not interested under § 1.23 solely because the director receives or has an expectation of continuing to receive reasonable director's fees or because the director wants to continue the directorship for nonpecuniary reasons, or because a particular transaction in control threatens the loss of the position as a director and therefore of usual and customary directors' fees.

————

Under RMBCA § 8.31(c), a majority of the disinterested directors on the board of directors or on a committee of the board can constitute a quorum to authorize, approve, or ratify a conflict of interest transaction, but more than one director must approve a transaction. The presence of an interested director at the meeting does not affect the validity of action taken by disinterested directors. § 8.31 does not define "interested" or a "direct" interest, although § 8.31(b) does define the concept of "indirect" interest to include an entity in which the director has a financial or managerial interest.

N.Y.B.C.L. § 713(a)(1) provides that if there are insufficient disinterested directors to approve the transaction under normal quorum requirements, the transaction may be authorized by unanimous vote of the disinterested directors. DGCL § 144(a) requires only that the transaction be authorized "by the affirmative votes of a majority of the disinterested directors, even though the disinterested directors be less than a quorum." It could be argued that under either of these provisions a "unanimous" or "majority" vote of one director would suffice to meet the requirements for disinterested director approval. Would you counsel reliance on such an interpretation, particularly in light of RMBCA § 8.31(c)?

b. Domination

Even if a director is "disinterested" in the transaction, board approval will not validate the transaction if the otherwise disinterested directors were "dominated" by a party interested in the transaction. "Domination" is largely defined by judicial decisions.

In *Shlensky*, the court stated, "[I]t is not the mere number of common directors which determines whether approval has been given by an independent and disinterested majority of directors, but rather whether a majority of the directors are dominated by an individual or group." 19 Ill.2d 268, 284, 166 N.E.2d 793, 802 (1960). The problem is especially acute where the interested director is also a major or controlling shareholder.

Globe Woolen Co. v. Utica Gas & Electric Co., 224 N.Y. 483, 121 N.E. 378 (1918) involved a contract between Globe Woolen and Utica Gas, a utility company. Maynard, the president of Globe Woolen also was a controlling shareholder of, and the dominant figure on the Utica Gas board. He had negotiated the challenged contract which had proved to be disastrously disadvantageous to Utica Gas. The court found that Maynard dominated the Utica Gas board and that he was "interested" in the transaction. Although his refusal to vote gave the transaction the form and presumption of propriety, the court held that the transaction unfair and voidable by Utica Gas. Judge Cardozo wrote:

[As a result of the contract, Utica Gas has] supplied the plaintiff with electric current for nothing, and owes, if the contract stands, about $11,000 for the privilege. These elements of unfairness, Mr. Maynard must have known, if indeed his knowledge be material. He may not have known how great the loss would be. He may have trusted to the superior technical skill of Mr. Greenidge [an employee of Utica Gas] to compute with approximate accuracy the comparative cost of steam and electricity. But he cannot have failed to know that he held a one-sided contract, which left the defendant at his mercy. He was not blind to the likelihood that in a term of ten years there would be changes in the business. The swiftness with which some of the changes followed permits the inference that they were premeditated. * * * But whether these and other changes were premeditated or not, at least they were recognized as possible. With that recognition, no word of warning was uttered to Greenidge or to any of the defendant's officers. There slumbered within these contracts a potency of profit which the plaintiff neither ignored in their making nor forgot in their enforcement.

It is no answer to say that this potency, if obvious to Maynard, ought also to have been obvious to other members of the committee. They did not know, as he did, the likelihood or the significance of changes in the business. There was need, too, of reflection and analysis before the dangers stood revealed. For the man who framed the contracts there was opportunity to consider and to judge. His fellow members, hearing them for the first time, and trustful of his loyalty, would have no thought of latent peril. That they had none is sufficiently attested by the fact that the contracts were approved. There was inequality, therefore, both in knowledge and in the opportunity for knowledge. It is not important in such circumstances whether the trustee foresaw the precise evils that developed. The inference that he did, might not be unsupported by the evidence. But the indefinite possibilities of hardship, the opportunity in changing circumstances to wrest unlooked-for profits and impose unlooked-for losses, these must have been foreseen. Foreseen or not, they were there, and their presence permeates the contracts with oppression and inequity.

We hold, therefore, that the refusal to vote does not nullify as of course an influence and predominance exerted without a vote. We hold that the constant duty rests on a trustee to seek no harsh advantage to the detriment of his trust, but rather to protest and renounce if through the blindness of those who treat with him he gains what is unfair. And because there is evidence that in the making of these contracts, that duty was ignored, the power of equity was fittingly exercised to bring them to an end.

————

Closely related to the *Globe Woolen* case are transactions in which the interested director represents both the corporation and himself in the bargaining process. One court has suggested that "[i]ndispensable to liability for violation of his fiduciary obligation as to any personal transaction with the corporation is the demonstration that a director has acted in a dual capacity—for himself as well as the corporation." Borden v. Guthrie, 23 A.D.2d 313, 260 N.Y.S.2d 769, 774 (1965), aff'd 17 N.Y.2d 571, 268 N.Y.S.2d 330, 215 N.E.2d 511 (1966). *Cf.* David J. Greene & Co. v. Dunhill International, Inc., 249 A.2d 427, 430–31 (Del.Ch.1969), in which the court indicated that

[i]n the absence of divided interests, the judgment of the majority stockholders and/or the board of directors * * * is presumed made in good faith and inspired by a bona fides of purpose. But when the persons * * * who control the making of a transaction and the fixing of its terms, are on both sides, then the presumption and deference to sound business judgment are no longer present.

Note: The Cleveland Browns Case

In Gries Sports Enterprises, Inc. v. Cleveland Browns Football Co., Inc., 26 Ohio St.3d 15, 496 N.E.2d 959 (1986), the court held that the directors of the corporation that owned the Cleveland Browns football team who approved the purchase of all of the stock of the Cleveland Stadium Corp. (CSC) were neither disinterested nor independent and that the acquisition was unfair to the Browns' minority shareholders. The Browns' board consisted of Gries (who owned 43 percent of the outstanding stock of the Browns), Modell (who owned 53 percent of the stock of the Browns and who was president and chief executive officer of the Browns), Modell's wife, Bailey (general counsel and a full-time employee of the Browns), Berick (outside legal counsel for the Browns and owner of less than 1 percent of the stock of the Browns), Cole and Wallack (full-time employees of the Browns). Modell owned 80 percent of the stock of CSC; the remaining 20 percent was owned by various individuals including Berick, Bailey, Cole and Wallack. Modell was president and Bailey was secretary and general counsel of CSC. In connection with the issues of interested directors and domination, the court concluded that the Browns' directors, Bailey, Berick, Cole and Wallack, were "interested" "because they had received a personal financial benefit from the challenged transaction" which was not equally shared by the stockholders. It also held that under Delaware case law, Berick was dominated because it was his job to do what Modell request-ed.

In analyzing the position of Berick and Bailey, one dissenting justice questioned what he called "the majority's simplistic analysis that merely because Berick was an officer in the Browns, and functioned accordingly, that he was not an independent director."

Berick's disinterest is * * * attacked by asserting that he, as outside legal counsel through his law firm, planned and prepared both transactions. As a matter of law, the presence of outside directors enhances the presumption of validity attributable to a director's actions. See, e.g., Puma v. Marriott, 283 A.2d 693 (Del. Ch.1971). In this case, the fee ultimately paid to Berick's firm for legal services was approximately twenty to twenty-five thousand dollars, which is asserted by appellants to be a financial interest in the outcome of the transaction. It is also asserted that because Modell offered to buy Berick's shares of Browns stock, that Berick was dominated by Modell.

However, the fee for services paid to Berick's firm was not at all dependent on the transactions at issue. Payment was owed and would have been made, despite the outcome of the board's vote. Nor was the law firm dependent on the Browns, since the Browns constituted less than one percent of that firm's business. Also, Berick refused to sell his shares of stock to Modell. Although Berick was enthusiastic concerning the acquisition of CSC, nothing about his opinion indicates anything other than a personal viewpoint. The fact that Berick sits as a director on the boards of a number of corporations, public and private, indicates a professional attitude. Thus, there was no dominance or tainting self-interest in his vote.

The majority fully misstates the law of Delaware by its state-ment that "Bailey's dual positions as an officer and general counsel for both corporations make him an 'interested' director." There are no Delaware cases which support this view. In fact, the cases utilized by the majority would agree that an interested director is one who is on both sides of the transaction, and who somehow wrongfully receives a benefit.

Bailey, who is in-house counsel to the Browns, is said to be an interested director because he helped to structure the two transac-tions. It was also alleged that Modell dominated him because he was presented to the board by Modell for the position of director and, at times, Modell sent Bailey to negotiate for him.

The law of Delaware makes it clear that positional relationships, without more, do not rise to disqualification of the director's vote. In the view of the Delaware Supreme Court, "it is not enough to charge that a director was nominated by or elected at the behest of those controlling the outcome of a corporate election. That is the usual way a person becomes a corporate director. It is the care, attention and sense of individual responsibility to the performance of one's duties, not the method of election, that generally touches on independence." [Aronson v. Lewis, 473 A.2d 805 (Del.1984).] "Such contentions do not support any claim under Delaware law that * * * directors lack independence." Id. at 815. Instead, it must be demonstrated that the directors "through personal or other relationships * * * are beholden to the controlling person. See Mayer v. Adams, Del.Ch., 167 A.2d 729, 732 * * *." Id.

Because of Bailey's position, he would naturally have negotiated for the Browns and, consequently, Modell. He was approved as a director by the entire board, including Gries. At no time was there proof of any self-dealing by Bailey. He personally believed the Browns should acquire CSC so as to control the team's playing facilities. Mere like-mindedness on issues hardly rises to the level of domination or self-interest.

496 N.E.2d at 977–78.

––––––––

It is important to note that courts have generally refused to find that "structural bias," alone, resulting from long-term non-financial relations of trust among directors, amounts to domination. Domination always appears to require an element of financial dependence on the "dominating" director, for example, in the form of employment or future business.

c. Timing of Approval

Should a different standard be applied to board action authorizing directors to enter into a transaction than to board action ratifying a transaction already consummated? Professor Buxbaum suggests that it is only in the former situation that directors should be able to avail themselves of the benefits of disinterested director approval. Richard M. Buxbaum, Conflict–of–Interest Statutes and the Need for a Demand on Directors in Derivative Actions, 68 Cal.L.Rev. 1122 (1980). Even if such a reading is not compelled by the statutory language. Professor Buxbaum concludes that:

[t]his distinction intuitively makes sense. One need not totally accept * * * comments about the difficult position of nominally independent directors who are expected coolly to judge their fellow directors' behavior to embrace the narrower proposition implicit in these statutes: that however difficult it may be to restrain fellow directors from a proposed course of conduct, it is excessively difficult to repudiate a transaction already effected by one's fellow directors, thereby subjecting them, among other things, to financial sanctions.

Id. at 1127.

The ALI has partially accepted Professor Buxbaum's view. See ALI, Principles of Corporate Governance: Analysis and Recommendations, § 5.02(a)(2)(C) (1994).

d. Shareholder Approval

An interested director transaction can also be found to be procedurally fair if it has been approved or subsequently ratified by shareholder vote provided that the material facts as to the transaction and the director's interest were disclosed to the shareholders. At common law, many cases held that if the terms of the transaction were substantively fair, the shares of the interested director could be voted in favor of ratification. Other decisions held that such shares could not be voted because interested directors could not ratify their own contracts with the corporation. Courts were divided as to whether a majority of informed shareholders could ratify a fraudulent transaction, or whether such ratification required unanimous approval. Where those issues did not arise, shareholder ratification created a presumption that the transaction was fair. Thus, some courts indicated that shareholder ratification has the effect of shifting the burden of proof to the party challenging the transaction to show that the terms were so unequal as to amount to waste. See Gottlieb v. Heyden Chemical Corp., 33 Del.Ch. 177, 91 A.2d 57 (1952); Eliasberg v. Standard Oil Co., 23 N.J.Super. 431, 92 A.2d 862 (Ch.Div.1952), aff'd 12 N.J. 467, 97 A.2d 437 (1953). Where, however, the interested directors own a majority of the shares, shareholder ratification generally does not shift the burden of proving unfairness to the challenging party. See Brundage v. New Jersey Zinc Co., 48 N.J. 450, 226 A.2d 585 (1967); Pappas v. Moss, 393 F.2d 865 (3d Cir.1968); David J. Greene & Co. v. Dunhill International, Inc., 249 A.2d 427 (Del.Ch.1968).

It appears that the shareholder approval provision of the interested director statutes, at least as interpreted by *Remillard Brick* and other decisions, codify the common law. Thus an interested director transaction is not void or voidable if the director's interest is disclosed to the shareholders and the shareholders approve the transaction. However, technical compliance with the statutory procedures will not immunize a transaction from scrutiny for fairness where the interested directors are also majority shareholders who vote in favor of the transaction. Would the rationale of *Remillard Brick* apply where the interested directors own a controlling but less than majority interest in the corporation? Where they own less than a controlling interest, but their votes are necessary for majority approval of a transaction?

To avoid the uncertainty of whether shareholder approval is valid if the interested directors vote their shares, it is now common to obtain "majority of the minority" shareholder approval as a condition of the transaction, particularly in controlled mergers. See Weinberger v. UOP, Inc., 457 A.2d 701 (Del.1983), discussed in Chapter 23. Cal.Corp.Code § 310(a)(1)) adopts the "majority of the minority" approach in transactions in which the directors have a material financial interest. Two commentators criticize this provision for having the effect of validating the transaction, thus precluding judicial scrutiny for fairness. Ahmed Bulbulia and Arthur R. Pinto, Statutory Responses to Interested Directors' Transactions: A Watering Down of Fiduciary Standards?, 53 Notre Dame Law. 201, 220 (1977).

The ALI's definition of an "interested" shareholder is narrower than its definition of an "interested" director. Thus, § 1.23(b) defines a shareholder as "interested" in a transaction "if either the shareholder or, to the shareholder's knowledge, an associate of the shareholder is a party to the transaction or the shareholder is also an interested director with respect to the same transaction." The ALI explains the difference by stating that "due to the practical difficulties that may arise in seeking to determine whether shareholders in a publicly owned corporation have an interest in a transaction, the test whether a shareholder is interested has been framed more narrowly than in the case of a director." ALI, Principles of Corporate Governance (1994), Comment to § 1.23. Is this explanation persuasive, or does the difference arise from the different roles that shareholders and directors generally play in a corporate governance system?

In that connection, consider the views of Harold Marsh:

> The rule [permitting shareholder approval of an interested director transaction after full disclosure] has been justified on the basis that where there is shareholder ratification the case is precisely analogous to that of a trustee dealing with his cestui que trust after full disclosure, and is not at all a case of a trustee dealing with himself. However, the validity of this analogy may be seriously questioned. When a trustee deals with his cestui que trust who is an individual that is sui juris, after full disclosure, then the cestui que trust is able to negotiate for himself and there is no more danger of fraud or over-reaching than in any other business transaction. However, when the shareholders of a publicly-held company are asked to ratify a transaction with interested directors they cannot as a practical matter *negotiate* for the corporation. They are, they must be, limited to rejecting or accepting the deal formulated by the interested directors. Even if it be assumed that the deal is fair, that is not what the shareholders are entitled to. They are entitled to have someone negotiate the best deal obtainable for their corporation, fair or unfair. This the interested directors cannot do. As the New Hampshire court said, it is "impossible for common directors to procure the lowest rates for one party and the highest rates for the other. * * * They were not arbitrators, called in to adjust conflicting claims. * * *"

Harold Marsh, Are Directors Trustees? Conflict of Interest and Corporate Morality, 22 Bus.Law. 35, 48–49 (1966).

e. *Disclosure*

Procedural fairness requires adequate disclosure of the existence of a conflict, and of other "material" information concerning the substance of the transaction, to the disinterested directors or to the shareholders from whom approval of the transaction is sought.

In State ex rel. Hayes Oyster Co. v. Keypoint Oyster Co., 64 Wash.2d 375, 391 P.2d 979 (1964), the president, a director and substantial shareholder, arranged for the sale of corporate properties to another corporation in which he was to have an interest. The transaction was submitted to the shareholders for their approval, but without disclosure of the director's interest. The director voted a majority of the stock, including his own, in favor of the sale. In invalidating the transaction, the court stated:

> [T]his court has abolished the mechanical rule whereby any transaction involving corporate property in which a director has an interest is voidable at the option of the corporation. Such a contract cannot be voided if the director or officer can show that the transaction was fair to the corporation. However, non-disclosure by an interested director or officer is, in itself, unfair. This wholesome rule can be applied automatically without any of the unsatisfactory results which flowed from a rigid bar against any self-dealing.

* * *

> [The] shareholders and directors had the right to know of Hayes' interest in [the properties] in order to intelligently determine the advisability of retaining Hayes as president and manager under the circumstances, and to determine whether or not it was wise to enter into the contract at all, in view of Hayes' conduct. In all fairness, they were entitled to know that their president and director might be placed in a position where he must choose between the interest[s of the two corporations in conducting their business with one another.]

391 P.2d at 984.

Although this language suggests that only the existence of the director's interest in the transaction need be disclosed, the court also said that the director was obligated to disclose fully all relevant or material information concerning the transaction to the directors and shareholders. This statement reflects the views of most common law courts. The question of what is "material information" will be considered more closely in Chapter 18.

f. Charter Provisions

Might the possibility of a successful attack on an interested director transaction be minimized by including a provision in the corporate charter that such transactions are valid for all purposes if ratified by the board of directors upon disclosure of the directors' interest? Can the shareholder elect not to subject interested director transactions to the duty of loyalty?

As we saw in Chapter 16, in states whose director exculpation statutes exclude the duty of loyalty, such a provision clearly would be invalid. At common law, however, the few cases that considered the impact of such a clause are in conflict. In Everett v. Phillips, 288 N.Y.

227, 43 N.E.2d 18, 22 (1942) (decided before adoption of the New York interested director statute) the court indicated that while transactions in which directors have acted in a dual capacity should be carefully scrutinized, the existence of the clause shifted the burden of proof on the question of fairness to the plaintiffs.   The court held that a charter provision "expressly authorizing the directors to act even in matters where they have dual interest, has the effect of exonerating the directors, at least in part, 'from adverse inferences which might otherwise be drawn against them.' "   But in both Abeles v. Adams Engineering Co., 35 N.J. 411, 173 A.2d 246 (1961) and Pappas v. Moss, 393 F.2d 865 (3d Cir.1968), the courts held that such charter provisions only authorized the directors to enter into conflict of interest transactions, and placed the burden of proving fairness on the interested directors.

Charter provisions also have been found to be effective in rebutting adverse inferences generally attaching to other aspects of conflict of interest transactions.   Thus, in Sterling v. Mayflower Hotel Corp., 33 Del.Ch. 20, 89 A.2d 862 (1952), the court found that despite the common law rule that a transaction would be voidable if interested directors were counted in determining the presence of a quorum, where a charter provision authorized interested directors to be counted for such purposes, the board's approval of the transaction was not invalid, at least where the transaction would subsequently be submitted to the shareholders for approval, and where the transaction was fair to the corporation.   Cf. Piccard v. Sperry Corp., 48 F.Supp. 465 (S.D.N.Y.1943), aff'd 152 F.2d 462 (2d Cir.1946), cert. denied 328 U.S. 845, 66 S.Ct. 1024, 90 L.Ed. 1619 (1946), upholding board action under such a provision even in the absence of shareholder ratification.

2. SUBSTANTIVE FAIRNESS

The elements of substantive fairness set out in *Shlensky* stress a comparison of the fair market value of the transaction to the price the corporation actually paid, as well as the corporation's need for and ability to consummate the transaction.   The test has often been articulated as "whether the proposition submitted would have commended itself to an independent corporation."   International Radio Telegraph Co. v. Atlantic Communication Co., 290 Fed. 698 (2d Cir.1923).   To the extent that this formulation contemplates independent arms-length negotiation as providing the basis for fair market value, fairness is not limited to a single number; a range of potential values could satisfy the test of substantive fairness.   But even this concept may become problematic in situations where it is difficult or impossible to determine a reliable fair market value, as, for example, would be the case with an intangible asset like undeveloped patent rights.   Because of the difficulties in defining substantive fairness precisely, courts sometimes are influenced in their determination of whether a transaction was substantively fair by whether there were procedural irregularities in the interested director's efforts to validate the transaction. In such a case, the presence or absence of procedural safeguards may lead to the inference of substantive fairness or unfairness in the transaction.

3. FAIRNESS AND THE BURDEN OF PROOF

Most commentators who have considered the interested director statutes agree that compliance with the procedures for board or shareholder approval of interested director transactions will not completely immunize those transactions from judicial scrutiny. See, Ahmed Bulbulia and Arthur R. Pinto, Statutory Responses to Interested Directors' Transactions: A Watering Down of Fiduciary Standards?, 53 Notre Dame Law. 201 (1977); Note, The Status of the Fairness Test Under Section 713 of the New York Business Corporation Law, 76 Colum.L.Rev. 1156 (1976); Alan M. Hoffman, Israels on Corporate Practice § 6.13 (4th ed., 1983). But there is no consensus among either the commentators or the courts as to what is or should be the effect of compliance. Much of the dispute appears to boil down to questions of burdens of proof (both burden of coming forward and of persuasion) and of standards of proof.

In a case in which there is no self-dealing, the directors start with a presumption that they have exercised the appropriate business judgment. The burden is on the plaintiff to show that there has been a breach of the duty of care, or, assuming, that there has not been, that the transaction was tantamount to a waste of corporate assets.

If the plaintiff alleges in the complaint that one or more of the directors has a conflict of interest, any interested director generally loses the presumption of business judgment and must show that the transaction was fair to the corporation. If the interested director can show that the transaction was approved by a disinterested majority of the directors or shareholders, the burden of proof usually shifts back to the plaintiff to show that the transaction was unfair. In this situation, the transaction will be presumed fair and the plaintiff will face a heavy burden.

The language courts use to articulate standards of proof is hopelessly vague. Courts have stated that to uphold or to invalidate a transaction, a party will be required to prove the presence or absence of: fairness; good faith; a bona fide business purpose; reasonableness; intrinsic fairness; constructive fraud; waste; or fraud. What is the quantum of proof required to satisfy each standard, and how does the quantum differ among standards? It may at times be difficult to avoid the conclusion that the court has made its decision by considering the merits of a case and thereafter has buttressed its decision by articulating a particular standard of proof that has or has not been met.

E. CONTEMPORARY STATUTORY REFORM: SUBCHAPTER F AND THE ALI PRINCIPLES OF CORPORATE GOVERNANCE

As we have seen, case law interpreting statutes similar to RMBCA § 8.31 is less clear than a mountain lake. Two major efforts have attempted to clarify the law relating to conflict of interest transactions. In 1989, the Committee on Corporate Laws of the American Bar Association adopted a new Subchapter F to replace the existing § 8.31. The basic provisions of the new sections do not differ materially from existing law in many respects, but they try are designed to preserve the disjunctive force of the word "or" and to provide specific "bright line" definitions of who is an "interested" director and what constitutes a "transaction" to which Subchapter F is applicable. If directors follow the prescribed procedures, the transaction will be subject only to the business judgment rule and not to a fairness standard. The ALI, by contrast, continues to provide a more pro-active role for courts in reviewing the fairness of the transaction. The ALI modifies existing statutes; Subchapter F revamps them.

ALI, PRINCIPLES OF CORPORATE GOVERNANCE (1994)

§ 5.02. Transactions With the Corporation

(a) *General Rule.* A director or senior executive who enters into a transaction with the corporation (other than a transaction involving the payment of compensation) fulfills the duty of fair dealing with respect to the transaction if:

(1) disclosure concerning the conflict of interest and the transaction is made to the corporate decisionmaker who authorizes in advance or ratifies the transaction; and

(2)(A) the transaction is fair to the corporation when entered into; or

(B) the transaction is authorized in advance, following disclosure concerning the conflict of interest and the transaction, by disinterested directors or, in the case of a senior executive who is not a director, authorized in advance by a disinterested superior, who could reasonably have concluded that the transaction was fair to the corporation at the time of such authorization; or

(C) the transaction is ratified, following such disclosure, by disinterested directors who could reasonably have concluded that the transaction was fair to the corporation at the time it was entered into, provided (i) a corporate decisionmaker who is not interested in the transaction acted for the corporation in the transaction and could have reasonably concluded the transaction to be fair to the corporation; (ii) the interested director or senior executive made disclosure to such decisionmaker pursuant to Subsection (a)(1) to the extent he or she then knew of the material facts; (iii) the interested director or senior executive did not act unreasonably in failing to seek advance authorization of the transaction by disinterested directors or a disinterested superior; and (iv) the failure to obtain advance authorization of the transaction from disinterested directors or a disinterested superior did not adversely affect the interests of the corporation in a significant way.

(D) the transaction is authorized in advance or ratified, following such disclosure, by disinterested shareholders and does not constitute a waste of corporate assets at the time of the shareholder action.

(b) *Burden of Proof.* A party who challenges a transaction between a director or senior executive and the corporation has the burden of proof, except that if such party establishes that the requirements of Subsections (a)(2)(B), (a)(2)(C), or (a)(2)(D) are not met, the director or the senior executive has the burden of proving that the transaction was fair to the corporation.

(c) *Ratification of Disclosure or Nondisclosure.* The disclosure requirements of § 5.02(a)(1) will be deemed to be satisfied if at any time (but no later than a reasonable time after suit is filed challenging the transaction) the transaction is ratified, following such disclosure, by the directors, the shareholders, or the corporate decisionmaker who initially approved the transaction or such decisionmaker's successor.

---

1. "INTERESTED" DIRECTORS AND "CONFLICT OF INTEREST" TRANSACTIONS

Sections 8.60 and 8.61 of Subchapter F attempt to frame the definition of who is "interested" in a transaction, and what constitutes a "conflict of interest transaction" much more tightly than does § 8.31. The Official Comment to § 8.31 states:

For purposes of section 8.31 a director should normally be viewed as interested in a transaction if he or the immediate members of his family have a financial interest in the transaction *or a relationship with the other parties to the transaction such that the relationship might reasonably be expected to affect his judgment in the particular matter in a manner adverse to the corporation.* (emphasis added).

The Official Comment to Subchapter F describes the italicized language as overly broad and leading to uncertainty by corporate directors at best, and vague and destabilizing at worst. Subchapter F takes a markedly different approach.

Section 8.61(a) is a key component in the design of subchapter F. It draws a bright-line circle, declaring that the definitions of section 8.60 wholly occupy and preempt the field of directors' conflicting interest transactions. Of course, outside this circle there is a penumbra of director interests, desires, goals, loyalties, and prejudices that may, in a particular context, run at odds with the best interests of the corporation, but section 8.61(a) forbids a court to ground remedial action on any of them. If a plaintiff charges that a director had a conflict of interest with respect to a transaction of the corporation because the other party was his cousin, the answer of the court should be: "No. A cousin as such and without more, is not included in section 8.60(3) as a related person—and under section 8.61(a), I have no authority to reach out farther." If a plaintiff contends that the director had a conflict of interest in a corporate transaction because the other party is president of the golf club the director wants desperately to join, the court should respond: "No. The only director's conflicting interest on the basis of which I can set aside a corporate transaction or impose other sanctions is a financial interest as defined by section 8.60."

Official Comment to Section 8.61.

The ALI differs philosophically with this approach. The ALI acknowledges that the definition of "related person" in RMBCA § 8.60 is narrower than is provided in its Principles but argues:

> The Model Act bases its bright-line test approach on the need for certainty in the area of conflict of interest transactions. The Reporters believe that in the area of avoidable conflict of interest transactions the desirability of affording certainty to a person with a potentially conflicting interest is outweighed by the desirability of encouraging oversight by disinterested directors in cases where a director has a relationship with a person transacting business with the corporation that is sufficiently substantial that it would reasonably be expected to affect the director's judgment with respect to the transaction in a manner adverse to the corporation.

ALI, Principles of Corporate Governance (1994), § 5.02, Reporter's Note 13.

Section 8.60's narrowly circumscribed definition of "related person" clearly is intended to leave a number of questionable situations immune from judicial scrutiny on the ground that "the legislative draftsman who chooses to suppress marginal anomalies by resorting to generalized statements of principle will pay a cost in terms of predictability." Recall the debate between Professor Cary and Judge Winter in Chapter 8. What factors should be considered in a cost-benefit analysis? Should such an analysis be the basis for the normative judgments found in a statute? If not, on what should such a normative judgment be based?

2. FAIRNESS

In many ways, Subchapter F takes the same approach as modern interested director statutes in evaluating substantive fairness. "[A] 'fair' price is any price in that broad range which an unrelated party might have been willing to pay or willing to accept * * * following a normal arm's-length business negotiation, in the light of the knowledge that would have been reasonably acquired in the course of such negotiations. * * *" Official Comment to § 8.61.

This range of fairness is narrower than the range of discretion to which directors' decisions are entitled under the business judgment standard of Section 8.30. The Official Comment to § 8.61 also points out that courts must consider "whether the transaction was one reasonably likely to yield favorable results * * * from the perspective of furthering the corporation's business activities" in addition to scrutinizing the price and terms of the transaction.

The most important element of fairness in Subchapter F is that Section 8.61(b)(3) appears to provide that a transaction which is "fair" should be upheld, whether or not it was approved by directors or shareholders in compliance with §§ 8.62 and 8.63. However, the Official Comment states:

> [i]n some circumstances, the behavior of the director having the conflicting interest can itself affect the finding and content of "fairness." The most obvious illustration of unfair dealing arises out of the director's failure to disclose fully his interest or hidden defects known to him regarding the transaction. Another illustration could be the exertion of improper pressure by the director upon the other directors. When the facts of such unfair dealing become known, the court should offer the corporation its option as to whether to rescind the transaction on grounds of "unfairness" even if it appears that the terms were "fair" by market standards and the corporation profited from it. * * * Thus, the course of dealing—or process—is a key component to a "fairness" determination under subsection (b)(3).

Official Comment to Section 8.61.

Another part of the Official Comment also suggests that the protection of the business judgment rule may not be as absolute under Subchapter F as it is in other contexts:

> * * * Consider, for example, a situation in which it is established that the board of a manufacturing corporation approved a cash loan to a director where the duration, security and interest terms of the loan were at prevailing commercial rates, but (i) the loan was not made in the course of the corporation's business activities and (ii) the loan required a commitment of limited working capital that would otherwise have been used in furtherance of the corporation's business activities. Such a loan transaction would not be afforded safe-harbor protection by section 8.62(b)(1) since the board did not comply with the requirement in section 8.30(a) that the board's action be, in its reasonable judgment, in the best interests of the corporation—that is, that the action will, as the board judges the circumstances at hand, yield favorable results (or

reduce detrimental results) as judged from the perspective of furthering the corporation's business activities.

If a determination is made that the terms of a director's conflicting interest transaction, judged according to the circumstances at the time of commitment, were manifestly unfavorable to the the corporation, that determination would be relevant to an allegation that the directors' action was not taken in good faith and therefore did not comply with section 8.30(a).

Official Comment to Section 8.61.

Does this comment thrust the courts back into determining fairness, notwithstanding Subchapter F's attempt to limit judicial intervention? Or should Subchapter F be read to shield a conflict of interest transaction whose terms are fair by market standards and from which the corporation benefits, even if the interested director failed to disclose material facts about the transaction? This result would overrule decisions such as *Hayes Oyster*, which held that disclosure is an indispensable element of fairness. Is this a good result?

The ALI clearly thinks not. It squarely takes the position that "fairness" is impossible without full disclosure of material facts. It acknowledges that fairness is often a range, but it argues that "[i]f an undisclosed material fact had been disclosed. * * * the corporation might have declined to transact at that high price, or might have bargained the price down lower in the range." ALI, Principles of Corporate Governance (1994), Part V Introductory Note.

3. JUDICIAL REVIEW

Subchapter F attempts to extend the business judgment rule to conflict of interest transactions that have been approved after full disclosure by disinterested directors or shareholders. It is here that the ALI differs most profoundly with Subchapter F. The Comment to § 5.02(a)(2)(B) states:

> * * * There are several reasons why a self-interested transaction should be subject to a closer scrutiny than is required by the business judgment rule even if the transaction has been [approved by disinterested directors].

> First, transactions of the types covered by § 5.02 are as a matter of accepted business practice normally regarded as deserving of closer scrutiny than in the case of transactions with unrelated third parties. In fact, corporate codes of conduct adopted by many public companies prohibit transactions between the corporation and its officers and employees. The New York Stock Exchange, which no longer seeks to prohibit such transactions and leaves their evaluation to company management, nevertheless states in its Listed Company Manual [§ 307.00] that: "The Exchange continues to believe that a publicly owned company of the size and character appropriate for listing on the Exchange should be able to operate on

its own merit and credit standing free from the suspicions that may arise when business transactions are consummated with insiders."

Second, the presence of close relationships among colleagues on the board or in management, particularly in smaller corporations, may sometimes interfere with the ability of directors or superiors to deal with a colleague with the degree of wariness that is employed in arm's length transactions.

Third, a court may under appropriate facts have cause to inquire whether the process of approval produced an unfair result— because, for example, the approval was obtained by improper pressure exerted on the decisionmakers by the interested director or senior executive.

Fourth, for the reasons set forth above, courts are likely to consider the fairness of self-interested transactions no matter what the test is said to be, where the circumstances suggest that the transaction is unfair to the corporation. If the test were framed in terms of the business judgment rule, there is a substantial risk that courts would unduly enlarge the scope of review under that rule in order to provide a fairness review with the potential for a similar result in settings where the business judgment rule is applied outside Part V.

While a greater degree of scrutiny of transactions subject to § 5.02 is appropriate than that afforded by the business judgment rule, § 5.02(a)(2)(B) accords two very significant effects to approval of such transactions by disinterested directors or a disinterested superior.

First, advance approval by disinterested directors * * * shifts the burden of proof to the party attacking the transaction. Where a self-interested transaction has not been approved by disinterested directors * * * the burden of proof is on the self-interested director * * * to show that the transaction was fair.

Second, advance approval by disinterested directors * * * changes the standard by which the self-interested transaction is measured. Under § 5.02(a)(2)(B) * * * a person attacking the transaction has the burden of proving not simply that the transaction is unfair, but that the terms of the transaction are so clearly outside the range of reasonableness that the directors * * * who authorized the transaction could not reasonably have concluded at the time of such authorization that the transaction was fair to the corporation. This test is intended to be substantially easier for the interested director * * * to satisfy than a pure fairness test, although not as easy to satisfy as the rationality test of the business judgment standard.

Some commentators argue that the ALI's approach is inconsistent with current law. See Charles Hansen, John F. Johnson & Frederick H. Alexander, The Role of Disinterested Directors in "Conflict" Transactions: The ALI Corporate Governance Project and Existing Law, 45 Bus. Law. 2083 (1990). Professor Michael Dooley suggests that the ALI approach and that of Subchapter F reflect two fundamentally different approaches to corporate law. Michael P. Dooley, Two Models of Corporate Governance, 47 Bus. Law. 461 (1992). To date, only Georgia, Mississippi, and Washington have adopted Subchapter F.

F. CORPORATE OPPORTUNITY

The corporate opportunity doctrine is a branch of the duty of loyalty. The doctrine forbids a director, officer, or managerial employee from diverting to herself a business opportunity that "belongs" to the corporation. As one of the leading cases, Guth v. Loft, 5 A.2d 503, 511 (Del.1939), noted, a corporate fiduciary cannot take a business opportunity for herself if it is one that the corporation can financially undertake; is within the line of the corporation's business and is advantageous to the corporation; and is one in which the corporation has an interest or a reasonable expectancy.

As with so much else in the duty of loyalty, the proposition is relatively simple to state and difficult to apply. The problem is to separate "opportunities" that should be turned over to the corporation from those that can properly be exploited by the individual. The issue arises because a corporation can only act through its agents, some of whom may have interests outside the corporation. When a business opportunity is presented to such a person (usually a director or officer), is she free to accept it for herself, or must she first offer it to the corporation? And which opportunities that belong to the corporation may she nevertheless take because the corporation, for some reason, is unable to do so?

To answer these questions, one must balance a number of interests. First, the corporation must ensure that its managers and its resources are directed to furthering its own legitimate business interests. Those in positions of trust and confidence cannot be permitted to abuse their positions to further their own economic interests at the expense of their employers. On the other hand, by cordoning off a class of business opportunities as belonging to the corporation, the doctrine effectively prohibits managers from competing with the corporation by using those opportunities, even in the absence of an explicit non-competition agreement. Larger social interests are, therefore, implicated as well. Society benefits when the party best able to take advantage of an opportunity is permitted to pursue it. If the definition of a corporate opportunity is too broad, society suffers because competition is chilled. Those with specialized abilities to recognize entrepreneurial opportunities will be forced by artificial pressures to forego exploiting them.

The corporate opportunity doctrine differs from other types of fiduciary duties with respect to the harm that the corporation suffers. In every other breach of fiduciary duty, actual harm to the corporation must be shown. With a corporate opportunity, however, the harm to the corporation is not actual; the breach arises because the corporate manager took the opportunity for herself and failed to present it to the corporation. Had she presented it, the corporation might have rejected it; had the corporation accepted it, the opportunity might not have been profitable. This last aspect of the doctrine is most relevant in determining the appropriate remedy for the unlawful taking of a corporate opportunity.

PROBLEM
MILTON CORPORATION—PART II

A little over a year ago, the Milton Corporation, which constructs, owns and operates hotels and restaurants throughout the United States, began to discuss the possibility of buying or building a gambling casino. After a management presentation to the directors on the advantages and disadvantages of such a step, the board authorized the officers to begin an active search for specific prospects. Management's initial investigations in the United States turned up nothing that seemed appropriate.

Robert White, a director of the Milton Corporation, has extensive personal investments in a variety of fields, including substantial real estate holdings. He is also the president and chairman of the board of Petro Investments, Inc., a holding company whose assets are invested primarily in real estate. Shortly after the board meeting at which the directors of Milton were informed of management's initial investigations, White met an old business acquaintance while on a trip to the Bahamas. White's friend told him that a casino there had just come on the market at what the friend said was a very attractive price. The friend further advised White that if he acted quickly the seller would take $10 million in cash for the casino. White immediately called the real estate broker who was handling the casino, and within two days signed a contract on behalf of Petro to purchase it. Twelve months later, Petro resold the casino at a $6 million profit.

Beatrice Parker, a shareholder in the Milton Corporation, who has recounted essentially these facts and has asked you about the possibility of success of a derivative suit against White. How should you advise her under the traditional corporate opportunity doctrine? The ALI's version of the corporate opportunity doctrine? What additional information would you need to know?

1. TRADITIONAL CORPORATE OPPORTUNITY DOCTRINE

FARBER v. SERVAN LAND COMPANY, INC.
662 F.2d 371 (5th Cir.1981).

[In 1959, Charles Serianni and other investors formed Servan Land Company,(Servan) to build and operate a golf course and country club near Fort Lauderdale, Florida. Serianni and A.I. Savin owned a majority of the stock and were Servan's principal officers. There were eight other stockholders, including Jack Farber, the plaintiff in this action. Servan acquired 160 acres of land on which to build the course and, shortly thereafter acquired an additional twenty acres abutting the course.

At the 1968 annual stockholders' meeting, a Servan director and stockholder said that James Farquhar, the vendor of the twenty acre tract, was willing to sell another 160 acres of abutting land to the corporation that was suitable for use as an additional golf course. After some discussion, the stockholders took no action to authorize the purchase of the land. In March 1969, Serianni and Savin, in their individual capacities, bought the 160 acres that had been discussed at the stockholders' meeting.

There was no discussion of the purchase at the 1969 annual stockholders' meeting, held in April 1969. In 1970, Farber learned of the purchase from a third party, and at the annual stockholders' meeting, he inquired about it. Savin and Serianni acknowledged the purchase, but there is conflicting evidence as to whether the stockholders ratified the purchase.

In 1973, Serianni, Savin and the corporation entered into an agreement with a purchaser to sell as a package the corporation's assets and the 160 acres of adjoining land Serianni and Savin had bought; each contract of sale was conditioned upon execution of the other. Of the aggregate sales price, the defendants allocated $5,000,000 to the corporation and $3,353,700 to Savin and Serianni, though this division was not based on any appraisal of the respective properties.

At a special directors' and stockholders' meeting, all the stockholders except Farber approved the sale and voted to liquidate Servan. After the sale was completed Farber brought a derivative suit alleging that Savin and Serianni's purchase constituted the taking of a corporate opportunity. Farber also sought appointment of an appraiser to determine the proper allocation of the purchase price.

The district court found that Serianni had been the "driving force" of Servan from its inception. The court also found that, although there was a possibility of real estate development, such development was not one of the purposes for which Servan had been formed. After reviewing the events of the 1968 stockholders' meeting, the court said that Serianni and Savin should have called a special stockholders' meeting to give the stockholders the opportunity to have the corporation purchase the land before Serianni and Savin did so individually. The court noted, however, that the corporation benefitted from their purchase because the entire package was worth more when the assets and real estate were sold in 1973. Finally, the court found that Farber was entitled to an appraisal to determine whether the corporation should have received a larger portion of the total sale price of the properties than the $5 million allocated by Serianni and Savin.

The appraiser subsequently valued the corporation's properties at $4,065,915, and the Serianni–Savin property at $3,950,925. Thus Serianni and Savin had allotted to the corporation a greater percentage of the proceeds of the sale than would have been allocated using the appraiser's figures.

After the appraisal, the district court issued a memorandum opinion which set forth its earlier findings and incorporated the results of the appraisal. The court again noted that Servan had profited from the purchase by Serianni and Savin. It also found that the acreage did not constitute a corporate opportunity because the property bore no substantial relationship to Servan's primary purpose of operating a golf course. Thus the purchase was not "antagonistic to any significant corporate purpose."]

TJOFLAT, CIRCUIT JUDGE:

I

* * *

Farber appealed the district court's decision, and this court vacated and remanded it for clarification, stating: "if, as seems to be clearly expressed, there was no corporate opportunity, why should, as is three times stated, Serianni and Savin have offered the 160 adjacent acres to the corporation? The holdings are inconsistent." Farber v. Servan Land Co., Inc., 541 F.2d 1086, 1088 (5th Cir.1976). * * * We stated:

> If the corporate opportunity doctrine is otherwise applicable it is not made inapplicable by the realization of a substantial gain from a fortuitous sale of its assets at the same time as the sale of the property asserted to be a corporate opportunity to a lone buyer who would not have bought either property without the other. If a corporate opportunity existed the corporation and its stockholders would have been entitled to the profits from the sale of both parcels.

Id.

On remand, the district court failed to explain why it found that Serianni and Savin had a duty to offer the opportunity to purchase the 160 acres to the corporation, but it reaffirmed its finding that "Seriani (sic) and Savin had satisfactorily sustained the burden of establishing the propriety of the transaction." * * *

Farber appeals once again.

II

In reviewing the district court's decision we must evaluate its resolution of four key issues: whether a corporate opportunity existed; whether the stockholders declined the opportunity by failing to act; whether the stockholders ratified Serianni and Savin's purchase; and whether the subsequent benefit the corporation received in selling its assets in conjunction with Serianni and Savin's 160 acres rectifies any wrong it might have suffered through the defendants' initial purchase of the land.

A. *The Existence of a Corporate Opportunity*

In Florida, a corporate director or officer "occupies a quasi-fiduciary relation to the corporation and the existing stockholders. He is bound to act with fidelity and the utmost good faith." Flight Equipment & Engineering Corp. v. Shelton, 103 So.2d 615, 626 (Fla.1958). Because he "occupies a fiduciary relationship to the corporation, (he) will not be allowed to act in hostility to it by acquiring for his own benefit any intangible assets of the corporation * * *. He cannot make a private profit from his position or, while acting in that capacity, acquire an interest adverse to that of the corporation * * *." Pruyser v. Johnson, 185 So.2d 516, 521 (Fla.App.1966).

If one occupying a fiduciary relationship to a corporation acquires, "in opposition to the corporation, property in which the corporation has an interest or tangible expectancy or which is essential to its existence," he violates what has come to be known as the "doctrine of 'corporate opportunity'." * * * Florida has long recognized the doctrine of corporate opportunity, and has described a corporate opportunity as a business opportunity in which the corporation has an interest for a "valid and significant corporate purpose." Pan American Trading & Trapping v. Crown Paint, Inc., 99 So.2d 705, 706 (Fla.1957). The opportunity need not be "of the utmost importance to the welfare of the corporation," Pan American, 99 So.2d at 706, to be protected from preemption by the corporation's directors and officers. As we elaborated in the first appeal of this case, however, the opportunity must "fit into the present activities of the corporation or fit into an established corporate policy which the acquisition of the opportunity would forward." Farber, 541 F.2d at 1088.

In its initial opinion the district court found that no corporate opportunity existed:

> The court finds the possibility of real estate development was contemplated by the stockholders. For example, Mr. Forman testified, via deposition, that scarcely a meeting of the stockholders occurred without discussing the acquiring of additional property from Mr. Farquhar. However, the possibility of real estate development would always be in the minds of a group of affluent businessmen. This does not mean that real estate development was actually part of the corporate purpose and the court specifically finds that real estate development was not a purpose for which the corporation was formed * * *.

> The mere fact that the land was adjacent to the corporate land in itself does not support a conclusion that therefore the acreage was a corporate opportunity. The property had no substantial relation to the corporation's primary purpose of operating a golf course and the individual purpose was not antagonistic to any significant corporate purpose and thus the facts do not fall within the general proposition that an officer of a corporation cannot acquire title to or an interest in property prejudicial to the corporation.

Farber v. Servan Land Co., Inc., 393 F.Supp. at 635, 638. We find that the district court's findings of fact do not support its legal conclusion that the opportunity to buy Farquhar's 160 acres was not a corporate opportunity.

It should be noted that the district court not only found that the stockholders frequently discussed acquisition of Mr. Farquhar's land at their meetings; it also found that the stockholders had discussed this matter at the last meeting, just shortly before Serianni and Savin made their purchase, and that they had "indicated a sense of approval to the idea of acquiring abutting land from Mr. Farquhar." Further, the court heard testimony that the corporation needed the land on the perimeter of the golf course, and evidence that the corporation had bought additional land from Mr. Farquhar in the past and that it had bought and operated a lodge located on part of that land. These facts make it clear that the opportunity to acquire the Farquhar land was an advantageous one that fit into a present, significant corporate purpose, as well as an ongoing corporate policy, and that the corporation had an active interest in it. Accordingly, the opportunity to buy the land constituted a corporate opportunity.

B. Whether the Stockholders Declined the Opportunity

In addition to finding that no corporate opportunity existed, the district court found that if one did exist, "it was rejected by the corporation." The court apparently reached this conclusion because after deciding at their annual meeting that the opportunity to purchase the land should be investigated, the stockholders did not vote, at that meeting, to commit the funds available from the refinancing to purchase the Farquhar property. We find that this failure does not indicate a decision to refrain from pursuing the opportunity to purchase. Indeed, since the stockholders apparently lacked specific information about Mr. Farquhar's terms of sale, it would have been illogical to make a commitment of funds at that time. It is true that there is no evidence to indicate that the stockholders undertook formal investigation of the potential purchase between the time of the meeting and the time of Serianni and Savin's purchase. It should be noted, however, that Serianni was the president of the corporation and the only active director. The other stockholders customarily relied upon him to exercise the executive powers of the corporation, since most of them resided in other states. Because the other stockholders relied upon Serianni to initiate the investigation on the corporation's behalf, he may not now translate his own inaction into a corporate rejection of the opportunity, thus allowing him to buy the land personally. The district court's finding that the corporation rejected the opportunity is clearly erroneous.

C. Ratification of the Purchase

As another ground for its decision, the district court held that the stockholders ratified Serianni and Savin's purchase at their May 9, 1970 meeting. Farber attacks this finding on two grounds. First, he argues that it was clearly erroneous to rely on the corporate minutes, which indicated a vote to ratify, rather than on his court reporter's transcript of the meeting, which indicates no ratification attempt.

The district court received adequate evidence that the corporate minutes were valid and reliable. This left it with an issue of credibility, and this court, on appeal, cannot say that the district judge's decision to rely on the corporate minutes was clearly erroneous. This is especially so since official minutes of corporate meetings are generally considered the best evidence of corporate business transacted.

Farber also argues that even if the ratification vote did take place, it cannot be used to prohibit his derivative action. We agree. When ratification is possible and the proceedings are proper, stockholders may sanction the act of a corporate officer or director and thus abolish any cause of action that the corporation might have against that individual. Not all acts may be ratified, and the Florida courts have not indicated whether stockholders are capable of ratifying a director or officer's breach of fiduciary duty. We do not need to decide whether ratification was possible here, however, because even if it was, the manner of ratification in this case renders the ratification a nullity.

According to the corporate minutes, all of the directors present at the annual meeting, except the plaintiff, voted to ratify the land purchase. Both of the purchasing directors were present, and between the two of them, they held four-sevenths of the stock. While it is true that directors ordinarily may vote their stock on measures in which they have a personal interest, most authorities agree that " '(t)he violation of their duty by corporate directors cannot be ratified by the action of those who were guilty of participation in the wrongful acts, even though they constitute a majority of the directors or of the stockholders.' " Chesapeake Construction Corp. v. Rodman, 256 Md. 531, 537, 261 A.2d 156, 159 (Md.App.1970) (quoting 19 C.J.S. Corporations § 763(b) at p. 112). Thus, Serianni and Savin may not bind Farber by ratifying their own inappropriate acts. Farber is entitled to bring a derivative action.

D.   The Effect of Benefit to the Corporation

Finally, in finding in favor of the defendants, the district court relied heavily on the notion that by valuing the two properties favorably for the corporation when they were sold jointly, and by selling the properties together, thus raising the value of each, Serianni and Savin benefitted the corporation. This benefit, according to the court, precluded any recovery for breach of fiduciary duty in obtaining the Farquhar acres in the first place.

As we stated in the first appeal, however:

> If the corporate opportunity doctrine is otherwise applicable it is not made inapplicable by the realization of a substantial gain from a fortuitous sale of its assets at the same time as the sale of the property asserted to be a corporate opportunity to a lone buyer who would not have bought either property without the other. *If a*

corporate opportunity existed the corporation and its stockholders would have been entitled to the profits from the sale of both parcels. Farber, 541 F.2d at 1088 (emphasis added).

Further, it has already been established that Serianni and Savin apportioned the proceeds of the joint sale without the benefit of an appraisal of the individual properties. While it may be to their credit that they overvalued the corporate property in the apportionment, they have not contended, nor has the district court found, that this overvaluation constituted a deliberate settlement between the parties for damages incurred in the defendants' acquisition of the Farquhar property. Despite the undervaluation of their own property relative to the corporation's assets, Serianni and Savin made a handsome profit on the sale. The two directors must hold those profits in trust for the corporation.

III

We find that the opportunity to buy Mr. Farquhar's 160 acres constituted a corporate opportunity and that the defendants, Serianni and Savin, breached their fiduciary duties to the corporation by preempting that opportunity. We also find that the attempted ratification of the preemption does not preclude Farber from bringing a derivative suit on behalf of the corporation.

The corporation is entitled to the profits of the directors' subsequent sale of the 160 acres. We remand the case to the district court to determine the proper amount of damages and the appropriate method for distributing those damages.

REVERSED AND REMANDED.

2. WHAT IS A CORPORATE OPPORTUNITY?

Courts have traditionally used one or more tests to determine whether a corporate opportunity exists: (1) interest or expectancy; (2) line of business; (3) fairness; and (4) a combination of these tests.

a. Interest or Expectancy

The interest or expectancy analysis is the earliest to have developed. See, e.g., Lagarde v. Anniston Lime & Stone Co., 126 Ala. 496, 28 So. 199 (1900). This is the test applied in *Farber.* In Litwin v. Allen, 25 N.Y.S.2d 667, 686 (Sup.Ct.1940) the court suggested how to discern whether the corporation has an interest or expectancy:

> This corporate right or expectancy, this mandate upon directors to act for the corporation, may arise from various circumstances, such as, for example, the fact that directors had undertaken to negotiate in the field on behalf of the corporation, or that the corporation was in need of the particular business opportunity to the knowledge of the directors, or that the business opportunity was seized and developed at the expense, and with the facilities of the corporation. It is noteworthy that in cases which have imposed this type of liability upon fiduciaries, the thing determined by the court

to be the subject of the trust was a thing of special and unique value to the [beneficiary]; for example, real estate, a proprietary formula valuable to the corporation's business, patents indispensable or valuable to its business, a competing enterprise or one required for the growth and expansion of the corporation's business or the like.

Because of its indeterminacy, the "interest or expectancy" standard has proved difficult to apply. The concept appears to be "something much less tenable than ownership—less than a legal right to exclude independent third parties from acquiring the project; and less even contingent contractual claims." Victor Brudney and Robert Charles Clark, A New Look at Corporate Opportunities, 94 Harv.L.Rev. 997, 1013–14 (1981) ("Brudney and Clark").

b. Line of Business

Under the line of business test, a corporation has a prior claim to a business opportunity presented to an officer or director that falls within the firm's line of business. The test is closely related to the "interest or expectancy" standard; indeed, some courts use both terms in determining the existence of a corporate opportunity. In Guth v. Loft, 23 Del.Ch. 255, 5 A.2d 503, 514 (1939), the court explained the concept as follows:

> The phrase is not within the field of precise definition, nor is it one that can be bounded by a set formula. It has a flexible meaning, which is to be applied reasonably and sensibly to the facts and circumstances of the particular case. Where a corporation is engaged in a certain business, and an opportunity is presented to it embracing an activity as to which it has fundamental knowledge, practical experience and ability to pursue, which, logically and naturally is adaptable to its business having regard for its financial position, and is one that is consonant with its reasonable needs and aspirations for expansion, it may be properly said that the opportunity is in the line of the corporation's business.

Courts typically apply the test to extend beyond a corporation's existing operations. The rationale for such an application is simple. Courts recognize that corporations are dynamic entities. Furthermore, shareholders reasonably expect that a corporation will go beyond the status quo and take advantage of highly profitable, but safe, opportunities. Note, When Opportunity Knocks: An Analysis of the Brudney and Clark and ALI Principles of Corporate Governance Proposals for Deciding Corporate Opportunity Claims, 11 J.Corp.L. 255, 258 (1986).

The line of business test also is problematic in many situations. It often may be difficult to determine whether the corporation's shareholders reasonably expected that every opportunity within the corporation's line of business would first be offered to the corporation.

BURG v. HORN

380 F.2d 897 (2d Cir.1967).

LUMBARD, CHIEF JUSTICE:

Darand was incorporated in September 1953 with a capital of $5500, subscribed equally by the three stockholders, Mrs. Burg and George and Max Horn, all of whom became directors, and immediately purchased a low-rent building in Brooklyn. The Horns, who were engaged in the produce business and had already acquired three similar buildings in Brooklyn through wholly-owned corporations, urged the Burgs, who were close friends then also residing in Brooklyn, to 'get their feet wet' in real estate, and the result was the formation of Darand. The Burgs testified that they expected the Horns to offer any low-rent properties they found in Brooklyn to Darand, but that there was not discussion or agreement to that effect. The Horns carried on the active management of Darand's properties.   * * *

Darand sold its first property and acquired another in 1956, and purchased two more buildings in 1959. From 1953 to 1963, nine similar properties were purchased by the Horns, individually or through wholly-owned corporations.   * * *

In 1962 the Burgs moved to California, and disagreements thereafter arose between them and the Horns concerning the accounting for rent receipts and expenditures of Darand. This action seeking an accounting for receipts and expenditures and the imposition of a constructive trust on the alleged corporate opportunities was brought in 1964. After a six-day trial, [the trial judge] held that the Horns had failed to account for $7,893.36 of rent receipts for 1961–1964. This holding has not been appealed. He found, however, that there was no agreement that all low-rent buildings found by the Horns should be offered to Darand, and that the Burgs were aware of the purposes of the loans from Darand and Louis Burg and of at least some of the Horns' post- 1953 acquisitions. He therefore declined to hold that those acquisitions were corporate opportunities of Darand.   * * *

[There is no evidence that the properties in question were sought by or offered to Darand, or necessary to its success.] Plaintiff apparently contends that defendants were as a matter of law under a duty to acquire for Darand further properties like those it was operating. She is seemingly supported by several commentators, who have stated that any opportunity within a corporation's 'line of business' is a corporate opportunity. E.g., Note, Corporate Opportunity, 74 Harv.L.Rev. 765, 768–69 (1961); Note, A Survey of Corporate Opportunity, 45 Geo.L.J. 99, 100–01 (1956). This statement seems to us too broad a generalization. We think that under New York law a court must determine in each case, by considering the relationship between the director and the corporation, whether a duty to offer the corporation all opportunities within its 'line of business' is fairly to be implied. Had the Horns been full-time employees of Darand with no prior real estate ventures of their own, New York law might well uphold a finding that they were subject to such an implied duty. But as they spent most of their time in unrelated produce and real estate enterprises and already owned corporations holding similar properties when Darand was formed, as plaintiff knew, we agree with [the trial judge] that a duty to offer Darand all such properties coming to their attention cannot be implied absent some further evidence of an agreement or understanding to that effect.

* * *

HAYS, CIRCUIT JUDGE (dissenting):

I dissent.

My brothers hold that the scope of a director's duty to his corporation must be measured by the facts of each case. However, although they are unable to find any New York case presenting the same facts as those before us, they conclude that New York law does not support the imposition of liability in the circumstances of this case. I do not agree.

In an often quoted passage, the New York Court of Appeals laid down the principles of fiduciary conduct:

> Many forms of conduct permissible in a workaday world for those acting at arm's length, are forbidden to those bound by fiduciary ties. A trustee is held to something stricter than the morals of the market place. Not honest alone, but the punctilio of an honor the most sensitive, is then the standard of behavior. As to this there has developed a tradition that is unbending an inveterate. Uncompromising rigidity has been the attitude of courts of equity when petitioned to undermine the rule of undivided loyalty by the "disintegrating erosion" of particular exceptions. Only thus has the level of conduct for fiduciaries been kept at a level higher than that trodden by the crowd. Meinhard v. Salmon, 249 N.Y. 458, 464, 164 N.E. 545, 546, 62 A.L.R.1 (1928).

Applying these standards to the instant case it seems clear that in the absence of a contrary agreement or understanding between the parties, the Horns, who were majority stockholders and managing officers of the Darand Corporation and whose primary function was to locate suitable properties for the company were under a fiduciary obligation to offer such properties to Darand before buying the properties for themselves. That the Horns used Darand's funds to effectuate certain of these purchases reinforces the conclusion that their conduct was improper and failed to comport with the standards established by law.

Since the Horns were under a fiduciary duty imposed by law not to take advantage for themselves of corporate opportunities, it is irrelevant that, as the district court found, there was no agreement under which "the Horns would contract their real estate activities or offer every property they located to Darand." A fortiori the Horns were not free to select the best properties for themselves.

———

c. *Fairness: Alone Or In Combination With Other Standards*

Some courts prefer a fairness test. In Durfee v. Durfee & Canning, Inc., 323 Mass. 187, 199, 80 N.E.2d 522, 529 (1948), the court stated:

> [T]he true basis of the governing doctrine [of corporate opportunity] rests fundamentally on the unfairness in the particular circumstances of a director, whose relation to the corporation is fiduciary, taking advantage of an opportunity * * * when the interests of the corporation justly call for protection. This calls for the application of ethical standards of what is fair and equitable * * * [in] particular sets of facts.

The fairness test is premised on removing the temptation for officers and directors to breach their fiduciary duty by making such breaches profitless. 323 Mass. at 198–99, 80 N.E.2d at 528–29. However, an amorphous fairness test produces uncertainty in application and unpredictability in result. Thus, the test does not provide a reliable guide to an officer or director concerning the scope of her duty to offer a specific opportunity to the corporation.

As a consequence of this uncertainty, some courts have attempted to combine the line of business doctrine with the fairness test. In Miller v. Miller, 301 Minn. 207, 224, 222 N.W.2d 71, 81 (1974), the court first determined when an opportunity was a corporate opportunity under the line of business test. If this test was satisfied, then under the second test, the officer or director would be liable unless she could sustain the burden of showing she did not violate her duties of good faith, loyalty, and fair dealing. The court stated that the following factors would be relevant in determining whether the taking of an opportunity was fair to the corporation:

> [T]he nature of the officer's relationship to the management and control of the corporation; whether the opportunity was presented to him in his official or individual capacity; his prior disclosure of the opportunity to the board of directors or shareholders and their response; whether or not he used or exploited corporate facilities, assets, or personnel in acquiring the opportunity; whether his acquisition harmed or benefited the corporation; and all other facts and circumstances bearing on an officer's good faith and whether he exercised the diligence, devotion, care and fairness toward the corporation which ordinarily prudent men would exercise under similar circumstances in like position.

301 Minn. at 226, 222 N.W.2d at 81–82.

The *Miller* approach appears to give an officer or director who may have usurped a corporate opportunity another line of defense under the fairness rubric. Commentators have criticized the *Miller* approach as "add[ing] only a new layer of confusion to an already murky area of the law, without forwarding the analysis in any significant fashion." Brudney and Clark at 999 n.2. Because of the multitude of factors a trier of fact considers in determining "fairness", particularly whether an individual's usurpation of the opportunity harmed the corporation, the *Miller* test is not useful as a planning vehicle or litigation predictor. Cf. Southeast Consultants, Inc. v. McCrary Engineering Corp., 246 Ga. 503, 273 S.E.2d 112 (1980) (substituting interest or expectancy test for line of business test in first step of the *Miller* analysis).

d. Multiple Corporations: To Whom Is The Duty Owed?

The difficulties involved in applying the line of business test are exacerbated when a director or officer holds positions in two or more corporations or is a corporate manager in one corporation and a substantial shareholder in another and dominates the latter through her ability to select its officers and directors.

COMMENT, CORPORATE OPPORTUNITY
74 Harv.L.Rev. 765, 770–771 (1961).

In resolving the conflict of loyalties that may confront an executive participating in the affairs of several corporations, the initial step should be to determine which, if any, of the corporations has under the line-of-business test a prior claim to the opportunity as against the executive. If only one of the corporations has a prior claim, the executive would seem to violate his duty to that corporation as much by delivering the opportunity to a different corporation as by appropriating it for himself. However, if the opportunity is within the line of business of more than one of his corporations, two determinations must be made: first, whether the executive should ever be permitted to resolve the conflict by delivering the opportunity to one of the corporations, rather than disclosing it to the corporations and letting them compete for it; second, whether within the area of the line of business, there are degrees of obligation the existence of which will under certain circumstances compel the executive to recognize a paramount duty to one of the corporations. There does appear to be at least one functional criterion for distinguishing between corporate claimants, namely whether the opportunity is essential to the successful performance of the present operations of one of the corporations. To put this criterion in a slightly different form, the inquiry should be whether one corporation has a claim to the opportunity under the old definition of corporate opportunity while the others must rely on the modern definition to support their claims. Another possible criterion is whether the opportunity will relieve one corporation from serious financial difficulties while it would merely augment the profits of the other claimants. But this criterion is a questionable one, since profit and loss are on the same continuum, and to the corporation and its shareholders the loss of a possible profit may not appear intrinsically different from the loss which would result from the corporation's falling into insolvency.

Even if the suggested criterion for determining degrees of obligation is adopted, there will undoubtedly be cases where all the potentially interested corporations fall within or without it. Under those circumstances, it might seem fairest to require disclosure to all of them. Disclosure, however, may lead to competitive bidding which will drive up the cost of the opportunity. When the shareholders of the competing corporations are not substantially identical, each corporation would seemingly prefer the risk of a higher price to the risk of losing the opportunity. But where most of the stock of each corporation is held by the same group of shareholders, and the management groups are different enough to make competition likely, the interests of the vast majority of shareholders may be best served by permitting a common officer or director to allocate the opportunity at his discretion, as long as he acts in good faith.

Where the applicable law is uncertain, a corporation could perhaps assure its executives freedom to allocate opportunities among the corporations to which they are obligated by adoption of a charter provision. Such a provision might stipulate that "officers and directors of this corporation may hold positions as officers and directors of other corporations in related businesses and their efforts to advance such corporations will not constitute a breach of fiduciary loyalty to this corporation in the absence of a showing of bad faith." This type of provision should ordinarily be effective to relieve an executive of his obligation to make disclosure to all the corporations with which he is connected, although a court might not be inclined to construe it to allow him to ignore a paramount duty arising under the criterion mentioned above.

In Johnston v. Greene, 35 Del.Ch. 479, 121 A.2d 919 (Del.1956), Odlum, a financier, who was an officer and director of numerous corporations, was offered, in his individual capacity, the chance to acquire the stock of Nutt–Shel, a corporation 100% owned by Hutson, and several patents pertaining to its business. The business of Nutt–Shel had no close relation to the business of Airfleets, Inc., of which Odlum was president. Odlum turned over to Airfleets the opportunity to buy the stock of Nutt–Shel, but purchased the patents for his friends and associates and, to a limited extent, for himself. Airfleets, a corporation with a large amount of cash, possessed the financial capability to buy the patents. The board of Airfleets, dominated by Odlum, voted to buy only the stock. In a shareholders' derivative action against Odlum and the directors. the Delaware Supreme Court found that Odlum had not breached his duty in the sale of the patents. In discussing the problem of multiple conflicting loyalties, the court stated:

* * * At the time when the Nutt–Shel business was offered to Odlum, his position was this: He was the part-time president of Airfleets. He was also president of Atlas—an investment company. He was a director of other corporations and a trustee of foundations interested in making investments. If it was his fiduciary duty, upon being offered any investment opportunity, to submit it to a corporation of which he was a director, the question arises, Which corporation? Why Airfleets instead of Atlas? Why Airfleets instead of one of the foundations? So far as appears, there was no specific tie between the Nutt–Shel business and any of these corporations or foundations. Odlum testified that many of his companies had money to invest, and this appears entirely reasonable. How, then, can it be said that Odlum was under any obligation to offer the opportunity to one particular corporation? And if he was not under such an obligation, why could he not keep it for himself?

Plaintiff suggests that if Odlum elects to assume fiduciary relationships to competing corporations he must assume the obligations that are entailed by such relationships. So he must, but what are the obligations? The mere fact of having funds to invest does not ordinarily put the corporations "in competition" with each other, as that phrase is used in the law of corporate opportunity. There is nothing inherently wrong in a man of large business and financial interests serving as a director of two or more investment companies, and both Airfleets and Atlas (to mention only two companies) must reasonably have expected that Odlum would be free either to offer to any of his companies any business opportunity that came to him personally, or to retain it for himself—provided always that there was no tie between any of such companies and the new venture or any specific duty resting upon him with respect to it.

It is clear to us that the reason why the Nutt–Shel business was offered to Airfleets was because Odlum, having determined that he did not want it for himself, chose to place the investment in that one of his companies whose tax situation was best adapted to receive it. He chose to do so, although he could probably have sold the stock to an outside company at a profit to himself. If he had done so, who could have complained? If a stockholder of Airfleets could have done so, why not a stockholder of Atlas as well?

121 A.2d at 924–925.

3. WHEN MAY A CORPORATE MANAGER TAKE AN OPPORTUNITY FOR HERSELF?

Even if a manager has taken a "corporate opportunity" as determined by the foregoing tests, her conduct may not constitute a breach of duty to the corporation if she can demonstrate that the offer came to her in her personal capacity rather than as a manager of the corporation; that the corporation was precluded from taking advantage of the opportunity; or that the corporation rejected the opportunity. Among the facts that courts consider in determining whether an officer or director may personally take an opportunity are whether:

1.   The corporation is financially unable to take advantage of the opportunity either because of financial difficulty or a lack of liquid assets. Actual financial insolvency leaves the corporate manager free to act. In Irving Trust Co. v. Deutsch, 73 F.2d 121, 124 (2d Cir.1934), reversing in part 2 F.Supp. 971 (S.D.N.Y.1932), cert. denied 294 U.S. 708, 55 S.Ct. 405, 79 L.Ed. 1243 (1935), the court stated:

> Nevertheless, [these facts which raise some question whether the corporation actually lacked the funds or credit necessary for carrying out a contract] tend to show the wisdom of a rigid rule forbidding directors of a solvent corporation to take over for their own profit a corporate contract on the plea of the corporation's financial inability to perform. If the directors are uncertain whether the corporation can make the necessary outlays, they need not embark it upon the venture; if they do, they may not substitute themselves for the corporation any place along the line and divert possible benefits into their own pockets.

Id. at 124.

Other jurisdictions are less rigid. In such jurisdictions, corporate managers may retain an opportunity because the corporation did not then "have the liquid funds available" to take advantage of it. Corporate managers must use their best efforts to uncover the financing needed by their corporation to acquire an opportunity. A director or officer, however, need not advance funds to enable a corporation to take advantage of a business opportunity. A.C. Petters Co. v. St. Cloud Enterprises, Inc., 301 Minn. 261, 222 N.W.2d 83 (1974). See also Gauger v. Hintz, 262 Wis. 333, 55 N.W.2d 426 (1952).

With respect to the relevance of corporate inability to undertake an opportunity, Brudney and Clark conclude:

> There is no reason to allow the diverters to exploit opportunities that they claim the corporation is unable to exploit, if the claimed inability may be feasibly eliminated. To permit claims of disability to become the subject of judicial controversy when they can only be disproved by outsiders with great difficulty and at considerable expense is to tempt participants to actions whose impropriety is visible but rarely subject to effective challenge. Availability of the defense of corporate incapacity reduces the incentive to solve corporate financing and other problems.

> The argument against the defense of incapacity or disability may be less forceful for close corporations than for public corporations because of the greater familiarity of the participants with the affairs of the firm, their better access to relevant information, and the relative manageability of the problems. But the arguments against the defense are not without power in the close corporation context as well, as several courts have noted. Moreover, the possi-

bility of obtaining consent to non-pro rata participation in a venture that the corporation appears unable to exploit should remove the seeming harshness of a rule that does not allow the defense of corporate incapacity. Indeed, rejection by the other participants of a request to assist in curing the incapacity might occur in circumstances that imply consent to the requesting person's taking the opportunity.

Brudney and Clark, at 1022. Is it possible that if the corporation is simply in serious financial difficulty or lacks liquid assets but is still a going concern, "the very existence of a prospective profitmaking venture may generate additional financial backing and may convince creditors to be less importunate in their demands." Comment, Corporate Opportunity, 74 Harv.L.Rev. 765, 772–73 (1961).

2. The opportunity has been offered to and rejected by an independent board of directors after full disclosure. Gaynor v. Buckley, 203 F.Supp. 620 (D.Or.1962), aff'd on other grounds 318 F.2d 432 (9th Cir.1963). As a prerequisite to developing an opportunity personally, an officer or director must generally tender the opportunity to the corporation. See, e.g., Kerrigan v. Unity Savings Ass'n, 58 Ill.2d 20, 27–29, 317 N.E.2d 39, 43–44 (1974). After an officer or director has tendered an opportunity to the corporation, it may accept or reject the opportunity. By accepting the opportunity, the corporation precludes an officer or director from developing it individually. Rejection of an opportunity by a disinterested board usually is dispositive of a subsequent claim that the officer or director usurped a corporate opportunity.

The question may arise whether an interested corporate manager dominated the board. As discussed earlier in this chapter, domination usually refers to the actual use of stock ownership to control or influence the board. Daniel Walker, Legal Handles Used to Open or Close the Corporate Opportunity Door, 56 Nw.U.L.Rev. 608, 622 (1961). However, an interested party may bring pressure, overt or implicit, on her fellow directors. See Johnston v. Greene, supra.

The taking of an opportunity which has been rejected by a controlled board may be validated if the rejection is otherwise fair to the corporation. See, e.g., Turner v. American Metal Co., 268 App.Div. 239, 251, 50 N.Y.S.2d 800, 812 (1944). See also Johnston v. Greene, supra. However, should an officer or director be allowed to prevail on a showing of fairness? One commentator has stated:

> Allowing the fiduciary to attempt to show the fairness of the diversion in these circumstances gives undeserved weight to board action that bears no resemblance to a rejection based on unfettered business judgment. Moreover, an inability to establish board domination which in fact existed would cloak the rejection with the protection of the business judgment rule. * * * Given the difficulty of proving that the board is dominated, the rejection of an opportunity by a dominated board may give the diverting party the protection of the business judgment rule. If the board is shown to be

interested or dominated, the director still has the opportunity to prove the fairness of the diversion. Because of the amorphous nature of the fairness test, the diverting fiduciary may prevail even when the corporation's interests cry out for protection.

Note, When Opportunity Knocks: An Analysis of the Brudney & Clark and ALI Principles of Corporate Governance for Deciding Corporate Opportunity Claims, 11 J.Corp.L. 255, 272–73 (1986).

3. The opportunity has been presented to and rejected by the shareholders after full disclosure. In the context of the publicly held corporation, Brudney and Clark argue that the proxy process usually will not result in truly informed consent. They maintain that "consent to the officer's taking a corporate opportunity approaches the kind of waste for which unanimous stockholder approval is traditionally required." Brudney and Clark at 1033. Thus, they conclude that all officers and directors, except outside directors, of public corporations should be precluded from taking any active, outside business opportunities. Several justifications are advanced for this rule. A strict rule would protect the usually powerless shareholders in public corporations from diversions of corporate assets. The scope of opportunities of public corporations suitable for exploitation is greater than in close corporations. The pursuit of active, outside business interests would distract full-time officers from corporate affairs. However, as to outside directors, a corporate opportunity would exist only when such a director has used corporate resources in acquiring or developing an opportunity. The narrower duty rests on the basis of the more limited responsibilities and remuneration of outside directors. Id. at 1023–25, 1042–1044. Alternatively, if "lawmakers decide that a safety valve is needed for the rare case in which genuine corporate consent [to a diversion] is available in the public corporation context, after the board rejects an opportunity, the shareholders would be required to approve the rejection before an officer or director could exploit the opportunity." Id. at 1035.

However, Brudney and Clark urge a more flexible approach for close corporations in light of the basically contractual nature of the venture. They reason:

> * * * Investors in public corporations are usually passive and widely scattered contributors of money to be managed by preselected officers to whom they effectively delegate full decision making power over operating matters. In contrast, investors in private ventures are fairly small in number and tend to know one another. They make more conscious choices when selecting managers from among themselves. They are likely to be active participants rather than merely passive contributors of funds. And they can consent in a more meaningful way to diversions of corporate assets by fellow participants, either when they form or join enterprises, or on the occasion of the diversion. Accordingly, such investors have less need of categorical strictures on such diversions.

Id. at 1003.

In proposing guidelines for the taking of opportunities by shareholders in closely held corporations, Brudney and Clark would permit the participants to consent, subject to certain limitations, in advance or contemporaneously to the diversion of a new project. Brudney and Clark suggest that "[a] requirement of contemporaneous consent [to a diversion] could be cast in terms either of board consent or of stockholder consent by vote, either unanimously or by a simple majority." Id. at 1011 n. 43.

It is important to recall, however, that not all close corporations fit Brudney and Clark's active participant model. Many contain passive participants in need of protections similar to those provided the shareholders of large, publicly held corporations. See, e.g., *Farber*, supra.

4. Corporate use of the opportunity is barred by state law or the corporation's articles of incorporation. Amending the articles may be a time consuming procedure thereby causing both the corporation and the corporate executive to lose the opportunity.

5. The third party refuses to deal with the corporation, but only if the corporate manager has not instigated that refusal. See e.g., Crittenden & Cowler Co. v. Cowler, 66 App.Div. 95, 72 N.Y.S. 701 (1901). But see Energy Resources Corp., Inc. v. Porter, 14 Mass.App.Ct. 296, 438 N.E.2d 391, 394 (1982) (manager's failure to disclose third party unwillingness to deal with corporation prevents corporation from taking action to change third party's position and renders unwillingness to deal both too difficult to verify and too easy to procure).

4. REMEDIES FOR USURPING A CORPORATE OPPORTUNITY

In general, the remedy for any completed breach of fiduciary duty is the award of damages in the amount of the harm the corporation suffered from the breach. When dealing with the taking of a corporate opportunity, however, the problem of the appropriate remedy is somewhat more complex. Recall that the original harm in such a case is that the corporate manager took the opportunity for herself and failed to present it to the corporation. Had she presented it, the corporation might have rejected it; had the corporation accepted it, there is no evidence as to how successful the corporation would have been in developing and using it. Thus the gain realized by the offending manager is not necessarily co-extensive with the actual harm suffered by the corporation. Indeed, to establish a breach of duty for taking a corporate opportunity, unlike any other breach of fiduciary duty, it is not necessary to show that the corporation suffered *actual* harm from the taking. The harm is that the corporation was deprived of the right to take the opportunity for itself.

One possible remedy is to assess damages in the amount of the profits realized by the usurping manager on the theory of unjust enrichment. Profit is generally easy to measure if the manager has already sold the opportunity, although as *Farber* illustrates, valuation problems may arise. This is all the more true if the manager's profit results from reselling the opportunity to the corporation from which she took it.

The traditional remedy is the imposition of a constructive trust upon the manager's new business. This approach eliminates messy valuation problems and effectively permits the corporation to recover any lost profits which it might otherwise have realized. The offending manager, however, is entitled to expenditures she have made in pursuing the opportunity, including her reasonable compensation. See generally Phoenix Airline Services, Inc. v. Metro Airlines, Inc., 194 Ga.App. 120, 390 S.E.2d 219, 227 (1989) (Pope, J. concurring), rev'd on other grounds 260 Ga. 584, 397 S.E.2d 699 (1990).

5. A NEW APPROACH TO CORPORATE OPPORTUNITY: ALI PRINCIPLES OF CORPORATE GOVERNANCE

KLINICKI v. LUNDGREN
298 Or. 662, 695 P.2d 906 (1985).

JONES, JUSTICE.

The factual and legal background of this complicated litigation was succinctly set forth by Chief Judge Joseph in the Court of Appeals opinion as follows:

"In January, 1977, plaintiff Klinicki conceived the idea of engaging in the air transportation business in Berlin, West Germany. He discussed the idea with his friend, defendant Lundgren. At that time, both men were furloughed Pan American pilots stationed in West Germany. They decided to enter the air transportation business, planning to begin operations with an air taxi service and later to expand into other service, such as regularly scheduled flights or charter flights. In April, 1977, they incorporated Berlinair, Inc., as a closely held Oregon corporation. Plaintiff was a vice-president and a director. Lundgren was the corporation's president and a director. Each man owned 33 percent of the company stock. Lelco, Inc., a corporation owned by Lundgren and members of his family, owned 33 percent of the stock. The corporation's attorney owned the remaining one percent of the stock. Berlinair obtained the necessary governmental licenses, purchased an aircraft and in November, 1977, began passenger service.

"As president, Lundgren was responsible, in part, for developing and promoting Berlinair's transportation business. Plaintiff was in charge of operations and maintenance. In November, 1977, plaintiff and Lundgren, as representatives of Berlinair, met with representatives of the Berliner Flug Ring (BFR), a consortium of Berlin travel agents that contracts for charter flights to take sallow German tourists to sunnier climes. The BFR contract was considered a lucrative business opportunity by those familiar with the air transportation business, and plaintiff and defendant had contemplated pursuing the contract when they formed Berlinair. After the initial meeting, all subsequent contacts with BFR were made by Lundgren or other Berlinair employes acting under his directions.

"During the early stages of negotiations, Lundgren believed that Berlinair could not obtain the contract because BFR was then satisfied with its carrier. In early June, 1978, however, Lundgren learned that there was a good chance that the BFR contract might be available. He informed a BFR representative that he would make a proposal on behalf of a new company. On July 7, 1978, he incorporated Air Berlin Charter Company (ABC) and was its sole owner. On August 20, 1978, ABC presented BFR with a contract proposal, and after a series of discussions it was awarded the contract on September 1, 1978. Lundgren effectively concealed from plaintiff his negotiations with BFR and his diversion of the BFR contract to ABC, even though he used Berlinair working time, staff, money and facilities.

"Plaintiff, as a minority stockholder in Berlinair, brought a derivative action against ABC for usurping a corporate opportunity of Berlinair. He also brought an individual claim against Lundgren for compensatory and punitive damages based on breach of fiduciary duty.

"The trial court found that ABC, acting through Lundgren, had wrongfully diverted the BFR contract, which was a corporate opportunity of Berlinair. The court imposed a constructive trust on ABC in favor of Berlinair, ordered an accounting by ABC and enjoined ABC from transferring its assets. The trial court also found that Lundgren, as an officer and director of Berlinair, had breached his fiduciary duties of good faith, fair dealing and full disclosure owed to plaintiff individually and to Berlinair. The court did not award plaintiff any actual damages on the breach of fiduciary duty claim. All the issues were tried to the court, except that a jury was empaneled to try the punitive damages issue. It returned a verdict in favor of plaintiff and assessed punitive damages against Lundgren in the amount of $750,000. Lundgren then moved to dismiss plaintiff's claim for punitive damages. The court granted the motion to dismiss and, sua sponte, entered judgment in favor of Lundgren notwithstanding the verdict on the punitive damages claim." Klinicki v. Lundgren, 67 Or.App. 160, 162–63, 678 P.2d 1250, 1251–52 (1984) (footnote omitted).

ABC appealed to the Court of Appeals contending that it did not usurp a corporate opportunity of Berlinair. Plaintiff cross-appealed from the trial court's dismissal of the punitive damages claim and from the entry of judgment in favor of Lundgren notwithstanding the verdict on that issue. The Court of Appeals affirmed the trial court on all issues.

I. The Appeal by Air Berlin Charter Co. (ABC)

ABC petitions for review to this court contending that the concealment and diversion of the BFR contract was not a usurpation of a corporate opportunity, because Berlinair did not have the financial ability to undertake that contract. ABC argues that proof of financial ability is a necessary part of a corporate opportunity case and that plaintiff had the burden of proof on that issue and did not carry that burden.

There is no dispute that the corporate opportunity doctrine precludes corporate fiduciaries from diverting to themselves business opportunities in which the corporation has an expectancy, property interest or right, or which in fairness should otherwise belong to the corporation. The doctrine follows from a corporate fiduciary's duty of undivided loyalty to the corporation. ABC agrees that, unless Berlinair's financial inability to undertake the contract makes a difference, the BFR contract was a corporate opportunity of Berlinair.

We first address the issue, resolved by the Court of Appeals in Berlinair's favor, of the relevance of a corporation's financial ability to undertake a business opportunity to proving a diversion of corporate opportunity claim. This is an issue of first impression in Oregon.

The Court of Appeals held that a corporation's financial ability to undertake a business opportunity is not a factor in determining the existence of a corporate opportunity unless the defendant demonstrates that the corporation is technically or de facto insolvent. Without defining these terms, the Court of Appeals specifically placed the burden of proof as to this issue on the fiduciary by saying: "To avoid liability for usurping a corporate opportunity on the basis that the corporation was insolvent, the fiduciary must prove insolvency." 67 Or.App. at 165, 678 P.2d at 1254. The Court of Appeals then concluded "that ABC usurped a corporate opportunity belonging to Berlinair when, acting through Lundgren, the BFR contract was diverted" because nothing in Lundgren's testimony or otherwise in the record suggested that Berlinair was insolvent or was no longer a viable corporate entity. 67 Or.App. at 166, 678 P.2d at 1254. Accordingly, the Court of Appeals held that the constructive trust, injunction, duty to account and other relief granted by the trial court against ABC were appropriate remedies.

* * *

Before proceeding further our initial task must be to define what is meant by "corporate opportunity," and to determine when, if ever, a corporate fiduciary may take personal advantage of such an opportunity. Our resolution of this case will be limited to announcing a rule to be applied when allegations of usurpation of a corporate opportunity are made against a director of a close corporation. The determination of a rule to apply to similar situations arising between a director and a publicly held corporation presents problems and concepts which may not necessarily require us to apply an identical rule in that similar but distinguishable context.

As we mentioned at the outset, this issue is a matter of first impression in this state. While courts universally stress the high standard of fiduciary duty owed by directors and officers to their corporation, there are distinct schools of thought on the circumstances in which business opportunities may be taken for personal advantage. One group of jurisdictions severely restricts the corporate official's freedom to take advantage of opportunities by saying that the ability to undertake the opportunity is irrelevant and usurpation is essentially prohibited; other jurisdictions use a test which gives relatively wide latitude to the corporate official on the theory that financial ability to undertake a corporate opportunity is a prerequisite to the existence of a corporate opportunity. * * *

Counsel for defendant, relying on Miller, contends there is no corporate opportunity if there is no capacity to take advantage of the corporate opportunity. We reject this argument. By the same token, we reject plaintiff's contention, relying on Irving Trust, that financial ability is totally irrelevant in an unlawful taking of a corporate opportunity. * * *

On April 13, 1984, the American Law Institute published its "Tentative Draft No. 3" concerning "Principles of Corporate Governance: Analysis and Recommendations." The draft, of course, does not represent the position of the ALI, but it does contain definitions and rules which we find helpful in resolving the main issue in this case. Section 5.12 of the draft, which contains the proposed general rule and definition, reads as follows *:

"(a) *General Rule:*

"A director or principal senior executive may not take a corporate opportunity for himself or an associate unless:

(1) The corporate opportunity has first been offered to the corporation, and disclosure has been made to the corporate decisionmaker of all material facts known to the director or principal senior executive concerning his conflict of interest and the corporate opportunity (unless the corporate decisionmaker is otherwise aware of such material facts); and

(2) The corporate opportunity has been rejected by the corporation in a manner that meets one of the following standards:

(A) In the case of a rejection of a corporate opportunity that was authorized by disinterested directors following such disclosure, the directors who authorized the rejection acted in a manner that meets the standards of the business judgment rule set forth in § 4.01(d);

---

* Section 5.05 of the Principles of Corporate Governance, as adopted, is substantially the same as Section 5.12 as set forth in the opinion—Eds.

(B) In the case of a rejection that was authorized or ratified by disinterested shareholders following such disclosure, the rejection was not equivalent to a waste of corporate assets; and

(C) In the case of a rejection that was not authorized or ratified in the manner contemplated in § 5.12(a)(2)(A) or (B) or permitted by the terms of a [validly adopted] standard of the corporation * * *, the taking of the opportunity was fair to the corporation.

"(b) *Definition of a Corporate Opportunity:*

"A corporate opportunity means any opportunity to engage in a business activity (including acquisition or use of any contract right or other tangible or intangible property) that:

(1) In the case of a principal senior executive or any director, is an opportunity that is communicated or otherwise made available to him either:

(A) in connection with the performance of his obligations as a principal senior executive or director or under circumstances that should reasonably lead him to believe that the person offering the opportunity expects him to offer it to the corporation, or

(B) through the use of corporate information or property, if the resulting opportunity is one that the principal senior executive or director should reasonably be expected to believe would be of interest to the corporation; or

(2) In the case of a principal senior executive or a director who is a full-time employee of the corporation, is an opportunity that he knows or reasonably should know is closely related to the business in which the corporation is engaged or may reasonably be expected to engage."   (Bracketed section references omitted.)

Section 5.12 presents an approach very similar to that suggested by Chief Judge Joseph in the Court of Appeals decision rendered in this case.   Section 5.12 generally would require an opportunity that could be advantageous to the corporation to be offered to the corporation by a director or principal senior executive before he takes it for himself. Section 5.12 declines to adopt the rigid rule expressed in Irving Trust Co. v. Deutsch, *supra*, which precludes a person subject to the duty of loyalty from pursuing a rejected opportunity.   The proposed rule permits a director or principal senior executive to deal with his corporation so long as he deals fairly with full disclosure and bears the burden of proving fairness unless the corporate opportunity was rejected by disinterested directors or shareholders.

The comment to Section 5.12(a) reads:

"Section 5.12(a) sets forth the general rule requiring a director or principal senior executive to first offer an opportunity to the corporation before taking it for himself.   If the opportunity is not offered to the corporation, the director or principal senior executive will have violated § 5.12(a).

> "Section 5.12(a) contemplates that a corporate opportunity will be promptly offered to the corporation, and that the corporation will promptly accept or reject the opportunity. Failure to accept the opportunity promptly will be considered tantamount to a rejection. * * * "

and that

> " * * * Rejection in the context of § 5.12(a)(2) may be based on one or more of a number of factors, such as lack of interest of the corporation in the opportunity, *its financial inability to acquire the opportunity*, legal restrictions on its ability to accept the opportunity, or unwillingness of a third party to deal with the corporation. * * * " (Emphasis added.)

* * *

Section 5.12(c) would allocate the burden of proof in corporate opportunity cases as follows:

> (c) *Burden of Proof:* "In any proceeding in which there is a challenge under § 5.12(a), the challenging party has the burden of proof, except if the rejection of a corporate opportunity was not authorized or ratified in the manner contemplated in § 5.12(a)(2)(A) or (B) or permitted by the terms of a [validly adopted] standard of the corporation * * *, the director or principal senior executive has the burden of proving that his taking of the opportunity was fair to the corporation. If a good faith attempt has been made to achieve the disclosure contemplated by § 5.12(a)(1) in connection with rejection of a corporate opportunity, the burden of proof remains on the challenging party even if the disclosure failed to so comply, so long as the rejection is ratified by disinterested directors or shareholders after complete disclosure has been made. *If the challenging party satisfies the burden of proving that a corporate opportunity was taken without being offered to the corporation, the challenging party will prevail.*" (Emphasis added.)

The comment to Section 5.12(c) reads in part:

> "The burden of coming forward with evidence and the ultimate burden of proof will be upon the person attacking a director's or principal senior executive's conduct to prove that (1) the director of principal senior executive acquired a corporate opportunity * * *. The complainant will also have the burden of proof with respect to all other aspects of the transaction, including lack of disclosure to the corporate decisionmaker and establishing that the requisite number of directors or shareholders who approved or ratified the transaction were not disinterested. *However, if disinterested directors or shareholders have not approved or ratified the rejection of the opportunity, the director or principal senior executive will have the burden of proving that his taking of the opportunity was fair and*

that the rejection of the opportunity was fair to the corporation at the time of the rejection. * * * " (Emphasis added.)

Whether the rejection was fair or not includes consideration of whether the corporation was financially or otherwise incapacitated from undertaking the corporate opportunity. We agree with the proposed ALI Principles of Corporate Governance, *supra,* as to the following rules for application in close corporation corporate opportunity cases.

Where a director or principal senior executive of a close corporation wishes to take personal advantage of a "corporate opportunity," as defined by the proposed rule, the director or principal senior executive must comply strictly with the following procedure:

(1) the director or principal senior executive must promptly offer the opportunity and disclose all material facts known regarding the opportunity to the disinterested directors or, if there is no disinterested director, to the disinterested shareholders. If the director or principal senior executive learns of other material facts after such disclosure, the director or principal senior executive must disclose these additional facts in a like manner before personally taking the opportunity.

(2) The director or principal senior executive may take advantage of the corporate opportunity only after full disclosure and only if the opportunity is rejected by a majority of the disinterested directors or, if there are no disinterested directors, by a majority of the disinterested shareholders. If, after full disclosure, the disinterested directors or shareholders unreasonably fail to reject the offer,[13] the interested director or principal senior executive may proceed to take the opportunity if he can prove the taking was otherwise "fair" to the corporation. Full disclosure to the appropriate corporate body is, however, an absolute condition precedent to the validity of any forthcoming rejection as well as to the availability to the director or principal senior executive of the defense of fairness.

(3) An appropriation of a corporate opportunity may be ratified by rejection of the opportunity by a majority of disinterested directors or a majority of disinterested shareholders, after full disclosure subject to the same rules as set out above for prior offer, disclosure and rejection. Where a director or principal senior executive of a close corporation appropriates a corporate opportunity without first fully disclosing the opportunity and offering it to the corporation, absent ratification, that director or principal senior executive holds the opportunity in trust for the corporation.

Applying these rules to the facts in this case, we conclude:

13. A valid acceptance of the offer by the disinterested directors or shareholders would bar the fiduciary from appropriating the opportunity. An acceptance of the offer by the disinterested directors which failed to meet the standards of the business judgment rule, or an acceptance by the disinterested shareholders which was the equivalent of a waste of corporate assets would have the same effect as an unreasonable failure to reject. The corporate fiduciary could appropriate the opportunity only upon a showing that the taking was fair to the corporation. See ALI, Principles of Corporate Governance and Structure § 5.12(a)(2) (Tent.Draft No. 3 1984).

(1) Lundgren, as director and principal executive officer of Berlinair, owed a fiduciary duty to Berlinair.

(2) The BFR contract was a "corporate opportunity" of Berlinair.

(3) Lundgren formed ABC for the purpose of usurping the opportunity presented to Berlinair by the BFR contract.

(4) Lundgren did not offer Berlinair the BFR contract.

(5) Lundgren did not attempt to obtain the consent of Berlinair to his taking of the BFR corporate opportunity.

(6) Lundgren did not fully disclose to Berlinair his intent to appropriate the opportunity for himself and ABC.

(7) Berlinair never rejected the opportunity presented by the BFR contract.

(8) Berlinair never ratified the appropriation of the BFR contract.

(9) Lundgren, acting for ABC, misappropriated the BFR contract.

Because of the above, the defendant may not now contend that Berlinair did not have the financial ability to successfully pursue the BFR contract. As stated in proposed Section 5.12(c) of the Principles of Corporate Governance, *supra*, "If the challenging party satisfies the burden of proving that a corporate opportunity was taken without being offered to the corporation, the challenging party will prevail."

* * *

The Court of Appeals is affirmed.

———

For an interesting critique of both the traditional and ALI formulations of the corporate opportunity doctrine, see Pat K. Chew, Competing Interests in the Corporate Opportunity Doctrine, 67 N.C. L. Rev. 435 (1989). Chew asserts that courts focus too narrowly on the corporation's interest in most decisions. This focus has led corporations to use the corporate opportunity doctrine in lieu of negotiating consensual non-competition agreements with their managers. As a consequence, courts have failed to recognize the individual manager's rights to pursue her own line of expertise once she has left her corporation. Such a failure, in turn, unnecessarily chills competition and the creation of experimental ventures and small businesses. Professor Chew notes:

> In generations of cases, courts applying the corporate opportunity doctrine have focused on the protection of the corporation's interest. The cases cast the corporation as the surprised, vulnerable, and righteous victim of unscrupulous directors and officers who succumb to their personal greed in derogation of their proper corporate duties. A closer and more thoughtful analysis of actual corporate

opportunity disputes and their consequences reveals that this picture is simplistic and unrealistic. * * *

[T]he practical consequences for corporate fiduciaries are drastic. In many instances fiduciaries who lose corporate opportunity lawsuits are effectively prohibited from competing with their former corporations. This results even though the fiduciaries have not signed noncompetition agreements. Such de facto restraints are contrary to individuals' rights to pursue freely their interests and talents and to society's long-standing goal of promoting competition. This consequence is especially worrisome because the categories of individuals subject to the doctrine, and hence subject to a prohibition against competition, are expanding.

Id. at 436–38.

Chew expresses particular concern that the corporate opportunity doctrine has been expanded to cover "key employees," who are not on notice that they are subject to the fiduciary duties the doctrine is designed to enforce. For a case in which Chew contends that the competing corporate, individual, and social interests were appropriately balanced, see Science Accessories Corp. v. Summagraphics Corp., 425 A.2d 957, 963 (Del.1980) (opportunity in line of business of electronics manufacturer held not corporate when developed off-hours by corporation's chief engineer, head of R & D, and supervisor of manufacturing who made only de minimis use of corporate facilities and resources).

G. THE RESPONSIBILITIES OF CONTROLLING STOCKHOLDERS

Thus far, our discussion of fiduciary duties has focused exclusively on directors and officers. But no analysis of fiduciary duties, and particularly the duty of loyalty, would be complete without examining the position of controlling stockholders. As we have seen, directors and officers generally manage the corporation's business, but they owe their position to the stockholders who have selected them. Thus, a stockholder who has the power to select a majority of the board of directors in effect controls the corporation even if she herself is not an officer or director.

One obvious example of a controlling stockholder is a parent corporation that owns all or a majority of the stock of a subsidiary. Similarly, an individual who owns more than 50% of of a corporation's voting stock will be considered to be its controlling stockholder.

A long line of cases supports the proposition that a stockholder may vote her stock as she pleases and has no fiduciary obligation to her fellow stockholders. Nevertheless, courts also treat the actions of controlling stockholders as similar to those of directors and officers, at least when those stockholders engage in transactions with the corporations they control. In concept this approach makes sense because the directors of the controlled corporations, who must approve or authorize such transactions, may be viewed as agents of the controlling shareholders. Thus the Supreme Court has said of dominant and controlling stockholders:

> Their powers are powers in trust. * * * Their dealings with the corporation are subjected to rigorous scrutiny and where any of their contracts or engagements with the corporation is challenged the burden is on the director or stockholder not only to prove the good faith of the transaction but also to show its inherent fairness from the view point of the corporation and those interested therein.

Pepper v. Litton, 308 U.S. 295, 306, 60 S.Ct. 238, 245, 84 L.Ed. 281 (1939).

Corporate statutes generally do not address transactions between corporations and their controlling stockholders. Thus there is no provision analogous to DGCL § 144. The ALI would impose a duty of loyalty on controlling stockholders that will be satisfied if: "(1) the transaction is fair to the corporation when entered into; or (2) the transaction is authorized in advance or ratified by disinterested shareholders following disclosure concerning the conflict of interest and the transaction does not constitute a waste of corporate assets at the time of the shareholder action." ALI, Principles of Corporate Governance, § 5.10 (1994). Unlike interested director transactions, approval by a majority of disinterested directors will not affect the standard by which the transaction is reviewed but it will shift the burden of proof to a shareholder challenging the transaction if there has been such approval.

Notwithstanding the foregoing analysis, it is important to keep in mind that the relationship between a controlling stockholder and her corporation is not precisely the same as that between a director or officer and the corporation. Directors and officers have voluntarily assumed the role of fiduciary that is inherent in a corporate office; controlling stockholders have never formally contracted with the minority stockholders to whom they may be held to owe a fiduciary duty. What, then, are the reasonable expectations of a stockholder who invests in a corporation that already has a controlling stockholder or who becomes a minority stockholder through no volitional act of her own? And how do those expectations affect the nature of the duty owed to the minority stockholder? For example, does a minority stockholder in a subsidiary expect that the parent will refrain from transactions with the subsidiary? If not, what should be the terms of such transactions? Does she expect that the parent is permanently locked into the existing relationship and cannot later decide to eliminate the minority interests? Does "self-dealing," as we have used the term earlier in this chapter, mean the same thing when we are talking about parent-subsidiary transactions? This section addresses some of these questions; others are considered in Chapters 21 and 23.

PROBLEM
MILTON CORPORATION—PART III

Review Part I of the problem for information about the Milton Corporation and its arrangements with RIC.

The Milton Corporation has operated at a loss for the past two years, largely for two reasons. First, because of new construction, there has been a surplus of hotel rooms in many of the cities where the corporation operates its hotels. Second, business travel, and the associated demand for hotel rooms has been seriously affected by the slump in the economy.

In the same period, RIC has earned record profits. Its revenues from its leases with Milton Corporation have declined modestly, but RIC has more than offset those losses by refinancing the mortgages on the land it owns at substantially lower interest rates. In accord with prevailing practices in the real estate industry, those leases provide for rent increases if certain costs that are beyond the control of RIC, such as local taxes, increase, but the leases contain no provision for rent reductions if RIC reduces its own interest expense.

Beatrice Parker has filed a derivative suit against the Milton family as controlling shareholders of Milton Corporation, seeking to recover all or a major share of RIC's profits for the past two years. You are an associate in the law firm representing the Milton family. The partner in charge has sent you a memorandum setting forth the above facts and noting that one possible line of defense is that the Milton family does not control Milton Corporation because the family only owns 40 percent of the outstanding stock. The partner has asked you what defenses would be available if a court found that the family does in fact control the corporation.

SINCLAIR OIL CORP. v. LEVIEN
280 A.2d 717 (Del.1971).

WOLCOTT, CHIEF JUSTICE:

This is an appeal by the defendant, Sinclair Oil Corporation (hereafter Sinclair), from an order of the Court of Chancery, in a derivative action requiring Sinclair to account for damages sustained by its subsidiary, Sinclair Venezuelan Oil Company (hereafter Sinven), organized by Sinclair for the purpose of operating in Venezuela, as a result of dividends paid by Sinven, the denial to Sinven of industrial development, and a breach of contract between Sinclair's wholly-owned subsidiary, Sinclair International Oil Company, and Sinven.

Sinclair, operating primarily as a holding company, is in the business of exploring for oil and of producing and marketing crude oil and oil products. At all times relevant to this litigation, it owned about 97% of Sinven's stock. The plaintiff owns about 3000 of 120,000 publicly held shares of Sinven. Sinven, incorporated in 1922, has been engaged in petroleum operations primarily in Venezuela and since 1959 has operated exclusively in Venezuela.

Sinclair nominates all members of Sinven's board of directors. The Chancellor found as a fact that the directors were not independent of Sinclair. Almost without exception, they were officers, directors, or employees of corporations in the Sinclair complex. By reason of Sinclair's domination, it is clear that Sinclair owed Sinven a fiduciary duty. Sinclair concedes this.

The Chancellor held that because of Sinclair's fiduciary duty and its control over Sinven, its relationship with Sinven must meet the test of intrinsic fairness. The standard of intrinsic fairness involves both a high degree of fairness and a shift in the burden of proof. Under this standard the burden is on Sinclair to prove, subject to careful judicial scrutiny, that its transactions with Sinven were objectively fair.

Sinclair argues that the transactions between it and Sinven should be tested, not by the test of intrinsic fairness with the accompanying shift of the burden of proof, but by the business judgment rule under which a court will not interfere with the judgment of a board of directors unless there is a showing of gross and palpable overreaching. Meyerson v. El Paso Natural Gas Co., 246 A.2d 789 (Del.Ch.1967). A board of directors enjoys a presumption of sound business judgment, and its decisions will not be disturbed if they can be attributed to any rational business purpose. A court under such circumstances will not substitute its own notions of what is or is not sound business judgment.

We think, however, that Sinclair's argument in this respect is misconceived. When the situation involves a parent and a subsidiary, with the parent controlling the transaction and fixing the terms, the test of intrinsic fairness, with its resulting shifting of the burden of proof, is applied. The basic situation for the application of the rule is the one in which the parent has received a benefit to the exclusion and at the expense of the subsidiary.

Recently, this court dealt with the question of fairness in parent-subsidiary dealings in Getty Oil Co. v. Skelly Oil Co. [267 A.2d 883 (Del.1970)]. In that case, both parent and subsidiary were in the business of refining and marketing crude oil and crude oil products. The Oil Import Board ruled that the subsidiary, because it was controlled by the parent, was no longer entitled to a separate allocation of imported crude oil. The subsidiary then contended that it had a right to share the quota of crude oil allotted to the parent. We ruled that the business judgment standard should be applied to determine this contention. Although the subsidiary suffered a loss through the administration of the oil import quotas, the parent gained nothing. The parent's quota was derived solely from its own past use. The past use of the subsidiary did not cause an increase in the parent's quota. Nor did the parent usurp a quota of the subsidiary. Since the parent received nothing from the subsidiary to the exclusion of the minority stockholders of the subsidiary, there was no self-dealing. Therefore, the business judgment standard was properly applied.

A parent does indeed owe a fiduciary duty to its subsidiary when there are parent-subsidiary dealings. However, this alone will not evoke the intrinsic fairness standard. This standard will be applied only when the fiduciary duty is accompanied by self-dealing—the situation when a parent is on both sides of a transaction with its subsidiary. Self-dealing occurs when the parent, by virtue of its domination of the subsidiary, causes the subsidiary to act in such a way that the parent receives something from the subsidiary to the exclusion of, and detriment to, the minority stockholders of the subsidiary.

We turn now to the facts. The plaintiff argues that, from 1960 through 1966, Sinclair caused Sinven to pay out such excessive dividends that the industrial development of Sinven was effectively prevented, and it became in reality a corporation in dissolution.

From 1960 through 1966, Sinven paid out $108,000,000 in dividends ($38,000,000 in excess of Sinven's earnings during the same period). The Chancellor held that Sinclair caused these dividends to be paid during a period when it had a need for large amounts of cash. Although the dividends paid exceeded earnings, the plaintiff concedes that the payments were made in compliance with 8 Del.C. § 170, authorizing payment of dividends out of surplus or net profits. However, the plaintiff attacks these dividends on the ground that they resulted from an improper motive—Sinclair's need for cash. The Chancellor, applying the intrinsic fairness standard, held that Sinclair did not sustain its burden of proving that these dividends were intrinsically fair to the minority stockholders of Sinven.

Since it is admitted that the dividends were paid in strict compliance with 8 Del.C. § 170, the alleged excessiveness of the payments alone would not state a cause of action. Nevertheless, compliance with the applicable statute may not, under all circumstances, justify all dividend payments. If a plaintiff can meet his burden of proving that a dividend cannot be grounded on any reasonable business objective, then the courts can and will interfere with the board's decision to pay the dividend.

Sinclair contends that it is improper to apply the intrinsic fairness standard to dividend payments even when the board which voted for the dividends is completely dominated. In support of this contention, Sinclair relies heavily on American District Telegraph Co. [ADT] v. Grinnell Corp., (N.Y.Sup.Ct.1969) aff'd. 33 A.D.2d 769, 306 N.Y.S.2d 209 (1969). Plaintiffs were minority stockholders of ADT, a subsidiary of Grinnell. The plaintiffs alleged that Grinnell, realizing that it would soon have to sell its ADT stock because of a pending anti-trust action, caused ADT to pay excessive dividends. Because the dividend payments conformed with applicable statutory law, and the plaintiffs could not prove an abuse of discretion, the court ruled that the complaint did not state a cause of action. Other decisions seem to support Sinclair's contention.

We do not accept the argument that the intrinsic fairness test can never be applied to a dividend declaration by a dominated board, although a dividend declaration by a dominated board will not inevitably demand the application of the intrinsic fairness standard. If such a dividend is in essence self-dealing by the parent, then the intrinsic fairness standard is the proper standard. For example, suppose a parent dominates a subsidiary and its board of directors. The subsidiary has outstanding two classes of stock, X and Y. Class X is owned by the parent and Class Y is owned by minority stockholders of the subsidiary. If the subsidiary, at the direction of the parent, declares a dividend on its Class X stock only, this might well be self-dealing by the parent. It would be receiving something from the subsidiary to the exclusion of and detrimental to its minority stockholders. This self-dealing, coupled with the parent's fiduciary duty, would make intrinsic fairness the proper standard by which to evaluate the dividend payments.

Consequently it must be determined whether the dividend payments by Sinven were, in essence, self-dealing by Sinclair. The dividends resulted in great sums of money being transferred from Sinven to Sinclair. However, a proportionate share of this money was received by the minority shareholders of Sinven. Sinclair received nothing from Sinven to the exclusion of its minority stockholders. As such, these dividends were not self-dealing. We hold therefore that the Chancellor erred in applying the intrinsic fairness test as to these dividend payments. The business judgment standard should have been applied.

We conclude that the facts demonstrate that the dividend payments complied with the business judgment standard and with 8 Del.C. § 170. The motives for causing the declaration of dividends are immaterial unless the plaintiff can show that the dividend payments resulted from improper motives and amounted to waste. The plaintiff contends only that the dividend payments drained Sinven of cash to such an extent that it was prevented from expanding.

The plaintiff proved no business opportunities which came to Sinven independently and which Sinclair either took to itself or denied to Sinven. As a matter of fact, with two minor exceptions which resulted in losses, all of Sinven's operations have been conducted in Venezuela, and Sinclair had a policy of exploiting its oil properties located in different countries by subsidiaries located in the particular countries.

From 1960 to 1966 Sinclair purchased or developed oil fields in Alaska, Canada, Paraguay, and other places around the world. The plaintiff contends that these were all opportunities which could have been taken by Sinven. The Chancellor concluded that Sinclair had not proved that its denial of expansion opportunities to Sinven was intrinsically fair. He based this conclusion on the following findings of fact. Sinclair made no real effort to expand Sinven. The excessive dividends paid by Sinven resulted in so great a cash drain as to effectively deny to Sinven any ability to expand. During this same period Sinclair actively pursued a company-wide policy of developing through its subsidiaries new sources of revenue, but Sinven was not permitted to participate and was confined in its activities to Venezuela.

However, the plaintiff could point to no opportunities which came to Sinven. Therefore, Sinclair usurped no business opportunity belonging to Sinven. Since Sinclair received nothing from Sinven to the exclusion of and detriment to Sinven's minority stockholders, there was no self-dealing. Therefore, business judgment is the proper standard by which to evaluate Sinclair's expansion policies.

Since there is no proof of self-dealing on the part of Sinclair, it follows that the expansion policy of Sinclair and the methods used to achieve the desired result must, as far as Sinclair's treatment of Sinven is concerned, be tested by the standards of the business judgment rule. Accordingly, Sinclair's decision, absent fraud or gross overreaching, to achieve expansion through the medium of its subsidiaries, other than Sinven, must be upheld.

Even if Sinclair was wrong in developing these opportunities as it did, the question arises, with which subsidiaries should these opportunities have been shared? No evidence indicates a unique need or ability of Sinven to develop these opportunities. The decision of which subsidiaries would be used to implement Sinclair's expansion policy was one of business judgment with which a court will not interfere absent a showing of gross and palpable overreaching. Meyerson v. El Paso Natural Gas Co., 246 A.2d 789 (Del.Ch.1967). No such showing has been made here.

Next, Sinclair argues that the Chancellor committed error when he held it liable to Sinven for breach of contract.

In 1961 Sinclair created Sinclair International Oil Company (hereafter International), a wholly owned subsidiary used for the purpose of coordinating all of Sinclair's foreign operations. All crude purchases by Sinclair were made thereafter through International.

On September 28, 1961, Sinclair caused Sinven to contract with International whereby Sinven agreed to sell all of its crude oil and refined products to International at specified prices. The contract provided for minimum and maximum quantities and prices. The plaintiff contends that Sinclair caused this contract to be breached in two respects. Although the contract called for payment on receipt, International's payments lagged as much as 30 days after receipt. Also, the contract required International to purchase at least a fixed minimum amount of crude and refined products from Sinven. International did not comply with this requirement.

Clearly, Sinclair's act of contracting with its dominated subsidiary was self-dealing. Under the contract Sinclair received the products produced by Sinven, and of course the minority shareholders of Sinven were not able to share in the receipt of these products. If the contract was breached, then Sinclair received these products to the detriment of Sinven's minority shareholders. We agree with the Chancellor's finding that the contract was breached by Sinclair, both as to the time of payments and the amounts purchased.

Although a parent need not bind itself by a contract with its dominated subsidiary, Sinclair chose to operate in this manner. As Sinclair has received the benefits of this contract, so must it comply with the contractual duties.

Under the intrinsic fairness standard, Sinclair must prove that its causing Sinven not to enforce the contract was intrinsically fair to the minority shareholders of Sinven. Sinclair has failed to meet this burden. Late payments were clearly breaches for which Sinven should have sought and received adequate damages. As to the quantities purchased, Sinclair argues that it purchased all the products produced by Sinven. This, however, does not satisfy the standard of intrinsic fairness. Sinclair has failed to prove that Sinven could not possibly have produced or someway have obtained the contract minimums. As such, Sinclair must account on this claim.

Finally, Sinclair argues that the Chancellor committed error in refusing to allow it a credit or setoff of all benefits provided by it to Sinven with respect to all the alleged damages. The Chancellor held that setoff should be allowed on specific transactions, e.g., benefits to Sinven under the contract with International, but denied an over all setoff against all damages claimed. We agree with the Chancellor, although the point may well be moot in view of our holding that Sinclair is not required to account for the alleged excessiveness of the dividend payments.

We will therefore reverse that part of the Chancellor's order that requires Sinclair to account to Sinven for damages sustained as a result of dividends paid between 1960 and 1966, and by reason of the denial to Sinven of expansion during that period. We will affirm the remaining portion of that order and remand the cause for further proceedings.

The *Meyerson* case referred to in *Sinclair* concerned the fairness of a parent corporation's filing a consolidated tax return with its subsidiary and using the losses of the subsidiary to offset the parent's income and reduce the parent's tax. The court rejected a minority shareholder's contention that this practice was unfair. Does the ruling of the court leaving that decision to the judgment of the board reflect a view that there is no self-dealing involved, or is the court saying that there are no established legal standards to invoke?

TRANS WORLD AIRLINES, INC. v. SUMMA CORP.
374 A.2d 5 (Del.Ch.1977).

[Howard Hughes owned all the stock of Hughes Tool Company ("Toolco") which owned 78% of the stock of TWA. While competitive airlines were acquiring jet aircraft from Boeing and Douglas in the late 1950's, TWA was not allowed to negotiate for the purchase of planes by itself but instead was forced to rely on Toolco which was unable to arrange financing for a long while. TWA sought an accounting and damages for the delay it suffered from Toolco's refusal to allow TWA to bargain for itself, which it charged was motivated by Toolco's desire to secure a tax advantage from the transaction. Toolco said that this was not a self-dealing transaction because the parent derived no benefit to the detriment of the minority.]

MARVEL, CHANCELLOR:

* * *

First of all, I am satisfied that the mere fact that Toolco engaged in the acquisition, financing, leasing, and ultimately in the sale of jet aircraft is not, in itself, of significance in this case because a parent company may concern itself with the purchase and sale of equipment to be used by a subsidiary, the basic question being rather whether or not TWA suffered injury by reason of being barred from dealing in such area on its own.

I conclude that the basic prerequisites to the application of the intrinsic fairness rule are found in the instant case. First of all, it is conceded that Toolco and Hughes exercised control over the affairs of TWA during the period in question, particularly in the area of the financing and acquisition of jet aircraft, the policy for which over a substantial period was dictated by the defendants, jet aircraft having been leased by Toolco to TWA on a day to day basis prior to agreement on a satisfactory financing arrangement. Furthermore, while Toolco ultimately turned over to TWA the jet aircraft in question once a financing plan was agreed upon, there is no doubt but that the defendants bargained on both sides of such transactions, causing TWA to act in such a way as to cause defendants to derive advantages at the expense of TWA to the exclusion of and to the detriment of the latter's minority shareholders. Accordingly, by refusing to allow TWA to select and finance the purchase of its own jet aircraft, the defendants were in a position to mete out to TWA such jet aircraft as they chose. In other words, by preventing TWA from making its own arrangements for the acquisition of jet planes, the defendants retained the capability of arranging the terms of such acquisitions so as to benefit themselves. In addition, in the event of the development of problems in connection with such acquisitions, as ultimately came to pass, in the task of obtaining long term financing for TWA, the defendants remained free to dispose of such aircraft to other air carriers.

Thus, it is clear on the present record that the minority shareholders of TWA received nothing in exchange for the strictures imposed by defendants on plaintiff's operations and that such stockholders may have suffered injury as a result of the loss of TWA's freedom to compete. As charged in the complaint, TWA might well have been able to earn substantially more income for its minority as well as majority stockholders through increased business activity during the period of its being dominated had it not been subject to the strictures imposed by the defendants.

The saga of Howard Hughes and TWA appears to have come to an end, Summa Corp. v. Trans World Airlines, Inc., 540 A.2d 403 (Del. 1988), and as Justice Moore noted in that opinion, the case in length of time, if in no other respect, is most reminiscent of *Jarndyce* and *Jarndyce* in Charles Dickens' *Bleak House*. The Delaware Supreme Court affirmed the Court of Chancery's finding that Toolco had breached its fiduciary duties to TWA. The court cited Weinberger v. UOP, Inc. (Chapter 23) and Sinclair v. Levien as providing the appropriate analytic framework and concluded that Toolco's conduct "hardly comports with basic concepts of fair dealing under the fiduciary standards of Delaware corporation law." The court rejected Toolco's argument that TWA did not need certain aircraft and that it should not be held liable for TWA's lost profits arising from Toolco's failure to order such aircraft. As the court noted, "this argument, like Toolco's others, ignores the fact that the intrinsic fairness test placed the burden upon Toolco to prove that it was not the cause of TWA's lost profits. * * * The trial court found, and we agree, that Toolco failed to meet that burden." Thus the court affirmed the Court of Chancery's award of $48,349,022.48 in damages and interest.

Chapter 18

DUTY OF DISCLOSURE TO SHAREHOLDERS

If fiduciary duties are one of the critical elements in the relationship between shareholders and management, it fairly may be said that disclosure lies at the heart of much of the law of fiduciary duties. We have already seen the importance of disclosure to the corporate decision-maker in a number of contexts. A director must be fully informed in order to gain the protection of the business judgment rule; disinterested shareholders or directors must be fully informed in a conflict of interest transaction in order to validate the transaction or to shift the burden of proof in litigation challenging the transaction; a director may be guilty of appropriating a corporate opportunity if she does not disclose the opportunity to the board before taking it for herself. And, clearly, full disclosure is paramount in the shareholder voting process.

In this latter connection, we have also seen that the proxy solicitation has become the substitute for the shareholders meeting in public corporations even though, as a formal matter, the meeting is actually held. The proxy process, in turn, reflects the intersection of state and federal law. Thus, when considering the duty of disclosure owed to the shareholder as decision-maker, it is necessary to examine how that duty has developed under both federal and state law and how those two bodies of law interrelate.

PROBLEM
NATIONAL METAL PRODUCTS
I

National Metal Products, Inc. ("National") is a Delaware corporation whose common stock is traded on the New York Stock Exchange. The company manufactures specialized metal products. Its sales for the most recent year were $500 million.

In February, the board of directors approved a merger with International Petroleum Corporation ("IPC") whereby National would issue additional shares of its common stock equal to 25% of the outstanding shares. The transaction required shareholder approval by both companies under state law. The proxy material sought approval of the merger and the election of directors. The candidates for election were the incumbent directors of National and Sanford, the CEO of IPC. At the meeting in May, the shareholders voted overwhelmingly to approve the merger and management's slate of directors.

The proxy statement contained all the information required by SEC rules concerning the merger and the candidates for election to the board. Among the statements made about the merger was the following: "The board of directors recommends approval of the merger. The board's recommendation is based upon its review of management's report and recommendations and the financial statements of IPC. It is the board's judgment, premised on this information, that the merger is in the best interests of the company and its shareholders."

Several months later, the following facts became known:

A. The merger was negotiated between Meacham, the CEO of National, and Sanford, the CEO of IPC. It was taken up by National's board at a regular meeting where Meacham and other members of management made a brief presentation and answered questions. Financial statements of IPC had been given to each member of the board two days before the meeting. After about 30 minutes of discussion, the board voted unanimously in favor of the merger. This was the same procedure that National had followed with three other acquisitions during the past two years.

B. The acquisition has proven costly to National, largely because of a price-fixing scheme that has recently come to light. Several years before the merger, management of IPC learned that its field managers had engaged in the scheme with several other independent oil producers. Senior management ordered the practice halted. Sanford informed Meacham of these past practices during the negotiations, and explained that it was common in the industry, but Meacham made no mention of these facts and his conversation with Sanford to the National board, nor was he asked any questions relating to possible price fixing.

Several months after the merger, it was revealed that the price-fixing practices had continued even after the merger with National. As a result, substantial contracts between National (through IPC) and some refineries were cancelled, and there was a likelihood both of large private suits under the anti-trust laws and criminal prosecutions. National has decided to dismiss some key managers who were engaged in this activity.

No mention of the past activity was made in the proxy statement.

C. National entered into a settlement of a claim by two local environmental protection agencies that the company violated their rules on emission controls. The violations were caused by furnaces in two older smelting plants of National, where management had decided to attempt compliance by patching up old emission control systems rather than replacing them with new and expensive electronic equipment. The company was fined $500,000. At the time the proxy statement was issued, the board was aware of management's decision on the furnaces and the risks but decided, on advice of counsel, that no disclosure was necessary in the proxy statement.

Rogers, the owner of 1,000 shares of National common stock believes that the proxy statement for the meeting was materially false and misleading in violation of Rule 14a–9 of the SEC proxy rules.

Questions

1. Assuming there were violations of rule 14a–9, can Rogers, after learning of the facts, bring suit based on federal law to obtain relief for those violations? What type of relief may be available?

2. Are there any material misstatements or omissions in the proxy statement in violation of Rule 14a–9?

3. Assuming that there are material misstatements or omissions, what causal connection can Rogers show between the violations he can establish and the injury of which he complains?

4. Suppose that Rogers believes that even if there were no material misstatements or omissions in the proxy statement, the merger was unfair because National paid too much to acquire IPC. Does Rogers have a valid claim under either the proxy rules or Rule 10b–5, either before or after the shareholder vote, based on a showing that the terms of the merger were unfair and that the unfairness was not directly disclosed?

5. Does Rogers have a claim under state law in connection with the proxy solicitation? If so, against whom? What must Rogers prove to prevail on his claim?

A. IMPLIED PRIVATE RIGHTS OF ACTION UNDER THE PROXY RULES

Note: A Student Guide to J.I. Case Co. v. Borak

The case that follows this note, the *Borak* case, is one of the most significant decisions in the interpretation of the federal securities laws and one of the most important landmarks at the intersection of corporate and securities law. Understanding its full significance, however, requires some background in the business and procedural aspects of the case.

Plaintiff Carl Borak was a stockholder in J.I. Case Co., a company that proposed to merge with American Tractor Corp. Borak contended that the merger involved improper self-dealing by the managers of his corporation and that the minority shareholders were treated unfairly.

Borak brought suit in federal district court to enjoin the merger. Jurisdiction was based on diversity of citizenship. The court denied the injunction, the merger was consummated and Borak's old corporation ceased to exist. A threshold issue was the capacity in which Borak was suing. Was the suit a class action, brought directly on behalf of the stockholders, or a derivative suit on behalf of the corporation? As we saw in Chapter 3 (and will see again in detail in Chapter 20), a derivative suit is one to enforce a right on behalf of the corporation that the corporation itself has not asserted. With rare exceptions, any damages that are awarded or amounts paid in settlement go to the corporation. A direct action, by contrast, alleges that the shareholders suffered direct injury in their capacity as shareholders.

The proxy solicitation used in approving the merger affects a corporate transaction (the merger between two corporations); thus any harm in the solicitation is arguably to the corporation. But the solicitation is also used to enable a shareholder to exercise her individual right to vote. Thus there are both direct and derivative elements in an action challenging the validity of the proxy solicitation

A key question in *Borak* involved the applicability of state substantive law. If the suit were brought only as a derivative suit, Borak would have had to comply with the state procedural requirements in derivative suits, including posting security for litigation expenses borne by defendant. These expenses include court costs and, in the court's discretion, the defendant's attorneys' fees. This requirement applies to diversity cases if it is required by the law of the forum state, which, in turn, may refer to the law of the state of incorporation. The purpose of this requirement is to protect the corporation and the individual defendants from the expense of defending frivolous suits. Although the bond itself may be expensive, the principal risk is that a plaintiff may have to make good on the bond and pay the underlying expenses if the litigation is unsuccessful.

Wisconsin had a security-for-expenses provision that would have been applicable to the common law suit, if it were derivative but not if the suit were a direct action. The district court characterized the suit as derivative and, because Borak refused to post security, dismissed the complaint. Thereafter, Borak amended his complaint to seek relief under § 14(a) of the Securities Exchange Act of 1934 and Rule 14a–9 of the SEC proxy rules. He also claimed that the state procedural requirements did not apply to his federal claim; thus he could not be required to post a bond.

In ruling on the amended complaint, the district court held that Borak's federal claim entitled him only to prospective or declaratory relief, i.e., an injunction or a ruling on the law. The court dismissed the other pleas for relief because Borak refused to post security. The district court reasoned that insofar as Borak requested the kind of relief under federal law that could be obtained only from his common law claim, such as damages, rescission or an order undoing or amending the terms of the merger, his request converted his federal claim into a state law claim. Borak appealed from all these rulings.

The Seventh Circuit reversed the district court. It held that the common law claim was both derivative and direct and thus was not subject to the security for expenses requirements. More important, the court held that the relief available under the federal count, as to which no security could be demanded, could be either prospective or retrospective, whichever was necessary to make the federal substantive requirements effective. Consequently, plaintiff could obtain the relief he sought even if the state claim were dropped. The decision created a conflict with the Sixth Circuit which had earlier ruled that only prospective relief could be granted for violation of the proxy rules. Dann v. Studebaker–Packard Corp., 288 F.2d 201 (6th Cir.1960).

If the action is held to be a class or direct action, the issue of security for expenses vanishes, but the question as to the scope of available relief remains. The district court's view as to the narrow scope of relief available under federal law is important if the available state law remedies are narrow. As a class claimant, however, Borak would be able to press both the common law and federal claim, and whatever relief could *not* be granted under federal law might still be granted under common law.

Under the district court's interpretation of federal remedies, it is not clear whether a court could dispense all the relief Borak requested, even if it had the powers of both federal and state courts. The reason for that is that Borak would be made to rely, very largely, on state remedies, and hope that state law would grant a full sweep of remedies in this context. The result might vary from state to state; some states might not allow damages or post-merger equitable relief. Other differences might exist between the relief that could be obtained from a federal court with full remedial powers and a state court. The statute of limitations might not be the same. The burden of proof might differ. Therefore, Borak sought to have the suit construed as a class action, so that he could press both federal and state claims. He also hoped to have the court rule that under both federal and state law, he would be entitled to both prospective relief and retrospective relief (damages).

J.I. CASE CO. v. BORAK
377 U.S. 426, 84 S.Ct. 1555, 12 L.Ed.2d 423 (1964).

MR. JUSTICE CLARK delivered the opinion of the Court.

This is a civil action brought by respondent, a stockholder of petitioner J.I. Case Company, charging deprivation of the pre-emptive rights of respondent and other shareholders by reason of a merger between Case and the American Tractor Corporation. It is alleged that the merger was effected through the circulation of a false and misleading proxy statement by those proposing the merger. The complaint was in two counts, the first based on diversity and claiming a breach of the directors' fiduciary duty to the stockholders. The second count alleged a violation of § 14(a) of the Securities Exchange Act of 1934 with reference to the proxy solicitation material. The trial court held that as to this count it had no power to redress the alleged violations of the Act but was limited solely to the granting of declaratory relief thereon under

§ 27 of the Act.[2] * * * On interlocutory appeal the Court of Appeals reversed. * * * We granted certiorari. We consider only the question of whether § 27 of the Act authorizes a federal cause of action for rescission or damages to a corporate stockholder with respect to a consummated merger which was authorized pursuant to the use of a proxy statement alleged to contain false and misleading statements violative of § 14(a) of the Act. * * *

I.

Respondent, the owner of 2,000 shares of common stock of Case acquired prior to the merger, brought this suit based on diversity jurisdiction seeking to enjoin a proposed merger between Case and the American Tractor Corporation (ATC) on various grounds, including breach of the fiduciary duties of the Case directors, self-dealing among the management of Case and ATC and misrepresentations contained in the material circulated to obtain proxies. The injunction was denied and the merger was thereafter consummated. * * * The claims pertinent to the asserted violation of the Securities Exchange Act were predicated on diversity jurisdiction as well as on § 27 of the Act. They alleged: that petitioners, or their predecessors, solicited or permitted their names to be used in the solicitation of proxies of Case stockholders for use at a special stockholders' meeting at which the proposed merger with ATC was to be voted upon; that the proxy solicitation material so circulated was false and misleading in violation of § 14(a) of the Act and Rule 14a–9 which the Commission had promulgated thereunder; that the merger was approved at the meeting by a small margin of votes and was thereafter consummated; that the merger would not have been approved but for the false and misleading statements in the proxy solicitation material; and that Case stockholders were damaged thereby. The respondent sought judgment holding the merger void and damages for himself and all other stockholders similarly situated, as well as such further relief "as equity shall require." The District Court ruled that the Wisconsin security for expenses statute did not apply to Count 2 since it arose under federal law. However, the court found that its jurisdiction was limited to declaratory relief in a private, as opposed to a government, suit alleging violation of § 14(a) of the Act. * * *

2. Section 27 of the Act, 48 Stat. 902–903, 15 U.S.C.A. § 78aa, provides in part: "The district courts of the United States, the Supreme Court of the District of Columbia, and the United States courts of any Territory or other place subject to the jurisdiction of the United States shall have exclusive jurisdiction of violations of this title or the rules and regulations thereunder, and of all suits in equity and actions at law brought to enforce any liability or duty created by this title or the rules and regulations thereunder. Any criminal proceeding may be brought in the district wherein any act or transaction constituting the violation occurred. Any suit or action to enforce any liability or duty created by this title or rules and regulations thereunder, or to enjoin any violation of such title or rules and regulations, may be brought in any such district or in the district wherein the defendant is found or is an inhabitant or transacts business, and process in such cases may be served in any other district of which the defendant is an inhabitant or wherever the defendant may be found."

II.

It appears clear that private parties have a right under § 27 to bring suit for violation of § 14(a) of the Act. Indeed, this section specifically grants the appropriate District Courts jurisdiction over "all suits in equity and actions at law brought to enforce any liability or duty created" under the Act. The petitioners make no concessions, however, emphasizing that Congress made no specific reference to a private right of action in § 14(a); that, in any event, the right would not extend to derivative suits and should be limited to prospective relief only. In addition, some of the petitioners argue that the merger can be dissolved only if it was fraudulent or non-beneficial, issues upon which the proxy material would not bear. But the causal relationship of the proxy material and the merger are questions of fact to be resolved at trial, not here. We therefore do not discuss this point further.

III.

While the respondent contends that his Count 2 claim is not a derivative one, we need not embrace that view, for we believe that a right of action exists as to both derivative and direct causes.

The purpose of § 14(a) is to prevent management or others from obtaining authorization for corporate action by means of deceptive or inadequate disclosure in proxy solicitation. The section stemmed from the congressional belief that "[f]air corporate suffrage is an important right that should attach to every equity security bought on a public exchange." H.R.Rep. No. 1383, 73d Cong., 2d Sess., 13. It was intended to "control the conditions under which proxies may be solicited with a view to preventing the recurrence of abuses which * * * [had] frustrated the free exercise of the voting rights of stockholders." Id., at 14. "Too often proxies are solicited without explanation to the stockholder of the real nature of the questions for which authority to cast his vote is sought." S.Rep. No. 792, 73d Cong., 2d Sess., 12. These broad remedial purposes are evidenced in the language of the section which makes it "unlawful for any person * * * to solicit or to permit the use of his name to solicit any proxy or consent or authorization in respect of any security * * * registered on any national securities exchange in contravention of such rules and regulations as the Commission may prescribe as necessary or appropriate in the public interest *or for the protection of investors.*" (Italics supplied.) While this language makes no specific reference to a private right of action, among its chief purposes is "the protection of investors," which certainly implies the availability of judicial relief where necessary to achieve that result.

The injury which a stockholder suffers from corporate action pursuant to a deceptive proxy solicitation ordinarily flows from the damage done the corporation, rather than from the damage inflicted directly upon the stockholder. The damage suffered results not from the deceit practiced on him alone but rather from the deceit practiced on the stockholders as a group. To hold that derivative actions are not within the sweep of the section would therefore be tantamount to a denial of private relief.   Private enforcement of the proxy rules provides a necessary supplement to Commission action.   As in anti-trust treble damage litigation, the possibility of civil damages or injunctive relief serves as a most effective weapon in the enforcement of the proxy requirements. The Commission advises that it examines over 2,000 proxy statements annually and each of them must necessarily be expedited.   Time does not permit an independent examination of the facts set out in the proxy material and this results in the Commission's acceptance of the representations contained therein at their face value, unless contrary to other material on file with it.   Indeed, on the allegations of respondent's complaint, the proxy material failed to disclose alleged unlawful market manipulation of the stock of ATC, and this unlawful manipulation would not have been apparent to the Commission until after the merger.

We, therefore, believe that under the circumstances here it is the duty of the courts to be alert to provide such remedies as are necessary to make effective the congressional purpose.   As was said in Sola Electric Co. v. Jefferson Electric Co., 317 U.S. 173, 176, 63 S.Ct. 172, 174, 87 L.Ed. 165 (1942):

> When a federal statute condemns an act as unlawful, the extent and nature of the legal consequences of the condemnation, though left by the statute to judicial determination, are nevertheless federal questions, the answers to which are to be derived from the statute and the federal policy which it has adopted.

It is for the federal courts "to adjust their remedies so as to grant the necessary relief" where federally secured rights are invaded.   "And it is also well settled that where legal rights have been invaded, and a federal statute provides for a general right to sue for such invasion, federal courts may use any available remedy to make good the wrong done." Bell v. Hood, 327 U.S. 678, 684, 66 S.Ct. 773, 777, 90 L.Ed. 939 (1946). Section 27 grants the District Courts jurisdiction "of all suits in equity and actions at law brought to enforce any liability or duty created by this title * * *."   In passing on almost identical language found in the Securities Act of 1933, the Court found the words entirely sufficient to fashion a remedy to rescind a fraudulent sale, secure restitution and even to enforce the right to restitution against a third party holding assets of the vendor.   Deckert v. Independence Shares Corp., 311 U.S. 282, 61 S.Ct. 229, 85 L.Ed. 189 (1940).   This significant language was used:

> The power *to enforce* implies the power to make effective the right of recovery afforded by the Act.   And the power to make the right of recovery effective implies the power to utilize any of the procedures or actions normally available to the litigant according to the exigencies of the particular case.   At 288 of 311 U.S., at 233 of 61 S.Ct.

Nor do we find merit in the contention that such remedies are limited to prospective relief.   This was the position taken in Dann v. Studebaker–Packard Corp., 6 Cir., 288 F.2d 201, where it was held that the "preponderance of questions of state law which would have to be interpreted and applied in order to grant the relief sought * * * is so great that the federal question involved * * * is really negligible in comparison." But we believe that the overriding federal law applicable here would, where the facts required, control the appropriateness of redress despite the provisions of state corporation law, for it "is not uncommon for federal courts to fashion federal law where federal rights are concerned." Textile Workers Union of America v. Lincoln Mills, 353 U.S. 448, 457, 77 S.Ct. 912, 918, 1 L.Ed.2d 972 (1957). In addition, the fact that questions of state law must be decided does not change the character of the right; it remains federal. * * *

Moreover, if federal jurisdiction were limited to the granting of declaratory relief, victims of deceptive proxy statements would be obliged to go into state courts for remedial relief. And if the law of the State happened to attach no responsibility to the use of misleading proxy statements, the whole purpose of the section might be frustrated. Furthermore, the hurdles that the victim might face (such as separate suits, as contemplated by Dann v. Studebaker–Packard Corp., *supra*, security for expenses statutes, bringing in all parties necessary for complete relief, etc.) might well prove insuperable to effective relief.

IV.

Our finding that federal courts have the power to grant all necessary remedial relief is not to be construed as any indication of what we believe to be the necessary and appropriate relief in this case. We are concerned here only with a determination that federal jurisdiction for this purpose does exist. Whatever remedy is necessary must await the trial on the merits.

The other contentions of the petitioners are denied.

Affirmed.

Note: Implied Private Rights of Action

Although seemingly straightforward, the Court's opinion in *Borak* is curious in several ways. Note that Section 14(a) provides no express cause of action for those injured by a violation of the section; if one exists, it must be judicially implied. Because the action is one "arising under the laws of the United States," and therefore is predicated on legislative authority, it is curious that the Court did not analyze Congressional intent in the enactment of § 14(a). In fact, the legislative history is sparse and does not indicate whether Congress contemplated that private suits could or could not be brought under § 14(a), an omission which subsequent courts have found significant in deciding whether to imply a private right of action under other statutory provisions.

The Court also does not discuss the carefully detailed pattern of express remedies provided in the Securities Exchange Act of 1934 and its companion statute, the Securities Act of 1933, or the effect that implied remedies would have on those provisions. The 1934 Act authorizes the

SEC to seek injunctive relief for a violation of any provision of the Act. It also provides express remedies for investors who are injured by manipulation (§ 9), for corporations whose insiders engage in buying and selling the company's stock (§ 16) and, most important, for investors who are injured as a result of any false or misleading information contained in a document filed with the SEC (§ 18). These remedies were carefully constructed and balanced; they extended relief beyond common law protections, but the tradeoff was the imposition of tight procedural restrictions and a short statute of limitations. Implied remedies, of course, were not the subject of that bargain. Because the proxy statement which was the basis of the suit was a document filed with the SEC and subject to liability under § 18, the Court might have found that a private right should not be implied where an express remedy was already available, even though the plaintiff could not avail himself of the remedy in this particular case.

Rather than using either of these approaches, the Court chose to base its decision on § 27, which confers exclusive jurisdiction on the federal courts for violations of the statute and provides for service of process and venue. Section 27 is necessary, whether or not private rights of action are implied, because jurisdiction and venue must be provided for both SEC enforcement actions and the express remedies in the statute. Had there been no express remedies, of course, § 27 could be read as indicating either that Congress intended that remedies be implied or that the SEC have exclusive enforcement power.

The Court could have adopted a different methodology—the statutory tort theory—in deciding whether to imply a private right of action, but to do so would have forced the Court to answer the question it so carefully avoided in the actual opinion: the capacity in which the plaintiff was suing. The statutory tort theory can be traced back to Dean Ezra Ripley Thayer's seminal article, Public Wrong and Private Action, 27 Harv.L.Rev. 317 (1914), which argued that it was unreasonable conduct for a defendant to violate a statute. Since a statutory violation was negligence per se, the courts upheld private recovery based upon such violation. Not every violation would lead to an implied private cause of action under this theory, however. As the American Law Institute emphasized in the Restatement of Torts, § 286, the plaintiff must also be part of the class the statute was intended to protect.

The Supreme Court and lower federal courts used a statutory tort analysis both before and after *Borak*. See Texas & Pacific Railway v. Rigsby, 241 U.S. 33, 36 S.Ct. 482, 60 L.Ed. 874 (1916). Wyandotte Transportation Co. v. United States, 389 U.S. 191, 88 S.Ct. 379, 19 L.Ed.2d 407 (1967). In the securities laws, a federal district court implied a private right of action under Rule 10b–5 under the 1934 Act, which prohibits false or misleading statements, or deceptive or manipulative acts or practices in connection with the purchase or sale of securities. Kardon v. National Gypsum Co., 69 F.Supp. 512 (E.D.Pa.

1946). The court found that the violation of the statute was a tort and granted relief for the plaintiff who was a member of the protected class.

Borak also raises the question of the proper role of federal courts in determining the substantive standard of conduct to which persons governed by a statute are subject. That role, of course, was altered by Erie Railroad Co. v. Tompkins, 304 U.S. 64, 58 S.Ct. 817, 82 L.Ed. 1188 (1938), which held that there was no federal general common law. Thereafter, federal courts develop their own body of federal law only when there is a federal statute that does not spell out the rights of private parties. In so doing, the courts analyze Congressional intent.

How is Congressional intent determined? Does a court ask whether Congress specifically intended that the federal courts would create federal common law, including private rights of action, under a particular statute, or should the court determine whether there is a private right of action on the basis of Congress' policy or purpose in a particular federal program and the need for a private remedy? See Wheeldin v. Wheeler, 373 U.S. 647, 83 S.Ct. 1441, 10 L.Ed.2d 605 (1963). Some commentators have urged that Congressional intent be examined in light of the traditional tort theory. Professor Louis Loss, the leading scholar of securities law, argued that Congressional silence about implied private rights of action in the face of "accepted" doctrine was best understood as justifying the conclusion that Congress intended the courts to follow this doctrine, thereby creating private rights of action. IX Louis Loss and Joel Seligman, Securities Regulation 4333–4334 (3d ed. 1992). Virtually none of this analysis is found in the *Borak* opinion.

The Supreme Court continued to support implied private rights of action under the federal securities laws in the years immediately following the *Borak* decision. In Mills v. Electric Auto–Lite Co., 396 U.S. 375, 90 S.Ct. 616, 24 L.Ed.2d 593 (1970), private stockholder actions to enforce the substantive provisions of the securities laws were hailed as "corporate therapeutics," 396 U.S. at 396, 90 S.Ct. at 627. In Superintendent of Insurance v. Bankers Life & Casualty Co., 404 U.S. 6, 13 (n. 9), 92 S.Ct. 165, 169, 30 L.Ed.2d 128 (1971), the Court acknowledged the existence of an implied right of action under Rule 10b–5 without any discussion in the main body of the opinion.

In the mid–1970's, the Supreme Court began to curtail the availability of implied private rights of action under federal law. Most important was Cort v. Ash, 422 U.S. 66, 95 S.Ct. 2080, 45 L.Ed.2d 26 (1975), where a unanimous Court refused to imply a private right of action under the Federal Election Campaign Law. A stockholder of Bethlehem Steel Corporation asserted that the corporation had illegally expended funds in the 1972 Presidential election, and brought a derivative suit to recover the expenditures. In rejecting the stockholder's claim, the Court laid down four factors for determining whether an implied private right of action exists:

1. Is the plaintiff one of the class for whose *especial* benefit the statute was enacted?

2.   Is there any indication of legislative intent, explicit or implicit, either to create or deny the private remedy?

3.   Is it consistent with the underlying purposes of the legislative scheme to imply such a remedy?

4.   Is the cause of action one traditionally relegated to state law in an area basically the concern of the states, so that it would be inappropriate to infer a cause of action based solely on federal law?

Cort moves away from the *Borak* analysis and attempts to incorporate the Court's various concerns about the growing role of, and burden on, federal courts.   Further, by instructing the courts to look at state law in interpreting a federal statute, the Court was advocating an approach antithetical to the approach followed by the Court from *Rigsby* to *Borak*.   Since *Cort*, the Supreme Court has struggled to find an appropriate analysis for when to imply a private right of action under a federal statute, and generally has been reluctant to imply such rights. See Robert H.A. Ashford, Implied Causes of Action Under Federal Laws: Calling the Court Back to Borak, 79 N.W.U.L.Rev. 227 (1984).

B.   STATE LAW REGULATION OF PROXY SOLICITATIONS

State regulation of proxy solicitations is a logical outgrowth of state statutes governing notice to shareholders of shareholder meetings. States have regulated proxy solicitations longer than has the federal government, yet far fewer cases have arisen under state law because of "judicial reluctance squarely to meet the problem of adequate disclosure in proxy solicitation."   Note, Standards of Disclosure in Proxy Solicitation of Unlisted Securities, 1960 Duke L.J. 623, 628 (1960).   State courts have been reluctant to embroil themselves in the "internal affairs" of corporations and have viewed any judicial intervention in the proxy process as an extraordinary measure.   It was this reluctance that the Court noted in *Borak* when it observed that some states might attach no responsibility to misleading proxy statements.

The common law standards for the validity of a proxy solicitation evolved slowly.   At the turn of the century, it appears that the principal test for validity was whether the shareholder had given the proxy voluntarily.   Unless an individual shareholder could prove "that he gave [his proxy] under any constraint or misapprehension or otherwise than as a matter of his own free will and personal preference," a suit objecting to the use of a proxy given in response to a request for it was certain to fail.   State ex rel. Pugh v. Meredith, 167 N.W. 626 (Iowa 1918).   The proxy solicitor, over time, came to be held to owe a fiduciary duty to the shareholder from whom she solicits proxies not to make false or misleading communications in doing so.

Prior to *Borak*, voluntariness gave way in state courts to concepts of fairness and common law fraud and misrepresentation.   The following excerpt from the dissenting opinion in Brown v. Ward, 593 P.2d 247 (Alaska 1979) summarizes the evolution of state law principles.

Ward contends that since Congress intended state law to control, in the absence of a statute, the elements of common law fraud and misrepresentation should control. However, the few courts which have addressed this issue have not so held. Rather, they have taken a compromise position between the federal standard and the common law tort of misrepresentation. See "Standards of Disclosure in Proxy Solicitation of Unlisted Securities," [1960 Duke L.J. 623 (1960)] n. 6, at 623; Aranow and Einhorn, "State Court Review of Corporate Elections," 56 Col.L.Rev. 155 (1956).

New York has had the most case law in this area. In Re Scheuer, 59 N.Y.S.2d 500 (Sup.1942), was an action by an aggrieved shareholder to have proxies invalidated because the solicitation material reported that certain new equipment expenditures had been deducted from gross earnings when, in fact, they were charged to capital. The court found that the actions of those engaged in securing the proxies had deviated from "the exacting standards of fairness" required in proxy solicitation and were misleading, whether done "carelessly, recklessly, or deliberately." 59 N.Y.S.2d at 501. Unfortunately, these standards were not further described. Continental Bank & Trust Co. v. 200 Madison Ave. Corp., 43 N.Y.S.2d 402 (Sup.1943), added that the alleged misrepresentation must be material such as to "influence any layman to give a proxy where he would not otherwise have done so." 43 N.Y.S.2d at 407–8. Wyatt v. Armstrong, 186 Misc. 216, 59 N.Y.S.2d 502 (1945), reasserted the Scheuer test. It held that proxies solicited without notification that the nominees, if elected, intended to resign was a concealment tantamount to fraud and misrepresentation. The test was whether the solicitation was "so clouded with doubt or tainted with questionable circumstances that the standards of fair dealing" were abused, depriving shareholders of the knowing freedom to vote. 59 N.Y.S.2d at 505, 508.

The last in this line of cases was In Re R. Hoe & Co., 14 Misc.2d 500, 137 N.Y.S.2d 142 (1954), aff'd, 309 N.Y. 719, 128 N.E.2d 420 (1955). After an election of directors, the displaced management sought to have the election set aside because the winning shareholder insurgents had made misrepresentations about management in their proxy solicitation material. The court found that there was a factual basis for the shareholders allegations against management. Management had fully availed itself of the opportunity to present its view to the shareholders. And, though the fight was bitter, the solicitation was not so tainted with fraud as to require judicial intervention to avoid an inequitable result. The court noted that "a certain amount of innuendo, misstatement, exaggeration and puffing must be allowed as a natural by-product of a bitter campaign." 137

N.Y.S.2d at 147–48. See also, Bresnick v. Home Title Guaranty Company, 175 F.Supp. 723 (S.D.N.Y.1959).

The view that shareholders would be better protected if the standard of proof for misleading proxy solicitation material were less rigorous than common law misrepresentation was best stated in Willoughby v. Port, 182 F.Supp. 496 (S.D.N.Y.1960). There, two directors sought a preliminary injunction against another director's use of proxies he had solicited, claiming that the director had misstated the attitude of the corporate counsel. The court said:

"Those who seek the proxies of their fellow corporate shareholders assume a fiduciary obligation. Even if the publicity here was defective only in that it did not tell the whole truth, the failure to make a full disclosure would have been a breach of fiduciary obligation. As things stand, I cannot find that any stockholder who sends defendants his proxy is doing so uninfluenced by the false impression. * * * Defendants are responsible for any such false impression and consequently cannot have the advantage of the proxies obtained thereby." (citations omitted) 182 F.Supp. at 499.

593 P.2d at 255–256.

———

Only three states, Alaska, Illinois and South Carolina, have enacted statutes regulating proxy solicitations. No cases directly construing these statutes have arisen, and many of the same questions that arose in connection with *Borak* remain.

Alaska enacted a statute in 1977 which prohibits false and misleading proxy solicitations. Alaska Stat. § 45.55.160 (1992). The statute establishes an agency to prosecute violations. Id. at § 45.55.200. Section 139 specifically requires those corporations organized under the Alaska Native Claims Settlement Act to file their proxy solicitation materials with the agency. Although the statute does not provide an express private right of action, the majority in Brown v. Ward, supra, implicitly recognized such an action under the statute so long as the corporation was required to file with the enforcing agency. 593 P.2d 247, 249 (Alaska 1979).

The Illinois and South Carolina statutes also prohibit the use of false and misleading statements when soliciting proxies, using language which closely resembles rule 14a–9 of the federal proxy rules. Unlike Alaska, Illinois and South Carolina do not set up an agency to enforce the statute or provide explicit penalties for violators. Like the Alaska statute, these statutes do not establish a private cause of action, and there are no cases construing them.

C.   MATERIALITY

TSC INDUSTRIES, INC. v. NORTHWAY, INC.
426 U.S. 438, 96 S.Ct. 2126, 48 L.Ed.2d 757 (1976).

[National Industries acquired 34% of TSC Industries stock by purchase from the founding family, and then placed five of its nominees on TSC's board of directors. The two companies agreed to a sale of TSC's assets to National in exchange for stock and warrants of National. A joint proxy statement was issued by the two companies. A shareholder of TSC sued for violation of Section 14(a) of the Securities Exchange Act of 1934 and Rule 14a–9. The shareholder claimed, among other things, that the proxy statement failed to state that purchase of the 34% block of stock, which was disclosed, gave it control of TSC. The District Court found no material omissions from the proxy statement, but the Court of Appeals reversed.]

Mr. Justice Marshall delivered the opinion of the Court.

* * *

The question of materiality, it is universally agreed, is an objective one, involving the significance of an omitted or misrepresented fact to a reasonable investor. Variations in the formulation of a general test of materiality occur in the articulation of just how significant a fact must be or, put another way, how certain it must be that the fact would affect a reasonable investor's judgment.

The Court of Appeals in this case concluded that material facts include "all facts which a reasonable shareholder *might* consider important." 512 F.2d at 330 (emphasis added). This formulation of the test of materiality has been explicitly rejected by at least two courts as setting too low a threshold for the imposition of liability under Rule 14a–9. Gerstle v. Gamble–Skogmo, Inc., 478 F.2d 1281, 1301–1302 (C.A.2 1973); Smallwood v. Pearl Brewing Co., 489 F.2d 579, 603–604 (C.A.5 1974). In these cases, panels of the Second and Fifth Circuits opted for the conventional tort test of materiality—whether a reasonable man *would* attach importance to the fact misrepresented or omitted in determining his course of action. * * *

In arriving at its broad definition of a material fact as one that a reasonable shareholder *might* consider important, the Court of Appeals in this case relied heavily upon language of this Court in Mills v. Electric Auto–Lite Co., *supra.* That reliance was misplaced. The *Mills* Court did characterize a determination of materiality as at least "embod[ying] a conclusion that the defect was of such a character that it might have been considered important by a reasonable shareholder who was in the process of deciding how to vote." But if any language in *Mills* is to be read as suggesting a general notion of materiality, it can only be the opinion's subsequent reference to materiality as a "requirement that the defect have a significant *propensity* to affect the voting process." For it was that requirement that the Court said "adequately serves the purpose of ensuring that a cause of action cannot be established by proof of a defect so trivial, or so unrelated to the transaction for which approval is sought, that correction of the defect or imposition of liability would not further the interests protected by § 14(a)." Even this language must be read, however, with appreciation that the Court specifically declined to consider the materiality of the omissions in *Mills*. The references to materiality were simply preliminary to our consideration of the sole question in the case—whether proof of the materiality of an omission from a proxy statement must be supplemented by a showing that the defect actually caused the outcome of the vote. It is clear, then, that *Mills* did not intend to foreclose further inquiry into the meaning of materiality under Rule 14a–9.

C

In formulating a standard of materiality under Rule 14a–9, we are guided, of course, by the recognition in *Borak* and *Mills* of the Rule's broad remedial purpose. That purpose is not merely to ensure by judicial means that the transaction, when judged by its real terms, is fair and otherwise adequate, but to ensure disclosures by corporate management in order to enable the shareholders to make an informed choice. As an abstract proposition, the most desirable role for a court in a suit of this sort, coming after the consummation of the proposed transaction, would perhaps be to determine whether in fact the proposal would have been favored by the shareholders and consummated in the absence of any misstatement or omission. But as we recognized in *Mills,* such matters are not subject to determination with certainty. Doubts as to the critical nature of information misstated or omitted will be commonplace. And particularly in view of the prophylactic purpose of the Rule and the fact that the content of the proxy statement is within management's control, it is appropriate that these doubts be resolved in favor of those the statute is designed to protect.

We are aware, however, that the disclosure policy embodied in the proxy regulations is not without limit. Some information is of such dubious significance that insistence on its disclosure may accomplish more harm than good. The potential liability for Rule 14a–9 violation can be great indeed, and if the standard of materiality is unnecessarily low, not only may the corporation and its management be subjected to liability for insignificant omissions or misstatements, but also management's fear of exposing itself to substantial liability may cause it simply to bury the shareholders in an avalanche of trivial information—a result that is hardly conducive to informed decisionmaking. Precisely these dangers are presented, we think, by the definition of a material fact adopted by the Court of Appeals in this case—a fact which a reasonable shareholder *might* consider important. We agree with Judge Friendly, speaking for the Court of Appeals in *Gerstle,* that the "might" formulation is "too suggestive of mere possibility, however unlikely."

The general standard of materiality that we think best comports with the policies of Rule 14a–9 is as follows: An omitted fact is material if there is a substantial likelihood that a reasonable shareholder would consider it important in deciding how to vote. This standard is fully consistent with *Mills* general description of materiality as a requirement that "the defect have a significant *propensity* to affect the voting process." It does not require proof of a substantial likelihood that disclosure of the omitted fact would have caused the reasonable investor to change his vote. What the standard does contemplate is a showing of a substantial likelihood that, under all the circumstances, the omitted fact would have assumed actual significance in the deliberations of the reasonable shareholder. Put another way, there must be a substantial likelihood that the disclosure of the omitted fact would have been viewed by the reasonable investor as having significantly altered the "total mix" of information made available.

* * * In considering whether summary judgment on the issue is appropriate, we must bear in mind that the underlying objective facts, which will often be free from dispute, are merely the starting point for the ultimate determination of materiality. The determination requires delicate assessments of the inferences a "reasonable shareholder" would draw from a given set of facts and the significance of those inferences to him, and these assessments are peculiarly ones for the trier of fact. Only if the established omissions are "so obviously important to an investor, that reasonable minds cannot differ on the question of materiality" is the ultimate issue of materiality appropriately resolved "as a matter of law" by summary judgment.

III

The omissions found by the Court of Appeals to have been materially misleading as a matter of law involved two general issues—the degree of National's control over TSC at the time of the proxy solicitation, and the favorability of the terms of the proposed transaction to TSC shareholders.

A. *National's Control of TSC*

The Court of Appeals concluded that two omitted facts relating to National's potential influence, or control, over the management of TSC were material as a matter of law. First, the proxy statement failed to state that at the time the statement was issued, the chairman of the TSC board of directors was Stanley Yarmuth, National's president and chief executive officer, and the chairman of the TSC executive committee was Charles Simonelli, National's executive vice president. Second the statement did not disclose that in filing reports required by the SEC, both TSC and National had indicated that National "may be deemed to be a 'parent' of TSC as that term is defined in the Rules and Regulations under the Securities Act of 1933." The Court of Appeals noted that TSC shareholders were relying on the TSC board of directors to negotiate on their behalf for the best possible rate of exchange with National. It then concluded that the omitted facts were material because they were "persuasive indicators that the TSC board was in fact under the control of National, and that National thus 'sat on both sides of the table' in setting the terms of the exchange."

We do not agree that the omission of these facts, when viewed against the disclosures contained in the proxy statement, warrants the entry of summary judgment against TSC and National on this record. Our conclusion is the same whether the omissions are considered separately or together.

The proxy statement prominently displayed the facts that National owned 34% of the outstanding shares in TSC, and that no other person owned more than 10%. App. 262–263, 267. It also prominently revealed that 5 out of 10 TSC directors were National nominees, and it recited the positions of those National nominees with National—indicating, among other things, that Stanley Yarmuth was president and a director of National, and that Charles Simonelli was executive vice president and a director of National. These disclosures clearly revealed the nature of National's relationship with TSC and alerted the reasonable shareholder to the fact that National exercised a degree of influence over TSC. In view of these disclosures, we certainly cannot say that the additional facts that Yarmuth was chairman of the TSC board of directors and Simonelli chairman of its executive committee were, on this record, so obviously important that reasonable minds could not differ on their materiality.

* * *

[The Court also found that the other omissions were not material as a matter of law. It reversed the entry of summary judgment for the plaintiff and remanded to allow a fact-finder to determine the materiality of the omissions discussed above.]

Note: Materiality Under Federal Law

As the Court makes clear in *TSC*, not every misstatement or omission is material. Must the omission or false or misleading statement have played a significant role in bringing about the matter submitted to a vote? Do only those errors which bear upon the financial soundness of the investment have bearing on a shareholder's decision to grant a proxy? Do other factors, not easily quantifiable, have anything to do with a shareholder's decision? Do the proxy rules have any aim other than the protection of the shareholder's interest?

These questions have jurisdictional significance. To the extent that a company may be held liable for failing to disclose information that is material in relation to some goal other than investor protection, great sweep is given to the federal securities laws and to the SEC's power to govern corporate conduct. Section 14(a) of the Securities Exchange Act of 1934 gives the Commission power to prescribe rules and regulations it deems "necessary or appropriate in the public interest or for the protection of investors." Presumably the words "in the public interest" have some meaning that, according to one writer, "would seem at least to permit the Commission to take into account the broader public interest when acting in areas near the margins of investor protection * * *." Russell B. Stevenson, Jr., The SEC and Foreign Bribery, 32 Bus.Law. 53 (1976). However, the Supreme Court in NAACP v. Federal Power Commission, 425 U.S. 662, 96 S.Ct. 1806, 48 L.Ed.2d 284 (1976) held that similar language in another statute should be read to confine the agency's power close to its main purposes, which in the case of the SEC means the protection of investors. And, as we saw in Chapter 14, the Court of Appeals in *Business Roundtable* strongly suggested that there were limits to the SEC's authority under Section 14(a) in areas of traditional state corporate governance.

To what extent is the failure to disclose violations of the law a material omission? One answer might be that the violation of law is material if the penalty imposed on the corporation is financially significant so as to be relevant to a traditional investment analysis. But suppose the violation results in relatively insignificant penalties or, even better from the company's standpoint, was incurred in the course of obtaining substantial benefits for the company. For example, a company might have violated some environmental law which enabled it to dispose of waste products at a great saving. Or it might have bribed a public official in return for which it received substantial economic benefits which it retains. Are investors interested in requiring disclosure of that information especially where the disclosure might deter the company from securing the economic advantage? Should there be liability under the proxy rules for omitting these facts? Or would it constitute a compounding of the original violation, brought within the scope of securities laws because of a failure to disclose that violation?

The cases that deal with these questions do not always arise under Section 14(a), but they are relevant to interpreting that section. Thus, the SEC found that United States Steel Corporation had violated the reporting requirements of Section 13(a) of the Securities Exchange Act of 1934 when it failed to disclose the company's frequent violations of environmental requirements, which resulted in fines to the company. In the Matter of United States Steel Corporation, Rel. No. 34–16223 (Sept. 27, 1979). It was the *pattern* of the company's behavior combined with its intransigent attitude toward the environmental violations rather than the isolated violation, that probably caused the SEC to charge disclosure violations.

In Levine v. NL Industries, Inc., 926 F.2d 199 (2d Cir.1991), plaintiffs argued that the failure to disclose the costs of failing to comply with environmental regulations constituted a violation of Rule 10b–5. Noting both SEC rules and the decision in *United States Steel,* the court acknowledged that such information would normally be material and thus required to be disclosed. In this case, however, the court found that there had been no breach of the duty to disclose because the United States government had indemnified the company against such costs.

For an expression of the SEC's concern about the adequacy of disclosure of environmental liability, see SEC Staff Accounting Bulletin 92 (June 8, 1993).

In the Report of the Securities and Exchange Commission on Questionable and Illegal Corporate Payments and Practices, submitted to the Senate Banking, Housing and Urban Affairs Committee in 1976, the SEC contended that questionable or illegal payments were material facts regardless of the size of the payments or their impact on the corporations' business. The Commission argued that the disclosure requirements are intended to facilitate the stockholders' evaluation of management's stewardship, and that "investors should be vitally interested in the quality and integrity of management." Several courts have endorsed this approach, albeit in particular contexts. In SEC v. Kalvex, Inc., 425 F.Supp. 310 (S.D.N.Y.1975), the court held that the proxy statement's failure to disclose that a candidate for director had arranged for illegal kick-backs of a small amount was a material omission because of the bearing that the information had on the candidate's integrity. Similarly, in Cooke v. Teleprompter Corp., 334 F.Supp. 467 (S.D.N.Y. 1971), the court found that it was a material omission to fail to disclose that a candidate for the board had been convicted of bribing public officials. Teleprompter's operations depended upon receiving an FCC license, heightening the importance of information the FCC might deem important. In SEC v. Jos. Schlitz Brewing Co., 452 F.Supp. 824 (E.D.Wis.1978) the court found that the failure to disclose illegal or improper payments made to induce the sale of the company's products was material because of the bearing it had on the integrity of management.

The SEC and the courts now limit disclosure about management integrity to those situations where the rules specifically mandate disclosure or where the conduct has had a materially adverse *economic* impact on the corporation. A former SEC Commissioner has written that self-dealing by directors and officers is a material fact, particularly in the context of proxy statements where directors are standing for office. Bevis Longstreth, SEC Disclosure Policy Regarding Management Integrity, 38 Bus.Law. 1413 (1983). But both the Commission and the courts have moved away from an earlier position that it was material to disclose whether directors or officers had engaged in illegal conduct even if they did not receive any personal benefit. Gaines v. Haughton, 645 F.2d 761 (9th Cir.1981). Disclosure of "material" facts does not require directors and officers to accuse themselves of antisocial or illegal policies in the proxy statement. Alleged violations of banking laws or labor laws, for example, supposedly revealing questionable moral or ethical conduct, are not "material" for purposes of the proxy rules. The emphasis of the disclosure requirements is on quantitatively significant information, not qualitative information except for self-dealing conduct.

In addition to providing a sufficient basis for a voting decision, disclosure may deter wrongful conduct. That is, disclosure can have a therapeutic effect. The Advisory Committee on Corporate Disclosure to the SEC recommended (with one of the authors of this book dissenting) that "the Commission should not adopt disclosure requirements which have as their principal objective the regulation of corporate conduct." In commenting upon that report the Commission said "it does not believe, however, that the benefits to be derived from such a statement would, on balance outweigh the difficulties which it might create * * *. Decisions as to whether to require disclosure frequently do affect conduct and Congress was well aware of this consequence and thought it would often be beneficial." Preliminary Responses of the Commission to the Recommendations of the Advisory Committee on Corporate Disclosure, Securities Act Release No. 5906, Feb. 15, 1978, Fed.Sec.L.Rept. (CCH) ¶ 81,505.

In some cases, the real focus of the shareholder's attack is management's conduct; the claim of inadequate disclosure in violation of the proxy rules becomes the vehicle for plaintiffs' obtaining federal jurisdiction rather than attempting to establish a breach of fiduciary duty under state law. For example, if the proxy statement for a patently unfair merger contained materially false and misleading statements, but the shareholders rejected the merger, no suit under Section 14(a) could be maintained. In such a case, the shareholder could not show how any loss was caused by the violation. The more likely scenario, however, is the converse: the facts establishing the unfairness of the merger were fully and painfully disclosed, but the shareholders approved. The loss is plain enough—the transaction was unfair—but has there been a violation of the proxy rules? Must the unfairness be identified and the merger characterized as unfair? In other words, do the rules require more than disclosure of facts from which the decision maker can draw her own conclusions? If so, the result would appear to be the federalization of state law fiduciary duties in the guise of implementing the full disclosure policy of the federal securities laws. Keep these questions in mind in reading the materials in Section E.

In Golub v. PPD Corp., 576 F.2d 759 (8th Cir.1978), plaintiffs alleged that a corporation's sale of assets to a related person was unfair, and that the proxy statement did not disclose management's improper motives. The court upheld dismissal of the complaint, stating:

> [The] plaintiffs are not complaining about any absence of facts in the proxy statement. Their complaint is that those who prepared the statement did not "disclose" what the plaintiffs say was the true motivation of * * * management in selling the assets of the company, and did not characterize the bonus aspects of the transaction as plaintiffs would have it characterized. Under the ['34] Act and

regulations plaintiffs were not entitled to have such a "disclosure" or such a characterization.

It is quite possible that plaintiffs may have a claim against the defendants or some of them under applicable state law. If so, plaintiffs are free to pursue that claim in an appropriate forum. * * *

576 F.2d at 764–65.

Similarly, in Wallerstein v. Primerica Corp., 701 F.Supp. 393 (E.D.N.Y.1988), the court rejected plaintiff's claim that the company's proxy statement was materially false and misleading because it stated that the board of directors had "carefully reviewed" the terms of a proposed merger when the board had not. The court noted that, absent anything more, a breach of fiduciary duty did not give rise to a claim under the federal securities laws. The court also found that the plaintiffs had suggested that the directors had not exercised reasonable diligence in connection with the transaction. Accordingly, the court concluded that plaintiffs' assertion "advanced as a 14a–9 claim * * * is a thinly but unsuccessfully disguised breach of fiduciary duty claim." 701 F.Supp. at 397.

Although the test for materiality is keyed to the "reasonable shareholder," the context in which the question of materiality arises often will influence the answer. In Justin Industries, Inc. v. Choctaw Securities, L.P., 920 F.2d 262 (5th Cir.1990), the target of a takeover bid, as a defensive tactic, amended its bylaws to include a supermajority provision for the removal of directors. The company failed to disclose the amendments in various SEC filings in violation of the 1934 Act. The amendments were subsequently rescinded. While the bylaws were in force, the directors were re-elected in an unopposed election. The bidder sued to set aside the election and to have a new election ordered in which it could run its own candidates. The district court denied the motion for an injunction, holding that the failure to disclose the amendments was not material because a "typical investor" would not have found them significant.

Although affirming the denial of the preliminary injunction, the Fifth Circuit reversed on the question of materiality and questioned the use of the "typical investor" standard. Noting that changes in the relative power of shareholders and directors were fundamental to the corporate governance system, the court suggested that "striking changes" in that relationship strongly suggested materiality. Here, the context mattered. Although not every change in the bylaws would be material, where the company had recently signaled its opposition to any hostile takeover, "the average investor mulling the future value of his or her stake and considering for whom to vote in the director elections could well consider the bylaw changes material." 920 F.2d at 267.

D. CAUSATION

MILLS v. ELECTRIC AUTO-LITE CO.
396 U.S. 375, 90 S.Ct. 616, 24 L.Ed.2d 593 (1970).

MR. JUSTICE HARLAN delivered the opinion of the Court.

This case requires us to consider a basic aspect of the implied private right of action for violation of § 14(a) of the Securities Exchange Act of 1934, recognized by this Court in J.I. Case Co. v. Borak, 377 U.S. 426 (1964). As in *Borak* the asserted wrong is that a corporate merger was accomplished through the use of a proxy statement that was materially false or misleading. The question with which we deal is what causal relationship must be shown between such a statement and the merger to establish a cause of action based on the violation of the Act.

I

Petitioners were shareholders of the Electric Auto–Lite Company until 1963, when it was merged into Mergenthaler Linotype Company. They brought suit on the day before the shareholders' meeting at which the vote was to take place on the merger against Auto–Lite, Mergenthaler, and a third company, American Manufacturing Company, Inc. The complaint sought an injunction against the voting by Auto–Lite's management of all proxies obtained by means of an allegedly misleading proxy solicitation; however, it did not seek a temporary restraining order, and the voting went ahead as scheduled the following day. Several months later petitioners filed an amended complaint, seeking to have the merger set aside and to obtain such other relief as might be proper.

In Count II of the amended complaint, which is the only count before us, petitioners predicated jurisdiction on § 27 of the 1934 Act. They alleged that the proxy statement sent out by the Auto–Lite management to solicit shareholders' votes in favor of the merger was misleading, in violation of § 14(a) of the Act and SEC Rule 14a–9 thereunder. Petitioners recited that before the merger Mergenthaler owned over 50% of the outstanding shares of Auto–Lite common stock, and had been in control of Auto–Lite for two years. American Manufacturing in turn owned about one-third of the outstanding shares of Mergenthaler, and for two years had been in voting control of Mergenthaler and, through it, of Auto–Lite. Petitioners charged that in light of these circumstances the proxy statement was misleading in that it told Auto–Lite shareholders that their board of directors recommended approval of the merger without also informing them that all 11 of Auto–Lite's directors were nominees of Mergenthaler and were under the "control and domination of Mergenthaler." Petitioners asserted the right to complain of this alleged violation both derivatively on behalf of Auto–Lite and as representatives of the class of all its minority shareholders.

On petitioners' motion for summary judgment with respect to Count II, the District Court for the Northern District of Illinois ruled as a matter of law that the claimed defect in the proxy statement was, in light of the circumstances in which the statement was made, a material omission. The District Court concluded, from its reading of the *Borak* opinion, that it had to hold a hearing on the issue whether there was "a causal connection between the finding that there has been a violation of the disclosure requirements of § 14(a) and the alleged injury to the plaintiffs" before it could consider what remedies would be appropriate.

After holding such a hearing, the court found that under the terms of the merger agreement, an affirmative vote of two-thirds of the Auto–Lite shares was required for approval of the merger, and that the respondent companies owned and controlled about 54% of the outstanding shares. Therefore, to obtain authorization of the merger, respondents had to secure the approval of a substantial number of the minority shareholders. At the stockholders' meeting, approximately, 950,000 shares, out of 1,160,000 shares outstanding were voted in favor of the merger. This included 317,000 votes obtained by proxy from the minority shareholders, votes that were "necessary and indispensable to the approval of the merger." The District Court concluded that a causal relationship had thus been shown, and it granted an interlocutory judgment in favor of petitioners on the issue of liability, referring the case to a master for consideration of appropriate relief.

The District Court made the certification required by 28 U.S.C. § 1292(b), and respondents took an interlocutory appeal to the Court of Appeals for the Seventh Circuit. That court affirmed the District Court's conclusion that the proxy statement was materially deficient, but reversed on the question of causation. The court acknowledged that, if an injunction had been sought a sufficient time before the stockholders' meeting, "corrective measures would have been appropriate." 403 F.2d 429, 435 (1968). However, since this suit was brought too late for preventive action, the courts had to determine "whether the misleading statement and omission caused the submission of sufficient proxies," as a prerequisite to a determination of liability under the Act. If the respondents could show, "by a preponderance of probabilities, that the merger would have received a sufficient vote even if the proxy statement had not been misleading in the respect found," petitioners would be entitled to no relief of any kind. *Id.*, at 436.

The Court of Appeals acknowledged that this test corresponds to the common law fraud test of whether the injured party relied on the misrepresentation. However, rightly concluding that "[r]eliance by thousands of individuals, as here, can scarcely be inquired into" (*id.*, at 436 n. 10), the court ruled that the issue was to be determined by proof of the fairness of the terms of the merger. If respondents could show that the merger had merit and was fair to the minority shareholders, the trial court would be justified in concluding that a sufficient number of shareholders would have approved the merger had there been no deficiency in the proxy statement. In that case respondents would be entitled to a judgment in their favor.

Claiming that the Court of Appeals has construed this Court's decision in *Borak* in a manner that frustrates the statute's policy of enforcement through private litigation, the petitioners then sought review in this Court. We granted certiorari, believing that resolution of this basic issue should be made at this stage of the litigation and not postponed until after a trial under the Court of Appeals' decision.

II

As we stressed in *Borak,* § 14(a) stemmed from a congressional belief that "[f]air corporate suffrage is an important right that should attach to every equity security bought on a public exchange." * * * The decision below, by permitting all liability to be foreclosed on the basis of a finding that the merger was fair, would allow the stockholders to be bypassed, at least where the only legal challenge to the merger is a suit for retrospective relief after the meeting has been held. A judicial appraisal of the merger's merits could be substituted for the actual and informed vote of the stockholders.

The result would be to insulate from private redress an entire category of proxy violations—those relating to matters other than the terms of the merger. Even outrageous misrepresentations in a proxy solicitation, if they did not relate to the terms of the transaction, would give rise to no cause of action under § 14(a). Particularly if carried over to enforcement actions by the Securities and Exchange Commission itself, such a result would subvert the congressional purpose of ensuring full and fair disclosure to shareholders.

Further, recognition of the fairness of the merger as a complete defense would confront small shareholders with an additional obstacle to making a successful challenge to a proposal recommended through a defective proxy statement. The risk that they would be unable to rebut the corporation's evidence of the fairness of the proposal, and thus to establish their cause of action, would be bound to discourage such shareholders from the private enforcement of the proxy rules that "provides a necessary supplement to Commission action." J.I. Case Co. v. Borak, 377 U.S., at 432, 84 S.Ct. at 1560.[5]

5. The Court of Appeals' ruling that "causation" may be negated by proof of the fairness of the merger also rests on a dubious behavioral assumption. There is no justification for presuming that the shareholders of every corporation are willing to accept any and every fair merger offer put before them; yet such a presumption is implicit in the opinion of the Court of Appeals. That court gave no indication of what evidence petitioners might adduce, once respondents had established that the merger proposal was equitable, in order to show that the shareholders would neverthe-less have rejected it if the solicitation had not been misleading. Proof of actual reliance by thousands of individuals would, as the court acknowledged, not be feasible, see R. Jennings & H. Marsh, Securities Regulation, Cases and Materials 1001 (2d ed. 1968) * * *. In practice, therefore, the objective fairness of the proposal would seemingly be determinative of liability. But in view of the many other factors that might lead shareholders to prefer their current position to that of owners of a larger, combined enterprise, it is pure conjecture to

Such a frustration of the congressional policy is not required by anything in the wording of the statute or in our opinion in the *Borak* case. Section 14(a) declares it "unlawful" to solicit proxies in contravention of Commission rules, and SEC Rule 14a–9 prohibits solicitations "containing any statement which * * * is false or misleading with respect to any material fact, or which omits to state any material fact necessary in order to make the statements therein not false or misleading * * *." Use of a solicitation that is materially misleading is itself a violation of law, as the Court of Appeals recognized in stating that injunctive relief would be available to remedy such a defect if sought prior to the stockholders' meeting. In *Borak,* which came to this Court on a dismissal of the complaint, the Court limited its inquiry to whether a violation of § 14(a) gives rise to "a federal cause of action for rescission or damages," 377 U.S., at 428, 84 S.Ct. at 1558. Referring to the argument made by petitioners there "that the merger can be dissolved only if it was fraudulent or non-beneficial, issues upon which the proxy material would not bear," the Court stated: "But the causal relationship of the proxy material and the merger are questions of fact to be resolved at trial, not here. We therefore do not discuss this point further." *Id.,* at 431, 84 S.Ct. at 1559. In the present case there has been a hearing specifically directed to the causation problem. The question before the Court is whether the facts found on the basis of that hearing are sufficient in law to establish petitioners' cause of action, and we conclude that they are.

Where the misstatement or omission in a proxy statement has been shown to be "material," as it was found to be here, that determination itself indubitably embodies a conclusion that the defect was of such a character that it might have been considered important by a reasonable shareholder who was in the process of deciding how to vote.[6] This requirement that the defect have a significant *propensity* to affect the voting process is found in the express terms of Rule 14a–9, and it adequately serves the purpose of ensuring that a cause of action cannot be established by proof of a defect so trivial, or so unrelated to the transaction for which approval is sought, that correction of the defect or imposition of liability would not further the interests protected by § 14(a).

assume that the fairness of the proposal will always be determinative of their vote.

6. In this case, where the misleading aspect of the solicitation involved failure to reveal a serious conflict of interest on the part of the directors, the Court of Appeals concluded that the crucial question in determining materiality was "whether the minority shareholders were sufficiently alerted to the board's relationship to their adversary to be on their guard." 403 F.2d, at 434. An adequate disclosure of this relationship would have warned the stockholders to give more careful scrutiny to the terms of the merger than they might to one recommended by an entirely disinterested board. Thus, the failure to make such a disclosure was found to be a material defect "as a matter of law," thwarting the informed decision at which the statute aims, regardless of whether the terms of the merger were such that a reasonable stockholder would have approved the transaction after more careful analysis. See also Swanson v. American Consumer Industries, Inc., 415 F.2d 1326 (C.A.7th Cir.1969).

There is no need to supplement this requirement, as did the Court of Appeals, with a requirement of proof of whether the defect actually had a decisive effect on the voting. Where there has been a finding of materiality, a shareholder has made a sufficient showing of causal relationship between the violation and the injury for which he seeks redress, if, as here, he proves that the proxy solicitation itself, rather than the particular defect in the solicitation materials, was an essential link in the accomplishment of the transaction. This objective test will avoid the impracticalities of determining how many votes were affected, and, by resolving doubts in favor of those the statute is designed to protect, will effectuate the congressional policy of ensuring that the shareholders are able to make an informed choice when they are consulted on corporate transactions.[7] * * *

III

Our conclusion that petitioners have established their case by showing that proxies necessary to approval of the merger were obtained by means of a materially misleading solicitation implies nothing about the form of relief to which they may be entitled. We held in *Borak* that upon finding a violation the courts were "to be alert to provide such remedies as are necessary to make effective the congressional purpose," noting specifically that such remedies are not to be limited to prospective relief. 377 U.S., at 433, 434. In devising retrospective relief for violation of the proxy rules, the federal courts should consider the same factors that would govern the relief granted for any similar illegality or fraud. One important factor may be the fairness of the terms of the merger. Possible forms of relief will include setting aside the merger or granting other equitable relief, but, as the Court of Appeals below noted, nothing in the statutory policy "requires the court to unscramble a corporate transaction merely because a violation occurred." 403 F.2d, at 436. In selecting a remedy the lower courts should exercise " 'the sound discretion which guides the determinations of courts of equity,' " keeping in mind the role of equity as "the instrument for nice adjustment and reconciliation between the public interest and private needs as well as between competing private claims." Hecht Co. v. Bowles, 321 U.S. 321, 329–330 (1944), quoting from Meredith v. Winter Haven, 320 U.S. 228, 235 (1943). * * *

Monetary relief will, of course, also be a possibility. Where the defect in the proxy solicitation relates to the specific terms of the merger, the district court might appropriately order an accounting to ensure that the shareholders receive the value that was represented as coming to them. On the other hand, where, as here, the misleading

---

7. We need not decide in this case whether causation could be shown where the management controls a sufficient number of shares to approve the transaction without any votes from the minority. Even in that situation, if the management finds it necessary for legal or practical reasons to solicit proxies from minority shareholders, at least one court has held that the proxy solicitation might be sufficiently related to the merger to satisfy the causation requirement, see Laurenzano v. Einbender, 264 F.Supp. 356 (D.C.E.D.N.Y.1966).

aspect of the solicitation did not relate to terms of the merger, monetary relief might be afforded to the shareholders only if the merger resulted in a reduction of the earnings or earnings potential of their holdings. In short, damages should be recoverable only to the extent that they can be shown. If commingling of the assets and operations of the merged companies makes it impossible to establish direct injury from the merger, relief might be predicated on a determination of the fairness of the terms of the merger at the time it was approved. These questions, of course, are for decision in the first instance by the District Court on remand, and our singling out of some of the possibilities is not intended to exclude others. * * *

IV

Although the question of relief must await further proceedings in the District Court, our conclusion that petitioners have established their cause of action indicates that the Court of Appeals should have affirmed the partial summary judgment on the issue of liability. The result would have been not only that respondents, rather than petitioners, would have borne the costs of the appeal, but also, we think, that petitioners would have been entitled to an interim award of litigation expenses and reasonable attorneys' fees. We agree with the position taken by petitioners, and by the United States as *amicus,* that petitioners, who have established a violation of the securities laws by their corporation and its officials, should be reimbursed by the corporation or its survivor for the costs of establishing the violation. * * *

While the general American rule is that attorneys' fees are not ordinarily recoverable as costs, both the courts and Congress have developed exceptions to this rule for situations in which overriding considerations indicate the need for such a recovery. A primary judge-created exception has been to award expenses where a plaintiff has successfully maintained a suit, usually on behalf of a class, that benefits a group of others in the same manner as himself. To allow the others to obtain from the plaintiff's efforts without contributing equally to the litigation expenses would be to enrich the others unjustly at the plaintiff's expense. This suit presents such a situation. The dissemination of misleading proxy solicitations was a "deceit practiced on the stockholders as a group," J.I. Case Co. v. Borak, 377 U.S. at 482, 84 S.Ct. at 1560, and the expenses of petitioners' lawsuit have been incurred for the benefit of the corporation and the other shareholders.

The fact that this suit has not yet produced, and may never produce, a monetary recovery from which the fees could be paid does not preclude an award based on this rationale. * * *

In many suits under § 14(a), particularly where the violation does not relate to the terms of the transaction for which proxies are solicited, it may be impossible to assign monetary value to the benefit. Nevertheless, the stress placed by Congress on the importance of fair and informed corporate suffrage leads to the conclusion that, in vindicating the statutory policy, petitioners have rendered a substantial service to the corporation and its shareholders. Whether petitioners are successful in showing a need for significant relief may be a factor in determining whether a further award should later be made. But regardless of the relief granted, private stockholders' actions of this sort "involve corporate therapeutics," and furnish a benefit to all shareholders by providing an important means of enforcement of the proxy statute. To award attorneys' fees in such a suit to a plaintiff who has succeeded in establishing a cause of action is not to saddle the unsuccessful party with the expenses but to impose them on the class that has benefited from them and that would have had to pay them had it brought the suit.

For the foregoing reasons we conclude that the judgment of the Court of Appeals should be vacated and the case remanded to that court for further proceedings consistent with this opinion.

It is so ordered.

Note: Subsequent Developments in Mills

On remand, the fairness of the transaction became relevant to the question of relief. The District Court found that the merger was unfair to the minority shareholders and awarded damages of $1,233,918. The Court of Appeals reversed, again holding that the merger was fair to Auto–Lite's minority shareholders. 552 F.2d 1239 (7th Cir.1977), cert. denied 434 U.S. 922, 98 S.Ct. 398, 54 L.Ed.2d 279 (1977). The court also held that plaintiff's attorneys would be entitled to fees from the corporation only for the period up to the Supreme Court decision. Lead counsel was awarded a fee of $250,000, not an overly generous amount considering the time devoted to the case.

E. DISCLOSURE AND FIDUCIARY STANDARDS UNDER FEDERAL LAW

Thus far, we have examined situations where shareholders have acted as decision-makers. In such cases, if there is a material misstatement or omission, the shareholder may be deceived when voting. Put differently, accurate information is necessary in order to preserve the integrity of the voting process. More difficult questions arise when a transaction does not require shareholder decision-making. Can a shareholder be deceived in such a situation? If so, how does the "deception" occur? Moreover, if the shareholder is not a decision-maker, how can there be causation, even if a material misstatement is made? Or, indeed, if there is *no* disclosure at all?

These question often arise in connection with transactions that, at least arguably, involve some financial unfairness. As we have seen, proof of financial unfairness may not be sufficient to establish a breach of fiduciary duty. State law principles, at times, insulate from judicial scrutiny transactions that arguably are unfair, especially if those transactions have been approved by independent directors or independent shareholders. In addition, state law often makes it difficult to maintain class actions or to sue defendants domiciled in different states.

In order to avoid litigating their claims under state law, or to obtain procedural advantages available to plaintiffs in actions brought under the federal securities laws, aggrieved shareholders often used those laws to challenge transactions they believed were unfair. When proxies had been solicited and the proxy solicitation constituted an "essential link" in effectuating the transaction, their task was simple—they sued under § 14(a) and Rule 14a–9. Where no proxy solicitation occurred, their task became more complex. The most attractive alternative often was a suit under § 10(b) of the 1934 Act and SEC Rule 10b–5.

Rule 10b–5 is concerned with decisions to purchase or sell stock, rather than with decisions about how to vote. It prohibits both false and misleading statements and fraudulent acts and practices in connection with the purchase or sale of any security. As noted above, federal courts have for years implied a private cause of action for damages under Rule 10b–5.

The earliest cases brought under Rule 10b–5 all involved traditional informational fraud. Then plaintiffs attempted to rely on Rule 10b–5 to challenge unfair or "constructively fraudulent," transactions. The courts at first rebuffed their efforts. See Birnbaum v. Newport Steel Corp., 193 F.2d 461 (2d Cir.1952), cert. denied 343 U.S. 956, 72 S.Ct. 1051, 96 L.Ed. 1356 (1952); Pappas v. Moss, 393 F.2d 865 (3d Cir.1968).

Then came Schoenbaum v. Firstbrook, 405 F.2d 215 (2d Cir.1968). A shareholder of Banff brought suit under Rule 10b–5, alleging that Banff had sold some of its stock to Aquitaine, its majority shareholder, at an unfair price in a transaction approved unanimously by Banff's non-Aquitaine directors. No shareholder vote was required in the transaction. The Second Circuit, *en banc*, reversed the dismissal of the shareholder's complaint, reasoning:

> In the present case it is alleged that Aquitaine exercised a controlling influence over the issuance to it of treasury stock of Banff for a wholly inadequate consideration. If it is established that the transaction took place as alleged, it constituted a violation of Rule 10b–5, Subdivision (3) because Aquitaine engaged in an "act, practice or course of business which operates or would operate as a fraud or deceit upon any person, in connection with the purchase or sale of any security." Moreover, Aquitaine and the directors of Banff were guilty of deceiving the stockholders of Banff (other than Aquitaine).

405 F.2d at 219–20.

This passage engendered considerable debate. Had the court ruled that it was sufficient, to state a claim under Rule 10b–5, to allege that a controlling shareholder had breached its fiduciary duty by purchasing stock from its majority-owned subsidiary at an unfair price? Or had the court upheld the complaint on the ground that Banff's shareholders (other than Aquitaine) were deceived? And, if the latter was the case, how had they been deceived, since the stock sale did not require shareholder approval? The theory for finding deception apparently is based on the view that the non-Aquitaine directors of Banff were the surrogates for the Banff shareholders in the transaction. Thus, if the directors were deceived, so were the shareholders, even though the latter did not participate in the transaction.

Superintendent of Insurance v. Bankers Life & Casualty Co., 404 U.S. 6, 92 S.Ct. 165, 30 L.Ed.2d 128 (1971), deepened the confusion. Through a complex series of transactions, the principal defendant Begole stole $5 million that Manhattan Casualty Co. should have received for selling certain Treasury bonds and used that money to finance his purchase of all Manhattan's stock. When Begole thereafter looted Manhattan, New York's Superintendent of Insurance brought suit under Rule 10b–5 against several parties who allegedly had aided and abetted Begole's scheme. The Court upheld the Superintendent's complaint, stating "Manhattan was injured as an investor through a deceptive device" because it received nothing for its Treasury bonds. But, in the view of most observers, the case really involved not informational fraud but simple theft by a corporate insider—a classic breach of fiduciary duty.

The high-water mark for the expanded view of Rule 10b–5 was reached in Green v. Santa Fe Industries, Inc., 533 F.2d 1283 (2d Cir.1976), involving a transaction in which a majority shareholder cashed out the minority interest in a short-form merger at a price far below the asset value of the corporation's stock. No vote by minority shareholders was required under Delaware law, and no advance notice of the merger was provided to the minority shareholders. As in *Schoenbaum*, it was difficult to argue that the minority shareholders had been deceived. Moreover, under Delaware law at that time, it appeared that appraisal was the exclusive remedy for minority shareholders in such a transaction, and they were advised of their ability to exercise their appraisal rights. Nevertheless, the Second Circuit interpreted *Schoenbaum* and *Superintendent of Insurance* to hold that Rule 10b–5 provided a remedy for constructive fraud and reversed dismissal of a claim that the majority shareholder had violated Rule 10b–5, stating: "Lest there be any lingering doubt on this point, we now hold that [in cases involving a breach of fiduciary duty], including the one now before us, no allegation or proof of misrepresentation or non-disclosure is necessary." 533 F.2d, at 1287.

1. INFORMATIONAL vs. CONSTRUCTIVE FRAUD

SANTA FE INDUSTRIES, INC. v. GREEN
430 U.S. 462, 97 S.Ct. 1292, 51 L.Ed.2d 480 (1977).

MR. JUSTICE WHITE delivered the opinion of the Court.

The issue in this case involves the reach and coverage of § 10(b) of the Securities Exchange Act of 1934 and Rule 10b–5 thereunder in the context of a Delaware short-form merger transaction used by the majority stockholder of a corporation to eliminate the minority interest.

I

In 1936, petitioner Santa Fe Industries, Inc. (Santa Fe), acquired control of 60% of the stock of Kirby Lumber Corp. (Kirby), a Delaware corporation. Through a series of purchases over the succeeding years, Santa Fe increased its control of Kirby's stock to 95%; the purchase prices during the period 1968–1973 ranged from $65 to $92.50 per share. In 1974, wishing to acquire 100% ownership of Kirby, Santa Fe availed itself of § 253 of the Delaware Corporation Law, known as the "short-form merger" statute. Section 253 permits a parent corporation owning at least 90% of the stock of a subsidiary to merge with that subsidiary, upon approval by the parent's board of directors, and to make payment in cash for the shares of the minority stockholders. The statute does not require the consent of, or advance notice to, the minority stockholders. However, notice of the merger must be given within 10 days after its effective date, and any stockholder who is dissatisfied with the terms of the merger may petition the Delaware Court of Chancery for a decree ordering the surviving corporation to pay him the fair value of his shares, as determined by a court-appointed appraiser subject to review by the court.

Santa Fe obtained independent appraisals of the physical assets of Kirby—land, timber, buildings, and machinery—and of Kirby's oil, gas, and mineral interests. These appraisals, together with other financial information, were submitted to Morgan Stanley & Co. (Morgan Stanley), an investment banking firm retained to appraise the fair market value of Kirby stock. Kirby's physical assets were appraised at $320 million (amounting to $640 for each of the 500,000 shares); Kirby's stock was valued by Morgan Stanley at $125 per share. Under the terms of the merger, minority stockholders were offered $150 per share.

The provisions of the short-form merger statute were fully complied with. The minority stockholders of Kirby were notified the day after the merger became effective and were advised of their right to obtain an appraisal in Delaware court if dissatisfied with the offer of $150 per share. They also received an information statement containing, in addition to the relevant financial data about Kirby, the appraisals of the value of Kirby's assets and the Morgan Stanley appraisal concluding that the fair market value of the stock was $125 per share.

Respondents, minority stockholders of Kirby, objected to the terms of the merger, but did not pursue their appraisal remedy in the Delaware Court of Chancery. Instead, they brought this action in federal court on behalf of the corporation and other minority stockholders, seeking to set aside the merger or to recover what they claimed to be the fair value of their shares. The amended complaint asserted that, based on the fair market value of Kirby's physical assets as revealed by the appraisal included in the information statement sent to minority shareholders, Kirby's stock was worth at least $772 per share. The complaint alleged further that the merger took place without prior notice to minority stockholders; that the purpose of the merger was to appropriate the difference between the "conceded pro rata value of the physical assets," and the offer of $150 per share—to "freez[e] out the minority stockholders at a wholly inadequate price," and that Santa Fe, knowing the appraised value of the physical assets, obtained a "fraudulent appraisal" of the stock from Morgan Stanley and offered $25 above that appraisal "in order to lull the minority stockholders into erroneously believing that [Santa Fe was] generous." This course of conduct was alleged to be "a violation of Rule 10b–5 because defendants employed a 'device, scheme, or artifice to defraud' and engaged in an 'act, practice or course of business which operates or would operate as a fraud or deceit upon any person, in connection with the purchase or sale of any security.' " Morgan Stanley assertedly participated in the fraud as an accessory by submitting its appraisal of $125 per share although knowing the appraised value of the physical assets.

The District Court dismissed the complaint for failure to state a claim upon which relief could be granted. 391 F.Supp. 849 (S.D.N.Y. 1975). * * *

A divided Court of Appeals for the Second Circuit reversed. 533 F.2d 1283 (1976). It first agreed that there was a double aspect to the case; first, the claim that gross undervaluation of the minority stock itself violated Rule 10b–5; and second, that "without any misrepresentation or failure to disclose relevant facts, the merger itself constitutes a violation of Rule 10b–5" because it was accomplished without any corporate purpose and without prior notice to the minority stockholders. Id., at 1285. As to the first aspect of the case, the Court of Appeals did not disturb the District Court's conclusion that the complaint did not allege a material misrepresentation or nondisclosure with respect to the value of the stock; and the court declined to rule that a claim of gross undervaluation itself would suffice to make out a Rule 10b–5 case. With respect to the second aspect of the case, however, the court fundamentally disagreed with the District Court as to the reach and coverage of Rule 10b–5. The Court of Appeals' view was that, although the Rule plainly reached material misrepresentations and nondisclosures in connection with the purchase or sale of securities, neither misrepresentation nor nondisclosure was a necessary element of a Rule 10b–5 action; the Rule reached "breaches of fiduciary duty by a majority against minority shareholders without any charge of misrepresentation or lack of disclosure." * * *

III

[The Court held that § 10(b) of the Act and, consequently, Rule 10b–5 prohibits only conduct involving manipulation or deception.]

As we have indicated, the case comes to us on the premise that the complaint failed to allege a material misrepresentation or material failure to disclose. The finding of the District Court, undisturbed by the Court of Appeals, was that there was no "omission" or "misstatement" in the information statement accompanying the notice of merger.   On the basis of the information provided, minority shareholders could either accept the price offered or reject it and seek an appraisal in the Delaware Court of Chancery.   Their choice was fairly presented, and they were furnished with all relevant information on which to base their decision.[14]

We therefore find inapposite the cases relied upon by respondents and the court below, in which the breaches of fiduciary duty held violative of Rule 10b–5 included some element of deception.   * * * [Those] cases do not support the proposition, adopted by the Court of Appeals below and urged by respondents here, that a breach of fiduciary duty by majority stockholders, without any deception, misrepresentation, or nondisclosure, violates the statute and the Rule.

It is also readily apparent that the conduct alleged in the complaint was not "manipulative" within the meaning of the statute.   "Manipulation" is "virtually a term of art when used in connection with securities markets."   Ernst & Ernst, 425 U.S., at 199, 96 S.Ct., at 1384.   * * * No doubt Congress meant to prohibit the full range of ingenious devices that might be used to manipulate securities prices.   But we do not think it would have chosen this "term of art" if it had meant to bring within the scope of § 10(b) instances of corporate mismanagement such as this, in which the essence of the complaint is that shareholders were treated unfairly by a fiduciary.

IV

The language of the statute is, we think, "sufficiently clear in its context" to be dispositive here, but even if it were not, there are additional considerations that weigh heavily against permitting a cause of action under Rule 10b–5 for the breach of corporate fiduciary duty alleged in this complaint.   Congress did not expressly provide a private cause of action for violations of § 10(b).   Although we have recognized an implied cause of action under that section in some circumstances, Superintendent of Insurance v. Bankers Life & Cas. Co., *supra*, 404 U.S., at 13 n. 9, 92 S.Ct., at 169, we have also recognized that a private cause of action under the antifraud provisions of the Securities Exchange Act should not be implied where it is "unnecessary to ensure the fulfillment of Congress' purposes" in adopting the Act.   Piper v. Chris–Craft Industries, 430 U.S., at 41, 97 S.Ct., at 949.   Cf. J.I. Case Co. v. Borak, 377

14. In addition to their principal argument that the complaint alleges a fraud under clauses (a) and (c) of Rule 10b–5, respondents also argue that the complaint alleges nondisclosure and misrepresentation in violation of clause (b) of the Rule.   Their major contention in this respect is that the majority stockholder's failure to give the minority advance notice of the merger was a material nondisclosure, even though the Delaware short-form merger statute does not require such notice.   Brief for Respondents 27.   But respondents do not indicate how they might have acted differently had they had prior notice of the merger.   Indeed, they accept the conclusion of both courts below that under Delaware law they could not have enjoined the merger because an appraisal proceeding is their sole remedy in the Delaware courts for any alleged unfairness in the terms of the merger.   Thus, the failure to give advance notice was not a material nondisclosure within the meaning of the statute or the Rule.   *Cf.* TSC Industries, Inc. v. Northway, Inc., 426 U.S. 438, 96 S.Ct. 2126, 48 L.Ed.2d 757 (1976).

U.S. 426, 431–433, 84 S.Ct. 1555, 12 L.Ed.2d 423 (1964). As we noted earlier, the Court repeatedly has described the "fundamental purpose" of the Act as implementing a "philosophy of full disclosure"; once full and fair disclosure has occurred, the fairness of the terms of the transaction is at most a tangential concern of the statute. As in Cort v. Ash, 422 U.S. 66, 78, 80, 95 S.Ct. 2080, 2087, 2090, 45 L.Ed.2d 26 (1975), we are reluctant to recognize a cause of action here to serve what is "at best a subsidiary purpose" of the federal legislation.

A second factor in determining whether Congress intended to create a federal cause of action in these circumstances is "whether 'the cause of action [is] one traditionally relegated to state law * * *.'" Piper v. Chris–Craft Industries, Inc., 430 U.S., at 40, 97 S.Ct., at 949, quoting Cort v. Ash, *supra,* at 78, 95 S.Ct., at 2087. The Delaware Legislature has supplied minority shareholders with a cause of action in the Delaware Court of Chancery to recover the fair value of shares allegedly undervalued in a short-form merger. Of course, the existence of a particular state-law remedy is not dispositive of the question whether Congress meant to provide a similar federal remedy, but as in *Cort* and *Piper,* we conclude that "it is entirely appropriate in this instance to relegate respondent and others in his situation to whatever remedy is created by state law." 422 U.S., at 84, 95 S.Ct., at 2091; 430 U.S., at 41, 97 S.Ct., at 949.

The reasoning behind a holding that the complaint in this case alleged fraud under Rule 10b–5 could not be easily contained. It is difficult to imagine how a court could distinguish, for purposes of Rule 10b–5 fraud, between a majority stockholder's use of a short-form merger to eliminate the minority at an unfair price and the use of some other device, such as a long-form merger, tender offer, or liquidation, to achieve the same result; or indeed how a court could distinguish the alleged abuses in these going private transactions from other types of fiduciary self-dealing involving transactions in securities. The result would be to bring within the Rule a wide variety of corporate conduct traditionally left to state regulation. In addition to posing a "danger of vexatious litigation which could result from a widely expanded class of plaintiffs under Rule 10b–5," Blue Chip Stamps v. Manor Drug Stores, 421 U.S., at 740, 95 S.Ct., at 1927, this extension of the federal securities laws would overlap and quite possibly interfere with state corporate law. Federal courts applying a "federal fiduciary principle" under Rule 10b–5 could be expected to depart from state fiduciary standards at least to the extent necessary to ensure uniformity within the federal system. Absent a clear indication of congressional intent, we are reluctant to federalize the substantial portion of the law of corporations that deals with transactions in securities, particularly where established state policies of corporate regulation would be overridden. As the Court stated in Cort v. Ash, *supra:* "Corporations are creatures of state law, and investors commit their funds to corporate directors on the understanding that, except where federal law *expressly* requires certain responsibilities of directors with respect to stockholders, state law will govern the internal affairs of the corporation."   422 U.S., at 84, 95 S.Ct., at 2091 (emphasis added).

We thus adhere to the position that "Congress by § 10(b) did not seek to regulate transactions which constitute no more than internal corporate mismanagement."   Superintendent of Insurance v. Bankers Life & Cas. Co., 404 U.S., at 12, 92 S.Ct., at 169.   There may well be a need for uniform federal fiduciary standards to govern mergers such as that challenged in this complaint.   But those standards should not be supplied by judicial extension of § 10(b) and Rule 10b–5 to "cover the corporate universe."

The judgment of the Court of Appeals is reversed, and the case is remanded for further proceedings consistent with this opinion.

So ordered.

MR. JUSTICE BRENNAN dissents and would affirm for substantially the reasons stated in the majority and concurring opinions in the Court of Appeals, 533 F.2d 1283 (CA2 1976).

Note: From Santa Fe to Virginia Bankshares

In *Santa Fe* the plaintiffs conceded that disclosure to shareholders would have served no function, not only because they had no vote but because their only remedy was appraisal.   Hence, there could be no "material" omission in the failure to disclose.   Under this approach, therefore, the availability of a federal cause of action under Rule 10b–5 seems to turn on whether there may also be a state cause of action, presumably for breach of fiduciary duty.

Goldberg v. Meridor, 567 F.2d 209 (2d Cir.1977), cert. denied 434 U.S. 1069, 98 S.Ct. 1249, 55 L.Ed.2d 771 (1978), involved such a situation.   Goldberg, a stockholder of Universal Gas & Oil Company, Inc. (UGO), brought suit against UGO's controlling parent, Maritimecor, S.A. and a number of other parties, challenging Maritimecor's sale of essentially all of its assets to UGO in exchange for up to 4,200,000 shares of UGO stock and the assumption by UGO of Maritimecor's debts.   Goldberg alleged that this transaction, for which shareholder approval was neither required or solicited, violated Rule 10b–5.

The essence of the amended complaint was that the exchange was unfair to UGO because Maritimecor had huge current liabilities and few liquid assets.   Thus, UGO was likely to be rendered insolvent by the challenged transaction.   The defendants moved to dismiss, on the ground that the amended complaint failed to allege the deception or non-disclosure needed to state a claim under rule 10b–5.   In response, plaintiff's counsel submitted an affidavit which asserted that "insofar as plaintiff Goldberg, a minority shareholder, is concerned, there has been no disclosure to him of the fraudulent nature of the transfer of Maritimecor assets and liabilities for stock of UGO."   Annexed to the affidavit were two press releases describing the agreement.   It was asserted that these two press releases failed to disclose certain conflicts of interest;   that current liabilities of Maritimecor exceeded the shareholder's net equity; and that Maritimecor had, in fact, overstated its assets since they showed a higher value than appropriate for UGO shares.

The Second Circuit held that the complaint should be treated as if it had alleged that the press releases were materially misleading and that one of UGO's directors was deceived or not fully informed as to the effects of the transaction. Judge Friendly stated:

> Here the complaint alleged "deceit * * * upon UGO's minority shareholders" and, if amendment had been allowed as it should have been, would have alleged misrepresentation as to the UGO–Maritimecor transaction at least in the sense of failure to state material facts "necessary in order to make the statements made, in the light of the circumstances under which they were made, not misleading," Rule 10b–5(b). The nub of the matter is that the conduct attacked in [*Santa Fe*] did not violate the "fundamental purpose" of the Act as implementing a "philosophy of full disclosure", 430 U.S. at 478, 97 S.Ct. at 1303; the conduct here attacked does.

> Defendants contend that even if all this is true, the failure to make a public disclosure or even the making of a misleading disclosure would have no effect, since no action by stockholders to approve the UGO–Maritimecor transaction was required. * * *

> * * * Here there is surely a significant likelihood that if a reasonable director of UGO had known the facts alleged by plaintiff rather than the barebones of the press releases, he would not have voted for the transaction with Maritimecor.

> Beyond this Goldberg and other minority shareholders would not have been without remedy if the alleged facts had been disclosed. The doubts entertained by our brother as to the existence of injunctive remedies in New York, * * * are unfounded. * * * [There have been a number of New York cases involving] suits by stockholders acting in their own behalf to enjoin the sale of all corporate assets or a merger transaction as to which New York afforded dissenters the remedy of an appraisal. Where an appraisal remedy is not available, the courts of New York have displayed no hesitancy in granting injunctive relief. * * *

> The availability of injunctive relief if the defendants had not lulled the minority stockholders of UGO into security by a deceptive disclosure, as they allegedly did, is in sharp contrast to [*Santa Fe,*] where the disclosure following the merger transaction was full and fair, and, as to the premerger period, respondents accepted "the conclusion of both courts below that under Delaware law they could not have enjoined the merger because an appraisal proceeding is their sole remedy in the Delaware courts for any alleged unfairness in the terms of the merger."

567 F.2d at 218–220.

Goldberg leaves open the question of precisely what plaintiffs must show concerning the availability of a state law remedy. Subsequent courts have divided on this issue. The Third Circuit, in Healey v. Catalyst Recovery of Pennsylvania, 616 F.2d 641 (3d Cir.1980), held that there must be a reasonable probability that the shareholder could have used the information to obtain an injunction. The Fifth Circuit, in Alabama Farm Bureau Mutual Casualty Co., Inc. v. American Fidelity Life Insurance Co., 606 F.2d 602 (5th Cir.1979), cert. denied 449 U.S. 820, 101 S.Ct. 77, 66 L.Ed.2d 22 (1980), held that "all that is required to establish 10b–5 liability is a showing that state law remedies are available, and that the facts shown make out a prima facie case for relief; it is not necessary to go further and prove that the state action would have been successful." 606 F.2d at 614.

However, both the Seventh and Ninth Circuits have demanded a higher threshold, insisting that the plaintiff show both the availability of a claim under state law, and that the state court would have granted the requested relief. Wright v. Heizer Corp., 560 F.2d 236 (7th Cir.1977), cert. denied 434 U.S. 1066, 98 S.Ct. 1243, 55 L.Ed.2d 767 (1978); Kidwell ex rel. Penfold v. Meikle, 597 F.2d 1273 (9th Cir.1979).

The latter approach has been criticized as unsound. One commentator observed that because the state law claim ultimately turns on the fairness of the transaction, a federal court ruling on the availability of a rule 10b–5 cause of action would be required to make its own determination of fairness—precisely what *Santa Fe* sought to avoid. See Note, Suits for Breach of Fiduciary Duty Under Rule 10b–5 after Santa Fe Industries Inc. v. Green, 91 Harv.L.Rev. 1874 (1978). See Ralph C. Ferrara and Marc I. Steinberg, A Reappraisal of Santa Fe: Rule 10b–5 and the New Federalism, 129 U.Pa.L.Rev. 263 (1980). On the other hand, under the approach of the Third and Fifth Circuits, plaintiff may have a remedy under Rule 10b–5 even if no relief would be available under state law—a result that also seems at odds with *Santa Fe*.

Goldberg can also be viewed as an effort by the Second Circuit (whose decision in *Santa Fe* the Supreme Court had reversed) to bring back into federal court issues that the Court had indicated were more properly left to state law. In Field v. Trump, 850 F.2d 938 (2d Cir.1988), cert. denied 489 U.S. 1012, 109 S.Ct. 1122, 103 L.Ed.2d 185 (1989), the Second Circuit limited its holding in *Goldberg* in a manner that addresses the federalism concerns of *Santa Fe*. The court reaffirmed *Goldberg*'s holding that a misstatement would be material if shareholders were lulled into foregoing an injunction that was available under state law and necessary to prevent irreparable injury to the corporation. However, the court limited application of this theory to cases involving "willfull misconduct of a self-serving nature" and not simple mismanagement or breaches of fiduciary duty. The court justified this limitation by noting that *Goldberg* "involved out-and-out 'looting' and 'stealing,'" under facts that did not require it "to distinguish between conduct that is 'reasonable' and 'unreasonable,' or 'informed' and 'uninformed,' distinctions that are the hallmarks of state fiduciary law." Id. at 948–49.

VIRGINIA BANKSHARES, INC. v. SANDBERG
___ U.S. ___, 111 S.Ct. 2749, 115 L.Ed.2d 929 (1991).

JUSTICE SOUTER delivered the opinion of the Court.

Section 14(a) of the Securities Exchange Act of 1934, authorizes the Securities and Exchange Commission to adopt rules for the solicitation of proxies, and prohibits their violation. In *J.I. Case Co. v. Borak,* we first recognized an implied private right of action for the breach of § 14(a) as implemented by SEC Rule 14a–9, which prohibits the solicitation of proxies by means of materially false or misleading statements.

The questions before us are whether a statement couched in conclusory or qualitative terms purporting to explain directors' reasons for recommending certain corporate action can be materially misleading within the meaning of Rule 14a–9, and whether causation of damages compensable under § 14(a) can be shown by a member of a class of minority shareholders whose votes are not required by law or corporate bylaw to authorize the corporate action subject to the proxy solicitation. We hold that knowingly false statements of reasons may be actionable even though conclusory in form, but that respondents have failed to demonstrate the equitable basis required to extend the § 14(a) private action to such shareholders when any indication of congressional intent to do so is lacking.

I

In December 1986, First American Bankshares, Inc., (FABI), a bank holding company, began a "freeze-out" merger, in which the First American Bank of Virginia (Bank) eventually merged into Virginia Bankshares, Inc., (VBI), a wholly owned subsidiary of FABI. VBI owned 85% of the Bank's shares, the remaining 15% being in the hands of some 2,000 minority shareholders. FABI hired the investment banking firm of Keefe, Bruyette & Woods (KBW) to give an opinion on the appropriate price for shares of the minority holders, who would lose their interests in the Bank as a result of the merger. Based on market quotations and unverified information from FABI, KBW gave the Bank's executive committee an opinion that $42 a share would be a fair price for the minority stock. The executive committee approved the merger proposal at that price, and the full board followed suit.

Although Virginia law required only that such a merger proposal be submitted to a vote at a shareholders' meeting, and that the meeting be preceded by circulation of a statement of information to the shareholders, the directors nevertheless solicited proxies for voting on the proposal at the annual meeting set for April 21, 1987. In their solicitation, the directors urged the proposal's adoption and stated they had approved the plan because of its opportunity for the minority shareholders to achieve a "high" value, which they elsewhere described as a "fair" price, for their stock.

Although most minority shareholders gave the proxies requested, respondent Sandberg did not, and after approval of the merger she sought damages in the United States District Court for the Eastern District of Virginia from VBI, FABI, and the directors of the Bank. She pleaded two counts, one for soliciting proxies in violation of § 14(a) and Rule 14a–9, and the other for breaching fiduciary duties owed to the minority shareholders under state law. Under the first count, Sandberg alleged, among other things, that the directors had not believed that the price offered was high or that the terms of the merger were fair, but had recommended the merger only because they believed they had no alternative if they wished to remain on the board. At trial, Sandberg invoked language from this Court's opinion in *Mills v. Electric AutoLite Co.*, to obtain an instruction that the jury could find for her without a showing of her own reliance on the alleged misstatements, so long as they were material and the proxy solicitation was an "essential link" in the merger process.

The jury's verdicts were for Sandberg on both counts, after finding violations of Rule 14a–9 by all defendants and a breach of fiduciary duties by the Bank's directors. The jury awarded Sandberg $18 a share, having found that she would have received $60 if her stock had been valued adequately.   * * *

On appeal, the United States Court of Appeals for the Fourth Circuit affirmed the judgments, holding that certain statements in the proxy solicitation were materially misleading for purposes of the Rule, and that respondents could maintain their action even though their votes had not been needed to effectuate the merger. 891 F.2d 1112 (1989). We granted certiorari because of the importance of the issues presented. 495 U.S. ___ (1990).

* * *

A

We consider first the actionability per se of statements of reasons, opinion or belief. Because such a statement by definition purports to express what is consciously on the speaker's mind, we interpret the jury verdict as finding that the directors' statements of belief and opinion were made with knowledge that the directors did not hold the beliefs or opinions expressed, and we confine our discussion to statements so made.[5] That such statements may be materially significant raises no serious question. The meaning of the materiality requirement for liability under § 14(a) was discussed at some length in *TSC Industries, Inc. v. Northway, Inc.*, where we held a fact to be material "if there is a substantial likelihood that a reasonable shareholder would consider it

---

5. In *TSC Industries, Inc. v. Northway, Inc.*, we reserved the question whether scienter was necessary for liability generally under § 14(a). We reserve it still.

important in deciding how to vote." We think there is no room to deny that a statement of belief by corporate directors about a recommended course of action, or an explanation of their reasons for recommending it, can take on just that importance. Shareholders know that directors usually have knowledge and expertness far exceeding the normal investor's resources, and the directors' perceived superiority is magnified even further by the common knowledge that state law customarily obliges them to exercise their judgment in the shareholders' interest. * * * Naturally, then, the share owner faced with a proxy request will think it important to know the directors' beliefs about the course they recommend, and their specific reasons for urging the stockholders to embrace it.

1

But, assuming materiality, the question remains whether statements of reasons, opinions, or beliefs are statements "with respect to * * * material fact[s]" so as to fall within the strictures of the Rule. Petitioners argue that we would invite wasteful litigation of amorphous issues outside the readily provable realm of fact if we were to recognize liability here on proof that the directors did not recommend the merger for the stated reason. * * *

Attacks on the truth of directors' statements of reasons or belief, however, need carry no such threats. Such statements are factual in two senses: as statements that the directors do act for the reasons given or hold the belief stated and as statements about the subject matter of the reason or belief expressed. In neither sense does the proof or disproof of such statements implicate the concerns expressed in *Blue Chip Stamps.** The root of those concerns was a plaintiff's capacity to manufacture claims of hypothetical action, unconstrained by independent evidence. Reasons for directors' recommendations or statements of belief are, in contrast, characteristically matters of corporate record subject to documentation, to be supported or attacked by evidence of historical fact outside a plaintiff's control. Such evidence would include not only corporate minutes and other statements of the directors themselves, but circumstantial evidence bearing on the facts that would reasonably underlie the reasons claimed and the honesty of any statement that those reasons are the basis for a recommendation or other action, a point that becomes especially clear when the reasons or beliefs go to valuations in dollars and cents.

It is no answer to argue, as petitioners do, that the quoted statement on which liability was predicated did not express a reason in dollars and cents, but focused instead on the "indefinite and unverifia-

---

* In Blue Chip Stamps v. Manor Drug Stores, 421 U.S. 723 (1975), discussed in Chapter 19, the Court held that a private action for damages under Rule 10b–5 can only be maintained by a person who actually purchased or sold securities. The Court justified its holding in large part by pointing to the speculative nature of a claim brought by a person who can only allege that, had she known the truth, she would have purchased or sold securities, and to the vexatious potential of litigation based on such a claim.—Eds.

ble" term, "high" value, much like the similar claim that the merger's terms were "fair" to shareholders.[7] The objection ignores the fact that such conclusory terms in a commercial context are reasonably understood to rest on a factual basis that justifies them as accurate, the absence of which renders them misleading. Provable facts either furnish good reasons to make a conclusory commercial judgment, or they count against it, and expressions of such judgments can be uttered with knowledge of truth or falsity just like more definite statements, and defended or attacked through the orthodox evidentiary process that either substantiates their underlying justifications or tends to disprove their existence. * * * In this case, whether $42 was "high," and the proposal "fair" to the minority shareholders depended on whether provable facts about the Bank's assets, and about actual and potential levels of operation, substantiated a value that was above, below, or more or less at the $42 figure, when assessed in accordance with recognized methods of valuation.

Respondents adduced evidence for just such facts in proving that the statement was misleading about its subject matter and a false expression of the directors' reasons. Whereas the proxy statement described the $42 price as offering a premium above both book value and market price, the evidence indicated that a calculation of the book figure based on the appreciated value of the Bank's real estate holdings eliminated any such premium. The evidence on the significance of market price showed that KBW had conceded that the market was closed, thin and dominated by FABI, facts omitted from the statement. There was, indeed, evidence of a "going concern" value for the Bank in excess of $60 per share of common stock, another fact never disclosed. However conclusory the directors' statement may have been, then, it was open to attack by garden-variety evidence, subject neither to a plaintiff's control nor ready manufacture, and there was no undue risk of open-ended liability or uncontrollable litigation in allowing respondents the opportunity for recovery on the allegation that it was misleading to call $42 "high."

2

Under § 14(a), then, a plaintiff is permitted to prove a specific statement of reason knowingly false or misleadingly incomplete, even when stated in conclusory terms. In reaching this conclusion, we have considered statements of reasons of the sort exemplified here, which

---

7. Petitioners are also wrong to argue that construing the statute to allow recovery for a misleading statement that the merger was "fair" to the minority shareholders is tantamount to assuming federal authority to bar corporate transactions thought to be unfair to some group of shareholders. It is, of course, true that we said in Santa Fe Industries, Inc. v. Green, 430 U.S. 462, 479 (1977), that " '[c]orporations are creatures of state law, and investors commit their funds to corporate directors on the understanding that, except

where federal law expressly requires certain responsibilities of directors with respect to stockholders, state law will govern the internal affairs of the corporation,' " quoting Cort v. Ash, 422 U.S. 66, 84 (1975). But § 14(a) does impose responsibility for false and misleading proxy statements. Although a corporate transaction's "fairness" is not, as such, a federal concern, a proxy statement's claim of fairness presupposes a factual integrity that federal law is expressly concerned to preserve. * * *

misstate the speaker's reasons and also mislead about the stated subject matter (e.g., the value of the shares). A statement of belief may be open to objection only in the former respect, however, solely as a misstatement of the psychological fact of the speaker's belief in what he says. * * *

The question arises, then, whether disbelief, or undisclosed belief or motivation, standing alone, should be a sufficient basis to sustain an action under § 14(a), absent proof by the sort of objective evidence described above that the statement also expressly or impliedly asserted something false or misleading about its subject matter. We think that proof of mere disbelief or belief undisclosed should not suffice for liability under § 14(a), and if nothing more had been required or proven in this case we would reverse for that reason. * * *

* * * [T]o recognize liability on mere disbelief or undisclosed motive without any demonstration that the proxy statement was false or misleading about its subject would authorize § 14(a) litigation confined solely to what one skeptical court spoke of as the "impurities" of a director's "unclean heart." This, we think, would cross the line that *Blue Chip Stamps* sought to draw. * * * We, therefore, hold disbelief or undisclosed motivation, standing alone, insufficient to satisfy the element of fact that must be established under § 14(a).

C

Petitioners' fall-back position assumes the same relationship between a conclusory judgment and its underlying facts that we described in Part II–B–1, *supra*. Thus, petitioners argue that even if conclusory statements of reason or belief can be actionable under § 14(a), we should confine liability to instances where the proxy material fails to disclose the offending statement's factual basis. There would be no justification for holding the shareholders entitled to judicial relief, that is, when they were given evidence that a stated reason for a proxy recommendation was misleading, and an opportunity to draw that conclusion themselves.

The answer to this argument rests on the difference between a merely misleading statement and one that is materially so. While a misleading statement will not always lose its deceptive edge simply by joinder with others that are true, the true statements may discredit the other one so obviously that the risk of real deception drops to nil. Since liability under § 14(a) must rest not only on deceptiveness but materiality as well (i.e., it has to be significant enough to be important to a reasonable investor deciding how to vote), petitioners are on perfectly firm ground insofar as they argue that publishing accurate facts in a proxy statement can render a misleading proposition too unimportant to ground liability.

But not every mixture with the true will neutralize the deceptive. If it would take a financial analyst to spot the tension between the one and the other, whatever is misleading will remain materially so, and liability should follow. The point of a proxy statement, after all, should be to inform, not to challenge the reader's critical wits. Only when the inconsistency would exhaust the misleading conclusion's capacity to influence the reasonable shareholder would a § 14(a) action fail on the element of materiality.

* * *

III

The second issue before us, left open in *Mills v. Electric Auto–Lite Co.*, 396 U.S. at 385, n. 7, is whether causation of damages compensable through the implied private right of action under § 14(a) can be demonstrated by a member of a class of minority shareholders whose votes are not required by law or corporate bylaw to authorize the transaction giving rise to the claim. * * *

Although a majority stockholder in *Mills* controlled just over half the corporation's shares, a two-thirds vote was needed to approve the merger proposal. * * * [The] Court found the solicitation essential, as contrasted with one addressed to a class of minority shareholders without votes required by law or by-law to authorize the action proposed, and left it for another day to decide whether such a minority shareholder could demonstrate causation.

In this case, respondents address *Mills'* open question by proffering two theories that the proxy solicitation addressed to them was an "essential link" under the *Mills* causation test. They argue, first, that a link existed and was essential simply because VBI and FABI would have been unwilling to proceed with the merger without the approval manifested by the minority shareholders' proxies, which would not have been obtained without the solicitation's express misstatements and misleading omissions. On this reasoning, the causal connection would depend on a desire to avoid bad shareholder or public relations, and the essential character of the causal link would stem not from the enforceable terms of the parties' corporate relationship, but from one party's apprehension of the ill will of the other.

In the alternative, respondents argue that the proxy statement was an essential link between the directors' proposal and the merger because it was the means to satisfy a state statutory requirement of minority shareholder approval, as a condition for saving the merger from voidability resulting from a conflict of interest on the part of one of the Bank's directors, Jack Beddow, who voted in favor of the merger while also serving as a director of FABI. * * * On this theory, causation would depend on the use of the proxy statement for the purpose of obtaining votes sufficient to bar a minority shareholder from commencing proceedings to declare the merger void.

Although respondents have proffered each of these theories as establishing a chain of causal connection in which the proxy statement is claimed to have been an "essential link," neither theory presents the proxy solicitation as essential in the sense of *Mills'* causal sequence, in which the solicitation links a directors' proposal with the votes legally required to authorize the action proposed. As a consequence, each theory would, if adopted, extend the scope of *Borak* actions beyond the ambit of *Mills,* and expand the class of plaintiffs entitled to bring *Borak* actions to include shareholders whose initial authorization of the transaction prompting the proxy solicitation is unnecessary.

* * * The rule that has emerged in the years since *Borak* and *Mills* came down is that recognition of any private right of action for violating a federal statute must ultimately rest on congressional intent to provide a private remedy. From this the corollary follows that the breadth of the right once recognized should not, as a general matter, grow beyond the scope congressionally intended.

[Justice Souter reviews the text and legislative history of the Securities Exchange Act of 1934 and concludes that they provide no guidance with respect to the intended scope of a private right of action.]

The congressional silence that is thus a serious obstacle to the expansion of cognizable *Borak* causation is not, however, a necessarily insurmountable barrier. [In *Blue Chip Stamps*], we looked to policy reasons for deciding where the outer limits of the right should lie. We may do no less here, in the face of respondents' pleas for a private remedy to place them on the same footing as shareholders with votes necessary for initial corporate action.

A

The same threats of speculative claims and procedural intractability [that were present in *Blue Chip Stamps*] are inherent in respondents' theory of causation linked through the directors' desire for a cosmetic vote. Causation would turn on inferences about what the corporate directors would have thought and done without the minority shareholder approval unneeded to authorize action. * * * The issues would be hazy, their litigation protracted, and their resolution unreliable. Given a choice, we would reject any theory of causation that promised such prospects, and we reject this one.

B

The theory of causal necessity derived from the requirements of Virginia law dealing with postmerger ratification seeks to identify the essential character of the proxy solicitation from its function in obtaining the minority approval that would preclude a minority suit attacking the merger. Since the link is said to be a step in the process of barring a class of shareholders from resort to a state remedy otherwise available, this theory of causation rests upon the proposition of policy that § 14(a) should provide a federal remedy whenever a false or misleading proxy statement results in the loss under state law of a shareholder plaintiff's state remedy for the enforcement of a state right. * * *

This case does not, however, require us to decide whether § 14(a) provides a cause of action for lost state remedies, since there is no indication in the law or facts before us that the proxy solicitation resulted in any such loss. The contrary appears to be the case. Assuming the soundness of respondents' characterization of the proxy statement as materially misleading, the very terms of the Virginia statute indicate that a favorable minority vote induced by the solicitation would not suffice to render the merger invulnerable to later attack on the ground of the conflict. The statute bars a shareholder from seeking to avoid a transaction tainted by a director's conflict if, inter alia, the minority shareholders ratified the transaction following disclosure of the material facts of the transaction and the conflict. Va.Code § 13.1–691(A)(2) (1989). Assuming that the material facts about the merger and Beddow's interests were not accurately disclosed, the minority votes were inadequate to ratify the merger under state law, and there was no loss of state remedy to connect the proxy solicitation with harm to minority shareholders irredressable under state law. Nor is there a claim here that the statement misled respondents into entertaining a false belief that they had no chance to upset the merger, until the time for bringing suit had run out.[14]

IV

The judgment of the Court of Appeals is reversed.

JUSTICE SCALIA, concurring in part and concurring in the judgment.

As I understand the Court's opinion, the statement "In the opinion of the Directors, this is a high value for the shares" would produce liability if in fact it was not a high value and the Directors knew that. It would not produce liability if in fact it was not a high value but the Directors honestly believed otherwise. The statement "The Directors voted to accept the proposal because they believe it offers a high value" would not produce liability if in fact the Directors' genuine motive was quite different—except that it would produce liability if the proposal in fact did not offer a high value and the Directors knew that.

I agree with all of this. However, not every sentence that has the word "opinion" in it, or that refers to motivation for Directors' actions, leads us into this psychic thicket. Sometimes such a sentence actually represents facts as facts rather than opinions—and in that event no more need be done than apply the normal rules for § 14(a) liability. I think that is the situation here. In my view, the statement at issue in this case is most fairly read as affirming separately both the fact of the Directors' opinion and the accuracy of the facts upon which the opinion was assertedly based. It reads as follows:

14. Respondents do not claim that any other application of a theory of lost state remedies would avail them here. It is clear, for example, that no state appraisal remedy was lost through a § 14(a) violation in this case. Respondent Weinstein and others did seek appraisal under Virginia law in the Virginia courts; their claims were rejected on the explicit grounds that although "[s]tatutory appraisal is now considered the exclusive remedy for stockholders opposing a merger," "dissenting stockholders in bank mergers do not even have this solitary remedy available to them," because "Va. Code § 6.1–43 specifically excludes bank mergers from application of § 13.1–730 [the Virginia appraisal statute]." Weinstein does not claim that the Virginia court was wrong and does not rely on this claim in any way. Thus, the § 14(a) violation could have had no effect on the availability of an appraisal remedy, for there never was one.

"The Plan of Merger has been approved by the Board of Directors because it provides an opportunity for the Bank's public shareholders to achieve a high value for their shares." * * *

Had it read "because in their estimation it provides an opportunity, etc." it would have set forth nothing but an opinion. As written, however, it asserts both that the Board of Directors acted for a particular reason and that that reason is correct. This interpretation is made clear by what immediately follows: "The price to be paid is about 30% higher than the [last traded price immediately before announcement of the proposal]. * * * [T]he $42 per share that will be paid to public holders of the common stock represents a premium of approximately 26% over the book value. * * * [T]he bank earned $24,767,000 in the year ended December 31, 1986. * * *" Id., at 53a–54a. These are all facts that support—and that are obviously introduced for the purpose of supporting—the factual truth of the "because" clause, i.e., that the proposal gives shareholders a "high value."

If the present case were to proceed, therefore, I think the normal § 14(a) principles governing misrepresentation of fact would apply.

JUSTICE STEVENS, with whom JUSTICE MARSHALL joins, concurring in part and dissenting in part.

* * * The case before us today involves a merger that has been found by a jury to be unfair, not fair. The interest in providing a remedy to the injured minority shareholders therefore is stronger, not weaker, than in *Mills.* The interest in avoiding speculative controversy about the actual importance of the proxy solicitation is the same as in *Mills.* Moreover, as in *Mills,* these matters can be taken into account at the remedy stage in appropriate cases. Accordingly, I do not believe that it constitutes an unwarranted extension of the rationale of *Mills* to conclude that because management found it necessary—whether for "legal or practical reasons"—to solicit proxies from minority shareholders to obtain their approval of the merger, that solicitation "was an essential link in the accomplishment of the transaction." In my opinion, shareholders may bring an action for damages under § 14(a) of the Securities Exchange Act of 1934 whenever materially false or misleading statements are made in proxy statements. That the solicitation of proxies is not required by law or by the bylaws of a corporation does not authorize corporate officers, once they have decided for whatever reason to solicit proxies, to avoid the constraints of the statute. I would therefore affirm the judgment of the Court of Appeals.

JUSTICE KENNEDY, with whom JUSTICE MARSHALL, JUSTICE BLACKMUN, and JUSTICE STEVENS join, concurring in part and dissenting in part.

I am in general agreement with Parts I and II of the majority opinion, but do not agree with the views expressed in Part III regarding the proof of causation required to establish a violation of § 14(a). With respect, I dissent from Part III of the Court's opinion. * * *

II

A

The severe limits the Court places upon possible proof of nonvoting causation in a § 14(a) private action are justified neither by our precedents nor any case in the courts of appeals. These limits are said to flow from a shift in our approach to implied causes of action that has occurred since we recognized the § 14(a) implied private action in *J.I. Case Co. v. Borak*.

* * * According to the Court, acceptance of non-voting causation theories would "extend the scope of *Borak* actions beyond the ambit of *Mills*." But *Mills* did not purport to limit the scope of *Borak* actions, and as footnote 7 of *Mills* indicates, some courts have applied nonvoting causation theories to *Borak* actions for at least the past 25 years.

To the extent the Court's analysis considers the purposes underlying § 14(a), it does so with the avowed aim to limit the cause of action and with undue emphasis upon fears of "speculative claims and procedural intractability." The result is a sort of guerrilla warfare to restrict a well established implied right of action. If the analysis adopted by the Court today is any guide, Congress and those charged with enforcement of the securities laws stand forewarned that unresolved questions concerning the scope of those causes of action are likely to be answered by the Court in favor of defendants.

B

The Court seems to assume, based upon the footnote in *Mills* reserving the question, that Sandberg bears a special burden to demonstrate causation because the public shareholders held only 15 percent of the Bank's stock. Here, First American Bankshares, Inc. (FABI) and Virginia Bankshares, Inc. (VBI) retained the option to back out of the transaction if dissatisfied with the reaction of the minority shareholders, or if concerned that the merger would result in liability for violation of duties to the minority shareholders. The merger agreement was conditioned upon approval by two-thirds of the shareholders and VBI could have voted its shares against the merger if it so decided. To this extent, the Court's distinction between cases where the "minority" shareholders could have voted down the transaction and those where causation must be proved by nonvoting theories is suspect. Minority shareholders are identified only by a post hoc inquiry. The real question ought to be whether an injury was shown by the effect the nondisclosure had on the entire merger process, including the period before votes are cast.

The Court's distinction presumes that a majority shareholder will vote in favor of management's proposal even if proxy disclosure suggests that the transaction is unfair to minority shareholders or that the board of directors or majority shareholder are in breach of fiduciary duties to the minority. If the majority shareholder votes against the transaction in order to comply with its state law duties, or out of fear of liability, or upon concluding that the transaction will injure the reputation of the business, this ought not to be characterized as nonvoting causation. Of course, when the majority shareholder dominates the voting process, as was the case here, it may prefer to avoid the embarrassment of voting against its own proposal and so may cancel the meeting of shareholders at which the vote was to have been taken. For practical purposes, the result is the same: because of full disclosure the transaction does not go forward and the resulting injury to minority shareholders is avoided. The Court's distinction between voting and nonvoting causation does not create clear legal categories.

III

Our decision in *Mills* rested upon the impracticality of attempting to determine the extent of reliance by thousands of shareholders on alleged misrepresentations or omissions. If minority shareholders hold sufficient votes to defeat a management proposal and if the misstatement or omission is likely to be considered important in deciding how to vote, then there exists a likely causal link between the proxy violation and the enactment of the proposal; and one can justify recovery by minority shareholders for damages resulting from enactment of management's proposal.

If, for sake of argument, we accept a distinction between voting and nonvoting causation, we must determine whether the *Mills* essential link theory applies where a majority shareholder holds sufficient votes to force adoption of a proposal. The merit of the essential link formulation is that it rests upon the likelihood of causation and eliminates the difficulty of proof. Even where a minority lacks votes to defeat a proposal, both these factors weigh in favor of finding causation so long as the solicitation of proxies is an essential link in the transaction. * * *

B

There is no authority whatsoever for limiting § 14(a) to protecting those minority shareholders whose numerical strength could permit them to vote down a proposal. One of Section 14(a)'s "chief purposes is 'the protection of investors.'" Those who lack the strength to vote down a proposal have all the more need of disclosure. The voting process involves not only casting ballots but also the formulation and withdrawal of proposals, the minority's right to block a vote through court action or the threat of adverse consequences, or the negotiation of an increase in price. The proxy rules support this deliberative process. These practicalities can result in causation sufficient to support recovery.

The facts in the case before us prove this point. Sandberg argues that had all the material facts been disclosed, FABI or the Bank likely would have withdrawn or revised the merger proposal. The evidence in the record, and more that might be available upon remand meets any reasonable requirement of specific and nonspeculative proof.

* * * I conclude that causation is more than plausible; it is likely, even where the public shareholders cannot vote down management's

proposal. Causation is established where the proxy statement is an essential link in completing the transaction, even if the minority lacks sufficient votes to defeat a proposal of management.

IV

The majority avoids the question whether a plaintiff may prove causation by demonstrating that the misrepresentation or omission deprived her of a state law remedy. * * * The majority asserts that respondents show no loss of a state law remedy, because if "the material facts of the transaction and Beddow's interest were not accurately disclosed, then the minority votes were inadequate to ratify the merger under Virginia law." This theory requires us to conclude that the Virginia statute governing director conflicts of interest, incorporates the same definition of materiality as the federal proxy rules. I find no support for that proposition. If the definitions are not the same, then Sandberg may have lost her state law remedy. For all we know, disclosure to the minority shareholders that the price is $42 per share may satisfy Virginia's requirement. If that is the case, then approval by the minority without full disclosure may have deprived Sandberg of the ability to void the merger.

* * * I would affirm the judgment of the Court of Appeals.

Note: Virginia Bankshares, Inc. v. Sandberg

1. Justice Scalia suggests that directors can reduce their exposure to liability if they make clear they are expressing opinions, not facts. This would seem to follow from his observation that with the addition of the bracketed words, the following sentence would "set forth nothing but an opinion."

> The Plan of Merger has been approved by the Board of Directors because [in their estimation] it provides an opportunity for the Bank's public shareholders to achieve a high value for their shares.

Is this reading of the Court's opinion accurate, or would the Court hold that the quoted sentence constituted a misstatement of material fact so long as documentary or circumstantial evidence demonstrated the merger did not provide "a high value" to the Bank's public shareholders?

2. In Shapiro v. UJB Financial Corp., 964 F.2d 272 (3d Cir.1992), the Third Circuit addressed some of the federalism concerns raised in *Virginia Bankshares* and *Santa Fe*. Shareholders in a financially troubled bank holding company brought a class action suit against the company and its officers and directors alleging that they suffered economic losses as a result of public statements that portrayed UJB in a "falsely optimistic manner." The shareholders alleged that defendants had stated that UJB's "loan loss reserves were adequate, loan review procedures and policies were stringently and continuously applied, lending opportunities were balanced appropriately against risks, and financial results were positive" when, in fact, none of these things were true.

The district court held that the alleged misrepresentations or omissions involved simple mismanagement and not fraud, and consequently were not actionable under the federal securities laws.

The Third Circuit reversed. It first stated that "a reasonable investor would be influenced significantly by knowledge that a bank has knowingly or recklessly hidden its true financial status by deliberately misstating its level of non-performing loans, failing to provide adequate reserves, and indulging its problem loan customers." Id. at 281. It then agreed with the district court that the failure to provide adequate reserves by itself is not actionable under the federal securities laws. The court also stated that if a defendant has not commented on the nature and quality of its management practices, there is no violation of the federal securities laws for failing to characterize them as poor. Nevertheless, in this case, plaintiffs alleged that the defendants did in fact address the quality of its management practices, thereby declaring the subjects of their representations to be material to reasonable shareholders. Once the defendants put the subjects "in play," they were bound to speak truthfully about them. The court went on to hold that *Virginia Bankshares* permitted plaintiffs to prove that the defendants' conclusory statements about the soundness of UJB's management practices were knowingly false or misleading. The court, however, directed plaintiffs to refile their complaint because the language of their complaint, as filed, failed adequately to distinguish the securities law violations from the mismanagement. "It is difficult to discern whether plaintiffs are alleging that defendants made material statements that the reserves were adequate when in fact they were not, or whether plaintiffs are merely alleging that the reserves were inadequate." Id. at 284.

Assuming that the plaintiffs in *Shapiro* are able to reformulate their complaint in a satisfactory manner, will the evidence they present in the federal securities law case differ substantially from the evidence they would have to present in a state trial alleging that the defendants violated their duty of care? Recall the concerns voice by some commentators at the close of the discussion of Goldberg v. Meridor. Are these criticisms not equally relevant to Note 7 of *Virginia Bankshares*?

3. In *Virginia Bankshares*, the Court suggests that "corporate minutes or other statements of the directors themselves" may support claims that directors' recommendations or statements of opinion were false. Rarely, however, will minutes of board meetings or other formal corporate records contain evidence that explicitly conflicts with or undermines directors' recommendations. Consequently, shareholders generally will have to rely on circumstantial evidence to prove such claims. Mendell v. Greenberg, 938 F.2d 1528 (2d Cir.1991), interpreted *Virginia Bankshares* to require that a hearing be held on the fair value of the stock of a corporation involved in a merger as the first step in determining whether directors' recommendation that shareholders approve the merger consideration was false or misleading. If this interpretation is correct, claims relating to directors' recommendations ultimately may be

decided on the basis of judgments relating to a transaction's "fairness." Does Note 7 of the Court's opinion deal adequately with this possibility?

4. In *Mills*, the Court held that plaintiffs could maintain their action under Rule 14a–9 and recover reasonable attorney fees, even if the trial court ultimately determined the merger they had voted to approve was fair. In *Virginia Bankshares*, the Court upheld a finding that the proxy statement was materially misleading, tacitly accepting the trial court's finding that the Bank's shareholders had received $42 for stock worth $60 per share, but nonetheless held plaintiffs could not maintain an action under Rule 14a–9. The Court seems to justify this holding by pointing out that, assuming plaintiffs could prove these elements of their case in a state court, "there was no loss of state remedy to connect the proxy solicitation with harm to shareholders irredressable under state law," i.e., the plaintiffs could recover their losses under Virginia law.

Justice Kennedy questions the Court's assumption that Virginia law incorporates the same definition of materiality as the federal proxy rules. This question appears to have some validity, especially given the uncertainty that existed prior to *Virginia Bankshares* as to when, if ever, directors' recommendations constituted statements of material fact. In addition, the Court's approach is difficult to reconcile with the statement in *Borak* that "if the law of the State happened to attach no responsibility to the use of misleading proxy statements, the whole purpose of the section might be frustrated." On the other hand, in the years since *Borak,* state courts have tended to impose on corporate managers a duty of disclosure similar to the duty imposed by Section 14(a) and Rule 14a–9. If that aspect of the policy considerations supporting the decision in *Borak* no longer has much force, to what extent does the Court's holding on the causation issue in *Sandberg* foreshadow further attrition of the private right of action under § 14(a)? The nature of the state law duty of disclosure will be considered in the last section of this chapter.

Note: Causation

In *Virginia Bankshares*, the Court's holding that the Bank's proxy solicitation was not an "essential link" in effectuating the merger appears to be grounded in its finding that the minority shareholders' votes were "not required by law or corporate bylaw to authorize the transaction giving rise to the claim." In many other settings, corporations solicit shareholder approval of transactions although such approval is "not required by law or corporate bylaw." These include transactions that directors have the authority to approve, but nonetheless submit to shareholders for approval or ratification; transactions involving the issuance of substantial amounts of stock, where New York Stock Exchange rules require shareholder approval if the new stock is to be listed; and agreements between parent companies and controlled subsidiaries that are made subject to the approval of a majority of the subsidiary's minority shareholders. Are proxy solicitations in connection with such transactions "essential," for purposes of demonstrating that some violation of Rule 14a–9 caused some cognizable injury to shareholders who were solicited?

"Causation" is one of the law's most central, yet most troublesome concepts. Indeed, philosophy students will recall that it has been a problematic concept in that discipline at least since the work of David Hume. In the more prosaic discipline of law, however, problems with the concept arise primarily not because of epistemological quandaries, but because its meaning may differ in different contexts. As applied to the tort of misrepresentation (or deceit), the Restatement (Second) of Torts (1977) speaks of Causation in Fact (Section 546) and Legal Causation (Section 548). Causation in Fact occurs when one's actual reliance was a substantial factor in determining the course of conduct resulting in loss, while Legal Causation, and consequently liability, arises only if the loss might reasonably be expected to result from the reliance.

There is a "but for" element to causation under this widely accepted formulation. Although that element is needed to establish causation in fact, it is not sufficient to establish liability. The missing element is referred to as "legal" cause or "proximate" cause. For instance, "but for" a misrepresentation, plaintiff might not have bought the property sold by defendant; her loss, nevertheless, might have resulted from a general economic decline. *See* ALI Fed.Sec.Code, Section 202(19), Comment 3(c) (1980).

The Court in *Mills* refused to make reliance an element of the test of causation, finding that a showing of materiality was sufficient to show that there was a relationship between violation and injury, so long as the solicitation of proxies was "an essential link in the accomplishment of the transaction." This is a policy choice, and its consequence is to facilitate private enforcement of violations of the proxy rules. See Note, Causation and Liability in Private Actions for Proxy Violations, 81 Yale L.J. 107 (1970).

As applied to liability under the main anti-fraud provisions of the federal securities laws, the concept of causation increasingly has been separated into two tests: *transaction* causation and *loss* causation. Loss causation is relatively easy to demonstrate—the transaction caused harm to the plaintiff. In *Borak*, the shareholders of the disappearing company received less for their shares than the shares were worth. Transaction causation, which is harder to prove, requires the plaintiff to show that the defendant's violation caused the company to engage in the transaction in question. Thus, in *Mills*, the loss was occasioned by the merger and the merger was caused by the solicitation of proxies to secure sufficient votes for its approval.

Where is the causal relationship between allegedly improper transactions such as illegal payments by the corporation or a breach of fiduciary duty by corporate managers, and any false or misleading statements in the proxy material? The harm can be shown in the form of the illegal or wasteful payments and their side effects. These payments, or their excessive nature were not disclosed in the proxy material sent to shareholders. Because the shareholders did not vote to approve the transactions that caused the loss, transaction causation was lacking in these circumstances. Abbey v. Control Data Corp., 603 F.2d 724 (8th Cir. 1979).

On the other hand, where shareholders challenged the election of directors alleging that the proxy material failed to disclose their cover up of illegal payments, transaction causation was established because the issue of the election of directors had been submitted to the shareholders. Of course, plaintiff still must show that the omission was material. Weisberg v. Coastal States Gas Corp., 609 F.2d 650 (2d Cir.1979). In contrast with *Abbey,* the plaintiff in *Weisberg* did not challenge the illegal payments, but only the election of directors.

The Ninth Circuit carried the foregoing analysis further in Gaines v. Haughton, 645 F.2d 761 (9th Cir.1981). Agreeing that when the plaintiff attacks the election, not the improper payments, the analysis shifts from causation to materiality, the court drew a distinction between non-disclosure of self-dealing conduct, which is presumptively material, and "allegations of simple breach of fiduciary duty/waste of corporate assets—the non-disclosure of which is never material for § 14(a) purposes."

The court elaborated on this latter point:

Many corporate actions taken by directors in the interest of the corporation might offend and engender controversy among some stockholders. Investors share the same diversity of social and political views that characterize the polity as a whole. The tenor of a company's labor relations policies, economic decisions to relocate or close established plants, commercial dealings with foreign countries which are disdained in certain circles, decisions to develop (or not to develop) particular natural resources or forms of energy technology, and the promulgation of corporate personnel policies that reject (or embrace) the principle of affirmative action, are just a few examples of business judgments, soundly entrusted to the broad discretion of the directors, which may nonetheless cause shareholder dissent and provoke claims of "wasteful," "unethical," or even "immoral" business dealings. Should corporate directors have a duty under § 14(a) to disclose all such corporate decisions in proxy solicitations for their re-election? We decline to extend the duty of disclosure under § 14(a) to these situations. While we neither condone nor condemn these and similar types of corporate conduct (including the now illegal practice of questionable foreign payments), we believe the aggrieved shareholders have sufficient recourse to state law claims against the responsible directors and, if all else fails, can sell or trade their stock in the offending corporation in favor of an enterprise more compatible with their own personal goals and values.

645 F.2d at 778–79.

The question of causation also arises when the alleged wrongdoer owns sufficient stock to assure approval of the transaction in question. The Court left this issue open in footnote 7 in *Mills* and subsequently resolved it in *Virginia Bankshares*.

2. LOST STATE REMEDIES

Recall that *Goldberg* and its progeny raised questions about the relationship between a cause of action under Rule 10b–5 and the availability of state law remedies in an allegedly unfair transaction. In that connection, *Virginia Bankshares* raises several new problems. It seems to render uncertain the holding in *Goldberg* that minority shareholders state a cause of action under Rule 10b–5 when claiming that they were lulled into not seeking to enjoin a merger because of the board's deceptive disclosures. First, the Court rejected the minority shareholders' theory of causation on the grounds that the theory "would turn on inferences about what the corporate directors might have done without the minority shareholder approval unneeded to authorize action." A major criticism of *Goldberg* has been its implicit presumption that but for the omission of material information, the plaintiffs would have rushed to state court to seek, and could have obtained, an injunction to prevent the merger. Is the Court's refusal in *Virginia Bankshares* to speculate about 'what might have been' equally pertinent to a *Goldberg* claim?

Second, *Virginia Bankshares* implicitly raises the question of what constitutes the "loss" of a state law remedy. Does being lulled by a deceptive disclosure into not seeking an injunction until it is too late constitute such a loss? Note that *Virginia Bankshares* closes with the caveat that there was no "claim here that the statement misled respondents into entertaining a false belief that they had no chance to upset the merger, until the time for bringing suit had run out." Does this statement save *Goldberg* or does it introduce a completely new methodology which focuses on whether the time has passed to seek a state law remedy rather than on whether such remedy was available at the time of the omission or misstatement?

WILSON v. GREAT AMERICAN INDUSTRIES, INC.
979 F.2d 924 (2d Cir.1992).

[Following the merger of Chenango Industries into Great American Industries, minority shareholders of Chenango sued Great American, Chenango, and various officers and directors connected with those corporations. The shareholders alleged that defendants violated, *inter alia*, Rule 14a–9 because of omissions and material misrepresentations in a joint proxy statement/prospectus issued in 1979 in connection with the merger. After a protracted series of court decisions, it was held that these proxy materials did contain material misrepresentations in violation of Rule 14a–9, and plaintiffs were awarded damages for the losses they claimed to have suffered. Defendants and plaintiffs appealed the district court decisions awarding damages. After these appeals were filed, the Supreme Court handed down its decision in Virginia Bankshares, Inc. v. Sandberg. The defendants then requested that the district court reconsider its prior decisions awarding damages in light of *Virginia Bankshares*. Defendants claimed that the plaintiffs' suit should have been dismissed on the ground that, as minority shareholders without power to influence the proposed merger, they suffered no compensable damages under section 14(a) of the Securities Exchange Act of 1934, notwithstanding that their votes were solicited by proxies containing material misrepresentations. The district court granted reconsideration, but declined to depart from its prior holdings that because the fact that the plaintiffs in this case may have been deprived of appraisal rights and other forms of equitable relief under state law, *Virginia Bankshares* was not controlling and did not clearly indicate that the plaintiffs had no cause of action.

CARDAMONE, CIRCUIT JUDGE:

* * * Under rules set forth in that case, defendants continue, minority shareholders situated as are plaintiffs can prove no damages from proxy misrepresentations under § 14(a). In addition, § 14(a) does not provide a private cause of action for lost state remedies—such as appraisal rights—and, even if a federal private cause of action is available, it does not provide greater relief than that provided under state law. As to that, defendants declare, plaintiffs cannot prove the defective proxy caused them to lose any state remedies. In the discussion that follows that leads us to affirm the district court in part, reverse it in part, and remand this case once again, we readily acknowledge our share of responsibility for its necessity.

DISCUSSION

I

A. Intervening Supreme Court Decision

The Supreme Court in Virginia Bankshares did not hold that minority shareholders whose votes number too few to affect the outcome of a shareholder vote may never recover damages under § 14(a) or that no implied private cause of action for such shareholders is provided under that section of the Act. And, it expressly declined to decide whether § 14(a) provides an implied federal remedy for minority shareholders deprived of certain state remedies as a result of deceptive proxy solicitations. ___ U.S. at ___ & n. 14, 111 S.Ct. at 2766 & n. 14. To the extent that this Circuit recognizes such a remedy, defendants incorrectly contend therefore that Virginia Bankshares precludes plaintiffs from seeking such relief. * * *

One theory of causation advanced by the plaintiffs in Virginia Bankshares was that, but for the defective proxies, the minority shareholders would not have voted in favor of the merger. In that event, dissenting votes would have preserved their right to pursue under Virginia law avoidance of the merger based on an alleged conflict of interest on the part of one the Bank's directors. Recognizing the possibility that a sufficient causal relationship might be established between a materially deceptive proxy and lost state remedies to support an implied right of recovery, the Court reasoned that causation under this theory could not be established because plaintiffs had not proved any loss.

Virginia law barred suits seeking to avoid a merger tainted by a director's conflict of interest only if the ratifying vote was procured pursuant to full disclosure of the material facts of the transaction, including the conflict of interest. Plaintiffs' contention that the proxy contained material misrepresentations necessarily prevented their loss of relief under this state law. Plaintiffs failed to allege any other lost state remedy. Hence, since plaintiffs failed to establish the necessary injury required under a theory of causation alleging lost state remedies, they could not succeed under such theory. The Supreme Court therefore found it unnecessary to decide whether § 14(a) provided such implied relief.

B. Plaintiff's Theories of Recovery

Plaintiffs in the present action seek recovery under four separate federal securities law provisions. In reversing the trial court's dismissal, we imposed liability only under § 14(a), without commenting on plaintiffs' other three causes of action. The necessary implication of our imposing liability under § 14(a) is the recognition of an implied private cause of action for minority shareholders who cannot affect the outcome of a corporate vote. In doing so, we did not comment on what theory of causation defendants' liability rested. Perhaps we presumed that plaintiffs had suffered an injury causally related to the defective proxy because defendants in Wilson I had not contested—and the district court found—causation.

Plaintiffs set forth two theories of causation to support their claims. They assert first that an implied action under any of the four securities law provisions pleaded should be recognized because 85 percent of the voting shares, or 12 percent of the minority shareholders in addition to the controlling majority shareholders, had to approve the merger in order for the exchange of stock to take place without tax consequences. * * * [W]e reject this theory of causation.

Plaintiffs' second theory of causation—one with more merit and upon which § 14(a) causes of action have been sustained in the past—is that their deceptively procured vote in favor of the merger deprived them of their state appraisal rights under N.Y.Bus.Corp.Law §§ 623 (a)(b) (McKinney 1986); § 910(a)(1) (McKinney Supp.1992). We and other courts have recognized that plaintiffs might prevail on such a § 14(a) theory. See Cole v. Schenley Indus., Inc., 563 F.2d 35, 39–40 (2d Cir.1977) (on a motion to dismiss complaint, implied right recognized when insignificant minority shareholders had state law alternatives to accepting merger); Schlick v. Penn–Dixie Cement Corp., 507 F.2d 374, 381–84 (2d Cir.1974) (though insignificant minority shareholders had no appraisal rights under state law, deprivation of measures other than casting proxies may support implied right to recovery under § 14(a)). See also Swanson v. American Consumers Indus., Inc., 475 F.2d 516, 520–21 (7th Cir.1973) (insignificant minority shareholders entitled to recovery for lost state appraisal rights under § 10(b)). Cf. Scattergood v. Perelman, 945 F.2d 618, 626 n. 4 (3d Cir.1991) (noting possibility that implied right of recovery might exist for lost state remedies).

As noted, Virginia Bankshares left open the possibility that § 14(a) might include this type of implied right to recover and did not address whether the causal relationship between a deceptive proxy and lost state remedies was sufficient to support a federal remedy. Defendants, having failed to contest causation prior to the present appeal * * * should hardly be allowed to argue the point now, especially when to permit such puts them in a better position than if they had made this objection earlier and lost.

We continue to believe that a minority shareholder, who has lost his right to a state appraisal because of a materially deceptive proxy, may make "a sufficient showing of causal relationship between the violation and the injury for which he seeks redress." Mills, 396 U.S. at 385, 90 S.Ct. at 622. The transaction effected by a proxy involves not only the merger of the corporate entities, and the attendant exchange of stock, but also the forfeiture of shareholders' appraisal rights. The injury sustained by a minority shareholder powerless to affect the outcome of the merger vote is not the merger but the loss of his appraisal right. The deceptive proxy plainly constitutes an "essential link" in accomplishing the forfeiture of this state right.

That the causal nexus between the merger and the proxy is absent when the minority stockholder's vote cannot affect the merger decision does not necessarily mean a causal link between the proxy and some other injury may not exist. We recognize that loss causation or economic harm to plaintiffs must be shown, as well as proof that the misrepresentations induced plaintiffs to engage in the subject transaction, that is, transaction causation. Here loss causation may be established when a proxy statement prompts a shareholder to accept an unfair exchange ratio for his shares rather than recoup a greater value through a state appraisal. And transaction causation may be shown when a proxy statement, because of material misrepresentations, causes a shareholder to forfeit his appraisal rights by voting in favor of the proposed corporate merger.

Even though the proxy was not legally required in this case, when defendants choose to issue a proxy plaintiffs have a right to a truthful one. With the Securities Exchange Act of 1934, Congress sought to promote fair corporate suffrage with respect to " 'every equity security' " by requiring an " 'explanation to the stockholder of the real nature of the questions for which authority to cast his vote is sought.' " Mills, 396 U.S. at 381, 90 S.Ct. at 620 (quoting H.R.Rep. No. 1383, 73d Cong., 2d Sess. 13–14 (1934)); see also J.I. Case Co. v. Borak, 377 U.S. 426,

431–32, 84 S.Ct. 1555, 1559–60, 12 L.Ed.2d 423 (1964). Congress' interest in the protection of investors and the " 'free exercise of [their] voting rights,' " Borak, 377 U.S. at 431, 84 S.Ct. at 1559 (quoting H.R.Rep. No. 1383, 73d Cong., 2d Sess. 14 (1934)), should not vary in degree according to the ability of the shareholder to affect the merger, if the vote nevertheless may result in a different sort of injury which full disclosure might have avoided.

The statute does not suggest that the prohibition of material misrepresentation in a proxy extends only to necessary proxies that are mailed to shareholders the solicitation of whose votes may affect the outcome of the proposed corporate action. That a controlling group of shareholders may accomplish any corporate change they want does not insulate them from liability for injury occasioned when they commit the sort of fraud that § 14(a) seeks to prevent. See Swanson v. American Consumer Indus., Inc., 415 F.2d 1326, 1331–32 (7th Cir.1969). To decline to extend the protection of § 14(a) to plaintiffs, we think, might sanction overreaching by controlling shareholders when the minority shareholders most need § 14(a)'s protection. At the same time, allowing the action does not pose a threat of "speculative claims and procedural intractability," Virginia Bankshares, ___ U.S. at ___, 111 S.Ct. at 2765, because the forfeiture of state appraisal rights is a question separate from the effectuation of the merger and does not require courts to guess how or whether the majority shareholders would have proceeded in the face of minority dissent.

Although a finding of materiality in a proxy solicitation may satisfy the elements of loss and transaction causation for forfeited state appraisal rights, plaintiffs must also prove that they in fact lost state appraisal rights. See *Virginia Bankshares*, ___ U.S. at ___ & n. 14, 111 S.Ct. at 2766 & n. 14. * * * Accordingly, we must remand this matter for the limited purpose of determining whether the proxy solicitation actually resulted in the loss of any remedies available to plaintiffs under New York law.

In *Mills*, the Court assumed without discussion that the "transaction" to which the "essential link" related was the allegedly unfair merger. And in *Santa Fe*, the Court found that there could be no deception (and, therefore, no causation) where appraisal was the only remedy available to a dissatisfied shareholder. In *Wilson*, however, the Second Circuit found that there could be causation if there were a link between "the proxy and *some other injury*" rather than between the proxy and the merger (emphasis added). Moreover, there can be transaction causation where a materially misleading proxy statement "causes a shareholder to forfeit his appraisal rights by voting in favor of the proposed corporate merger." Is *Wilson* consistent with either *Mills* or *Santa Fe*, or does it create a new definition of "transaction" in determining whether there is causation?

For an extensive discussion of *Virginia Bankshares* in a case involving Rule 13–3 under the 1934 Act, see Howing Co. v. Nationwide Corp., 972 F.2d 700 (6th Cir.1992), cert. denied ___ U.S. ___, 113 S.Ct. 1645, 123 L.Ed.2d 266 (1993).

F. FAULT

In Footnote 5 of *Virginia Bankshares*, the Court left open the question of whether the standard of culpability to which the directors will be held in a Section 14(a) action is negligence or scienter (the traditional fraud standard). The language of Section 14(a), which simply prohibits the solicitation of proxies in violation of the SEC's rules, provides no guidance nor does the legislative history. The two principal liability provisions of the federal securities laws, Section 11 of the Securities Act of 1933 and Rule 10b–5 provide different answers: Section 11 contains an explicit negligence standard, while Rule 10b–5 requires the more exacting test of scienter. *See* Ernst & Ernst v. Hochfelder, 425 U.S. 185, 96 S.Ct. 1375, 47 L.Ed.2d 668 (1976).

Lower federal courts are also divided. In Gould v. American Hawaiian Steamship Co., 535 F.2d 761 (3d Cir.1976), the court held that an outside director "was responsible with his fellow directors for the action of the board in which he participated as well as for his acts or failure to act * * *. The [lower] court held that in any event [the outside director would have known that the proxy statement in its final form was false if he had read it, which it was his duty to do as a member of the board of directors which was issuing the document to solicit the shareholders' proxies. The [lower] court concluded that under these circumstances the [outside director] was liable for the materially false and misleading proxy statement * * *. As we have seen, the District Court held negligence to be the appropriate standard under § 14(a) and we agree." 535 F.2d at 776–77.

By contrast, in Adams v. Standard Knitting Mills, 623 F.2d 422 (6th Cir.1980) the court held that scienter was the appropriate standard, at least with respect to the corporation's outside accountants. The court stated that "[a]lthough we are not called on in this case to decide the standard of liability of the corporate issuer of proxy material, we are influenced by the fact that the accountant here, unlike the corporate issuer, does not directly benefit from the proxy vote and is not in privity with the stockholder. Unlike the corporate issuer, the preparation of financial statements to be appended to proxies and other reports is the daily fare of accountants, and the accountant's potential liability for relatively minor mistakes would be enormous under a negligence standard. * * * [I]n the instant case there was no proof of investor reliance on the notes to the financial statements which erroneously described the restriction on payment of dividends. We can see no reason for a different standard of liability for accountants under the proxy provisions than under 10(b). 623 F.2d at 429. Perhaps the high threshold for the accountant's liability can be explained by the firm's lack of financial involvement in the transaction, but what justifies the relatively low standard for the outside directors' liability? See Fradkin v. Ernst, 571 F.Supp. 829 (N.D.Ohio 1983).

In Herskowitz v. Nutri/System, Inc., 857 F.2d 179 (3d Cir.1988) the court extended the *Gould* negligence standard for directors to outside advisers to the corporation such as accountants and investment bankers. The court rejected the scienter standard in *Adams* because it was bound by *Gould*. However, as the court noted, "since an investment banker rendering a fairness opinion in connection with a leveraged buyout knows full well that it will be used to solicit shareholder approval, and is well paid for the service it performs, we see no convincing reason for not holding it to the same standard of liability as the management it is assisting." 857 F.2d at 190.

G. STATE LAW DUTY OF DISCLOSURE

Delaware and other states, to a lesser degree, have not limited their regulation of corporate communications to proxy solicitations. A growing body of state law mandates that all communications between corporate fiduciaries and shareholders fully disclose all material information on the subject of the communication. The principal difference between regulation of disclosure and regulation of proxy solicitation is that only corporate fiduciaries owe the broader duty of disclosure, while the duties owed in connection with a proxy solicitation attach to anyone soliciting proxies, whether or not a corporate fiduciary.

1. ORIGINS AND EVOLUTION OF THE DUTY OF DISCLOSURE

The Delaware duty of disclosure can be traced ultimately to a now repealed state statute: 8 Del.C. § 144 (1953). That section held directors and officers jointly and severally liable for damages resulting from their knowing distribution or publication of materially false written statements about the condition of the corporation. While the statute on its face mandated no affirmative duty to disclose, a court held that it required a director making a written statement to shareholders concerning the condition of the corporation to "disclose all material facts." Hall v. John S. Isaacs & Sons Farms, 37 Del.Ch. 530, 146 A.2d 602, 609–10 (1958). Nine years after the decision in *Hall*, Section 144 was repealed without explanation; however, Kelly v. Bell, 254 A.2d 62, 71 (Del.Ch. 1969), aff'd, 266 A.2d 878 (Del.1970) decided after the repeal, reaffirmed the principle of *Hall* regarding disclosure.

The principal evolution of the state law duty of disclosure began in 1977 with the Delaware Supreme Court's decision in Lynch v. Vickers Energy Corp., 383 A.2d 278 (Del.1977). Among other things, *Lynch* expanded the class of those owing the duty to include majority shareholders and further defined the affirmative aspects of the duty. In *Lynch*, the majority shareholder, Vickers, made a tender offer at $12 per share for the remaining shares of Transocean that Vickers did not own. The offer included a circular made jointly by Vickers and the directors of Transocean which did not disclose that: (1) a "highly qualified" petroleum engineer who was a member of Transocean's management appraised the company to be worth more than Vickers' offer and (2) Vickers' management had authorized open market purchases of Transocean's shares during the period immediately preceding the offer for bids of up to $15 a share. The court held that Vickers in this context owed a duty of "complete candor" to disclose all "germane facts" to the minority shareholders. The court feared that majority shareholders, as insiders, could use their special knowledge to the detriment of those on the outside. Thus, the duty to disclose seemed to emanate from the duty of loyalty owed by controlling shareholders.

While *Lynch* marked the beginning of the rapid evolution of the state law duty to disclose, it left open three important questions: (1) Under what circumstances does the duty arise? (2) Who, specifically, owes the duty? and (3) What must be disclosed?

2.   UNDER WHAT CIRCUMSTANCES DOES THE DUTY ARISE?

The duty to disclose arises traditionally when a fiduciary (generally, the corporation's management or controlling shareholder) communicates to the shareholders, soliciting shareholder action. A duty exists when (1) a fiduciary asks shareholders to act as the corporate decision-maker (e.g., ratification of the board's decision), or (2) a fiduciary asks or forces shareholders to make a decision concerning the sale or appraisal of their shares (e.g., tender offers and freeze-out mergers). Recent authority suggests, however, that any communication by a fiduciary to shareholders must disclose all material information, whether or not the fiduciary is seeking shareholder action.

a.   *Shareholder as Corporate Decision-maker*

The duty to disclose arises when a fiduciary asks the shareholders to act as corporate decision-maker. Stroud v. Grace, 606 A.2d 75 (Del. 1992) clearly affirms that principle but slightly limits its scope. In *Stroud* the board of directors of a closely held corporation approved controversial by-law amendments that established new qualifications for board membership. The board then sought shareholder ratification at the annual meeting. The notice of the meeting which was sent to the shareholders included a copy of the amended by-laws but did not explain the purpose of these amendments. The board, however, did explain their purpose at the meeting. In upholding the actions of the board, the court reaffirmed the principle that "directors of Delaware corporations are under a fiduciary duty to disclose fully and fairly all material information within the board's control when it seeks shareholder action." 606 A.2d at 84.

Under most circumstances, application of this principle would have meant that the board's failure to explain the purpose of the proposed amendments constituted a material omission in breach of its fiduciary duty. Here, however, the court limited the principle, holding that the common law duty of disclosure did not override the specific disclosure requirements for the notice of meeting that were specifically set out in the statute, i.e., the time and place of the meeting and a copy or summary of any amendment to the corporation's certificate of incorporation. The effect of this limitation is likely to be slight; few statutory provisions contain explicit disclosures that would override the general duty to disclose.

Stroud might be thought to allow a board to bypass the duty to disclose by foregoing a proxy solicitation in the hope of passing a controversial measure at a lightly attended annual meeting. The court suggested, however, that *Schnell* (Chapter 3) would forbid such conduct if it was intended to manipulate the shareholder vote inequitably.

b. Mergers and Tender Offers

Courts have held that both directors and controlling shareholders have a duty to disclose when they place the shareholder in a position in which she has to decide whether to sell her stock or seek appraisal, whether in a traditional merger, a tender offer by a controlling shareholder or a tender offer by the corporation for its own shares (a self-tender). See *Lynch*, supra; Glassman v. Wometco Cable Television, 1989 WL 1160 (Del.Ch.1989); Eisenberg v. Chicago Milwaukee Corp., 537 A.2d 1051 (Del.Ch.1987).

The courts have extended the duty to disclose to short-form mergers,even though no shareholder vote is required. In Shell Petroleum, Inc. v. Smith, 606 A.2d 112 (Del.1992) a majority shareholder initiated a short-form merger and distributed documents to minority shareholders regarding the financial health of the company. The court held that the majority "bears the burden of showing complete disclosure of all material facts relevant to a minority shareholders' decision whether to accept the short-form merger consideration or seek an appraisal." 606 A.2d at 114.

c. A Comprehensive Duty of Disclosure?

It may be that the duty to disclose applies to *all* communications by fiduciaries to shareholders, regardless of whether shareholder action is required. Because the duty arises specifically out of fiduciary responsibilities to shareholders, disclosure obligations would seem to attach whenever a fiduciary discloses information to shareholders. In Marhart, Inc. v. CalMat Co., 1992 WL 82365, Fed.Sec.L.Rep. (CCH) ¶ 96,655 (Del.Ch.1992), CalMat announced in an allegedly misleading press release that it had rejected a $40 per share takeover bid because the price was inadequate and that it was engaging in a restructuring program that would make CalMat stock worth more than $40 per share. The press release allegedly was intended to encourage investors to purchase and hold CalMat stock at prices $40 per share or more. The court held that under these facts, defendant-directors had a duty to disclose all material facts, even though no shareholder action was directly solicited. The court stated that "fiduciaries who undertake the responsibility of informing stockholders about corporate affairs [are] required to do so honestly." Id. On rehearing, the court stressed that its decision did not extend the fiduciary duty of full disclosure to nonstockholders, to whom fiduciary duties do not run. 1992 WL 82365 at * 3 (Del.Ch.1992). But cf. In re Rexene Corp. Shareholders Litig., 1991 WL 77529 Fed.Sec. L.Rep. (CCH) ¶¶ 96,010, 90,059 n.1 (Del.Ch.1991), which suggests that the duty to disclose applies to all public communications, not only those distributed to stockholders.

d. "Voluntary" Disclosures

What duty does a fiduciary owe to shareholders when a vote is sought but not required or needed to accomplish a contemplated transaction? You will recall *Mills* and *Virginia Bankshares* in which proxies were solicited even though management had sufficient votes to approve the transaction without the vote of the minority shareholders. Although *Virginia Bankshares* found causation lacking under Section 14(a) of the 1934 Act in such a situation, Delaware has not yet directly addressed the question as a matter of state law. The Delaware Supreme Court has indicated, however, that a duty of full and fair disclosure arises whenever directors are either required to seek a shareholder vote or elect to do so. Stroud v. Milliken Enterprises, Inc., 552 A.2d 476, 480 (Del.1989).

In light of Delaware's seeming willingness to impose the duty to disclose when a board "voluntarily" seeks approval of a transaction by a majority of the minority shareholders, how much insulation does *Virginia Bankshares* give the board, even if no action can be brought under federal law? How realistic is the Court's concern in *Borak* that if a victim of a deceptive proxy statement were "obliged to go into state courts for remedial relief * * * [and] the law of the State happened to attach no responsibility to the use of misleading proxy statements, the whole purpose of [federal proxy regulation] might be frustrated?" For further discussion of the interrelationship between federal and state law on disclosure after *Virginia Bankshares*, see Jesse A. Finkelstein, Mark J. Gentile and J. Michael Christopher, The Potential Implications of Virginia Bankshares for Delaware Law, Insights, May 1992, 26.

3. WHO OWES THE DUTY?

Those who are in a fiduciary relationship to the shareholders owe the duty, including at least directors and controlling shareholders. The court in Lacos Land Co. v. Arden Group, 517 A.2d 271, 279 (Del.Ch. 1986) stated that, "it is, of course, well-established in our law that an element of the fiduciary duty that directors owe to shareholders is the duty, arising when the board is required or elects to seek shareholder action, to disclose fully and fairly pertinent information within the board's control." In *Lacos Land* the board solicited proxies to obtain shareholder approval of a recapitalization that would effectively place voting control in the hands of the controlling shareholder. The proxy statement led one to think that the controlling shareholder was a "restricted person" when in reality she was not. The court found that the board had violated its disclosure duty.

The duty of disclosure also applies to controlling shareholders. Kahn v. Household Acquisition Corp., 591 A.2d 166 (Del.1991). In *Kahn*, Household Acquisition Corporation ("HAC"), the controlling shareholder of Wien, attempted to merge with Wien by either having the minority approve the merger or tender their shares. The proxy statement HAC sent to the minority shareholders did not disclose that Wien had moved forward in its negotiations with the Civil Aeronautics Board regarding the amount of subsidies Wien would receive for the coming year. The court found that the controlling shareholder had a duty to disclose the information, a duty emanating from the controlling shareholder's duty of fair dealing owed to the minority shareholders.

As a general rule, those not in a fiduciary relationship with shareholders do not owe them a duty of disclosure. Zirn v. VLI Corp., 1992 WL 136450 (Del.Ch.1992) rev'd on other grounds 621 A.2d 773 (Del. 1993). The Delaware Court of Chancery held that the third party tender offeror was not responsible under the state law duty of disclosure for a misleading proxy statement sent to shareholders of a corporation it was attempting to purchase. The court noted, however, that once the third party tender offeror, here AHP, became the controlling shareholder as a result of its tender offer, the duty to disclose arose and applied to all subsequent communications by AHP. The court found, however, that AHP had not breached this duty. Additionally, corporate fiduciaries are not responsible for the failures of non-fiduciaries to disclose. In Citron v. Fairchild Camera & Instrument Corp., 569 A.2d 53 (Del.1989), a third party did not disclose allegedly "material" information in his tender offer to Fairchild. The Delaware Supreme Court upheld the Court of Chancery's finding that the Fairchild board was not legally responsible for the third party's alleged violations "absent some proof that the two * * * engaged in joint conduct to mislead the shareholders." 569 A.2d at 70.

While a person must be a corporate fiduciary in order to owe the duty to disclose, it is still possible to violate the duty vicariously under an aiding and abetting standard; thus, a third party can violate the duty if she "knowingly" helps a fiduciary violate the duty. In re Shoetown, 1990 WL 13475 (Del.Ch.1990). The non-fiduciary does not have to exert an influence over the fiduciary. In *Shoetown* the court ultimately dismissed on other grounds plaintiff's claim of a violation of the duty of disclosure by an investment banking firm that assisted management in buying out the corporation by finding a financier and preparing a fairness opinion for management. However, the court recognized that there could be liability under a "knowing" standard. It may be, as noted in the discussion of *Citron*, that corporate fiduciaries are also responsible for a third party's misleading communications under an aiding and abetting standard.

When shareholders bring suit charging breach of the duty to disclose, the corporation itself is frequently named as a defendant. Does such an action make sense as a matter of doctrine? Can the corporation per se, as opposed to its directors or controlling shareholder, owe a duty to its shareholders? Delaware courts have indicated that because a corporation *qua* corporate entity cannot stand in a fiduciary relationship to its stockholders, it cannot be liable for breach of a fiduciary duty to disclose. See In re Dataproducts Corp. Shareholders Litig., 1991 WL 165301, Fed.Sec.L.Rep. (CCH) ¶ 96,227 (Del.Ch.1991). The court went on to explain, however, that it

> [i]s not to say that a corporation owes no duty or can never be held liable under Delaware law if it promulgates false and misleading disclosures to its shareholders. Rather, it means that under Delaware law any disclosure duty owed by the corporation to its shareholders must be predicated upon a theory of legal or equitable fraud. * * * Legal (i.e., common law) fraud requires (1) a false representation (usually of fact) by the defendant, (2) the defendant's knowledge or belief that the representation was false or made with reckless indifference to the truth, (3) an intent to induce the plaintiff to act or refrain from acting, (4) the plaintiff's action or inaction taken in justifiable reliance upon the representation, and (5) damage to the plaintiff as a result of such reliance. Equitable fraud requires a showing of those same elements, except for element (2). That is, in equity the defendant does not have to know or believe that his statement was false or have acted in reckless disregard of the truth. Rather, equitable fraud can be founded upon a negligent or an innocent misrepresentation.

Id. at 91,183. See also, Gaffin v. Teledyne, Inc., 611 A.2d 467 (Del. 1992). How do the theories of legal or equitable fraud differ from the fiduciary duty to disclose material information to shareholders?

4. MATERIALITY UNDER STATE LAW

Fiduciaries must disclose "all material information." In Rosenblatt v. Getty Oil Co., 493 A.2d 929, 944 (Del.1985), the Delaware Supreme Court expressly adopted the Supreme Court's definition of materiality set forth in in *TSC, supra.* Because of language in Lynch v. Vickers and subsequent decisions to the effect that the "duty of candor" required the disclosure of all "germane" information, there was some initial confusion as to the extent to which the federal and Delaware standards were coextensive The Delaware Supreme Court resolved this confusion in *Stroud* when it emphasized that:

> [t]he term "duty of candor" does not import a unique or special rule of disclosure. It represents nothing more than the well-recognized proposition that directors of Delaware corporations are under a fiduciary duty to disclose fully and fairly all material information within the board's control when it seeks shareholder action. * * * Thus, the term "duty of candor" has no well accepted meaning in

the disclosure context. Its use is both confusing and imprecise given the well-established principles and duties of disclosure that otherwise exist. Thus, it is more appropriate for our courts to speak of a duty of disclosure based on a materiality standard rather than the unhelpful language that has crept into Delaware court decisions as a "duty of candor." This is entirely consistent with our prior statements of Delaware law regarding the duty and standard of disclosure.

606 A.2d at 84.

In determining whether a fiduciary's omission of information or false statement in a disclosure is material, whether the directors acted in good faith appears to be irrelevant. In Shell Petroleum, Inc. v. Smith, 606 A.2d 112 (Del.1992), the controlling shareholder released erroneous information to the shareholders concerning the value of the corporation. Although the error was inadvertent, the court nonetheless held the controlling shareholder liable for the omission because it controlled the preparation of the materials and thus had constructive knowledge of the error. "It is only logical that a majority shareholder who directs a subsidiary to prepare certain disclosure materials and then distributes those materials to minority shareholders should be held accountable for any errors contained therein." 606 A.2d at 116.

In effect, fiduciaries are held to a standard of strict liability for violations of the duty to disclose: they are liable for its breach whether or not they are acting in good faith. How is the business judgement rule for director decisions affected by what approaches a strict liability disclosure standard? In In re Anderson, Clayton Shareholders Litig., 519 A.2d 669 (Del.Ch.1986), the court held that:

> [T]he question whether shareholders have, under the circumstances, been provided with appropriate information upon which an informed choice on a matter of fundamental corporate importance may be made, is not a decision concerning the management of business and affairs of the enterprise (8 Del.C. § 141(a)) of the kind the business judgement rule is intended to protect; it is rather a matter relating to the directors' duty to shareholders who are technically outside the corporation.

519 A.2d at 675.

Although the Delaware and federal definitions of materiality are the same, it is not clear that the different courts would apply them identically. See J. Robert Brown, Jr., The Regulation of Corporate Disclosure, pp. 278.21–22 (1993 Supp.).

Chapter 19

REGULATION OF SECURITIES TRADING

We study the regulation of securities trading in a corporations course for at least two reasons. Securities trading often involves corporate management and thus necessarily involves the fiduciary duties we have studied previously; securities trading also affects the market for a corporation's stock and thus implicates the corporation's relationship with actual and potential investors. In this chapter we will consider some of the legal problems associated with securities transactions taking place in the public trading markets. Federal law, particularly the Securities Exchange Act of 1934, is the most important source of the rules governing these transactions. State law also may apply, and knowledge of state law is important in any event to understand federal law. Before studying these subjects, however, it is useful to review how securities markets operate, the significance of information to those markets and how the two are linked.

A. INTRODUCTION TO SECURITIES TRADING

There are two types of organized securities markets: stock exchanges and the over-the-counter (OTC) market. A stock exchange has a physical central marketplace, the "floor" of the exchange, where a limited number of broker-dealers who are members of the exchange buy and sell securities that are listed on the exchange ("listed securities") for the accounts of their customers and for their own accounts. The principal exchanges are the New York Stock Exchange and the American Stock Exchange; several regional exchanges mostly handle trades in the shares of smaller companies.

An investor who wishes to buy or sell listed securities places an order with a broker which, if it is a member of an exchange on which the issue is traded, will handle the transaction itself; otherwise the broker will forward the order to a firm that is an exchange member. The commission broker that handles the execution of the order sends it to a floor trader who is physically present on the floor of the exchange. The floor trader goes to the place on the floor at which the security is traded (the "post") where the order is executed. At the post are always a number of other floor traders (the "crowd") and a "specialist" who is required to maintain a continuous market in the security. The specialist trades both for her own account (in which case she is acting as a "dealer") and for the accounts of others who have given her orders to execute (in which case she is acting as a "broker"). The specialist's role is an important one; her market-making furnishes liquidity in the trading of the security, permitting easier matching of buy and sell orders and causing the price of the stock to move more smoothly.

There are two principal types of customers' orders: "limit orders" and "market orders." The former direct the broker to buy or sell at a particular price. The latter call for a trade at the prevailing price. When a market order is brought to the post it is executed immediately at the prevailing market price. It may be matched with a countervailing order held by another broker in the crowd, or, if there is no such order, it will be accepted by the specialist either for her own account or carrying out a limit order. The specialist maintains a limit order book to keep track of limit orders left with her by brokers who cannot always be continuously present at one post.

The OTC market consists of a network of telephone lines and a computerized quotation system through which broker-dealers trade in securities that are, for the most part, not listed on an exchange. One or more broker-dealers may make a market in a given OTC security by giving continuous quotations of prices at which they will buy and sell. Thus the price of an OTC security is usually given in the form "20 bid, 20½ asked." That is, the market-maker is offering to buy a reasonable number of shares for $20 per share and to sell a reasonable number at $20.50 per share. (The difference between the bid and asked prices may vary, but it is usually under $1.) These quotations are communicated to other broker-dealers either through the National Association of Securities Dealers Automated Quotation System (NASDAQ), a computerized network that furnishes continuous quotations, or through printed "sheets" that are revised daily. There may be no market-maker for lightly traded securities; for more heavily-traded issues there may be several.

Like the specialist in the exchanges, a market-maker provides liquidity for a security. The degree of liquidity depends on the number of shares, on balance, bought or sold, the size of the market-maker's spread (that is, the difference between the bid and asked prices), and the effect of the market-maker's transactions on succeeding quotations and transactions.

Transactions in the OTC market are usually negotiated and consummated by telephone, not on the floor of an exchange. A broker-dealer may act as a broker for its customer on an agency basis and negotiate with the market-maker offering the best price quotation in a relevant stock. A broker-dealer may also act as a dealer (principal) and match public orders from its own inventory. In confirming a transaction, a broker-dealer will state whether it acted as a broker or a dealer. The name of the person or entity from whom the market-maker or the dealer acquired the shares is not indicated. Transactions on stock exchanges or on the OTC market, therefore, are faceless transactions.

B. ECONOMIC THEORY, THE SECURITIES MARKETS AND SECURITIES TRANSACTIONS

1. THE EFFICIENT CAPITAL MARKET HYPOTHESIS

One question central to the entire functioning of the securities markets is whether it is possible on a systematic basis to make money through investing in those markets. Certainly enough time, effort and money is devoted to discovering new information about corporations in an attempt to do so. The following excerpt discusses an economic model which suggests that it is very difficult for investors systematically to outperform the market.

a. *The Efficient Capital Market Hypothesis (ECMH): What It Is*

CHRISTOPHER PAUL SAARI, NOTE, THE EFFICIENT CAPITAL MARKET HYPOTHESIS, ECONOMIC THEORY AND THE REGULATION OF THE SECURITIES INDUSTRY
29 Stan.L.Rev. 1031, 1035–1040 (1977).

The statement that security prices fully reflect available information—which is to say that capital markets are efficient—is of great significance in two respects. On a societal level, it implies that the market uses all available information to allocate resources. Capital will flow to the most profitable investments which, in a market economy, are reflections of society's values. Market efficiency at the same time is significant to the individual investor. Under conditions of efficiency, no investor, using only information also generally available to other investors, can systematically identify and acquire undervalued (or overvalued) securities.

Despite its significance as a general assertion, the statement that security prices fully reflect available information is not sufficiently precise as such to be empirically tested and verified. To provide an empirically testable assertion, three factors must be specified with particularity: the determinants of security values, the processes of security price formation and the characteristics of prices that "fully reflect" available information.

Investors may purchase assets, including securities, for many reasons. Nothing theoretically compels investors to value assets by any particular method. Thus, assumptions must be made about investor behavior to develop any theory of asset valuation. Economists often hypothesize that investors value assets according to the future monetary rewards—or "expected returns"—associated with those assets, after adjusting for "risk," the degree of certainty with which the expected returns can be predicted. Based on this assumption, economists have developed what is known as portfolio theory, which can be combined with other economic theory to explain price determination in capital markets. The implications of portfolio theory for security price determination combined with the ECMH assertion that prices fully reflect all available information yield the proposition that, in an efficient market, all available information is used to determine expected returns on securities, and therefore to establish security prices. If all available information is incorporated into security prices, investors cannot use available information to identify mispriced securities. Prices that reflect all available information are sometimes referred to as "fair game prices."

If securities markets operate in accordance with the ECMH, securities prices are such that the expected returns are equal for all securities having the same degree of risk. The *realized* returns on all securities in the same risk category need not be equal; realized returns may and will vary. Nevertheless, *ex ante,* all securities in the same risk category have the same chances of gain or loss; their *expected* returns are equal.

The ECMH and the theory of security price movement just articulated imply two salient characteristics of security prices in efficient markets: first, prices adjust rapidly and without bias to new information, and second, prices move randomly. If price adjustments to new information were not rapid and without bias, intertemporal security price movements would exhibit trends upon which astute market observers could profit. If adjustments were gradual, security prices would not reflect fully all available information because during the adjustment process the prices would not reflect fully the information implicit in the price adjustment itself. Similarly, if price adjustments to new information exhibited bias, that is, a systematic pattern of overadjustment or underadjustment to new information, investors could trade advantageously on such biased adjustments to earn above average returns.

Random movements of security prices, a second characteristic of market efficiency, is similarly essential to the ECMH. If security prices did not move randomly, an investor aware of systematic price movements could use that information to generate above average returns through propitious trading. The random characteristic of security price movements in an efficient market has been the subject not only of logical argument but also of mathematical proof.

b. Levels of Market Efficiency

An important conclusion flowing from the ECMH is that neither information describing a security's past prices nor information concerning the financial well-being of a corporation is likely to help an investor determine which securities are over or undervalued. In short, the ECMH leads to the conclusion that a security's market price is the best estimate of that security's value, based on all available information relating to that security. One frequently debated question, discussed in the following excerpt, is whether stock markets efficiently incorporate all information, including nonpublic or "inside" information, into the market price of a security. The answer to this question is of obvious importance in considering what, if anything, should be done about insider trading. Specifically, if inside information is accurately reflected in the market price of a security, even an insider trading on the basis of such information would be unable consistently to achieve extraordinary returns and there might be no reason to regulate such trading.

JAMES D. COX, FINANCIAL INFORMATION, ACCOUNTING AND THE LAW
181, 183–188 (1980).

The different forms or levels of market efficiency are distinguished by the kinds of information that equilibrium market prices are hypothesized to fully reflect. The weak form of the hypothesis states that prices fully reflect all information contained in the historical pattern of market prices. The semi-strong form states that prices reflect all public information, including that in financial statements. The strong form states that prices fully reflect all information, including nonpublic or "inside" information. There is no significant empirical evidence that contradicts the weak form of the hypothesis that is not subject to substantive criticism about methodology. Some evidence appears to contradict the semi-strong form, but it is not yet clear whether the results are valid contradictions or whether they stem from flaws in the research. Many observers agree that existing evidence confirms that market prices fully reflect all information that is publicly available—that is, that the New York Stock Exchange is efficient in the weak and semi-strong forms. Evidence on the other markets (American Stock Exchange, Over-the-Counter) is less complete, but the evidence available suggests that those markets are also efficient at the semi-strong level.

On the other hand, capital market efficiency to the extent of public information is not universally accepted. In part, it is rejected because it contradicts traditional views. The hypothesis does not reflect the experience of some investors and analysts who have earned excess returns and do not accept the explanation that such results can occur in an efficient market because of insider information or simply through good fortune. And, in part, it reflects the fact that the theory and its implications are not fully understood because it is both new and complex. Thus, a large fraction of the investment community ignores the hypothesis and the related research and continues to seek excess returns (returns significantly higher than those available on a market-based portfolio of comparable risk) as in the past. In general, those who are disposed to accept the hypothesis find all of the support they need in existing evidence, while those who reject it also find support for their beliefs.

The weak form of market efficiency has been investigated by the study of the interrelationships of successive price changes for individual securities. The research has been fairly consistent in finding that successive price changes are independent of one another, i.e., they are randomly distributed, so that a stock's future price cannot be extrapolated from only its past price changes. Evidence that all stock price changes follow a random walk, however, is not inconsistent with the belief that stocks have an intrinsic value and that their value responds to financially significant events or information. A logical explanation of why stock prices follow a random walk is that the stock prices quickly impound successive pieces of new information as they become available (i.e., the stock's price is increased/decreased by the effect the information has on investor behavior). If stock prices responded slowly to new information, it would be expected that stock price changes would be dependent not independent. Such bits of information change daily and are independently related. Hence, the stock price changes which mirror the information changes can also be expected to be independent of one another.

To document the theorem that stock prices are random because publicly available information changes daily, requires an association of stock prices and information to be established. A finding that stock price changes are associated with the release of new information and that such response occurs rapidly is consistent with the conditions that should be present if security markets are efficient in the semi-strong form. The only way the empiricist can determine whether securities markets are efficient in the semi-strong form is to investigate whether conditions consistent with a market which is efficient in the semi-strong form exist.

Evidence supporting the semi-strong form of market efficiency is found in the empirical research of stock price changes in response to earnings and dividend announcements. The semi-strong form of market efficiency holds that all public information is impounded rapidly in a stock's price, so that an extraordinary return can not be made by analysis of public information. The researcher, therefore, is interested in whether stock prices do respond to financially significant information as well as how rapidly they respond.

The initial research of the semi-strong form of market efficiency entailed the reaction of stock prices to annual earnings announcements. At first glance this may appear to be documenting the obvious. The studies are important because they offer significant proof that the annual earnings report prepared according to generally accepted accounting principles are indeed used by investors (an assumption challenged by those who believe accounting information to be largely irrelevant). Furthermore, the studies offer invaluable insight into stock price behavior.

Professors Ball and Brown found that stock prices anticipate favorable and unfavorable annual earnings as early as 12 months before the earnings are publicly announced. A finding that substantial price changes occur before the annual report is consistent with the semi-strong form of market efficiency. It demonstrates that alternative sources of information exist, such as quarterly reports, press releases, and the like, which are used by investors to supplement the annual report in assessing the company's stock. Professors Ball and Brown concluded that no more than 10–15% of the information in the annual earnings announcement has not been anticipated by the month of the announcement.

Professor Beaver in a more detailed investigation of the relationship of stock prices and the annual earnings announcement also found that stock prices did anticipate by many months the earnings ultimately announced for the year. However, he found the greatest price change occurred during the week the annual earnings were announced. In view of the magnitude of the price change during the week the earnings were announced, he concluded that, although the investors' judgments were found to forecast yearly earnings using information from a variety of sources, they were not very efficient predictors of the earnings ultimately announced.

If investors were efficient forecasters, the significant price change during the week of the earnings announcement would not have occurred. Studies of cash and stock dividends, as well as quarterly reports, have further documented that stock prices anticipate by many months favorable and unfavorable information. Furthermore, the studies have shown that within a few days following announcement of a dividend the stock's price fully impounds the information so that an extraordinary return can no longer be made using the publicly announced information. Therefore, conditions consistent with the semi-strong form of market efficiency appear to exist. Stock prices respond to financially significant information, the response occurs rapidly, and following public announcement it is no longer possible to make an extraordinary return on the basis of such publicly available information.

* * *

The final form of market efficiency is the *strong form* which holds that all information, public *and nonpublic,* is impounded in a security's price so that no abnormal returns are available, even upon inside information. Although the research investigating the strong form of market efficiency is not nearly as extensive as that for the weak or semi-strong forms, preliminary indications are that securities markets are not efficient in the strong form.

The strong form of market efficiency is counter to the popular belief that corporate insiders enrich themselves by frequently trading in their corporation's stock before release of news affecting the stock's price. An outgrowth of this sentiment is § 16 of the Securities Exchange Act of

1934 which requires insiders of most large corporations to report trading activities in their corporation's stock. Insiders are defined in § 16 as officers, directors, or owners of more than 10% of that corporation's equity securities.

Professors Lorie and Neiderhoffer studied the insider trading reports compelled by § 16 to determine whether insiders in fact were able to outperform the market. They concluded that insiders were superior forecasters of large changes in the price of their corporation's stock. For example, following an insider's purchase, the odds in favor of a large increase in a stock's price were about 2.5:1. The insiders' superior ability to capture an abnormal return is apparently explained solely by their possession of nonpublic information, a conclusion inconsistent with the strong form of market efficiency.

Further evidence inconsistent with the strong form of market efficiency is the study by Professor Collins of the trading advantages afforded by nonpublic information. In 1970 the SEC required registered corporations with more than one product line to disclose the profits and sales of each product line. The prior practice was that sales and profits of all the product lines were consolidated. Knowledge of the operations of individual product lines enables the analyst to more accurately project future operations. The requirement was made retroactive for the years 1967–1969. Collins investigated whether an abnormal return could have been earned during 1967–1969 if an investor had exclusive access to the product line information for those years. He concluded that knowledge of this nonpublic information would have yielded an abnormal return. After 1970, when this information was public, superior trading results were no longer possible by the use of the sales and profits of each product line. Therefore, the market was efficient with respect to public information, but not for nonpublic information.

c. Critique of the ECMH

A number of scholars have begun to question whether the ECMH accurately describes the way in which the stock market functions. Indeed, Professor (and Nobel laureate) James Tobin has suggested that there are, in fact, two types of market efficiency. He calls the semi-strong version of the ECMH "information-arbitrage" efficiency and essentially accepts that the market is efficient in that sense. On the other hand, he notes that stock prices should reflect the discounted present value of future dividends and other payouts. A market which reflected such values would be "fundamental-valuation" efficient. James Tobin argues that efficiency in this latter sense "is by no means implied by the * * * efficiency [reflecting all public information] * * * There are good reasons to be skeptical." James Tobin, On the Efficiency of the Financial System, 153 Lloyds Bank Rev. 1 (1984).

Professor Wang builds on Professor Tobin's analysis and argues that the market may not be fully efficient in either sense. William K. S. Wang, Some Arguments That the Stock Market Is Not Efficient, 19 U.C.Davis L.Rev. 341 (1986) ("Wang"). In support of his argument,

Wang points to some convertible securities which sell at their conversion value without reflecting any premium for conversion. He also notes that, contrary to expectation, some packages of dual purpose mutual fund shares sell below their net asset value. Looking at other evidence, Professor Lowenstein reaches the same conclusion as Wang. Louis Lowenstein, Pruning Deadwood in Hostile Takeovers: A Proposal for Legislation, 83 Colum.L.Rev. 249 (1986). Lowenstein notes that the premiums paid in going private transactions and leveraged buyouts (see Chapters 21 and 23) indicate that the market undervalued the shares being purchased. He also points to the takeovers of natural resource companies whose reserves were undervalued by the stock market. For a critique of the use of the ECMH in a variety of corporate law contexts see generally Louis Lowenstein, What's Wrong With Wall Street (1988).

Scholars have further developed the critique of the stock market's ability to properly account for a company's assets when pricing shares. Professor Kraakman notes that critiques of share pricing generally fall into one of two categories. Some question whether a single valuation model should apply to the markets for firms and shares, since each market may discount asset values differently depending on the interests at stake. For example, shareholders and traders may place a different value on a firm's liquid assets depending on the importance each places on liquidity. Others pose the theory that stock prices often reflect persistent biases from uninformed traders, such as misconceived strategies, fads and erroneous valuation assumptions. Renier Kraakman, Taking Discounts Seriously: The Implications of "Discounted" Share Prices as an Acquisition Motive, 88 Colum.L.Rev. 891, 898–901 (1988).

The theory underpinning the second category of arguments generally is identified as "noise" theory. Noise theorists assert that stock markets are infected by a substantial amount of trading based on information unrelated to fundamental asset values. The popularity of the noise theory, as well as other factors, lead Professor Langevoort, among others, to question the validity of the ECMH. Donald C. Langevoort, Theories, Assumptions, and Securities Regulation: Market Efficiency Revisited, 140 U.Pa.L.Rev. 851, 866–72 (1992). Langevoort notes that the origins of the noise theory go back to Keynes, who hypothesized that investors were more concerned with owning shares others felt was the best, rather than owning the stock they thought was the best. The most prominent noise theorist today is Robert J. Schiller, who believes that investors rely on many sub-optimal considerations when purchasing stocks. Much of this results from investors who have neither the capacity nor the desire to utilize the available information in making investment decisions. As a result, rumors and fads are disseminated widely and lead to inefficient decisions made on hunches and emotions. See generally, Robert J. Schiller, Market Volatility (1989).

Other economists question how great an effect irrational investors actually have on the market. While most accept the idea that some "noise" does affect stock prices, they feel that its impact is mainly short-term. For the most part, economists maintain that there are many informed investors who take advantage of the arbitrage opportunities caused by sub-optimal behavior, and, in the end, efficiency prevails most of the time. Burton G. Malkiel, A Random Walk Down Wall Street, 210–211 (5th ed. 1990). However, two well-respected economists hypothesize that arbitrage is risky and limited and, therefore, does not fully counter noisy behavior. See Andrei Shleifer and Lawrence H. Summers, The Noise Trader Approach to Finance, 4 J.Econ.Persp. 19 (Spring 1990).

Other studies challenging the validity of the ECMH have come from financial analysts and economists. Perhaps the most famous of these studies is one which demonstrated that an investor who followed the Value Line Investor Survey ranking system could achieve above-normal returns. Fischer Black, Yes, Virginia, There Is Hope: Tests of the Value Line Ranking System, 29 Fin.Analysts J. 10 (1973) (but see "Paying the Piper," Forbes, October 19, 1987, 208, suggesting that actual results would not be as successful because of timing problems and transaction costs).

Perhaps one reason why there is so much criticism of the ECMH is that if the ECMH is valid, much of the effort expended by investment analysts would be worthless. Or, as Wang has put it, "[i]f the pure form of the semi-strong hypothesis were correct, one would have to conclude that the market for investment research was extremely inefficient." Wang, supra at 375.

Without deciding that question, a better reason for examining the ECMH closely is that we do not fully understand the process by which the market *becomes* efficient. Moreover, there is increasing reason to believe that this process is not uniform for every security. Indeed, because there are different speeds for processing different types of information, there may be momentary inefficiencies in the market for any given security during which investors have the opportunity to realize above-average returns. For most investors, however, the difficulty arises in identifying *ex ante* the securities in which such inefficiencies exist.

The validity of the ECMH has taken on greater significance because of the role it has assumed in financial economics and the regulation of the securities markets. As Professors Gilson and Kraakman observe in an important article on the nature of market efficiency:

> "Of all recent developments in financial economics, the efficient market hypothesis * * * has achieved the widest acceptance by the legal culture. It now commonly informs the academic literature on a variety of topics; it is addressed by major law school casebooks and textbooks on business law; it structures debate over the future of securities regulation both within and without the Securities and Exchange Commission; it has served as the intellectual premise for a major revision of the disclosure system administered by the Commission; and it has even begun to influence judicial decisions and the actual practice of law. In short, the ECMH is now the

context in which serious discussion of the regulation of financial markets takes place."

Ronald Gilson & Renier Kraakman, The Mechanisms of Market Efficiency, 70 Va.L.Rev. 549, 549–50 (1984).

In Basic Inc. v. Levinson, 485 U.S. 224, 108 S.Ct. 978, 99 L.Ed.2d 194 (1988), the Supreme Court relied on the efficient capital market hypothesis to support a presumption that investors rely on the efficiency of market prices when they purchase stock. The majority commented, "Recent empirical studies have tended to confirm Congress' premise that market price of shares traded on well developed market reflects all publicly available information, and hence, any material misrepresentations." (485 U.S. at 246, 108 S.Ct. 991). The Court stopped short of endorsing the empirical studies; instead it took a sort of judicial notice of the behavior of market professionals and its effect on prices:

> "We need not determine by adjudication what economists and social scientists have debated through the use of sophisticated statistical analysis and the application of economic theory. For purposes of accepting the presumption of reliance in this case, we need only believe that market professionals generally consider most publicly announced material statements about companies, thereby affecting stock market prices." Id.

The dissenters in *Basic* objected to the novelty of the underlying economic theory. They argued, "Confusion and contradiction in court rulings are inevitable when traditional legal analysis is replaced with economic theorization by the federal courts." 485 U.S. at 252, 108 S.Ct. at 994.

The dissenters also challenged the Court's as well as lower courts' competence to adopt an economic theory supporting the fraud on the market theory, believing that a task for Congress:

> "But with no staff economists, no experts schooled in the 'efficient-capital-market-hypothesis,' no ability to test the validity of empirical market studies, we are not well equipped to embrace novel constructions of a statute based on contemporary microeconomic theory. * * * The Congress, with its superior resources and expertise, is far better equipped than the federal courts for the task of determining how modern economic theory and global financial markets require that established legal notions of fraud be modified." 485 U.S. at 253–254, 108 S.Ct. at 994–995.

This leads to the question of whether market efficiency should be the goal of securities regulation. In analyzing market efficiency, be aware of two aspects of a efficiency: 1) informational efficiency which is related to the speed with which stock prices adjust to new information and 2) allocational efficiency which focuses on the allocation of resources to their best use. Professor Stout argues that market efficiency should be abandoned as a goal of securities regulation, mainly because she believes that stock markets are not allocatively efficient. She bases her conclusion on evidence of mispricing which often occurs in public offerings, the limited influence of secondary stock market prices on the proceeds received by corporations making equity offerings, and the general unimportance of equity as a source of corporate capital. She further argues that if the market is not allocationally efficient, then it is socially wasteful to absorb the high cost of informational efficiency, and the pursuit of the efficient market should be abandoned. Lynn Stout, The Unimportance of Being Efficient: An Economic Analysis of Stock Market Pricing and Securities Regulation, 87 Mich.L.Rev. 613 (1988). But see John C. Coffee, Jr., Market Failure and the Economic Case for a Mandatory Disclosure System, 70 Va.L.Rev. 717, 725–33 (1984) who asserts that the SEC's mandatory disclosure system provides a low cost method of correcting the market's failure to provide adequate information regarding securities and serves as a means of economizing on information costs.

Professor Langevoort argues that the SEC has used the ECMH as a facade for its disclosure initiatives. For the most part, Langevoort feels that the ECMH is used to buttress the point that markets are informationally efficient in a broad sense, a point he believes is highly uncontroversial. However, the continued use of ECMH rhetoric by the courts and the SEC may lend more weight to the theory than is deserved, especially in light of its many critics. This, Langevoort fears, may lead to an overconfidence in the ECMH, which may lead to a quelling of other ideas, such as the noise theory, which may be worth examining. Donald C. Langevoort, Theories, Assumptions, and Securities Regulation: Market Efficiency Revisited, 140 U.Pa.L.Rev. 851, 886–920 (1992).

2. AN OVERVIEW OF THE ISSUES

This chapter deals mainly with insider trading and its impact on market efficiency. The paradigm case of insider trading is simple: the president of a large corporation whose stock is traded on the New York Stock Exchange learns that the corporation has just made a major technological breakthrough which will revolutionize the industry, and produce substantially greater earnings than previously had been expected. Before the corporation discloses this information, the president purchases a large block of stock on the New York Stock Exchange at the then prevailing market price. Immediately after disclosure, the stock price rises sharply and remains at the higher level. You will read a great deal about the law regulating the president's conduct (and variations on that conduct which implicate other actors). Before assessing the judicial and legislative responses to this conduct and without regard to what the law is or should be, consider the following questions and the readings which shed light on them.

1. Who is hurt by the president's purchases?

    a. The person who sold the stock to the president.

    b. All the stockholders in the corporation.

    c. The corporation itself.

    d. The "market."

  2. If there was harm, how did it occur?

    a. Through the president's purchase.

    b. Through the corporation's non-disclosure.

    c. Through the combination of these.

  3. If the president must pay damages, who should recover?

    a. The person who sold the stock to the president.

    b. All those who sold stock at or about the same time the president purchased.

    c. All those who sold stock from the time the president purchased to the time the corporation disclosed the discovery.

    d. The corporation.

  4. How much should the president pay in damages?

    a. The amount of the profit he realized (but suppose he still owns the stock?).

    b. The amount of the losses suffered by those who were harmed (how are those losses to be measured?).

    c. An amount sufficient to deter others from engaging in the same type of conduct.

3. ECONOMIC THEORY AND INSIDER TRADING

For many years, there was little debate over the foregoing questions; courts, the S.E.C. and commentators all generally condemned insider trading. Although Henry Manne's defense of the practice in his book, Insider Trading and the Stock Market (1966) ("Manne"), sparked some discussion in the late 1960's, little scholarly analysis explored the phenomenon in depth.* To many people, insider trading resembled playing cards with a marked deck; little attention was paid to the precise nature of the cheating. Although most writers still oppose insider trading, some recent scholars, particularly those who bring the "law and economics" perspective to the question, have argued that insider trading is beneficial to investors and to the market and should not be prohibited. Their arguments, while not generally accepted, have led to a scholarly re-examination of many conclusions which had previously seemed axiomatic and a questioning of premises which had appeared to be self-evident. Although the wave of insider trading scandals of the late 1980s changed the atmosphere in which this debate occurred, the theoretical underpinnings of the debate are still significant in assessing the regulatory structure of insider trading.

Harm to Investors from Insider Trading. At first blush, it seems simple to identify what is wrong with insider trading and who is hurt by

---

* See Roy A. Schotland, Unsafe at any Price: A Reply to Manne, Insider Trading and the Stock Market, 53 Va.L.Rev. 1425 (1966), Henry G. Manne, Insider Trading and the Law Professors, 23 Vand.L.Rev. 547 (1970).

it. It is unfair to permit insiders who have an informational advantage which other investors cannot overcome to benefit personally from that advantage, particularly when the information has been generated for a corporate purpose rather than for their own individual gain. Thus, when an investor enters the market, it would seem axiomatic that he would be harmed by a trade with someone who had inside information. The insider knows the real value of the stock, and can exploit this information when trading with an outsider. See Victor Brudney, Insiders, Outsiders, and Informational Advantages Under the Federal Securities Laws, 93 Harv.L.Rev. 322, 356–57 (1979).

Closer analysis reveals certain problems with this intuitive argument. Trading in the securities of publicly-held companies does not occur in face-to-face transactions. Rather, it occurs in anonymous markets where buyers and sellers are randomly matched with each other. Moreover, as Professor Cox has noted: "Insider trading is at most a fortuity for the investor because the investor is no worse off when the insider trades than when the insider does not trade. The investor's decision to sell or purchase is unaffected by whether the insider is also secretly buying or selling shares in the open market. If the insider neither trades nor discloses his confidential material information, one can nevertheless expect the investor to pursue his trading plan. Sellers naturally are disadvantaged by the nondisclosure of good news, just as buyers are disadvantaged by the nondisclosure of bad news. These considerations, however, cast no light on why the insider's decision to trade should prompt disclosure." James D. Cox, Insider Trading and Contracting: A Critical Response to the "Chicago School," 1986 Duke L.J. 628, 635 (1986) ("Cox"). Notwithstanding this criticism, the intuitive argument remains popular. See James Brooks, The Takeover Game, 316–17 (1987).

Among the more innovative theories of the harm from insider trading is that of Professor Wang, whose analysis is based on a phenomenon which he calls "The Law of Conservation of Securities." William K. S. Wang, Trading on Material, Non Public Information on Impersonal Markets: Who is Harmed, and Who Can Sue Whom Under SEC Rule 10b–5?, 54 S.Cal.L.Rev. 1217 (1981). Wang argues that insider trading harms specific individuals, although the investors who trade with insiders are not necessarily the people who are harmed. He maintains that the insider's trades preempt (and thereby injure) those who would otherwise have been able to trade the shares acquired or sold by the insider. He further contends that an insider may also cause injury by inducing trades that otherwise would not have occurred without his participation in the market. Under Wang's analysis, investors who are induced to sell are harmed because they fail to realize the price increase that results from the subsequent announcement of good news. Similarly, investors who are induced to buy, suffer a price decrease when bad news is ultimately disclosed. Id. at 1234–35.

Under Wang's theory, disclosure will not always prevent potential victims from being harmed. Wang argues that disclosure prevents harm to induced traders but does not protect the preempted trader because the latter's transaction might otherwise have been precluded by new transactions at prices reflecting the disclosure. In short, public disclosure improves the position of one type of potential victim but not the other. Id. at 1252.

Like other theories, Wang's argument is valid only if the insider's trading significantly increases the trading activity in the stock. And, as Professor Cox has noted, even in such a case, "the harm in the preempted price situation is likely to be small; in the increased trading situation, the insider's trading causes the parallel trader to dispose of a dog or acquire a pearl." Cox, supra, at 635, n. 33.

Delayed Disclosure. Many writers argue that one consequence of legalizing insider trading is that it will interfere with the market's allocational efficiency because insiders will delay disclosure of material information so that they can benefit from it prior to public disclosure. Professor Haft also notes that because information flows up the corporate ladder through many stages, the possibility of delay is magnified as those at each stage take advantage of it before passing it along. Robert J. Haft, The Effect of Insider Trading Rules on the Internal Efficiency of the Large Corporation, 80 Mich.L.Rev. 1051 (1982).

The extent to which disclosure will be delayed may turn on whether the undisclosed information is good news or bad news. Professor Scott argues that insiders who can profit from delayed disclosure have more incentive to cause the corporation to disclose information when the information is positive than when it is negative. Positive news about the firm benefits all stockholders, including the insiders, so that insiders will be anxious to profit from it, whereas they can delay the impact of negative news by simply not trading. Scott believes that the price movements which ordinarily signal the market that undisclosed information is present and which are said to dampen price shocks when that information is ultimately released do not occur in the case of bad news. He therefore concludes that a regime which allows insider trading encourages prompt disclosure of good news and, in the case of bad news, permits at least some information to reach the market sooner than it would have if such trading were banned. Kenneth E. Scott, Insider Trading: Rule 10b–5, Disclosure and Corporate Privacy, 9 J. Legal Stud. 801, 810–11 (1980).

Judge (formerly Professor) Easterbrook agrees in principle that insider trading allows some types of information to reach the market but disagrees with Scott's argument that a firm's incentive to disclose depends on whether the news is positive or negative. Instead, he contends that firms need to be credible in communicating to investors and that this credibility is furthered only if the firm promptly releases bad news along with the good. Frank H. Easterbrook, Insider Trading, Secret Agents, Evidentiary Privileges, and the Production of Information, 1981 Sup.Ct.Rev. 309, 327 (1981) ("Easterbrook").

One response to Easterbrook's argument might be that because prohibiting insider trading reduces the ability of insiders to profit on favorable developments, the prohibition may also diminish incentives to communicate all information to investors. Scott, supra, at 813. This diminished incentive would bring a concomitant reduction in the likelihood that the corporation would release any information to securities analysts, whose livelihood depends on assembling and organizing information for their clients. Because the analysts' information-gathering process enhances the efficiency of the market, prohibiting insider trading would reduce that efficiency. Michael P. Dooley, Enforcement of Insider Trading Restrictions, 66 Va.L.Rev. 1 (1980).

Portfolio Theory and the Cost of Capital. Another series of arguments against insider trading is based on portfolio theory. Because insider trading occurs randomly, investors do not know *ex ante* which firms will have material inside information or which firm's insiders will trade on that information. Because investors cannot make such distinctions accurately, and because they believe that insider trading is harmful, they must assume that every investment presents the same risk of insider trading as does the market as a whole. Accordingly, while some investors will refrain completely from investing, most will discount the value of any individual firm by the average agency costs of all firms. The consequence of such discounting is that the risk of insider trading, while seemingly non-systemic (i.e., related to a specific company or industry and thus capable of being protected against through portfolio diversification) is in fact systemic (i.e., inherent in every security). Because the risk is systematic, diversification cannot reduce it; indeed, increased diversification will simply guarantee that the investor's risk is that of the entire market.

If this theory is correct, an investor is not harmed by insider trading because he can self-insure against such behavior by discounting all stocks by the risk of such trading for all firms. This discounting protects him in his inability to distinguish firms in which insider trading occurs from those in which it does not. And if his portfolio is efficiently diversified, his losses from insider trading will be offset by increased returns in corporations where such trading does not occur, even though the investor could not have known in advance which firms would fall into each category.

The consequence of the foregoing argument is that insider trading will harm firms rather than investors because it will increase their cost of capital by the amount that investors discount the price of their securities. To reduce this discount, firms may seek to incur bonding and monitoring costs (see Chapter 12) which will enable them to signal investors that they have a lower likelihood of insider trading. However, as we have previously seen, despite such efforts, it is impossible to eliminate insider trading completely because it will not be economical for a firm to do so at any cost. Thus, if firms cannot engage in meaningful signaling, investors will not distinguish among firms on the basis of whether insider trading occurs and will continue discounting the price they pay for their investments.

Professors Carlton and Fischel reject the argument that investors prefer to invest in companies that forbid insider trading. They argue that if investors had such a preference, a competitive market for capital would lead firms to ban such trading so that they could signal investors that they had reduced their agency costs. Carlton and Fischel conclude that the absence of widespread efforts by firms to prohibit insider trading through employment contracts or corporate charters suggests either that investors are indifferent to such trading or, in some circumstances, they may believe it is beneficial. Dennis W. Carlton & Daniel R. Fischel, The Regulation of Insider Trading, 35 Stan.L.Rev. 857, 858 (1983) ("Carlton & Fischel").

Judge Posner is doubtful. He notes the high costs of enforcing any prohibition and the many opportunities to evade such a ban and concludes that these, as well as "the more fundamental one that insider trading is inherently easy to conceal may explain why corporations have made little effort on their own to ban the practice, leaving this function to public regulation instead * * * [i]f the probability of detection is so low that heavy penalties * * * would be necessary to curtail the practice, it might not pay companies to try to curtail it." Richard A. Posner, Economic Analysis of the Law, 418 (4th Ed. 1992) ("Posner"). See, also, Easterbrook, supra at 333–34.

Effect of Insider Trading on Stock Prices. Perhaps the most strongly held view in support of insider trading is that it will permit smoother changes in stock prices until the stock reaches its equilibrium price after the inside information has been publicly disclosed. Manne, supra, at 78–104. To the extent that insider trading affects stock prices, those who trade with the insider will sell at higher prices on good news or purchase at a lower price on bad news than if the insider had not traded. Moreover, not all information is in a form which is immediately communicable to the market; in those situations, increased trading volume attributable to insider trading signals the market that there is undisclosed information which is not being reflected in the share price. In some cases, this information may be confidential information that a firm would otherwise not wish to disclose to its competitors; insider trading conveys at least some of this information to the market. Carlton & Fischel, supra, at 879. Similarly, where other market participants are able to determine that insider trading is occurring, additional information may be conveyed to the market. Frank H. Easterbrook & Daniel R. Fischel, The Economic Structure of Corporate Law 256–57 (1991) ("Easterbrook & Fischel").

In light of the pervasiveness of this argument, it is surprising that there has been relatively little attempt to challenge its premises and conclusions. Professor Cox has argued vigorously that the argument is seriously flawed. He points out that for the investor who trades with the insider, smoother prices are a poor second choice to having the information being disclosed prior to the trade. As he notes, "[t]he insider's opposite is far better off with the price established by the insider's disclosure of the information than he is with a price that has been modestly nudged by the insider's secret trading. In the case of the insider's non-disclosure of bad news, the opposite trader emerges owning a stock that has a lower price after disclosure than its purchase price; and in the case of good news, the insider's opposite emerges having sold the security for an amount substantially below its price following disclosure." Moreover, he argues that price changes occur much more quickly and efficiently through public disclosure than through trading because there are too many other factors affecting a stock price to permit an investor to discern clearly that there is undisclosed inside information reflected in that price. Cox, supra, at 646.

Cox also contends that the stock price argument proves too much. "If accepted, this position justifies massive trading and tipping to ensure that sufficient trading occurs to propel the stock to the equilibrium price appropriate for the nondisclosed information. Such widespread trading, however, compromises the corporate interest that justified nondisclosure in the first place." Id. at 648.

It should also be noted that some trades are time-induced and would benefit from smoother price movements. Other trades, however, are induced by changes in volume or price; these latter would more likely be harmed by the price movements caused by the insider's trading.

Insider Trading as Management Compensation. Some scholars argue that insider trading should not be regulated because it compensates managers and provides them with an additional incentive to take risks that will benefit investors. Originally propounded by Manne, supra, at 138–143, this argument had been generally rejected because it appeared to permit managers to benefit from bad news which could have the product of their own mistakes. However, Carlton and Fischel have revived it. They contend that because managements are inherently risk-averse, it is necessary to provide them with incentives to make business decisions which have the potential to increase the value of the firm substantially. If the firm's value does increase, all investors—insiders and outsiders—will share in the growth. Thus Carlton and Fischel argue that the insiders do not secure their gains at the expense of outsiders because the total wealth of the firm has increased. Put differently, they maintain that insider trading does not cause outsiders to get a smaller piece of the pie; rather, all investors benefit from a substantially larger pie. Carlton & Fischel, supra at 870–873.

Easterbrook and Fischel expand upon the argument that insider trading should be permitted as a means of managerial compensation. Allowing insider trading in effect permits the manager to renegotiate his compensation package with his every stock transaction. Thus, a "manager who observes an investment for the firm * * * will be more inclined to pursue this opportunity if rewarded on success. * * * Basing compensation in part on trading is one method for distinguishing superior from inferior managers." Easterbrook & Fischel, supra, at 258.

For Carlton and Fischel, permitting managers to profit from bad news is consistent with the theory of insider trading as a compensation device; a manager will be more willing to take risks if he knows that he can profit by selling short prior to public disclosure of the failure. Insider trading, whether on good or bad news, is thus a means of rewarding entrepreneurial risk-taking, whether or not those risks succeed.

There are serious problems with this latter argument. If a manager can profit from either success or failure, why should he care which occurs? He is far more likely to be concerned with his own interests than with maximizing the value of the firm for the shareholders, and he will end by being risk-neutral rather than risk-preferring. Cox, supra, at 651. See also, Posner, supra at 417.

Professor Cox uses the foregoing response to Carlton and Fischel as the basis for maintaining that continuing external regulation of insider trading is warranted. He contends that there is no reason to believe that permitting such trading is in the shareholders' interest. He points out that managers control the amount of such trading and can thus distort the costs and benefits to investors. Consequently, shareholders have little to gain and much to lose by permitting insider trading; a ban would be consistent with what the parties would have negotiated were negotiations feasible.

Cox offers three other reasons to support his conclusion. First, he argues that knowledge of a manager's sources of compensation is essential to understand his discretionary behavior and that investors will be better protected when compensation is tied to performance rather than to the ability to profit from external events. Second, he maintains that an assessment of a manager's performance is possible only when an investor has knowledge of the manager's costs and the firm's productivity. Finally, he notes that shareholders expect managers to concentrate on the shareholders' best interests rather than their own private investments; the prohibition against insider trading "stems from the shareholders' expectation that a manager is paid to look after the shareholders' welfare, not his own." Cox, supra, at 657–58.

For contrasting views on the theoretical aspects of insider trading see Louis Loss & Joel Seligman, Securities Regulation 3448–3466 (3rd ed.) and Frank H. Easterbrook and Daniel R. Fischel, The Economic Structure of Corporate Law 256–262 (1991).

PROBLEM
STANDARD ELECTRONICS CORPORATION

Standard Electronics Corporation (Standard) is a Delaware corporation. It manufactures a wide variety of products which are used in high technology communications industries. It has assets of $500 million and, in its most recent fiscal year, had sales of $550 million and earnings of $30 million. The company went public six years ago and its common stock is now listed on the New York Stock Exchange. In the last year, Standard's stock has traded between $19 and $28 per share and has recently been trading at about $25 per share. In order to provide incentives for its staff, it introduced an employee stock option plan almost immediately after going public and, to provide stock for that plan, Standard has been purchasing its own stock on the New York Stock Exchange on alternate Fridays pursuant to a prearranged schedule. The three trustees of the plan are the company's president, Herbert Jones, its treasurer, and one of its outside directors.

The industry is highly capital intensive and intensely competitive; Standard has succeeded because of its ability to develop new products. In March of this year, its laser division discovered a process which would enable it to produce laser discs on which both graphics and large amounts of text could be stored. This process would also permit the company to produce the discs in far greater quantity and at far lower prices than at present. On April 1, the division's research team advised Jones that to develop the product to its full potential, heavy capital investments would be required. They indicated that with adequate financing, the company could gain a significant head start over its competitors.

On April 2, Jones met with the company's general counsel, Abigail Benedict, to discuss the stock market implications of the new process. The two decided that the information was to be kept highly confidential within the company and was to be referred to only by the code name "Nirvana." Benedict reminded Jones that the company had a code of conduct requiring senior officers to obtain advance clearance from her office for their securities transactions. She recommended that clearance be denied to all senior management and that an embargo be placed on all transactions by those working on the Nirvana project until the project had been made public. Jones accepted this recommendation and, on the same day, circulated a confidential memorandum to all Nirvana project employees notifying them of the embargo.

Three days after this memorandum was issued, Steve Davis, a marketing vice-president, asked Benedict's office for permission to buy some stock. He was told that senior management was temporarily barred from trading but was not told why. Nevertheless, he bought 3,000 shares at about $26 per share on the same day. In addition, on April 7, without asking anyone, Amy Stevens, the research director of the Nirvana project, bought 5,000 shares at $24 per share.

On April 5, Jones met with the board of directors to discuss how best to finance the development of the new product. Jones again stressed the need for secrecy and the use of Nirvana as a code name. In addition to the full board, the meeting was attended by Ted Long, a partner of Goldwin & Co., a well-established investment banking firm which had underwritten the company's public offering and which continued to give it financial advice. Long proposed several alternative means of financing the project, including, among others, a merger with a company with substantial capital or the sale of a large block of stock. The Board reached no decision and retained Goldwin to advise how best to finance the development. Long advised the Board that it would be necessary for the company, even at the preliminary stage, to prepare a disclosure document which might be shown to potential investors. The board instructed Benedict to work with Potter & Moore, Goldwin's counsel, in preparing such a document.

On May 5, one week before the company's annual meeting of stockholders, Long reported to the board that Goldwin was engaged in confidential discussions with several possible investors but that it was not prepared to present a formal recommendation. At the annual meeting, a stockholder asked Jones about new developments or products. Jones replied that "there is nothing I can report on now, although we are always hopeful that something exciting will emerge from the company's on-going research." His statement was accurately quoted on the Dow Jones News Service and in the Wall Street Journal.

On June 7, Long presented Goldwin's formal report to the full board. In that report, Goldwin stated that if the new product could be fully developed commercially, Goldwin projected Standard's value at between $40 and $45 per share. Long also told the board that because of the project's degree of risk, a sale of a large block of stock could not be made at prices reflecting fair value, but that Goldwin had approached Universal Products, Inc. (Universal), a diversified high technology company whose shares are listed on the New York Stock Exchange, concerning a merger between the two companies at a price of $45–50 per share. After discussing Goldwin's report, the board authorized Jones to enter into formal negotiations with Universal and to furnish any necessary confidential information to Universal.

From June 15–30, representatives of Standard and Universal met to review and discuss confidential and public financial data concerning Standard. At the end of the June 30 meeting, Universal's president said that he would seek authorization from his board to acquire Standard at a price of slightly more than $50 per share for each share of Standard stock. Later that day, both companies received calls from the New York Stock Exchange, asking them to comment on the large number of rumors that were circulating concerning a possible merger. On advice of counsel, the companies advised the Exchange that they were not in a position to comment because they had not reached a definitive agreement as to the price to be paid or the form the acquisition might take.

On July 7 both boards approved a merger in which Universal would issue stock having a value of $51 per share for 100% of the stock of Standard. The final agreement was signed on July 10 and, at the request of both companies, the New York Stock Exchange halted trading in both companies' stock until the companies issued a joint press release disclosing the terms of the merger. When trading resumed the following day, Standard stock traded at $43 per share.

You are an associate in a prominent law firm which specializes in corporate and securities law matters and which has represented Standard for a number of years. The senior partner has just sent you a memorandum detailing the above facts which he has developed from a series of meetings with Jones. He has concluded his memo as follows:

"I certainly hope we don't have another *Texas Gulf Sulphur* on our hands. Certainly we have advised the company on how best to deal with the whole problem of 10b–5 and insider trading. The merger with Universal hasn't closed yet and I need to know how serious the problems are. By the way, even though we probably won't represent everyone, I would like to know about personal as well as corporate liability. In your memo, I would like you to cover the following issues:

"1) Let's begin at the beginning. Before there was a Rule 10b–5 (difficult as that may to be imagine), there was some common law dealing with insider trading and, as I recall, there have been some common law decisions recently, although some of the cases may have been brought in federal court. Is there any common law liability on these facts and, if so, who could recover? How serious is the possibility that someone might be liable for damages under both common and federal law?

"2) I understand that materiality is an essential element of a Rule 10b–5 violation, but the facts here confuse me. Depending on whose conduct we are looking at, there are several possible material facts—the embargo, the discovery or the merger (or some combination of these). At what point, if ever, was the information about the new product or the merger material? It seems to me that if everyone was just speculating about future profits, there may be no problem with any of what transpired. What additional information do we need to know?

"3) I am concerned about Davis and Stevens. Neither of them are directors of Standard, but might they be considered insiders for purposes of 10b–5 liability? Look at Darke in the *Texas Gulf Sulphur* case. What is the requisite culpable state of mind?

"4) Long has told me that after a squash game with Bill Baker, one of his partners, in response to a casual question about Standard, Long said that it looks like they've hit the jackpot in a deal with Universal. Long says it was inadvertent, and I am inclined to believe him. You know that Goldwin has a large number of institutional clients, many of whom are handled by Baker. Who knows whether and what they may have been told or what they may have done with the information? I once thought that everyone in this chain would be liable, but now, frankly, I'm not so sure.

"a) Look at footnote 14 in *Dirks*. Are Goldwin, Long and Baker "insiders" for purposes of this deal?

"b) Baker surely was fortunate to have stumbled into this information and some internal antenna should have cautioned him against doing anything with it. But, in fact, he had nothing to do with the deal. Does the misappropriation theory apply to him? If so, who can recover from him?

"c) On any theory, analyze the potential liability of any of Goldwin's clients who traded after talking to Baker.

"d) We don't know what Baker told his clients. Could he or Goldwin be liable for the clients' trades if Baker recommended the purchase of Standard stock but did not specifically disclose material non-public information?

"5) It now appears that Pamela Hobbes, one of the lawyers at Potter and Moore who was working on the disclosure document, upon learning of the discovery, bought 1,000 shares of Standard stock for herself and told various members of her family who bought an additional 5,000 shares.

"a) Could Hobbes be considered an insider in these circumstances even though she was not directly retained by Standard?

"b) Does the misappropriation theory apply to Hobbes and, if so, who could bring suit against her? What damages or other relief might be granted?

"c) How does the tipper-tippee analysis apply to Hobbes and her family?

"6) I'm unclear about the corporate obligation to disclose. Did Standard have any legal duty to do so? After all, they weren't buying or selling stock on the basis of that information, unless you count that stock option plan. Don't we get some comfort from the fact that there was a regular stock buying program unrelated to the discovery? I'm not delighted with what Jones said at the annual meeting, but what else could he have done, given the need to keep the information confidential? Has the law evolved to a point where such confidence is illegal? What ever happened to the old doctrines of reliance and causation to say nothing of a culpable state of mind? I'm sure that Universal's counsel will want our views on the response to the New York Stock Exchange. I understand that the SEC may disagree with us; how much danger does that pose?"

"7) Four months before purchasing Standard stock, Davis had sold 1,000 shares which he then owned. Is he liable under Section 16(b) of the 1934 Act and, if so, what are the consequences?

C. THE COMMON LAW

1. INTRODUCTION

The law governing the trading of securities is today largely federal law and, more specifically, law developed under § 10(b) of the Securities Exchange Act of 1934 and Rule 10b–5. That state law has largely been supplanted in this area is due in part to the procedural advantages of suing under the 1934 Act, as we noted in Chapter 14 in connection with suits under the proxy rules. Perhaps the most important advantages are the provisions of § 27 that allow worldwide service of process on the defendant and an extremely liberal choice of venue. Suing under federal law in federal court also overcomes obstacles to derivative suits, often posed by state law. In addition federal discovery rules are often more liberal than their state counterparts.

The development of the law under Rule 10b–5 is also, however, a result of the unsatisfactory nature of the substantive rights afforded by the common law, which depend in large measure on the tort action of fraud or deceit.

The contours of the common law tort of deceit vary considerably from one state to another, and contain a host of qualifications and conditions that depend on the particular fact pattern. It is nevertheless useful to review the basic outlines of the traditional common law tort, to understand both why it proved an inadequate tool for dealing with securities fraud and how the federal courts have constructed their analysis of Rule 10b–5 by omitting or modifying the elements of the common law action for deceit.

The traditional action for deceit required the plaintiff to prove five elements: (1) The plaintiff justifiably relied (2) to his detriment (3) on a misrepresentation of a material fact (4) made by the defendant with the knowledge of its falsity or with reckless disregard for the truth and (5) with the intention that the plaintiff rely.

When applied to fraud in securities transactions, the traditional action for deceit suffered from several serious drawbacks. First, there was often no affirmative misrepresentation; rather, the defendant *omitted* material information when dealing with the plaintiff. Thus the plaintiff was required to prove that the defendant had a duty to disclose the omitted material information prior to trading in order to satisfy the fraud requirement of a misrepresentation. A second problem arose from the reliance requirement. Even when a plaintiff could establish a duty to disclose, it was difficult to prove that he had relied on the omitted fact. Moreover, the reliance requirement limited actions to those where the plaintiff and defendant had dealt directly; a plaintiff could not establish reliance when the transaction occurred through the impersonal medium of a securities exchange.

2. DUTY TO SHAREHOLDERS AND INVESTORS

GOODWIN v. AGASSIZ
283 Mass. 358, 186 N.E. 659 (1933).

RUGG, CHIEF JUSTICE.

[A stockholder of the Cliff Mining Company, the stock of which was listed on the Boston Stock Exchange, sought relief for losses suffered in the sale through the exchange of 700 shares of the company's stock to the defendants, who were officers and directors of the corporation. The court accepted the trial judge's findings that Cliff had started exploration for copper on its land in 1925, acting on certain geological surveys. The exploration was not successful, however, and the company removed its equipment in May, 1926.

Meanwhile, in March, 1926, an experienced geologist wrote a report theorizing as to the existence of copper deposits in the region of the company's holdings. The defendants, believing there was merit to the theory, secured options to land adjacent to the copper belt. Also, anticipating an increase in the value of the stock if the theory proved correct, the defendants purchased shares of the company's stock through an agent.

When the plaintiff learned of the termination of the original exploratory operations from a newspaper article—for which defendants were in no way responsible—he immediately sold his stock.]

The contention of the plaintiff is that the purchase of his stock in the company by the defendants without disclosing to him as a stockholder their knowledge of the geologist's theory, their belief that the theory was true, had value, the keeping secret the existence of the theory, discontinuance by the defendants of exploratory operations begun in 1925 on property of the Cliff Mining Company and their plan ultimately to test the value of the theory, constitute actionable wrong for which he as stockholder can recover.

The trial judge ruled that conditions may exist which would make it the duty of an officer of a corporation purchasing its stock from a stockholder to inform him as to knowledge possessed by the buyer and not by the seller, but found, on all the circumstances developed by the trial and set out at some length by him in his decision, that there was no fiduciary relation requiring such disclosure by the defendants to the plaintiff before buying his stock in the manner in which they did.

The question presented is whether the decree dismissing the bill rightly was entered on the facts found.

The directors of a commercial corporation stand in a relation of trust to the corporation and are bound to exercise the strictest good faith in respect to its property and business. The contention that directors also occupy the position of trustee toward individual stockholders in the corporation is plainly contrary to repeated decisions of this court and cannot be supported. In Smith v. Hurd, 12 Metc. 371, 384, 46 Am.Dec. 690, it was said by Chief Justice Shaw: "There is no legal privity, relation, or immediate connexion, between the holders of shares in a bank, in their individual capacity, on the one side, and the directors of the bank on the other. The directors are not the bailees, the factors, agents or trustees of such individual stockholders." * * *

The principle thus established is supported by an imposing weight of authority in other jurisdictions. A rule holding that directors are trustees for individual stockholders with respect to their stock prevails in comparatively few states; but in view of our own adjudications it is not necessary to review decisions to that effect.

While the general principle is as stated, circumstances may exist requiring that transactions between a director and a stockholder as to stock in the corporation be set aside. The knowledge naturally in the possession of a director as to the condition of a corporation places upon him a peculiar obligation to observe every requirement of fair dealing when directly buying or selling its stock. Mere silence does not usually amount to a breach of duty, but parties may stand in such relation to each other that an equitable responsibility arises to communicate facts. Wellington v. Rugg, 243 Mass. 30, 35, 136 N.E. 831. Purchases and sales of stock dealt in on the stock exchange are commonly impersonal affairs. An honest director would be in a difficult situation if he could neither buy nor sell on the stock exchange shares of stock in his corporation without first seeking out the other actual ultimate party to the transaction and disclosing to him everything which a court or jury might later find that he then knew affecting the real or speculative value of such shares. Business of that nature is a matter to be governed by practical rules. Fiduciary obligations of directors ought not to be made so onerous that men of experience and ability will be deterred from accepting such office. Law in its sanctions is not coextensive with morality. It cannot undertake to put all parties to every contract on an equality as to knowledge, experience, skill and shrewdness. It cannot undertake to relieve against hard bargains made between competent parties without fraud. On the other hand, directors cannot rightly be allowed to indulge with impunity in practices which do violence to prevailing standards of upright businessmen. Therefore, where a director personally seeks a stockholder for the purpose of buying his shares without making disclosure of material facts within his peculiar knowledge and not within reach of the stockholder, the transaction will be closely scrutinized and relief may be granted in appropriate instances. Strong v. Repide, 213 U.S. 419, 29 S.Ct. 521, 53 L.Ed. 853 * * *.

The precise question to be decided in the case at bar is whether on the facts found the defendants as directors had a right to buy stock of the plaintiff, a stockholder. Every element of actual fraud or misdoing by the defendants is negatived by the findings. Fraud cannot be presumed; it must be proved. Brown v. Little, Brown & Co., Inc., 269 Mass. 102, 117, 168 N.E. 521. The facts found afford no ground for inferring fraud or conspiracy. The only knowledge possessed by the defendants not open to the plaintiff was the existence of a theory formulated in a thesis by a geologist as to the possible existence of copper deposits where certain geological conditions existed common to the property of the Cliff Mining Company and that of other mining companies in its neighborhood. This thesis did not express an opinion that copper deposits would be found at any particular spot or on property of any specified owner. Whether that theory was sound or fallacious, no one knew, and so far as appears has never been demonstrated. The defendants made no representations to anybody about the theory. No facts found placed upon them any obligation to disclose the theory. A few days after the thesis expounding the theory was brought to the attention of the defendants, the annual report by the directors of the Cliff Mining Company for the calendar year 1925, signed by Agassiz for the directors, was issued. It did not cover the time when the theory was formulated. The report described the status of the operations under the exploration which had been begun in 1925. At the annual meeting of the stockholders of the company held early in April, 1926, no reference was made to the theory. It was then at most a hope, possibly an expectation. It had not passed the nebulous stage. No disclosure was made of it. The Cliff Mining Company was not harmed by the nondisclosure. There would have been no advantage to it, so far as appears, from a disclosure.

The disclosure would have been detrimental to the interests of another mining corporation in which the defendants were directors. In the circumstances there was no duty on the part of the defendants to set forth to the stockholders at the annual meeting their faith, aspirations and plans for the future. Events as they developed might render advisable radical changes in such views. Disclosure of the theory, if it ultimately was proved to be erroneous or without foundation in fact, might involve the defendants in litigation with those who might act on the hypothesis that it was correct. The stock of the Cliff Mining Company was bought and sold on the stock exchange. The identity of buyers and sellers of the stock in question in fact was not known to the parties and perhaps could not readily have been ascertained. The defendants caused the shares to be bought through brokers on the stock exchange. They said nothing to anybody as to the reasons actuating them. The plaintiff was no novice. He was a member of the Boston stock exchange and had kept a record of sales of Cliff Mining Company stock. He acted upon his own judgment in selling his stock. He made no inquiries of the defendants or of other officers of the company. The result is that the plaintiff cannot prevail.

Decree dismissing bill affirmed with costs.

Note: Common Law Rules

Goodwin sets out what is generally described as the "majority rule": directors and officers owe a fiduciary duty only to the corporation and, accordingly, are under no affirmative obligation to disclose material nonpublic information when dealing in securities with others who are unaware of it.

A second rule, developed in reaction to the sometimes harsh consequences of this approach, is the "special facts doctrine" enunciated in Strong v. Repide, 213 U.S. 419, 29 S.Ct. 521, 53 L.Ed. 853 (1909). Under this doctrine, although an insider normally owes no fiduciary duty to individual shareholders, a plaintiff may be afforded a remedy when, in particular circumstances, non-disclosure amounts to unconscionable behavior by the insider.

In *Strong,* the defendant was a director, the majority stockholder, and general manager of the corporation. He was authorized by the board of directors to conduct negotiations leading to the sale to the United States government of otherwise worthless land that was one of the corporation's principal assets. At the time of the transaction in question, he alone knew that the successful completion of the negotiations was near at hand. Without revealing his identity, he purchased, through an agent, the shares of another stockholder for one-tenth what the shares were to become worth when the property was sold three months later. The Supreme Court granted rescission of the sale of stock, saying, "That the defendant was a director of the corporation is but one of the facts upon which the liability is asserted, the existence of all the others in addition making such a combination as rendered it the plain duty of the defendant to speak." 213 U.S. at 431, 29 S.Ct. at 525. Other courts have invoked the "special facts doctrine" often enough to erode significantly the strict majority rule.

According to the third "rule," one that has steadily attracted more adherents among state courts, officers and directors owe a fiduciary duty to individual shareholders as well as to the corporation, regardless of whether there are special circumstances. Thus they have a duty to disclose material nonpublic information in any face-to-face stock transaction with a shareholder. This duty "exists because the stockholders have placed the directors in a strategic position where they can secure firsthand knowledge of important developments. * * * [T]he detailed information a director has of corporate affairs is in a very real sense property of the corporation, and * * * no director should be permitted to use such information for his own benefit at the expense of his stockholders." Taylor v. Wright, 69 Cal.App.2d 371, 159 P.2d 980, 984–85 (1945).

This "strict" or "Kansas" rule had its origin in Hotchkiss v. Fischer, 136 Kan. 531, 16 P.2d 531 (1932). The plaintiff, an impoverished widow from Burr Oak, Kansas, came to Topeka shortly before a board meeting to inquire of the defendant, who was president and a director of the corporation, whether she could expect a dividend. If not, she believed she would have to sell her stock. The president replied that he could not say whether a dividend would be declared until the board met. He showed her the corporation's financial statements, explained them, but maintained a rather pessimistic stance. The widow sold her stock to him for $1.25 per share. Three days later, the corporation declared a dividend of $1 per share. The court held that in such a transaction, the officer or director "acts in a relation of scrupulous trust and confidence," and his behavior is therefore subject to the closest scrutiny.

Whether a jurisdiction adopted the "special facts" doctrine or the "Kansas rule," the fiduciary duty of the insider, narrowly conceived, would apply only in dealings with an existing shareholder. It could therefore be thought to impose an obligation to disclose only when the plaintiff was selling stock to the insider since a buyer of stock would not usually become a stockholder until after the transaction. Moreover, any common law duty applied only in a transaction in which the parties dealt directly with each other rather than on a stock exchange. At common law, had Mrs. Hotchkiss' stock been listed on the New York Stock Exchange and her trade effected there, she could not have recovered from the corporation's president even if she could have demonstrated that he purchased the actual shares which she sold; the fact that he did not make any affirmative misrepresentations directly to her would have relieved him from liability.

One court has found that when a director solicits a shareholder to purchase his stock and fails to disclose material information bearing on the value of that stock, there is very little difference between the three rules. In such a case, the court held that the director will be liable to the shareholder who may either recover damages or rescind the sale. Bailey v. Vaughan, 178 W.Va. 371, 359 S.E.2d 599 (1987).

3. DUTY TO THE CORPORATION

DIAMOND v. OREAMUNO
24 N.Y.2d 494, 301 N.Y.S.2d 78, 248 N.E.2d 910 (1969).

Fuld, Chief Judge.

Upon this appeal from an order denying a motion to dismiss the complaint as insufficient on its face, the question presented—one of first impression in this court—is whether officers and directors may be held accountable to their corporation for gains realized by them from transactions in the company's stock as a result of their use of material inside information.

The complaint was filed by a shareholder of Management Assistance, Inc. (MAI) asserting a derivative action against a number of its officers and directors to compel an accounting for profits allegedly acquired as a result of a breach of fiduciary duty. It charges that two of the defendants—Oreamuno, chairman of the board of directors, and Gonzalez, its president—had used inside information, acquired by them solely by virtue of their positions, in order to reap large personal profits from the sale of MAI shares and that these profits rightfully belong to the corporation. Other officers and directors were joined as defendants on the ground that they acquiesced in or ratified the assertedly wrongful transactions.

MAI is in the business of financing computer installations through sale and lease back arrangements with various commercial and industrial users. Under its lease provisions, MAI was required to maintain and repair the computers but, at the time of this suit, it lacked the capacity to perform this function itself and was forced to engage the manufacturer of the computers, International Business Machines (IBM), to service the machines. As a result of a sharp increase by IBM of its charges for such service, MAI's expenses for August of 1966 rose considerably and its net earnings declined from $262,253 in July to $66,233 in August, a decrease of about 75%. This information, although earlier known to the defendants, was not made public until October of 1966. Prior to the release of the information, however, Oreamuno and Gonzalez sold off a total of 56,500 shares of their MAI stock at the then current market price of $28 a share.

After the information concerning the drop in earnings was made available to the public, the value of a share of MAI stock immediately fell from the $28 realized by the defendants to $11. Thus, the plaintiff alleges, by taking advantage of their privileged position and their access to confidential information, Oreamuno and Gonzalez were able to realize $800,000 more for their securities than they would have had this inside information not been available to them. * * * A motion by the defendants to dismiss the complaint * * * for failure to state a cause of action was granted by the court at Special Term. * * *

It is well established, as a general proposition, that a person who acquires special knowledge or information by virtue of a confidential or fiduciary relationship with another is not free to exploit that knowledge or information for his own personal benefit but must account to his principal for any profits derived therefrom. This, in turn, is merely a corollary of the broader principle, inherent in the nature of the fiduciary relationship, that prohibits a trustee or agent from extracting secret profits from his position of trust.

In support of their claim that the complaint fails to state a cause of action, the defendants take the position that, although it is admittedly wrong for an officer or director to use his position to obtain trading profits for himself in the stock of his corporation, the action ascribed to them did not injure or damage MAI in any way. Accordingly, the defendants continue, the corporation should not be permitted to recover the proceeds. They acknowledge that, by virtue of the exclusive access which officers and directors have to inside information, they possess an unfair advantage over other shareholders and, particularly, the persons who had purchased the stock from them but, they contend, the corporation itself was unaffected and, for that reason, a derivative action is an inappropriate remedy.

It is true that the complaint before us does not contain any allegation of damages to the corporation but this has never been considered to be an essential requirement for a cause of action founded on a breach of fiduciary duty. This is because the function of such an action, unlike an ordinary tort or contract case, is not merely to compensate the plaintiff for wrongs committed by the defendant but, as this court declared many years ago (Dutton v. Willner, 52 N.Y. 312, 319) "to *prevent* them, by removing from agents and trustees all inducement to attempt dealing for their own benefit in matters which they have undertaken for others, or to which their agency or trust relates." (Emphasis supplied.)

Just as a trustee has no right to retain for himself the profits yielded by property placed in his possession but must account to his beneficiaries, a corporate fiduciary, who is entrusted with potentially valuable information, may not appropriate that asset for his own use even though, in so doing, he causes no injury to the corporation. The primary concern, in a case such as this, is not to determine whether the corporation has been damaged but to decide, as between the corporation and the defendants, who has a higher claim to the proceeds derived from the exploitation of the information. In our opinion, there can be no justification for permitting officers and directors, such as the defendants, to retain for themselves profits which, it is alleged, they derived solely from exploiting information gained by virtue of their inside position as corporate officials.

In addition, it is pertinent to observe that, despite the lack of any specific allegation of damage, it may well be inferred that the defendants' actions might have caused some harm to the enterprise. Although the corporation may have little concern with the day-to-day transactions in its shares, it has a great interest in maintaining a reputation of integrity, an image of probity, for its management and in insuring the continued public acceptance and marketability of its stock. When officers and directors abuse their position in order to gain personal profits, the effect may be to cast a cloud on the corporation's name, injure stockholder relations and undermine public regard for the corporation's securities. As Presiding Justice Botein aptly put it, in the course of his opinion for the Appellate Division, "[t]he prestige and good will of a corporation, so vital to its prosperity, may be undermined by the revelation that its chief officers had been making personal profits out of corporate events which they had not disclosed to the community of stockholders." (29 A.D.2d at p. 287, 287 N.Y.S.2d at p. 303.)

The defendants maintain that extending the prohibition against personal exploitation of a fiduciary relationship to officers and directors of a corporation will discourage such officials from maintaining a stake in the success of the corporate venture through share ownership, which, they urge, is an important incentive to proper performance of their duties. There is, however, a considerable difference between corporate officers who assume the same risks and obtain the same benefits as other shareholders and those who use their privileged position to gain special advantages not available to others. The sale of shares by the defendants for the reasons charged was not merely a wise investment decision which any prudent investor might have made. Rather, they were assertedly able in this case to profit solely because they had information which was not available to any one else—including the other shareholders whose interests they, as corporate fiduciaries, were bound to protect.

Although no appellate court in this State has had occasion to pass upon the precise question before us, the concept underlying the present cause of action is hardly a new one. (See, e.g., Securities Exchange Act of 1934 [48 U.S.Stat. 881], § 16[b]; U.S.Code, tit. 15, § 78p, subd. [b]; Brophy v. Cities Serv. Co., 31 Del.Ch. 241; Restatement, 2d, Agency, § 388, comment c.) Under Federal law (Securities Exchange Act of 1934, § 16[b]), for example, it is conclusively presumed that, when a director, officer or 10% shareholder buys and sells securities of his corporation within a six-month period, he is trading on inside information. The remedy which the Federal statute provides in that situation is precisely the same as that sought in the present case under State law, namely, an action brought by the corporation or on its behalf to recover all profits derived from the transactions.

In providing this remedy, Congress accomplished a dual purpose. It not only provided for an efficient and effective method of accomplishing its primary goal—the protection of the investing public from unfair treatment at the hands of corporate insiders—but extended to the corporation the right to secure for itself benefits derived by those insiders from their exploitation of their privileged position.   * * *

Although the provisions of section 16(b) may not apply to all cases of trading on inside information, it demonstrates that a derivative action can be an effective method for dealing with such abuses which may be used to accomplish a similar purpose in cases not specifically covered by the statute. In Brophy v. Cities Serv. Co. (31 Del.Ch. 241, 70 A.2d 5, *supra*), for example, the Chancery Court of Delaware allowed a similar remedy in a situation not covered by the Federal legislation. One of the defendants in that case was an employee who had acquired inside information that the corporate plaintiff was about to enter the market and purchase its own shares. On the basis of this confidential information, the employee, who was not an officer and, hence, not liable under Federal law, bought a large block of shares and, after the corporation's purchases had caused the price to rise, resold them at a profit. The court sustained the complaint in a derivative action brought for an accounting, stating that "[p]ublic policy will not permit an employee occupying a position of trust and confidence toward his employer to abuse that relation to his own profit, regardless of whether his employer suffers a loss" (31 Del.Ch., at p. 246, 70 A.2d, at p. 8). And a similar view has been expressed in the Restatement, 2d Agency (§ 388, comment c):

> c. *Use of confidential information.* An agent who acquires confidential information in the course of his employment or in violation of his duties has a duty * * * to account for any profits made by the use of such information, although this does not harm the principal. * * * So, if [a corporate officer] has "inside" information that the corporation is about to purchase or sell securities, or to declare or to pass a dividend, profits made by him in stock transactions undertaken because of his knowledge are held in constructive trust for the principal.

In the present case, the defendants may be able to avoid liability to the corporation under section 16(b) of the Federal law since they had held the MAI shares for more than six months prior to the sales. Nevertheless, the alleged use of the inside information to dispose of their stock at a price considerably higher than its known value constituted the same sort of "abuse of a fiduciary relationship" as is condemned by the

Federal law. Sitting as we are in this case as a court of equity, we should not hesitate to permit an action to prevent any unjust enrichment realized by the defendants from their allegedly wrongful act.

The defendants recognize that the conduct charged against them directly contravened the policy embodied in the Securities Exchange Act but, they maintain, the Federal legislation constitutes a comprehensive and carefully wrought plan for dealing with the abuse of inside information and that allowing a derivative action to be maintained under State law would interfere with the Federal scheme. Moreover, they urge, the existence of dual Federal and State remedies for the same act would create the possibility of double liability.

An examination of the Federal regulatory scheme refutes the contention that it was designed to establish any particular remedy as exclusive. In addition to the specific provisions of section 16(b), the Securities and Exchange Act contains a general anti-fraud provision in section 10(b) (U.S.Code, tit. 15, § 78j, subd. [b]) which, as implemented by rule 10b–5 (Code of Fed.Reg., tit. 17, § 240.10b–5) under that section, renders it unlawful to engage in a variety of acts considered to be fraudulent. In interpreting this rule, the Securities and Exchange Commission and the Federal courts have extended the common-law definition of fraud to include not only affirmative misrepresentations, relied upon by the purchaser or seller, but also a failure to disclose material information which might have affected the transaction.

Accepting the truth of the complainant's allegations, there is no question but that the defendants were guilty of withholding material information from the purchasers of the shares and, indeed, the defendants acknowledge that the facts asserted constitute a violation of rule 10b–5. The remedies which the Federal law provides for such violation, however, are rather limited. An action could be brought, in an exceptional case, by the SEC for injunctive relief. This, in fact, is what happened in the *Texas Gulf Sulphur* case (401 F.2d 833). The purpose of such an action, however, would appear to be more to establish a principle than to provide a regular method of enforcement. A class action under the Federal rule might be a more effective remedy but the mechanics of such an action have, as far as we have been able to ascertain, not yet been worked out by the Federal courts and several questions relating thereto have never been resolved. These include the definition of the class entitled to bring such an action, the measure of damages, the administration of the fund which would be recovered and its distribution to the members of the class. Of course, any individual purchaser, who could prove an injury as a result of a rule 10b–5 violation can bring his own action for rescission but we have not been referred to a single case in which such an action has been successfully prosecuted where the public sale of securities is involved. The reason for this is that sales of securities, whether through a stock exchange or over-the-counter, are characteristically anonymous transactions, usually handled through brokers, and the matching of the ultimate buyer with the ultimate seller presents virtually insurmountable obstacles. Thus, unless a section 16(b) violation is also present, the Federal law does not yet provide a really effective remedy.

In view of the practical difficulties inherent in an action under the Federal law, the desirability of creating an effective common-law remedy is manifest. "Dishonest directors should not find absolution from retributive justice", Ballantine observed in his work on Corporations ([rev.ed., 1946], p. 216), "by concealing their identity from their victims under the mask of the stock exchange." There is ample room in a situation such as is here presented for a "private Attorney General" to come forward and enforce proper behavior on the part of corporate officials through the medium of the derivative action brought in the name of the corporation. Only by sanctioning such a cause of action will there be any effective method to prevent the type of abuse of corporate office complained of in this case.

There is nothing in the Federal law which indicates that it was intended to limit the power of the States to fashion additional remedies to effectuate similar purposes. Although the impact of Federal securities regulation has on occasion been said to have created a "Federal corporation law," in fact, its effect on the duties and obligations of directors and officers and their relation to the corporation and its shareholders is only occasional and peripheral. The primary source of the law in this area ever remains that of the State which created the corporation. Indeed, Congress expressly provided against any implication that it intended to pre-empt the field by declaring, in section 28(a) of the Securities Exchange Act of 1934 (48 U.S.Stat. 903), that "[t]he rights and remedies provided by this title shall be in addition to any and all other rights and remedies that may exist at law or in equity".

Nor should we be deterred, in formulating a State remedy, by the defendants' claim of possible double liability. Certainly, as already indicated, if the sales in question were publicly made, the likelihood that a suit will be brought by purchasers of the shares is quite remote. But, even if it were not, the mere possibility of such a suit is not a defense nor does it render the complaint insufficient. It is not unusual for an action to be brought to recover a fund which may be subject to a superior claim by a third party. If that be the situation, a defendant should not be permitted to retain the fund for his own use on the chance that such a party may eventually appear. A defendant's course, if he wishes to protect himself against double liability, is to interplead any and all possible claimants and bind them to the judgment.

In any event, though, no suggestion has been made either in brief or on oral argument that any purchaser has come forward with a claim against the defendants or even that anyone is in a position to advance such a claim. As we have stated, the defendants' assertion that such a party may come forward at some future date is not a basis for permitting them to retain for their own benefit the fruits of their allegedly wrongful acts. For all that appears, the present derivative action is the only effective remedy now available against the abuse by these defendants of their privileged position.

* * *

The order appealed from should be affirmed, with costs, and the question certified answered in the affirmative.

FREEMAN v. DECIO
584 F.2d 186 (7th Cir.1978).

Wood, Jr., Circuit Judge.

* * *

I.
Diamond v. Oreamuno and Indiana Law

Both parties agree that there is no Indiana precedent directly dealing with the question of whether a corporation may recover the profits of corporate officials who trade in the corporation's securities on the basis of inside information. However, the plaintiff suggests that were the question to be presented to the Indiana courts, they would adopt the holding of the New York Court of Appeals in Diamond v. Oreamuno, 24 N.Y.2d 494, 301 N.Y.S.2d 78, 248 N.E.2d 910 (1969). There, building on the Delaware case of Brophy v. Cities Service Co., 31 Del.Ch. 241, 70 A.2d 5 (1949), the court held that the officers and directors of a corporation breached their fiduciary duties owed to the corporation by trading in its stock on the basis of material non-public information acquired by virtue of their official positions and that they should account to the corporation for their profits from those transactions. Since *Diamond* was decided, few courts have had an opportunity to consider the problem there presented. In fact, only one case has been brought to our attention which raised the question of whether *Diamond* would be followed in another jurisdiction. In Schein v. Chasen, 478 F.2d 817 (2d Cir.1973), vacated and remanded sub nom., Lehman Bros. v. Schein, 416 U.S. 386, 94 S.Ct. 1741, 40 L.Ed.2d 215 (1974), on certification to the Fla.Sup.Ct., 313 So.2d 739 (Fla.1975), the Second Circuit, sitting in diversity, considered whether the Florida courts would permit a *Diamond*-type action to be brought on behalf of a corporation. The majority not only tacitly concluded that Florida would adopt *Diamond,* but that the *Diamond* cause of action should be extended so as to permit recovery of the profits of non-insiders who traded in the corporation's stock on the basis of inside information received as tips from insiders. Judge Kaufman, dissenting, agreed with the policies underlying a *Diamond*-type cause of action, but disagreed with the extension of liability to outsiders. He also failed to understand why the panel was not willing to utilize Florida's certified question statute so as to bring the question of law before the Florida Supreme Court. Granting *certiorari,* the United States Supreme Court agreed with the dissent on this last point and on remand the case was certified to the Florida Supreme Court. That court not only stated that it would not "give the unprecedented expansive reading to *Diamond* sought by appellants" but that, furthermore, it did not "choose to adopt the innovative ruling of the New York Court of Appeals in *Diamond* [itself]." 313 So.2d 739, 746 (Fla.1975). Thus, the question here is whether the Indiana courts are more likely to follow the New York Court of Appeals or to join the Florida Supreme Court in refusing to undertake such a change from existing law.

It appears that from a policy point of view it is widely accepted that insider trading should be deterred because it is unfair to other investors who do not enjoy the benefits of access to inside information. The goal is not one of equality of possession of information—since some traders will always be better "informed" than others by dint of greater expenditures of time and resources, greater experience, or greater analytical abilities—but rather equality of access to information. Thus, in *Cady, Roberts & Co.*, 40 S.E.C. 907, 912 (1961), the SEC gave the following explanation of its view of the obligation of corporate insiders to disclose material inside information when trading in the corporation's stock:

> Analytically, the obligation rests on two principal elements: first, the existence of a relationship giving access, directly or indirectly, to information intended to be available only for a corporate purpose and not for the personal benefit of anyone, and second, the inherent unfairness involved where a party takes advantage of such information knowing it is unavailable to those with whom he is dealing.

Yet, a growing body of commentary suggests that pursuit of this goal of "market egalitarianism" may be costly. In addition to the costs associated with enforcement of the laws prohibiting insider trading, there may be a loss in the efficiency of the securities markets in their capital allocation function. The basic insight of economic analysis here is that securities prices act as signals helping to route capital to its most productive uses and that insider trading helps assure that those prices will reflect the best information available (i.e., inside information) as to where the best opportunities lie.[13] However, even when confronted with the possibility of a trade-off between fairness and economic efficiency, most authorities appear to find that the balance tips in favor of discouraging insider trading.

Over 40 years ago Congress was stirred by examples of flagrant abuse of inside information unearthed during the hearings preceding the 1933 and 1934 Securities Acts to include in the latter a section aimed at insider trading. Section 16(b) provides for the automatic recovery by corporations of profits made by insiders in short-swing transactions within a six-month period. This automatic accountability makes the

---

13. However, it has been suggested that insider trading may harm the securities markets in indirect ways. For one thing, outsiders might be less willing to invest in securities markets marked by the preva- lence of a practice which they consider unfair. In addition an equal, if not greater degree of allocative efficiency can normally be achieved if the inside information is made public.

rule one of relatively easy application and avoids very difficult problems concerning the measurement of damages, yet upon occasion leads to harsh results. The section has been characterized as a "crude rule of thumb." It is too narrow in that only short-swing trading and short selling are covered, leaving untouched other ways of profiting from inside information in the securities market. It is too broad in that short-swing trades not actually made on the basis of inside information are also caught in the Section's web of liability.

The SEC has also used its full panoply of powers to police insider trading through enforcement actions and civil actions. The agency has relied, *inter alia,* on Section 17(a) of the 1933 Act, Section 15(c)(1) of the 1934 Act, and Rule 10b–5. The relief obtained has included not only injunctions and suspension orders, but also disgorgement of profits earned in insider trading.

Lastly, the "victims" of insider trading may recover damages from the insiders in many instances. Absent fraud, the traditional common law approach has been to permit officers and directors of corporations to trade in their corporation's securities free from liability to other traders for failing to disclose inside information. However, there has been a movement towards the imposition of a common law duty to disclose in a number of jurisdictions, at least where the insider is dealing with an existing stockholder. A few jurisdictions now require disclosure where certain "special facts" exist, and some even impose a strict fiduciary duty on the insider *vis-à-vis* the selling shareholder. But the most important remedies available to those injured by insider trading are found in the federal securities laws and in particular Rule 10b–5. Judicial development of a private right of action under that rule has led to significant relaxation of many of the elements of common law fraud, including privity, reliance, and the distinction between misrepresentation and non-disclosure. The rule has proven a favorite vehicle for damage suits against insiders for failing to disclose material information while trading in their corporation's stock. Section 17(a) of the 1933 Act may also provide a means of recovering damages from insiders in some cases. Lastly, persons injured by insider trading may be able to take advantage of the liability sections of state securities laws. A number of states, including Indiana, have enacted laws containing antifraud provisions modeled on Rule 10b–5. See Burns Ind.Stat.Ann. § 23–2–1–12.

Yet, the New York Court of Appeals in *Diamond* found the existing remedies for controlling insider trading to be inadequate. Although the court felt that the device of a class action under the federal securities laws held out hope of a more effective remedy in the future, it concluded that "the desirability of creating an effective common-law remedy is manifest." 301 N.Y.S.2d at 85, 248 N.E.2d at 915. It went on to do so by engineering an innovative extension of the law governing the relation between a corporation and its officers and directors. The court held that corporate officials who deal in their corporation's securities on the basis of non-public information gained by virtue of their inside position commit a breach of their fiduciary duties to the corporation. This holding represents a departure from the traditional common law approach, which was that a corporate insider did not ordinarily violate his fiduciary duty to the corporation by dealing in the corporation's stock, unless the corporation was thereby harmed.

* * *

There are a number of difficulties with the *Diamond* court's ruling. Perhaps the thorniest problem was posed by the defendants' objection that whatever the ethical status of insider trading, there is no injury to the corporation which can serve as a basis for recognizing a right of recovery in favor of the latter. The Court of Appeals' response to this argument was two-fold, suggesting first that no harm to the corporation need be shown and second that it might well be inferred that the insiders' activities did in fact cause some harm to the corporation. * * * Some might see the *Diamond* court's decision as resting on a broad, strict-trust notion of the fiduciary duty owed to the corporation: no director is to receive any profit, beyond what he receives from the corporation, solely because of his position. Although once accepted, this basis for the *Diamond* rule would obviate the need for finding a potential for injury to the corporation, it is not at all clear that current corporation law contemplates such an extensive notion of fiduciary duty. It is customary to view the *Diamond* result as resting on a characterization of inside information as a corporate asset. The lack of necessity for looking for an injury to the corporation is then justified by the traditional "no inquiry" rule with respect to profits made by trustees from assets belonging to the trust *res*. However, to start from the premise that all inside information should be considered a corporate asset may presuppose an answer to the inquiry at hand. It might be better to ask whether there is any potential loss to the corporation from the use of such information in insider trading before deciding to characterize the inside information as an asset with respect to which the insider owes the corporation a duty of loyalty (as opposed to a duty of care). This approach would be in keeping with the modern view of another area of application of the duty of loyalty—the corporate opportunity doctrine. Thus, while courts will require a director or officer to automatically account to the corporation for diversion of a corporate opportunity to personal use, they will first inquire to see whether there was a possibility of a loss to the corporation—i.e., whether the corporation was in a position to potentially avail itself of the opportunity—before deciding that a corporate opportunity in fact existed. Similarly, when scrutinizing transactions between a director or officer and the corporation under the light of the duty of loyalty, most courts now inquire as to whether there was any injury to the corporation, i.e., whether the transaction was fair and in good faith, before permitting the latter to avoid the transaction. An analogous question might be posed with respect to the *Diamond* court's unjust enrichment analysis: is it proper to conclude that an insider has been unjustly enriched *vis-à-vis* the corporation (as compared to other traders in the market) when there is no way that the corporation could have used the information to its own profit, just because the insider's trading was made possible by virtue of his corporate position?

Not all information generated in the course of carrying on a business fits snugly into the corporate asset mold. Information in the form of trade secrets, customer lists, etc., can easily be categorized as a valuable or potentially valuable corporate "possession," in that it can be directly used by the corporation to its own economic advantage. However, most information involved in insider trading is not of this ilk, e.g., knowledge of an impending merger, a decline in earnings, etc. If the corporation were to attempt to exploit such non-public information by dealing in its own securities, it would open itself up to potential liability under federal and state securities laws, just as do the insiders when they engage in insider trading. This is not to say that the corporation does not have any interests with regard to such information. It may have an interest in either preventing the information from becoming public or in regulating the timing of disclosure. However, insider trading does not entail the disclosure of inside information, but rather its use in a manner in which the corporation itself is prohibited from exploiting it.

Yet, the *Diamond* court concluded that it might well be inferred that insider trading causes some harm to the corporation * * *. It must be conceded that the unfairness that is the basis of the wide-spread disapproval of insider trading is borne primarily by participants in the securities markets, rather than by the corporation itself. By comparison, the harm to corporate goodwill posited by the *Diamond* court pales in significance. At this point, the existence of such an indirect injury must be considered speculative, as there is no actual evidence of such a reaction. Furthermore, it is less than clear to us that the nature of this harm would form an adequate basis for an action for an accounting based on a breach of the insiders' duty of loyalty, as opposed to an action for damages based on a breach of the duty of care. The injury hypothesized by the *Diamond* court seems little different from the harm to the corporation that might be inferred whenever a responsible corporate official commits an illegal or unethical act using a corporate asset. Absent is the element of loss of opportunity or potential susceptibility to outside influence that generally is present when a corporate fiduciary is required to account to the corporation.

The *Brophy* case is capable of being distinguished on this basis. Although the court there did not openly rely on the existence of a potential harm to the corporation, such a harm was possible. Since the corporation was about to begin buying its own shares in the market, by purchasing stock for his own account the insider placed himself in direct competition with the corporation. To the degree that his purchases might have caused the stock price to rise, the corporation was directly injured in that it had to pay more for its purchases. The other cases cited by the *Diamond* court also tended to involve an agent's competition with his principal, harm to it, disregard for its instructions, or the like.
* * *

A second problem presented by the recognition of a cause of action in favor of the corporation is that of potential double liability. The *Diamond* court thought that this problem would seldom arise, since it thought it unlikely that a damage suit would be brought by investors where the insiders traded on impersonal exchanges. * * *. The Second Circuit also gave consideration to the possibility of double liability in Schein v. Chasen, 478 F.2d at 824–25, but concluded that double liability could be avoided by methods such as that employed in SEC v. Texas Gulf Sulphur Co., 312 F.Supp. 77, 93 (S.D.N.Y.1970), where the defendants' disgorged profits were placed in a fund subject first to the claims of injured investors, with the residue payable to the corporation. The efficacy of the *Diamond* court's suggestion of resort to an interpleader action is open to question. The creation of a fund subject to the superior claims of injured investors also poses some difficulties. Although some observers have suggested that double liability be imposed so as to more effectively deter insider trading and that it is analytically justifiable since the two causes of action involved are based on separate legal wrongs, the *Diamond* and *Schein* courts' concern for avoiding double liability may implicitly reflect the view that a right of recovery in favor of the corporation was being created because of the perceived likelihood that the investors who are the true victims of insider trading would not be able to bring suit. When the latter in fact bring an action seeking damages from the insiders, thereby creating the possibility of double liability, the need for a surrogate plaintiff disappears and the corporation's claim is implicitly relegated to the back seat.

Since the *Diamond* court's action was motivated in large part by its perception of the inadequacy of existing remedies for insider trading, it is noteworthy that over the decade since *Diamond* was decided, the 10b–5 class action has made substantial advances toward becoming the kind of effective remedy for insider trading that the court of appeals hoped that it might become. Most importantly, recovery of damages from insiders has been allowed by, or on the behalf of, market investors even when the insiders dealt only through impersonal stock exchanges, although this is not yet a well-settled area of the law. In spite of other recent developments indicating that such class actions will not become as easy to maintain as some plaintiffs had perhaps hoped, it is clear the remedies for insider trading under the federal securities laws now constitute a more effective deterrent than they did when *Diamond* was decided.

* * * [H]aving carefully examined the decision of the New York Court of Appeals in *Diamond*, we are of the opinion that although the court sought to ground its ruling in accepted principles of corporate common law, that decision can best be understood as an example of judicial securities regulation. Although the question is a close one, we believe that were the issue to be presented to the Indiana courts at the present time, they would most likely join the Florida Supreme Court in refusing to adopt the New York court's innovative ruling.

* * *

The judgment of the district court is affirmed.

For further discussion, see In re ORFA Securities Litigation, 654 F.Supp. 1449 (D.N.J.1987) where the court denied a motion to dismiss a shareholder's derivative suit claim for injury to the corporation resulting from insider trading by corporate officers. The complaint alleged substantial harm to the corporation.

Section 5.04 of the ALI's Principles of Corporate Governance provides that a director or senior executive generally may not use corporate property, material non-public information, or her corporate position to secure a pecuniary benefit. Section 5.04(a)(3) contains an exception for the use of corporate information which "is not in connection with trading of the corporation's securities, is not a use of proprietary information of the corporation, and does not harm the corporation * * *." Section 5.04 follows the result in *Diamond* and rejects the approach of *Freeman*. Comment d(2)(a) to § 5.04 states:

> * * * Section 5.04(a) would also permit the corporation to seek damages for any actual harm it suffers as a result of the unauthorized use of material inside information. However, § 5.04(a) does not authorize the corporation to seek damages on behalf of shareholders who may have a claim based on harm suffered by them. Furthermore, to the extent that shareholders assert harm to themselves in violation of § 5.04(a) as a result of insider trading, the primary right to recovery would be in the shareholders, and under § 5.04(c) the corporation would not also be entitled to obtain recovery on the same facts for a violation of § 5.04(a) on a theory of unjust enrichment.

* * *

The cases uniformly reject the conclusion that unrelated third parties who have been given information by the corporation or who have received information as a tippee are subject to a duty of loyalty to the corporation. Such persons may nevertheless be liable to the corporation or its shareholders on a theory of participation in a breach of the duty of fair dealing owed by a director or senior executive who wrongfully supplies the inside information, or on a theory of breach of duty owed by an agent to a principal, or under a theory of breach of an agreement to hold the information received confidential, or for violation of federal or state securities laws. *See* Dirks v. Securities and Exchange Commission, 463 U.S. 646, 77 L.Ed.2d 911 (1983).

D.   FEDERAL REGULATION—RULE 10b-5

1.   INTRODUCTION

The SEC's Rule 10b-5 is "a judicial oak which has grown from little more than a legislative acorn." Blue Chip Stamps v. Manor Drug

Stores, 421 U.S. 723, 95 S.Ct. 1917, 44 L.Ed.2d 539 (1975). It is responsible for a large portion of that body of law that is often referred to as "federal corporation law"—almost always in quotation marks because of the implications of such a phrase in a post-Erie legal system.

The authority for the adoption of the rule is § 10(b) of the Securities Exchange Act of 1934, itself no more than a brief statement of a broad anti-fraud principle. The legislative history of that section is described in SEC v. Texas Gulf Sulphur Co., 401 F.2d 833, 859 (2d Cir.1968):

> Section 10(b) of the Act * * * was taken by the Conference Committee from Section 10(b) of the proposed Senate bill, S. 3420, and taken from it verbatim insofar as here pertinent. The only alteration made by the Conference Committee was to substitute the present closing language of Section 10(b), " * * * in contravention of such rules and regulations as the Commission may prescribe as necessary or appropriate in the public interest or for the protection of investors" for the closing language of the original Section 10(b) of S. 3420, " * * * which the Commission may declare to be detrimental to the interests of investors." 78 Cong.Rec. 10261 (1934).

> The Report of the Senate Committee which presented S. 3420 to the Senate summarized Section 10(b) as follows:

> Subsection (b) authorizes the Commission by rules and regulations to prohibit or regulate the use of *any other manipulative or deceptive practices which it finds detrimental to the interests of the investor.* (Emphasis supplied.)

> S.Rep. No. 792, 73rd Cong., 2d Sess. 18 (1934).

> Indeed, from its very inception, Section 10(b), and the proposed sections in H.R. 1383 and S. 3420 from which it was derived, have always been acknowledged as catchalls. See Bromberg, Securities Law: SEC Rule 10b–5, p. 19 (1967). In the House Committee hearings on the proposed House bill, Thomas G. Corcoran, Counsel with the Reconstruction Finance Corporation and a spokesman for the Roosevelt Administration, described the broad prohibitions contained in § 9(c), the section which corresponded to Section 10(b) of S. 3420 and eventually to Section 10(b) of the Act, as follows: "Subsection (c) says, 'Thou shalt not devise any other cunning devices' * * * Of course subsection (c) is a catchall clause to prevent manipulative devices. I do not think there is any objection to that kind of a clause. The Commission should have the authority to deal with new manipulative devices." Stock Exchange Regulation, Hearings before the House Committee on Interstate and Foreign Commerce, 73rd Cong., 2d Sess. 115 (1934). Although several other witnesses objected to the breadth of the proposed prohibition that Corcoran was supporting, the section as enacted did not in any way limit the broad scope of the "in connection with" phrase. See 3 Loss, Securities Regulation, 1424 n. 7 (2d ed. 1961).

The SEC probably had no idea when it adopted Rule 10b–5 in 1942 what the courts would make of its briefly worded prohibition against fraud and deceit. The rule was first held to support an implied private action in Kardon v. National Gypsum Co., 69 F.Supp. 512 (E.D.Pa.1946). The principal parties in the suit were two family groups, each of which owned 50 percent of the stock of a corporation. The defendants learned that National Gypsum was interested in purchasing the corporation and bought the shares of the plaintiffs without telling them of that fact. The defendants then conveyed the corporation's assets to National Gypsum, reaping a substantial profit. Plaintiffs asserted that the defendants were guilty of fraud and deceit in connection with the purchase of their stock. The court held that, although neither § 10(b) nor Rule 10b–5 explicitly provided a private remedy for a violation of their prohibitions, it was appropriate for the court to create one, citing the principle of tort law that the violation of a statute resulting in an injury to another is a tort. The lower courts generally followed *Kardon* in implying a private right of action for damages under Rule 10b–5, and the Supreme Court finally confirmed it in Superintendent of Insurance v. Bankers Life & Casualty Co., 404 U.S. 6, 13 n. 9, 92 S.Ct. 165, 169 n. 9, 30 L.Ed.2d 128 (1971). *See* Note on Implied Remedies in Chapter 18.

In 1961, the S.E.C. ushered in the era of insider trading analysis under Rule 10b–5 in the seminal case of *In re Cady, Roberts & Co.,* 40 S.E.C. 907 (1961). The Commission brought the action against the brokerage firm of Cady, Roberts & Co. and Gintel, one of its partners. On November 25, 1959, the directors of Curtiss–Wright Corp. met to consider the declaration of a dividend. The stock price had recently moved up and Gintel had purchased a substantial number of shares for his clients. He had also begun to dispose of some of those shares on the day before the meeting. The directors voted to cut the dividend and Cowdin, a director of Curtiss–Wright and an associate at Cady, Roberts, left the meeting after this decision but prior to its public disclosure which was inadvertently delayed. Cowdin informed Gintel of Curtiss–Wright's decision; Gintel immediately thereafter sold his customers' shares and those in a trust for his children and sold short for his own account.

The Commission held that Gintel violated Rule 10b–5 and announced the principle that a corporate insider who had material, nonpublic information concerning that corporation was under a duty either to abstain from trading in that corporation's securities, or first to disclose the nonpublic information. Chairman Cary's opinion pointed out that:

> [a]nalytically, the obligation rests on two principal elements; first, the existence of a relationship giving access, directly or indirectly, to information intended to be available only for a corporate purpose and not for the personal benefit of anyone, and second, the inherent unfairness involved where a party takes advantage of such information knowing it is unavailable to those with whom he is dealing.

40 S.E.C. at 912.

The SEC held that both Gintel and Cady, Roberts had violated Rule 10b–5 on the basis of Gintel's trading activity. The Commission concluded that:

> [t]he facts here impose on Gintel the responsibilities of those commonly referred to as "insiders." He received the information prior to its public release from a director of Curtiss–Wright, Cowdin, who was associated with [Cady, Roberts.] Cowdin's relationship to the company clearly prohibited him from selling the securities affected by the information without disclosure. By logical sequence, it should prohibit Gintel, a partner of [Cady, Roberts.]

40 S.E.C. at 912.

2. THE SCOPE OF THE RULE

Rule 10b–5 gives rise to two distinct sets of duties: (1) a duty not to trade on inside information and (2) a duty relating to the disclosure of material information. The next case frames both sets of issues and serves as a point of reference for the cases and materials that follow.

SECURITIES AND EXCHANGE COMMISSION v. TEXAS GULF SULPHUR CO.
401 F.2d 833 (2d Cir.1968), cert. denied 394 U.S. 976, 89 S.Ct. 1454, 22 L.Ed.2d 756 (1969).

Before LUMBARD, CHIEF JUDGE, and WATERMAN, MOORE, FRIENDLY, SMITH, KAUFMAN, HAYS, ANDERSON and FEINBERG, CIRCUIT JUDGES.

WATERMAN, CIRCUIT JUDGE:

This action was commenced in the United States District Court for the Southern District of New York by the Securities and Exchange Commission (the SEC) pursuant to Sec. 21(e) of the Securities Exchange Act of 1934 (the Act), 15 U.S.C. § 78u(e), against Texas Gulf Sulphur Company (TGS) and several of its officers, directors and employees *, to enjoin certain conduct by TGS and the individual defendants said to violate Section 10(b) of the Act, 15 U.S.C. Section 78j(b), and Rule 10b–5 (17 CFR 240.10b–5) (the Rule), promulgated thereunder, and to compel the rescission by the individual defendants of securities transactions assertedly conducted contrary to law. The complaint alleged (1) that defendants Fogarty, Mollison, Darke, Murray, Huntington, O'Neill, Clayton, Crawford, and Coates had either personally or through agents purchased TGS stock or calls thereon from November 12, 1963 through April 16, 1964 on the basis of material inside information concerning the

---

* The positions in TGS held by each of the defendants were: Claude O. Stephens, President and Director; Charles F. Fogarty, Executive Vice President and Director; Thomas S. Lamont, Director; Francis G. Coates, Director; Harold B. Kline, Vice President and General Counsel; Richard D. Mollison, Vice President; David M. Crawford, Secretary; Richard H. Clayton, Engineer; Walter Holyk, Chief Geologist; Kenneth H. Darke, Geologist; Earl L. Huntington, Attorney; John A. Murray, Office Manager.—Eds.

results of TGS drilling in Timmins, Ontario, while such information remained undisclosed to the investing public generally or to the particular sellers **; (2) that defendants Darke and Coates had divulged such information to others for use in purchasing TGS stock or calls [3] or recommended its purchase while the information was undisclosed to the public or to the sellers; [3] that defendants Stephens, Fogarty, Mollison, Holyk, and Kline had accepted options to purchase TGS stock on Feb. 20, 1964 without disclosing the material information as to the drilling progress to either the Stock Option Committee or the TGS Board of Directors * * *. The case was tried at length before Judge Bonsal of the Southern District of New York, sitting without a jury. Judge Bonsal in a detailed opinion decided, *inter alia,* that the insider activity prior to April 9, 1964 was not illegal because the drilling results were not "material" until then; that Clayton and Crawford had traded in violation of law because they traded after that date; that Coates had committed no violation as he did not trade before disclosure was made * * *" 258 F.Supp. 262, at 292–296 (SDNY 1966). Defendants Clayton and Crawford appeal from that part of the decision below which held that they had violated Sec. 10(b) and Rule 10b–5 and the SEC appeals from the remainder of the decision which dismissed the complaint against defendants TGS, Fogarty, Mollison, Holyk, Darke, Stephens, Kline, Murray, and Coates.

* * *

The Factual Setting

This action derives from the exploratory activities of TGS begun in 1957 on the Canadian Shield in eastern Canada. In March of 1959, aerial geophysical surveys were conducted over more than 15,000 square miles of this area by a group led by defendant Mollison, a mining engineer and a Vice President of TGS. The group included defendant Holyk, TGS's chief geologist, defendant Clayton, an electrical engineer and geophysicist, and defendant Darke, a geologist. These operations resulted in the detection of numerous anomalies, i.e., extraordinary variations in the conductivity of rocks, one of which was on the Kidd 55 segment of land located near Timmins, Ontario.

On October 29 and 30, 1963, Clayton conducted a ground geophysical survey on the northeast portion of the Kidd 55 segment which confirmed the presence of an anomaly and indicated the necessity of diamond core drilling for further evaluation. Drilling of the initial hole, K–55–1, at the strongest part of the anomaly was commenced on November 8 and terminated on November 12 at a depth of 655 feet. Visual estimates by Holyk of the core of K–55–1 indicated an average

---

** TGS stock was purchased by insiders at prices between $17–5/8 and $18–1/8 in November. The price rose steadily to about $33 on April 12, 1964, the date of the first press release issued by TGS. It then dipped to about $30 per share.—Eds.

3. A "call is a negotiable option contract by which the bearer has the right to buy from the writer of the contract a certain number of shares of a particular stock at a fixed price on or before a certain agreed-upon date.

copper content of 1.15% and an average zinc content of 8.64% over a length of 599 feet. This visual estimate convinced TGS that it was desirable to acquire the remainder of the Kidd 55 segment, and in order to facilitate this acquisition TGS President Stephens instructed the exploration group to keep the results of K–55–1 confidential and undisclosed even as to other officers, directors, and employees of TGS. The hole was concealed and a barren core was intentionally drilled off the anomaly. Meanwhile, the core of K–55–1 had been shipped to Utah for chemical assay which, when received in early December, revealed an average mineral content of 1.18% copper, 8.26% zinc, and 3.94% ounces of silver per ton over a length of 602 feet. These results were so remarkable that neither Clayton, an experienced geophysicist, nor four other TGS expert witnesses, had ever seen or heard of a comparable initial exploratory drill hole in a base metal deposit. So, the trial court concluded, "There is no doubt that the drill core of K–55–1 was unusually good and that it excited the interest and speculation of those who knew about it." Id. at 282. By March 27, 1964, TGS decided that the land acquisition program had advanced to such a point that the company might well resume drilling, and drilling was resumed on March 31.

During this period, from November 12, 1963 when K–55–1 was completed, to March 31, 1964 when drilling was resumed, certain of the individual defendants listed in fn. 2, supra, and persons listed in fn. 4, supra, said to have received "tips" from them, purchased TGS stock or calls thereon. Prior to these transactions these persons had owned 1135 shares of TGS stock and possessed no calls; thereafter they owned a total of 8235 shares and possessed 12,300 calls.

On February 20, 1964, also during this period, TGS issued stock options to 26 of its officers and employees whose salaries exceeded a specified amount, five of whom were the individual defendants Stephens, Fogarty, Mollison, Holyk, and Kline. Of these, only Kline was unaware of the detailed results of K–55–1, but he, too, knew that a hole containing favorable bodies of copper and zinc ore had been drilled in Timmins. At this time, neither the TGS Stock Option Committee nor its Board of Directors had been informed of the results of K–55–1, presumably because of the pending land acquisition program which required confidentiality. All of the foregoing defendants accepted the options granted them.

When drilling was resumed on March 31, hole K–55–3 was commenced 510 feet west of K–55–1 and was drilled easterly at a 45° angle so as to cross K–55–1 in a vertical plane. Daily progress reports of the drilling of this hole K–55–3 and of all subsequently drilled holes were sent to defendants Stephens and Fogarty (President and Executive Vice President of TGS) by Holyk and Mollison. Visual estimates of K–55–3 revealed an average mineral content of 1.12% copper and 7.93% zinc over 641 of the hole's 876–foot length. On April 7, drilling of a third hole, K–55–4, 200 feet south of and parallel to K–55–1 and westerly at a 45° angle, was commenced and mineralization was encountered over 366 of its 579–foot length. Visual estimates indicated an average content of

1.14% copper and 8.24% zinc.   Like K–55–1, both K–55–3 and K–55–4 established substantial copper mineralization on the eastern edge of the anomaly.   On the basis of these findings relative to the foregoing drilling results, the trial court concluded that the vertical plane created by the intersection of K–55–1 and K–55–3, which measured at least 350 feet wide by 500 feet deep extended southward 200 feet to its intersection with K–55–4, and that "There was real evidence that a body of commercially minable ore might exist."   Id. at 281–82.

On April 8 TGS began with a second drill rig to drill another hole, K–55–6, 300 feet easterly of K–55–1.   This hole was drilled westerly at an angle of 60° and was intended to explore mineralization beneath K–55–1.   While no visual estimates of its core were immediately available, it was readily apparent by the evening of April 10 that substantial copper mineralization had been encountered over the last 127 feet of the hole's 569–foot length.   On April 10, a third drill rig commenced drilling yet another hole, K–55–5, 200 feet north of K–55–1, parallel to the prior holes, and slanted westerly at a 45° angle.   By the evening of April 10 in this hole, too, substantial copper mineralization had been encountered over the last 42 feet of its 97–foot length.

Meanwhile, rumors that a major ore strike was in the making had been circulating throughout Canada.   On the morning of Saturday, April 11, Stephens at his home in Greenwich, Conn. read in the New York Herald Tribune and in the New York Times unauthorized reports of the TGS drilling which seemed to infer a rich strike from the fact that the drill cores had been flown to the United States for chemical assay. Stephens immediately contacted Fogarty at his home in Rye, N.Y., who in turn telephoned and later that day visited Mollison at Mollison's home in Greenwich to obtain a current report and evaluation of the drilling progress.   The following morning, Sunday, Fogarty again telephoned Mollison, inquiring whether Mollison had any further information and told him to return to Timmins with Holyk, the TGS Chief Geologist, as soon as possible "to move things along."   With the aid of one Carroll, a public relations consultant, Fogarty drafted a press release designed to quell the rumors, which release, after having been channeled through Stephens and Huntington, a TGS attorney, was issued at 3:00 P.M. on Sunday, April 12, and which appeared in the morning newspapers of general circulation on Monday, April 13.   It read in pertinent part as follows:

> NEW YORK, April 12—The following statement was made today by Dr. Charles F. Fogarty, executive vice president of Texas Gulf Sulphur Company, in regard to the company's drilling operations near Timmins, Ontario, Canada.   Dr. Fogarty said:
>
> > "During the past few days, the exploration activities of Texas Gulf Sulphur in the area of Timmins, Ontario, have been widely reported in the press, coupled with rumors of a substantial copper discovery there.   These reports exaggerate the scale of operations, and mention plans and statistics of size and grade

of ore that are without factual basis and have evidently originated by speculation of people not connected with TGS.

"The facts are as follows. TGS has been exploring in the Timmins area for six years as part of its overall search in Canada and elsewhere for various minerals—lead, copper, zinc, etc. During the course of this work, in Timmins as well as in Eastern Canada, TGS has conducted exploration entirely on its own, without the participation by others. Numerous prospects have been investigated by geophysical means and a large number of selected ones have been core-drilled. These cores are sent to the United States for assay and detailed examination as a matter of routine and on advice of expert Canadian legal counsel. No inferences as to grade can be drawn from this procedure.

"Most of the areas drilled in Eastern Canada have revealed either barren pyrite or graphite without value; a few have resulted in discoveries of small or marginal sulphide ore bodies.

"Recent drilling on one property near Timmins has led to preliminary indications that more drilling would be required for proper evaluation of this prospect. The drilling done to date has not been conclusive, but the statements made by many outside quarters are unreliable and include information and figures that are not available to TGS.

"The work done to date has not been sufficient to reach definite conclusions and any statement as to size and grade of ore would be premature and possibly misleading. When we have progressed to the point where reasonable and logical conclusions can be made, TGS will issue a definite statement to its stockholders and to the public in order to clarify the Timmins project."

* * *

The release purported to give the Timmins drilling results as of the release date, April 12. From Mollison, Fogarty had been told of the developments through 7:00 P.M. on April 10, and of the remarkable discoveries made up to that time, detailed supra, which discoveries, according to the calculations of the experts who testified for the SEC at the hearing, demonstrated that TGS had already discovered 6.2 to 8.3 million tons of proven ore having gross assay values from $26 to $29 per ton. TGS experts, on the other hand, denied at the hearing that proven or probable ore could have been calculated on April 11 or 12 because there was then no assurance of continuity in the mineralized zone.

The evidence as to the effect of this release on the investing public was equivocal and less than abundant. On April 13 the New York Herald Tribune in an article head-noted "Copper Rumor Deflated" quoted from the TGS release of April 12 and backtracked from its original April 11 report of a major strike but nevertheless inferred from the TGS release that "recent mineral exploratory activity near Timmins, Ontario, has provided preliminary favorable results, sufficient at least to require a step-up in drilling operations." Some witnesses who testified at the hearing stated that they found the release encouraging. On the other hand, a Canadian mining security specialist, Roche, stated that "earlier in the week [before April 16] we had a Dow Jones saying that they [TGS] didn't have anything basically" and a TGS stock specialist for the Midwest Stock Exchange became concerned about his long position in the stock after reading the release. The trial court stated only that "While, in retrospect, the press release may appear gloomy or incomplete, this does not make it misleading or deceptive on the basis of the facts then known." Id. at 296.

Meanwhile, drilling operations continued. By morning of April 13, in K–55–5, the fifth drill hole, substantial copper mineralization had been encountered to the 580 foot mark, and the hole was subsequently drilled to a length of 757 feet without further results. Visual estimates revealed an average content of 0.82% copper and 4.2% zinc over a 525–foot section. Also by 7:00 A.M. on April 13, K–55–6 had found mineralization to the 946–foot mark. On April 12 a fourth drill rig began to drill K–55–7, which was drilled westerly at a 45° angle, at the eastern edge of the anomaly. The next morning the 137 foot mark had been reached, fifty feet of which showed mineralization. By 7:00 P.M. on April 15, the hole had been completed to a length of 707 feet but had only encountered additional mineralization during a 26–foot length between the 425 and 451–foot marks. A mill test hole, K–55–8, had been drilled and was complete by the evening of April 13 but its mineralization had not been reported upon prior to April 16. K–55–10 was drilled westerly at a 45° angle commencing April 14 and had encountered mineralization over 231 of its 249–foot length by the evening of April 15. It, too, was drilled at the anomaly's eastern edge.

While drilling activity ensued to completion, TGS officials were taking steps toward ultimate disclosure of the discovery. On April 13, a previously-invited reporter for The Northern Miner, a Canadian mining industry journal, visited the drillsite, interviewed Mollison, Holyk and Darke, and prepared an article which confirmed a 10 million ton ore strike. This report, after having been submitted to Mollison and returned to the reporter unamended on April 15, was published in the April 16 issue. A statement relative to the extent of the discovery, in substantial part drafted by Mollison, was given to the Ontario Minister of Mines for release to the Canadian media. Mollison and Holyk expected it to be released over the airways at 11 P.M. on April 15th, but, for undisclosed reasons, it was not released until 9:40 A.M. on the 16th. An official detailed statement, announcing a strike of at least 25 million tons of ore, based on the drilling data set forth above, was read to representatives of American financial media from 10:00 A.M. to 10:10 or 10:15 A.M. on April 16, and appeared over Merrill Lynch's private wire at 10:29 A.M. and, somewhat later than expected, over the Dow Jones ticker tape at 10:54 A.M.

Between the time the first press release was issued on April 12 and the dissemination of the TGS official announcement on the morning of April 16, the only defendants before us on appeal who engaged in market activity were Clayton and Crawford and TGS director Coates. Clayton ordered 200 shares of TGS stock through his Canadian broker on April 15 and the order was executed that day over the Midwest Stock Exchange. Crawford ordered 300 shares at midnight on the 15th and another 300 shares at 8:30 A.M. the next day, and these orders were executed over the Midwest Exchange in Chicago at its opening on April 16. Coates left the TGS press conference and called his broker son-in-law Haemisegger shortly before 10:20 A.M. on the 16th and ordered 2,000 shares of TGS for family trust accounts of which Coates was a trustee but not a beneficiary; Haemisegger executed this order over the New York and Midwest Exchanges, and he and his customers purchased 1500 additional shares.

During the period of drilling in Timmins, the market price of TGS stock fluctuated but steadily gained overall. On Friday, November 8, when the drilling began the stock closed at 17 3/8; on Friday, November 15, after K–55–1 had been completed, it closed at 18. After a slight decline to 16 3/8 by Friday, November 22, the price rose to 20 7/8 by December 13, when the chemical assay results of K–55–1 were received, and closed at a high of 24 1/8 on February 21, the day after the stock options had been issued. It had reached a price of 26 by March 31, after the land acquisition program had been completed and drilling had been resumed, and continued to ascend to 30 1/8 by the close of trading on April 10, at which time the drilling progress up to then was evaluated for the April 12th press release. On April 13, the day on which the April 12 release was disseminated, TGS opened at 30 1/8, rose immediately to a high of 32 and gradually tapered off to close at 30 7/8. It closed at 30 1/4 the next day, and at 29 3/8 on April 15. On April 16, the day of the official announcement of the Timmins discovery, the price climbed to a high of 37 and closed at 36 3/8. By May 15, TGS stock was selling at 58 1/4.

I. The Individual Defendants

A. Introductory

* * *

Rule 10b–5 was promulgated pursuant to the grant of authority given the SEC by Congress in Section 10(b) of the Securities Exchange Act of 1934 (15 U.S.C. § 78j(b)). By that Act Congress proposed to prevent inequitable and unfair practices and to insure fairness in securities transactions generally, whether conducted face-to-face, over the counter, or on exchanges, see 3 Loss, Securities Regulation 1455–56 (2d ed. 1961). The Act and the Rule apply to the transactions here, all of which were consummated on exchanges. Whether predicated on traditional fiduciary concepts, see, e.g., Hotchkiss v. Fisher, 136 Kan. 530, 16 P.2d 531 (Kan.1932), or on the "special facts" doctrine, see, e.g., Strong v. Repide, 213 U.S. 419, 29 S.Ct. 521, 53 L.Ed. 853 (1909), the Rule is based in policy on the justifiable expectation of the securities market-place that all investors trading on impersonal exchanges have relatively equal access to material information, see Cary, Insider Trading in Stocks, 21 Bus.Law. 1009, 1010 (1966), Fleischer, Securities Trading and Corporation Information Practices: The Implications of the Texas Gulf Sulphur Proceeding, 51 Va.L.Rev. 1271, 1278–80 (1965). The essence of the Rule is that anyone who, trading for his own account in the securities of a corporation has "access, directly or indirectly, to information intended to be available only for a corporate purpose and not for the personal benefit of anyone" may not take "advantage of such information knowing it is unavailable to those with whom he is dealing," i.e., the investing public. Matter of Cady, Roberts & Co., 40 SEC 907, 912 (1961). Insiders, as directors or management officers are, of course, by this Rule, precluded from so unfairly dealing, but the Rule is also applicable to one possessing the information who may not be strictly termed an "insider" within the meaning of Sec. 16(b) of the Act. Cady, Roberts, supra. Thus, anyone in possession of material inside information must either disclose it to the investing public, or, if he is disabled from disclosing it in order to protect a corporate confidence, or he chooses not to do so, must abstain from trading in or recommending the securities concerned while such inside information remains undisclosed. So, it is here no justification for insider activity that disclosure was forbidden by the legitimate corporate objective of acquiring options to purchase the land surrounding the exploration site; if the information was, as the SEC contends, material, its possessors should have kept out of the market until disclosure was accomplished. Cady, Roberts, supra at 911.

B. Material Inside Information

An insider is not, of course, always foreclosed from investing in his own company merely because he may be more familiar with company operations than are outside investors. An insider's duty to disclose information or his duty to abstain from dealing in his company's securities arises only in "those situations which are essentially extraordinary in nature and which are reasonably certain to have a substantial effect on the market price of the security if [the extraordinary situation is] disclosed." Fleischer, Securities Trading and Corporate Information Practices: The Implications of the Texas Gulf Sulphur Proceeding, 51 Va.L.Rev. 1271, 1289.

Nor is an insider obligated to confer upon outside investors the benefit of his superior financial or other expert analysis by disclosing his educated guesses or predictions. The only regulatory objective is that access to material information be enjoyed equally, but this objective requires nothing more than the disclosure of basic facts so that outsiders may draw upon their own evaluative expertise in reaching their own investment decisions with knowledge equal to that of the insiders.

This is not to suggest, however, as did the trial court, that "the test of materiality must necessarily be a conservative one, particularly since many actions under Section 10(b) are brought on the basis of hindsight," 258 F.Supp. 262 at 280, in the sense that the materiality of facts is to be assessed solely by measuring the effect the knowledge of the facts would have upon prudent or conservative investors. As we stated in List v. Fashion Park, Inc., 340 F.2d 457, 462, "The basic test of materiality * * * is whether a *reasonable* man would attach importance * * * in determining his choice of action in the transaction in question. Restatement, Torts § 538(2)(a); accord Prosser, Torts 554–55; I. Harper & James, Torts 565–66." (Emphasis supplied.) This, of course, encompasses any fact " * * * which in reasonable and objective contemplation *might* affect the value of the corporation's stock or securities * * *." List v. Fashion Park, Inc., supra at 462, quoting from Kohler v. Kohler Co., 319 F.2d 634, 642 (7 Cir.1963). (Emphasis supplied.) Such a fact is a material fact and must be effectively disclosed to the investing public prior to the commencement of insider trading in the corporation's securities. The speculators and chartists of Wall and Bay Streets are also "reasonable" investors entitled to the same legal protection afforded conservative traders. Thus, material facts include not only information disclosing the earnings and distributions of a company but also those facts which affect the probable future of the company and those which may affect the desire of investors to buy, sell, or hold the company's securities.

In each case, then, whether facts are material within Rule 10b–5 when the facts relate to a particular event and are undisclosed by those persons who are knowledgeable thereof will depend at any given time upon a balancing of both the indicated probability that the event will occur and the anticipated magnitude of the event in light of the totality of the company activity. Here, notwithstanding the trial court's conclusion that the results of the first drill core, K–55–1, were "too 'remote' * * * to have had any significant impact on the market, i.e., to be deemed material," 258 F.Supp. at 283, knowledge of the possibility, which surely was more than marginal, of the existence of a mine of the vast magnitude indicated by the remarkably rich drill core located rather close to the surface (suggesting minability by the less expensive open-pit method) within the confines of a large anomaly (suggesting an extensive region of mineralization) might well have affected the price of TGS stock and would certainly have been an important fact to a reasonable, if speculative, investor in deciding whether he should buy, sell, or hold. After all, this first drill core was "unusually good and * * * excited the interest and speculation of those who knew about it." 258 F.Supp. at 282.

Our disagreement with the district judge on the issue does not, then, go to his findings of basic fact, as to which the "clearly erroneous" rule would apply, but to his understanding of the legal standard applicable to them. Our survey of the facts found below conclusively establishes that knowledge of the results of the discovery hole, K–55–1, would have been important to a reasonable investor and might have affected the price of the stock.[12] On April 16, The Northern Miner, a trade publication in wide circulation among mining stock specialists, called K–55–1, the discovery hole, "one of the most impressive drill holes completed in modern times." Roche, a Canadian broker whose firm specialized in mining securities, characterized the importance to investors of the results of K–55–1. He stated that the completion of "the first drill hole" with "a 600 foot drill core is very very significant * * * anything over 200 feet is considered very significant and 600 feet is just beyond your wildest imagination." He added, however, that it "is a natural thing to buy more stock once they give you the first drill hole." Additional testimony revealed that the prices of stocks of other companies, albeit less diversified, smaller firms, had increased substantially solely on the basis of the discovery of good anomalies or even because of the proximity of their lands to the situs of a potentially major strike.

Finally, a major factor in determining whether the K–55–1 discovery was a material fact is the importance attached to the drilling results by those who knew about it. In view of other unrelated recent developments favorably affecting TGS, participation by an informed person in a regular stock-purchase program, or even sporadic trading by an informed person, might lend only nominal support to the inference of the materiality of the K–55–1 discovery; nevertheless, the timing by those who knew of it, of their stock purchases and their purchases of *short-term* calls—purchases in some cases by individuals who had never before purchased calls or even TGS stock—virtually compels the inference that the insiders were influenced by the drilling results. This insider trading activity, which surely constitutes highly pertinent evidence and the only truly objective evidence of the materiality of the K–55–1 discovery, was apparently disregarded by the court below in favor of the testimony of defendants' expert witnesses, all of whom "agreed that one drill core does not establish an ore body, much less a mine," 258 F.Supp. at 282–283. Significantly, however, the court below, while relying upon what these defense experts said the defendant insiders *ought* to have thought about the worth to TGS of the K–55–1 discovery, and finding that from November 12, 1963 to April 6, 1964 Fogarty, Murray, Holyk and Darke spent more than $100,000 in purchasing TGS stock and calls on that stock, made no finding that the insiders were motivated by any factor other than the extraordinary K–55–1 discovery when they bought their stock and their calls. No reason appears why outside investors, perhaps better acquainted with speculative modes of investment and with, in

---

12. We do not suggest that material facts must be disclosed immediately; the timing of disclosure is a matter for the business judgment of the corporate officers entrusted with the management of the corporation within the affirmative disclosure requirements promulgated by the exchanges and by the SEC. Here, a valuable corporate purpose was served by delaying the publication of the K–55–1 discovery. We do intend to convey, however, that where a corporate purpose is thus served by withholding the news of a material fact, those persons who are thus quite properly true to their corporate trust must not during the period of nondisclosure deal personally in the corporation's securities or give to outsiders confidential information not generally available to all the corporations' stockholders and to the public at large.

many cases, perhaps more capital at their disposal for intelligent specu-lation, would have been less influenced, and would not have been similarly motivated to invest if they had known what the insider inves-tors knew about the K–55–1 discovery.

Our decision to expand the limited protection afforded outside investors by the trial court's narrow definition of materiality is not at all shaken by fears that the elimination of insider trading benefits will deplete the ranks of capable corporate managers by taking away an incentive to accept such employment. Such benefits, in essence, are forms of secret corporate compensation, see Cary, Corporate Standards and Legal Rules, 50 Calif.L.Rev. 408, 409–10 (1962), derived at the expense of the uninformed investing public and not at the expense of the corporation which receives the sole benefit from insider incentives. Moreover, adequate incentives for corporate officers may be provided by properly administered stock options and employee purchase plans of which there are many in existence. In any event, the normal motivation induced by stock ownership, i.e., the identification of an individual with corporate progress, is ill-promoted by condoning the sort of speculative insider activity which occurred here; for example, some of the corpora-tion's stock was sold at market in order to purchase short-term calls upon that stock, calls which would never be exercised to increase a stockholder equity in TGS unless the market price of that stock rose sharply.

The core of Rule 10b–5 is the implementation of the Congressional purpose that all investors should have equal access to the rewards of participation in securities transactions. It was the intent of Congress that all members of the investing public should be subject to identical market risks,—which market risks include, of course, the risk that one's evaluative capacity or one's capital available to put at risk may exceed another's capacity or capital. The insiders here were not trading on an equal footing with the outside investors. They alone were in a position to evaluate the probability and magnitude of what seemed from the outset to be a major ore strike; they alone could invest safely, secure in the expectation that the price of TGS stock would rise substantially in the event such a major strike should materialize, but would decline little, if at all, in the event of failure, for the public, ignorant at the outset of the favorable probabilities would likewise be unaware of the unproduc-tive exploration, and the additional exploration costs would not signifi-cantly affect TGS market prices. Such inequities based upon unequal access to knowledge should not be shrugged off as inevitable in our way of life, or, in view of the congressional concern in the area, remain uncorrected.

We hold, therefore, that all transactions in TGS stock or calls by individuals apprised of the drilling results of K–55–1 were made in violation of Rule 10b–5. Inasmuch as the visual evaluation of that drill core (a generally reliable estimate though less accurate than a chemical assay) constituted material information, those advised of the results of the visual evaluation as well as those informed of the chemical assay traded in violation of law. The geologist Darke possessed undisclosed material information and traded in TGS securities. Therefore we reverse the dismissal of the action as to him and his personal transactions. The trial court also found, 258 F.Supp. at 284, that Darke, after the drilling of K–55–1 had been completed and with detailed knowledge of the results thereof, told certain outside individuals that TGS "was a good buy." These individuals thereafter acquired TGS stock and calls. The trial court also found that later, as of March 30, 1964, Darke not only used his material knowledge for his own purchases but that the substantial amounts of TGS stock and calls purchased by these outside individuals on that day, was "strong circumstantial evidence that Darke must have passed the word to one or more of his 'tippees' that drilling on the Kidd 55 segment was about to be resumed." 258 F.Supp. at 284. Obviously if such a resumption were to have any meaning to such "tippees," they must have previously been told of K–55–1.

Unfortunately, however, there was no definitive resolution below of Darke's liability in these premises for the trial court held as to him, as it held as to all the other individual defendants, that this "undisclosed information" never became material until April 9. As it is our holding that the information acquired after the drilling of K–55–1 was material, we, on the basis of the findings of direct and circumstantial evidence on the issue that the trial court has already expressed, hold that Darke violated Rule 10b–5(3) and Section 10(b) by "tipping" and we remand, pursuant to the agreement of the parties, for a determination of the appropriate remedy. As Darke's "tippees" are not defendants in this action, we need not decide whether, if they acted with actual or constructive knowledge that the material information was undisclosed, their conduct is as equally violative of the Rule as the conduct of their insider source, though we note that it certainly could be equally reprehensible.

With reference to Huntington, the trial court found that he "had no detailed knowledge as to the work" on the Kidd–55 segment, 258 F.Supp. 281. Nevertheless, the evidence shows that he knew about and participated in TGS's land acquisition program which followed the receipt of the K–55–1 drilling results, and that on February 26, 1964 he purchased 50 shares of TGS stock. Later, on March 16, he helped prepare a letter for Dr. Holyk's signature in which TGS made a substantial offer for lands near K–55–1, and on the same day he, who had never before purchased calls on any stock, purchased a call on 100 shares of TGS stock. We are satisfied that these purchases in February and March, coupled with his readily inferable and probably reliable, understanding of the highly favorable nature of preliminary operations on the Kidd segment, demonstrate that Huntington possessed material inside information such as to make his purchase violative of the Rule and the Act.

C. When May Insiders Act?

Appellant Crawford, who ordered the purchase of TGS stock shortly before the TGS April 16 official announcement, and defendant Coates, who placed orders with and communicated the news to his broker immediately after the official announcement was read at the TGS-called press conference, concede that they were in possession of material information. They contend, however, that their purchases were not proscribed purchases for the news had already been effectively disclosed. We disagree.

Crawford telephoned his orders to his Chicago broker about midnight on April 15 and again at 8:30 in the morning of the 16th, with instructions to buy at the opening of the Midwest Stock Exchange that morning. The trial court's finding that "he sought to, and did, 'beat the news,' " 258 F.Supp. at 287, is well documented by the record. The rumors of a major ore strike which had been circulated in Canada and, to a lesser extent, in New York, had been disclaimed by the TGS press release of April 12, which significantly promised the public an official detailed announcement when possibilities had ripened into actualities. The abbreviated announcement to the Canadian press at 9:40 A.M. on the 16th by the Ontario Minister of Mines and the report carried by The Northern Miner, parts of which had sporadically reached New York on the morning of the 16th through reports from Canadian affiliates to a few New York investment firms, are assuredly not the equivalent of the official 10–15 minute announcement which was not released to the American financial press until after 10:00 A.M. Crawford's orders had been placed before that. Before insiders may act upon material information, such information must have been effectively disclosed in a manner sufficient to insure its availability to the investing public. Particularly here, where a formal announcement to the entire financial news media had been promised in a prior official release known to the media, all insider activity must await dissemination of the promised official announcement.

Coates was absolved by the court below because his telephone order was placed shortly before 10:20 A.M. on April 16, which was after the announcement had been made even though the news could not be considered already a matter of public information. 258 F.Supp. at 288. This result seems to have been predicated upon a misinterpretation of dicta in *Cady, Roberts,* where the SEC instructed insiders to "keep out of the market until the established procedures for public release of the information are *carried out* instead of hastening to execute transactions in advance of, and in frustration of, the objectives of the release," 40 S.E.C. at 915 (emphasis supplied). The reading of a news release, which prompted Coates into action, is merely the first step in the process of dissemination required for compliance with the regulatory objective of providing all investors with an equal opportunity to make informed investment judgments. Assuming that the contents of the official release could instantaneously be acted upon,[18] at the minimum Coates

---

18. Although the only insider who acted after the news appeared over the Dow Jones broad tape is not an appellant and therefore we need not discuss the necessity of considering the advisability of a "reasonable waiting period" during which outsiders may absorb and evaluate disclosures, we note in passing that, where the news is of a

should have waited until the news could reasonably have been expected to appear over the media of widest circulation, the Dow Jones broad tape, rather than hastening to insure an advantage to himself and his broker son-in-law.

* * *

II. The Corporate Defendant

Introductory

At 3:00 P.M. on April 12, 1964, evidently believing it desirable to comment upon the rumors concerning the Timmins project, TGS issued the press release quoted in pertinent part in the text. * * * The SEC argued below and maintains on this appeal that this release painted a misleading and deceptive picture of the drilling progress at the time of its issuance, and hence violated Rule 10b–5(2). TGS relies on the holding of the court below that "The issuance of the release produced no unusual market action" and "In the absence of a showing that the purpose of the April 12 press release was to affect the market price of TGS stock to the advantage of TGS or its insiders, the issuance of the press release did not constitute a violation of Section 10(b) or Rule 10b–5 since it was not issued 'in connection with the purchase or sale of any security' " and, alternatively, "even if it had been established that the April 12 release was issued in connection with the purchase or sale of any security, the Commission has failed to demonstrate that it was false, misleading or deceptive." 258 F.Supp. at 294.

Before further discussing this matter it seems desirable to state exactly what the SEC claimed in its complaint and what it seeks. The specific SEC allegation in its complaint is that this April 12 press release " * * * was materially false and misleading and was known by certain of defendant Texas Gulf's officers and employees, including defendants Fogarty, Mollison, Holyk, Darke and Clayton, to be materially false and misleading."

The specific relief the SEC seeks is, pursuant to Section 21(e) of Securities Exchange Act of 1934, 15 U.S.C.A. § 78u(e), a permanent injunction restraining the issuance of any further materially false and misleading publicly distributed informative items.

B.   The "In Connection With * * * " Requirement.

In adjudicating upon the relationship of this phrase to the case before us it would appear that the court below used a standard that does not reflect the congressional purpose that prompted the passage of the Securities Exchange Act of 1934.

sort which is not readily translatable into investment action, insiders may not take advantage of their advance opportunity to evaluate the information by acting immediately upon dissemination. In any event, the permissible timing of insider transactions after disclosures of various sorts is one of the many areas of expertise for appropriate exercise of the SEC's rule-making power, which we hope will be utilized in the future to provide some predictability of certainty for the business community.

The dominant congressional purposes underlying the Securities Exchange Act of 1934 were to promote free and open public securities markets and to protect the investing public from suffering inequities in trading, including, specifically, inequities that follow from trading that has been stimulated by the publication of false or misleading corporate information releases. * * *

Therefore it seems clear from the legislative purpose Congress expressed in the Act, and the legislative history of Section 10(b) that Congress when it used the phrase "in connection with the purchase or sale of any security" intended only that the device employed, whatever it might be, be of a sort that would cause reasonable investors to rely thereon, and, in connection therewith, so relying, cause them to purchase or sell a corporation's securities. There is no indication that Congress intended that the corporations or persons responsible for the issuance of a misleading statement would not violate the section unless they engaged in related securities transactions or otherwise acted with wrongful motives; indeed, the obvious purposes of the Act to protect the investing public and to secure fair dealing in the securities markets would be seriously undermined by applying such a gloss onto the legislative language. Absent a securities transaction by an insider it is almost impossible to prove that a wrongful purpose motivated the issuance of the misleading statement. The mere fact that an insider did not engage in securities transactions does not negate the possibility of wrongful purpose; perhaps the market did not react to the misleading statement as much as was anticipated or perhaps the wrongful purpose was something other than the desire to buy at a low price or sell at a high price. Of even greater relevance to the Congressional purpose of investor protection is the fact that the investing public may be injured as much by one's misleading statement containing inaccuracies caused by negligence as by a misleading statement published intentionally to further a wrongful purpose. We do not believe that Congress intended that the proscriptions of the Act would not be violated unless the makers of a misleading statement also participated in pertinent securities transactions in connection therewith, or unless it could be shown that the issuance of the statement was motivated by a plan to benefit the corporation or themselves at the expense of a duped investing public.

* * *

* * * Accordingly, we hold that Rule 10b–5 is violated whenever assertions are made, as here, in a manner reasonably calculated to influence the investing public, e.g., by means of the financial media, if such assertions are false or misleading or are so incomplete as to mislead irrespective of whether the issuance of the release was motivated by corporate officials for ulterior purposes. It seems clear, however, that if corporate management demonstrates that it was diligent in ascertaining that the information it published was the whole truth and that such

diligently obtained information was disseminated in good faith, Rule 10b–5 would not have been violated.

C. Did the Issuance of the April 12 Release Violate Rule 10b–5?

Turning first to the question of whether the release was misleading, i.e., whether it conveyed to the public a false impression of the drilling situation at the time of its issuance, we note initially that the trial court did not actually decide this question. Its conclusion that "the Commission has failed to demonstrate that it was false, misleading or deceptive," 258 F.Supp. at 294, seems to have derived from its views that "The defendants are to be judged *on the facts known to them* when the April 12 release was issued," 258 F.Supp. at 295 (emphasis supplied), that the draftsmen "exercised reasonable business judgment under the circumstances," 258 F.Supp. at 296, and that the release was not "misleading or deceptive *on the basis of the facts then known,*" 258 F.Supp. at 296 (emphasis supplied) rather than from an appropriate primary inquiry into the meaning of the statement to the reasonable investor and its relationship to truth. While we certainly agree with the trial court that "in retrospect, the press release may appear gloomy or incomplete," 258 F.Supp. at 296, we cannot, from the present record, by applying the standard Congress intended, definitively conclude that it was deceptive or misleading to the reasonable investor, or that he would have been misled by it. Certain newspaper accounts of the release viewed the release as confirming the existence of preliminary favorable developments, and this optimistic view was held by some brokers, so it could be that the reasonable investor would have read between the lines of what appears to us to be an inconclusive and negative statement and would have envisioned the actual situation at the Kidd segment on April 12. On the other hand, in view of the decline of the market price of TGS stock from a high of 32 on the morning of April 13 when the release was disseminated to 29–3/8 by the close of trading on April 15, and the reaction to the release by other brokers, it is far from certain that the release was generally interpreted as a highly encouraging report or even encouraging at all. Accordingly, we remand this issue to the district court that took testimony and heard and saw the witnesses for a determination of the character of the release in the light of the facts existing at the time of the release, by applying the standard of whether the reasonable investor, in the exercise of due care, would have been misled by it.

In the event that it is found that the statement was misleading to the reasonable investor it will then become necessary to determine whether its issuance resulted from a lack of due diligence. The only remedy the Commission seeks against the corporation is an injunction, and therefore we do not find it necessary to decide whether just a lack of due diligence on the part of TGS, absent a showing of bad faith, would subject the corporation to any liability for damages. We have recently stated in a case involving a private suit under Rule 10b–5 in which damages and an injunction were sought, " 'It is not necessary in a suit for equitable or prophylactic relief to establish all the elements required in a suit for monetary damages.' "   Mutual Shares Corp. v. Genesco, Inc., 384 F.2d 540, 547, quoting from SEC v. Capital Gains Research Bureau, Inc., 375 U.S. 180, 193, 84 S.Ct. 275, 11 L.Ed.2d 237 (1963).

We hold only that, in an action for injunctive relief, the district court has the discretionary power under Rule 10b–5 and Section 10(b) to issue an injunction, if the misleading statement resulted from a lack of due diligence on the part of TGS.   The trial court did not find it necessary to decide whether TGS exercised such diligence and has not yet attempted to resolve this issue.   While the trial court concluded that TGS had exercised "reasonable *business* judgment under the circumstances," 258 F.Supp. at 296 (emphasis supplied) it applied an incorrect *legal* standard in appraising whether TGS should have issued its April 12 release on the basis of the facts known to its draftsmen at the time of its preparation, 258 F.Supp. at 295, and in assuming that disclosure of the full underlying facts of the Timmins situation was not a viable alternative to the vague generalities which were asserted.   258 F.Supp. at 296.

It is not altogether certain from the present record that the draftsmen could, as the SEC suggests, have readily obtained current reports of the drilling progress over the weekend of April 10–12, but they certainly should have obtained them if at all possible for them to do so.   However, even if it were not possible to evaluate and transmit current data in time to prepare the release on April 12, it would seem that TGS could have delayed the preparation a bit until an accurate report of a rapidly changing situation was possible.   See 258 F.Supp. at 296.   At the very least, if TGS felt compelled to respond to the spreading rumors of a spectacular discovery, it would have been more accurate to have stated that the situation was in flux and that the release was prepared as of April 10 information rather than purporting to report the progress "to date."   Moreover, it would have obviously been better to have specifically described the known drilling progress as of April 10 by stating the basic facts.   Such an explicit disclosure would have permitted the investing public to evaluate the "prospect" of a mine at Timmins without having to read between the lines to understand that preliminary indications were favorable—in itself an understatement.

The choice of an ambiguous general statement rather than a summary of the specific facts cannot reasonably be justified by any claimed urgency.   The avoidance of liability for misrepresentation in the event that the Timmins project failed, a highly unlikely event as of April 12 or April 13, did not forbid the accurate and truthful divulgence of detailed results which need not, of course, have been accompanied by conclusory assertions of success.   Nor is it any justification that such an explicit disclosure of the truth might have "encouraged the rumor mill which they were seeking to allay."   258 F.Supp. at 296.

We conclude, then, that, having established that the release was issued in a manner reasonably calculated to affect the market price of TGS stock and to influence the investing public, we must remand to the district court to decide whether the release was misleading to the reasonable investor and if found to be misleading, whether the court in its discretion should issue the injunction the SEC seeks.

* * *

CONCLUSION

In summary, therefore, we affirm the finding of the court below that appellants Richard H. Clayton and David M. Crawford have violated 15 U.S.C.A. § 78j(b) and Rule 10b–5; we reverse the judgment order entered below dismissing the complaint against appellees Charles F. Fogarty, Richard H. Clayton, Richard D. Mollison, Walter Holyk, Kenneth H. Darke, Earl L. Huntington, and Francis G. Coates, as we find that they have violated 15 U.S.C.A. § 78j(b) and Rule 10b–5. As to these eight individuals we remand so that in accordance with the agreement between the parties the Commission may notice a hearing before the court below to determine the remedies to be applied against them. We reverse the judgment order dismissing the complaint against Claude O. Stephens, Charles F. Fogarty, and Harold B. Kline as recipients of stock options, direct the district court to consider in its discretion whether to issue injunction orders against Stephens and Fogarty, and direct that an order issue rescinding the option granted Kline and that such further remedy be applied against him as may be proper by way of an order of restitution * * *.

* * * [W]e reverse the judgment dismissing the complaint against Texas Gulf Sulphur Company, remand the cause as to it for further determination below, in light of the approach explicated by us in the foregoing opinion, as to whether, in the exercise of its discretion the injunction against it which the Commission seeks should be ordered.

On remand, the district court ordered those TGS insiders who had, prior to April 16, purchased TGS stock or recommended its purchase to others to disgorge their profits and those of their tippees to the corporation. The profits were held to be "the difference between the mean average price of TGS common stock on the New York Stock Exchange on April 17, 1964, which has been stipulated by the parties to be 40 3/8, and the purchase price of their shares." SEC v. Texas Gulf Sulphur Co., 312 F.Supp. 77 (S.D.N.Y.1970), aff'd 446 F.2d 1301 (2d Cir.1971). The decree made no provision for attempting to contact the defrauded sellers from whom the defendants or their tippees had bought. The damages paid by the defendants were, however, to be held in an escrow account, subject to court order, for five years after which any amount that had not been paid out to private claimants would become the property of the corporation. The settlement of some of the private actions arising from the insider trading aspects of the case is set forth in Cannon v. Texas Gulf Sulphur Co., 55 F.R.D. 308 (S.D.N.Y.1972).

3. REGULATION OF INSIDER TRADING

CHIARELLA v. UNITED STATES
445 U.S. 222, 100 S.Ct. 1108, 63 L.Ed.2d 348 (1980).

MR. JUSTICE POWELL delivered the opinion of the Court.

The question in this case is whether a person who learns from the confidential documents of one corporation that it is planning an attempt to secure control of a second corporation violates § 10(b) of the Securities Exchange Act of 1934 if he fails to disclose the impending takeover before trading in the target company's securities.

I

Petitioner is a printer by trade. In 1975 and 1976, he worked as a "markup man" in the New York composing room of Pandick Press, a financial printer. Among documents that petitioner handled were five announcements of corporate takeover bids. When these documents were delivered to the printer, the identities of the acquiring and target corporations were concealed by blank spaces or false names. The true names were sent to the printer on the night of the final printing.

The petitioner, however, was able to deduce the names of the target companies before the final printing from other information contained in the documents. Without disclosing his knowledge, petitioner purchased stock in the target companies and sold the shares immediately after the takeover attempts were made public. By this method, petitioner realized a gain of slightly more than $30,000 in the course of 14 months. Subsequently, the Securities and Exchange Commission (Commission or SEC) began an investigation of his trading activities. In May 1977, petitioner entered into a consent decree with the Commission in which he agreed to return his profits to the sellers of the shares. On the same day, he was discharged by Pandick Press.

In January 1978, petitioner was indicted on 17 counts of violating § 10(b) of the Securities Exchange Act of 1934 (1934 Act) and SEC Rule 10b–5. After petitioner unsuccessfully moved to dismiss the indictment, he was brought to trial and convicted on all counts.

The Court of Appeals for the Second Circuit affirmed petitioner's conviction. 588 F.2d 1358 (1978). We granted certiorari, 441 U.S. 942, 99 S.Ct. 2158, 60 L.Ed.2d 1043 (1979), and we now reverse.

II

* * *

This case concerns the legal effect of the petitioner's silence. The District Court's charge permitted the jury to convict the petitioner if it found that he willfully failed to inform sellers of target company securities that he knew of a forthcoming takeover bid that would make their shares more valuable. In order to decide whether silence in such circumstances violates § 10(b), it is necessary to review the language and legislative history of that statute as well as its interpretation by the Commission and the federal courts.

Although the starting point of our inquiry is the language of the statute, Ernst & Ernst v. Hochfelder, 425 U.S. 185, 197, 96 S.Ct. 1375, 1382, 47 L.Ed.2d 668 (1976), § 10(b) does not state whether silence may constitute a manipulative or deceptive device. Section 10(b) was designed as a catchall clause to prevent fraudulent practices. *Id.*, at 202, 206. But neither the legislative history nor the statute itself affords specific guidance for the resolution of this case. When Rule 10b–5 was promulgated in 1942, the SEC did not discuss the possibility that failure to provide information might run afoul of § 10(b).

The SEC took an important step in the development of § 10(b) when it held that a broker-dealer and his firm violated that section by selling securities on the basis of undisclosed information obtained from a director of the issuer corporation who was also a registered representative of the brokerage firm. In *Cady, Roberts & Co.*, 40 S.E.C. 907 (1961), the Commission decided that a corporate insider must abstain from trading in the shares of his corporation unless he has first disclosed all material inside information known to him. The obligation to disclose or abstain derives from

> [a]n affirmative duty to disclose material information[,] [which] has been traditionally imposed on corporate "insiders," particular officers, directors, or controlling stockholders. We, and the courts have consistently held that insiders must disclose material facts which are known to them by virtue of their position but which are not known to persons with whom they deal and which, if known, would affect their investment judgment. *Id.*, at 911.

The Commission emphasized that the duty arose from (i) The existence of a relationship affording access to inside information intended to be available only for a corporate purpose, and (ii) the unfairness of allowing a corporate insider to take advantage of that information by trading without disclosure. *Id.*, at 912, and n. 15.

That the relationship between a corporate insider and the stockholders of his corporation gives rise to a disclosure obligation is not a novel twist of the law. At common law, misrepresentation made for the purpose of inducing reliance upon the false statement is fraudulent. But one who fails to disclose material information prior to the consummation of a transaction commits fraud only when he is under a duty to do so. And the duty to disclose arises when one party has information "that the other [party] is entitled to know because of a fiduciary or similar relation of trust and confidence between them." In its *Cady, Roberts* decision, the Commission recognized a relationship of trust and confidence between the shareholders of a corporation and those insiders who have obtained confidential information by reason of their position with that corporation. This relationship gives rise to a duty to disclose because of the "necessity of preventing a corporate insider from [taking] * * * unfair advantage of the uninformed minority stockholders." Speed v. Transamerica Corp., 99 F.Supp. 808, 829 (D.Del.1951).

The Federal courts have found violations of § 10(b) where corporate insiders used undisclosed information for their own benefit. *E.g.,* SEC v. Texas Gulf Sulphur Co., 401 F.2d 833 (CA2 1968), cert. denied, 404 U.S. 1005, 92 S.Ct. 561, 30 L.Ed.2d 558 (1972). The cases also have emphasized, in accordance with the common-law rule, that "[t]he party charged with failing to disclose market information must be under a duty to disclose it." Frigitemp Corp. v. Financial Dynamics Fund, Inc., 524 F.2d 275, 282 (CA2 1975). Accordingly, a purchaser of stock who has no duty to a prospective seller because he is neither an insider nor a fiduciary has been held to have no obligation to reveal material facts.

This Court followed the same approach in Affiliated Ute Citizens v. United States, 406 U.S. 128, 92 S.Ct. 1456, 31 L.Ed.2d 741 (1972). A group of American Indians formed a corporation to manage joint assets derived from tribal holdings. The corporation issued stock to its Indian shareholders and designated a local bank as its transfer agent. Because of the speculative nature of the corporate assets and the difficulty of ascertaining the true value of a share, the corporation requested the bank to stress to its stockholders the importance of retaining the stock. *Id.,* at 146, 92 S.Ct., at 1468. Two of the bank's assistant managers aided the shareholders in disposing of stock which the managers knew was traded in two separate markets—a primary market of Indians selling to non-Indians through the bank and a resale market consisting entirely of non-Indians. Indian sellers charged that the assistant managers had violated § 10(b) and Rule 10b–5 by failing to inform them of the higher prices prevailing in the resale market. The Court recognized that no duty of disclosure would exist if the bank merely had acted as a transfer agent. But the bank also had assumed a duty to act on behalf of the shareholders, and the Indian sellers had relied upon its personnel when they sold their stock. *Id.,* at 152, 92 S.Ct., at 1471. Because these officers of the bank were charged with a responsibility to the shareholders, they could not act as market makers inducing the Indians to sell their stock without disclosing the existence of the more favorable non-Indian market. *Id.,* at 152–153, 92 S.Ct., at 1471–1472.

Thus, administrative and judicial interpretations have established that silence in connection with the purchase or sale of securities may operate as a fraud actionable under § 10(b) despite the absence of statutory language or legislative history specifically addressing the legality of nondisclosure. But such liability is premised upon a duty to disclose arising from a relationship of trust and confidence between parties to a transaction. Application of a duty to disclose prior to trading guarantees that corporate insiders, who have an obligation to place the shareholder's welfare before their own, will not benefit personally through fraudulent use of material nonpublic information.[12]

---

12. "Tippees" of corporate insiders have been held liable under § 10(b) because they have a duty not to profit from the use of inside information that they know is

III

In this case, the petitioner was convicted of violating § 10(b) although he was not a corporate insider and he received no confidential information from the target company. Moreover, the "market information" upon which he relied did not concern the earning power or operations of the target company, but only the plans of the acquiring company. Petitioner's use of that information was not a fraud under § 10(b) unless he was subject to an affirmative duty to disclose it before trading. In this case, the jury instructions failed to specify any such duty. In effect, the trial court instructed the jury that petitioner owed a duty to everyone; to all sellers, indeed, to the market as a whole. The jury simply was told to decide whether petitioner used material, nonpublic information at a time when "he knew other people trading in the securities market did not have access to the same information." Record, at 677.

The Court of Appeals affirmed the conviction by holding that "*[a]nyone*—corporate insider or not—who regularly receives material nonpublic information may not use that information to trade in securities without incurring an affirmative duty to disclose." 588 F.2d 1358, 1365 (CA2 1978) (emphasis in original). Although the court said that its test would include only persons who regularly receive material nonpublic information, *id.,* at 1366, its rationale for that limitation is unrelated to the existence of a duty to disclose.[14] The Court of Appeals, like the trial court, failed to identify a relationship between petitioner and the sellers that could give rise to a duty. Its decision thus rested solely upon its belief that the federal securities laws have "created a system providing equal access to information necessary for reasoned and intelligent invest-

---

confidential and know or should know came from a corporate insider, Shapiro v. Merrill Lynch, Pierce, Fenner & Smith, 495 F.2d 228, 237–238 (CA2 1974). The tippee's obligation has been viewed as arising from his role as a participant after the fact in the insider's breach of a fiduciary duty. Subcommittees of American Bar Association Section of Corporation, Banking, and Business Law, Comment Letter on Material, Non–Public Information (Oct. 15, 1973) reprinted in BNA, Securities Regulation & Law Report No. 233, at D–1, D–2 (Jan. 2, 1974).

14. The Court of Appeals said that its "regular access to market information" test would create a workable rule embracing "those who occupy * * * strategic places in the market mechanism." United States v. Chiarella, 588 F.2d 1358, 1365 (CA2 1978). These considerations are insufficient to support a duty to disclose. A duty arises from the relationship between parties, see n. 9, *supra,* and accompanying text, and not merely from one's ability to acquire information because of his position in the market.

The Court of Appeals also suggested that the acquiring corporation itself would not be a "market insider" because a tender offeror creates, rather than receives, information and takes a substantial economic risk that its offer will be unsuccessful. *Id.,* at 1366–1367. Again, the Court of Appeals departed from the analysis appropriate to recognition of a duty. The Court of Appeals for the Second Circuit previously held, in a manner consistent with our analysis here, that a tender offeror does not violate § 10(b) when it makes preannouncement purchases precisely because there is no relationship between the offeror and the seller. "We know of no rule of law * * * that a purchaser of stock, who was not an 'insider' and had no fiduciary relation to a prospective seller, had any obligation to reveal circumstances that might raise a seller's demands and thus abort the sale." General Time Corp. v. Talley Industries, 403 F.2d 159, 164 (CA2 1968), cert. denied, 393 U.S. 1026, 89 S.Ct. 631, 21 L.Ed.2d 570 (1969).

ment decisions." 588 F.2d, at 1362. The use by anyone of material information not generally available is fraudulent, this theory suggests, because such information gives certain buyers or sellers an unfair advantage over less informed buyers and sellers.

This reasoning suffers from two defects. First not every instance of financial unfairness constitutes fraudulent activity under § 10(b). See Santa Fe Industries Inc. v. Green, 430 U.S. 462, 474–477, 97 S.Ct. 1292, 1301–1303, 51 L.Ed.2d 480 (1977). Second, the element required to make silence fraudulent—a duty to disclose—is absent in this case. No duty could arise from petitioner's relationship with the sellers of the target company's securities, for petitioner had no prior dealings with them. He was not their agent, he was not a fiduciary, he was not a person in whom the sellers had placed their trust and confidence. He was, in fact, a complete stranger who dealt with the sellers only through impersonal market transactions.

We cannot affirm petitioner's conviction without recognizing a general duty between all participants in market transactions to forgo actions based on material, nonpublic information. Formulation of such a broad duty, which departs radically from the established doctrine that duty arises from a specific relationship between two parties, see n. 9, *supra*, should not be undertaken absent some explicit evidence of congressional intent.

As we have seen, no such evidence emerges from the language or legislative history of § 10(b). Moreover, neither the Congress nor the Commission ever has adopted a parity-of-information rule. Instead the problems caused by misuse of market information have been addressed by detailed and sophisticated regulation that recognizes when use of market information may not harm operation of the securities markets. For example, the Williams Act limits but does not completely prohibit a tender offeror's purchases of target corporation stock before public announcement of the offer. Congress' careful action in this and other areas contrasts, and is in some tension, with the broad rule of liability we are asked to adopt in this case.

Indeed, the theory upon which the petitioner was convicted is at odds with the Commission's view of § 10(b) as applied to activity that has the same effect on sellers as the petitioner's purchases. "Warehousing" takes place when a corporation gives advance notice of its intention to launch a tender offer to institutional investors who then are able to purchase stock in the target company before the tender offer is made public and the price of shares rises. In this case, as in warehousing, a buyer of securities purchases stock in a target corporation on the basis of market information which is unknown to the seller. In both of these situations, the seller's behavior presumably would be altered if he had the nonpublic information. Significantly, however, the Commission has acted to bar warehousing under its authority to regulate tender offers after recognizing that action under § 10(b) would rest on a "somewhat different theory" than that previously used to regulate insider trading as fraudulent activity.

We see no basis for applying such a new and different theory of liability in this case. As we have emphasized before, the 1934 Act cannot be read "'more broadly than its language and the statutory scheme reasonably permit.'" Touche Ross & Co. v. Redington, 442 U.S. 560, 578, 99 S.Ct. 2479, 2490, 61 L.Ed.2d 82 (June 18, 1979), quoting SEC v. Sloan, 436 U.S. 103, 116, 98 S.Ct. 1702, 1711, 56 L.Ed.2d 148 (1978). Section 10(b) is aptly described as a catch-all provision, but what it catches must be fraud. When an allegation of fraud is based upon nondisclosure, there can be no fraud absent a duty to speak. We hold that a duty to disclose under § 10(b) does not arise from the mere possession of nonpublic market information. The contrary result is without support in the legislative history of § 10(b) and would be inconsistent with the careful plan that Congress has enacted for regulation of the securities markets. Cf. Santa Fe Industries Inc. v. Green, 430 U.S., at 479, 97 S.Ct., at 1304.

* * *

IV

In its brief to this Court, the United States offers an alternative theory to support petitioner's conviction. It argues that petitioner breached a duty to the acquiring corporation when he acted upon information that he obtained by virtue of his position as an employee of a printer employed by the corporation. The breach of this duty is said to support a conviction under § 10(b) for fraud perpetrated upon both the acquiring corporation and the sellers.

We need not decide whether this theory has merit for it was not submitted to the jury. * * *

The jury instructions demonstrate that petitioner was convicted merely because of his failure to disclose material, nonpublic information to sellers from whom he bought the stock of target corporations. The jury was not instructed on the nature or elements of a duty owed by petitioner to anyone other than the sellers. Because we cannot affirm a criminal conviction on the basis of a theory not presented to the jury, Rewis v. United States, 401 U.S. 808, 814 (1971), see Dunn v. United States, 442 U.S. 100, 106 (1979), we will not speculate upon whether such a duty exists, whether it has been breached, or whether such a breach constitutes a violation of § 10(b).

The judgment of the Court of Appeals is reversed.

MR. CHIEF JUSTICE BURGER, dissenting.

I believe that the jury instructions in this case properly charged a violation of § 10(b) and Rule 10b–5, and I would affirm the conviction.

I

As a general rule, neither party to an arm's-length business transaction has an obligation to disclose information to the other unless the parties stand in some confidential or fiduciary relation. See W. Prosser, Law of Torts § 106 (2d ed. 1955). This rule permits a businessman to capitalize on his experience and skill in securing and evaluating relevant information; it provides incentive for hard work, careful analysis, and astute forecasting. But the policies that underlie the rule also should limit its scope. In particular, the rule should give way when an informational advantage is obtained, not by superior experience, foresight, or industry, but by some unlawful means. One commentator has written:

> "[T]he way in which the buyer acquires the information which he conceals from the vendor should be a material circumstance. The information might have been acquired as the result of his bringing to bear a superior knowledge, intelligence, skill or technical judgment; it might have been acquired by mere chance; or it might have been acquired by means of some tortious action on his part. * * * *Any time information is acquired by an illegal act it would seem that there should be a duty to disclose that information.*" Keeton, Fraud—Concealment and Non–Disclosure, 15 Texas L.Rev. 1, 25–26 (1936) (emphasis added).

I would read § 10(b) and Rule 10b–5 to encompass and build on this principle: to mean that a person who has misappropriated nonpublic information has an absolute duty to disclose that information or to refrain from trading.

The language of § 10(b) and of Rule 10b–5 plainly support such a reading. By their terms, these provisions reach *any* person engaged in *any* fraudulent scheme. This broad language negates the suggestion that congressional concern was limited to trading by "corporate insiders" or to deceptive practices related to "corporate information." Just as surely Congress cannot have intended one standard of fair dealing for "white collar" insiders and another for the "blue collar" level. The very language of § 10(b) and Rule 10b–5 "by repeated use of the word 'any' [was] obviously meant to be inclusive." Affiliated Ute Citizens v. United States, 406 U.S. 128, 151, 92 S.Ct. 1456, 1471, 31 L.Ed.2d 741 (1972).

The history of the statute and of the Rule also supports this reading. The antifraud provisions were designed in large measure "to assure that dealing in securities is fair and without undue preferences or advantages among investors." H.R.Conf.Rep. No. 94–229, p. 91 (1975). These provisions prohibit "those manipulative and deceptive practices which have been demonstrated to fulfill no useful function." S.Rep. No. 792, 73d Cong., 2d Sess., 6 (1934). An investor who purchases securities on the basis of misappropriated nonpublic information possesses just such an "undue" trading advantage; his conduct quite clearly serves no useful function except his own enrichment at the expense of others.

This interpretation of § 10(b) and Rule 10b–5 is in no sense novel. It follows naturally from legal principles enunciated by the Securities and Exchange Commission in its seminal *Cady, Roberts* decision. 40 S.E.C. 907 (1961). There, the Commission relied upon two factors to impose a duty to disclose on corporate insiders: (1) " * * * access * * * to information intended to be available only for a corporate purpose *and not for the personal benefit of anyone* " (emphasis added); and (2) the unfairness inherent in trading on such information when it is inaccessible to those with whom one is dealing. Both of these factors are present whenever a party gains an informational advantage by unlawful means. Indeed, in In re Blyth & Co., 43 S.E.C. 1037 (1969), the Commission applied its *Cady, Roberts* decision in just such a context. In that case a broker-dealer had traded in Government securities on the basis of confidential Treasury Department information which it received from a Federal Reserve Bank employee. The Commission ruled that the trading was "improper use of inside information" violative of § 10(b) and Rule 10b–5. 43 S.E.C., at 1040. It did not hesitate to extend *Cady, Roberts* to reach a "tippee" of a Government insider.

Finally, it bears emphasis that this reading of § 10b and Rule 10b–5 would not threaten legitimate business practices. So read, the antifraud provisions would not impose a duty on a tender offeror to disclose its acquisition plans during the period in which it "tests the water" prior to purchasing a full 5% of the target company's stock. Nor would it proscribe "warehousing." See generally SEC, Institutional Investor Study Report, H.R.Doc. No. 92–64, pt. 4, p. 2273 (1971). Likewise, market specialists would not be subject to a disclose-or-refrain requirement in the performance of their everyday market functions. In each of these instances, trading is accomplished on the basis of material, nonpublic information, but the information has not been unlawfully converted for personal gain.

II

The Court's opinion, as I read it, leaves open the question whether § 10(b) and Rule 10b–5 prohibit trading on misappropriated nonpublic information. Instead, the Court apparently concludes that this theory of the case was not submitted to the jury. In the Court's view, the instructions given the jury were premised on the erroneous notion that the mere failure to disclose nonpublic information, however acquired, is a deceptive practice. And because of this premise, the jury was not instructed that the means by which Chiarella acquired his informational advantage—by violating a duty owed to the acquiring companies—was an element of the offense. See *ante,* at 1118.

The Court's reading of the District Court's charge is unduly restrictive. Fairly read as a whole and in the context of the trial, the instructions required the jury to find that Chiarella obtained his trading advantage by misappropriating the property of his employer's customers. * * *

[T]he evidence shows beyond all doubt that Chiarella, working literally in the shadows of the warning signs in the printshop, misappropriated—stole to put it bluntly—valuable nonpublic information entrusted to him in the utmost confidence. He then exploited his ill-gotten informational advantage by purchasing securities in the market. In my view, such conduct plainly violates § 10(b) and Rule 10b–5. Accordingly, I would affirm the judgment of the Court of Appeals.

SECURITIES AND EXCHANGE COMMISSION v. CLARK

915 F.2d 439 (9th Cir.1990).

CYNTHIA HOLCOMB HALL, CIRCUIT JUDGE:

In an enforcement action brought by the Securities and Exchange Commission ("SEC"), a jury determined that John Naylor Clark, III ("Clark") violated § 10(b) of the Securities and Exchange Act of 1934, and Rule 10b–5, by misappropriating and using material nonpublic information regarding his employer's plans to acquire another company. The jury also found that Clark's stockbroker, Russell Van Moppes, who had executed Clark's trades and had traded upon Clark's information, had not violated federal securities laws. The district court ordered, inter alia, that Clark disgorge the profits he and Van Moppes realized. Clark appeals both the finding of liability and the disgorgement order. We * * * affirm.

I

Until late 1983, Clark was president of Rolyan Manufacturing Company, Inc. ("Rolyan"), a Wisconsin corporation which produced and sold various medical supplies. In December of that year, Smith & Nephew, plc ("SN"), a London-based multinational corporation, acquired Rolyan and renamed it Smith & Nephew Rolyan ("SNR"). SN decided to keep Clark on as president of SNR.

SN's successful acquisition of Rolyan whetted its appetite for other medical supply manufacturers in North America. Consequently, it set up an acquisitions team to keep an eye out for appetizing takeover targets. Clark was a member of this team and attended regular meetings to discuss possible acquisition candidates. Team members were well aware that SN considered all information regarding takeovers as confidential and forbade the disclosure or personal use of such information.

Curtis Easter, SN's vice president of finance for North American operations, was also a member of the acquisitions team. Beginning in the middle of 1984, Easter become involved in the team's investigation of, and subsequent negotiations with, Affiliated Health Products, Inc. ("AHP"), a surgical glove manufacturer. Clark had no connection with the AHP project.

On December 12, Easter, who had just returned from a tour of AHP's midwestern manufacturing plants, dropped into Clark's office at SNR. Clark told Easter that he had heard that SN was planning to buy a surgical glove company. Easter, figuring that Clark knew all about the AHP project, told him that SN planned to acquire AHP in the near future. He added that SN planned to offer roughly $35 for each share of AHP's stock.

At that point, Clark made a quick telephone call to find out the market price for AHP stock. Upon learning that the current price was about $17, he and Easter "bantered back and forth" about how much money they could make by trading in AHP stock. After a few minutes of wishful thinking, Easter ended the conversation by saying that life was "too short" to try such a scheme.

That very day, Clark made a telephone call to Bellevue, Washington. He told one of his stockbrokers, Russell Van Moppes, that he wanted to buy 2,000 shares of AHP stock because he knew that AHP was the target of a takeover attempt.[1] He also told Van Moppes that he wanted to hide his trading from his employer. After discussing various options, they concluded that the best way would be to place the AHP shares in a new account bearing someone else's name. Clark decided to open an AHP account in his wife's maiden name, Teresa Ann Dale. Van Moppes' assistant misspelled Dale's last name as "Bale." Van Moppes purchased the stock on December 13 and 14. Several days later Clark, in an effort to further "bury" his trading from SN's view, had Van Moppes' assistant change the address for the Bale account from his Wisconsin home to his in-laws' Minnesota address. He then placed another order for 1,000 shares of AHP stock. Altogether, Clark purchased 3,000 shares of AHP stock at prices ranging from $17.875 to $19.75 per share.

Clark was not the only one to trade upon the basis of SN's confidential plans to acquire AHP. On December 13, Dale, at her husband's urging, bought 100 shares of AHP stock at $17.65 per share. On December 26, Van Moppes bought himself 500 shares of AHP stock at $19.50 per share.

SN's designs on AHP soon reached the public. On January 4, 1985, AHP announced that it had begun preliminary discussions with a company interested in acquiring it. Ten days later, SN announced that it had agreed to purchase AHP. Specifically, SN stated that it had agreed to buy roughly three-quarters of AHP's stock from United Industrial Corporation, AHP's parent company. In addition, SN stated that it would purchase the remaining AHP stock from the public at $36 per share, payable in cash.

Shortly thereafter, Clark, Dale, and Van Moppes sold all of their holdings in AHP stock and realized profits of $47,466.32, $1,664.67, and $7,812, respectively.

On May 20, 1987, the SEC, acting pursuant to its authority under § 21(d) of the Exchange Act, filed a complaint against Clark and Van Moppes which alleged that Clark's misappropriation and use of SN's material non-public information violated Rule 10b–5. * * *

---

1. Van Moppes testified at trial that he   spoke to him.
had not even heard of AHP until Clark

After a five-day trial, the jury returned a special verdict finding that only Clark had violated Rule 10b–5. The remedy stage of the SEC's proceeding was left to the equitable discretion of the district court. The court entered an order (1) enjoining Clark from future Rule 10b–5 violations; (2) requiring Clark to disgorge profits which he, Dale, and Van Moppes realized from their AHP trades; and (3) imposing a $75,000 penalty on Clark pursuant to the Insider Trading Sanctions Act [§ 20A of Securities Exchange Act of 1934].

Clark appeals his liability under the misappropriation theory. In the alternative, he appeals the order requiring him to disgorge the profits made by Van Moppes, who the jury found had not violated the federal securities laws.

II

Clark's central claim on appeal is that misappropriation and trading on SN's confidential information does not violate § 10(b) and Rule 10b–5. Whether the misappropriation theory should apply to this case involves questions of law and thus calls for de novo review. This is so even though the legal analysis becomes mixed with factual details.

* * *

Our task is to determine whether Congress, in enacting § 10(b), empowered the SEC to promulgate rules which would encompass the misappropriation theory. In addition, we must determine whether Rule 10b–5 was drafted such that the theory may legitimately be implied.

A

Until recently, the bulk of trading cases involving § 10(b) and Rule 10b–5 involved a defendant who had a fiduciary or similar relationship to the shareholders of the company in whose stock he traded. This common scenario gave rise to what may be called the "classical" theory of Rule 10b–5 liability. The classical theory, as refined by the Supreme Court in Chiarella v. United States, 445 U.S. 222, 100 S.Ct. 1108, 63 L.Ed.2d 348 (1980), and Dirks v. SEC, 463 U.S. 646, 103 S.Ct. 3255, 77 L.Ed.2d 911 (1983), provides that

> a person violates Rule 10b–5 by buying or selling securities on the basis of material nonpublic information if (1) he owes a fiduciary or similar duty to the other party to the transaction; (2) he is an insider of the corporation in whose shares he trades, and thus owes a fiduciary duty to the corporation's shareholders; or (3) he is a tippee who received his information from an insider of the corporation and knows, or should know, that the insider breached a fiduciary duty in disclosing the information to him.

Significantly, the classical theory does not extend to trading on material nonpublic information by "outsiders," i.e. persons who are neither insiders of the companies whose shares are being traded, nor tippees of such insiders. Under this definition, Clark is an "outsider."

Unlike the classical theory, the misappropriation theory extends to trading by outsiders. Generally speaking, the theory provides that Rule 10b–5 is violated when a person (1) misappropriates material nonpublic information (2) by breaching a duty arising out of a relationship of trust and confidence and (3) uses that information in a securities transaction, (4) regardless of whether he owed any duties to the shareholders of the traded stock. *See, e.g.*, SEC v. Materia, 745 F.2d 197, 201–02 (2d Cir.1984), cert. denied, 471 U.S. 1053, 105 S.Ct. 2112, 85 L.Ed.2d 477 (1985). Significantly, this analysis determines only whether there is a Rule 10b–5 violation; it does not determine whether a private party may obtain relief therefrom.

The government first advanced the misappropriation theory a decade ago in *Chiarella*, 445 U.S. 222, 100 S.Ct. 1108. * * * The government argued that Chiarella, by breaching a duty of confidentiality to the acquiring corporations, had misappropriated and traded upon information from his employer and thus had committed fraud on his employer's clients and the sellers of the target companies' securities. Id. at 235–36, 100 S.Ct. at 1118–19.

Writing for the majority, Justice Powell declined to address the merits of the government's new theory because it had not been submitted to the jury. Id. at 236, 100 S.Ct. at 1118. However, five Justices indicated in dictum varying degrees of support for the theory.

Apparently heartened by this reception (particularly by the Chief Justice's strongly-worded dissent), the government made a second attempt in United States v. Newman, 664 F.2d 12 (2d Cir.1981), cert. denied, 464 U.S. 863, 104 S.Ct. 193, 78 L.Ed.2d 170 (1983). In *Newman*, two employees of different investment banking firms had, at Newman's behest, misappropriated confidential tender offer information which had been entrusted to the firms' corporate clients. Id. at 15. The two employees secretly conveyed this valuable information to Newman, a securities trader, who then told two confederates. The Newman trio immediately bought stock in the target companies and sold it at substantial premiums after the tender offers became public. They then shared their profits with the two investment bank employees who had stolen the information. Id. The district court dismissed the indictment on the grounds that Newman had defrauded neither a purchaser nor a seller of the relevant securities. Id. at 14, 19.

The Second Circuit reversed. Citing portions of Chief Justice Burger's *Chiarella* dissent, the *Newman* court expressly adopted the misappropriation theory. The court concluded that Newman and his cohorts defrauded the investment banking firms entrusted with the information "as surely as if they took their money," notwithstanding the fact that the firms had not traded in the relevant stock. Id. at 17. The court also observed that the defendants had wronged the firms' corporate clients because their secret trading had artificially inflated the target companies' stock prices. Id. at 17–18.

Significantly, although the Second Circuit referred to Chief Justice Burger's *Chiarella* dissent, it did not endorse the Chief Justice's view of the theory. To the Chief Justice, the Rule 10b–5 fraud consisted of the defendant's failure to disclose the material nonpublic information to the parties with whom he trades. * * * To the *Newman* court however, the fraud consisted of the defendant's use of the material nonpublic information despite his implicit representation not to do so. 664 F.2d at 17–18. It is *Newman*'s view of the theory which survives today.

The Second Circuit revisited the misappropriation theory in SEC v. Materia, 745 F.2d 197 (2d Cir.1984), cert. denied, 471 U.S. 1053, 105 S.Ct. 2112, 85 L.Ed.2d 477 (1985). Like *Chiarella*, *Materia* involved an employee of a financial printer who had misappropriated and traded upon confidential information regarding proposed tender offers by the printer's corporate clients. Id. at 199. Unlike *Chiarella*, the misappropriation theory was properly preserved for appeal.

The Second Circuit noted that *Newman* controlled the case, but nonetheless undertook a more elaborate analysis of the misappropriation theory. The court first noted that misappropriating and trading upon information communicated in the utmost confidence fit comfortably within the meaning of "fraud or deceit" in Rule 10b–5. Id. at 201. It also observed that the legislative history negated any suggestion that § 10(b) of the Exchange Act was "aimed solely at the eradication of fraudulent trading by corporate insiders." Id. From there the court concluded that because Materia's breach of confidentiality and subsequent trading had damaged the reputation of the printing firm, Materia had perpetrated a fraud upon it. Id. at 202.

Next, the *Materia* court addressed the question of whether § 10(b) and Rule 10b–5 fraud is limited to cases where the defendant has a duty to disclose her nonpublic information to the persons with whom she trades. Noting that the *Chiarella* Court had avoided this question, the Second Circuit concluded that a duty to disclose is relevant only to determine whether an injured buyer or seller has standing to recover damages in a private cause of action; it does not touch upon the threshold question of whether Rule 10b–5 has been violated. Id.[10]

10. The Second Circuit made this distinction two years earlier in Moss v. Morgan Stanley, Inc., 719 F.2d 5 (2d Cir.1983), cert. denied, 465 U.S. 1025, 104 S.Ct. 1280, 79 L.Ed.2d 684 (1984). Arising out of the same facts as in *Newman*, *Moss* involved an action by the shareholders of the target companies' stock who had unwittingly sold their undervalued shares to Newman and his associates. The Second Circuit held that because there was no fiduciary relationship between the bank's corporate clients and the target firm's shareholders, there could be no derivative relationship between the banking firm (or its employees) and the sellers. Thus, the court concluded, the sellers could not allege that the banking firm breached a duty to disclose to them nonpublic material information. Id. at 13, 15–16.

[The Insider Trading and Securities Fraud Enforcement Act of 1988 (Section 20A of the 1934 Act) creates a private right of action on behalf of contemporaneous traders against insiders, tippers, tippees, and their controlling persons thereby reversing the *Moss* decision.—Eds.]

The Second Circuit extended the misappropriation theory in United States v. Carpenter, 791 F.2d 1024 (2d Cir.1986) aff'd by an equally divided court, 484 U.S. 19, 108 S.Ct. 316, 98 L.Ed.2d 275 (1987). *Carpenter* concerned the exploits of R. Foster Winans, co-author of The Wall Street Journal's influential "Heard on the Street" column. Winans had entered into a scheme with two stockbrokers wherein he provided information regarding the timing and content of forthcoming columns in exchange for a share of profits resulting from trades based upon that information. Id. at 1026. The government had prosecuted the defendants for violating § 10(b) and Rule 10b–5, as well as the federal mail and wire fraud statutes.

Carpenter differed from the normal misappropriation theory case in two respects. First, there was no allegation that the information was not available to the public in one form or another. Id. at 1031–32. Second, the source of the information, a financial newspaper, neither traded in the securities nor received its information from corporate clients which intended to do so. Nonetheless, a divided Second Circuit applied the misappropriation theory and affirmed the convictions.

An eight-member panel of the Supreme Court affirmed the Rule 10b–5 convictions only because it had divided evenly on them. See 484 U.S. at 24, 108 S.Ct. 316. Because the sole opinion in that decision does not state the basis for the division, we cannot know whether the four justices who voted to overturn the Rule 10b–5 convictions did so because they rejected the misappropriation theory in general or merely its novel application in that case.[11]

Nonetheless, the Second Circuit has continued to apply the misappropriation theory.

District courts within the Second Circuit have also contributed to the development of the misappropriation theory. SEC v. Musella (Musella I), 578 F.Supp. 425 (S.D.N.Y.1984), concerned the activities of Alan Ihne, an office services manager for the law firm of Sullivan & Cromwell ("Sullivan"). By virtue of his position at Sullivan, Ihne learned of numerous tender offers planned by the firm's corporate clients. On at least four occasions, he communicated this material nonpublic information to ten of his friends, who immediately bought shares in the target companies and resold them immediately after the tender offers were announced. Id. at 431–34.[12] The government had prosecuted Ihne and

---

11. One commentator has observed that [d]ifferent legal experts reacted quite differently to the Court's four-to-four deadlock on the question of whether the *Carpenter* defendants had committed securities fraud. A member of the Securities and Exchange Commission insisted that the Justices had left the misappropriation theory "alive and well." A prominent law professor, on the other hand, thought that the decision indicated "pretty strongly" that the theory was "a fairly dubious proposition." Perhaps the least controversial appraisal was offered by a former SEC official: "The fact that it's four to four shows there is a split in the Court." Aldave, The Misappropriation Theory: Carpenter and its Aftermath, 49 Ohio St.L.J. 373, 374 (1988) (footnotes omitted).

12. * * * Sullivan had given Ihne several memoranda emphasizing the importance of maintaining absolute secrecy of tender offer information. Ihne acknowledged that he knew it was wrong to steal the informa-

his friends on both the classical and misappropriation theories of Rule 10b–5 liability. The district court noted that because none of the defendants had a fiduciary relationship to the shareholders of the target companies, they were not liable under the classical theory. Id. at 436–37. However, the court concluded that because Ihne owed Sullivan and its clients a duty to remain silent about the proposed tender offers, he and his tippees were instead liable under the misappropriation theory. Id. at 438–39. The court further stated that by adopting the misappropriation theory, "the Second Circuit gave legal effect to the commonsensical view that trading on the basis of improperly obtained information is fundamentally unfair, and that distinctions premised on the source of the information undermine the prophylactic intent of the securities laws." Id. at 438.

* * *

United States v. Reed, 601 F.Supp. 685 (S.D.N.Y.) rev'd on other grounds, 773 F.2d 477 (2d Cir.1985), offers a different perspective on the misappropriation theory. There the defendant had allegedly misappropriated from his own father, a director of Amax Petroleum Corporation, confidential information regarding Amax's proposed merger with Standard Oil Company of California. Id. at 689. Although the court's lengthy discussion of the confidential relationship between father and son, id. at 703–18, does not concern us, its focus on the misappropriation theory's consonance with common law principles of fraud and deceit is instructive:

> Stripped to its essentials, outsider trading liability is premised on the common law principle that when a fiduciary profits from confidential information that he had received because of his fiduciary status, he breaches a legal duty to the person or entity that entrusted him with the information. The misappropriation of secret information for personal aggrandizement in breach of such a relationship constitutes fraud. The origins of this approach can be traced to the law of restitution. A person who receives confidential information from another and misappropriates it for personal benefit is deemed to hold the proceeds of the misappropriation in a constructive trust for the benefit of the entrusting party. The misappropriator thus becomes the trustee ex maleficio, or quasi-fiduciary, of the entrustor. In the context of the securities laws, it does not matter for purposes of assessing liability whether the recipient of the information is actually trading in the securities issued by the source of the information. Rather, the duty is breached by the misappropriation and resulting profit, and a constructive trust attaches.

Id. at 700 (citations and footnote omitted).

Further insight into how misappropriation and trading operates as fraud was recently provided in United States v. Willis, 737 F.Supp. 269

tion but made a "conscious decision" to do so anyway.

(S.D.N.Y.1990). In another novel application of the misappropriation theory, the government prosecuted a psychiatrist who had traded on confidential information communicated to him by one of his patients, the wife of a corporate insider. In holding that the indictment sufficiently alleged culpability under the misappropriation theory, the court observed:

> The underlying rationale of the misappropriation theory is that a person who receives secret business information from another because of an established relationship of trust and confidence between them has a duty to keep that information confidential. By breaching that duty and appropriating the confidential information for his own advantage, the fiduciary is defrauding the confider who was entitled to rely on the fiduciary's tacit representation of confidentiality.

Id. at 274.*

Thus *Willis* makes explicit what had been assumed by earlier decisions: that by becoming part of a fiduciary or similar relationship, an individual is implicitly stating that she will not divulge or use to her own advantage information entrusted to her in the utmost confidence. She deceives the other party by playing the role of the trustworthy employee or agent; she defrauds it by actually using the stolen information to its detriment.

In the few instances the misappropriation theory has been advanced outside of the Second Circuit, it has been welcomed by circuit and district courts alike. *See* Rothberg v. Rosenbloom, 771 F.2d 818, 822 (3d Cir.1985) ("An insider on either side of a proposed transaction violates ... [§ 10(b)] when he uses insider information in violation of the fiduciary duty owed to the corporation to which he owes a duty of confidentiality.") * * *.

In short, the amount of careful thought that has gone into the misappropriation theory is considerable, and the consistency with which

---

* Subsequently, in United States v. Willis, 778 F.Supp. 205 (S.D.N.Y.1991) the court rejected claims by Dr. Willis that dismissal was required by the en banc decision in United States v. Chestman, 947 F.2d 551 (2d Cir.1991), cert. denied 112 S.Ct. 1759 (1992). Dr. Willis claimed that the government failed to prove a relationship of trust and confidence between his patient and her insider husband. He also contended that there must be an unbroken chain of confidentiality and that once the chain is broken through disclosure by an insider to a person who is not in a fiduciary relationship to the insider, the person who subsequently receives the information in a fiduciary capacity cannot be a misappropriator even if the person trades on the information in breach of the person's duty of trust and confidence. The court stated that the government had not been given a chance to prove the relationship between Dr. Willis and his patient. In addition, the court held that the key relationship for purposes of the misappropriation theory is between the misappropriator (here, the psychiatrist) and the person to whom he owes an obligation of confidentiality (here, the confiding patient). The psychiatrist's relationship to his patient, the court added, is clearly one of trust and confidence. "A treating psychiatrist's relationship to his patient," the court stated, "is a traditional inherent fiduciary relationship." The court concluded that Dr. Willis provided no basis for his theory of an unbroken chain of confidentiality.—Eds.

it has been applied is impressive. Nonetheless, we now turn to the legislative and administrative materials themselves.

B

Rule 10b–5 has been described as a "catchall" antifraud provision. *See Chiarella,* 445 U.S. at 226, 100 S.Ct. at 1113 (citing *Hochfelder,* 425 U.S. at 202, 206, 96 S.Ct. at 1387). There are two distinct senses in which this claim is true. First, the language of the rule explicitly encompasses *any* purchase or sale by *any* person of *any* security. There are no exemptions. The rule applies to publicly-held and privately-held companies—regardless of whether they are registered under the 1934 Exchange Act—so long as they issue something that can be called a "security."

Second, Rule 10b–5 is a catchall because its terms are notoriously vague. Words and phrases like "fraud," "deceit," and "device, scheme or artifice" provide a broad linguistic frame within which a large number of practices may fit. Moreover, such practices merely have to be "in connection with" security purchases or sales.

1

For guidance in determining whether the misappropriation theory fits within the concept of "fraud" in § 10(b) and Rule 10b–5, we look to the mail and wire fraud statutes, which contain similar language. It is well settled that misappropriation and use of confidential information in breach of a fiduciary or similar duty amounts to fraud within the meaning of those statutes. *See, e.g., Carpenter,* 484 U.S. at 27–28, 108 S.Ct. at 321–22 (misappropriation of confidential newspaper information). * * *

The Supreme Court's decision in *Carpenter* is particularly illuminating in this respect. The petitioner there argued that R. Foster Winans, the Wall Street Journal columnist who had misappropriated and disclosed information to his cohorts regarding the contents and timing of his column, had not committed fraud but had merely violated a few workplace rules. 484 U.S. at 27, 108 S.Ct. at 321. However, a unanimous Court had "little trouble" in finding Winans' conduct a "scheme to defraud" within the ambit of the mail and wire fraud statutes. Id. at 28, 108 S.Ct. at 321. The Court observed:

> The concept of "fraud" includes the act of embezzlement, which is the " 'fraudulent appropriation to one's own use of the money or goods entrusted to one's care by another.' " Grin v. Shine, 187 U.S. 181, 189, 23 S.Ct. 98, 102, 47 L.Ed. 130 (1902).

* * *

The Journal's business information that it intended to be kept confidential was its property; the declaration to that effect in the employee manual merely removed any doubts on that score and made the finding of specific intent to defraud that much easier. Winans continued in the employ of the Journal, appropriating its confidential business information for his own use, all the while pretending to perform his duty of safeguarding it. In fact, he told his editors twice about leaks of confidential information not related to the stock-trading scheme, demonstrating both his knowledge that the Journal viewed information concerning the "Heard" column as confidential and his deceit as he played the role of a loyal employee.

Id. at 27–28, 108 S.Ct. at 321–22 (citation omitted) (emphasis added).

We find no linguistic reason not to apply this conception of fraud to the securities context. Thus we conclude that the misappropriation theory fits comfortably within the meaning of "fraud" in § 10(b) and Rule 10b–5.

2

Section 10(b) and Rule 10b–5 do not proscribe all frauds occurring in the business world, but only those "in connection with the purchase or sale of any security." In other words, the fraud must somehow "touch" upon securities transactions. *See* Superintendent of Ins. of N.Y. v. Bankers Life & Cas. Co., 404 U.S. 6, 12–13, 92 S.Ct. 165, 168–69, 30 L.Ed.2d 128 (1971). Thus the question here is whether there is some nexus between Clark's misappropriation of SN's confidential information and any securities transactions.

Purely as a matter of linguistic construction, we have little trouble concluding that there is. The evidence indicated that Clark's sole purpose in obtaining the nonpublic information about SN's plans to acquire AHP was to make a fast buck by trading in its securities. To deny a connection between the misappropriation and the subsequent trading would be disingenuous. *See Materia*, 745 F.2d at 203; *Newman*, 664 F.2d at 18.

C

Although we find that the misappropriation theory fits comfortably within the broad linguistic frame of § 10(b) and Rule 10b–5, we must ensure that our interpretation "effectuate[s] the policies underlying the federal securities laws." Securities Inv. Protection Corp. v. Vigman, 764 F.2d 1309, 1313 (9th Cir.1985). To do so, we turn to both the contemporaneous and subsequent history of § 10(b) and Rule 10b–5.

* * *

2

Our inquiry does not stop there, however. Our search for legislative purpose is complete only when we have considered Congress' intent when it enacted legislation affecting the scheme of which § 10(b) and Rule 10b–5 are a part. * * *

When it passed the Insider Trading Sanctions Act of 1984, Pub.L. No. 98–376, 98 Stat. 1264 [hereinafter ITSA] to amend various provisions of the 1934 Exchange Act, Congress found the misappropriation theory consistent with § 10(b) and Rule 10b–5. The House Report accompanying the bill noted that "[s]ince its creation, the [SEC] has * * * appropriately used the antifraud provisions to remedy unlawful trading and tipping by persons in a variety of positions of trust and confidence who have illegally acquired or illegally used material non-public information." H.R.Rep. No. 355, 98th Cong., 2d Sess. 4, reprinted in 1984 U.S.Code Cong. & Admin.News 2274, 2277. Referring to cases such as *Newman*, which first adopted the misappropriation theory, the report continued,

> [I]n certain widely-publicized instances, agents of tender offerors and persons contemplating a merger or acquisition have used for personal gain information entrusted to them solely for a business purpose. Such conversion for personal gain of information lawfully obtained abuses relationships of trust and confidence and is no less reprehensible than the outright theft of nonpublic information.

Id. at 2277–78 (footnote omitted) (emphasis added). Then, echoing the Second Circuit in *Newman,* the report stated, "In other areas of the law, deceitful misappropriation of confidential information by a fiduciary, whether described as theft, conversion, or breach of trust, has consistently been held to be unlawful. The Congress has not sanctioned a less rigorous code of conduct under the federal securities laws." Id. at 2278 (footnotes omitted).

Perhaps more significantly, Congress passed up an opportunity to supply a definition of "insider trading" at least partially because it considered contemporary Rule 10b–5 jurisprudence, which included the misappropriation theory, "sufficiently well-developed at this time to provide adequate guidance." Id. at 2286 (footnote omitted) (citing *Newman*).

Four years later, Congress reaffirmed its belief that the misappropriation theory was consistent with § 10(b) and Rule 10b–5. The Insider Trading and Securities Fraud Enforcement Act of 1988, Pub.L. 100–704, 102 Stat. 4677 [hereinafter ITSFEA] was Congress' reaction to the stock market crash of October 19, 1987, viewed by many of its members as linked to continued insider and outsider trading despite stiff ITSA penalties. See H.R.Rep. No. 910, 7, 11 reprinted in 1988 U.S.Code.Cong. & Admin. News 6043, 6044, 6048. The House Committee reporting on the bill acknowledged that the misappropriation theory had split the Supreme Court in *Carpenter*, yet nonetheless endorsed the theory as consistent with the broad objectives of § 10(b) and Rule 10b–5. Id. at 6047. Furthermore, in discussing an amendment to the 1934 Exchange Act [Section 20A] expressly creating a private right of action for various securities violations, the Committee noted:

> [T]he codification of a right of action for contemporaneous traders is specifically intended to overturn court cases which have precluded recovery for plaintiffs where the defendant's violation is premised upon the misappropriation theory. See, e.g., Moss v. Morgan Stanley, 719 F.2d 5 (2d Cir.1983). The Committee believes that this

result is inconsistent with the remedial purposes of the Exchange Act, and that the misappropriation theory fulfills appropriate regulatory objectives in determining when communicating or trading while in possession of material nonpublic information is unlawful.

Id. at 6063–64 (emphasis added).

D

The "peculiar blend of legislative, administrative, and judicial history" surrounding § 10(b) and Rule 10b–5, Blue Chip Stamps v. Manor Drug Stores, 421 U.S. 723, 749, 95 S.Ct. 1917, 1931, 44 L.Ed.2d 539 (1975), provides strong evidence that the misappropriation theory is compatible with the broad language of those provisions. Although the Supreme Court has yet to recognize the theory, we nonetheless adopt it as it was prosecuted in this case. Specifically, we hold that an employee's knowing misappropriation and use of his employer's material nonpublic information regarding its intention to acquire another firm constitutes a violation of § 10(b) and Rule 10b–5.

Clark first objects to our adoption of the theory on the basis that § 10(b) and Rule 10b–5 "require that at least the person defrauded be an investor in the securities involved." While that argument may raise interesting questions in more novel applications of the theory, it has little merit in a garden-variety misappropriation case such as this, for there is no question that the victim of the misappropriation, SN, traded in AHP's stock and thus was defrauded by the trading activities of Clark and his tippees.

Clark next claims that adopting the theory in this case would introduce a "parity-of-information" rule which has been previously rejected by the Supreme Court as inconsistent with § 10(b) and Rule 10b–5, *see Dirks*, 463 U.S. at 654, 103 S.Ct. at 3261; *Chiarella*, 445 U.S. at 233, 100 S.Ct. at 1117.[25] We disagree. The misappropriation theory, as we have adopted it today, applies only where the misappropriation occurs by means of a violation of fiduciary or similar duty.[26] Thus it does not run afoul of Supreme Court precedent.

* * *

IV

For these reasons, the judgment of the district court is AFFIRMED.

———

S.E.C. v. Cherif, 933 F.2d 403 (7th Cir.1991), cert. denied ___ U.S. ___, 112 S.Ct. 966, 117 L.Ed.2d 131 (1992), is interesting because the

25. However, by its adoption of the ITS-FEA, Congress appears to have introduced the parity-of-information rule into securities regulation.

26. The fact that SN had no written confidentiality policy is of little moment. Clark admitted at trial that he and the other acquisition team members well understood that they were not to divulge or use information regarding SN's takeover plans. Moreover, Clark's knowledge of this fact is evidenced by his conduct in concealing his purchases of AHP.

defendant's misappropriation and subsequent trading occurred after the defendant had ceased to be an employee of the company from whom he misappropriated the information. The court found that the termination of his employment did not relieve him from liability under Rule 10b–5 because he had breached a continuing duty to his former employer by using confidential information that he had obtained while an employee.

Note: The Misappropriation Theory: Its Rationale and Reach

Considering the Supreme Court's flirtation with the misappropriation theory in *Chiarella* and *Carpenter*, its treatment by the respective circuits, and its support in the Insider Trading and Securities Fraud Enforcement Act of 1988, it is natural to ask where the misappropriation theory stands as a means for expanding the reach of Section 10(b) and Rule 10b–5. How important is the misappropriation theory in combating insider trading? What is the actual reach and role of the misappropriation theory? Does the misappropriation theory go too far, to the point where it no longer serves as a justifiable rationale for proscribing insider trading? Specifically, how is it that a misappropriation is actually deceptive? What interests does the misappropriation theory protect?

There is no doubt that the misappropriation theory offers the potential to greatly expand the ability of the courts to assail the use of material nonpublic information by those who do not fall within the traditional definition of an insider or a tippee. As one commentator, Professor Aldave, has stated, "[w]ithout the aid of the misappropriation theory, section 10(b) and rule 10b–5 would lose much of their efficacy as weapons against trading on nonpublic information, since they would no longer extend to trading by 'outsiders'." Barbara Bader Aldave, The Misappropriation Theory: Carpenter and Its Aftermath, 49 Ohio St. L. J. 373, 380 (1988). The misappropriation theory thus allows the courts to fill in the gaps left in the abstain or disclose theory mandated by *Chiarella* and *Dirks*, to reach behavior which falls in the cracks of the current law, but which strikes judges as being unlawful. Behavior that otherwise might be left untouched, can be reached using a misappropriation theory.

While it is clear that the misappropriation theory extends the reach of Rule 10b–5, the question arises whether the misappropriation theory is the proper vehicle for enforcing Section 10(b) and Rule 10b–5. Some commentators feel that the misappropriation theory represents a natural extension of Rule 10b–5 and implore the Supreme Court to give it support. Professor Aldave, for example, believes that the Court should have unanimously supported the misappropriation theory prong of the *Carpenter* case. She believes that the Court was reticent to support the theory because of an erroneous belief that the only victim of fraud in that case was the newspaper, not any market participant. Therefore, she asserts the Court was not comfortable in concluding that the fraud occurred in connection with a "purchase or sale of securities," and decided that as a matter of policy Rule 10b–5 should not be used to protect the interests of a party that was neither a buyer or seller of securities.   However, Aldave reasons that a defendant who trades in securities, using the misappropriated information, creates the connection to the market.   She contends that such a defendant inflicts concrete economic injuries on innocent investors, who suffer net losses in the amount of a defendant's illicit gains.   That there may be no specific plaintiff that can sue the misappropriators should not, according to Aldave, obscure the fact that such a defendant committed a fraud on investors.   Id. at 375–380.

4.   TIPPING

Note: A Guide to Tipping (or When 15% Is Not Enough)

Whatever subtleties may arise in particular cases, the general parameters of the law of insider trading are reasonably well established when the person who has traded is either a traditional insider or is an employee of the corporation whose position disqualifies him from trading on the material nonpublic information (Darke, in *Texas Gulf Sulphur,* for example).   Those parameters are not at all clear when the person who has traded is not such a person but has obtained the information from someone who is.   The Supreme Court has twice attempted to determine the applicability of 10b–5 to such persons and twice has rejected broad theories of liability without providing clear direction to lower courts.   As a guide to this section, consider the following model.

A.   Terminology

    1.   Tipper. A tipper is a person who discloses material nonpublic information.

    2.   Tippee. A tippee is a person who receives material nonpublic information from a tipper.   If the tippee subsequently discloses the information, he becomes a tipper as well as a tippee and the person to whom he discloses becomes a:

    3.   Sub-tippee.

B.   Categories of People Involved

    1.   The tipper is an insider or employee of the corporation.

    2.   The tipper is not an employee but has a confidential relationship with the corporation.

    3.   The tippee is a complete outsider.

    4.   The tippee has an intermediate position arising from the nature of her profession and its relationship to the corporation, i.e., securities analyst.

C.   Situations Covered

    1.   The tipper tips but does not trade; the tippee trades.

    2.   The tipper trades and tips; the tippee trades.

    3.   Neither the tipper nor the tippee trade; the tippee tips; the sub-tippee trades.

4. The chain in situations 1–3 is extended to more remote sub-tippees with the same conduct.

D. Possible Theories of Tipper and/or Tippee Liability

   1. Parity of Information

   2. Equal Access to Information

   3. Fairness

   4. Breach of Fiduciary Duty to Disclose or Abstain

   5. Misappropriation

As you read the following materials, remember the discussion of the importance of information as the basis of an efficient market and the need to permit the development of new information on which efficient pricing can be based. One of the problems with which the courts struggle is how to permit such development without giving those who develop it an unfair advantage with respect to its use.

DIRKS v. SECURITIES AND EXCHANGE COMMISSION

463 U.S. 646, 103 S.Ct. 3255, 77 L.Ed.2d 911 (1983).

JUSTICE POWELL delivered the opinion of the Court.

Petitioner Raymond Dirks received material nonpublic information from "insiders" of a corporation with which he had no connection. He disclosed this information to investors who relied on it in trading in the shares of the corporation. The question is whether Dirks violated the antifraud provisions of the federal securities laws by this disclosure.

I

In 1973, Dirks was an officer of a New York broker-dealer firm who specialized in providing investment analysis of insurance company securities to institutional investors. On March 6, Dirks received information from Ronald Secrist, a former officer of Equity Funding of America. Secrist alleged that the assets of Equity Funding, a diversified corporation primarily engaged in selling life insurance and mutual funds, were vastly overstated as the result of fraudulent corporate practices. Secrist also stated that various regulatory agencies had failed to act on similar charges made by Equity Funding employees. He urged Dirks to verify the fraud and disclose it publicly.

Dirks decided to investigate the allegations. He visited Equity Funding's headquarters in Los Angeles and interviewed several officers and employees of the corporation. The senior management denied any wrongdoing, but certain corporation employees corroborated the charges of fraud. Neither Dirks nor his firm owned or traded any Equity Funding stock, but throughout his investigation he openly discussed the information he had obtained with a number of clients and investors. Some of these persons sold their holdings of Equity Funding securities, including five investment advisers who liquidated holdings of more than $16 million.[2]

While Dirks was in Los Angeles, he was in touch regularly with William Blundell, the *Wall Street Journal'* s Los Angeles bureau chief. Dirks urged Blundell to write a story on the fraud allegations. Blundell did not believe, however, that such a massive fraud could go undetected and declined to write the story. He feared that publishing such damaging hearsay might be libelous.

During the two-week period in which Dirks pursued his investigation and spread word of Secrist's charges, the price of Equity Funding stock fell from $26 per share to less than $15 per share. This led the New York Stock Exchange to halt trading on March 27. Shortly thereafter California insurance authorities impounded Equity Funding's records and uncovered evidence of the fraud. Only then did the Securities and Exchange Commission (SEC) file a complaint against Equity Funding[3] and only then, on April 2, did the *Wall Street Journal* publish a front-page story based largely on information assembled by Dirks. Equity Funding immediately went into receivership.

The SEC began an investigation into Dirks' role in the exposure of the fraud. After a hearing by an administrative law judge, the SEC found that Dirks had aided and abetted violations of § 17(a) of the Securities Act of 1933, 15 U.S.C. § 77q(a), § 10(b) of the Securities Exchange Act of 1934, 15 U.S.C. § 78j(b), and SEC Rule 10b–5, 17 CFR § 240.10b–5 (1982), by repeating the allegations of fraud to members of the investment community who later sold their Equity Funding stock. The SEC concluded: "Where 'tippees'—regardless of their motivation or occupation—come into possession of material 'information that they know is confidential and know or should know came from a corporate insider,' they must either publicly disclose that information or refrain from trading." 21 S.E.C. Docket 1401, 1407 (1981) (footnote omitted) (quoting Chiarella v. United States, 445 U.S. 222, 230 n. 12, 100 S.Ct. 1108, 1116 n. 12, 63 L.Ed.2d 348 (1980)). Recognizing, however, that Dirks "played an important role in bringing [Equity Funding's] massive fraud to light," 21 S.E.C. Docket, at 1412, the SEC only censured him.

Dirks sought review in the Court of Appeals for the District of Columbia Circuit. The court entered judgment against Dirks "for the reasons stated by the Commission in its opinion." App. to Pet. for Cert.

2. Dirks received from his firm a salary plus a commission for securities transactions above a certain amount that his clients directed through his firm. See 21 S.E.C. Docket, at 1402, n. 3. But "[i]t is not clear how many of those with whom Dirks spoke promised to direct some brokerage business through [Dirks' firm] to compensate Dirks, or how many actually did so." 220 U.S.App.D.C., at 316, 681 F.2d, at 831. The Boston Company Institutional Investors, Inc., promised Dirks about $25,000 in commissions, but it is unclear whether Boston actually generated any brokerage business for his firm. * * *

3. As early as 1971, the SEC had received allegations of fraudulent accounting practices at Equity Funding. Moreover, on March 9, 1973, an official of the California Insurance Department informed the SEC's regional office in Los Angeles of Secrist's charges of fraud. Dirks himself voluntarily presented his information at the SEC's regional office beginning on March 27.

C–2. Judge Wright, a member of the panel, subsequently issued an opinion. Judge Robb concurred in the result and Judge Tamm dissented; neither filed a separate opinion. Judge Wright believed that "the obligations of corporate fiduciaries pass to all those to whom they disclose their information before it has been disseminated to the public at large." 220 U.S.App.D.C. 309, 324, 681 F.2d 824, 839 (1982). Alternatively, Judge Wright concluded that, as an employee of a broker-dealer, Dirks had violated "obligations to the SEC and to the public completely independent of any obligations he acquired" as a result of receiving the information. *Id.,* at 325, 681 F.2d, at 840.

In view of the importance to the SEC and to the securities industry of the question presented by this case, we granted a writ of certiorari. 459 U.S. 1014, 103 S.Ct. 371, 74 L.Ed.2d 506 (1982). We now reverse.

II

In the seminal case of In re Cady, Roberts & Co., 40 S.E.C. 907 (1961), the SEC recognized that the common law in some jurisdictions imposes on "corporate 'insiders,' particularly officers, directors, or controlling stockholders" an "affirmative duty of disclosure * * * when dealing in securities." *Id.,* at 911, and n. 13. The SEC found that not only did breach of this common-law duty also establish the elements of a Rule 10b–5 violation, but that individuals other than corporate insiders could be obligated either to disclose material nonpublic information before trading or to abstain from trading altogether. *Id.,* at 912. In *Chiarella,* we accepted the two elements set out in *Cady, Roberts* for establishing a Rule 10b–5 violation: "(i) the existence of a relationship affording access to inside information intended to be available only for a corporate purpose, and (ii) the unfairness of allowing a corporate insider to take advantage of that information by trading without disclosure." 445 U.S., at 227, 100 S.Ct., at 1114. In examining whether Chiarella had an obligation to disclose or abstain, the Court found that there is no general duty to disclose before trading on material nonpublic information, and held that "a duty to disclose under § 10(b) does not arise from the mere possession of nonpublic market information." *Id.,* at 235, 100 S.Ct., at 1118. Such a duty arises rather from the existence of a fiduciary relationship. See *id.,* at 227–235, 100 S.Ct. at 1114–1118.

Not "all breaches of fiduciary duty in connection with a securities transaction," however, come within the ambit of Rule 10b–5. Santa Fe Industries, Inc. v. Green, 430 U.S. 462, 472, 97 S.Ct. 1292, 1300, 51 L.Ed.2d 480 (1977). There must also be "manipulation or deception." *Id.,* at 473, 97 S.Ct., at 1300. In an inside-trading case this fraud derives from the "inherent unfairness involved where one takes advantage" of "information intended to be available only for a corporate purpose and not for the personal benefit of anyone." In re Merrill Lynch, Pierce, Fenner & Smith, Inc., 43 S.E.C. 933, 936 (1968). Thus, an insider will be liable under Rule 10b–5 for inside trading only where he fails to disclose material nonpublic information before trading on it and thus makes "secret profits." *Cady, Roberts,* 40 S.E.C., at 916, n. 31.

III

We were explicit in *Chiarella* in saying that there can be no duty to disclose where the person who has traded on inside information "was not [the corporation's] agent, * * * was not a fiduciary, [or] was not a person in whom the sellers [of the securities] had placed their trust and confidence." 445 U.S., at 232, 100 S.Ct., at 1116. Not to require such a fiduciary relationship, we recognized, would "depar[t] radically from the established doctrine that duty arises from a specific relationship between two parties" and would amount to "recognizing a general duty between all participants in market transactions to forego actions based on material, nonpublic information." *Id.*, at 232, 233, 100 S.Ct., at 1116, 1117. This requirement of a specific relationship between the shareholders and the individual trading on inside information has created analytical difficulties for the SEC and courts in policing tippees who trade on inside information. Unlike insiders who have independent fiduciary duties to both the corporation and its shareholders, the typical tippee has no such relationships.[14] In view of this absence, it has been unclear how a tippee acquires the *Cady, Roberts* duty to refrain from trading on inside information.

A

The SEC's position, as stated in its opinion in this case, is that a tippee "inherits" the *Cady, Roberts* obligation to shareholders whenever he receives inside information from an insider:

> "In tipping potential traders, Dirks breached a duty which he had assumed as a result of knowingly receiving confidential information from [Equity Funding] insiders. Tippees such as Dirks who received non-public material information from insiders become 'subject to the same duty as [the] insiders.' Shapiro v. Merrill Lynch, Pierce, Fenner & Smith, Inc. [495 F.2d 228, 237 (CA2 1974) (quoting Ross v. Licht, 263 F.Supp. 395, 410 (SDNY 1967))]. Such a tippee breaches the fiduciary duty which he assumes from the insider when the tippee knowingly transmits the information to someone who will probably trade on the basis thereof. * * * Presumably, Dirks'

---

14. Under certain circumstances, such as where corporate information is revealed legitimately to an underwriter, accountant, lawyer, or consultant working for the corporation, these outsiders may become fiduciaries of the shareholders. The basis for recognizing this fiduciary duty is not simply that such persons acquired nonpublic corporate information, but rather that they have entered into a special confidential relationship in the conduct of the business of the enterprise and are given access to information solely for corporate purposes. See SEC v. Monarch Fund, 608 F.2d 938, 942 (CA2 1979); In re Investors Management Co., 44 S.E.C. 633, 645 (1971); In re Van Alstyne, Noel & Co., 43 S.E.C. 1080, 1084–1085 (1969); In re Merrill Lynch, Pierce, Fenner & Smith, Inc., 43 S.E.C. 933, 937 (1968); Cady, Roberts, 40 S.E.C., at 912. When such a person breaches his fiduciary relationship, he may be treated more properly as a tipper than a tippee. See Shapiro v. Merrill Lynch, Pierce, Fenner & Smith, Inc., 495 F.2d 228, 237 (CA2 1974) (investment banker had access to material information when working on a proposed public offering for the corporation). For such a duty to be imposed, however, the corporation must expect the outsider to keep the disclosed nonpublic information confidential, and the relationship at least must imply such a duty.

informants were entitled to disclose the [Equity Funding] fraud in order to bring it to light and its perpetrators to justice. However, Dirks—standing in their shoes—committed a breach of the fiduciary duty which he had assumed in dealing with them, when he passed the information on to traders." 21 S.E.C. Docket, at 1410, n. 42.

This view differs little from the view that we rejected as inconsistent with congressional intent in *Chiarella*. In that case, the Court of Appeals agreed with the SEC and affirmed Chiarella's conviction, holding that " '[a]nyone—corporate insider or not—who regularly receives material nonpublic information may not use that information to trade in securities without incurring an affirmative duty to disclose.' " United States v. Chiarella, 588 F.2d 1358, 1365 (CA2 1978) (emphasis in original). Here, the SEC maintains that anyone who knowingly receives nonpublic material information from an insider has a fiduciary duty to disclose before trading.

In effect, the SEC's theory of tippee liability in both cases appears rooted in the idea that the antifraud provisions require equal information among all traders. This conflicts with the principle set forth in *Chiarella* that only some persons, under some circumstances, will be barred from trading while in possession of material nonpublic information. Judge Wright correctly read our opinion in *Chiarella* as repudiating any notion that all traders must enjoy equal information before trading: "[T]he 'information' theory is rejected. Because the disclose-or-refrain duty is extraordinary, it attaches only when a party has legal obligations other than a mere duty to comply with the general antifraud proscriptions in the federal securities laws." 220 U.S.App.D.C., at 322, 681 F.2d, at 837. See *Chiarella*, 445 U.S., at 235, n. 20, 100 S.Ct., at 1118, n. 20. We reaffirm today that "[a] duty [to disclose] arises from the relationship between parties * * * and not merely from one's ability to acquire information because of his position in the market." 445 U.S., at 232–233, n. 14, 100 S.Ct., at 1116, n. 14.

Imposing a duty to disclose or abstain solely because a person knowingly receives material nonpublic information from an insider and trades on it could have an inhibiting influence on the role of market analysts, which the SEC itself recognizes is necessary to the preservation of a healthy market.[17] It is commonplace for analysts to "ferret out and analyze information," 21 S.E.C., at 1406, and this often is done by meeting with and questioning corporate officers and others who are

---

17. The SEC expressly recognized that "[t]he value to the entire market of [analysts'] efforts cannot be gainsaid; market efficiency in pricing is significantly enhanced by [their] initiatives to ferret out and analyze information, and thus the analyst's work redounds to the benefit of all investors." 21 S.E.C., at 1406. The SEC asserts that analysts remain free to obtain from management corporate information for purposes of "filling in the 'interstices in analysis' * * *." Brief for Respondent 42 (quoting *Investors Management Co.*, 44 S.E.C., at 646). But this rule is inherently imprecise, and imprecision prevents parties from ordering their actions in accord with legal requirements. Unless the parties have some guidance as to where the line is between permissible and impermissible disclosures and uses, neither corporate insiders nor analysts can be sure when the line is crossed. Cf. Adler v. Klawans, 267 F.2d 840, 845 (CA2 1959) (Burger, J., sitting by designation).

insiders. And information that the analysts obtain normally may be the basis for judgments as to the market worth of a corporation's securities. The analyst's judgment in this respect is made available in market letters or otherwise to clients of the firm. It is the nature of this type of information, and indeed of the markets themselves, that such information cannot be made simultaneously available to all of the corporation's stockholders or the public generally.

B

The conclusion that recipients of inside information do not invariably acquire a duty to disclose or abstain does not mean that such tippees always are free to trade on the information. The need for a ban on some tippee trading is clear. Not only are insiders forbidden by their fiduciary relationship from personally using undisclosed corporate information to their advantage, but they may not give such information to an outsider for the same improper purpose of exploiting the information for their personal gain. See 15 U.S.C. § 78t(b) (making it unlawful to go indirectly "by means of any other person" any act made unlawful by the federal securities laws). Similarly, the transactions of those who knowingly participate with the fiduciary in such a breach are "as forbidden" as transactions "on behalf of the trustee himself." Mosser v. Darrow, 341 U.S. 267, 272, 71 S.Ct. 680, 682, 95 L.Ed. 927 (1951). As the Court explained in *Mosser,* a contrary rule "would open up opportunities for devious dealings in the name of the others that the trustee could not conduct in his own." 341 U.S., at 271, 71 S.Ct., at 682. See SEC v. Texas Gulf Sulphur, Co., 446 F.2d 1301, 1308 (CA2), cert. denied, 404 U.S. 1005, 92 S.Ct. 561, 30 L.Ed.2d 558 (1971). Thus, the tippee's duty to disclose or abstain is derivative from that of the insider's duty. See Tr. of Oral Ar. 38. Cf. *Chiarella,* 445 U.S., at 246, n. 1, 100 S.Ct., at 1124, n. 1 (Blackmun, J., dissenting). As we noted in *Chiarella,* "[t]he tippee's obligation has been viewed as arising from his role as a participant after the fact in the insider's breach of a fiduciary duty." 445 U.S., at 230, n. 12, 100 S.Ct., at 1116, n. 12.

Thus, some tippees must assume an insider's duty to the shareholders not because they receive inside information, but rather because it has been made available to them *improperly.* And for Rule 10b-5 purposes, the insider's disclosure is improper only where it would violate his *Cady, Roberts* duty. Thus, a tippee assumes a fiduciary duty to the shareholders of a corporation not to trade on material nonpublic information only when the insider has breached his fiduciary duty to the shareholders by disclosing the information to the tippee and the tippee knows or should know that there has been a breach. As Commissioner Smith perceptively observed in *Investors Management Co.*: "[T]ippee responsibility must be related back to insider responsibility by a necessary finding that the tippee knew the information was given to him in breach of a duty by a person having a special relationship to the issuer not to disclose the information * * *." 44 S.E.C., at 651 (concurring in the result). Tipping thus properly is viewed only as a means of indirectly violating the *Cady, Roberts* disclose-or-abstain rule.

C

In determining whether a tippee is under an obligation to disclose or abstain, it thus is necessary to determine whether the insider's "tip" constituted a breach of the insider's fiduciary duty. All disclosures of confidential corporate information are not inconsistent with the duty insiders owe to shareholders. In contrast to the extraordinary facts of this case, the more typical situation in which there will be a question whether disclosure violates the insider's *Cady, Roberts* duty is when insiders disclose information to analysts. In some situations, the insider will act consistently with his fiduciary duty to shareholders, and yet release of the information may affect the market. For example, it may not be clear—either to the corporate insider or to the recipient analyst— whether the information will be viewed as material nonpublic information. Corporate officials may mistakenly think the information already has been disclosed or that it is not material enough to affect the market. Whether disclosure is a breach of duty therefore depends in large part on the purpose of the disclosure. This standard was identified by the SEC itself in *Cady, Roberts:* a purpose of the securities laws was to eliminate "use of inside information for personal advantage." 40 S.E.C., at 912, n. 15. Thus, the test is whether the insider personally will benefit, directly or indirectly, from his disclosure. Absent some personal gain, there has been no breach of duty to stockholders. And absent a breach by the insider, there is no derivative breach. As Commissioner Smith stated in *Investors Management Co.:* "It is important in this type of case to focus on policing insiders and what they do * * * rather than on policing information *per se* and its possession * * *." 44 S.E.C., at 648 (concurring in the result).

The SEC argues that, if inside-trading liability does not exist when the information is transmitted for a proper purpose but is used for trading, it would be a rare situation when the parties could not fabricate some ostensibly legitimate business justification for transmitting the information. We think the SEC is unduly concerned. In determining whether the insider's purpose in making a particular disclosure is fraudulent, the SEC and the courts are not required to read the parties' minds. Scienter in some cases is relevant in determining whether the tipper has violated his *Cady, Roberts* duty. But to determine whether the disclosure itself "deceive[s], manipulate[s], or defraud[s]" shareholders, Aaron v. SEC, 446 U.S. 680, 686, 100 S.Ct. 1945, 1950, 64 L.Ed.2d 611 (1980), the initial inquiry is whether there has been a breach of duty by the insider. This requires courts to focus on objective criteria, *i.e.,* whether the insider receives a direct or indirect personal benefit from the disclosure, such as a pecuniary gain or a reputational benefit that will translate into future earnings. Cf. 40 S.E.C., at 912, n. 15; Brudney, Insiders, Outsiders, and Informational Advantages Under the Federal Securities Laws, 93 Harv.L.Rev. 324, 348 (1979) ("The theory * * * is that the insider, by giving the information out selectively, is in effect selling the information to its recipient for cash, reciprocal information or other things of value for himself * * * ''). There are objective facts and circumstances that often justify such an inference. For example, there may be a relationship between the insider and the recipient that suggests a *quid pro quo* from the latter, or an intention to benefit the particular recipient. The elements of fiduciary duty and exploitation of nonpublic information also exist when an insider makes a gift of confidential information to a trading relative or friend. The tip and trade resemble trading by the insider himself followed by a gift of the profits to the recipient.

Determining whether an insider personally benefits from a particular disclosure, a question of fact, will not always be easy for courts. But it is essential, we think, to have a guiding principle for those whose daily activities must be limited and instructed by the SEC's inside-trading rules, and we believe that there must be a breach of the insider's fiduciary duty before the tippee inherits the duty to disclose or abstain. In contrast, the rule adopted by the SEC in this case would have no limiting principle.

IV

Under the inside-trading and tipping rules set forth above, we find that there was no actionable violation by Dirks. It is undisputed that Dirks himself was a stranger to Equity Funding, with no pre-existing fiduciary duty to its shareholders. He took no action, directly or indirectly, that induced the shareholders or officers of Equity Funding to repose trust or confidence in him. There was no expectation by Dirks' sources that he would keep their information in confidence. Nor did Dirks misappropriate or illegally obtain the information about Equity Funding. Unless the insiders breached their *Cady, Roberts* duty to shareholders in disclosing the nonpublic information to Dirks, he breached no duty when he passed it on to investors as well as to the *Wall Street Journal*.

It is clear that neither Secrist nor the other Equity Funding employees violated their *Cady, Roberts* duty to the corporation's shareholders by providing information to Dirks.[18] The tippers received no monetary

---

18. In this Court, the SEC appears to contend that an insider invariably violates a fiduciary duty to the corporation's shareholders by transmitting nonpublic corporate information to an outsider when he has reason to believe that the outsider may use it to the disadvantage of the shareholders. * * *

The dissent argues that "Secrist violated his duty to Equity Funding shareholders by transmitting material nonpublic information to Dirks with the intention that Dirks would cause his clients to trade on that information." *Post,* at 12. By perceiving a breach of fiduciary duty whenever inside information is intentionally disclosed to securities traders, the dissenting opinion effectively would achieve the same result as the SEC's theory below, *i.e.,* mere possession of inside information while trading would be viewed as a Rule 10b–5 violation. But *Chiarella* made it explicitly clear there is no general duty to forego market transactions "based on material, nonpublic information." 445 U.S., at 233, 100 S.Ct., at 1117. Such a duty would "depar[t] radically from the established doctrine that duty arises from a specific relationship between two parties." *Ibid.*

or personal benefit for revealing Equity Funding's secrets, nor was their purpose to make a gift of valuable information to Dirks. As the facts of this case clearly indicate, the tippers were motivated by a desire to expose the fraud. See *supra,* at 1–2. In the absence of a breach of duty to shareholders by the insiders, there was no derivative breach by Dirks. See n. 20, *supra.* Dirks therefore could not have been "a participant after the fact in [an] insider's breach of a fiduciary duty." *Chiarella,* 445 U.S., at 230, n. 12, 100 S.Ct., at 1116, n. 12.

V

We conclude that Dirks, in the circumstances of this case, had no duty to abstain from use of the inside information that he obtained. The judgment of the Court of Appeals therefore is

Reversed.

JUSTICE BLACKMUN, with whom JUSTICE BRENNAN and JUSTICE MARSHALL join, dissenting.

The Court today takes still another step to limit the protections provided investors by § 10(b) of the Securities Exchange Act of 1934. See Chiarella v. United States, 445 U.S. 222, 246, 100 S.Ct. 1108, 1123, 63 L.Ed.2d 348 (1980) (dissenting opinion). The device employed in this case engrafts a special motivational requirement on the fiduciary duty doctrine. This innovation excuses a knowing and intentional violation of an insider's duty to shareholders if the insider does not act from a motive of personal gain. Even on the extraordinary facts of this case, such an innovation is not justified.

* * *

II

A.

No one questions that Secrist himself could not trade on his inside information to the disadvantage of uninformed shareholders and pur-

---

Moreover, to constitute a violation of Rule 10b–5, there must be fraud. See Ernst & Ernst v. Hochfelder, 425 U.S. 185, 199, 96 S.Ct. 1375, 1383, 47 L.Ed.2d 668 (1976) (statutory words "manipulative," "device," and "contrivance * * * connot[e] intentional or willful conduct designed to *deceive or defraud* investors by controlling or artificially affecting the price of securities") (emphasis added). There is no evidence that Secrist's disclosure was intended to or did in fact "deceive or defraud" anyone. Secrist certainly intended to convey relevant information that management was unlawfully concealing, and—so far as the record shows—he believed that persuading Dirks to investigate was the best way to disclose the fraud. Other efforts had proved fruitless. Under any objective standard, Secrist received no direct or indirect personal benefit from the disclosure.

The dissenting opinion focuses on shareholder "losses," "injury," and "damages," but in many cases there may be no clear causal connection between inside trading and outsiders' losses. In one sense, as market values fluctuate and investors act on inevitably incomplete or incorrect information, there always are winners and losers; but those who have "lost" have not necessary been defrauded. On the other hand, inside trading for personal gain is fraudulent, and is a violation of the federal securities laws. * * *. Thus, there is little legal significance to the dissent's argument that Secrist and Dirks created new "victims" by disclosing the information to persons who traded. In fact, they prevented the fraud from continuing and victimizing many more investors.

chasers of Equity Funding securities. See Brief for United States as *Amicus Curiae* 19, n. 12. Unlike the printer in *Chiarella,* Secrist stood in a fiduciary relationship with these shareholders. As the Court states, *ante,* at 5, corporate insiders have an affirmative duty of disclosure when trading with shareholders of the corporation. See *Chiarella,* 445 U.S., at 227, 100 S.Ct., at 1114. This duty extends as well to purchasers of the corporation's securities. *Id.,* at 227, n. 8, 100 S.Ct., at 1114, n. 8 citing Gratz v. Claughton, 187 F.2d 46, 49 (CA2), cert. denied, 341 U.S. 920, 71 S.Ct. 741, 95 L.Ed. 1353 (1951).

The Court also acknowledges that Secrist could not do by proxy what he was prohibited from doing personally. Mosser v. Darrow, 341 U.S. 267, 272, 71 S.Ct. 680, 682, 95 L.Ed. 927 (1951). But this is precisely what Secrist did. Secrist used Dirks to disseminate information to Dirks' clients, who in turn dumped stock on unknowing purchasers. Secrist thus intended Dirks to injure the purchasers of Equity Funding securities to whom Secrist had a duty to disclose. Accepting the Court's view of tippee liability, it appears that Dirks' knowledge of this breach makes him liable as a participant in the breach after the fact.

B

The Court holds, however, that Dirks is not liable because Secrist did not violate his duty; according to the Court, this is so because Secrist did not have the improper purpose of personal gain. In so doing, the Court imposes a new, subjective limitation on the scope of the duty owed by insiders to shareholders. The novelty of this limitation is reflected in the Court's lack of support for it.

The insider's duty is owed directly to the corporation's shareholders. See Langevoort, Insider Trading and the Fiduciary Principle: A Post-*Chiarella* Restatement, 70 Calif.L.Rev. 1, 5 (1982); 3A W. Fletcher, Private Corporations § 1168.2, pp. 288–289 (1975). As *Chiarella* recognized, it is based on the relationship of trust and confidence between the insider and the shareholder. 445 U.S., at 228, 100 S.Ct., at 1114. That relationship assures the shareholder that the insider may not take actions that will harm him unfairly. The affirmative duty of disclosure protects against this injury. See Pepper v. Litton, 308 U.S. 295, 307, n. 15, 60 S.Ct. 238, 245, n. 15, 84 L.Ed. 281 (1939); Strong v. Rapide, 213 U.S. 419, 431–434, 29 S.Ct. 521, 524–525, 53 L.Ed. 853 (1909); see also *Chiarella,* 445 U.S., at 228, n. 10, 100 S.Ct., at 1114, n. 10; cf. *Pepper,* 308 U.S., at 307, 60 S.Ct., at 245 (fiduciary obligation to corporation exists for corporation's protection).

C

The fact that the insider himself does not benefit from the breach does not eradicate the shareholder's injury. Cf. Restatement (Second) of Trusts § 205, Comments c and d (1959) (trustee liable for acts causing diminution of value of trust); 3 A. Scott on Trusts § 205, p. 1665 (1967) (trustee liable for any losses to trust caused by his breach). It makes no difference to the shareholder whether the corporate insider gained or intended to gain personally from the transaction; the shareholder still has lost because of the insider's misuse of nonpublic information. The duty is addressed not to the insider's motives, but to his actions and their consequences on the shareholder. Personal gain is not an element of the breach of this duty.[11]

This conclusion is borne out by the Court's decision in Mosser v. Darrow, 341 U.S. 267, 71 S.Ct. 680, 95 L.Ed. 927 (1951). There, the Court faced an analogous situation: a reorganization trustee engaged two employee-promoters of subsidiaries of the companies being reorganized to provide services that the trustee considered to be essential to the successful operation of the trust. In order to secure their services, the trustee expressly agreed with the employees that they could continue to trade in the securities of the subsidiaries. The employees then turned their inside position into substantial profits at the expense both of the trust and of other holders of the companies' securities.

The Court acknowledged that the trustee neither intended to nor did in actual fact benefit from this arrangement; his motives were completely selfless and devoted to the companies. 341 U.S., at 275, 71 S.Ct., at 684. The Court, nevertheless, found the trustee liable to the estate for the activities of the employees he authorized. The Court described the trustee's defalcation as "a willful and deliberate setting up of an interest in employees adverse to that of the trust." *Id.*, at 272. The breach did not depend on the trustee's personal gain, and his motives in violating his duty were irrelevant; like Secrist, the trustee intended that others would abuse the inside information for their personal gain. Cf. Dodge v. Ford Motor Co., 204 Mich. 459, 506–509, 170 N.W. 668, 684–685 (1919) (Henry Ford's philanthropic motives did not permit him to set Ford Motor Company dividend policies to benefit public at expense of shareholders).

As *Mosser* demonstrates, the breach consists in taking action disadvantageous to the person to whom one owes a duty. In this case, Secrist

---

11. The Court seems concerned that this case bears on insiders' contacts with analysts for valid corporate reasons. It also fears that insiders may not be able to determine whether the information transmitted is material or nonpublic. When the disclosure is to an investment banker or some other adviser, however, there is normally no breach because the insider does not have scienter: he does not intend that the inside information be used for trading purposes to the disadvantage of shareholders. Moreover, if the insider in good faith does not believe that the information is material or nonpublic, he also lacks the necessary scienter. Ernst & Ernst v. Hochfelder, 425 U.S. 185, 197 (1976). In fact, the scienter requirement functions in part to protect good faith errors of this type.

Should the adviser receiving the information use it to trade, it may breach a separate contractual or other duty to the corporation not to misuse the information. Absent such an arrangement, however, the adviser is not barred by Rule 10b–5 from trading on that information if it believes that the insider has not breached any duty to his shareholders. See Walton v. Morgan Stanley & Co., 623 F.2d 796, 798–799 (CA2 1980).

The situation here, of course, is radically different. *Ante*, at 11, n. 17 (Dirks received information requiring no analysis "as to its market relevance"). Secrist divulged the information for the precise purpose of causing Dirks' clients to trade on it. I fail to understand how imposing liability on Dirks will affect legitimate insider-analyst contacts.

owed a duty to purchasers of Equity Funding shares. The Court's addition of the bad purpose element to a breach of fiduciary duty claim is flatly inconsistent with the principle of *Mosser*. I do not join this limitation of the scope of an insider's fiduciary duty to shareholders.

III

The improper purpose requirement not only has no basis in law, but it rests implicitly on a policy that I cannot accept. The Court justifies Secrist's and Dirks' action because the general benefit derived from the violation of Secrist's duty to shareholders outweighed the harm caused to those shareholders, see Heller, *Chiarella,* SEC Rule 14e–3 and *Dirks:* "Fairness" versus Economic Theory, 37 Bus.Lawyer 517, 550 (1982); Easterbrook, Insider Trading, Secret Agents, Evidentiary Privileges, and the Production of Information, 1981 S.Ct.Rev. 309, 338—in other words, because the end justified the means. Under this view, the benefit conferred on society by Secrist's and Dirks' activities may be paid for with the losses caused to shareholders trading with Dirks' clients.[14]

Although Secrist's general motive to expose the Equity Funding fraud was laudable, the means he chose were not. Moreover, even assuming that Dirks played a substantial role in exposing the fraud, he and his clients should not profit from the information they obtained from Secrist. Misprision of a felony long has been against public policy. Branzburg v. Hayes, 408 U.S. 665, 696–697, 92 S.Ct. 2646, 2664, 33 L.Ed.2d 626 (1972); see 18 U.S.C. § 4. A person cannot condition his transmission of information of a crime on a financial award. As a citizen, Dirks had at least an ethical obligation to report the information to the proper authorities. See *ante,* at 13, n. 20. The Court's holding is deficient in policy terms not because it fails to create a legal norm out of that ethical norm, see *ibid.,* but because it actually rewards Dirks for his aiding and abetting.

Dirks and Secrist were under a duty to disclose the information or to refrain from trading on it. I agree that disclosure in this case would have been difficult. I also recognize that the SEC seemingly has been less than helpful in its view of the nature of disclosure necessary to satisfy the disclose-or-refrain duty. The Commission tells persons with inside information that they cannot trade on that information unless they disclose; it refuses, however, to tell them how to disclose. See In re Faberge, Inc., 45 S.E.C. 249, 256 (1973) (disclosure requires public release through public media designed to reach investing public general-

---

14. This position seems little different from the theory that insider trading should be permitted because it brings relevant information to the market. See H. Manne, Insider Trading and the Stock Market 59–76, 111–146 (1966); Manne, Insider Trading and the Law Professors, 23 Vand.L.Rev. 547, 565–576 (1970). The Court also seems to embrace a variant of that extreme theory, which postulates that insider trading causes no harm at all to those who pur-chase from the insider. Both the theory and its variant sit at the opposite end of the theoretical spectrum from the much maligned equality-of-information theory, and never have been adopted by Congress or ratified by this Court. See Langevoort, 70 Calif.L.Rev., at 1 and n. 1. The theory rejects the existence of any enforceable principle of fairness between market participants.

ly). This seems to be a less than sensible policy, which it is incumbent on the Commission to correct. The Court, however, has no authority to remedy the problem by opening a hole in the congressionally mandated prohibition on insider trading, thus rewarding such trading.

IV

In my view, Secrist violated his duty to Equity Funding shareholders by transmitting material nonpublic information to Dirks with the intention that Dirks would cause his clients to trade on that information. Dirks, therefore, was under a duty to make the information publicly available or to refrain from actions that he knew would lead to trading. Because Dirks caused his clients to trade, he violated § 10(b) and Rule 10b–5. Any other result is a disservice to this country's attempt to provide fair and efficient capital markets. I dissent.

Note: Life After Dirks

Chiarella, Clark and *Dirks* provide broad guidelines for determining when a person violates Section 10(b) and Rule 10b–5 by trading on the basis of material, nonpublic information. *Chiarella* held that such a violation occurs when there is a duty to disclose arising from a fiduciary duty or relationship of trust and confidence between the parties to the transaction. *Dirks* suggested that an outsider may owe a fiduciary duty to a corporation's shareholders when he receives nonpublic corporate information with the expectation that it will be kept confidential. In footnote 14, the Court noted that outsiders who might be in such a position include underwriters, accountants, lawyers or consultants working for the corporation. *Clark* and the other decisions applying the misappropriation theory establish that misuse of confidential information can constitute a breach of duty even if the misappropriator owes no duty to the person with whom she trades.

Dirks also held that tipping constitutes a breach of fiduciary duty if "the insider will benefit, directly or indirectly, from his disclosure." Finally, *Dirks* held that a "tippee" violates the Rule "when an insider has breached a fiduciary duty to the shareholders by disclosing the information to the tippee and the tippee knows or should know that there has been a breach." If the misappropriation theory is valid, the same would appear to be true when information that has been misappropriated is disclosed to a tippee and the tippee knows or should know of the misappropriation.

The lower courts have been left with the often difficult task of interpreting and applying these broad guidelines. This note will examine the principal cases dealing with the following questions:

(i) What constitutes a benefit to the tipper such that the tip would constitute a breach of fiduciary duty requiring a tippee who knew or should have known of the breach to abstain or disclose?;

(ii) Under what circumstances can an outsider be held to have a duty to the corporation's shareholders under the *Dirks* footnote 14 test?;

(iii) Under what circumstances can outsiders, including family members, be held to have violated Rule 10b–5 based on a misappropriation theory?; and

(iv) To establish liability on the part of tippees, is it sufficient they trade while they knowingly possessed material inside information, or must the trading be causally connected with the misappropriated information?

1. Benefit to Tipper

In S.E.C. v. Switzer, 590 F.Supp. 756 (W.D.Okl.1984), Switzer, while attending a track meet, overheard Platt, the Chairman and chief executive officer of Phoenix Resources Company ("Phoenix"), tell his wife that he might be out of town the following week because there was a possibility that Phoenix would be liquidated. The court found that Platt's purpose in telling his wife of the trip was so that child care arrangements could be made. The court also found that the Platts did not know that Switzer was on a bench behind them during this conversation.

Based on the information regarding Phoenix's possible liquidation, Switzer, who knew of Platt's position with Phoenix, and several of Switzer's friends, made substantial investments in Phoenix. The SEC argued that Switzer and his friends were liable under Rule 10b–5 as tippees.

The court held, however, that Platt did not breach a fiduciary duty to Phoenix's shareholders by disclosing this information since he did not personally benefit, directly or indirectly, from the disclosure. Accordingly, under the *Dirks* test, Switzer and his friends were held to have owed no duty to Phoenix's stockholders, and thus were not liable as tippees.

The case suggests a difficulty with *Dirks'* requirement that a tipper must receive a benefit from his tip before Rule 10b–5 liability may be imposed on a tippee trading on the basis of that tip. It can be argued that the combination of Platt's imprudent disclosure (arguably a breach of fiduciary duty) and Switzer's knowledge of the nonpublic nature of that information should be enough to constitute a 10b–5 violation. But *Dirks* requires more. It requires the tipper, or corporate insider, also to have benefitted from the breach. Moreover, while the Court is not explicit on this point, it appears that *Dirks* also requires the tipper's benefit to be connected in some way with the tippee's trading. In *Switzer*, for instance, it is probable that any benefit Platt received from the disclosure to his wife by arranging for child care was not the type of benefit contemplated by *Dirks*. Specifically, it is difficult to see how Platt's disclosure to his wife conferred a benefit on him which is related to Switzer's trading; the benefit, if any, to Platt was peace of mind about child care.

United States v. Libera, 989 F.2d 596 (2d Cir.1993), was one of numerous insider trading cases based on access to advance copies of *Business Week* magazine. The tippees received their copies of the magazine from employees of the company that printed it. That company had a policy prohibiting its employees from disclosing the magazine's contents before it reached the public. The Second Circuit concluded that, as a matter of law, the employer-employee relationship was sufficient to establish a duty not to disclose and that the printer's employees breached by providing advance copies of the magazine to others.

The court also held that a tipper could be found liable even if the tipper did not know that the tippee would trade on the basis of the misappropriated information. The fact that a tipper knows she is breaching a duty to the owner of the information "suffices to establish the tipper's expectation that the breach will lead to some kind of misuse of the information." "This is so," the court reasoned, "because it may be presumed that the tippee's interest in the information is, in contemporary jargon, not for nothing." "To allow a tippee to escape liability because the government cannot prove to a jury's satisfaction that the tipper knew exactly what misuse would result from the tipper's wrongdoing would not fulfill the purpose of the misappropriation theory, which is to protect property rights to information * * *. Indeed," the court indicated, "such a requirement would serve no purpose other than to create a loophole for such misuse." 989 F.2d at 600.

2. *Constructive Insiders*

In S.E.C. v. Lund, 570 F.Supp. 1397 (C.D.Cal.1983), Lund, the chief executive officer, president and Chairman of the Board of Directors of Verit Industries was asked by Horowitz, a member of Verit's board, and the chief executive officer, president and chairman of P & F Industries, ("P & F"), if Verit would be interested in providing $600,000 capital for a joint venture involving a gambling casino between P & F and Jockey Club Casino Corporation. Soon after, but apparently prior to any public disclosure regarding the venture, Lund purchased 10,000 shares of P & F stock, which he subsequently sold at a profit. The court concluded that under *Dirks,* Lund could not be liable as a tippee because Horowitz had not breached a fiduciary duty to P & F's shareholders by disclosing information concerning the venture to Lund. The court did hold, however, that Lund was liable as a "temporary insider," since the "information was made available to Lund solely for corporate purposes." Consider whether the latter conclusion is correct. *Dirks* footnote 14 states that to qualify as a constructive insider, an outsider must know the corporation expects her to keep the information confidential. Was that the situation in *Lund*?

3. *Family Relationships*

In United States v. Chestman, 947 F.2d 551 (2d Cir.1991) cert. denied ___ U.S. ___, 112 S.Ct. 1759, 118 L.Ed.2d 422 (1992) (en banc), a divided Second Circuit reversed the insider trading conviction of stockbroker Robert Chestman.* Chestman had learned from a client, Keith Loeb, that the Great Atlantic & Pacific Tea Co. (A & P) planned to acquire the Waldbaum supermarket chain. Loeb's mother-in-law was the sister of Ira Waldbaum, the CEO of Waldbaum. Ira told his sister that he had agreed to sell the Waldbaum chain to A & P and cautioned her that the information was confidential. His sister passed the news on to her daughter, Keith's wife, who then conveyed the information to her husband but told him to treat it as confidential. Keith proceeded to tell Chestman that he had received "definite * * * accurate" information regarding the sale of Waldbaum for a substantial premium over its current market price and to place an order to purchase Waldbaum stock. Chestman also bought Waldbaum stock for his own account.

Chestman was convicted of aiding and abetting Loeb's misappropriation of material nonpublic information in breach of a duty Loeb owed to the Waldbaum family and to his wife and of trading as a "tippee" on the basis of that same misappropriated information. The government conceded that conviction under both theories required proof that Loeb had breached a fiduciary duty to his wife or to the Waldbaum family, and that Chestman knew that Loeb had done so. The court had "little trouble finding the evidence insufficient to establish a fiduciary relationship or its functional equivalent between Keith Loeb and the Waldbaum family." It held that "[k]inship alone does not create the necessary relationship," 947 F.2d at 570, and concluded that "because Keith [Loeb] owed neither [his wife] nor the Waldbaum family a fiduciary duty or its functional equivalent, he did not defraud them by disclosing news of the pending tender offer to Chestman. Absent a predicate act of fraud by Keith Loeb, the alleged misappropriator, Chestman could not be derivatively liable as Loeb's tippee or as an aider and abettor." Id. at 571.

Judge Ralph Winter, joined by five other judges, dissented from the reversal of Chestman's conviction for violating Rule 10b–5. According to the dissent, "When members of a family have benefitted from the family's control of a corporation and are in a position to acquire such information in the ordinary course of family interactions, that position comes with it a duty not to trade. * * * Such a duty is of course based on mutual understandings among family members * * * and owed to the family. However, the duty originates in the corporation and is ultimately intended to protect the corporation and its public shareholders." Id. at 579 (Winter, J., dissenting). The dissent also saw "no room for argument over whether there was sufficient evidence for the jury to find that Chestman knew Keith Loeb was violating an obligation. The record fairly brims with Chestman's consciousness that Keith Loeb was behaving improperly." Id. at 580–81 (Winter, J., dissenting).

4. *Tippee's State of Mind*

United States v. Teicher, 987 F.2d 112 (2d Cir.1993), involved the question of whether proof a tippee traded while in possession of material,

---

* However, the court affirmed Chestman's conviction under SEC Rule 14e–3(a), which prohibits trading on the basis of ma-   terial, non-public information about a pending tender offer.

nonpublic information is sufficient to establish causation in an insider trading case, or whether the government must prove defendants traded on the basis of that information. A young attorney had provided defendants with information about ongoing or contemplated transactions involving clients of the law firm that employed him. The defendants were arbitrageurs whose business involved gathering information ranging from rumors to public reports about publicly traded companies.

The Second Circuit held that a violation of Rule 10b–5 occurs "when a trade is conducted in 'knowing possession' of material nonpublic information obtained in breach of a fiduciary or similar duty." Id. at 120. In addition to relying on the fact that the SEC has consistently endorsed the interpretation that Rule 10b–5 only requires "knowing possession," the court set forth three factors which favor a "knowing possession" standard.

First, both Section 10(b) and Rule 10b–5 require that a deceptive practice be conducted in connection with the purchase or sale of a security. The "in connection with" clause has been construed flexibly, the court asserted, to include deceptive practices "touching" the sale of securities, a very tenuous relationship.

Second, the "knowing possession" standard "comports with the oft-quoted maxim that one with a fiduciary or similar duty to hold material nonpublic information in confidence must either disclose or abstain with regard to trading." Thus, an insider who has a fiduciary obligation not to disclose material nonpublic information must abstain from trading. It "would be consistent with the disclose or abstain rule that a tippee acquire the same duty as his fiduciary tipper." Id.

Third, a "knowing possession" test has the "attribute of simplicity." The test "recognizes that one who trades while knowingly possessing material inside information has an information advantage over other traders." Id. This advantage may manifest itself in a variety of forms, including trading on the information, rescinding a previously decided transaction, or proceeding with a previously planned transaction. In contrast, "a requirement of causal connection between the information and the trade could frustrate attempts to distinguish between legitimate trades and those conducted in connection with inside information." Id.

Note: Remedies for Insider Trading Violations

Section 20A of the 1934 Act creates a private right of action on behalf of contemporaneous traders against insiders, constructive insiders, tippers, and tippees (as well as their controlling persons) who trade on the basis of material nonpublic information. The liability of defendants in actions by contemporaneous traders is limited to the actual profits realized or losses avoided, reduced by the amount of any disgorgement obtained by the SEC under its broad authority to seek injunctive relief. Courts have generally followed the same disgorgement of insiders' gains. Elkind v. Liggett & Myers, Inc., 635 F.2d 156 (2d Cir.1980). The liability of controlling persons is governed by section 20(a) of the

1934 Act which permits such persons to defend by showing that they acted in good faith and did not know of the violation of their controlled person.

Pursuant to section 21A of the 1934 Act, the SEC is authorized to seek judicially imposed civil penalties against insiders, constructive insiders, tippers, and tippees of up to three times the profits gained or the losses avoided in unlawful insider trading. These civil penalties are *in addition* to other remedies. Thus, an insider, tipper, or tippee may be required to disgorged her profits, whether in an SEC or private action, and pay a treble damage penalty. The civil penalty can be imposed only at the instance of the SEC.

Section 21A(b) also permits the imposition of civil penalties on controlling persons, such as employers, of up to $1 million or three times the insider's profits (whichever is greater) if the controlling person knowingly or recklessly disregards the insider trading by persons under its control. Section 21A(e) of the 1934 Act also encourages private watchdogs by providing for the payment of bounties to people who provide information concerning insider trading.

The penalties for criminal securities violations include sentences of up to a maximum of ten years and maximum fines of $1 million for individuals and $2 million for nonnatural persons. Section 32(a) of the 1934 Act.

The Securities Enforcement and Penny Stock Act of 1990, which amended Section 8 of the 1933 Act and Section 21 of the 1934 Act, gives the SEC administrative "cease and desist" authority, and authorizes the SEC to impose civil penalties under Section 21B of the 1934 Act.

5. THE AFFIRMATIVE DUTY TO DISCLOSE

SECURITIES EXCHANGE ACT RELEASE
No 34–8995 (1970).

The Securities and Exchange Commission today reiterated the need for publicly held companies to make prompt and accurate disclosure of information, both favorable and unfavorable, to security holders and the investing public. Companies subject to the reporting requirements of the Securities Exchange Act of 1934 are, at the present time, generally required to file annual reports within 120 days after the end of their fiscal years, semi-annual reports within 45 days after the end of the 6-month period and current reports within 10 days after the end of the month in which a reportable event has occurred * * *.

Notwithstanding the fact a company complies with such reporting requirements, it still has an obligation to make full and prompt announcements of material facts regarding the company's financial condition. The responsibility for making such announcement rests, and properly so, with the management of the company. They are intimately aware of the factors affecting the operations of the business. Management of noninvestment companies are cognizant of factors affecting profits and losses, such as curtailment of operations, decline of orders, or costs overruns on major contracts. They are also cognizant of liquidity problems such as a decreased inflow of collections from sales to customers, the availability or lack of availability of credit from suppliers, banks, and other financial institutions, and the inability to meet maturing obligations when they fall due * * *.

The policy of prompt corporate disclosure of material business events is embodied in the rules and directives of the major exchanges. It should be noted that unless adequate and accurate information is available, a company may not be able to purchase its own securities or make acquisitions using its securities, and its insiders may not be able to trade its securities without running a serious risk of violating Section 10(b) of the Securities Exchange Act of 1934 and Rule 10b–5 thereunder.

Corporate managements are urged to review their policies with respect to corporate disclosure and endeavor to set up procedures which will insure that prompt disclosure be made of material corporate developments, both favorable and unfavorable, so that investor confidence can be maintained in an orderly and effective securities market.

NEW YORK STOCK EXCHANGE LISTED COMPANY MANUAL, SECTION 2: DISCLOSURE AND REPORTING MATERIAL INFORMATION

202.01 Internal Handling of Confidential Corporate Matters

Unusual market activity or a substantial price change has on occasion occurred in a company's securities shortly before the announcement of an important corporate action or development. Such incidents are extremely embarrassing and damaging to both the company and the Exchange since the public may quickly conclude that someone acted on the basis of inside information.

Negotiations leading to mergers and acquisitions, stock splits, the making of arrangements preparatory to an exchange or tender offer, changes in dividend rates or earnings, calls for redemption, and new contracts, products, or discoveries are the type of developments where the risk of untimely and inadvertent disclosure of corporate plans are most likely to occur. Frequently, these matters require extensive discussion and study by corporate officials before final decisions can be made. Accordingly, extreme care must be used in order to keep the information on a confidential basis.

Where it is possible to confine formal or informal discussions to a small group of the top management of the company or companies involved, and their individual confidential advisors where adequate security can be maintained, premature public announcement may properly be avoided. In this regard, the market action of a company's securities should be closely watched at a time when consideration is being given to important corporate matters. If unusual market activity should arise, the company should be prepared to make an immediate public announcement of the matter.

At some point it usually becomes necessary to involve other persons to conduct preliminary studies or assist in other preparations for contemplated transactions, e.g., business appraisals, tentative financing arrangements, attitude of large outside holders, availability of major blocks of stock, engineering studies and market analyses and surveys. Experience has shown that maintaining security at this point is virtually impossible. Accordingly, fairness requires that the company make an immediate public announcement as soon as disclosures relating to such important matters are made to outsiders.

The extent of the disclosures will depend upon the stage of discussions, studies, or negotiations. So far as possible, public statements should be definite as to price, ratio, timing and/or any other pertinent information necessary to permit a reasonable evaluation of the matter. As a minimum, they should include those disclosures made to outsiders. Where an initial announcement cannot be specific or complete, it will need to be supplemented from time to time as more definitive or different terms are discussed or determined.

Corporate employees, as well as directors and officers, should be regularly reminded as a matter of policy that they must not disclose confidential information they may receive in the course of their duties and must not attempt to take advantage of such information themselves.

In view of the importance of this matter and the potential difficulties involved, the Exchange suggests that a periodic review be made by each company of the manner in which confidential information is being handled within its own organization. A reminder notice of the company's policy to those in sensitive areas might also be helpful.

A sound corporate disclosure policy is essential to the maintenance of a fair and orderly securities market. It should minimize the occasions where the Exchange finds it necessary to temporarily halt trading in a security due to information leaks or rumors in connection with significant corporate transactions.

While the procedures are directed primarily at situations involving two or more companies, they are equally applicable to major corporate developments involving a single company.

202.03 Dealing With Rumors or Unusual Market Activity

The market activity of a company's securities should be closely watched at a time when consideration is being given to significant corporate matters. If rumors or unusual market activity indicate that information on impending developments has leaked out, a frank and explicit announcement is clearly required. If rumors are in fact false or inaccurate, they should be promptly denied or clarified. A statement to the effect that the company knows of no corporate developments to account for the unusual market activity can have a salutary effect. It is obvious that if such a public statement is contemplated, management should be checked prior to any public comment so as to avoid any embarrassment or potential criticism. If rumors are correct or there are developments, an immediate candid statement to the public as to the state of negotiations or of development of corporate plans in the rumored area must be made directly and openly. Such statements are essential despite the business inconvenience which may be caused and even though the matter may not as yet have been presented to the company's Board of Directors for consideration.

* * *

202.05 Timely Disclosure of Material News Developments

A listed company is expected to release quickly to the public any news or information which might reasonably be expected to materially affect the market for its securities. This is one of the most important and fundamental purposes of the listing agreement which the company enters into with the Exchange.

A listed company should also act promptly to dispel unfounded rumors which result in unusual market activity or price variations.

STATE TEACHERS RETIREMENT
BOARD v. FLUOR CORP.
654 F.2d 843 (2d Cir.1981).

[The plaintiff, a public pension fund, sued Fluor Corporation, a large engineering and construction firm, for alleged violations of Rule 10b–5 and of the New York Stock Exchange Listing Agreement and Company Manual. On February 28, 1975 Fluor signed a $1 billion contract to build a large coal gasification plant in South Africa known as SASOL II. The agreement provided for an "embargo" on all publicity about the contract until March 10, 1975, apparently to allow the South African party to complete delicate negotiations with the French government for financing.

During the week of March 3, the volume of trading in Fluor stock grew and the price moved up slightly. Rumors began to circulate that Fluor had received a large contract, and several securities professionals called the company to inquire about them. On March 6 a representative of the New York Stock Exchange contacted Fluor and suggested that it might be advisable to suspend trading. Fluor agreed, and trading was suspended on March 7.

Meanwhile, between March 3 and March 6, State Teachers sold, according to a decision made in January, some $6.4 million worth of Fluor stock.

The Court of Appeals held, among other things, that Fluor had not breached a duty to disclose its contract or to halt trading in its stock pending an announcement and that there is no implied private right of action under the portions of the New York Stock Exchange Company

Manual set forth above. The section of the opinion dealing with the former issue follows.]

1. Duty to Disclose or Halt Trading

State Teachers asserts that Fluor had a duty to disclose the signing of the SASOL II contract during the week of March 3 when rumors became rampant and the price and volume of its stock shot upward. We disagree. Under all the circumstances, and particularly in light of its agreement with SASOL to make no announcement until March 10, Fluor was under no obligation to disclose the contract. A company has no duty to correct or verify rumors in the marketplace unless those rumors can be attributed to the company. Elkind v. Liggett & Myers, Inc., 635 F.2d 156 (2d Cir.1980). There is no evidence that the rumors affecting the volume and price of Fluor stock can be attributed to Fluor. Fluor responded to inquiries from analysts between March 4 and March 6 without comment on the veracity of the rumors and without making any material misrepresentation.

Moreover, even if the facts here give rise to a duty to disclose, there is no showing of any intent to defraud investors or any conduct which was reckless in any degree. Fluor's actions between March 3 and March 6 were made in a good faith effort to comply with the publicity embargo. The record completely lacks any evidence of *scienter*—a prerequisite to liability under section 10(b). Ernst & Ernst v. Hochfelder, *supra*. Indeed, at oral argument, counsel for State Teachers conceded that Fluor may not have had a duty to disclose the SASOL II contract under the circumstances.

State Teachers argues that, in any event, Fluor was under a duty to do what it could to halt trading in its stock once it learned that rumors regarding the SASOL II contract were affecting the price of the stock. This issue was not specifically addressed by the district court. State Teachers now argues that once an issuer decides as a matter of business judgment to withhold material information, it then assumes a duty to protect that news from selective disclosure which may disrupt the public market in its stock. In such a circumstance, the issuer must notify the Exchange and request a trading suspension until the news may be made public. State Teachers argues that this duty arises where, as here, the issuer becomes aware that the precise details of the material information are circulating in the market. It submits that this duty (i) is assumed by any issuer who has its stock traded on a public stock exchange and (ii) is consonant with the purpose of the Securities Exchange Act of 1934 to insure the integrity of the marketplace.

* * * State Teachers further argues that an issuer who fails to fulfill this duty to request a halt in trading, knowing that a selling stockholder may suffer a loss, is reckless; therefore, the *scienter* requirement for liability to attach in a section 10(b) private action is satisfied.

Under the circumstances presented in this case, we find that Fluor had no duty under section 10(b) to notify the Exchange and request that trading in its shares be suspended. Fluor first heard of rumors in the marketplace regarding the SASOL II contract on March 4. At that point, the volume of trading in Fluor stock had increased over previous weeks but there was no significant change in price. It was not until March 6 that the volume of trading in the stock and its price increased dramatically. The record indicates that no one at Fluor knew the reason for these market developments. That day, Fluor told the New York Stock Exchange that the signing of the SASOL II contract might be an explanation for the activity, and it agreed to the suggestion of the Exchange that trading be suspended. There was no trading on March 7. These facts obviate any suggestion that Fluor acted recklessly, much less with the fraudulent intent necessary for liability under section 10(b). *See, e.g.,* Chiarella v. United States, 445 U.S. 222, 100 S.Ct. 1108, 63 L.Ed.2d 348 (1980); Ernst & Ernst v. Hochfelder, *supra.* Fluor acted scrupulously when it revealed to the Exchange that the signing of the SASOL II contract might be an explanation for what the Exchange perceived as unusual market activity in Fluor stock. Fluor's good faith is further evidenced by its endorsement of the Exchange's decision to halt trading. For us to say that Fluor should have notified the Exchange at some earlier time would be to create a standard of liability under section 10(b) which gives undue weight to hindsight.

In addition to the absence of an intent to defraud investors, the difficulty of establishing causation also supports our conclusion that a section 10(b) claim does not exist here for Fluor's failure to request a halt in trading. *See* Affiliated Ute Citizens v. United States, 406 U.S. 128, 154, 92 S.Ct. 1456, 1472, 31 L.Ed.2d 741 (1972). Although the Exchange likely would have honored a request by Fluor to halt trading, the decision rests entirely in the hands of the Exchange. It would be impossible for State Teachers to show on the record before us that had Fluor acted sooner to request a halt in trading the Exchange would have suspended trading before March 7.

* * *

Note: Business Judgment and the Duty to Disclose

In Financial Industrial Fund, Inc. v. McDonnell Douglas Corp., 474 F.2d 514 (10th Cir.1973), a mutual fund bought shares of Douglas Aircraft (which later merged to become McDonnell Douglas) a week before the company issued a press release that revealed its profits would be substantially below previously published forecasts. The decline was due to shortages of materials and skilled workers and incorrect costing estimates. Plaintiff argued that management knew about, and should have disclosed, the shortfall well before it issued the press release. McDonnell Douglas responded that the timing of the disclosure of negative performance was, under the facts, within management's discretion.

The court held that material information must be "available and ripe for publication" before a duty to disclose arises. In the instant case, while management had an inkling of the situation prior to disclosure, it did not have reliable specific figures. The court further held that the defendant exercised "good faith and due diligence" in ascertaining and verifying the information. In essence, the court suggested that a company would not be held liable so long as its management had exercised reasonable business judgment in deciding on the timing of disclosure.

BASIC INCORPORATED v. LEVINSON
485 U.S. 224, 108 S.Ct. 978, 99 L.Ed.2d 194 (1988).

JUSTICE BLACKMUN delivered the opinion of the Court.

This case requires us to apply the materiality requirement of § 10(b) of the Securities Exchange Act of 1934, and the Securities and Exchange Commission's Rule 10b–5, promulgated thereunder, in the context of preliminary corporate merger discussions.* * * *

I

Prior to December 20, 1978, Basic Incorporated was a publicly traded company primarily engaged in the business of manufacturing chemical refractories for the steel industry. As early as 1965 or 1966, Combustion Engineering, Inc., a company producing mostly alumina-based refractories, expressed some interest in acquiring Basic, but was deterred from pursuing this inclination seriously because of antitrust concerns it then entertained. In 1976, however, regulatory action opened the way to a renewal of Combustion's interest. The "Strategic Plan," dated October 25, 1976, for Combustion's Industrial Products Group included the objective: "Acquire Basic Inc. $30 million."

Beginning in September 1976, Combustion representatives had meetings and telephone conversations with Basic officers and directors, including petitioners here, concerning the possibility of a merger. During 1977 and 1978, Basic made three public statements denying that it was engaged in merger negotiations.[4] On December 18, 1978, Basic

---

* The portion of the opinion dealing with the fraud-on-the-market theory is set out in Section B–1 of this Chapter—Eds.

4. On October 21, 1977, after heavy trading and a new high in Basic stock, the following news item appeared in the Cleveland Plain Dealer:

"[Basic] President Max Muller said the company knew no reason for the stock's activity and that no negotiations were under way with any company for a merger. He said Flintkote recently denied Wall Street rumors that it would make a tender offer of $25 a share for control of the Cleveland-based maker of refractories for the steel industry." App. 363.

On September 25, 1978, in reply to an inquiry from the New York Stock Ex-

change, Basic issued a release concerning increased activity in its stock and stated that

"management is unaware of any present or pending company development that would result in the abnormally heavy trading activity and price fluctuation in company shares that have been experienced in the past few days." Id., at 401.

On November 6, 1978, Basic issued to its shareholders a "Nine Months Report 1978." This Report stated:

"With regard to the stock market activity in the Company's shares we remain unaware of any present or pending developments which would account for the high volume of trading and price fluctuations in recent months." Id., at 403.

asked the New York Stock Exchange to suspend trading in its shares and issued a release stating that it had been "approached" by another company concerning a merger. On December 19, Basic's board endorsed Combustion's offer of $46 per share for its common stock, and on the following day publicly announced its approval of Combustion's tender offer for all outstanding shares.

Respondents are former Basic shareholders who sold their stock after Basic's first public statement of October 21, 1977, and before the suspension of trading in December 1978. Respondents brought a class action against Basic and its directors, asserting that the defendants issued three false or misleading public statements and thereby were in violation of § 10(b) of the 1934 Act and of Rule 10b–5. Respondents alleged that they were injured by selling Basic shares at artificially depressed prices in a market affected by petitioners' misleading statements and in reliance thereon.

The District Court adopted a presumption of reliance by members of the plaintiff class upon petitioners' public statements that enabled the court to conclude that common questions of fact or law predominated over particular questions pertaining to individual plaintiffs. The District Court therefore certified respondents' class. On the merits, however, the District Court granted summary judgment for the defendants. It held that, as a matter of law, any misstatements were immaterial: there were no negotiations ongoing at the time of the first statement, and although negotiations were taking place when the second and third statements were issued, those negotiations were not "destined, with reasonable certainty, to become a merger agreement in principle."

The United States Court of Appeals for the Sixth Circuit affirmed the class certification, but reversed the District Court's summary judgment, and remanded the case. 786 F.2d 741 (1986). The court reasoned that while petitioners were under no general duty to disclose their discussions with Combustion, any statement the company voluntarily released could not be " 'so incomplete as to mislead.' " Id., at 746, quoting SEC v. Texas Gulf Sulphur Co., 401 F.2d 833, 862 (CA2 1968) (en banc), cert. denied *sub nom.* Coates v. SEC, 394 U.S. 976 (1969). In the Court of Appeals' view, Basic's statements that no negotiations were taking place, and that it knew of no corporate developments to account for the heavy trading activity, were misleading. With respect to materiality, the court rejected the argument that preliminary merger discussions are immaterial as a matter of law, and held that "once a statement is made denying the existence of any discussions, even discussions that might not have been material in absence of the denial are material because they make the statement made untrue." 786 F.2d, at 749.

The Court of Appeals joined a number of other circuits in accepting the "fraud-on-the-market theory" to create a rebuttable presumption that respondents relied on petitioners' material misrepresentations, noting that without the presumption it would be impractical to certify a class. * * * See 786 F.2d, at 750–751.

We granted certiorari, to resolve the split, see Part III, *infra,* among the Courts of Appeals as to the standard of materiality applicable to preliminary merger discussions, and to determine whether the courts below properly applied a presumption of reliance in certifying the class, rather than requiring each class member to show direct reliance on Basic's statements.

II

The 1934 Act was designed to protect investors against manipulation of stock prices. See S.Rep. No. 792, 73d Cong., 2d Sess., 1–5 (1934). Underlying the adoption of extensive disclosure requirements was a legislative philosophy: "There cannot be honest markets without honest publicity. Manipulation and dishonest practices of the market place thrive upon mystery and secrecy." H.R.Rep. No. 1383, 73d Cong., 2d Sess., 11 (1934). This Court "repeatedly has described the 'fundamental purpose' of the Act as implementing a 'philosophy of full disclosure.'" Santa Fe Industries, Inc. v. Green, 430 U.S. 462, 477–478 (1977), quoting SEC v. Capital Gains Research Bureau, Inc., 375 U.S. 180, 186 (1963).

Pursuant to its authority under § 10(b) of the 1934 Act, the Securities and Exchange Commission promulgated Rule 10b-5. Judicial interpretation and application, legislative acquiescence, and the passage of time have removed any doubt that a private cause of action exists for a violation of § 10(b) and Rule 10b-5, and constitutes an essential tool for enforcement of the 1934 Act's requirements.

The Court previously has addressed various positive and common-law requirements for a violation of § 10(b) or of Rule 10b-5. * * * The Court also explicitly has defined a standard of materiality under the securities laws, see TSC Industries, Inc. v. Northway, Inc., 426 U.S. 438 (1976), concluding in the proxy-solicitation context that "[a]n omitted fact is material if there is a substantial likelihood that a reasonable shareholder would consider it important in deciding how to vote." *Id.,* at 449. Acknowledging that certain information concerning corporate developments could well be of "dubious significance," *id.,* at 448, the Court was careful not to set too low a standard of materiality; it was concerned that a minimal standard might bring an overabundance of information within its reach, and lead management "simply to bury the shareholders in an avalanche of trivial information—a result that is hardly conducive to informed decisionmaking." *Id.,* at 448–449. It further explained that to fulfill the materiality requirement "there must be a substantial likelihood that the disclosure of the omitted fact would have been viewed by the reasonable investor as having significantly altered the "total mix' of information made available." *Id.,* at 449. We now expressly adopt the *TSC Industries* standard of materiality for the § 10(b) and Rule 10b-5 context.

III

The application of this materiality standard to preliminary merger discussions is not self-evident. Where the impact of the corporate development on the target's fortune is certain and clear, the *TSC Industries* materiality definition admits straightforward application. Where, on the other hand, the event is contingent or speculative in nature, it is difficult to ascertain whether the "reasonable investor" would have considered the omitted information significant at the time. Merger negotiations, because of the ever-present possibility that the contemplated transaction will not be effectuated, fall into the latter category.

A

Petitioners urge upon us a Third Circuit test for resolving this difficulty. Under this approach, preliminary merger discussions do not become material until "agreement-in-principle" as to the price and structure of the transaction has been reached between the would-be merger partners. See Greenfield v. Heublein, Inc., 742 F.2d 751, 757 (CA3 1984), cert. denied, 469 U.S. 1215 (1985). By definition, then, information concerning any negotiations not yet at the agreement-in-principle stage could be withheld or even misrepresented without a violation of Rule 10b–5.

Three rationales have been offered in support of the "agreement-in-principle" test. The first derives from the concern expressed in *TSC Industries* that an investor not be overwhelmed by excessively detailed and trivial information, and focuses on the substantial risk that preliminary merger discussions may collapse: because such discussions are inherently tentative, disclosure of their existence itself could mislead investors and foster false optimism. See Greenfield v. Heublein, Inc., 742 F.2d, at 756; Reiss v. Pan American World Airways, Inc., 711 F.2d 11, 14 (CA2 1983). The other two justifications for the agreement-in-principle standard are based on management concerns: because the requirement of "agreement-in-principle" limits the scope of disclosure obligations, it helps preserve the confidentiality of merger discussions where earlier disclosure might prejudice the negotiations; and the test also provides a usable, bright-line rule for determining when disclosure must be made.

None of these policy-based rationales, however, purports to explain why drawing the line at agreement-in-principle reflects the significance of the information upon the investor's decision. The first rationale, and the only one connected to the concerns expressed in *TSC Industries,* stands soundly rejected, even by a Court of Appeals that otherwise has accepted the wisdom of the agreement-in-principle test. "It assumes that investors are nitwits, unable to appreciate—even when told—that mergers are risky propositions up until the closing." Flamm v. Eberstadt, 814 F.2d, at 1175. Disclosure, and not paternalistic withholding of accurate information, is the policy chosen and expressed by Congress. We have recognized time and again, a "fundamental purpose" of the various securities acts, "was to substitute a philosophy of full disclosure for the philosophy of *caveat emptor* and thus to achieve a high standard of business ethics in the securities industry." SEC v. Capital Gains

Research Bureau, Inc., 375 U.S. 180, 186 (1963).   The role of the materiality requirement is not to "attribute to investors a child-like simplicity, an inability to grasp the probablistic significance of negotiations," Flamm v. Eberstadt, 814 F.2d, at 1175, but to filter out essentially useless information that a reasonable investor would not consider significant, even as part of a larger "mix" of factors to consider in making his investment decision.   TSC Industries, Inc. v. Northway, Inc., 426 U.S., at 448–449.

The second rationale, the importance of secrecy during the early stages of merger discussions, also seems irrelevant to an assessment whether their existence is significant to the trading decision of a reasonable investor.   To avoid a "bidding war" over its target, an acquiring firm often will insist that negotiations remain confidential, see, *e.g.,* In re Carnation Co., Exchange Act Release No. 22214, 33 SEC Docket 1025 (1985), and at least one Court of Appeals has stated that "silence pending settlement of the price and structure of a deal is beneficial to most investors, most of the time."   Flamm v. Eberstadt, 814 F.2d, at 1177.

We need not ascertain, however, whether secrecy necessarily maximizes shareholder wealth—although we note that the proposition is at least disputed as a matter of theory and empirical research—for this case does not concern the *timing* of a disclosure;   it concerns only its accuracy and completeness.   We face here the narrow question whether information concerning the existence and status of preliminary merger discussions is significant to the reasonable investor's trading decision.   Arguments based on the premise that some disclosure would be "premature" in a sense are more properly considered under the rubric of an issuer's duty to disclose.   The "secrecy" rationale is simply inapposite to the definition of materiality.

The final justification offered in support of the agreement-in-principle test seems to be directed solely at the comfort of corporate managers. A bright-line rule indeed is easier to follow than a standard that requires the exercise of judgment in the light of all the circumstances.   But ease of application alone is not an excuse for ignoring the purposes of the securities acts and Congress' policy decisions.   Any approach that designates a single fact or occurrence as always determinative of an inherently fact-specific finding such as materiality, must necessarily be over- or underinclusive.   In *TSC Industries* this Court explained: "The determination [of materiality] requires delicate assessments of the inferences a 'reasonable shareholder' would draw from a given set of facts and the significance of those inferences to him. * * *" 426 U.S., at 450.   After much study, the Advisory Committee on Corporate Disclosure cautioned the SEC against administratively confining materiality to a rigid formula.   Courts also would do well to heed this advice.

We therefore find no valid justification for artificially excluding from the definition of materiality information concerning merger discussions, which would otherwise be considered significant to the trading decision of a reasonable investor, merely because agreement-in-principle as to price and structure has not yet been reached by the parties or their representative.

B

The Sixth Circuit explicitly rejected the agreement-in-principle test, as we do today, but in its place adopted a rule that, if taken literally, would be equally insensitive, in our view, to the distinction between materiality and the other elements of an action under Rule 10b–5:

> "When a company whose stock is publicly traded makes a statement, as Basic did, that 'no negotiations' are underway, and that the corporation knows of 'no reason for the stock's activity,' and that 'management is unaware of any present or pending corporate development that would result in the abnormally heavy trading activity,' information concerning ongoing acquisition discussions becomes material *by virtue of the statement denying their existence.*

* * *

> "In analyzing whether information regarding merger discussions is material such that it must be affirmatively disclosed to avoid a violation of Rule 10b–5, the discussions and their progress are the primary considerations. However, once a statement is made denying the existence of any discussions, even discussions that might not have been material in absence of the denial are material because they make the statement made untrue." 786 F.2d, at 748–749 (emphasis in original).

This approach, however, fails to recognize that, in order to prevail on a Rule 10b–5 claim, a plaintiff must show that the statements were *misleading* as to a *material* fact. It is not enough that a statement is false or incomplete, if the misrepresented fact is otherwise insignificant.

C

Even before this Court's decision in *TSC Industries,* the Second Circuit had explained the role of the materiality requirement of Rule 10b–5, with respect to contingent or speculative information or events, in a manner that gave that term meaning that is independent of the other provisions of the Rule. Under such circumstances, materiality "will depend at any given time upon a balancing of both the indicated probability that the event will occur and the anticipated magnitude of the event in light of the totality of the company activity." Interestingly, neither the Third Circuit decision adopting the agreement-in-principle test nor petitioners here take issue with this general standard. Rather, they suggest that with respect to preliminary merger discussions, there are good reasons to draw a line at agreement on price and structure.

In a subsequent decision, the late Judge Friendly, writing for a Second Circuit panel, applied the *Texas Gulf Sulphur* probability/magnitude approach in the specific context of preliminary merger negotiations.

After acknowledging that materiality is something to be determined on the basis of the particular facts of each case, he stated:

> "Since a merger in which it is bought out is the most important event that can occur in a small corporation's life, to wit, its death, we think that inside information, as regards a merger of this sort, can become material at an earlier stage than would be the case as regards lesser transactions—and this even though the mortality rate of mergers in such formative stages is doubtless high."

SEC v. Geon Industries, Inc., 531 F.2d 39, 47–48 (CA2 1976). We agree with that analysis.[16]

Whether merger discussions in any particular case are material therefore depends on the facts. Generally, in order to assess the probability that the event will occur, a factfinder will need to look to indicia of interest in the transaction at the highest corporate levels. Without attempting to catalog all such possible factors, we note by way of example that board resolutions, instructions to investment bankers, and actual negotiations between principals or their intermediaries may serve as indicia of interest. To assess the magnitude of the transaction to the issuer of the securities allegedly manipulated, a factfinder will need to consider such facts as the size of the two corporate entities and of the potential premiums over market value. No particular event or factor short of closing the transaction need be either necessary or sufficient by itself to render merger discussions material.[17]

As we clarify today, materiality depends on the significance the reasonable investor would place on the withheld or misrepresented information.[18] The fact-specific inquiry we endorse here is consistent

---

16. The SEC in the present case endorses the highly fact-dependent probability/magnitude balancing approach of *Texas Gulf Sulphur*. It explains: "The *possibility* of a merger may have an immediate importance to investors in the company's securities even if no merger ultimately takes place." Brief for SEC as *Amicus Curiae* 10. The SEC's insights are helpful, and we accord them due deference. See TSC Industries, Inc. v. Northway, Inc., 426 U.S., at 449, n. 10.

17. To be actionable, of course, a statement must also be misleading. Silence, absent a duty to disclose, is not misleading under Rule 10b–5. "No comment" statements are generally the functional equivalent of silence. See *In re Carnation Co., supra*. See also New York Stock Exchange Listed Company Manual § 202.01 * * * (premature public announcement may properly be delayed for valid business purpose and where adequate security can be maintained); American Stock Exchange Company Guide §§ 401–405 * * * (similar provisions).

It has been suggested that given current market practices, a "no comment" statement is tantamount to an admission that merger discussions are underway. See Flamm v. Eberstadt, 814 F.2d, at 1178. That may well hold true to the extent that issuers adopt a policy of truthfully denying merger rumors when no discussions are underway, and of issuing "no comment" statements when they are in the midst of negotiations. There are, of course, other statement policies firms could adopt; we need not now advise issuers as to what kind of practice to follow, within the range permitted by law. Perhaps more importantly, we think that creating an exception to a regulatory scheme founded on a prodisclosure legislative philosophy, because complying with the regulation might be "bad for business," is a role for Congress, not this Court. * * *

18. We find no authority in the statute, the legislative history, or our previous decisions, for varying the standard of materiality depending on who brings the action or whether insiders are alleged to have profit-with the approach a number of courts have taken in assessing the materiality of merger negotiations. Because the standard of materiality we have adopted differs from that used by both courts below, we remand the case for reconsideration of the question whether a grant of summary judgment is appropriate on this record.

* * *

V

In summary:

1. We specifically adopt, for the § 10(b) and Rule 10b–5 context, the standard of materiality set forth in TSC Industries, Inc. v. Northway, Inc., 426 U.S., at 449.

2. We reject "agreement-in-principle as to price and structure" as the bright-line rule for materiality.

3. We also reject the proposition that "information becomes material by virtue of a public statement denying it."

4. Materiality in the merger context depends on the probability that the transaction will be consummated, and its significance to the issuer of the securities. Materiality depends on the facts and thus is to be determined on a case-by-case basis.

* * *

The judgement of the Court of Appeals is vacated and the case is remanded to that court for further proceedings consistent with this opinion.

It is so ordered.

Taylor v. First Union Corporation of South Carolina, 857 F.2d 240 (4th Cir.1988), cert. denied 489 U.S. 1080, 109 S.Ct. 1532, 103 L.Ed.2d

ed. See *e.g.,* Pavlidis v. New England Patriots Football Club, Inc., 737 F.2d 1227, 1231 (CA1 1984) ("A fact does not become more material to the shareholder's decision because it is withheld by an insider, or because the insider might profit by withholding it"); cf. Aaron v. SEC, 446 U.S. 680, 691 (1980) ("scienter is an element of a violation of § 10(b) and Rule 10b–5, regardless of the identity of the plaintiff or the nature of the relief sought").

We recognize that trading (and profit making) by insiders can serve as *an* indication of materiality, see SEC v. Texas Gulf Sulphur Co., 401 F.2d, at 851; General Portland, Inc. v. LaFarge Coppee S.A., CCH Fed.Sec.L.Rep. (1982–1983 Transfer Binder) ¶ 99,148, p. 95,544 (ND Tex.1981). We

are not prepared to agree, however, that "[i]n cases of the disclosure of inside information to a favored few, determination of materiality has a different aspect than when the issue is, for example, an inaccuracy in a publicly disseminated press release." SEC v. Geon Industries, Inc., 531 F.2d 39, 48 (CA2 1976). Devising two different standards of materiality, one for situations where insiders have traded in abrogation of their duty to disclose or abstain (or for that matter when any disclosure duty has been breached), and another covering affirmative misrepresentations by those under no duty to disclose (but under the ever-present duty not to mislead), would effectively collapse the materiality requirement into the analysis of defendant's disclosure duties.

837 (1989), involved the application of *Basic* to a merger between Southern Bancorporation and First Union Corp. Plaintiff sold her stock to First Union and, after the merger, brought suit, alleging that Southern and First Union had conspired to withhold information about the merger from her and her husband in order to acquire their stock at less than its true value.

The court found that defendants' silence as to the merger talks was neither misleading nor material under Rule 10b–5. Generally, silence, absent a duty to disclose is not misleading under Rule 10b–5. "Plaintiff has failed to identify any statements made misleading by the defendants' nondisclosure of their merger discussions," the court stated. Furthermore, "[t]here is no allegation that defendants had previously denied the possibility of a merger at some future time."

Applying Basic's "facts and circumstances" test, the court rejected the argument that the merger talks were material. It found that there was no agreement regarding the price or structure of the deal. The court noted that although, after *Basic*, this finding alone is not dispositive of the materiality question, "it is certainly not irrelevant to the circumstances test articulated in that case." In addition, the court stated, neither the factual nor the legal predicates for a merger were in place; there was no evidence of board resolutions, actual negotiations, or instructions to investment bankers to facilitate a merger. Because the U.S. Supreme Court had yet to rule on the constitutionality of interstate banking, a merger between Southern and First Union was contingent on events beyond the parties' control.

The court concluded that any relationship between Southern and First Union at the time plaintiff sold her stock was of a "fickle and changeable character" and was not subject to disclosure. To hold that disclosure of such speculative and tentative discussions was required, the court said, "would result in endless and bewildering guesses as to the need for disclosure, operate as a deterrent to the legitimate conduct of corporate operations, and threaten to 'bury the shareholders in an avalanche of trivial information.'"

In Release No. 33–6835 (May 18, 1989), the SEC stated that corporations need not disclose merger discussions in the Management Discussion & Analysis (MD & A) section of their annual Form 10–K report to the Commission if doing so would jeopardize the transaction and if other conditions were met. The MD & A section requires a corporation to explain in narrative form its current financial situation and future prospects. Corporations must disclose known material changes, trends and uncertainties that they reasonably expect will materially impact on future sales and long-term analysis of the corporation's business. According to the release, to determine if a particular matter should be discussed in its MD & A, a company's officials (1) must determine if a known trend or uncertainty is likely to come to fruition; (2) must assess the potential impact of the trend or uncertainty on the company's operations; and (3) must assess whether the potential impact would be material. Regarding preliminary merger negotiations, the SEC stated that a company need not discuss merger talks in its MD & A, provided it has not made any prior disclosures about merger talks, such disclosure is not required by other SEC rules, and management determines that disclosure would jeopardize the transaction's completion.

6. ELEMENTS OF A 10b–5 ACTION FOR DISCLOSURE FRAUD

The SEC's enforcement action in *Texas Gulf Sulphur*, spawned an explosion of private actions in Rule 10b–5 cases and forced the courts to consider more closely the elements of such an action. In Mitchell v. Texas Gulf Sulphur Co., 446 F.2d 90 (10th Cir.1971), cert. denied 404 U.S. 1004, 92 S.Ct. 564, 30 L.Ed.2d 558 (1971), reh. denied 404 U.S. 1064, 92 S.Ct. 734, 30 L.Ed.2d 754 (1972), the court noted that in a "civil action instituted on the basis of 10b–5 violations, the keynote of which is fraud, the full panoply of common law fraud elements— misrepresentation or nondisclosure, materiality, scienter, intent to defraud, reliance and causation—have crept in and played varying roles of significance." Neither Section 10(b) nor Rule 10b–5 explicitly contain these requirements and the course, while paying deference to the general analytical structure of the traditional common law action, have reshaped them so that, as the court said in *Mitchell*, "a number of these elements have diminished in importance." More recent Supreme Court decisions indicate these elements have continuing vitality. We now examine the key elements in a private action for damages: (1) standing, (2) scienter, and (3) privity, reliance, and causation.

a. *Standing*

In Blue Chip Stamps v. Manor Drug Stores, 421 U.S. 723, 95 S.Ct. 1917, 44 L.Ed.2d 539 (1975), the Supreme Court held that a plaintiff in a private damage action under Rule 10b–5 had to be an actual purchaser or seller of securities. In so doing, the Court followed the rule first enunciated in Birnbaum v. Newport Steel Corp., 193 F.2d 461 (2d Cir.1952), cert. denied 343 U.S. 956, 72 S.Ct. 1051, 96 L.Ed. 1356 (1952), and which had been adopted by virtually every lower court to have considered the issue, including the Ninth Circuit in *Blue Chip* itself.

In *Blue Chip,* defendant Blue Chip Stamps made a stock offering to certain retailers pursuant to an antitrust consent decree. Unlike most stock offerings, it was in the defendant's interest to discourage purchases of the stock; thus it prepared and distributed a prospectus which allegedly was intentionally overly pessimistic. The plaintiffs contended that they were discouraged from accepting a bargain offer so that Blue Chip could later offer the rejected shares to the public at a higher price. The plaintiffs further alleged that they had been induced not to buy shares because of defendants' misrepresentations.

In denying plaintiffs standing, the Court first noted the longstanding acceptance of *Birnbaum* and Congress' failure to reject *Birnbaum* 's interpretation of the "in connection with the purchase or sale" language of Section 10(b). The Court then observed that because a private action under 10b–5 is judicially created action, the Court could not discern any Congressional intent concerning the contours of such an action. Thus, the Court turned to policy considerations in an attempt to define those contours.

The Court began its policy analysis by observing that the *Birnbaum* rule barred three classes of potential plaintiffs. First are potential purchasers of shares who allege that they did not purchase because of an unduly pessimistic assessment of the corporation's prospects. Second are actual shareholders who allege that they decided not to sell because of an unduly optimistic assessment of the corporation's prospects. Third are shareholders, creditors, and others who suffer a loss in the value of their investment because of corporate or insider activities which violate Rule 10b–5.

The Court observed that while shareholder members of the second and third classes could satisfy the *Birnbaum* rule by bringing a derivative action on behalf of the corporation if the corporation was itself a purchaser or seller of securities, the first class (of which Blue Chip was a member) would be entirely precluded from maintaining a 10b–5 action by the *Birnbaum* rule.

The Court acknowledged that this preclusion might be a disadvantage but concluded that this disadvantage was outweighed by the fact that Rule 10b–5 presents a danger of vexatious litigation different in degree and kind from that which accompanies litigation in general.

The Court suggested two distinct grounds for this conclusion. First, the Court believed that a 10b–5 complaint which had very little chance of success at trial might nonetheless have a settlement value out of proportion to its prospects of success. The Court noted that largely groundless suits could be used to frustrate or delay the normal business activity of defendants through the extensive use of discovery devices, thus representing "an *in terrorem* increment of the settlement value, rather than a reasonably founded hope that the process will reveal relevant evidence." 421 U.S. at 741, 95 S.Ct. at 1928.

The Court stated that without the *Birnbaum* rule, even improbable 10b–5 allegations would be virtually impossible to dispose of prior to trial because determination of the facts would depend largely on how the jury credited the oral testimony presented at trial. The Court believed that the *Birnbaum* rule would bar many of these cases prior to trial, since the requirement that a plaintiff actually purchased or sold securities could be demonstrated by documentation, and did not depend solely upon oral testimony.

The second reason the Court gave for its conclusion that the *Birnbaum* rule prevented vexatious 10b–5 litigation was that absent the *Birnbaum* rule, the trier of fact would be forced to determine "rather hazy issues of fact the truth of which depended almost entirely on oral testimony." Because there can be no documentation of why a plaintiff failed to purchase stock, proof of those reasons would often rely entirely upon a plaintiff's uncorroborated oral testimony. The Court reasoned that:

> In the absence of the *Birnbaum* doctrine, bystanders to the securities marketing process could await developments on the sidelines without risk, claiming that inaccuracies in disclosure caused non-selling in a falling market and that unduly pessimistic predictions by the issuer followed by a rising market caused them to allow retrospectively golden opportunities to pass. 421 U.S. at 747, 95 S.Ct. at 1931.

By contrast, the *Birnbaum* rule, which requires a plaintiff at least to demonstrate the often objectively verifiable fact of having purchased or sold securities, arguably mitigates the possibility of suits being filed by riskless bystanders.

By itself, the decision in *Blue Chip* was neither surprising nor disturbing. What made it significant was the tone of Justice Rehnquist's opinion. In just five years, the Court had moved from the "corporate therapeutics" of Mills v. Electric Auto–Lite, to the "vexatious litigation" of *Blue Chip*. In so doing, the Court called into question the carefully constructed system of exceptions to *Birnbaum* and foreshadowed a more restrictive interpretation of the federal securities laws.

b. Scienter

In Ernst & Ernst v. Hochfelder, 425 U.S. 185, 96 S.Ct. 1375, 47 L.Ed.2d 668 (1976), the Supreme Court held that one element of a 10b–5 action is that the plaintiff prove scienter—the intent to deceive, manipulate or defraud. In *Hochfelder,* defendant Ernst & Ernst, an accounting firm, was retained as an auditor by First Securities Company of Chicago ("First Securities"). First Securities' president induced the plaintiffs to invest in non-existent "escrow" accounts and converted the funds to his own use. The president's fraud came to light when he committed suicide, and left a note that described First Securities as bankrupt and the escrow accounts as "spurious."

Plaintiffs alleged that the escrow scheme violated Section 10(b) and Rule 10b–5 and that Ernst & Ernst had aided and abetted the violations by failing to conduct proper audits of First Securities. Plaintiffs' case rested on a theory of negligent nonfeasance: Ernst & Ernst's failure to use appropriate auditing procedures had led to its failure to discover certain irregular internal practices of the company which had interfered with the audit. Significantly, the plaintiffs did not accuse Ernst & Ernst of fraud or intentional misconduct, but instead of inexcusable negligence.

The Court began its analysis by examining the language of Section 10(b). After observing that the Section makes unlawful the use or employment of "any manipulative or deceptive device or contrivance" which violates SEC rules, the court noted:

> The words "manipulative or deceptive," when used in conjunction with "device or contrivance," strongly suggest that § 10(b) was intended to proscribe knowing or intentional misconduct. * * *

[T]he use of the words "manipulative," "device" and "contrivance" * * * make unmistakable a congressional intent to proscribe a type of conduct quite different from negligence. Use of the word "manipulative" is especially significant. It is and was virtually a term of art when used in connection with securities markets. It connotes intentional or willful conduct designed to deceive or defraud investors by controlling or artificially affecting the price of securities. 425 U.S. at 197–199, 96 S.Ct. at 1382–83.

The Court then discussed the legislative history and found it

* * * difficult to believe that any lawyer, legislative draftsman, or legislator would use these words if the intent was to create liability for merely negligent acts or omissions. Neither the legislative history nor the briefs supporting respondents identify any usage or authority for construing "manipulative [or cunning] devices' to include negligence. 425 U.S. at 203, 96 S.Ct. at 1385.

The Court also found "no indication that Congress intended anyone to be liable for [manipulative] practices unless he acted other than in good faith. The catchall provision of § 10(b) should be interpreted no more broadly." 425 U.S. at 206, 96 S.Ct. at 1387.

Finally, the Court responded to the S.E.C.'s argument that Rule 10b–5(2) and (3) encompass negligent as well as intentional behavior. The Court concluded that because Rule 10b–5 was adopted pursuant to the authority granted under Section 10(b), its scope could not exceed that authority. Having interpreted the language and history of Section 10(b) as limiting the Commission's authority to the prevention of intentional wrongdoing, the Court would not extend the scope of the statute to validate a rule which might be based on negligent conduct.

The *Hochfelder* court left open two important questions: whether reckless misconduct satisfies the scienter requirement and whether scienter is required in an S.E.C. injunctive action as well as a private damage action. The Court answered the second question affirmatively in its very next term in Aaron v. SEC, 446 U.S. 680, 100 S.Ct. 1945, 64 L.Ed.2d 611 (1980). Relying on *Hochfelder'*s discussion of the use of the terms "manipulative," "device" and "contrivance," the Court held that scienter is a required element of a Rule 10b–5 offense, no matter who the plaintiff is or what remedy is being sought.

The Supreme Court has yet to decide whether reckless conduct is sufficient to meet the 10b–5 scienter requirement. In an action for deceit at common law, as the Court noted, recklessness was often held to be sufficient to satisfy the scienter requirements and most lower courts have so held. But see Schlanger v. Four–Phase Systems, Inc., 582 F.Supp. 128 (S.D.N.Y.1984) (actual intent to deceive required under 10b–5.) However, what constitutes reckless conduct, is far from clear. In SEC v. Southwest Coal & Energy Co., 624 F.2d 1312, 1321 n. 17 (5th Cir.1980) the Fifth Circuit held that reckless conduct will satisfy the scienter requirement for 10b–5 purposes only if that conduct constitutes "an extreme departure from the standards of ordinary care, * * * which presents a danger of misleading buyers or sellers that is either known to the defendant or is so obvious that the actor must have been aware of it." See also McLean v. Alexander, 599 F.2d 1190 (3d Cir.1979) ("a conscious deception or * * * a misrepresentation so recklessly made that the culpability attaching to such reckless conduct closely approaches that which attaches to conscious deception"). Other courts have adopted less stringent tests and it is difficult to articulate a standard that would be accepted by most courts. As one court has noted, "the conduct covered by the term recklessness is not easy to define, given that recklessness standards of varying strictness have been applied in [the Second] Circuit." duPont v. Brady, 646 F.Supp. 1067, 1073 (S.D.N.Y.1986), reversed on other grounds 828 F.2d 75 (2d Cir.1987).

c. Privity, Reliance and Causation

Because Rule 10b–5 only proscribes conduct that occurs "in connection with the purchase or sale of any security," courts have had to decide what connection is necessary between plaintiff and defendant in order to find a violation of the rule. The question of the required connection can be broken down into two separate issues: what conduct is sufficient to satisfy the "in connection with" requirement *and* what constitutes legal causation for purposes of determining whether there has been civil liability. This latter question, in turn, is relevant in deciding the scope of damages, assuming that all the other elements of a Rule 10b–5 violation can be established. Review the discussion in Chapter 18 of the difference between transaction causation and loss causation.

Texas Gulf Sulphur addressed the "in connection with" requirement in the corporate publicity aspect of the case. The SEC alleged that the corporation violated the rule by issuing a materially false or misleading press release. The corporation responded that because it was not trading in the market, its conduct was not "in connection with the purchase or sale of securities" as the rule requires. The court rejected the corporation's argument and held that the "in connection with" requirement was satisfied whenever a statement was made in a manner reasonably calculated to influence the investing public even though the defendant was not trading. In Heit v. Weitzen, 402 F.2d 909 (2d Cir.1968), decided shortly after *Texas Gulf Sulphur,* the Second Circuit extended the "in connection with" requirement to cover a situation where the corporation's disclosure was not made directly to the market or with the intent of misleading investors. All that was required to satisfy Rule 10b–5 was that the corporation's statements be reasonably calculated to influence investors. *Heit* is particularly important because, unlike *Texas Gulf Sulphur,* it involved a private suit for damages rather than an SEC action for an injunction.

In addition to the "in connection with" requirement, courts have grappled with the necessity for plaintiffs to show reliance and causation. The Supreme Court attempted to deal with these issues in the context of face-to-face transactions in Affiliated Ute Citizens v. United States, 406

U.S. 128, 92 S.Ct. 1456, 31 L.Ed.2d 741 (1972). In that case, members of a large class of stockholders alleged that in selling their stock, they had relied on the advice of two employees of the bank where they had deposited their stock and that the employees had failed to disclose the stock's true value and their position as market makers in the stock. The plaintiffs were held to have a right to expect that the defendants would disclose all material information:

> Under the circumstances of this case, involving primarily a failure to disclose, positive proof of reliance is not a prerequisite to recovery. All that is necessary is that the facts withheld be material in the sense that a reasonable investor might have considered them important in the making of this decision. * * * This obligation to disclose and this withholding of a material fact establish the requisite element of causation in fact.

406 U.S. at 154, 92 S.Ct. at 1472.

The problem becomes more complex in an open market non-disclosure situation. In a face-to-face transaction, plaintiff relies on what he is told and assumes that nothing material is being omitted; in that sense, there is reliance on an omission. In an open-market transaction, the insider is not misrepresenting because normally he is not saying anything; if anyone is disclosing anything, it is the corporation.

In an effort to deal with the problems of proving reliance in open-market transactions, some courts developed the theory of "fraud on the market." That theory utilizes the efficient capital market hypothesis as the basis either for holding that reliance is not required or for redefining the nature of reliance. As one court explained:

> The fraud on the market theory is based on the hypothesis that, in an open and developed securities market, the price of a company's stock is determined by the available material information regarding the company and its business. Misleading statements will therefore defraud purchasers of stock even if the purchasers do not directly rely on the misstatements. The misstatements may affect the price of the stock, and thus defraud purchasers who rely on the price as an indication of the stock's value. By artificially inflating the price of the stock, the misrepresentations defraud purchasers who rely on the price as an indication of the stock's value. The causal connection between the defendants' fraud and the plaintiffs' purchase of stock in such a case is no less significant than in a case of direct reliance on misrepresentations. In both cases, defendants' fraudulent statements or omissions cause plaintiffs to purchase stock they would not have purchased absent defendants' misstatements and/or omissions.

Peil v. Speiser, 806 F.2d 1154, 1160–61 (3d Cir.1986).

The Supreme Court embraced one version of the fraud-on-the-market theory in Basic, Inc. v. Levinson, 485 U.S. 224, 108 S.Ct. 978, 99

L.Ed.2d 194 (1988), a case involving affirmative misrepresentations.*
The Court stated:

IV

A

We turn to the question of reliance and the fraud-on-the-market
theory.

* * *

Our task, of course, is not to assess the general validity of the
theory, but to consider whether it was proper for the courts below to
apply a rebuttable presumption of reliance, supported in part by the
fraud-on-the-market theory.

This case required resolution of several common questions of law
and fact concerning the falsity or misleading nature of the three public
statements made by Basic, the presence or absence of scienter, and the
materiality of the misrepresentations, if any. In their amended complaint, the named plaintiffs alleged that in reliance on Basic's statements
they sold their shares of Basic stock in the depressed market created by
petitioners. Requiring proof of individualized reliance from each member of the proposed plaintiff class effectively would have prevented
respondents from proceeding with a class action, since individual issues
then would have overwhelmed the common ones. * * *

Petitioners and their *amici* complain that the fraud-on-the-market
theory effectively eliminates the requirement that a plaintiff asserting a
claim under Rule 10b–5 prove reliance. They note that reliance is and
long has been an element of common-law fraud and argue that because
the analogous express right of action includes a reliance requirement,
see, *e.g.*, § 18(a) of the 1934 Act, as amended, so too must an action
implied under § 10(b).

We agree that reliance is an element of a Rule 10b–5 cause of action.
Reliance provides the requisite causal connection between a defendant's
misrepresentation and a plaintiff's injury. There is, however, more than
one way to demonstrate the causal connection. Indeed, we previously
have dispensed with a requirement of positive proof of reliance, where a
duty to disclose material information had been breached, concluding that
the necessary nexus between the plaintiffs' injury and the defendant's
wrongful conduct had been established. See Affiliated Ute Citizens v.
United States, 406 U.S., at 153–154. Similarly, we did not require proof
that material omissions or misstatements in a proxy statement decisively
affected voting, because the proxy solicitation itself, rather than the
defect in the solicitation materials, served as an essential link in the
transaction. See Mills v. Electric Auto–Lite Co., 396 U.S. 375, 384–385
(1970).

---

* The portion of the Court's opinion dealing with the duty to disclose preliminary
merger negotiations was set out earlier in
this chapter.—Eds.

The modern securities markets, literally involving millions of shares changing hands daily, differ from the face-to-face transactions contemplated by early fraud cases, and our understanding of Rule 10b–5's reliance requirement must encompass these differences.[22]

* * *

B

Presumptions typically serve to assist courts in managing circumstances in which direct proof, for one reason or another, is rendered difficult. The courts below accepted a presumption, created by the fraud-on-the-market theory and subject to rebuttal by petitioners, that persons who had traded Basic shares had done so in reliance on the integrity of the price set by the market, but because of petitioners' material misrepresentations that price had been fraudulently depressed. Requiring a plaintiff to show a speculative state of facts, *i. e.*, how he would have acted if omitted material information had been disclosed or if the misrepresentation had not been made would place an unnecessarily unrealistic evidentiary burden on the Rule 10b–5 plaintiff who has traded on an impersonal market.

Arising out of considerations of fairness, public policy, and probability, as well as judicial economy, presumptions are also useful devices for allocating the burdens of proof between parties. The presumption of reliance employed in this case is consistent with, and, by facilitating Rule 10b–5 litigation, supports, the congressional policy embodied in the 1934 Act. In drafting that Act, Congress expressly relied on the premise that securities markets are affected by information, and enacted legislation to facilitate an investor's reliance on the integrity of those markets:

> "No investor, no speculator, can safely buy and sell securities upon the exchanges without having an intelligent basis for forming his judgment as to the value of the securities he buys or sells. The idea of a free and open public market is built upon the theory that competing judgments of buyers and sellers as to the fair price of a security brings [*sic*] about a situation where the market price reflects as nearly as possible a just price. Just as artificial manipulation tends to upset the true function of an open market, so the hiding and secreting of important information obstructs the opera-

---

22. Actions under Rule 10b–5 are distinct from common-law deceit and misrepresentation claims, see Blue Chip Stamps v. Manor Drug Stores, 421 U.S. 723, 744–745 (1975), and are in part designed to add to the protections provided investors by the common law, see Herman & MacLean v. Huddleston, 459 U.S. 375, 388–389 (1983).

"In face-to-face transactions, the inquiry into an investor's reliance upon information is into the subjective pricing of that information by that investor. With the presence of a market, the market is interposed between seller and buyer and, ideally, transmits information to the investor in the processed form of a market price. Thus the market is performing a substantial part of the valuation process performed by the investor in a face-to-face transaction. The market is acting as the unpaid agent of the investor, informing him that given all the information available to it, the value of the stock is worth the market price." In re LTV Securities Litigation, 88 F.R.D. 134, 143 (ND Tex.1980).

tion of the markets as indices of real value." H.R.Rep. No. 1383, *supra*, at 11.

See Lipton v. Documation, Inc., 734 F.2d 740, 748 (CA11 1984), cert. denied, 469 U.S. 1132 (1985).

The presumption is also supported by common sense and probability. Recent empirical studies have tended to confirm Congress' premise that the market price of shares traded on well-developed markets reflects all publicly available information, and, hence, any material misrepresentations.[24] It has been noted that "it is hard to imagine that there ever is a buyer or seller who does not rely on market integrity. Who would knowingly roll the dice in a crooked crap game?" Schlanger v. Four–Phase Systems Inc., 555 F.Supp. 535, 538 (SDNY 1982). Indeed, nearly every court that has considered the proposition has concluded that where materially misleading statements have been disseminated into an impersonal, well-developed market for securities, the reliance of individual plaintiffs on the integrity of the market price may be presumed. Commentators generally have applauded the adoption of one variation or another of the fraud-on-the-market theory. An investor who buys or sells stock at the price set by the market does so in reliance on the integrity of that price. Because most publicly available information is reflected in market price, an investor's reliance on any public material misrepresentations, therefore, may be presumed for purposes of a Rule 10b–5 action.

C

The Court of Appeals found that petitioners "made public, material misrepresentations and [respondents] sold Basic stock in an impersonal, efficient market. Thus, the class, as defined by the district court, has established the threshold facts for proving their loss." 786 F.2d at 751.[27] The court acknowledged that petitioners may rebut proof of the elements giving rise to the presumption, or show that the misrepresentation in fact did not lead to a distortion of price or that an individual plaintiff

---

24. See In re LTV Securities Litigation, 88 F.R.D. 134, 144 (ND Tex.1980) (citing studies); Fischel, Use of Modern Finance Theory in Securities Fraud Cases Involving Actively Traded Securities, 38 Bus.Law. 1, 4, n. 9 (1982) (citing literature on efficient-capital-market theory); Dennis, Materiality and the Efficient Capital Market Model: A Recipe for the Total Mix, 25 Wm. & Mary L.Rev. 373, 374–381, and n. 1 (1984). We need not determine by adjudication what economists and social scientists have debated through the use of sophisticated statistical analysis and the application of economic theory. For purposes of accepting the presumption of reliance in this case, we need only believe that market professionals generally consider most publicly announced material statements about companies, thereby affecting stock market prices.

27. The Court of Appeals held that in order to invoke the presumption, a plaintiff must allege and prove: (1) that the defendant made public misrepresentations; (2) that the misrepresentations were material; (3) that the shares were traded on an efficient market; (4) that the misrepresentations would induce a reasonable, relying investor to misjudge the value of the shares; and (5) that the plaintiff traded the shares between the time the misrepresentations were made and the time the truth was revealed. See 786 F.2d at 750.

Given today's decision regarding the definition of materiality as to preliminary merger discussions, elements (2) and (4) may collapse into one.

traded or would have traded despite his knowing the statement was false. *Id.*, at 750, n. 6.

Any showing that severs the link between the alleged misrepresentation and either the price received (or paid) by the plaintiff, or his decision to trade at a fair market price, will be sufficient to rebut the presumption of reliance. For example, if petitioners could show that the "market makers" were privy to the truth about the merger discussions here with Combustion, and thus that the market price would not have been affected by their misrepresentations, the causal connection could be broken: the basis for finding that the fraud had been transmitted through market price would be gone.[28] Similarly, if, despite petitioners' allegedly fraudulent attempt to manipulate market price, news of the merger discussions credibly entered the market and dissipated the effects of the misstatements, those who traded Basic shares after the corrective statements would have no direct or indirect connection with the fraud.[29] Petitioners also could rebut the presumption of reliance as to plaintiffs who would have divested themselves of their Basic shares without relying on the integrity of the market. For example, a plaintiff who believed that Basic's statements were false and that Basic was indeed engaged in merger discussions, and who consequently believed that Basic stock was artificially underpriced, but sold his shares nevertheless because of other unrelated concerns, *e.g.*, potential antitrust problems, or political pressures to divest from shares of certain businesses, could not be said to have relied on the integrity of a price he knew had been manipulated.

Notably, the Court accepted the fraud on the market theory largely to lessen the plaintiff's burden of proof. Under this theory, the plaintiff must merely prove that the material misstatement or omission had an effect on the stock price. It is not necessary for the plaintiff to prove individual reliance on the misstatement or omission in the context of an open market transaction. Instead, the fraud on the market theory establishes the element of reliance by the market. Following Basic Inc. v. Levinson, one court explained this theory as "posit[ing] that in well-developed capital markets, investors may be presumed to rely on material misrepresentations because those misrepresentations will affect the market price of the relevant stock." In re Columbia Securities Litiga-

---

28. By accepting this rebuttable presumption, we do not intend conclusively to adopt any particular theory of how quickly and completely publicly available information is reflected in market price. Furthermore, our decision today is not to be interpreted as addressing the proper measure of damages in litigation of this kind.

29. We note there may be a certain incongruity between the assumption that Ba-

sic shares are traded on a well-developed, efficient, and information-hungry market, and the allegation that such a market could remain misinformed, and its valuation of Basic shares depressed, for 14 months, on the basis of the three public statements. Proof of that sort is a matter for trial. * * *

tion, 747 F.Supp. 237, 246 (S.D.N.Y.1990). Therefore, "[t]o the extent that the defendant's misrepresentations artificially altered the price of the stock and defrauded the market, causation is presumed." In re Control Data Corp. Securities Litigation, 933 F.2d 616, 619–20 (8th Cir.1991) (stating that CDC would be liable if its improper accounting practices affected its stock price). An investor's sophistication does not render inapplicable the fraud on the market presumption of reliance. As the Ninth Circuit stated in Blackie v. Barrack, 524 F.2d 891, 905 (9th Cir.1975), cert. denied 429 U.S. 816, 97 S.Ct. 57, 50 L.Ed.2d. 75 (1976), "Differences in sophistication, etc., among purchasers have no bearing in the impersonal market fraud context, because dissemination of false information necessarily translates through market mechanisms into price inflation which harms each purchaser identically."

The rationale for permitting the fraud on the market theory to satisfy the reliance element turns on the premise that investors trading stock in an efficient market can rely on the integrity of the market to establish the price of the security. In an efficient capital market, most (if not all) material public information is immediately reflected in a firm's stock price. Therefore, to utilize the fraud on the market theory, plaintiffs must establish that their transactions were made on an efficient and developed market. Peil v. Speiser, 806 F.2d 1154, 1160–61 (3d Cir.1986). Among the factors courts consider in determining whether there is an efficient market for the purpose of applying the fraud on the market theory are: a large weekly trading volume; the existence of a significant number of reports by security analysts; and the existence of market makers in the security. Freeman v. Laventhol & Horwath, 915 F.2d 193 (6th Cir.1990).

The assertion that large national securities markets are presumed (or conceded by defendants to be) efficient (see, e.g., In re Laidlaw Securities Litigation, 1992 WL 68341 (E.D.Pa.1992)) has been disputed. Rather the determination of efficiency is much more complex. Macey and Miller explain that courts must consider the type of information conveyed, the type of security, the issuer's identity and the market on which its securities trade when determining whether an efficient capital market existed. Not only is the market for some types of stocks less efficient than for others, but also the market adjusts to some classes of information less rapidly than to other information. Jonathan R. Macey & Geoffrey P. Miller, Good Finance, Bad Economics: An Analysis of the Fraud-on-the-Market Theory, 42 Stan.L.Rev. 1059, 1084–87 (1990).

In addition to the reliance element (transaction causation), the plaintiff must also establish loss causation. To show loss causation, the plaintiff must prove that, if the defendant had not violated Rule 10b–5 by misstating or failing to disclose material facts, the plaintiff would not suffered the injury for which damages are sought. Loss causation is shown if the defendant's misstatements or omissions of material facts touch on the actual reasons why the plaintiff suffered an investment loss. Loss causation is not established if the plaintiff suffered an investment loss for reasons that are unrelated to the defendant's misrepresentations or nondisclosures. Bastian v. Petren Resources Corp., 892 F.2d 680, 684–85 (7th Cir.1990), cert. denied 490 U.S. 906, 110 S.Ct. 2590, 110 L.Ed.2d 270 (1990).

Applying the Supreme Court's decision in Virginia Bankshares Inc. v. Sandberg (Chapter 18), the court in Booth v. Connelly Containers, Inc., Fed.Sec.L.Rep. (CCH) ¶ 96,213, 1991 WL 171450 (E.D.Pa.1991) dismissed a Section 10(b) action brought by minority shareholders claiming fraud in the proxy solicitation for a merger transaction. Members of the Connelly family, who controlled a majority of the shares on Connelly Containers, Inc. (CCI), proposed acquiring 100 percent of CCI's stock through the merger of a new entity into CCI. CCI's public shareholders would receive $20 per share. After CCI's board approved the plan, the board issued a proxy statement in connection with the merger to CCI's shareholders who approved the transaction at a special meeting.

A class of minority shareholders sued alleging violations of Sections 10(b) and 14(a). The plaintiffs claimed, among other things, that the defendants (1) deliberately undervalued CCI's assets on its balance sheet prior to the merger and that the defendants were aware of the undervaluation and (2) know that the investment adviser's fairness opinion was "flawed" because it omitted to state that CCI's stock was worth more than $20 per share.

In granting the defendant's motion for summary judgment on the Section 10(b) claim, the court noted that to prevail in a private action under Section 10(b), a plaintiff must show both transaction and loss causation. Transaction causation, the court explained, "is satisfied if the plaintiff proves that the allegedly fraudulent acts caused the plaintiff to purchase or sell securities." Loss causation is shown by establishing a "causal nexus between a defendant's fraudulent action and a plaintiff's economic harm." This nexus "must not * * * by attenuated; rather, the fraudulent action must be responsible for the loss in some reasonable direct or proximate way." As a policy matter, the court noted, the federal securities laws are not to be construed "to establish an insurance plan for every security purchased or sold in reliance on a material misstatement or omission."

The plaintiffs in the *Virginia Bankshares* case claimed they were a "causal link" in the merger there because the defendant banks and their directors would not have been willing to proceed with the merger without the approval of the proxies of the minority shareholders. This approval, the plaintiffs in Virginia Bankshares argued, would not have been obtained without the material misrepresentations forming the basis of the controversy. The Supreme Court stated that if it adopted this reasoning causation would turn on unreliable inferences as to what the directors would have thought and done without the approval of the minority shareholders whose votes were not needed to authorize the merger.

The Booth court said that the same reasoning applies to limit the expansion of loss causation in a private Section 10(b) suit. Even if the fraud allegedly occurred, the court found that the defendants had sufficient shareholder support to complete the transaction at $20 per share. Thus, the plaintiffs' votes "were unneeded, and any nexus between defendants' alleged fraudulent actions and plaintiffs' economic loss is too attenuated to satisfy the element of loss causation under § 10(b) and Rule 10b–5."

E. FEDERAL REGULATION—SECTION 16

Insider trading was one of the principal problems Congress addressed in the 1934 Act. The practice was so widespread that, although publicly condemned, it had come to be accepted by many in the financial world as one of the forms of compensation to which corporate officials were entitled. This view was abetted by the common law, which, as we have seen, did little to prevent insider trading. Moreover, even had the common law prohibited it, the prohibition would have been difficult to enforce in the anonymity of the stock exchanges.

Although determined to make a strong statement against insider trading, Congress did not establish a general rule against trading on the basis of material nonpublic information, or an enforcement mechanism for such a rule. Rather, Congress simply attacked one narrow type of stock trading often associated with the misuse of inside information. At the time, it was thought that in many, if not most of the more flagrant cases of insider trading, the insider bought and sold (or, more rarely sold and bought) stock of his company within a relatively short period of time. Since the capital gains period of the tax laws was then six months, there was good reason to suspect that in most cases someone with access to inside information who bought and sold within six months (and therefore forewent the favorable tax treatment available for profits made on trades separated by a longer period) was doing so to take advantage of some special knowledge. It was only a step from this perception to the simple and readily enforceable, if crude, principle of Section 16(b), which provides that any profits realized by an insider (as defined) on a purchase followed by a sale, or a sale followed by a purchase, within a six-month period, "shall inure to and be recoverable by the issuer." Although the section explicitly states that its purpose is "preventing the unfair use of information which may have been obtained by [the insider] by reason of his relationship to the issuer," there is no need to show any such "unfair use." All that is necessary is offsetting trades within six months by someone with the necessary relationship to the corporation.

Section 16 applies to the directors and officers of a corporation and to any person who is the "beneficial owner" of more than ten percent of a class of equity securities of the corporation registered under Section 12 of the 1934 Act. To ensure that potential plaintiffs can learn about violations of Section 16(b), Section 16(a) requires those covered by the statute to file reports with the SEC disclosing the ownership of their equity securities as well as any changes in that ownership. The latter report must be filed within ten days after the end of the month in which the transaction takes place. The Commission publishes a monthly compilation of these reports, and summaries appear regularly in a number of financial publications.

Section 16(b) has a self-contained remedy provision with its own procedures which make it a hybrid form of derivative suit. Thus, the security holder, who need not be a contemporaneous owner, must make a demand on the directors unless demand would be futile. Thereafter, the corporation has sixty days to decide whether to institute suit. If it does not, the action may be maintained by the holder at the time of suit who remains such through the trial. The contemporaneous ownership requirement of F.R.C.P. 23.1 does not apply. See Thomas Lee Hazen, The Law of Securities Regulation 629–630 (2d ed. 1990).

A security holder will have little incentive to bring an action under Section 16(b) when the proceeds will go to the corporation whose gain will normally be of only the remotest benefit to him. And, as with conventional derivative suits, the moving force in Section 16(b) actions is generally plaintiff's counsel who seeks the fees that are awarded in a successful action. Indeed, courts have held that it is no defense to a Section 16(b) action that the suit was motivated primarily by the desire to obtain such fees. Magida v. Continental Can Co., Inc., 231 F.2d 843 (2d Cir.1956).

Notwithstanding the benefits that a Section 16(b) action can confer on a corporation, the stockholder's attorney will not always be able to recover her fees when the corporation has recovered the profits from the insider. In Portnoy v. Gold Reserve Corp., 711 F.Supp. 565 (E.D.Wash. 1989), the company became aware of the Section 16(b) violation when it filed the insider's reporting form and took immediate steps to recover his profits directly. After the report was made public, a number of demands were made upon the company to recover the profits and a derivative suit was instituted to achieve the same end. Upon being advised that the company had already received the profits, plaintiff's attorney applied for counsel fees for the benefit his work had conferred on the company. The court rejected the application, holding that the attorney's efforts "were not a substantial or motivating factor in [the company's] eventual pursuit and recovery of the short-swing profits." In addition, the court noted that there were substantial policy considerations militating against the payment of fees in cases where the corporation itself had been vigilant in enforcing its own rights.

Note: Interpretative Problems Under Section 16

1. Who is an "Officer"?

The definition of "officer" includes executive officers and chief financial or accounting officers as well as any person, regardless of title, who performs significant "policy-making functions." Rule 16a–1(f). Or, as an early case stated, whether a person is "a corporate employee performing important executive duties of such character that he would be likely, in discharging these duties, to obtain confidential information about the company's affairs that would aid him if he engaged in personal market transactions." Colby v. Klune, 178 F.2d 872, 873 (2d Cir.1949). The definition of "officer" makes it clear that a person's functions determine the applicability of Section 16. An officer includes any person who is engaged in a significant policy-making function for the corporation (Rule 16a–1(f)). In Merrill Lynch, Pierce, Fenner & Smith, Inc. v. Livingston, 566 F.2d 1119 (9th Cir.1978), the Ninth Circuit held that where a company had three hundred and fifty "executive vice presidents," the title created an inference that there were opportunities to obtain confidential information; the court found that the defendant vice-president had not violated Section 16(b) because he was able to prove that his title was merely honorary and did not carry with it the executive responsibilities which might be assumed. Id. at 1122–1123. At a time when corporate law has increasingly held officers and directors to a high standard of care, does *Livingston* constitute strong precedent for deciding who is an officer?

How far down the corporate structure does Section 16 reach? In Lee National Corp. v. Segur, 281 F.Supp. 851 (E.D.Pa.1968), the court held that an officer of a subsidiary of the issuer was not subject to Section 16(b) liability unless he was actually performing the functions of an officer of the parent corporation. Does that analysis give too much weight to the external formalities of corporate organization?

2. Who is a "Beneficial Owner"?

Beneficial ownership, solely for purposes of determining a person's status as a 10% shareholder, is defined with reference to the framework of Section 13(d) of the 1934 Act. Rule 16a–1(a)(1). For all other purposes under Section 16, beneficial ownership is determined by whether a Section 16 insider has a pecuniary interest (as defined) in the security. Rule 16a–1(a)(2).

In Whiting v. Dow Chemical Co., 523 F.2d 680 (2d Cir.1975), the court stated that the term "beneficial owner" should be read "more expansively than it [is] in the law of trusts." The court went on to say that "[f]or purposes of the family unit, shares to which legal title is held by one spouse may be said to be 'beneficially owned' by the other, the insider, if the ordinary rewards are used for their joint benefit * * * While we cannot earmark the proceeds of Mrs. Whiting's particular sales as going to household and family support, we know from the findings that the larger part of their joint maintenance came from her estate, the bulk of it in Dow stock. We also know that they engaged in joint estate planning. So that while it is true that if they ever separated, Mrs. Whiting would take her Dow shares, it is also true that while they continue to live as a married couple, there is hardly anything Mrs. Whiting gets out of the ownership that appellant does not share." Id. at 688. See also, Whittaker v. Whittaker Corp., 639 F.2d 516 (9th Cir. 1981) (corporate insider who exercised virtually complete control over his mother's affairs through a power of attorney held to be "beneficial owner" of her securities since he enjoyed "benefits substantially equivalent to those of ownership.'') See Rules 16a–1(a)(2)(i) and (ii)(A) and 16a–1(e).

Not every court stretches the concept of "beneficial ownership" that far. The Seventh Circuit has held that profits accruing to an insider's grown children who were beneficiaries of a trust were not necessarily subject to the short swing recovery provision. In CBI Industries, Inc. v. Horton, 682 F.2d 643 (7th Cir.1982), a corporate executive sold 3000 shares of stock, and within six months bought 2000 shares for his sons' trusts. The court limited the concept of "profit" under Section 16(b) by concluding that it meant only direct pecuniary benefit to the insider and not the sense of enhanced well being that comes from the increased pecuniary wealth of his children. The insider, although a co-trustee of his children's trusts, could not use trust assets or income to pay his personal expenses. Today, Section 16(b) would not apply to a person's interest in securities held in trust except if the ownership requirements of Rule 16a–8 are met.

In computing the requisite ten percent ownership, it is necessary to count the beneficial ownership of all equity securities, including those securities which could be acquired through the exercise of conversion rights. Rule 16a–2(b). This computation is based on the assumption that there is a full conversion of all rights by all holders. The term "equity security" includes convertible securities, but convertibles themselves do not constitute a separate class of equity securities for Section 16(b) purposes. Chemical Fund, Inc. v. Xerox Corp., 377 F.2d 107 (2d Cir.1967). The actual conversion is exempt from the definition of "purchase" and "sale" under Rule 16b–9.

In a complicated case, one court has held that seven corporations, all controlled by the same individual were not joint beneficial owners of stock owned by any of the corporations for purposes of Section 16(b) liability. Mayer v. Chesapeake Insurance Company Limited, 877 F.2d 1154 (2d Cir.1989). In that case, Victor Posner controlled APL Corp. and six other related corporations, all of which owned stock in Peabody International Corp. APL had clearly made short-swing profits in Peabody stock. Plaintiff argued that because Posner controlled the other companies, their stock should be aggregated so as to make APL a ten percent owner at an earlier date, thereby increasing its liability for trading within the six-month period. With one dissent, the court rejected this argument, finding that no entity other than APL was able to use the proceeds from APL's sale of its Peabody stock. The court declined to extend the "group" concept of Section 13(d) of the 1934 Act to Section 16(b). What would be the result in this case under Rule 16a–1(a)(1)?

3. Who Is a "Director?"

A partnership or corporation may be deemed to be a director if one of its members or officers serves as a director of the corporation whose shares it trades and is found to have been "deputized" to represent the partnership or corporation. Deputization is a question of fact and must be proved by the plaintiff. Where a partner had not been deputized to represent the partnership on a corporate board, liability under Section 16(b) will attach only to his or her share of the partnership's profits from the partnership's trading activities. Blau v. Lehman, 368 U.S. 403, 82 S.Ct. 451, 7 L.Ed.2d 403 (1962); Feder v. Martin Marietta Corp., 406 F.2d 260 (2d Cir.1969).

4. The Timing of Purchases and Sales: When Does Liability Attach?

An officer or director is subject to the strictures of Section 16(b) even though he may not have been in office at the time of both purchase and sale. Feder v. Martin Marietta Corp., 406 F.2d 260 (2d Cir.1969); Adler v. Klawans, 267 F.2d 840 (2d Cir.1959). By contrast, a beneficial owner may be liable only if he owned more than ten percent of the stock at the time of both purchase and sale. Thus where a ten percent shareholder, within six months, sells enough shares to reduce his holdings to a fraction less than ten percent and then in a separate transaction, sells the remaining shares, the profit realized from the first sale is recoverable by the corporation but the profit from the second is not. Reliance Electric Co. v. Emerson Electric Co., 404 U.S. 418, 92 S.Ct. 596, 30 L.Ed.2d 575 (1972). Applying the same principle, one who purchases enough shares to become a ten percent shareholder and then sells some shares within six months is not liable for any profit realized. Foremost McKesson, Inc. v. Provident Securities Co., 423 U.S. 232, 96 S.Ct. 508, 46 L.Ed.2d 464 (1976). Because Section 16(b) refers to transactions in a period of "less than six months," there will be no liability if the transactions are *exactly* six months apart. Morales v. Reading & Bates Offshore Drilling Co., 392 F.Supp. 41 (N.D.Okl.1975).

The reason for treating officers and directors differently from owners of more than ten percent of the stock is that "officers and directors have more ready access to the intimate business secrets of corporations and factors which can affect the market value of stock. * * * Moreover, a director or officer can usually stimulate more directly actions which affect stock values * * *." Adler v. Klawans, supra at 845.

5. Computation of "Profits Realized."

In order to increase the deterrent effect of the statute, courts compute the "profits" from a series of several purchases and sales within six months so as to produce the maximum damages. In the leading case of Smolowe v. Delendo Corp., 136 F.2d 231 (2d Cir.1943), the defendants argued that their profits should be computed as they would be for income tax purposes, i.e., stock certificate numbers should be used to determine the actual profits earned from the purchase and sale of particular shares; if the certificate numbers are not known, profits should be calculated on a first-in-first-out basis. The court rejected this approach, holding that to give the statute its full effect, the shares with the lowest purchase price should be matched against those with the highest sale price, ignoring any losses this would produce. This method has achieved some bizarre results. In one case the defendant was required to pay $300,000 to the corporation for "profits" earned over several six month periods of trading although he had actually incurred a net loss of $400,000 on the transactions. Gratz v. Claughton, 187 F.2d 46 (2d Cir.1951), cert. denied 341 U.S. 920, 71 S.Ct. 741, 95 L.Ed. 1358 (1951).

6. *Definition of "Purchase" and "Sale".*

The problems that have generated the greatest amount of litigation under Section 16(b) are those related to the definitions of "purchase" and "sale." Where a transaction involves cash for stock, no questions arise. Where, however, the transaction is "unorthodox," the analysis is more difficult. In a merger transaction, for example, the shareholders of the acquired corporation normally exchange their shares for shares of the surviving corporation. It is not clear under Section 16(b), however, whether this exchange involves a "sale" of the stock of the old corporation and "purchase" of shares of the new. When faced with this question, the courts have generally taken a pragmatic approach, depending on the presence or absence of the potential for speculative abuse in the transaction. See e.g., Kern County Land Co. v. Occidental Petroleum Corp., 411 U.S. 582, 93 S.Ct. 1736, 36 L.Ed.2d 503 (1973). Thus when officers or directors of the acquired corporation become officers or directors of the acquiring corporation after the merger, the exchange is a "purchase" because of their access to inside information. Gold v. Sloan, 486 F.2d 340 (4th Cir.1973). See also Newmark v. RKO General, Inc., 425 F.2d 348 (2d Cir.1970). On the other hand, when a successful bidder in a tender offer thereafter causes a merger with the target company, the exchange in the merger by the losing offeror of the target company's stock it had previously acquired is not a "sale." Kern County Land Co. v. Occidental Petroleum Corp., supra.

In Colan v. Mesa Petroleum Co., 951 F.2d 1512 (9th Cir.1991), cert. denied ___ U.S. ___, 112 S.Ct. 1943, 118 L.Ed.2d 548 (1992), the Ninth Circuit held that a beneficial owner's exchange of its common stock for nonconvertible debt securities in a self-tender is a "sale" triggering short-swing profits liability. Subsequent to the decision in Unocal Corp. v. Mesa Petroleum Co. (Chapter 23), Mesa entered into an agreement to exchange the 7.8 million shares of Unocal common stock that it owned for negotiable debt securities which it later sold for about $589 million. A Unocal shareholder filed suit on behalf of Unocal alleging violations of Section 16(b) seeking to recover Mesa's short-swing profits.

The Court of Appeals held that Mesa's exchange constituted a "sale" that triggered short-swing liability under Section 16(b). The court distinguished *Kern County Land* case in which the Supreme Court had held that an exchange of stock did not constitute a Section 16 sale because the exchange had been required pursuant to a merger and thus was involuntary. In *Colan*, the court noted, Mesa "had the choice of participating in the tender offer or holding onto [its] stock."

The court also rejected Mesa's argument that a voluntary exchange may be exempt from the reach of Section 16 if a beneficial owner is coerced economically into participating or suffering a financial loss. The court concluded that this line of reasoning would contravene the "intent of Congress in enacting the bright-line, flat rule set forth in Section 16(b) requiring disgorgement of profits."

Other transactions that have been held not to be purchases or sales include: gifts, Shaw v. Dreyfus, 172 F.2d 140 (2d Cir.1949); certain stock reclassifications, Roberts v. Eaton, 212 F.2d 82 (2d Cir.1954); and some conversions of securities, Petteys v. Butler, 367 F.2d 528 (8th Cir.1966), cert. denied 385 U.S. 1006, 87 S.Ct. 712, 17 L.Ed.2d 545 (1967), and Blau v. Lamb, 363 F.2d 507 (2d Cir.1966), cert. denied 385 U.S. 1002, 87 S.Ct. 707, 17 L.Ed.2d 542 (1967).

7. *Derivative Securities.*

The rules define the application of Section 16 to standardized options (puts and calls) and other derivative securities. Rule 16a–4(a). Under these rules, insiders will not be able to avoid liability for short-swing profits under Section 16(b) by resorting to purchases and sales of derivative securities. Transactions in derivative securities can be matched against transactions in the underlying securities and against each other. Short-swing profits obtained by insiders through the use of derivative securities are, therefore, recoverable under Section 16(b).

Chapter 20

SHAREHOLDER LITIGATION

A. INTRODUCTION

A derivative suit is an action on behalf of another "person" brought by one who has an interest in that person but is not its normal decision maker. We have already encountered derivative suits as the vehicle through which fiduciary duties are enforced. In the typical derivative suit, a shareholder is allowed to act for the corporation on the theory that the board of directors, which is charged with that responsibility, has failed to do so. Any recovery from a derivative suit belongs to the corporation, the real party in interest, rather than to the plaintiff-shareholder. Plaintiff's counsel looks to the corporation for her fee on the theory that she is entitled to compensation for conferring a benefit on the corporation.

The modern derivative suit originated in mid–19th century English equity and trust theory, as a means of allowing shareholders to challenge management abuses. Professor Bert Prunty notes that as corporations grew larger, "[t]he resulting concentration of power produced abuses * * *. The evolution of the derivative suit is the record of the efforts of judges and lawyers to enforce * * * [management] responsibility without destroying the right of a majority of the members of a corporate body to govern the affairs of that body and without assuming the burden of all intra-corporate conflict." Bert S. Prunty, The Shareholders' Derivative Suit: Notes on its Derivation, 32 N.Y.U. L.Rev. 980, 992–93 (1957). American courts adopted and refined the derivative suit, focusing from the start on the relationship between corporate directors and shareholders.

The stockholder-plaintiff in a derivative suit acts in a representative capacity for all the injured shareholders. Indeed, F.R.C.P. 23.1 requires that the plaintiff must "fairly and adequately represent the interests of the shareholders * * * similarly situated in enforcing the rights of the corporation." Courts stress the obligations that fall on a stockholder when she initiates a derivative suit. The Supreme Court has characterized the stockholder as assuming "a position, not technically as a trustee perhaps, but one of a fiduciary character. He sues, not for himself alone, but as representative of a class comprising all who are similarly situated * * * He is a self-chosen representative and a volunteer champion." Cohen v. Beneficial Industrial Loan Corp., 337 U.S. 541, 549, 69 S.Ct. 1221, 1227, 93 L.Ed. 1528 (1949). Having assumed that role, the plaintiff cannot later abandon it for personal benefit. Cf. Young v. Higbee Co., 324 U.S. 204, 213, 65 S.Ct. 594, 599, 89 L.Ed. 890 (1945). See also Heckmann v. Ahmanson, 168 Cal.App.3d 119, 214 Cal.Rptr. 177 (1985) (stockholder-plaintiff's agreement to dismiss individual claim and not oppose dismissal of derivative suit as a condition of sale of stock to defendant-corporation at a substantial premium could constitute stockholder's use of position as class representative for its own financial advantage).

ALI, PRINCIPLES OF CORPORATE GOVERNANCE (1994)
Part VII, Chapter 1, Introductory Note.

THE DERIVATIVE ACTION

* * * [It must be recognized] that the derivative action is neither the initial nor the primary protection for shareholders against managerial misconduct. A variety of social and market forces also operate to hold corporate officials accountable: the professional standards of managers, oversight by outside directors, the disciplinary power of the market, and shareholder voting—all these mechanisms plus the regulatory authority of governmental agencies would constitute significant protections in the absence of private litigation. Even if dissatisfied shareholders had no other recourse than to sell their shares, such action, taken collectively, might also inhibit managerial overreaching, to the extent it depressed the value of the corporation's stock, which management typically also holds. Yet, no single technique of accountability (including market and legal remedies) is likely to be optimal under all circumstances. Each has its characteristic and well-known limitations, and, as a result, shareholders are best served by an overlapping system of protections. When properly structured, the derivative action should enhance the capabilities of these other mechanisms of accountability by (1) ensuring a measure of judicial oversight, (2) providing for a remedy that does not depend upon the ability of widely dispersed shareholders to take coordinated action, and (3) protecting the market for corporate control from unreasonable interferences. In addition, the derivative action may offer the only effective remedy in those circumstances where a control group has the ability to engage in self-dealing transactions with the corporation.

The social utility of the derivative action must also be judged in terms of the alternative of greater public regulation, to which society would likely turn if private mechanisms of enforcement proved inadequate. Over the long run, the availability of private enforcement should reduce the need for public enforcement and bureaucratic oversight of corporate conduct. Moreover, private enforcement multiplies society's enforcement resources, and also probably minimizes enforcement costs, because the private enforcer is typically compensated only when he is successful. In this light, [the ALI's] focus on private litigation remedies reflects a preference for private ordering and a desire to minimize the need for governmental regulation.

Nonetheless, private enforcement, as represented by the derivative action, should not be idealized. Experience suggests that the social costs associated with intracorporate litigation can sometimes outweigh the benefits. In overview, two problems stand out: First, the threat of liability for violations of the duty of care may reduce managerial incentives to take business risks, with resulting loss to shareholders and to the economy generally. * * * Second, in both class and derivative litigation, incentives exist for a private enforcer to bring a non-meritorious action for its nuisance or settlement value. Even in meritorious cases, a private enforcer can reach an inadequate or even collusive settlement that exchanges a low corporate recovery for a high award of attorneys' fees that is paid by the corporation. * * * In light of these problems associated with private enforcement, [the ALI] assigns only a limited role to the derivative action as a mechanism of corporate accountability.

B. POLICY OBJECTIVES

1. THE PARTIES' INCENTIVES

To understand fully the policy issues that derivative suits raise, one must appreciate the economic incentives of the principal players in these suits and the conflicts that these incentives create. Because any recovery in a derivative suit goes to the corporation, the nominal shareholder-plaintiff receives no direct pecuniary benefit from successful litigation; her benefit comes from an increase in the corporation's stock price attributable to the recovery. Thus, the plaintiff wants to maximize the size of that recovery, an interest shared by the corporation itself. The defendant, usually a senior executive or director, seeks to minimize her costs, which consist of monies paid in judgment or settlement and attorneys' fees. As in any contingent fee litigation, plaintiff's counsel will receive a fee if the suit results in a favorable judgment or a settlement; she earns nothing if the plaintiff loses. The size of the fee will be based either on the time spent on the litigation or on a percentage of the total recovery.

Unlike most litigation in which the plaintiff's gain comes at the defendant's expense, a derivative suit is not a zero-sum game; in fact, both plaintiff *and* defendant can recover many of their litigation costs from the corporation. The defendant in a derivative suit, particularly if she is a director, is not like a defendant in other actions. As we saw in Chapter 16, under most state corporate laws, a corporation may indemnify a director for her expenses in a derivative suit if she has not been *adjudged* to have breached her duty to the corporation and otherwise meets the standards for indemnification. These expenses include attorneys' fees, which can be substantial, and, in some jurisdictions, even the amounts paid in settlement. Thus, a risk-averse defendant has a strong incentive to agree to a relatively small settlement and be indemnified for substantially all her expenses rather than risk an adverse judicial decision. To the extent that the monetary settlement is reduced through the inclusion of non-pecuniary relief, the defendant's economic risk is lessened still further. Because indemnification usually is paid by insurance which the corporation purchases at its own expense, a settlement may result in the shareholders paying part of the cost of the defense, notwithstanding that the defendant may have breached her duty to the corporation.

Similarly, the plaintiff in a derivative suit is not like most plaintiffs, and her relationship with her lawyer is not like most lawyer-client relationships in contingent fee litigation. Counsel generally must operate within the bounds set by her client. When the client tells counsel to litigate, counsel litigates; when the client prefers to settle, the lawyer settles. By contrast, the shareholder in a derivative suit has only a nominal economic interest and usually gives no directions. Additionally, in most contingent litigation the client knows she has been injured and seeks out a lawyer; in the derivative suit, it is not uncommon for the lawyer to seek out the client and advise her of the wrong that has occurred. Indeed, one commentator has called plaintiff's counsel "the engine that drives the derivative action." John C. Coffee, Jr., American Law Institute's Corporate Governance Project: Remedies: Litigation and Corporate Governance: An Essay on Steering Between Scylla and Charybdis, 52 Geo.Wash.L.Rev. 789, 800 (1984). Finally, in a derivative suit, the lawyer has far more at stake than the plaintiff shareholder. Thus, plaintiff's counsel has an incentive to agree to settlements that shareholders collectively might view as inadequate, in order to assure that she receives a fee for her work.

Some of the problems described above are present in any form of contingent litigation. They are more troublesome here because of the representative nature of the derivative suit. Nuisance suits are not peculiar to the corporate setting. Nevertheless, in order to discourage abuses by people purporting to act on the corporation's behalf, the law has singled out derivative suits for the imposition of special procedural restrictions and judicial oversight. Among other things, this chapter examines the reasons for these restrictions, how they operate, and how to evaluate their efficacy and desirability. The class action is another tool of shareholder litigation, but it is a device with broader applicability and will not be examined here.

2. RATIONALES FOR THE DERIVATIVE SUIT

The original rationale for the derivative suit appears to have been compensatory; the corporation has been harmed by the defendant's acts and can be made whole if the defendant pays the appropriate damages. There are, however, several problems with such a rationale. First, because the recovery goes to the corporation, whose shareholder body is changing constantly, those who were shareholders when the wrong occurred and have subsequently sold their shares at a price which reflects that wrong do not share in the subsequent recovery. Similarly, those who purchased at the depressed price receive a windfall when the recovery ultimately occurs.

A second problem is that the amount of the corporate injury may not be the same as that suffered by the shareholders. As Professors Coffee and Schwartz have noted: "Even assuming an efficient securities market that automatically translates any injury suffered by the corporation into a decline in its share values, it is still plausible that the stockholders' aggregate loss will exceed that of the corporation—basically because the events will be seen by the marketplace as creating a risk of repetition * * * [F]or legal purposes, the corporation's loss is a historical concept, measured by accounting conventions and limited to injuries that have actually occurred; in contrast, the shareholder's loss may be greater, because in a securities market that discounts future possibilities, predictions of future loss are immediately converted into a present decline in share values." John C. Coffee, Jr. & Donald E. Schwartz, The Survival of the Derivative Suit: An Evaluation and a Proposal for Legislative Reform, 81 Colum. L. Rev. 261, 304 (1981). Still another problem with the compensatory rationale is that because the corporation pays indemnification and the plaintiff's attorneys fees, the corporation can never be fully compensated for the wrong, particularly when the suit is settled.

Coffee and Schwartz argue that deterrence rather than compensation should be the principal rationale for the derivative suit. However, as they recognize, there are also serious problems with the deterrence rationale. To begin with, the plaintiff is cast in the role of a "bounty hunter," seeking a reward for assuring that the deterrence function has been performed. Indeed, the role of plaintiff in a deterrence system is such that anyone, regardless of the nature of her interest in the corporation, could play it. Moreover, even if it were possible to limit appropriate plaintiffs, the litigation costs that the corporation incurred might exceed its recovery. The excess could be rationalized as necessary to achieve the desired level of deterrence.

Recent scholarship has used agency cost literature and portfolio theory in analyzing the rationale for the derivative suit. Professor Cox, who basically favors a compensatory approach, notes that these can be used to support a deterrence rationale:

The important teaching of portfolio theory explains the beneficial effects of holding an efficient portfolio. An efficient portfolio requires investments in a large number of firms in different industries. A fully diversified investor assumes the risk of the market as a whole, generally referred to as systematic risk, and avoids the risk specific to each individual firm. The preceding discussion of agency costs suggested that the average agency cost for all firms constitutes one source of systematic risk reflected in any firm's cost of capital.

So viewed, an important contribution of derivative suits is their potential impact upon the level of systematic risk by deterring managerial misbehavior and not simply compensating the specific firm whose managers have misbehaved. Consequently, management misbehavior that affects a specific firm, arguably, does not harm investors holding an efficient portfolio because the misconduct's impact is offset by the randomness of firm-specific gains and losses, which sum to zero. Therefore, under this view, resources expended to redress a corporation's injury are not efficiently employed because they consume rather than increase wealth. On the other hand, if derivative suits have the collateral effect of widely mitigating agency costs so that the threat of suit effectively reduces systematic risk, they are economically justified. With this reduction, the investor can make sharper comparisons between investments, including risk-free assets and non-managed risky assets.

James D. Cox, Compensation, Deterrence and the Market, 52 Geo. Wash. L. Rev. 745, 748–9 (1984).

Professor Coffee pursues the implications of this argument in analyzing whether it is appropriate for a corporation to incur more in litigation costs than the maximum possible recovery. Under Professor Cox's analysis, if corporate expenditures reduce average agency costs by deterring potential wrongdoers, the fully diversified shareholder will benefit in a case where $300,000 is expended to recover $200,000. Notwithstanding his sympathy for a deterrence rationale, Coffee is troubled by this result. He notes that, "it is open-ended: one does not know whether expenditures of $400,000, $500,000 or even more would also produce a deterrent benefit in excess of the costs incurred. Nor can one begin to estimate the marginal deterrent benefit, if any, of each additional successful derivative action." John C. Coffee, Jr., Litigation and Corporate Governance: An Essay on Steering Between Scylla and Charybdis, 52 Geo. Wash. L. Rev. 789, 807–8 (1984). For Coffee, however, the greatest problem with using the average agency cost analysis is that most shareholders are not fully diversified and thus would lose, rather than gain, when corporate expenditures exceeded the corporate recovery, even if a deterrent surplus were created that would benefit all diversified investors.

A more serious question is whether derivative suits, either as compensation or deterrent, actually improve corporate governance through their effects on corporate managers' behavior. See Roberta Romano, The Shareholder Suit: Litigation Without Foundation?, 7 J. of Law, Econ. & Org. 55 (1991). Sampling a number of shareholder suits, including both derivative and class-action proceedings, Romano concluded that "shareholder litigation is a weak, if not ineffective, instrument of corporate governance." Id. at 84. Plaintiffs rarely prevail in derivative lawsuits, and any monetary settlement is extremely small on a per share basis (recovery is significantly higher for class actions than derivative suits). Negotiated settlements sometimes include changes in board structure or composition, but Romano argues that these changes usually are cosmetic, so that even indirect benefits from derivative suits are minimal. Shareholder suits do not deter managers from improper actions, because insurance and indemnification provisions normally cover their expenses. Romano suggests that the main beneficiaries of shareholder suits are the attorneys who collect fees for pursuing them.

Questions as to the underlying rationale and incentives of derivative suits are of more than academic interest; they also raise issues of practicality and public policy. How much of a deviation from the normal principles of corporate governance should be allowed in the conduct of a derivative suit? How does one balance the costs of derivative suits against the burdens? These large questions are subsumed in smaller ones: What are the requirements for standing? What preliminary steps does the law require to be taken before the suit may be brought? What objections can be raised to the right of the particular plaintiff to act for the corporation? Can the directors prevent the suit from proceeding? How can settlement of a suit be achieved? Who pays the counsel fees? What are the special responsibilities of lawyers in this type of litigation? As you read the following materials, consider how the courts and legislatures have grappled with these questions. Decide whether you think the derivative suit is appropriately viewed as an effective weapon in the arsenal of corporate governance or whether the old appellation, "strike suit," is still appropriate.

PROBLEM
MILTON CORPORATION—PART IV

Reread the facts of Part I of the Milton Corporation problem in Chapter 17.

Acting on advice of counsel, the Corporation submitted the proposed lease transaction between it and RIC to the shareholders, who approved it overwhelmingly. The proxy statement estimated that the amounts that would be paid under the clause in the lease giving RIC a percentage of the profits of the concessionaires would equal approximately 50 percent of the base rent.

It is now three years later, and the hotel has been extremely successful. As a result of several new concessions, the percentage of the concessionaires' profits paid to RIC under the lease in the last two years was twice the percentage that had been estimated in the proxy statement.

In answering the following questions, assume that the applicable law is that of:

a) Delaware

b) Columbia

A

Herman Patterson is a retired businessman who owns a few shares of stock in many public corporations, including 10 shares of the stock of

Milton Corporation. This stock is held in the name of Herman's brokerage firm. Your firm has represented Herman for many years, and he has been the named plaintiff in many shareholder suits in which your firm has been lead counsel. You have recently talked to Herman and advised him of your belief that the transactions with RIC might constitute a breach of fiduciary duty as well as a violation of the federal proxy rules. Specifically, you have told him that the Corporation's management may have known that the revenues that would be paid under the lease were likely to exceed the estimates given in the proxy statement and that the payments to RIC are so high as to be unfair to the Corporation and the minority shareholders. At your request, he has agreed to be the plaintiff in a derivative suit challenging the lease transactions and the related proxy disclosure.

Pamela Gilbert, the partner for whom you work, has asked you to analyze several questions:

1. It appears that the most promising causes of action involve unfair self-dealing transactions and possible proxy violations under state and federal law. Should the suit be brought as a derivative suit or a direct suit (probably in the form of a class action)?

2. Does Herman have standing to bring a derivative suit?

3. If the action is cast as a derivative suit, must Herman first make a demand on the directors?

B

Assume that you are an associate at the firm that has done the Corporation's corporate and securities work for some time. Robert Carey, the partner for whom you work, advised Milton on the transaction in question. He discussed it with James Milton and with other top company officials and reviewed the lease and various other corporate documents.

Herman has filed suit in the federal district court in Columbia, alleging both that the lease transaction violated state law and that its approval violated the federal proxy rules. The complaint further alleged that no demand was made on the Board because it would have been futile to do so. Carey has asked you to research the following questions:

4. Suppose the Board appointed Brown, Grey and White to serve as a special litigation committee, with Frank Berger, formerly a justice of the state supreme court, as special counsel. The committee's function would be to consider both the merits of the claim and, if the claim was meritorious, whether it would be in the best interest of the corporation to pursue it. If the committee, after investigating Herman's allegations, concluded that it would not be in the best interest of the corporation for the suit to continue, and the corporation moved to dismiss, what would be the likely result?

5. If the Corporation moves to require the posting of security for expenses, will Herman have to comply if the suit is brought in New

York? In Columbia? In Delaware? Does it matter whether the cause of action is based on federal or state law?

6. Can your firm represent both the Corporation and James Milton in the lawsuit? If not, who, if anyone, can it represent?

7. Will Herman be able to depose Carey concerning his conversations with James Milton about the transaction? Will Herman be able to obtain discovery of the opinion of Carey's firm provided to the Board concerning the fairness of the lease?

C

You are clerk to Judge Crater, to whom the case has been assigned. After preliminary discovery by plaintiff, the parties have submitted a proposed settlement of the suit in which they agree to the following terms:

A. The lease will be reformed so that RIC will receive a percentage of the concessionaires' profits for a period which is the earlier of the termination of the lease or 10 years.

B. The participation in the concessionaires' profits will not exceed 50 percent of the base rental. The parties estimate that this will provide RIC with $250,000 annually over the base rent, which is less than half the amount paid in recent years.

C. All subsequent contracts between the Corporation and its officers and directors must be approved by a majority of all the unaffiliated directors.

D. Counsel fees of $500,000 are to be paid by the Corporation to Gilbert.

8. What procedures must be followed before the settlement is approved?

9. Would you recommend that the judge approve the settlement?

C. WHAT IS A DERIVATIVE SUIT?

COWIN v. BRESLER
741 F.2d 410 (D.C.Cir.1984).

BORK, CIRCUIT JUDGE:

Bresler & Reiner, Inc. is a publicly-owned company incorporated in the State of Delaware and engaged in the development and management of residential and commercial properties in the District of Columbia. In late 1980, Daniel Cowin, a Bresler & Reiner shareholder, sued the company and its directors on his own behalf. Cowin has a minority interest in the company. The individual directors-appellees, with their families, own in excess of 79% of the company's stock. Appellees Bresler and Reiner together hold more than 70% of the company's outstanding shares, and their control of the corporation is undisputed.

The thrust of Cowin's charges is that the appellees have manipulated the business for their personal profit at the expense of the minority shareholders. The complaint alleges numerous instances of corporate mismanagement, fraud, and self-dealing, all in breach of the common law fiduciary duty owed by the directors of the company to the appellant as a shareholder. Several of the challenged transactions involve deals between the company and certain limited partnerships in which the appellees, including Bresler and Reiner, have significant interests. The complaint also charges Bresler and Reiner with forcing the company to engage in a stock repurchase program at a time when the company was in default on its notes payable and having severe cash flow problems. Cowin alleges that appellees used, and are still using, the repurchase plan to "severely limit[] the public market for trading in Company stock"; according to appellant, their ultimate intent is to "convert[] the Company to a private corporation owned solely by" them for their own benefit. To remedy the alleged common law violations, Cowin seeks damages for the diminished value of his stock and injunctions against the allegedly wrongful transactions. He also requests the appointment of a receiver to liquidate the company for his benefit and the benefit of the other shareholder.

The remainder of the complaint charges appellees with violations of the federal securities laws, primarily in connection with the transactions detailed above. * * *

In its first order, entered December 23, 1981, the district court ruled that while Cowin could legally seek the appointment of a receiver for a solvent corporation in his individual capacity, he had failed to allege the "extreme circumstances showing imminent danger of great loss" necessary to support such drastic relief. The court then dismissed appellant's common law claims because, in its view, both federal and common law required Cowin to "bring * * * a derivative suit to recover damages for a decline in the value of stock" due to alleged corporate mismanagement and fraud. *Id.* at 35. The court would "not permit [Cowin] to elevate form over substance in order to escape the requirements of a derivative suit merely by attaching an unjustified request for the appointment of a receiver * * * to his complaint." *Id.* at 36.

* * *

We agree with the district court's holding that appellant's common law claims for damages and injunctive relief must be pursued, if at all, on a derivative basis. Both case law and sound policy support this conclusion. In Bokat v. Getty Oil Co., 262 A.2d 246, 249 (Del.1970), plaintiff shareholder charged that Getty Oil had, among other things, forced its wholly-owned subsidiary to purchase oil from Getty at an inflated price. Delaware's highest court characterized this claim as one "seek[ing] money damages for improper management" and held that such claims belonged to the corporation and not to its minority stockholders:

When an injury to corporate stock falls equally upon all stockholders, then an individual stockholder may not recover for the injury to his stock alone, but must seek recovery derivatively in behalf of the corporation.

Id. at 249 (emphasis added). The court concluded that "mismanagement which depresses the value of stock is a wrong to the corporation; i.e., the stockholders collectively, to be enforced by a derivative action." *Id.*

The logic of *Bokat* is compelling. Claims of corporate mismanagement must be brought on a derivative basis because no shareholder suffers a harm independent of that visited upon the corporation and the other shareholders. Because each shareholder has been injured in proportion to his equity ownership, "each will be made whole if the corporation obtains compensation or restitution from the wrongdoer." Empire Life Insurance Co. v. Valdak Corp., 468 F.2d 330, 335 (5th Cir.1972). A contrary rule "would authorize multitudinous litigation and ignore the corporate entity." Sutter v. General Petroleum Corp., 28 Cal. 2d 525, 530, 170 P.2d 898, 901 (1946). Requiring derivative enforcement of claims belonging in the first instance to the corporation also prevents an individual shareholder from incurring a benefit at the expense of other shareholders similarly situated.

This general rule is the law of several jurisdictions. There are, however, certain circumstances in which a shareholder may proceed against his company on an individual basis. In Elster v. American Airlines, Inc., the Delaware chancery court stated:

There are cases, of course, in which there is injury to the corporation and also *special injury* to the individual stockholder. In such cases a stockholder, if he should so desire, may proceed on his claim for the protection of his individual rights rather than in the right of the corporation. The action would then not constitute a derivative action.

34 Del.Ch. at 99, 100 A.2d at 222 (emphasis added).

A fair reading of the "special injury" cases shows that a personal cause of action is properly pursued in two situations—where the allegedly wrongful conduct violates a duty to the complaining shareholder independent of the fiduciary duties owed that party along with all other shareholders, or, where the conduct causes an injury to the shareholders distinct from any injury to the corporation itself. In cases of the first sort, the complaining shareholder may sue as an individual only because he stands, and has been injured in his relationship to the corporation, in a capacity other than that of a shareholder. In Sedco International, S.A. v. Cory, 522 F.Supp. 254 (S.D.Iowa 1981), aff'd, 683 F.2d 1201 (8th Cir.), cert. denied, 459 U.S. 1017, 74 L.Ed. 2d 512, 103 S.Ct. 379 (1982), for example, a shareholder was permitted to bring a personal action against the company because he was injured in his capacity as a creditor of the corporation; his status as a shareholder was irrelevant to his right to pursue a creditor's remedy. * * *

The second category of harms which may be remedied on an individual basis consists of "wrong[s] inflicted upon [the stockholder] alone * * * or wrong[s] affecting * * * the stockholders and not the corporation * * *" *Elster*, 34 Del.Ch. at 99, 100 A.2d at 222. Wrongful withholding of dividends, for example, gives rise to an individual cause of action. Because dividends are an incident of stock ownership, an action to compel the payment of dividends withheld will not inure to the benefit of the corporation; the shareholders alone will gain by a judgment in their favor and, therefore, each shareholder may sue for his own account.

Condec Corp. v. Lunkenheimer Co., 43 Del Ch. 353, 230 A.2d 769 (1967), is also representative of this second category. In that case, the company's directors denied a controlling corporate shareholder its right to exercise voting control over the company. This claim was properly remedied on an individual basis because the injury was the shareholder's alone, not shared by the corporation or other equity owners. * * *

Appellant's allegations do not fall within the "special injury" exception articulated above. Although Cowin generally argues that appellees—through their conduct—have breached fiduciary duties owed directly to the minority shareholders, he has not shown, and indeed could not show, that these duties are distinct from those owed the corporation. His claims that appellees caused the company to enter into a series of "unfair" transactions that have "involved self-dealing" and "diverting assets" are fundamentally claims belonging to the corporation and to Cowin only derivatively. Cowin's charge that the deceptive and incomplete reports issued by the company in an attempt to "artificially deflate * * * the market price of [the company's] common stock" is also an allegation of harm primarily to the corporation shared by each stockholder proportionate to their holdings. While the underlying value of the corporation's assets may be unaffected by this wrongful act, the attractiveness of the corporation as an investment and its ability to compete for capital funds have been impaired. That these deceptive reports may have prevented the company stock from being traded in a "perfect" market causes similar injury to the corporation. In these circumstances, then, because "each [shareholder] will be made whole if the corporation obtains compensation or restitution from the wrongdoer,"468 F.2d at 335, appellant must pursue his common law claims for damages and injunctive relief on a derivative basis.

B.

Cowin's request for the appointment of a receiver to liquidate the company, as distinct from his state law claims for damages and injunctive relief, was properly before the district court in a personal action. The court found, however, that Cowin had failed to meet the pleading requirements necessary to support such relief. We disagree. Although a request for a court-appointed receiver "to wind up a solvent going business is rarely granted," Berwald v. Mission Development Co., 40 Del.Ch. 509, 512, 185 A.2d 480, 482 (Sup. Ct. 1962), and the court's power to do so must "always [be] exercised with great restraint," Hall v.

John S. Isaacs & Sons Farms, Inc. 39 Del.Ch. 244, 253, 163 A.2d 288, 293 (Sup. Ct. 1960), we believe that Cowin has sufficiently plead the requisite elements to support his claim.

* * *

Note: Features of a Derivative Suit

1. *Derivative or Direct.*

Determining whether an action is direct or derivative sometimes can be complicated. It is an important distinction primarily because of the procedural hurdles that the stockholder-plaintiff in a derivative action must overcome. These include limitations on standing, the need for demand on the corporation's board of directors, the ability of the board to seek dismissal of the action before trial, and the posting of a bond as security for the expenses.

ALI, PRINCIPLES OF CORPORATE GOVERNANCE (1994)

§ 7.01. *Direct and Derivative Actions Distinguished*

Comment:

 c. *Characterization of an action.* * * * [A] wrongful act that depletes corporate assets and thereby injures shareholders only indirectly, by reason of the prior injury to the corporation, should be seen as derivative in character; conversely, a wrongful act that is separate and distinct from any corporate injury, such as one that denies or interferes with the rightful incidents of share ownership, gives rise to a direct action. Sometimes this result has been justified in terms of an "injury" test that looks to whose interests were more directly damaged; at other times, the test has been phrased in terms of the respective rights of the corporation and its shareholders; but regardless of the verbal formula employed, the results have been substantially similar.

 Although some discrepancies exist in the case law, most courts have properly considered actions such as the following as direct actions: (1) actions to enforce the right to vote, to protect preemptive rights, to prevent the improper dilution of voting rights, or to enjoin the improper voting of shares; (2) actions to compel dividends or to protect accrued dividend arrearages; (3) actions challenging the use of corporate machinery or the issuance of stock for a wrongful purpose (such as an attempt to perpetuate management in control or to frustrate voting power legitimately acquired by existing shareholders); (4) actions to enjoin an ultra vires or unauthorized act; (5) actions to prevent oppression of, or fraud against, minority shareholders; (6) actions to compel dissolution, appoint a receiver, or obtain similar equitable relief; (7) actions challenging the improper expulsion of shareholders through mergers, redemptions, or other means; (8) actions to inspect corporate books and records; (9) actions to require the holding of a shareholders' meeting or the sending of notice thereof; and (10) actions to hold controlling shareholders liable for acts undertaken in their individual capacities that depress the value of the minority's shares. In some instances, actions that essentially involve the structural relationship of the shareholder to the corporation (which thus should be seen as direct actions) may also give rise to a derivative action when the corporation suffers or is threatened with a loss. * * * In such cases, the plaintiff may opt to plead either a direct or a derivative action, or to bring both actions simultaneously, unless the court finds that the plaintiff is unable to provide fair and adequate representation. * * *

JOHN W. WELCH, SHAREHOLDERS INDIVIDUAL AND DERIVATIVE ACTIONS: UNDERLYING RATIONALES AND THE CLOSELY HELD CORPORATION
9 J. Corp. L. 147 (1984).

* * * How a given action is classified may vary from one jurisdiction to another.

As such, the following actions are frequently mentioned as being, by definition, actionable only derivatively: actions for misfeasance or misappropriation of corporate property; actions for the enforcement of corporate contracts with third parties; actions against corporate directors for competing with the corporation; suits alleging that corporate officers received excessive salaries; third party torts against the corporation; and actions to correct false entries by directors in the records of the corporation.

2. *Individual Recovery.*

Because a derivative suit asserts a cause of action belonging to the corporation, any monetary recovery usually goes directly to the corporation. Creditors and shareholders benefit indirectly by the strengthening of the corporation. If recovery were awarded to individual shareholders, it would in effect, be a distribution of corporate assets to the shareholders either as a dividend or in partial liquidation of the corporation, something that courts do not usually do. Eshleman v. Keenan, 22 Del.Ch. 82, 194 A. 40 (1937), aff'd 23 Del.Ch. 234, 2 A.2d 904 (1938) (where the corporation is a going concern conducting a profitable business, individual recovery in a derivative action is inappropriate because it would interfere with the management responsibilities of the directors).

Occasionally courts have held that special circumstances require that a monetary judgment be awarded directly to the shareholders on a pro rata basis. In Perlman v. Feldmann, 219 F.2d 173 (2d Cir.1955), cert. denied 349 U.S. 952, 75 S.Ct. 880, 99 L.Ed. 1277 (1955), (Chapter 21) minority shareholders brought a derivative suit against Feldmann, who had sold his 37% controlling interest in a steel manufacturer. The court awarded damages in the amount of the premium paid to Feldmann and ordered that they be be paid pro rata to the injured stockholders. If the corporation had received the award, the syndicate that purchased the shares would have recovered some of the premium it paid for the controlling shares. *See* Note, Individual Pro Rata Recovery in Stockholders' Derivative Suits, 69 Harv.L.Rev. 1314 (1956).

Courts have awarded individual recovery in other limited circumstances. See Eaton v. Robinson, 19 R.I. 146, 31 A. 1058 (1895) (majority shareholders/directors voted themselves excessive salaries in a scheme to deprive derivative action plaintiffs of their share in a judgment if their litigation were successful); Matthews v. Headley Chocolate Co., 130 Md. 523, 100 A. 645 (1917) (successor controlling stockholders purchased their stock with full knowledge of excessive salaries paid by the corporation to their predecessor controlling stockholders); Di Tomasso v. Loverro, 250 App.Div. 206, 293 N.Y.S. 912 (1937), aff'd 276 N.Y. 551, 12 N.E.2d 570 (1937) (the wrongdoers were themselves substantial shareholders of the corporation); Sale v. Ambler, 335 Pa. 165, 6 A.2d 519 (1939) (the corporation no longer was a going concern and the parties to the suit owned all the shares of the corporation).

Glenn v. Hoteltron Systems, 74 N.Y.2d 386, 547 N.Y.S.2d 816, 547 N.E.2d 71 (1989), involved an action between the only two shareholders in a close corporation. The plaintiff alleged that the defendant had diverted corporate assets and opportunities for his own benefit. The court held that the damages should be awarded to the corporation, rather than to the plaintiff even though the defendant who had caused the injury would benefit from the payment in his capacity as a 50 percent owner of the corporation. The court conceded that it was an "anomaly" that the wrongdoer-shareholder would ultimately share in the damages awarded but concluded that this factor was not sufficiently important to justify a judicial exception to the general rule that the corporation should receive the benefits from a successful derivative action. The court recognized that its holding might not sufficiently deter wrongdoing but noted that other interests were also at stake. Thus, for example, the rights of a corporate creditor whose claims were superior to those of the shareholder might be impaired if the court were to award an asset that had been diverted from the corporation directly to the shareholder.

3. *Close Corporations.*

The policy reasons for imposing the procedural requirements of a derivative suit where a publicly held corporation is concerned may be absent in a suit involving a close corporation. When minority shareholders bring an action that would typically be derivative in nature, the procedural requirements such as demand on the directors are futile, because the managers, owners, and directors often are the same people. See John W. Welch, Shareholders, Individual and Derivative Actions: Underlying Rationales and the Closely Held Corporation, 9 J. Corp. L. 147, 170 (1984). Thus, in a close corporation the likelihood of a strike suit is much smaller, because the suit is very often a personal dispute between minority and majority stockholders. Nevertheless, there may be other reasons for requiring that the action be maintained as a derivative suit; as *Glenn* indicates, creditors may need protection by having the damages awarded to the corporation rather than to an individual shareholder.

Courts divide on whether derivative claims that arise in a close corporation should be maintained as a derivative or direct action. In *Watson v. Button*, 235 F.2d 235 (9th Cir.1956), the court balanced the interests in favor of a direct action against the policy reasons for requiring a derivative suit. The court looked at three factors in permitting the suit to be maintained as a direct action: 1) the possibility of a multiplicity of suits against the corporation, 2) adequate protection of creditors, and 3) promotion of an equal distribution of the recovery. The ALI has adopted the *Watson* test, thus permitting a court in its discretion to allow an action to be maintained as a direct rather than a derivative suit when a close corporation is involved. ALI, Principles of Corporate Governance (1994) § 7.01(d).

4. *Jury Trial.*

The derivative suit was originally a remedy available in equity, allowing shareholders to enforce a corporate cause of action against officers, directors or third parties. As with all suits in equity, parties had no right to a jury trial. When the Seventh Amendment, which preserves the right to a jury trial in suits at common law, was adopted, a corporation's suit to enforce a legal right was an action carrying the right to a jury trial. The derivative suit's status under the Seventh Amendment was uncertain until *Ross v. Bernhard*, 396 U.S. 531, 90 S.Ct. 733, 24 L.Ed.2d 729 (1970). In *Ross*, shareholders brought suit against the directors of an investment company, Lehman Corporation and its broker, Lehman Brothers, alleging breach of fiduciary duty, breach of contract, gross negligence and violations of the Investment Company Act. The Supreme Court held that a shareholder-plaintiff was entitled to a jury trial in a derivative action as to those issues on which the corporation would have been entitled to a jury trial had it sued in its own right.

The Court set forth a three part test to determine the legal or equitable nature of an issue. "The 'legal' nature of an issue is determined by considering, first, the pre-merger [of law and equity] custom with reference to such questions; second, the remedy sought; and third, the practical abilities and limitations of juries." 396 U.S. at 538 n.10, 90 S.Ct. at 738 n.10, 24 L.Ed.2d at 736 n.10. The Court found that the breach of contract and gross negligence claims would have entitled the corporation to a jury trial. The Court did not decide if a claim for breach of fiduciary duty, by itself, was properly triable to a jury. However, subsequent courts have found that some actions based solely on a breach of fiduciary duty are wholly equitable and not triable to a jury, because the remedy is restitutionary in nature. Maldonado v.

Flynn, 477 F.Supp. 1007, (S.D.N.Y.1979). This holding, however, does not reflect judicial consensus, and courts have not used *Ross* to determine whether specific issues are legal or equitable. In most cases, a court's analysis relies most heavily on the type of remedy sought.

Most derivative suits are brought in state court where the Seventh Amendment does not apply. Minneapolis & St. Louis Railroad Co. v. Bombolis, 241 U.S. 211, 217, 36 S.Ct. 595, 596, 60 L.Ed. 961, 963 (1916). Thus, the right to a jury trial in state court becomes a question of state constitutional law. Some state courts have specifically adopted *Ross*. Others treat a derivative action as involving an equitable remedy and reject the right to a jury trial, although many states, including Delaware, have not directly addressed the issue. Deborah DeMott, Shareholder Derivative Actions: Law and Practice, § 4.18 (1992).

D. STANDING

BANGOR PUNTA OPERATIONS, INC. v. BANGOR & AROOSTOOK RAILROAD CO.
417 U.S. 703, 94 S.Ct. 2578, 41 L.Ed.2d 418 (1974).

MR. JUSTICE POWELL delivered the opinion of the Court.

This case involves an action by a Maine railroad corporation seeking damages from its former owners for violations of federal antitrust and securities laws, applicable state statutes, and common-law principles. The complaint alleged that the former owners had engaged in various acts of corporate waste and mismanagement during the period of their control. The shareholder presently in control of the railroad acquired more than 99% of the railroad's shares from the former owners long after the alleged wrongs occurred. We must decide whether equitable principles applicable under federal and state law preclude recovery by the railroad in these circumstances.

I

Respondent Bangor & Aroostook Railroad Co. (BAR), a Maine corporation, operates a railroad in the northern part of the State of Maine. Respondent Bangor Investment Co., also a Maine corporation, is a wholly owned subsidiary of BAR. Petitioner Bangor Punta Corp. (Bangor Punta), a Delaware corporation, is a diversified investment company with business operations in several areas. Petitioner Bangor Punta Operations, Inc. (BPO), a New York corporation, is a wholly owned subsidiary of Bangor Punta.

On October 13, 1964, Bangor Punta, through its subsidiary BPO, acquired 98.3% of the outstanding stock of BAR. * * * On October 2, 1969, Bangor Punta, again through its subsidiary, sold all of its stock for $5,000,000 to Amoskeag Co., a Delaware investment corporation. Amoskeag assumed responsibility for the management of BAR and later acquired additional shares to give it ownership of more than 99% of all the outstanding stock.

In 1971, BAR and its subsidiary filed the present action against Bangor Punta and its subsidiary in the United States District Court for the District of Maine. The complaint specified 13 counts of alleged mismanagement, misappropriation, and waste of BAR's corporate assets occurring during the period [when] Bangor Punta controlled BAR. Damages were sought in the amount of $7,000,000 for violations of both federal and state laws. * * *

The District Court granted petitioners' motion for summary judgment and dismissed the action. 353 F.Supp. 724 (1972). The court first observed that although the suit purported to be a primary action brought in the name of the corporation, the real party in interest and hence the actual beneficiary of any recovery, was Amoskeag, the present owner of more than 99% of the outstanding stock of BAR. The court then noted that Amoskeag had acquired all of its BAR stock long after the alleged wrongs occurred and that Amoskeag did not contend that it had not received full value for its purchase price, or that the purchase transaction was tainted by fraud or deceit. Thus, any recovery on Amoskeag's part would constitute a windfall because it had sustained no injury. With this in mind, the court then addressed the claims based on federal law and determined that Amoskeag would have been barred from maintaining a shareholder derivative action because of its failure to satisfy the "contemporaneous ownership" requirement of Fed Rule Civ Proc 23.1(1).[3] * * *.

The United States Court of Appeals for the First Circuit reversed. 482 F.2d 865 (1973). * * *

We granted petitioners' application for certiorari. 414 U.S. 1127, 94 S.Ct. 863, 38 L.Ed.2d 752 (1974). We now reverse.

II

A

We first turn to the question whether respondent corporations may maintain the present action under § 10 of the Clayton Act, 15 U.S.C. § 20, and § 10(b) of the Securities Exchange Act of 1934, 15 U.S.C.A. § 78j(b), and Rule 10b–5, 17 CFR § 240.10b–5. The resolution of this issue depends upon the applicability of the settled principle of equity that a shareholder may not complain of acts of corporate mismanagement if he acquired his shares from those who participated or acquiesced in the allegedly wrongful transactions. This principle has been invoked with special force where a shareholder purchases all or substantially all the shares of a corporation from a vendor at a fair price, and then seeks to have the corporation recover against that vendor for prior corporate

---

3. Rule 23.1(1), which specifies the requirements applicable to shareholder derivative actions, states that the complaint shall aver that "the plaintiff was a shareholder or member at the time of the transaction of which he complains * * *." This provision is known as the "contemporaneous ownership" requirement. See 3B J. Moore, Federal Practice ¶ 23.1 et seq. (2d ed 1974).

mismanagement. The equitable considerations precluding recovery in such cases were explicated long ago by Dean (then Commissioner) Roscoe Pound in Home Fire Insurance Co. v. Barber [67 Neb. 644, 93 N.W. 1024 (1903).] Dean Pound, writing for the Supreme Court of Nebraska, observed that the shareholders of the plaintiff corporation in that case had sustained no injury since they had acquired their shares from the alleged wrongdoers after the disputed transactions occurred and had received full value for their purchase price. Thus, any recovery on their part would constitute a windfall, for it would enable them to obtain funds to which they had no just title or claim. Moreover, it would in effect allow the shareholders to recoup a large part of the price they agreed to pay for their shares, notwithstanding the fact that they received all they had bargained for. Finally, it would permit the shareholders to reap a profit from wrongs done to others, thus encouraging further such speculation. Dean Pound stated that these consequences rendered any recovery highly inequitable and mandated dismissal of the suit.

The considerations supporting the *Home Fire* principle are especially pertinent in the present case. As the District Court pointed out, Amoskeag, the present owner of more than 99% of the BAR shares, would be the principal beneficiary of any recovery obtained by BAR. Amoskeag, however, acquired 98.3% of the outstanding shares of BAR from petitioner Bangor Punta in 1969, well after the alleged wrongs were said to have occurred. Amoskeag does not contend that the purchase transaction was tainted by fraud or deceit, or that it received less than full value for its money. Indeed, it does not assert that it has sustained any injury at all. Nor does it appear that the alleged acts of prior mismanagement have had any continuing effect on the corporations involved or the value of their shares. Nevertheless, by causing the present action to be brought in the name of respondent corporations, Amoskeag seeks to recover indirectly an amount equal to the $5,000,000 it paid for its stock, plus an additional $2,000,000. All this would be in the form of damages for wrongs petitioner Bangor Punta is said to have inflicted, not upon Amoskeag, but upon respondent corporations during the period in which Bangor Punta owned 98.3% of the BAR shares. In other words, Amoskeag seeks to recover for wrongs Bangor Punta did to *itself* as owner of the railroad. At the same time it reaps this windfall, Amoskeag desires to retain all its BAR stock. Under *Home Fire,* it is evident that Amoskeag would have no standing in equity to maintain the present action.[8]

---

8. Conceding the lack of equity in any recovery by Amoskeag, the dissent argues that the present action can nevertheless be maintained because there are 20 minority shareholders, holding less than 1% of the BAR stock, who owned their shares "during the period from 1960 through 1967 when the transactions underlying the railroad's complaint took place, and who still owned that stock in 1971 when the complaint was filed." Post, at 722, 41 L.Ed.2d, at 432. The dissent would conclude that the existence of these innocent minority shareholders entitles BAR, and hence Amoskeag, to recover the entire $7,000,000 amount of alleged damages.

Aside from the illogic of such an approach, the dissent's position is at war with the precedents, for the Home Fire principle

We are met with the argument, however, that since the present action is brought in the name of respondent corporations, we may not look behind the corporate entity to the true substance of the claims and the actual beneficiaries. The established law is to the contrary. Although a corporation and its shareholders are deemed separate entities for most purposes, the corporate form may be disregarded in the interests of justice where it is used to defeat an overriding public policy. In such cases, courts of equity, piercing all fictions and disguises, will deal with the substance of the action and not blindly adhere to the corporate form. Thus, where equity would preclude the shareholders from maintaining an action in their own right, the corporation would also be precluded. It follows that Amoskeag, the principal beneficiary of any recovery and itself estopped from complaining of petitioners' alleged wrongs, cannot avoid the command of equity through the guise of proceeding in the name of respondent corporations which it owns and controls. * * *

III

In reaching the contrary conclusion, the Court of Appeals stated that it could not accept the proposition that Amoskeag would be the "sole beneficiary" of any recovery by BAR. 482 F.2d, at 868. The court noted that in view of the railroad's status as a "quasi-public" corporation and the essential nature of the services it provides, the public had an identifiable interest in BAR's financial health. Thus, any recovery by BAR would accrue to the benefit of the public through the improvement in BAR's economic position and the quality of its services. The court thought that this factor rendered any windfall to Amoskeag irrelevant.

At the outset, we note that the Court of Appeals' assumption that any recovery would necessarily benefit the public is unwarranted. As that court explicitly recognized, any recovery by BAR could be diverted to its shareholders, namely Amoskeag, rather than reinvested in the railroad for the benefit of the public. Nor do we believe this possibility can be avoided by respondents' suggestion that the District Court impose limitations on the use BAR might make of the recovery. There is no support for such a result under either federal or state law. BAR would be entitled to distribute the recovery in any lawful manner it may choose, even if such distribution resulted only in private enrichment. In sum, there is no assurance that the public would receive any benefit at all from these funds.

The Court of Appeals' position also appears to overlook the fact that Amoskeag, the actual beneficiary of any recovery through its ownership of more than 99% of the BAR shares, would be unjustly enriched since it has sustained no injury. It acquired substantially all the BAR shares

has long been applied to preclude full recovery by a corporation even where there are innocent minority shareholders who acquired their shares prior to the alleged wrongs. * * * The dissent also mistakes the factual posture of this case, since the respondent corporations did not institute this action for the benefit of the minority shareholders. See discussion at n.15, infra.

from Bangor Punta subsequent to the alleged wrongs and does not deny that it received full value for its purchase price. No fraud or deceit of any kind is alleged to have been involved in the transaction. The equitable principles of *Home Fire* preclude Amoskeag from reaping a windfall by enhancing the value of its bargain to the extent of the entire purchase price plus an additional $2,000,000. Amoskeag would in effect have acquired a railroad worth $12,000,000 for only $5,000,000. Neither the federal antitrust or securities laws nor the applicable state laws contemplate recovery by Amoskeag in these circumstances.

The Court of Appeals further stated that it was important to insure that petitioners would not be immune from liability for their wrongful conduct and noted that BAR's recovery would provide a needed deterrent to mismanagement of railroads. Our difficulty with this argument is that it proves too much. If deterrence were the only objective, then in logic any plaintiff willing to file a complaint would suffice. No injury or violation of a legal duty to the particular plaintiff would have to be alleged. The only prerequisite would be that the plaintiff agree to accept the recovery, lest the supposed wrongdoer be allowed to escape a reckoning. Suffice it to say that we have been referred to no authority which would support so novel a result, and we decline to adopt it.

We therefore conclude that respondent corporations may not maintain the present action.[15] The judgment of the Court of Appeals is reversed.

So ordered.

Mr. Justice Marshall, with whom Mr. Justice Douglas, Mr. Justice Brennan, and Mr. Justice White join, dissenting.

* * *

I cannot agree. Having read the precedents relied upon by the majority, I respectfully submit that they not only do not support, but indeed directly contradict the result reached today. While purporting to rely on settled principles of equity, the Court sadly mistakes the facts of this case and the established powers of an equity court. In my view, no windfall recovery to Amoskeag is inevitable, or even likely, on the facts of this case. But even if recovery by respondents would in fact be a windfall to Amoskeag, the Court disregards the interests of the railroad's

---

15. Our decision rests on the conclusion that equitable principles preclude recovery by Amoskeag, the present owner of more than 99% of the BAR shares. The record does not reveal whether the minority shareholders who hold the remaining fraction of 1% of the BAR shares stand in the same position as Amoskeag. Some courts have adopted the concept of a pro-rata recovery where there are innocent minority shareholders. Under this procedure, damages are distributed to the minority shareholders individually on a proportional basis, even though the action is brought in the name of the corporation to enforce primary rights. See, e.g., Matthews v. Headley Chocolate Co., 130 Md. 523, 536–540, 100 A. 645, 650–652 (1917). In the present case, respondents have expressly disavowed any intent to obtain a pro-rata recovery on behalf of the 1% minority shareholders of BAR. We therefore do not reach the question whether such recovery would be appropriate. * * *

creditors, as well as the substantial public interest in the continued financial viability of the Nation's railroads which have been so heavily plagued by corporate mismanagement, and ignores the powers of the court to impose equitable conditions on a corporation's recovery so as to insure that these interests are protected. The Court's decision is also inconsistent with prior decisions of this Court limiting the application of equitable defenses when they impede the vindication, through private damage actions, of the important policies of the federal antitrust laws. * * *

     * * * Although first Bangor Punta and then Amoskeag owned the great majority of the shares of respondent railroad, the record shows that there are many minority shareholders who owned BAR stock during the period from 1960 through 1967 when the transactions underlying the railroad's complaint took place, and who still owned that stock in 1971 when the complaint was filed. Any one of these minority shareholders would have had the right, during the 1960–1967 period, as well as thereafter, to bring a derivative action on behalf of the corporation against the majority shareholder for misappropriation of corporate assets.

* * *

     * * * To begin with, it is not at all clear from the record that any recovery had by the railroad will in fact be a windfall to Amoskeag, its present majority shareholder.

     But let us assume that the majority is correct in finding some windfall recovery to Amoskeag inevitable in this case. This is still but one of several factors which a court of equity should consider in determining whether the public interest would best be served by piercing the corporate veil in order to bar this action. The public interest against windfall recoveries is no doubt a significant factor which a court of equity should consider. But in this case it is clearly outweighed by other considerations, equally deserving the recognition of a court of equity, supporting the maintenance of the railroad's action against those who have defrauded it of its assets. Equity should take into account, for example, the railroad's relationships with its creditors. BAR owes a debt of approximately $23 million, indicating almost 90% debt ownership of the enterprise. App. 7. If the allegations of the complaint are true, the conversion and misappropriation of corporate assets committed by petitioners placed the railroad close to the brink of bankruptcy, to the certain detriment of its creditors. * * *

     Surely the corporation, as an entity independent of its shareholders, has an interest of its own in assuring that it can meet its responsibility to its creditors. And I do not see how it can do so unless it remains free to bring suit against those who have defrauded it of its assets. The Court's result, I fear, only gives added incentive to abuses of the corporate form which equity has long sought to discourage—allowing a majority shareholder to take advantage of the protections of the corporate form while bleeding the corporation to the detriment of its creditors, and then permitting the majority shareholder to sell the corporation and remain free from any liability for its wrongdoing.

More importantly, equity should take into account the public interest at stake in this litigation. * * *

The significance of the public interest in the financial well-being of railroads should be self-evident in these times, with many of our Nation's railroads in dire financial straits and with some of the most important lines thrown into reorganization proceedings. Indeed, the prospect of large-scale railroad insolvency in the Northeast United States was deemed by Congress to present a national emergency, prompting enactment of the Regional Rail Reorganization Act of 1973, in which the Federal Government, for the first time, committed tax dollars to a long-term commitment to preserve adequate railroad service for the Nation. * * *

The Court gives short shrift, however, to the public interest. While recognizing that respondents' complaint is based primarily on federal antitrust and securities statutes designed to benefit the public, and while conceding that the statutorily designated plaintiffs are respondent corporations, the Court nevertheless holds that these plaintiffs cannot maintain this action because any recovery by Amoskeag would violate established principles of equity. I cannot agree, for the public interest and the legislative purpose should always be heavily weighed by a court of equity. As this Court has frequently recognized, equity should pierce the corporate veil only when necessary to serve some paramount public interest, or "where it otherwise would present an obstacle to the due protection or enforcement of public or private rights." New Colonial Ice Co. v. Helvering, 292 U.S., at 442, 54 S.Ct. at 791. Here, however, it is the failure to recognize the railroad's own right to maintain this suit which undercuts the public interest.

Note: The Standing Requirement

1. General

Because a derivative suit seeks to enforce a right in the name of the corporation, standing generally has been limited to those with an ownership interest in the corporation. The rationale is that it is the owners who have suffered most directly from the harm to the corporation and it is they who should have a right to assert the corporation's right to redress. Simple ownership generally is not sufficient. In almost all jurisdictions, the plaintiff also must have been a shareholder at the time of the wrong complained of and at the time of the suit and must remain a shareholder throughout the litigation. Taken together, these requirements are designed to assure that the corporation's rights will be vigorously prosecuted by someone whose harm is actual and who is interested in a successful outcome.

The standing requirements, like the Court's argument in *Bangor Punta*, assume that the principal purpose of the derivative suit is compensation. Were it deterrence, as the Court noted, no need would exist for the contemporaneous ownership requirement; "any plaintiff willing to file a complain would suffice. No injury or violation of a legal duty to the particular plaintiff would have to be alleged." If, however, the primary purpose of derivative suits is deterrence, the analysis changes. It then would matter less who brings the suit, so long as the plaintiff has a sufficient incentive to pursue the claim. Standing would be expanded to increase deterrence of breaches of fiduciary duty.

The standing requirements in most states are generally similar. See RMBCA § 7.40; N.Y.B.C.L. § 626. These requirements may be found in the corporate statute or, more logically, in the procedure statute or the applicable court rules. See F.R.C.P. 23.1.

2. Security Ownership

In most jurisdictions, a derivative suit may be brought by either a holder of record or a beneficial owner of stock; only a few jurisdictions adhere to an earlier requirement that the shareholder be a holder of record or a registered owner. RMBCA § 7.40(e) includes in its definition of "shareholder" a person whose shares are held in a voting trust as well as the more traditional "street name" owner of shares. The meaning of "beneficial owner", however, is not entirely clear. The ALI would give standing to a "holder of an equity security" and defines "holder" as a person with "a substantial beneficial interest" in the stock, leaving the determination of "substantial beneficial interest" to judicial development. ALI, Principles of Corporate Governance (1994), § 7.02; § 1.22.

Suppose the plaintiff is not and never was a shareholder of the corporation that was a party to in the transaction of which she complains, but instead owns stock in a corporation that owns stock of that corporation. The action would then be a double derivative suit, or possibly a triple derivative suit. In Brown v. Tenney, 125 Ill.2d 348, 126 Ill.Dec. 545, 532 N.E.2d 230 (1988), the court found standing for a stockholder in P Corporation who claimed an injury to S Corporation, a wholly owned subsidiary of P Corporation. There was no doubt that the plaintiff's interest in P Corporation was economically affected by what happened to S Corporation. The justification for allowing a remote derivative suit is that both the corporation that suffered the wrong and its parent corporation which had the right to bring the derivative suit, were controlled by those charged with inflicting the injury. United States Lines v. United States Lines Co., 96 F.2d 148 (2d Cir.1938). The ALI would allow multiple derivative suits but only "where the shareholder's corporation holds at least a *de facto* controlling interest in the injured subsidiary." ALI, Principles of Corporate Governance (1994) § 7.02 Comment f.

3. Creditor Standing

In most jurisdictions, only those holding equity securities may institute a derivative suit. See, e.g., RMBCA § 7.40. Common and preferred stock are clearly equity securities; the difficult problem is in classifying convertible debt securities. As we saw in Chapter 9, a convertible debt security is a hybrid which contains elements of both debt and equity. The holder of a convertible security has the protections of a debt holder, but the interest paid on the security is less because of the holder's right to convert her investment into equity. In Harff v. Kerkorian, 324 A.2d 215 (Del.Ch.1974), the court held that a holder of convertible subordinated debentures had no standing to sue because only a person who was a shareholder could maintain a derivative action. Although the court noted that an equitable owner of stock would be considered a shareholder, it held that the owner of convertible debentures was a holder of a debt instrument rather than the equitable owner of the shares into which the debentures were convertible until such time as she actually converted her debentures. By contrast, in Hoff v. Sprayregan, 52 F.R.D. 243 (S.D.N.Y.1971), the court held that the holder of convertible debentures satisfied the F.R.C.P. 23.1 "shareholder" requirement in a suit alleging a violation of Rule 10b–5 under the Securities Exchange Act of 1934. In reaching its decision, the court relied on the fact that the 1934 Act defined "equity security" to include convertible debentures. See Note, Derivative Actions—Harff v. Kerkorian—Standing of Convertible Holders in Delaware, 1 J.Corp.L. 413 (1976).

The reason that creditors do not have standing to bring derivative suits is that they are not the owners of the corporation. The theory appears to be based on two major premises. First, the perspective of creditors is different from that of stockholders; because creditors are more risk-averse, they are more likely to challenge management decisions which might be properly considered as within an acceptable range of business risks. Second, creditors can negotiate contractual provisions restricting managers' discretion and thus do not need the added protection of the derivative suit. Only when the corporation has become insolvent or if a director has acted with an intent to defraud the creditor have courts been willing to permit a creditor to maintain a derivative suit.

Some commentators have argued for a more relaxed rule. See Lawrence E. Mitchell, The Fairness Rights of Bondholders, 65 N.Y.U. L. Rev. 1165 (1990); Morey McDaniel, Bondholders and Stockholders, 14 J. Corp. L. 205 (1988); Morey McDaniel, Bondholders and Corporate Governance, 41 Bus.Law. 413 (1986); Note, Creditors' Derivative Suits on Behalf of Solvent Corporations, 88 Yale L.J. 1299 (1979). These writers note that while large creditors may be able to protect themselves contractually against an increased risk of default arising after the loan has been made, smaller creditors often do not have the economic leverage to negotiate such protection. Moreover, as the indenture protecting the creditor has become more stylized, it has become increasingly difficult for even large creditors to obtain the protections they might need. McDaniel notes that the distinction between creditor and shareholder has become blurred with the creation of an increasing number of hybrid securities and low grade bonds which resemble equity. He contends that the difference between shareholders and bondholders is no longer in the ownership of the corporation but in the amount of risk each assumes in supplying needed amounts of capital. He also argues that directors should have fiduciary duties to creditors and that creditors should have standing to bring a derivative suit where stockholder action is unlikely to occur or it is necessary to provide adequate protection to creditors. Whatever the theoretical force of these arguments, courts have almost universally rejected them. See, e.g., Metropolitan Life Insurance Co. v. RJR Nabisco, Inc., 716 F.Supp. 1504 (S.D.N.Y.1989); Simons v. Cogan, 542 A.2d 785 (Del.Ch.1987), aff'd 549 A.2d 300 (Del.1988); Katz v. Oak Industries, 508 A.2d 873 (Del.Ch.1986). For the argument that these cases misunderstand the nature of the indenture and the contracting process, see Martin Riger, The Trust Indenture as Bargained Contract: The Persistence of Myth, 16 J. Corp. Law 211 (1991).

As with other aspects of the standing question, whether creditors should have standing may turn on the purpose of the derivative suit. Creditors are particularly well suited to monitor corporate management. Moreover, because derivative suits often are motivated by the economic incentives of plaintiff's counsel, there might not be a large risk of an increase in frivolous suits if creditors were permitted to sue. On the other hand, as the ALI has noted in rejecting creditor standing, the interests of creditors generally depart substantially from those of shareholders and the possibility of "creditor suits based on broad concepts of fiduciary duty might chill the board's willingness to accept desirable business risks." ALI, Principles of Corporate Governance (1994), § 7.02, Reporter's Note 2. For an extensive bibliography on the rights of bondholders, see Victor Brudney and William W. Bratton, Brudney and Chirelstein's Corporate Finance: Cases and Materials (4th ed. 1993), 225.

4. Contemporaneous Ownership

Many jurisdictions require that the plaintiff have been a shareholder at the time of the wrong complained of or that she acquired her shares by operation of law from such a person. RMBCA § 7.40(a); F.R.C.P. 23.1; N.Y.B.C.L. § 626. This requirement ensures that the plaintiff acting on the corporation's behalf actually have suffered some form of economic harm. Were there no such requirement, a person could purchase her stock at a price which reflected the harm already done to the corporation and, if the suit succeeded, receive a windfall through the corporation's recovery of damages. Thus, in *Bangor Punta* (which the Court analyzed as if it were a derivative suit), the Court found that the plaintiff-shareholder had no standing because it had received what it had bargained for and was not entitled to a windfall recovery of damages, although there were minority shareholders of the railroad who were owners at the time of the wrong. Bear in mind that the main purpose of the contemporaneous ownership requirement is to prevent persons from "buying lawsuits."

Some jurisdictions have relaxed the strict contemporaneous ownership requirement. California permits a suit if "there is a strong prima facie case in favor of the claim asserted on behalf of the corporation * * * [and] the plaintiff acquired the shares before there was disclosure to the public or to the plaintiff of the wrongdoing of which plaintiff complains" and certain other criteria are satisfied. Cal.Corp.Code § 800(b)(1)(1977). See also Pa. Bus. Corp. Law § 1516 (Purdon 1967) and ALI, Principles of Corporate Governance (1994), § 7.02(a)(1). Where the security is publicly traded, the harm to the corporation has not been reflected in the stock price until there has been public disclosure of the alleged wrongdoing. Hence, permitting a person who purchased after the wrongdoing but before its public disclosure will not do violence to the basic rationale of the contemporaneous ownership requirement.

Some courts also have permitted suit when the plaintiff could show that the original misconduct had a continuing effect on the corporation and hence on the value of the shares. The cases are not clear, however, on what constitutes a continuing effect or when the so-called "continuing wrong" doctrine should apply. In Nickson v. Filtrol Corp., 262 A.2d 267 (Del.Ch.1970), the corporation's managers caused the corporation to purchase certain bonds before the plaintiff became a shareholder. The court rejected plaintiff's argument that the purchase price was unfair and that the retention of the bonds continued the wrong which had occurred through the purchase. The court held that the only actionable wrong was the purchase of the bonds and reasoned that were the retention also to be actionable, the contemporaneous ownership requirement would be eviscerated.

Not all courts have reached the same result. In Forbes v. Wells Beach Casino, Inc., 307 A.2d 210 (Me.1973), plaintiff was denied a contractual right to purchase property from a corporation, a right which he claimed was improperly diverted to the defendant at a price below plaintiff's bid. As in Nickson, the defendant retained the property. Plaintiff then bought stock in the corporation and brought a derivative suit for the loss to the corporation. The court held that under the "continuing wrong" doctrine, a plaintiff who purchased shares after a wrongful taking of property but remained a shareholder while the wrongful holding continued was not barred from bringing suit. Similarly, in Palmer v. Morris, 316 F.2d 649 (5th Cir.1963), the "continuing wrong" theory prevented dismissal of a derivative suit which challenged a contract entered into prior to the shareholder's purchase of stock but under which payments were still being made. The attack was not against the initial transaction but against the current payments.

The "continuing wrong" doctrine is difficult to understand conceptually. In order to recover, the plaintiff must attack the original transaction but she is not permitted to recover for any part of that transaction which occurred before she acquired her stock. If she acquired her shares at a price which has discounted the harm of the original transaction, why should she be permitted to challenge that transaction? If not, why should she be able to challenge its subsequent effects? After all, any plaintiff lacking standing to challenge the original misconduct can always argue that it has had some continuing effect.

5. *Continuing Interest*

Either directly or by implication from the applicable statute, many jurisdictions require that the plaintiff maintain an interest in her shares throughout the litigation. Thus, although F.R.C.P. 23.1 does not explicitly require a continuing interest, courts have inferred the requirement from the provision that "a derivative action may not be maintained if it appears that the plaintiff does not fairly and adequately represent the interests of the shareholders * * * similarly situated in enforcing the rights of the corporation." A continuing interest is required to protect against the possibility that a plaintiff (and her attorney) who can no longer benefit from a corporate recovery might have an incentive to accept a low settlement or to prosecute the litigation less vigorously. See Lewis v. Chiles, 719 F.2d 1044 (9th Cir.1983).

The issue often arises when shareholders attempt to assert a claim on behalf of a corporation which has been merged out of existence or on behalf of the surviving corporation. In Basch v. Talley Industries, Inc., 53 F.R.D. 9 (S.D.N.Y.1971), the court, applying Delaware law, found that the merged corporation and its shareholders lost their capacity to sue on behalf of the original corporation. By virtue of the merger, the original corporation's rights, privileges and identity were merged into the surviving corporation. However, where a corporation sold its assets to another corporation and subsequently dissolved, the shareholders were found to have standing to sue the erstwhile directors of their now dissolved corporation. Independent Investor Protective League v. Time, Inc., 50 N.Y.2d 259, 428 N.Y.S.2d 671, 406 N.E.2d 486 (1980). The difference in result appears to turn on the statutory provision applicable to the underlying transaction. The New York statute governing dissolution recognizes that shareholders in a dissolved corporation have a continuing interest in securing the full benefits of the dissolution. By contrast, merger statutes provide that the rights of the merged corporation are transferred to the surviving corporation by operation of law. Recall the analysis in Chapter 12. Is the distinction between the two cases sensible if there is no economic significance to the choice of form of the transaction?

In Alford v. Shaw, 327 N.C. 526, 398 S.E.2d 445 (1990), defendants argued that plaintiffs lost standing to sue because the corporation on whose behalf they had been suing had merged into another corporation. The North Carolina court rejected this argument, noting that nothing in the statute requires that plaintiffs remain shareholders after the suit has been brought. The court also found that the facts of the case, involving a challenge to the conduct surroundings the merger itself, permitted an equitable exception to the continuous ownership principle. Thus the court held that "under these facts, * * * if in the course of a shareholder derivative suit defendants' actions terminate the plaintiffs' shareholder status and these actions are closely related to the grounds for the derivative suit, the plaintiffs would retain standing to continue prosecution of the suit they initiated. To hold otherwise, that is to hold that a merged corporation or its shareholders loses standing to sue in a situation in which the allegedly wrongful activities of the defendants forced the plaintiffs to lose their status would be highly inequitable." 398 S.E.2d at 451–52.

In Blasband v. Rales, 971 F.2d 1034 (3d Cir.1992), the plaintiff was a stockholder in Easco Hand Tools, Inc. which merged with Danaher Corp., becoming its wholly-owned subsidiary. Easco shareholders, including the plaintiff, received Danaher stock in the merger as consideration for their Easco stock. The plaintiff filed a derivative suit on Easco's behalf, alleging that an investment that Easco had made in junk bonds prior to the merger constituted a breach of the directors' fiduciary duty to the Easco shareholders. The Third Circuit reversed the district court's holding that the plaintiff did not have standing to sue because he no longer owned shares in Easco. The court compared the case to a double derivative suit. It reasoned that if a subsidiary is harmed, its parent company is also harmed and is entitled to seek relief. Easco's cause of action against its directors for the junk bond transaction passed to Danaher with the merger. As a shareholder in the parent company, Danaher, Blasband retained an indirect economic interest in its subsidiary, Easco. This interest gave him standing to sue derivatively on Easco's behalf if both boards failed to pursue the claim. If Blasband had received shares in the post-merger Easco, he would have retained standing to file a derivative suit on its behalf. The fact that he received shares in its parent company instead was deemed irrelevant to his standing.

The ALI would permit a suit to be maintained where the plaintiff's interest has been involuntarily eliminated through a cash-out merger or other similar technique after the suit has been brought or where no shareholder of the surviving corporation can assert the corporate claim. In the latter situation, the ALI would permit a contemporaneous owner of the merged corporation who has been eliminated voluntarily to bring suit rather than have the right be forfeited. ALI, Principles of Corporate Governance (1994), § 7.02(a)(2).

6. *Auctioning Derivative Suits*

If one accepts the deterrence rationale, a derivative suit should be brought by the party with the greatest incentive to litigate the case fully. One proposal that would expand the class of persons who could bring a derivative suit is to auction the right to pursue such suits to the highest bidder. See Jonathan R. Macey and Geoffrey P. Miller, The Plaintiff's Attorney's Role in Class Action and Derivative Litigation: Economic Analysis and Recommendations for Reform, 58 U. Chi. L. Rev. 1 (1991). An auction is an attractive alternative if the judge finds that: 1) there is a large number of claimants, each with a small amount at stake so that none individually has the incentive to litigate; 2) multiple lawsuits have been filed, so that their consolidation would increase efficiency; 3) the claims are similar enough to be combined into a single lawsuit; and 4) the case does not necessitate active participation by the class members, so that the winning bidder can assume control of the suit completely and litigate it effectively.

After deciding that an auction is appropriate for a particular case, the judge has the task of defining the claim, although this definition remains subject to later amendment. After appropriate notice, the highest sealed bid that meets a preset minimum is awarded the right to pursue the suit. The class members need not be involved after this stage; the winning bidder will simply litigate in the name of a "Jane Doe" or "Richard Roe" plaintiff. The attorney who filed the claim initially will be compensated for her services from this bid amount, even though she surrenders all rights in the suit to the winning bidder. The defendant is allowed to bid; if she wins the auction, the case is essentially over. If another party wins, the case continues much as any other.

The proposal to auction derivative lawsuits is not without drawbacks, as Macey and Miller acknowledge. Prior to bids being made, the claim itself needs to be defined precisely to establish claim preclusion. The trial court overseeing the auction will be allowed to order limited discovery of the defendant, both to define the claim and enable the potential purchasers to ascertain exactly for what they are bidding. Macey and Miller admit that the uncertainty surrounding the claim might discount the value of the suit. An auction is not feasible if the plaintiffs seek injunctive rather than monetary relief; for example, no one will bid to ensure that civil rights are enforced. Additionally, a possibility exists that bidders will collude to manipulate the bidding process and keep the price of the suit artificially low. Ethics and the threat of disbarment, however, should prevent such collusion. Courts will need to develop new procedures for ensuring that all members of the plaintiff class cooperate with the auction winner in the suit and that all potential claims are consolidated in a single case.

Perhaps the largest obstacle to the auction proposal is finding enough bidders who will compete to ensure a sufficiently high price. The potentially huge recoveries will attract bidders with large financial resources to the auctions. As a solution to the limited class of bidders with the financial resources to bid on these claims, Macey and Miller argue that *anyone* should be allowed to bid. including venture capitalists, investors, limited partnerships or even the corporation itself. As the auction system develops, the authors suggest that specialized financial arrangements will be created to provide enough bidders to keep the auction prices sufficiently high to reflect the suits' value. As an alternative, if not enough financing appears, Macey and Miller propose that courts auction the litigation rights to these suits, rather than the claim itself, to the lawyer who will pursue the case for the lowest percentage of the recovery. This alternative, however, reintroduces agency costs; lawyers will once again have an incentive to settle cases prematurely to assure themselves of at least some fees. For an argument that auctions will not necessarily result in the highest possible price for the claim because bidders will recognize the superior position and greater information possessed by the defendant and discount their bids, see Randall S. Thomas and Robert G. Hansen, Auctioning Class Action and Derivative Lawsuits: A Critical Analysis, 87 Nw. L. Rev. 423 (1993); see also Jonathan R. Macey and Geoffrey P. Miller, Auctioning Class Action and Derivative Suits: A Rejoinder, 87 Nw. L. Rev. 458 (1993).

E. INTERNAL CORPORATE PROCEDURES

Directors, not shareholders, manage the corporation. Certainly individual, self-appointed shareholder-plaintiffs do not manage the corporation. Generally, courts will not interfere in a decision by a board of directors that establishes or carries out corporate policy. This doctrine of noninterference stems from the business judgment rule, which carries with it a presumption of reasonableness. Decisions to litigate are managerial judgments, at least as the norm. In recognition of the fact that derivative suits depart from this norm, courts and legislatures require shareholders to exhaust their intra-corporate remedies before bringing suit on behalf of the corporation. This requirement acknowledges, in effect, the practical reality that litigation is both time-consuming and expensive and that it is socially desirable to seek alternative methods for redressing wrongs allegedly committed against the corporation. Moreover, it recognizes that given the incentives to initiate derivative suits, there is a risk that frivolous and wasteful suits will be brought. A need exists to screen out frivolous suits and permit the meritorious ones to proceed. The problem is in finding a screening device with the right mesh.

All jurisdictions require, as a condition to bringing a shareholder derivative suit, that the plaintiff make a demand on directors to take appropriate corrective action to remedy alleged misconduct. A few jurisdictions require that demand also be made on shareholders. Demand has been described as a substantive right of the corporation, and not simply a procedural prerequisite. Haber v. Bell, 465 A.2d 353, 357 (Del.Ch.1983), Cottle v. Hilton Hotels Corp., 635 F.Supp. 1094, 1097 (N.D.Ill.1986). However, the necessity for demand is stated as a pleading requirement, in both F.R.C.P. 23.1, and state corporation laws. See, e.g., RMBCA § 7.40(b). Most jurisdictions excuse such demand if it would be "futile." The requirement for demand on directors is rarely explicit; rather, the plaintiff must *plead* that demand has been made or specifically state why demand would be futile. From this requirement, two questions arise. Under what circumstances is demand "futile?" If a board of directors rejects demand, may the suit proceed nonetheless?

These questions focus on the function of demand. Courts have often stated that the purpose of demand is to bring allegations of wrongdoing to the attention of the board and allow the directors an opportunity to take corrective action. However, as a practical matter, the claims described in the demand are almost always well-known to the directors and their prior and continuing silence or inaction bespeaks their attitude about the possible suit. Demand would seem to serve mainly as a warning that the suit is about to be brought. Plaintiffs' counsel is anxious to file the suit quickly because delay only serves the defendants' interests. Moreover, counsel wishes to act before other similar suits are filed, in order to strengthen her claim to be lead counsel.

The demand requirement has become increasingly controversial in the past two decades. Plaintiffs assert that demand is an extraneous procedural hurdle that allows defendant directors to shield their misdeeds behind the business judgment rule. Defendants argue that the process of considering demand amounts to a corporate decision on the merits and wisdom of the litigation. They contend that this process is an important aspect of the board's governance role, to be respected by courts as any other business decision, to be left undisturbed unless the decision was clearly wrongful.

1. DEMAND ON DIRECTORS

ARONSON v. LEWIS
473 A.2d 805 (Del.1984).

MOORE, JUSTICE:

[W]hen is a stockholder's demand upon a board of directors, to redress an alleged wrong to the corporation, excused as futile prior to the filing of a derivative suit? We granted this interlocutory appeal to the defendants, Meyers Parking System, Inc. (Meyers), a Delaware corporation, and its directors, to review the Court of Chancery's denial of their motion to dismiss this action, pursuant to Chancery Rule 23.1, for the plaintiff's failure to make such a demand or otherwise demonstrate its futility. The Vice Chancellor ruled that plaintiff's allegations raised a "reasonable inference" that the directors' action was unprotected by the business judgment rule. Thus, the board could not have impartially considered and acted upon the demand. See Lewis v. Aronson, Del.Ch., 466 A.2d 375, 381 (1983).

We cannot agree with this formulation of the concept of demand futility. In our view demand can only be excused where facts are alleged with particularity which create a reasonable doubt that the directors' action was entitled to the protections of the business judgment rule. Because the plaintiff failed to make a demand, and to allege facts with particularity indicating that such demand would be futile, we reverse the Court of Chancery and remand with instructions that plaintiff be granted leave to amend the complaint.

II.

The issues of demand futility rest upon the allegations of the complaint. The plaintiff, Harry Lewis, is a stockholder of Meyers. The defendants are Meyers and its ten directors, some of whom are also company officers.

In 1979, Prudential Building Maintenance Corp. (Prudential) spun off its shares of Meyers to Prudential's stockholders. Prior thereto Meyers was a wholly owned subsidiary of Prudential. Meyers provides parking lot facilities and related services throughout the country. Its stock is actively traded over-the-counter.

This suit challenges certain transactions between Meyers and one of its directors, Leo Fink, who owns 47% of its outstanding stock. Plaintiff claims that these transactions were approved only because Fink personally selected each director and officer of Meyers.

Prior to January 1, 1981, Fink had an employment agreement with Prudential which provided that upon retirement he was to become a consultant to that company for ten years. This provision became operable when Fink retired in April 1980. Thereafter, Meyers agreed with Prudential to share Fink's consulting services and reimburse Prudential for 25% of the fees paid Fink. Under this arrangement Meyers paid Prudential $48,332 in 1980 and $45,832 in 1981.

On January 1, 1981, the defendants approved an employment agreement between Meyers and Fink for a five year term with provision for automatic renewal each year thereafter, indefinitely. Meyers agreed to pay Fink $150,000 per year, plus a bonus of 5% of its pre-tax profits over $2,400,000. Fink could terminate the contract at any time, but Meyers could do so only upon six months' notice. At termination, Fink was to become a consultant to Meyers and be paid $150,000 per year for the first three years, $125,000 for the next three years, and $100,000 thereafter for life. Death benefits were also included. Fink agreed to devote his best efforts and substantially his entire business time to advancing Meyers' interests. The agreement also provided that Fink's compensation was not to be affected by any inability to perform services on Meyers' behalf. Fink was 75 years old when his employment agreement with Meyers was approved by the directors. There is no claim that he was, or is, in poor health.

Additionally, the Meyers board approved and made interest-free loans to Fink totalling $225,000. These loans were unpaid and outstanding as of August 1982 when the complaint was filed. At oral argument defendants' counsel represented that these loans had been repaid in full.

The complaint charges that these transactions had "no valid business purpose", and were a "waste of corporate assets" because the amounts to be paid are "grossly excessive", that Fink performs "no or little services", and because of his "advanced age" cannot be "expected to perform any such services". The plaintiff also charges that the existence of the Prudential consulting agreement with Fink prevents him from providing his "best efforts" on Meyers' behalf. Finally, it is alleged that the loans to Fink were in reality "additional compensation" without any "consideration" or "benefit" to Meyers.

The complaint alleged that no demand had been made on the Meyers board because:

13. * * * such attempt would be futile for the following reasons:

(a) All of the directors in office are named as defendants herein and they have participated in, expressly approved and/or acquiesced in, and are personally liable for, the wrongs complained of herein.

(b) Defendant Fink, having selected each director, controls and dominates every member of the Board and every officer of Meyers.

(c) Institution of this action by present directors would require the defendant-directors to sue themselves, thereby placing the conduct of this action in hostile hands and preventing its effective prosecution.

Complaint, at 13.

The relief sought included the cancellation of the Meyers–Fink employment contract and an accounting by the directors, including Fink, for all damage sustained by Meyers and for all profits derived by the directors and Fink. * * *

V.

A.

A cardinal precept of the General Corporation Law of the State of Delaware is that directors, rather than shareholders, manage the business and affairs of the corporation. 8 Del.C. § 141(a). Section 141(a) states in pertinent part:

"The *business and affairs* of a corporation organized under this chapter *shall be managed by or under the direction* of a board of directors except as may be otherwise provided in this chapter or in its certificate of incorporation."

8 Del.C. § 141(a) (Emphasis added). The existence and exercise of this power carries with it certain fundamental fiduciary obligations to the corporation and its shareholders. Moreover, a stockholder is not powerless to challenge director action which results in harm to the corporation. The machinery of corporate democracy and the derivative suit are potent tools to redress the conduct of a torpid or unfaithful management. The derivative action developed in equity to enable shareholders to sue in the corporation's name where those in control of the company refused to assert a claim belonging to it. The nature of the action is two-fold. First, it is the equivalent of a suit by the shareholders to compel the corporation to sue. Second, it is a suit by the corporation, asserted by the shareholders on its behalf, against those liable to it.

By its very nature the derivative action impinges on the managerial freedom of directors. Hence, the demand requirement of Chancery Rule 23.1 exists at the threshold, first to insure that a stockholder exhausts his intracorporate remedies, and then to provide a safeguard against strike suits. Thus, by promoting this form of alternate dispute resolution, rather than immediate recourse to litigation, the demand requirement is a recognition of the fundamental precept that directors manage the business and affairs of corporations.

In our view the entire question of demand futility is inextricably bound to issues of business judgment and the standards of that doctrine's applicability. The business judgment rule is an acknowledgment of the managerial prerogatives of Delaware directors under Section 141(a). It is a presumption that in making a business decision the directors of a corporation acted on an informed basis, in good faith and in the honest belief that the action taken was in the best interests of the company. Absent an abuse of discretion, that judgment will be respected by the courts. The burden is on the party challenging the decision to establish facts rebutting the presumption.

The function of the business judgment rule is of paramount significance in the context of a derivative action. It comes into play in several ways—in addressing a demand, in the determination of demand futility, in efforts by independent disinterested directors to dismiss the action as inimical to the corporation's best interests, and generally, as a defense to the merits of the suit. However, in each of these circumstances there are certain common principles governing the application and operation of the rule.

First, its protections can only be claimed by disinterested directors whose conduct otherwise meets the tests of business judgment. From the standpoint of interest, this means that directors can neither appear on both sides of a transaction nor expect to derive any personal financial benefit from it in the sense of self-dealing, as opposed to a benefit which devolves upon the corporation or all stockholders generally. Sinclair Oil Corp. v. Levien, Del.Supr., 280 A.2d 717, 720 (1971); Cheff v. Mathes, Del.Supr., 199 A.2d 548, 554 (1964). See also 8 Del.C. § 144. Thus, if such director interest is present, and the transaction is not approved by a majority consisting of the disinterested directors, then the business judgment rule has no application whatever in determining demand futility. See 8 Del.C. § 144(a)(1).

Second, to invoke the rule's protection directors have a duty to inform themselves, prior to making a business decision, of all material information reasonably available to them. Having become so informed, they must then act with requisite care in the discharge of their duties. While the Delaware cases use a variety of terms to describe the applicable standard of care, our analysis satisfies us that under the business judgment rule director liability is predicated upon concepts of gross negligence.

However, it should be noted that the business judgment rule operates only in the context of director action. Technically speaking, it has no role where directors have either abdicated their functions, or absent a conscious decision, failed to act. But it also follows that under applicable principles, a conscious decision to refrain from acting may nonetheless be a valid exercise of business judgment and enjoy the protections of the rule. * * *

Delaware courts have addressed the issue of demand futility on several earlier occasions. * * * The rule emerging from these decisions is that where officers and directors are under an influence which sterilizes their discretion, they cannot be considered proper persons to conduct litigation on behalf of the corporation. Thus, demand would be futile.

However, those cases cannot be taken to mean that any board approval of a challenged transaction automatically connotes "hostile interest" and "guilty participation" by directors, or some other form of sterilizing influence upon them. Were that so, the demand requirements of our law would be meaningless, leaving the clear mandate of Chancery Rule 23.1 devoid of its purpose and substance.

The trial court correctly recognized that demand futility is inextricably bound to issues of business judgment, but stated the test to be based on allegations of fact, which, if true, "show that there is a reasonable inference" the business judgment rule is not applicable for purposes of a pre-suit demand.

The problem with this formulation is the concept of reasonable inferences to be drawn against a board of directors based on allegations in a complaint. As is clear from this case, and the conclusory allegations upon which the Vice Chancellor relied, demand futility becomes virtually automatic under such a test. Bearing in mind the presumptions with which director action is cloaked, we believe that the matter must be approached in a more balanced way.

Our view is that in determining demand futility the Court of Chancery in the proper exercise of its discretion must decide whether, under the particularized facts alleged, a reasonable doubt is created that: (1) the directors are disinterested and independent and (2) the challenged transaction was otherwise the product of a valid exercise of business judgment. Hence, the Court of Chancery must make two inquiries, one into the independence and disinterestedness of the directors and the other into the substantive nature of the challenged transaction and the board's approval thereof. As to the latter inquiry the court does not assume that the transaction is a wrong to the corporation requiring corrective steps by the board. Rather, the alleged wrong is substantively reviewed against the factual background alleged in the complaint. As to the former inquiry, directorial independence and disinterestedness, the court reviews the factual allegations to decide whether they raise a reasonable doubt, as a threshold matter, that the protections of the business judgment rule are available to the board. Certainly, if this is an "interested" director transaction, such that the business judgment rule is inapplicable to the board majority approving the transaction, then the inquiry ceases. In that event futility of

demand has been established by any objective or subjective standard.[8]
* * *

However, the mere threat of personal liability for approving a questioned transaction, standing alone, is insufficient to challenge either the independence or disinterestedness of directors, although in rare cases a transaction may be so egregious on its face that board approval cannot meet the test of business judgment, and a substantial likelihood of director liability therefore exists. In sum the entire review is factual in nature. The Court of Chancery in the exercise of its sound discretion must be satisfied that a plaintiff has alleged facts with particularity which, taken as true, support a reasonable doubt that the challenged transaction was the product of a valid exercise of business judgment. Only in that context is demand excused.

B.

Having outlined the legal framework within which these issues are to be determined, we consider plaintiff's claims of futility here: Fink's domination and control of the directors, board approval of the Fink–Meyers employment agreement, and board hostility to the plaintiff's derivative action due to the directors' status as defendants.

Plaintiff's claim that Fink dominates and controls the Meyers' board is based on: (1) Fink's 47% ownership of Meyers' outstanding stock, and (2) that he "personally selected" each Meyers director. Plaintiff also alleges that mere approval of the employment agreement illustrates Fink's domination and control of the board. In addition, plaintiff argued on appeal that 47% stock ownership, though less than a majority, constituted control given the large number of shares outstanding, 1,245,-745.

Such contentions do not support any claim under Delaware law that these directors lack independence. In Kaplan v. Centex Corp., Del.Ch., 284 A.2d 119 (1971), the Court of Chancery stated that "[s]tock ownership alone, at least when it amounts to less than a majority, is not sufficient proof of domination or control". *Id.* at 123. Moreover, in the demand context even proof of majority ownership of a company does not strip the directors of the presumptions of independence, and that their acts have been taken in good faith and in the best interests of the corporation. There must be coupled with the allegation of control such facts as would demonstrate that through personal or other relationships the directors are beholden to the controlling person. To date the principal decisions dealing with the issue of control or domination arose only after a full trial on the merits. Thus, they are distinguishable in

---

8. We recognize that drawing the line at a majority of the board may be an arguably arbitrary dividing point. Critics will charge that we are ignoring the structural bias common to corporate boards throughout America, as well as the other unseen socialization processes cutting against independent discussion and decisionmaking in the boardroom. The difficulty with structural bias in a demand futile case is simply one of establishing it in the complaint for purposes of Rule 23.1. We are satisfied that discretionary review by the Court of Chancery of complaints alleging specific facts pointing to bias on a particular board will be sufficient for determining demand futility.

the demand context unless similar particularized facts are alleged to meet the test of Chancery Rule 23.1. * * *

The requirement of director independence inheres in the conception and rationale of the business judgment rule. The presumption of propriety that flows from an exercise of business judgment is based in part on this unyielding precept. Independence means that a director's decision is based on the corporate merits of the subject before the board rather than extraneous considerations or influences. While directors may confer, debate, and resolve their differences through compromise, or by reasonable reliance upon the expertise of their colleagues and other qualified persons, the end result, nonetheless, must be that each director has brought his or her own informed business judgment to bear with specificity upon the corporate merits of the issues without regard for or succumbing to influences which convert an otherwise valid business decision into a faithless act.

Thus, it is not enough to charge that a director was nominated by or elected at the behest of those controlling the outcome of a corporate election. That is the usual way a person becomes a corporate director. It is the care, attention and sense of individual responsibility to the performance of one's duties, not the method of election, that generally touches on independence.

We conclude that in the demand-futile context a plaintiff charging domination and control of one or more directors must allege particularized facts manifesting "a direction of corporate conduct in such a way as to comport with the wishes or interests of the corporation (or persons) doing the controlling". *Kaplan,* 284 A.2d at 123. The shorthand shibboleth of "dominated and controlled directors" is insufficient. In recognizing that *Kaplan* was decided after trial and full discovery, we stress that the plaintiff need only allege specific facts; he need not plead evidence. Otherwise, he would be forced to make allegations which may not comport with his duties under Chancery Rule 11.

Here, plaintiff has not alleged any facts sufficient to support a claim of control. The personal-selection-of-directors allegation stands alone, unsupported. At best it is a conclusion devoid of factual support. The causal link between Fink's control and approval of the employment agreement is alluded to, but nowhere specified. The director's approval, alone, does not establish control, even in the face of Fink's 47% stock ownership. The claim that Fink is unlikely to perform any services under the agreement, because of his age, and his conflicting consultant work with Prudential, adds nothing to the control claim. Therefore, we cannot conclude that the complaint factually particularizes any circumstances of control and domination to overcome the presumption of board independence, and thus render the demand futile.

C.

Turning to the board's approval of the Meyers–Fink employment agreement, plaintiff's argument is simple: all of the Meyers directors are named defendants, because they approved the wasteful agreement; if plaintiff prevails on the merits all the directors will be jointly and severally liable; therefore, the directors' interest in avoiding personal liability automatically and absolutely disqualifies them from passing on a shareholder's demand.

Such allegations are conclusory at best. In Delaware mere directorial approval of a transaction, absent particularized facts supporting a breach of fiduciary duty claim, or otherwise establishing the lack of independence or disinterestedness of a majority of the directors, is insufficient to excuse demand. Here, plaintiff's suit is premised on the notion that the Meyers–Fink employment agreement was a waste of corporate assets. So, the argument goes, by approving such waste the directors now face potential personal liability, thereby rendering futile any demand on them to bring suit. Unfortunately, plaintiff's claim fails in its initial premise. The complaint does not allege particularized facts indicating that the agreement is a waste of corporate assets. Indeed, the complaint as now drafted may not even state a cause of action, given the directors' broad corporate power to fix the compensation of officers.

In essence, the plaintiff alleged a lack of consideration flowing from Fink to Meyers, since the employment agreement provided that compensation was not contingent on Fink's ability to perform any services. The bare assertion that Fink performed "little or no services" was plaintiff's conclusion based solely on Fink's age and the *existence* of the Fink–Prudential employment agreement. As for Meyers' loans to Fink, beyond the bare allegation that they were made, the complaint does not allege facts indicating the wastefulness of such arrangements. Again, the mere existence of such loans, given the broad corporate powers conferred by Delaware law, does not even state a claim.

In sustaining plaintiff's claim of demand futility the trial court relied on Fidanque v. American Maracaibo Co., Del.Ch., 92 A.2d 311, 321 (1952), which held that a contract providing for payment of consulting fees to a retired president/director was a waste of corporate assets. *Id.* In *Fidanque,* the court found after trial that the contract and payments were in reality compensation for past services. *Id.* at 320. This was based upon facts not present here: the former president/director was a 70 year old stroke victim, neither the agreement nor the record spelled out his consulting duties at all, the consulting salary equalled the individual's salary when he was president and general manager of the corporation, and the contract was silent as to continued employment in the event that the retired president/director again became incapacitated and unable to perform his duties. *Id.* at 320–21. Contrasting the facts of *Fidanque* with the complaint here, it is apparent that plaintiff has not alleged facts sufficient to render demand futile on a charge of corporate waste, and thus create a reasonable doubt that the board's action is protected by the business judgment rule.

D.

Plaintiff's final argument is the incantation that demand is excused because the directors otherwise would have to sue themselves, thereby placing the conduct of the litigation in hostile hands and preventing its effective prosecution. This bootstrap argument has been made to and dismissed by other courts. Its acceptance would effectively abrogate Rule 23.1 and weaken the managerial power of directors. Unless facts are alleged with particularity to overcome the presumptions of independence and a proper exercise of business judgment, in which case the directors could not be expected to sue themselves, a bare claim of this sort raises no legally cognizable issue under Delaware corporate law.

VI.

In sum, we conclude that the plaintiff has failed to allege facts with particularity indicating that the Meyers directors were tainted by interest, lacked independence, or took action contrary to Meyers' best interests in order to create a reasonable doubt as to the applicability of the business judgment rule. Only in the presence of such a reasonable doubt may a demand be deemed futile, hence, we reverse the Court of Chancery's denial of the motion to dismiss, and remand with instructions that plaintiff be granted leave to amend his complaint to bring it into compliance with Rule 23.1 based on the principles we have announced today.

* * *

Reversed and remanded.

RALES v. BLASBAND
Cite as, Del.Supr., 634 A.2d 927 (1993)

VEASEY, CHIEF JUSTICE:

This certified question of law comes before the Court pursuant to Article IV, Section 11(9) of the Delaware Constitution and Supreme Court Rule 41. The question of law was certified by the United States District Court for the District of Delaware (the "District Court"), and was accepted by this Court on June 16, 1993.

The underlying action pending in the District Court is a stockholder derivative action filed on March 25, 1991, by Alfred Blasband ("Blasband") on behalf of Danaher Corporation, a Delaware corporation ("Danaher"). Following Blasband's filing of an amended complaint (the "amended complaint"), the defendants filed a motion to dismiss and moved to certify the following question of law to this Court:

> In the context of this novel action, which is neither a simple derivative suit nor a double derivative suit, but which the United States Court of Appeals for the Third Circuit describes as a "first cousin to a double derivative suit," has plaintiff Alfred Blasband, in accordance with the substantive law of the State of Delaware, alleged facts to show that demand is excused on the board of directors of Danaher Corporation, a Delaware corporation?

After consideration of the allegations of the amended complaint, the briefs, and the oral argument of the parties in this Court, it is our conclusion that the certified question must be answered in the affirmative. Because the amended complaint does not challenge a decision of the board of directors of Danaher (the "Board"), the test enunciated in *Aronson v. Lewis,* Del.Supr., 473 A.2d 805 (1984) is not implicated. In the unusual context of this case, demand on the Board is excused because the amended complaint alleges particularized facts creating a reasonable doubt that a majority of the Board would be disinterested or independent in making a decision on a demand.

I. FACTS

Blasband is currently a stockholder of Danaher. Prior to 1990 Blasband owned 1100 shares of Easco Hand Tools, Inc., a Delaware corporation ("Easco"). Easco entered into a merger agreement with Danaher in February 1990 whereby Easco became a wholly-owned subsidiary of Danaher (the "Merger").

Steven M. Rales and Mitchell P. Rales (the "Rales brothers") have been directors, officers, or stockholders of Easco and Danaher at relevant times. Prior to the merger, the Rales brothers were directors of Easco, and together owned approximately 52 percent of Easco's common stock. They continued to serve as directors of Easco after the Merger.

The Rales brothers also own approximately 44 percent of Danaher's common stock. Prior to the Merger, Mitchell Rales was President and Steven Rales was Chief Executive Officer of Danaher. The Rales brothers resigned their positions as officers of Danaher in early 1990, but continued to serve as members of the Board. The Board consists of eight members. The other six members are Danaher's President and Chief Executive Officer, George Sherman ("Sherman"), Donald E. Ehrlich ("Ehrlich"), Mortimer Caplin ("Caplin"), George D. Kellner ("Kellner"), A. Emmett Stephenson, Jr. ("Stephenson"), and Walter Lohr ("Lohr"). A number of these directors have business relationships with the Rales brothers or with entities controlled by them.

The central focus of the amended complaint is the alleged misuse by the Easco board of the proceeds of a sale of that company's 12.875% Senior Subordinated Notes due 1998 (the "Notes"). On or about September 1, 1988, Easco sold $100 million of the Notes in a public offering (the "Offering"). * * * The prospectus [for the Offering] stated that "[p]ending such uses, the Company will invest the balance of the net proceeds from this offering in government and other marketable securities which are expected to yield a lower rate of return than the rate of interest borne by the Notes."

Blasband alleges that the defendants did not invest in "government and other marketable securities," but instead used over $61.9 million of the proceeds to buy highly speculative "junk bonds" offered through Drexel Burnham Lambert Inc. ("Drexel"). Blasband alleges that these junk bonds were bought by Easco because of the Rales brothers' desire to help Drexel at a time when it was under investigation and having trouble selling such bonds. * * *

The amended complaint alleges that these investments have declined substantially in value, resulting in a loss to Easco of at least $14 million. Finally, Blasband complains that the Easco and Danaher boards of directors refused to comply with his request for information regarding the investments.

II. Scope and Standard of Review

* * *

The parties have raised a threshold issue regarding this Court's ability to consider the legal standards which are applicable to the certified question. Blasband contends that the role of this Court in responding to the certified question is limited to a mechanical application of the two-part test set forth in *Aronson*. The defendants disagree, and argue that the Court should apply a test more stringent than the *Aronson* test to protect corporations against strike suits.

* * * The certified question does not limit the issue presented to the mere application of the *Aronson* test, but instead calls upon this Court to decide whether Blasband's amended complaint establishes that demand is excused under the "substantive law of the State of Delaware." It is therefore necessary for this Court to determine what the applicable "substantive law" is before we can decide whether demand on the Board should be excused. Accordingly, the language of the question certified to this Court requires a consideration of the appropriate legal principles, including the applicability of the *Aronson* test in this unusual context, so that we may properly decide the issue presented to us.

III. The Standards for Determining Whether Demand Is Excused in This Derivative Suit

* * *

Because derivative suits challenge the propriety of decisions made by directors pursuant to their managerial authority, we have repeatedly held that the stockholder plaintiffs must overcome the powerful presumptions of the business judgment rule before they will be permitted to pursue the derivative claim. * * *

Although [the *Aronson*] standards are well-established, they cannot be applied in a vacuum. Not all derivative suits fall into the paradigm addressed by *Aronson* and its progeny. The essential predicate for the *Aronson* test is the fact that a *decision* of the board of directors is being challenged in the derivative suit. * * *

Under the unique circumstances of this case, an analysis of the Board's ability to consider a demand requires a departure here from the standards set forth in *Aronson*. The Board did not approve the transaction which is being challenged by Blasband in this action. In fact, the

Danaher directors have made no decision relating to the subject of this derivative suit. Where there is no conscious decision by directors to act or refrain from acting, the business judgment rule has no application. The absence of board action, therefore, makes it impossible to perform the essential inquiry contemplated by *Aronson*—whether the directors have acted in conformity with the business judgment rule in approving the challenged transaction.

Consistent with the context and rationale of the *Aronson* decision, a court should not apply the *Aronson* test for demand futility where the board that would be considering the demand did not make a business decision which is being challenged in the derivative suit. This situation would arise in three principal scenarios: (1) where a business decision was made by the board of a company, but a majority of the directors making the decision have been replaced;[8] (2) where the subject of the derivative suit is not a business decision of the board;[9] and (3) where, as here, the decision being challenged was made by the board of a different corporation.

Instead, it is appropriate in these situations to examine whether the board that would be addressing the demand can impartially consider its merits without being influenced by improper considerations. Thus, a court must determine whether or not the particularized factual allegations of a derivative stockholder complaint create a reasonable doubt that, as of the time the complaint is filed, the board of directors could have properly exercised its independent and disinterested business judgment in responding to a demand. If the derivative plaintiff satisfies this burden, then demand will be excused as futile.

8. This first scenario was addressed by the Court of Chancery in *Harris v. Carter,* Del.Ch., 582 A.2d 222 (1990):

In the special case, however, where there is a change in board control between the date of the challenged transaction and the date of suit, it might open the way to error to focus on the board existing at the time of the challenged transaction. What, in the end, is relevant is not whether the board that approved the challenged transaction was or was not interested in that transaction but whether the present board is or is not disabled from exercising its right and duty to control corporate litigation.

I do not consider that *Aronson* intended to determine that demand under Rule 23.1 upon an independent board that has come into existence after the time of the "challenged transaction" would be excused if the board that approved the challenged transaction did not qualify for business judgment protection.

Id. at 230 (emphasis added). Because the new board in *Harris* was not yet in place at the time of the original complaint in that case, the Court of Chancery did not need to determine how, or if, *Aronson* would apply where there was a change in the board prior to the derivative suit being filed.

9. For example, if a stockholder brings a derivative suit alleging that a third party breached a contract with the corporation, demand should not be excused simply because the subject matter of the suit—the third party's breach of contract—does not implicate the business judgment rule. Similarly, where directors are sued derivatively because they have failed to do something (such as a failure to oversee subordinates), demand should not be excused automatically in the absence of allegations demonstrating why the board is incapable of considering a demand. Indeed, requiring demand in such circumstances is consistent with the board's managerial prerogatives because it permits the board to have the opportunity to take action where it has not previously considered doing so.

In so holding, we reject the defendants' proposal that, for purposes of this derivative suit and future similar suits, we adopt either a universal demand requirement or a requirement that a plaintiff must demonstrate a reasonable probability of success on the merits. The defendants seek to justify these stringent tests on the need to discourage "strike suits" in situations like the present one. This concern is unfounded.

A plaintiff in a double derivative suit is still required to satisfy the *Aronson* test in order to establish that demand on the *subsidiary's* board is futile. The *Aronson* test was designed, in part, with the objective of preventing strike suits by requiring derivative plaintiffs to make a threshold showing, through the allegation of particularized facts, that their claims have some merit. Moreover, defendants' proposal of requiring demand on the parent board in all double derivative cases, even where a board of directors is interested, is not the appropriate protection against strike suits. While defendants' alternative suggestion of requiring a plaintiff to demonstrate a reasonable probability of success is more closely related to the prevention of strike suits, it is an extremely onerous burden to meet at the pleading stage without the benefit of discovery.[10] Because a plaintiff must satisfy the *Aronson* test in order to show that demand is excused on the subsidiary board, there is no need to create an unduly onerous test for determining demand futility on the parent board simply to protect against strike suits.

IV. WHETHER THE BOARD IS INTERESTED OR LACKS INDEPENDENCE

In order to determine whether the Board could have impartially considered a demand at the time Blasband's original complaint was filed, it is appropriate to examine the nature of the decision confronting it. A stockholder demand letter would, at a minimum, notify the directors of the nature of the alleged wrongdoing and the identities of the alleged wrongdoers. The subject of the demand in this case would be the alleged breaches of fiduciary duty by the Easco board of directors in connection with Easco's investment in Drexel "junk bonds." The alle-

---

10. Although derivative plaintiffs may believe it is difficult to meet the particularization requirement of *Aronson* because they are not entitled to discovery to assist their compliance with Rule 23.1, *see Levine,* 591 A.2d at 208–10, they have many avenues available to obtain information bearing on the subject of their claims. For example, there is a variety of public sources from which the details of a corporate act may be discovered, including the media and governmental agencies such as the Securities and Exchange Commission. In addition, a stockholder who has met the procedural requirements and has shown a specific proper purpose may use the summary procedure embodied in 8 *Del.C.* § 220 to investigate the possibility of corporate wrongdoing. *Compaq Computer Corp. v. Horton,* Del.Supr., 631 A.2d 1 (1993). *See* n. 4, *supra.* Surprisingly, little use has been made of section 220 as an information-gathering tool in the derivative context. Perhaps the problem arises in some cases out of an unseemly race to the court house, chiefly generated by the "first to file" custom seemingly permitting the winner of the race to be named lead counsel. The result has been a plethora of superficial complaints that could not be sustained. Nothing requires the Court of Chancery, or any other court having appropriate jurisdiction, to countenance this process by penalizing diligent counsel who has employed these methods, including section 220, in a deliberate and thorough manner in preparing a complaint that meets the demand excused test of *Aronson.*

gations of the amended complaint, which must be accepted as true in this procedural context, claim that the investment was made solely for the benefit of the Rales brothers, who were acting in furtherance of their business relationship with Drexel and not with regard to Easco's best interests. Such conduct, if proven, would constitute a breach of the Easco directors' duty of loyalty.

The task of a board of directors in responding to a stockholder demand letter is a two-step process. First, the directors must determine the best method to inform themselves of the facts relating to the alleged wrongdoing and the considerations, both legal and financial, bearing on a response to the demand. If a factual investigation is required, it must be conducted reasonably and in good faith. Second, the board must weigh the alternatives available to it, including the advisability of implementing internal corrective action and commencing legal proceedings. * * * In carrying out these tasks, the board must be able to act free of personal financial interest and improper extraneous influences. We now consider whether the members of the Board could have met these standards.

A. Interest

The members of the Board at the time Blasband filed his original complaint were Steven Rales, Mitchell Rales, Sherman, Ehrlich, Caplin, Kellner, Stephenson, and Lohr. The Rales brothers and Caplin were also members of the Easco board of directors at the time of the alleged wrongdoing. Blasband's amended complaint specifically accuses the Rales brothers of being the motivating force behind the investment in Drexel "junk bonds." The Board would be obligated to determine whether these charges of wrongdoing should be investigated and, if substantiated, become the subject of legal action.

A director is considered interested where he or she will receive a personal financial benefit from a transaction that is not equally shared by the stockholders. Directorial interest also exists where a corporate decision will have a materially detrimental impact on a director, but not on the corporation and the stockholders. In such circumstances, a director cannot be expected to exercise his or her independent business judgment without being influenced by the adverse personal consequences resulting from the decision.

We conclude that the Rales brothers and Caplin must be considered interested in a decision of the Board in response to a demand addressing the alleged wrongdoing described in Blasband's amended complaint. Normally, "the mere threat of personal liability for approving a questioned transaction, standing alone, is insufficient to challenge either the independence or disinterestedness of directors...." *Aronson,* 473 A.2d at 815. Nevertheless, the Third Circuit has already concluded that "Blasband has pleaded facts raising at least a reasonable doubt that the [Easco board's] use of proceeds from the Note Offering was a valid exercise of business judgment." *Blasband* I, 971 F.2d at 1052. This determination is part of the law of the case, *Blasband* II, 979 F.2d at

328, and is therefore binding on this Court. Such determination indicates that the potential for liability is not "a mere threat" but instead may rise to "a substantial likelihood." *See Aronson,* 473 A.2d at 815.

Therefore, a decision by the Board to bring suit against the Easco directors, including the Rales brothers and Caplin, could have potentially significant financial consequences for those directors. Common sense dictates that, in light of these consequences, the Rales brothers and Caplin have a disqualifying financial interest that disables them from impartially considering a response to a demand by Blasband.

B. Independence

Having determined that the Rales brothers and Caplin would be interested in a decision on Blasband's demand, we must now examine whether the remaining Danaher directors are sufficiently independent to make an impartial decision despite the fact that they are presumptively disinterested. As explained in *Aronson,* "[i]ndependence means that a director's decision is based on the corporate merits of the subject before the board rather than extraneous considerations or influences." 473 A.2d at 816. To establish lack of independence, Blasband must show that the directors are "beholden" to the Rales brothers or so under their influence that their discretion would be sterilized. *Id.* at 815; *Levine,* 591 A.2d at 205; *Kaplan v. Centex Corp.,* Del.Ch., 284 A.2d 119, 123 (1971); *Lewis v. Aronson,* Del.Ch., C.A. No. 6919, Hartnett, V.C. (May 1, 1985) (on remand) (holding that demand was excused because the plaintiff's amended complaint alleged sufficient specific facts to create a reasonable doubt regarding the board's independence because it was beholden to a 47 percent stockholder). We conclude that the amended complaint alleges particularized facts sufficient to create a reasonable doubt that Sherman and Ehrlich, as members of the Board, are capable of acting independently of the Rales brothers.

Sherman is the President and Chief Executive Officer of Danaher. His salary is approximately $1 million per year. Although Sherman's continued employment and substantial remuneration may not hinge solely on his relationship with the Rales brothers, there is little doubt that Steven Rales' position as Chairman of the Board of Danaher and Mitchell Rales' position as Chairman of its Executive Committee place them in a position to exert considerable influence over Sherman. In light of these circumstances, there is a reasonable doubt that Sherman can be expected to act independently considering his substantial financial stake in maintaining his current offices.

Ehrlich is the President of Wabash National Corp. ("Wabash"). His annual compensation is approximately $300,000 per year. Ehrlich also has two brothers who are vice presidents of Wabash. The Rales brothers are directors of Wabash and own a majority of its stock through an investment partnership they control. As a result, there is a reasonable doubt regarding Ehrlich's ability to act independently since it can be inferred that he is beholden to the Rales brothers in light of his employment.

Therefore, the amended complaint pleads particularized facts raising a reasonable doubt as to the independence of Sherman and Ehrlich. Because of their alleged substantial financial interest in maintaining their employment positions, there is a reasonable doubt that these two directors are able to consider impartially an action that is contrary to the interests of the Rales brothers.

V. Conclusion

We conclude that, under the "substantive law" of the State of Delaware, the *Aronson* test does not apply in the context of this double derivative suit because the Board was not involved in the challenged transaction. Nevertheless, we do not agree with the defendants' argument that a more stringent test should be applied to deter strike suits. Instead, the appropriate inquiry is whether Blasband's amended complaint raises a reasonable doubt regarding the ability of a majority of the Board to exercise properly its business judgment in a decision on a demand had one been made at the time this action was filed. Based on the existence of a reasonable doubt that the Rales brothers and Caplin would be free of a financial interest in such a decision, and that Sherman and Ehrlich could act independently in light of their employment with entities affiliated with the Rales brothers, we conclude that the allegations of Blasband's amended complaint establish that DEMAND IS EXCUSED on the Board. The certified question is therefore answered in the AFFIRMATIVE.

Note: The Demand Requirement

A. Post–Aronson Delaware Law on Demand Futility

1. Until *Rales*, it had generally been thought that *Aronson* created serious hurdles for plaintiffs to overcome, particularly at the pleading stage without discovery of facts that could rebut the presumption of the business judgment rule. Indeed, one important line of cases did demonstrate the difficulty of proving futility in Delaware. These cases involved derivative suits by shareholders of General Motors, to force the board to rescind a repurchase of stocks and notes from Ross Perot for $742 million. Grobow v. Perot, 526 A.2d 914 (Del.Ch.1987), aff'd 539 A.2d 180 (Del.1988); Levine v. Smith, 591 A.2d 194 (Del.1991). In *Grobow*, the plaintiffs charged that the price that General Motors paid Perot for his shares was excessive, amounting to a waste of corporate assets. They alleged that demand was futile because the repurchase was essentially an attempt by the board to entrench themselves in office and rid the board of Perot and his public criticism of their management of the company.

The trial court held that the "reasonable doubt" standard required the plaintiffs to plead particularized facts sufficient to sustain a "judicial finding" either that the directors were interested, lacked independence or failed to exercise business judgment. The court also found that the fairness of the challenged transaction was a "pivotal question" in an *Aronson* analysis. On appeal, the Delaware Supreme Court stated:

* * * The test for demand futility should be whether the well-pleaded facts of the particular complaint support a reasonable doubt of business judgment protection, not whether the facts support a judicial finding that the directors' actions are not protected by the business judgment rule.

* * * The facts necessary to support a finding of reasonable doubt either of director disinterest or independence, or whether proper business judgment was exercised in the transaction will vary with each case. Reasonable doubt must be decided by the trial court on a case-by-case basis employing an objective analysis. Were we to adopt a standard criterion * * * the test for demand excusal would, in all likelihood, become rote and inelastic.

Finally, since a Rule 23.1 motion normally precedes rather than follows discovery, a plaintiff may be able in one case and without formal discovery to plead facts sufficient to raise a reasonable doubt of business judgment protection, but be unable in another case without such discovery to plead facts sufficient to support a judicial finding of the lack of business judgment protection. On the other hand, if a derivative complaint alleges facts which would support a judicial finding of a lack of business judgment protection, then such facts would more than satisfy *Aronson*'s reasonable doubt standard.

Therefore, we decline to approve the use of a "judicial finding" standard as the minimum criterion below which presuit demand will not be excused. We think it sufficient simply to say that the Court of Chancery must weigh the presumption of the business judgment rule that attaches to a board of directors' decision against the well-pleaded facts alleged in a plaintiff's demand-futility complaint. In that respect, the suggestion in the Trial Court's Opinion that a transaction is first analyzed from the standpoint of fairness is erroneous. Fairness becomes an issue only if the presumption of the business judgment is defeated.

539 A.2d at 186–87. *Grobow* made clear also that the two-part test for determining demand futility set forth in *Aronson* is disjunctive. Id. at 186.

Thereafter, *Grobow* was consolidated with another derivative suit challenging the same repurchase, Levine v. Smith, 591 A.2d 194 (Del. 1991). Although the plaintiff in *Levine* did make demand, the Delaware Supreme Court's second opinion addresses both the "demand excused" and "demand refused" aspects of the demand requirement and contains a full exposition of the Delaware law on demand. Commenting on the circumstances that could lead to dismissal of demand as futile, the court wrote that the "premise of a shareholder claim of futility of demand is that a majority of the board of directors either has a financial interest in the challenged transaction or lacks independence or otherwise failed to exercise due care. On either showing, it may be inferred that the board is *incapable* of exercising its power and authority to pursue the derivative claims directly." Id. at 205. *Levine* essentially reaffirms prior decisions and clarifies that plaintiffs must satisfy the demand requirement without discovery, regardless of whether demand is excused or refused.

The implications of *Aronson*, *Grobow* and *Levine* for the continued efficacy of the derivative suit are profound. At one level, the decisions vest substantial power in the trial court to determine, solely on the basis of the pleadings, whether the lawsuit can be maintained. Given the standards of a business judgment rule review, plaintiffs face a high burden in drafting a complaint that will demonstrate futility. In *Grobow* and *Levine*, the court may well have viewed the litigation as an attempt to procure a settlement by keeping alive a well publicized intracorporate dispute that General Motors had already spent $750 million to resolve. These cases, however, will also be precedent in situations in which the potential for abuse may not be so obvious.

Of equal significance, it appears that, under the court's formulation, demand will not be excused, and hence the litigation may not be able to continue, if a self-dealing transaction has been approved by a disinterested board even if, the underlying transaction would not be insulated from review by the business judgment rule. Nor will discovery be available to assist in establishing reasonable doubt. In *Aronson*, for example, plaintiffs alleged that the transactions with Fink constituted a breach of *his* fiduciary duty of loyalty and that the rest of the board had, independently, breached *their* fiduciary duties by approving those transactions. Because the plaintiffs were unable to show that the board was not independent, the court viewed the challenged transaction as being within the protection of the business judgment rule. It never considered whether, as to Fink, the challenge should receive a hearing on the merits because *he* would not be protected by the business judgment rule. It is difficult to understand why the court should protect the transaction from potential judicial scrutiny at the demand stage of the litigation. Such protection, in effect, converts the board of directors into the ultimate decisionmaker as to the desirability of proceeding with a self-dealing case and would seem to be contrary to the statement by the Delaware Court of Chancery that "under our system of law, courts and not litigants should decide the merits of litigation." Maldonado v. Flynn, 413 A.2d 1251, 1263 (Del.Ch.1980). The analysis of the directors' interest and independence in *Rales* suggests, however, that the Delaware Supreme Court may, in fact, be more sympathetic to demand futility in duty of loyalty cases than these earlier cases might indicate.

One court has observed: "When faced with a demand by a shareholder, the directors have a number of options. They can exercise their discretion to accept the demand and prosecute the action, to resolve the grievance internally without resort to litigation, or to refuse the demand. It is at this point that the business judgment rule comes into play." Weiss v. Temporary Investment Fund, Inc., 692 F.2d 928, 941 (3d Cir.1982). Thus, even when the suit involves corporate insiders, a court may find an independent board's decision not to sue is a valid exercise of business judgment. This view can make the arguments over demand futility, outcome-determinative. If the business judgment rule applies, the plaintiff will seldom be able to convince a court that that the rejection of demand was wrongful. Allison on Behalf of GMC v. General Motors Corp., 604 F.Supp. 1106 (D.Del.1985), aff'd without op. 782 F.2d 1026 (3d Cir.1985). See Dennis J. Block, Nancy E. Barton & Stephen A. Radin, The Business Judgment Rule (3rd ed 1989).

2. In Kaplan v. Peat, Marwick, Mitchell & Co., 540 A.2d 726 (Del.1988), the Delaware Supreme Court considered two previously undecided aspects of the demand requirement. Plaintiffs brought a derivative action on behalf of Chase Manhattan Corp. against its independent auditor for allegedly negligent conduct in two investment transactions. The auditor, Peat, Marwick, moved to dismiss for failure to satisfy the demand requirement or, alternatively, for summary judgment on the ground that Chase made a business judgment not to sue Peat, Marwick.

In deciding the first part of the motion, the court held that because of the importance of presuit demand in the Delaware corporate governance system, a defendant other than the corporation has standing to raise the failure to make demand. The second part of the motion raised the question of whether the corporation can be neutral as to the maintenance of a derivative suit and, if so, whether such neutrality excuses demand. With respect to the latter, the court stated:

> When a corporation takes a position regarding a derivative action asserted on its behalf, it cannot effectively stand neutral. Because of the inherent nature of the derivative action, a corporation's failure to object to a suit brought on its behalf must be viewed as an approval for the shareholders' capacity to sue derivatively. We hold, therefore, that when a corporation chooses to take a position in regards to a derivative action asserted on its behalf, it must affirmatively object to or support the continuation of the litigation.

540 A.2d at 731. Hence, a position of neutrality is viewed as tacit approval of the continuation of the litigation, excusing demand by the plaintiff.

B. *Other Standards for Futility*

1. Because demand is excused only when it is clear from particularized pleadings that the business judgment rule does not apply to the case, courts tend to insist that demand be made. The plaintiff must show that the elements of the business judgment rule are not present; i.e., that there was self-dealing, a biased decision maker or an egregious transaction that transcends rationality. See Note, The Demand and Standing Requirements in Stockholder Derivative Actions, 44 U.Chi. L.Rev. 168 (1976). Some jurisdictions are stricter than Delaware in allowing exceptions to demand. In re Kauffman Mutual Fund Actions, 479 F.2d 257 (1st Cir.1973), cert. denied 414 U.S. 857, 94 S.Ct. 161, 38 L.Ed.2d 107 (1973), required a showing that the defendant directors were charged with self-dealing (not established by their having approved

the transaction) and that the transaction was "completely undirected to a corporate purpose."   479 F.2d at 265.

Although most courts rely on standards similar to Delaware's, states vary regarding what is necessary to prove futility.   California excuses demand if "the directors are involved or not disinterested in the actions for which plaintiff seeks relief."   Country Nat. Bank v. Mayer, 788 F.Supp. 1136, 1144 (E.D.Cal.1992).   Additionally, allegations of the board's domination by a member who is adverse to the plaintiff's position are sufficient to demonstrate futility.   Id. at 1145.   Maryland excuses demand as futile if the suit would cause the directors to sue themselves, because their interests would be "antagonistic" to the plaintiff's interests.   Burt on Behalf of McDonnell Douglas v. Danforth, 742 F.Supp. 1043, 1047 (E.D.Mo.1990).   Although naming all the directors as defendants will not excuse demand, under Maryland law demand is futile if "a majority of the board of directors is charged with actively participating in the wrongdoing," or if a majority of the shareholders could not have ratified the alleged wrong, as with fraud.   Id. Whatever phrasing is used to determine when demand is futile, as one commentator notes, "Inevitably, under any standard, the question of demand futility is fact-oriented and for this reason some courts appear unwilling to commit themselves to rigid application of an exacting standard."   Deborah DeMott, Shareholder Derivative Actions: Law and Practice (1992) § 5:13.

2.   A lawsuit may allege that directors neglected their oversight functions rather than that they engaged in misconduct in connection with a business decision.   For example, the complaint may assert breach of the duty of care by reason of a failure to monitor the business adequately, See Brane v. Roth and Hoye v. Meek in Chapter 16.   Given the confusing relationship between the duty of care and the business judgment rule, what must be pleaded to demonstrate demand futility in such a case?   What is the relevance of the "reasonable doubt" standard?

3.   Plaintiffs often plead that demand should be excused because all or a majority of the board of directors approved the challenged transaction or were otherwise involved in the wrongdoing.   One of the leading cases in this area, Lewis v. Graves, 701 F.2d 245 (2d Cir.1983), applying Delaware law, held that the mere naming of a majority, or even all of the directors, as defendants because they approved the transaction at issue will not excuse demand.   Plaintiff alleged that the directors of J. Ray McDermott & Co., Inc., ("McDermott") all of whom were named as defendants, had approved the issuance of stock under an executive compensation plan to a minority of the directors who were officers and, further, that the board had approved McDermott's acquisition of Babcock & Wilcox to ensure their positions with the company.   The complaint offered no facts as to how the acquisition would entrench their positions.   No further specific facts of participation were alleged.   Plaintiff sued all the directors and asserted that demand would be futile because it would be asking the directors to institute suit against themselves.   The court held that "absent specific allegations of self-dealing or

bias on the part of a majority of the board, mere approval and acquiescence are insufficient to render demand futile." 701 F.2d at 248. Further:

> The fact that a corporation's directors have previously approved transactions subsequently challenged in a derivative suit does not inevitably lead to the conclusion that those directors, bound by their fiduciary obligations to the corporation, will refuse to take up the suit. This is particularly true where the directors' prior acquiescence was obtained through fraud or where the dealings in question otherwise went sour for the corporation. Moreover, Rule 23.1 would be substantially diluted if prior board approval standing alone established futility. Derivative suits are almost invariably directed at major, allegedly illegal, corporate transactions. By virtue of their offices, directors ordinarily participate in the decision making involved in such transactions. Excusing demand on the mere basis of prior board acquiescence, therefore, would obviate the need for demand in practically every case.

* * *

> * * * If a derivative plaintiff could show self-interest in a transaction by mere conclusory allegations that the defendant directors approved a business acquisition simply to secure their own positions, without providing any logical or factual nexus between the transaction and the asserted entrenchment, the demand requirement of Rule 23.1 would again become virtually meaningless.

Id. at 248–50. See also, Elgin v. Alfa Corp., 598 So.2d 807, 815 (Ala.1992), ("our case law clearly indicates, and has so indicated for nearly a century, that where the majority of the directors are themselves the alleged wrongdoers, a derivative action plaintiff can be excused from director-demand because such a demand can be deemed futile.")

4. New York may have taken a different approach in Barr v. Wackman, 36 N.Y.2d 371, 368 N.Y.S.2d 497, 329 N.E.2d 180 (1975). The New York Court of Appeals sustained the excusing of demand under N.Y. B.C.L. § 626(c) in a case charging self-dealing by the officer-directors of Talcott National Corporation ("Talcott") and breaches of the duty of due care (but no self-dealing) against the outside directors, who were a majority of the board. The complaint charged that after the boards of Talcott and Gulf & Western ("G & W") agreed in principle on G & W's acquisition of Talcott, the latter's board approved a number of transactions made for the benefit of Talcott's inside directors and G & W, but not Talcott or its shareholders. These transactions included approval of favorable employment contracts for Talcott officers, approval of an allegedly excessive finder's fee, and the sale of a Talcott subsidiary at a loss. The defendants claimed that at most the complaint indicated erroneous business judgment.

Judge Fuchsberg explained:

The basic question is whether from the particular circumstances of the liability charged it may be inferred that the making of such a demand will be excused where the alleged wrongdoers control or comprise a majority of the directors. * * * And, while justification for failure to give directors notice prior to the institution of a derivative action is not automatically to be found in bare allegations which merely set forth prima facie personal liability of directors without spelling out some detail, such justification may be found when the claim of liability is based on formal action of the board in which the individual directors were participants.

It is not sufficient, however, merely to name a majority of the directors as parties defendant with conclusory allegations of wrong-doing or control by wrongdoers. This pleading tactic would only beg the question of actual futility and ignore the particularity requirement of the statute. The complaint here does much more than simply name the individual board members as defendants. It sets out, with particularity, a series of transactions allegedly for the benefit of Gulf & Western and the affiliated directors. Though there are no allegations that the unaffiliated directors personally benefited from the transactions, they are claimed to have disregarded Talcott's interests for the sole purpose of accommodating Gulf & Western, which, in turn, would allegedly reciprocate by promoting the self-interest of the affiliated directors. Acting officially, the board, qua board, is claimed to have participated or acquiesced in assertedly wrongful transactions * * *

If true, the allegations of the complaint * * * state a cause of action against the defendants, including the unaffiliated directors, for breach of their duties of due care and diligence to the corporation. Plaintiff may prove that the exercise of reasonable diligence and independent judgment under all the circumstances by the unaffiliated directors, at least to meaningfully check the decisions of the active corporate managers, would have put them on notice of the claimed self-dealing of the affiliated directors and avoided the alleged damage to Talcott. If the unaffiliated directors abdicated their responsibility, they may be liable for their omissions. Taking their potential liability from the face of the complaint, plaintiff's failure to make a demand on the board was warranted.

We reject appellants' proposition that allegations of directorial fraud or self-interest is, in every case, a prerequisite to excusing a derivative shareholder from making a demand on a board. * * * Directors undertake affirmative duties of due care and diligence to a corporation and its shareholders in addition to their obligation merely to avoid self-dealing. That unaffiliated directors may not have personally profited from challenged actions does not necessarily end the question of their potential liability to the corporation and the consequent unlikelihood that they would prosecute the action. * * *

As a consequence, a derivative shareholder's complaint may, in a particular case, withstand a motion to dismiss for failure to make a demand upon the board, even though a majority of the board are not individually charged with fraud or self-dealing. Particular allegations of formal board participation in and approval of active wrongdoing may, as here, suffice to defeat a motion to dismiss. We believe the better approach in these cases is to rest the determination of the necessity for a demand in the sound discretion of the court to which the issue is first presented, to be determined from the sufficiency of the complaint, liberally construed.

368 N.Y.S.2d at 505–08.

Is the allegation of participation in *Barr* any more particularized in its description of wrongful conduct than the allegation in *Graves*? Are these cases two of a kind or do they represent different approaches to the demand requirement?

C. Successful Pleading of Demand Futility

1. In re NVF Company Litigation, 1989 WL 146237 (Del.Ch.1989) (Unpublished Case), involved a challenge to the board's decision, taken at an emergency meeting, to sell the company's major asset, a large block of stock of APL Corporation which was controlled by Victor Posner. Posner was also chairman of NVF. In determining whether plaintiffs were justified in believing that a demand would be futile, the court focused on whether the directors had divided loyalties. The plaintiffs alleged that the directors who approved the APL stock sale had conflicting loyalties because at least five of the six directors received compensation as NVF directors and as directors of other Posner-affiliated firms. In addition, three of the six had family relationships with Posner. In concluding that these considerations raised a reasonable doubt as to the directors' interest in the challenged transaction, the court stated: "While this is not to say necessarily that Posner controls and dominates the board, it is to say that a reasonable doubt exists whether the board's interest is divided between the interest of the corporation and that of Posner."

The court also examined the substantive nature of the challenged stock sale and the board's approval to see if a reasonable doubt existed that the directors used valid business judgment. The defendants asserted that an emergency situation existed because of threatened bank foreclosure of a $1.8 million unpaid loan. The court recognized that an emergency might affect the determination of what constituted reasonable conduct but would not excuse a director from satisfying her fiduciary duties. Specifically, a director must assess each transaction, such as the stock sale in question, with a critical eye. The court concluded that the record disclosed no evidence that the directors did anything but vote for the sale of the APL stock. The alleged emergency was the result of a two-year old loan, as the board faced an on-going concern when asked to consider the stock sale. Thus a reasonable doubt existed whether the board validly exercised its business judgment in hastily approving the stock sale at a brief board meeting.

2. Pleadings are more likely to raise a reasonable doubt that directors are disinterested and independent if the directors are alleged to have engaged in conduct that violates a specific statute rather than simply constituting a breach of fiduciary duty. For example, in Shields v. Erikson, Fed.Sec.L.Rep. (CCH) ¶ 94,723, 1989 WL 100001 (D.C. N.D.Ill 1989), the court applied Delaware law to excuse demand as futile when the plaintiff alleged that the directors received "numerous gifts and goodies" wrongfully charged to the United States government. The plaintiff charged that each director, or at least a majority of them, had participated in these illegal acts, which had resulted in fines and penalties against the corporation. The court held that the allegations were sufficient to create a reasonable doubt that the defendant directors were independent and disinterested.

3. Another context in which plaintiffs have often been successful in proving futility is when directors may be unable to be reimbursed for their liability to the corporation through insurance or indemnification. In First American Bank and Trust by Levitt v. Frogel, 726 F.Supp. 1292 (S.D.Fla.1989), the plaintiff sued a bank and several of its officers and directors for violations of the federal securities laws and for breaches of fiduciary duty. Applying Florida law (which uses Delaware law for guidance), the court focused on the plaintiff's allegations "that the officers and directors' liability insurance policy contains a provision which prohibits the board from instituting or authorizing any suit on behalf of the Bank against an officer or a director. Insurance coverage would cease if such a suit were brought or authorized by the Bank or the directors." Id. at 1298. Consequently, the court concluded that demand was futile because directors could not be expected to bring a derivative lawsuit when they had no protection against personal liability.

In Grill v. Hoblitzell, 771 F.Supp. 709 (D.Md.1991), applying Maryland law, plaintiff argued that demand would be futile because the corporation's director and officer indemnification policy covered damages awarded in a derivative suit brought by a shareholder but not one instituted by the board. The court granted the defendants' motion to dismiss for failure to make demand, but permitted the plaintiff to amend his complaint to plead with greater particularity the specifics of the corporation's insurance policy. The court noted that the original charges, if true, could mean that "it may very well be that a demand upon the directors to institute an action seeking monetary relief from any present or past director would be futile. * * * [S]ince a recovery under an insurance policy is self-evidently different from recovery against personal assets, if what the plaintiff alleges is true, the directors may have deprived themselves of the ability to exercise independent judgment as to the advisability of instituting an action against any officer or director for mismanagement and thereby divested themselves of the power to govern this aspect of the corporation's affairs." Id. at 713.

D.   Consequences of the Board's Refusal to Sue

Suppose demand is made. How long must a plaintiff wait before bringing suit? The prevailing view is that the board must respond within a reasonable time. The board needs an opportunity to study the matter, and a complex transaction may entail a lengthy investigation. The case may be in a state of suspended animation for months. If the board refuses to bring suit after demand, does the shareholder still have a right to sue? Remember, if demand is "accepted," the derivative suit is automatically barred, since the directors will bring suit or negotiate a settlement directly in the name of the corporation.

In Rubin v. Posner, 701 F.Supp. 1041 (D.Del.1988), suit was filed one month after demand had been received and defendants moved to dismiss partly on the ground, that the corporation had not had adequate time to reply to the demand. The court denied the motion, finding that the corporation had not acted reasonably in its response to the demand. The court noted that, the suit did not involve complex technological issues, a large number of defendants, or a difficult factual situation. In addition, the court found that the board had apparently taken no action between receipt of the demand and the filing of the suit.

RMBCA § 7.42 bars suit for 90 days from the date of demand unless the shareholder has been notified earlier that her demand was rejected or irreparable injury would result from waiting the full time period.

E.   Universal Demand

1. Most jurisdictions follow Delaware's pattern of requiring demand except when it would be futile. Universal demand, in contrast, eliminates the futility exception; a plaintiff must always make demand prior to filing a derivative suit. The ALI has adopted such a requirement, although it permits a narrow exception for "irreparable injury to the corporation." The ALI offers three rationales for universal demand. First, it will reduce threshold litigation to determine whether demand is actually futile and therefore should be excused. Second, universal demand is a form of alternative dispute resolution that allows the board an opportunity to correct any wrong that may have occurred. Moreover, making demand is relatively easy and adds little to the plaintiff's burden in bringing a claim. Third, universal demand provides a single, clear standard of judicial review for demand-excused and demand-refused cases. Today, Delaware and other courts are more deferential to the decisions of boards and committees in demand required cases than when demand is excused. ALI, Principles of Corporate Governance (1994), § 7.03, Comment e. See Zapata Corp. v. Maldonado, 430 A.2d 779 (Del.1981), infra. Additionally, the ALI notes that the entire area of law is confusing because there is no consensus as to what constitutes "futility." The ALI criticizes Delaware particularly for requiring too much judicial subjectivity in interpreting the "reasonable doubt" standard established in *Aronson*.

RMBCA § 7.42 also established a universal demand requirement, for the first two reasons offered by the ALI. Several states, including

Florida, Georgia, Michigan, Virginia and Wisconsin, have adopted the RMBCA's universal demand requirement.

2. Kamen v. Kemper Financial Services, 500 U.S. 90, 111 S.Ct. 1711, 114 L.Ed.2d 152 (1991), involved the question of whether demand was required in a derivative suit under Section 20(a) of the Investment Company Act of 1940. Plaintiff had alleged that demand would have been futile. The district court dismissed the complaint on the ground that plaintiff had failed to allege sufficient facts to demonstrate futility. The Seventh Circuit affirmed on different grounds. 908 F.2d 1338 (7th Cir.1990) It adopted, as a rule of federal common law, the ALI's universal demand requirement, noting that the futility exception had produced "gobs" of litigation involving speculation about a board's inchoate action.

The Supreme Court reversed and held that in an action under a federal statute such as the Investment Company Act of 1940, a federal court must apply the demand futility exception as defined by the law of the defendant corporation's state of incorporation. The Court stated:

> Because the contours of the demand requirement—when it is required, and when excused—determine *who* has the power to control corporate litigation, we have little trouble concluding that this aspect of state law relates to the allocation of governing powers within the corporation. * * *

> KFS contends that the scope of a federal common law demand requirement need not be tied to the allocation of power to control corporate litigation. This is so, KFS suggests, because a court adjudicating a derivative action based on federal law could sever the requirement of shareholder demand from the standard used to review the directors' decision to bar initiation of, or to terminate, the litigation. Drawing on the ALI's Principles of Corporate Governance, the Court of Appeals came to this same conclusion. Freed from the question of the directors' power to control the litigation, the universal-demand requirement, KFS maintains, would force would-be derivative suit plaintiffs to exhaust their intracorporate remedies before filing suit and would spare both the courts and the parties the expense associated with the often protracted threshold litigation that attends the collateral issue of demand futility.

> We reject this analysis. Whatever its merits as a matter of legal reform, we believe that KFS' proposal to detach the demand standard from the standard for reviewing board action would require a quantum of federal common lawmaking that exceeds federal courts' interstitial mandate. Under state law, the determination whether a derivative representative can initiate a suit without making demand typically is made at the outset of the litigation and is based on the application of the State's futility doctrine to circumstances as they then exist. Under KFS' proposal, federal courts would be obliged to develop a body of principles that would replicate the substantive effect of the State's demand futility doctrine but that would be

applied *after* demand has been made and refused. The ALI, for example, has developed an elaborate set of standards that calibrates the deference afforded the decision of the directors to the character of the claim being asserted by the derivative plaintiff. See ALI, Principles of Corporate Governance § 7.08 (Tent.Draft No. 8, Apr. 15, 1988); id., § 7.08, Comment *c*, p. 120 (noting that Principles "dra[w] a basic distinction between the standard of review applicable to actions that are founded on a breach of the duty of care and the standard of review applicable to actions that are founded on a breach of the duty of loyalty"). Whether a federal court adopts the ALI's standards wholesale or instead attempts to devise postdemand review standards more finely tuned to the distinctive allocation of managerial decisionmaking power embodied in any given jurisdiction's demand futility doctrine, KFS' suggestion would impose upon federal courts the very duty "to fashion an entire body of federal corporate law" that *Burks* sought to avoid.

3. Under the ALI's approach, the board will always be required to respond to the demand. If, as is likely, the board refuses the demand, its refusal may increase the plaintiffs' burden in another manner. The ALI would allow the board to include a statement with its demand refusal that asserts that the board was "not interested in the transaction or conduct * * * and that such directors constituted a majority of the entire board and were capable as a group of objective judgment in the circumstances * * *" ALI, Principles of Corporate Governance (1994), § 7.04(a)(2). If a board includes such a statement and provides specific reasons in support, the plaintiff must plead, with particularity, facts that, if true, raise a "significant prospect" that 1) the board's statement is false; 2) if the business judgment rule applies, the defendants fail to meet its standards; or 3) if a standard other than the business judgment rule applies, the disinterested directors could not have reasonably determined that demand refusal was in the corporation's best interests. Id. at § 7.04(a)(2)(A-C). If the plaintiff fails to plead such particularized facts, the defendants are entitled to dismissal of the complaint prior to discovery, and will normally move to dismiss. The ALI's definition of "interested" when applied to derivative suits provides that a director is not necessarily considered "interested" because she is a defendant in the case if the complaint is 1) based only on the director's approval or acquiescence of the transaction at issue, and 2) does not allege particularized facts that, if, true, raise a significant prospect that the director is liable to the corporation or the shareholders. Id. at § 1.23(c). The ALI's requirement, adopted after the Institute had formally adopted the entire Project, was highly controversial. See Paul H. Dawes and Mark W. Smith, The Demand Requirement and the Special Litigation Committee in Derivative Actions, 26 Rev. Sec. and Comm. Reg. 77 (1993).

F. Demand on Stockholders

Although all jurisdictions require that a shareholder make demand on directors unless it is excused as futile, most have abandoned an earlier requirement that demand also be made on shareholders. Delaware, for example, amended its law in 1967 to eliminate this requirement. S. Solomont & Sons Trust, Inc. v. New England Theatres Operating Corp., 326 Mass. 99, 93 N.E.2d 241 (1950), exemplifies the so-called "Massachusetts" or "strict" rule which always requires demand on shareholders as a precondition to the bringing of a derivative suit; only a few other states follow the Massachusetts rule. Deborah DeMott, Demand in Derivative Actions: Problems of Interpretation and Function, 19 U.Cal.Davis 461, 476–7 (1986). In cases involving federal claims, such as those arising under the federal securities laws, demand on shareholders is not "necessary." See F.R.C.P. Rule 23.1. In fact, the courts see demand on shareholders as presenting an impermissible barrier to a federal remedy. Levitt v. Johnson, 334 F.2d 815 (1st Cir.1964), cert. denied 379 U.S. 961, 85 S.Ct. 649, 13 L.Ed.2d 556 (1965).

2. TERMINATING DERIVATIVE SUITS

One internal procedure that defendants have used after demand has been made or a suit has begun is the creation of a special litigation committee. Appointed by the board and comprised of directors disinterested in the transactions at issue, such a committee has the task of determining whether the litigation should be terminated. Arguably it must address two business decisions: whether the lawsuit has merit and whether the corporation has more to gain or to lose from its prosecution. Should the court view those decisions as simply another exercise of business judgment or should it take a fresh look?

Gall v. Exxon, 418 F.Supp. 508 (S.D.N.Y.1976), was the first case in which a decision by a special litigation committee was used as a basis for seeking dismissal of the suit. In July 1975, an Exxon shareholder made a demand on the board, alleging illegal foreign political contributions and bribes that wasted corporate assets. Exxon's board established a special litigation committee consisting of three board members. The committee retained as counsel the retired chief justice of the New Jersey Supreme Court. The committee found that Exxon had authorized the expenditure of approximately $27 million in questionable payments, but noted that no Exxon officials had engaged in bribery. The committee then decided not to bring suit. When a suit was later filed and the plaintiff challenged the committee's determination, the court held that the suit would be dismissed if the decision was in fact a bona fide business judgment by independent directors. Plaintiff challenged the independence of the committee and the bona fides of its determination, but the court sustained the committee on both these issues.

Burks v. Lasker, 441 U.S. 471, 99 S.Ct. 1831, 60 L.Ed.2d 404 (1979), gave added impetus to the use of special litigation committees. *Burks* was a derivative suit by shareholders of a mutual fund against several directors of the fund and its investment adviser. Plaintiffs alleged that the fund's substantial purchases of the commercial paper of Penn Central just prior to Penn Central's insolvency violated the Investment Company Act of 1940 and the directors' duty of care. The complaint did not allege any self-dealing on the part of defendants. Five members of the eleven-person board who were not affiliated with the fund's investment adviser and not defendants in the suit convened as a quorum pursuant to the company's bylaws and retained a retired chief judge of the New York Court of Appeals as independent counsel. On the basis of their investigation, they decided that the litigation was adverse to the company's best interest and moved to dismiss. After permitting discovery on the question of the directors' independence, the district court granted the motion. The Court of Appeals for the Second Circuit reversed.

The Supreme Court sustained the dismissal. It held that state law governed the question of whether disinterested directors possess the power to terminate a derivative suit if they conclude that the litigation is adverse to the corporation's best interest. However, the Court acknowledged that even if state law permitted such a decision, circumstances could exist in which such a state law was inconsistent with a federal policy underlying the cause of action. It did not find any conflict between the federal statute involved and the board action in *Burks*.

Gall and *Burks* encouraged the use of independent committees as a device to obtain dismissal of derivative suits. More importantly, these cases strengthened assertions by boards that they possess the power to terminate derivative suits in the exercise of their business judgment. A quick succession of cases upheld determinations by special litigation committees to terminate derivative suits.

The use of special litigation committees raises important questions of corporate governance. Judicial deference to decisions of these committees has the potential to curtail almost totally the availability of a shareholder's right to use courts for redress of alleged breaches of fiduciary duty, including the duty of loyalty. Those who oppose the use of this mechanism argue that litigation is for courts to resolve, not for committees potentially dominated by defendants. However, considerable savings may be achieved when independent, diligent directors perform their accustomed role of protecting the corporate interest. They may be able to screen wasteful litigation effectively without shielding managers who may have breached their fiduciary duties. If the use of such committees is a permissible technique, the law must decide in what categories of cases it may be used, what procedures must be followed, what opportunity the plaintiff should be given to discover facts, what role the courts will play when the motion to terminate the litigation is made and whether there should be any limitations as to the types of defendants who may utilize this procedure.

ZAPATA CORP. v. MALDONADO
430 A.2d 779 (Del.1981).

[In 1970, Zapata Corporation granted options to certain of its officers and directors to purchase stock at $12.15 per share. The options could be exercised in installments, with the final installment exercisable not before July 14, 1974. At around that time, when the stock had reached a price of between $18–19, the Company planned to make a tender offer for its own shares at $25.00 per share. The company planned to announce the tender offer just prior to July 14, 1974. The effect of the announcement would be to increase the market value of the shares to approximately $25.00 per share. As a result, there would be an additional federal income tax liability on persons who exercised the option, since the tax liability was measured as the difference between the option price ($12.15) and the market price at the time of exercise (about $25).

It was alleged that in order to reduce their individual income tax liability, the board of directors voted to accelerate the exercise date to a time prior to the announcement of the tender offer. The optionees could then exercise when a lower market price prevailed. However, this had the further effect of reducing the corporation's corresponding tax deduction for officers' compensation because the corporation could deduct only $18.00 per share although the price would appreciate on announcement of the offer to $25.00. In effect, the option holders and the corporation were caught in a zero sum game: one could not win without the other losing. A majority of the directors had a direct interest in the outcome of the game since they were option holders.

In 1975, derivative suits were filed in both state and federal courts, alleging breach of fiduciary duty by directors who voted to accelerate the option exercise date and federal proxy rule violations in connection with the re-election of the directors who had so benefitted at the expense of the Corporation. Both of these suits were styled Maldonado v. Flynn.

Four years after the filing of these suits, the Zapata Board appointed two new directors and constituted them as the "Independent Investigation Committee of Zapata Corporation." The committee retained as counsel the law firm of one of the directors. Within three months of their appointment, the Committee filed a "Report and Determination" to the effect that all of the law suits should be dismissed. At their direction, the Corporation's counsel then moved for dismissal of the action.

The Federal District Court in New York concluded that the board of a Delaware corporation had authority to terminate derivative litigation. The court observed, with respect to the exercise of business judgment in this case:

> [T]he Committee labored under no compulsion to conclude that the actions were lacking in merit. Such a finding is not a prerequisite to the exercise of business judgment though of course it is a factor that may well be considered. To the contrary, the essence of the business judgment rule in this context is that directors may freely find that certain *meritorious* actions are not in the corporation's best interests to pursue. Indeed, here liability is not a foregone conclusion as the issue of materiality remains for trial determination.

The final substantive judgment whether a particular lawsuit should be maintained requires a balance of many factors—ethical, commercial, promotional, public relations, employee relations, fiscal as well as legal. The factors to be taken into account and their evaluation are for the Committee expressly appointed to consider them and are beyond the judicial reach. In the last analysis the decision required to be made and that in fact was made is not a legal but a business judgment. * * *

The court found no conflict with the policy of the federal proxy rules. Maldonado v. Flynn, 485 F.Supp. 274 (S.D.N.Y.1980).

The Delaware Chancery Court held otherwise and ruled that the case could not be dismissed. Maldonado v. Flynn, 413 A.2d 1251 (Del.Ch.1980).]

QUILLEN, JUSTICE.

* * * We limit our review in this interlocutory appeal to whether the Committee has the power to cause the present action to be dismissed.

We begin with an examination of the carefully considered opinion of the Vice Chancellor which states, in part, that the "business judgment" rule does not confer power "to a corporate board of directors to terminate a derivative suit", 413 A.2d at 1257. His conclusion is particularly pertinent because several federal courts, applying Delaware law, have held that the business judgment rule enables boards (or their committees) to terminate derivative suits, decisions now in conflict with the holding below.

As the term is most commonly used, and given the disposition below, we can understand the Vice Chancellor's comment that "the business judgment rule is irrelevant to the question of whether the Committee has the authority to compel the dismissal of this suit." 413 A.2d at 1257. Corporations, existing because of legislative grace, possess authority as granted by the legislature. Directors of Delaware corporations derive their managerial decision making power, which encompasses decisions whether to initiate, or refrain from entering, litigation, from 8 Del.C. § 141(a). This statute is the fount of directorial powers. The "business judgment" rule is a judicial creation that presumes propriety, under certain circumstances, in a board's decision. Viewed defensively, it does not create authority. In this sense the "business judgment" rule is not relevant in corporate decision making until after a decision is made. It is generally used as a defense to an attack on the decision's soundness. The board's managerial decision making power, however, comes from § 141(a). The judicial creation and legislative grant are related because the "business judgment" rule evolved to give recognition and deference to directors' business expertise when exercising their managerial power under § 141(a).

In the case before us, although the corporation's decision to move to dismiss or for summary judgment was, literally, a decision resulting from an exercise of the directors' (as delegated to the Committee) business judgment, the question of "business judgment", in a defensive sense, would not become relevant until and unless the decision to seek termination of the derivative lawsuit was attacked as improper. This question was not reached by the Vice Chancellor because he determined that the stockholder had an individual right to maintain this derivative action.

Thus, the focus in this case is on the power to speak for the corporation as to whether the lawsuit should be continued or terminated. As we see it, this issue in the current appellate posture of this case has three aspects: the conclusions of the Court below concerning the continuing right of a stockholder to maintain a derivative action; the corporate power under Delaware law of an authorized board committee to cause dismissal of litigation instituted for the benefit of the corporation; and the role of the Court of Chancery in resolving conflicts between the stockholder and the committee.

Accordingly, we turn first to the Court of Chancery's conclusions concerning the right of a plaintiff stockholder in a derivative action. We find that its determination that a stockholder, once demand is made and refused, possesses an independent, individual right to continue a derivative suit for breaches of fiduciary duty over objection by the corporation, as an absolute rule, is erroneous. * * *

Moreover, McKee v. Rogers, Del.Ch., 156 A. 191 (1931), stated "as a general rule" that "a stockholder cannot be permitted * * * to invade the discretionary field committed to the judgment of the directors and sue in the corporation's behalf when the managing body refuses. This rule is a well settled one." 156 A. at 193.

The *McKee* rule, of course, should not be read so broadly that the board's refusal will be determinative in every instance. Board members, owing a well-established fiduciary duty to the corporation, will not be allowed to cause a derivative suit to be dismissed when it would be a breach of their fiduciary duty. Generally disputes pertaining to control of the suit arise in two contexts.

Consistent with the purpose of requiring a demand, a board decision to cause a derivative suit to be dismissed as detrimental to the company, after demand has been made and refused, will be respected unless it was wrongful.[10] A claim of a wrongful decision not to sue is thus the first exception and the first context of dispute. Absent a wrongful refusal, the stockholder in such a situation simply lacks legal managerial power.

---

10. In other words, when stockholders, after making demand and having their suit rejected, attack the board's decision as improper, the board's decision falls under the "business judgment" rule and will be respected if the requirements of the rule are met. That situation should be distinguished from the instant case, where demand was not made, and the *power* of the board to seek a dismissal, due to disqualification, presents a threshold issue. We recognize that the two contexts can overlap in practice.

But it cannot be implied that, absent a wrongful board refusal, a stockholder can never have an individual right to initiate an action. For, as is stated in *McKee,* a "well settled" exception exists to the general rule.

[A] stockholder may sue in equity in his derivative right to assert a cause of action in behalf of the corporation, *without prior demand* upon the directors to sue, when it is apparent that a demand would be futile, that the officers are under an influence that sterilizes discretion and could not be proper persons to conduct the litigation.

156 A. at 193 (emphasis added). This exception, the second context for dispute, is consistent with the Court of Chancery's statement below, that "[the stockholder's individual right to bring the action does not ripen, however, * * * unless he can show a demand to be futile." *Maldonado,* 413 A.2d at 1262.

These comments in *McKee* and in the opinion below make obvious sense. A demand, when required and refused (if not wrongful), terminates a stockholder's legal ability to initiate a derivative action. But where demand is properly excused, the stockholder does possess the ability to initiate the action on his corporation's behalf.

These conclusions, however, do not determine the question before us. Rather, they merely bring us to the question to be decided. It is here that we part company with the Court below. * * * We see no inherent reason why the "two phases" of a derivative suit, the stockholder's suit to compel the corporation to sue and the corporation's suit should automatically result in the placement in the hands of the litigating stockholder sole control of the corporate right throughout the litigation. To the contrary, it seems to us that such an inflexible rule would recognize the interest of one person or group to the exclusion of all others within the corporate entity. Thus, we reject the view of the Vice Chancellor as to the first aspect of the issue on appeal.

The question to be decided becomes: When, if at all, should an authorized board committee be permitted to cause litigation, properly initiated by a derivative stockholder in his own right, to be dismissed? As noted above, a board has the power to choose not to pursue litigation when demand is made upon it, so long as the decision is not wrongful. If the board determines that a suit would be detrimental to the company, the board's determination prevails. Even when demand is excusable, circumstances may arise when continuation of the litigation would not be in the corporation's best interests. Our inquiry is whether, under such circumstances, there is a permissible procedure under § 141(a) by which a corporation can rid itself of detrimental litigation. If there is not, a single stockholder in an extreme case might control the destiny of the entire corporation. This concern was bluntly expressed by the Ninth Circuit in Lewis v. Anderson, 9th Cir., 615 F.2d 778, 783 (1979), cert. denied, 449 U.S. 869, 101 S.Ct. 206, 66 L.Ed.2d 89 (1980): "To allow one shareholder to incapacitate an entire board of directors merely by leveling charges against them gives too much leverage to dissident shareholders.'' But, when examining the means, including the committee mechanism examined in this case, potentials for abuse must be recognized. This takes us to the second and third aspects of the issue on appeal.

Before we pass to equitable considerations as to the mechanism at issue here, it must be clear that an independent committee possesses the corporate power to seek the termination of a derivative suit. Section 141(c) allows a board to delegate all of its authority to a committee. Accordingly, a committee with properly delegated authority would have the power to move for dismissal or summary judgment if the entire board did.

Even though demand was not made in this case and the initial decision of whether to litigate was not placed before the board, Zapata's board, it seems to us, retained all of its corporate power concerning litigation decisions. If Maldonado had made demand on the board in this case, it could have refused to bring suit. Maldonado could then have asserted that the decision not to sue was wrongful and, if correct, would have been allowed to maintain the suit. The board, however, never would have lost its statutory managerial authority. The demand requirement itself evidences that the managerial power is retained by the board. When a derivative plaintiff is allowed to bring suit after a wrongful refusal, the board's authority to choose whether to pursue the litigation is not challenged although its conclusion—reached through the exercise of that authority—is not respected since it is wrongful. Similarly, Rule 23.1, by excusing demand in certain instances, does not strip the board of its corporate power. It merely saves the plaintiff the expense and delay of making a futile demand resulting in a probable tainted exercise of that authority in a refusal by the board or in giving control of litigation to the opposing side. But the board entity remains empowered under § 141(a) to make decisions regarding corporate litigation. The problem is one of member disqualification, not the absence of power in the board.

The corporate power inquiry then focuses on whether the board, tainted by the self-interest of a majority of its members, can legally delegate its authority to a committee of two disinterested directors. We find our statute clearly requires an affirmative answer to this question. As has been noted, under an express provision of the statute, § 141(c), a committee can exercise all of the authority of the board to the extent provided in the resolution of the board. Moreover, at least by analogy to our statutory section on interested directors, 8 Del.C. § 141, it seems clear that the Delaware statute is designed to permit disinterested directors to act for the board.

We do not think that the interest taint of the board majority is per se a legal bar to the delegation of the board's power to an independent committee composed of disinterested board members. The committee can properly act for the corporation to move to dismiss derivative litigation that is believed to be detrimental to the corporation's best interest.

Our focus now switches to the Court of Chancery which is faced with a stockholder assertion that a derivative suit, properly instituted, should continue for the benefit of the corporation and a corporate assertion, properly made by a board committee acting with board authority, that the same derivative suit should be dismissed as inimical to the best interests of the corporation.

At the risk of stating the obvious, the problem is relatively simple. If, on the one hand, corporations can consistently wrest bona fide derivative actions away from well-meaning derivative plaintiffs through the use of the committee mechanism, the derivative suit will lose much, if not all, of its generally-recognized effectiveness as an intra-corporate means of policing boards of directors. If, on the other hand, corporations are unable to rid themselves of meritless or harmful litigation and strike suits, the derivative action, created to benefit the corporation, will produce the opposite, unintended result. It thus appears desirable to us to find a balancing point where bona fide stockholder power to bring corporate causes of action cannot be unfairly trampled on by the board of directors, but the corporation can rid itself of detrimental litigation.

As we noted, the question has been treated by other courts as one of the "business judgment" of the board committee. If a "committee, composed of independent and disinterested directors, conducted a proper review of the matters before it, considered a variety of factors and reached, in good faith, a business judgment that [the] action was not in the best interest of [the corporation", the action must be dismissed. The issues become solely independence, good faith, and reasonable investigation. The ultimate conclusion of the committee, under that view, is not subject to judicial review.

We are not satisfied, however, that acceptance of the "business judgment" rationale at this stage of derivative litigation is a proper balancing point. While we admit an analogy with a normal case respecting board judgment, it seems to us that there is sufficient risk in the realities of a situation like the one presented in this case to justify caution beyond adherence to the theory of business judgment.

The context here is a suit against directors where demand on the board is excused. We think some tribute must be paid to the fact that the lawsuit was properly initiated. It is not a board refusal case. Moreover, this complaint was filed in June of 1975 and, while the parties undoubtedly would take differing views on the degree of litigation activity, we have to be concerned about the creation of an "Independent Investigation Committee" four years later, after the election of two new outside directors. Situations could develop where such motions could be filed after years of vigorous litigation for reasons unconnected with the merits of the lawsuit.

Moreover, notwithstanding our conviction that Delaware law entrusts the corporate power to a properly authorized committee, we must be mindful that directors are passing judgment on fellow directors in the same corporation and fellow directors, in this instance, who designated them to serve both as directors and committee members. The question naturally arises whether a "there but for the grace of God go I" empathy might not play a role. And the further question arises whether inquiry as to independence, good faith and reasonable investigation is sufficient safeguard against abuse, perhaps subconscious abuse. * * *.

It seems to us that there are two other procedural analogies that are helpful in addition to reference to Rules 12 and 56. There is some analogy to a settlement in that there is a request to terminate litigation without a judicial determination of the merits. "In determining whether or not to approve a proposed settlement of a derivative stockholders' action [when directors are on both sides of the transaction], the Court of Chancery is called upon to exercise its own business judgment." Neponsit Investment Co. v. Abramson, Del.Supr., 405 A.2d 97, 100 (1979). In this case, the litigating stockholder plaintiff facing dismissal of a lawsuit properly commenced ought, in our judgment, to have sufficient status for strict Court review.

Finally, if the committee is in effect given status to speak for the corporation as the plaintiff in interest, then it seems to us there is an analogy to Court of Chancery Rule 41(a)(2) where the plaintiff seeks a dismissal after an answer. Certainly, the position of record of the litigating stockholder is adverse to the position advocated by the corporation in the motion to dismiss. Accordingly, there is perhaps some wisdom to be gained by the direction in Rule 41(a)(2) that "an action shall not be dismissed at the plaintiff's instance save upon order of the Court and upon such terms and conditions as the Court deems proper."

Whether the Court of Chancery will be persuaded by the exercise of a committee power resulting in a summary motion for dismissal of a derivative action, where a demand has not been initially made, should rest, in our judgment, in the independent discretion of the Court of Chancery. We thus steer a middle course between those cases which yield to the independent business judgment of a board committee and this case as determined below which would yield to unbridled plaintiff stockholder control. In pursuit of the course, we recognize that "[t]he final substantive judgment whether a particular lawsuit should be maintained requires a balance of many factors—ethical, commercial, promotional, public relations, employee relations, fiscal as well as legal." Maldonado v. Flynn, *supra*, 485 F.Supp. at 285. But we are content that such factors are not "beyond the judicial reach" of the Court of Chancery which regularly and competently deals with fiduciary relationships, disposition of trust property, approval of settlements and scores of similar problems. We recognize the danger of judicial overreaching but the alternatives seem to us to be outweighed by the fresh view of a judicial outsider. Moreover, if we failed to balance all the interests involved, we would in the name of practicality and judicial economy foreclose a judicial decision on the merits. At this point, we are not convinced that is necessary or desirable.

After an objective and thorough investigation of a derivative suit, an independent committee may cause its corporation to file a pretrial motion to dismiss in the Court of Chancery. The basis of the motion is the best interests of the corporation, as determined by the committee. The motion should include a thorough written record of the investigation and its findings and recommendations. Under appropriate Court supervision, akin to proceedings on summary judgment, each side should have an opportunity to make a record on the motion. As to the limited issues presented by the motion noted below, the moving party should be prepared to meet the normal burden under Rule 56 that there is no genuine issue as to any material fact and that the moving party is entitled to dismiss as a matter of law. The Court should apply a two-step test to the motion.

First, the Court should inquire into the independence and good faith of the committee and the bases supporting its conclusions. Limited discovery may be ordered to facilitate such inquiries. The corporation should have the burden of proving independence, good faith and a reasonable investigation, rather than presuming independence, good faith and reasonableness. If the Court determines either that the committee is not independent or has not shown reasonable bases for its conclusions, or, if the Court is not satisfied for other reasons relating to the process, including but not limited to the good faith of the committee, the Court shall deny the corporation's motion. If, however, the Court is satisfied under Rule 56 standards that the committee was independent and showed reasonable bases for good faith findings and recommendations, the Court may proceed, in its discretion, to the next step.

The second step provides, we believe, the essential key in striking the balance between legitimate corporate claims as expressed in a derivative stockholder suit and a corporation's best interests as expressed by an independent investigating committee. The Court should determine, applying its own independent business judgment, whether the motion should be granted.[18] This means, of course, that instances could arise where a committee can establish its independence and sound bases for its good faith decisions and still have the corporation's motion denied. The second step is intended to thwart instances where corporate actions meet the criteria of step one, but the result does not appear to satisfy its spirit, or where corporate actions would simply prematurely terminate a stockholder grievance deserving of further consideration in the corporation's interest. The Court of Chancery of course must carefully consider and weigh how compelling the corporate interest in dismissal is when faced with a non-frivolous lawsuit. The Court of Chancery should, when appropriate, give special consideration to matters of law and public policy in addition to the corporation's best interests.

---

18. This step shares some of the same spirit and philosophy of the statement by the Vice Chancellor: "Under our system of law, courts and not litigants should decide the merits of litigation." 413 A.2d at 1263.

If the Court's independent business judgment is satisfied, the Court may proceed to grant the motion, subject, of course, to any equitable terms or conditions the Court finds necessary or desirable.

The interlocutory order of the Court of Chancery is reversed and the cause is remanded for further proceedings consistent with this opinion.

Note: Terminating Derivative Suits

1. The court in *Zapata* distinguished between a case where demand on directors was required and one where demand was excused. Only in the latter situation did the full force of the opinion apply. No demand was made in *Zapata,* nor did the defendants urge its necessity. Thus the *Zapata* court was not called upon to explore the question of when demand was required. That issue is what *Aronson* and its progeny address. *Zapata* did, however, reserve a role for the courts in reviewing a special committee's motion to terminate a derivative suit and rejected reliance on the business judgment rule as the appropriate standard for such review.

2. In Auerbach v. Bennett, 47 N.Y.2d 619, 419 N.Y.S.2d 920, 393 N.E.2d 994 (1979) New York adopted a different approach. A derivative suit was brought against directors and the independent auditor of General Telephone and Electronics Corporation following disclosure that the company had made illegal payments and bribes, and that some of the individual defendants had been personally involved. The board appointed a special litigation committee consisting of three directors, all of whom had joined the board after the incidents in question and one of whom was appointed to the board after the suit was brought. The committee concluded that none of the defendants had breached the duty of due care, that none had profited personally and that it was not in the best interest of the corporation for the derivative suit to proceed. The trial court granted the committee's motion for summary judgment. An intermediate appellate court reversed, but the Court of Appeals reversed again and affirmed the trial court's decision.

The Court of Appeals observed that the "disposition on the merits turns on the proper application of the business judgment doctrine." 419 N.Y.S.2d at 926, 393 N.E.2d at 999. Since the case presented a "special instance of the application of the business judgment rule [sic]" the court had to inquire whether the "rule" applied with full vigor and precluded judicial scrutiny of the merits.

> The business judgment rule does not foreclose inquiry by the courts into the disinterested independence of those members of the board chosen by it to make the corporate decision on its behalf— here the members of the special litigation committee. Indeed the rule shields the deliberations and conclusions of the chosen representatives of the board only if they possess a disinterested independence and do not stand in a dual relation which prevents an

unprejudicial exercise of judgment. 419 N.Y.S.2d at 927, 393 N.E.2d at 1001.

After the court found that plaintiff had failed to produce evidence calling into question the independence of the committee members, it considered how far its review of the committee's action should extend.

> First, there was the selection of procedures appropriate in the pursuit of its charge, and second there was the ultimate substantive decision, predicated on the procedures chosen and the data produced thereby, not to pursue the claims advanced in the shareholders' derivative actions. The latter, substantive decision falls squarely within the embrace of the business judgment doctrine, involving as it did the weighing and balancing of legal, ethical, commercial, promotional, public relations, fiscal and other factors familiar to the resolution of many if not most corporate problems. To this extent the conclusion reached by the special litigation committee is outside the scope of our review. Thus, the courts cannot inquire as to which factors were considered by that committee or the relative weight accorded them in reaching that substantive decision * * *. Inquiry into such matters would go to the very core of the business judgment made by the committee. To permit judicial probing of such issues would be to emasculate the business judgment doctrine as applied to actions and determinations of the special litigation committee. Its substantive evaluation of the problems posed and its judgment in their resolution are beyond our reach.

419 N.Y.S.2d at 928, 393 N.E.2d at 1002.

However, the court added that review of the methodologies and procedures followed by the committee were areas for which the courts are "well equipped by long and continuing experience to make determinations. In fact they are better qualified in this regard than are corporate directors in general * * *. While the court may properly inquire as to the adequacy and appropriateness of the committee's investigative procedures and methodologies, it may not under the guise of consideration of such factors trespass in the domain of business judgment." Id.

One commentator has attacked *Auerbach* for limiting judicial review to procedural issues. See Charles W. Murdock, Corporate Governance— The Role of Special Litigation Committees, 68 Wash. L. Rev. 79 (1993). Murdock argues that courts should scrutinize the substantive conclusions of a special litigation committee rather than limiting their inquiry to whether the investigation was conducted properly. Although the business judgment rule is designed to protect corporate boards from judicial interference in corporate management, allowing termination of a derivative suit before the court reviews its merits shields directors even when they are grossly negligent. Murdock would also preclude courts from deferring to boards or special litigation committees when the alleged wrong involves a breach of the duty of loyalty, as was the case in *Zapata*.

Auerbach does not seem to contemplate *Zapata*'s discretionary second-step, which allows the court to dismiss the committee's recommendation that the suit be terminated even though the committee was independent, disinterested and conducted a thorough investigation with reasonable bases for its conclusions. The decision involved—whether to allow a lawsuit to proceed—is different in analytical process and risk exposure from the ordinary business decision. When considering what to do about the possible suit, the board or committee takes a backward look, much as it does when it considers ratification of a self-dealing act by a director, rather than a risk-laden forward look.

Nevertheless, some courts feel the need to install a kind of screening device against excessive, costly and time consuming litigation. If functioning properly (as *Auerbach* conceives it), the special litigation committee can be an alternative dispute resolution mechanism that provides quick and satisfactory common-sense answers to the charges raised in a derivative suit. Critics of the committee process cannot ignore the strong desire to avoid these costly lawsuits that may not have substantial merit.

3. Notice that the *Auerbach* court sometimes refers to the business judgment *rule* and at other times speaks of the business judgment *doctrine.* The business judgment rule, as we have seen, is a policy of judicial abstinence that shields directors from liability for their business decisions. It comes into play when a shareholder seeks to impose liability on the directors for having made a costly and erroneous decision. The *doctrine* fulfills another goal. It functions not as a shield but rather as a sword, recognizing the decisionmaking primacy of the board. It is an expression of corporate governance, not liability. See Joseph Hinsey IV, Business Judgment and the American Law Institute's Corporate Governance Project: the Rule, the Doctrine, and the Reality, 52 Geo. Wash.L.Rev. 609, 611 (1984).

Thus in *Auerbach,* two decisions were involved. The first concerned illegal payments and the second concerned a decision to terminate the suit to recover those payments. The plaintiff sued to recover the loss arising from the first decision. He was met by the second decision, which he challenged, but he did not seek to impose liability on those that made the decision. The *rule* would govern the question of whether anyone would be liable for her decision, an issue arising only with respect to the first decision. The *doctrine* applies only to the second decision, where the issue was whether the court should defer to the decision not to sue those who made the first decision and paid the bribes. The conduct involved in the first decision was conceivably protected by the business judgment rule, (although arguably not if an illegal act was involved). Yet if the doctrine applied to the second decision, a shareholder would be precluded from recovering the corporate loss resulting from the first decision.

4. *Zapata* 's two-step approach to demand has not been universally applauded by the lower courts that must apply it. Indeed, the elaborate procedures that flow from the full application of *Zapata* were described in Kaplan v. Wyatt, 484 A.2d 501 (Del.Ch.1984), aff'd 499 A.2d 1184

(Del.1985), as a "legal mouthful." *Kaplan* involved a derivative suit brought by a shareholder of Coastal Corporation against the chief executive officer, alleging self-dealing and excessive compensation. A special litigation committee consisting of two members was appointed. One member of the committee was a substantial shareholder of other companies that had extensive business dealings with Coastal. Independent counsel and auditors were named to assist the committee. The committee found that the suit had no merit and concluded that it was not in the best interests of the corporation to proceed with the litigation. It therefore filed a motion to dismiss the suit.

The Chancellor granted the motion after finding that the committee was independent and that the procedural requirements of *Zapata* had been satisfied. He emphasized that even if a committee was independent and its investigation reasonably supported, a court reviewing a committee's recommendation to dismiss a suit could reject the recommendation if, in its own business judgment, dismissal would not be in the corporation's best interest.

The court also discussed the problems of a board using a special litigation committee to investigate a derivative suit and the court relying on the committee's recommendation. After a thorough review of what it interpreted as the *Zapata* requirements, the Chancellor wrote:

> I fail to see how the Special Litigation Committee procedure can be taken lightly or stated any less explicitly given that which is at stake. For it must be kept in mind that the entire procedure is designed to provide a means, if warranted, to throw a derivative plaintiff out of Court before he has an opportunity to engage in any discovery whatever in support of the merits of his cause of action purportedly brought on the corporation's behalf. In fact, the *Zapata* procedure takes the case away from the plaintiff, turns his allegations over to special agents appointed on behalf of the corporation for the purpose of making an informal, internal investigation of his charges, and places the plaintiff on the defensive once a motion to dismiss is filed by the Special Litigation Committee, leaving him to snipe away at the bona fides of the Committee and its extra-judicial investigation in a last-ditch effort to salvage a right to present the case on the corporation's behalf as he sees it. The procedure also asks the Court to consider dismissing the case prior to the time that the facts pertaining to the plaintiff's allegations are developed in an adversarial context unlike the procedure that has existed heretofore. As to whether this new departure in derivative litigation is good or bad I offer no judgment. Certainly, it has its justification in legal theory as is ably expressed in *Zapata*. However, it is fraught with practical complications at the trial court level. It certainly does not speed up the course of derivative litigation and, based upon what I have seen so far, it is doubtful that it reduces the expense or inconvenience of derivative litigation to the corporation.

484 A.2d at 509–10.

In fact, the court noted, the *Zapata* requirements actually increase the amount of litigation and judicial resources necessary to decide whether a derivative suit should be terminated. The use of a special litigation committee adds at least three hearings to the court's calendar. The first such hearing is a motion, upon the committee's appointment, for a stay of perhaps many months until the committee conducts its investigation. Such a stay must be granted by the court as a "foregone conclusion" because *Zapata* recognized the board's inherent right to manage and protect the corporation. Second, at least a "reasonable likelihood" exists that the committee will recommend that the suit be dismissed. If such a recommendation is made, the court must hold a hearing to determine, in its discretion, whether to grant the plaintiff limited discovery to determine the independence and good faith of the committee. Moreover, the court must read the committee's report, which is often lengthy, apparently to demonstrate the committee's thoroughness and good faith. The plaintiff in turn seeks as much discovery as possible to attack the committee and its findings. Third, the court must consider the actual motion made by the committee to dismiss the suit. By this point, the plaintiff may present any number of legal arguments, however poorly grounded, in a last attempt to keep her claim alive. The board will respond with an all-out effort to terminate the suit and its demands on the board's time and energy. The court must then decide whether to agree with the committee that pursuing the lawsuit is not in the best interests of the corporation or, in its discretion, substitute its own business judgment for that of the committee.

The Chancellor concluded *Kaplan* with this comment on *Zapata*:

"In short, the new *Zapata* procedure, while perhaps laudatory in legal concept, has the pragmatic effect of setting up a form of litigation within litigation. (At this point in this case, we are some three years after the amended complaint was filed, we have had three full-scale, briefed arguments, we have had all of the investigation and activity previously mentioned, and as yet we have not reached the point of any of the normal discovery and motion practice permitted by the Court Rules.) The *Zapata* procedure adds, in effect, a new party to derivative litigation—the Special Litigation Committee—and a new battery of lawyers—counsel for the Committee—with the attendant expense to the corporation. It sidetracks derivative litigation as we have heretofore known it for approximately two years at a minimum while the Committee goes through its functions and while the plaintiff passively awaits his chances to resist them. And in the process the *Zapata* procedure has imposed substantial additional burdens at the trial court level in each such derivative suit in which it has been employed." 484 A.2d at 505–512.

5. North Carolina, after initially embracing *Auerbach*, emphatically rejected it in Alford v. Shaw, 320 N.C. 465, 358 S.E.2d 323 (1987). The case concerned alleged looting of an insurance company by its controlling persons. After suit was filed, the board elected two new members and constituted them as a special litigation committee with authority to act for the corporation. The committee investigated the derivative suit, and

then recommended settlement of two minor claims and dismissal of the
rest. The trial court, applying the business judgment rule, granted the
motion, but an intermediate Court of Appeals held that the directors
could not confer upon the committee the power to terminate the suit.
However, the Supreme Court again reversed, found that *Auerbach* was
the appropriate standard, (modified by imposing the burden of proof on
defendants), and dismissed the case. 318 N.C. 289, 349 S.E.2d 41
(1986). In so doing, the court took note of North Carolina's commercial
and industrial growth, and observed, "A favorable business climate can
be fostered in part by recognizing the importance of traditional intra-
corporate relationships and by providing a measure of protection against
"strike suits' (nuisance suits brought to extort settlement)." 349 S.E.2d
at 51.

However, the Supreme Court changed its mind on rehearing and
reversed its earlier decision. Remanding the case to the trial court, the
court observed a trend away from *Auerbach*. It held that North Carolina's "liberal" derivative suit provisions, requiring judicial approval for
dismissal or settlement of a derivative suit, compelled judicial examination of the substance of the proposed action. "To rely blindly on the
report of a corporation-appointed committee which assembled such materials on behalf of the corporation is to abdicate the judicial duty to
consider the interests of shareholders imposed by the statute. This
abdication is particularly inappropriate in a case such as this one, where
shareholders allege serious breaches of fiduciary duties owed to them by
the directors controlling the corporation." 358 S.E.2d at 327.

Unlike *Zapata*, the court did not limit inquiry into the merits to
cases where demand was futile and therefore excused. "Thus, court
approval is required for disposition of *all* derivative suits, even where the
directors are not charged with fraud or self-dealing, or where the
plaintiff and the board agree to discontinue, dismiss, compromise, or
settle the lawsuit." Id.

Moreover, the court observed that the statutory requirement imposing the burden of proving fairness on interested persons in self-dealing
cases requires that "the court must make a fair assessment of the report
* * *, along with all other facts and circumstances in the case, in order
to determine whether the defendants will be able to show that the
transaction complained of was just and reasonable to the corporation."
Id. at 328. On remand, the trial court undertook the modified *Zapata*
analysis of the special litigation committee's report and, after a hearing,
entered judgment for the defendants. The North Carolina Supreme
Court affirmed that judgment.

6. Both *Zapata* and *Auerbach*, in perhaps only slightly varying
degrees, rely upon the ability of independent directors to make a fair and
impartial decision on behalf of the corporation. Other courts have
expressed skepticism about whether directors can be truly independent
when asked to function in this manner.

In Joy v. North, 692 F.2d 880, 888 (2d Cir.1982), cert. denied 460 U.S. 1051, 103 S.Ct. 1498, 75 L.Ed.2d 930 (1983), the court held that Connecticut would follow *Zapata,* but noted:

[t]he reality is * * * that special litigation committees created to evaluate the merits of certain litigation are appointed by defendants to that committee. It is not cynical to expect that such committees will tend to view derivative actions against the other directors with skepticism. Indeed if the involved directors expected any results other than a recommendation of termination, at least as to them, they would probably never establish the committee.

Suspicion about the nature of the special litigation committee caused the Iowa Supreme Court to reject both *Zapata* and *Auerbach.* In Miller v. Register and Tribune Syndicate, Inc., 336 N.W.2d 709, 716 (Iowa 1983), the court commented:

It is tacitly, if not expressly, conceded by the defendant corporation and the defendant directors, in the present case that the board itself could not seek dismissal of the action against the majority of its own members by invoking the business judgment rule. The question which naturally arises is whether, given this circumstance, the board has the power to delegate to a committee the authority to do that which it may not do itself. * * *

The central theme of these concerns [about special litigation committees] has been focused on the "structural bias' approach, which suggests that it is unrealistic to assume that the members of independent committees are free from personal, financial or moral influences which flow from the directors who appoint them. The argument is made that this is all the more so where, as in the present derivative action, the members of the special committee are fellow directors.

The court denied power to Iowa corporations to create special litigation committees to bind the corporation in its conduct of the litigation. However, the court held that the corporation could apply to the court for appointment of a "special panel" to make an investigation and take binding action on behalf of the corporation. See also Will v. Engebretson & Co., Inc., 213 Cal.App.3d 1033, 261 Cal.Rptr. 868 (1989), (even a special litigation committee made up entirely of outside directors has an "inherent structural bias" that warrants judicial review of the committee's independence and good faith in urging the dismissal of a derivative suit).

7. Professors James Cox, a law professor, and Harry Munsinger, a psychologist, offer the following analysis in support of suspicions of "structural bias:"

The directors called upon to evaluate a derivative suit against their colleagues are not, and generally have not been, isolated from the suit's defendants. As members of the board of directors they continue to interact with the defendants, who usually remain directors or officers of the corporation. Even members of a special litigation committee who were appointed *after* the derivative suit was initiated are legally bound under the organic requirements for committee membership to serve as directors on the full board. The new special litigation committee members and the defendant directors therefore serve as colleagues on the same corporate board in addressing an array of nonderivative suit issues. Consequently, the judges and those to be judged associate on a regular basis in discharging their many tasks as corporate directors during the preliminary derivative suit skirmishes. In doing so, they share a mutual duty to serve the corporate interest, and they often adopt a common view of that corporate interest. Analogous studies suggest that the effect of these shared experiences is not only to bond the directors and the defendants together but also to form a basis upon which the directors can be expected to give greater weight to the defendant's values, attitudes, and perceptions than to those of outgroup members like the plaintiff. Indeed, the greater the interaction between the defendants and directors, in terms of frequency and degree of task complexity, the stronger the favoritism the directors can be expected to express toward the defendants. While this favoritism does not necessarily cause the outgroup member (the plaintiff) to be held at a lower level of esteem, in an absolute sense, than when there was no interaction between ingroup members, on a relative scale a greater regard results for ingroup members than for outgroup members.

More is involved in the dynamics of intergroup discrimination in the demand or special litigation committee context than the seemingly simple categorization of the nondefendant directors as "directors," a category which also includes the defendants. As seen earlier, individuals place great value on their selection to and membership on a corporation's board: They are attracted to their colleagues and value greatly the associations they reap from the directorship. The relative attractiveness and rewards of board membership to the nondefendant director are important considerations in the director's ability to be an impartial arbitrator of a colleague's behavior.

A variety of psychological factors contributes to ingroup bias. Not only does each of these biasing factors, such as continued association, competition from without, complexity of shared tasks, and mutual attraction, contribute its individual influence to the overall strength of ingroup biasing, but when several complementary psychological factors occur together within the same person, they tend to exert extra psychological force by their coexistence. This enhanced effect is commonly referred to as synergism wholeness; it means that the total influence of a coherent system of psychological factors is more than the simple sum of its components. Rather, when several compatible psychological factors come together as a *whole system,* they jointly enhance total ingroup bias, so the effect is greater than we would expect on the bias of a simple additive model alone. This synergetic *whole system* has been observed frequently in the psychological literature. It is as if a coherent attitudinal system takes on a life of its own, and the *wholeness* enhances the influence of each individual factor. As a coherent, congruent system within the single person, this synergism creates compelling psychological forces toward ingroup biases within the board or the special litigation committee.

James D. Cox and Harry Munsinger, Bias in the Boardroom: Psychological Foundations and Legal Implications of Corporate Cohesion, 48 Law & Contemp. Probs., Summer 1985, at 83, 103–4.

Aronson rejects the structural bias argument, absent a showing of specific facts. And in Kaplan v. Wyatt, 499 A.2d 1184 (Del.1985), aff'g 484 A.2d 501 (Del.Ch.1984), following *Aronson,* the fact that a corporate director had investments and affiliations with companies that did substantial business with the defendant corporation was not enough to establish bias because there was no showing of "personal dealings" or other impairment to the director's independence.

The Delaware Court of Chancery did find bias in Lewis v. Fuqua, 502 A.2d 962 (Del.Ch.1985), appeal refused 504 A.2d 571 (Del.1986), where all but one member of the board were sued for appropriating a corporate opportunity. That director (former Governor, then president of Duke University, and later Senator Terry Sanford) was then appointed as a one-person special litigation committee. The court found that he was not independent because:

> He was a member of the Board of Directors of Fuqua Industries at the time the challenged actions took place; he is one of the defendants in this suit; he has had numerous political and financial dealings with J.B. Fuqua who is the chief executive officer of Fuqua Industries and who allegedly controls the Board; he is President of Duke University which is a recent recipient of a $10 million pledge from Fuqua Industries and J.B. Fuqua; and J.B. Fuqua has, in the past, made several contributions to Duke University and is a Trustee of the University.

502 A.2d at 966–67.

8. *Zapata* assigns several important roles to the courts. The traffic cop function with respect to discovery is analyzed in *Kaplan.* The court's more important function, however, is to exercise its own business judgment as to the ultimate question—should the lawsuit be terminated?

If the standard of the business judgment rule does not govern the issue, how should the court analyze the question of whether it is in the best interests of the corporation to maintain the lawsuit? Judge Winter, in Joy v. North, supra, analyzed the question as follows:

> [T]he function of the court's review is to determine the balance of probabilities as to likely future benefit to the corporation, not to render a decision on the merits, fashion the appropriate legal

principles or resolve issues of credibility. Where the legal rule is unclear and the likely evidence in conflict, the court need only weigh the uncertainties, not resolve them. The court's function is thus not unlike a lawyer's determining what a case is "worth" for purposes of settlement.

Where the court determines that the likely recoverable damages discounted by the probability of a finding of liability are less than the costs to the corporation in continuing the action it should dismiss the case. The costs which may properly be taken into account are attorney's fees and other out-of-pocket expenses related to the litigation and time spent by corporate personnel preparing for and participating in the trial. The court should also weigh indemnification which is mandatory under corporate bylaws, private contracts or Connecticut law, discounted of course by the probability of liability for such sums. We believe indemnification the corporation may later pay as a matter of discretion should not be taken into account since it is an avoidable cost. The existence or non-existence of insurance should not be considered in the calculation of costs, since premiums have previously been paid. The existence of insurance is relevant to the calculation of potential benefits.

Where, having completed the above analysis, the court finds a likely net return to the corporation which is not substantial in relation to shareholder equity, it may take into account two other items as costs. First, it may consider the impact of distraction of key personnel by continued litigation. Second, it may take into account potential lost profits which may result from the publicity of a trial.

Judicial scrutiny of special litigation committee recommendations should thus be limited to a comparison of the direct costs imposed upon the corporation by the litigation with the potential benefits. We are mindful that other less direct costs may be incurred such as a negative impact on morale and upon the corporate image. Nevertheless, we believe that such factors, with the two exceptions noted, should not be taken into account. Quite apart from the elusiveness of attempting to predict such effects, they are quite likely to be directly related to the degree of wrongdoing, a spectacular fraud being generally more newsworthy and damaging to morale than a mistake in judgment as to the strength of consumer demand.

We do recognize two exceptions, however. First, where the likely net return is not substantial in relation to shareholder equity, the court can consider the degree to which key personnel may be distracted from corporate business by continuance of the litigation. We appreciate that litigation can disrupt the decisionmaking process and thereby impose unforeseen and undetected costs. These are not measurable and we limit consideration of them to cases where the likely return to the corporation is not great. Where that is the case and many of the key directors and officers will be heavily involved in the litigation, a court may take such potential costs into account.

Second, where the corporation deals with the general public and its level of business is dependent upon public identification and acceptance of the corporate product or service, we believe the court ought to take potential business lost as a consequence of a trial into account when the likely net return to the corporation is not substantial in relation to total shareholder equity. In such a case, there is less likelihood of a direct relationship between impact on business and degree of misconduct. Where the likely return to the corporation from the litigation is higher, however, we believe the uncertainty as to the kind of publicity which will attend a trial precludes consideration of that impact. Moreover, when potential lost profits are taken into account, the basis for calculating them must be something more solid than the conclusory opinions of alleged experts, e.g., verifiable examples in similar firms.

692 F.2d at 892–93.

Does Judge Winter take into account all of the appropriate cost and benefit factors that should bear upon the decision? Given the high cost of litigation, could he ever overturn a decision by a committee not to pursue a relatively small prospective recovery?

9. As noted above, both the ALI and the RMBCA adopt a universal demand requirement, but they differ substantially in their treatment of judicial review of the subsequent use of a Special Litigation Committee to dismiss the litigation. The ALI adheres to none of the approaches to special litigation committees described above. It bifurcates the judicial standard of review based on whether the claim charges a breach of the duty of loyalty or the duty of care. If the duty of care is involved, the court should uphold a recommendation to dismiss a claim unless the decision by the board or committee fails the business judgment rule. If the claim alleges a breach of the duty of loyalty, the ALI recommends stricter judicial scrutiny. In such cases, the board or committee must determine that dismissal is in the best interests of the corporation; this determination must be "based on grounds that the court deems to warrant reliance." In deciding whether the findings "warrant reliance," a court should examine the adequacy of the investigation, the level of the board's involvement in the transaction, the plausibility of the reasons presented by the board or committee to support dismissal and, most importantly, the nature of the claim. Scrutiny should be more stringent if the nature of the claim involves charges of "knowing and culpable violations of the law," including those acts that are "morally reprehensible under generally prevailing standards."

The ALI imposes a stiff burden of proof on defendants if they retain a "significant improper benefit" from the challenged transaction. Strict scrutiny of these cases is designed to deter such conduct, although the defendants can overcome their burden even here if the injury to the corporation caused by allowing the case to continue outweighs the harm to the public interest resulting from terminating the lawsuit. ALI, Principles of Corporate Governance (1994), §§ 7.08, 7.10.

Houle v. Low, 407 Mass. 810, 556 N.E.2d 51 (1990) followed the ALI's approach rather than adopting either *Zapata* or *Auerbach*. After an extensive review of the case law in other jurisdictions, the court concluded that such committees were permitted under Massachusetts law. The court noted, however, that because of the danger of "structural bias" and the lack of independence, "a great deal of judicial oversight is necessary in each case," and held that the burden of proving independence, a lack of bias and good faith falls on the corporation. In the case, the committee consisted of one director who had a close professional relationship with the defendants and other shareholders and depended on them for her future economic success. Under those circumstances, the court remanded for a further determination of her independence.

Assuming that the committee was independent, the court found that the second step requires a trial judge to determine "whether the committee reached a reasonable and principled decision. Even in those cases where a committee is independent and conducts a thorough investigation, the judge may conclude that the committee's decision is contrary to the great weight of the evidence." 556 N.E.2d at 59. Citing the ALI Principles of Corporate Governance § 7.08 (T.D. No. 8, 1988), the court said that the trial court should look to factors such as "the likelihood of a judgment in the plaintiff's favor, the expected recovery as compared to out-of-pocket costs, whether the corporation itself took corrective action, whether the balance of corporate interests warrants dismissal, and whether dismissal would allow any defendant who has control of the corporation to retain a significant improper benefit." Id.

10. By contrast, RMBCA § 7.44 requires dismissal of a derivative suit if an appropriate decision-maker concludes, after "reasonable inquiry on which its conclusions are based that the maintenance of the [suit] is not in the best interests of the corporation." The determination must be made by a majority vote of either the independent directors constituting a quorum or a committee consisting of two or more independent directors who have been appointed by a majority of independent directors, regardless of whether the latter constitute a quorum.

As the Official Comment makes clear, § 7.44 is not intended to modify the general standard of conduct of directors, and the analysis that we undertook in Chapter 16 applies to the decision-making process used in determining whether to dismiss a derivative suit. Most important, the court will not review the reasonableness of the determination if the directors who make the decision are independent.

The question of the independence of the directors who are members of the committee and those who appoint them directly implicates the issue of structural bias. The Official Comment states:

The decisions which have examined the qualifications of directors making the determination have required that they be both "disinterested" in the sense of not having a personal interest in the transaction being challenged as opposed to a benefit which devolves upon the corporation or all shareholders generally, and "independent" in the sense of not being influenced in favor of the defendants by reason of personal or other relationships. Only the word "independent" has been used in section 7.44(b) because it is believed that this word necessarily also includes the requirement that a person have no interest in the transaction. The concept of an independent director is not intended to be limited to non-officer or "outside" directors but may in appropriate circumstances include directors who are also officers.

Many of the special litigation committees involved in the reported cases consisted of directors who were elected after the alleged wrongful acts by the directors who were named as defendants in the action. Subsection (c)(1) makes it clear that the participation of non-independent directors or shareholders in the nomination or election of a new director shall not prevent the new director from being considered independent. This sentence therefore rejects the concept that the mere appointment of new directors by the non-independent directors makes the new directors not independent in making the necessary determination because of an inherent structural bias. Clauses (2) and (3) also confirm the decisions by a number of courts that the mere fact that a director has been named as a defendant or approved the action being challenged does not cause the director to be considered not independent. * * *

The structure of § 7.44 places great weight on who has the burden of proof concerning the independence of the directors recommending dismissal. The Official Comment states:

Since section 7.42 requires demand in all cases, the distinction between demand excused and demand required cases does not apply. Subsections (d) and (e) of section 7.44 carry forward the distinction, however, by establishing pleading rules and allocating the burden of proof depending on whether there is a majority of independent directors. Subsection (d), like Delaware law, assigns the plaintiff the threshold burden of alleging facts establishing that a majority of the board is not independent. If there is an independent majority, the burden remains with the plaintiff to plead and establish that the requirements of section 7.44(a) have not been met. If there is no independent majority, the burden is on the corporation on the issues delineated in section 7.44(a). In this case, the corporation must prove both the independence of the decisionmakers and the propriety of the inquiry and determination.

Subsections (d) and (e) of section 7.44 thus follow the first *Aronson* standard in allocating the burden of proof depending on whether the majority of the board is independent. The Committee decided, however, not to adopt the second *Aronson* standard for excusing demand (and thus shifting the burden to the corporation) based on whether the decision of the board that decided the challenged transaction is protected by the business judgment rule. The Committee believes that the only appropriate concern in the context of derivative litigation is whether the board considering the demand has a disabling conflict.

Note: Demand, Special Litigation Committees and Conceding Futility or a Lack of Independence

In Stotland v. GAF Corp., 469 A.2d 421 (Del.1983), the court held that plaintiff, by making demand on the board mooted his claim that demand was futile. And in Abbey v. Computer & Communications Technology, 457 A.2d 368 (Del.Ch.1983), the court found that the board of directors, by appointing a special litigation committee, had conceded that they were interested in the transaction and not protected by the business judgment rule. Finally, in Allison on Behalf of GMC v. General Motors Corp., 604 F.Supp. 1106 (D.Del.1985), aff'd without op. 782 F.2d 1026 (3d Cir.1985), the board successfully avoided this latter holding by delegating to a committee only the power to investigate and recommend while retaining final decisionmaking power itself.

In Spiegel v. Buntrock, 1988 WL 124324 (Del.Ch.1988) (Unpublished Case), aff'd 571 A.2d 767 (Del.1990), the Court of Chancery concluded that a disinterested board that referred a derivative plaintiff's demand to a special litigation committee did not abandon the protection of the "plain vanilla business judgment rule." The court stated that the more elaborate procedures enunciated in *Zapata* in which the court applies its own independent business judgment before terminating the litigation, were inapplicable. The court refused to interpret *Abbey* as requiring that "the act of appointing a special committee itself, in all instances" compels the conclusion that the board was disabled. The court read *Abbey* as merely drawing a "factual inference" and not establishing a legal proposition that the appointment of a special litigation committee to function for the board necessarily triggers application of the *Zapata* test "even if the original complaint did not allege facts excusing the demand." The court noted that *Zapata* is "a narrow exception to the business judgment form of judicial review that ordinarily precludes courts from exercising substantive judgment about the wisdom or fairness of business decisions made advisedly by independent boards in good faith." Thus, the *Zapata* form of review applies only where demand on the board is excused. In *Spiegel,* the plaintiff did not allege facts sufficient to "raise a reasonable doubt" that the board was disabled from determining whether it was in the corporation's interest to pursue the claim at issue.

In Peller v. Southern Co., 911 F.2d 1532 (11th Cir.1990), the court permitted a derivative suit to proceed against the boards of an electric utility and its wholly-owned subsidiary despite the failure to make demand and despite the subsequent recommendation of an independent litigation committee that the case be dismissed. Georgia Power Co., a Georgia corporation, was a wholly-owned subsidiary of Southern Co., a Delaware corporation. Plaintiff, a shareholder of the parent, alleged that the two companies and their directors had acted negligently in connection with the construction of a nuclear power plant and a storage facility. Plaintiff also alleged that demand would have been futile because the defendant directors were insiders who participated in the challenged conduct.

At this point, the timing of events becomes significant. In July 1986, the court stayed the litigation pending the appointment and report of an independent litigation committee to investigate plaintiff's claims. The committee was chosen in September 1986 and given the sole authority to evaluate the merits of the litigation. Its report was due on November 30, 1987. At the same time, the Georgia Public Service Commission, in connection with a rate case, investigated much of the same evidence that the committee considered. The Commission's report, issued on October 2, 1987, concluded that the two companies had made a number of imprudent management decisions and disallowed $300 million from the rate base. The litigation committee's report, issued one day before the Commission's report, concluded that the challenged decisions were either correct or reasonable business judgments when they were made. Thus, as a matter of business judgment, the committee determined that the derivative suit was not in the best interests of the companies or the shareholders and that it should be dismissed.

On October 13, 1987, the companies moved to dismiss or, alternatively, for summary judgment on the plaintiff's suit on the ground that, because demand was not excused, the business judgment rule required the court to defer to the committee's decision to dismiss the suit. The district court held that demand was excused and that, after subsequent discovery, the motion to dismiss should be denied.

Applying Delaware law, the court considered the interplay between *Abbey* and *Spiegel*. *Under Abbey,* if a board responds to a derivative suit by appointing a special litigation committee with the sole authority to decide whether to pursue the litigation *before* moving to dismiss for failure to make demand, the board has conceded its disqualification and demand is excused. By contrast, under *Spiegel,* if the committee is established *after* the motion to dismiss, no such concession is made. By appointing the committee before moving to dismiss for failure to make demand, defendants had conceded that demand was excused. The court of appeals noted that the order of events was "completely different from the order in *Spiegel* and virtually identical to the order in *Abbey.*"

F.   SECURITY FOR EXPENSES

1. Fifteen states provide that the plaintiff may be required to post security for expenses in a derivative action if her financial stake in the corporation is below a minimum threshold. Such a provision requires the plaintiff to secure a bond to cover anticipated expenses in the litigation. "Expenses" entail far more than the "costs" that the losing party is frequently assessed; the main item is attorney's fees. Costs related to discovery may also be included. While the cost of the bond

itself may not be great, the real risk is in having to pay the amount of expenses it secures if the court chooses to impose them, a risk that often will appear too costly for a plaintiff with little to gain personally from the suit. The minimum holding to avoid posting security may be expressed as a percentage of ownership (5 percent in New York) or a dollar amount ($50,000 in New York and $25,000 in New Jersey). California and Texas leave it to the discretion of the courts. Neither Delaware nor the RMBCA provide for the posting of security.

Who is served by the elimination of security for expenses requirement? Professors Jonathan Macey and Geoffrey Miller in Toward an Interest–Group Theory of Delaware Corporate Law, 65 Tex. L. Rev. 469 (1987), argue that the corporate bar benefits most from the elimination of a security for expense provision, at least in Delaware, and that it is in the economic interest of the Delaware bar to encourage derivative litigation to occur in Delaware. The elimination of procedural hurdles, such as security for expenses, is one way of achieving this goal.

2. The policy considerations underlying security for expenses legislation were summarized by Mr. Justice Jackson in Cohen v. Beneficial Industrial Loan Corp., 337 U.S. 541, 69 S.Ct. 1221, 93 L.Ed. 1528 (1949), in which the Supreme Court upheld such statutes against a constitutional attack and furthermore found that the *Erie* doctrine required their application in diversity suits. Mr. Justice Jackson wrote:

> Unfortunately, the remedy [of stockholder derivative suits] itself provided opportunity for abuse, which was not neglected. Suits sometimes were brought not to redress real wrongs, but to realize upon their nuisance value. They were bought off by secret settlements in which any wrongs to the general body of share owners were compounded by the suing stockholder, who was mollified by payments from corporate assets. These litigations were aptly characterized in professional slang as "strike suits." And it was said that these suits were more commonly brought by small and irresponsible than by large stockholders, because the former put less to risk and a small interest was more often within the capacity and readiness of management to compromise than a large one.

3. Derivative suit abuses led New York to adopt the first security for expenses statute in 1944. This statute followed the Wood Report, a study of derivative suit litigation sponsored by the New York State Chamber of Commerce that listed the "common and principal abuses" of derivative suits. The Report found that most such actions were brought by stockholders having so little stake in any possible recovery that it was not credible that they would prosecute the case on their own. Indeed, only attorneys were likely to profit substantially in the event of success. Under the old New York rule, suits were brought by plaintiffs who purchased stock immediately prior to suit to gain standing. A few attorneys controlled the bulk of the litigation, suggesting that they also instigated it. Plaintiffs, defendants, and their attorneys treated deriva-

tive suits as their private concern, without regard to the impact on the corporation or its shareholders.

4. The impact of the legislation has been less than expected. One reason is that a plaintiff confronted with a motion for security may request a shareholder list for the purpose of circularizing the stockholder body to enlist co-plaintiffs who will own in the aggregate enough stock to avoid the statute's application. See Baker v. MacFadden Publications, 300 N.Y. 325, 90 N.E.2d 876 (1950). Corporate management, when they are defendants, are likely to blanch at the idea of the circulation of a letter to shareholders describing, in forceful terms, their alleged misdeeds. A public corporation would be required to make these disclosures in a proxy statement thereby giving added publicity to the alleged wrongdoing.

5. Finally, it is important to note that state security for expenses statutes are inapplicable in federal courts where the action is founded on a federal question. Fielding v. Allen, 181 F.2d 163 (2d Cir.1950), cert. denied 340 U.S. 817, 71 S.Ct. 46, 95 L.Ed. 600 (1950). McClure v. Borne Chemical Co., 292 F.2d 824 (3d Cir.1961), cert. denied 368 U.S. 939, 82 S.Ct. 382, 7 L.Ed.2d 339 (1961). Where the plaintiff also asserts a claim arising under state law, relying either on pendent jurisdiction or diversity of citizenship to establish jurisdiction, the usual practice is to require the posting of security for only that portion of the costs expected to arise out of the defense of the state law portion of the complaint. See, e.g., Epstein v. Solitron Devices, Inc., 388 F.2d 310 (2d Cir.1968); Fielding v. Allen, supra. Recall that this was a major issue in *Borak*.

G. SETTLEMENT

1. INTRODUCTION

The settlement of lawsuits has always played a major role in the American judicial system. Few ever go to trial or reach final judgment; most are dismissed or settled. Because settlement generally saves both time and money and reflects the compromise agreed to by the parties to the suit themselves, courts generally look with favor on the settlement process and are reluctant to interfere with the parties' own arrangements. In addition, settlement prevents ceaseless litigation being brought by shareholders. Judicial approval of a derivative suit settlement acts as res judicata and bars any further adjudication of the issues raised.

Settlements occur no less frequently in derivative suits than in other cases, but the nature of a derivative suit creates problems that do not often arise elsewhere. As noted at the beginning of the chapter, the interests of plaintiffs and their counsel can diverge widely. Shareholders, who do not gain directly from the recovery in a derivative suit, are primarily interested in the impact of the recovery on the value of their shares. In contrast, plaintiff's counsel has at least three incentives: to maximize fees, minimize the amount of time needed to generate those fees, and reduce the risk of the complete loss of any fee. Thus, she may prefer to share in a smaller, speedier but more certain settlement than to risk a trial, where the outcome is necessarily unclear and where she may wind up uncompensated for many years of work. Because of these conflicts, the fact that the parties to the litigation favor a settlement does not carry the normal assurance that the settlement reflects their discounted best estimate of the likely result if the case went to trial. Consequently, F.R.C.P. 23.1, RMBCA § 7.40 and many state statutes require judicial approval of any settlement, compromise, discontinuance or dismissal of a derivative suit.

In addition to the divergent interests and incentives of plaintiffs and their attorneys, other factors may prevent derivative suit settlements from accurately reflecting the actual merits of a case. See Janet Cooper Alexander, Do The Merits Matter? A Study of Settlements in Securities Class Actions, 43 Stan. L. Rev. 497 (1991). Professor Alexander argues that settlements traditionally have been favored because they conserve judicial time and resources. Also, settlements are thought to represent what the parties voluntarily think are the merits of their respective cases. Although the first factor is certainly true—settlements demand less attention by a court than a full trial—the second reason for favoring settlements may not be correct. Alexander asserts that settlements in large categories of cases are neither voluntarily entered into by the parties nor an accurate reflection of the merits.

To support her hypothesis, Professor Alexander studied a group of securities class actions that shared common factors. These cases involved initial public offerings for a new company in the computer industry, each was filed within the same six-month time period, and each involved a similar claim of fraud. Given the common features shared by these cases, the only variable was the relative merits of each case. If the merits varied, the settlements of the cases should also have varied. In fact, however, Alexander found that almost all the cases settled for approximately one-quarter of the damages sought. As she notes, "[A] strong case * * * appears to have been worth no more than a weak one." Id. at 500.

Alexander argues that an explanation for these results is that the judicial system essentially denies parties both the incentive and access to settlement. Defendants, particularly individuals, are especially risk-averse in securities actions because of the large amounts at stake, amounts that often exceed the available indemnification and insurance coverage. Nevertheless, indemnification and liability insurance remain a potential source of funds available to the defendants in event of settlement but not for a judgment against them. If they settle, defendants can shift the costs of the litigation to others. Moreover, securities litigation is generally more expensive for defendants than for plaintiffs, adding to the incentive for defendants to settle early. As described above, plaintiffs' attorneys are eager to settle because their often substantial fees are then assured. These attorneys, not their clients, control the litigation and decide whether to settle.

Alexander contends that her analysis of these securities suits and conclusion that their merits are irrelevant to their settlements are applicable also to derivative suits, nearly all of which tend to settle and result in little benefit to corporations. For additional criticism of problems with the current system of derivative suits and their settlement, see Roberta Romano, The Shareholder Suit: Litigation Without Foundation?, 7 J. of Law, Econ. & Org. 55 (1991).

As you read the following materials, consider whether settlement of derivative suits is driven by the merits. Why does it matter if a case reaches trial so that its merits are, in fact, ultimately determined? Does the judicial system suffer if some defendants pay unwarranted expenses and plaintiffs see little compensation while lawyers reap the benefits? Can a judge protect the plaintiffs' interest in the absence of an advocate for the plaintiffs, if plaintiffs' attorneys appear to be more concerned with their own economic return? Should courts and the legal rules encourage settlements so much, or would it be better to allow more cases go to trial? As Alexander notes, if more cases were heard in court, there would be at least the benefit of more precedent upon which later litigants could base their determinations of what a case is truly worth. If the merits do not matter in the settlement negotiations, do derivative suits provide enough of a deterrent to management to justify furthering such suits?

2. JUDICIAL REVIEW OF SETTLEMENTS

SHLENSKY v. DORSEY

574 F.2d 131 (3d Cir.1978).

Maris, Circuit Judge.

* * *

The eight actions comprising the consolidated derivative suit now before us were instituted between March and November of 1975 in five separate district courts, including the District Court for the Western District of Pennsylvania to which the suits were eventually transferred and there consolidated. Named as defendants are Gulf, eighteen of its present and former officers and directors, an officer of a former Gulf subsidiary, and Price Waterhouse, Gulf's former independent certified public accountant and auditor. The shareholders seek recovery on behalf of Gulf of allegedly illegally expended corporate funds in excess of $18,800,000, incidental monetary damages and costs incurred by Gulf, equitable relief and the plaintiffs' litigation expenses.

The derivative suits arose out of public revelations in 1973 and 1975 by Gulf officials and the Securities and Exchange Commission of alleged illegal corporate action. Investigation by the Watergate Special Prosecution Force into the activities of the Finance Committee to Re–Elect the President (in 1972) precipitated Gulf's disclosure in 1973 that its vice president in charge of government relations, Claude C. Wild, Jr., had, in 1971 and 1972, donated out of corporate funds $100,000, $15,000 and $10,000 to the 1972 presidential election campaigns of President Nixon, Representative Mills and Senator Jackson, respectively. The contributions amounting to $125,000 were subsequently returned to Gulf. In November 1973 Gulf and Wild pleaded guilty to criminal charges of violations of the Federal Election Campaign Act, 18 U.S.C. § 610. Gulf was fined $5,000 and Wild, $1,000. * * *

Opting to settle the case rather than proceed to trial, the parties, with the exception of Price Waterhouse, entered into a "Stipulation of Compromise and Settlement" and on September 29, 1976, petitioned the district court for its approval. * * *

Gulf agreed to reimburse and indemnify the settling defendants * * * as to their reasonable expenses, including counsel fees, incurred in connection with the consolidated action or any other action, judgment or penalty arising out of the matters * * *. Gulf also agreed to the adoption of and further implementation of already initiated internal auditing and reporting procedures designed to avoid a recurrence of unlawful political contributions.

The North River Insurance Company, the insurance carrier under Gulf's directors' and officers' liability and corporate reimbursement policy, agreed to pay $2,000,000 to Gulf conditioned on the execution of releases by Gulf and the defendants named as insured in the policy.

Certain of the individual defendants agreed not to contest the rescission by Gulf's board of directors on July 13, 1976, of stock option rights and attendant stock appreciation rights previously granted them under the 1974 stock option plan and the board's denial of incentive compensation awards for 1975 amounting to $370,000. Gulf agreed to refuse delivery to other defendants of Gulf stock valued at $250,000 previously awarded them. Other Gulf employees, not defendants, consented to the denial of incentive compensation due them aggregating $23,882.28. A retired employee * * * was denied all future payments to him under a 1964 agreement with Gulf. Gulf admitted reimbursement by recipients of illegal or unauthorized contributions from Gulf funds amounting to $57,261.55.

Lastly, based upon the complexity of the litigation, the competence of the attorneys and accountants involved and the benefits to Gulf and its shareholders from the compromise and settlement of the case, Gulf agreed not to oppose an application, with supporting data, to the district court by the plaintiffs' attorneys and accountants for payment by Gulf of their reasonable fees and reimbursement of their expenses in an amount not to exceed $600,000 for fees and $25,000 for expenses.

A summary of the settlement terms was sent to the more than 300,000 Gulf shareholders of record with directions to file in advance of a settlement hearing to be held November 18, 1976, their written objections, if any, to the settlement and notice of their intention to appear if they desired to do so. * * *

* * * [T]he district court conducted a hearing on the plaintiffs' application for accountants' and attorneys' fees and expenses. The district court found the objective value of the time spent by the persons involved in representing the plaintiffs to be in the aggregate $407,-429.50. That amount was increased by the court by $167,570.50 in consideration of such factors as the contingent nature of success in the litigation, the benefits achieved by the settlement terms and the quality of the services performed. The court accordingly found $575,000 to be representative of fair and reasonable fees. The court also approved reimbursement of the attorneys' and accountants' expenses in the amount of $32,777.95 and directed by order entered November 19, 1976, payment by Gulf of a total of $607,777.95 for fees and reimbursement of expenses of the plaintiffs' accountants and attorneys.

* * *

Turning to the district court's determination that the settlement was fair and reasonable, we bear in mind that the scope of our review is very limited. For the district court has wide discretion in making that decision * * *.

The principal factor to be considered in determining the fairness of a settlement concluding a shareholders' derivative action is the extent of the benefit to be derived from the proposed settlement by the corporation, the real party in interest. The adequacy of the recovery provided the corporation by the settlement must be considered in the light of the best possible recovery, of the risks of establishing liability and proving damages in the event the case is not settled, and of the cost of prolonging the litigation.

Given the amount of unlawfully disbursed corporate funds alleged to total $18,800,000 and taking into consideration the risks of establishing liability and damages, set forth at length in the district court's findings of fact and conclusions of law, we cannot say that it was an abuse of the district court's discretion to conclude that $3,500,000 represented a fair and reasonable settlement amount even without taking into consideration the additional nonmonetary benefits to Gulf referred to but not valued by the district court. * * *

One of the factors to be considered in determining the fairness of a settlement disposing of a class action is the reaction of the members of the class. * * * Here the overwhelming majority of Gulf shareholders have not objected to the settlement and Gulf, for the benefit of which the suit was filed, has agreed to its terms.

Bearing in mind all of the factors—the $2,000,000 contribution to Gulf by its insurer under a directors' and officers' liability insurance policy in exchange for its release from further liability under the policy, the agreements of the individual defendants to give up their claims against Gulf for compensation and stock option rights valued by the district court at approximately $1,500,000, the additional cost of protracted litigation, the risk of successful prosecution of the claims given up, the fact that so very few shareholders objected to the settlement, the corporation's approval of the settlement, and the fact that the settlement provides a substantial net benefit to Gulf after payment of plaintiffs' counsel fees and expenses—we cannot say that the district court abused its discretion in approving the settlement as a fair compromise and settlement of the action before it.

Note: Judicial Review of Settlements

When a settlement is presented to the court, the burden of proof as to its fairness rests with its proponents. As *Shlensky* indicates, a court will be most concerned with the extent of the net benefit which the settlement confers upon the corporation. In most cases, the court will give greatest weight to the adequacy of the proposed financial settlement when compared to the potential recovery if the plaintiff succeeded at trial. To make such an evaluation, the court must discount the possible recovery at trial by the time value of money over the period during which recovery will be delayed and by the risk factors inherent in any litigation. The court also should, but does not always, consider the amount of plaintiffs' counsel fees and indemnification that may be paid under both alternatives. See ALI, Principles of Corporate Governance (1994), § 7.14(b). The following standard reflects the general approach of federal courts when evaluating settlements:

> First, the proponents have the burden of proving that (1) the settlement is not collusive but was reached after arm's length negotiation; (2) the proponents are counsel experienced in similar cases; (3) there has been sufficient discovery to enable counsel to act intelligently; and (4) the number of objectants or their relative interest is small. If the proponents establish these propositions, the burden of attacking the settlement then shifts to the objectants, if any. Finally, the court must approve the settlement only after finding it to be reasonable in light of the plaintiffs' ultimate probability of success in the lawsuit.
>
> In determining reasonableness, the courts in this circuit have not applied any single, inflexible test. Instead, they have considered the amount of the settlement in light of all the circumstances, including such factors as (1) the best possible recovery; (2) the likely recovery if the claims were fully litigated; (3) the complexity, expense and probable duration of continued litigation; (4) the risk of maintaining the class action throughout trial; (5) the risk of establishing damages; * * * (8) the stage of the proceedings and (9) the ability of the defendants to withstand a greater judgment.

Desimone v. Industrial Bio–Test Laboratories, Inc., 83 F.R.D. 615 (S.D.N.Y.1979).

Evaluating the fairness of the settlement becomes more difficult when the settlement provides nonpecuniary benefits to the corporation. Often, outside directors will be added to the board or independent audit and nominating committees will be created. Similarly, settlements will include provisions requiring directors to surrender stock options or to sell their shares back to the corporation. Recent empirical studies have shown that such relief has become increasingly common. See Roberta Romano, The Shareholder Suit: Litigation Without Foundation?, 7 J. Law & Econ. Org. 55 (1991). Professor Romano found that approximately one-half of the derivative suit settlements included structural relief. In contrast, the corporation appeared to receive monetary relief in about 20 percent of these settlements. While internal corrective measures are useful to the corporation in remedying past misdeeds, they raise a separate problem: in the words of the ALI, "such therapeutic relief can sometimes represent a counterfeit currency by which the parties can increase the apparent value of the settlement and thereby justify higher attorney's fees for plaintiff's counsel, who is often the real party in interest." To deal with this problem, the ALI recommends that the court review the value of non-pecuniary relief both when evaluating the settlement and when computing plaintiff's counsel fees. ALI, Principles of Corporate Governance (1994), § 7.14, Comment c. See Girsh v. Jepson, 521 F.2d 153 (3d Cir.1975).

Judicial approval of a proposed settlement seems to be necessary to protect stockholders but a number of factors may hinder the court's review. Because the parties to the suit have already agreed to the settlement, they will be reluctant to point out its weaknesses. The court thus may be forced to scrutinize the settlement without the benefit of any adversarial review. The nature of the proceeding may lead the court to place too much weight on the therapeutic non-pecuniary aspects of the settlement, given the materials provided by the parties involved. It is not that the court cannot ask the right questions; rather, the danger is that the court will not know what the right questions are.

Courts have dealt with these problems in a number of ways. In some cases, they have undertaken their own investigation into the merits or have appointed special masters to do so. On occasion, they have asked for expert advice from governmental agencies such as the SEC. The most common solution, however, is to afford notice and an opportunity for a hearing to stockholders who wish to object to the settlement. In the federal courts and many state courts, judicial approval of the settlement must be preceded by notice to affected stockholders. The nature of the notice provisions and when notice may be excused, however, vary considerably. F.R.C.P. 23.1 only requires notice "in such manner as the court directs," and many states have statutes or court rules that track this language. RMBCA § 7.40 is somewhat more specific, requiring notice when the proposed settlement "will substantially affect the interest of the corporation's shareholders or a class of shareholders." The most critical concern to the parties in giving notice is who will bear its cost. Where the case involves a large public corporation with millions of shares and thousands of stockholders, these costs may be prohibitive. In recent years, courts have sought flexible approaches to the problem and have permitted parties to provide notice either through publication or by notifying a random and representative number of shareholders rather than requiring individual written notice to be mailed to all shareholders.

When notice has been given to shareholders, courts may provide for a hearing on the fairness of the settlement at which objecting stockholders may seek to demonstrate why the settlement should be rejected. While the shareholders' failure to object to the settlement should not be construed as implying approval, courts often will approve the settlement if no opposition is presented. A shareholder who does wish to object to the settlement faces substantial hurdles. Generally, she lacks detailed information about the merits of the action and the manner in which the settlement was negotiated. To obtain this information, she may have to challenge plaintiff's counsel who is nominally representing all the shareholders but who has a vested interest in having the settlement approved. The stockholder usually must also act within a fairly limited time period between the notice and the hearing.

In Saylor v. Lindsley, 456 F.2d 896 (2d Cir.1972), after hearing evidence introduced from objecting stockholders, the court conducted a mini-trial on the merits of the settlement and found it was unfair to the corporation. The extent to which stockholders can introduce evidence is a matter of judicial discretion. Courts have permitted limited discovery and the introduction of evidence through interrogatories, depositions, affidavits and expert testimony. The mini-trial is also not uncommon, although, as the court in *Saylor* noted, it is intended to focus only on the terms of the settlement and not on the merits of the original claim.

Even when courts express skepticism about the benefits of a proposed settlement, they are reluctant to overturn a settlement. Bell Atlantic Corp. v. Bolger, 2 F.3d 1304 (3d Cir.1993), involved a derivative suit against a corporation that, in settlement of consumer fraud claims, agreed to pay $40 million to customers, contribute to a consumer education fund and pay the state's legal costs. Plaintiffs sought to recover these payments from the corporation's officers and certain directors. Under the settlement, the corporation agreed to include information about the lawsuit in its next proxy statement. The company also agreed to install new employee monitoring procedures and pay plaintiffs' counsel up to $450,000. The district court upheld the settlement over the objection of twenty-five shareholders.

On appeal, the Third Circuit noted that the value of the benefits to a corporation of structural, nonpecuniary changes is difficult to quantify. Nevertheless, such changes can support judicial approval of a settlement as fair. The settlement in *Bell Atlantic* was not very beneficial to the company partly because of the weakness of the plaintiffs' case. To prove that the defendant directors breached their fiduciary duties, the plaintiffs needed to overcome the business judgment rule. The directors also were protected by an indemnification agreement with Bell Atlantic, allowed by DGCL § 102(b)(7). These agreements raised the plaintiffs' burden of establishing the defendants' liability from breach of fiduciary duty under the business judgment rule to reckless and intentional misconduct. Even if the settlement netted the company a small benefit, it constituted "fair consideration" given the merits of the plaintiffs' claims.

One court rejected a proposed settlement because the directors lacked sufficient independence. In re Oracle Securities Litigation, 829 F.Supp. 1176 (N.D.Cal.1993). Consolidated class action and derivative plaintiffs charged directors of Oracle Systems Corporation with insider trading and mismanagement, and the directors appointed a special litigation committee to review the plaintiffs' demand. The court held that the directors on the committee had not acted independently and in good faith, because they were advised by Oracle's own general counsel. Such representation could amount to a conflict of interest because the corporation's general counsel is likely to be responsive to the board and thus will almost inevitably protect the interests of the defendant directors at the expense of the corporation. Although a settlement approved under such circumstances is not per se unreasonable, the court found it impossible to rely on the approval of directors, who themselves relied on biased counsel, to determine whether the settlement was in the corporation's best interests. The court required the company to retain truly independent counsel before proceeding with the lawsuit.

A Vice Chancellor of the Delaware Court of Chancery recently studied judicial approval of shareholder litigation settlements in that court. See Carolyn Berger and Darla Pomeroy, Settlement Fever, Vol. 2, No. 1 Business Law Today 7 (Sept./Oct. 1992). In a 2 1/2 year period, the Court of Chancery approved 96 of 98 proposed class action and derivative settlements, with 95% being approved as submitted. One settlement was rejected because it conferred no benefit on the shareholders; the other case was awaiting notice to the class members. Fee awards to attorneys averaged 92% of the amount requested, with two-thirds granted in full.

Given the conflicts between plaintiffs and their counsel, should Vice Chancellor Berger's statistics give plaintiffs reason for concern or for thanks when they consider how well the courts protect their interests in the settlement process? How useful is the requirement of judicial approval when courts can express as much doubt about a settlement's value as was done in *Kahn*, discussed in Chapter 5, and yet still grant approval? Do we want or need courts to spend a great deal of time reviewing settlements to which the parties have voluntarily agreed? Will this time spent simply reduce the conservation of judicial resources that is seen as a primary benefit of avoiding litigation?

If, as happens rarely, the corporation assumes control of the litigation, the courts are removed from the settlement process. In Wolf v. Barkes, 348 F.2d 994 (2d Cir.1965), the plaintiff in a derivative suit sought to enjoin a settlement of the underlying allegations by the corporation with the defendant-officers. The plaintiff's concern was that the corporate settlement would constitute a presumptively valid defense to the derivative suit, on the basis of which the defendants could move to dismiss it even though the settlement between the corporation and the defendants had been without judicial approval.

The court held that the notice and approval provisions of F.R.C.P. 23.1 did not apply to the settlement because the corporation was not settling a derivative suit. The court recognized the plaintiff's concerns, but pointed out that a corporation always retains the power to settle its own litigation directly. The court noted that the plaintiff still could attack the settlement in a separate action on the ground that it constituted waste or fraud in a self-dealing transaction. Would a court give the same type of review to the settlement in that suit that it would when considering whether to approve a settlement? What are the consequences to plaintiff's counsel from the decision in this case?

3. ATTORNEYS' FEES

Under the "American" rule which generally applies in litigation in the United States, the successful party is not entitled to recover attorneys' fees from the losing party absent statutory authorization. However, the courts, exercising equitable powers, have permitted a plaintiff whose efforts have led to the creation of a fund benefitting others as well as herself to recover some of the costs of the litigation, including attorneys' fees, from that fund. In a derivative suit, although the corporation which receives the fund is not the direct client of plaintiff's counsel, counsel will be awarded a fee if the corporation has derived a benefit, either monetary or nonmonetary, from the successful prosecution or settlement of the suit.

Recent cases have examined the extent of the benefit that must be conferred before fees will be awarded and the relationship between the benefit and the fees. Perhaps the most unusual was Tandycrafts, Inc. v. Initio Partners, 562 A.2d 1162 (Del.1989) where the court sustained the award of counsel fees to an individual shareholder who had voluntarily dismissed an individual action against a corporation and its directors after the corporation had taken corrective action to cure allegedly false and misleading disclosure in a proxy statement. The Court of Chancery determined that the litigation, although moot, had conferred a significant benefit on the corporation and had awarded counsel fees, notwithstanding that the plaintiff had neither sued derivatively nor on behalf of a class.

In affirming, the Delaware Supreme Court noted that a corporate benefit need not be defined solely in economic terms and that changes in corporate policy or, as in this case, greater disclosure, might justify the award of counsel fees. The court then stated that "[O]nce it is determined that action benefitting the corporation chronologically followed the filing of a meritorious suit, the burden is upon the corporation to demonstrate 'that the lawsuit did not in any way cause their action.' " (Citation omitted).

562 A.2d at 1165.

The court also addressed the need for a derivative or class suit as a prerequisite to granting attorneys fees and noted:

> * * * If, as here, the shareholder commences an individual action with consequential benefit for all other members of a class, or for the corporation itself, there is no justification for denying recourse to the fee shifting standard which has evolved for the therapeutic purpose of rewarding individual effort which flows to a class. We believe the better reasoned approach to be that there is no class action or derivative suit prerequisite to an award of attorneys' fees under the common benefit exception * * * "The form of suit is not a deciding factor; rather the question to be determined is whether a plaintiff, in bringing a suit either individually or representatively, has conferred a benefit on others." (Citation omitted).

562 A.2d at 1166.

Shortly thereafter, in Zlotnick v. Metex, Inc. 1989 WL 150767 (Del.Ch.1989) (Unpublished Case) the Court of Chancery reluctantly followed *Tandycrafts*. Plaintiff had sued to enjoin a proposed merger on the grounds that the merger price was grossly unfair. After suit was filed, an improved offer was accepted by both parties to the merger as a result of actions of a special committee of the board of the target company. In reviewing the request for attorneys' fees, the court noted the holding in *Tandycrafts* that placed the burden on the defendant to show that the lawsuit did not cause the improved offer. The difficulty, as the court correctly pointed out, is that more than one cause may have led to the improved offer. Nevertheless, the defendants failed to meet their burden of proof and thus had to pay a fee of $60,000, an amount that the court noted, "considering the meager services rendered, is generous." See also, Robert M. Bass Group v. Evans, 1989 WL 137936 (Del.Ch.) (Unpublished Case).

In Weinberger v. Great Northern Nekoosa Corp., 801 F.Supp.804 (D.Me.1992), the district court took these cases to their inexorable extreme, awarding *no* fees to plaintiff's counsel in a class action that had been brought in connection with a tender offer. The court found that counsel had failed to show that their efforts "were substantial or material factors" in conferring benefits on the Great Northern shareholders.

In Lindy Brothers Builders, Inc. of Philadelphia v. American Radiator & Standard Sanitary Corp., 487 F.2d 161 (3d Cir.1973), appeal following remand 540 F.2d 102 (3d Cir.1976), the Third Circuit established the so-called "lodestar" test for computing attorneys' fees. This test is favored by the Federal Judicial Manual for Complex Litigation. A recent task force of the Third Circuit has described the "lodestar" method as follows:

> * * * First, the court must determine the hours reasonably expended by counsel that created, protected, or preserved the fund. Second, the number of compensable hours is multiplied by a reasonable

hourly rate for the attorney's services. Hourly rates may vary according to the status of the attorney who performed the work (that is, the attorney's experience, reputation, practice, qualifications, and similar factors) or the nature of the services provided. This multiplication of the number of compensable hours by the reasonable hourly rate [constitutes] the "lodestar" of the court's fee determination.

The "lodestar" then could be increased or decreased based upon the contingent nature or risk in the particular case involved and the quality of the attorney's work. An increase or decrease of the lodestar amount is referred to as a "multiplier." In determining whether to increase the lodestar to reflect the contingent nature of the case, * * * "the district court should consider any information that may help to establish the probability of success." However, "[t]he court may find that the contingency was so slight or the amount found to constitute reasonable compensation for the hours worked was so large a proportion of the total recovery that an increased allowance for the contingent nature of the fee would be minimal." As to the quality multiplier, it was to be employed only for "an unusual degree of skill, superior or inferior, exhibited by counsel in the specific case before the court."

Report of the Third Circuit Task Force, Court Awarded Attorney Fees, 3–4 (1985). See also, Silberman v. Bogle, 683 F.2d 62 (3d Cir.1982).

The alternative to the "lodestar" method is the "salvage value" approach, pursuant to which courts calculate the fee as a percentage of the total recovery. Under this latter method, awards generally range between 20%–35% when the award is below $1 million and 15%–20% when it is more.

Neither approach is entirely successful in resolving the structural conflicts inherent in settlements. If the lodestar formula is used, it is obviously in plaintiff's counsel's interest to prolong the suit and maximize the time spent on the case. Thus, counsel would prefer to reject an early settlement offer or negotiate its terms for a prolonged period of time. Defendants who also have a strong incentive to settle will often tacitly acquiesce in this scenario by extending the time needed to negotiate the settlement. This structural collusion may benefit counsel, but it works against the plaintiff-shareholders and the corporation whose interest is to settle the case as favorably and quickly as possible.

The risk of implicit structural collusion exists even when, prior to the settlement, there have been no negotiations as to plaintiff's counsel fees. See John C. Coffee, Jr., Understanding the Plaintiff's Attorney: The Implications of Economic Theory for Private Enforcement of Law Through Class and Derivative Actions, 86 Colum.L.Rev. 669 (1986). The very use of the lodestar formula may make it difficult to separate the fees from the rest of the settlement. Because the amount of counsel's fee is not directly linked to the amount of the award, counsel who has expended a substantial amount of time on the case will have an incentive to settle for an amount which is less than the shareholders might want to accept. This incentive is increased at the time when the hours which counsel has spent exceed the gain which she expected from the case *ex ante* based upon her estimate of the odds of success.

While the lodestar test seems to encourage plaintiff's counsel to diverge from the best interests of her client, the percentage of the recovery method is similarly problematic. Often, plaintiff's counsel will seek to settle the case very early so as to avoid expending too much effort and time. Since the marginal value of the settlement decreases as the amount of time invested by plaintiff's counsel rises, counsel will attempt to delay any serious investment of time in discovery, and, instead, negotiate a settlement that may be premature and possibly inadequate. Under the percentage of recovery method, plaintiff's counsel also may be reluctant to include non-pecuniary benefits in a settlement because no value will be attached to those benefits in determining the amount of her fees.

The percentage of recovery value method also tends to increase case splitting and fee splitting among different counsel. By diversifying the risks involved in any one case among a number of different lawyers, the lead counsel can reduce the effort put into the case and, hence, the costs that would be incurred if the case is not settled or litigated successfully. Such case splitting both decreases the incentive for plaintiff's counsel to settle early and reduces the effectiveness of counsel's work, thereby weakening the likelihood of a large recovery for the corporation. See John C. Coffee, Jr., The Unfaithful Champion: The Plaintiff as Monitor of Shareholder Litigation, 48 Law and Contemp. Prob. 5 (1985); John C. Coffee, Jr., Rescuing the Private Attorney General: Why the Model of the Lawyer as Bounty Hunter is Not Working, 42 Md.L.Rev. 215 (1983).

The difficulties with both approaches led the Third Circuit, the creator of the lodestar method, to appoint a Task Force to re-examine the problems arising from court awarded attorney fees. The Task Force report notes that when the question of attorneys' fees arises, the role of plaintiff's counsel changes from that of fiduciary for her client to a claimant against the fund created for her client's benefit. In such a situation, the role of the judge also changes; she must now act as a fiduciary for the fund's beneficiaries because there is no one else in the proceedings who is likely to do so.

To obviate the conflicts and problems described above, the Task Force recommended that "at the earliest practicable moment," the court, either on motion or its own initiative, attempt to establish a percentage fee which will be satisfactory to both the court and plaintiff's counsel. In making such an attempt, the court should appoint a representative on behalf of the putative fund beneficiaries to negotiate a fee arrangement with plaintiff's counsel in the same way that any contingent fee would be negotiated. The agreement would then be submitted to the court for its approval; if the parties could not agree on the fee structure, the court would then attempt to work out a solution which would be satisfactory to plaintiff's counsel. The Task Force assumes that in most cases, the fee would be a sliding scale based on the estimated ultimate recovery with the percentage decreasing as the size of the recovery increased. To promote an early settlement, the fee arrangement could provide incentives based on how quickly and efficiently the case was resolved. The Task Force believes that its recommendations may deal effectively with two of the principal problems caused by the lodestar approach. First, by establishing the fee early in the case, counsel has less of an inducement to increase the hours spent on the case as Lindy would have encouraged. Second, there will be a greater incentive for plaintiff's counsel to settle cases more quickly because delay will not increase his compensation. Report of the Third Circuit Task Force, Court Awarded Attorney Fees, 21–26 (1985).

The concern of the Third Circuit Task Force is shared by at least one court. In In re Activision Securities Litigation, 723 F.Supp. 1373, 1378 (N.D.Cal.1989), the court held that in future cases involving a common fund (whether derivative or class), absent extraordinary circumstances, the percentage of recovery for plaintiffs' counsel will always be set at 30 percent of the fund. The court also noted that its review of recent reported common fund cases disclosed that the fee awards almost always ranged around this amount. Hence the court concluded that the lodestar approach did not achieve "the stated purposes of proportionality, predictability and protection of the class. [They] encourage abuses such as unjustified work and protracting the litigation. [They] add to the work load of already overworked district courts. In short, [they] do not encourage efficiency, but rather * * * add inefficiency to the process."

In another interesting attempt to deal with attorneys fees, a federal district court required numerous plaintiffs' counsel to submit competitive bids to determine lead counsel. Four bids were submitted, all of which were based on the percentage of recovery that the law firm would accept with variations for contingencies such as the size of recovery and the amount of time spent on litigation. The judge made the selection by determining which bid provided the prospect of the best recovery for the plaintiff class. In re Oracle Securities Litigation, 131 F.R.D. 688 (N.D.Cal.1990); In re Oracle Securities Litigation, 132 F.R.D. 538 (N.D.Cal.1990).

H. ROLE OF COUNSEL

Can the lawyer who has represented the corporation now represent the individual directors—who very often will be the management of the corporation—in a derivative suit? While it is true that counsel represented the corporation, it is also the fact that she rendered advice to the individuals relating to the transaction being challenged. It is natural for those individuals now to turn to that lawyer and ask that she represent them when litigation arises. But is such representation in conflict with the lawyer's responsibility to the corporation—which has been her client? Will representation of the individual defendants necessarily cause the counsel to reveal confidences of the corporation in breach of her professional responsibility?

DEVELOPMENTS IN THE LAW—CONFLICTS OF INTEREST IN THE LEGAL PROFESSION
94 Harv.L.Rev. 1244, 1339–1342 (1981).

SHAREHOLDER DERIVATIVE SUITS

A derivative suit is nominally brought "to enforce a right of the corporation against a third party, and recovery in the suit must generally go to the corporation. But it may nevertheless be in the entity's interest to oppose a derivative suit. The entity's decision to oppose the suit or merely remain a passive bystander is of more than academic interest, because various potentially decisive procedural defenses can be raised only by the entity. The corporate attorney directed by management to resist such a suit, when the real defendant to the suit is a corporate insider, must be concerned that opposing the suit may be in the insider's—but not in the shareholders'—best interest.

The possibility for conflict of interest here is universally recognized. Although early cases found joint representation permissible where no conflict of interest was obvious, the emerging rule is against dual representation in all derivative actions. Outside counsel must thus be retained to represent one of the defendants. The cases and ethics opinions differ on whether there must be separate representation from the outset or merely from the time the corporation seeks to take an active role. Furthermore, this restriction on dual representation should not be waivable by consent in the usual way; the corporation should be presumptively incapable of giving valid consent.

It has been suggested that the outside lawyer should represent the individual defendants, perhaps as an indirect means of ensuring that their legal fees are not borne by the corporation. The better rule is to require that outside counsel represent the corporation, while the corporate attorney represents the insider defendant; the question of expenses would be decided separately. This rule recognizes that while the in-house attorney is nominally the representative of the corporation, his personal loyalties will inevitably be to the individual executives who hired him.

A corollary of the principle that the entity interests do not necessarily coincide with the position taken by the plaintiff in a derivative suit is that a former corporate attorney may not represent a shareholder in a derivative suit against the same corporation. If one looks only to the form of the suit, there would appear to be no conflict here—after all, the derivative suit purportedly seeks to advance the interests of the attorney's former client—but in reality these suits are often opposed to the entity's true interests.

CANNON v. UNITED STATES ACOUSTICS CORP.
398 F.Supp. 209 (N.D.Ill.1975), aff'd in relevant part
per curiam 532 F.2d 1118 (7th Cir.1976).

[This case was a stockholder's derivative suit in which the plaintiff alleged that the individual defendants committed numerous violations of the federal securities laws: granting themselves illegal stock options; causing the corporation to issue them additional shares based upon false claims that the stock was paid for rent, services and other expenses; usurpation of corporate opportunities; and the payment of illegal compensation.

Plaintiff sought to disqualify the law firm that represented both the corporation and the individual defendants. The defendants asserted that the conflict was theoretical only, and that if any real conflict did arise, they would withdraw.

The court disqualified counsel from representing the corporation. It found the thrust of the rules to be that "The interest of the corporate client is paramount and should not be influenced by any interest of the individual corporate officials." It summarized the law as follows:]

MARSHALL, DISTRICT JUDGE.

* * * These are serious charges. If they are proved, the corporations stand to gain substantially. The CPR unquestionably prohibits one lawyer from representing multiple clients when their interests are in conflict. The code goes so far as to say that if the clients' interests are potentially differing, the preferable course is for the lawyer to refuse the employment initially. In addition, at least one influential bar association has issued an opinion stating that dual representation is subject to conflicts of interest even when the corporation takes a passive role in the litigation. The case law on the question is not consistent; older cases hold dual representation is not improper, while more recent decisions hold that it is, both in derivative shareholder suits and in suits under 29 U.S.C.A. § 501 (1970).

As previously discussed the court is bound to apply the CPR to lawyers practicing before it. The code is clear that multiple representation is improper when the client's interests are adverse. Nevertheless, defendants' counsel argue there is no present conflict and should one arise they will withdraw their representation of the individual defendants and represent only the corporations. There are a number of problems with this solution. First, the complaint on its face establishes a conflict that cannot be ignored despite counsel's good faith representations. Second, counsel overlooks the hardship on the court and the parties if in the middle of this litigation new counsel must be obtained because a conflict arises. Lastly, although counsel offers to withdraw its representation of the individual defendants and remain counsel for the corporations if a conflict should arise, the appropriate course, as suggested by [Lewis v. Shaffer Stores Co., 218 F.Supp. 238 (S.D.N.Y.1963)] and

[Murphy v. Washington American League Base Ball Club, Inc., 324 F.2d 394 (D.C.Cir.1963)], is for the corporation to retain independent counsel. Under this procedure, once counsel has examined the evidence, a decision can be made regarding the role the corporation will play in the litigation. This decision will be made without the possibility of any influence emanating from the representation of the individual defendants, and will also eliminate the potential problem of confidences and secrets reposed by the individual defendants being used adverse to their interests by former counsel should new counsel have had to have been selected under the approach suggested by defense counsel. This solution, concededly, is not without its disabilities. The corporations' rights to counsel of their choice are infringed and in a closely held corporation, as here, the financial burden is increased. Nevertheless, on balance, the corporations must obtain independent counsel.

Although *Cannon* reflects the prevailing view as to the propriety of joint representation, there has been much litigation dealing with the disqualification of attorneys in a variety of contexts and it is difficult to draw definite conclusions about when joint representation will be permitted in derivative suits. See Annotation, Representation of Conflicting Interests As Disqualifying Attorney From Acting in a Civil Case, 31 ALR3d 715 (1970); Annotation, Disqualification of Law Firm From Representing Party in Federal Civil Suit Involving Former Client of That Firm, 56 ALR Fed. 194 (1982). See also, Opinion 842, Committee on Professional Ethics of Association of Bar of the City of New York (1960).

Note: Attorney-Client Privilege

Perhaps the most difficult operational questions for counsel concern the scope of the attorney-client privilege and the work product doctrine. The attorney-client privilege exists to protect a client's confidential communications to her attorney. Where the client is a natural person, it is easier to identify the situations in which the need for the privilege arises than it is in the corporate setting. In the latter, counsel often has consulted with individual members of management in her role as counsel to the corporation. Were those conversations privileged? Was counsel engaged in a meeting with the "client" when she spoke to the managers? Is a memorandum from the chief executive officer to field employees concerning business practices privileged if it is designed to elicit information which will be furnished to counsel but lacks the formal trappings of confidentiality? An action brought by a shareholder—either a derivative suit or a class action—makes the analysis of these questions still more complex because such a suit involves a dispute among different parts of the corporate whole. In such a case, what does it mean to say that the "corporation" is the client?

In Garner v. Wolfinbarger, 430 F.2d 1093 (5th Cir.1970), counsel asserted that the attorney-client privilege prevented him from testifying as to the advice he gave the "corporation" in a transaction involving the sale of securities. The sale was attacked in a shareholder suit alleging fraud under the federal securities laws. The court stated:

> It is urged that disclosure is injurious to both the corporation and the attorney. Corporate management must manage. It has the duty to do so and requires the tools to do so. Part of the managerial task is to seek legal counsel when desirable, and, obviously, management prefers that it confer with counsel without the risk of having the communications revealed at the instance of one or more dissatisfied stockholders. The managerial preference is a rational one, because it is difficult to envision the management of any sizeable corporation pleasing all of its stockholders all of the time, and management desires protection from those who might second-guess or even harass in matters purely of judgment.

> But in assessing management assertions of injury to the corporation it must be borne in mind that management does not manage for itself and that the beneficiaries of its action are the stockholders. Conceptualistic phrases describing the corporation as an entity separate from its stockholders are not useful tools of analysis. They serve only to obscure the fact that management has duties which run to the benefit ultimately of the stockholders. For example, it is difficult to rationally defend the assertion of the privilege if all, or substantially all, stockholders desire to inquire into the attorney's communications with corporate representatives who have only nominal ownership interests, or even none at all. There may be reasonable differences over the manner of characterizing in legal terminology the duties of management, and over the extent to which corporate management is less of a fiduciary than the common law trustee. There may be many situations in which the corporate entity or its management, or both, have interests adverse to those of some or all stockholders. But when all is said and done management is not managing for itself.

> The representative and the represented have a mutuality of interest in the representative's freely seeking advice when needed and putting it to use when received. This is not to say that management does not have allowable judgment in putting advice to use. But management judgment must stand on its merits, not behind an ironclad veil of secrecy which under all circumstances preserves it from being questioned by those for whom it is, at least in part, exercised.

* * *

In summary, we say this. The attorney-client privilege still has viability for the corporate client. The corporation is not barred from asserting it merely because those demanding information enjoy the status of stockholders. But where the corporation is in suit against its stockholders on charges of acting inimically to stockholder interests, protection of those interests as well as those of the corporation and of the public require that the availability of the privilege be subject to the right of the stockholders to show cause why it should not be invoked in the particular instance.

There are many indicia that may contribute to a decision of presence or absence of good cause, among them the number of shareholders and the percentage of stock they represent; the bona fides of the shareholders; the nature of the shareholders' claim and whether it is obviously colorable; the apparent necessity or desirability of the shareholders having the information and the availability of it from other sources; whether, if the shareholders' claim is of wrongful action by the corporation, it is of action criminal, or illegal but not criminal, or of doubtful legality; whether the communication related to past or to prospective actions; whether the communication is of advice concerning the litigation itself; the extent to which the communication is identified versus the extent to which the shareholders are blindly fishing; the risk of revelation of trade secrets or other information in whose confidentiality the corporation has an interest for independent reasons.

Professor Hazard has said of the court's good cause test that it "circumscribes the problem rather nicely but does not progress much toward comprehending it." Geoffrey Hazard, Triangular Lawyer Relationships, 1 Geo. J. Leg. Ethics 15, 31 (1987). See Keith W. Johnson, Evidence: *Fausek v. White*: The Sixth Circuit Garners Support For A Good Cause Exception To The Attorney–Client Privilege, 18 U. Dayton L. Rev. 313 (1993) *and* Note, The Shareholders' Derivative–Claim Exception to the Attorney–Client Privilege, 48 L. & Contemp. Prob. 199 (Summer 1985).

Bailey v. Meister Brau, Inc., 55 F.R.D. 211 (N.D.Ill.1972) was a class action against the officers and directors of the corporation in which the plaintiff was a shareholder in the acquisition of that corporation by Meister Brau. The officer whose communications with counsel were sought was an officer of both the acquiring and the acquired corporations. In asserting the attorney-client privilege, he argued that he had been wearing his "Meister Brau hat" during the discussions of the purchase of the acquired company. The court rejected this argument, holding that "[a] fiduciary cannot turn his responsibilities on and off like a faucet * * * As long as that [fiduciary duty] existed, so did the concomitant interest of the [acquired company's] shareholders in knowing his legal communications concerning the future of their company." 55 F.R.D. at 214.

In Valente v. Pepsico, Inc., 68 F.R.D. 361 (D.Del.1975), the court extended *Garner* to permit minority shareholders of Wilson Sporting Goods Co., the acquired corporation in a merger with Pepsico, to compel the production of certain documents prepared by Pepsico's attorney concerning the possible tax consequences of the merger. The court held that documents prepared by counsel for directors of Pepsico who were also directors of Wilson were not protected by the attorney-client privilege because of the rule that where an attorney serves two clients, otherwise confidential communications are not privileged in a subsequent controversy between the two. The court also held that documents prepared by both house counsel and outside counsel for Pepsico were not protected because of Pepsico's fiduciary obligations as a controlling shareholder to the minority shareholder.

Garner rests on the "joint client" exception to the attorney-client privilege. In shareholder actions, that exception is premised upon the fiduciary duties owed by corporate management to the shareholders and the status of the shareholders as beneficiaries of management's operation of corporate affairs. This rationale is clearly well suited to derivative suits in which the plaintiff is seeking to assert the corporation's interest. Should it apply in a class action where the interests of the plaintiff shareholders and the corporation are opposed? Some courts have so held. See Cohen v. Uniroyal, Inc., 80 F.R.D. 480 (E.D.Pa.1978); In re Transocean Tender Offer Securities Litigation, 78 F.R.D. 692 (N.D.Ill.1978). One court has applied the *Garner* rule in litigation between a corporation and its debenture holders. Broad v. Rockwell International Corp., [1976–77 Transfer Binder], Fed.Sec.L.Rep. (CCH) ¶ 95,894 (N.D.Tex.1977). In *Garner* itself, the court indicated that the form of the suit was not relevant to its decision. 430 F.2d at 1097, n. 11.

Garner suggests that the interests of a corporation and its shareholders are never inconsistent or adversarial. But suppose that the corporation has more than one class of stock. Are the interests of preferred stockholders, for example, always consistent with those of the common stockholders? Consider the materials in Chapter 9. See Note, The Attorney–Client Privilege and the Corporation in Shareholder Litigation, 50 So.Cal.L.Rev. 303 (1977).

In re Bairnco Corp. Securities Litigation, 148 F.R.D. 91 (S.D.N.Y. 1993) concerned plaintiffs' ability to overcome a corporation's attorney-client privilege under the *Garner* good cause standard. Plaintiffs sued Bairnco under Rule 10b–5 for misleading statements made by its wholly owned subsidiary, Keene, that discounted the potential liability arising from asbestos litigation. After Keene later admitted its uncertainty concerning the impact of the litigation on its profitability, Bairnco's stock fell more than 50 percent. Some of the documents that plaintiffs sought in discovery to prove that the misstatements were designed to inflate the company's stock artificially included advice from counsel to the corporation. The court, relying on *Garner*, ordered the documents to be produced because of "the existence of a fiduciary duty or mutuality of interest between the corporation and its shareholders at the time of the communications sought to be discovered," led the court to order the documents produced. Id. at 98.

The extent of the privilege was interpreted in Upjohn Co. v. United States, 449 U.S. 383, 101 S.Ct. 677, 66 L.Ed.2d 584 (1981). Counsel undertook an investigation of reports that the company had made questionable payments to foreign officials to secure business. Counsel sent questionnaires to foreign managers and conducted interviews. The government subpoenaed the resulting documents, and counsel resisted the subpoena on the basis of the attorney-client privilege. The Sixth Circuit rejected the claim on grounds that it was limited to discussions with members of the "control group" of the corporation. The Supreme Court stated:

> In the case of the individual client the provider of information and the person who acts on the lawyer's advice are one and the same. In the corporate context, however, it will frequently be employees beyond the control group as defined by the court below— "officers and agents * * * responsible for directing [the company's] actions in response to legal advice"—who will possess the information needed by the corporation's lawyers. Middle-level—and indeed lower-level—employees can, by actions within the scope of their employment, embroil the corporation in serious legal difficulties, and it is only natural that these employees would have the relevant information needed by corporate counsel if he is adequately to advise the client with respect to such actual or potential difficulties. * * *

> The control group test adopted by the court below thus frustrates the very purpose of the privilege by discouraging the communication of relevant information by employees of the client to attorneys seeking to render legal advice to the client corporation. The attorney's advice will also frequently be more significant to noncontrol group members than to those who officially sanction the advice, and the control group test makes it more difficult to convey full and frank legal advice to the employees who will put into effect the client corporation's policy.

> The narrow scope given the attorney-client privilege by the court below not only makes it difficult for corporate attorneys to formulate sound advice when their client is faced with a specific legal problem but also threatens to limit the valuable efforts of corporate counsel to ensure their client's compliance with the law. In light of the vast and complicated array of regulatory legislation confronting the modern corporation, corporations, unlike most individuals, "constantly go to lawyers to find out how to obey the law," Burnham, The Attorney–Client Privilege in the Corporate Arena, 24 Bus.Law. 901, 913 (1969), particularly since compliance with the law in this area is hardly an instinctive matter * * *. The test adopted by the court below is difficult to apply in practice, though no abstractly formulated and unvarying "test" will necessarily enable courts to decide questions such as this with mathematical precision. But if the purpose of the attorney-client privilege is to be served, the attorney and client must be able to predict with some degree of certainty whether particular discussions will be protected. An uncertain privilege, or one which purports to be certain but results in

widely varying applications by the courts, is little better than no privilege at all. The very terms of the test adopted by the court below suggest the unpredictability of its application. The test restricts the availability of the privilege to those officers who play a "substantial role" in deciding and directing a corporation's legal response.

Despite *Upjohn*'s broad scope, *Garner* and its progeny continue to survive, albeit with some limitations. Thus in In re LTV Securities Litigation, 89 F.R.D. 595 (N.D.Tex.1981), the first reported case after *Upjohn* to address the availability of the attorney-client privilege in shareholder actions, the court upheld the attorney-client privilege for various materials relating to counsel's internal investigation and report to the company as well as materials prepared for the litigation at issue. Although supporting the "free interchange" idea of *Upjohn,* the court also sustained the "good cause" standard of *Garner.* The court's decision was based largely on a "temporal distinction"; all the materials had been prepared after the events which were the subject matter of the litigation. See also, Quintel Corp., N.V. v. Citibank, N.A., 567 F.Supp. 1357 (S.D.N.Y.1983) (fiduciary relationship outweighed interests protected by attorney-client privilege).

Notwithstanding *Garner* and *Upjohn,* the availability of the privilege may be difficult to determine when the communications between the lawyer and his corporate client involve questions of both business and law, a situation which is most likely to arise when counsel is also a director or officer of the corporation. See S.E.C. v. Gulf & Western Industries, Inc., 518 F.Supp. 675 (D.D.C.1981) (where counsel was also director and member of pension fund investment committee requiring him to spend considerable time at corporation's offices, "it cannot be assumed that all of his discussions with corporate officials involved legal advice").

For an extensive discussion of the attorney-client privilege, see Herbert E. Milstein, Attorney–Client Privilege and Work–Product Doctrine: Corporate Applications, Bureau of National Affairs, Corporate Practice Series No. 22–2nd (1994).

Note: Sanctions

We have already seen that critics of derivative suits view them as a device for unscrupulous lawyers to threaten or institute frivolous litigation in the hope of obtaining a settlement from which they will personally benefit. Blue Chip Stamps v. Manor Drug Stores, 421 U.S. 723, 95 S.Ct. 1917, 44 L.Ed.2d 539 (1975). While such conduct may always have been possible, a number of existing mechanisms now make it more difficult to succeed. First, courts have always had the inherent power to impose monetary sanctions on an attorney whose conduct constitutes an abuse of judicial process. Roadway Express, Inc. v. Piper, 447 U.S. 752, 100 S.Ct. 2455, 65 L.Ed.2d 488 (1980). Secondly, Rule 11 of the Federal Rules of Civil Procedure was amended in 1983 to require attorneys to believe, after reasonable inquiry, that every pleading, motion or other paper filed in court be well grounded in fact, be based on a reasonable interpretation of law and not interposed for an improper purpose such as harassment, unnecessary delay or needless increase in the cost of litigation. If the Rule is violated, the court is required to impose sanctions, which may include opposing counsel's fees, on the person who signed the document, his client, or both. There has been an increasing volume of litigation under Rule 11 and courts have shown a willingness to impose sanctions on offending lawyers, including representatives of major law firms. See Note, The 1983 Amendments to Rule 11: Answering the Critics' Concern with Judicial Self- Restraint, 61 Notre Dame L.Rev. 798 (1986); Note, The Dynamics of Rule 11: Preventing Frivolous Litigation by Demanding Professional Responsibility, 61 N.Y.U.L.Rev. 300 (1986).

Rule 11 is not the only source of sanctions that may be imposed on lawyers who initiate frivolous lawsuits; such conduct can also lead to sanctions for violating state bar rules on professional conduct. Greenfield v. U.S. Healthcare, Inc., 146 F.R.D. 118 (E.D.Pa.1993) concerned a lawyer who was referred to the Pennsylvania Disciplinary Board for possible formal disciplinary proceedings because he maintained a "stable" of potential plaintiffs in derivative and class action litigation. After reading an article suggesting that corporate insiders had engaged in insider trading, the attorney telephoned a shareholder in the company to ask if he would serve as a representative in a class action lawsuit against the company. This shareholder had been the named plaintiff in six earlier class action suits for the lawyer's firm and had provided the firm with a list of his shareholdings. The shareholder agreed to be the plaintiff in an action against U.S. Healthcare, and the lawyer filed the suit without explaining the suit further or inquiring whether the shareholder had a potential conflict of interest in the action. After realizing that he knew nothing about the allegations and that he had a conflict of interest because he was a director of a company that did business with the defendant corporation, the plaintiff withdrew.

The Pennsylvania rule provided that "A lawyer shall explain a matter to the extent necessary to permit the client to make informed decisions regarding the representation." The court found a "strong basis" for concluding that the lawyer's conduct violated this rule because the attorney had failed to make disclosure that would enable his client to make an "informed decision" about the lawsuit. Additionally, the telephone call that the lawyer had made to the shareholder shortly after learning of the possible insider trading demonstrated that the attorney was simply interested in being the first to file a lawsuit, thus increasing his chance to become lead counsel for all the class action plaintiffs and receive the largest fee. The court was "troubled" by a practice under which a firm "apparently initiates lawsuits by creating plaintiffs." The court noted that this practice might not be illegal, but it raised ethical questions and suggested that the lawyer "put his pecuniary interests above that of his client."

Chapter 21

SALE OF CONTROL

A. INTRODUCTION

"Control," as used in this and the following chapter, means the power to determine the policies of a corporation's business. Control arises in two ways, First, absent special voting rules applicable to the board of directors or to shareholders, a person who owns more than 50 percent of a corporation's stock controls that corporation because she can select a majority of the board of directors. In addition, as we saw in Chapter 17, a person who owns a large block of stock that is less than 50 percent often has *de facto* control, because she usually is in the best position to mobilize sufficient votes to elect a majority of the board unless another person owns a comparable block. If that is the case, no one may be able to exercise control through stock ownership.

Control also can arise from incumbency. In public corporations where ownership is fragmented among thousands or millions of shareholders, incumbent directors and managers usually possess *de facto* control because of their power to choose management's candidates for election as directors. They also can use corporate resources to support election of those candidates. As you read the following materials, consider which type of control is at issue.

Control is valuable; the power to dictate how corporate resources should be used makes it possible for a controlling person to eliminate many of the agency costs associated with the divorce of ownership from control. Persons who control a company often can command a premium price when they seek to sell their stock, because of the power to exercise control. In addition, a non-controlling person who believes those who currently control a company are not managing it efficiently may find it attractive to purchase control, even at a substantial premium over current market prices, with a view to better employing the company's assets and thereby increasing the company's profits. Similarly, an outsider may pay a premium to acquire control of a company whose operations she believes she can efficiently integrate with the operations of other companies she controls.

Acquiring control also may be attractive for less legitimate reasons. Control can be exploited. A controlling person may find it easy to misappropriate a corporation's assets, to appoint herself and her associates to corporate offices and pay themselves excessive compensation, or to cause the corporation to transact business on unfair terms with other entities that she or her associates own or control. To be sure, the duties of care and loyalty apply to a controlling person's decisions regarding these and similar matters. But breaches of those duties often are difficult to detect, challenge, or remedy. Consequently, when control is sold at a premium price, one must consider whether the transaction serves some legitimate end, or whether the acquiror is paying the premium as a kind of "bribe" to obtain a position in which she can enrich herself at the expense of a corporation's remaining shareholders and, if she bankrupts the corporation, at the expense of creditors as well.

The difficulty comes in distinguishing between legitimate and improper transfers of control. Every sale of stock by a controlling person, if it is accompanied by the departure of the controlling person from the company, necessarily carries with it a change in management and dominion over the company's assets. If more than 50% of the stock is sold, the investment properties and the control properties of that stock are inseparable. It is impossible to sell one without selling the other. It almost defies nature to say that, in such circumstances, one can sell stock but cannot sell control.

Transactions involving a sale of stock accompanied by a sale of control have troubled legal commentators for years. Professor Adolf A. Berle theorized that the control element of a controlling person's stock is an asset belonging to the corporation. He observed that the value of control stemmed from the fact that corporations may act without the consent of all shareholders, so long as the requisite majority approves the action in question. Therefore, he maintained, the corporate mechanism imparts value to some stock, when combined in sufficient numbers, that is not possessed by other stock. This added value, he concluded, should belong to the corporation. See Adolf A. Berle, Jr. and Gardiner Means, The Modern Corporation and Private Property 207–52 (rev. ed. 1968). The implication of Berle's theory is that the premium that the seller of a control block is entitled to keep is limited to the relatively modest cost of assembling the control block. Any excess belongs to the corporation.

Other commentators believe that exploitation of minority shareholders presents the greatest danger. William D. Andrews, The Stockholder's Right to Equal Opportunity in the Sale of Shares, 78 Harv. L.Rev. 505 (1965), argues that "a controlling shareholder should not be free to sell, at least to an outsider, except pursuant to a purchase offer made equally available to other shareholders." Id. at 506. Other commentators maintain that the law should impose few if any restrictions on transfers of control because most such transfers are beneficial; they move corporate resources into the hands of those who value them most highly and therefore are apt to utilize them most efficiently. Frank E.

Easterbrook & Daniel R. Fischel, Corporate Control Transactions, 91 Yale L.J. 698, 698 (1982) assert "that those who produce a gain [through a transfer of control] should be allowed to keep it, subject to the constraint that other parties to the transaction be at least as well off as before the transaction." Consequently, [a]ny attempt to require sharing simply reduces the likelihood that there will be gains to share." Id.

More recently, Einer Elhauge has pointed out that the rules advanced by Andrews and by Easterbrook and Fischel both may serve useful purposes, but that both also have drawbacks. Any rule designed to facilitate transfers of control also is certain to facilitate some potentially exploitative transactions, while any rule designed to discourage all exploitative transfers of control surely will deter some potentially beneficial transactions. Consequently, Professor Elhauge suggests, the debate should focus not on absolutes, but on the trade-offs involved. See Einer Elhauge, The Triggering Function of Sale of Control Doctrine, 59 U. Chi. L. Rev. 1465 (1992).

Courts also largely have rejected the extreme positions. The basic rule is that control can be sold at a premium price. Only in special circumstances does this rule not apply. The New York Court of Appeals has summarized this rule as follows:

> Recognizing that those who invest the capital necessary to acquire a dominant position in the ownership of a corporation have the right of controlling that corporation, it has long been settled law that, absent looting of corporate assets, conversion of a corporate opportunity, fraud or other acts of bad faith, a controlling stockholder is free to sell, and a purchaser is free to buy, that controlling interest at a premium price.

Zetlin v. Hanson Holdings, Inc., 48 N.Y.2d 684, 685, 421 N.Y.S.2d 877, 878, 397 N.E.2d 387, 388 (1979).

PROBLEM
GOTHAM TRIBUNE

Gotham Tribune, Inc. (GTI), publisher of the Gotham Tribune, is a publicly owned Columbia corporation whose stock is traded on the New York Stock Exchange. In recent months the price of the stock has been fairly stable at about $15 per share. Burt and Ernie, sons of the founder of the paper, each owns 15 percent of the stock and holds office as co-chief executive of GTI. GTI has 10 million shares of common stock outstanding.

GTI Timber, Inc., a wholly-owned subsidiary of GTI, owns substantial timber property in Canada and is a large producer of newsprint. Timber supplies all of the Tribune's needs and sells to other users as well. The Tribune pays the same price as Timber's other customers. There is a growing shortage of newsprint and prices are on the rise. For this reason and others, the Tribune has contributed a relatively declining amount to GTI's profits and Timber has contributed increasingly more. GTI earned $15 million, or $1.50 per share last year, of which $5 million was contributed by Timber. Were it not for Timber, GTI stock probably would sell for six or seven times its remaining earnings of $1.00 per share. Timber, as an independent company, probably would sell for $8.00 to $9.00 per share. However, the Tribune is the pride of GTI's management and is generally acclaimed to be one of the region's finest papers.

World Publishers, Inc. publishes more than 50 newspapers. Most of them are highly profitable; all are very different from the Tribune. Some of the differences suggest why those papers are more profitable than the Tribune. The papers are directed at a mass market; they emphasize the sensational; and they rely heavily on wire services, rather than separate and expensive news gathering bureaus, for national and international news.

World recently offered to buy Timber from GTI for $50 million in cash and long-term debentures, subject to a commitment to continue supplying newsprint of the Tribune. GTI's board, composed of Burt, Ernie, GTI's attorney, the president of Timber and five business people who have no other connection with GTI, voted unanimously to reject World's offer as inadequate, since it was only ten times Timber's earnings for the prior year.

World then approached Burt and Ernie and offered to buy their stock for $21 per share, or a total of $63 million. Burt wanted to accept the offer; he is anxious to get out of the newspaper business and enter politics. Ernie, however, initially decided not to sell. That appeared to scuttle the deal, since World's offer was for both their shares.

Ernie subsequently became apprehensive that World might make another offer to Burt or might make a tender offer directly to GTI's public shareholders, which could leave him as a minority stockholder with little influence over GTI. Moreover, World agreed that if Ernie stepped down as co-CEO, it would continue him as a director and as publisher of the Tribune, at a salary higher than his present salary. Under these circumstances, Ernie tentatively agreed with Burt to accept World's $63 million offer.

As part of their contract with World, Burt and Ernie also would have to arrange for GTI's other directors to resign seriatim and for a slate of candidates suggested by World to be elected in their stead.* Burt and Ernie know little about any of World's candidates. They are aware that World's CEO has a reputation as a flamboyant entrepreneur. They also are familiar with the details of an exposé the Tribune published last year linking World's second-in-command to payoffs of labor racketeers tied to newspaper distribution companies.

Before proceeding to sign a contract with World, Ernie has sought the advice of counsel. The partner in charge of this matter has sent you a memorandum setting forth the facts stated above and further noting:

---

* Seriatim replacement of directors works as follows: If the board consists of A, B and C, who agree to elect X, Y and Z in their place, first A resigns and B and C elect X. Then B resigns and C and X elect Y. C then resigns and X and Y elect Z.

This is the kind of situation for which shareholder's suits are made, and I have advised our client of the high probability of litigation. I asked Ernie whether World could be induced to pay the same price for all GTI stock now held by public shareholders; he said World has made clear they are not willing to proceed in that fashion. That eliminates what probably would be the best way to minimize litigation problems.

Assume that Ernie wants to go forward only if we conclude that he is likely to prevail in any lawsuits that may be brought by GTI shareholders. The threshold issue is whether this transaction involves a sale of control. Assuming it does, could shareholders sustain claims of looting, sale of corporate office, or usurpation of corporate opportunity or other breaches of fiduciary duty. Is there anything that Ernie should do prior to closing to protect himself against such claims? Does he have any responsibility for what happens to GTI or its shareholders after World assumes control? Could a shareholder successfully claim that by giving World control of Timber, Ernie has converted a corporate opportunity into a personal profit? Even if we assume that Ernie will take any protective actions that we believe are necessary, can he nonetheless be required to give up some or all of the premium he will receive for his stock? If so, is there some other way to restructure the deal so as to avoid such liability?

Prepare to respond to the partner's questions.

B. THE DUTY OF CARE IN THE SALE OF CONTROL

SWINNEY v. KEEBLER CO.
480 F.2d 573 (4th Cir.1973).

WINTER, CIRCUIT JUDGE.

[Plaintiffs were holders of defaulted debentures of Meadors, Inc. who brought a class action against Meadors and prior owners of its stock to obtain payment of the debentures or recover damages equal to the amounts unpaid. The district court found for plaintiffs.]

Since Keebler is the only defendant who has appealed, we will confine our consideration to the case against it. The district court found that, in connection with the successive sales of Meadors' stock from Keebler to Atlantic to Flora Mir Distributing, Meadors had been looted by Atlantic and its corporate assets dissipated, with the result, among others, that the interest and principal of the debentures were in default. Although the district court made no finding that Keebler had looted Meadors and, indeed, made no finding of any intentional wrongdoing on the part of Keebler, it nevertheless held Keebler liable for violation of its obligation to Meadors and Meadors' debenture holders "[i]n light of all the circumstances known to Keebler * * * to conduct such investigation of the purchaser [Atlantic] as would convince a reasonable man that the sale was legitimate, or to refrain from making the sale." Swinney v. Keebler Company, 329 F.Supp. 216, 224 (D.S.C.1971).

We disagree that the circumstances were such as to give rise to an obligation on the part of Keebler to conduct an investigation of Atlantic beyond that which was actually conducted or to refrain from making the sale. Accordingly, we reverse and direct the entry of judgment for Keebler.

I.

* * *

Briefly stated, Keebler bought the stock of Meadors, a candy manufacturer, on August 7, 1963. At the time of the purchase, Meadors was in serious financial trouble and its debentures had a book value of less than one-half of their principal amount. Keebler operated Meadors, manufacturing and distributing candy and causing it to engage in other profitable operations so as to utilize a substantial tax loss carryback. By February, 1968, Meadors had total assets of $581,491, including cash of $321,337, and a net worth of $230,000.

Prior to February, 1968, Keebler decided to withdraw from the manufacture of candy, but not its sale and distribution, and it concluded to sell Meadors. It employed a broker to find a buyer and subsequently began negotiations with Flora Mir Candy.

Negotiations with Flora Mir Candy proceeded to the point where the buyer was preparing to purchase Meadors for $176,000, although not all aspects of the transaction had been agreed upon, when on February 9, 1968, a Keebler officer, Mr. Chester Burchsted, received a telephone call from a broker, Mr. Olen, who indicated that Atlantic might be interested in purchasing Meadors.

* * *

Burchsted and Olen met in the Newark airport on the morning of February 14, 1968, and as a result of the meeting an afternoon session was arranged in New York at the offices of Keebler's lawyers between Atlantic's counsel, Ivan Ezrine, Esquire, and several representatives of Keebler, including Edward Vincek, Esquire, Keebler's general counsel. In the meantime, Keebler's negotiations with Flora Mir Candy were suspended.

During the afternoon meeting, Keebler's various representatives questioned Ezrine concerning Atlantic, its financing structure and its corporate and financial history. Ezrine told Keebler that Atlantic was a prospering small holding company which was becoming a conglomerate and wanted to diversify by expanding into the candy business. Ezrine gave Keebler recent unaudited financial statements, prepared by certified public accountants, which showed that Atlantic had a net worth of

$997,000 as of December 31, 1967, and net income of $158,588 for that calendar year.

At the February 14 meeting, Keebler and Atlantic negotiated an agreement for the sale of Meadors' stock, and the agreement was executed that day or the next. The contract documents were patterned largely on those which had been prepared while the negotiations with Flora Mir Candy were continuing. Among other things, the following agreements were reached: (1) the sales price was set at $235,000, (2) Atlantic represented its financial statement of December 31, 1967 as true, correct, and prepared in accordance with generally accepted accounting principles, (3) Atlantic promised, as a condition of the sale, that its financial strength on the closing date would be substantially the same or better than shown in its December 31, 1967 statements, (4) Atlantic agreed to guarantee Meadors' accounts payable and accruals, (5) Atlantic agreed to guarantee payment of the interest and principal of the Meadors' seven percent subordinated debentures, and (6) Atlantic agreed to indemnify Keebler from any liability arising out of the sale.

Keebler, for its part, warranted as true and correct its representations including the Meadors' balance sheet, the list of outstanding contracts and the list of Meadors' tangible properties. Keebler promised to use its best efforts to retain Meadors' personnel except officers and directors who were Keebler's nominees, and it agreed to purchase $562,000 worth of candy from Meadors within the ensuing nine-month period.

The closing was held in Greenville, South Carolina, on February 19. Prior thereto, Atlantic sent its certified public accountant to the Meadors' plant twice to inspect it. The accountant found a minor discrepancy in the properties of Meadors and the parties agreed to a $5,000 reduction in the ultimate purchase price paid by Atlantic on that account. Once at the negotiating session and once prior to the closing, Ezrine inquired of Vincek as to the possibility of making some arrangement to avoid Atlantic's bringing the funds for consummation of the transaction from New York. Both times Vincek rejected the suggestion and advised Ezrine that it was Atlantic's responsibility to finance the purchase.

At the closing, various documents were executed and delivered, including a licensing agreement which permitted Meadors to use Keebler's "Kitchen Rich" trademark under which Meadors' candy had been sold, and a detailed bill of sale conveying to Meadors all machinery and equipment theretofore on lease from Keebler. Although there was no evidence to show that Keebler was aware of what had transpired, Atlantic made a one-day borrowing of $235,000 from the People's National Bank, a bank in Greenville where Meadors had its account. Atlantic deposited the loan proceeds in an account in its name, then bought a $230,000 banker's check drawn on a New York bank in favor of Keebler for the adjusted purchase price. After the closing, Atlantic transferred $310,000 from the Meadors' account to its own account and repaid the loan. The transfer of funds was shown on Meadors' books as a loan to Atlantic—an account receivable—and on Atlantic's books as a loan from Meadors—an account payable.

Keebler had nothing further to do with Meadors after the closing except for the purchase of candy pursuant to the candy contract.

Atlantic retained ownership of Meadors for approximately four months and repaid approximately $33,200 of its loan. During this period, Meadors paid its trade accounts and made a profit of approximately $19,000. Atlantic's efforts to build up an independent sales force and find markets for its candy other than Keebler were largely unsuccessful, and Atlantic then sold the stock to Flora Mir Distributing, a subsidiary of Flora Mir Candy, on June 25, 1968, for a purchase price of $352,000. At that closing, Atlantic's accounts payable to Meadors was repaid; but Flora Mir Distributing, perpetuating the pattern established by Atlantic, thereafter withdrew funds from Meadors, reflected on Meadors' books as a loan to Flora Mir Distributing. Flora Mir Distributing acquired other candy companies, and Flora Mir Distributing treated itself and its subsidiaries as a single company, transferring monies and properties from one to the other. Initially, the group experienced success with their combined operations, but ultimately the combination became short of working capital and went into bankruptcy.

II.

The parties do not seriously dispute the applicable law. The district court correctly, we think, drew upon the leading case of Insuranshares Corporation v. Northern Fiscal Corporation, 35 F.Supp. 22 (E.D.Pa. 1940), which held the sellers of a controlling interest in a corporation liable to the corporation when the buyers proceeded to loot it after their acquisition of control. Liability was predicated upon breach of a duty not to transfer control since the circumstances surrounding the transfer were "such as to awaken suspicion and put a prudent man on his guard—unless a reasonably adequate investigation discloses such facts as would convince a reasonable person that no fraud is intended or likely to result." 35 F.Supp. at 25.

In *Insuranshares,* the suspicious circumstances included (1) the defendants' probable knowledge that the purchase was to be financed by a pledge of the corporation's assets, (2) the corporation's president's clear predisposition to allow a sale to be financed by pledging those assets as security, (3) defendants' awareness of the purchasers' plan to have a large part of the corporation's assets converted into cash prior to the sale, (4) the inflated price or premium paid for control, especially given the nature of the business which was an investment trust with no physical assets but only the ready equivalent of cash in the form of marketable securities, (5) warnings from the sellers' attorneys as to their potential liabilities for dealing with little-known purchasers, and (6) the fact that the corporation had been looted five years before by a different group who had gained control by using the same method of financing.

The standard of conduct to which *Insuranshares* holds controlling transferors had been widely accepted. Generally, the owner of corporate stock may dispose of his shares as he sees fit. A dominant or majority stockholder does not become a fiduciary for other stockholders *merely* by owning stock. In selling their stock, the stockholders necessarily act for themselves, and not as trustees for the other stockholders. But majority stockholders who assume the management of the corporation, as Keebler did here, can be said to stand in fiduciary relation to the minority under certain circumstances. Thus, while the majority is not an absolute insurer against any wrongs which may be done to the corporation after the transfer of control or against any decisions by the new owners that may not be in the best interest of the minority, if the sellers of control are in a position to foresee the likelihood of fraud on the corporation, including its creditors, or on the remaining stockholders, at the hands of the transferee, their fiduciary duty imposes a positive duty to investigate the motives and reputation of the would-be purchaser; and unless such a reasonable investigation shows that to a reasonable man no fraud is intended or likely to result, the sellers must refrain from the transfer of control.

III.

In light of the facts and applicable law, plaintiffs' right to recover turns on whether Keebler had sufficient knowledge to foresee the likelihood of fraud so as to give rise to a duty to conduct a further investigation and to satisfy itself, by the test of a reasonable man, that no fraud was intended or likely to result before it consummated the sale of control. The district court identified essentially seven circumstances which "might have indicated [to Keebler] that Atlantic Services had no intention of operating Meadors * * *." 329 F.Supp. at 220. These factors were: (1) no one from Atlantic had any experience in the candy business, (2) at the time the contract was executed no one from Atlantic had inspected the "Meadors operation," (3) by the time of the closing, only Atlantic's accountant had examined Meadors to "any appreciable extent and he was interested principally in the books and inventory," (4) Meadors had no market of its own and the "profit as shown could not have been accepted at face value by an outsider," (5) prior to the closing Atlantic had no negotiations with Meadors' key employees concerning the continuation of the business, (6) the sale was consummated with dispatch, and (7) Atlantic had inquired as to the availability of Meadors' funds for payment of the purchase price. Although the district court concluded that the first five factors were "not necessarily inconsistent with a legitimate sale of a business the size of Meadors," it held that when coupled with facts six and seven, they "were more than sufficient to arouse the suspicion of Keebler."

We think that the findings of fact relied on by the district court to conclude that Keebler was liable to Meadors' debenture holders were insufficient to support that result. We will comment on them seriatim.

From Keebler's point of view, the fact that no one from Atlantic had any experience in the candy business should not have been suspicious. Atlantic was represented to Keebler as a holding and investment company which did business through subsidiaries. A conglomerate, which Atlantic professed to be aspiring, regularly acquires diverse businesses; and in any event, it is not unusual for any corporation to venture into a new business field. Meadors was an integrated functioning enterprise with management and equipment in place, and Keebler agreed, except with respect to Meadors' officers and directors, which were Keebler personnel, to use its best efforts to maintain intact other personnel of Meadors then on Meadors' payroll. As a result of Keebler's agreement to purchase candy for a nine-month period, Keebler could assume that Meadors would have, at least for the short run, a ready market for candy and an opportunity to recruit and train a sales force.

No suspicion should have been aroused from the fact that no one from Atlantic inspected the Meadors' operation prior to execution of the contract, and that at the time of closing, only Atlantic's accountant had examined Meadors to any appreciable extent. Atlantic's broker, Olen, who first telephoned Keebler's Burchsted, had some familiarity with Meadors, albeit apparently obtained from the broker retained by Keebler. Keebler made extensive warranties concerning the plant and its financial operations and were these warranties untrue, Atlantic might have rescinded the sale or sued for damages. A sufficient inspection prior to closing was made so that the parties agreed to a $5,000 reduction in the purchase price. From Keebler's point of view, Atlantic's reliance on its broker, on Keebler's warranties, and on Atlantic's accountant's inspections was hardly a circumstance indicative of an intention not to operate, much less of an intention to loot.

We see nothing suspicious in the fact that Meadors had no market of its own, and we do not agree that the profit as shown on Meadors' financial statements could not have been accepted at face value by an outsider. While Meadors' past profit history may have been somewhat questionable, its operation by Keebler was profitable, and Keebler warranted Meadors' balance sheet at the time of closing. There is no question but that Keebler's agreement to purchase candy provided Meadors with a substantial initial market, and Keebler could have reasonably assumed that during the period and with the financial support of its purchase of candy, Meadors could build up its own market. Keebler cannot be held liable as a result of its failure to sell Meadors to a company with a candy market already well developed. Only a small portion of the business community could live under such a restrictive rule with regard to the purchase and sale of business enterprises.

Nor do we find significant the fact that prior to closing, Atlantic conducted no negotiations with key employees then operating Meadors relative to their continuation of the business. Keebler contracted to use its best efforts to retain them as employees, and Atlantic did retain them after it took over. The wisdom of Atlantic's failure to negotiate with them prior to closing is not in issue—only its impact on Keebler as a "suspicious circumstance" is significant. Since Keebler owned Meadors, had full power to sell the company, and agreed to do its part in keeping the enterprise intact, we do not think that Keebler was confronted with a suspicious circumstance.

The dispatch with which the sale was consummated was not suspicious. In the first place, no reason to delay closing has been suggested. In any event, any haste was principally that of Keebler's making and not that of Atlantic. Keebler had been prepared to sell Meadors to Flora Mir Candy; active negotiations were being carried on and legal papers to consummate the transaction were in the course of preparation when Atlantic appeared on the scene. When agreement with Atlantic was reached, Keebler was pressing to consummate a more profitable transaction in lieu of a less profitable one before the latter was irrevocably lost.

The inquiries made by Atlantic with regard to the availability of Meadors' funds for payment of the purchase price were not such as to provide a basis on which Keebler could suspect how payment would be made, especially since Keebler made its position clear that Atlantic must consummate the purchase with its own funds. It is true that the record shows that Atlantic did not do so, but the record does not disclose an evidentiary basis to find, nor did the district court find, that Keebler knew or had reason to know of Atlantic's one-day loan and its immediate repayment with Meadors' funds. Whatever inkling Keebler may have had that Atlantic was interested in using Meadors' cash did not rise to a level sufficient to necessitate further investigation, especially in light of Atlantic's seemingly strong financial position and its apparent ability to finance the transaction with its own monies.

Overall, we conclude that the seven factors considered singly or in concert, were not sufficient to suggest to Keebler that Atlantic did not intend to operate Meadors, but rather intended to loot it. As our discussion of the findings relied on to support the contrary conclusion discloses, there were many positive indications that Atlantic intended to operate Meadors and to operate it profitably. In addition, Atlantic's guarantee of the payment of principal of and interest on Meadors' debentures was significant, especially in the light of Atlantic's apparent financial ability to fulfill that commitment. It follows, we think, that Keebler's obligation to conduct a further investigation sufficient to satisfy a reasonable man that no fraud was intended or likely to result, or to refrain from the transfer of control, did not arise. The obligation could not have been breached, so that there was therefore no basis to impose liability on Keebler.

Reversed.

Note: Liability for Looting

Why should the *seller* rather than the buyer be liable if there is subsequent looting? In Harris v. Carter, 582 A.2d 222 (Del.Ch.1990), Chancellor Allen suggested that the principle of *Insuranshares*, on which the court relied in Swinney v. Keebler Co, is grounded in tort law:

[I]t does not follow from the proposition that ordinarily a shareholder has a right to sell her stock to whom and on such terms as she deems expedient, that no duty may arise from the particular circumstances to take care in the exercise of that right. It is established American legal doctrine that, unless privileged, each person owes a duty to those who may foreseeably be harmed by her action to take such steps as a reasonably prudent person would take in similar circumstances to avoid such harm to others. While this principle arises from the law of torts and not the law of corporations or of fiduciary duties, that distinction is not, I think, significant unless the law of corporations or of fiduciary duties somehow privileges a selling shareholder by exempting her from the reach of this principle. The principle itself is one of great generality and, if not negated by privilege, would apply to a controlling shareholder who negligently places others foreseeably in the path of injury.

That a shareholder may sell her stock (or that a director may resign his office) is a right that, with respect to the principle involved, is no different, for example, than the right that a licensed driver has to operate a motor vehicle upon a highway. The right exists, but it is not without conditions and limitations, some established by positive regulation, some by common-law. Thus, to continue the parallel, the driver owes a duty of care to her passengers because it is foreseeable that they may be injured if, through inattention or otherwise, the driver involves the car she is operating in a collision. In the typical instance a seller of corporate stock can be expected to have no similar apprehension of risks to others from her own inattention. But, in some circumstances, the seller of a control block of stock may or should reasonably foresee danger to other shareholders; with her sale of stock will also go control over the corporation and with it the opportunity to misuse that power to the injury of such other shareholders. Thus, the reason that a duty of care is recognized in any situation is fully present in this situation. I can find no universal privilege arising from the corporate form that exempts a controlling shareholder who sells corporate control from the wholesome reach of this common-law duty. * * *

Thus, I conclude that while a person who transfers corporate control to another is surely not a surety for his buyer, when the circumstances would alert a reasonably prudent person to a risk that his buyer is dishonest or in some material respect not truthful, a duty devolves upon the seller to make such inquiry as a reasonably prudent person would make, and generally to exercise care so that others who will be affected by his actions should not be injured by wrongful conduct.

Id. at 234–35.

One question, of course, is in what circumstances "may or should [a selling shareholder] reasonably foresee danger to other shareholders?" In particular, does a purchaser's payment of a large premium trigger a duty to investigate? Clagett v. Hutchison, 583 F.2d 1259, 1262 (4th Cir.1978), held that payment of $34.75 per share for a majority interest in a race track corporation whose shares had been trading for $7.50 to $10.00 could "not be said to be so unreasonable as to place [the seller] on notice of the likelihood of fraud * * *." The court found it "farfetched" that a purchaser would pay a 400% premium to acquire control of a corporation simply to loot it. Do you agree?

It should be noted that computation of the liability of a shareholder who wrongfully sells control to a looter is consistent with a tort rationale. That is, the liability of the selling shareholder is equal to the loss suffered by the corporation, not merely to the premium she received.

C. SALE OF CORPORATE OFFICE

ESSEX UNIVERSAL CORP. v. YATES
305 F.2d 572 (2d Cir.1962).

[Plaintiff contracted to purchase defendant's 28.3% interest in Republic Pictures for $8 per share, approximately $2 above the price at which the stock sold on the New York Stock Exchange. The contract required the seller to deliver resignations of a majority of Republic's directors and to cause the election of persons designated by the buyer. The seller refused to go ahead with this condition and claimed as a defense in a suit for breach of contract that to do so would be illegal.

The court unanimously reversed a judgment for defendant, but its decision is reflected in three separate opinions.]

LUMBARD, CHIEF JUDGE.

* * *

It is established beyond question under New York law that it is illegal to sell a corporate office or management control by itself (that is, accompanied by no stock or insufficient stock to carry voting control). The rationale of the rule is undisputable: persons enjoying management control hold it on behalf of the corporation's stockholders, and therefore may not regard it as their own personal property to dispose of as they wish. Any other rule would violate the most fundamental principle of corporate democracy, that management must represent and be chosen by, or at least with the consent of, those who own the corporation.

Essex was, however, contracting with Yates for the purchase of a very substantial percentage of Republic stock. If, by virtue of the voting power carried by this stock, it could have elected a majority of the board of directors, then the contract was not a simple agreement for the sale of office to one having no ownership interest in the corporation, and the question of its legality would require further analysis. Such stock voting control would incontestably belong to the owner of a majority of the voting stock, and it is commonly known that equivalent power usually accrues to the owner of 28.3% of the stock. For the purpose of this analysis, I shall assume that Essex was contracting to acquire a majority of the Republic stock, deferring consideration of the situation where, as here, only 28.3% is to be acquired.

Republic's board of directors at the time of the aborted closing had fourteen members divided into three classes, each class being "as nearly as may be" of the same size. Directors were elected for terms of three years, one class being elected at each annual shareholder meeting on the first Tuesday in April. Thus, absent the immediate replacement of directors provided for in this contract, Essex as the hypothetical new majority shareholder of the corporation could not have obtained managing control in the form of a majority of the board in the normal course of events until April 1959, some eighteen months after the sale of the stock. The first question before us then is whether an agreement to accelerate the transfer of management control, in a manner legal in form under the corporation's charter and by-laws, violates the public policy of New York.

There is no question of the right of a controlling shareholder under New York law normally to derive a premium from the sale of a controlling block of stock. In other words, there was no impropriety *per se* in the fact that Yates was to receive more per share than the generally prevailing market price for Republic stock.

The next question is whether it is legal to give and receive payment for the immediate transfer of management control to one who has achieved majority share control but would not otherwise be able to convert that share control into operating control for some time. I think that it is.

* * *

A fair generalization from these cases may be that a holder of corporate control will not, as a fiduciary, be permitted to profit from facilitating actions on the part of the purchasers of control which are detrimental to the interests of the corporation or the remaining shareholders. There is, however, no suggestion that the transfer of control over Republic to Essex carried any such threat to the interests of the corporation or its other shareholders.

Given this principle that it is permissible for a seller thus to choose to facilitate immediate transfer of management control, I can see no objection to a contractual provision requiring him to do so as a condition of the sale. Indeed, a New York court has upheld an analogous contractual term requiring the board of directors to elect the nominees of the purchasers of a majority stock interest to officerships. San Remo Copper Mining Co. v. Moneuse, 149 App.Div. 26, 133 N.Y.S. 509 (1st Dept.1912). The court said that since the purchaser was about to acquire "absolute control" of the corporation, "it certainly did not destroy the validity of the contract that by one of its terms defendant was to be invested with this power of control at once, upon acquiring the stock, instead of waiting for the next annual meeting."

* * *

The easy and immediate transfer of corporate control to new interests is ordinarily beneficial to the economy and it seems inevitable that such transactions would be discouraged if the purchaser of a majority stock interest were required to wait some period before his purchase of control could become effective. Conversely it would greatly hamper the efforts of any existing majority group to dispose of its interest if it could not assure the purchaser of immediate control over corporation operations. I can see no reason why a purchaser of majority control should not ordinarily be permitted to make his control effective from the moment of the transfer of stock.

* * *

Because 28.3 per cent of the voting stock of a publicly owned corporation is usually tantamount to majority control, I would place the burden of proof on this issue on Yates as the party attacking the legality of the transaction. Thus, unless on remand Yates chooses to raise the question whether the block of stock in question carried the equivalent of majority control, it is my view that the trial court should regard the contract as legal and proceed to consider the other issues raised by the pleadings. If Yates chooses to raise the issue, it will, on my view, be necessary for him to prove the existence of circumstances which would have prevented Essex from electing a majority of the Republic board of directors in due course. It will not be enough for Yates to raise merely hypothetical possibilities of opposition by the other Republic shareholders to Essex' assumption of management control. Rather, it will be necessary for him to show that, assuming neutrality on the part of the retiring management, there was at the time some concretely foreseeable reason why Essex' wishes would not have prevailed in shareholder voting held in due course. In other words, I would require him to show that there was at the time of the contract some other organized block of stock of sufficient size to outvote the block Essex was buying, or else some circumstance making it likely that enough of the holders of the remaining Republic stock would band together to keep Essex from control.

Reversed and remanded for further proceedings not inconsistent with the judgment of this court.

CLARK, CIRCUIT JUDGE (concurring in the result).

Since Barnes v. Brown, 80 N.Y. 527, teaches us that not all contracts like the one before us are necessarily illegal, summary judgment seems definitely improper and the action should be remanded for trial. But particularly in view of our lack of knowledge of corporate realities and the current standards of business morality, I should prefer to avoid too precise instructions to the district court in the hope that if the action again comes before us the record will be generally more instructive on this important issue than it now is. I share all the doubts and questions stated by my brothers in their opinions and perhaps have some additional ones of my own. My concern is lest we may be announcing abstract moral principles which have little validity in daily business practice other than to excuse a defaulting vendor from performance of his contract of sale. Thus for fear of a possible occasional contract inimical to general stockholder interest we may be condemning out of hand what are more often normal and even desirable business relationships. As at present advised I would think that the best we can do is to consider each case on its own facts and with the normal presumption that he who asserts illegality must prove it.

* * *

FRIENDLY, CIRCUIT JUDGE (concurring).

Chief Judge Lumbard's thoughtful opinion illustrates a difficulty, inherent in our dual judicial system, which has led at least one state to authorize its courts to answer questions about its law that a Federal court may ask. Here we are forced to decide a question of New York law, of enormous importance to all New York corporations and their stockholders, on which there is hardly enough New York authority for a really informed prediction what the New York Court of Appeals would decide on the facts here presented.

I have no doubt that many contracts, drawn by competent and responsible counsel, for the purchase of blocks of stock from interests thought to "control" a corporation although owning less than a majority, have contained provisions like paragraph 6 of the contract * *sub judice.* However, developments over the past decades seem to me to show that such a clause violates basic principles of corporate democracy. To be sure, stockholders who have allowed a set of directors to be placed in office, whether by their vote or their failure to vote, must recognize that death, incapacity or other hazard may prevent a director from serving a full term, and that they will have no voice as to his immediate successor. But the stockholders are entitled to expect that, in that event, the remaining directors will fill the vacancy in the exercise of their fiduciary responsibility. A mass seriatim resignation directed by a selling stockholder, and the filling of vacancies by his henchmen at the dictation of a purchaser and without any consideration of the character of the latter's nominees, are beyond what the stockholders contemplated or should have been expected to contemplate. This seems to me a wrong to the corporation and the other stockholders which the law ought not countenance, whether the selling stockholder has received a premium or not. Right in this Court we have seen many cases where sudden shifts of

---

* Paragraph 6 provided for the resignation of the old board and the election of new directors designated by the purchaser.

corporate control have caused serious injury. To hold the seller for delinquencies of the new directors only if he knew the purchaser was an intending looter is not a sufficient sanction. The difficulties of proof are formidable even if receipt of too high a premium creates a presumption of such knowledge, and, all too often, the doors are locked only after the horses have been stolen. Stronger medicines are needed—refusal to enforce a contract with such a clause, even though this confers an unwarranted benefit on a defaulter, and continuing responsibility of the former directors for negligence of the new ones until an election has been held. Such prophylactics are not contraindicated, as Judge Lumbard suggests, by the conceded desirability of preventing the dead hand of a former "controlling" group from continuing to dominate the board after a sale, or of protecting a would-be purchaser from finding himself without a majority of the board after he has spent his money. A special meeting of stockholders to replace a board may always be called, and there could be no objection to making the closing of a purchase contingent on the results of such an election. I perceive some of the difficulties of mechanics such a procedure presents, but I have enough confidence in the ingenuity of the corporate bar to believe these would be surmounted.

Hence, I am inclined to think that if I were sitting on the New York Court of Appeals, I would hold a provision like Paragraph 6 violative of public policy save when it was entirely plain that a new election would be a mere formality—i.e., when the seller owned more than 50% of the stock. I put it thus tentatively because, before making such a decision, I would want the help of briefs, including those of *amici curiae,* dealing with the serious problems of corporate policy and practice more fully than did those here, which were primarily devoted to argument as to what the New York law has been rather than what it ought to be. Moreover, in view of the perhaps unexpected character of such a holding, I doubt that I would give it retrospective effect.

As a judge of this Court, my task is the more modest one of predicting how the judges of the New York Court of Appeals would rule, and I must make this prediction on the basis of legal materials rather than of personal acquaintance or hunch. Also, for obvious reasons, the prospective technique is unavailable when a Federal court is deciding an issue of state law. Although Barnes v. Brown, 80 N.Y. 527 (1880), dealt with the sale of a majority interest, I am unable to find any real indication that the doctrine there announced has been thus limited. True, there are New York cases saying that the sale of corporate offices is forbidden; but the New York decisions do not tell us what this means and I can find nothing, save perhaps one unexplained sentence in the opinion of a trial court in Ballantine v. Ferretti, 28 N.Y.S.2d 668, 682 (Sup.Ct.N.Y.Co.1941), to indicate that New York would not apply Barnes v. Brown to a case where a stockholder with much less than a majority conditioned a sale on his causing the resignation of a majority of the directors and the election of the purchaser's nominees.

Chief Judge Lumbard's proposal goes part of the way toward meeting the policy problem I have suggested. Doubtless proceeding from what, as it seems to me, is the only justification in principle for permitting even a majority stockholder to condition a sale on delivery of control of the board—namely that in such a case a vote of the stockholders would be a useless formality, he sets the allowable bounds at the line where there is "a practical certainty" that the buyer would be able to elect his nominees and, in this case, puts the burden of disproving that on the person claiming illegality.

Attractive as the proposal is in some respects, I find difficulties with it. One is that I discern no sufficient intimation of the distinction in the New York cases, or even in the writers, who either would go further in voiding such a clause. * * * When an issue does arise, the "practical certainty" test is difficult to apply. * * * Judge Lumbard correctly recognizes that, from a policy standpoint, the pertinent question must be the buyer's prospects of election, not the seller's—yet this inevitably requires the court to canvass the likely reaction of stockholders to a group of whom they know nothing and seems rather hard to reconcile with a position that it is "right" to insert such a condition if a seller has a larger proportion of the stock and "wrong" if he has a smaller. At the very least the problems and uncertainties arising from the proposed line of demarcation are great enough, and its advantages small enough, that in my view a Federal court would do better simply to overrule the defense here, thereby accomplishing what is obviously the "just" result in this particular case, and leave the development of doctrine in this area to the State, which has primary concern for it.

I would reverse the grant of summary judgment and remand for consideration of defenses other than a claim that the inclusion of paragraph 6 *ex mero motu* renders the contract void.

Note: Selling Corporate Office

In Carter v. Muscat, 21 A.D.2d 543, 251 N.Y.S.2d 378 (1st Dept. 1964), the directors of Republic Corporation chose a new majority of the board in connection with the sale of 9.7 percent of the stock, by Republic's former management, at a price slightly above market. The sale occurred approximately nine months before the next regularly scheduled shareholders' meeting; an interim report on the board's action was furnished to shareholders. At their next meeting, the shareholders reelected the new directors. A dissident shareholder then petitioned to set the directors' election aside.

The court rejected the petition, remarking: "When a situation involving less than 50% of the ownership of stock exists, the question of what percentage of stock is sufficient to constitute working control is likely to be a matter of fact, at least in most circumstances." The interim notice and subsequent election establish that there was no deception of Republic's shareholders.

Brecher v. Gregg, 89 Misc.2d 457, 392 N.Y.S.2d 776 (1975), involved the sale by Gregg, the president of Lin Broadcasting Corporation, of his 4 percent stock interest to the Saturday Evening Post. Gregg also promised to resign and cause the Post's president and two others to be elected directors of Lin and the Post's president to be elected Lin's president.

A Lin shareholder sued to recover from Gregg and the other directors the premium paid by the Post. The court held Gregg, but not the other directors, liable, reasoning as follows:

> The Court concludes as a matter of law that the agreement insofar as it provided for a premium in exchange for a promise of control, with only 4% of the outstanding shares actually being transferred, was contrary to public policy and illegal.

> * * *

> In summary, an officer's transfer of fewer than a majority of his corporation's shares, at a price in excess of that prevailing in the market, accompanied by his promise to effect the transfer of offices and control in the corporation to the vendee, is a transaction which breaches the fiduciary duty owed the corporation and upon application to a court of equity; the officer will be made to forfeit that portion of his profit ascribable to the unlawful promise as he has been unjustly enriched; and an accounting made on behalf of the corporation, since it is, of the two, the party more entitled to the proceeds.

> Since there has been no showing that the actions of any directors other than Gregg either led to any pecuniary loss to the corporation or to the realization of any personal profit or gain to themselves, it follows that they cannot be held liable jointly, or severally, with Gregg for the payment of the premium over to the corporation.

392 N.Y.S.2d at 779–82.

Note: What Constitutes "Control"?

Claims of sale of office, almost by definition, are brought only against shareholders who possess the ability to transfer control. Do similar rules apply to a large shareholder, even a director, who is not a controlling person?

Treadway Companies, Inc. v. Care Corp., 638 F.2d 357 (2d Cir.1980), involved a claim against Cowin, the largest shareholder and a director of Treadway Companies, Inc., who owned 14 percent of its stock. Treadway became the target of a takeover bid by Care Corporation. While negotiating with Care concerning sale of his stock, Cowin accepted renomination for election to Treadway's board. He also rejected an invitation to sell his stock back to Treadway because he did not think the company could afford the purchase and because he questioned whether it was proper for a director to resell his stock to the company at a premium price. Cowin subsequently sold his shares to Care for consideration having a present value of $8 a share, equal to a 35 percent premium over market.

Treadway sued to recover from Cowin his profits on the sale of his stock. The court rejected its claim:

> We also conclude that Cowin breached no duty in selling his own shares to Care at a premium. Apparently Treadway's argument is that Cowin had a duty to afford the other shareholders an opportunity to participate in the sale, either because he was a director or because he was Treadway's "largest shareholder." We find both theories unpersuasive.

> Treadway has pointed us to no case, and we know of none, in which a director was required, solely by reason of his status as director to account to the shareholders for profits earned on the sale of his shares.

> > Ordinarily a director possesses the same right as any other stockholder to deal freely with his shares of stock and to dispose of them at such a price as he may be able to obtain, provided the director acts in good faith, since the corporation as such has no interest in its outstanding stock or in dealing in its shares among its stockholders.

> 3 Fletcher, [Cyclopedia of the Law of Private Corporations at § 900]. There is no indication that Cowin acted other than in good faith toward Treadway and its shareholders. The district court found that Cowin did not misuse confidential information and that he did not usurp any corporate opportunity. Cowin's sale permitted Care to increase its stake in Treadway, but the district court found that neither Treadway nor its shareholders were thereby harmed in any way. Thus, we see nothing that would take this case outside the general principle that a director is free to sell his stock at whatever price he may obtain.

> Nor do we find that Cowin's status as Treadway's "largest shareholder" carried with it a duty to share his premium with the other shareholders. It is true that in certain circumstances, a *controlling* shareholder may be required to account to the minority shareholders for the "control premium" he obtains upon selling his controlling shares. But Cowin was not a controlling shareholder. At the time of his sale, Cowin owned only 14% of Treadway's outstanding stock; the district court specifically found that Cowin did not have control of the corporation. Since Cowin therefore did not transfer control, he was under no duty to account for the premium he obtained.

See, also, In re Sea–Land Corporation Shareholders Litigation, Fed.Sec. L.Rep. (CCH) [1988–89 Transfer Binder] ¶ 93,923, 1988 WL 49126 (Del.Ch.1988) (holding that shareholder that participated in purchase of 39.5% of Sea–Land through hostile takeover bid, but never exercised domination or control of Sea–Land, owed no fiduciary duty to Sea–Land's shareholders when it later sold its Sea–Land stock at premium price.)

D. SHAREHOLDER'S DUTY OF LOYALTY AND THE SALE OF CONTROL

PERLMAN V. FELDMANN

219 F.2d 173 (2d Cir.1955), cert. denied 349 U.S.
952, 75 S.Ct. 880, 99 L.Ed. 1277 (1955).

CLARK, CHIEF JUDGE.

This is a derivative action brought by minority stockholders of Newport Steel Corporation to compel accounting for, and restitution of, allegedly illegal gains which accrued to defendants as a result of the sale in August, 1950, of their controlling interest in the corporation. The principal defendant, C. Russell Feldmann, who represented and acted for the others, members of his family [owning a total of 37%], was at that time not only the dominant stockholder, but also the chairman of the board of directors and the president of the corporation. Newport, an Indiana corporation, operated mills for the production of steel sheets for sale to manufacturers of steel products, first at Newport, Kentucky, and later also at other places in Kentucky and Ohio. The buyers, a syndicate organized as Wilport Company, a Delaware corporation, consisted of end-users of steel who were interested in securing a source of supply in a market becoming ever tighter in the Korean War. Plaintiffs contend that the consideration paid for the stock included compensation for the sale of a corporate asset, a power held in trust for the corporation by Feldmann as its fiduciary. This power was the ability to control the allocation of the corporate product in a time of short supply, through control of the board of directors; and it was effectively transferred in this sale by having Feldmann procure the resignation of his own board and the election of Wilport's nominees immediately upon consummation of the sale.

* * *

The essential facts found by the trial judge are not in dispute. Newport was a relative newcomer in the steel industry with predominantly old installations which were in the process of being supplemented by more modern facilities. Except in times of extreme shortage Newport was not in a position to compete profitably with other steel mills for customers not in its immediate geographical area. Wilport, the purchasing syndicate, consisted of geographically remote end-users of steel who were interested in buying more steel from Newport than they had been able to obtain during recent periods of tight supply. The price of $20 per share was found by Judge Hincks to be a fair one for a control block of stock, although the over-the-counter market price had not exceeded

$12 and the book value per share was $17.03. But this finding was limited by Judge Hincks' statement that "[w]hat value the block would have had if shorn of its appurtenant power to control distribution of the corporate product, the evidence does not show." It was also conditioned by his earlier ruling that the burden was on plaintiffs to prove a lesser value for the stock.

Both as director and as dominant stockholder, Feldmann stood in a fiduciary relationship to the corporation and to the minority stockholders as beneficiaries thereof. Although there is no Indiana case directly in point, the most closely analogous one emphasizes the close scrutiny to which Indiana subjects the conduct of fiduciaries when personal benefit may stand in the way of fulfillment of trust obligations. * * *

In Indiana, then, as elsewhere, the responsibility of the fiduciary is not limited to a proper regard for the tangible balance sheet assets of the corporation, but includes the dedication of his uncorrupted business judgment for the sole benefit of the corporation, in any dealings which may adversely affect it. * * *

It is true, as defendants have been at pains to point out, that this is not the ordinary case of breach of fiduciary duty. We have here no fraud, no misuse of confidential information, no outright looting of a helpless corporation. But on the other hand, we do not find compliance with that high standard which we have just stated and which we and other courts have come to expect and demand of corporate fiduciaries. In the often-quoted words of Judge Cardozo: "Many forms of conduct permissible in a workaday world for those acting at arm's length, are forbidden to those bound by fiduciary ties. A trustee is held to something stricter than the morals of the market place. Not honesty alone, but the punctilio of an honor the most sensitive, is then the standard of behavior. As to this there has developed a tradition that is unbending and inveterate. Uncompromising rigidity has been the attitude of courts of equity when petitioned to undermine the rule of undivided loyalty by the 'disintegrating erosion' of particular exceptions." Meinhard v. Salmon, supra, 249 N.Y. 458, 464, 164 N.E. 545, 546, 62 A.L.R. 1. The actions of defendants in siphoning off for personal gain corporate advantages to be derived from a favorable market situation do not betoken the necessary undivided loyalty owed by the fiduciary to his principal.

The corporate opportunities of whose misappropriation the minority stockholders complain need not have been an absolute certainty in order to support this action against Feldmann. If there was possibility of corporate gain, they are entitled to recover. * * *

This rationale is equally appropriate to a consideration of the benefits which Newport might have derived from the steel shortage. In the past Newport had used and profited by its market leverage by operation of what the industry had come to call the "Feldmann Plan." This consisted of securing interest-free advances from prospective purchasers of steel in return for firm commitments to them from future production. The funds thus acquired were used to finance improvements in existing plants and to acquire new installations. In the summer of 1950 Newport had been negotiating for cold-rolling facilities which it needed for a more fully integrated operation and a more marketable product, and Feldmann plan funds might well have been used toward this end.

Further, as plaintiffs alternatively suggest, Newport might have used the period of short supply to build up patronage in the geographical area in which it could compete profitably even when steel was more abundant. Either of these opportunities was Newport's, to be used to its advantage only. Only if defendants had been able to negate completely any possibility of gain by Newport could they have prevailed. It is true that a trial court finding states: "Whether or not, in August, 1950, Newport's position was such that it could have entered into 'Feldmann Plan' type transactions to procure funds and financing for the further expansion and integration of its steel facilities and whether such expansion would have been desirable for Newport, the evidence does not show." This, however, cannot avail the defendants, who—contrary to the ruling below—had the burden of proof on this issue, since fiduciaries always have the burden of proof in establishing the fairness of their dealings with trust property.

Defendants seek to categorize the corporate opportunities which might have accrued to Newport as too unethical to warrant further consideration. It is true that reputable steel producers were not participating in the gray market brought about by the Korean War and were refraining from advancing their prices, although to do so would not have been illegal. But Feldmann plan transactions were not considered within this self-imposed interdiction; the trial court found that around the time of the Feldmann sale Jones & Laughlin Steel Corporation, Republic Steel Company, and Pittsburgh Steel Corporation were all participating in such arrangements. In any event, it ill becomes the defendants to disparage as unethical the market advantages from which they themselves reaped rich benefits.

We do not mean to suggest that a majority stockholder cannot dispose of his controlling block of stock to outsiders without having to account to his corporation for profits or even never do this with impunity when the buyer is an interested customer, actual or potential for the corporation's product. But when the sale necessarily results in a sacrifice of this element of corporate good will and consequent unusual profit to the fiduciary who has caused the sacrifice, he should account for his gains. So in a time of market shortage, where a call on a corporation's product commands an unusually large premium, in one form or another, we think it sound law that a fiduciary may not appropriate to himself the value of this premium. Such personal gain at the expense of his coventurers seems particularly reprehensible when made by the trusted president and director of his company. In this case the violation of duty seems to be all the clearer because of this triple role in which Feldmann appears, though we are unwilling to say, and are not to be understood as saying, that we should accept a lesser obligation for any one of his roles alone.

Hence to the extent that the price received by Feldmann and his codefendants included such a bonus, he is accountable to the minority stockholders who sue here. And plaintiffs, as they contend, are entitled to a recovery in their own right, instead of in right of the corporation (as in the usual derivative actions), since neither Wilport nor their successors in interest should share in any judgment which may be rendered. Defendants cannot well object to this form of recovery, since the only alternative, recovery for the corporation as a whole, would subject them to a greater total liability.

The case will therefore be remanded to the district court for a determination of the question expressly left open below, namely, the value of defendants' stock without the appurtenant control over the corporation's output of steel. We reiterate that on this issue, as on all others, relating to a breach of fiduciary duty, the burden of proof must rest on the defendants. Judgment should go to these plaintiffs and those whom they represent for any premium value so shown to the extent of their respective stock interests.

The judgment is therefore reversed and the action remanded for further proceedings pursuant to this opinion.

Swan, Circuit Judge (dissenting).

With the general principles enunciated in the majority opinion as to the duties of fiduciaries I am, of course, in thorough accord. But, as Mr. Justice Frankfurter stated in Securities and Exchange Comm. v. Chenery Corp., 318 U.S. 80, 85, 63 S.Ct. 454, 458, 87 L.Ed. 626, "to say that a man is a fiduciary only begins analysis; it gives direction to further inquiry. To whom is he a fiduciary? What obligations does he owe as a fiduciary? In what respect has he failed to discharge these obligations?" My brothers' opinion does not specify precisely what fiduciary duty Feldmann is held to have violated or whether it was a duty imposed upon him as the dominant stockholder or as a director of Newport. Without such specification I think that both the legal profession and the business world will find the decision confusing and will be unable to foretell the extent of its impact upon customary practices in the sale of stock.

The power to control the management of a corporation, that is, to elect directors to manage its affairs, is an inseparable incident to the ownership of a majority of its stock, or sometimes, as in the present instance, to the ownership of enough shares, less than a majority, to control an election. Concededly a majority or dominant shareholder is ordinarily privileged to sell his stock at the best price obtainable from the purchaser. In so doing he acts on his own behalf, not as an agent of the corporation. If he knows or has reason to believe that the purchaser intends to exercise to the detriment of the corporation the power of management acquired by the purchase, such knowledge or reasonable suspicion will terminate the dominant shareholder's privilege to sell and will create a duty not to transfer the power of management to such purchaser. The duty seems to me to resemble the obligation which everyone is under not to assist another to commit a tort rather than the obligation of a fiduciary. But whatever the nature of the duty, a violation of it will subject the violator to liability for damages sustained by the corporation. Judge Hincks found that Feldmann had no reason to think that Wilport would use the power of management it would acquire by the purchase to injure Newport, and that there was no proof that it ever was so used. Feldmann did know, it is true, that the reason Wilport wanted the stock was to put in a board of directors who would be likely to permit Wilport's members to purchase more of Newport's steel than they might otherwise be able to get. But there is nothing illegal in a dominant shareholder purchasing from his own corporation at the same prices it offers to other customers. That is what the members of Wilport did, and there is no proof that Newport suffered any detriment therefrom.

My brothers say that "the consideration paid for the stock included compensation for the sale of a corporate asset", which they describe as "the ability to control the allocation of the corporate product in a time of short supply, through control of the board of directors; and it was effectively transferred in this sale by having Feldmann procure the resignation of his own board and the election of Wilport's nominees immediately upon consummation of the sale." The implications of this are not clear to me. If it means that when market conditions are such as to induce users of a corporation's product to wish to buy a controlling block of stock in order to be able to purchase part of the corporation's output at the same mill list prices as are offered to other customers, the dominant stockholder is under a fiduciary duty not to sell his stock, I cannot agree. For reasons already stated, in my opinion Feldmann was not proved to be under any fiduciary duty as a stockholder not to sell the stock he controlled.

Notes

1. The Court of Appeals' opinion makes no reference to the following finding of fact contained in the District Court's opinion:

> Since the Wilport nominees took over the management of Newport on August 31, 1950, substantial improvements have been made in Newport's property and the corporation has enjoyed continued prosperity. Although the Wilport stockholders have purchased substantial quantities of steel from Newport, no sales were made at less than Newport's quoted mill prices. There is no evidence of any sort that Newport has suffered from mismanagement or inefficient management since August 31, 1950, or that it has suffered or is likely hereafter to suffer any harm whatever at the hands of its new management, or that its new management has in any way failed to do anything which should have been done for the good of the corporation.

129 F.Supp. 162, 175–76 (D.Conn.1952).

In light of this finding, which the appellate court did not find to be clearly erroneous, on what did the appellate court base its reversal of the trial court's decision?

2. Robert Hamilton, Private Sale of Control Transactions: Where We Stand Today, 36 Case W.Res.L.Rev. 248, 275 (1985), argues that *Perlman* involves the wrongful appropriation of a corporate opportunity. Other commentators have interpreted *Perlman* to establish a duty to share a control premium with all of a corporation's shareholders. See, e.g., Andrews, 78 Harv. L. Rev. at 514–15, 524–26. Professor Elhauge suggests the key to understanding *Perlman* lies in the existence of a market shortage created by the informal, Korean–War–period system of price controls. Wilport, once in control of Newport, could arrange to purchase more of the steel Newport was producing at the ethically fixed price. A Newport shareholder, however, would find it difficult to prove Newport was injured by such sales, since no court was likely to rule that Newport had a duty to evade the wartime system of price controls. The court's ruling, viewed in this light, is based not on some general equal sharing principle, but represents a particularized holding that Feldmann, Newport's controlling shareholder, had a duty to share with Newport's other shareholders any premium attributable to the existence of these special market conditions. Elhauge, 59 U.Chi.L.Rev. at 1516–17.

Elhauge's interpretation appears consistent with the Court of Appeals' ruling on damages. On remand, the District Court computed the investment value of Newport's common stock based on a capitalization of its earnings, and then ordered Feldmann to distribute to Newport's public shareholders their *pro rata* share of the amount by which the purchase price he received exceeded that figure. 154 F.Supp. 436 (D.C.Conn.1957).

3. Professors Easterbrook and Fischel, in contrast, critique *Perlman* as follows:

> The Second Circuit held in *Perlman* that the seller of the control block had a duty to share the control premium with the other shareholders. The court's holding * * * was based on a belief that the steel shortage allowed Newport to finance needed expansion via the "Plan," and that the premium represented an attempt by Wilport to divert a corporate opportunity—to secure for itself the benefits resulting from the shortage. The court stated that "[o]nly if defendants had been able to negate completely any possibility of gain by Newport could they have prevailed."

> There are several problems with this treatment. Foremost is the assumption that the gain resulting from the "Plan" was not widely reflected in the price of Newport's stock. Newport stock was widely traded, and the existence of the Feldmann Plan was known to investors. The going price of Newport shares prior to the transaction therefore reflected the full value of Newport, including the valued of advances under the Feldmann Plan. The Wilport

syndicate paid some two-thirds more than the going price and thus could not profit from the deal unless (a) the sale of control resulted in an increase in the value of Newport, or (b) Wilport's control of Newport was the equivalent of looting. * * *

Hence, the court's proposition that Wilport extracted a corporate opportunity from Newport—the functional equivalent of looting—has testable implications. Unless the price of Newport's outstanding shares plummeted, the Wilport syndicate could not be extracting enough to profit. In fact, however, the value of Newport's shares rose substantially after the transaction [even after adjusting for price increases in steel company shares generally]. The data refute the court's proposition that Wilport appropriated a corporate opportunity from Newport.

Easterbrook & Fischel, 91 Yale L.J. at 718.

JONES v. H.F. AHMANSON & CO.
1 Cal.3d 93, 81 Cal.Rptr. 592, 460 P.2d 464 (1969).

[Plaintiff, the owner of 25 shares of United Savings and Loan Association (Association) brought a class action on behalf of herself and all similarly situated stockholders. Defendants were H.F. Ahmanson & Co. (Ahmanson) and other persons who had controlled Association prior to transferring 85% of Association's stock to a holding company known as United Financial Corporation (United Financial), which defendants also controlled.

Association, originally organized as a mutual savings and loan company, became a stock corporation in 1956 when is issued 6,568 shares, including 987 shares (14.8%) purchased by plaintiff and other depositors. In May 1958, Ahmanson acquired a majority of Association's shares, and by May 1959 it owned 63.5% of Association's stock.

From 1958 to 1962, the price of stock in most publicly traded savings and loan companies increased sharply. Association stock did not participate in this trend, largely because the trading market in its stock was very thin. With a book value of more than $1,000 per share, a small number of shares outstanding, and little information about the company available because the federal securities laws as they then existed did not oblige Association to furnish periodic reports to shareholders, there was little investor demand for Association shares.

In 1959, Ahmanson and other defendants formed United Financial and transferred the 85% of Association stock that they owned to it, receiving 250 shares of United Financial stock (a "derived block") for each share of Association. Defendants did not offer Association's minority shareholders an opportunity to exchange their shares. Following the exchange, defendants controlled United Financial and, through it, continued to control Association.

In June 1960, United Financial raised $7.2 million through a public offering of units consisting of shares of its stock and a debenture. In connection with this offering, United Financial also acknowledged that it would need to rely on dividends from Association, which accounted for approximately 85% of United Financial assets, to service the debentures. Following the offering, United Financial distributed $6.2 million of the proceeds (an amount equal to $927.50 for each derived block) as a return of capital to defendants, who remained in control of United Financial. Eight months later, United Financial made a secondary offering of 600,000 shares of the derived stock, including 568,190 shares sold by defendants, for a total of $15,275,000. During this period, trading in Association stock declined from about 170 shares per year, prior to the formation of United Financial, to about 85 shares per year.

Shortly after United Financial's first public offering, at a time when Association stock had a book value of $1,411 per share and earnings of $301 per share, defendants caused United Financial to offer to purchase up to 350 shares of Association stock at $1,100 per share. By way of comparison, at that time a derived block of United Financial had a market value of $3,700, in addition to the $927.50 received as a return of capital. United Financial acquired an additional 130 Association shares through this offer.

Association had paid extra dividends of $75 and $57 per share in 1959 and 1960, but in December 1960, after United made its $1,100 per share offer, defendants caused Association to notify each of its minority stockholders that for the foreseeable future Association would pay only a regular $4 per share annual dividend.

United Financial thereafter proposed to exchange 51 shares of United Financial stock with each of the minority shares of Association. Association shares then had a book value of $1,700 per share and the earnings of $615 per share. Fifty-one United Financial shares had a market value of $2,400, a book value of $210 and earnings of $134. Defendant's derived blocks were then worth approximately $8,800 each. When Association's minority shareholders objected, United Financial withdrew its offer.

Plaintiff then brought suit, alleging that defendants had breached the fiduciary duty they owed as majority or controlling shareholders by rendering Association stock unmarketable and then refusing to purchase it at a fair price or to allow plaintiff to exchange it for United Financial stock on the same terms as had defendants. Defendants responded that they had "an absolute right to use and dispose of their stock as they saw fit so long as they violated no right of the corporation or the other stockholders." They asserted that they had no duty to permit minority shareholders to participate on an equal basis in the disposition of their stock.

The trial court ruled for defendants and an intermediate appellate court affirmed, observing: "To act in good faith one does not have to be a 'good neighbor' nor does the law demand of a fiduciary that he should in all matters do unto his beneficiary as he would be done by." Jones v.

H.F. Ahmanson & Co., 76 Cal.Rptr. 293, 297 (Cal.App.1969), vacated 1 Cal.3d 93, 81 Cal.Rptr. 592, 460 P.2d 464 (1969).]

TRAYNOR, J.

I

Plaintiff's Capacity to Sue

We are faced at the outset with defendants' contention that if a cause of action is stated, it is derivative in nature since any injury suffered is common to all minority stockholders of the Association. Therefore, defendants urge, plaintiff may not sue in an individual capacity or on behalf of a class made up of stockholders excluded from the United Financial exchange, and in any case may not maintain a derivative action without complying with Financial Code, section 7616. * * *

It is clear from the stipulated facts and plaintiff's allegations that she does not seek to recover on behalf of the corporation for injury done to the corporation by defendants. Although she does allege that the value of her stock has been diminished by defendants' actions, she does not contend that the diminished value reflects an injury to the corporation and resultant depreciation in the value of the stock. Thus the gravamen of her cause of action is injury to herself and the other minority stockholders.

II

Majority Shareholders' Fiduciary Responsibility

Defendants take the position that as shareholders they owe no fiduciary obligation to other shareholders, absent reliance on inside information, use of corporate assets, or fraud. This view has long been repudiated in California. The Courts of Appeal have often recognized that majority shareholders, either singly or acting in concert to accomplish a joint purpose, have a fiduciary responsibility to the minority and to the corporation to use their ability to control the corporation in a fair, just, and equitable manner. Majority shareholders may not use their power to control corporate activities to benefit themselves alone or in a manner detrimental to the minority. Any use to which they put the corporation or their power to control the corporation must benefit all shareholders proportionately and must not conflict with the proper conduct of the corporation's business.

* * *

Defendants assert, however, that in the use of their own shares they owed no fiduciary duty to the minority stockholders of the Association. They maintain that they made full disclosure of the circumstances surrounding the formation of United Financial, that the creation of United Financial and its share offers in no way affected the control of the Association, that plaintiff's proportionate interest in the Association was not affected, that the Association was not harmed, and that the market for Association stock was not affected. Therefore, they conclude, they have breached no fiduciary duty to plaintiff and the other minority stockholders.

Defendants would have us retreat from a position demanding equitable treatment of all shareholders by those exercising control over a corporation to a philosophy much criticized by commentators and modified by courts in other jurisdictions as well as our own. In essence defendants suggest that we reaffirm the so-called "majority" rule reflected in our early decisions. This rule, exemplified by the decision in Ryder v. Bamberger, 172 Cal. 791, 158 P. 753 but since severely limited, recognized the "perfect right [of majority shareholders] to dispose of their stock * * * without the slightest regard to the wishes and desires or knowledge of the minority stockholders; * * * " (p. 806, 158 P. p. 759) and held that such fiduciary duty as did exist in officers and directors was to the corporation only. The duty of shareholders as such was not recognized unless they, like officers and directors, by virtue of their position were possessed of information relative to the value of the corporation's shares that was not available to outside shareholders. In such case the existence of special facts permitted a finding that a fiduciary relationship to the corporation and other shareholders existed. (Hobart v. Hobart Estate Co., 26 Cal.2d 412, 159 P.2d 958.)

* * * The rule applies alike to officers, directors, and controlling shareholders in the exercise of powers that are theirs by virtue of their position and to transactions wherein controlling shareholders seek to gain an advantage in the sale or transfer or use of their controlling block of shares. Thus we held in In re Security Finance, 49 Cal.2d 370, 317 P.2d 1, that majority shareholders do not have an absolute right to dissolve a corporation, although ostensibly permitted to do so by Corporations Code, section 4600, because their statutory power is subject to equitable limitations in favor of the minority. We recognized that the majority had the right to dissolve the corporation to protect their investment *if* no alternative means were available *and* no advantage was secured over other shareholders, and noted that "there is nothing sacred in the life of a corporation that transcends the interests of its shareholders, but because dissolution falls with such finality on those interests, above all corporate powers it is subject to equitable limitations." (49 Cal.2d 370, 377, 317 P.2d 1, 5.)

* * *

The increasingly complex transactions of the business and financial communities demonstrate the inadequacy of the traditional theories of fiduciary obligation as tests of majority shareholder responsibility to the minority. These theories have failed to afford adequate protection to minority shareholders and particularly to those in closely held corporations whose disadvantageous and often precarious position renders them particularly vulnerable to the vagaries of the majority. Although courts have recognized the potential for abuse or unfair advantage when a controlling shareholder sells his shares at a premium over investment value (Perlman v. Feldmann, 219 F.2d 173, 50 A.L.R.2d 1134) or in a controlling shareholder's use of control to avoid equitable distribution of corporate assets (Zahn v. Transamerica Corporation (3rd Cir.1946) 162 F.2d 36, 172 A.L.R. 495 [use of control to cause subsidiary to redeem stock prior to liquidation and distribution of assets]), no comprehensive rule has emerged in other jurisdictions. Nor have most commentators approached the problem from a perspective other than that of the advantage gained in the sale of control. Some have suggested that the price paid for control shares over their investment value be treated as an asset belonging to the corporation itself (Berle and Means, The Modern Corporation and Private Property (1932) p. 243), or as an asset that should be shared proportionately with all shareholders through a general offer (Jennings, Trading in Corporate Control (1956) 44 Cal.L.Rev. 1, 39), and another contends that the sale of control at a premium is always evil (Bayne, The Sale–of–Control Premium: the Intrinsic Illegitimacy (1969) 47 Tex.L.Rev. 215).

* * * The case before us, in which no sale or transfer of actual control is directly involved, demonstrates that the injury anticipated by these authors can be inflicted with impunity under the traditional rules and supports our conclusion that the comprehensive rule of good faith and inherent fairness to the minority in any transaction where control of the corporation is material properly governs controlling shareholders in this state.

We turn now to defendants' conduct to ascertain whether this test is met.

III

Formation of United Financial and Marketing Its Shares

Defendants created United Financial during a period of unusual investor interest in the stock of savings and loan associations. They then owned a majority of the outstanding stock of the Association. This stock was not readily marketable owing to a high book value, lack of investor information and facilities, and the closely held nature of the Association. The management of the Association had made no effort to create a market for the stock or to split the shares and reduce their market price to a more attractive level. Two courses were available to defendants in their effort to exploit the bull market in savings and loan stock. Both were made possible by defendants' status as controlling stockholders. The first was either to cause the Association to effect a stock split (Corp.Code, § 1507) and create a market for the Association stock or to create a holding company for Association shares and permit all stockholders to exchange their shares before offering holding company shares to the public. All stockholders would have benefited alike had this been done, but in realizing their gain on the sale of their stock the majority stockholders would of necessity have had to relinquish some of their control shares. Because a public market would have been created, however, the minority stockholders would have been able to extricate themselves without sacrificing their investment had they elected not to remain with the new management.

The second course was that taken by defendants. A new corporation was formed whose major asset was to be the control block of Association stock owned by defendants, but from which minority shareholders were to be excluded. The unmarketable Association stock held by the majority was transferred to the newly formed corporation at an exchange rate equivalent to a 250 for 1 stock split. The new corporation thereupon set out to create a market for its own shares. Association stock constituted 85 percent of the holding company's assets and produced an equivalent proportion of its income. The same individuals controlled both corporations. It appears therefrom that the market created by defendants for United Financial shares was a market that would have been available for Association stock had defendants taken the first course of action.

After United Financial shares became available to the public it became a virtual certainty that no equivalent market could or would be created for Association stock. United Financial had become the controlling stockholder and neither it nor the other defendants would benefit from public trading in Association stock in competition with United Financial shares. Investors afforded an opportunity to acquire United Financial shares would not be likely to choose the less marketable and expensive Association stock in preference. Thus defendants chose a course of action in which they used their control of the Association to obtain an advantage not made available to all stockholders. They did so without regard to the resulting detriment to the minority stockholders and in the absence of any compelling business purpose. Such conduct is not consistent with their duty of good faith and inherent fairness to the minority stockholders. Had defendants afforded the minority an opportunity to exchange their stock on the same basis or offered to purchase them at a price arrived at by independent appraisal, their burden of establishing good faith and inherent fairness would have been much less. At the trial they may present evidence tending to show such good faith or compelling business purpose that would render their action fair under the circumstances. On appeal from the judgment of dismissal after the defendants' demurrer was sustained we decide only that the complaint states a cause of action entitling plaintiff to relief.

Defendants gained an additional advantage for themselves through their use of control of the Association when they pledged that control over the Association's assets and earnings to secure the holding company's debt, a debt that had been incurred for their own benefit.[14] In so doing the defendants breached their fiduciary obligation to the minority

14. Should it become necessary to encumber or liquidate Association assets to service this debt or to depart from a dividend policy consistent with the business needs of the Association, damage to the Association itself may occur. We need not resolve here, but note with some concern, the problem facing United Financial, which owes the same fiduciary duty to its own shareholders as to those of the Association. Any decision regarding use of Association assets and earnings to service the holding company debt must be made in the context of these potentially conflicting interests.

once again and caused United Financial and its controlling shareholders to become inextricably wedded to a conflict of interest between the minority stockholders of each corporation. Alternatives were available to them that would have benefited all stockholders proportionately. The course they chose affected the minority stockholders with no less finality than does dissolution (In re Security Finance, *supra,* 49 Cal.2d 370, 317 P.2d 1) and demands no less concern for minority interests.

In so holding we do not suggest that the duties of corporate fiduciaries include in all cases an obligation to make a market for and to facilitate public trading in the stock of the corporation. But when, as here, no market exists, the controlling shareholders may not use their power to control the corporation for the purpose of promoting a marketing scheme that benefits themselves alone to the detriment of the minority. Nor do we suggest that a control block of shares may not be sold or transferred to a holding company. We decide only that the circumstances of any transfer of controlling shares will be subject to judicial scrutiny when it appears that the controlling shareholders may have breached their fiduciary obligation to the corporation or the remaining shareholders.

IV

Damages

From the perspective of the minority stockholders of the Association, the transfer of control under these circumstances to another corporation and the resulting impact on their position as minority stockholders accomplished a fundamental corporate change as to them. Control of a closely held savings and loan association, the major portion of whose earnings had been retained over a long period while its stockholders remained stable, became an asset of a publicly held holding company. The position of the minority shareholder was drastically changed thereby. His practical ability to influence corporate decision-making was diminished substantially when control was transferred to a publicly held corporation that was in turn controlled by the owners of more than 750,000 shares. The future business goals of the Association could reasonably be expected to reflect the needs and interest of the holding company rather than the aims of the Association stockholders thereafter. In short, the enterprise into which the minority stockholders were now locked was not that in which they had invested.

* * *

Appraisal rights protect the dissenting minority shareholder against being forced to either remain an investor in an enterprise fundamentally different than that in which he invested or sacrifice his investment by sale of his shares at less than a fair value. Plaintiff here was entitled to no less. But she was entitled to more. In the circumstances of this case she should have been accorded the same opportunity to exchange her Association stock for that of United Financial accorded the majority.

Although a controlling shareholder who sells or exchanges his shares is not under an obligation to obtain for the minority the consideration that he receives in all cases, when he does sell or exchange his shares the transaction is subject to close scrutiny. When the majority receives a premium over market value for its shares, the consideration for which that premium is paid will be examined. If it reflects payment for that which is properly a corporate asset all shareholders may demand to share proportionately. (Perlman v. Feldmann, *supra,* 219 F.2d 173.) Here the exchange was an integral part of a scheme that the defendants could reasonably foresee would have as an incidental effect the destruction of the potential public market for Association stock. The remaining stockholders would thus be deprived of the opportunity to realize a profit from those intangible characteristics that attach to publicly marketed stock and enhance its value above book value. Receipt of an appraised value reflecting book value and earnings alone could not compensate the minority shareholders for the loss of this potential. Since the damage is real, although the amount is speculative, equity demands that the minority stockholders be placed in a position at least as favorable as that the majority created for themselves.

If, after trial of the cause, plaintiff has established facts in conformity with the allegations of the complaint and stipulation, then upon tender of her Association stock to defendants she will be entitled to receive at her election either the appraised value of her shares on the date of the exchange, May 14, 1959, with interest at 7 percent a year from the date of this action or a sum equivalent to the fair market value of a "derived block" of United Financial stock on the date of this action with interest thereon from that date, and the sum of $927.50 (the return of capital paid to the original United Financial shareholders) with interest thereon from the date United Financial first made such payments to its original shareholders, for each share tendered. The appraised or fair market value shall be reduced, however, by the amount by which dividends paid on Association shares during the period from May 14, 1959 to the present exceeds the dividends paid on a corresponding block of United Financial shares during the same period.

* * *

Chapter 22

PROTECTING CONTROL

A. INTRODUCTION

Most changes in control are negotiated. One corporation "buys" another corporation. The managements of the two corporations bargain at arm's length over the terms, conditions, future management, and precise legal form of the transaction. If no deal is struck, that usually is the end of the matter.

In a negotiated transaction, shareholders' interests are represented by the managements of the companies involved. Although corporate law may require shareholder approval, and federal securities law may require full disclosure to shareholders, the deal is the work of managers, directors and their advisers. In a truly arm's length transaction, the business judgment rule largely insulates directors from liability. As long as the board exercises due care and no self dealing is involved, directors have little to fear from a stockholder suit.

If the management of a corporation that another company wants to acquire (the *target* company) is unable to agree to terms with the would-be acquiror (the *bidder*) or is unwilling (or believed to be unwilling) to negotiate at all, the latter may launch a "hostile" takeover bid, seeking to gain control by going over the heads of management and appealing directly to the target company's stockholders. The bidder can select the form of challenge—either a proxy contest or a tender offer. The two have different economic consequences. If the bidder succeeds in a proxy contest, it will gains managerial control; if it succeeds through a tender offer, it will also obtain ownership control. The bidder's objectives will determine which it chooses; does it seek managerial control alone or does it want to own the target as well?

Proxy contests occur with less frequency than tender offers although, relatively speaking, they are much easier to mount. One explanation for this phenomenon is that bidders generally have found it more difficult to gain control of target companies through proxy contests than through tender offers. Not surprisingly, it is easier to convince investors to sell out at a premium price than to vote for a change in management. Moreover, proxy contests may ultimately prove to be more costly. If the bidder fails, it will not be able to recoup the expenses it incurred mounting the proxy contest, unless it can convince (or coerce) the target to buy it off. But a bidder in a tender offer, although it may spend a great deal more in an effort to purchase a control block of the target's stock, often will earn a large profit even if the bid falls short because it will be able to sell its stock to the successful bidder at a profit.

The focus of this chapter is not on bidders but on issues relating to the target management's efforts to fend off hostile takeover bids. However, it is difficult to appreciate those issues fully without some understanding of how proxy contests and tender offers are conducted and regulated. The next two sections deal with those questions.

B. PROXY CONTESTS

A proxy contest provides stockholders a choice in the selection of directors, and ultimately in management. Stockholders receive proxy statements and proxy voting forms from two different slates of candidates, one favored by the target's incumbent management and the other favored by the bidder. In addition, both sides may contact shareholders directly and run newspaper advertisements that make strenuous appeals for votes.

The goal of a proxy contest is to win the voting support of the stockholders, not to acquire their shares, although bidders often also seek to increase their own holdings of target company stock. A challenger must frame the issues and select her candidates. Traditionally, shareholders tend to vote in favor of management. Waging an effective campaign to overcome this tendency requires time. But time may be limited, due to the pendency of the target's annual meeting and the problems involved in calling a special meeting. In addition, management has some ability to manipulate the corporate machinery to its advantage. Recall Chapters 3 and 12. If state law and the target's articles of incorporation permit (see DGCL § 228), the challenger may simply solicit consents to remove incumbent directors without cause and replace them with its nominees.

Although proxy contests are fought openly, challengers often hope to get organized before the target's management knows much about them or their plans. They want to contact potential supporters and to launch their effort before management can put takeover defenses in place. The SEC's rules, however, may make it difficult for a challenger to proceed secretly. As discussed in Chapter 14, Section 13(d) of the 1934 Act requires any "person" that acquired more than 5% of the stock of a public company to file a Schedule 13D within 10 days after reaching the 5% threshold. "Person" includes a "group" and the SEC rules state that a "group" is deemed to have "acquired" the shares of its members when the "group" is formed. Thus, although the proxy rules allow limited contact without any disclosure, under § 13(d) the same conduct may trigger a filing obligation.

Management begins a proxy contest with certain distinct advantages. We have already mentioned the shareholders' usual propensity to vote for management. In addition, management has a ready source of funds—the corporate treasury. The limits on how much corporate money managers may use are not very stringent. Although a bidder may be able to recover its expenses if it wins the contest, while the contest is in process, management usually has a substantial financial edge.

Management also maintains the shareholder list and thus knows who the shareholders are and how many shares they own. A bidder may have a right to obtain a copy of the list as a matter of state law. Recall Chapter 12. But even if the bidder has a proper purpose for seeking the list, management may question that purpose and force the bidder to sue, thereby delaying delivery of the list. If the proxy contest has already begun, delay can be very damaging.

Bidders often also have to deal with costly litigation, which frequently is financed on the target's side by the corporate treasury. SEC Rule 14a–9 prohibits false and misleading statements in connection with the solicitation of a proxy. In most proxy contests, each side closely reads the soliciting material of the other side and then tries to convince the staff of the SEC to seek to enjoin its' opponent's solicitations as false and misleading. Failing that, the parties—especially the target's management—is likely to go to court on their own to seek injunctive relief.

Finally, bidders have to be prepared to engage in several rounds of soliciting activity. Proxies are revocable; a later executed proxy often revokes all earlier executed proxies. Hence, a bidder must be prepared to counter efforts by the target's management to wean away support the bidder has obtained, as well as to make second, third and fourth efforts to secure the votes of shareholders who have resisted the bidders' previous blandishments.

In the end, both sides are likely to target most of their efforts on large institutional investors, whose votes are likely to determine the outcome of most proxy contests. Here, too, proxy contests pose hazards greater than those posed by tender offers. An institution, especially one concerned about its own interests as well as those of its beneficiaries, may well find it easier to justify voting in favor of an incumbent management, even one whose performance has been poor, than to explain why it is not tendering shares it owns for a price that represents a substantial premium over market. Money talks.

C. TENDER OFFERS

In a tender offer, a bidder typically offers to buy stock in a publicly held target corporation at a price substantially above the price at which that stock currently is trading. The consideration offered may be cash, stock, other securities, or some combination. The offer may be for some portion of the target company's stock or for all the outstanding shares. Almost all tender offers contain one or more conditions that must be satisfied before the bidder will be obligated to purchase any tendered stock.

Notwithstanding the high probability of success, acquiring another company in a tender offer entails substantial risks for a bidder. One is surprise. In a negotiated purchase, a would-be acquiror generally can arrange to investigate fully the business of the proposed target company. In a tender offer, a hostile bidder often flies blind; it has no opportunity to learn about the target from the inside. Moreover, if a contest for control develops, a bidder may find itself overpaying for its prize. As in any auction, the party who prevails is the one who, rightly or wrongly, places the highest value on the company to be acquired.

A bidder contemplating a possible tender offer begins by selecting its prospective target which may be a company that has the potential to prosper under new and better management, a company whose business might efficiently be combined with that of the bidder, or a company whose stock the bidder believes is selling for less that the "true value" of the company's assets. Economists generally believe that the stock market is "efficient," that stock prices represent the most accurate available prediction of the present value of the future earnings or cash flow that a company will generate under its present management. Believers in efficient capital markets predict that targets will tend to be poorly managed companies, and that tender offers consequently have the potential to increase real wealth. Critics hotly dispute this point. They claim that the market places undue emphasis on short-term factors and that stock prices do not necessarily reflect a company's fundamental, or inherent value. They also point to evidence that targets of hostile tender offers have been well-managed companies, not deadwood.

Whatever the general merit of these competing arguments, it does seem clear that, in the recent past, some targets were the financial equivalent of an "attractive nuisance." That is, they had large pools of liquid assets which anyone who purchased those companies could use, after acquiring control, to pay off a large part of the purchase price. For example, some targets have had substantially overfunded pension plans, retirement funds with more in assets than actuarially necessary to pay pensions to all anticipated retirees. Bidders acquiring such companies terminated the pension plans, drawn off the excess assets, and had enough left over to provide for the beneficiaries.

The bidder must arrange to finance the tender offer. This is perhaps the most critical aspect of planning; it is not uncommon for a takeover bid to exceed a billion dollars. Bidders sometimes are large well financed companies that do not require extensive outside financing. If the bidder needs outside funding, it often will turn to commercial banks or investment banks. Commercial banks generally charge commitment fees when they agree to provide financing for a takeover bid.

In the 1980s, investment banks often had networks of wealthy investors who were willing to finance takeover bids. Thus, they could furnish potential bidders with letters stating that they were "highly confident" they could raise the funds needed to finance the offer. Since the bidder will need the funds only if and when its bid succeeds, proceeding on the basis of such a letter can reduce a bidder's costs. At other times, investment banks will commit to providing "bridge loans" with their own funds to finance clients' takeover bids. At still others, investment banks ally themselves with their clients, becoming co-bidders with a view to participating as equity holders if the target is acquired.

A bidder typically forms a shell corporation to make the tender offer. If the bid is successful, the bidder often will merge the shell with the target company in a second step transaction designed to eliminate that company's remaining public shareholders. (See Chapter 23.) In part, the bidder's ability to cause the second step transaction helps to create an atmosphere in which shareholders of the target company feel compelled to tender their stock, even if they believe that present management best serves their long term interests, or that a better deal is possible given enough time. A tactic that effectively creates such pressure is the so-called two-tier tender offer: a bidder offers $50 cash per share for buy 51% of the stock of a target company selling at $30 per share and simultaneously announces that if its bid succeeds, it will effectuate a second step merger in which the target's remaining shareholders will receive $40 per share in debt securities. The offer presents shareholders with a "prisoner's dilemma." Even if they would prefer to reject the offer entirely, believing the "blended" price of $45 per share to be inadequate, they are unwilling to risk having other shareholders accept the $50 per share front end and being left with the $40 per share back end payment. Consequently, shareholders hasten to accept the front end offer, assuring both its success and the ensuing merger.

Bidders' ability to put pressure on target shareholders has been reduced by developments in the law. Shareholders may wait out the bid until the last minute without prejudice. Whether the offer is for any and all shares tendered or only for some of the shares, it must remain open for 20 business days (Rule 14e–1). Shares that are tendered may be withdrawn at any time during the offer (Section 14(d)(5) and Rule 14d–7) which gives the target about a month to come up with a better alternative. A new offer, or an increase in the price of the original offer, will extend the duration of the offer and the withdrawal period by ten business days. If the offer is for less than all the shares, acceptance must be on a pro-rata basis, not first-come, first-served. (Section 14(d)(6) and Rule 14d–8) An increase in the offer must apply retroactively. (Section 14(d)(7)) But even though these rules allow shareholders to take their time and change their minds, most sell unless a better deal is presented because they realize that if they do not, the market after the offer is likely to be inactive and the stock's price is likely to retreat to pre-offer levels. Many will not even wait for the offer period to end.

Rather, they sell their shares soon after the offer is made, pocketing a sure profit rather than waiting to see if the offer succeeds.

During the time in which the tender offer is open, the dominant purchasers in the market are arbitrageurs, or "arbs," who are professional risk takers. Often they are brokers who purchase from the public at a price below the tender offer price (sometimes higher if the arbs are convinced that an auction is about to ensue), with the expectation that they will tender to the bidder at the higher price and make a profit on the spread. The reason for the spread is because of the risk that the target will be able to prevent consummation of the tender offer by some means and send the price back to its pre-tender offer level. The arbitrageur assumes the risk of failure of the offer in return for the expected profit.

Consequently, a large percentage of the shares tendered to most bidder are owned by arbs. This presents the misleading impression that tender offers mainly benefit the arbs, overlooking the fact that the arbs acquired their stock from shareholders who willingly sold to them at a discount rather than incur the risk that the offer would fail. Arbs will be alert to the possibility that a competing bidder may offer a higher price, providing them with an opportunity for a greater than expected profit. However, arbs lose money as well, and when they do, their losses are large. The game is not for the faint of heart or nerve.

Ultimately the tender offer will run its course. Several possible outcomes exist. First, the bidder may succeed on approximately the terms originally offered. Second, the target may have agreed to be acquired by a suitor of its choice, a "white knight." Shareholders will do at least as well under this arrangement as they would have under the original offer, and management may do considerably better. Third, the target's management may make a competing bid or may propose a financial restructuring, usually with the target financing a substantial distribution to its shareholders with borrowed funds. Fourth, the bidder and the target may reach a compromise, perhaps compelled by the strength of the target's defenses, whereby the bidder increases the price it is offering and, sometimes, provides some job security to the target's management. Finally, and least likely, the target will be able to thwart the bid entirely on some legal objection, or through its internal defenses, and remain largely intact.

D.   FEDERAL SECURITIES LAW PROVISIONS RELATING TO PROXY CONTESTS AND TENDER OFFERS

The Securities Exchange Act of 1934 has always authorized the regulation of proxy solicitations and since 1954, the Securities and Exchange Commission has had special rules dealing with proxy contests. In 1968, Congress passed the Williams Act, which added provisions regulating tender offers to the Securities Exchange Act of 1934.

1. PROXY CONTESTS

All the provisions of the proxy rules, including Rule 14a–9 which prohibits materially false or misleading statements in proxy solicitations, apply to proxy contests as well as to the types of solicitations discussed in Chapter 14.

Rule 14a–7 provides that an issuer must make available to a shareholder who seeks to solicit proxies from the issuer's other shareholders an estimate of the number of record holders and beneficial owners whose shares are owned in street name, and an estimate of the cost of mailing proxy materials to those holders. If the shareholder defrays the reasonable costs of mailing, the issuer must promptly mail the shareholders' proxy materials to all other shareholders. In lieu of that mailing, an issuer may furnish the shareholder with a list that sets forth names and addresses of all shareholders, but that need not list the number of shares each shareholder owns. Because the issuer retains the choice and always elects to mail, the challengers rarely avail themselves of the Rule.

Rule 14a–11 is a special rule that deals with election contests, which are defined as solicitations in opposition to another candidate for director. Under that Rule 14a–11, all "participants" in an election contest—including the issuer, directors, nominees, committees or groups soliciting proxies or financing the solicitation must disclose in their proxy statement biographical information about the participant and any interest in the securities of the subject company.

2. TENDER OFFERS

Section 14(d)(1) prohibits the making of a "tender offer" (a term the statute does not define) for a class of securities registered under section 12, if the bidder would then own 5% of that class, unless certain information is filed with the SEC and sent to the target when the offer is first made. There are no pre-offer filing requirements. Schedule 14D–1, the required form, calls for information similar to that set forth in Schedule 13D, including the description of the bidder's purposes and plans for the target. In addition, when the bidder is a corporation and its financial condition is material to the target company shareholder's decision to accept the offer, certain financial information about the bidder is required.

Section 14(d)(5) permits a security holder to withdraw any shares she has tendered until seven days after the commencement of the tender offer and after 60 days from the commencement of the tender offer. Rule 14d–7 extends this right. A shareholder now can withdraw her shares any time a tender offer remains open. Rule 14e–1 requires that a tender offer be held open for a minimum of 20 business days. If a bidder increases the consideration or the soliciting dealer's fee, the offer must remain open for 10 business days after the increase.

Section 14(d)(6) provides that if a tender offer is for less than all of a class of securities and a greater number are tendered, then the bidder is required to purchase tendered shares on a pro-rata basis from all shareholders who tendered their shares within ten days of the date the offer was made. Rule 14d–8 effectively extends this pro rata period by providing that shares tendered while an offer was open must be purchased on a pro-rata basis.

Section 14(d)(7) provides that if a bidder increases the consideration offered before the offer expires, then the increased consideration must be paid to those who previously tendered their shares.

Rule 14d–9 requires certain persons to file a Schedule 14D–9 with the Commission when they publish or send a solicitation or recommendation with respect to a tender offer. These persons include the subject company, its management, affiliates, the bidder and persons acting on the bidder's behalf. Rule 14e–2 requires a target company to disclose its position with respect to a tender offer to its security holders in a statement no later than ten business days from the dissemination of a tender offer. The statement must include the reasons for the company's position. If the company takes no position on the offer, it must explain why. A target company may issue a "stop-look-and-listen" communication to security holders without filing a Schedule 14D–9, but it must then inform shareholders of a date by which it will advise them of its position on the tender offer.

Rule 14d–10 is known as the "all holders rule." It requires that a tender offer must be open to all security holders of the class subject to the offer and that the consideration paid to all holders must be the highest consideration paid to any other security holder of that class during the tender offer. The latter requirement does not prohibit offering a choice of form of consideration.

Section 14(e) makes it unlawful "for any person to make any untrue statement of a material fact or omit to state any material fact necessary in order to make the statements made, in the light of the circumstances under which they are made, not misleading, or to engage in any fraudulent, deceptive, or manipulative acts or practices, in connection with any tender offer or request or invitation for tenders, or any solicitation of security holders in opposition to or in favor of any such offer, request or invitation."

Rules 14e–1 and 14e–2, both noted above, have been issued pursuant to § 14(e). Rule 14e–3 addresses the problem of persons who have advance knowledge of a pending tender offer, where the bidder has taken substantial steps to commence an offer. Except for the bidder and a few others, Rule 14e–3 declares it to be a fraudulent, deceptive or manipulative act or practice for a person possessing knowledge gained from the bidder, the issuer or an officer, director or employee of such person, to buy or sell shares of the target unless the information has been publicly disclosed a reasonable time before the purchase. The rule contains a number of detailed operational provisions.

E. POLICY QUESTIONS

1. CORPORATE GOVERNANCE

Earlier chapters of the book have presented some of the legal and corporate governance issues that tender offers raise, but it is well to review some of them at this point. The initial regulatory question is the extent to which federal law should control. CTS Corporation v. Dynamics Corporation of America (Chapter 4) suggests states have considerable, but not unlimited, scope to regulate takeover bids. It is also clear that Congress has the constitutional power to preempt state law affecting tender offers and defenses against them. Justice Scalia's concurring comment in *CTS* that "a law can be both economic folly and constitutional" may dictate the Court's deference to the legislature, but not Congress'. Thus, the issue is one of policy, not power. If both the federal government and the states are to retain jurisdiction in this field, is it desirable for them to pursue different objectives? If not, how should their objectives be harmonized?

The substantive issues of corporate governance arise in the context of responses to takeovers. Powerful defenses have been created to deter tender offers, or at least slow down the process. In countering takeover bids, targets have undertaken major corporate transactions, such as massive restructuring or recapitalization, that would not have occurred but for the tender offer. Corporations have incurred heavy debt to fend off a raid. Enhancing the power of the board of directors and management to defeat a bid may weaken the shareholders' ability to hold directors and managers accountable. This weakening is troublesome if one views takeover defenses as essentially self-serving. But if tender offers serve shareholders well, does resistance serve them even better? Courts have wrestled with the proper standard to apply to takeover defenses, whether it is the business judgment rule (or doctrine), intrinsic fairness or something in between. The legal question is related to the underlying economic issue of whether takeovers function as effective governors of management conduct, which in turn may be dependent upon empirical studies of which companies become targets of tender offers.

The ultimate question is how much freedom should a target company board have to resist a takeover bid that it determines is not in the best interests of the corporation? Should the board be denied all discretion, allowed to employ tactics designed to extract a higher price for shareholders, or empowered to decide that the company is "not for sale" to anyone regardless of price or the bidder's capabilities.

2. ECONOMIC THEORY

The fundamental issue is whether tender offers create or simply redistribute wealth. If wealth is created, what is the source? Economists Michael Jensen and Richard Ruback in The Market for Corporate

Control: The Scientific Evidence, 11 J.Fin.Econ. 5 (1983), referring to stock prices, point to the great gains by shareholders of target companies and the slight gains by shareholders of bidder companies, and conclude that the evidence plainly demonstrates that tender offers have created wealth. Moreover, although Jensen and Ruback are uncertain as to the source, they believe that the gains do not result from monopoly profits. To them, the clear public policy implication is that no impediments to hostile takeover bids should be allowed.

However, the economic and political issues concern a broader spectrum of interests than shareholders. Even assuming the validity of Jensen and Ruback's conclusions, is the public policy directive so clear? Do the objectively measurable stock gains they find reflect the gains and losses of other with an interest in the corporation—the employees, the suppliers, the communities where the corporation operates? There is a political question as well: does a dollar of shareholder gain justify imposing a loss of 80 cents on employees, suppliers, customers and the community combined (assuming those figures are correct)? The marginal value of the added wealth to shareholders, given the demographics of that body, may not be as "important" as the marginal losses to the others.

Economists Andrei Shleifer and Lawrence Summers, in their paper Hostile Takeovers as Breaches of Trust (Feb. 20, 1987), contend that society *can* be worse off from a takeover bid that benefits shareholders. For example, bidders may be willing to terminate implicit long-term contracts with other stakeholders (employees, suppliers and the community) that existing management would honor. Sometimes these terminations result in benefits to the community as well as to stockholders, when the stakeholders can replace their old relationships without cost. In that event, assets have been moved to more productive users. The stock gains measure society's gain. In other situations, the stakeholders' losses may equal shareholder gains, in which event society has not gained, nor has it lost. But at times the stakeholder losses may exceed shareholder gains, if the consequences of job and supplier losses produce a ripple effect of further community losses.

Clearly, some politicians are not convinced that reference to stock prices alone provides clear, unbiased proof of the value of tender offers. Much of the legislative effort has been directed to preventing the stakeholder losses. When T. Boone Pickens raised an eyebrow in the direction of Boeing, a Delaware corporation that employs over 100,000 workers in the state of Washington, the Washington legislature quickly rallied to the support of the company despite serious misgivings about its constitutional authority to do so.

The public policy analysis must determine how efficient is the market, and whether the short term price studies are sufficient to measure the wealth creation of the event. There is political content to the claims of market efficiency, since the argument concludes that no regulation is necessary absent a market failure. Some market participants consistently gain from that approach, while others are exposed to losses. That result has led to a curious call for regulation from large business organizations, like the Business Roundtable, who normally abhor Congressional intrusion into the market place. However, they claim that tender offers have forced them into a short term business strategy designed to maintain high stock prices without regard to the long term welfare of their companies.

3. MANAGEMENT DISCIPLINE

Are hostile takeovers a useful discipline for managers of publicly traded corporations? Does this discipline improve the efficiency of those corporations? No issue affecting tender offers has been debated more heatedly.

In Chapter 14, we saw that the market for corporate control plays a central role in the nexus-of-contracts theory of the corporation. Chapter 6 of the 1985 Economic Report of the President contains a good exposition of the supporters of this theory. Focusing on maximizing shareholder wealth, the Report asserts that the market aligns management interests with those of the shareholders through the labor market for management services and through the external market for corporate control. There are important limits to the effectiveness of the labor market. Most notably, it allows poorly performing entrenched managers to remain in control if they believe they are performing efficiently. What is needed, therefore, is an objective means of measuring management performance. The stock market provides this function by its efficient pricing of corporate stock.

Management's best assurance that it will retain control is to keep the stock price high relative to outsiders' estimates of the potential value of the shares. By contrast, a low stock price attracts bidders who seek to gain control, displace management, and achieve the potential value. In this fashion, the market for corporate control disciplines managers who have failed to maximize share values.

The Report observes that available evidence indicates that target company shareholders gain from 16–34% over pre-bid stock values and bidder shareholders gain approximately 2% when tender offers are made. The Report presents five hypotheses concerning the source of these gains. First, there may be production and distribution economies. Second, acquisitions may permit technology transfers that would otherwise be unavailable. Third, there may be cost-reducing effects to companies that have larger market shares. Fourth, assets may be shifted to higher valued uses. Finally, gains may come from improved management. So as not to overstate the last point, the Report notes that not all targets are poorly managed, but that poor management is one motive for takeovers, and that restraints on takeovers can protect managers from the discipline of the marketplace.

In A Guide to Takeovers: Theory, Evidence, and Regulation, 9 Yale J. Reg. 119 (1992), Professor Roberta Romano surveys the empirical evidence for explanations of takeovers. She finds that the data on returns from takeovers corresponds to those in the Economic Report of the President. Takeovers do create an overall gain when bidder and target returns are aggregated. Romano finds, however, that the data for bidder returns is more ambiguous than that in the Report, at least during the 1980's. She agrees with the Report that management discipline provides an explanation for takeovers, but argues that there are other explanations.

Romano divides the possible causes into two groups. First, there are value-maximizing sources in which the desire to increase the equity share price of the bidder motivates the acquisition. These explanations can be divided into efficiency, wealth transfer or expropriation, and market inefficiency categories. Second, there are non-wealth-maximizing explanations in which management's desire to maximize its own utility at the expense of shareholder wealth cause the takeover.

Romano finds the strongest empirical support for efficiency-enhancing value-maximizing causes of takeovers. Not surprisingly, there is more than one explanation of takeovers with strong empirical support, an indication that takeovers occur for a variety of reasons. She concludes that replacement of inefficient management has empirical support as one source of takeover gains. Statistics indicate that poorly managed corporations are often targets, and that targets typically have lower profitability relative to their industry peers prior to being acquired. Asset productivity, as measured by cash flow, improves after an acquisition regardless of whether the bidder and target are in related or unrelated industries. The absence of any difference in the rate of improvement suggests that the gains from takeovers do not rely solely on operating synergies, which should be higher when the bidder and target engage in related businesses.

Operating synergies provide another source of efficiency gains in takeovers. Economies of scale allow the acquirer to spread overhead expenses across a bigger business. Economies of scope allow bidder and target to combine complementary assets to raise their productivity. The bidder's management expertise can be extended and transferred to the target. Finally, the takeover may lower the target's cost of capital, because it can use the acquirer's internally generated funds to finance its capital expenditures rather than relying on more expensive external borrowings.

Romano does not find significant empirical support for other value-maximizing theories of takeovers based on either market inefficiency or expropriation. There is no evidence that the stock market consistently undervalues takeover targets nor that stock market myopia creates targets by penalizing long-term projects or research and development. She concludes that gains from takeovers cannot be traced to wealth transfers to target shareholders by labor, bondholders, consumers, or taxpayers. Although tax benefits from interest deductions may account for the premiums in going-private transactions, the net effect for taxpayers is ambiguous, because those benefits are offset by taxes paid by target shareholder on their gains. Consumers may fear that increasing industry concentration will raise prices, but Romano finds no support for this. Bondholders may suffer in takeovers as the value of bonds drop, because the target's indebtedness increases, but that loss in value does not account for gain to shareholders. Romano also sees no linkage between takeovers and employment levels except for top and middle managers.

Romano concludes that the data relied on to support theories that takeovers are not value-maximizing are ambiguous. Some data suggest that management may engage in takeovers to promote its own welfare at the expense of shareholder wealth. The fact, however, that the data show that there are net gains from takeovers demonstrates that takeovers do increase overall wealth. Therefore, non-value-maximizing theories cannot explain the majority of takeovers. Takeovers occur for a variety and combination of reasons. No single theory can explain all takeovers. Non-value-maximizing theories explain an isolated number of takeovers. In the majority of takeovers, Romano finds that efficiency-enhancing, value-maximizing theories of takeovers provide the best explanation for the gains created.

The wealth-creating nature of takeovers suggests to Romano that some takeover regulation should be reconsidered. Regulations that seek to protect employees or other constituencies in takeovers do not protect the public interest. Because the empirical support for claims that takeovers expropriate wealth from labor or other groups is weak, while the evidence does support claims that takeovers serve to eliminate inefficient management, such regulation may simply transfer wealth from shareholders to management. Similarly, restrictive state takeover laws have a negative stock price effect, harming shareholders with little benefit for other groups except management. Romano finds that regulations favoring auctions have an ambiguous impact. Auctions do raise premiums for target shareholders, but the increased competition may lower bidder returns and therefore make the threat of hostile takeovers a less effective disciplinary device. The data, however, do not make clear whether legal rules promoting auctions have a negative impact on the number of takeovers, and it is possible that by reducing search costs or allowing the highest valuing-bidder to acquire the target, those rules have a beneficial effect.

A related question is whether the rapid decline in takeover activity after 1989, which followed a long gradual increase that began in 1975, was caused by the proliferation in antitakeover defenses. By 1991, 87% of all exchange-listed firms were protected against an uninvited takeover bid by either a poison pill, a business combination statute, a control share statute, or some combination of the three. Robert Comment & G. William Schwert, Poison or Placebo? Evidence on the Deterrent And Wealth Effects of Modern Antitakeover Measures 3 (NBER Working Paper No. 4316 (1993). Despite the strong correlation between the proliferation of antitakeover defenses and the demise of takeover activity, Professors Comment and Schwert found no "direct evidence" that antitakeover measures caused the decline. Id. at 37. That led them to "conclude that the demise of the 1980s market for corporate control was caused by secular trends [i.e., "the 1990 recession and cash crunch"] and not the introduction, spread, and legal acceptance of poison pill rights plans, control share statutes, or business combination statutes." Id.

F. PROTECTION OF CONTROL

PROBLEM
GENERAL INDUSTRIES CORPORATION—PART I

General Industries Corporation (GIC) is a Columbia corporation whose stock is listed on the New York Stock Exchange. GIC's authorized capital is 100 million shares of common stock, of which 50 million shares are outstanding. GIC develops and produces high technology medical products. Its headquarters and principal laboratories are located in a medium size city in Connecticut, where GIC employs 3,000 people.

GIC has long been a research-oriented firm. It enjoys an excellent reputation for innovative, high quality work. Many of its employees are scientists, and GIC has always spent substantial amounts on research and development. R&D expenditures have grown in recent years, but few commercially successful products have been developed. GIC has reported losses for the last several years and its stock price has declined from a high of $90 to a current price of $34 per share.

GIC's 15 member board consists of seven management and eight non-management directors. The chairman of the board and chief executive officer is Abigail Andrews. Among the eight non-management directors is William Post, a partner in the company's outside law firm. Members of the board own a total of 5% of the outstanding stock.

Several months ago, GIC announced that it had negotiated a large contract with the National Institutes of Health (NIH) to work on development of new treatments for breast and prostate cancer. The contract calls for GIC to commit substantial resources to further investigate and test experimental technologies initially developed by NIH. Profits, if any, will come only if GIC develops commercially viable treatment technologies. Then, GIC will have exclusive rights to market any products it develops. GIC's board, after having been briefed on the contract and the potential impact of the technologies involved, unanimously approved the contract, even though in the short term its financial impact on GIC will be negative.

Charles Danton, a wealthy real estate investor, has owned 400,000 shares of GIC for several years and recently has become quite concerned about the company's declining earnings. After GIC announced the NIH contract, Danton decided the time had come to seek control of GIC. He is prepared to commit about $300 million of his personal funds and has been told by his investment bank, Merrill, Stanley & Co., that it can arrange a line of credit to provide the additional funds Danton would need to acquire 51% of GIC's stock at a price of up to $60 per share. Danton's plan is to make GIC more profitable by emphasizing consumer and industrial uses of its technology, eliminating some of the less profitable and riskier research, attempting to abrogate the NIH contract, and moving GIC's headquarters to Tucson, where his real estate investment firm is headquartered and where he is a trustee of the University Medical Center.

After receiving the commitment from Merrill, Stanley, Danton purchased an additional 600,000 shares of GIC stock on the open market at an average price of $32 per share, bringing his holdings to 2% of the outstanding stock. GIC's investment banker, First Prudential (First Pru), became aware of increased activity and managed to determine that Danton was the buyer. Through an intermediary, First Pru also learned about Danton's plans for GIC and also learned that he probably would be willing to sell his one million shares for $45 million, slightly more than his total cost for those shares.

First Pru has brought all this information to the attention of Ms. Andrews. It also has pointed out that to finance the purchase of Danton's stock, GIC probably would have to borrow $45 million at slightly over the prime rate. The GIC board has scheduled a meeting to consider how to proceed. Both Post and representatives of First Pru are scheduled to make presentations. Post has asked you, an associate in his law firm, to brief him on the following questions.

1. Can GIC purchase Danton's stock at an above market price? If the purchase is made, should GIC seek a commitment from Danton that he will not turn around and make another takeover bid?

2. If it decides not to buy Danton's stock, what other measures might GIC take in anticipation of the expected bid? What measures the board implement on its own and what measures require shareholder approval?

1. BUSINESS JUDGMENT OR SELF-DEALING?

CHEFF v. MATHES
41 Del.Ch. 494, 199 A.2d 548 (1964).

CAREY, JUSTICE.

This is an appeal from the decision of the Vice–Chancellor in a derivative suit holding certain directors of Holland Furnace Company liable for loss allegedly resulting from improper use of corporate funds to purchase shares of the company. Because a meaningful decision upon review turns upon a complete understanding of the factual background, a somewhat detailed summary of the evidence is required.

Holland Furnace Company, a corporation of the State of Delaware, manufactures warm air furnaces, air conditioning equipment, and other home heating equipment. At the time of the relevant transactions, the board of directors was composed of the seven individual defendants. Mr. Cheff had been Holland's Chief Executive Officer since 1933, received an annual salary of $77,400, and personally owned 6,000 shares of the company. He was also a director. Mrs. Cheff, the wife of Mr. Cheff, was a daughter of the founder of Holland and had served as a director since 1922. She personally owned 5,804 shares of Holland and owned 47.9 percent of Hazelbank United Interest, Inc. Hazelbank is an investment vehicle for Mrs. Cheff and members of the Cheff–Landwehr family group, which owned 164,950 shares of the 883,585 outstanding shares of Holland. As a director, Mrs. Cheff received a compensation of $200.00 for each monthly board meeting, whether or not she attended the meeting.

The third director, Edgar P. Landwehr, is the nephew of Mrs. Cheff and personally owned 24,010 shares of Holland and 8.6 percent of the outstanding shares of Hazelbank. He received no compensation from Holland other than the monthly director's fee.

Robert H. Trenkamp is an attorney who first represented Holland in 1946. In May 1953, he became a director of Holland and acted as general counsel for the company. During the period in question, he received no retainer from the company, but did receive substantial sums for legal services rendered the company. Apart from the above-described payments, he received no compensation from Holland other than the monthly director's fee. He owned 200 shares of Holland Furnace stock. Although he owned no shares of Hazelbank, at the time relevant to this controversy, he was serving as a director and counsel of Hazelbank.

John D. Ames was then a partner in the Chicago investment firm of Bacon, Whipple & Co. and joined the board at the request of Mr. Cheff. During the periods in question, his stock ownership varied between ownership of no shares to ownership of 300 shares. He was considered by the other members of the Holland board to be the financial advisor to the board. He received no compensation from Holland other than the normal director's fee.

Mr. Ralph G. Boalt was the Vice President of J.R. Watkins Company, a manufacturer and distributor of cosmetics. In 1953, at the request of Mr. Cheff, he became a member of the board of directors. Apart from the normal director's fee, he received no compensation from Holland for his services.

Mr. George Spatta was the President of Clark Equipment Company, a large manufacturer of earth moving equipment. In 1951, at the request of Mr. Cheff, he joined the board of directors of Holland. Apart from the normal director's fee, he received no compensation from the company.

* * *

Prior to the events in question, Holland employed approximately 8500 persons and maintained 400 branch sales offices located in 43 states. The volume of sales had declined from over $41,000,000 in 1948 to less than $32,000,000 in 1956. Defendants contend that the decline in earnings is attributable to the artificial post-war demand generated in the 1946–1948 period. In order to stabilize the condition of the company, the sales department apparently was reorganized and certain unprofitable branch offices were closed. By 1957 this reorganization had been completed and the management was convinced that the changes were manifesting beneficial results. The practice of the company was to directly employ the retail salesman, and the management considered that practice—unique in the furnace business—to be a vital factor in the company's success.

During the first five months of 1957, the monthly trading volume of Holland's stock on the New York Stock Exchange ranged between 10,300 shares to 24,200 shares. In the last week of June 1957, however, the trading increased to 37,800 shares, with a corresponding increase in the market price. In June of 1957, Mr. Cheff met with Mr. Arnold H. Maremont, who was President of Maremont Automotive Products, Inc. and Chairman of the boards of Motor Products Corporation and Allied Paper Corporation. Mr. Cheff testified, on deposition, that Maremont generally inquired about the feasibility of merger between Motor Products and Holland. Mr. Cheff testified that, in view of the difference in sales practices between the two companies, he informed Mr. Maremont that a merger did not seem feasible. In reply, Mr. Maremont stated that, in the light of Mr. Cheff's decision, he had no further interest in Holland nor did he wish to buy any of the stock of Holland.

None of the members of the board apparently connected the interest of Mr. Maremont with the increased activity of Holland stock. However, Mr. Trenkamp and Mr. Staal, the Treasurer of Holland, unsuccessfully made an informal investigation in order to ascertain the identity of the purchaser or purchasers. The mystery was resolved, however, when Maremont called Ames in July of 1957 to inform the latter that Maremont then owned 55,000 shares of Holland stock. At this juncture, no requests for change in corporate policy were made, and Maremont made no demand to be made a member of the board of Holland.

Ames reported the above information to the board at its July 30, 1957 meeting. Because of the position now occupied by Maremont, the board elected to investigate the financial and business history of Maremont and corporations controlled by him. Apart from the documentary evidence produced by this investigation, which will be considered infra, Staal testified, on deposition, that "leading bank officials" had indicated that Maremont "had been a participant, or had attempted to be, in the liquidation of a number of companies." * * *

On August 23, 1957, at the request of Maremont, a meeting was held between Mr. Maremont and Cheff. At this meeting, Cheff was informed that Motor Products then owned approximately 100,000 shares of Holland stock. Maremont then made a demand that he be named to the board of directors, but Cheff refused to consider it. Since considerable controversy has been generated by Maremont's alleged threat to liquidate the company or substantially alter the sales force of Holland, we believe it desirable to set forth the testimony of Cheff on this point: "Now we have 8500 men, direct employees, so the problem is entirely different. He indicated immediately that he had no interest in that type of distribution, that he didn't think it was modern, that he felt furnaces could be sold as he sold mufflers, through half a dozen salesmen in a wholesale way."

Testimony was introduced by the defendants tending to show that substantial unrest was present among the employees of Holland as a result of the threat of Maremont to seek control of Holland. * * * Moreover, at approximately this time, the company was furnished with a Dun and Bradstreet report, which indicated the practice of Maremont to achieve quick profits by sales or liquidations of companies acquired by him. The defendants were also supplied with an income statement of Motor Products, Inc., showing a loss of $336,121.00 for the period in 1957.

On August 30, 1957, the board was informed by Cheff of Maremont's demand to be placed upon the board and of Maremont's belief that the retail sales organization of Holland was obsolete. The board was also informed of the results of the investigation by Cheff and Staal. Predicated upon this information, the board authorized the purchase of company stock on the market with corporate funds, ostensibly for use in a stock option plan.

Subsequent to this meeting, substantial numbers of shares were purchased and, in addition, Mrs. Cheff made alternate personal purchases of Holland stock. As a result of purchases by Maremont, Holland and Mrs. Cheff, the market price rose. * * * On September 4th, Maremont proposed to sell his current holdings of Holland to the corporation for $14.00 a share. However, because of delay in responding to this offer, Maremont withdrew the offer. At this time, Mrs. Cheff was obviously quite concerned over the prospect of a Maremont acquisition, and had stated her willingness to expend her personal resources to prevent it.

On September 30, 1957, Motor Products Corporation, by letter to Mrs. Bowles, made a buy-sell offer to Hazelbank. Although Mrs. Bowles and Mrs. Putnam were opposed to any acquisition of Holland stock by Hazelbank, Mr. Landwehr conceded that a majority of the board were in favor of the purchase. Despite this fact, the finance committee elected to refer the offer to the Holland board on the grounds that it was the primary concern of Holland.

Thereafter, Mr. Trenkamp arranged for a meeting with Maremont, which occurred on October 14–15, 1957, in Chicago. Prior to this meeting, Trenkamp was aware of the intentions of Hazelbank and Mrs. Cheff to purchase all or portions of the stock then owned by Motor Products if Holland did not so act. As a result of the meeting, there was a tentative agreement on the part of Motor Products to sell its 155,000 shares at $14.40 per share. On October 23, 1957, at a special meeting of the Holland board, the purchase was considered. All directors, except Spatta, were present. The dangers allegedly posed by Maremont were again reviewed by the board. Trenkamp and Mrs. Cheff agree that the latter informed the board that either she or Hazelbank would purchase part or all of the block of Holland stock owned by Motor Products if the Holland board did not so act. The board was also informed that in order for the corporation to finance the purchase, substantial sums would have to be borrowed from commercial lending institutions. A resolution authorizing the purchase of 155,000 shares from Motor Products was adopted by the board. The price paid was in excess of the market price prevailing at the time, and the book value of the stock was approximately $20.00 as compared to approximately $14.00 for the net quick asset value. The transaction was subsequently consummated. The stock option plan mentioned in the minutes has never been implemented. In 1959, Holland stock reached a high of $15.25 a share.

On February 6, 1958, plaintiffs, owners of 60 shares of Holland stock, filed a derivative suit in the court below naming all of the individual directors of Holland, Holland itself and Motor Products Corporation as defendants. The complaint alleged that all of the purchases of stock by Holland in 1957 were for the purpose of insuring the perpetuation of control by the incumbent directors. The complaint requested that the transaction between Motor Products and Holland be rescinded and, secondly, that the individual defendants account to Holland for the alleged damages. Since Motor Products was never served with process, the initial remedy became inapplicable. Ames was never served nor did he enter an appearance.

After trial, the Vice Chancellor found the following facts: (a) Holland directly sells to retail consumers by means of numerous branch offices. There were no intermediate dealers. (b) Immediately prior to the complained-of transactions, the sales and earnings of Holland had declined and its marketing practices were under investigation by the Federal Trade Commission. (c) Mr. Cheff and Trenkamp had received substantial sums as Chief Executive and attorney of the company, respectively. (d) Maremont, on August 23rd, 1957, demanded a place on the board. (e) At the October 14th meeting between Trenkamp, Staal and Maremont, Trenkamp and Staal were authorized to speak for Hazelbank and Mrs. Cheff as well as Holland. Only Mr. Cheff, Mrs. Cheff, Mr. Landwehr, and Mr. Trenkamp clearly understood, prior to the October 23rd meeting, that either Hazelbank or Mrs. Cheff would have utilized their funds to purchase the Holland stock if Holland had not acted. (g) There was no real threat posed by Maremont and no substantial evidence of intention by Maremont to liquidate Holland. (h) Any employee unrest could have been caused by factors other than Maremont's intrusion and "only one important employee was shown to have left, and his motive for leaving is not clear." (i) The Court rejected the stock option plan as a meaningful rationale for the purchase from Maremont or the prior open market purchases.

The Court then found that the actual purpose behind the purchase was the desire to perpetuate control, but because of its finding that only the four above-named directors knew of the "alternative", the remaining directors were exonerated. No appeal was taken by plaintiffs from that decision.

* * *

Under the provisions of 8 Del.C. § 160, a corporation is granted statutory power to purchase and sell shares of its own stock. The charge here is not one of violation of statute, but the allegation is that the true motives behind such purchases were improperly centered upon perpetuation of control. In an analogous field, courts have sustained the use of proxy funds to inform stockholders of management's views upon the policy questions inherent in an election to a board of directors, but have not sanctioned the use of corporate funds to advance the selfish desires of directors to perpetuate themselves in office. Similarly, if the actions of the board were motivated by a sincere belief that the buying out of the dissident stockholder was necessary to maintain what the board believed to be proper business practices, the board will not be held liable for such decision, even though hindsight indicates the decision was not the wisest course. See Kors v. Carey, Del.Ch., 158 A.2d 136. On the other hand, if the board has acted solely or primarily because of the desire to perpetuate themselves in office, the use of corporate funds for such purposes is improper. See Bennett v. Propp, Del., 187 A.2d 405, and Yasik v. Wachtel, 25 Del.Ch. 247, 17 A.2d 309.

Our first problem is the allocation of the burden of proof to show the presence or lack of good faith on the part of the board in authorizing the purchase of shares. Initially, the decision of the board of directors in authorizing a purchase was presumed to be in good faith and could be overturned only by a conclusive showing by plaintiffs of fraud or other misconduct. In Kors, cited supra, the court merely indicated that the directors are presumed to act in good faith and the burden of proof to show to the contrary falls upon the plaintiff. However, in Bennett v. Propp, supra, we stated:

> We must bear in mind the inherent danger in the purchase of shares with corporate funds to remove a threat to corporate policy when a threat to control is involved. The directors are of necessity confronted with a conflict of interest, and an objective decision is difficult. * * * Hence, in our opinion, the burden should be on the directors to justify such a purchase as one primarily in the corporate interest. (187 A.2d 409, at page 409).

* * *

To say that the burden of proof is upon the defendants is not to indicate, however, that the directors have the same "self-dealing interest" as is present, for example, when a director sells property to the corporation. The only clear pecuniary interest shown on the record was held by Mr. Cheff, as an executive of the corporation, and Trenkamp, as its attorney. The mere fact that some of the other directors were substantial shareholders does not create a personal pecuniary interest in the decisions made by the board of directors, since all shareholders would presumably share the benefit flowing to the substantial shareholder. Accordingly, these directors other than Trenkamp and Cheff, while called upon to justify their actions, will not be held to the same standard of proof required of those directors having personal and pecuniary interest in the transaction.

* * *

Plaintiffs urge that the sale price was unfair in view of the fact that the price was in excess of that prevailing on the open market. However, as conceded by all parties, a substantial block of stock will normally sell at a higher price than that prevailing on the open market, the increment being attributable to a "control premium". Plaintiffs argue that it is inappropriate to require the defendant corporation to pay a control premium, since control is meaningless to an acquisition by a corporation of its own shares. However, it is elementary that a holder of a substantial number of shares would expect to receive the control premium as part of his selling price, and if the corporation desired to obtain the stock, it is unreasonable to expect that the corporation could avoid paying what any other purchaser would be required to pay for the stock. In any event, the financial expert produced by defendant at trial indicated that the price paid was fair and there was no rebuttal.

The question then presented is whether or not defendants satisfied the burden of proof of showing reasonable grounds to believe a danger to corporate policy and effectiveness existed by the presence of the Maremont stock ownership. It is important to remember that the directors satisfy their burden by showing good faith and reasonable investigation; the directors will not be penalized for an honest mistake of judgment, if the judgment appeared reasonable at the time the decision was made.

* * *

[W]e are of the opinion that the evidence presented in the court below leads inevitably to the conclusion that the board of directors, based upon direct investigation, receipt of professional advice, and personal observations of the contradictory action of Maremont and his explanation of corporate purpose, believed, with justification, that there was a reasonable threat to the continued existence of Holland, or at least existence in its present form, by the plan of Maremont to continue building up his stock holdings. We find no evidence in the record sufficient to justify a contrary conclusion. The opinion of the Vice Chancellor that employee unrest may have been engendered by other factors or that the board had no grounds to suspect Maremont is not supported in any manner by the evidence.

As noted above, the Vice–Chancellor found that the purpose of the acquisition was the improper desire to maintain control, but, at the same time, he exonerated those individual directors whom he believed to be unaware of the possibility of using non-corporate funds to accomplish this purpose. Such a decision is inconsistent with his finding that the motive was improper, within the rule enunciated in Bennett. If the actions were in fact improper because of a desire to maintain control, then the presence or absence of a non-corporate alternative is irrelevant, as corporate funds may not be used to advance an improper purpose even if there is no non-corporate alternative available. Conversely, if the actions were proper because of a decision by the board made in good faith that the corporate interest was served thereby, they are not rendered improper by the fact that some individual directors were willing to advance personal funds if the corporation did not. It is conceivable that the Vice Chancellor considered this feature of the case to be of significance because of his apparent belief that any excess corporate funds should have been used to finance a subsidiary corporation. That action would not have solved the problem of Holland's over-capitalization. In any event, this question was a matter of business judgment, which furnishes no justification for holding the directors personally responsible in this case.

Accordingly, the judgment of the court below is reversed and remanded with instruction to enter judgment for the defendants.

Note: Evaluating Defensive Tactics:
An Introduction

1. Courts usually avoid inquiry into directors' motives for making corporate decisions. If no conflict of interest is shown, courts assume directors acted in good faith and that their decisions reflect valid business judgments. If a conflict is shown, courts assume directors were motivated by their personal financial interests and require that they demonstrate their decisions were fair. This analytic framework breaks down, however, with regard to decisions that have the effect of protecting control. On the one hand, a board must decide whether a change in control is in the corporation's best interest. On the other, management (especially inside directors and officers) has an interest in safeguarding its jobs. See Ronald J. Gilson, A Structural Approach to Corporations: The Case Against Defensive Tactics in Tender Offers, 33 Stan.L.Rev. 819, 826–827 (1981).

One could argue that because of management's interest, the business judgment rule should not apply and that fairness must be proved. But Professor Gilson points out that fairness is not an effective standard in terms of which to evaluate a decision to protect control. A transaction usually is considered "fair" if its terms are equivalent to those that disinterested parties would reach in an arm's-length transaction. When a defensive tactic such as a share repurchase is being evaluated, the real question is whether the decision to repurchase shares was justified, *not* whether the repurchase price was fair. Judicial review should focus on whether shareholders were better off after the repurchase than they were before. It is difficult to answer this question using a fairness standard, but a court also must examine "factors which the business judgment rule excludes from consideration." Id. at 827.

Professor Gilson suggests that the *Cheff* court attempted to deal with this problem by focusing on the Holland directors' motives for repurchasing Maremont's stock. He notes that courts are accustomed to examining motive in a variety of other contexts, which may have made the court comfortable with this approach. What the court actually held was that if Holland's directors had reasonable grounds to believe that Maremont's stock ownership threatened corporate policy and effectiveness, the court would not second guess the board's decision. The court further stated that it would treat the board's determination that a threat existed as a business judgment if it found the board had acted in good faith and after reasonable investigation. The board's showing that it had policy difference with Maremont satisfied this requirement.

Cheff can be read as implying that so long as a corporation's management can identify some policy difference between itself and a potential bidder, courts will not evaluate whether the tactics it employs to eliminate that "threat" are either reasonable or fair even though management has a conflict of interest. The rule is a little different than in a standard business judgment situation, in that directors have the burden of proving that their determination a threat existed was based on a reasonable investigation. But consider the evidence on which the court relied to hold that Holland's directors had satisfied that burden.

2. ENHANCED BUSINESS JUDGMENT RULE

UNOCAL CORPORATION v. MESA PETROLEUM CO.
493 A.2d 946 (Del.1985).

MOORE, JUSTICE.

We confront an issue of first impression in Delaware—the validity of a corporation's self-tender for its own shares which excludes from participation a stockholder making a hostile tender offer for the company's stock.

The Court of Chancery granted a preliminary injunction to the plaintiffs, Mesa Petroleum Co., Mesa Asset Co., Mesa Partners II, and Mesa Eastern, Inc. (collectively "Mesa") * enjoining an exchange offer of the defendant, Unocal Corporation (Unocal) for its own stock. The trial court concluded that a selective exchange offer, excluding Mesa, was

---

* T. Boone Pickens, Jr., is President and Chairman of the Board of Mesa Petroleum and President of Mesa Asset and controls the related Mesa entities.

legally impermissible. We cannot agree with such a blanket rule. The factual findings of the Vice Chancellor, fully supported by the record, establish that Unocal's board, consisting of a majority of independent directors, acted in good faith, and after reasonable investigation found that Mesa's tender offer was both inadequate and coercive. Under the circumstances the board had both the power and duty to oppose a bid it perceived to be harmful to the corporate enterprise. On this record we are satisfied that the device Unocal adopted is reasonable in relation to the threat posed, and that the board acted in the proper exercise of sound business judgment. We will not substitute our views for those of the board if the latter's decision can be "attributed to any rational business purpose." Sinclair Oil Corp. v. Levien, Del.Supr., 280 A.2d 717, 720 (1971). Accordingly, we reverse the decision of the Court of Chancery and order the preliminary injunction vacated.

I.

The factual background of this matter bears a significant relationship to its ultimate outcome.

On April 8, 1985, Mesa, the owner of approximately 13% of Unocal's stock, commenced a two-tier "front loaded" cash tender offer for 64 million shares, or approximately 37%, of Unocal's outstanding stock at a price of $54 per share. The "back-end" was designed to eliminate the remaining publicly held shares by an exchange of securities purportedly worth $54 per share. However, pursuant to an order entered by the United States District Court for the Central District of California on April 26, 1985, Mesa issued a supplemental proxy statement to Unocal's stockholders disclosing that the securities offered in the second-step merger would be highly subordinated, and that Unocal's capitalization would differ significantly from its present structure. Unocal has rather aptly termed such securities "junk bonds".

Unocal's board consists of eight independent outside directors and six insiders. It met on April 13, 1985, to consider the Mesa tender offer. Thirteen directors were present, and the meeting lasted nine and one-half hours. The directors were given no agenda or written materials prior to the session. However, detailed presentations were made by legal counsel regarding the board's obligations under both Delaware corporate law and the federal securities laws. The board then received a presentation from Peter Sachs on behalf of Goldman Sachs & Co. (Goldman Sachs) and Dillon, Read & Co. (Dillon Read) discussing the bases for their opinions that the Mesa proposal was wholly inadequate. Mr. Sachs opined that the minimum cash value that could be expected from a sale or orderly liquidation for 100% of Unocal's stock was in excess of $60 per share. In making his presentation, Mr. Sachs showed slides outlining the valuation techniques used by the financial advisors, and others, depicting recent business combinations in the oil and gas industry. The Court of Chancery found that the Sachs presentation was designed to apprise the directors of the scope of the analyses performed rather than the facts and numbers used in reaching the conclusion that Mesa's tender offer price was inadequate.

Mr. Sachs also presented various defensive strategies available to the board if it concluded that Mesa's two-step tender offer was inadequate and should be opposed. One of the devices outlined was a self-tender by Unocal for its own stock with a reasonable price range of $70 to $75 per share. The cost of such a proposal would cause the company to incur $6.1—6.5 billion of additional debt, and a presentation was made informing the board of Unocal's ability to handle it. The directors were told that the primary effect of this obligation would be to reduce exploratory drilling, but that the company would nonetheless remain a viable entity.

The eight outside directors, comprising a clear majority of the thirteen members present, then met separately with Unocal's financial advisors and attorneys. Thereafter, they unanimously agreed to advise the board that it should reject Mesa's tender offer as inadequate, and that Unocal should pursue a self-tender to provide the stockholders with a fairly priced alternative to the Mesa proposal. The board then reconvened and unanimously adopted a resolution rejecting as grossly inadequate Mesa's tender offer. Despite the nine and one-half hour length of the meeting, no formal decision was made on the proposed defensive self-tender.

On April 15, the board met again with four of the directors present by telephone and one member still absent. This session lasted two hours. Unocal's Vice President of Finance and its Assistant General Counsel made a detailed presentation of the proposed terms of the exchange offer. A price range between $70 and $80 per share was considered, and ultimately the directors agreed upon $72. The board was also advised about the debt securities that would be issued, and the necessity of placing restrictive covenants upon certain corporate activities until the obligations were paid. The board's decisions were made in reliance on the advice of its investment bankers, including the terms and conditions upon which the securities were to be issued. Based upon this advice, and the board's own deliberations, the directors unanimously approved the exchange offer. Their resolution provided that if Mesa acquired 64 million shares of Unocal stock through its own offer (the Mesa Purchase Condition), Unocal would buy the remaining 49% outstanding for an exchange of debt securities having an aggregate par value of $72 per share. The board resolution also stated that the offer would be subject to other conditions that had been described to the board at the meeting, or which were deemed necessary by Unocal's officers, including the exclusion of Mesa from the proposal (the Mesa exclusion). Any such conditions were required to be in accordance with the "purport and intent" of the offer.

Unocal's exchange offer was commenced on April 17, 1985, and Mesa promptly challenged it by filing this suit in the Court of Chancery. On April 22, the Unocal board met again and was advised by Goldman

Sachs and Dillon Read to waive the Mesa Purchase Condition as to 50 million shares. This recommendation was in response to a perceived concern of the shareholders that, if shares were tendered to Unocal, no shares would be purchased by either offeror. The directors were also advised that they should tender their own Unocal stock into the exchange offer as a mark of their confidence in it.

Another focus of the board was the Mesa exclusion. Legal counsel advised that under Delaware law Mesa could only be excluded for what the directors reasonably believed to be a valid corporate purpose. The directors' discussion centered on the objective of adequately compensating shareholders at the "back-end" of Mesa's proposal, which the latter would finance with "junk bonds". To include Mesa would defeat that goal, because under the proration aspect of the exchange offer (49%) every Mesa share accepted by Unocal would displace one held by another stockholder. Further, if Mesa were permitted to tender to Unocal, the latter would in effect be financing Mesa's own inadequate proposal.

Meanwhile, on April 22, 1985, Mesa amended its complaint in this action to challenge the Mesa exclusion. A preliminary injunction hearing was scheduled for May 8, 1985. However, on April 23, 1985, Mesa moved for a temporary restraining order in response to Unocal's announcement that it was partially waiving the Mesa Purchase Condition. After expedited briefing, the Court of Chancery heard Mesa's motion on April 26.

On April 29, 1985, the Vice Chancellor temporarily restrained Unocal from proceeding with the exchange offer unless it included Mesa. The trial court recognized that directors could oppose, and attempt to defeat, a hostile takeover which they considered adverse to the best interests of the corporation. However, the Vice Chancellor decided that in a selective purchase of the company's stock, the corporation bears the burden of showing: (1) a valid corporate purpose, and (2) that the transaction was fair to all of the stockholders, including those excluded.

* * *

II.

The issues we address involve these fundamental questions: Did the Unocal board have the power and duty to oppose a takeover threat it reasonably perceived to be harmful to the corporate enterprise, and if so, is its action here entitled to the protection of the business judgment rule?

Mesa contends that the discriminatory exchange offer violates the fiduciary duties Unocal owes it. Mesa argues that because of the Mesa exclusion the business judgment rule is inapplicable, because the directors by tendering their own shares will derive a financial benefit that is not available to *all* Unocal stockholders. Thus, it is Mesa's ultimate contention that Unocal cannot establish that the exchange offer is fair to *all* shareholders, and argues that the Court of Chancery was correct in concluding that Unocal was unable to meet this burden.

Unocal answers that it does not owe a duty of "fairness" to Mesa, given the facts here. Specifically, Unocal contends that its board of directors reasonably and in good faith concluded that Mesa's $54 two-tier tender offer was coercive and inadequate, and that Mesa sought selective treatment for itself. Furthermore, Unocal argues that the board's approval of the exchange offer was made in good faith, on an informed basis, and in the exercise of due care. Under these circumstances, Unocal contends that its directors properly employed this device to protect the company and its stockholders from Mesa's harmful tactics.

III.

We begin with the basic issue of the power of a board of directors of a Delaware corporation to adopt a defensive measure of this type. Absent such authority, all other questions are moot. Neither issues of fairness nor business judgment are pertinent without the basic underpinning of a board's legal power to act.

The board has a large reservoir of authority upon which to draw. Its duties and responsibilities proceed from the inherent powers conferred by 8 Del.C. § 141(a), respecting management of the corporation's "business and affairs". Additionally, the powers here being exercised derive from 8 Del.C. § 160(a), conferring broad authority upon a corporation to deal in its own stock. From this it is now well established that in the acquisition of its shares a Delaware corporation may deal selectively with its stockholders, provided the directors have not acted out of a sole or primary purpose to entrench themselves in office.

Finally, the board's power to act derives from its fundamental duty and obligation to protect the corporate enterprise, which includes stockholders, from harm reasonably perceived, irrespective of its source. Thus, we are satisfied that in the broad context of corporate governance, including issues of fundamental corporate change, a board of directors is not a passive instrumentality.

Given the foregoing principles, we turn to the standards by which director action is to be measured. In Pogostin v. Rice, Del.Supr., 480 A.2d 619 (1984), we held that the business judgment rule, including the standards by which director conduct is judged, is applicable in the context of a takeover. *Id.* at 627. The business judgment rule is a "presumption that in making a business decision the directors of a corporation acted on an informed basis, in good faith and in the honest belief that the action taken was in the best interests of the company." Aronson v. Lewis, Del.Supr., 473 A.2d 805, 812 (1984). A hallmark of the business judgment rule is that a court will not substitute its judgment for that of the board if the latter's decision can be "attributed to any rational business purpose." Sinclair Oil Corp. v. Levien, Del. Supr., 280 A.2d 717, 720 (1971).

When a board addresses a pending takeover bid it has an obligation to determine whether the offer is in the best interests of the corporation and its shareholders. In that respect a board's duty is no different from any other responsibility it shoulders, and its decisions should be no less entitled to the respect they otherwise would be accorded in the realm of business judgment. *See also* Johnson v. Trueblood, 629 F.2d 287, 292–293 (3d Cir.1980). There are, however, certain caveats to a proper exercise of this function. Because of the omnipresent specter that a board may be acting primarily in its own interests, rather than those of the corporation and its shareholders, there is an enhanced duty which calls for judicial examination at the threshold before the protections of the business judgment rule may be conferred.

This Court has long recognized that:

> We must bear in mind the inherent danger in the purchase of shares with corporate funds to remove a threat to corporate policy when a threat to control is involved. The directors are of necessity confronted with a conflict of interest, and an objective decision is difficult.

Bennett v. Propp, Del.Supr., 187 A.2d 405, 409 (1962). In the face of this inherent conflict directors must show that they had reasonable grounds for believing that a danger to corporate policy and effectiveness existed because of another person's stock ownership. Cheff v. Mathes, 199 A.2d at 554–55. However, they satisfy that burden "by showing good faith and reasonable investigation. * * *" *Id.* at 555. Furthermore, such proof is materially enhanced, as here, by the approval of a board comprised of a majority of outside independent directors who have acted in accordance with the foregoing standards.

IV.

A.

In the board's exercise of corporate power to forestall a takeover bid our analysis begins with the basic principle that corporate directors have a fiduciary duty to act in the best interests of the corporation's stockholders. Guth v. Loft, Inc., Del.Supr., 5 A.2d 503, 510 (1939). As we have noted, their duty of care extends to protecting the corporation and its owners from perceived harm whether a threat originates from third parties or other shareholders. But such powers are not absolute. A corporation does not have unbridled discretion to defeat any perceived threat by any Draconian means available.

The restriction placed upon a selective stock repurchase is that the directors may not have acted solely or primarily out of a desire to perpetuate themselves in office. *See* Cheff v. Mathes, 199 A.2d at 556; Kors v. Carey, 158 A.2d at 140. Of course, to this is added the further caveat that inequitable action may not be taken under the guise of law. Schnell v. Chris–Craft Industries, Inc., Del.Supr., 285 A.2d 437, 439 (1971). The standard of proof established in Cheff v. Mathes and discussed *supra,* is designed to ensure that a defensive measure to thwart or impede a takeover is indeed motivated by a good faith concern for the welfare of the corporation and its stockholders, which in all circumstances must be free of any fraud or other misconduct. Cheff v. Mathes, 199 A.2d at 554–55. However, this does not end the inquiry.

B.

A further aspect is the element of balance. If defensive measure is to come within the ambit of the business judgment rule, it must be reasonable in relation to the threat posed. This entails an analysis by the directors of the nature of the takeover bid and its effect on the corporate enterprise. Examples of such concerns may include: inadequacy of the price offered, nature and timing of the offer, questions of illegality, the impact on "constituencies" other than shareholders (*i.e.,* creditors, customers, employees, and perhaps even the community generally), the risk of nonconsummation, and the quality of securities being offered in the exchange. *See* Lipton and Brownstein, Takeover Responses and Directors' Responsibilities: An Update, p. 7, ABA National Institute on the Dynamics of Corporate Control (December 8, 1983). While not a controlling factor, it also seems to us that a board may reasonably consider the basic stockholder interests at stake, including those of short term speculators, whose actions may have fueled the coercive aspect of the offer at the expense of the long term investor.[11] Here, the threat posed was viewed by the Unocal board as a grossly inadequate two-tier coercive tender offer coupled with the threat of greenmail.

Specifically, the Unocal directors had concluded that the value of Unocal was substantially above the $54 per share offered in cash at the front end. Furthermore, they determined that the subordinated securities to be exchanged in Mesa's announced squeeze out of the remaining shareholders in the "back-end" merger were "junk bonds" worth far less than $54. It is now well recognized that such offers are a classic coercive measure designed to stampede shareholders into tendering at the first tier, even if the price is inadequate, out of fear of what they will receive at the back end of the transaction. Wholly beyond the coercive aspect of an inadequate two-tier tender offer, the threat was posed by a corporate raider with a national reputation as a "green-mailer".[13]

11. There has been much debate respecting such stockholder interests. One rather impressive study indicates that the stock of over 50 percent of target companies, who resisted hostile takeovers, later traded at higher market prices than the rejected offer price, or were acquired after the tender offer was defeated by another company at a price higher than the offer price. *See* Lipton, *supra* 35 Bus.Law. at 106–109, 132–133. Moreover, an update by Kidder Peabody & Company of this study involving the stock prices of target companies that have defeated hostile tender offers during the period from 1973 to 1982 demonstrates that in a majority of cases the target's shareholders benefited from the defeat. The stock of 81% of the targets studied has, since the tender offer, sold at prices higher than the tender offer price. When adjusted for the time value of money, the figure is 64%. *See* Lipton & Brownstein, *supra* ABA Institute at 10. The thesis being that this strongly supports application of the business judgment rule in response to takeover threats. There is, however, a rather vehement contrary view. *See* Easterbrook & Fischel, *supra* 36 Bus.Law. at 1739–1745.

13. The term "greenmail" refers to the practice of buying out a takeover bidder's stock at a premium that is not available to other shareholders in order to prevent the takeover. The Chancery Court noted that "Mesa has made tremendous profits from

In adopting the selective exchange offer, the board stated that its objective was either to defeat the inadequate Mesa offer, or, should the offer still succeed, provide the 49% of its stockholders, who would otherwise be forced to accept "junk bonds", with $72 worth of senior debt. We find that both purposes are valid.

However, such efforts would have been thwarted by Mesa's participation in the exchange offer. First, if Mesa could tender its shares, Unocal would effectively be subsidizing the former's continuing effort to buy Unocal stock at $54 per share. Second, Mesa could not, by definition, fit within the class of shareholders being protected from its own coercive and inadequate tender offer.

Thus, we are satisfied that the selective exchange offer is reasonably related to the threats posed. It is consistent with the principle that "the minority stockholder shall receive the substantial equivalent in value of what he had before." Sterling v. Mayflower Hotel Corp., Del.Supr., 93 A.2d 107, 114 (1952). *See also* Rosenblatt v. Getty Oil Co., Del.Supr., 493 A.2d 929, 940 (1985). This concept of fairness, while stated in the merger context, is also relevant in the area of tender offer law. Thus, the board's decision to offer what it determined to be the fair value of the corporation to the 49% of its shareholders, who would otherwise be forced to accept highly subordinated "junk bonds", is reasonable and consistent with the directors' duty to ensure that the minority stockholders receive equal value for their shares.

V.

Mesa contends that it is unlawful, and the trial court agreed, for a corporation to discriminate in this fashion against one shareholder. It argues correctly that no case has ever sanctioned a device that precludes a raider from sharing in a benefit available to all other stockholders. However, as we have noted earlier, the principle of selective stock repurchases by a Delaware corporation is neither unknown nor unauthorized. The only difference is that heretofore the approved transaction was the payment of "greenmail" to a raider or dissident posing a threat to the corporate enterprise. All other stockholders were denied such favored treatment, and given Mesa's past history of greenmail, its claims here are rather ironic.

However, our corporate law is not static. It must grow and develop in response to, indeed in anticipation of, evolving concepts and needs. Merely because the General Corporation Law is silent as to a specific matter does not mean that it is prohibited. *See* Providence and Worcester Co. v. Baker, Del.Supr., 378 A.2d 121, 123–124 (1977). In the days when *Cheff, Bennett, Martin* and *Kors* were decided, the tender offer, while not an unknown device, was virtually unused, and little was

its takeover activities although in the past few years it has not been successful in acquiring any of the target companies on an unfriendly basis." Moreover, the trial court specifically found that the actions of the Unocal board were taken in good faith to eliminate both the inadequacies of the tender offer and to forestall the payment of "greenmail".

known of such methods as two-tier "front-end" loaded offers with their coercive effects. Then, the favored attack of a raider was stock acquisition followed by a proxy contest. Various defensive tactics, which provided no benefit whatever to the raider, evolved. Thus, the use of corporate funds by management to counter a proxy battle was approved. Hall v. Trans–Lux Daylight Picture Screen Corp., Del.Supr., 171 A. 226 (1934); Hibbert v. Hollywood Park, Inc., Del.Supr., 457 A.2d 339 (1983). Litigation, supported by corporate funds, aimed at the raider has long been a popular device.

More recently, as the sophistication of both raiders and targets has developed, a host of other defensive measures to counter such ever mounting threats has evolved and received judicial sanction. These include defensive charter amendments and other devices bearing some rather exotic, but apt, names: Crown Jewel, White Knight, Pac Man, and Golden Parachute. Each has highly selective features, the object of which is to deter or defeat the raider.

Thus, while the exchange offer is a form of selective treatment, given the nature of the threat posed here the response is neither unlawful nor unreasonable. If the board of directors is disinterested, has acted in good faith and with due care, its decision in the absence of an abuse of discretion will be upheld as a proper exercise of business judgment.

To this Mesa responds that the board is not disinterested, because the directors are receiving a benefit from the tender of their own shares, which because of the Mesa exclusion, does not devolve upon *all* stockholders equally. *See* Aronson v. Lewis, Del.Supr., 473 A.2d 805, 812 (1984). However, Mesa concedes that if the exclusion is valid, then the directors and all other stockholders share the same benefit. The answer of course is that the exclusion is valid, and the directors' participation in the exchange offer does not rise to the level of a disqualifying interest. The excellent discussion in Johnson v. Trueblood, 629 F.2d at 292–293, of the use of the business judgment rule in takeover contests also seems pertinent here.

Nor does this become an "interested" director transaction merely because certain board members are large stockholders. As this Court has previously noted, that fact alone does not create a disqualifying "personal pecuniary interest" to defeat the operation of the business judgment rule. Cheff v. Mathes, 199 A.2d at 554.

Mesa also argues that the exclusion permits the directors to abdicate the fiduciary duties they owe it. However, that is not so. The board continues to owe Mesa the duties of due care and loyalty. But in the face of the destructive threat Mesa's tender offer was perceived to pose, the board had a supervening duty to protect the corporate enterprise, which includes the other shareholders, from threatened harm.

Mesa contends that the basis of this action is punitive, and solely in response to the exercise of its rights of corporate democracy. Nothing precludes Mesa, as a stockholder, from acting in its own self-interest.

See e.g., Dupont v. Dupont, 251 Fed. 937 (D.Del.1918), aff'd 256 Fed. 129 (3d Cir.1918); Ringling Bros.-Barnum & Bailey Combined Shows, Inc. v. Ringling, Del.Supr., 53 A.2d 441, 447 (1947); Heil v. Standard Gas & Electric Co., Del.Ch., 151 A. 303, 304 (1930). *But see,* Allied Chemical & Dye Corp. v. Steel & Tube Co. of America, Del.Ch., 120 A. 486, 491 (1923) (majority shareholder owes a fiduciary duty to the minority shareholders). However, Mesa, while pursuing its own interests, has acted in a manner which a board consisting of a majority of independent directors has reasonably determined to be contrary to the best interests of Unocal and its other shareholders. In this situation, there is no support in Delaware law for the proposition that, when responding to a perceived harm, a corporation must guarantee a benefit to a stockholder who is deliberately provoking the danger being addressed. There is no obligation of self-sacrifice by a corporation and its shareholders in the face of such a challenge.

Here, the Court of Chancery specifically found that the "directors' decision [to oppose the Mesa tender offer] was made in the good faith belief that the Mesa tender offer is inadequate." Given our standard of review under Levitt v. Bouvier, Del.Supr., 287 A.2d 671, 673 (1972), and Application of Delaware Racing Association, Del.Supr., 213 A.2d 203, 207 (1965), we are satisfied that Unocal's board has met its burden of proof. Cheff v. Mathes, 199 A.2d at 555.

VI.

In conclusion, there was directorial power to oppose the Mesa tender offer, and to undertake a selective stock exchange made in good faith and upon a reasonable investigation pursuant to a clear duty to protect the corporate enterprise. Further, the selective stock repurchase plan chosen by Unocal is reasonable in relation to the threat that the board rationally and reasonably believed was posed by Mesa's inadequate and coercive two-tier tender offer. Under those circumstances the board's action is entitled to be measured by the standards of the business judgment rule. Thus, unless it is shown by a preponderance of the evidence that the directors' decisions were primarily based on perpetuating themselves in office, or some other breach of fiduciary duty such as fraud, overreaching, lack of good faith, or being uninformed, a Court will not substitute its judgment for that of the board.

In this case that protection is not lost merely because Unocal's directors have tendered their shares in the exchange offer. Given the validity of the Mesa exclusion, they are receiving a benefit shared generally by all other stockholders except Mesa. In this circumstance the test of Aronson v. Lewis, 473 A.2d at 812, is satisfied. *See also* Cheff v. Mathes, 199 A.2d at 554. If the stockholders are displeased with the action of their elected representatives, the powers of corporate democracy are at their disposal to turn the board out. Aronson v. Lewis, Del.Supr., 473 A.2d 805, 811 (1984). *See also* 8 Del.C. §§ 141(k) and 211(b).

With the Court of Chancery's findings that the exchange offer was based on the board's good faith belief that the Mesa offer was inadequate, that the board's action was informed and taken with due care, that Mesa's prior activities justify a reasonable inference that its principle objective is greenmail, and implicitly, that the substance of the offer itself was reasonable and fair to the corporation and its stockholders if Mesa were included, we cannot say that the Unocal directors have acted in such a manner as to have passed an "unintelligent and unadvised judgment". Mitchell v. Highland–Western Glass Co., Del.Ch., 167 A. 831, 833 (1933). The decision of the Court of Chancery is therefore REVERSED, and the preliminary injunction is VACATED.

Note: Corporate Defensive Tactics

During the 1980s as the number of hostile takeovers rose, corporate boards adopted a variety of tactics to protect their shareholders and their corporations. Aided by corporate lawyers and investment bankers, companies implemented a variety of innovative defensive techniques including self-tender offers, defensive mergers, leveraged management-buyouts, poison pills, supermajority voting provisions, and corporate restructurings. No technique created an absolute bar to hostile takeovers. Each one, however, helped deter a hostile transaction by slowing the process, raising the economic cost to the bidder, or providing shareholders with an attractive alternative to the takeover bid. In assessing the efficacy of the defenses outlined below, consider what the rationale is for each. Is it to maintain the independence of the target? Is it meant to produce negotiations with the bidder? Is it designed to initiate an auction? Or is it intended to bring about a business combination with another partner?

Further, in thinking about what view the law should take with respect to takeover defenses, consider what weight should be given to the market effects of particular defensive tactics. The Office of the Chief Economist of the SEC has studied different takeover defenses and has found that anti-takeover amendments, poison pills and targeted share repurchases (greenmail) reduce shareholder wealth as measured by their immediate impact on the market place of affected companies' stock. This conclusion is consistent with the argument advanced by Frank H. Easterbrook and Daniel R. Fischel, The Proper Role of a Target Management in Responding to a Tender Offer, 94 Harv.L.Rev. 1161 (1981), that any resistance to takeovers injures shareholders' interests. A contrary view holds that shareholders are not so foolish as to approve takeover defenses that are injurious, and that certain defenses allow shareholders to act in a coordinated way, avoid the prisoner's dilemma and thereby improve their welfare. William J. Carney, Shareholder Coordination Costs, Shark Repellents, and Takeout Mergers: The Case Against Fiduciary Duties, 1983 Am.B.Found Res.J. 341.

For any defensive measure, advance planning is essential. Many defenses require shareholder approval, which often is difficult to obtain after a tender offer has commenced. Where measures do not require shareholder approval, the existence of a tender offer will make heightened judicial scrutiny likely; an inadequate record supporting adoption of a defensive measure will make it vulnerable to injunctive relief and could even result in liability for directors.

a. Poison Pills

One of the most common and effective defensive techniques has been shareholder rights plans or "poison pills." A rights plan grants to each shareholder, typically as a dividend, a contingent right to purchase stock or other securities at any time within a long time period, generally 10 years. Because the right is not exercisable until a triggering event occurs, it has little present value to the holder. The events that trigger poison pills typically are a tender offer for the company that the incumbent board of directors has not approved (a hostile tender offer) or the acquisition of common stock by a third party above a certain threshold, usually 20% or 30% of the outstanding common stock. Until the triggering event occurs, the board retains the power to redeem the rights for a nominal payment.

A poison pill can have "flip-over" rights, "flip-in" rights or both. A flip-over right issued by the target company allows the target company's shareholders (but not any bidder who purchases their stock) to purchase shares of the *bidder's* stock at half-price if the bidder (or a corporation controlled by the bidder) merges with the target after the tender offer. Such second-step mergers are common, and will be essential if the bidder plans to use the assets of the target to finance, or secure financing for, the cost of the acquisition. If a flip-over plan is in place and a substantial portion of the target's shareholders do not tender their stock, their ability to purchase shares in the merged entity at half price, will have the effect of diluting the value of stock held by the bidder's other shareholders, often to the point where the overall cost of the acquisition will become prohibitive. However, a flip-over plan will not deter an acquiror who does not plan on effectuating a second-step merger. Thus, Crown Zellerbach was acquired even though it had a flip-over poison pill because Sir James Goldsmith, who purchased the controlling interest, did not plan a second-step merger.

Flip-in poison pills were developed to overcome this problem. A flip-in pill allows a rights holder, other than the bidder, to purchase stock or other securities of the *target* company at a below-market price. When such rights are exercised, the overall cost of the takeover is raised to an uneconomic level.

Another variant of poison pills is a "back-end" plan. These plans allow target company directors to designate a "fair price" for target company stock and give shareholders the right to require the target to purchase their shares at that price if the bidder does not do so after it obtains control. A back-end plan protects shareholders from coercive two-tier tender offers in which a bidder offers a high price for a control block and then offers a lower price on the back-end to purchase the remaining shares. The back-end right ensures shareholders that they will not be penalized in the second step, and thus effectively eviscerates the coercive component of a two-tier bid.

A key element of all three types of poison pills is that the target company's board of directors retains the right to redeem the pill before a triggering event has occurred. This provides a powerful incentive for a potential bidder to negotiate with the target's board, before going forward with a tender offer, to have the poison pill redeemed. The board can use this bargaining leverage to seek a better deal for shareholders, or for other, arguably less legitimate purposes.

Moran v. Household International, Inc., 500 A.2d 1346 (Del.1985) held a flip-over pill to be valid under Delaware law. Household's board had adopted the pill out of concern that the company was vulnerable to a hostile bid although no bid had yet been made. Plaintiff sought to have the pill declared invalid on the grounds that it deprived shareholders of their right to receive a subsequent tender offer.

The Delaware Supreme Court upheld the validity of the poison pill. The court found that DGCL § 157 authorized the board to issue rights to purchase the company's stock, although it acknowledged that § 157 had never been used to create the rights such as those Household had created. The court also noted that flip-over provisions were analogous to "anti-dilution" or "anti-destruction" provisions which were customary provisions of corporate securities that protect the security holder in a merger. Pointing to the Crown Zellerbach takeover and the Household board's ability to redeem the rights, the court rejected the argument that the poison pill precluded all future tender offers. It noted that a potential bidder could avoid triggering the pill by not effectuating a second-step merger, could condition its offer on redemption of the poison pill by Household's board of directors, or could seek to remove Household's board through a proxy solicitation and then have the new board redeem the rights.

The court emphasized that it was only holding that adoption of the poison pill constituted legitimate corporate planning that was reasonable under a *Unocal* standard. It made clear, however, that the fact that a pill had been validly adopted did not preclude subsequent judicial scrutiny of a board's decision as to whether to redeem the pill. It stated that such a decision would be evaluated at the appropriate time, again using the *Unocal* test.

For an interesting discussion of poison pills in the context of a proxy contest, see Randall S. Thomas, Judicial Review of Defensive Tactics in Proxy Contests: When Is Using A Rights Plan Right?, 46 Vand.L.Rev 503 (1993).

b. *Using the Corporate Machinery*

As *Moran* indicates, directors have became adept at using their control over existing corporate machinery to deter hostile takeovers. One critical issue involves the standard courts will use to evaluate such actions, assuming the board has lawful authority to take them. Because there was no pending bid, the *Moran* court had little difficulty with the Household board's decision to deploy a poison pill, but made clear that *Unocal* mandates more rigorous review of an action designed to defeat an outstanding hostile bid. As we saw in Chapter 12, courts have tended to analyze even more closely defensive actions designed to frustrate pending corporate electoral challenges. Recall *Blasius* and *Stahl*.

There are measures that a board can take before a proxy contest or tender offer that may make a hostile takeover bid less likely. By amending its charter, a company can stagger the terms of its directors, so that only one-third are elected each year. A bidder then faces the prospect of having to win two successive proxy contests to gain control. Rarely, however, will staggered boards deter a determined bidder. Directors usually are unwilling to remain on a board once a proxy contest has been lost or a new majority shareholder has requested their resignation. Other charter amendments can make directors removable only for good cause; allow directors but not shareholders to call special shareholder meetings; or eliminate shareholder power to act without a meeting. These deterrents have the potential to slow down a bidder seeking control, but are unlikely to stop an aggressive bidder prepared to make an all-cash tender offer.

A supermajority voting requirement may constitute a more useful tender offer defense. A corporation's charter can be amended to require that all mergers be approved by 80 percent of the shares, instead of the usual majority, if the other party to the transaction owns more than 5 % of the corporation's stock. For a bidder to gain complete control of the corporation, it thus will need to acquire the support of at least 80 percent of the stock. A supermajority provision can prove to be an especially effective deterrent if a company's insiders own enough stock to block a merger.

The SEC only has jurisdiction to regulate disclosure in proxy statements seeking approval of shark-repellent measures, but in Rel. No. 34–15230 (Oct. 13, 1978), the Commission revealed more general concern about the propriety of defensive provisions. In addition, it made clear that to constitute adequate disclosure, a proxy should explain the reasons management has proposed the measure and "the factors and/or principles supporting" those reasons. In particular the proxy should disclose whether the proposal is the result of knowledge of a specific effort to obtain control of the company or accumulate its securities. If the proposal is not a response to some special effort, management must explain its reasons for making the proposal at this time. In addition, the proxy should describe the effect of the proposal on management's tenure and the proposals ability "to render more difficult or to discourage a merger, tender offer or proxy contest, the assumption of control by a holder of a larger block of the corporation's securities and the removal of incumbent management."

c. Corporate Restructuring

In some cases, companies have chosen to preempt bidders by restructuring the corporation so as to confer value on the shareholders in excess of the bidder's offer. In a restructuring, the potential target offers shareholders a package of securities (usually debt or preferred stock) and cash either as an extraordinary dividend without shareholder approval or through an exchange offer, merger, corporate reclassification, or a spin-off which does require shareholder approval. After the transaction, the company usually will have more debt and shareholders will have received a payment of cash and/or securities while maintaining a greatly reduced equity interest in the company.

To finance a restructuring, a company often will take actions similar to those taken by a prospective bidder. It will borrow much of the money it needs, thus increasing the leverage in its financial structure, and also sell non-essential assets and attempt to streamline its remaining business. A restructuring resembles a leveraged buy-out, in which a bidder borrows against the target's assets to finance the acquisition. Instead, the target borrows against its own assets, but its shareholders continue to maintain an equity interest in the now more leveraged company. Management, to survive, will have to find a way to both service the debt and maintain the viability of the company's operations. Recall Chapter 9, Section D.

A restructuring undertaken in the face of a takeover may raise duty of loyalty problems. If management's equity interest in the restructured company will increase, because shareholders are given a choice of receiving cash or securities for their stock and management plans to take additional equity, the possibility arises that management is enriching itself at shareholders' expense. Moreover, analysis is complicated by the difficulty of valuing precisely the securities to be issued as part of the restructuring.

In AC Acquisitions v. Anderson, Clayton & Co., 519 A.2d 103 (Del.Ch.1986), the court held invalid a restructuring that was coercive in design. In Robert M. Bass Group, Inc. v. Evans, 552 A.2d 1227 (Del.Ch. 1988), the court enjoined a restructuring proposal developed by Macmillan's management in response to a hostile takeover bid. The court found first that the hostile bid, although originally arguably inadequate, had been raised to a level that Macmillan's own advisors found fair. A reasonable response to the offer would have been a higher offer or, at the very least, a proposal giving shareholders a choice between equivalent values in different forms. In concluding that the management restructuring offered neither, the court stated, "Not only does it offer inferior value to the shareholders, it also forces them to accept it. No shareholder vote is afforded; no choice given. The restructuring is crafted to take the form of a dividend, requiring only director approval. On that basis alone * * * the restructuring is a coercive, and economically inferior, response to the Bass Group 'threat.' " 552 A.2d at 1242. On the other hand, in GAF Corp. v. Union Carbide Corp., 624 F.Supp. 1016 (S.D.N.Y. 1985), the court upheld a restructuring involving substantial asset sales as a valid business judgment, in part because Union Carbide's independent directors believed that the prospective takeover would be injurious to the corporation and its shareholders.

d. Defensive Mergers

The "white knight" defense, in which the target searches for a more compatible merger partner, offers an alternative to restructuring the company. Shareholders still receive an attractive price for their shares, but managers are likely to keep their jobs. A friendly transaction often encourages closer communication between buyer and seller, which can increase the price. However, the haste with which the target seeks to attract an alternate suitor creates its own danger. Acquisitions require careful study to determine whether they make sense and how they should be priced. A hostile bidder may have studied the target for months before launching its bid. In contrast, the target may have only a few weeks to find a white knight and conclude an acquisition agreement. The white knight, caught up in the excitement of a battle for corporate control, may discover that the business it has acquired is not exactly the business it thought it was buying.

e. Issuance of Stock

A corporation's board of directors has authority to issue previously authorized stock to acquire assets, to effect a merger, to fund an employee stock ownership plan (ESOP), or in exchange for stock or cash. Issuance of stock to an investor friendly to management can have a decisive effect in a takeover contest. In simple terms, if enough additional shares are issued to persons friendly to management, the bidder will not be able to obtain control.

Judicial decisions as to the propriety of a stock issuance in the context of a takeover bid have been heavily influenced by the surrounding facts and circumstances. Compare Condec Corp. v. Lunkenheimer Co., 43 Del.Ch. 353, 230 A.2d 769 (1967) (sale enjoined where primary purpose was to prevent transfer of control to a suitor who had acquired more than 50 percent of common stock in two tender offers) and Klaus v. Hi–Shear Corp., 528 F.2d 225 (9th Cir.1975) (voting of shares transferred to Employee Stock Ownership Trust enjoined where management failed to establish a compelling business reason for transfer at a time so clearly advantageous to it) with Cummings v. United Artists Theatre Circuit, Inc., 237 Md. 1, 204 A.2d 795 (1964) (sale not enjoined where "principal motive was not related to control, and the effect on control caused by the board's action is not of compelling significance").

The sale of a large block of stock to an ESOP has become a popular defensive tactic. ESOPs provide valuable business benefits to the corporation in the form of lower benefit costs due to special tax advantages and improved employee performance by aligning employee interests with those of shareholders. However, because management often controls the right to vote some or all of the shares in the ESOP, and since employees often vote with management in any event, a potential conflict of interest exists. In Buckhorn, Inc. v. Ropak Corp., 656 F.Supp. 209 (S.D.Ohio 1987), the court observed:

However, it is clear that when shares of corporate stock are purchased for an ESOP and placed under director or management control during the course of a tender offer, as in the present case, the same conflict of interest which arises in more obvious defensive measures is also inherent in the creation of an ESOP. * * * Thus, while it is certainly permissible for the directors to adopt measures for the benefit of the employees during the midst of a corporate control struggle, the directors must show that "there are rationally related benefits accruing to the stockholders from adopting such measures." *Revlon,* supra at 182. Furthermore, the Court believes that it is appropriate to look at such factors as "the timing of the ESOP's establishment, the financial impact upon the company, the identity of the trustees and the voting control of the ESOP shares" in determining whether the ESOP was created to benefit the employees and not simply to further entrench management. [Norlin Corp. v. Rooney, Pace Inc., 744 F.2d 255 (2d Cir.1984)] at 266.

656 F.Supp. at 231–32.

In Shamrock Holdings, Inc. v. Polaroid Corp., 559 A.2d 257 (Del.Ch. 1989), Polaroid transferred stock to an ESOP after receiving a threatening letter from Shamrock. Shamrock sought to abrogate that transaction. The court held that Polaroid was required to demonstrate the fairness of its action. But after analyzing the timing of the ESOP, its structure and operation and its purpose and probable impact, the court concluded that the ESOP was fair to Polaroid and its shareholders, largely because it did not constitute an insurmountable obstacle ot Shamrock's takeover bid.

In NCR Corp. v. American Telephone & Telegraph Co., 761 F.Supp. 475 (S.D.Ohio 1991), NCR Corp. adopted an ESOP as part of its defense against a takeover bid by AT & T, which was attempting to remove all or a majority of the NCR board of directors at a special meeting of NCR shareholders. The court found that the plan was an improper attempt by NCR management to perpetuate its control. It also held that the NCR directors were not protected by the business judgment rule because they had reached their decision to fund the ESOP on the basis of "grossly inadequate information." Consequently, the court enjoined NCR from voting the ESOP's stock at the special shareholders meeting.

f. Share Repurchases and Greenmail

A corporation generally has the power to repurchase its own stock, so long as such action does not violate the applicable legal capital rules. Repurchases often serve valid financial purposes. On those occasions where the corporation must issue stock, such as the exercise of options and warrants, the conversion of convertible securities, the acquisition of assets, or a merger, a stock repurchase will allow the subsequent issuance of shares without diluting current stockholders. Further, if the stock's market price falls below what the board believes is the stock's fair value, a stock repurchase will allow those shareholders who do not want to sell to increase their proportionate interest in the company without having to use their own cash, and will provide a market for those shareholders who want to exit.

When a contest for control is in progress, a stock repurchase also can be used to end the threat to incumbent management. As in *Cheff*, the corporation can eliminate the bidder by paying a premium price. In most cases, the target's board will be concerned that the bidder will turn around and use the proceeds of its resale of stock to the corporation to launch another bid, especially if, as is frequently the case, the target's stock price falls after the repurchase is announced. Consequently, before actually repurchasing the bidder's stock, the target will require the bidder to enter into a standstill agreement—an agreement not to purchase or bid for the target's shares for a specified period of time.

The willingness of some companies to resolve takeover threats by repurchasing their shares at a premium made it attractive for entrepreneurial investors to acquire substantial blocks of stock in potential targets and then threaten a takeover bid in the hope that the target would offer to repurchase the stock instead. In the jargon of the takeover world, such payments became known as "greenmail" and investors who sought them became known as "greenmailers." In most cases where greenmail has been paid, the stock price has declined after the repurchase, leaving the bidder enriched, the shareholders unhappy, and the target company's treasury somewhat depleted.

In Heckman v. Ahmanson, 168 Cal.App.3d 119, 214 Cal.Rptr. 177 (2 Dist.1985), the Steinberg Group purchased more than two million shares and declared its intention to make a tender offer for Disney stock at $67.50 per share. Disney responded by agreeing to repurchase the Steinberg Group's stock at $77 per share. The Steinberg Group also abandoned a suit it had brought against the Disney directors relating to their resistance to the forthcoming tender offer. Following announcement of the repurchase, the trading price of Disney stock declined to $49 per share. A Disney shareholder sued and obtained a preliminary injunction barring the Steinberg Group from using the repurchase proceeds until the case was heard on the merits. The court noted that "[w]hile there may be many valid reasons why corporate directors would purchase another company or repurchase the corporation's shares, the naked desire to retain their positions of power and control over the corporation is not one of them. * * * If the Disney directors breached their fiduciary duty to the stockholders, the Steinberg Group could be held jointly liable as an aider and abettor." 214 Cal.Rptr. at 182.

In contrast, the Delaware Court of Chancery sustained a settlement of litigation challenging Texaco's repurchase of 9.9% of its stock from the Bass Brothers at $49 per share, approximately $10 above the market. The court held that repurchasing stock to avoid a contest for control is sometimes in a corporation's best interests. See Polk v. Good, 507 A.2d 531 (Del.1986).

Scholars are not of one mind on the propriety of greenmail. Most criticize it as self-serving, but some believe that greenmail often confers benefits on shareholders by facilitating an auction for the target's shares. It signals important information to the market place while at the same time enabling the company to rid itself of an unwanted suitor. Jonathan R. Macey and Fred S. McChesney, A Theoretical Analysis of Corporate Greenmail, 95 Yale L.J. 13 (1985). Studies by the Office of the Chief Economist of the SEC and by the Office of Management and Budget differ in their assessment of greenmail, with the former offering evidence that share prices significantly decline after a greenmail payment (Study dated September 11, 1984) and the latter contending that shareholders benefit. Memorandum from Douglas H. Ginsburg, dated September 13, 1984.

3. CHANGES IN CONTROL

PROBLEM

GENERAL INDUSTRIES CORPORATION—PART II

A

At the meeting anticipated in Part I, the GIC board adopted a Stock Rights Plan pursuant to which the holder of each share of GIC stock received a right to purchase one additional share of GIC stock for one-half the closing price of that stock on the New York Stock Exchange on the last trading day before the date on which any person became the owner of 20% or more of GIC's outstanding stock without the prior approval of GIC's board of directors. GIC can redeem the rights at any time, for $.01 per share. The board also asked First Pru to consider alternative transactions that GIC might pursue if Danton made a tender offer, including a defensive merger, but the board also stressed the importance of GIC's retaining its ability to continue its most important research projects. Finally, GIC advised Danton that it was not interested in entering into any transactions with him or any company that he controls.

One month later, First Pru advised GIC's management that Mercury Industries, Inc., a large diversified corporation, was interested in acquiring GIC in a friendly transaction because Mercury is extremely supportive of GIC's corporate goals. Mercury has acquired other companies in negotiated transactions, after which it usually has left existing management in place and has tried to avoid layoffs and relocations. But Mercury owes its success to a management system that requires managers of acquired companies to meet ambitious earnings targets and removes those who fail. Mercury has indicated that, subject to an opportunity to conduct a reasonable investigation of GIC, including an examination of budgets, forecasts, and certain other confidential information, it is prepared to offer $55 cash per share for all GIC stock in a tender offer and second step cash merger. First Pru has provided the GIC board with its opinion that the fair value of GIC stock is from $52 to $64 per share and, accordingly, that the Mercury offer is fair from a financial point of view.

1. Before announcing the Mercury transaction, what are GIC's obligations, if any, to negotiate with Danton or inquire further of First Pru as to whether any other company might offer a higher price for GIC? Are such obligations those of GIC's management? Its outside directors?

2. Assume that Mercury has proposed the following conditions to its offer:

> (a) GIC will not make available to any other potential bidder the confidential documents that it will make available to Mercury (the "no shop" clause);

> (b) GIC will pay Mercury $25 million if for any reason Mercury does not succeed in acquiring GIC (the "topping fee"); and

> (c) GIC will grant Mercury an option to purchase 10 million shares of authorized but unissued GIC stock for $35 per share (the current price on the New York Stock Exchange) (the "option").

What obligations, if any, must GIC's management or outside directors meet before GIC can agree to these conditions?

B

Assume that GIC agreed to all of Mercury's conditions and that Mercury made its offer to GIC as described above. In response, Danton announced a $60 per share cash tender offer, to be made by Danton Acquisition Corp. (Acquisition), for all outstanding GIC stock, subject to (i) GIC redeeming the rights; (ii) the Mercury conditions being declared invalid; and (iii) at least 24 million shares being tendered. Danton also announced that if Acquisition's offer was successful, he intended to effect a second-step merger of GIC and Acquisition as soon as practicable, in which all remaining public shareholders of GIC would receive $60 per share in cash. He further disclosed that he plans to finance the proposed transactions with $300 million of his own funds and approximately $2.5 billion in bank loans and a line of credit for which he has firm commitments.

The day after Danton's announcement, the GIC board held an all-day meeting with counsel and First Pru to evaluate the offer and decide how to proceed. First Pru acknowledged that Danton's offer was at a fair price, but several members of the board questioned Danton's ability to manage a sophisticated, research-oriented company like GIC. They also made clear that they had no interest in negotiating a better deal with Danton.

1. Advise the board as to its responsibilities concerning Danton's tender offer. In particular, does the board have any obligation to redeem the rights, negotiate with Danton to see if he will pay a higher price, or seek a higher bid from either Mercury or other third parties?

2. What is the likely outcome of a suit by Danton or a GIC shareholder challenging the validity of the no shop clause, the topping fee, and the option?

C

Assume that, in response to Danton's bid, Mercury advised GIC that it would not raise the amount of cash that it would pay ($55), but that it also would issue a new class of stock to the GIC shareholders whose value would depend on GIC's performance after the acquisition. Mercury stated that if GIC met the projections that its management had given to Mercury, the stock would have a value of no less than $7 per share. However, First Pru and other investment bankers with whom GIC has consulted have advised GIC that the stock is not likely to have an initial market value of more than $3 per share.

1. Can GIC support Mercury's offer by approving the acquisition of GIC stock by Mercury but not by Danton, thus leaving the rights in effect with respect to Danton's bid?

2. What other responsibilities, if any, do GIC's management or its outside directors have with respect to the two competing bids?

REVLON, INC. v. MacANDREWS & FORBES HOLDINGS, INC.

506 A.2d 173 (Del.1986).

[Revlon, Inc. (Revlon) was a Delaware corporation. It had a 14 member board of directors, six of whom held senior management positions and two others who owned significant blocks of Revlon stock. Four of the remaining six directors had been associated with entities that had business relationships with Revlon.

In June 1985, Ronald O. Perelman, the chief executive officer of Pantry Pride, Inc. (Pantry Pride) met with Michel C. Bergerac, Revlon's chief executive officer to discuss a friendly acquisition of Revlon by Pantry Pride at a price in the $40–$50 range. Bergerac, who developed a strong personal antipathy toward Perelman, rejected the offer as being far below Revlon's intrinsic value. In mid-August, Perlman offered to acquire Revlon in a negotiated transaction at $42–$43 per share or in a hostile tender offer at $45. Again, Bergerac rejected any possible Pantry Pride acquisition.

On August 19, the Revlon board met with counsel and with Lazard Freres, its investment banker, to consider the impending hostile tender offer. The board voted to repurchase up to 5 million shares of its common stock and to adopt a Note Purchase Rights plan. The plan permitted the rights holders to exchange their stock for a $65 one-year note unless someone acquired all the Revlon stock at $65 per share.

On August 23, Pantry Pride made an all cash, all shares tender offer at $47.50 per share, subject to obtaining financing and to the redemption of the rights. On August 26, the Revlon board rejected the offer and, three days later, offered to exchange notes for 10 million shares of common stock. The notes contained various covenants, the most important of which was a covenant against incurring future debt. Ultimately Revlon accepted the full 10 million shares in the exchange offer.

On September 16, Pantry Pride announced a revised offer at $42 per share, conditioned on receiving 90% of the stock (or less, if Revlon removed the rights). Because of the exchange offer, the revised offer was the economic equivalent of Pantry Pride's earlier higher bid. Again the Revlon board rejected the offer. On September 27, Pantry Pride increased its bid to $50 per share, and on October 1 raised it again to $53.

Meanwhile, the Revlon board agreed to a leveraged buyout in the form of a merger with Forstmann Little (Forstmann) in which the Revlon shareholders would receive $56 per share, Forstmann would assume the debt incurred in the exchange offer, and Revlon would redeem the rights and waive the note covenants for Forstmann or any offer superior to Forstmann's. Immediately after the announcement of the merger, the market price of the notes fell substantially.

On October 7, Pantry Pride raised its bid to $56.25, subject to cancellation of the rights and the waiver of the note covenants. Two days later, it declared its intention to top any competing bid.

On October 12, Forstmann offered $57.25 per share and agreed to support the market price of the notes after the covenants were removed. The offer also required Revlon to grant Forstmann a lock-up option on two of its divisions at a price well below Lazard Frere's valuation if anyone else acquired 40% of the Revlon stock. Finally Revlon was to pay a $25 million cancellation fee if the merger agreement was terminated or anyone else acquired more than 19.9% of the Revlon stock. The Revlon board accepted the offer because the price exceeded Pantry Pride's bid, the noteholders were protected against a decline in the value of their notes, and Forstmann's financing was secure.

Pantry Pride promptly sued to invalidate the agreement and, on October 22, raised its bid to $58, conditioned upon the nullification of the rights, the waiver of the note covenants, and the granting of an injunction against the lock-up.]

MOORE, JUSTICE:

In this battle for corporate control of Revlon, the Court of Chancery enjoined certain transactions designed to thwart the efforts of Pantry Pride to acquire Revlon.[1] The defendants are Revlon, its board of directors, and Forstmann Little & Co. and the latter's affiliated limited partnership (collectively, Forstmann). The injunction barred consummation of an option granted Forstmann to purchase certain Revlon assets (the lock-up option), a promise by Revlon to deal exclusively with Forstmann in the face of a takeover (the no-shop provision), and the payment of a $25 million cancellation fee to Forstmann if the transaction was aborted. The Court of Chancery found that the Revlon directors had breached their duty of care by entering into the foregoing transac-

---

1. The nominal plaintiff, MacAndrews & Forbes Holdings, Inc., is the controlling stockholder of Pantry Pride. For all practical purposes their interests in this litigation are virtually identical, and we hereafter will refer to Pantry Pride as the plaintiff.

tions and effectively ending an active auction for the company. The trial court ruled that such arrangements are not illegal *per se* under Delaware law, but that their use under the circumstances here was impermissible. We agree. *See* MacAndrews & Forbes Holdings, Inc. v. Revlon, Inc., Del.Ch., 501 A.2d 1239 (1985). Thus, we granted this expedited interlocutory appeal to consider for the first time the validity of such defensive measures in the face of an active bidding contest for corporate control. Additionally, we address for the first time the extent to which a corporation may consider the impact of a takeover threat on constituencies other than shareholders. *See* Unocal Corp. v. Mesa Petroleum Co., Del.Supr., 493 A.2d 946, 955 (1985).

In our view, lock-ups and related agreements are permitted under Delaware law where their adoption is untainted by director interest or other breaches of fiduciary duty. The actions taken by the Revlon directors, however, did not meet this standard. Moreover, while concern for various corporate constituencies is proper when addressing a takeover threat, that principle is limited by the requirement that there be some rationally related benefit accruing to the stockholders. We find no such benefit here.

Thus, under all the circumstances we must agree with the Court of Chancery that the enjoined Revlon defensive measures were inconsistent with the directors' duties to the stockholders. Accordingly, we affirm.

* * *

II.

To obtain a preliminary injunction, a plaintiff must demonstrate both a reasonable probability of success on the merits and some irreparable harm which will occur absent the injunction. Gimbel v. Signal Companies, Del.Ch., 316 A.2d 599, 602 (1974), aff'd Del.Supr., 316 A.2d 619 (1974). Additionally, the Court shall balance the conveniences of and possible injuries to the parties. *Id.*

A.

We turn first to Pantry Pride's probability of success on the merits. The ultimate responsibility for managing the business and affairs of a corporation falls on its board of directors. 8 Del.C. § 141(a). In discharging this function the directors owe fiduciary duties of care and loyalty to the corporation and its shareholders. Guth v. Loft, Inc., 23 Del.Supr. 255, 5 A.2d 503, 510 (1939); Aronson v. Lewis, Del.Supr., 473 A.2d 805, 811 (1984). These principles apply with equal force when a board approves a corporate merger pursuant to 8 Del.C. § 251(b); Smith v. Van Gorkom, Del.Supr., 488 A.2d 858, 873 (1985); and of course they are the bedrock of our law regarding corporate takeover issues. Pogostin v. Rice, Del.Supr., 480 A.2d 619, 624 (1984); Unocal Corp. v. Mesa Petroleum Co., Del.Supr., 493 A.2d 946, 953, 955 (1985); Moran v. Household International, Inc., Del.Supr., 500 A.2d 1346, 1350 (1985). While the business judgment rule may be applicable to the actions of corporate directors responding to takeover threats, the principles upon which it is founded—care, loyalty and independence—must first be satisfied. Aronson v. Lewis, 473 A.2d at 812.[10]

If the business judgment rule applies, there is a "presumption that in making a business decision the directors of a corporation acted on an informed basis, in good faith and in the honest belief that the action taken was in the best interests of the company." Aronson v. Lewis, 473 A.2d at 812. However, when a board implements anti-takeover measures there arises "the omnipresent specter that a board may be acting primarily in its own interests, rather than those of the corporation and its shareholders. * * *" Unocal Corp. v. Mesa Petroleum Co., 493 A.2d at 954. This potential for conflict places upon the directors the burden of proving that they had reasonable grounds for believing there was a danger to corporate policy and effectiveness, a burden satisfied by a showing of good faith and reasonable investigation. *Id.* at 955. In addition, the directors must analyze the nature of the takeover and its effect on the corporation in order to ensure balance—that the responsive action taken is reasonable in relation to the threat posed. *Id.*

B.

The first relevant defensive measure adopted by the Revlon board was the Rights Plan, which would be considered a "poison pill" in the current language of corporate takeovers—a plan by which shareholders receive the right to be bought out by the corporation at a substantial premium on the occurrence of a stated triggering event. See generally Moran v. Household International, Inc., Del.Supr., 500 A.2d 1346 (1985). By 8 *Del.C.* §§ 141 and 157, the board clearly had the power to adopt the measure. See Moran v. Household International, Inc., 500 A.2d at 1351. Thus, the focus becomes one of reasonableness and purpose.

The Revlon board approved the Rights Plan in the face of an impending hostile takeover bid by Pantry Pride at $45 per share, a price which Revlon reasonably concluded was grossly inadequate. Lazard Freres had so advised the directors, and had also informed them that Pantry Pride was a small, highly leveraged company bent on a "bust-up" takeover by using "junk bond" financing to buy Revlon cheaply, sell the acquired assets to pay the debts incurred, and retain the profit for

---

10. One eminent corporate commentator has drawn a distinction between the business judgment rule, which insulates directors and management from personal liability for their business decisions, and the business judgment doctrine, which protects the decision itself from attack. The principles upon which the rule and doctrine operate are identical, while the objects of their protection are different. *See* Hinsey, Business Judgment and the American Law Institute's Corporate Governance Project: The Rule, the Doctrine and the Reality, 52 Geo.Wash.L.Rev. 609, 611–13 (1984). In the transactional justification cases, where the doctrine is said to apply, our decisions have not observed the distinction in such terminology. *See* Polk v. Good & Texaco, Del.Supr., ___ A.2d ___, ___ (1986); Moran v. Household International, Inc., Del.Supr., 500 A.2d 1346, 1356 (1985); Unocal Corp. v. Mesa Petroleum Co., Del.Supr., 493 A.2d 946, 953–55 (1985); Rosenblatt v. Getty Oil Co., Del.Supr., 493 A.2d 929, 943 (1985). Under the circumstances we do not alter our earlier practice of referring only to the business judgment rule, although in transactional justification matters such reference may be understood to embrace the concept of the doctrine.

itself.[12] In adopting the Plan, the board protected the shareholders from a hostile takeover at a price below the company's intrinsic value, while retaining sufficient flexibility to address any proposal deemed to be in the stockholders' best interests.

To that extent the board acted in good faith and upon reasonable investigation. Under the circumstances it cannot be said that the Rights Plan as employed was unreasonable, considering the threat posed. Indeed, the Plan was a factor in causing Pantry Pride to raise its bids from a low of $42 to an eventual high of $58. At the time of its adoption the Rights Plan afforded a measure of protection consistent with the directors' fiduciary duty in facing a takeover threat perceived as detrimental to corporate interests. Far from being a "show-stopper," as the plaintiffs had contended in *Moran,* the measure spurred the bidding to new heights, a proper result of its implementation.

* * *

C.

The second defensive measure adopted by Revlon to thwart a Pantry Pride takeover was the company's own exchange offer for 10 million of its shares. The directors' general broad powers to manage the business and affairs of the corporation are augmented by the specific authority conferred under 8 Del.C. § 160(a), permitting the company to deal in its own stock. *Unocal,* 493 A.2d at 953–54; Cheff v. Mathes, 41 Del.Supr. 494, 199 A.2d 548, 554 (1964); Kors v. Carey, 39 Del.Ch. 47, 158 A.2d 136, 140 (1960). However, when exercising that power in an effort to forestall a hostile takeover, the board's actions are strictly held to the fiduciary standards outlined in *Unocal.* These standards require the directors to determine the best interests of the corporation and its stockholders, and impose an enhanced duty to abjure any action that is motivated by considerations other than a good faith concern for such interests. *Unocal,* 493 A.2d at 954–55; *see* Bennett v. Propp, 41 Del. Supr. 14, 187 A.2d 405, 409 (1962).

The Revlon directors concluded that Pantry Pride's $47.50 offer was grossly inadequate. In that regard the board acted in good faith, and on an informed basis, with reasonable grounds to believe that there existed a harmful threat to the corporate enterprise. The adoption of a defensive measure, reasonable in relation to the threat posed, was proper and fully accorded with the powers, duties, and responsibilities conferred upon directors under our law. *Unocal,* 493 A.2d at 954; Pogostin v. Rice, 480 A.2d at 627.

D.

However, when Pantry Pride increased its offer to $50 per share, and then to $53, it became apparent to all that the break-up of the

---

12. As we noted in *Moran,* a "bust-up" takeover generally refers to a situation in which one seeks to finance an acquisition by selling off pieces of the acquired company, presumably at a substantial profit. *See Moran,* 500 A.2d at 1349, n. 4.

company was inevitable. The Revlon board's authorization permitting management to negotiate a merger or buyout with a third party was a recognition that the company was for sale. The duty of the board had thus changed from the preservation of Revlon as a corporate entity to the maximization of the company's value at a sale for the stockholders' benefit. This significantly altered the board's responsibilities under the *Unocal* standards. It no longer faced threats to corporate policy and effectiveness, or to the stockholders' interests, from a grossly inadequate bid. The whole question of defensive measures became moot. The directors' role changed from defenders of the corporate bastion to auctioneers charged with getting the best price for the stockholders at a sale of the company.

III.

This brings us to the lock-up with Forstmann and its emphasis on shoring up the sagging market value of the Notes in the face of threatened litigation by their holders. Such a focus was inconsistent with the changed concept of the directors' responsibilities at this stage of the developments. The impending waiver of the Notes covenants had caused the value of the Notes to fall, and the board was aware of the noteholders' ire as well as their subsequent threats of suit. The directors thus made support of the Notes an integral part of the company's dealings with Forstmann, even though their primary responsibility at this stage was to the equity owners.

The original threat posed by Pantry Pride—the break-up of the company—had become a reality which even the directors embraced. Selective dealing to fend off a hostile but determined bidder was no longer a proper objective. Instead, obtaining the highest price for the benefit of the stockholders should have been the central theme guiding director action. Thus, the Revlon board could not make the requisite showing of good faith by preferring the noteholders and ignoring its duty of loyalty to the shareholders. The rights of the former already were fixed by contract. Wolfensohn v. Madison Fund, Inc., Del.Supr., 253 A.2d 72, 75 (1969); Harff v. Kerkorian, Del.Ch., 324 A.2d 215 (1974). The noteholders required no further protection, and when the Revlon board entered into an auction-ending lock-up agreement with Forstmann on the basis of impermissible considerations at the expense of the shareholders, the directors breached their primary duty of loyalty.

The Revlon board argued that it acted in good faith in protecting the noteholders because *Unocal* permits consideration of other corporate constituencies. Although such considerations may be permissible, there are fundamental limitations upon that prerogative. A board may have regard for various constituencies in discharging its responsibilities, provided there are rationally related benefits accruing to the stockholders. *Unocal*, 493 A.2d at 955. However, such concern for non-stockholder interests is inappropriate when an auction among active bidders is in progress, and the object no longer is to protect or maintain the corporate enterprise but to sell it to the highest bidder.

Revlon also contended that by Gilbert v. El Paso Co., Del.Ch., 490 A.2d 1050, 1054–55 (1984), it had contractual and good faith obligations to consider the noteholders. However, any such duties are limited to the principle that one may not interfere with contractual relationships by improper actions. Here, the rights of the noteholders were fixed by agreement, and there is nothing of substance to suggest that any of those terms were violated. The Notes covenants specifically contemplated a waiver to permit sale of the company at a fair price. The Notes were accepted by the holders on that basis, including the risk of an adverse market effect stemming from a waiver. Thus, nothing remained for Revlon to legitimately protect, and no rationally related benefit thereby accrued to the stockholders. Under such circumstances we must conclude that the merger agreement with Forstmann was unreasonable in relation to the threat posed.

A lock-up is not *per se* illegal under Delaware law. Its use has been approved in an earlier unpublished case. Thompson v. Enstar Corp., Del.Ch. (1984). Such options can entice other bidders to enter a contest for control of the corporation, creating an auction for the company and maximizing shareholder profit. Current economic conditions in the takeover market are such that a "white knight" like Forstmann might only enter the bidding for the target company if it receives some form of compensation to cover the risks and costs involved. Note, Corporations–Mergers—"Lock–up" Enjoined Under Section 14(e) of Securities Exchange Act—Mobil Corp. v. Marathon Oil Co., 669 F.2d 366 (6th Cir. 1981), 12 Seton Hall L.Rev. 881, 892 (1982). However, while those lock-ups which draw bidders into the battle benefit shareholders, similar measures which end an active auction and foreclose further bidding operate to the shareholders' detriment. Note, Lock-up Options: Toward a State Law Standard, 96 Harv.L.Rev. 1068, 1081 (1983).

Recently, the United States Court of Appeals for the Second Circuit invalidated a lock-up on fiduciary duty grounds similar to those here. Hanson Trust PLC, et al. v. ML SCM Acquisition Inc., et al., 781 F.2d 264 (2nd Cir.1986). Citing Thompson v. Enstar Corp., *supra,* with approval, the court stated:

> In this regard, we are especially mindful that some lock-up options maybe beneficial to the shareholders, such as those that induce a bidder to compete for control of a corporation, while others may be harmful, such as those that effectively preclude bidders from competing with the optionee bidder.

In *Hanson Trust,* the bidder, Hanson, sought control of SCM by a hostile cash tender offer. SCM management joined with Merrill Lynch to propose a leveraged buy-out of the company at a higher price, and Hanson in turn increased its offer. Then, despite very little improvement in its subsequent bid, the management group sought a lock-up option to purchase SCM's two main assets at a substantial discount. The SCM directors granted the lock-up without adequate information as to the size of the discount or the effect the transaction would have on the company. Their action effectively ended a competitive bidding situation. The Hanson Court invalidated the lock-up because the directors failed to fully inform themselves about the value of a transaction in which management had a strong self-interest. "In short, the Board appears to have failed to ensure that negotiations for alternative bids were conducted by those whose only loyalty was to the shareholders."

The Forstmann option had a similar destructive effect on the auction process. Forstmann had already been drawn into the contest on a preferred basis, so the result of the lock-up was not to foster bidding, but to destroy it. The board's stated reasons for approving the transaction were: (1) better financing, (2) noteholder protection, and (3) higher price. As the Court of Chancery found, and we agree, any distinctions between the rival bidders' methods of financing the proposal were nominal at best, and such a consideration has little or no significance in a cash offer for any and all shares. The principal object, contrary to the board's duty of care, appears to have been protection of the noteholders over the shareholders' interests.

While Forstmann's $57.25 offer was objectively higher than Pantry Pride's $56.25 bid, the margin of superiority is less when the Forstmann price is adjusted for the time value of money. In reality, the Revlon board ended the auction in return for very little actual improvement in the final bid. The principal benefit went to the directors, who avoided personal liability to a class of creditors to whom the board owed no further duty under the circumstances. Thus, when a board ends an intense bidding contest on an insubstantial basis, and where a significant by-product of that action is to protect the directors against a perceived threat of personal liability for consequences stemming from the adoption of previous defensive measures, the action cannot withstand the enhanced scrutiny which *Unocal* requires of director conduct. *See Unocal*, 493 A.2d at 954–55.

In addition to the lock-up option, the Court of Chancery enjoined the no-shop provision as part of the attempt to foreclose further bidding by Pantry Pride. MacAndrews & Forbes Holdings, Inc. v. Revlon, Inc., 501 A.2d at 1251. The no-shop provision, like the lock-up option, while not *per se* illegal, is impermissible under the *Unocal* standards when a board's primary duty becomes that of an auctioneer responsible for selling the company to the highest bidder. The agreement to negotiate only with Forstmann ended rather than intensified the board's involvement in the bidding contest.

It is ironic that the parties even considered a no-shop agreement when Revlon had dealt preferentially, and almost exclusively, with Forstmann throughout the contest. After the directors authorized management to negotiate with other parties, Forstmann was given every negotiating advantage that Pantry Pride had been denied: cooperation from management, access to financial data, and the exclusive opportunity to present merger proposals directly to the board of directors. Favoritism for a white knight to the total exclusion of a hostile bidder might be justifiable when the latter's offer adversely affects shareholder interests, but when bidders make relatively similar offers, or dissolution of the company becomes inevitable, the directors cannot fulfill their enhanced *Unocal* duties by playing favorites with the contending factions. Market forces must be allowed to operate freely to bring the target's shareholders the best price available for their equity. Thus, as the trial court ruled, the shareholders' interests necessitated that the board remain free to negotiate in the fulfillment of that duty.

IV.

Having concluded that Pantry Pride has shown a reasonable probability of success on the merits, we address the issue of irreparable harm. The Court of Chancery ruled that unless the lock-up and other aspects of the agreement were enjoined, Pantry Pride's opportunity to bid for Revlon was lost. The court also held that the need for both bidders to compete in the marketplace outweighed any injury to Forstmann. Given the complexity of the proposed transaction between Revlon and Forstmann, the obstacles to Pantry Pride obtaining a meaningful legal remedy are immense. We are satisfied that the plaintiff has shown the need for an injunction to protect it from irreparable harm, which need outweighs any harm to the defendants.

V.

In conclusion, the Revlon board was confronted with a situation not uncommon in the current wave of corporate takeovers. A hostile and determined bidder sought the company at a price the board was convinced was inadequate. The initial defensive tactics worked to the benefit of the shareholders, and thus the board was able to sustain its *Unocal* burdens in justifying those measures. However, in granting an asset option lock-up to Forstmann, we must conclude that under all the circumstances the directors allowed considerations other than the maximization of shareholder profit to affect their judgment, and followed a course that ended the auction for Revlon, absent court intervention, to the ultimate detriment of its shareholders. No such defensive measure can be sustained when it represents a breach of the directors' fundamental duty of care. *See* Smith v. Van Gorkom, Del.Supr., 488 A.2d 858, 874 (1985). In that context the board's action is not entitled to the deference accorded it by the business judgment rule. The measures were properly enjoined. The decision of the Court of Chancery, therefore, is affirmed.

Note: Auctions

In *Revlon*, the court held that the responsibility of the board of directors changes when the company is "for sale." Long-term considerations disappear; the short-term selling price becomes paramount. "The directors' role change[s] from defenders of the corporate bastion to auctioneers charged with getting the best price for the stockholders at a sale of the company." 506 A.2d at 182. Concerns over threats to corporate policy or shareholder interests from an inadequate bid become moot.

What does it mean to say that a company is "for sale?" In *Revlon*, a moment arrived when "it became apparent to all that the break-up of the company was inevitable," and at that moment an auction was required. In the context of a hostile tender offer in which Revlon's management sought to remain independent and undertook extensive defensive measures to achieve that end, it is easy to understand the court's analysis. But does *every* acquisition transaction, even when voluntarily negotiated, constitute a "sale" that requires the selling corporation to conduct an auction before closing the transaction? If so, *Revlon* would have profound consequences for ordinary corporate acquisitions.

The law in this area continues to evolve; the most recent Delaware cases, Paramount Communications, Inc. v. Time, Inc., 571 A.2d 1140 (Del.1989) and Paramount Communications, Inc. v. QVC Network, Inc., 637 A.2d 34 (Del.1994), are set out at the end of this Section. This note traces the evolution of the law from *Revlon* to those opinions.

a. Triggering the Auction

Two years after *Revlon,* in City Capital Associates L.P. v. Interco, 551 A.2d 787 (Del.Ch.1988), the Court of Chancery noted that *Revlon* did not "require * * * that before every corporate merger agreement can validly be entered into, the constituent corporations must be 'shopped' or, more radically, an auction process undertaken, even though a merger may be regarded as a sale of the Company." The court did stress the need for a board to be informed as to possible alternatives and found that if it did so and was thus "in a position to act advisedly * * * the *Revlon* holding [does not require] it to turn to an auction alternative, if it has arrived at a good faith, informed determination that a recapitalization or other form of transaction is more beneficial to shareholders." Similarly, in Barkan v. Amsted Industries, Inc., 567 A.2d 1279 (Del. 1989), the court commented:

> * * * *Revlon* does not demand that every change in the control of a Delaware corporation be preceded by a heated bidding contest. *Revlon* is merely one of an unbroken line of cases that seek to prevent the conflicts of interest that arise in the field of mergers and acquisitions by demanding that directors act with scrupulous concern for fairness to shareholders. When multiple bidders are competing for control, this concern for fairness forbids directors from using defensive mechanisms to thwart an auction or to favor one bidder over another. When the board is considering a single offer and has no reliable grounds upon which to judge its adequacy, this concern for fairness demands a canvas of the market to determine if higher bids may be elicited. When, however, the directors possess a body of reliable evidence with which to evaluate the fairness of a transaction, they may approve that transaction without conducting an active survey of the market. As the Chancellor recognized, the

circumstances in which this passive approach is acceptable are limited. "A decent respect for reality forces one to admit that * * * advice [of an investment banker] is frequently a pale substitute for the dependable information that a canvas of the relevant market can provide." The need for adequate information is central to the enlightened evaluation of a transaction that a board must make. Nevertheless, there is no single method that a board must employ to acquire such information. Here, the Chancellor found that the advice of the Special Committee's investment bankers, when coupled with the special circumstances surrounding the negotiation and consummation of the MBO [management-sponsored leveraged buy-out], supported a finding that Amsted's directors had acted in good faith to arrange the best possible transaction for shareholders. Our own review of the record leads us to rule that the Chancellor's finding was well within the scope of his discretion.

What happens when the transfer of control involves a sale of less than all of the company's stock? In Black & Decker Corp. v. American Standard, Inc., 682 F.Supp. 772 (D.Del.1988), American Standard's board approved a management sponsored recapitalization in which shareholders kept their shares but in which the ownership by management and the employees increased from 5% to approximately 55%. The court held the recapitalization constituted a decision to sell the corporation under *Revlon*. Thus the court enjoined a severance plan and certain amendments to American Standard's retirement and savings plans adopted by the board which were found to favor management's recapitalization without any corresponding benefit to the shareholders. Earlier in Ivanhoe Partners v. Newmont Mining Corp., 535 A.2d 1334 (Del.1987), Newmont's board adopted a restructuring plan in response to a hostile tender offer for 42% of the company's shares. The restructuring plan included a special dividend which allowed a friendly shareholder to increase its stake to 49.9%. However, the court found that a sale was not inevitable because the friendly shareholder had signed a standstill agreement with Newmont which limited it to selecting no more than 40% of Newmont's board and because no bidding contest had occurred.

b. Best Price and the Conduct of the Auction

Revlon may best be viewed as an elaboration of *Unocal*. Once it is clear that a company is for sale, the only reasonable actions a board can take are those directed at obtaining what the Delaware Supreme Court now terms the "best value reasonably available" for shareholders. *QVC*, infra. Moreover, because *Unocal* applies, directors' conduct of an auction will be scrutinized under *Unocal*'s enhanced business judgment rule. A board may rely on corporate officers, employees, and outside advisers who have been selected with reasonable care, but the board retains ultimate responsibility for ensuring the integrity of the auction. It cannot delegate this responsibility to others, although it can create a special committee of independent directors to conduct the auction. Indeed, if some board members have an interest in a potential transaction, use of an independent special committee of the board will increase materially the proof that a defensive tactic was reasonable. *Moran*, supra.

In deciding what is the best value, the board must look at more than the asserted nominal value of the offer. In an art auction, each bidder bids on the same terms with the same consideration: cash payment at the end of the auction. In a corporate auction, bidders may pay in one transaction or several; they may use cash, their own stock, or other securities. The value of this consideration may be a source of debate between the buyer, the seller and their respective investment bankers. Under these conditions, the board may decide that the highest available price for shareholders is not the transaction with the highest nominal price. In Citron v. Fairchild Camera and Instrument Corp., [1988–89 Transfer Binder] Fed.Sec.L.Rep. (CCH) ¶ 93,915, 1988 WL 53322 (Del. Ch.1988) (Unpublished Case), the Court of Chancery held that the Fairchild board did not breach its *Revlon* duty by accepting Schlumberger's offer to acquire all Fairchild shares for $66 per share in cash and rejecting an offer by Gould to acquire 42% of the shares for $70 per share in cash and the balance for preferred stock to be valued at $70 per share. The court held that the board's duty under *Revlon* is not simply to get the highest price, but the best available transaction for the shareholders. The court concluded that a decision to reject a seemingly higher offer in favor of an all-cash offer with an arguably lower value does not by itself constitute a breach of the duty of loyalty, absent evidence of a breach of duty in the decision-making process. The court found that the board's decision to accept the Schlumberger offer was protected by the business judgment rule because the offer was for all cash and required no financing whereas Gould was unclear on the precise nature of the second step of its offer.

On appeal, the Delaware Supreme Court refused to remove the protection of the business judgment rule from the board's decision. Citron v. Fairchild Camera and Instrument Corp., 569 A.2d 53 (Del. 1989). The court noted that although the Fairchild board chairman did "exhibit some animus toward Gould," the record supported a finding that the chairman did not dominate the board so as to interfere with the exercise of its business judgment. Furthermore, there was "ample evidence" of the board's active and direct role in the sale process. The court noted that the board received investment advice from four leading investment banking firms, commissioned financial evaluations from three of them, shopped the company to other potential buyers, and discussed the sale of the company at three separate board meetings over the course of three weeks.

In In re RJR Nabisco, Inc. Shareholders Litigation, [1988–89 Transfer Binder] Fed.Sec.L.Rep. (CCH) ¶ 94,194, 1989 WL 7036 (Del.Ch.1989) (Unpublished Case), the court held that a board's decision to accept one of two substantially equivalent bids for a company without initiating further bidding was entitled to the protection of the business judgment rule and did not violate the board's *Revlon* duties. In that case, a committee of the directors of RJR, conducting an auction for the sale of the company, received a bid from a management group and one from KKR which the directors' financial advisers determined were substantially equivalent and fair to the RJR shareholders. The committee endorsed the KKR bid without seeking further bidding. The court found that this decision did not indicate bad faith and was entitled to the protection of the business judgment rule. Moreover, the court concluded that the decision of whether to incur the risks associated with further bidding was itself a business judgment protected by the rule.

In order to obtain the best possible price, the board may negotiate with potential bidders, but need not negotiate with them on identical terms. The duties created by *Revlon* are owed by the board to shareholders and not to potential suitors. In re J.P. Stevens & Co., Inc. Shareholder Litigation, 542 A.2d 770 (Del.Ch.1988) arose out of the contest for control of J.P. Stevens between West–Point Pepperell and Odyssey Partners. After several rounds of bidding, West Point had indicated its willingness to increase its offer to $64 per share. Stevens then entered into a merger agreement with Odyssey at $64 per share in which Stevens agreed to reimburse Odyssey for some of its expenses and pay a fee if the winning bid exceeded $64. West Point sued to invalidate the agreement to pay expenses and the fee on the ground that, under *Revlon,* the Stevens' board could not favor Odyssey in the auction but was limited to obtaining the highest available price.

The Court of Chancery rejected this argument, holding that *Revlon* did not purport to restrict a disinterested board from entering into agreements such as the one between J.P. Stevens and Odyssey if the board acted in good faith and with appropriate care. The fact that such agreements "have the effect of tilting the playing field * * * does not establish that they necessarily are not in the best interest of shareholders" because "it is the shareholders to whom the board owes a duty of fairness, not the person seeking to acquire the Company." Thus, the court concluded, "the board may tilt the playing field if, but only if, it is in the shareholders' interest to do so." 542 A.2d at 782. Since West Point had already indicated a willingness to increase its offer to $64 per share, the court held that it was not unreasonable for the Stevens board to agree to the topping fee and expense reimbursement as an inducement to Odyssey to make its own $64 bid. Only by so acting could it create a possibility that a still higher bid would be made.

Mills Acquisition Co. v. Macmillan, Inc., 559 A.2d 1261 (Del.1989), which involved an auction for control of Macmillan between KKR and Robert Maxwell, shows the limits of unequal treatment. During the auction, Macmillan's management and investment bankers provided KKR with significant assistance not offered to Maxwell. This assistance included greater access to confidential information, tipping KKR to the terms of Maxwell's bid, and giving additional bidding instructions to KKR on how to structure its bid to obtain board approval. In addition, despite Maxwell's stated willingness to increase his $89 all cash bid if it were not the highest bid for the company, Macmillan's advisers negotiated a lockup option with KKR which would allow KKR to purchase several of Macmillan's core assets if KKR's bid for the entire company was topped. In exchange for this lockup, KKR submitted a bid of $90.05 consisting of cash and securities. The terms of the lockup effectively terminated the auction.

The Delaware Supreme Court held that the Macmillan board had breached its fiduciary duties in the conduct of the auction by not "scrupulously [adhering] to ordinary principles of fairness." Fairness did not require equal treatment, but it did require that "stockholder interests are enhanced, rather than diminished, in the conduct of an auction for sale of corporate control." Because Macmillan failed to demonstrate that its special arrangements with KKR promoted stockholder interests or that they were done in good faith, the court enjoined the lock-up.

Macmillan's board failed to exercise active oversight of the auction. Instead, it allowed management which had an interest in KKR's bid and its investment bankers to control the auction. Further, rather than delegating oversight to a special committee of independent directors, the entire board including its interested members maintained nominal oversight. To the court, the lack of oversight along with fiduciary lapses by management and the investment bankers "irremediably taint[ed] * * * the transaction" and removed the protection of the business judgment rule.

Macmillan also redefined the auctioneer's duty; it is not to obtain the highest price available, but to obtain the "highest value reasonably attainable for shareholders" provided that "it was offered by a reputable and responsible bidder." In evaluating competing bids, a board can consider:

> [T]he adequacy and terms of the offer; its fairness and feasibility; the proposed or actual financing for the offer, and the consequences of that financing; questions of illegality; the impact of both the bid and the potential acquisition on other constituencies, provided that it bears some reasonable relationship to general shareholder interests; the risk of nonconsummation; the basic stockholder interests at stake; the bidder's identity, prior background and other business venture experiences; and the bidder's business plans for the corporation and their effects on stockholder interests.

559 A.2d. at 1282 n. 29.

These factors indicate a board may examine more than price or value during an auction. At a minimum, the board appears to have the power to exclude certain bidders from participation in the auction. But what factors would support such exclusion? Could a board defend a decision to not accept the highest bidder because it had doubts about a bidder's reputation or because it did not like its business plans? Should a board be able to determine to whom shareholders may sell their stock? If the Medical Committee had presented Dow Chemical (see Chapter 14) with a fully-financed cash tender offer for all Dow's stock, would Dow's board have been free to reject in favor of another offer at a lower price? Could it have rejected both bids, if both were fair from a financial point of view?

To answer those questions, one must first consider whether *Revlon* applies. *Macmillan* states that "not every offer or transaction affecting the corporate structure invokes *Revlon* duties." A board's refusal to entertain an unsolicited offer when the company is not for sale may in some circumstances be protected by the business judgment rule. Valid reasons for rebuffing an offer may include:

> [T]he nature and timing of the offer; its legality, feasibility and effect on the corporation and the stockholders; the alternatives available and their effect on the various constituencies, particularly the stockholders; the company's long term strategic plans; and any special factors bearing on stockholder and public interests.

559 A.2d at 1285 n. 35.

Do these factors permit a board, relying on "special factors bearing on the stockholder and public interests" to employ defensive measures against a fully-financed all-cash tender offer at a fair price? Or should shareholders be allowed to determine what is in their interest?

Note: Poison Pills as a Defensive Tactic

In the 1980s, the poison pill became a favorite defensive measure. Courts gave boards of directors considerable freedom to use poison pills to delay a hostile takeover bids while they attempted to negotiate better deals from bidders or explored alternative transactions that had the potential to produce a higher value for shareholders. In CRTF Corp. v. Federated Department Stores, 683 F.Supp. 422 (S.D.N.Y.1988), the court described a poison pill as providing "the directors with a shield to fend off coercive offers and with a gavel to run an auction." Accepting this rationale, Delaware courts held that a board may refuse to redeem a pill if the offer is inadequate, or because an auction for the company exists. See Facet Enterprises, Inc. v. Prospect Group, 1988 WL 36140 (Del.Ch. 1988) (Unpublished Case); Nomad Acquisition Corp. v. Damon Corporation, 1988 WL 96192 (Del.Ch.1988) (Unpublished Case); Doskocil Companies, Inc. v. Griggy, 1988 WL 105751 (Del.Ch.1988) (Unpublished Case); BNS, Inc. v. Koppers Company, Inc., 683 F.Supp. 458 (D.Del. 1988).

Moran had made clear that a board did not have "unfettered discretion in refusing to redeem the Rights." 500 A.2d at 1354. Bidders and target company shareholders both brought numerous suits, seeking to force boards to redeem poison pills after a tender offer had been made. The issue which caused the courts most difficulty was whether a target company board must provide shareholders with an alternative to the hostile bid, or whether a decision to "just say no" can ever be considered reasonable.

Analytically, the courts used *Unocal* 's enhanced business judgment test to examine decisions concerning the redemption of poison pills, focusing on whether a board's refusal to redeem was a reasonable response to a perceived threat to the corporation. In AC Acquisitions Corp. v. Anderson, Clayton & Co., 519 A.2d 103 (Del.Ch.1986), the court held that management had breached its *Unocal* duty by precluding shareholders from considering a non-coercive hostile bid that represented an alternative to a management recapitalization plan. Other decisions, however, suggested that courts might give greater weight to business judgments not to redeem poison pills when hostile tender offers were coercive or inadequate. See Desert Partners, L.P. v. USG Corporation, 686 F.Supp. 1289 (N.D.Ill.1988); Ivanhoe Partners v. Newmont Mining Corp., 535 A.2d 1334 (Del.1987); John C. Coffee, Jr., Proportionality after *Pillsbury:* The New Delaware Common Law on Defensive Tactics, 1 M & A L.Rep. 982 (1989).

Two cases, however, suggested that a board cannot hide behind a pill indefinitely when faced with a non-coercive all-cash tender offer for all shares at an adequate price. In City Capital Associates L.P. v. Interco, Inc., 551 A.2d 787 (Del.Ch.1988), the Rales brothers made a hostile $74 all-cash, all-shares offer for Interco, subject to the redemption of Interco's poison pill. The Interco board determined that the price was inadequate and, as an alternative, proposed a restructuring plan that would offer shareholders a package of cash and securities worth a minimum of $76 per share. Interco contended that its decision not to redeem the pill was necessary to guard the company and its shareholders from the threat posed by the inadequate offer and to protect the higher-valued restructuring. The court rejected this argument, finding that the offer was not coercive because it was an all-cash offer for all the shares. Although recognizing that such an offer could be a "threat" under *Unocal* if it was for an inadequate price, the court stated that the value of Interco's own plan was an "inherently * * * debatable proposition." Thus, the court concluded that a shareholder might well prefer an immediate cash payment of $74 to receiving the package that might be worth $76. For the court, the shareholder's ability to make this choice—rather than the choice itself—was pivotal. The court held that the Rales offer did not pose a sufficiently significant threat to warrant preventing shareholders from accepting it if they so desired. In *Unocal* terms, the refusal to redeem the pill was not reasonable in relation to the threat presented by the offer.

In Grand Metropolitan Public Ltd. Co. v. Pillsbury Co., 558 A.2d 1049 (Del.Ch.1988), the "just say no" defense arose more squarely. Grand Met made a $63 all-cash, all-shares offer for Pillsbury that the Pillsbury board determined was inadequate. In response, the board developed (or announced that it would develop) a restructuring plan involving the spin-off and sale of some of its assets in a time frame stretching from six months to five years. Pillsbury's investment bankers advised that, giving effect to such restructuring, Pillsbury had a present value of between $68 and $73 per share. The Court of Chancery found that the Grand Met offer was for a fair price and that, for a shareholder to realize the higher price, it would be necessary "to be patient and endure for a long time, perhaps until 1992 or 1993." Even then, the higher price would depend on economic conditions that were beyond Pillsbury's control. Thus the court held that the "threat" posed by Grand Met's offer did not justify the Pillsbury board's refusal to redeem the poison pill. Although the court did not directly address the question of whether a target company board could leave a pill in place simply because it believed a non-coercive offer was not in the best interests of the corporation or its shareholders, the court's decision seemed to imply that there comes a time in the life of every company when poison pills and other impediments to shareholder acceptance of a hostile tender offer must be swept away.

In TW Services, Inc. v. SWT Acquisition Corp., Fed.Sec.L.Rep. (CCH) ¶ 94,334, 1989 WL 20290 (Del.Ch.1989) (Unpublished Case), the Court of Chancery appeared to back away from this implication of *Interco* and *Pillsbury*. SWT made an all-cash, all-shares offer for TW, subject to the somewhat unusual conditions that the TW board of directors redeem its poison pill, approve SWT's offer and enter into a merger agreement with SWT. TW argued that SWT's offer was simply an invitation to the board to enter into merger negotiations, not a bona fide offer to acquire the company. Further, TW argued that it was entitled to manage the corporation in the best long-range interests of the shareholder and was not required to come up with an alternative value-enhancing plan in opposition to an unsolicited offer. The court acknowledged this latter argument but found it unnecessary to resolve the issue. Rather, it held that because of SWT's conditions, the offer "involves *both* a proposal to negotiate a merger and a conditional tender offer precluded by a poison pill." Insofar as the offer concerned merger negotiations, the refusal to negotiate was fully protected by the business judgment rule. Because the board's actions were proper under such an analysis, the court refused to order the board to redeem the pill.

Delaware is not the universe, however, and other jurisdictions have also had occasion to consider the refusal to redeem a poison pill. The New York courts invalidated the poison pill that Irving Bank Corporation adopted as part of its defense against the Bank of New York on the grounds that the pill constituted a breach of the directors' fiduciary duties. See Bank of New York Co., Inc. v. Irving Bank Corp., 142 Misc.2d 145, 536 N.Y.S.2d 923 (1988), aff'd without opinion 143 A.D.2d 1075, 533 N.Y.S.2d 412 (1988); and 139 Misc.2d 665, 528 N.Y.S.2d 482 (1988). See also, Georgia–Pacific Corp. v. Great Northern Nekoosa Corp., 728 F.Supp. 807 (D.Me.1990) (stock purchase rights plan valid under Maine law) and Avon Products, Inc., v. Chartwell Associates L.P., 907 F.2d 322 (2d Cir.1990) (shareholder rights plan invalid under New York law). For an analysis of how Wisconsin would apply the *Unocal* standard, see Amanda Acquisition Corp. v. Universal Foods Corp., 708 F.Supp. 984 (E.D.Wis.1989), aff'd on other grounds 877 F.2d 496 (7th

Cir.1989), cert. denied 493 U.S. 955, 110 S.Ct. 367, 107 L.Ed.2d 353 (1989).

Note: Other Constituencies

Recall Chapter 5 in which we saw that constituency statutes often were enacted to give directors an additional weapon against hostile takeovers. These statutes permit directors to consider the effects of their actions (including the adoption of defensive techniques) on a broad range of non-shareholder constituencies and afford the protection of the business judgment rule to directors when they do so.

Must there be specific statutory authorization before directors can consider other constituencies in the context of a takeover? Consider the following amendment to Control Data Corporation's certificate of incorporation adopted in 1978:

> Tenth: The Board of Directors of the Corporation, when evaluating any offer of another party to (a) make a tender or exchange offer for any equity security of the Corporation, (b) merge or consolidate the Corporation with another corporation, or (c) purchase or otherwise acquire all or substantially all of the properties and assets of the Corporation, shall, in connection with the exercise of its judgment in determining what is in the interests of the Corporation and its stockholders, give due notice to all relevant factors, including without limitation the social and economic effects on the employees, customers, suppliers and other constituents of the Corporation and its subsidiaries and on the communities in which the Corporation and its subsidiaries operate or are located.

The cynical reaction is that Control Data's management is cleverly trying to give itself the broadest possible latitude to fend off a hostile tender offer, should one appear. Better still, by serving strong notice to any prospective bidder that it will face a fight to the finish, the company hopes to deter possible tender offers. On the other hand, isn't Control Data doing precisely what many corporate critics, including the cynics, are demanding of modern management, which is displaying sensitivity to a community of interests larger than its stockholders?

Lacking a constituency statute, the Delaware courts have taken a somewhat narrower view of the directors' power. In *Unocal*, the Delaware Supreme Court stated that the board of directors could consider other constituencies such as "creditors, customers, employees, and perhaps even the community generally" when selecting reasonable defensive measures to a takeover which threatens the corporation. In *Revlon*, the court limited the consideration of these other constituencies to the extent that the directors' consideration is "rationally related to benefits accruing to the stockholders." Consideration of non-stockholder constituencies, in those circumstances, does not violate a director's duty of loyalty and will allow directors to retain the protection of the business judgment rule.

Generally, consideration of other constituencies will be rationally related to stockholder interests. Stockholders may have an interest in maintaining and increasing the long run value of the corporation even if its short run value may suffer. That value can often be improved when the board considers the interest of other constituencies. However, when the board reaches the decision to sell the company and terminate the interests of current stockholders, concern for the company's long run value disappears. The interests of stockholders is limited to obtaining the highest price possible for their shares. In addition, unlike *Unocal*, the ability to consider other constituencies is circumscribed by *Revlon*'s obligation that the board act to further the shareholders' best interests.

Herald Co. v. Seawell, 472 F.2d 1081 (10th Cir.1972), which involved a struggle for control of the company that published the Denver Post newspaper, took a different approach. The Denver Post is a large metropolitan newspaper with a long tradition of local ownership. The Bonfils family had had a large ownership interest in the Post, and Helen Bonfils, the daughter of one of the Post's founders, was both an officer and director. In May 1960, Samuel Newhouse, the owner of one of the nation's largest newspaper chains purchased 18 percent of the outstanding common stock of the Denver Post with the intent of acquiring the newspaper. On July 7, 1960, the Post purchased 19,574 shares of its stock (about 21 percent of that outstanding) held by the U.S. National Bank as trustee for Children's Hospital at $260 per share. For several years prior to this purchase, the Post board of directors had contemplated establishing an employee stock ownership plan. After the purchase, the board implemented an employee stock trust plan, transferring approximately 3400 treasury shares to the trust. Helen Bonfils donated 1600 shares from her personal holdings. By December 1969, 415 of the eligible 1159 employees had purchased shares from the trust.

More than eight years after the purchase of the Children's Hospital stock, the Herald Company, which was owned by Newhouse, brought a derivative action on behalf of the Post against its officers and directors for misconduct, breach of trust and misuse of corporate assets. The plaintiff claimed that the board and the trustees of the employee stock trust had conspired to acquire sufficient shares of stock to vest control in Helen Bonfils. Among the numerous acts which the defendants allegedly committed was the creation of an "illusory stock trust" from which the defendants sold shares at prices which resulted in a decrease in the Post's surplus.

The district court determined that management's primary obligation was to earn profits for the company's shareholders, and ordered the public sale of several blocks of Post shares, including those remaining in the treasury from the Children's Hospital purchase and those transferred to the trust.

The Tenth Circuit reversed. The evidence established that the directors feared a Newhouse takeover would adversely affect the character and quality of the Post. The directors believed that local independent ownership was preferable and superior to chain ownership. They also knew that Newhouse had a reputation among his employees for having poor relations with labor. Significantly, the court noted that a newspaper had a threefold obligation—to the stockholders, to the employees, and to the public—that was greater than the duty to increase profits.

> Such a newspaper is endowed with an important public interest. It must adhere to the ethics of the great profession of journalism. The readers are entitled to a high quality of accurate news coverage of local, state, national and international events. The newspaper management has an obligation to assume leadership, when needed, for the betterment of the area served by the newspaper. Because of these relations with the public, a corporation publishing a great newspaper such as the Denver Post is, in effect, a quasi-public institution.

472 F.2d at 1095.

Because the board had the power to adopt the stock trust plan, the court refused to substitute its own judgment for that of the board and upheld the transaction.

4. STRATEGIC TRANSACTIONS

The foregoing materials raise difficult conceptual and practical questions. Is a target company ever free to enter into a transaction that its management believes is in the best interest of the corporation without first being subject to *Revlon* duties? Put differently, can there be such a thing as a "friendly" deal without considering other potential or actual bidders? Are there circumstances under which the target's board can effectively preclude its shareholders from accepting a non-coercive tender offer? More succinctly, absent coercion, can directors "just say no?" Consider the extent to which the following cases answer these questions.

PARAMOUNT COMMUNICATIONS, INC. v. TIME, INC.

571 A.2d 1140 (Del.1989).

[Time, Inc. (Time) was a Delaware corporation whose traditional business was the publication of magazines and books. It owned cable television franchises and provided pay television programming through its Home Box Office and Cinemax subsidiaries. In 1983, Time began to consider expanding into the entertainment industry and in 1987, a special committee of Time executives endorsed expansion into ownership and creation of video programming.

Some of Time's outside directors viewed such a move as a threat to the editorial integrity and journalistic focus of Time. Their primary concern was the preservation of the "Time Culture." They believed that Time was recognized as an institution built upon a foundation of journalistic integrity. To protect this reputation, Time's management had refrained from involvement in Time's editorial policy. The outside directors feared that a merger with an entertainment company would divert Time's focus from news journalism and would weaken the separation of the editorial policy from the business side of Time.

In June 1988, management distributed to the board a comprehensive long-range plan that examined strategies for the 1990s. The plan included Warner as potential acquisition candidate. J. Richard Munro, Time's chairman and CEO, and N.J. Nicholas, Jr., president and chief operating officer then met with each outside director to discuss long-term strategies and specifically a combination with Warner Communications (Warner) whose business complemented Time better than other potential merger candidates. After these discussions, Time's board approved in principle a strategic plan for expansion and authorized continuing merger discussions with Warner.

Talks between Time and Warner began in August, 1988. Although Time had preferred an acquisition involving all cash or cash and securities, it agreed to a stock-for-stock exchange so that Warner's stockholders could retain an equity interest in the new corporation. Time also insisted on control of the board in order to preserve "a management committed to Time's journalistic integrity." Negotiations broke down when the parties failed to agree on the top executives of the new corporation, and Time then pursued other merger alternatives.

In January, 1988, Time resumed its talks with Warner after the parties agreed on the governance issues. Many of the details of the original agreement remained intact, and on March 3, 1989, Time's board approved a stock-for-stock merger with Warner. The merger would give Warner shareholders 62% of the combined company. The new company would have a 24–member board with Time and Warner each initially represented by 12 directors. The board would have both an entertainment and editorial committee controlled respectively by Warner and Time directors. The rules of the New York Stock Exchange (NYSE) required Time's shareholders to approve the merger, although, because the transaction was cast as a triangular merger (see Chapter 12), Delaware law did not.

At the March 3 meeting, Time's board adopted several defensive tactics. It agreed to an automatic share exchange with Warner which gave Warner the right to receive 11.1% of Time's outstanding common stock. Time also sought and paid for "confidence letters" from its banks in which the banks agreed to not finance a hostile acquisition of Time. Time agreed to a no-shop clause preventing it from considering any other consolidation proposal regardless of the merits. After the announcement of the transaction, Time publicized the lack of debt in the transaction as being one of its chief benefits. Time scheduled the shareholder vote for June 23 and sent out its proxy materials for the merger on May 24.

On June 7, Paramount Communications (Paramount) announced a $175 per share, all-cash, all-shares "fully-negotiable" offer for Time. Time's board found that Paramount's offer was subject to three conditions: that Time terminate its merger agreement and share exchange agreement with Warner; that Paramount obtain acceptable cable franchise transfers from Time; and that DGCL § 203 (the anti-takeover statute) not apply to any subsequent Time–Paramount merger. Time believed that it would take at least several months to satisfy these conditions.

Although, Time's financial advisors informed the board that Time's per share value was materially higher than Paramount's $175 offer, the board was concerned that shareholders would not appreciate the long-term benefits of the Warner merger if given the opportunity to accept the Paramount offer. Therefore, Time sought the NYSE's approval to complete the merger without stockholder approval. The NYSE refused.

On June 8, Time formally rejected Paramount's offer. Because it continued to believe that the offer presented a threat to Time's control of its own destiny and the "Time Culture", the board chose to recast the form of the Warner transaction. Under the new proposal, Time would make an immediate all-cash offer for 51% of Warner's outstanding stock at $70 per share. The remaining 49% would be purchased at some later date for a mixture of cash and securities worth $70 per share. Time would fund the acquisition of Warner by incurring $7–10 billion of debt, despite its original assertion that the debt-free nature of the combination was one of its principal benefits. Time also agreed to pay $9 billion to Warner for its goodwill. As a condition of accepting the revised transaction, Warner received a control premium and guarantee that the corporate governance provisions in the original merger agreement would remain. Time agreed to not employ its poison pill against Warner, and unless enjoined, to complete the transaction.

On June 23, 1989, Paramount raised its offer to $200 per share while continuing to maintain that all aspects of the offer were negotiable. On June 26, Time's board rejected the second offer on the grounds that it was still inadequate and that Time's acquisition of Warner "offered a greater long-term value for the stockholders and, unlike Paramount, was not a threat to Time's survival and its 'culture.'"

Two groups of Time shareholders ("Shareholder Plaintiffs") and Paramount sought to enjoin Time's tender offer. The Court of Chancery denied plaintiffs' motions. Plaintiffs appealed.]

HORSEY, JUSTICE.

* * *

II.

The Shareholder Plaintiffs first assert a *Revlon* claim. They contend that the March 4 Time–Warner agreement effectively put Time up for sale, triggering *Revlon* duties, requiring Time's board to enhance short-term shareholder value and to treat all other interested acquirers on an equal basis. The Shareholder Plaintiffs base this argument on two facts: (i) the ultimate Time–Warner exchange ratio of .465 favoring Warner, resulting in Warner shareholders' receipt of 62% of the combined company; and (ii) the subjective intent of Time's directors as evidenced in their statements that the market might perceive the Time–Warner merger as putting Time up "for sale" and their adoption of various defensive measures.

The Shareholder Plaintiffs further contend that Time's directors, in structuring the original merger transaction to be "takeover-proof," triggered *Revlon* duties by foreclosing their shareholders from any prospect of obtaining a control premium. In short, plaintiffs argue that Time's board's decision to merge with Warner imposed a fiduciary duty to maximize immediate share value and not erect unreasonable barriers to further bids. Therefore, they argue, the Chancellor erred in finding: that Paramount's bid for Time did not place Time "for sale"; that Time's transaction with Warner did not result in any transfer of control; and that the combined Time–Warner was not so large as to preclude the possibility of the stockholders of Time–Warner receiving a future control premium.

Paramount asserts only a *Unocal* claim in which the shareholder plaintiffs join. Paramount contends that the Chancellor, in applying the first part of the *Unocal* test, erred in finding that Time's board had reasonable grounds to believe that Paramount posed both a legally cognizable threat to Time shareholders and a danger to Time's corporate policy and effectiveness. Paramount also contests the court's finding that Time's board made a reasonable and objective investigation of Paramount's offer so as to be informed before rejecting it. Paramount further claims that the court erred in applying *Unocal*'s second part in finding Time's response to be "reasonable." Paramount points primarily to the preclusive effect of the revised agreement which denied Time shareholders the opportunity both to vote on the agreement and to respond to Paramount's tender offer. Paramount argues that the underlying motivation of Time's board in adopting these defensive measures was management's desire to perpetuate itself in office.

The Court of Chancery posed the pivotal question presented by this case to be: Under what circumstances must a board of directors abandon an in-place plan of corporate development in order to provide its shareholders with the option to elect and realize an immediate control premium? As applied to this case, the question becomes: Did Time's board, having developed a strategic plan of global expansion to be launched through a business combination with Warner, come under a fiduciary duty to jettison its plan and put the corporation's future in the hands of its shareholders?

While we affirm the result reached by the Chancellor, we think it unwise to place undue emphasis upon long-term versus short-term corporate strategy. Two key predicates underpin our analysis. First,

Delaware law imposes on a board of directors the duty to manage the business and affairs of the corporation. 8 *Del.C.* § 141(a). This broad mandate includes a conferred authority to set a corporate course of action, including time frame, designed to enhance corporate profitability.[12] Thus, the question of "long-term" versus "short-term" values is largely irrelevant because directors, generally, are obliged to charter a course for a corporation which is in its best interests without regard to a fixed investment horizon. Second, absent a limited set of circumstances as defined under *Revlon,* a board of directors, while always required to act in an informed manner, is not under any *per se* duty to maximize shareholder value in the short term, even in the context of a takeover. In our view, the pivotal question presented by this case is: "Did Time, by entering into the proposed merger with Warner, put itself up for sale?" A resolution of that issue through application of *Revlon* has a significant bearing upon the resolution of the derivative *Unocal* issue.

A.

We first take up plaintiffs' principal *Revlon* argument, summarized above. In rejecting this argument, the Chancellor found the original Time–Warner merger agreement not to constitute a "change of control" and concluded that the transaction did not trigger *Revlon* duties. The Chancellor's conclusion is premised on a finding that "[b]efore the merger agreement was signed, control of the corporation existed in a fluid aggregation of unaffiliated shareholders representing a voting majority—in other words, in the market." The Chancellor's findings of fact are supported by the record and his conclusion is correct as a matter of law. However, we premise our rejection of plaintiffs' *Revlon* claim on broader grounds, namely, the absence of any substantial evidence to conclude that Time's board, in negotiating with Warner, made the dissolution or breakup of the corporate entity inevitable, as was the case in *Revlon.*

Under Delaware law there are, generally speaking and without excluding other possibilities, two circumstances which may implicate *Revlon* duties. The first, and clearer one, is when a corporation initiates an active bidding process seeking to sell itself or to effect a business reorganization involving a clear break-up of the company. See, e.g., Mills Acquisition Co. v. Macmillan, Inc., Del.Supr., 559 A.2d 1261 (1988). However, *Revlon* duties may also be triggered where, in response to a bidder's offer, a target abandons its long-term strategy and seeks an alternative transaction also involving the breakup of the company. Thus, in *Revlon,* when the board responded to Pantry Pride's offer by contemplating a "bust-up" sale of assets in a leveraged acquisition, we imposed upon the board a duty to maximize immediate shareholder value and an obligation to auction the company fairly. If, however, the

---

12. In endorsing this finding, we tacitly accept the Chancellor's conclusion that it is not a breach of faith for directors to determine that the present stock market price of shares is not representative of true value or that there may indeed be several market values for any corporation's stock. We have so held in another context. *See Van Gorkom,* 488 A.2d at 876.

board's reaction to a hostile tender offer is found to constitute only a defensive response and not an abandonment of the corporation's continued existence, *Revlon* duties are not triggered, though *Unocal* duties attach.[14] See, e.g., Ivanhoe Partners v. Newmont Mining Corp., Del. Supr., 535 A.2d 1334, 1345 (1987).

The plaintiffs insist that even though the original Time–Warner agreement may not have worked "an objective change of control," the transaction made a "sale" of Time inevitable. Plaintiffs rely on the subjective intent of Time's board of directors and principally upon certain board members' expressions of concern that the Warner transaction *might* be viewed as effectively putting Time up for sale. Plaintiffs argue that the use of a lock-up agreement, a no-shop clause, and so-called "dry-up" agreements prevented shareholders from obtaining a control premium in the immediate future and thus violated *Revlon*.

We agree with the Chancellor that such evidence is entirely insufficient to invoke *Revlon* duties; and we decline to extend *Revlon* 's application to corporate transactions simply because they might be construed as putting a corporation either "in play" or "up for sale." See Citron v. Fairchild Camera, Del.Supr., 569 A.2d 53 (1989); *Macmillan,* 559 A.2d at 1285 n. 35. The adoption of structural safety devices alone does not trigger *Revlon*. Rather, as the Chancellor stated, such devices are properly subject to a *Unocal* analysis.

Finally, we do not find in Time's recasting of its merger agreement with Warner from a share exchange to a share purchase a basis to conclude that Time had either abandoned its strategic plan or made a sale of Time inevitable.[16] The Chancellor found that although the merged Time–Warner company would be large (with a value approaching approximately $30 billion), recent takeover cases have proven that acquisition of the combined company might nonetheless be possible. The legal consequence is that *Unocal* alone applies to determine whether the business judgment rule attaches to the revised agreement. Plaintiffs' analogy to *Macmillan* thus collapses and plaintiffs' reliance on *Macmillan* is misplaced.

B.

We turn now to plaintiffs' *Unocal* claim. We begin by noting, as did the Chancellor, that our decision does not require us to pass on the wisdom of the board's decision to enter into the original Time–Warner

---

14. Within the auction process, any action taken by the board must be reasonably related to the threat posed or reasonable in relation to the advantage sought, see Mills Acquisition Co. v. Macmillan, Inc., Del. Supr., 559 A.2d 1261, 1288 (1988). Thus, a *Unocal* analysis may be appropriate when a corporation is in a *Revlon* situation and *Revlon* duties may be triggered by a defensive action taken in response to a hostile offer. Since *Revlon,* we have stated that differing treatment of various bidders is not actionable when such action reasonably relates to achieving the best price available for the stockholders. *Macmillan,* 559 A.2d at 1286–87.

16. We note that, although Time's advisors presented the board with such alternatives as an auction or sale to a third party bidder, the board rejected those responses, preferring to go forward with its pre-existing plan rather than adopt an alternative to Paramount's proposal.

agreement. That is not a court's task. Our task is simply to review the record to determine whether there is sufficient evidence to support the Chancellor's conclusion that the initial Time–Warner agreement was the product of a proper exercise of business judgment. *Macmillan,* 559 A.2d at 1288.

We have purposely detailed the evidence of the Time board's deliberative approach, beginning in 1983–84, to expand itself. Time's decision in 1988 to combine with Warner was made only after what could be fairly characterized as an exhaustive appraisal of Time's future as a corporation. After concluding in 1983–84 that the corporation must expand to survive, and beyond journalism into entertainment, the board combed the field of available entertainment companies. By 1987 Time had focused upon Warner; by late July 1988 Time's board was convinced that Warner would provide the best "fit" for Time to achieve its strategic objectives. The record attests to the zealousness of Time's executives, fully supported by their directors, in seeing to the preservation of Time's "culture," i.e., its perceived editorial integrity in journalism. We find ample evidence in the record to support the Chancellor's conclusion that the Time board's decision to expand the business of the company through its March 3 merger with Warner was entitled to the protection of the business judgment rule. See Aronson v. Lewis, Del. Supr., 473 A.2d 805, 812 (1984).

The Chancellor reached a different conclusion in addressing the Time–Warner transaction as revised three months later. He found that the revised agreement was defense-motivated and designed to avoid the potentially disruptive effect that Paramount's offer would have had on consummation of the proposed merger were it put to a shareholder vote. Thus, the court declined to apply the traditional business judgment rule to the revised transaction and instead analyzed the Time board's June 16 decision under *Unocal.* The court ruled that *Unocal* applied to all director actions taken, following receipt of Paramount's hostile tender offer, that were reasonably determined to be defensive. Clearly that was a correct ruling and no party disputes that ruling.

In *Unocal,* we held that before the business judgment rule is applied to a board's adoption of a defensive measure, the burden will lie with the board to prove (a) reasonable grounds for believing that a danger to corporate policy and effectiveness existed; and (b) that the defensive measure adopted was reasonable in relation to the threat posed. *Unocal,* 493 A.2d 946. Directors satisfy the first part of the *Unocal* test by demonstrating good faith and reasonable investigation. We have repeatedly stated that the refusal to entertain an offer may comport with a valid exercise of a board's business judgment. *See, e.g., Macmillan,* 559 A.2d at 1285 n. 35; *Van Gorkom,* 488 A.2d at 881; Pogostin v. Rice, Del.Supr., 480 A.2d 619, 627 (1984).

Unocal involved a two-tier, highly coercive tender offer. In such a case, the threat is obvious: shareholders may be compelled to tender to avoid being treated adversely in the second stage of the transaction. In subsequent cases, the Court of Chancery has suggested that an all-cash, all-shares offer, falling within a range of values that a shareholder might reasonably prefer, cannot constitute a legally recognized "threat" to shareholder interests sufficient to withstand a *Unocal* analysis. AC Acquisitions Corp. v. Anderson, Clayton & Co., Del.Ch., 519 A.2d 103 (1986); see Grand Metropolitan, PLC v. Pillsbury Co., Del.Ch., 558 A.2d 1049 (1988); City Capital Associates v. Interco, Inc., Del.Ch., 551 A.2d 787 (1988). In those cases, the Court of Chancery determined that whatever danger existed related only to the shareholders and only to price and not to the corporation.

From those decisions by our Court of Chancery, Paramount and the individual plaintiffs extrapolate a rule of law that an all-cash, all-shares offer with values reasonably in the range of acceptable price cannot pose any objective threat to a corporation or its shareholders. Thus, Paramount would have us hold that only if the value of Paramount's offer were determined to be clearly inferior to the value created by management's plan to merge with Warner could the offer be viewed—objectively—as a threat.

Implicit in the plaintiffs' argument is the view that a hostile tender offer can pose only two types of threats: the threat of coercion that results from a two-tier offer promising unequal treatment for nontendering shareholders; and the threat of inadequate value from an all-shares, all-cash offer at a price below what a target board in good faith deems to be the present value of its shares. See, e.g., *Interco*, 551 A.2d at 797; see also BNS, Inc. v. Koppers, D.Del., 683 F.Supp. 458 (1988). Since Paramount's offer was all-cash, the only conceivable "threat," plaintiffs argue, was inadequate value.[17] We disapprove of such a narrow and rigid construction of *Unocal,* for the reasons which follow.

Plaintiffs' position represents a fundamental misconception of our standard of review under *Unocal* principally because it would involve the court in substituting its judgment for what is a "better" deal for that of a corporation's board of directors. To the extent that the Court of Chancery has recently done so in certain of its opinions, we hereby reject such approach as not in keeping with a proper *Unocal* analysis. See, e.g., *Interco*, 551 A.2d 787, and its progeny; but see TW Services, Inc. v. SWT Acquisition Corp., Del.Ch., 1989 WL 20290 (March 2, 1989).

---

17. Some commentators have suggested that the threats posed by hostile offers be categorized into not two but three types: "(i) *opportunity loss* * * * [where] a hostile offer might deprive target shareholders of the opportunity to select a superior alternative offered by target management [or, we would add, offered by another bidder]; (ii) *structural coercion,* * * * the risk that disparate treatment of non-tendering shareholders might distort shareholders' tender decisions; and * * * (iii) *substantive coer-* cion, * * * the risk that shareholders will mistakenly accept an underpriced offer because they disbelieve management's representations of intrinsic value." The recognition of substantive coercion, the authors suggest, would help guarantee that the *Unocal* standard becomes an effective intermediate standard of review. Gilson & Kraakman, Delaware's Intermediate Standard for Defensive Tactics: Is There Substance to Proportionality Review?, 44 The Business Lawyer, 247, 267 (1989).

The usefulness of *Unocal* as an analytical tool is precisely its flexibility in the face of a variety of fact scenarios. *Unocal* is not intended as an abstract standard; neither is it a structured and mechanistic procedure of appraisal. Thus, we have said that directors may consider, when evaluating the threat posed by a takeover bid, the "inadequacy of the price offered, nature and timing of the offer, questions of illegality, the impact on contingencies other than shareholders, the risk of nonconsummation and the quality of securities being offered in the exchange." 493 A.2d at 955. The open-ended analysis mandated by *Unocal* is not intended to lead to a simple mathematical exercise: that is, of comparing the discounted value of Time–Warner's expected trading price at some future date with Paramount's offer and determining which is the higher. Indeed, in our view, precepts underlying the business judgment rule mitigate against a court's engaging in the process of attempting to appraise and evaluate the relative merits of a long-term versus a short-term investment goal for shareholders. To engage in such an exercise is a distortion of the *Unocal* process and, in particular, the application of the second part of *Unocal*'s test, discussed below.

In this case, the Time board reasonably determined that inadequate value was not the only legally cognizable threat that Paramount's all-cash, all-shares offer could present. Time's board concluded that Paramount's eleventh hour offer posed other threats. One concern was that Time shareholders might elect to tender into Paramount's cash offer in ignorance or a mistaken belief of the strategic benefit which a business combination with Warner might produce. Moreover, Time viewed the conditions attached to Paramount's offer as introducing a degree of uncertainty that skewed a comparative analysis. Further, the timing of Paramount's offer to follow issuance of Time's proxy notice was viewed as arguably designed to upset, if not confuse, the Time stockholders' vote. Given this record evidence, we cannot conclude that the Time board's decision of June 6 that Paramount's offer posed a threat to corporate policy and effectiveness was lacking in good faith or dominated by motives of either entrenchment or self-interest.

Paramount also contends that the Time board had not duly investigated Paramount's offer. Therefore, Paramount argues, Time was unable to make an informed decision that the offer posed a threat to Time's corporate policy. Although the Chancellor did not address this issue directly, his findings of fact do detail Time's exploration of the available entertainment companies, including Paramount, before determining that Warner provided the best strategic "fit." In addition, the court found that Time's board rejected Paramount's offer because Paramount did not serve Time's objectives or meet Time's needs. Thus, the record does, in our judgment, demonstrate that Time's board was adequately informed of the potential benefits of a transaction with Paramount. We agree with the Chancellor that the Time board's lengthy pre-June investigation of potential merger candidates, including Paramount, mooted any obligation on Time's part to halt its merger process with Warner to reconsider Paramount. Time's board was under no obligation to negotiate with Paramount. *Unocal*, 493 A.2d at 954–55; see also *Macmillan*, 559 A.2d at 1285 n. 35. Time's failure to negotiate cannot be fairly found to have been uninformed. The evidence supporting this finding is materially enhanced by the fact that twelve of Time's sixteen board members were outside independent directors. *Unocal*, 493 A.2d at 955; Moran v. Household Intern., Inc., Del.Supr., 500 A.2d 1346, 1356 (1985).

We turn to the second part of the *Unocal* analysis. The obvious requisite to determining the reasonableness of a defensive action is a clear identification of the nature of the threat. As the Chancellor correctly noted, this "requires an evaluation of the importance of the corporate objective threatened; alternative methods of protecting that objective; impacts of the "defensive' action, and other relevant factors." In Re: Time Incorporated Shareholder Litigation, Del.Ch., 565 A.2d 281 (1989). It is not until both parts of the *Unocal* inquiry have been satisfied that the business judgment rule attaches to defensive actions of a board of directors. *Unocal*, 493 A.2d at 954.[18] As applied to the facts of this case, the question is whether the record evidence supports the Court of Chancery's conclusion that the restructuring of the Time–Warner transaction, including the adoption of several preclusive defensive measures, was a *reasonable response* in relation to a perceived threat.

Paramount argues that, assuming its tender offer posed a threat, Time's response was unreasonable in precluding Time's shareholders from accepting the tender offer or receiving a control premium in the immediately foreseeable future. Once again, the contention stems, we believe, from a fundamental misunderstanding of where the power of corporate governance lies. Delaware law confers the management of the corporate enterprise to the stockholders' duly elected board representatives. 8 Del.C. § 141(a). The fiduciary duty to manage a corporate enterprise includes the selection of a time frame for achievement of corporate goals. That duty may not be delegated to the stockholders. *Van Gorkom*, 488 A.2d at 873. Directors are not obliged to abandon a deliberately conceived corporate plan for a short-term shareholder profit unless there is clearly no basis to sustain the corporate strategy. See, e.g., *Revlon*, 506 A.2d 173.

Although the Chancellor blurred somewhat the discrete analyses required under *Unocal*, he did conclude that Time's board reasonably perceived Paramount's offer to be a significant threat to the planned Time–Warner merger and that Time's response was not "overly broad." We have found that even in light of a valid threat, management actions that are coercive in nature or force upon shareholders a management-

---

18. Some commentators have criticized *Unocal* by arguing that once the board's deliberative process has been analyzed and found not to be wanting in objectivity, good faith or deliberateness, the so-called "enhanced" business judgment rule has been satisfied and no further inquiry is undertaken. See generally Johnson and Siegel, Corporate Mergers: Redefining the Role of Target Directors, 136 U.Pa.L.Rev. 315 (1987). We reject such views.

sponsored alternative to a hostile offer may be struck down as unreasonable and nonproportionate responses. *Macmillan,* 559 A.2d 1261; *AC Acquisitions Corp.,* 519 A.2d 103.

Here, on the record facts, the Chancellor found that Time's responsive action to Paramount's tender offer was not aimed at "cramming down" on its shareholders a management-sponsored alternative, but rather had as its goal the carrying forward of a pre-existing transaction in an altered form. Thus, the response was reasonably related to the threat. The Chancellor noted that the revised agreement and its accompanying safety devices did not preclude Paramount from making an offer for the combined Time–Warner company or from changing the conditions of its offer so as not to make the offer dependent upon the nullification of the Time–Warner agreement. Thus, the response was proportionate. We affirm the Chancellor's rulings as clearly supported by the record. Finally, we note that although Time was required, as a result of Paramount's hostile offer, to incur a heavy debt to finance its acquisition of Warner, that fact alone does not render the board's decision unreasonable so long as the directors could reasonably perceive the debt load not to be so injurious to the corporation as to jeopardize its well being.

B.

Conclusion

Applying the test for grant or denial of preliminary injunctive relief, we find plaintiffs failed to establish a reasonable likelihood of ultimate success on the merits. Therefore, we affirm.

The *Time* decision triggered an avalanche of comment. Many believe *Time* endorses a "just say no" defense that allows a board of directors to ignore shareholder wealth maximization so as to pursue what the board believes are the corporation's interests. Consider the following excerpt:

> In effect, the Supreme Court holds that, as long as the "corporation's continued existence" is not being abandoned by the board, no *Revlon* duties attach. As with the Court's discussion of the "long-term/short-term" issue, we again see the emphasis on director duties to the *corporate enterprise,* rather than more narrowly to *shareholder* interests. Duty to the enterprise is paramount; only when the enterprise's configuration is to be substantially diminished do shareholder interests assume primacy.
>
> [W]hat warrants emphasis about the Supreme Court's * * * opinion is that, *absent* the limiting circumstances of *Revlon, Unocal's* focus is wholly on director duty to the continuing enterprise, not on satisfying the desires or enhancing the well-being of shareholders. The net effect * * * is to integrate *Revlon* into the larger

body of corporate law jurisprudence while, at the same time, blunting its force by treating it as a "special" case.

Lyman Johnson and David Millon, The Case Beyond *Time*, 45 Bus.Law. 2105 (1990)(emphasis in original).

Others read *Time* more narrowly.

The court appears to have been very impressed * * * with the effort Time's management had devoted to planning and negotiating the merger with Warner; with the Time outside director's determination * * * to stick to their original plan and resist the Paramount bid; and with the possibility that those directors reasonably believed Paramount, after disrupting the Time–Warner merger, would rely on the other conditions in its bid to abandon its bid and leave Time's shareholders holding the bag. Operating very much within the framework of the two-part *Unocal* test, the court was not willing to term unreasonable either the directors' belief that Paramount's offer threatened the well-being of Time and its shareholders, or the directors's decision to employ a non-coercive defense to counter that threat. In short, while *Time* may suggest that corporations have more latitude to respond to noncoercive bids than one might infer from *Revlon* and *Mills*, *Time* surely does not signify that the Delaware court has abandoned its effort to develop a principled approach that allows courts to meaningfully review corporations' responses to uninvited takeover bids.

Elliott J. Weiss, Whose Rules Should Govern Takeovers: Delaware's, The ALI's, or Martin Lipton's?, 33 Ariz.L.Rev. 761 (1991).

Note: The ALI Project

Time was decided just as the takeover boom of the 1980s seemed to run out of gas. Whether the abatement of takeover activity was due to poison pills, *Time* and state antitakeover laws, or to a combination of market and economic forces, is itself subject to considerable controversy. In any event, the ALI's Corporate Governance Project was also drawing to a close and, after considerable controversy, the ALI adopted a proposal concerning when directors can properly resist hostile takeover bids that ostensibly reflected the teachings of Delaware caselaw from *Unocal* through *Time*.

ALI, PRINCIPLES OF CORPORATE GOVERNANCE (1994)

§ 6.02. ACTION OF DIRECTORS THAT HAS THE FORESEEABLE EFFECT OF BLOCKING UNSOLICITED TENDER OFFERS

(a) The board of directors may take an action that has the foreseeable effect of blocking an unsolicited tender offer, if the action is a reasonable response to the offer.

(b) In considering whether its action is a reasonable response to the offer:

(1) the board may take into account all factors relevant to the best interests of the corporation and shareholders including, among other things, questions of legality and whether the offer, if successful, would threaten the corporation's essential economic prospects; and

(2) the board may, in addition to the analysis under § 6.02(b)(1), have regard for interests or groups (other than shareholders) with respect to which the corporation has a legitimate concern if to do so would not significantly disfavor the long-term interests of shareholders.

(c) A person who challenges an action of the board on the ground that it fails to satisfy the standards of Subsection (a) has the burden of proof that the board's action is an unreasonable response to the offer.

(d) An action that does not meet the standards of Subsection (a) may be enjoined or set aside, but directors who authorize such an action are not subject to liability for damages if their conduct meets the standard of the business judgment rule.

ELLIOTT J. WEISS, WHOSE RULES SHOULD GOVERN TAKEOVERS: DELAWARE'S, THE ALI'S, OR MARTIN LIPTON'S?
33 Ariz. L. Rev. 761, 797–800 (1991).

[The most significant provisions are Sections 6.02(b)(1), 6.02(b)(2) and 6.02(c).] At first blush, section 6.02(c) appears to be the most troublesome. This provision is flatly inconsistent with *Unocal's* requirement that directors bear the burden of proving that a defensive action was reasonable. The ALI attempts to justify this deviation by offering the circular argument that section 6.02(c) "reflects the premise that credence should be given to the determinations made by directors * * *." It makes no other effort to refute the *Unocal* court's widely-credited observation that directors should bear the burden of proving a defensive action is reasonable "[b]ecause of the omnipresent specter that a board may be acting in its own interests, rather than those of the corporation and its shareholders * * *." Neither does the ALI explain why directors' decisions to block tender offers should receive any more credence than do shareholders' decisions to sell their shares.

Concerns about this recommendation may be alleviated somewhat by the ALI's discussion of how a plaintiff can meet her burden of proof. After pointing out that non-coercive defenses which provide shareholders with alternatives, and defenses that protect shareholders from coercive partial tender offers generally should be permitted, the Comment observes:

On the other hand, where the plaintiff has made a prima facie showing that the directors' action was not in the best interests of the corporation and its shareholders, the directors who took the preclusive action are in the best position to know the facts * * * and the directors must then come forward with evidence supporting their conclusion, although the plaintiff will bear the ultimate burden of persuasion on the point.

This explanation, though not a model of clarity, suggests that a plaintiff will meet her initial burden of production by introducing evidence that a board action will foreseeably preclude shareholders from accepting a non-coercive tender offer. At that point, defendant directors will be required to produce evidence sufficient to convince the court that their action was a reasonable response to the tender offer. Because, as the Comment points out, the directors will possess most of the relevant facts, and because how the directors' action affects shareholders is not likely to be in dispute, who bears "the ultimate burden of persuasion" may not matter a great deal.

Note the conditional nature of this conclusion. Whether relieving directors of the burden of persuasion matters a great deal will depend in large part on the nature of the ultimate question a court is required to decide. If the court must compare the impact a defensive action will have to the objectively ascertainable impact of a tender offer on a corporation and its shareholders—that is, whether the price bid is fair and whether the offer is coercive—the evaluative process should be relatively straightforward, and who bears the burden of persuasion generally should not matter a great deal. But if the court must consider more subjective factors, the ALI's recommendation that plaintiffs bear the burden of persuasion becomes considerably more worrisome. The more nebulous the factors a court must evaluate, the harder it will be for a plaintiff to convince the court that the director's decision to take defensive action was unreasonable.

This shifts the focus of analysis to section 6.02(b), which authorizes directors to consider two essentially subjective factors when they respond to an uninvited tender offer—whether the offer "would threaten the corporation's essential economic prospects," and whether a defense designed to protect non-shareholder groups "would not significantly disfavor the long-term interests of shareholders." Some glimmerings as to how the ALI intends section 6.02(b) to be interpreted, not all of them reassuring, can be garnered from the Comment. It makes clear that the reference in section 6.02(b)(1) to an offer that would "threaten the corporation's essential economic prospects" is directed at offers that directors conclude would saddle their companies with too much debt. The Comment does not explain, though, why a target company's board has any legitimate reason to be concerned about the impact post-takeover debt will have on that company, at least where the offeror is prepared to purchase all the company's stock for cash. Excessive debt may lead to losses for those who lend to the offeror, but it would be more than curious for the ALI to authorize directors to sacrifice the interests of target company shareholders in order to protect an offeror's lenders. To be sure, excessive debt also may create problems for employees or other constituencies of a corporation, but section 6.02(b)(2) authorizes directors to consider the interests of those groups. Consequently, it remains unclear whether section 6.02(b)(1) is devoid of content, or whether it serves some more nefarious purpose.

One possibility, not specifically negated by the Comment, is that section 6.02(b)(1) creates a huge loophole in a provision that otherwise seems designed to restrict directors' authority to block unsolicited tender offers. Whenever a tender offer is made that relies on substantial debt financing, directors should find it easy to locate a reputable investment banker who will be prepared to opine that the debt associated with the offer will "threaten the target company's essential economic prospects." If courts were to treat such opinions as sufficient to justify preclusive defensive actions, section 6.02(b)(1) would work a major, unwelcome change in the law. Directors would then be able to block tender offers made by all but the most solvent bidders.

Since section 6.02(b)(1) clearly could be construed to allow this result, one must hope that either the ALI or the courts will reject this interpretation. One basis for doing so would be to read section 6.02(b)(2) as implicitly limiting the scope of section 6.02(b)(1).

Subsection (b)(2) authorizes directors to take account of the interests of non-shareholder constituencies, but only if so doing will not significantly disfavors shareholders' long-term economic interests. The ALI's illustrations of situations where directors properly can rely on this provision suggests its scope is limited. Directors are allowed to act where a company's charter includes the goal of maintaining a clean environment or insuring the well-being of communities in which the company operates—provisions found in the charters of few business corporations. Absent such a charter provision, directors are authorized to protect groups other than shareholders only if the economic burden on shareholders will be slight.

* * * The illustrations and section 6.02(b)(2)'s limitation * * * suggests the reporters' intent is that this new provision not make much of a change in current law.

PARAMOUNT COMMUNICATIONS INC. v. QVC NETWORK INC.

637 A.2d 34 (Del.1994).

VEASEY, C.J.

In this appeal we review an order of the Court of Chancery * * * preliminarily enjoining certain defensive measures designed to facilitate a so-called strategic alliance between Viacom Inc. ("Viacom") and Paramount Communications Inc. ("Paramount") approved by the board of directors of Paramount (the "Paramount Board" or the "Paramount directors") and to thwart an unsolicited, more valuable, tender offer by QVC Network Inc. ("QVC"). In affirming, we hold that the sale of control in this case, which is at the heart of the proposed strategic alliance, implicates enhanced judicial scrutiny of the conduct of the Paramount Board under Unocal Corp. v. Mesa Petroleum Co., Del.Supr.,

493 A.2d 946 (1985), and Revlon, Inc. v. MacAndrews & Forbes Holdings, Inc., Del.Supr., 506 A.2d 173 (1986). We further hold that the conduct of the Paramount Board was not reasonable as to process or result.

QVC and certain stockholders of Paramount commenced separate actions (later consolidated) in the Court of Chancery seeking preliminary and permanent injunctive relief against Paramount, certain members of the Paramount Board, and Viacom. This action arises out of a proposed acquisition of Paramount by Viacom through a tender offer followed by a second-step merger (the "Paramount–Viacom transaction"), and a competing unsolicited tender offer by QVC. The Court of Chancery granted a preliminary injunction. * * *

The Court of Chancery found that the Paramount directors violated their fiduciary duties by favoring the Paramount–Viacom transaction over the more valuable unsolicited offer of QVC. The Court of Chancery preliminarily enjoined Paramount and the individual defendants (the "Paramount defendants") from amending or modifying Paramount's stockholder rights agreement (the "Rights Agreement"), including the redemption of the Rights, or taking other action to facilitate the consummation of the pending tender offer by Viacom or any proposed second-step merger, including the Merger Agreement between Paramount and Viacom dated September 12, 1993 (the "Original Merger Agreement"), as amended on October 24, 1993 (the "Amended Merger Agreement"). Viacom and the Paramount defendants were enjoined from taking any action to exercise any provision of the Stock Option Agreement between Paramount and Viacom dated September 12, 1993 (the "Stock Option Agreement"), as amended on October 24, 1993. The Court of Chancery did not grant preliminary injunctive relief as to the termination fee provided for the benefit of Viacom in Section 8.05 of the Original Merger Agreement and the Amended Merger Agreement (the "Termination Fee").

Under the circumstances of this case, the pending sale of control implicated in the Paramount–Viacom transaction required the Paramount Board to act on an informed basis to secure the best value reasonably available to the stockholders. Since we agree with the Court of Chancery that the Paramount directors violated their fiduciary duties, we have AFFIRMED the entry of the order of the Vice Chancellor granting the preliminary injunction and have REMANDED these proceedings to the Court of Chancery for proceedings consistent herewith.

* * *

I. FACTS

* * *

Paramount is a Delaware corporation with its principal offices in New York City. Approximately 118 million shares of Paramount's common stock are outstanding and traded on the New York Stock

Exchange. The majority of Paramount's stock is publicly held by numerous unaffiliated investors. Paramount owns and operates a diverse group of entertainment businesses, including motion picture and television studios, book publishers, professional sports teams, and amusement parks.

There are 15 persons serving on the Paramount Board. Four directors are officer-employees of Paramount [including] Martin S. Davis ("Davis"), Paramount's Chairman and Chief Executive Officer since 1983 [and] Donald Oresman ("Oresman"), Executive Vice–President, Chief Administrative Officer, and General Counsel * * *. Paramount's 11 outside directors are distinguished and experienced business persons who are present or former senior executives of public corporations or financial institutions.

* * * Viacom is controlled by Sumner M. Redstone ("Redstone"), its Chairman and Chief Executive Officer, who owns indirectly approximately 85.2 percent of Viacom's voting Class A stock and approximately 69.2 percent of Viacom's nonvoting Class B stock through National Amusements, Inc. ("NAI"), an entity 91.7 percent owned by Redstone. Viacom has a wide range of entertainment operations, including a number of well-known cable television channels such as MTV, Nickelodeon, Showtime, and The Movie Channel. Viacom's equity co-investors in the Paramount–Viacom transaction include NYNEX Corporation and Blockbuster Entertainment Corporation.

* * * QVC has several large stockholders, including Liberty Media Corporation, Comcast Corporation, Advance Publications, Inc., and Cox Enterprises Inc. Barry Diller ("Diller"), the Chairman and Chief Executive Officer of QVC, is also a substantial stockholder. QVC sells a variety of merchandise through a televised shopping channel. QVC has several equity co-investors in its proposed combination with Paramount including BellSouth Corporation and Comcast Corporation.

Beginning in the late 1980s, Paramount investigated the possibility of acquiring or merging with other companies in the entertainment, media, or communications industry. Paramount considered such transactions to be desirable, and perhaps necessary, in order to keep pace with competitors in the rapidly evolving field of entertainment and communications. Consistent with its goal of strategic expansion, Paramount made a tender offer for Time Inc. in 1989, but was ultimately unsuccessful. See Paramount Communications, Inc. v. Time Inc., Del. Supr., 571 A.2d 1140 (1990) ("Time–Warner").

Although Paramount had considered a possible combination of Paramount and Viacom as early as 1990, * * * serious negotiations began taking place in early July [1993].

* * * After a short hiatus [because of a disagreement as to the terms of the transaction], the parties negotiated in earnest in early September, and performed due diligence with the assistance of their financial advisors, Lazard Freres & Co. ("Lazard") for Paramount and Smith Barney for Viacom. On September 9, 1993, the Paramount Board was informed about the status of the negotiations and was provided

information by Lazard, including an analysis of the proposed transaction.

On September 12, 1993, the Paramount Board met again and unanimously approved the Original Merger Agreement whereby Paramount would merge with and into Viacom. The terms of the merger provided that each share of Paramount common stock would be converted into 0.10 shares of Viacom Class A voting stock, 0.90 shares of Viacom Class–B nonvoting stock, and $9.10 in cash. In addition, the Paramount Board agreed to amend its "poison pill" Rights Agreement to exempt the proposed merger with Viacom. The Original Merger Agreement also contained several provisions designed to make it more difficult for a potential competing bid to succeed. We focus, as did the Court of Chancery, on three of these defensive provisions: a "no-shop" provision (the "No–Shop Provision"), the Termination Fee, and the Stock Option Agreement.

First, under the No–Shop Provision, the Paramount Board agreed that Paramount would not solicit, encourage, discuss, negotiate, or endorse any competing transaction unless: (a) a third party "makes an unsolicited written, bona fide proposal, which is not subject to any material contingencies relating to financing"; and (b) the Paramount Board determines that discussions or negotiations with the third party are necessary for the Paramount Board to comply with its fiduciary duties.

Second, under the Termination Fee provision, Viacom would receive a $100 million termination fee if: (a) Paramount terminated the Original Merger Agreement because of a competing transaction; (b) Paramount's stockholders did not approve the merger; or (c) the Paramount Board recommended a competing transaction.

The third and most significant deterrent device was the Stock Option Agreement, which granted to Viacom an option to purchase approximately 19.9 percent (23,699,000 shares) of Paramount's outstanding common stock at $69.14 per share if any of the triggering events for the Termination Fee occurred. In addition to the customary terms that are normally associated with a stock option, the Stock Option Agreement contained two provisions that were both unusual and highly beneficial to Viacom: (a) Viacom was permitted to pay for the shares with a senior subordinated note of questionable marketability instead of cash, thereby avoiding the need to raise the $1.6 billion purchase price (the "Note Feature"); and (b) Viacom could elect to require Paramount to pay Viacom in cash a sum equal to the difference between the purchase price and the market price of Paramount's stock (the "Put Feature"). Because the Stock Option Agreement was not "capped" to limit its maximum dollar value, it had the potential to reach (and in this case did reach) unreasonable levels.

After the execution of the Original Merger Agreement and the Stock Option Agreement on September 12, 1993, Paramount and Viacom announced their proposed merger. In a number of public statements, the parties indicated that the pending transaction was a virtual certainty. Redstone described it as a "marriage" that would "never be torn asunder" and stated that only a "nuclear attack" could break the deal. Redstone also called Diller and John Malone of Tele–Communications Inc., a major stockholder of QVC, to dissuade them from making a competing bid.

Despite these attempts to discourage a competing bid, Diller sent a letter to Davis on September 20, 1993, proposing a merger in which QVC would acquire Paramount for approximately $80 per share, consisting of 0.893 shares of QVC common stock and $30 in cash. QVC also expressed its eagerness to meet with Paramount to negotiate the details of a transaction. When the Paramount Board met on September 27, it was advised by Davis that the Original Merger Agreement prohibited Paramount from having discussions with QVC (or anyone else) unless certain conditions were satisfied. In particular, QVC had to supply evidence that its proposal was not subject to financing contingencies. The Paramount Board was also provided information from Lazard describing QVC and its proposal.

On October 5, 1993, QVC provided Paramount with evidence of QVC's financing. The Paramount Board then held another meeting on October 11, and decided to authorize management to meet with QVC. Davis also informed the Paramount Board that Booz–Allen & Hamilton, a management consulting firm, had been retained to assess, inter alia, the incremental earnings potential from a Paramount–Viacom merger and a Paramount–QVC merger. Discussions proceeded slowly, however, due to a delay in Paramount signing a confidentiality agreement. In response to Paramount's request for information, QVC provided two binders of documents to Paramount on October 20.

On October 21, 1993, QVC filed this action and publicly announced an $80 cash tender offer for 51 percent of Paramount's outstanding shares (the "QVC tender offer"). Each remaining share of Paramount common stock would be converted into 1.42857 shares of QVC common stock in a second-step merger. The tender offer was conditioned on, among other things, the invalidation of the Stock Option Agreement, which was worth over $200 million by that point. QVC contends that it had to commence a tender offer because of the slow pace of the merger discussions and the need to begin seeking clearance under federal antitrust laws.

Confronted by QVC's hostile bid, which on its face offered over $10 per share more than the consideration provided by the Original Merger Agreement, Viacom realized that it would need to raise its bid in order to remain competitive. Within hours after QVC's tender offer was announced, Viacom entered into discussions with Paramount concerning a revised transaction. These discussions led to serious negotiations concerning a comprehensive amendment to the original Paramount–Viacom transaction. In effect, the opportunity for a "new deal" with Viacom was at hand for the Paramount Board. With the QVC hostile bid offering greater value to the Paramount stockholders, the Paramount Board had considerable leverage with Viacom.

At a special meeting on October 24, 1993, the Paramount Board approved the Amended Merger Agreement and an amendment to the Stock Option Agreement. The Amended Merger Agreement was, however, essentially the same as the Original Merger Agreement, except that it included a few new provisions. One provision related to an $80 per share cash tender offer by Viacom for 51 percent of Paramount's stock, and another changed the merger consideration so that each share of Paramount would be converted into 0.20408 shares of Viacom Class A voting stock, 1.08317 shares of Viacom Class B nonvoting stock, and 0.20408 shares of a new series of Viacom convertible preferred stock. The Amended Merger Agreement also added a provision giving Paramount the right not to amend its Rights Agreement to exempt Viacom if the Paramount Board determined that such an amendment would be inconsistent with its fiduciary duties because another offer constituted a "better alternative." Finally, the Paramount Board was given the power to terminate the Amended Merger Agreement if it withdrew its recommendation of the Viacom transaction or recommended a competing transaction.

Although the Amended Merger Agreement offered more consideration to the Paramount stockholders and somewhat more flexibility to the Paramount Board than did the Original Merger Agreement, the defensive measures designed to make a competing bid more difficult were not removed or modified. In particular, there is no evidence in the record that Paramount sought to use its newly-acquired leverage to eliminate or modify the No–Shop Provision, the Termination Fee, or the Stock Option Agreement when the subject of amending the Original Merger Agreement was on the table.

Viacom's tender offer commenced on October 25, 1993, and QVC's tender offer was formally launched on October 27, 1993. Diller sent a letter to the Paramount Board on October 28 requesting an opportunity to negotiate with Paramount, and Oresman responded the following day by agreeing to meet. The meeting, held on November 1, was not very fruitful, however, after QVC's proposed guidelines for a "fair bidding process" were rejected by Paramount on the ground that "auction procedures" were inappropriate and contrary to Paramount's contractual obligations to Viacom.

On November 6, 1993, Viacom unilaterally raised its tender offer price to $85 per share in cash and offered a comparable increase in the value of the securities being proposed in the second-step merger. At a telephonic meeting held later that day, the Paramount Board agreed to recommend Viacom's higher bid to Paramount's stockholders.

QVC responded to Viacom's higher bid on November 12 by increasing its tender offer to $90 per share and by increasing the securities for its second-step merger by a similar amount. In response to QVC's latest offer, the Paramount Board scheduled a meeting for November 15, 1993.

Prior to the meeting, Oresman sent the members of the Paramount Board a document summarizing the "conditions and uncertainties" of QVC's offer. One director testified that this document gave him a very negative impression of the QVC bid.

At its meeting on November 15, 1993, the Paramount Board determined that the new QVC offer was not in the best interests of the stockholders. The purported basis for this conclusion was that QVC's bid was excessively conditional. The Paramount Board did not communicate with QVC regarding the status of the conditions because it believed that the No–Shop Provision prevented such communication in the absence of firm financing. Several Paramount directors also testified that they believed the Viacom transaction would be more advantageous to Paramount's future business prospects than a QVC transaction. Although a number of materials were distributed to the Paramount Board describing the Viacom and QVC transactions, the only quantitative analysis of the consideration to be received by the stockholders under each proposal was based on then-current market prices of the securities involved, not on the anticipated value of such securities at the time when the stockholders would receive them.[8]

The preliminary injunction hearing in this case took place on November 16, 1993. On November 19, Diller wrote to the Paramount Board to inform it that QVC had obtained financing commitments for its tender offer and that there was no antitrust obstacle to the offer. On November 24, 1993, the Court of Chancery issued its decision granting a preliminary injunction in favor of QVC and the plaintiff stockholders. This appeal followed.

II. APPLICABLE PRINCIPLES OF ESTABLISHED DELAWARE LAW

The General Corporation Law of the State of Delaware and the decisions of this Court have repeatedly recognized the fundamental principle that the management of the business and affairs of a Delaware corporation is entrusted to its directors, who are the duly elected and authorized representatives of the stockholders. Under normal circumstances, neither the courts nor the stockholders should interfere with the managerial decisions of the directors. The business judgment rule embodies the deference to which such decisions are entitled.

Nevertheless, there are rare situations which mandate that a court take a more direct and active role in overseeing the decisions made and actions taken by directors. In these situations, a court subjects the directors' conduct to enhanced scrutiny to ensure that it is reasonable. The decisions of this Court have clearly established the circumstances where such enhanced scrutiny will be applied. The case at bar implicates two such circumstances: (1) the approval of a transaction resulting in a sale of control, and (2) the adoption of defensive measures in response to a threat to corporate control.

---

8. The market prices of Viacom's and QVC's stock were poor measures of their actual values because such prices constantly fluctuated depending upon which company was perceived to be the more likely to acquire Paramount.

A. The Significance of a Sale or Change [10] of Control

When a majority of a corporation's voting shares are acquired by a single person or entity, or by a cohesive group acting together, there is a significant diminution in the voting power of those who thereby become minority stockholders. Under the statutory framework of the General Corporation Law, many of the most fundamental corporate changes can be implemented only if they are approved by a majority vote of the stockholders. Such actions include elections of directors, amendments to the certificate of incorporation, mergers, consolidations, sales of all or substantially all of the assets of the corporation, and dissolution. Because of the overriding importance of voting rights, this Court and the Court of Chancery have consistently acted to protect stockholders from unwarranted interference with such rights.

In the absence of devices protecting the minority stockholders, stockholder votes are likely to become mere formalities where there is a majority stockholder. For example, minority stockholders can be deprived of a continuing equity interest in their corporation by means of a cash-out merger. Absent effective protective provisions, minority stockholders must rely for protection solely on the fiduciary duties owed to them by the directors and the majority stockholder, since the minority stockholders have lost the power to influence corporate direction through the ballot. The acquisition of majority status and the consequent privilege of exerting the powers of majority ownership come at a price. That price is usually a control premium which recognizes not only the value of a control block of shares, but also compensates the minority stockholders for their resulting loss of voting power.

In the case before us, the public stockholders (in the aggregate) currently own a majority of Paramount's voting stock. Control of the corporation is not vested in a single person, entity, or group, but vested in the fluid aggregation of unaffiliated stockholders. In the event the Paramount–Viacom transaction is consummated, the public stockholders will receive cash and a minority equity voting position in the surviving corporation. Following such consummation, there will be a controlling stockholder who will have the voting power to: (a) elect directors; (b) cause a break-up of the corporation; (c) merge it with another company; (d) cash-out the public stockholders; (e) amend the certificate of incorporation; (f) sell all or substantially all of the corporate assets; or (g) otherwise alter materially the nature of the corporation and the public stockholders' interests. Irrespective of the present Paramount Board's vision of a long-term strategic alliance with Viacom, the proposed sale of control would provide the new controlling stockholder with the power to alter that vision.

Because of the intended sale of control, the Paramount–Viacom transaction has economic consequences of considerable significance to

---

10. For purposes of our December 9 Order and this Opinion, we have used the terms "sale of control" and "change of control" interchangeably without intending any doctrinal distinction.

the Paramount stockholders. Once control has shifted, the current Paramount stockholders will have no leverage in the future to demand another control premium. As a result, the Paramount stockholders are entitled to receive, and should receive, a control premium and/or protective devices of significant value. There being no such protective provisions in the Viacom–Paramount transaction, the Paramount directors had an obligation to take the maximum advantage of the current opportunity to realize for the stockholders the best value reasonably available.

B.   The Obligations of Directors in a Sale or Change of Control Transaction

The consequences of a sale of control impose special obligations on the directors of a corporation.[13] In particular, they have the obligation of acting reasonably to seek the transaction offering the best value reasonably available to the stockholders. The courts will apply enhanced scrutiny to ensure that the directors have acted reasonably. The obligations of the directors and the enhanced scrutiny of the courts are well-established by the decisions of this Court. The directors' fiduciary duties in a sale of control context are those which generally attach. * * *

In the sale of control context, the directors must focus on one primary objective—to secure the transaction offering the best value reasonably available for the stockholders—and they must exercise their fiduciary duties to further that end. The decisions of this Court have consistently emphasized this goal. * * *

In pursuing this objective, the directors must be especially diligent. In particular, this Court has stressed the importance of the board being adequately informed in negotiating a sale of control: "The need for adequate information is central to the enlightened evaluation of a transaction that a board must make." *Barkan,* 567 A.2d at 1287. This requirement is consistent with the general principle that "directors have a duty to inform themselves, prior to making a business decision, of all material information reasonably available to them." *Aronson,* 473 A.2d at 812. Moreover, the role of outside, independent directors becomes particularly important because of the magnitude of a sale of control transaction and the possibility, in certain cases, that management may not necessarily be impartial.

---

13. We express no opinion on any scenario except the actual facts before the Court, and our precise holding herein. Unsolicited tender offers in other contexts may be governed by different precedent. For example, where a potential sale of control by a corporation is not the consequence of a board's action, this Court has recognized the prerogative of a board of directors to resist a third party's unsolicited acquisition proposal or offer. See *Pogostin,* 480 A.2d at 627; *Time–Warner,* 571 A.2d at 1152; Bershad v. Curtiss–Wright Corp., Del.Supr., 535 A.2d 840, 845 (1987); *Macmillan,* 559 A.2d at 1285 n. 35. The decision of a board to resist such an acquisition, like all decisions of a properly-functioning board, must be informed, *Unocal,* 493 A.2d at 954–55, and the circumstances of each particular case will determine the steps that a board must take to inform itself, and what other action, if any, is required as a matter of fiduciary duty.

Barkan teaches some of the methods by which a board can fulfill its obligation to seek the best value reasonably available to the stockholders. These methods are designed to determine the existence and viability of possible alternatives. They include conducting an auction, canvassing the market, etc. Delaware law recognizes that there is "no single blueprint" that directors must follow. [567 A.2d] at 1286–87.

In determining which alternative provides the best value for the stockholders, a board of directors is not limited to considering only the amount of cash involved, and is not required to ignore totally its view of the future value of a strategic alliance. Instead, the directors should analyze the entire situation and evaluate in a disciplined manner the consideration being offered. Where stock or other non-cash consideration is involved, the board should try to quantify its value, if feasible, to achieve an objective comparison of the alternatives. In addition, the board may assess a variety of practical considerations relating to each alternative, including:

> [an offer's] fairness and feasibility; the proposed or actual financing for the offer, and the consequences of that financing; questions of illegality; * * * the risk of non-consum[m]ation; * * * the bidder's identity, prior background and other business venture experiences; and the bidder's business plans for the corporation and their effects on stockholder interests.

Macmillan, 559 A.2d at 1282 n. 29. These considerations are important because the selection of one alternative may permanently foreclose other opportunities. While the assessment of these factors may be complex, the board's goal is straightforward: Having informed themselves of all material information reasonably available, the directors must decide which alternative is most likely to offer the best value reasonably available to the stockholders.

C. Enhanced Judicial Scrutiny of a Sale or Change of Control Transaction

Board action in the circumstances presented here is subject to enhanced scrutiny. Such scrutiny is mandated by: (a) the threatened diminution of the current stockholders' voting power; (b) the fact that an asset belonging to public stockholders (a control premium) is being sold and may never be available again; and (c) the traditional concern of Delaware courts for actions which impair or impede stockholder voting rights. * * *

The key features of an enhanced scrutiny test are: (a) a judicial determination regarding the adequacy of the decisionmaking process employed by the directors, including the information on which the directors based their decision; and (b) a judicial examination of the reasonableness of the directors' action in light of the circumstances then existing. The directors have the burden of proving that they were adequately informed and acted reasonably.

Although an enhanced scrutiny test involves a review of the reasonableness of the substantive merits of a board's actions, a court should not ignore the complexity of the directors' task in a sale of control. There are many business and financial considerations implicated in investigating and selecting the best value reasonably available. The board of directors is the corporate decisionmaking body best equipped to make these judgments. Accordingly, a court applying enhanced judicial scrutiny should be deciding whether the directors made a reasonable decision, not a perfect decision. If a board selected one of several reasonable alternatives, a court should not second-guess that choice even though it might have decided otherwise or subsequent events may have cast doubt on the board's determination. Thus, courts will not substitute their business judgment for that of the directors, but will determine if the directors' decision was, on balance, within a range of reasonableness.

D.   Revlon and Time–Warner Distinguished

The Paramount defendants and Viacom assert that the fiduciary obligations and the enhanced judicial scrutiny discussed above are not implicated in this case in the absence of a "break-up" of the corporation, and that the order granting the preliminary injunction should be reversed. This argument is based on their erroneous interpretation of our decisions in *Revlon* and *Time–Warner.*

In *Revlon,* we reviewed the actions of the board of directors of Revlon, Inc. ("Revlon"), which had rebuffed the overtures of Pantry Pride, Inc. and had instead entered into an agreement with Forstmann Little & Co. ("Forstmann") providing for the acquisition of 100 percent of Revlon's outstanding stock by Forstmann and the subsequent break-up of Revlon. Based on the facts and circumstances present in Revlon, we held that "[t]he directors' role changed from defenders of the corporate bastion to auctioneers charged with getting the best price for the stockholders at a sale of the company." 506 A.2d at 182. We further held that "when a board ends an intense bidding contest on an insubstantial basis, * * * [that] action cannot withstand the enhanced scrutiny which Unocal requires of director conduct." Id. at 184.

It is true that one of the circumstances bearing on these holdings was the fact that "the break-up of the company * * * had become a reality which even the directors embraced." Id at 182. It does not follow, however, that a "break-up" must be present and "inevitable" before directors are subject to enhanced judicial scrutiny and are required to pursue a transaction that is calculated to produce the best value reasonably available to the stockholders. In fact, we stated in *Revlon* that "when bidders make relatively similar offers, or dissolution of the company becomes inevitable, the directors cannot fulfill their enhanced *Unocal* duties by playing favorites with the contending factions." Id. at 184 (emphasis added). *Revlon* thus does not hold that an inevitable dissolution or "break-up" is necessary.

The decisions of this Court following *Revlon* reinforced the applicability of enhanced scrutiny and the directors' obligation to seek the best value reasonably available for the stockholders where there is a pending sale of control, regardless of whether or not there is to be a break-up of the corporation. In *Macmillan,* this Court held:

> We stated in *Revlon,* and again here, that *in a sale of corporate control* the responsibility of the directors is to get the highest value reasonably attainable for the shareholders.

559 A.2d at 1288 (emphasis added).

Although *Macmillan* and *Barkan* are clear in holding that a change of control imposes on directors the obligation to obtain the best value reasonably available to the stockholders, the Paramount defendants have interpreted our decision in *Time–Warner* as requiring a corporate break-up in order for that obligation to apply. The facts in *Time–Warner,* however, were quite different from the facts of this case, and refute Paramount's position here. In *Time–Warner,* the Chancellor held that there was no change of control in the original stock-for-stock merger between Time and Warner because Time would be owned by a fluid aggregation of unaffiliated stockholders both before and after the merger:

> If the appropriate inquiry is whether a change in control is contemplated, the answer must be sought in the specific circumstances surrounding the transaction. Surely under some circumstances a stock for stock merger could reflect a transfer of corporate control. That would, for example, plainly be the case here if Warner were a private company. But where, as here, the shares of both constituent corporations are widely held, corporate control can be expected to remain unaffected by a stock for stock merger. This in my judgment was the situation with respect to the original merger agreement. When the specifics of that situation are reviewed, it is seen that, aside from legal technicalities and aside from arrangements thought to enhance the prospect for the ultimate succession of [Nicholas J. Nicholas, Jr., president of Time], neither corporation could be said to be acquiring the other. *Control of both remained in a large, fluid, changeable and changing market.*
>
> The existence of a control block of stock in the hands of a single shareholder or a group with loyalty to each other does have real consequences to the financial value of "minority" stock. The law offers some protection to such shares through the imposition of a fiduciary duty upon controlling shareholders. *But here, effectuation of the merger would not have subjected Time shareholders to the risks and consequences of holders of minority shares. This is a reflection of the fact that no control passed to anyone in the transaction contemplated.* The shareholders of Time would have "suffered" dilution, of course, but they would suffer the same type of dilution upon the public distribution of new stock.

Paramount Communications Inc. v. Time Inc., Del.Ch., No. 10866, Allen, C. (July 17, 1989), reprinted at 15 Del.J.Corp.L. 700, 739 (emphasis added). Moreover, the transaction actually consummated in *Time–Warner* was not a merger, as originally planned, but a sale of Warner's stock to Time.

In our affirmance of the Court of Chancery's well-reasoned decision, this Court held that "The Chancellor's findings of fact are supported by the record *and his conclusion is correct as a matter of law*." 571 A.2d at 1150 (emphasis added). Nevertheless, the Paramount defendants here have argued that a break-up is a requirement and have focused on the following language in our *Time–Warner* decision:

> However, we premise our rejection of plaintiffs' *Revlon* claim on different grounds, namely, the absence of any substantial evidence to conclude that Time's board, in negotiating with Warner, made the dissolution or break-up of the corporate entity inevitable, as was the case in *Revlon.*

> Under Delaware law there are, generally speaking and *without excluding other possibilities*, two circumstances which may implicate *Revlon* duties. The first, and clearer one, is when a corporation *initiates an active bidding process seeking to sell itself* or to effect a business reorganization involving a clear break-up of the company. However, *Revlon* duties may also be triggered where, in response to a bidder's offer, a target abandons its long-term strategy and seeks an alternative transaction involving the breakup of the company.

Id. at 1150 (emphasis added) (citation and footnote omitted).

The Paramount defendants have misread the holding of *Time–Warner*. Contrary to their argument, our decision in *Time–Warner* expressly states that the two general scenarios discussed in the above-quoted paragraph are not the *only* instances where "*Revlon* duties" may be implicated. The Paramount defendants' argument totally ignores the phrase "without excluding other possibilities." Moreover, the instant case is clearly within the first general scenarios set forth in *Time–Warner*. The Paramount Board, albeit unintentionally, had "initiate[d] an active bidding process seeking to sell itself" by agreeing to sell control of the corporation to Viacom in circumstances where another potential acquiror (QVC) was equally interested in being a bidder.

The Paramount defendants' position that *both* a change of control and a break-up are *required* must be rejected. Such a holding would unduly restrict the application of *Revlon*, is inconsistent with this Court's decisions in *Barkan* and *Macmillan*, and has no basis in policy. There are few events that have a more significant impact on the stockholders than a sale of control or a corporate break-up. Each event represents a fundamental (and perhaps irrevocable) change in the nature of the corporate enterprise from a practical standpoint. It is the significance of each of these events that justifies: (a) focusing on the directors' obligation to seek the best value reasonably available to the stockholders; and (b) requiring a close scrutiny of board action which could be contrary to the stockholders' interests.

Accordingly, when a corporation undertakes a transaction which will cause: (a) a change in corporate control; or (b) a break-up of the corporate entity, the directors' obligation is to seek the best value reasonably available to the stockholders. This obligation arises because the effect of the Viacom–Paramount transaction, if consummated, is to shift control of Paramount from the public stockholders to a controlling stockholder, Viacom. Neither *Time–Warner* nor any other decision of this Court holds that a "break-up" of the company is essential to give rise to this obligation where there is a sale of control.

III. BREACH OF FIDUCIARY DUTIES BY PARAMOUNT BOARD

We now turn to duties of the Paramount Board under the facts of this case and our conclusions as to the breaches of those duties which warrant injunctive relief.

A. *The Specific Obligations of the Paramount Board*

Under the facts of this case, the Paramount directors had the obligation: (a) to be diligent and vigilant in examining critically the Paramount–Viacom transaction and the QVC tender offers; (b) to act in good faith; (c) to obtain, and act with due care on, all material information reasonably available, including information necessary to compare the two offers to determine which of these transactions, or an alternative course of action, would provide the best value reasonably available to the stockholders; and (d) to negotiate actively and in good faith with both Viacom and QVC to that end.

Having decided to sell control of the corporation, the Paramount directors were required to evaluate critically whether or not all material aspects of the Paramount–Viacom transaction (separately and in the aggregate) were reasonable and in the best interests of the Paramount stockholders in light of current circumstances, including:. the change of control premium, the Stock Option Agreement, the Termination Fee, the coercive nature of both the Viacom and QVC tender offers, the No–Shop Provision, and the proposed disparate use of the Rights Agreement as to the Viacom and QVC tender offers, respectively.

These obligations necessarily implicated various issues, including the questions of whether or not those provisions and other aspects of the Paramount–Viacom transaction (separately and in the aggregate): (a) adversely affected the value provided to the Paramount stockholders; (b) inhibited or encouraged alternative bids; (c) were enforceable contractual obligations in light of the directors' fiduciary duties; and (d) in the end would advance or retard the Paramount directors' obligation to secure for the Paramount stockholders the best value reasonably available under the circumstances.

The Paramount defendants contend that they were precluded by certain contractual provisions, including the No–Shop Provision, from negotiating with QVC or seeking alternatives. Such provisions, whether or not they are presumptively valid in the abstract, may not validly define or limit the directors' fiduciary duties under Delaware law or prevent the Paramount directors from carrying out their fiduciary duties under Delaware law. To the extent such provisions are inconsistent with those duties, they are invalid and unenforceable.

Since the Paramount directors had already decided to sell control, they had an obligation to continue their search for the best value reasonably available to the stockholders. This continuing obligation included the responsibility, at the October 24 board meeting and thereafter, to evaluate critically both the QVC tender offers and the Paramount–Viacom transaction to determine if: (a) the QVC tender offer was, or would continue to be, conditional; (b) the QVC tender offer could be improved; (c) the Viacom tender offer or other aspects of the Paramount–Viacom transaction could be improved; (d) each of the respective offers would be reasonably likely to come to closure, and under what circumstances; (e) other material information was reasonably available for consideration by the Paramount directors; (f) there were viable and realistic alternative courses of action; and (g) the timing constraints could be managed so the directors could consider these matters carefully and deliberately.

B. The Breaches of Fiduciary Duty by the Paramount Board

The Paramount directors made the decision on September 12, 1993, that, in their judgment, a strategic merger with Viacom on the economic terms of the Original Merger Agreement was in the best interests of Paramount and its stockholders. Those terms provided a modest change of control premium to the stockholders. The directors also decided at that time that it was appropriate to agree to certain defensive measures (the Stock Option Agreement, the Termination Fee, and the No–Shop Provision) insisted upon by Viacom as part of that economic transaction. Those defensive measures, coupled with the sale of control and subsequent disparate treatment of competing bidders, implicated the judicial scrutiny of *Unocal, Revlon, Macmillan,* and their progeny. We conclude that the Paramount directors' process was not reasonable, and the result achieved for the stockholders was not reasonable under the circumstances.

When entering into the Original Merger Agreement, and thereafter, the Paramount Board clearly gave insufficient attention to the potential consequences of the defensive measures demanded by Viacom. The Stock Option Agreement had a number of unusual and potentially "draconian" provisions, including the Note Feature and the Put Feature. Furthermore, the Termination Fee, whether or not unreasonable by itself, clearly made Paramount less attractive to other bidders, when coupled with the Stock Option Agreement. Finally, the No–Shop Provision inhibited the Paramount Board's ability to negotiate with other potential bidders, particularly QVC which had already expressed an interest in Paramount.

Throughout the applicable time period, and especially from the first QVC merger proposal on September 20 through the Paramount Board meeting on November 15, QVC's interest in Paramount provided the opportunity for the Paramount Board to seek significantly higher value for the Paramount stockholders than that being offered by Viacom. QVC persistently demonstrated its intention to meet and exceed the Viacom offers, and frequently expressed its willingness to negotiate possible further increases.

The Paramount directors had the opportunity in the October 23–24 time frame, when the Original Merger Agreement was renegotiated, to take appropriate action to modify the improper defensive measures as well as to improve the economic terms of the Paramount–Viacom transaction. Under the circumstances existing at that time, it should have been clear to the Paramount Board that the Stock Option Agreement, coupled with the Termination Fee and the No–Shop Clause, were impeding the realization of the best value reasonably available to the Paramount stockholders. Nevertheless, the Paramount Board made no effort to eliminate or modify these counterproductive devices, and instead continued to cling to its vision of a strategic alliance with Viacom. Moreover, based on advice from the Paramount management, the Paramount directors considered the QVC offer to be "conditional" and asserted that they were precluded by the No–Shop Provision from seeking more information from, or negotiating with, QVC.

By November 12, 1993, the value of the revised QVC offer on its face exceeded that of the Viacom offer by over $1 billion at then current values. This significant disparity of value cannot be justified on the basis of the directors' vision of future strategy, primarily because the change of control would supplant the authority of the current Paramount Board to continue to hold and implement their strategic vision in any meaningful way. Moreover, their uninformed process had deprived their strategic vision of much of its credibility.

When the Paramount directors met on November 15 to consider QVC's increased tender offer, they remained prisoners of their own misconceptions and missed opportunities to eliminate the restrictions they had imposed on themselves. Yet, it was not "too late" to reconsider negotiating with QVC. The circumstances existing on November 15 made it clear that the defensive measures, taken as a whole, were problematic: (a) the No–Shop Provision could not define or limit their fiduciary duties; (b) the Stock Option Agreement had become "draconian"; and (c) the Termination Fee, in context with all the circumstances, was similarly deterring the realization of possibly higher bids. Nevertheless, the Paramount directors remained paralyzed by their uninformed belief that the QVC offer was "illusory." This final opportunity to negotiate on the stockholders' behalf and to fulfill their obligation to seek the best value reasonably available was thereby squandered.

IV. VIACOM'S CLAIM OF VESTED CONTRACT RIGHTS

Viacom argues that it had certain "vested" contract rights with respect to the No–Shop Provision and the Stock Option Agreement. In effect, Viacom's argument is that the Paramount directors could enter into an agreement in violation of their fiduciary duties and then render Paramount, and ultimately its stockholders, liable for failing to carry out an agreement in violation of those duties. Viacom's protestations about vested rights are without merit. This Court has found that those defensive measures were improperly designed to deter potential bidders, and that such measures do not meet the reasonableness test to which they must be subjected. They are consequently invalid and unenforceable under the facts of this case.

The No–Shop Provision could not validly define or limit the fiduciary duties of the Paramount directors. To the extent that a contract, or a provision thereof, purports to require a board to act or not act in such a fashion as to limit the exercise of fiduciary duties, it is invalid and unenforceable. Despite the arguments of Paramount and Viacom to the contrary, the Paramount directors could not contract away their fiduciary obligations. Since the No–Shop Provision was invalid, Viacom never had any vested contract rights in the provision.

As discussed previously, the Stock Option Agreement contained several "draconian" aspects, including the Note Feature and the Put Feature. While we have held that lock-up options are not per se illegal, no options with similar features have ever been upheld by this Court. Under the circumstances of this case, the Stock Option Agreement clearly is invalid. Accordingly, Viacom never had any vested contract rights in that Agreement.

Viacom, a sophisticated party with experienced legal and financial advisors, knew of (and in fact demanded) the unreasonable features of the Stock Option Agreement. It cannot be now heard to argue that it obtained vested contract rights by negotiating and obtaining contractual provisions from a board acting in violation of its fiduciary duties. As the Nebraska Supreme Court said in rejecting a similar argument in Con-Agra, Inc. v. Cargill, Inc., Neb.Supr., 382 N.W.2d 576, 587–88 (1986), "To so hold, it would seem, would be to get the shareholders coming and going." Likewise, we reject Viacom's arguments and hold that its fate must rise or fall, and in this instance fall, with the determination that the actions of the Paramount Board were invalid.

V. CONCLUSION

The realization of the best value reasonably available to the stockholders became the Paramount directors' primary obligation under these facts in light of the change of control. That obligation was not satisfied, and the Paramount Board's process was deficient. The directors' initial hope and expectation for a strategic alliance with Viacom was allowed to dominate their decisionmaking process to the point where the arsenal of defensive measures established at the outset was perpetuated (not modified or eliminated) when the situation was dramatically altered. QVC's unsolicited bid presented the opportunity for significantly greater value for the stockholders and enhanced negotiating leverage for the directors. Rather than seizing those opportunities, the Paramount directors chose to wall themselves off from material information which was reasonably available and to hide behind the defensive measures as a rationalization for refusing to negotiate with QVC or seeking other alternatives. Their view of the strategic alliance likewise became an empty rationalization as the opportunities for higher value for the stockholders continued to develop.

It is the nature of the judicial process that we decide only the case before us—a case which, on its facts, is clearly controlled by established Delaware law. Here, the proposed change of control and the implications thereof were crystal clear. In other cases they may be less clear. The holding of this case on its facts, coupled with the holdings of the principal cases discussed herein where the issue of sale of control is implicated, should provide a workable precedent against which to measure future cases.

* * *

G. CODA

ANDREW G.T. MOORE II, THE 1980s—DID WE
SAVE THE STOCKHOLDERS WHILE THE
CORPORATION BURNED?
70 Wash. Univ. L.Q. 277, 287–288 (1992).

Obviously, the [Delaware Supreme] Court played a significant role in the battles for corporate control. What is not clear, however, is the nature of that role: did the decisions of the Court feed the takeover frenzy or serve to limit it?

There is no easy answer to this question because it is necessary to understand the type of controversy that typically was before the Court. We did not approach cases with the question of whether to allow the corporation to continue in its present form or to permit someone else to acquire the company. Typically, either management or a third-party had made an offer in response to an initial offer. Thus, the question before the Court was whether the directors acted properly in accepting or rejecting the competing offers. Regardless of the Court's decision, the resulting company would be dramatically different.

Although the Court could not stop a corporation from incurring huge debts, it could try to ensure that the directors acted in the shareholders' best interests. While sale to the corporation to the highest bidder satisfied the director's fiduciary duties, the stark fact often remained that the resulting corporation was so highly leveraged that its future was questionable. As long as the directors adhered to their fiduciary duties, it would have been most inappropriate for any court to intrude upon a board's business decision. No court has a role in disciplining directors for the proper exercise of business judgment, even if it turns out to be wrong.

However, based on the nature of the transactions before us and the scope of our review, we did establish the rules by which the battles were fought.

As we consider these matters in retrospect, it is rather staggering to realize that profound changes have occurred. Now we are paying the price for what happened to companies in the 1980s—all in the name of *saving* them from bidders who could easily muster the financial resources to put virtually any company in play. There is mounting evidence that the actions of bidders and their investment bankers were not in pursuit of the pious claim of returning value to the shareholders. It appears that frequently they were the naked display of awesome financial power fueled by greed and the basest of motives.

Clearly, we are left with many unanswered and dangerous questions with heavy portent for the nineties: did the intense focus on next quarter's earnings, at the expense of meeting competition and developing and selling a product, so divert American business that it suffered a disastrous decline in world markets? * * * Did courts lend balance to an otherwise run-away situation, or, according to their critics, abandon restraint to interfere either with the operations of a free market or the proper business decisions of corporate management?

We now have time to reflect on these questions. One can only hope that, as we try to discern the solutions, those who come after us will not have to relearn either the questions or their answers.

Chapter 23

CASH OUT MERGERS

A. INTRODUCTION

The previous two chapters dealt with problems that arise when those who control a corporation decide to sell or use corporate resources or authority to protect that control. This chapter, in contrast, deals with the issues raised by transactions in which the person (or persons) who controls a corporation seeks to terminate, or *cash out*, other shareholders' equity interest in that corporation, usually by forcing those shareholders to accept cash for their stock.

At first blush, the very concept that a shareholder can be forced to sell her stock at all may seem strange. After all, a person who owns a '56 Chevy convertible or an heirloom gold watch cannot be compelled to sell it. Why should stock be different?

The answer derives from the fact that corporate stock, as much as the corporate entity itself, is a creature of state law. Its attributes are those that state law assigns to it. As we saw in Chapter 12, state corporation laws typically provide that a merger agreement approved by a majority of a corporation's shareholders is binding on all the other shareholders. Like it or not, this latter group must accept the consideration paid in the merger (unless they dissent and seek appraisal). And, in virtually every state, cash (or debt securities or stock of some other corporation) can constitute valid consideration. See, e.g., RMBCA §§ 11.01(b)(3), 11.02; DGCL § 251.

Consequently, arranging to cash out unwanted shareholders in a controlled corporation is relatively straightforward. Typically, the person (P) who controls the corporation (S) organizes a new shell corporation (Newco) into which she transfers all her S stock. Next, P causes the boards of directors of S and Newco to enter into a merger agreement providing that, upon the merger of Newco into S, all the shareholders of S will receive cash for their S stock.* P then votes all the stock of Newco in favor of the merger. She also votes her S stock in its favor

---

* The issues are substantially the same if S's non-controlling shareholders receive Newco debt or P stock in the merger rather than cash.

1266

and, if necessary, uses her control of S (generally through the proxy machinery) to obtain the support of enough shares to approve the merger. The S shareholders who are dissatisfied with the terms of the merger cannot remain as shareholders of S. Under most corporate statutes, their only option is to exercise dissenters' rights and demand payment in cash of the "fair value" of their stock.

Cash out mergers are fraught with potential for abuse. If P owns a majority of S stock, she can dictate the terms on which S's minority shareholders will be cashed out through her control of S's board of directors and her ability to vote sufficient S stock to ensure shareholder approval of the cash out merger. Unless S's non-controlling shareholders can induce a court to intervene on equitable grounds, they will be powerless to alter the terms of the merger or to retain their equity interest in S.

If P has *de facto* but not *de jure* control of S, she will need the support of other S shareholders to accomplish the cash out. But three factors limit their ability to block, other than by judicial means, cash out mergers that they believe are unfair: collective action problems, the absence of real bargaining between P and S's non-controlling shareholders, and the obstacles non-controlling shareholders would face were they to seek to oust P from control of S.

These problems are exacerbated by the fact that P usually will have a better understanding than other shareholders of S's business, the character and value of S's assets, and whether S's past performance accurately indicates its future potential. P also generally will have made or approved all of S's significant business policy decisions for many years and will be aware of how changes in those policies could affect S's earnings, cash flows, and distributions to shareholders. Finally, P often will be in a position to time a cash out so as to take advantage of shifts in interest rates, fluctuations in S's stock price, or changes in the value of S's assets.

The availability of appraisal does not significantly mitigate the potential for P's abuse, even if one assumes that non-controlling shareholders will be satisfied if they receive a higher price for their stock in an appraisal proceeding. Consider the position of the owner of 1,000 shares of S stock who receives a proposal for a cash out merger at $9 per share and who believes that her stock is worth $12. With a maximum potential gain of an additional $3,000, she is likely to be reluctant to incur the legal fees, expert witness fees, and other costs involved in pursuing her dissenters' rights. Moreover, even if most of the non-controlling shareholders of S similarly valued their stock at $12, collective action problems similar to those discussed in Chapter 14 will impede those shareholders in coordinating their efforts to pursue appraisal in an amount that might have been a significant deterrent to P when determining the initial terms of the transaction. In other words, if the fear of a substantial award in an appraisal proceeding were a cogent threat before P presented her initial offer to the minority shareholders, that offer would be higher than it will be where P knows that collective action problems will minimize the number of shareholders who actually seek appraisal. Silent, if resentful, acquiescence in the terms of the cash out seems more likely.

Despite the potential for abuse, a cash out merger is not inevitably exploitative or unfair. P may have *bona fide* reasons for such a transaction. P may believe that there will be operating efficiencies from combining P and S. P may wish to engage in concededly fair transactions with S without the threat of litigation (recall Sinclair v. Levien in Chapter 17). Or P may wish to eliminate the expense of having public shareholders, including S's compliance with the reporting requirements of the Securities Exchange Act of 1934. Finally, of course, whatever the business reasons for the cash out, P may, in fact, offer the minority shareholders a fair price for their stock.

All that said, a number of factors almost guarantee that litigation will occur in every cash out merger: the conflicts of interest and inherent potential for abuse; the very large stakes involved; and the likelihood that any attorney who successfully challenges a cash out merger will receive a substantial contingency fee. Faced with continuing litigation, courts are sensitive to the need to provide corporate planners with some degree of certainty when planning cash out mergers which, after all, are authorized by law. Consequently, when considering challenges to such mergers, courts have attempted to consider both the potential for abuse in the merger *and* the possibility that the challenge to the merger is driven more by an attorney's desire to generate a substantial fee than by truly unfair conduct.

This chapter treats the most important issues that courts have considered. These are: (1) whether a control person must have a "proper purpose" before cashing out non-controlling shareholders and, if so, what constitutes such a purpose; (2) what other remedies, if any, a court should make available to a shareholder who has a statutory right to seek appraisal of her stock; (3) are there procedures that, if followed, make it more likely the terms of a cash out merger will be fair; (4) how, in the absence of market prices, a court can best determine whether the terms of a cash out are fair; and (5) what factors a court should consider to determine the "fair value" of a cashed out shareholder's stock. Because of the complexity of the subject, these issues are necessarily interrelated. Although separated here for organizational purposes, you should appreciate that each is a part of an integrated whole.

PROBLEM
PHILLIPS CORPORATION

Phillips Corporation (Phillips) is a diversified corporation, operating a wide variety of businesses directly and through subsidiaries. Phillips manufactures construction equipment, ball bearings, machine tools and computer equipment and operates retail stores, hotels and a travel agency. Its stock is listed on the New York Stock Exchange.

Phillips owns 12 million shares of common stock of Slick, Inc. (Slick), which operates a chain of supermarkets in a ten-state region. The remaining 8 million shares of Slick's stock are owned by about 22,500 public investors and are traded in the over-the- counter market on the NASDAQ system. Slick has a nine-member board of directors. Three directors also are officers and directors of Phillips and another two are officers but not directors of Phillips. Phillips acquired its holdings in Slick over a number of years in private transactions with members of the family that founded Slick and through purchases on the open market.

The price of Slick stock has declined from the $40–45 per share range at which it was selling three years ago to about $10–12 per share now. Slick's earnings also have declined from $4.00 per share three years ago to $2.40 per share last year. Analysts have attributed the decline to the fact that many of Slick's stores have become obsolete, are too small or have been managed inefficiently. Slick's shareholders have grown increasingly restive, especially because Slick's management appears to have done little to reverse these trends.

Phillips' board of directors became greatly concerned because Phillips' rate of return on its investment in Slick was lower than its return from any of its other divisions or subsidiaries. At the board's request, Phillips management commissioned Tolliver Brothers (Tolliver), an investment banking firm with expertise in the retail food industry, to conduct a study of the alternatives available to Phillips.

Tolliver prepared a report stating that Slick probably could be sold for $15 per share, but that Slick also could be made considerably more profitable if the following steps were taken:

    A. About one-fourth of Slick's stores should be closed and the real estate sold because the real estate on which those stores sit is worth more than are the stores on an operating basis.

    B. Slick could enhance the profitability of another one-fourth of its stores by enlarging and modernizing them. The cost would be substantial, but Slick could earn in excess of 20 percent per annum on the investment it would be required to make.

    C. The remaining half of Slick's stores do not require major investments, but their performance could be improved by better management. In addition, most need new computerized equipment that would lower labor costs, provide valuable information, and link the stores to each other and to Slick's headquarters.

The total cost of the proposed program would be around $150 million. Tolliver opined that financing would be available on reasonable terms, and that in five years Slick's earnings would double. Tolliver also suggested that, if Phillips decided to go forward with the investment in Slick, it should consider cashing out Slick's minority shareholders before doing so. Tolliver estimated that, assuming Phillips caused Slick to implement the rest of its recommendations, Phillips could increase its overall return on its investment in Slick to 25 percent by buying out the minority shareholders at $18 per share, a price more than 50 percent above the current market price of Slick stock.

One month later, Phillips management submitted a report to the board in which it recommended that Phillips cash out Slick's minority shareholders at $18 per share and then make the recommended investment in, and changes at, Slick. The form of the transaction would be a merger of Slick into New Slick, a new subsidiary of Phillips. In the merger, the minority shareholders of Slick would receive $18 in cash, and New Slick would acquire all the assets and assume the liabilities of Slick. Finally New Slick would change its name to Slick. Management also reported that Tolliver was prepared to opine that $18 was a fair price for the Slick stock, in light of Slick's current market price and its book value of $17.86 per share.

The report also noted that, based on management's own studies, the proceeds from closing Slick's obsolete stores and selling the real estate probably would be greater than Tolliver had estimated. Management also estimated that if the board decided to liquidate Slick and sell its assets rather than do a cash out merger, the Slick shareholders probably would realize $20–21 per share.

After reviewing and discussing management's recommendations and the Tolliver report, a copy of which was given to all Phillips directors prior to the board meeting, the Phillips board unanimously endorsed the plan to cash out Slick's minority shareholders and take the actions recommended by Tolliver to revive Slick's business. Two days later, Doris Knight, Phillips' CEO and a director of both Phillips and Slick, presented Phillips' offer to the Slick board of directors. Knight, acting on the advice of counsel, also gave a copy of the Tolliver report to all Slick directors. She did not give them Phillips' internal report. She recommended that the Slick board appoint a committee consisting of three Slick outside directors who had no other affiliation with Phillips to review the offer and represent Slick in its dealings with Phillips. The Slick board accepted this recommendation and authorized the new Special Negotiating Committee (SNC) to retain advisors and counsel as necessary and to represent Slick in negotiating the proposed merger with Phillips.

The SNC retained Blanchard & Co., investment bankers, to help it assess Phillips' offer. After two weeks of intensive research and analysis, Blanchard submitted a report concluding that the fair value of Slick, considered as a whole, was between $500 million and $600 million, or $25 to $30 per share. The SNC then advised Phillips that it was prepared to recommend a merger of Slick and New Slick only if Slick's minority shareholders would receive $27.50 per share. Knight, on behalf of Phillips, replied that Phillips was not prepared to offer more than $18. The SNC responded that, after further consideration, it might be prepared to recommend a merger at $26 per share and suggested that, if Phillips was not prepared to pay that price, it consider soliciting bids for all Slick stock, including the stock it owned. If no bid came in above the $18 Phillips was offering, the SNC said, it would be prepared to reconsider Phillips' offer of $18 per share.

After consulting with the Phillips board, Knight responded that Phillips was not prepared to improve its bid and had no intention of selling its Slick stock. Negotiations then ended, with the SNC stating that it was not prepared to make any further concessions.

Knight has now asked your firm for advice as to how to proceed. More specifically, she has asked:

1. Does Phillips have any obligation to sell its Slick stock if some third party is prepared to offer more than the $18 per share Phillips is prepared to pay for the minority interest in Slick?

2. Can Phillips lawfully effectuate the proposed merger of New Slick and Slick at $18 per share without the consent of the members of the SNC? What risks would be involved in so proceeding?

3. Alternatively, should Phillips, by means of a tender offer or open market purchases, seek to acquire sufficient additional shares of Slick to become a more than 90% shareholder and then cash out Slick's minority shareholders in a short form merger? What risks would be involved in so proceeding?

B. FRAMING THE ISSUES

The Delaware Supreme Court's decision in Weinberger v. UOP, Inc., reproduced below, addresses most of the major issues raised by cash out mergers. To adequately appreciate *Weinberger*, though, it is helpful to know something about that decision's antecedents.

Recall Santa Fe Industries, Inc. v. Green (Chapter 18), which involved a claim by cashed out shareholders of Kirby Lumber, a Delaware corporation, that they should be allowed to recover damages from Santa Fe, Kirby's majority shareholder, under Rule 10b–5. Plaintiffs claimed that a federal remedy was necessary because Delaware law did not adequately redress their injury. Specifically, plaintiffs contended that Delaware law (1) allowed Santa Fe to cash them out for any reason whatsoever, (2) provided that appraisal was their exclusive remedy, and (3) mandated an approach to determining fair value in an appraisal proceeding (known as the "Delaware block approach") that would not provide them with the fair market value of their stock. A number of Delaware decisions, including Stauffer v. Standard Brands, Inc., 41 Del. Ch. 7, 187 A.2d 78 (Del.1962) and David J. Greene & Co. v. Schenley Industries, Inc., 281 A.2d 30 (Del.Ch.1971), seemed to support plaintiffs' characterization of Delaware law. See *Santa Fe* at n. 14.

The Second Circuit agreed that the inadequacy of Delaware's appraisal remedy, combined with Santa Fe's alleged lack of a business purpose for cashing out Kirby's minority shareholders, constituted constructive fraud and was actionable under Rule 10b–5. Green v. Santa Fe

Indus., Inc., 533 F.2d 1283, 1291 (2d Cir.1976), rev'd and remanded, 430 U.S. 462, 97 S.Ct. 1292, 51 L.Ed.2d 480 (1977). The Supreme Court reversed on the ground that some evidence of deception or manipulation was necessary to make out a claim under Rule 10b–5. But the Court never questioned plaintiffs' claim that the merger involved "mismanagement" and a "breach of fiduciary duty." 430 U.S. at 479–80, 97 S.Ct. at 1304. Rather, the Court declined "to federalize the substantial portion of the law of corporations that deals with transactions in securities," observing that while "[t]here well may be a need for uniform federal fiduciary standards to govern mergers such as that challenged in this complaint * * * those standards should not be supplied by judicial extension of section 10(b) and Rule 10b–5 * * *." Id.

Three months later, the Delaware Supreme Court handed down its decision in Singer v. Magnavox Co., 380 A.2d 969 (Del.1977), a case that it had taken under submission before *Santa Fe* was decided. North American Phillips Corporation (NAP) had acquired 84% of the stock of Magnavox through a $9 per share cash tender offer that Magnavox management had supported. NAP then sought to acquire the remaining 16% of Magnavox stock, again at $9 per share, through a cash out merger. The Singers sued to enjoin that merger, alleging that NAP's sole purpose was to cash out Magnavox's minority shareholders at a grossly inadequate price.

The Court of Chancery, relying on *Stauffer* and *Schenley*, dismissed the complaint. The Delaware Supreme Court reversed, overruling *Stauffer* and *Schenley*. It held that a merger "made for the sole purpose of freezing-out minority stockholders is an abuse of the corporate process" and that, in any event, under the rule of Sterling v. Mayflower Hotel Corp., 33 Del.Ch. 293, 93 A.2d 107 (1952), NAP, as Magnavox's majority shareholder, bore the burden of demonstrating the "entire fairness" of the proposed merger. 380 A.2d at 980.

In *Singer* and two subsequent decisions, Tanzer v. International General Industries, Inc., 379 A.2d 1121 (Del.1977), and Roland International Corp. v. Najjar, 407 A.2d 1032 (Del.1979), the Delaware Supreme Court made clear that it wanted to provide minority shareholders with enhanced protection against unfair cash out mergers. These decisions, often referred to as the "*Singer* trilogy," established that a shareholder dissatisfied with the terms of a cash out merger would avoid being relegated to her appraisal remedy if she filed a complaint alleging that the sole purpose of the cash out merger was "to eliminate minority shareholders at a grossly inadequate price." However, the *Singer* trilogy provided little guidance as to when the court would consider a cash out merger to have a proper purpose or what criteria it would use to decide if such a merger was "entirely fair." Thus, the *Singer* trilogy served largely to make it substantially more likely that any given cash out merger would become the subject of extended litigation. An aggrieved shareholder could always allege that the merger had been effectuated "solely to cash out minority shareholders at an inadequate price," since one effect of cash out mergers always is to eliminate minority shareholders. The allegation would create an issue of fact as to whether the merger had a proper purpose. It would also shift to the majority shareholder the burden of proving that the terms of the merger were "entirely fair."

More importantly, an aggrieved shareholder generally would be able to challenge the cash out merger in a class action brought on behalf of all similarly situated shareholders, including those who had not objected to the merger. Such an action would eliminate the collective action problems that often make appraisal an unattractive remedy. The potential damages theoretically would be equal to the difference between the cash out price and whatever the plaintiff could establish to be the "fair value" of all shares previously owned by non-controlling shareholders. The potential for a large damage award would make it attractive for an entrepreneurial (or opportunistic) attorney to represent aggrieved shareholders on a contingency basis. Concern about this aspect of the *Singer* trilogy—the likelihood of increased litigation and the uncertainty that would result—led one member of the Delaware Supreme Court to criticize the *Singer* trilogy for creating an "unnecessary damage forum" and to suggest that the court should have sought to make appraisal a more effective remedy. See *Najjar*, 407 A.2d at 1040, n.12 (Quillen, J., dissenting).

WEINBERGER v. UOP, INC.
457 A.2d 701 (Del.1983).

MOORE, JUSTICE.

This post-trial appeal was reheard en banc from a decision of the Court of Chancery. It was brought by the class action plaintiff below, a former shareholder of UOP, Inc., who challenged the elimination of UOP's minority shareholders by a cash-out merger between UOP and its majority owner, The Signal Companies, Inc. Originally, the defendants in this action were Signal, UOP, certain officers and directors of those companies, and UOP's investment banker, Lehman Brothers Kuhn Loeb, Inc. The present Chancellor held that the terms of the merger were fair to the plaintiff and the other minority shareholders of UOP. Accordingly, he entered judgment in favor of the defendants.

Numerous points were raised by the parties, but we address only the following questions presented by the trial court's opinion:

1) The plaintiff's duty to plead sufficient facts demonstrating the unfairness of the challenged merger;

2) The burden of proof upon the parties where the merger has been approved by the purportedly informed vote of a majority of the minority shareholders;

3) The fairness of the merger in terms of adequacy of the defendants' disclosures to the minority shareholders;

4) The fairness of the merger in terms of adequacy of the price paid for the minority shares and the remedy appropriate to that issue; and

5) The continued force and effect of Singer v. Magnavox Co., Del.Supr., 380 A.2d 969, 980 (1977), and its progeny.

In ruling for the defendants, the Chancellor re-stated his earlier conclusion that the plaintiff in a suit challenging a cash-out merger must allege specific acts of fraud, misrepresentation or other items of misconduct to demonstrate the unfairness of the merger terms to the minority. We approve this rule and affirm it.

The Chancellor also held that even though the ultimate burden of proof is on the majority shareholder to show by a preponderance of the evidence that the transaction is fair, it is first the burden of the plaintiff attacking the merger to demonstrate some basis for invoking the fairness obligation. We agree with that principle. However, where corporate action has been approved by an informed vote of a majority of the minority shareholders, we conclude that the burden entirely shifts to the plaintiff to show that the transaction was unfair to the minority. But in all this, the burden clearly remains on those relying on the vote to show that they completely disclosed all material facts relevant to the transaction.

Here, the record does not support a conclusion that the minority stockholder vote was an informed one. Material information, necessary to acquaint those shareholders with the bargaining positions of Signal and UOP, was withheld under circumstances amounting to a breach of fiduciary duty. We therefore conclude that this merger does not meet the test of fairness, at least as we address that concept, and no burden thus shifted to the plaintiff by reason of the minority shareholder vote. Accordingly, we reverse and remand for further proceedings consistent herewith.

In considering the nature of the remedy available under our law to minority shareholders in a cash-out merger, we believe that it is, and hereafter should be, an appraisal under 8 Del.C. § 262 as hereinafter construed. We therefore overrule Lynch v. Vickers Energy Corp., Del. Supr., 429 A.2d 497 (1981) (*Lynch II*) to the extent that it purports to limit a stockholder's monetary relief to a specific damage formula. But to give full effect to section 262 within the framework of the General Corporation Law we adopt a more liberal, less rigid and stylized, approach to the valuation process than has heretofore been permitted by our courts. While the present state of these proceedings does not admit the plaintiff to the appraisal remedy per se, the practical effect of the remedy we do grant him will be co-extensive with the liberalized valuation and appraisal methods we herein approve for cases coming after this decision.

Our treatment of these matters has necessarily led us to a reconsideration of the business purpose rule announced in the trilogy of Singer v. Magnavox Co., *supra;* Tanzer v. International General Industries, Inc.,

Del.Supr., 379 A.2d 1121 (1977); and Roland International Corp. v. Najjar, Del.Supr., 407 A.2d 1032 (1979). For the reasons hereafter set forth we consider that the business purpose requirement of these cases is no longer the law of Delaware.

I.

The facts found by the trial court, pertinent to the issues before us, are supported by the record, and we draw from them as set out in the Chancellor's opinion.

Signal is a diversified, technically based company operating through various subsidiaries. Its stock is publicly traded on the New York, Philadelphia and Pacific Stock Exchanges. UOP, formerly known as Universal Oil Products Company, was a diversified industrial company engaged in various lines of business, including petroleum and petro-chemical services and related products, construction, fabricated metal products, transportation equipment products, chemicals and plastics, and other products and services including land development, lumber prod-ucts and waste disposal. Its stock was publicly held and listed on the New York Stock Exchange.

In 1974 Signal sold one of its wholly-owned subsidiaries for $420,-000,000 in cash. *See* Gimbel v. Signal Companies, Inc., Del.Ch., 316 A.2d 599, aff'd, Del.Supr., 316 A.2d 619 (1974). While looking to invest this cash surplus, Signal became interested in UOP as a possible acquisi-tion. Friendly negotiations ensued, and Signal proposed to acquire a controlling interest in UOP at a price of $19 per share. UOP's represen-tatives sought $25 per share. In the arm's length bargaining that followed, an understanding was reached whereby Signal agreed to pur-chase from UOP 1,500,000 shares of UOP's authorized but unissued stock at $21 per share.

This purchase was contingent upon Signal making a successful cash tender offer for 4,300,000 publicly held shares of UOP, also at a price of $21 per share. This combined method of acquisition permitted Signal to acquire 5,800,000 shares of stock, representing 50.5% of UOP's out-standing shares. The UOP board of directors advised the company's shareholders that it had no objection to Signal's tender offer at that price. Immediately before the announcement of the tender offer, UOP's common stock had been trading on the New York Stock Exchange at a fraction under $14 per share.

The negotiations between Signal and UOP occurred during April 1975, and the resulting tender offer was greatly oversubscribed. Howev-er, Signal limited its total purchase of the tendered shares so that, when coupled with the stock bought from UOP, it had achieved its goal of becoming a 50.5% shareholder of UOP.

Although UOP's board consisted of thirteen directors, Signal nomi-nated and elected only six. Of these, five were either directors or employees of Signal. The sixth, a partner in the banking firm of Lazard Freres & Co., had been one of Signal's representatives in the negotiations and bargaining with UOP concerning the tender offer and purchase price of the UOP shares.

However, the president and chief executive officer of UOP retired during 1975, and Signal caused him to be replaced by James V. Crawford, a long-time employee and senior executive vice president of one of Signal's wholly-owned subsidiaries. Crawford succeeded his predecessor on UOP's board of directors and also was made a director of Signal.

By the end of 1977 Signal basically was unsuccessful in finding other suitable investment candidates for its excess cash, and by February 1978 considered that it had no other realistic acquisitions available to it on a friendly basis. Once again its attention turned to UOP.

The trial court found that at the instigation of certain Signal management personnel, including William W. Walkup, its board chairman, and Forrest N. Shumway, its president, a feasibility study was made concerning the possible acquisition of the balance of UOP's outstanding shares. This study was performed by two Signal officers, Charles S. Arledge, vice president (director of planning), and Andrew J. Chitiea, senior vice president (chief financial officer). Messrs. Walkup, Shumway, Arledge and Chitiea were all directors of UOP in addition to their membership on the Signal board.

Arledge and Chitiea concluded that it would be a good investment for Signal to acquire the remaining 49.5% of UOP shares at any price up to $24 each. Their report was discussed between Walkup and Shumway who, along with Arledge, Chitiea and Brewster L. Arms, internal counsel for Signal, constituted Signal's senior management. In particular, they talked about the proper price to be paid if the acquisition was pursued, purportedly keeping in mind that as UOP's majority shareholder, Signal owed a fiduciary responsibility to both its own stockholders as well as to UOP's minority. It was ultimately agreed that a meeting of Signal's Executive Committee would be called to propose that Signal acquire the remaining outstanding stock of UOP through a cash-out merger in the range of $20 to $21 per share.

The Executive Committee meeting was set for February 28, 1978. As a courtesy, UOP's president, Crawford, was invited to attend, although he was not a member of Signal's executive committee. On his arrival, and prior to the meeting, Crawford was asked to meet privately with Walkup and Shumway. He was then told of Signal's plan to acquire full ownership of UOP and was asked for his reaction to the proposed price range of $20 to $21 per share. Crawford said he thought such a price would be "generous", and that it was certainly one which should be submitted to UOP's minority shareholders for their ultimate consideration. * * *

Thus, Crawford voiced no objection to the $20 to $21 price range, nor did he suggest that Signal should consider paying more than $21 per share for the minority interests. Later, at the Executive Committee meeting the same factors were discussed, with Crawford repeating the position he earlier took with Walkup and Shumway. Also considered was the 1975 tender offer and the fact that it had been greatly oversubscribed at $21 per share. For many reasons, Signal's management concluded that the acquisition of UOP's minority shares provided the solution to a number of its business problems.

Thus, it was the consensus that a price of $20 to $21 per share would be fair to both Signal and the minority shareholders of UOP. Signal's executive committee authorized its management "to negotiate" with UOP "for a cash acquisition of the minority ownership in UOP, Inc., with the intention of presenting a proposal to [Signal's] board of directors * * * on March 6, 1978". Immediately after this February 28, 1978 meeting, Signal issued a press release stating:

> The Signal Companies, Inc. and UOP, Inc. are conducting negotiations for the acquisition for cash by Signal of the 49.5 per cent of UOP which it does not presently own, announced Forrest N. Shumway, president and chief executive officer of Signal, and James V. Crawford, UOP president.

> Price and other terms of the proposed transaction have not yet been finalized and would be subject to approval of the boards of directors of Signal and UOP, scheduled to meet early next week, the stockholders of UOP and certain federal agencies.

The announcement also referred to the fact that the closing price of UOP's common stock on that day was $14.50 per share.

Two days later, on March 2, 1978, Signal issued a second press release stating that its management would recommend a price in the range of $20 to $21 per share for UOP's 49.5% minority interest. This announcement referred to Signal's earlier statement that "negotiations" were being conducted for the acquisition of the minority shares.

Between Tuesday, February 28, 1978 and Monday, March 6, 1978, a total of four business days, Crawford spoke by telephone with all of UOP's non-Signal, i.e., outside, directors. Also during that period, Crawford retained Lehman Brothers to render a fairness opinion as to the price offered the minority for its stock. He gave two reasons for this choice. First, the time schedule between the announcement and the board meetings was short (by then only three business days) and since Lehman Brothers had been acting as UOP's investment banker for many years, Crawford felt that it would be in the best position to respond on such brief notice. Second, James W. Glanville, a long-time director of UOP and a partner in Lehman Brothers, had acted as a financial advisor to UOP for many years. Crawford believed that Glanville's familiarity with UOP, as a member of its board, would also be of assistance in enabling Lehman Brothers to render a fairness opinion within the existing time constraints.

Crawford telephoned Glanville, who gave his assurance that Lehman Brothers had no conflicts that would prevent it from accepting the task. Glanville's immediate personal reaction was that a price of $20 to $21 would certainly be fair, since it represented almost a 50% premium over

UOP's market price. Glanville sought a $250,000 fee for Lehman Brothers' services, but Crawford thought this too much. After further discussions Glanville finally agreed that Lehman Brothers would render its fairness opinion for $150,000.

During this period Crawford also had several telephone contacts with Signal officials. In only one of them, however, was the price of the shares discussed. In a conversation with Walkup, Crawford advised that as a result of his communications with UOP's non-Signal directors, it was his feeling that the price would have to be the top of the proposed range, or $21 per share, if the approval of UOP's outside directors was to be obtained. But again, he did not seek any price higher than $21.

Glanville assembled a three-man Lehman Brothers team to do the work on the fairness opinion. These persons examined relevant documents and information concerning UOP, including its annual reports and its Securities and Exchange Commission filings from 1973 through 1976, as well as its audited financial statements for 1977, its interim reports to shareholders, and its recent and historical market prices and trading volumes. In addition, on Friday, March 3, 1978, two members of the Lehman Brothers team flew to UOP's headquarters in Des Plaines, Illinois, to perform a "due diligence" visit, during the course of which they interviewed Crawford as well as UOP's general counsel, its chief financial officer, and other key executives and personnel.

As a result, the Lehman Brothers team concluded that "the price of either $20 or $21 would be a fair price for the remaining shares of UOP". They telephoned this impression to Glanville, who was spending the weekend in Vermont.

On Monday morning, March 6, 1978, Glanville and the senior member of the Lehman Brothers team flew to Des Plaines to attend the scheduled UOP directors meeting. Glanville looked over the assembled information during the flight. The two had with them the draft of a "fairness opinion letter" in which the price had been left blank. Either during or immediately prior to the directors' meeting, the two-page "fairness opinion letter" was typed in final form and the price of $21 per share was inserted.

On March 6, 1978, both the Signal and UOP boards were convened to consider the proposed merger. Telephone communications were maintained between the two meetings. Walkup, Signal's board chairman, and also a UOP director, attended UOP's meeting with Crawford in order to present Signal's position and answer any questions that UOP's non-Signal directors might have. Arledge and Chitiea, along with Signal's other designees on UOP's board, participated by conference telephone. All of UOP's outside directors attended the meeting either in person or by conference telephone.

First, Signal's board unanimously adopted a resolution authorizing Signal to propose to UOP a cash merger of $21 per share as outlined in a certain merger agreement, and other supporting documents. This proposal required that the merger be approved by a majority of UOP's outstanding minority shares voting at the stockholders meeting at which the merger would be considered, and that the minority shares voting in favor of the merger, when coupled with Signal's 50.5% interest would have to comprise at least two-thirds of all UOP shares. Otherwise the proposed merger would be deemed disapproved.

UOP's board then considered the proposal. Copies of the agreement were delivered to the directors in attendance, and other copies had been forwarded earlier to the directors participating by telephone. They also had before them UOP financial data for 1974–1977, UOP's most recent financial statements, market price information, and budget projections for 1978. In addition they had Lehman Brothers' hurriedly prepared fairness opinion letter finding the price of $21 to be fair. Glanville, the Lehman Brothers partner, and UOP director, commented on the information that had gone into preparation of the letter.

Signal also suggests that the Arledge–Chitiea feasibility study, indicating that a price of up to $24 per share would be a "good investment" for Signal, was discussed at the UOP directors' meeting. The Chancellor made no such finding, and our independent review of the record, detailed *infra*, satisfies us by a preponderance of the evidence that there was no discussion of this document at UOP's board meeting. Furthermore, it is clear beyond peradventure that nothing in that report was ever disclosed to UOP's minority shareholders prior to their approval of the merger.

After consideration of Signal's proposal, Walkup and Crawford left the meeting to permit a free and uninhibited exchange between UOP's non-Signal directors. Upon their return a resolution to accept Signal's offer was then proposed and adopted. While Signal's men on UOP's board participated in various aspects of the meeting, they abstained from voting. However, the minutes show that each of them "if voting would have voted yes".

On March 7, 1978, UOP sent a letter to its shareholders advising them of the action taken by UOP's board with respect to Signal's offer. This document pointed out, among other things, that on February 28, 1978 "both companies had announced negotiations were being conducted".

Despite the swift board action of the two companies, the merger was not submitted to UOP's shareholders until their annual meeting on May 26, 1978. In the notice of that meeting and proxy statement sent to shareholders in May, UOP's management and board urged that the merger be approved. The proxy statement also advised:

> The price was determined after *discussions* between James V. Crawford, a director of Signal and Chief Executive Officer of UOP, and officers of Signal which took place during meetings on February 28, 1978, and in the course of several subsequent telephone conversations. (Emphasis added.)

In the original draft of the proxy statement the word "negotiations" had been used rather than "discussions". However, when the Securities and Exchange Commission sought details of the "negotiations" as part of its review of these materials, the term was deleted and the word "discussions" was substituted. The proxy statement indicated that the vote of UOP's board in approving the merger had been unanimous. It also advised the shareholders that Lehman Brothers had given its opinion that the merger price of $21 per share was fair to UOP's minority. However, it did not disclose the hurried method by which this conclusion was reached.

As of the record date of UOP's annual meeting, there were 11,488,-302 shares of UOP common stock outstanding, 5,688,302 of which were owned by the minority. At the meeting only 56%, or 3,208,652, of the minority shares were voted. Of these, 2,953,812, or 51.9% of the total minority, voted for the merger, and 254,840 voted against it. When Signal's stock was added to the minority shares voting in favor, a total of 76.2% of UOP's outstanding shares approved the merger while only 2.2% opposed it.

By its terms the merger became effective on May 26, 1978, and each share of UOP's stock held by the minority was automatically converted into a right to receive $21 cash.

II.

A.

A primary issue mandating reversal is the preparation by two UOP directors, Arledge and Chitiea, of their feasibility study for the exclusive use and benefit of Signal. This document was of obvious significance to both Signal and UOP. Using UOP data, it described the advantages to Signal of ousting the minority at a price range of $21–$24 per share. Mr. Arledge, one of the authors, outlined the benefits to Signal:

Purpose of the Merger

1) Provides an outstanding investment opportunity for Signal— (Better than any recent acquisition we have seen.)

2) Increases Signal's earnings.

3) Facilitates the flow of resources between Signal and its subsidiaries—(Big factor—works both ways.)

4) Provides cost savings potential for Signal and UOP.

5) Improves the percentage of Signal's "operating earnings" as opposed to "holding company earnings."

6) Simplifies the understanding of Signal.

7) Facilitates technological exchange among Signal's subsidiaries.

8) Eliminates potential conflicts of interest.

Having written those words, solely for the use of Signal it is clear from the record that neither Arledge nor Chitiea shared this report with their fellow directors of UOP. We are satisfied that no one else did either. This conduct hardly meets the fiduciary standards applicable to such a transaction * * *

The Arledge–Chitiea report speaks for itself in supporting the Chancellor's finding that a price of up to $24 was a "good investment" for Signal. It shows that a return on the investment at $21 would be 15.7% versus 15.5% at $24 per share. This was a difference of only two-tenths of one percent, while it meant over $17,000,000 to the minority. Under such circumstances, paying UOP's minority shareholders $24 would have had relatively little long-term effect on Signal, and the Chancellor's findings concerning the benefit to Signal, even at a price of $24, were obviously correct.

Certainly, this was a matter of material significance to UOP and its shareholders. Since the study was prepared by two UOP directors, using UOP information for the exclusive benefit of Signal, and nothing whatever was done to disclose it to the outside UOP directors or the minority shareholders, a question of breach of fiduciary duty arises. This problem occurs because there were common Signal–UOP directors participating, at least to some extent, in the UOP board's decision-making processes without full disclosure of the conflicts they faced.[7]

B.

In assessing this situation, the Court of Chancery was required to:

examine what information defendants had and to measure it against what they gave to the minority stockholders, in a context in which "complete candor' is required. In other words, the limited function of the Court was to determine whether defendants had disclosed all information in their possession germane to the transaction in issue. And by "germane' we mean, for present purposes, information such as a reasonable shareholder would consider important in deciding whether to sell or retain stock.

* * *

* * * Completeness, not adequacy, is both the norm and the mandate under present circumstances.

Lynch v. Vickers Energy Corp., Del.Supr., 383 A.2d 278, 281 (1977) (*Lynch I*). This is merely stating in another way the long-existing

---

7. Although perfection is not possible, or expected, the result here could have been entirely different if UOP had appointed an independent negotiating committee of its outside directors to deal with Signal at arm's length. *See, e.g.,* Harriman v. E.I. duPont de-Nemours & Co., 411 F.Supp. 133 (D.Del.1975). Since fairness in this context can be equated to conduct by a theoretical, wholly independent, board of directors acting upon the matter before them, it is unfortunate that this course apparently was neither considered nor pursued. Johnston v. Greene, Del.Supr., 121 A.2d 919, 925 (1956). Particularly in a parent-subsidiary context, a showing that the action taken was as though each of the contending parties had in fact exerted its bargaining power against the other at arm's length is strong evidence that the transaction meets the test of fairness. Getty Oil Co. v. Skelly Oil Co., Del.Supr., 267 A.2d 883, 886 (1970); Puma v. Marriott, Del.Ch., 283 A.2d 693, 696 (1971).

principle of Delaware law that these Signal designated directors on UOP's board still owed UOP and its shareholders an uncompromising duty of loyalty. * * *

Given the absence of any attempt to structure this transaction on an arm's length basis, Signal cannot escape the effects of the conflicts it faced, particularly when its designees on UOP's board did not totally abstain from participation in the matter. There is no "safe harbor" for such divided loyalties in Delaware. When directors of a Delaware corporation are on both sides of a transaction, they are required to demonstrate their utmost good faith and the most scrupulous inherent fairness of the bargain. Gottlieb v. Heyden Chemical Corp., Del.Supr., 91 A.2d 57, 57–58 (1952). The requirement of fairness is unflinching in its demand that where one stands on both sides of a transaction, he has the burden of establishing its entire fairness, sufficient to pass the test of careful scrutiny by the courts.

There is no dilution of this obligation where one holds dual or multiple directorships, as in a parent-subsidiary context. Levien v. Sinclair Oil Corp., Del.Ch., 261 A.2d 911, 915 (1969). Thus, individuals who act in a dual capacity as directors of two corporations, one of whom is parent and the other subsidiary, owe the same duty of good management to both corporations, and in the absence of an independent negotiating structure (see note 7, *supra*), or the directors' total abstention from any participation in the matter, this duty is to be exercised in light of what is best for both companies. The record demonstrates that Signal has not met this obligation.

C.

The concept of fairness has two basic aspects: fair dealing and fair price. The former embraces questions of when the transaction was timed, how it was initiated, structured, negotiated, disclosed to the directors, and how the approvals of the directors and the stockholders were obtained. The latter aspect of fairness relates to the economic and financial considerations of the proposed merger, including all relevant factors: assets, market value, earnings, future prospects, and any other elements that affect the intrinsic or inherent value of a company's stock. However, the test for fairness is not a bifurcated one as between fair dealing and price. All aspects of the issue must be examined as a whole since the question is one of entire fairness. However, in a non-fraudulent transaction we recognize that price may be the preponderant consideration outweighing other features of the merger. Here, we address the two basic aspects of fairness separately because we find reversible error as to both.

D.

Part of fair dealing is the obvious duty of candor required by *Lynch I, supra*. Moreover, one possessing superior knowledge may not mislead any stockholder by use of corporate information to which the latter is not privy. Delaware has long imposed this duty even upon persons who are not corporate officers or directors, but who nonetheless are privy to matters of interest or significance to their company. Brophy v. Cities Service Co., Del.Ch., 70 A.2d 5, 7 (1949). With the well-established Delaware law on the subject, and the Court of Chancery's findings of fact here, it is inevitable that the obvious conflicts posed by Arledge and Chitiea's preparation of their "feasibility study", derived from UOP information, for the sole use and benefit of Signal, cannot pass muster.

The Arledge–Chitiea report is but one aspect of the element of fair dealing. How did this merger evolve? It is clear that it was entirely initiated by Signal. The serious time constraints under which the principals acted were all set by Signal. It had not found a suitable outlet for its excess cash and considered UOP a desirable investment, particularly since it was now in a position to acquire the whole company for itself. For whatever reasons, and they were only Signal's, the entire transaction was presented to and approved by UOP's board within four business days. Standing alone, this is not necessarily indicative of any lack of fairness by a majority shareholder. It was what occurred, or more properly, what did not occur, during this brief period that makes the time constraints imposed by Signal relevant to the issue of fairness.

The structure of the transaction, again, was Signal's doing. So far as negotiations were concerned, it is clear that they were modest at best. Crawford, Signal's man at UOP, never really talked price with Signal, except to accede to its management's statements on the subject, and to convey to Signal the UOP outside directors' view that as between the $20–$21 range under consideration, it would have to be $21. The latter is not a surprising outcome, but hardly arm's length negotiations. Only the protection of benefits for UOP's key employees and the issue of Lehman Brothers' fee approached any concept of bargaining.

As we have noted, the matter of disclosure to the UOP directors was wholly flawed by the conflicts of interest raised by the Arledge–Chitiea report. All of those conflicts were resolved by Signal in its own favor without divulging any aspect of them to UOP.

This cannot but undermine a conclusion that this merger meets any reasonable test of fairness. The outside UOP directors lacked one material piece of information generated by two of their colleagues, but shared only with Signal. True, the UOP board had the Lehman Brothers' fairness opinion, but that firm has been blamed by the plaintiff for the hurried task it performed, when more properly the responsibility for this lies with Signal. There was no disclosure of the circumstances surrounding the rather cursory preparation of the Lehman Brothers' fairness opinion. Instead, the impression was given UOP's minority that a careful study had been made, when in fact speed was the hallmark, and Mr. Glanville, Lehman's partner in charge of the matter, and also a UOP director, having spent the weekend in Vermont, brought a draft of the "fairness opinion letter" to the UOP directors' meeting on March 6, 1978 with the price left blank. We can only conclude from the record that the rush imposed on Lehman Brothers by Signal's timetable contributed to the difficulties under which this investment banking firm attempted to perform its responsibilities. Yet, none of this was disclosed to UOP's minority.

Finally, the minority stockholders were denied the critical information that Signal considered a price of $24 to be a good investment. Since this would have meant over $17,000,000 more to the minority, we cannot conclude that the shareholder vote was an informed one. Under the circumstances, an approval by a majority of the minority was meaningless. Lynch I, 383 A.2d at 279, 281.

Given these particulars and the Delaware law on the subject, the record does not establish that this transaction satisfies any reasonable concept of fair dealing, and the Chancellor's findings in that regard must be reversed.

E.

Turning to the matter of price, plaintiff also challenges its fairness. His evidence was that on the date the merger was approved the stock was worth at least $26 per share. In support, he offered the testimony of a chartered investment analyst who used two basic approaches to valuation: a comparative analysis of the premium paid over market in ten other tender offer-merger combinations, and a discounted cash flow analysis.

In this breach of fiduciary duty case, the Chancellor perceived that the approach to valuation was the same as that in an appraisal proceeding. Consistent with precedent, he rejected plaintiff's method of proof and accepted defendants' evidence of value as being in accord with practice under prior case law. This means that the so-called "Delaware block" or weighted average method was employed wherein the elements of value, i.e., assets, market price, earnings, etc., were assigned a particular weight and the resulting amounts added to determine the value per share. This procedure has been in use for decades. However, to the extent it excludes other generally accepted techniques used in the financial community and the courts, it is now clearly outmoded. It is time we recognize this in appraisal and other stock valuation proceedings and bring our law current on the subject.

While the Chancellor rejected plaintiff's discounted cash flow method of valuing UOP's stock, as not corresponding with "either logic or the existing law" (426 A.2d at 1360), it is significant that this was essentially the focus, i.e., earnings potential of UOP, of Messrs. Arledge and Chitiea in their evaluation of the merger. Accordingly, the standard "Delaware block" or weighted average method of valuation, formerly employed in appraisal and other stock valuation cases, shall no longer exclusively control such proceedings. We believe that a more liberal approach must include proof of value by any techniques or methods which are generally considered acceptable in the financial community and otherwise admissible in court, subject only to our interpretation of 8 Del.C. § 262(h), *infra.* This will obviate the very structured and mechanistic procedure that has heretofore governed such matters. *See* Tri–Continental Corp. v. Battye, Del.Ch., 66 A.2d 910, 917–18 (1949).

Fair price obviously requires consideration of all relevant factors involving the value of a company. This has long been the law of Delaware as stated in *Tri–Continental Corp.,* 74 A.2d at 72:

> The basic concept of value under the appraisal statute is that the stockholder is entitled to be paid for that which has been taken from him, viz., his proportionate interest in a going concern. By value of the stockholder's proportionate interest in the corporate enterprise is meant the true or intrinsic value of his stock which has been taken by the merger. In determining what figure represents this true or intrinsic value, the appraiser and the courts must take into consideration all factors and elements which reasonably might enter into the fixing of value. Thus, market value, asset value, dividends, earning prospects, the nature of the enterprise and any other facts which were known or which could be ascertained as of the date of merger and which throw any light on *future prospects* of the merged corporation are not only pertinent to an inquiry as to the value of the dissenting stockholders' interest, but *must be considered* by the agency fixing the value. (Emphasis added.)

* * *

It is significant that section 262 now mandates the determination of "fair" value based upon "all relevant factors". Only the speculative elements of value that may arise from the "accomplishment or expectation" of the merger are excluded. We take this to be a very narrow exception to the appraisal process, designed to eliminate use of *pro forma* data and projections of a speculative variety relating to the completion of a merger. But elements of future value, including the nature of the enterprise, which are known or susceptible of proof as of the date of the merger and not the product of speculation, may be considered. When the trial court deems it appropriate, fair value also includes any damages, resulting from the taking, which the stockholders sustain as a class. If that was not the case, then the obligation to consider "all relevant factors" in the valuation process would be eroded. We are supported in this view not only by *Tri–Continental Corp.,* 74 A.2d at 72, but also by the evolutionary amendments to section 262.

* * *

Although the Chancellor received the plaintiff's evidence, his opinion indicates that the use of it was precluded because of past Delaware practice. While we do not suggest a monetary result one way or the other, we do think the plaintiff's evidence should be part of the factual mix and weighed as such. Until the $21 price is measured on remand by the valuation standards mandated by Delaware law, there can be no finding at the present stage of these proceedings that the price is fair.

Given the lack of any candid disclosure of the material facts surrounding establishment of the $21 price, the majority of the minority vote, approving the merger, is meaningless.

The plaintiff has not sought an appraisal, but rescissory damages of the type contemplated by Lynch v. Vickers Energy Corp., Del.Supr., 429 A.2d 497, 505–06 (1981) (*Lynch II*). In view of the approach to valuation that we announce today, we see no basis in our law for *Lynch II* 's exclusive monetary formula for relief. On remand the plaintiff will be permitted to test the fairness of the $21 price by the standards we herein establish, in conformity with the principle applicable to an appraisal—that fair value be determined by taking "into account all relevant factors" [*see* 8 *Del.C.* § 262(h), *supra*]. In our view this includes the elements of rescissory damages if the Chancellor considers them susceptible of proof and a remedy appropriate to all the issues of fairness before him. To the extent that *Lynch II, 429 A.2d at 505–06,* purports to limit the Chancellor's discretion to a single remedial formula for monetary damages in a cash-out merger, it is overruled.

While a plaintiff's monetary remedy ordinarily should be confined to the more liberalized appraisal proceeding herein established, we do not intend any limitation on the historic powers of the Chancellor to grant such other relief as the facts of a particular case may dictate. The appraisal remedy we approve may not be adequate in certain cases, particularly where fraud, misrepresentation, self-dealing, deliberate waste of corporate assets, or gross and palpable overreaching are involved. Under such circumstances, the Chancellor's powers are complete to fashion any form of equitable and monetary relief as may be appropriate, including rescissory damages. Since it is apparent that this long completed transaction is too involved to undo, and in view of the Chancellor's discretion, the award, if any, should be in the form of monetary damages based upon entire fairness standards, i.e., fair dealing and fair price.

Obviously, there are other litigants, like the plaintiff, who abjured an appraisal and whose rights to challenge the element of fair value must be preserved. Accordingly, the quasi-appraisal remedy we grant the plaintiff here will apply only to: (1) this case; (2) any case now pending on appeal to this Court; (3) any case now pending in the Court of Chancery which has not yet been appealed but which may be eligible for direct appeal to this Court; (4) any case challenging a cash-out merger, the effective date of which is on or before February 1, 1983; and (5) any proposed merger to be presented at a shareholders' meeting, the notification of which is mailed to the stockholders on or before February 23, 1983. Thereafter, the provisions of 8 Del.C. § 262, as herein construed, respecting the scope of an appraisal and the means for perfecting the same, shall govern the financial remedy available to minority shareholders in a cash-out merger. Thus, we return to the well established principles of Stauffer v. Standard Brands, Inc., Del.Supr., 187 A.2d 78 (1962) and David J. Greene & Co. v. Schenley Industries,

Inc., Del.Ch., 281 A.2d 30 (1971), mandating a stockholder's recourse to the basic remedy of an appraisal.

III.

Finally, we address the matter of business purpose. The defendants contend that the purpose of this merger was not a proper subject of inquiry by the trial court. The plaintiff says that no valid purpose existed—the entire transaction was a mere subterfuge designed to eliminate the minority. The Chancellor ruled otherwise, but in so doing he clearly circumscribed the thrust and effect of *Singer*. Weinberger v. UOP, 426 A.2d at 1342–43, 1348–50. This has led to the thoroughly sound observation that the business purpose test "may be * * * virtually interpreted out of existence, as it was in *Weinberger*." [9]

The requirement of a business purpose is new to our law of mergers and was a departure from prior case law. See Stauffer v. Standard Brands, Inc., *supra;* David J. Greene & Co. v. Schenley Industries, Inc., *supra.*

In view of the fairness test which has long been applicable to parent-subsidiary mergers, Sterling v. Mayflower Hotel Corp., Del.Supr., 93 A.2d 107, 109–10 (1952), the expanded appraisal remedy now available to shareholders, and the broad discretion of the Chancellor to fashion such relief as the facts of a given case may dictate, we do not believe that any additional meaningful protection is afforded minority shareholders by the business purpose requirement of the trilogy of *Singer, Tanzer, Najjar,* and their progeny. Accordingly, such requirement shall no longer be of any force or effect.

The judgment of the Court of Chancery, finding both the circumstances of the merger and the price paid the minority shareholders to be fair, is reversed. The matter is remanded for further proceedings consistent herewith. Upon remand the plaintiff's post-trial motion to enlarge the class should be granted.

* * *

Reversed and remanded.

On remand, the Court of Chancery seemed unimpressed with the Delaware Supreme Court's finding that Signal had dealt unfairly with the UOP minority shareholders. Weinberger v. UOP, Inc., 1985 WL 11546 (Del.Ch.1985). It interpreted the Supreme Court's holding as equating "to a finding that Signal was guilty of a misrepresentation," even though the court did not believe that Signal had committed deliberate fraud. Chancellor Brown stated that he felt free to make a

9. Weiss, The Law of Take Out Mergers: A Historical Perspective, 56 N.Y.U.L.Rev. 624, 671, n. 300 (1981).

damage award without reference to "the results of an appraisal of the value of a share of UOP stock either at the merger date or at some other date." Accordingly, he awarded $1 per share together with interest from the date of the Supreme Court's opinion. He declined to award rescissory damages because of the speculative nature of the offered proof.

Note: Other Approaches

Weinberger left unresolved important details concerning what constitutes fair dealing, how fair price should be determined, and when collateral attacks on cash out mergers will be allowed, but set forth a basic approach to regulating cash out mergers that many other courts have embraced. Nevertheless, a few of those courts have continued to require that cash out mergers have a proper purpose.

Alpert v. 28 William St. Corp., 63 N.Y.2d 557, 483 N.Y.S.2d 667, 473 N.E.2d 19 (1984), involved a cash out of minority shareholders in a corporation that owned a valuable building. After affirming that the merger was the product of fair dealing and involved a fair price, the court added:

> Fair dealing and fair price alone will not render the merger acceptable. As mentioned, there exists a fiduciary duty to treat all shareholders equally. * * * The fact remains, however, that in a freeze-out merger the minority shareholders are being treated in a different manner: the majority is permitted continued participation in the equity of the surviving corporation while the minority has no choice but to surrender their shares for cash. On its face, the majority's conduct would appear to breach this fiduciary obligation.
>
> * * *
>
> In the context of a freeze-out merger, variant treatment of the minority shareholders—i.e., causing their removal—will be justified when related to the advancement of a general corporate interest. The benefit need not be great, but it must be for the corporation. For example, if the sole purpose of the merger is reduction of the number of profit sharers—in contrast to increasing the corporation's capital or profits, or improving its management structure—there will exist no "independent corporate interest." * * * What distinguishes a proper corporate purpose from an improper one is that, with the former, removal of the minority shareholders furthers the objective of conferring some general gain upon the corporation. Only then will the fiduciary duty of good and prudent management of the corporation serve to override the concurrent duty to treat all shareholders fairly. * * *
>
> * * *
>
> Without passing on all of the business purposes cited by Supreme Court as underlying the merger, it is sufficient to note that at least one justified the exclusion of plaintiffs' interests: attracting additional capital to effect needed repairs of the building. There is proof that there was a good-faith belief that additional, outside capital was required. Moreover, this record supports the conclusion

that this capital would not have been available through the merger had not plaintiffs' interest in the corporation been eliminated. Id., at 676–77, 473 N.E.2d at 27–29.

Similarly, in Coggins v. New England Patriots Football Club, 397 Mass. 525, 492 N.E.2d 1112 (1986), the court held that, "[u]nlike the [*Weinberger*] court, * * * we believe that the 'business-purpose' test is an additional useful means under our statutes and case law for examining a transaction in which a controlling stockholder eliminates the minority interest in a corporation." 492 N.E.2d at 1117. The court then affirmed a trial court ruling that it was not proper for a controlling shareholder to effectuate a cash out merger solely to gain access to the corporation's assets for the purpose of repaying personal debts that he had incurred to finance his purchase of control. Id. at 1119.

The SEC advanced a disclosure-based approach to regulating certain cash out mergers by adopting Rule 13e–3, which applies to "going private transactions." See Rule 13e–3(a)(3). The person effectuating such a transaction must file with the SEC and distribute to shareholders a Schedule 13E that discusses, *inter alia,* the purpose and fairness of the cash out. More specifically, Item 7 of Schedule 13E requires that person to state the purpose of the transaction, to describe briefly any alternative means to accomplish that purpose that she considered, to explain why she rejected those alternatives, and to explain her reasons for structuring the transaction as a cash out. Item 8 of Schedule 13E requires that person to state whether she believes the terms of the merger are reasonably fair to the shareholders who will be cashed out and to discuss "in reasonable detail the material factors upon which the belief * * * is based, and, to the extent practicable, the weight assigned to each factor" in a list of valuation factors.

In Howing v. Nationwide Corp., 826 F.2d 1470 (6th Cir.1987) ("Howing I"), the Sixth Circuit held that a cashed out shareholder could maintain an implied private action for damages under § 13(e) of the 1934 Act and Rule 13e–3. The court also held that Rule 13e–3 requires a "reasonably detailed analysis of the various financial valuation methods discussed by the Rule and the weights attached thereto." Id. at 1479. In Howing v. Nationwide Corp., 927 F.2d 263 (6th Cir.1991) ("Howing II"), the court further held that the instructions to Item 8 of Schedule 13E create a presumption that a reasonable investor would consider a discussion of book, going concern and liquidation value to be important and, consequently, that any proxy statement that omits such information will be presumed to be materially misleading. The Supreme Court granted certiorari, but subsequently vacated Howing II and remanded for reconsideration in light of its intervening decision in Virginia Bankshares, Inc. v. Sandberg (Chapter 18). The Sixth Circuit interpreted *Sandberg* to allow a plaintiff to establish causation in an action under Rule 13e–3 by proving that a defendant's misleading disclosures had caused her to lose a state law remedy. Howing v. Nationwide Corp., 972 F.2d 700 (6th Cir.1992), cert. denied ___ U.S. ___, 113 S.Ct. 1645, 123

L.Ed.2d 266 (1993). Plaintiffs had lost their right to seek appraisal under Ohio law, which led the court to remand the case for trial on the merits.

C. EXCLUSIVITY OF APPRAISAL

In *Weinberger*, the court stated that although appraisal was to be considered the exclusive remedy for a dissenting shareholder, it might "not be adequate * * * where fraud, misrepresentation, self-dealing, deliberate waste of corporate assets, or gross and palpable overreaching are involved." In such a case, equitable relief or monetary damages would be appropriate. States are similarly divided as to whether appraisal is the exclusive remedy available to a shareholder dissatisfied with a cash out merger or any other transaction that gives rise to dissenters' rights. Yanow v. Teal Industries, Inc., 178 Conn. 262, 274–80, 422 A.2d 311, 317–18 (1979) interpreted Conn.Gen.Stat. § 33–373(f) as making appraisal exclusive. In re Jones & Laughlin Steel Corp., 488 Pa. 524, 530–31, 412 A.2d 1099, 1102–03 (1980) gave a similar reading to Pa.Bus.Corp.L. § 1515(K), but added that an aggrieved shareholder also could seek to enjoin a transaction fraught with "fraud or fundamental unfairness." On the other hand, some statutes explicitly allow shareholders to challenge a merger if it involves self-dealing and is unfair, see, e.g., Maine Bus. Corp. Act § 909(13); South Carolina Corporations, Partnerships and Associations § 33–11–270(k), and some courts have held that a shareholder entitled to seek appraisal nonetheless can maintain a collateral attack on an unfair transaction. See Vorenberg, Exclusiveness of the Dissenting Stockholder's Appraisal Right, 77 Harv. L.Rev. 1189 (1964).

California Corp.Code § 1312 makes appraisal the exclusive remedy unless: (1) the plaintiff alleges that the required number of shareholders did not vote to approve the challenged transaction or (2) the parties to that transaction were affiliated with each other (as is the case in a cash out merger). In Steinberg v. Amplica, Inc., 42 Cal.3d 1198, 233 Cal. Rptr. 249, 729 P.2d 683 (1986), a divided court held that appraisal was the exclusive remedy available to minority shareholders who claimed that their shares were undervalued in a merger that did not fall within the statutory exception. Analyzing the history of the merger and appraisal provisions of California corporation law, the court pointed out that one important benefit of the exclusivity provision was that it precluded obstructive "strike suits" by opportunistic minority shareholders.

Ohio's courts have adopted an approach that places even greater emphasis on certainty and predictability. Armstrong v. Marathon Oil Co., 32 Ohio St.3d 397, 513 N.E.2d 776 (1987), involved an appraisal proceeding brought by former shareholders of Marathon, which U.S. Steel had acquired in a two-tier takeover bid that Marathon's board had supported. U.S. Steel first acquired 51% of Marathon's stock by means of a $125 per share cash tender offer. Then U.S. Steel effected a second-step merger in which it exchanged a bond with a projected market value of $88 for each Marathon share that had not been accepted in the tender offer. The dissenting Marathon shareholders claimed they were entitled to considerably more—at least the "blended value" of U.S. Steel's offer, or roughly $106 per share, and preferably a much higher price that reflected the estimated market value of Marathon's huge oil reserves.

The court held that where a corporation's stock was actively traded prior to a merger, the benchmark for determining the "fair cash value" of that stock—the term used in Ohio's appraisal statute—is the price at which the stock traded on the day before the merger. The court explained:

> By utilizing the stock market price as the beginning point of analysis in cases such as those before us now, a great many advantages will result to shareholders and corporations alike. One obvious benefit is that the scope of analysis is fairly narrowed such that the parties may, to a reasonable degree, predict the outcome of the proceedings. Pre-appraisal settlement then becomes the better alternative to litigation. The harassment potential inherent within an appraisal remedy as well as vexatious lawsuits (by those whose real goal is simply to receive more money for their stock) will, under the within clarified standard, become much more unlikely. Further, costs to all shareholders will be ultimately reduced by this more straightforward proceeding.

> The dissenting shareholder will bear fewer costs to exercise his legal rights since the scope of discovery and concomitant courtroom presentations will be lessened. Also, the costs to the majority shareholders will decrease since less corporate funds will go toward participation in the appraisal proceeding. Finally, a less complicated valuation proceeding will advance the goal of streamlining corporate reorganizations and, at the same time, protect the liquidity and value of the dissenting shareholder's stock.

Id. at 409–10, 513 N.E.2d at 787–88.

The court further held that Ohio law required that the pre-merger market price of a company's stock be adjusted to eliminate the effects of a pending merger. Dissenting shareholders would not be entitled to any increase in value attributable to the pendency of the merger or any tender offer that has preceded it. Rather, if the pendency of the merger had caused the price of the company's stock to increase, a reduction from the pre-merger market price would be appropriate. Following this approach on remand, the trial court adjusted the pre-merger price of Marathon's stock, $75.75 per share, downward and found that its pre-merger "fair cash value" was $68.43 per share. See Armstrong v. Marathon Oil Co., 66 Ohio App.3d 127, 583 N.E.2d 462 (1990).

Stepak v. Schey, 51 Ohio St.3d 8, 553 N.E.2d 1072 (1990) involved the question of when a shareholder can maintain a class action challenging a cash out merger as unfair because it allegedly involved self-dealing. A former shareholder of Scott & Fetzer charged that company's directors with having agreed to a cash out merger with Berkshire Hathaway Inc., at a price lower than other bidders might have been prepared to pay, in exchange for Berkshire Hathaway's agreement to allow those directors to receive $30 million in "golden parachute" payments. A three-judge plurality of the Ohio Supreme Court held that the plaintiff could not maintain this action because his objection to the merger essentially related to the price he had received for his stock. Citing *Armstrong*, the plurality continued: "The obvious benefit of this approach is that it makes more unlikely vexatious lawsuits by those whose goal is simply to receive more money for their stock." Id. at 11, 553 N.E.2d at 1075. Two other justices concurred, reasoning that in the interest of promoting certainty and eliminating unnecessary litigation, a suit for breach of fiduciary duty of the kind alleged in the case should be allowed only if it was filed prior to the consummation of the merger. Id. at 11–16, 553 N.E.2d at 1075–79.

Two justices dissented, arguing that the majority's decision confronted the minority shareholders with a Catch–22 situation:

> If corporate management engages in a bid-rigging scheme which deprives shareholders of a premium over market price, a complaint cannot be made without challenging the price paid for the stock. But, dissatisfaction with the price paid does not automatically convert the action to a simple demand for the 'fair cash value' of a stockholder's shares. Here, the complaint clearly charges that the directors failed in their duty to obtain the best price possible for the sale of shares.
>
> * * * Had plaintiff pursued his action via appraisal, he would not have received any premium over market price. Armstrong v. Marathon Oil Co. (1987), 32 Ohio St.3d 397, 410, 513 N.E.2d 776, 788. Where the opportunity to obtain a premium price for sale of shares is destroyed by self-dealing officers of a corporation, there should be a remedy. Unfortunately, the majority's holding eliminates the possibility of remedy for that wrong.

Id. at 16–17, 553 N.E.2d at 1079–80.

RMBCA § 13.02(b) essentially adopts *Weinberger*'s approach. It provides that appraisal is a dissenting shareholder's exclusive remedy "unless the action [giving rise to dissenters' rights] is unlawful or fraudulent with respect to the shareholder or the corporation." The Official Comment to RMBCA § 13.02(b) explains:

> The theory underlying this section is as follows: when a majority of shareholders has approved a corporate change, the corporation should be permitted to proceed even if a minority considers the change unwise or disadvantageous, and persuades a court that this is correct. Since dissenting shareholders can obtain the fair value of their shares, they are protected from pecuniary loss. Thus in general terms an exclusivity principle is justified. But the prospect that shareholders may be "paid off" does not justify the corporation

in proceeding unlawfully or fraudulently.   If the corporation attempts an action in violation of the corporation law on voting, in violation of clauses in articles of incorporation prohibiting it, by deception of shareholders, or in violation of a fiduciary duty—to take some examples—the court's freedom to intervene should be unaffected by the presence or absence of dissenters' rights under this chapter.   Because of the variety of situations in which unlawfulness and fraud may appear, this section makes no attempt to specify particular illustrations.   Rather, it is designed to recognize and preserve the principles that have developed in the case law of Delaware, New York and other states with regard to the effect of dissenters' rights on other remedies of dissident shareholders.

Rabkin v. Philip A. Hunt Chemical Corp., 498 A.2d 1099 (Del.1985) attempted to clarify *Weinberger*'s ruling as to when a cash out merger can be challenged as unfair.   On March 1, 1983, Olin Corporation had purchased a 63.4% interest in Hunt, from Hunt's controlling shareholder, for $25 per share.   As part of that transaction, Olin agreed to pay the same price if it sought to purchase the minority interest in Hunt within one year.   Internal Olin documents made it clear that Olin always intended to acquire 100% of Hunt.   However, Olin waited until three weeks after the one-year period had expired to propose a second-step merger in which the minority shareholder in Hunt would be cashed out at $20 per share.

Hunt's board created a special committee of three outside directors, which then hired an investment banker.   The investment banker advised the committee that Hunt's stock had a fair value of between $19 and $25 a share and stated that Olin's offer therefore qualified as fair. The committee nonetheless sought an increase in the merger price.   Olin declined to increase its offer and the committee then unanimously approved the merger as fair to Hunt's minority shareholders.   All this was disclosed.   Three Hunt minority shareholders then filed class actions challenging the merger as unfair.

The Court of Chancery dismissed those actions, ruling that, absent deception, *Weinberger* made appraisal the exclusive remedy available to dissatisfied minority shareholders.   The Delaware Supreme Court reversed, stating that "the holding in *Weinberger* is broader than the scope accorded it by the trial court."   Id. at 1100.   The court continued:

[W]e find that the trial court erred in dismissing the plaintiffs' actions for failure to state a claim upon which relief could be granted.   As we read the complaints and the proposed amendments, they assert a conscious intent by Olin, as the majority shareholder of Hunt, to deprive the Hunt minority of the same bargain that Olin made with Hunt's former majority shareholder, Turner and Newall. But for Olin's allegedly unfair manipulation, the plaintiffs contend, this bargain also was due them.   In short, the defendants are charged with bad faith which goes beyond issues of "mere inadequacy of price."   Cole v. National Cash Credit Association, Del.Ch., 156

A. 183, 187–88 (1931). In *Weinberger* we specifically relied upon this aspect of *Cole* in acknowledging the imperfections of an appraisal where circumstances of this sort are present.

Necessarily, this will require the Court of Chancery to closely focus upon *Weinberger*'s mandate of entire fairness based on a careful analysis of both the fair price and fair dealing aspects of a transaction. We recognize that this can present certain practical problems, since stockholders may invariably claim that the price being offered is the result of unfair dealings. However, we think that plaintiffs will be tempered in this approach by the prospect that an ultimate judgment in defendants' favor may have cost plaintiffs their unperfected appraisal rights. Moreover, our courts are not without a degree of sophistication in such matters. A balance must be struck between sustaining complaints averring faithless acts, which taken as true would constitute breaches of fiduciary duties that are reasonably related to and have a substantial impact upon the price offered, and properly dismissing those allegations questioning judgmental factors of valuation. Otherwise, we face the anomalous result that stockholders who are eliminated without appraisal rights can bring class actions, while in other cases a squeezed-out minority is limited to an appraisal, provided there was no deception, regardless of the degree of procedural unfairness employed to take their shares. Without that balance, *Weinberger*'s concern for entire fairness loses all force.

Id. at 1107–08. However, the minority shareholders' triumph in *Rabkin* proved to be short lived. On remand, the Court of Chancery found for Olin, concluding that it had not deliberately timed the merger to avoid its one-year price commitment. Rabkin v. Olin Corp., Fed.Sec.L.Rep. (CCH) ¶ 95,255, 1990 WL 47648 (Del.Ch.1990).

Cede & Co. v. Technicolor, Inc., 542 A.2d 1182 (Del.1988), also addressed the relation between the appraisal remedy and an action alleging a cash out merger was unfair. A cashed out shareholder who had exercised dissenters' rights filed a second suit challenging the fairness of the cash out merger on the basis of a later-discovered fraud. In a decision allowing the second suit to proceed, the Delaware Supreme Court stated:

An appraisal proceeding is a limited legislative remedy intended to provide shareholders dissenting from a merger on grounds of inadequacy of the offering price with a judicial determination of the intrinsic worth (fair value) of their stock. Value was traditionally arrived at by determining "the true or intrinsic value" of the shareholders' proportionate interest in the company, valued on a going-concern rather than a liquidated basis. See Universal City Studios, Inc. v. Francis I. duPont & Co., Del.Supr., 334 A.2d 216 (1975); Tri–Continental Corp. v. Battye, Del.Supr., 74 A.2d 71, 72 (1950).

Weinberger broadens or liberalizes the process for determining the "fair value" of the company's outstanding shares by including all generally accepted techniques of valuation used in the financial community, thereby supplementing the previously employed rigid or stylized approach to valuation. See 457 A.2d at 712–13. *Weinberger* directs that this "liberalized approach" to appraisal shall be used to determine the value of a cashed-out minority's share interest on the day of the merger, reflecting all relevant information regarding the company and its shares. Id. at 713. This includes information concerning future events not arising solely "from the accomplishment or expectation of the merger," 8 Del.C. § 262(h), which, if made public, can affect the current value of the shares and "which are known or susceptible of proof as of the date of the merger.* * *'" 457 A.2d at 713; 8 Del.C. § 262(h).[8]

In contrast to appraisal, entire fairness—fair price and fair dealing—is the focal point against which the merger transaction and consideration arrived at can be measured. See *Rabkin,* 498 A.2d at 1106 (unfair dealing claims, based on breaches of the duties of loyalty and care, raise "issues which an appraisal cannot address"); *Weinberger,* 457 A.2d at 714 ("[t]he appraisal remedy * * * may not be adequate in certain cases, particularly where fraud, misrepresentation, self-dealing, deliberate waste of corporate assets, or gross and palpable overreaching are involved"). It is important to emphasize that "the test for fairness is not a bifurcated one as between fair dealing and price. *All aspects of the issue must be examined as a whole* since the question is one of *fairness.*" Id. at 711 (emphasis added).

To summarize, in a section 262 appraisal action the only litigable issue is the determination of the value of the appraisal petitioners' shares on the date of the merger, the only party defendant is the surviving corporation and the only relief available is a judgment against the surviving corporation for the fair value of the dissenters' shares. In contrast, a fraud action asserting fair dealing and fair price claims affords an expansive remedy and is brought against the alleged wrongdoers to provide whatever relief the facts of a particu-

---

8. Information and insight not communicated to the market may not be reflected in stock prices; thus, minority shareholders being cashed out may be deprived of part of the true investment value of their shares. See generally R. Clark, Corporate Law 507 (1986); Fama, Efficient Capital Markets: A Review of Theory and Empirical Work, 25 J.Fin. 383 (1970). The issue we are addressing is not the manipulation of the transaction, see *Rabkin,* 498 A.2d at 1104–05, nor the suppression or misstatement of material information by insiders defrauding the market, see Basic Inc. v. Levinson, __ U.S. __, 108 S.Ct. 978, 99 L.Ed.2d 194 (1988). Instead, we recognize that the ma-jority may have insight into their company's future based primarily on bits and pieces of nonmaterial information that have value as a totality. See Clark, supra at 508. It is this information that, if available in a statutory appraisal proceeding, the Court of Chancery must evaluate to determine if future earnings will affect the fair value of shares on the day of the merger. See 8 Del.C. § 262(h). To obtain this information the appraisal petitioner must be permitted to conduct a "detailed investigation into the facts that is warranted by the acute conflict of interest and the potential for investor harm that is inherent in freezeout transactions." Clark, supra at 508.

lar case may require. In evaluating claims involving violations of entire fairness, the trial court may include in its relief any damages sustained by the shareholders. See *Rabkin,* 498 A.2d at 1107; *Weinberger,* 457 A.2d at 713. In a fraud claim, the approach to determining relief may be the same as that employed in determining fair value under 8 Del.C. § 262. However, an appraisal action may not provide a complete remedy for unfair dealing or fraud because a damage award in a fraud action may include "rescissory damages if the [trier of fact] considers them susceptible of proof and a remedy appropriate to all issues of fairness before him." *Weinberger,* 457 A.2d at 714. *Weinberger* and *Rabkin* make this clear distinction in terms of the relief available in a section 262 action as opposed to a fraud in the merger suit.

Id. at 1186–88.

STRINGER v. CAR DATA SYSTEMS, INC.

314 Or. 576, 841 P.2d 1183 (1992).

PETERSON, JUSTICE.

This case involves what courts and commentators have described as a "cash-out merger," a "squeeze-out merger," or a "freeze-out merger." In this opinion, we will use the term "cash-out merger." Under ORS 60.551 to 60.594, majority shareholders may eliminate minority shareholders of a corporation by merger procedures that allow dissenting minority shareholders to receive "fair value" for their shares.

Plaintiffs were minority shareholders in Consumer Data Systems, Inc. (CDS), an Oregon corporation. They filed this action, claiming a violation of various rights incident to a cash-out merger involving CDS and another corporation, Car Data Systems, Inc. (Car Data). Plaintiffs allege that other CDS shareholders and directors breached a fiduciary duty owed to plaintiffs as minority shareholders. They seek compensatory and punitive damages. The trial court dismissed their complaint for failure to state a claim, ORCP 21 A(8), and the Court of Appeals affirmed. Stringer v. Car Data Systems, Inc., 108 Or.App. 523, 816 P.2d 677, modified on reconsideration, 110 Or.App. 14, 821 P.2d 418 (1991). We affirm the decision of the Court of Appeals, but on different grounds.

Before turning to the facts, a brief summary of cash-out mergers is appropriate.

At common law, each shareholder of a corporation was considered to have a "vested right" in the corporation. As a result, the rule in many jurisdictions was that a single shareholder could veto a proposed business combination.

Legislatures, courts, and commentators found that the right of a single shareholder to veto business transactions trammeled the concept of corporate democracy. The veto was therefore eliminated. The general rule today is that decision-making by the majority must take precedence over the objection of a lone dissenter. See Revised Model Business Corporation Act § 13.02 (1984) (the "Model Act"); ORS 60.554(1).

The rejection of a minority veto and the recognition of majority rule has not occurred without regard for the potential abuses of a majority's power directed against minority interests. The linchpin of a dissenter's protection in merger cases is found in the statutory appraisal remedy. This remedy is designed to provide statutory protection to those minority shareholders who do not concur with the decision of the majority shareholders.

One device commonly used to eliminate minority shareholders who disagree with the majority shareholders about corporate decision-making is the cash-out merger. * * * Undeniably, such mergers have a coercive element.

> "Freezeouts, by definition, are coercive: minority stockholders are bound by majority rule to accept cash or debt in exchange for their common shares, even though the price they receive may be less than the value they assign to those shares. But this alone does not render freezeouts objectionable. Majority rule always entails coercion. It is, nonetheless, an acceptable rule of governance if all members of the voting constituency share a common goal and if all will be identically affected by the outcome of the vote. In the ordinary arm's-length merger negotiated by the managements of two unrelated corporations, stockholders of the merged entity are properly viewed as having a common interest in maximizing the returns on their stock, whether through periodic dividends or through sale or liquidation of the firm. Once approved by a statutory majority, the terms of such a merger will apply equally to each of the merging company's stockholders, and the common decision will satisfy the principle that all members of the class be treated alike. Majority rule is thus an appropriate means of deciding whether an arm's-length merger should be allowed, and it is of course a universal feature of the corporate law. Despite the element of coercion, dissenters to such a merger are bound, or remitted to an appraisal proceeding, by vote of a majority of their class, because it is assumed that any disagreement among the stockholders involves nothing more than a practical judgment about the best way to achieve a common aim." Brudney & Chirelstein, A Restatement of Corporate Freezeouts, 87 Yale LJ 1354, 1357– 58 (1978).

Dissenters from a proposed merger have a right to demand payment for their shares. ORS 60.571. If they do so, the corporation is then required to pay each dissenter "the fair value of the shareholder's shares, plus accrued interest." ORS 60.577(1). If the parties do not agree as to fair value for the shares, the corporation "shall commence a proceeding * * * to determine the fair value of the shares and accrued interest." ORS 60.591(1). A court then determines the fair value of the shares. The appraisal procedure is the sole remedy for dissenting shareholders in the absence of "unlawful or fraudulent" conduct. ORS

60.554(2) provides: "A shareholder entitled to dissent and obtain payment for the shareholder's shares under ORS 60.551 to 60.594 may not challenge the corporate action creating the shareholder's entitlement unless the action is unlawful or fraudulent with respect to the shareholder or the corporation."

* * *

Plaintiffs' complaint alleges that plaintiffs Stringer and Schubert and two other shareholders owned 43 percent of the shares of CDS. Thirty-two individuals, including the six directors of CDS, owned the remaining 57 percent of CDS. According to the complaint, "[i]n late 1988 or early 1989, the CDS Directors and the larger CDS shareholders, Donald Smith, Mark Kallenberger and Lawrence Custer * * *, decided to squeeze the Minority Shareholders out of their ownership in CDS and to offer them a nominal sum for their stock, which sum was significantly below the fair market value of the stock." The directors and larger shareholders formed a new company that subsequently became Car Data, transferred their shares in CDS to Car Data in exchange for its stock, and solicited all the remaining shareholders, except for the four minority shareholders, to participate in their plan. A total of 32 CDS shareholders transferred their stock, amounting to 57 percent of the CDS shares, to Car Data. Car Data shareholders then voted for a merger between Car Data and CDS. Pursuant to the merger proposal, each CDS shareholder would receive $0.002 per share. As owner of 57 percent of CDS, Car Data voted for the merger. The merger was approved over the objections of plaintiffs and two other minority shareholders.

Plaintiffs claimed that their shares were worth at least $0.10 per share and refused to accept the $0.002 offered them. Car Data rejected plaintiffs demand for $0.10 per share and instituted an appraisal proceeding in the circuit court pursuant to ORS 60.591. Plaintiffs instituted this action in the circuit court against Car Data, CDS, the 32 individual former shareholders of CDS and the present shareholders of Car Data (the shareholder defendants), and the lawyers who represented both CDS and Car Data during the merger process. Plaintiffs' complaint contained * * * a claim for breach of fiduciary duty against all defendants, in which they prayed for rescission of the merger and appointment of a receiver, or, alternatively, for compensatory damages and an award of punitive damages against Car Data and the shareholder defendants * * *.

The circuit court stayed the proceedings in the present case pending trial of the appraisal case. The appraisal case was concluded, and this case then proceeded.*

* * *

* The court found that the fair value of CDS stock, as of the merger date, was $0.07 per share. Chrome Data Systems, Inc. v. Stringer, 109 Or.App. 513, 820 P.2d 831 (1991). [Eds.]

As stated above, ORS 60.554(2) provides that a dissenting shareholder "may not challenge the corporate action creating the shareholder's entitlement unless the action is unlawful or fraudulent with respect to the shareholder or the corporation." The dispositive question here is whether plaintiffs have alleged facts that would establish that defendants' conduct was "unlawful or fraudulent" within the meaning of ORS 60.554(2).

We start with the observation that this court may not question the wisdom of the Legislative Assembly in enacting the Oregon Business Corporation Act. That law drew upon the Model Business Corporation Act and contains procedures for majority shareholders to "squeeze out" minority shareholders. The legislative decision involved considerations affecting both majority shareholders and dissenting shareholders. "The accompanying proposals as a whole are designed to benefit both minority shareholders and controlling shareholders. Minority shareholders benefit because the assertion of their rights is made easier, and penalties are introduced for vexatious obstruction by corporate management. Controlling shareholders benefit directly and indirectly. They benefit directly by the added incentives for dissenters to settle without a judicial appraisal. They benefit indirectly because the provision of an adequate appraisal right diminishes the justification for courts to enjoin or set aside corporate changes because of the absence of an 'adequate remedy at law,' or because the corporate action 'would operate as a fraud.' " Conard, Amendments of Model Business Corporation Act Affecting Dissenters' Rights (Sections 73, 74, 80, and 81), 33 Bus.Law. 2587, 2593 (1978).

* * *

Plaintiffs' complaint in this case alleged neither fraud nor misleading representations that were relied upon by plaintiffs. From plaintiffs' complaint, one can infer only that the amount paid by CDS was unfair and unreasonably low, in an attempt to avoid paying fair value to plaintiffs for their shares.

Cases such as this are the very kind addressed by the statutory scheme. With the exception of punitive damages, every element of damages that plaintiffs seek herein is recoverable under ORS 60.551 to 60.594. The complaint contains no allegations of fact that, if proved, would support a punitive damages award. The legislative plan expressly provides for recovery of attorney fees and expenses and of expert fees and expenses for arbitrary or vexatious action, or actions "not in good faith" in connection with the cash-out merger. See 60.594(1) and (2). This provision suggests to us that the legislature intended that, even if the corporation offers too little money to the dissenters for their shares "arbitrarily, vexatiously or not in good faith," ORS 60.594(2), and if the disagreement is solely as to the value of the shares, statutory appraisal is the exclusive remedy.

The last clause of ORS 60.551(4) also is significant. To the extent, if any, that plaintiffs seek damages for "any appreciation or depreciation in anticipation of the corporate action," those damages can be considered if "exclusion would be inequitable." We agree with the Delaware Supreme Court that "there is a legislative intent to fully compensate shareholders for whatever their loss may be, subject only to the narrow limitation that one can not take speculative effects of the merger into account." Weinberger v. UOP, Inc., 457 A.2d 701, 714 (Del.1983). * * *

Plaintiffs' complaint clearly alleges a disagreement as to valuation, and we also can infer payment by Car Data of an unreasonably low price. Where the allegations show only a disagreement as to price, however, with no allegations that permit any inference of self-dealing, fraud, deliberate waste of corporate assets, misrepresentation, or other unlawful conduct, the remedy afforded by ORS 60.551 to 60.594 is exclusive. That is true even if the majority shareholders acted arbitrarily or vexatiously or not in good faith. Stepak v. Schey, 51 Ohio St.3d 8, 553 N.E.2d 1072, 1075 (1990) (remedy for breach of fiduciary duty involving only the price that a shareholder receives is limited to appraisal statute); Schloss Associates v. C & O Ry., 73 Md.App. 727, 536 A.2d 147, 158 (1988) ("What we have then is essentially a complaint over price—the amount and how it was established—for which the statutory appraisal right is a wholly adequate remedy."); Green v. Santa Fe Industries, Inc., 70 N.Y.2d 244, 519 N.Y.S.2d 793, 800, 514 N.E.2d 105, 112 (1987) ("Here, * * * all of the actions with which defendant corporations are charged relate to price; there are no claims asserted against individual defendants based on dual representation; and it cannot be said that the 'defendants are charged with bad faith which goes beyond issues of "mere inadequacy of price". Cole v. National Cash Credit Association 18 Del.Ch. 47, 156 A. 183, 187–88 [1931]' ").

It may be that the $0.002 offer was insulting to plaintiffs, and it may even have been motivated by bad faith. But, because the facts alleged in the complaint, if established, support no claim for damages apart from the fair value of the shares, we believe that the legislature intended that dissenting shareholders in the position of plaintiffs be limited to their remedies under the appraisal statutes.

The decision of the Court of Appeals and the judgment of the circuit court are affirmed.

UNIS, JUSTICE, concurring in part, dissenting in part.

The issue in this case is whether plaintiffs' complaint states a claim for breach of fiduciary duty and civil conspiracy. I cannot agree with the majority's holding that plaintiffs' complaint fails to state a claim under either theory. I would hold that plaintiffs' complaint states a claim for breach of fiduciary duty and civil conspiracy against all defendants except defendant attorneys. * * *

Because plaintiffs' complaint was dismissed for failure to state a claim pursuant to ORCP 21 A(8), this court must accept the allegations in the complaint as "true." Moreover, as the majority recognizes, we must give plaintiffs the benefit of all favorable inferences that may be drawn from the allegations. Applying these principles, the following seems to be a fair summary of those pleaded "facts" and favorable inferences to be drawn therefrom.

Plaintiffs Stringer and Schubert and three others founded CDS in 1986. Stock was sold in the corporation until, in 1989, there were 36 shareholders. Stringer and Schubert, along with the two nominal defendants in this case, retained about 43 percent of the stock. The stock was sold at about 10 cents a share during this period.

According to the complaint, CDS was successful during this period, and revenues were increasing faster than expenses. In early 1989, again according to the complaint, a third party made a written offer to purchase CDS at a price substantially above what was subsequently offered during the "squeeze-out" merger at issue here. CDS, by vote of the majority of shareholders, rejected the third party's offer.

The complaint alleges the following: "In late 1988 or early 1989, the CDS Directors and the larger CDS shareholders, Donald Smith, Mark Kallenberger and Lawrence Custer (collectively referred to herein as the 'Controlling Shareholders'), decided to squeeze the Minority Shareholders out of their ownership in CDS and to offer then a nominal sum for their stock, which sum was significantly below fair market value of the stock (the 'Plan'). *The principal purpose of the Plan was to deprive the Minority Shareholders of most of the present value of their stock in CDS* and to deprive the Minority Shareholders of their share of the anticipated significant rise in the value of CDS stock over the next few years." (Emphasis added). * * *

The complaint also alleges that, in furtherance of the plan, the CDS directors and the "Controlling Shareholders" transferred all their CDS stock to Car Data and then solicited the participation of all CDS shareholders, except plaintiffs and the two nominal defendants. Once Car Data had obtained by these means a majority of the stock of CDS, a merger was proposed between CDS and Car Data.

As majority shareholder of CDS, Car Data approved the merger with a stock value of $0.002 per share, a price far below that previously offered by the third party. The stockholders of Car Data, i.e., the board of directors of CDS and all the former shareholders of CDS except plaintiffs and the two nominal defendants, also approved the merger. Plaintiffs allege that, as a result of this vote, the minority shareholders received $9,900 for stock with a fair market value of $290,000.

BREACH OF FIDUCIARY DUTY CLAIM

In plaintiffs' claim for breach of fiduciary duty, plaintiffs allege that the above acts by the directors, the collective majority of CDS shareholders and Car Data, constitute a breach of their fiduciary duty to the minority shareholders, including plaintiffs. Plaintiffs seek, inter alia, rescission of the merger or, in the alternative, damages equal to the fair market value of plaintiffs' proportionate share of defendant Car Data on the date of trial, plus punitive damages.

The majority['s] * * * conclusion, in my judgment, ignores allegations that we must accept on an ORCP 21 A(8) motion as "true" pleaded "facts," and it ignores inferences favorable to plaintiffs that may be drawn from those allegations.

* * *

The statutory provisions relating to the appraisal procedure are subject to ORS 60.554(2) and must be read in conjunction with that provision. ORS 60.554(2), which is taken from RMBCA section 13.02(b), provides that a dissenting shareholder "may not challenge the corporate action creating the shareholder's entitlement *unless the action is unlawful or fraudulent with respect to the shareholder or the corporation.*" (Emphasis added.) * * *

* * *

* * * [N]one of the fiduciary obligations owed by corporate directors and majority shareholders were satisfied in this case. Plaintiffs Stringer and Schubert alleged that the directors of CDS, acting with three certain larger CDS shareholders, developed a plan to squeeze out plaintiffs for a nominal sum, a sum significantly below the fair market value of plaintiffs' shares. The squeeze-out merger was implemented just after the majority shareholders had rejected a third-party offer to purchase substantially all of CDS assets at a price substantially greater than the $0.002 per share price set in the squeeze-out merger. The squeeze-out merger would have permitted the majority shareholders, which includes the six directors of CDS, to sell the CDS assets at this higher price without sharing any of the proceeds with the minority shareholders.

Such conduct by directors and the large shareholders does not meet duties of good faith and fair dealing imposed by Oregon law. See, e.g., Zidell v. Zidell, Inc., 277 Or. 413, 418, 560 P.2d 1086 (1977) ("those in control of corporate affairs have fiduciary duties of good faith and fair dealing toward minority shareholders"). With respect to the minority shareholders of CDS and, in particular, plaintiffs, the allegations of the complaint are, in my view, sufficient to permit an inference of self-dealing and gross, palpable, overreaching conduct—a violation of the fiduciary duty owed to plaintiffs by CDS directors and majority shareholders. As such, the case should not have been dismissed at the pleading stage for failure to state a claim.

* * *

The inference fairly drawn from the complaint is that there was no "merger" in this case to which one could apply an appraisal remedy. Car Data, the complaint alleges, was no more than the alter ego of CDS's own directors and several of its largest shareholders. Its purpose, again according to the complaint, was to create a majority voting block to devalue the corporation's stock.

Had the three larger majority shareholders ("Controlling Shareholders") conspired with the CDS directors to reject a legitimate purchase offer and then sold all CDS's assets to Car Data at far below market value so that they could resell Car Data at a windfall price, I do not believe that the majority would find it as difficult to find "overreaching." Yet, in this case, an allegation that certain shareholders and the directors of CDS created a paper corporation in order to accomplish the same result through a "merger" is considered insufficient. I do not believe that the drafters of the RMBCA or the Oregon legislature intended to create a vehicle for this kind of business practice simply because they wished to facilitate legitimate business mergers when there is a disagreement among shareholders over the wisdom of the merger.

* * *

FADELEY, J., joins in this opinion.

———

Assuming plaintiffs had prevailed in *Stringer*, to what relief should they have been entitled, over and above the $7.00 per share they received in their appraisal action? Put differently, was the real issue here not whether appraisal was the exclusive remedy available to plaintiffs, but whether the valuation approach used in plaintiffs' appraisal action took account of all the factors that should have been considered in valuing plaintiffs' stock.

D. FAIR DEALING

Weinberger suggests that a court assessing the fairness of a cash out merger should consider whether the merger was the product of fair dealing and whether it involved a fair price. Fair dealing requires inquiry into the process by which the transaction was negotiated and approved. Fair price involves a review of the substantive terms of the merger.

Courts often seem more comfortable dealing with issues of process than with issues of price, especially when there is no ready market for the product in question (the stock of S, in a cash out merger). In that context, determining a fair price often calls for a type of business judgment that courts traditionally are reluctant to make. On the other hand, if there has been fair dealing, it is easier for a court to conclude that the price is also fair. In other words, a fair process may well be indicative, if not dispositive, of a fair price. Thus, it would seem to follow that if the parties to a cash out merger employed a process that replicated (or better yet involved) the operation of market forces, a court should conclude that the requirements of fair dealing and fair price both have been satisfied.

1. USING MARKET FORCES TO ENSURE FAIR DEALING

Two fundamental characteristics of cash out mergers increase the potential that they will be exploitative. In most cash out situations, the control person knows more about the corporation involved—i.e., the property to be sold—than do the shareholders who will be cashed out; in other transactions, the person selling property often knows (or is a position to know) more about that property than does the buyer. In addition, in most cash out situations, the control person can block or obstruct bids by others, while in most other settings, a person interested in selling property can solicit bids from as many potential buyers as she wishes and can decide not to sell if none of the bids pleases her.

In concept, these characteristics largely could be eliminated by treating every proposal for a cash out merger as the equivalent of a decision to sell the company and by making the company's control person subject to a *Revlon* duty to get the best price for all the the stockholders. Courts, however, have rejected this approach in situations where a corporation has a majority shareholder. Bershad v. Curtis–Wright Corp., 535 A.2d 840, 845 (Del.1987), held that the proposition that a majority shareholder has "an affirmative duty * * * to auction the corporation when seeking to cash-out the minority" was "unsupported by any accepted principle of law." The court explained:

> Stockholders in Delaware corporations have a right to control and vote their shares in their own interest. They are limited only by any fiduciary duty owed to their shareholders. * * * Clearly, a stockholder is under no duty to sell its holdings in a corporation, even if it is a majority shareholder, merely because the sale would profit the minority.

Id.

In contrast, when a group that owns less than a majority of a company's stock seeks to cash out that company's public shareholders, an auction is possible and, under *Revlon*, would seem to be required. See Paramount Communications, Inc. v. QVC Network, Inc. (Chapter 22).

ALI, PRINCIPLES OF CORPORATE GOVERNANCE (1994).

§ 5.15. TRANSFER OF CONTROL IN WHICH A DIRECTOR OR PRINCIPAL SENIOR EXECUTIVE IS INTERESTED

(a) If directors of principal senior executives of a corporation are interested in a transaction in control or a tender offer that results in a transfer of control of the corporation to another person, then those directors or principal senior executives have the burden of proving that the transaction was fair to the shareholders of the corporation unless (1) the transaction involves a transfer by a controlling shareholder or (2) the conditions of Subsection (b) are satisfied.

(b) If in connection with a transaction described in Subsection (a) involving a publicly held corporation:

(1) public disclosure of the proposed transaction is made;

(2) responsible persons who express an interest are provided relevant information concerning the corporation and given a reasonable opportunity to submit a competing proposal;

(3) the transaction is authorized in advance by disinterested directors after the procedures set forth in Subsections (1) and (2) have been complied with; and

(4) the transaction is authorized or ratified by disinterested shareholders (or, if the transaction is effected by a tender offer, the offer is accepted by disinterested shareholders), after disclosure concerning the conflict of interest and the transaction has been made;

then a party challenging the transaction has the burden of proving that the terms of the transaction are equivalent to a waste of corporate assets.

* * *

COMMENT:

* * *

* * * No recourse to the market for corporate control for price protection is possible in connection with a freeze-out transaction because the presence of a controlling shareholder eliminates the possibility of a competitive bid. In the context of a management buyout, however, the market for corporate control is potentially available to police the fairness of the non-arm's-length division of the gain from the management buyout transaction. If the price to be paid for the corporation is too low, the possibility exists that it will evoke a competing bid, thereby creating an incentive for management to fairly price the transaction in the first place.

Under current circumstances, there is substantial reason to doubt that bids competing with the management-sponsored bid will be forthcoming with sufficient frequency. Although announcement of the terms of proposed management buyout often has given rise to a competing bid, a party that might contemplate bidding against a management-sponsored group suffers under significant information and timing disadvantages. Most important, the management-sponsored group, and its financing sources, have access to substantial, often non-public, information concerning the corporation at essentially no cost. Additionally, even if the potential competing bidder has the means to develop independent sources of information, the opportunity for the management-sponsored group to choose the moment when it makes its offer, and to act first, puts any potential competitor at a disadvantage.

Section 5.15 sets out governance rules that will allow the market for corporate control to operate as a realistic protection against non-arm's-length division of gains from a transaction in control of the corporation to which its directors or principal senior executives are parties. Section 5.15(b) provides a safe harbor for transactions that are subjected to an adequate market test of the fairness of their terms. * * *

* * *

Section 5.15(b) reflects two basic premises. The first is that a market review of the fairness of the terms of a management buyout is preferable to judicial review. Thus, when the requirements of § 5.15(b) are satisfied, judicial review is limited to a waste standard in contrast to the fairness review contemplated by § 5.15(a). The second is that before the market for corporate control can serve as a meaningful check on the pricing of management buyout transactions, and thus serve as a substitute for a judicial fairness review, the disadvantages under which potential competitive bidders currently operate must be significantly reduced. To this end, § 5.15(b) establishes three transactional requirements that must be met before market review can be substituted for judicial review.

2. FAIR DEALING IN THE ABSENCE OF A MARKET

Weinberger gives some guidance as to how fair dealing can be promoted in parent-subsidiary mergers. Footnote 7 states that "fairness, in this context, can be equated to conduct by a theoretical, wholly independent board of directors," and notes that "[a]lthough perfection is not possible, or expected," the result could have been better "if UOP had appointed an independent negotiating committee of its outside directors to deal with Signal at arm's length." The court also held that if a merger is "approved by an informed vote of a majority of the minority shareholders, * * * the burden entirely shifts to the plaintiff to show that the transaction was unfair to the minority." The court also held that those relying on a shareholder vote to shift the burden of proof must show that they fully disclosed all material facts. Issues relating to directors' and controlling shareholders' disclosure obligations are discussed in Chapter 18.

As might be expected, subsequent to *Weinberger* it became common for corporations involved in cash out mergers to create "independent negotiating committees of [their] outside directors" to negotiate with controlling shareholders and to condition such mergers on the approval of a majority of the minority shareholders. Recall Virginia Bankshares v. Sandberg (Chapter 18). Post-*Weinberger* decisions have assessed the performance of such committees and have considered what weight to attach to shareholder approval.

Rosenblatt v. Getty Oil Company, 493 A.2d 929 (Del.1985) involved a challenge to the fairness of a merger between Getty Oil Company and its majority-owned subsidiary, Skelly Oil Company. Skelly had appointed a committee of unaffiliated directors to negotiate the merger. The committee and Getty's representatives differed sharply concerning the value of the two companies' assets. Finally, the negotiators asked DeGolyer & McNaughton, a highly respected petroleum engineering firm, to prepare an estimate of asset values. The two companies then agreed to a merger exchange ratio based on that firm's estimate.

A substantial majority of Skelly's minority shareholders subsequently approved the merger. As a consequence, the Delaware Supreme Court held, pursuant to *Weinberger*, that the shareholders challenging the merger bore the burden of proving the merger was unfair. But the court also held, without much explanation, that the standard applicable to the merger remained entire fairness, not waste.

Rosenblatt also addressed one procedural issue that had provoked controversy after *Weinberger* : the duty of the parent to disclose its own internal reports. In *Rosenblatt*, the plaintiffs argued that an internal Getty report, projecting reduced Getty earnings, was improperly withheld from Skelly, likening this action to the treatment of the Arledge–Chitiea report in *Weinberger*. The court cautioned, "While it has been suggested that *Weinberger* stands for the proposition that a majority shareholder must under all circumstances disclose its top bid to the minority, that clearly is a misconception of what we said there. The sole basis for our conclusions in *Weinberger* regarding the non-disclosure of the Arledge–Chitiea report was because Signal appointed directors on UOP's board, who thus stood on both sides of the transaction, violated their undiminished duty of loyalty to UOP. It had nothing to do with Signal's duty, as the majority stockholder, to the other shareholders of UOP." 493 A.2d at 939.

CITRON v. E.I. DUPONT de NEMOURS & COMPANY
584 A.2d 490, 498–502 (Del.Ch.1990).

[DuPont had owned a majority of the stock of Remington Arms Company for more than 40 years. In 1979, DuPont decided to acquire the approximately 30% of Remington's common stock it did not own, in order to facilitate the diversification of Remington's business and achieve certain economies.

In considering the basis on which to acquire the remaining Remington stock, DuPont was aware of its legal responsibilities as Remington's majority shareholder. It also knew that litigation challenging the acquisition was highly likely. Accordingly, one of DuPont's important objectives was to assure that the merger would be both fair to Remington's minority shareholders and economically justifiable to DuPont. In furtherance of that objective, DuPont made three critical decisions.

First, with one exception, DuPont decided not to formulate any merger terms on its own. Instead, it retained the investment banking firm of Morgan Stanley & Co. ("Morgan Stanley") to recommend merger terms that DuPont would then propose to Remington. The only exception was that the merger consideration would consist of DuPont stock rather than cash, so that Remington's shareholders would incur no immediate tax liability and could continue as DuPont stockholders if they chose.

Second, DuPont placed no constraints upon any valuation methodology that Morgan Stanley could use, or upon the terms that Morgan Stanley might ultimately recommend.

Third, the merger proposal would be made subject to approval by a majority of the shares voted by Remington's minority stockholders. In effect, DuPont gave the Remington minority the power to decide whether or not the merger should go forward.

Morgan Stanley conducted an extensive evaluation of the businesses, financial condition, prospects, and other relevant value-related aspects of Remington and DuPont. Based upon this analysis, Morgan Stanley advised DuPont that a merger exchange ratio of .52 shares of DuPont stock for each share of Remington—representing an implied cash value of approximately $22 per Remington share—would be fair to the shareholders of both companies. Morgan Stanley also opined that a merger on that basis would represent a 40% premium for Remington's minority stockholders over the market price in July 1979.

Based upon Morgan Stanley's recommendation and analysis, DuPont formally proposed a stock for stock merger to Remington in which DuPont would acquire the 30% Remington minority interest by exchanging .52 share of DuPont common stock for each share of Remington common stock.

Remington's Board of Directors responded to this proposal by creating a Merger Committee made up of independent directors, which then retained its own counsel and investment banker. That Committee rejected DuPont's offer. After extensive and sometimes tense negotiations, DuPont agreed to increase the merger consideration to .55 share of DuPont stock (worth about $24.50) for each share of Remington stock. That consideration would increase or decrease slightly if the market price of DuPont stock significantly depreciated or appreciated.

The merger was approved by 91% of the shares voted, representing 72% of the stock held by minority shareholders. Due to a decline in the price of DuPont stock, the merger consideration ultimately was .574 DuPont share, worth about $23.46 per Remington share.

JACOBS, VICE CHANCELLOR

* * *

It is undisputed that DuPont, as the majority stockholder standing on both sides of the transaction, would normally have the burden to prove that the merger was entirely fair. However, this case poses the question whether the validity of the merger and DuPont's liability should be reviewed under the less exacting business judgment standard, because of (a) ratification by Remington's minority stockholders, (b) negotiation and approval by a committee of disinterested, independent directors, or (c) both.

In reviewing the statutory and case law on this subject, a useful starting point is 8 Del.C. § 144. That statute essentially provides that an "interested" transaction between a corporation and its directors (or between the corporation and an entity in which the corporation's directors are also directors or have a financial interest) will not be void or voidable solely for that reason, if the transaction (i) is approved in good faith by a majority of informed, disinterested directors, or (ii) is ratified by an informed, good faith vote of shareholders, or (iii) is fair to the corporation at the time it is approved.

Section 144 was most recently construed in Marciano v. Nakash, Del.Supr., 535 A.2d 400, 403–05 (1987), a case involving a challenge, on fairness grounds, to the validity of a loan made to the corporation by certain of its directors. The Supreme Court, applying § 144, held that because neither shareholder ratification nor disinterested director approval could be obtained (due to a deadlock), the "intrinsic fairness" review standard would govern. However, the Court noted that: "[A]pproval by fully informed disinterested directors under section 144(a)(1) or disinterested stockholders under section 144(a)(2), permits invocation of the business judgment rule and limits judicial review to issues of gift or waste with the burden of proof upon the party attacking the transaction." Marciano, 535 A.2d at 405, n. 3.

Except in the case of parent-subsidiary mergers, our courts have applied the same analysis, and reached similar results, in interested transaction cases that were not decided under § 144. Puma v. Marriott, Del.Ch., 283 A.2d 693 (1971). The same result has been reached in cases involving mergers with acquirors who were fiduciaries but did not own a controlling stock interest in the corporation.

The question posed here is whether the business judgment form of review will also govern a parent-subsidiary merger that is either negotiated on behalf of the subsidiary by a committee of disinterested, independent directors, or is ratified by the informed vote of disinterested minority shareholders, or both. Although it did not decide that issue, Weinberger v. UOP, Inc., contains language from which that result (the application of the business judgment standard) might be inferred. However, subsequent case law confirms that that inference is erroneous.

In *Rosenblatt, supra,* a special committee of the subsidiary's independent directors negotiated (quite adversarially) a merger with the corporate parent. The merger was later ratified by the subsidiary's minority stockholders. The *Rosenblatt* court (citing Weinberger v. UOP, Inc., 457 A.2d at 703) held that minority stockholder ratification "shifts the burden of proving the unfairness of the merger entirely to the plaintiffs." 493 A.2d at 937, However, in evaluating the claims against the parent corporation, the Supreme Court did not apply the business judgment standard of review. Instead, it employed the "entire fairness" mode of analysis, imposing the ultimate burden of persuasion upon the plaintiff.

Rosenblatt indicates that minority stockholder ratification of a parent-subsidiary merger, will not cause the transaction to be evaluated under the business judgment review standard that normally applies to challenged stock options or the other above described corporate transactions. Rather, in a parent-subsidiary merger context, shareholder ratification operates only to shift the burden of persuasion, not to change the substantive standard of review (entire fairness). Nor does the fact that the merger was negotiated by a committee of independent, disinterested directors alter the review standard.

Thus, shareholder ratification and disinterested director intervention have a different procedural effect where the transaction is a parent-subsidiary merger, than in cases where the transaction is with a fiduciary that does not control the corporation. Although the Delaware cases do not articulate a distinction in those terms, a plausible basis exists for it. Parent-subsidiary mergers, unlike stock options, are proposed by a party that controls, and will continue to control, the corporation, whether or not the minority stockholders vote to approve or reject the transaction. The controlling stockholder relationship has the inherent potential to influence, however subtly, the vote of minority stockholders in a manner that is not likely to occur in a transaction with a non-controlling party.

Even where no coercion is intended, shareholders voting on a parent subsidiary merger might perceive that their disapproval could risk retaliation of some kind by the controlling stockholder. For example, the controlling stockholder might decide to stop dividend payments or to effect a subsequent cash out merger at a less favorable price, for which the remedy would be time consuming and costly litigation. At the very least, the potential for that perception, and its possible impact upon a shareholder vote, could never be fully eliminated. Consequently, in a merger between the corporation and its controlling stockholder—even one negotiated by disinterested, independent directors—no court could be certain whether the transaction terms fully approximate what truly independent parties would have achieved in an arm's length negotiation. Given that uncertainty, a court might well conclude that even minority shareholders who have ratified a parent-subsidiary merger need procedural protections beyond those afforded by full disclosure of all material facts. One way to provide such protections would be to adhere to the more stringent entire fairness standard of judicial review.

Accordingly, the *Rosenblatt* review standard will govern the Court's evaluation of DuPont's conduct and liability in the case at bar.

[The court concluded that the merger terms were "substantively fair to the Remington minority."]

WILLIAM T. ALLEN, INDEPENDENT DIRECTORS IN MBO TRANSACTIONS: ARE THEY FACT OR FANTASY?
45 Bus. Law. 2055 (1990).

* * * I want to inquire into the role of outside directors—special committees of outside directors—when the corporation is to be sold, and whether such committees can or do function adequately to protect appropriate interests in such a setting. Addressing that subject requires, as well, that one explore, a bit, the role of the investment bankers and lawyers who guide the board in a change of control transaction.

To relieve any suspense, I will report now that I am going to conclude that, as one who has reviewed in one way or another a fair number of special committees in a sale context, I remain open to the possibility that such committees can be employed effectively to protect corporate and shareholder interests. But I must confess a painful awareness of the ways in which the device may be subverted and rendered less than useful. I conclude, as well, that it is the lawyers and the investment bankers who in many cases hold the key to the effectiveness of the special committee.

Now, the foundation for an inquiry into whether special committees are worthy of respect by courts is the question whether outside directors can be expected to exercise independent judgment on matters in which the corporation's CEO has a conflicting interest—the paradigm case of such conflict and the one that I presently have in mind being the management affiliated leveraged buyout.

On this foundational question, there is a disturbing dichotomy of views. A prominent view is the view that outside directors serve a largely ornamental role in the month-to-month direction of the enterprise. * * *

Yet our statutory corporation law has long assumed that disinterested directors can exercise a business judgment unaffected by the fact that the CEO of the firm may be self-interested. Indeed, one of the principal threads in the development of corporation law over the past 20 years has been the emphasis on bringing more outside directors onto boards, and

the creation of more board committees comprised of outside directors.
* * *

What is going on here? How do we explain the dissonance between what the established organs of corporation law—statutes, court decrees, statements by the organized bar—imply, and what those who purport to be realists say, about the likelihood that outside directors will act as an effective constraint upon self-interested management?

* * *

Consider the outside director who is asked to serve on a special committee to preside over a sale of the company. While he may receive some modest special remuneration for this service, he and his fellow committee members are likely to be the only persons intensely involved in the process who do not entertain the fervent hope of either making a killing or earning a princely fee. Couple that with the pressure that the seriousness and urgency of the assignment generate; the unpleasantness that may be required if the job is done right; and, the fact that no matter what the director does he will probably be sued for it, and you have, I think, a fairly unappetizing assignment.

Combine these factors with those mentioned earlier that create feelings of solidarity with management directors, particularly the corporation's CEO, and it becomes, I would think, quite easy to understand how some special committees appear as no more than, in T.S. Eliot's phrase, "an easy tool, deferential, glad to be of use."

Only one factor stands against these pressures towards accommodation of the CEO: that is a sense of duty. When special committees have appeared to push and resist their colleagues, it has been, I submit, because the men and women who comprised the committee have understood that as a result of accepting this special assignment, they have a new duty and stand in a new and different relationship to the firm's management or its controlling shareholder. * * *

I fully appreciate that corrupt conduct does occur. But I believe—especially in the context of the larger public companies—that when outside directors serving on a special committee fail to meet our expectations, it is likely that they fail because they have not understood what was expected of them. Directors must know what is right before courts can expect them to do what is right.

Thus, I come to the role of the committee's advisors—the lawyers and investment bankers who guide the committee through the process of the sale of a public company. I regard the role of the advisors in establishing the integrity of this process as absolutely crucial. Indeed, the motives and performance of the lawyers and bankers who specialize in the field of mergers and acquisitions is to my mind the great, largely unexamined variable in the process. In all events, it is plain that quite often the special committee relies upon the advisors almost totally. It is understandable why. Frequently, the outside directors who find themselves in control of a corporate sale process have had little or no experience in the sale of a public company. They are in terra incognito. Naturally, they turn for guidance to their specialist advisors who will typically have had a great deal of relevant experience.

Thus, in my opinion, if the special committee process is to have integrity, it falls in the first instance to the lawyers to unwrap the bindings that have joined the directors into a single board; to instill in the committee a clear understanding of the radically altered state in which it finds itself and to lead the committee to a full understanding of its new duty.

* * *

Please don't mistake me. This is not a call to pay even greater attention to appearances; it is advice to abandon the theatrical and to accept and to implement the substance of an arm's-length process. To do this, the lawyers and the bankers must be independent of management. They must accept in their hearts that in the MBO or the auction context, their client is the committee and not management. They must clearly and emphatically remind their client that, at this juncture, the CEO and his associates are to be treated at arm's-length. And the lawyers and bankers must act on that view. That means that from the outset, the advisors must be prepared to forego future business. It comes to that.

* * *

My intuition is that the jury is still out on the question whether the special committee device works well enough, often enough, for the law to continue to accord it weight. I am sure, however, of this: if the future leads us to view that that process does offer to shareholders protections that are consistent with justice, it will in large measure be because lawyers have been true to their professional responsibilities and have used their talent and power to see that outside directors understand and strive to satisfy their duty.

3. FAIR DEALING IN TENDER OFFERS

As noted in Chapter 18, Eisenberg v. Chicago Milwaukee Corp., 537 A.2d 1051, 1057 (Del Ch. 1987), held that a controlled corporation making a tender offer for its own stock had a duty to make full disclosure "even 'more onerous' than in a contested offer." Barkan v. Armsted Industries, 567 A.2d 1279 (Del.1989), appeared to curtail *Eisenberg*, interpreting its concerns as a mere "admonishment" that "courts be particularly mindful of the danger of omissions and misrepresentations in situations in which directors are confronted with conflicts of interest," 567 A.2d at 1288, and noting that, "a recognition of these dangers does not affect the definition of materiality." Id. But other courts have followed *Eisenberg* 's approach, asserting that judicial review of disclosures is "especially rigorous" in the case of management buy-outs, where material information is often "exclusively within" the possession of management. Plaza Securities v. Freuhauf Corp., 643 F.Supp. 1535, 1544 (E.D.Mich.1986).

Whatever the nature of a majority shareholder's disclosure duties, it remains unclear whether a majority shareholder also has a duty to offer minority shareholders a "fair price" in a tender offer. Recall *Bershad*'s holding that a majority shareholder has no duty to sell her shares, even if a third party will pay more for them than the majority shareholder is prepared to offer minority shareholders in a cash out merger. It would seem inconsistent with this holding to require the majority shareholder to offer a given price for the minority shareholders' stock, particularly in a tender offer where, unlike a cash out merger, minority shareholders are free to refuse to sell at all. On the other hand, as the court pointed out in *Citron*, minority shareholders who must approve a cash out merger are likely to feel coerced, even if no coercion is intended. The same is likely to be true when a majority shareholder makes a tender offer.

Joseph v. Shell Oil Co., 1985 WL 150466 (Del.Ch.1985), aff'd on other grounds Selfe v. Joseph, 501 A.2d 409 (Del.1985) involved a claim that a majority shareholder does have a duty to offer a fair price in a tender offer. Royal Dutch Petroleum Company ("Royal Dutch") had for more than 60 years conducted most of its business in the United States through Shell Oil Company ("Shell"), a Delaware corporation. As of January 24, 1984, Royal Dutch controlled approximately 70 percent of Shell's stock. On that date, Royal Dutch proposed a cash out merger, at $55 per share, between Shell and a newly-created subsidiary, SPNV Holdings, Inc. ("Holdings"). The merger price was $2.00 per share more than the price that Morgan Stanley & Co., Royal Dutch's investment banker, on the basis of publicly available information, had opined was the fair value of Shell's minority stock It was also approximately $11 per share more than the price at which Shell stock was trading.

Shell's board of directors created a special committee, consisting of six outside directors, to evaluate Royal Dutch's merger proposal. The committee retained Goldman Sachs & Co., which estimated that the fair value of Shell stock was between $70.00 and $95.00 per share and that Shell had a liquidation value of $80.00 to $85.00 per share. Relying largely on this opinion, the special committee concluded unanimously that it would support a cash out merger only if the price was $75.00 per share.

Royal Dutch chose not to negotiate. Instead, it withdrew its merger proposal and, six days later, made a cash tender offer of $58.00 per share for the minority shares. It simultaneously announced that it would not make another tender offer for 18 months; that it intended eventually to acquire all the minority shares; that it would cash out any remaining minority shareholder at $58.00 per share in a short-form merger if after the tender offer it owned more than 90 percent of Shell's stock; and that if the tender offer did not result in its owning more than 90 percent of Shell, it might buy sufficient shares in the open market to reach the 90 percent level and then effect a short-form merger.

Shell's board of directors recommended that the minority shareholders not tender their stock. The board also circulated a Form 14D–9 to shareholders explaining its reasons for opposing the Royal Dutch offer and supporting a merger at $75.00 per share. Nonetheless, minority shareholders tendered more than 80 percent of the outstanding minority stock. Certain minority shareholders sought to enjoin Royal Dutch's tender offer and any subsequent short-form merger. They claimed that Royal Dutch had failed to disclose all material information and that Royal Dutch had breached its duty to deal fairly with the minority shareholders by offering a grossly inadequate price for their stock.

In Joseph v. Shell Oil Co., 482 A.2d 335 (Del.Ch.1984), the court enjoined consummation of the tender offer, ruling that it "did not satisfy the requirements of disclosure of all germane facts with complete candor." The court found that Royal Dutch had not disclosed (1) that it had denied Morgan Stanley access to information about Shell's probable oil reserves, (2) its internal estimates that Shell's going concern value was $91.00 per share, and (3) information about Shell's recent discovery of oil reserves potentially worth more than $3.90 per share. The court recommended that new valuation studies be undertaken and ordered Royal Dutch to circulate a supplemental disclosure document and afford all shareholders who had tendered an opportunity to withdraw their stock.

After this information, together with a letter from Morgan Stanley reiterating its earlier opinion as to the value of Shell stock, was circulated, the Shell shareholders withdrew only 363,000 shares, less than 0.5% of those that had been tendered. Through Holdings, Royal Dutch then purchased the remaining shares that had been tendered for $58.00 per share, increasing its ownership of Shell to 94.6%. About 17 million shares remained in the hands of public shareholders.

Litigation continued relating to the claim that Royal Dutch had violated its duty of fair dealing by offering a grossly inadequate price. Royal Dutch argued that its only duty was to disclose all material information it possessed, leaving the minority shareholders free to accept or reject its offer. The case was settled shortly before trial. Royal Dutch agreed to pay an additional $2.00 per share to all shareholders who had accepted its tender offer; to offer $58.00 per share in merger consideration, plus an additional $2.00 per share for agreeing not to seek an appraisal, to all remaining minority shareholders; and to pay $15 million in fees to plaintiffs' attorneys. In approving the settlement, the court found that there were serious questions as to the merit of plaintiffs' claims. The court also noted that it was unclear whether, even if plaintiffs prevailed, they would be entitled to any relief beyond being allowed to withdraw their shares, dissent from the planned short-form merger, and seek appraisal for their stock. Finally, the court pointed out that the proposed $190 million settlement was perhaps the largest recovery ever achieved in a shareholder class action.

E.   FAIR PRICE

Weinberger recognized that price often is "the preponderant consideration" in a cash out merger and held that the determination of a fair price "requires consideration of all relevant factors involving the value of a company," including "proof of value by any techniques or methods which are generally considered acceptable in the financial community and otherwise admissible in court * * *."   RMBCA § 13.01(3) is similarly open-ended, defining "fair value" for purposes of appraisal as "the value of the shares immediately before the effectuation of the corporate action to which the dissenter objects, excluding any appreciation or depreciation in anticipation of the corporate action unless exclusion would be inequitable."

The Official Comment to RMBCA § 13.01 states:

> The definition of "fair value" in section 13.01(3) leaves to the parties (and ultimately to the courts) the details by which "fair value" is to be determined within the broad outlines of the definition.   This definition thus leaves untouched the accumulated case law about market value, value based on prior sales, capitalized earnings value, and asset value.   It specifically preserves the former language excluding appreciation and depreciation in anticipation of the proposed corporate action, but permits an exception for equitable considerations.   The purpose of this exception * * * is to permit consideration of factors similar to those approved by the Supreme Court of Delaware in Weinberger v. UOP, Inc., 457 A.2d 701 (Del.1983), a case in which the court found that the transaction did not involve fair dealing or fair price * * *.   Consideration of appreciation or depreciation which might result from other corporate actions is permitted; these effects in the past have often been reflected either in market value or capitalized earnings value.

1.   SHARES OF STOCK OR INTEREST IN A COMPANY

IN RE VALUATION OF COMMON STOCK OF McLOON OIL CO.
565 A.2d 997 (Me.1989).

McKusick, Chief Justice.

Ten years ago we examined for the first time the principles to be applied in finding the "fair value" of a dissenting shareholder's stock under the recently enacted Maine Business Corporations Act.   See In re Valuation of Common Stock of Libby, McNeill & Libby, 406 A.2d 54 (Me.1979).   Libby involved a public corporation with common stock listed on the New York Stock Exchange.   In the present appeal we revisit the fair value question in an appraisal proceeding involving three Maine corporations with untraded stock owned entirely by the members of a single family.

* * *

FACTS AND PROCEDURAL HISTORY

McLoon, Morse Bros., and T–M Oil Companies were closely held companies entirely owned by the members of the Pescosolido family under the leadership of Carl Pescosolido, Sr. Two of his sons, Carl Jr. and Richard, each held 475 shares in McLoon, 800 shares in Morse Bros., and 350 shares in T–M. The combined holdings of Carl Jr. and Richard constituted 50% of the McLoon common stock, 50% of the Morse Bros. common stock, and 14.3% of the T–M common stock.

In December 1975 Carl Sr. proposed to merge all family-held companies into Lido, over which he would exercise sole voting control. Carl Jr. and Richard (hereinafter "Dissenters") objected in writing to the proposed merger. On December 6, 1976, the parties executed a merger agreement in which the Dissenters expressly preserved their appraisal rights under 13–A M.R.S.A. § 909. On December 15, 1976, the Dissenters individually wrote to each of the three Maine companies and requested payment for their shares. On January 8, 1977, Lido responded by offering each Dissenter $128,685.55 for his combined interests in all three companies. Within a week, both Dissenters formally rejected that offer.

Pursuant to 13–A M.R.S.A. § 909(9)(B), the Dissenters on April 1, 1977, filed a Superior Court suit nominally in Lido's name for valuation of their stock in all three companies. * * *

Ten years later, on May 22, 1987, acting pursuant to M.R.Civ.P. 53 and with the agreement of the parties, the Superior Court (Delahanty, J.) appointed Professor David P. Cluchey of the University of Maine School of Law to serve as referee to determine all issues in the case. * * *

* * *

FAIR VALUE WITH NO MINORITY OR NONMARKETABILITY DISCOUNT

Ten years ago in the *Libby* case we ruled that a stock's fair value under section 909 could appropriately be determined by weighing three factors—the stock's market price, the company's net asset value, and the company's investment value—with the weight to be accorded each factor depending on its reliability as an indicator of fair value. See In re Valuation of Common Stock of Libby, McNeill & Libby, 406 A.2d at 60. We recognized that the reliability of each factor will vary with the particular facts and circumstances of each case, so that "[t]he weighing of these interdependent elements of fair value is more akin to an artistic composition than to a scientific process. A judicial determination of fair value cannot be computed according to any precise mathematical formula." *Id.* However, the court should in each case consider all three elements of fair value, even if only to find one or more of them unreliable in the circumstances. *Id.*

* * *

[T]he referee held that the fair value of each Dissenter's stock was his proportionate share of the full value of each company, as determined from the expert appraisal testimony presented by the parties. The referee expressly rejected Lido's contention that he should discount the full value of each company because of the minority status and lack of marketability of the Dissenters' stock. On appeal Lido's only serious challenge to the referee's finding of fair value is directed at the referee's recognition of the Dissenters' full proportionate interest in the whole value of each company, free of any minority or nonmarketability discount. We find Lido's arguments for such discounts unpersuasive. In our view application of those discounts would run directly counter to our appraisal statute's purpose of protecting dissenting shareholders. The referee's finding of aggregate fair value of $334,925 for each Dissenter is fully supported by the evidence and by a correct application of legal principles.

The referee applied the three-factor valuation method used in Libby but noted that the method has come under some criticism since 1979, specifically citing Weinberger v. UOP, Inc., 457 A.2d 701 (Del.1983), for the proposition that the modern approach to valuation "must include proof of value by any techniques or methods which are generally considered acceptable in the financial community, and otherwise admissible in court." Id. at 712–13. *Weinberger* by its own terms broadened rather than changed the basic method of stock valuation used in *Libby*. * * *

Nothing in *Libby*, however, prevents the consideration and use of any other generally accepted and admissible valuation techniques. In the case at bar the evidence presented by the witnesses went toward establishing those same three criteria of value; even the discounted cash flow analysis used by Cooper deals essentially with investment value. Although Lido argues that the three-part test is outmoded, we find the approach as outlined in Libby entirely compatible with *Weinberger* and the broadening of the Delaware block method.

Lido tries to use *Weinberger* and its progeny as a basis upon which to introduce the use of minority and nonmarketability discounts as a generally accepted alternative method of valuation. As previously noted, however, Weinberger advocated the same definition of "fair value" of a single shareholder's stock as did *Libby* : "his proportionate interest in a going concern." 457 A.2d at 713. *Weinberger* stands for the simple proposition that the value of the business entity as a whole should be determined by the best available valuation methods. No one can quarrel with that proposition. It has nothing to do, however, with the critical issue raised by Lido's appeal, which arises only after completion of the valuation of the whole firm by the best available methods: Should the dissenting shareholder's proportionate part of that whole firm value as so determined be discounted because of the minority status and lack of marketability of his stock? The Delaware Supreme Court, the same court that decided *Weinberger*, has recently said no: Delaware emphatically rejects the application of those discounts in determining the fair value of a dissenting shareholder's stock. See Cavalier Oil Corp. v. Harnett, 564 A.2d 1137, 1141 (Del.1989) ("application of a discount to a minority shareholder is contrary to the requirement that the company be viewed as a going concern").

The appraisal remedy has deep roots in equity. The traditional rule through much of the 19th century was that any corporate transaction that changed the rights of common shareholders required unanimous consent. The appraisal remedy for dissenting shareholders evolved as it became clear that unanimous consent was inconsistent with the growth and development of large business enterprises. By the bargain struck in enacting an appraisal statute, the shareholder who disapproves of a proposed merger or other major corporate change gives up his right of veto in exchange for the right to be bought out—not at market value, but at "fair value." Methods used in valuing stock for tax, probate, ERISA, and like purposes in which market value is of the essence are inapposite to the determination of the fair value owed to dissenting shareholders. In the statutory appraisal proceeding, the involuntary change of ownership caused by a merger requires as a matter of fairness that a dissenting shareholder be compensated for the loss of his proportionate interest in the business as an entity. The valuation focus under the appraisal statute is not the stock as a commodity, but rather the stock only as it represents a proportionate part of the enterprise as a whole. The question for the court becomes simple and direct: What is the best price a single buyer could reasonably be expected to pay for the firm as an entirety? The court then prorates that value for the whole firm equally among all shares of its common stock. The result is that all of those shares have the same fair value.

Our view of the appraisal remedy is obviously inconsistent with the application of minority and nonmarketability discounts. Lido would have us discount the stock for minority status and lack of marketability in order to reflect what it calls the "real world" value of the stock to the Dissenters. * * * Especially in fixing the appraisal remedy in a close corporation, the relevant inquiry is what is the highest price a single buyer would reasonably pay for the whole enterprise, not what a willing buyer and a willing seller would bargain out as the sales price of a dissenting shareholder's shares in a hypothetical market transaction. Any rule of law that gave the shareholders less than their proportionate share of the whole firm's fair value would produce a transfer of wealth from the minority shareholders to the shareholders in control. Such a rule would inevitably encourage corporate squeeze-outs. As the Delaware Supreme Court stated recently in Cavalier Oil Corp. v. Harnett,

> to fail to accord to a minority shareholder the full proportionate value of his shares imposes a penalty for lack of control, and unfairly

enriches the majority shareholders who may reap a windfall from the appraisal process by cashing out a dissenting shareholder, a clearly undesirable result.

Cavalier Oil Corp. v. Harnett, 564 A.2d at 1141. We agree.

As noted in the discussion of exclusivity, Ohio courts allow a dissenting shareholder only the pre-transaction market value of her stock. Armstrong v. Marathon Oil Co., supra. Other courts also have held that, in certain circumstances, a minority discount should apply to avoid paying a dissenter as if she had a controlling interest. See Hernando Bank v. Huff, 609 F.Supp. 1124 (N.D.Miss.1985), aff'd 796 F.2d 803 (5th Cir.1986); Perlman v. Permonite Mfg. Co., 568 F.Supp. 222 (N.D.Ind.1983), aff'd 734 F.2d 1283 (7th Cir.1984); Atlantic States Constr., Inc. v. Beavers, 169 Ga.App. 584, 314 S.E.2d 245 (1984); Stanton v. Republic Bank, 144 Ill.2d 472, 163 Ill.Dec. 524, 581 N.E.2d 678 (1991); Moore v. New Ammest, Inc., 6 Kan.App.2d 461, 630 P.2d 167 (1981); Blasingame v. American Materials, Inc., 654 S.W.2d 659 (Tenn.1983).

A majority of courts, however, agree with *McLoon* 's argument that to allow a minority discount would provide an inappropriate incentive for controlling shareholders to effectuate cash out mergers. See, e.g., Woolf v. Universal Fidelity Life Ins. Co., 849 P.2d 1093 (Okl.App.1992); MT Properties, Inc. v. CMC Real Estate Corp., 481 N.W.2d 383 (Minn.App. 1992); Hunter v. Mitek Indus., Inc., 721 F.Supp. 1102 (E.D.Mo.1989); Brown v. Allied Corrugated Box Co., 91 Cal.App.3d 477, 154 Cal.Rptr. 170 (1979); Walter S. Cheesman Realty Co. v. Moore, 770 P.2d 1308 (Colo.App.1988); Woodward v. Quigley, 257 Iowa 1077, 133 N.W.2d 38 (1965), modified on other grounds 257 Iowa 1077, 136 N.W.2d 280 (1965); Columbia Management, 94 Or.App. 195, 765 P.2d 207; Charland v. Country View Golf Club, Inc., 588 A.2d 609 (R.I.1991).

In Rapid–American Corp. v. Harris, 603 A.2d 796 (Del.1992), the Delaware Supreme Court carried one step further the idea that a dissenting shareholder should receive her proportionate interest in the value of a company as a whole. Rapid–American was essentially a holding company with three operating subsidiaries. The Court of Chancery had valued Harris' Rapid American stock by estimating what the trading value of the subsidiaries' stock would have been if those subsidiaries had been public companies. Harris argued that Rapid–American could sell the subsidiaries at prices in excess of the projected trading value of their stock and that the "control premium" Rapid–American could receive should be counted in determining the "fair value" of Rapid American stock. On appeal, citing *Cavalier Oil*, the Delaware Supreme Court agreed. On remand, the Court of Chancery determined that the fair value of Rapid American stock, as of the date of the merger, was $73.29 per share, which was $22.29 per share more than the value the court had found without the control premium.   Harris v. Rapid-American Corp., 1992 WL 69614 (Del.Ch.1992).

2. THE RELATIONSHIP BETWEEN "FAIR DEALING" AND "FAIR PRICE"

In most cases where a court has concluded that a cash out merger was the product of fair dealing, it also has found that the merger price was fair.   See, e.g., *Rosenblatt,* supra; *Citron,* supra.   But that has not invariably been the case.   Kahn v. Household Acquisition Corp., 591 A.2d 166 (Del.1991), involved a challenge to a cash out merger of an 11.6% minority interest in Wien Air Alaska, Inc. at $6.00 per share. Household had previously purchased substantial blocks of Wien stock at $6.00 per share from Wien directors and a group of pilots and had acquired additional shares through tender offers at $6.00 and $6.50 per share.   The court found that the cash out merger involved no unfair dealing, but, relying on expert testimony, concluded that Wien stock had a fair value of $7.27 per share.

In Alabama By–Products Corp. v. Neal, 588 A.2d 255 (Del.1991), the Delaware Supreme Court made clear that a court should not consider claims of unfair dealing in connection with a cash out merger when determining the fair value of the dissenting shareholders' stock.   However, a court properly can treat evidence of unfair dealing as a "relevant factor" when it is assessing the credibility of the corporation's evidence concerning fair value.   The court distinguished breach of duty claims relating to the cash out merger from derivative claims for pre-merger breaches of fiduciary duty, noting that *Cavalier Oil* had held that the value of the latter should be considered in determining fair value in an appraisal proceeding.

BNE Massachusetts Corp. v. Sims, 32 Mass.App. 190, 588 N.E.2d 14 (1992), an appraisal action to determine the fair value of Charterbank stock, did not involve any claim of unfair dealing.   Charterbank had retained Merrill Lynch to solicit acquisition offers in the context of a "controlled auction."   Six substantial banking institutions made bids. Charterbank chose what it believed to be the best bid and agreed to be acquired by the Conifer/Essex Group, Inc. (Conifer) in a two-step transaction with a blended value of $95.35 per share—$101 in cash for 35% of Charterbank's stock and $92.25 in Conifer stock for the balance.   Certain Charterbank shareholders dissented and sought appraisal pursuant to M.G.L.A. c. 156B, § 92.

At trial, expert witnesses retained by the shareholders testified that the fair value of Charterbank's stock was $118.78 or $120.00.   Conifer's expert testified that the fair value of the stock was only $72.45.   The trial judge, using the "Delaware block" method, concluded that the stock had a fair value of $101.75 per share.   The appellate court reversed, pointing out that the trial court had not explained why he had assigned equal weight to market price, earnings value and asset value and had valued only the dissenters' minority interests rather than the value of

Charterbank as a whole. The court then suggested that where share-holders dissented from an arm's-length transaction, a different approach should be used to value their stock.

Assuming the plaintiff's statements are an accurate description of the transaction—an arm's-length merger agreement which was the product of a "controlled auction" among six qualified bidders and approved by the officers and directors who were free of any conflicting interest and who sought and obtained the advice of experienced investment bankers—the trial judge could appropriately consider whether the blended value of the merger price should be binding upon both parties. The plaintiff argues that the dissenting shareholders should be required to accept $22.90 less than the blended value of the merger terms, but its brief is silent as to why § 92 requires that dissenting stockholders be penalized for having dissented. Similarly, the defendants claim that they are entitled to more than the merger terms, but they suggest no reason in their cross-appeal why § 92 requires that dissenting stockholders be re-warded for having dissented. Given the untainted nature of this merger transaction—if that is the fact of the matter—we are unable to perceive any sound reason why dissenting stockholders should receive any more or less than the amount received by all other stockholders in a transaction approved by the board of directors upon the advice of investment bankers. The purpose of § 92, as we have said, is to assure minority stockholders that those in control of the enterprise will not obtain unfair advantage. In this case, neither party has suggested that unfair advantage was sought or obtained. Section 92 was not designed to provide sellers with an opportunity for a windfall or to provide buyers with an opportunity for a bargain. * * * The opinion of experts, who have analyzed the experience of comparable institutions and extrapolated the results to the behavior of an hypothesized willing buyer, cannot match the reality experienced by this institution in setting the terms of the merger with the actual buyer who prevailed over five competing institutions.

On remand, the trial judge should determine the blended value in cash of the merger price (unless the value is agreed to by the parties), and he should determine whether the [dissenters] are prepared to place before the court an offer of proof that the merger transaction was either (i) tainted by conflicting interests at the officer or board level, or (ii) for some other identified reason, not the genuine product of an arms-length bidding process among qualified, informed and willing bidders. Absent such proof, the judge should consider whether judgment may appropriately be entered for the dissenters in the amount of the blended cash value of the Conifer payment, with interest. If there is an offer of proof satisfactory to the judge, he should proceed to trial on that issue. If, at the conclusion of the trial, he is not persuaded by a preponderance of the evidence that the financial terms of the merger agreement should prevail, he should proceed to a determination of the fair value of the shares of the dissenters based on the expert testimony already received.

Id. at 200–02, 588 N.E.2d at 20–21. *See, also*, ALI Principles of Corporate Governance § 7.22 (1994), providing that when appraisal is sought in connection with a business combination not involving a controlling shareholder or other control person, "the aggregate price accepted by the board of directors of the subject corporation should be presumed to represent the fair value of the corporation * * *, unless the [dissenting shareholder] can prove otherwise by clear and convincing evidence."

Of course, when a court finds that a merger was not the product of arm's length bargaining, it has little choice but to rely on expert testimony to determine whether the merger price was fair. As the materials in Chapter 6 make clear, determining a corporation's value often requires many complex and highly subjective judgments. In a cash out merger, this determination is more difficult because plaintiffs and defendants can be expected to choose experts who will disagree sharply about the value of the corporation.

In re Appraisal of Shell Oil Co., 607 A.2d 1213 (Del.1992), involved just such a situation. The dissenting shareholders' expert valued Shell stock at $89.00 per share; Shell's expert said it was worth only $55.00. The court, after affirming the vice chancellor's decision that Shell stock had a fair value of $71.20 per share, commented:

> [W]e take the occasion to comment upon a recurring theme in recent appraisal cases—the clash of contrary, and often antagonistic, expert opinion on value. The presentation of widely divergent views reflecting partisan positions in appraisal proceedings adds to the burden of the Court of Chancery's task of fixing value. * * * We impute no impropriety to the participants in this or other appraisal litigation in their efforts to advance their respective positions. That is to be expected in an adversarial system. But if the Court is limited to the biased presentation of the parties, it is often forced to pick and choose from a limited record without the benefit of objective analysis and opinion. To compensate for this handicap, the Court of Chancery should consider, in a proper case, appointing its own expert witness.

> * * *

> We do not mandate the use of court appointed experts in any case, leaving such determination to the discretion of the trial judge, but we believe the time has come for the Court of Chancery to avail itself of such a practice whenever it believes that a more objective presentation of evidence is required, particularly in valuation matters. Finally, we suggest that the Court of Chancery consider adoption of a rule, modeled after Federal Rule[s of Evidence] 706, which will implement its inherent authority in this area.

Id. at 1222–23.

3. CHOICE OF REMEDIES

Weinberger specified a liberalized approach to determining "fair value" in appraisal proceedings and seemed to suggest that courts should use a similar approach when evaluating the fairness of the price paid in a cash out merger involving an alleged breach of fiduciary duty. In at least two instances where courts have found breaches of fiduciary duty in connection with such mergers, however, they have awarded plaintiff shareholders different amounts than they awarded to shareholders who dissented and sought appraisal.

a. The Shell Litigation

As noted above, Royal Dutch Petroleum acquired all but 17 million publicly held shares of Shell Oil Co. by means of a $58.00 per share cash tender offer and then paid an additional $2.00 per share to all shareholders who had tendered their stock to settle outstanding litigation. Royal Dutch also agreed to offer $58.00 per share in merger consideration, plus an additional $2.00 per share for agreeing not to seek an appraisal, to the remaining minority shareholders. Shortly thereafter, Royal Dutch effectuated a short-form merger and sent to the minority shareholders notice of that merger, updated disclosure documents, and notice that they could accept the $58.00 per share merger consideration and that they would receive an additional $2.00 per share payment if they promptly waived their right to seek appraisal. Alternatively, they could reject the merger consideration and seek appraisal of their stock. The disclosure documents reminded shareholders of Shell's previous internal evaluations indicating per share values "substantially higher than $60."

Holders of almost 16 million shares accepted the merger consideration and waived their right to dissent, while holders of slightly more than one million shares sought appraisal. However, certain shareholders who did not dissent brought a class action claiming the short form merger was unfair and succeeded in establishing that Royal Dutch's disclosure statement contained a material misstatement. A computer programming error by a Shell staff engineer led to an understatement of Shell's oil and gas reserves and a consequent understatement of Shell's estimated discounted future cash flows of about $1 billion, equal to about $3.00 per share of Shell stock. The error clearly was due to negligence, but the court found other defects in Holdings' disclosure documents were "indicative of a conscious intent [by Royal Dutch] * * * to be less than candid." Smith v. Shell Petroleum, Inc., 1990 WL 84218 (Del.Ch.1990).

At a hearing on remedies, Royal Dutch proposed that it provide class members with corrected disclosure documents and then require them to elect either to retain the merger consideration or to return it, with interest, in exchange for the right to receive whatever consideration the court awarded in the related appraisal proceeding that was then *sub judice*. Plaintiffs countered that class members should automatically receive any increase over the merger consideration that the court awarded in the appraisal proceeding then pending in the same court, but should not be required to remit any portion of the merger consideration or to accept less than $58 per share.

The court rejected plaintiffs' argument. Referring to the small number of tendered shares withdrawn after the court had required corrective disclosure in the original tender offer litigation, the court observed: "It seems highly likely that even if those shareholders of Shell who chose not to seek an appraisal [after the short-form merger] * * * had been provided with completely accurate disclosures, most of them would still have decided to accept the cash-out merger price rather than seek an appraisal." Id. at * 4. Finding Royal Dutch's proposed remedy also was inappropriate, because five years had passed since the merger and much had changed during that period, the court decided that the most suitable remedy was to award $2.00 per share in damages to each member of the plaintiff class. Royal Dutch appealed this ruling; the Delaware Supreme Court affirmed. Shell Petroleum, Inc. v. Smith, 606 A.2d 112 (Del.1992).

In the related appraisal action, the vice chancellor concluded the fair value of Shell stock on the date of the merger had been $71.20 per share and noted, "[f]or purposes of information only, * * * that this figure is not far from the $70 per share "low' value arrived at by [the Shell special committee's investment banker] in 1984 * * *." Again, the Delaware Supreme Court affirmed. In re the Appraisal of Shell Oil Co., 607 A.2d 1213 (Del.1992). Consequently, shareholders who accepted Shell's tender offer received a total of $60.00 per share for their stock, shareholders who did not tender but were cashed out in the short form merger and who waived their right to seek appraisal received $62.00 per share, and shareholders who dissented and sought appraisal were awarded $71.20 per share. However, as explained below, the vice chancellor's decision to award only simple interest to the dissenting shareholders reduced the economic value of the payment they received to approximately $61.13 per share.

b. *The Patriots' Litigation*

The Patriots litigation related to a merger by means of which William H. Sullivan cashed out at $15 per share all public shareholders in the New England Patriots Football Club (Patriots), the corporation that owned the New England Patriots football team. The purpose of the merger was to enable Sullivan to use Patriots' assets to pay off personal loans he had incurred to finance his purchase of all the Patriots voting stock. Under Massachusetts law, the public shareholders, who collectively owned 128,974 shares of non-voting stock, were entitled to vote on the merger. 71,644 shares were voted in favor; 34,535 were voted against; and 22,795 did not vote. Of the dissenters, the holders of 2,291 shares brought suit challenging the merger as unfair.

Coggins v. New England Patriots Football Club, 397 Mass. 525, 492 N.E.2d 1112 (1986), held that Sullivan was required to have, and had not had, a proper purpose for the merger. Id. at 1119. *Coggins* also held that although shareholders wrongfully cashed out of a corporation ordinarily might be entitled to rescission, the passage of time and other factors made that remedy inappropriate. Instead, the court awarded plaintiffs rescissory damages based on the current value of the Patriots. The court reasoned that to award plaintiffs only the value of their Patriots stock when they were cashed out in 1976 "would make this suit [finding Sullivan had cashed plaintiffs out to advance an improper purpose] a nullity, leaving the plaintiffs with no effective remedy except appraisal, a position we have already rejected." 492 N.E.2d at 1119–20. The award of rescissory damages appeared highly favorable to plaintiffs; the Patriots football team had just played in the Super Bowl and the corporation's value was at a peak.

After this decision, the *Coggins* defendants agreed to pay plaintiffs rescissory damages totalling $584,000, or $254.91 per share, plus interest from the date the settlement fund was created. Litigation continued over whether defendants also were liable for plaintiffs' attorneys fees and expenses. The trial court held that because the action involved direct rather than derivative claims, plaintiffs' fees and expenses should be paid out of the separate fund created by the settlement. Plaintiffs' attorneys said that their services were worth $816,500 but because this amount was more than the entire damage award, claimed only $380,000 in fees and expenses. In its final award, the court reduced this figure to $220,550. The Supreme Judicial Court affirmed. Coggins v. New England Patriots Football Club, 406 Mass. 666, 550 N.E.2d 141 (1990). Thus, plaintiffs ultimately received $158.64 per share, plus interest from the date of settlement, and plaintiffs' attorneys no doubt felt grossly undercompensated.

Other shareholders who voted against the merger pursued appraisal. By statute, they were entitled to the value of their stock on the day prior to the merger. The court found that their stock had a value of $80 per share as of that date, or less than one-third the per share value implicit in the *Coggins* settlement. But the dissenters also were awarded 9% interest, compounded annually, from the date of the merger and the Patriots had to pay the cost of the appraisal proceeding. Consequently, as of the date the Supreme Judicial Court affirmed the fair value determination, the dissenters were entitled to roughly $173.75 per share, or $15 per share more than the *Coggins* plaintiffs ultimately received. See Sarrouf v. New England Patriots Football Club, 397 Mass. 542, 492 N.E.2d 1122 (1986), decided on the same day as *Coggins*.

Yet another suit was brought in federal court claiming that the Patriots' proxy statement was materially misleading and that shareholders' approval of the merger therefore was invalid. The suit was a class action on behalf of shareholders who had voted for the merger, those who had abstained, and those who voted against the merger but did not seek appraisal or participate in *Coggins*. The district court initially rejected plaintiffs' disclosure claims, but the First Circuit reversed, holding that the district court had used an incorrect standard of materiality and remanded the case for reconsideration of the disclosure claims.

Pavlidis v. New England Patriots Football Club, Inc., 737 F.2d 1227 (1st Cir.1984). The First Circuit also pointed out that if the district court found disclosure fraud, it had "broad power to fashion appropriate relief * * *. It may, for example, restore the plaintiffs to the position they would have occupied as dissenters to the merger and allow them to receive the 'fair value' of their shares as determined in the appraisal proceeding now pending * * *; or it may grant other appropriate relief." 737 F.2d at 1338.

On remand, the district court again concluded that the Patriots' proxy statement had not been materially misleading. See Pavlidis v. New England Patriots Football Club, Inc., 675 F.Supp. 688 (D.Mass. 1986). Turning to plaintiffs' pendent state law claims the court, relying on *Coggins*, held that Sullivan had breached his fiduciary duty to minority shareholders by cashing them out for an improper purpose. Id. However, the court concluded that the shareholders who voted for the merger were estopped from asserting this breach of fiduciary duty; only those who had abstained and those who had dissented and neither sought appraisal nor participated in *Coggins* could recover. Pavlidis v. New England Patriots Football Club, Inc., 675 F.Supp. 701 (D.Mass. 1987).

The remaining plaintiffs argued that they were entitled to choose whether to accept the fair value of their stock as determined in *Sarrouf* or to recover rescissory damages as determined in *Coggins*. The Patriots contended that since plaintiffs' claims were based on breach of fiduciary duty, they were entitled only to rescissory damages. Agreeing with plaintiffs, the court allowed class members who had not turned in their stock to recover $80 per share, plus 9% interest compounded annually, and class members who had accepted the $15 per share merger consideration to recover $65 per share, plus 9% interest. Id. However, since their claims were made in a class action, rather than an appraisal proceeding, the court ordered that attorneys fees, equal to about 26% of the amount recovered, be paid out of the common fund created for class members. Pavlidis v. New England Patriots Football Club, Inc., 675 F.Supp. 707 (D.Mass.1987).

4. INTEREST IN APPRAISAL PROCEEDINGS

The history of the Shell and Patriots litigations makes clear that whether dissenting shareholders are awarded interest on the fair value of their stock, what rate of interest they receive, and whether interest is compound or simple can have a major impact on the attractiveness of the appraisal remedy. Decisions about whether to award interest and how it is to be computed generally are within the discretion of the trial court. A customary guideline is that dissenting shareholders should be compensated for their inability to use the money tied up in the stock being appraised, and that a defendant corporation should be required to pay a rate of interest equivalent to what it would have paid to borrow funds at the time of the transaction giving rise to the appraisal proceeding. In *Sarrouf*, the trial court used this approach and the appellate court affirmed an award of 9% compound interest as "not an abuse of the judge's discretion." *Sarrouf*, 492 N.E.2d at 1129.

In *McLoon Oil Co.*, supra, the Maine Supreme Court held that the trial court had abused its discretion in awarding dissenting shareholders simple rather than compound interest. It explained:

> As a matter of law, interest under the appraisal statute is not a mere procedural incentive but is a substantive right, intended to reimburse the Dissenters for the lost use of their money during the pendency of the appraisal proceeding while the corporation retained control and use of it. One commentator has forcefully noted that in the absence of compound interest, the corporation could force the dissenter to sell his shares at less than fair value. If the corporation initially makes a low settlement offer, lengthy appraisal proceedings are inevitable. However, the allowance of only simply interest on the appraisal award could, in some cases, result in a situation where it would be more profitable for the shareholder to accept the settlement offer and invest the money in a savings account, drawing compounded interest quarterly, rather than go through the lengthy appraisal process. This result is clearly inconsistent with the purpose of the appraisal statutes which is to guarantee the dissenting shareholder fair value of his shares and to encourage the corporation to make a fair settlement offer. Compounding the 8% interest rate selected in this case is the only fair and equitable way to compensate the Dissenters for the lost use of their funds for nearly thirteen years.

565 A.2d at 1007–08.

The Delaware Supreme Court has adopted a different approach. In Rapid American Corp. v. Harris, supra, the parties agreed that the appropriate rate of interest, representing what Rapid–American would have paid to borrow funds, was 12.75 percent. The Court of Chancery accepted that figure, but then ruled, without further explanation, that it would not depart from its standard practice of awarding simple interest.

On appeal, Harris pointed out that Rapid–American had had the use of the funds due to him since the merger was consummated and that no prudent investor would make an investment during that period for simple interest. He also argued that awarding simple interest provided corporations with an incentive to delay the resolution of appraisal proceedings. The Delaware Supreme Court rejected Harris' argument. It first recognized "that no Delaware case has ever explicitly considered the factors which determine whether a court should award either simple or compound interest." 603 A.2d at 808. It then held that DGCL § 262(i) gave the trial court discretion to determine whether simple or compound interest should be awarded and concluded that it had not been an abuse of discretion to award only simple interest.

This decision significantly reduced Harris's ultimate recovery. Rapid–American had cashed out its minority shareholders in January 1981 for approximately $28.00 per share. Harris dissented and the Court of Chancery eventually determined his stock had a fair value, as of the merger date, of $73.29 per share. Rapid American Corp. v. Harris, supra. Consequently, with 12.75% simple interest for approximately 11½ years, Harris received roughly $187 per share. Had the court awarded interest compounded annually, Harris would have received 55% more, or approximately $292 per share, for his stock.

Similarly, in In re Appraisal of Shell Oil Co., supra, the court affirmed an award of 10% per annum simple interest on a fair value of $71.20 per share. The court's decision not to award compound interest reduced the economic value of the dissenting shareholders' recovery to the equivalent of approximately $61.13 paid shortly after the short-form merger, plus 10 percent interest compounded semi-annually—or little more than the $60 per share received by the shareholders who accepted Royal Dutch's original $58 per share tender offer and were paid an additional $2 per share pursuant to the settlement in Joseph v. Shell Oil Co., supra. As Yogi Berra once said, "It's never over 'til its over."

*

Index

References are to Pages
